W9-BUA-500

Acknowledgments

This publication was made possible by the invaluable input of many people working in KPMG member firms worldwide. The overview of the requirements of IFRSs and the interpretive positions described reflect the work of both current and former members of the KPMG International Standards Group, for which the authors and editors are grateful.

Current members of the International Standards Group and a panel of reviewers from KPMG member firms around the world generously contributed their time for exhaustive and challenging reviews of this edition. A list of contributors to this edition is included on the following pages.

KPMG member firms' contributors

Principal editors

Heath Preston	Australia
Jeremy Sage	Canada
Sanel Tomlinson	New Zealand
Yin Wong	Canada

Authors and principal contributors

Daniel Armesto	Brazil
Ewa Bialkowska	United Kingdom
Darryl Briley	United States
Jim Calvert	Ireland
Ross Collins	United States
Regina Croucher	United States
Bruce Darton	United Kingdom
Eamon Dillon	Ireland
Phil Dowad	Canada
Egbert Eeftink	The Netherlands
Markus Fuchs	Germany
Danielle Handlan	United States
Eric Johnston	Australia
Hagit Keren	Israel
Joachim Kölschbach	Germany
Emmanuel Lahouste	France
Wolfgang Laubach	Germany
David Littleford	United Kingdom
Aditya Maheshwari	Canada
Jennifer Martin	United States
Steve McGregor	South Africa
Annie Mersereau	France
Mike Metcalf	United Kingdom
Astrid Montagnier	France
Catherine Morley	Hong Kong
Paul Munter	United States
Brian O'Donovan	United Kingdom
Masashi Oki	Japan
Joanna Osborne	United Kingdom
Kris Peach	Australia
Lynn Pearcy	United Kingdom
Nicole Perry	Australia

Nicolle Pietsch	Germany
Ingo Rahe	Germany
David Rizik	United States
Julie Santoro	United Kingdom
Thomas Schmid	Switzerland
Andrea Schriber	Switzerland
Johan Schrumpf	The Netherlands
Sylvia Smith	Canada
Chris Spall	United Kingdom
Sze Yen Tan	Singapore
Hirotaka Tanaka	Japan
Enrique Tejerina	United States
Mary Tokar	United States
Abhimanyu Verma	Canada
Andrew Vials	United Kingdom
David Ward	United Kingdom

Panel of reviewers
IFRS Panel

Esther Bay	Singapore
Reinhard Dotzlaw	Canada
Egbert Eeftink	The Netherlands
Gord Fowler	Canada
Ryoji Fujii	Japan
Ramon Jubels	Brazil
Michael Sten Larsen	Denmark
Wolfgang Laubach	Germany
Steve McGregor	South Africa
Reyaz Mihular	MESA
Paul Munter	United States
Carmel O'Rourke	Czech Republic
Emmanuel Paret	France
Kris Peach	Australia
Mary Tokar	United States
Mark Vaessen (Global IFRS network leader)	United Kingdom
Andrew Vials	United Kingdom

Business Combinations and Consolidation Topic Team

Mahesh Balasubramanian	MESA
Peter Carlson	Australia
Steven Douglas	Canada
Egbert Eeftink	The Netherlands
Ramon Jubels	Brazil
Wincey Lam	Hong Kong
Steve McGregor	South Africa
Paul Munter (Leader)	United States

Mike Metcalf (Deputy leader)	United Kingdom
Claus Nielsen	Russia
Emmanuel Paret	France
Julie Santoro	United Kingdom

Employee Benefits Topic Team

Kees Bergwerff	The Netherlands
Kim Bromfield	South Africa
Regina Croucher	United States
Bruce Darton	United Kingdom
Yusuf Hassan	MESA
Gale Kelly	Canada
Michael Sten Larsen	Denmark
Robert Malhotra	United States
Ralph Menschel	Mexico
Annie Mersereau (Deputy leader)	France
Takanobu Miwa	Japan
Lynn Pearcy (Leader)	United Kingdom
Mary Tokar	United States
Bruce Zirlen	Hong Kong

Financial Instruments Topic Team

Marco Andre Almeida	Brazil
Ewa Bialkowska	United Kingdom
Ana Cortez	Hong Kong
Jean-Francois Dande	France
Terry Harding	Germany
Gale Kelly	Canada
Agnes Lutukai	South Africa
Marina Malyutina	Russia
Chris Spall (Deputy leader)	United Kingdom
Patricia Stebbens	Australia
Enrique Tejerina (Deputy leader)	United States
Andrew Vials (Leader)	United Kingdom
Venkataramanan Vishwanath	India
Danny Vitan	Israel

Income Taxes Topic Team

Syed Anjum	Pakistan
Bruce Darton	United Kingdom
Jon Fehleison	United States
Ryoji Fujii	Japan
Johnny Guldborg Jensen	Russia
Benoit Lebrun	France
Rebecca Mak	China
Winfried Melcher	Germany

| Kensuke Sodekawa | Japan |
| Sanel Tomlinson | New Zealand |

Revenue Recognition and Provisions Topic Team

Bruce Darton	United Kingdom
Riaan Davel	South Africa
Phil Dowad (Leader)	Canada
Kim Heng	Australia
Graciela Laso	Argentina
Tamara Mathis	United States
Vijay Mathur	India
Catherine Morley (Deputy leader)	Hong Kong
Brian O'Donovan	United Kingdom
Carmel O'Rourke	Czech Republic
Thomas Schmid	Switzerland
Mary Tokar	United States
Sachiko Tsujino	Japan
Riccardo Zeni	Italy

Valuations and Impairment Topic Team

Jim Calvert	Ireland
Marc Castedello	Germany
Robert de Virion	Poland
Egbert Eeftink (Leader)	The Netherlands
Raphael Jacquemard	France
Wolfgang Laubach	Germany
Sylvie Leger	Canada
Omar Mahmood	MESA
Marcus McArdle	Australia
Paul Munter	United States
BJ Orzechowski	United States
Julie Santoro (Deputy leader)	United Kingdom
Elizabeth Sherratt	South Africa
Kuldip Singh	Panama
Orazio Vagnozzi	Italy
Beth Zhang	China

other member firm, nor does KPMG International have any such authority to obligate or bind any member firm, in any manner whatsoever.

Foreword

When we were updating *Insights into IFRS* a year ago we struggled to assess whether the IASB would be able to complete its heavy work plan as scheduled. Unfortunately we have only a little more visibility 12 months later.

The IASB has re-prioritised its work plan, emphasising areas in which improvements to financial reporting are most needed, especially in the areas of financial instruments, revenue recognition, insurance and fair value measurement. All of these projects are coordinated with the US Financial Accounting Standards Board (FASB). However, the IASB and FASB scaled back their convergence ambitions on a number of projects, moving from a "gold standard" objective of joint documents or fully aligned requirements to a "silver medal" of largely converged principles. In other words, with an eye on the clock for the end of 2011, the IASB is working to fulfil its commitment to the G20 leaders by prioritising work on standards that most need improvement and not letting the great (gold standard) be the enemy of the good (silver medal).

The IASB's agenda remains ambitious, even after its efforts to prioritise. It has more than 20 active projects scheduled for completion in the next 18 months. This furious pace places significant demands on the IASB's stakeholders for input as the standards are developed. With half a dozen major proposals due in the next six months, on top of two (revenue and insurance) currently open to comment, the demands on stakeholders has never been greater.

Against this backdrop of rapidly changing standards, we are pleased to provide you with the latest edition of *Insights into IFRS*. This publication focuses on interpretation and application of current IFRSs, and continues to draw on our experience with auditing and advising on the application of IFRSs around the world via our global network of KPMG member firms.

To ensure you have up-to-date resource at your fingertips when navigating your way through today's IFRSs, we have updated *Insights into IFRS* to incorporate both changes that are new requirements for 2010 reporting and also to introduce those changes that will become effective in 2011. We also have highlighted the areas that are likely to be changed by projects on the IASB's work plan.

We hope that *Insights into IFRS* will continue to be a valuable guide to the current standards and a useful warning for changes ahead.

KPMG International Standards Group

About this publication

Insights into IFRS, now in its seventh edition, emphasises the application of IFRSs in practice and explains the conclusions that we have reached on many interpretive issues. We have based *Insights into IFRS* on actual questions that have arisen in practice around the world. The guide includes many illustrative examples to elaborate or clarify the practical application of IFRSs.

This publication does not consider the requirements of IAS 26 *Accounting and Reporting by Retirement Benefit Plans*. In addition, this publication does not address the requirements included in the *IFRS for Small and Medium-sized Entities* (IFRS for SMEs), which was published in July 2009, other than in a brief summary of the IFRS for SMEs in 1.1.160.

While it includes an overview of the requirements of IFRSs, this publication is an interpretive guide to IFRSs that builds on those standards and should be read alongside them.

Organisation of the text

The publication is organised into topics, following the typical presentation of items in financial statements. Separate sections deal with **general issues** such as business combinations, specific **statement of financial position** and **statement of comprehensive income items**, and with **special topics** such as leases. A separate section is focused on issues relevant to those making the **transition to IFRSs**.

The overviews of the requirements of IFRSs and our interpretations of them are referenced to current IFRS literature, unless indicated otherwise. References in the left-hand column identify the relevant paragraphs of the standards or other literature (e.g. *IFRS 1.7* is IFRS 1 paragraph 7; *IAS 18.IE3* is IAS 18 illustrative example, paragraph 3). References to the IFRS Interpretations Committee decisions and IASB tentative decisions, addressed in their publications *IFRIC Update* and *IASB Update,* respectively, as issued by the IFRS Foundation, also are indicated (e.g. *IU 11-07* is *IFRIC Update* November 2007; *BU 05-09* is *IASB Update* May 2009).

Standards and interpretations

This seventh edition of *Insights into IFRS* reflects IFRSs that are in issue at 1 August 2010. The guidance differentiates between **currently effective requirements**, **forthcoming requirements** and possible **future developments**.

Currently effective requirements

The main text is based on IFRSs required to be applied by an entity with an annual reporting period beginning on 1 January 2010, i.e. an entity with an annual reporting date of 31 December 2010. These requirements are referred to as the **currently effective requirements**.

A list of the standards and interpretations that comprise the currently effective requirements, including the latest amendments to those standards and interpretations, is included in Appendix I.

Forthcoming requirements

When a significant change will occur as a result of an IFRS that has been issued at 1 August 2010, but which is not yet required to be adopted by an entity with an annual reporting date of 31 December 2010, it is marked with a # and the impact of these **forthcoming requirements** is explained in accompanying boxed text.

For example, IFRIC 19 *Extinguishing Financial Liabilities with Equity Intruments*, issued in November 2009, is effective for annual periods beginning on or after 1 July 2010. Therefore the impact of this interpretation is highlighted as a forthcoming requirement.

In addition, IFRS 9 *Financial Instruments* and IAS 24 *Related Parties* (2009) are the subjects of chapters 3.6A and 5.5A respectively. As the subjects of these chapters relate entirely to forthcoming requirements, both chapters are highlighted as forthcoming requirements.

A list of standards and interpretations that comprise forthcoming requirements is included in Appendix I.

Future developments

When significant changes to IFRSs in issue at 1 August 2010 are anticipated, for example, as a result of an exposure draft or active project of the IASB, it is marked with a * as an area that may be subject to **future developments** and a brief overview of the relevant project is provided at the end of that chapter.

Other ways KPMG professionals can help

This publication has been produced by the KPMG International Standards Group. We have a range of publications that can assist you further, including:

- IFRS Handbooks, which include extensive interpretative guidance and illustrative examples to elaborate or clarify the practical application of a standard;
- Illustrative financial statements for interim and annual periods;

- New on the Horizon publications, which discuss consultation papers;
- IFRS Practice Issues, which discuss specific requirements of pronouncements;
- First Impressions publications, which discuss new pronouncements;
- Newsletters, which highlight recent developments; and
- IFRS disclosure checklist.

IFRS-related technical information is available at www.kpmg.com/ifrs.

For access to an extensive range of accounting, auditing and financial reporting guidance and literature, visit KPMG's Accounting Research Online. This web-based subscription service can be a valuable tool for anyone who wants to stay informed in today's dynamic environment. For a free 15-day trial, go to www.aro.kpmg.com and register today.

Abbreviations

The following abbreviations are used often within this publication:

CEO	Chief Executive Officer
CGU	Cash-generating unit
DP	Discussion paper
E&E	Exploration and evaluation
EBITDA	Earnings before interest, taxes, depreciation and amortisation
EBIT	Earnings before interest and taxes
ED	Exposure draft
EITF	US Emerging Issues Task Force
EPS	Earnings per share
EU	European Union
FASB	US Financial Accounting Standards Board
Framework	The IASB's *Framework for the Preparation and Presentation of Financial Statements*
GAAP	Generally accepted accounting principles/practices
IASB	International Accounting Standards Board
IASs	International Accounting Standards
Interpretations Committee	IFRS Interpretations Committee
IFRSs	International Financial Reporting Standards
IT	Information technology
NCI	Non-controlling interests
Newco	New entity
R&D	Research and development
SIC	Standing Interpretations Committee
SPE	Special purpose entity

Table of concordance

Appendix II includes a table of concordance, which shows paragraphs that have either moved or have changed in numbering from the 2009/10 Edition to this edition of this publication.

Overview of contents

1.1 Introduction
(IFRS Foundation Constitution, Preface to IFRSs, IAS 1)

1. Background

1.1 Introduction
(IFRS Foundation Constitution, Preface to IFRSs, IAS 1)

Overview of currently effective requirements

- **IFRSs is the term used to indicate the whole body of IASB authoritative literature.**

- **IFRSs are designed for use by profit-oriented entities.**

- **Any entity claiming compliance with IFRSs complies with all standards and interpretations, including disclosure requirements.**

- **Both the bold- and plain-type paragraphs of IFRSs have equal authority.**

- **The overriding requirement of IFRSs is for the financial statements to give a fair presentation (or true and fair view).**

Currently effective requirements

This publication reflects IFRSs in issue at 1 August 2010. The currently effective requirements cover annual periods beginning on 1 January 2010. The requirements related to this topic are derived mainly from the *IFRS Foundation Constitution, Preface to IFRSs* and IAS 1 *Presentation of Financial Statements*.

Forthcoming requirements and future developments

When a currently effective requirement will be changed by a new requirement that is issued but is not yet effective, it is marked with a # as a **forthcoming requirement** and the impact of the change is explained in the accompanying boxed text. In respect of this topic no forthcoming requirements are noted.

When a significant change to the currently effective or forthcoming requirements is expected, it is marked with a * as an area that may be subject to **future developments** and a brief outline of the relevant projects is given in 1.1.170.

1.1.5 **International Financial Reporting Standards Foundation**

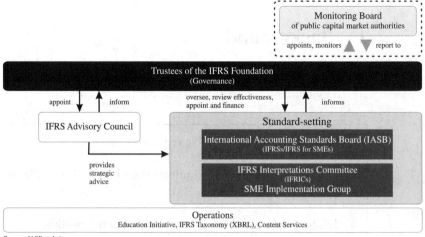

Source: IASB website

Constitution 1.1.5.10 The objectives of the International Financial Reporting Standards Foundation (IFRS
2 Foundation) (formerly the IASC Foundation), as stated in the revised constitution, are to:

- develop, in the public interest, a single set of high quality, understandable, enforceable and globally accepted financial reporting standards based upon clearly
articulated principles that require high quality, transparent and comparable information in financial statements and other financial reporting to help investors, other
participants in the world's capital markets and other users of financial information
make economic decisions;
- promote the use and rigorous application of those standards;
- consider the needs of a range of sizes and types of entities operating in diverse
economic settings; and
- promote and facilitate the adoption of IFRSs by converging IFRSs with national
accounting standards.

Constitution 1.1.5.20 The governance of the IFRS Foundation lies with the Trustees of the IFRS
3, 4, 6 Foundation (Trustees) and other governing bodies as may be appointed by the Trustees.
The Trustees are comprised of twenty-two individuals. The Trustees are required to commit to acting in the public interest in all matters and are comprised of:

- six Trustees appointed from the Asia/Oceania region;
- six Trustees appointed from Europe;
- six Trustees appointed from North America;
- one Trustee appointed from Africa;
- one Trustee appointed from South America; and
- two Trustees appointed from any area, subject to maintaining the overall geographical balance.

4

1.1.10 International Accounting Standards Board

1.1.20 *Formation*

1.1.20.10 The International Accounting Standards Board (IASB) started operations in April 2001 as the successor to the International Accounting Standards Committee (IASC). The IASB is the standard-setting body of the IFRS Foundation.

1.1.30 *Composition*

Constitution 1.1.30.10 The IASB currently comprises 15 full-time members, appointed by the Trustees
18-28 of the IFRS Foundation. The members come from a range of functional backgrounds. Some members also are responsible for formal liaison with national standard-setters in order to promote the convergence of national accounting standards and IFRSs. Although the selection of members is not based on geographical representation, the Trustees are required to ensure that the IASB is not dominated by any particular geographical interest. Members are appointed for a term of up to five years, which is renewable once.

Constitution 1.1.30.20 As a result of the amendments to the IFRS Foundation's Constitution in
24, 26 2009 and 2010, the size of the IASB is to be increased to 16 members by 1 July 2012, up to three of which can be part-time. The following geographical composition guidelines for IASB membership also were introduced: four members from each of Europe, North America and the Asia/Oceania region; one member from each of Africa and South America; and two other members from any area, subject to maintaining the overall geographical balance.

1.1.35 Monitoring Board

Constitution 1.1.35.10 The Monitoring Board, comprised of capital market authorities, was created
18 in 2009 to establish a formal link of public accountability between the Trustees and public authorities. The objective of the Monitoring Board is to enhance the public accountability of the IFRS Foundation, while at the same time maintain the operational independence of the IFRS Foundation and the IASB.

Constitution 1.1.35.20 The Monitoring Board is responsible for overseeing the Trustees' fulfilment of
19 their constitutional duties. Specific responsibilities of the Monitoring Board include:

- participating in the nomination process for Trustees of the IFRS Foundation and approving the appointment of Trustees;
- reviewing and providing advice to the Trustees on their fulfilment of their responsibilities; and
- meeting with the Trustees, or a subgroup of the Trustees, at least once annually, and more frequently, as appropriate. These meetings may include discussion of, and any IFRS Foundation or IASB proposed resolution of, issues that the Monitoring Board has referred for timely consideration by the IFRS Foundation or the IASB.

Constitution 1.1.35.30 The membership of the Monitoring Board is institutional and initially
21 comprises:

- the responsible member of the European Commission;
- the chair of the Emerging Markets Commission of the International Organization of Securities Commissions (IOSCO);
- the chair of IOSCO's Technical Committee;
- the commissioner of the Japan Financial Services Agency;
- the chairman of the US Securities and Exchange Commission; and
- as an observer, the chairman of the Basel Committee on Banking Supervision.

1.1.40 [Not used]

1.1.50 IFRS Advisory Council

Constitution 1.1.50.10 The IFRS Advisory Council (the Advisory Council) (formerly the Standards
44-46 Advisory Council or SAC), is a formal advisory body of the IASB. The Advisory Council comprises 30 (or more) organisations and individuals with an interest in standard setting and which represent relevant constituencies. The Advisory Council meets three times a year to advise the IASB on agenda decisions, work load priorities and other areas as appropriate. As stated in the IFRS Foundation's constitution, the objectives of the Advisory Council are to:

- provide advice to the IASB on agenda decisions and priorities in the IASB's work;
- inform the IASB of the views of the members of the Advisory Council on major standard-setting projects; and
- provide other advice to the IASB or Trustees.

1.1.60 IFRS Interpretations Committee

Constitution 1.1.60.10 The IFRS Interpretations Committee (Interpretations Committee) (formerly
39-43 the International Financial Reporting Interpretations Committee or IFRIC), was reconstituted in December 2001 as the successor to the Standing Interpretations Committee (SIC). Its 14 voting members are appointed by the Trustees of the IFRS Foundation for renewable terms of three years. The Interpretations Committee is responsible for providing interpretations of accounting issues that are likely to give rise to divergent or unacceptable treatments in the absence of authoritative guidance. In certain cases, the Interpretations Committee may decide that it is not able to conclude on an accounting issue and will inform the IASB and the public. The Interpretations Committee may recommend that the accounting issue be considered by the IASB.

1.1.65 Financial Crisis Advisory Group

1.1.65.10 The Financial Crisis Advisory Group (FCAG) comprises approximately 15 – 20 senior leaders with experience with international financial markets. The group focuses on:

- assisting investor confidence in financial markets through improvements to financial reporting; and
- identifying significant accounting issues that require attention of standard-setters, such as the IASB.

1.1.70 **International Financial Reporting Standards**

1.1.80 *Definition*

P.5 1.1.80.10 International Financial Reporting Standards (IFRSs) is the term used to indicate the whole body of IASB authoritative literature, and includes:

- IFRSs issued by the IASB;
- International Accounting Standards (IASs) issued by the IASC, or revisions thereof issued by the IASB;
- Interpretations of IFRSs and IASs developed by the Interpretations Committee and approved for issue by the IASB; and
- Interpretations of IASs developed by the SIC and approved for issue by the IASB or IASC.

1.1.80.20 The term IFRSs is used in this publication to indicate any of the material in 1.1.80.10.

P.9 1.1.80.30 IFRSs are designed for use by profit-oriented entities. Entities in the public sector should refer to the International Public Sector Accounting Standards issued by the International Federation of Accountants. Notwithstanding this, entities engaged in not-for-profit activities may find IFRSs useful, and may follow them if considered appropriate.*

1.1.80.40 IFRSs are not limited to a particular legal framework. Therefore, financial statements prepared under IFRSs often contain supplementary information required by local statute or listing requirements.

1.1.85 *Annual improvements process*

1.1.85.10 The annual improvements process is the IASB's process for dealing with non-urgent but necessary amendments to IFRSs, whereby such amendments are accumulated throughout a year and then processed collectively on an annual basis. As part of this process an exposure draft of proposed improvements will be published for comment in the second half of each year, with an associated comment period of 90 days. The final *Improvements to IFRSs* will be published by the second quarter of the following year. The Board will deal with effective dates, early application and transitional provisions on a standard-by-standard basis; the amendments generally will be effective from 1 July of the year the amendment is issued or 1 January the following year.

1.1.90 *Structure*

P.14 1.1.90.10 IFRSs comprise a series of bold-type and plain-type paragraphs. Generally the bold-type paragraphs outline the main principle, and the plain-type paragraphs provide further explanation. Both bold- and plain-type paragraphs have equal authority.

1.1.90.20 Some IFRSs contain appendices (e.g. IAS 7 *Statement of Cash Flows*). A statement at the top of each appendix clarifies its status. When an appendix is illustrative only and not an integral part of the standard, it does not have the same status as the standard itself. However, in our view, generally the guidance in an appendix should be followed except when it conflicts with the requirements of an IFRS, or when such guidance merely represents an illustrative example and it is clear that a standard or requirement can be complied with in different ways. For example, Appendix A of IAS 7 presents interest paid as part of operating activities, whereas the standard itself states clearly that interest paid may be classified as part of either operating or financing activities (see 2.3.50.20).

1.1.100 [Not used]

1.1.110 **Compliance with IFRSs**

1.1.120 *General*

IAS 1.16   1.1.120.10 Any entity claiming that a set of financial statements is in compliance with IFRSs complies with *all* such standards and related interpretations. An entity cannot claim that its financial statements are, for example, "materially" in compliance with IFRSs, or that it has complied with "substantially all" requirements of IFRSs. Compliance with IFRSs encompasses disclosure as well as recognition and measurement requirements.

1.1.120.20 The IASB does not carry out any inquiry or enforcement role regarding the application of its standards. However, often this is undertaken by local regulators and/or stock exchanges.

1.1.130 *Fair presentation*

IAS 1.15   1.1.130.10 The overriding requirement of IFRSs is for the financial statements to give a fair presentation (or true and fair view).

IAS 1.15   1.1.130.20 *Fair presentation* is the faithful representation of the effects of transactions, other events and conditions in accordance with the definitions and recognition criteria for assets, liabilities, income and expenses as set out in the IASB's conceptual framework *Framework for the Preparation and Presentation of Financial Statements* (Framework) (see 1.2). Compliance with IFRSs, including additional disclosure when necessary, is presumed to result in a fair presentation.

IAS 1.19-24   1.1.130.30 When compliance with a requirement of an IFRS would be so misleading that it would conflict with the objective of financial reporting set out in the Framework, an entity departs from the required treatment in order to give a fair presentation, unless the relevant regulator prohibits such an override. If an override cannot be used because it is prohibited by the regulator, then additional disclosure is required in the notes to the

8

financial statements to reduce the perceived misleading impact of compliance to the maximum extent possible.

1.1.130.40 Compliance with a requirement of an IFRS is misleading when it conflicts with the objective of financial statements as set out in the Framework (see 1.2.10).

IAS 1.19-21 1.1.130.50 The use of a true and fair override is very rare under IFRSs and such a course of action should not be taken lightly. In the rare case of an override, extensive disclosures are required, including the particulars of the departure, the reasons for the departure and its effect.

1.1.140 [Not used]

1.1.150 Private entities

1.1.150.10 An entity that claims compliance with IFRSs applies all IFRSs (see 1.1.70 and 110). However, as an alternative, a private entity may consider applying the *IFRS for Small and Medium-sized Entities* (the IFRS for SMEs).

1.1.160 IFRS for Small and Medium-sized Entities

1.1.160.10 In July 2009 the IASB published the IFRS for SMEs. The standard facilitates financial reporting by, and provides accounting standards suitable for, private entities that want to use international standards.

1.1.160.20 The IFRS for SMEs is a stand-alone document organised by topic. It does not follow the numbering of full IFRSs; it also does not contain cross references to full IFRSs, except for IAS 39 *Financial Instruments: Recognition and Measurement*. The IFRS for SMEs contains reduced guidance as compared to full IFRSs; therefore even when the general principles in the IFRS for SMEs appear to be the same as full IFRSs, differences in application may result. Therefore, financial statements prepared under the IFRS for SMEs cannot claim compliance with IFRSs.

1.1.160.30 The IFRS for SMEs is applicable for entities that publish general purpose financial statements for external users and that do not have public accountability. An entity would have public accountability if it files (or is in the process of filing) financial statements with a securities commission or other regulatory organisation for the purpose of issuing any class of instruments in a public market, or if it holds assets in a fiduciary capacity for a broad group of outsiders (e.g. a bank or insurance company). There are no quantitative thresholds in order to qualify as a SME.

1.1.170 Future developments

1.1.170.10 The IASB and the FASB are working on a joint project aimed at developing a common conceptual framework (see 1.2.120.10). One of the topics under considera- tion is the application of the standards to not-for-profit entities. The expected timing and initial type of document to be published for this phase of this project are yet to be determined by the IASB.

1.2   The Framework
(IASB Framework)

1.2 The Framework
(IASB Framework)

Overview of currently effective requirements

- The IASB uses its conceptual framework when developing new or revised IFRSs or amending existing IFRSs.

- The Framework is a point of reference for preparers of financial statements in the absence of specific guidance in IFRSs.

- IFRSs do not apply to items that are "immaterial".

- Transactions are accounted for in accordance with their substance, rather than only their legal form.

- Transactions with shareholders in their capacity as shareholders are recognised directly in equity.

Currently effective requirements

This publication reflects IFRSs in issue at 1 August 2010. The currently effective requirements cover annual periods beginning on 1 January 2010. The requirements related to this topic are derived mainly from the *Framework for the Preparation and Presentation of Financial Statements* (Framework) and several other standards that help to explain the basic principles of the Framework.

Forthcoming requirements and future developments

When a currently effective requirement will be changed by a new requirement that is issued but is not yet effective, it is marked with a # as a **forthcoming requirement** and the impact of the change is explained in the accompanying boxed text. In respect of this topic no forthcoming requirements are noted.

When a significant change to the currently effective or forthcoming requirements is expected, it is marked with a * as an area that may be subject to **future developments** and a brief outline of the relevant projects is given in 1.2.120.

1.2.10 **Introduction***

1.2.10.10 The Framework provides a broad discussion of the basis of preparing financial statements. It discusses the objectives of financial statements; their underlying assumptions and qualitative characteristics, such as relevance and reliability; and perhaps more importantly, it discusses the elements of financial statements, including assets, liabilities, equity, income and expenses, providing definitions and recognition criteria. The Framework also discusses in broad terms the measurement of assets and liabilities and the concepts of capital and capital maintenance.

1.2.10.20 The IASB uses the Framework when developing new or revised IFRSs or amending existing IFRSs. The Framework also provides a point of reference for preparers of financial statements in the absence of specific guidance in IFRSs on a particular subject (see 2.8.6); the purpose of this section is to highlight some of the Framework's key principles.

1.2.20 Assets and liabilities*

1.2.30 *Definitions*

F.49   1.2.30.10 In developing new standards and interpretations, the IASB relies on the following definitions of assets and liabilities, which are key elements of the financial statements:

- An *asset* is a resource controlled by the entity as a result of past events, from which future economic benefits are expected to flow to the entity.
- A *liability* is a present obligation of the entity arising from past events, the settlement of which is expected to result in an outflow from the entity of resources embodying economic benefits.

F.49, 70   1.2.30.20 The definitions of equity, income and expenses are derived from the definitions of assets and liabilities:

- *Equity* is the residual interest in the assets of the entity after deducting all of its liabilities.
- *Income* is an increase in economic benefits during the period in the form of inflows or enhancements of assets or decreases in liabilities that result in increases in equity, other than those related to contributions from equity participants.
- *Expenses* are decreases in economic benefits during the period in the form of outflows or depletions of assets or increases in liabilities that result in decreases in equity, other than those related to distributions to equity participants.

1.2.30.30 The Framework's emphasis on assets and liabilities, and the resulting influence that this has had on standard setting in general, means that in our view any entity analysing how a transaction should be accounted for should consider this "balance sheet" orientation.

1.2.40 *Recognition criteria*

F.83   1.2.40.10 An item that meets the definition of an asset or liability is recognised when:

- it is probable that any future economic benefits associated with the item will flow to the entity (in the case of an asset) or from the entity (in the case of a liability); and

14

- the asset or liability has a cost or value that can be measured reliably.

IAS 37.23   1.2.40.20 The term "probable" is not defined in the Framework, nor is it generally defined in the standards when it is used in such standards. However, IAS 37 *Provisions, Contingent Liabilities and Contingent Assets* specifies that, for the purpose of that standard, probable means "more likely than not" (see 3.12.30.10). While this interpretation of probable may be used in other areas in which there is no specific guidance, higher thresholds cannot be ruled out, e.g. in the recognition of deferred tax assets (see 3.13.170.40).

IAS 37.27-34   1.2.40.30 Contingent assets are not recognised in the statement of financial position because this may result in the recognition of income that never may be realised (see 3.14.40.10). Contingent liabilities are not recognised in the statement of financial position, unless assumed in a business combination (see 3.14.30.10). However, their disclosure may be required under the requirements for contingent assets and liabilities (see 3.14.60 and 70).

1.2.50 *Matching*

F.95   1.2.50.10 A typical objective in preparing financial statements is to match revenues and expenses. While matching historically has had a significant influence on the preparation of financial statements, it has been de-emphasised in recent standard setting as the predominance of the balance sheet approach has grown. Accordingly, expenses (or revenues) may be deferred in the statement of financial position only if they meet the definition of an asset (or liability).

1.2.50.20 For example, a football club may spend five months of the year incurring maintenance expenditure to prepare the grounds for the oncoming season. If the expense could be deferred and recognised at the same time as the revenue from ticket sales, then the entity might avoid showing a loss in the income statement during those five months and significant profits later. However, notwithstanding the uneven impact on the income statement, the maintenance expenditure is expensed as incurred since the maintenance expenditure does not meet the definition of an asset.

1.2.55 *Measurement basis*

F.99-101,   1.2.55.10 The Framework requires the selection of a basis of measurement for the
IAS 37.3   elements of the financial statements. IFRSs require financial statements to be prepared on a modified historical cost basis, with a growing emphasis on fair value (see 2.4).

1.2.60 *Executory contracts*

IAS 37.3   1.2.60.10 Although the Framework does not refer explicitly to executory contracts, they are an integral part of accounting under IFRSs. IAS 37 describes an executory contract as one in which neither party has performed any of its obligations or both parties have partially performed their obligations to an equal extent. For example, an entity enters into a contract to buy equipment in six months and agrees to pay 100 at that time. Initially this is an executory contract because the seller has the obligation to deliver the equipment and the buyer has the right to receive the equipment, but also has an obligation to pay 100, and neither party has performed its obligations.

IAS 37.66, 68 1.2.60.20 Even though the rights and obligations under executory contracts are outside the scope of IAS 39 *Financial Instruments: Recognition and Measurement* and they generally meet the definition and recognition criteria of assets and liabilities, current practice generally is not to recognise them in the financial statements to the extent that the rights and obligations have equal value, or the rights have a value greater than that of the obligations. When the unavoidable costs of meeting the obligations exceed the expected economic benefits, a provision for an onerous contract is recognised in accordance with IAS 37 (see 3.12.630). See 3.6.90 for a discussion of executory contracts within the scope of IAS 39.

1.2.70 Relevance vs reliability*

F.26, 31 1.2.70.10 Two of the qualitative characteristics of financial statements are relevance and reliability. Information is relevant if it assists users in making economic decisions, or in assessing past evaluations; information is reliable if it represents faithfully what it purports to represent or could reasonably be expected to represent.

1.2.70.20 In many cases there is a trade-off between the relevance and reliability of information. For example, knowing the fair value of an asset often is more relevant to users than historical cost; however, the measurement of historical cost typically is more reliable because it is based on an actual transaction to which the entity was a party, and therefore accurate information usually is available. In many cases IFRSs favour relevance over reliability, and the use of fair values in preparing financial statements is becoming more predominant (see 2.4.10).

1.2.80 Materiality

F.29, 30, 1.2.80.10 IFRSs do not apply to items that are "immaterial". The term is not defined
IAS 1.11, 8.5 explicitly, but the Framework and IFRSs define materiality by illustration. Omissions or misstatements of items are material if they could, individually or collectively, influence the economic decisions of users taken on the basis of the financial statements. Materiality depends on the size and nature of the omission or misstatement judged in the surrounding circumstances. Either the size or the nature of the item, or a combination of both, could be the determining factor. Consideration of materiality is relevant to judgements regarding both the selection and application of accounting policies, and to the omission or disclosure of information in the financial statements.

IAS 1.30, 31, 1.2.80.20 Materiality is a factor when making judgements about disclosure. For example,
86 materiality affects when items may be aggregated, the use of additional line items, headings and subtotals. Materiality also is relevant to the positioning of these disclosures: an item may be sufficiently material to warrant disclosure on the face of the financial statements, or only may require disclosure in the notes to the financial statements. Mate-

riality may mean that a specific disclosure requirement in a standard or an interpretation is not provided if the information is not material.

IAS 8.8   1.2.80.30 Accounting policies selected in accordance with IFRSs do not need to be applied when their effect is immaterial.

IAS 8.8, 41   1.2.80.40 Financial statements do not comply with IFRSs if they contain either material errors, or immaterial errors that are made intentionally to achieve a particular presentation of an entity's financial position, financial performance or cash flows.

1.2.85 Going concern

F.23,   1.2.85.10 Financial statements are prepared on a going concern basis, unless manage-
IAS 1.23   ment intends or has no alternative other than to liquidate the entity or stop trading. If the going concern assumption is not appropriate, then IFRSs are applied in a manner appropriate to the circumstances (see 2.4.15.10).

1.2.90 Prudence*

F.37   1.2.90.10 In preparing financial statements there may be a tendency to put greater emphasis on the possible negative outcomes of transactions and events rather than the possible positive outcomes. This could lead to a loss of neutrality and to the understatement of profit. The Framework makes it clear that prudence means exercising a degree of caution in making judgements under conditions of uncertainty, but that it should not lead to the creation of hidden reserves or excessive provisions.

1.2.100 Substance over form

F.35, IFRIC 4,   1.2.100.10 The Framework establishes a general requirement to account for transactions
SIC-27   in accordance with their substance, rather than only their legal form. This principle comes through clearly in many IFRSs. For example, revenue from the sale of goods is not recognised automatically at the stated effective date of a contract if the significant risks and rewards of ownership of the goods have not been transferred to the buyer (see 4.2.100). In addition, accounting for a transaction in the legal form of a lease should reflect its economic substance; and IAS 17 *Leases* applies when an arrangement conveys a right to use an asset for a specified period of time, regardless of whether the contract is structured legally as a lease (see 5.1).

1.2.110 Transactions with shareholders

F.70   1.2.110.10 The definitions of income and expenses exclude capital transactions with equity participants. Accordingly, such transactions for example, capital contributions from shareholders, are recognised directly in equity as are distributions made to shareholders. However, the position is less clear when the transaction with the shareholder equally could have been with a third party.

1.2.110.20 For example, an entity sells inventory at fair value to a shareholder. In this case the transaction is recognised in profit or loss because the transaction price (being at fair value) indicates that the shareholder is not acting in its capacity as a shareholder; rather, it is transacting with the entity in the same way as any other third party.

1.2.110.30 But suppose that the inventory is given without consideration to a shareholder. In this case it can be argued that the shareholder has received a benefit from the entity in its capacity as a shareholder because an independent third party would not have been given the inventory for free. In our view, and in the absence of any other pertinent facts, this transaction should be recognised directly in equity as a distribution to shareholders (see 3.11.450).

1.2.110.40 In another example, suppose the shareholder pays considerably more than fair value for the inventory. In such cases, it may be appropriate to split the transaction into a capital transaction and a revenue transaction. Proceeds equal to the fair value of the inventory would be recognised in profit or loss, with the remaining proceeds being recognised directly in equity as a contribution from shareholders.

1.2.110.45 In another example, Company M is an acquisition target of Company B and both entities are currently in negotiations. M signs a bonus agreement with senior management of M promising a bonus payment for successful completion of the transaction with B. The amount of the bonus is linked to the share price of M. The pre-existing shareholders of M were not a party to the bonus agreement. In our view, this bonus arrangement is not a transaction with shareholders and if the bonus is paid, then it should be expensed. We believe that the bonus paid would not represent a transaction with shareholders, as it is senior management's fiduciary duty/responsibility to act in the best interest of shareholders and in this role they are still employees and representatives of M. In addition, consideration should be given as to whether the transaction is within the scope of IFRS 2 *Share-based Payment*, as the payment varies depending on the share price of M (see 4.5).

1.2.110.50 Generally, IFRSs do not discuss the circumstances in which it would be appropriate for a transaction entered into by a shareholder on behalf of the reporting entity to be recognised in the financial statements of the reporting entity ("attribution"). However, IFRS 2 does require the attribution of expense for certain share-based payment transactions (see 4.5.10.100). In other instances judgement should be used in determining whether attribution is appropriate. IAS 24 *Related Party Disclosures* requires attribution for disclosure purposes in certain circumstances (see 5.5.110.30).

1.2.110.60 The key point is that transactions with shareholders, or any transactions that are made on behalf of the reporting entity, are considered carefully, having regard to all the facts and circumstances, in determining the appropriate accounting.

1.2.120 **Future developments**

1.2.120.10 In April 2004 the IASB and the FASB agreed to add to their agendas a joint project for the development of a common conceptual framework. The framework will be built upon the IASB's and the FASB's existing conceptual frameworks and will provide a basis for developing future accounting standards.

1.2.120.15 The IASB and FASB have identified the following phases of this project:

A. Objectives and qualitative characteristics;
B. Elements and recognition;
C. Measurement;
D. Reporting entity;
E. Presentation and disclosure;
F. Purpose and status;
G. Application to not-for-profit entities; and
H. Remaining issues, if any.

1.2.120.17 Of the phases noted, only phases A – D currently are active projects.

1.2.120.20 In May 2008, as a result of phase A of the project, the IASB published ED *An improved Conceptual Framework for Financial Reporting Chapter 1: The Objective of Financial Reporting Chapter 2: Qualitative Characteristics and Constraints of Decision-useful Financial Reporting Information.* The ED includes proposed new guidance on the objective of general purpose financial reporting for business entities in the private sector and the qualitative characteristics and constraints of decision-useful information. The ED proposes that the objective of general purpose financial reporting is to provide financial information that is useful to all decisions to be made by present and potential capital providers. In this context capital providers consist of all parties who have a claim on the entity's resources such as equity investors and lenders. A final chapter as a result of phase A is scheduled for the second quarter of 2010.

1.2.120.30 The IASB and FASB have started deliberating issues in phase B of the project, including focusing on the working definitions for "asset" and "liability". The expected timing of this phase is yet to be determined by the IASB.

1.2.120.40 In December 2009, as a result of phase C of the project, the IASB and FASB considered a staff paper outlining the measurement concepts for possible inclusion in a DP. A DP on phase C is scheduled for the fourth quarter of 2010/first quarter of 2011.

1.2.120.50 In March 2010, as a result of phase D of the project, the IASB published ED/2010/2 *Conceptual Framework for Financial Reporting: The Reporting Entity.* The objective of the ED is to develop a reporting entity concept consistent with the objective of general purpose financial reporting for inclusion in the common conceptual framework. A final chapter as a result of phase D is scheduled for the fourth quarter of 2010.

2.1 Form and components of financial statements
(IAS 1, IAS 27)

2. General issues

2.1 Form and components of financial statements
(IAS 1, IAS 27)

Overview of currently effective requirements

- The following are presented: a statement of financial position; a statement of comprehensive income; a statement of changes in equity; a statement of cash flows; and notes including accounting policies.

- In addition, a statement of financial position as at the beginning of the earliest comparative period is presented when an entity restates comparative information following a change in accounting policy, correction of an error or reclassification of items in the financial statements.

- Comparative information is required for the preceding period only, but additional periods and information may be presented.

- An entity with one or more subsidiaries presents consolidated financial statements unless specific criteria are met.

- An entity without subsidiaries but with an associate or jointly controlled entity prepares individual financial statements unless specific criteria are met.

- In its individual financial statements, generally an entity accounts for an investment in an associate using the equity method, and an investment in a jointly controlled entity using the equity method or proportionate consolidation.

- An entity is permitted, but not required, to present separate financial statements in addition to consolidated or individual financial statements.

Currently effective requirements

This publication reflects IFRSs in issue at 1 August 2010. The currently effective requirements cover annual periods beginning on 1 January 2010. The requirements related to this topic are derived mainly from IAS 1 *Presentation of Financial Statements* and IAS 27 *Consolidated and Separate Financial Statements*.

Forthcoming requirements and future developments

When a currently effective requirement will be changed by a new requirement that is issued but is not yet effective, it is marked with a # as a **forthcoming requirement** and the impact of the change is explained in the accompanying boxed text. In respect of this topic no forthcoming requirements are noted.

The currently effective requirements may be subject to **future developments** and a brief outline of the relevant project is given in 2.1.90.

2.1.10 Components of the financial statements

IAS 1.10   2.1.10.10 The following is presented as a complete set of financial statements:

- a statement of financial position (see 3.1);
- a statement of comprehensive income, presented either in a single statement of comprehensive income (which includes all components of profit or loss and other comprehensive income) or in the form of two statements, being an income statement (which displays components of profit or loss) followed immediately by a separate statement of comprehensive income (which begins with profit or loss as reported in the income statement and displays components of other comprehensive income to sum to total comprehensive income for the period) (see 4.1);
- a statement of changes in equity (see 2.2);
- a statement of cash flows (see 2.3);
- notes, comprising a summary of significant accounting policies and other explanatory information; and
- a statement of financial position as at the beginning of the earliest comparative period when an entity restates comparative information following a change in accounting policy, correction of an error or reclassification of items in the financial statements (see 2.1.35).

2.1.10.20 The statements presented outside of the notes to the financial statements generally are referred to as financial statements in IAS 1 (previously primary statements). For the purposes of this chapter, those financial statements are described when necessary as primary financial statements to distinguish them from the financial statements as a whole. While IAS 1 provides the titles for the primary financial statements as outlined in 2.1.10.10, those titles are not mandatory. Throughout this publication we use the titles provided in IAS 1 for each primary statement.

IAS 1.11   2.1.10.25 All financial statements within a complete set of financial statements are presented with equal prominence.

2.1.10.30 While IFRSs specify minimum disclosures to be made in the financial statements, they do not prescribe specific formats to be followed. In our experience, entities consider the presentation adopted by other entities in the same industry or country.

IAS 1.13, 54, 2.1.10.40 Although a number of disclosures are made in the primary financial
55, 82-85 statements, generally IFRSs allow significant flexibility in presenting additional line items and subtotals when necessary to ensure a fair presentation (see 4.1). In addition to the information required to be disclosed in the financial statements, many entities provide additional information outside of the financial statements, either voluntarily or because of local regulations or stock exchange requirements (see 5.8).

IAS 1.113, 2.1.10.50 Notes to the financial statements are presented in a systematic order and are
114(a)-(d), cross-referenced from items in the primary financial statements. Notes generally are
117 presented in the following order:

- a statement of compliance with IFRSs;
- the basis of preparation and the significant accounting policies applied;
- supporting information for items presented in the primary financial statements, in the order in which each statement and each line item is presented; and
- other disclosures, including contingencies, commitments and non-financial disclosures.

2.1.10.60 However, in some circumstances it may be appropriate to vary the order of specific items within the notes. For example, tax items in the statement of comprehensive income and the statement of financial position might be presented together, or an entity might combine information on changes in fair value recognised in profit or loss (disclosure related to the statement of comprehensive income) with information on the maturities of financial instruments (disclosure related to the statement of financial position). Nevertheless, an entity should have a systematic structure for the notes.

2.1.20 Reporting period

IAS 1.10, 2.1.20.05 A complete set of financial statements is presented for the period ending on the
IN11 date of the statement of financial position. Both of the terms "balance sheet date" and "reporting date" were replaced in IFRSs by the term "the end of the reporting period" by IAS 1. We use the terms "reporting date" and "the end of the reporting period" interchangeably.

IAS 1.36 2.1.20.10 The end of the annual reporting period may change only in exceptional circumstances, e.g. following a change of major shareholder or due to regulatory or taxation requirements. If the end of the annual reporting period does change, then the financial statements for that period will cover either more or less than 12 months, in which case disclosure of that fact is required. In such cases, comparative information is not adjusted. However, *pro forma* information for the comparable preceding reporting period might be presented (see 2.1.80).

2.1.20.15 IFRSs are silent on the approach to take when a subsidiary changes the end of its annual reporting period in order to align it with that of the parent. In our view,

25

the consolidated financial statements should include the results of the subsidiary from the end of its last reporting period to the end of its new reporting period. Therefore, the subsidiary's results included in the consolidated financial statements might cover a period of either more or less than 12 months (see 2.5.290.30).

2.1.30 Comparative information

IAS 1.38   2.1.30.10 Comparative information is required for the immediately preceding period. Unless there is a specific exemption provided in an IFRS, an entity discloses comparative information in respect of the previous period for all amounts reported in the current period's financial statements. Generally the previous period's related narrative and descriptive information is required only when relevant for an understanding of the current period's financial statements. For example, comparative segment information would be disclosed.

2.1.30.20 No particular format is required for the presentation of comparatives. In our experience, most entities reporting under IFRSs provide comparative information about the immediately preceding period alongside that for the current period.

2.1.30.30 More extensive comparatives may be presented voluntarily or to meet regulatory or stock exchange requirements. However, any additional comparatives included in the financial statements need not comply with IFRSs provided that those comparatives are labelled clearly and explanatory disclosures are included.

2.1.30.40 When an entity is adopting IFRSs for the first time, the comparatives required by IFRSs are prepared in accordance with IFRSs (see 6.1.30.120).

2.1.35 *Presentation of a third statement of financial position and related notes*

IAS 1.10, 39   2.1.35.10 An additional statement of financial position is presented as at the beginning of the earliest comparative period following a change in accounting policy, the correction of an error or the reclassification of items in the financial statements.

2.1.35.20 It is unclear from IAS 1 how the requirement addressed in 2.1.35.10 should be interpreted in certain circumstances. For example, the adoption of IFRS 8 *Operating Segments* is a change in accounting policy that does not affect the statement of financial position; the issue then arises as to whether the adoption of IFRS 8 means that a third statement of financial position should be presented in the year in which it is adopted.

IAS 1.39, 60,   2.1.35.30 In our view, the requirement to present a third statement of financial position
19.118   should be interpreted having regard to materiality based on the particular facts and circumstances (see 1.2.80.10). In other words, a third statement of financial position would be required when there is a material impact on the statement of financial position at the beginning of the earliest comparative period. Therefore, we believe for example, that the reclassification of expenses in the statement of comprehensive income might not require a third statement of financial position to be presented. However, if an entity decided to split its obligation for post-employment benefits into separate current and non-current

components in the statement of financial position, previously having presented the entire amount as non-current as allowed by IAS 19 *Employee Benefits*, then we believe that a third statement of financial position generally would be required. If there has been a change in accounting policy, the correction of an error or the reclassification of items in the financial statements, but a third statement of financial position is not presented on the basis that it is judged to be not material, then we recommend considering whether this fact should be disclosed. See 6.1 for the requirement to present a third statement of financial position and related notes for first-time adopters.

IFRS 6.13, 2.1.35.40 IAS 1 requires the presentation of related notes when a third statement of *IAS 1.39* financial position is presented. In our view, this requirement should be interpreted as requiring disclosure of those notes that are relevant to the reason why the third statement of financial position is presented, i.e. not all notes related to the third statement of financial position are required in every circumstance. For example, in 2010 an entity with a calendar reporting date makes a voluntary change in its accounting policy to capitalise certain exploration and evaluation (E&E) expenditures as allowed by IFRS 6 *Exploration for and Evaluation of Mineral Resources*; previously all such expenditures had been expensed as incurred. In this circumstance, we believe that the entity should present a third statement of financial position as of 1 January 2009 together with all notes affected by the capitalisation of the E&E expenditures.

2.1.40 Types of financial statements

2.1.40.10 IFRSs set out the requirements that apply to three distinct types of financial statements: consolidated financial statements, individual financial statements and separate financial statements. Most, but not all, recognition, measurement, presentation and disclosure requirements apply to all three types of financial statements.

2.1.40.20 It is the reporting entity's interests in subsidiaries, associates and jointly controlled entities that, subject to certain exemptions, determine which type of financial statements the entity is required to prepare.

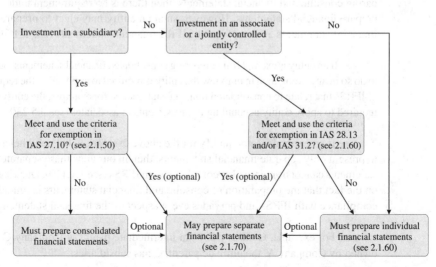

2.1.50 **Consolidated financial statements**

IAS 27.4   2.1.50.10 Consolidated financial statements are financial statements of a parent and its subsidiaries presented as a single economic entity.

IAS 27.9, 28.13, 31.28, 30   2.1.50.20 In consolidated financial statements, subsidiaries are consolidated (see 2.5). Unless they are held for sale (see 5.4.20), investments in associates are equity accounted and jointly controlled entities are either proportionately consolidated or equity accounted (see 3.5.230).

IAS 27.10   2.1.50.30 An entity with an investment in a subsidiary is exempt from preparing consolidated financial statements only if all of the following criteria are met:

- the parent is itself a wholly-owned subsidiary, or is a partially-owned subsidiary and its other owners (including those not otherwise entitled to vote) have been informed about, and do not object to, the parent not presenting consolidated financial statements;
- the parent's debt or equity instruments are not traded in a public market, including stock exchanges and over-the-counter markets;
- the parent did not file, and is not in the process of filing, its financial statements with a regulatory organisation for the purpose of issuing any class of instruments in a public market; and
- the ultimate or any intermediate parent of the parent produces consolidated financial statements that comply with IFRSs and are available for public use.

2.1.50.40 An entity that prepares consolidated financial statements (i.e. it does not meet and use the criteria in 2.1.50.30 for exemption) may elect to prepare separate financial statements in addition to its consolidated financial statements (see 2.1.70).

IAS 27.8   2.1.50.50 In our view, if an entity meets and uses the criteria for exemption from preparing consolidated financial statements, then there is no requirement under IFRSs to prepare financial statements. However, such an entity may elect to prepare separate financial statements as its only set of IFRS financial statements (see 2.1.70).

2.1.50.55 If an entity is exempt from preparing consolidated financial statements, but chooses to do so in any event, then in our view the entity is required to apply all of the requirements of IFRSs that relate to consolidated financial statements; for example, the entity would be required to apply equity accounting to investments in associates (see 3.5.230).

2.1.50.60 If an entity does not qualify for the above exemption, but nonetheless decides to present only separate financial statements, then in our view these separate financial statements cannot be regarded as complying with IFRSs (see 1.1.110). Our view is based on the fact that the preparation of consolidated financial statements is fundamental to compliance with IFRSs and pervades every aspect of the financial statements.

2.1.50.70 For example, Company B is an intermediate parent of Company C, and B is owned by Company A, the ultimate parent. C has subsidiaries.

2.1.50.80 C is not required to prepare consolidated financial statements when the following conditions are met:

- either A or B prepares consolidated financial statements in accordance with IFRSs and those consolidated financial statements are available to the users of the financial statements of C;
- C's debt or equity instruments are not traded in a public market, including stock exchanges and over-the-counter markets; and
- C did not file, and is not in the process of filing, its financial statements with a regulatory organisation for the purpose of issuing any class of instruments in a public market.

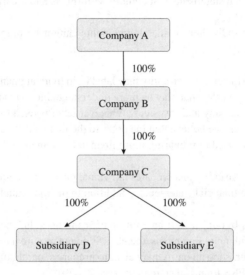

2.1.50.90 In our view, if an entity disposes of its last subsidiary during the current reporting period, then consolidated financial statements are not required to be prepared as the entity is no longer a parent at the end of the reporting period. In such cases we believe that the financial statements, including comparatives, should be presented as unconsolidated financial statements (i.e. individual or separate financial statements as appropriate (see 2.1.60 and 70 respectively)) unless the consolidated financial statements are required by a regulator. However, the entity may wish to present supplementary information on a consolidated basis (see 5.8).

2.1.60 Individual financial statements

IAS 28.13, 31.2 2.1.60.10 An entity that has no subsidiaries, but which has an investment in an associate and/or a jointly controlled entity, prepares individual financial statements, in which such investments are accounted for using the equity method, unless either of the following criteria is met:

- All such interests are classified as held for sale in accordance with IFRS 5 *Non-current Assets Held for Sale and Discontinued Operations* (see 5.4.20).

29

- All of the following criteria are satisfied:
    - the investor is a wholly-owned subsidiary, or is a partially-owned subsidiary and its other owners (including those not otherwise entitled to vote) have been informed and they do not object to the investor not applying the equity method;
    - the investor's debt or equity instruments are not traded in a public market, including a stock exchange or an over-the-counter market;
    - the investor did not file, nor is it in the process of filing, its financial statements with a regulatory organisation for the purpose of issuing any class of instruments in a public market; and
    - the ultimate or any intermediate parent of the investor produces consolidated financial statements that comply with IFRSs and are available for public use.

2.1.60.20 Individual financial statements cannot be prepared by an entity that has a subsidiary.

2.1.60.30 In our view, an entity may label its individual financial statements as such, or use alternative titles that may be more understandable to readers, e.g. financial statements of the company and investees. Whatever label is used to identify individual financial statements, we believe that the notes to the financial statements should explain clearly the basis used in preparing those financial statements.

2.1.60.40 An entity that prepares individual financial statements also may elect to prepare separate financial statements in addition to the individual financial statements.

2.1.60.50 In our view, if an entity meets and uses the exemption from preparing individual financial statements, then IFRSs do not require it to prepare financial statements. However, such an entity may elect to prepare separate financial statements as its only set of IFRS financial statements (see 2.1.70).

2.1.70 Separate financial statements

IAS 27.6, 8, 37, 28.4, 5, 31.5, 6   2.1.70.10 An entity that is not required to prepare consolidated financial statements (see 2.1.50.30) or individual financial statements (see 2.1.60.10) may prepare separate financial statements (see 3.5.810). Alternatively, separate financial statements may be prepared in addition to consolidated or individual financial statements. In separate financial statements interests in subsidiaries, associates and jointly controlled entities are accounted for at cost or as financial assets, unless they are classified as held for sale (see 5.4.20).

2.1.70.20 Separate financial statements prepared voluntarily by an entity that does not have an investment in a subsidiary, associate or a jointly controlled entity follow the same recognition and measurement requirements as the individual financial statements, and therefore could be considered to be both the separate and individual financial statements of the entity.

2.1.70.30 IFRSs do not contain a requirement to prepare separate financial statements; however, an entity may elect, or be required by local regulations, to prepare such statements.

2.1.70.35 IFRSs do not preclude an entity from including both consolidated and separate financial statements within the same report. If an entity chooses to do so, then there is no required format or order in which the financial statements should be presented. However, the information presented should be identified clearly as related to either the separate or consolidated financial statements.

2.1.70.40 If an entity prepares separate financial statements in accordance with IFRSs, then all relevant IFRSs apply equally to those separate financial statements (see 1.1.110).

IAS 27.43   2.1.70.50 All separate financial statements disclose:

- the fact that the financial statements are separate financial statements;
- a list of significant investments in subsidiaries, jointly controlled entities and associates, including the name, country of incorporation or residence, proportion of ownership interest and, if different, the proportion of voting power held; and
- a description of the method used to account for these investments.

IAS 27.42   2.1.70.60 Separate financial statements of a parent that meets and uses the criteria for exemption from preparing consolidated financial statements disclose in addition to requirements in 2.1.70.50:

- the fact that the exemption from consolidation has been used;
- the name and country of incorporation or residence of the entity whose consolidated financial statements that comply with IFRSs have been produced for public use; and
- the address at which those consolidated financial statements are obtainable.

IAS 27.43   2.1.70.70 Separate financial statements of an entity that is not exempt from preparing consolidated or individual financial statements (see 2.1.50.30 and 2.1.60.10) disclose the reason for preparing them if it is not required by law, and identify the related consolidated or individual financial statements.

2.1.80 Presentation of *pro forma* information

IFRS 3.   2.1.80.10 IFRSs generally are silent on the presentation of *pro forma* information within
B64(q)   the financial statements, with the exception of the requirement in IFRS 3 *Business Combinations* to present, following a business combination, revenue and profit or loss of the combined entity determined as if the acquisition had been effected at the beginning of the period.

2.1.80.20 In some cases an entity may wish to present *pro forma* information that is not required by IFRSs, for example *pro forma* comparative financial statements following a change in the end of its reporting period (see 2.1.20.10) or a *pro forma* statement of comprehensive income following significant changes in the composition of the entity. In our view, such additional information generally is acceptable to the extent that it is allowed by local regulations and relevant stock exchange rules, and provided that:

- the information is labelled clearly to distinguish it from the financial statements prepared in accordance with IFRSs and is marked clearly as unaudited if that is the case;
- the entity discloses the transaction or event that is reflected in the *pro forma* financial information, the source of the financial information on which it is based, the significant assumptions used in developing the *pro forma* adjustments, and any significant uncertainties about those adjustments; and
- the presentation indicates that the *pro forma* financial information should be read in conjunction with the financial statements and that the *pro forma* financial information is not necessarily indicative of the results that would have been attained if, for example, the transaction or event had taken place at a different date.

2.1.90 **Future developments**

2.1.90.10 In May 2010 the IASB published ED/2010/5 *Presentation of Items of Other Comprehensive Income – Proposed Amendments to IAS 1*, which proposes to:

- change the title of the statement of comprehensive income to statement of profit or loss and other comprehensive income; however, an entity is still allowed to use other titles;
- present comprehensive income and its components in a single statement of profit or loss and other comprehensive income, with items of other comprehensive income presented in a separate section from profit or loss within that statement, thereby eliminating the alternative permitted by current IAS 1 to present a separate income statement; and
- present separately the items of other comprehensive income that would be reclassified to profit or loss in the future from those that would never be reclassified to profit or loss.

2.1.90.20 The final amendments are scheduled for the fourth quarter of 2010.

2.1.90.30 The overall objective of the comprehensive financial statement presentation project is to establish a global standard that prescribes the basis for presentation of financial statements of an entity that are consistent over time, and that promote comparability between entities. The financial statement presentation project is conducted in three phases:

- Phase A was completed in September 2007 with the release of a revised IAS 1;
- Phase B is in progress and addresses the more fundamental issues related to financial statement presentation; and
- Phase C has not been initiated, but is expected to address issues related to interim financial statements.

2.1.90.40 In July 2010 the IASB posted a staff draft of a proposed ED reflecting tentative decisions made to date in respect of phase B to obtain further stakeholder feedback. An ED is scheduled for the first quarter of 2011.

2.2 Changes in equity
(IAS 1)

2.2 Changes in equity

(IAS 1)

Overview of currently effective requirements

- **An entity presents a statement of changes in equity as part of a complete set of financial statements.**

- **All owner-related changes in equity are presented in the statement of changes in equity, separately from non-owner changes in equity.**

Currently effective requirements

This publication reflects IFRSs in issue at 1 August 2010. The currently effective requirements cover annual periods beginning on 1 January 2010. The requirements related to this topic are derived mainly from IAS 1 *Presentation of Financial Statements*.

Forthcoming requirements and future developments

When a currently effective requirement will be changed by a new requirement that is issued but is not yet effective, it is marked with a # as a **forthcoming requirement** and the impact of the change is explained in the accompanying boxed text. The forthcoming requirements related to this topic are derived from the *Improvements to IFRSs 2010*. A brief outline of the impact of the *Improvements to IFRSs 2010* on this topic is given in 2.2.45, and a brief outline of the annual improvements process is given in 1.1.85.

When a significant change to the currently effective or forthcoming requirements is expected, it is marked with a * as an area that may be subject to **future developments** and a brief outline of the relevant project is given in 2.2.80.

2.2.10 – 30 [Not used]

2.2.40 Statement of changes in equity#*

IAS 1.106 2.2.40.10 A statement of changes in equity includes:

- total comprehensive income for the period, separately showing the total amounts attributable to owners of the parent and to non-controlling interests;
- for each component of equity, the effects of retrospective application or retrospective restatement recognised in accordance with IAS 8 *Accounting Policies, Changes in Accounting Estimates and Errors*;
- for each component of equity, a reconciliation between the carrying amount at the beginning and at the end of the period, separately disclosing each change resulting from:
  - profit or loss;
  - each item of other comprehensive income; and

     –   transactions with owners in their capacity as owners, showing separately contributions by and distributions to owners and changes in ownership interests in subsidiaries that do not result in a loss of control.

2.2.40.20 [Not used]

IAS 1.106,   2.2.40.30 In our view, the analysis of changes in equity attributable to each item of
IG6   other comprehensive income for the period may be presented either in the statement of changes in equity or in the notes.

IAS 1.107   2.2.40.40 IAS 1 requires all owner-related changes in equity to be presented in the statement of changes in equity, separately from non-owner changes in equity. As such, dividends and the related per-share amounts are disclosed either in the statement of changes in equity or in the notes to the financial statements. Such disclosures are not included in the statement of comprehensive income (see 4.1.190).

2.2.45 *Forthcoming requirements*

2.2.45.10 In the *Improvements to IFRSs 2010* the Board amended IAS 1 to state that for each component of equity a reconciliation from opening to closing balances is required to be presented in the statement of changes in equity. That reconciliation is required to show separately changes arising from items recognised in profit or loss, in other comprehensive income and from transactions with owners acting in their capacity as owners. Disaggregation of changes in each component of equity arising from transactions recognised in other comprehensive income also is required to be presented, but is permitted to be presented either in the statement of changes in equity or in the notes. This amendment is effective for annual periods beginning on or after 1 January 2011; early application is permitted.

2.2.50 – 60 [Not used]

2.2.70 *Changes in accounting policies and errors*

IAS 1.106(b),   2.2.70.10 A change in accounting policy or the correction of a prior period material
110   error generally is presented by adjusting the opening balance of each component of equity of the earliest period presented, and revising comparatives (see 2.8).

IAS 1.10(f)   2.2.70.20 In addition, a statement of financial position as at the beginning of the earliest comparative period is presented following a change in accounting policy, the correction of an error or the reclassification of items in the financial statements (see 2.1.35).

2.2.80 Future developments

2.2.80.10 The overall objective of the comprehensive financial statement presentation project is to establish a global standard that prescribes the basis for presentation of financial statements of an entity that are consistent over time, and that promote comparability between entities. The financial statement presentation project is conducted in three phases:

- Phase A was completed in September 2007 with the release of a revised IAS 1;
- Phase B is in progress and addresses the more fundamental issues related to financial statement presentation; and
- Phase C has not been initiated, but is expected to address issues related to interim financial statements.

2.2.80.20 In July 2010 the IASB posted a staff draft of a proposed ED reflecting tentative decisions made to date in respect of phase B to obtain further stakeholder feedback. An ED is scheduled for the first quarter of 2011.

2.3 Statement of cash flows
(IAS 7)

2.3 Statement of cash flows

(IAS 7)

Overview of currently effective requirements

- The statement of cash flows presents cash flows during the period classified by operating, investing and financing activities.

- Net cash flows from all three categories are totalled to show the change in cash and cash equivalents during the period, which then is used to reconcile opening and closing cash and cash equivalents.

- Cash and cash equivalents includes certain short-term investments and, in some cases, bank overdrafts.

- Cash flows from operating activities may be presented using either the direct method or the indirect method.

- Foreign currency cash flows are translated at the exchange rates at the dates of the cash flows (or using averages when appropriate).

- Generally all financing and investing cash flows are reported gross. Cash flows are offset only in limited circumstances.

Currently effective requirements

This publication reflects IFRSs in issue at 1 August 2010. The currently effective requirements cover annual periods beginning on 1 January 2010. The requirements related to this topic are derived mainly from IAS 7 *Statement of Cash Flows*.

Forthcoming requirements and future developments

When a currently effective requirement will be changed by a new requirement that is issued but is not yet effective, it is marked with a # as a **forthcoming requirement** and the impact of the change is explained in the accompanying boxed text. In respect of this topic no forthcoming requirements are noted.

When a significant change to the currently effective or forthcoming requirements is expected, it is marked with a * as an area that may be subject to **future developments** and a brief outline of the relevant project is given in 2.3.130.

2.3.10 Cash and cash equivalents

IAS 7.6 2.3.10.10 Cash comprises cash on hand and demand deposits. Cash equivalents are short-term highly liquid investments that are readily convertible to known amounts of cash and that are subject to an insignificant risk of changes in value.

2.3.10.20 Demand deposits are not defined in IFRSs, but in our view they should have the same level of liquidity as cash, and therefore should be able to be withdrawn at any time without penalty. In addition, in our view demand deposits need not be held with a financial institution; for example, monies held by solicitors for clients in separate and designated accounts could be considered demand deposits as long as they are not restricted. Even if a deposit fails to be classified as cash it still may meet the definition of cash equivalents.

IAS 7.7 2.3.10.30 Since the investments comprising cash equivalents must be readily convertible to known amounts of cash, in our view only debt securities and deposits can qualify for inclusion, subject to the other criteria being met. "Short-term" is not defined, but the standard encourages a cut-off of three months' maturity from the acquisition date. In our view, three months should be used as an absolute cut-off, and debt securities with a longer maturity should be regarded as part of investing activities.

IU 05-09 2.3.10.35 In our view, an investment that is redeemable at any time could be considered a cash equivalent but only if the amount of cash that would be received is known at the time of the initial investment, is subject to an insignificant risk of changes in value, and the other IAS 7 criteria for cash equivalents are met. The fact that an investment can be converted at the market price at any time does not mean that the "readily convertible to known amounts of cash" criterion has been met.

IAS 7.7 2.3.10.40 Investments with a longer maturity at acquisition do not become cash equivalents once their remaining maturity period falls to three months.

IAS 7.7 2.3.10.50 In practice much emphasis is placed on the above definitions. However, an overriding test is that cash equivalents are held for the purpose of meeting short-term cash commitments rather than for investment or other purposes. For example, an entity gives a three-month loan to a customer to assist the customer in managing its short-term liquidity position; in our view this loan is not a cash equivalent because it was given for a purpose other than for the entity to manage its own short-term cash commitments.

IAS 7.8, 32.42 2.3.10.60 Bank overdrafts repayable on demand are included as cash and cash equivalents to the extent that they form an integral part of the entity's cash management. However, even though a bank overdraft might be netted against cash and cash equivalents for purposes of the statement of cash flows, this is not permitted in the statement of financial position unless the offsetting criteria are met (see 3.1.50 and 5.6.490).

IAS 7.45 2.3.10.70 A reconciliation of cash and cash equivalents in the statement of cash flows to the equivalent amount presented in the statement of financial position is disclosed, and may be included in the notes to the financial statements.

2.3.20 Operating, investing and financing activities

IAS 7.6, 10 2.3.20.10 The statement of cash flows presents cash flows during the period classified by operating, investing and financing activities:

- Operating activities are the principal revenue-producing activities of the entity and other activities that are not investing or financing activities.
- Investing activities relate to the acquisition and disposal of long-term assets and other investments not included in cash equivalents.
- Financing activities relate to shareholders' equity and borrowings of the entity.

2.3.20.11 The wording of the definitions means that operating activities is the default classification when a cash flow does not meet the definition of either investing or financing cash flows.

IFRS 6.24, IAS 7.11, 16, 8.10 2.3.20.13 An entity presents its cash flows in the manner most appropriate to its business. For example, IFRS 6 *Exploration for and Evaluation of Mineral Resources* allows entities in the extractive industries to choose an accounting policy, to be applied consistently, in respect of qualifying E&E expenditure; such expenditure may be either capitalised as an asset or expensed as incurred (see 5.11.30). However, if such expenditure is capitalised, then the related cash flows are classified as investing activities, as only expenditures that result in the recognition of an asset can be classified as investing activities. If such expenditure is expensed, then the related cash flows are classified as operating activities in the statement of cash flows.

2.3.20.15 In our view, in the consolidated financial statements transaction costs associated with a business combination, although ancillary to the assets acquired, are classified as operating activities since the transaction costs are not capitalised.

2.3.20.17 – 19 [Not used]

IAS 7.12 2.3.20.20 The separate components of a single transaction each should be classified as operating, investing or financing; IFRSs do not allow a transaction to be classified based on its predominant characteristic. For example, a loan repayment comprises interest (which may be classified as operating or financing (see 2.3.50.20)) and principal repayment (which is classified as financing).

IAS 7.39-42 2.3.20.30 However, the aggregate net cash flows from obtaining and losing control of subsidiaries and other businesses are presented separately as a single line item as part of investing activities. For example, when a subsidiary is acquired, a single line item equal to the consideration paid by cash and cash equivalents, less any cash and cash equivalents held by the subsidiary at the time of acquisition, is shown as an investing cash outflow, rather than as separate cash outflows and inflows for the various net assets and liabilities acquired.

IAS 7.42A 2.3.20.35 A subsequent purchase of an additional interest or a sale by a parent of a subsidiary's equity instruments that does not result in a loss of control is classified as cash flows from financing activities because such changes in ownership interests are accounted for as transactions with equity holders (see 2.3.20.10 and 2.5.385.10).

IAS 7.43, 44 2.3.20.40 Non-cash investing or financing transactions (e.g. shares issued as consideration in a business combination, acquisition of assets via a finance lease) are not included in the statement of cash flows, but are disclosed in order to provide relevant information about investing and financing activities.

2.3.30 Direct vs indirect method*

IAS 7.18-20   2.3.30.10 Cash flows from operating activities may be presented either by the direct method (receipts from customers, payments to suppliers etc.) or by the indirect method (profit or loss for the period reconciled to the total net cash flow from operating activities). Although the standard encourages use of the direct method, in our experience the indirect method usually is used.

IAS 7.18, 20,   2.3.30.20 For an entity that elects to present operating cash flows using the indirect method,
A   often there is confusion about the correct starting point: should it be profit or loss (i.e. the final figure in the statement of comprehensive income) or can a different figure, such as profit before income tax, be used? The standard itself refers to profit or loss, but the example provided in the appendix to the standard starts with a different figure (i.e. profit before taxation). We prefer to follow the standard since the appendix is illustrative only and therefore does not have the same status as the standard (see 1.1.90.20).

IAS 7.20, A   2.3.30.30 Alternatively, an entity using the indirect method may choose to present its operating cash flows by showing revenues and expenses before working capital changes as the starting point, followed by changes during the period in inventories, and operating receivables and payables. However, in our experience, this approach is less common.

2.3.40 Classification issues

2.3.50 *Interest, dividends and taxes*

IAS 7.31-36   2.3.50.10 IFRSs require cash flows from interest and dividends received and paid, and income taxes paid, to be disclosed separately. In our view, this means that disclosure is required in the statement of cash flows rather than in the notes.

IAS 7.31-36   2.3.50.20 The standard does not, however, specify the classification of such cash flows, and an entity is required to choose its own policy for classifying each of interest and dividends paid as operating or financing activities and each of interest and dividends received as operating or investing activities. The presentation is selected to present these cash flows in a manner that is most appropriate for the business or industry (e.g. banking), if applicable, and the method selected is applied consistently. Taxes paid are classified as operating activities unless it is practicable to identify them with, and therefore classify them as, financing or investing activities.

2.3.50.30 With regard to the presentation of taxes paid, if an entity wants to classify certain taxes as investing or financing activities, then the standard is not clear as to whether *all* taxes paid must be allocated among the three categories of cash flows, or whether it is acceptable to allocate only certain taxes paid because they relate to transactions classified as investing or financing, leaving the balance in operating activities. In our view, it is acceptable to allocate only certain material tax cash flows, while leaving the balance in operating activities, as long as the approach taken is applied consistently and disclosed appropriately. We believe that allocating, for example, 60 percent of the tax cash flows as it represents the material tax cash flows known to be from investing or financing activities, with appropriate disclosure, provides better information than not allocating any.

IAS 7.12, 32   2.3.50.40 In our view, to the extent that borrowing costs are capitalised in respect of qualifying assets (see 4.6.350), the cost of acquiring those assets should be split in the statement of cash flows. For example, an entity constructs an asset and pays construction expenses of 1,000, which includes 50 of capitalised interest. In such circumstances, the interest paid of 50 will be included in operating or financing activities (depending on the entity's accounting policy for presenting interest paid in the statement of cash flows), and the remaining 950 will be included in investing activities. This is consistent with the requirement to classify separately the different components of a single transaction (see 2.3.20.20).

2.3.55 *Assets held for rental and subsequently held for sale*

IAS 7.14,   2.3.55.10 Generally cash flows related to the acquisition of an asset recognised in
16.68A   accordance with IAS 16 *Property Plant and Equipment* are cash flows from investing activities (see 2.3.20.10). However, cash payments to manufacture or acquire assets held for rental, which subsequently become held for sale (i.e. transferred to inventory) are cash flows from operating activities (see 3.2.440.37). Cash flows from rental payments and subsequent sales of these assets also are classified as operating.

2.3.60 *Hedging*

IAS 7.16   2.3.60.10 When a hedging instrument is accounted for as a hedge of an identifiable position (see 3.7), the cash flows of the hedging instrument are classified in the same manner as the cash flows of the position being hedged. See 5.6.270 for a discussion of the presentation of hedging instruments.

2.3.70 *Securitisation of receivables*

2.3.70.10 There is no specific guidance in IFRSs on presenting cash flows from securitisations, but in our view the classification of the proceeds from a securitisation of receivables should follow the underlying accounting (see 3.6.1310):

- If the receivables are not derecognised and the proceeds are recognised as a liability, then the proceeds should be classified as part of financing activities.
- If the receivables are derecognised, then we prefer that the proceeds are classified as part of operating activities even if the entity does not enter into such transactions regularly. This is because we believe that such proceeds do not fit clearly into the

definitions of either investing or financing activities (see 2.3.20); also, a securitisation resulting in derecognition is analogous to the early collection of amounts due from customers.

2.3.80 Foreign currency differences

IAS 7.25-28 2.3.80.10 Cash flows arising from an entity's foreign currency transactions are translated into the entity's functional currency (see 2.7.30) at the exchange rates at the dates of the cash flows; when exchange rates have been relatively stable, an appropriate average can be used. When the presentation currency is different from the functional currency, the functional currency cash flows are translated into the presentation currency at rates at the dates of the cash flows (or appropriate averages). For example, the functional currency cash flows of a foreign operation will need to be translated into the group presentation currency when preparing consolidated financial statements. The effect of exchange rate changes on the balances of cash and cash equivalents is presented as part of the reconciliation of movements therein.

2.3.90 *Cash held in a foreign currency*

2.3.90.10 The following example illustrates the calculation of the effect of exchange rate changes on the balances of cash and cash equivalents and its presentation in the statement of cash flows:

	Fx	Rate	Functional currency
Balance of cash held in foreign currency at 1 January 2010	100	1:1	100
Revenue	100	1.5:1	150
Expenses	(50)	1.6:1	(80)
Balance of cash held in foreign currency at 31 December 2010	150		170
Translated cash at the end of the reporting period	150	2:1	300
Gain on cash held in foreign currency			130

Statement of financial position

	Functional currency 2010	Functional currency 2009
Share capital	100	100
Retained earnings	200 (150 - 80 + 130)	-
	300	100
Cash	300	100

Statement of cash flows extract – direct method	
	2010
Receipts from customers (all receivables collected by the end of the reporting period)	150
Payments to suppliers (all invoices paid by the end of the reporting period)	(80)
Net increase in cash	70
Cash and cash equivalents at 1 January 2010	100
Effect of exchange rate fluctuations on cash held	130
Cash and cash equivalents at 31 December 2010	300

Statement of cash flows extract – indirect method	
	2010
Net profit	200
Unrealised foreign currency gain	(130)
Net increase in cash	70
Cash and cash equivalents at 1 January 2010	100
Effect of exchange rate fluctuations on cash held	130
Cash and cash equivalents at 31 December 2010	300

2.3.100 *Other foreign currency differences*

2.3.100.10 Assets and liabilities denominated in a foreign currency generally include an element of unrealised exchange differences at the end of the reporting period. We prefer that when applying the indirect method, the unrealised exchange difference should be presented as a single non-cash item within operating activities, rather than being left embedded in the asset or liability. The following example illustrates this point:

	Fx	*Rate*	*FC[1]*
Loan received during 2010 (converted to AC immediately)	250	1.5:1	375
Translate at the end of the reporting period	250	2:1	500

Statement of financial position (in AC)

	2010		2009
Share capital	100		100
Retained earnings	75	(200 - 125)	200
	175		300
Cash	675		300[1]
Loan	(500)		-
	175		300

Statement of cash flows extract – indirect method

	2010
Net loss	(125)
Unrealised foreign currency loss	125
Net cash from operating activities	-
Loan obtained (financing activities)	375
Net cash increase	375
Cash at 1 January 2010	300
Cash at 31 December 2010	675

Notes

(1) Cash on balance at the end of 2009 is held in its own functional currency (FC)

2.3.100.20 As there are no receipts from customers or payments to suppliers, net cash from operating activities also would be zero using the direct method.

2.3.110 Offsetting

IAS 7.21 2.3.110.10 Generally all financing and investing cash flows are reported gross.

2.3.110.20 For example, an entity obtains a loan of 2,000 during the reporting period and uses the proceeds to repay another loan of 2,000. The following should be presented as financing activities: proceeds from borrowings 2,000, and, separately, repayment of borrowings 2,000.

IAS 7.22, 23 2.3.110.25 Receipts and payments may be netted only when the items concerned, e.g. sale and purchase of investments, turn over quickly, the amounts are large, and the maturities are short; or when they are on behalf of customers and the cash flows reflect the activities of the customers.

IAS 7.24 2.3.110.30 In addition, a financial institution may report on a net basis certain advances, deposits and repayments thereof that form part of its operating activities. However, not all borrowings of a financial institution are part of operating activities; therefore the example in 2.3.110.20 in relation to financing activities applies equally to a financial institution.

2.3.110.40 In our view, if a group comprises a combination of financial institution and non-financial institution subsidiaries, then the offsetting requirements would apply separately to each subsidiary's cash flows as presented in the consolidated statement of cash flows.

2.3.120 Taxes collected on behalf of third parties

2.3.120.10 IAS 7 is silent on the classification of cash flows from taxes that are collected on behalf of third parties when the direct method is used to present cash flows from operating activities; examples include value added tax (VAT) and goods and services tax (GST).

2.3.120.20 In our view, taxes collected on behalf of third parties, when the direct method is used, may be either:

- included as separate line items to show the impact on cash flows of such taxes separately; or
- included in receipts from customers and payments to suppliers.

2.3.120.30 Although we prefer the first method in 2.3.120.20, in our experience generally these indirect taxes are included in receipts from customers and payments to suppliers as the impact on the statement of cash flows is generally immaterial (see 1.2.80).

2.3.120.40 The following example illustrates the alternatives:

Services rendered for cash during 2010 (excluding GST)	100	
GST paid to tax authorities	10	
GST payable to tax authorities (GST collected from customers is 20 of which 10 is paid and 10 remains outstanding to tax authorities)	10	

Statement of financial position		
	2010	*2009*
Share capital	100	100
Retained earnings	100	-
	200	100
Cash	210	100
GST payable	(10)	-
	200	100

Statement of cash flows extract – direct method option 1

	2010
Receipts from customers (all receivables collected by the end of the reporting period)	100
Indirect taxes collected	20
Indirect taxes paid	(10)
Net cash increase	110
Cash at 1 January 2010	100
Cash at 31 December 2010	210

Statement of cash flows extract – direct method option 2

	2010
Receipts from customers (all receivables collected by the end of the reporting period)	120
Payments to tax authorities (all invoices paid by the reporting period)	(10)
Net cash increase	110
Cash at 1 January 2010	100
Cash at 31 December 2010	210

Statement of cash flows extract – indirect method

	2010
Net profit	100
Increase in accounts payable	10
Net cash increase	110
Cash at 1 January 2010	100
Cash at 31 December 2010	210

2.3.125 Cash flow requirements of other standards

2.3.125.10 Other standards have certain cash flow disclosure requirements such as cash flows of discontinued operations (see 5.4.220.40 and 50) and cash flows arising from the exploration of mineral resources (see 5.11.165).

2.3.130 Future developments

2.3.130.10 The overall objective of the comprehensive financial statement presentation project is to establish a global standard that prescribes the basis for presentation of financial statements of an entity that are consistent over time, and that promote comparability between entities. The financial statement presentation project is conducted in three phases:

- Phase A was completed in September 2007 with the release of a revised IAS 1 *Financial Statement Presentation*;

- Phase B is in progress and addresses the more fundamental issues related to financial statement presentation; and
- Phase C has not been initiated, but is expected to address issues related to interim financial statements.

2.3.130.20 In July 2010 the IASB posted a staff draft of a proposed ED reflecting tentative decisions made to date in respect of phase B to obtain further stakeholder feedback. An ED is scheduled for the first quarter of 2011.

2.4   Basis of accounting
(IAS 1, IAS 21, IAS 29, IFRIC 7)

2.4 Basis of accounting
(IAS 1, IAS 21, IAS 29, IFRIC 7)

Overview of currently effective requirements

- **Financial statements are prepared on a modified historical cost basis with a growing emphasis on fair value.**

- **When an entity's functional currency is hyperinflationary, its financial statements should be adjusted to state all items in the measuring unit current at the reporting date.**

Currently effective requirements

This publication reflects IFRSs in issue at 1 August 2010. The currently effective require-ments cover annual periods beginning on 1 January 2010. The requirements related to this topic are derived mainly from IAS 1 *Presentation of Financial Statements*, IAS 21 *The Effects of Changes in Foreign Exchange Rates*, IAS 29 *Financial Reporting in Hyperinflationary Economies* and IFRIC 7 *Applying the Restatement Approach under IAS 29 Financial Reporting in Hyperinflationary Economies*.

Forthcoming requirements and future developments

When a currently effective requirement will be changed by a new requirement that is issued but is not yet effective, it is marked with a # as a **forthcoming requirement** and the impact of the change is explained in the accompanying boxed text. In respect of this topic no forthcoming requirements are noted.

The currently effective requirements may be subject to **future developments** and a brief outline of the relevant project is given in 2.4.190.

2.4.10 The modified historical cost convention

Glossary   2.4.10.10 IFRSs require financial statements to be prepared on a modified historical cost basis with a growing emphasis on fair value. Fair value is the amount for which an asset could be exchanged, or a liability settled, between knowledgeable, willing parties in an arm's length transaction. Issues associated with the determination of fair value are discussed throughout this publication in connection with the relevant asset or liability.

2.4.10.20 The following are examples of assets and liabilities whose carrying amounts are determined by reference to cost-based measurements subsequent to initial recognition (ignoring adjustments for impairment):

- property, plant and equipment and intangible assets that are not revalued (see 3.2 and 3.3);
- investment property that is not measured at fair value (see 3.4); and
- loans and receivables, held-to-maturity investments and financial liabilities other than those measured at fair value (see 3.6).

2.4.10.30 The carrying amounts of the following assets and liabilities are based on fair value measurements subsequent to initial recognition:

- All derivatives, all financial assets and financial liabilities held for trading or designated as at fair value through profit or loss, and all financial assets that are classified as available for sale are measured at fair value (see 3.6.790).
- Biological assets are measured at fair value less costs to sell (see 3.9.30).
- Whole classes of property, plant and equipment may be revalued to fair value subject to certain conditions (see 3.2.300).
- Certain intangible assets may be revalued to fair value (see 3.3.280).
- Investment property may be measured at fair value (see 3.4.140).

2.4.10.40 In addition, the following value-based measurements are an integral part of financial reporting under IFRSs:

- Recoverable amount, which is used in impairment testing for many assets (see 3.10.180), is the higher of an asset's value in use (estimated net future cash flows) and its fair value less costs to sell.
- Net realisable value (estimated selling price less costs of completion and disposal) is used as a ceiling test to avoid over-valuing inventory (see 3.8.110).
- Discounting is inherent in many IFRSs although the discount rate used varies. For example, defined benefit plans for employees are discounted using a corporate or government bond rate (see 4.4.300), whereas deferred payment related to the sale of goods may be discounted using either a market interest rate or a rate of interest that discounts the nominal amount payable to the current cash sales price (see 4.2.20).

2.4.15 Going concern

IAS 1.25, 26, 10.14 2.4.15.10 Financial statements are prepared on a going concern basis, unless management intends or has no alternative other than to liquidate the entity or stop trading. In assessing whether the going concern assumption is appropriate, management assesses all available information about the future for at least, but not limited to, 12 months from the reporting date. If the going concern assumption is not appropriate, then IFRSs are applied accordingly, with particular attention paid to the requirements of IFRS 5 *Non-current Assets Held for Sale and Discontinued Operations* (to the extent that assets are being held for sale and not abandoned), IAS 32 *Financial Instruments: Presentation* (with respect to the classification of the entity's debt and equity instruments), IAS 36 *Impairment of Assets* and IAS 37 *Provisions, Contingent Liabilities and Contingent Assets*. However, in our view there is no general dispensation from the measurement, recognition and disclosure requirements of IFRSs if the entity is not expected to continue as a going concern. In addition, if an entity ceases to be a going concern after its reporting date but before its financial statements are authorised for issue, then IAS 10 *Events after the Reporting Period* requires that it shall not prepare its financial statements on a going concern basis (see 2.9.20).

2.4.15.15 In the case of an entity in liquidation, all liabilities should continue to be recognised and measured in accordance with the applicable IFRS until the obligations are discharged, cancelled or expire. For example, Company C is in liquidation. If C has a financial liability in accordance with IAS 39 *Financial Instruments: Recognition and Measurement*, then this financial liability cannot be derecognised until the requirement of paragraph 39 of IAS 39 is met, i.e. the obligation specified in the related contract is discharged, cancelled or expires.

2.4.15.20 If a subsidiary is expected to be liquidated and its financial statements are prepared on a non-going concern basis, but the parent is expected to continue as a going concern, then in our view the consolidated financial statements should be prepared on a going concern basis. The subsidiary should continue to be consolidated until it is liquidated or otherwise disposed of, unless the exemption criteria in IAS 27 *Consolidated and Separate Financial Statements* are met (see 2.1.50).

2.4.20 Hyperinflation

IAS 21.43, 29.8   2.4.20.10 When an entity's functional currency (see 2.7.30) is hyperinflationary, its financial statements are adjusted to state all items in the measuring unit current at the reporting date (i.e. it should adopt the current purchasing power concept). Moreover, when an entity has foreign operations (e.g. a subsidiary, associate or jointly controlled entity) whose functional currency is hyperinflationary, the investee's financial statements should be adjusted before being translated and included in the investor's financial statements. Comparative amounts are excluded from the restatement requirement when the presentation currency of the ultimate financial statements into which they will be included is non-hyperinflationary (see 2.7.270).

2.4.30 *Indicators of hyperinflation*

IAS 29.3   2.4.30.10 Under IFRSs it is a matter of judgement as to when restatement for hyperinflation becomes necessary. Hyperinflation is indicated by the characteristics of an economy, which include but are not limited to the following:

- The general population prefers to keep its wealth in non-monetary assets or in a relatively stable foreign currency; amounts of local currency held are invested immediately to maintain purchasing power.
- The general population regards monetary amounts not in terms of the local currency but in terms of a relatively stable foreign currency; prices may be quoted in the stable currency.
- Sales and purchases on credit take place at prices that compensate for the expected loss of purchasing power during the credit period, even if the period is short.
- Interest rates, wages and prices are linked to a price index.
- The cumulative inflation rate over three years is approaching, or exceeds, 100 percent.

2.4.30.20 While the 100 percent numerical indicator is a key factor in identifying hyperinflation, it is not the only factor and should not be considered in isolation. Applying all of these factors could result in a country being considered hyperinflationary when its three-year cumulative inflation rate is, for example, only 80 percent.

IAS 29.4   2.4.30.30 While judgement is involved in determining the onset of hyperinflation in a particular case, a preference is stated in the standard for all affected entities to apply the standard from the same date.

2.4.30.40 Restatement for hyperinflation is not elective. For example, the standard cannot be adopted when an entity believes that the cumulative effects of inflation are significant and therefore that restatement would be helpful. In such cases the entity may consider presenting supplementary current cost information (see 5.8).

2.4.40 *Measuring the inflation rate*

2.4.50 *The appropriate price index*

2.4.50.10 For most countries there are two main indices that generally are used in measuring the general inflation rate: a consumer price index (CPI) and a producer or wholesale price index (PPI or WPI). The CPI measures the change in the cost of a fixed basket of products and services consumed by a "typical household", generally including housing, electricity, food and transportation. The PPI or WPI measures wholesale price levels.

IAS 29.37   2.4.50.20 IFRSs require the use of a general price index that reflects changes in *general* purchasing power. In addition, two of the indicators of hyperinflation refer to the *general* population rather than a specific sector. For these reasons, in our view the CPI is the most appropriate index to use in measuring the inflation rate, since it is a broad-based measurement across all consumers in an economy.

2.4.60 *The cumulative inflation rate*

IAS 29.3   2.4.60.10 IAS 29 refers to a cumulative inflation rate, but is silent as to whether the calculation should be done on a simple or compounded basis. In our view, a compounded inflation rate should be calculated because the simple rate aggregates three discrete results without viewing the three-year period itself on a cumulative basis.

2.4.60.20 For example, the inflation rate in three consecutive years is 20 percent, 30 percent and 40 percent respectively. The cumulative rate calculated on a simple basis is 90 percent (20 + 30 + 40). However, on a compounded basis the rate is 118 percent, which is calculated as follows:

- At the start of year one, assume the index to be 100.
- At the end of year one, the index is 120 (100 x 1.2).
- At the end of year two, the index is 156 (120 x 1.3).

- At the end of year three, the index is 218 (156 x 1.4), which gives a cumulative rate of 118 percent.

2.4.70 *No index available*

IAS 29.17   2.4.70.10 When there is no index available, the standard requires an index to be estimated; the example it provides is using an estimate based on exchange rate movements between the functional currency and a relatively stable foreign currency. Although the standard uses this example in the context of the restatement of property, plant and equipment, in our view this method could be used for the restatement of the entire financial statements in cases when no index is available. The same issue will arise when the official indices are considered unreliable, but this problem should be rare.

2.4.80 **Mechanics**

IAS 29.9   2.4.80.10 In adjusting for hyperinflation a general price index is applied to all non-monetary items in the financial statements (including equity) and the resulting gain or loss, which is the gain or loss on the entity's net monetary position, is recognised in profit or loss. The gain or loss is simply a multiplication exercise; the gain or loss on the net monetary position recognised in the comparative period is not recalculated.

2.4.80.20 The following example illustrates the process of restatement.

Index at the end of 2008	100	
Index at the end of 2009	150	
Index at the end of October 2010	180	
Index at the end of 2010	200	
Average index during 2010	175	
Statement of financial position before IAS 29 restatement		
	2010	*2009*
	Historical	*Historical*
	cost	*cost*
Share capital (contributed at the end of 2008)	100	100
Retained earnings	1,000	800
	1,100	900
Land (acquired at the end of 2009)	600	600
Investment securities held for trading	200	150
Inventories (acquired at the end of October 2010)	100	-
Trade receivables	500	200
Cash	100	350
Loan payable	(400)	(400)
Net assets	1,100	900

2.4 Basis of accounting

Statement of comprehensive income before IAS 29 restatement

	2010
Revenue	1,200
Expenses	(1,000)
	200

IAS 29.12 2.4.80.30 Items in the statement of financial position that are either money held or items to be received or paid in money (monetary items) are not restated because the carrying amount represents their value in terms of current purchasing power.

IAS 29.14, 2.4.80.40 All other items in the statement of financial position are non-monetary items;
15, 18 they include the components of equity (other than retained earnings) as well as items such as prepaid expenses and income received in advance. In general non-monetary items are restated from the acquisition or contribution date. However, if an asset or liability has been revalued, then it is restated only from the date of the valuation; if the item is stated at fair value at the reporting date, then no restatement is necessary.

IAS 29.24 2.4.80.50 Restated retained earnings is derived after all other amounts in the restated statement of financial position and profit or loss are calculated. Restated retained earnings should be split into net profit or loss, gain or loss on the net monetary position and other retained earnings. The schedule below illustrates these principles using the example in 2.4.80.20.

Statement of financial position

	2010 Historical	2010 Restatement	2010 Restated
Share capital	100	100	200[1]
Retained earnings	1,000	111[2]	1,111
Total equity	1,100	211	1,311
Land	600	200	800[3]
Investment securities held for trading	200		200
Inventories	100	11	111[4]
Trade receivable	500		500
Cash	100		100
Loan payable	(400)		(400)
Net assets	1,100	211	1,311

Notes
(1) Share capital contributed in 2008, calculated using 2008 index as 200 / 100 x 100
(2) Balancing figure
(3) Land purchased in 2009, calculated using 2009 index as 200 / 150 x 600
(4) Inventory purchased in October 2010, calculated using October 2010 index as 200 / 180 x 100

2.4.80.55 Following the principles illustrated above, the 2009 historical cost statement of financial position is restated as follows for presentation in the 2009 financial statements:

Statement of financial position

	2009 Historical	2009 Restatement	2009 Restated[1]
Share capital	100	50	150[2]
Retained earnings	800	(50)[3]	750
Total equity	900	-	900
Land	600	-	600[4]
Investment securities held for trading	150	-	150
Inventories (acquired at the end of October 2010)	-	-	-
Trade receivables	200	-	200
Cash	350	-	350
Loan payable	(400)	-	(400)
Net assets	900	-	900

Notes
(1) i.e. restated for the purposes of reporting in the 2009 financial statements
(2) Share capital contributed in 2008, calculated using 2008 and 2009 indexes as 150 / 100 x 100
(3) Balancing figure
(4) Land purchased at the end of 2009 is not adjusted

IAS 29.8, 34 2.4.80.60 In restating for the effects of hyperinflation, comparative information is restated so that it is expressed in the measuring unit current at the reporting date. In this example all assets and liabilities in the 2009 statement of financial position are divided by the index at the end of 2009 of 150 and multiplied by the index at the end of 2010 of 200.

Statement of financial position

	2009 Reported in prior period[1]	2009 Restated comparative[2]
Share capital (contributed at the end of 2008)	150	200
Retained earnings	750	1,000
	900	1,200
Land (acquired at the end of 2009)	600	800
Investment securities held for trading	150	200
Inventories (acquired at the end of October 2010)	-	-
Trade receivables	200	267
Cash	350	467
Loan payable	(400)	(534)
Net assets	900	1,200

> Notes
> (1) As included in the 2009 financial statements
> (2) As restated for inclusion as comparatives in the 2010 financial statements

IAS 29.26   2.4.80.70 Income and expenses recorded in the statement of comprehensive income are updated to reflect changes in the price index from the date that they are recorded initially in the financial statements. In this example an average index is applied. However, averages (i.e. annual, monthly etc.) can be applied only when the overall result is not materially different from the result that would be obtained by indexing individual items of income and expense based on the date at which the transaction took place.

Statement of comprehensive income

	2010 Historical	2010 Restatement	Restated
Revenue	1,200	171	1,371[1]
Expenses	(1,000)	(143)	(1,143)[2]
Net profit	200	28	228
Loss on net monetary position	-	(117)	(117)[3]
Total net profit/(loss)	200	(89)	111[4]

Notes
(1) Revenue calculated using average index for 2010 as 200 / 175 x 1,200
(2) Expenses calculated using average index for 2010 as 200 / 175 x 1,000
(3) Calculation of the loss on net monetary position is illustrated in 2.4.80.100
(4) Total net profit also can be calculated as a change in restated retained earnings (1,111 - 1,000)

IAS 29.9   2.4.80.80 Because the restatement of the financial statements involves only non-monetary items, it is not intuitive that the resulting gain or loss recognised in profit or loss actually relates to the monetary position (see example in 2.4.80.90).

2.4.80.90 For example, Company H is formed on 1 January 2010 and the shareholders contribute cash of 1,000. There are no transactions during 2010. At the end of the year the entity has share capital of 1,000, which is represented by cash. The index is 100 at 1 January, and 150 at 31 December. At the end of 2010 share capital is restated to 1,500 (150 / 100 x 1,000); the cash, being monetary, is not restated and a loss of 500 results. Superficially the 500 is a balancing number in the statement of financial position and results from the restatement of the non-monetary item (the share capital). However, it relates to the monetary position because the entity would need 1,500 of cash at 31 December in order to be in the same position as having 1,000 of cash at the start of the year, and a loss of 500 actually has occurred.

IAS 29.27   2.4.80.100 The loss on the net monetary position recognised in the 2010 financial statements in the example (beginning at 2.4.80.20) is determined as follows:

- For all items in the 2010 statement of financial position that originated in prior periods and were restated, compare the restated carrying amount to the prior period carrying amount.

- For transactions that occurred during 2010, compare the restated carrying amount to the amount at which the transaction originally was recorded.

Restated statement of financial position			
	Prior to restatement	*2010 Restated*	*Difference*
Share capital	150	200	(50)
Land	600	800	200
Opening retained earnings	750	1,000	(250)
Transactions during 2010			
Inventories	100	111	11
Revenues	1,200	1,371	(171)
Expenses	1,000	1,143	143
Loss on net monetary position			(117)

2.4.90 *First application of hyperinflationary accounting*

IFRIC 7.3   2.4.90.10 When an entity identifies that the economy of its functional currency is hyperinflationary, it applies IAS 29 retrospectively, as if the economy has always been hyperinflationary. Non-monetary assets and liabilities are restated for changes in prices from their dates of acquisition or incurrence (or revaluation, if applicable) until the closing date of the current reporting period.

2.4.90.20 IFRIC 7 provides guidance on the calculation of deferred tax in the opening statement of financial position of the first financial statements in which the functional currency is hyperinflationary. Deferred tax is calculated based on the nominal carrying amounts of non-monetary items under IAS 29 by applying the effect of inflation from the acquisition (or revaluation) date to the opening date of the current reporting period. Then to calculate the opening balances, deferred tax is remeasured by applying the effects of inflation from the opening date to the end of the reporting period. At the closing reporting date deferred taxes are calculated in accordance with IAS 12 *Income Taxes* (see 3.13).

IAS 21.42,   2.4.90.30 IAS 29 requires comparatives to be restated in the measuring unit current at
29.8   the reporting date (see 2.4.80.60). However, IAS 21 prohibits restatement of comparatives for the effects of inflation in the current period if the entity's presentation currency is that of a non-hyperinflationary economy (see 2.4.120.10 and 2.7.270.20). It is unclear whether on first application of hyperinflationary accounting the entity should restate its comparatives for price changes in prior periods if its presentation currency is that of a non-hyperinflationary economy. In our view, an entity should choose an accounting policy, to be applied consistently, as to whether it restates its comparatives in these cir-

cumstances. If an entity chooses not to restate its comparatives in these circumstances, then in our view the entity should recognise directly in equity the gain or loss on the net monetary position related to price changes in prior periods. This will ensure that the gain or loss on the net monetary position recognised in profit or loss in the current period is consistent with the amount that would have been recognised had the entity always applied restatement under IAS 29.

2.4.90.40 The example in 2.4.90.50 – 100 illustrates these alternative approaches.

2.4.90.50 Assume that Company M was incorporated on 1 January 2009 with a capital contribution of 300 in cash. On 1 January 2009, M purchased land for 200. M earned no income in 2009 and 2010. The consumer price index was as follows:

Index at the end of 2008	100
Index at the end of 2009	120
Index at the end of 2010	200

2.4.90.60 M's unrestated statements of financial positions would be as follows:

	2010	2009
Cash	100	100
Land	200	200
Capital	300	300

2.4.90.70 If M applies restatement under IAS 29 in 2010 for the first time, and its presentation currency is non-hyperinflationary, then, as discussed in 2.4.90.30, it will choose an accounting policy between the following methods.

2.4.95 Method 1: Comparatives are restated

	2010	2009
Statement of financial position		
Cash	100[1]	100[1]
Land	400[2]	240[3]
	500	340
Capital	600[2]	360[3]
Retained earnings	(100)[4]	(20)[4]
	500	340

64

Statement of comprehensive income

Loss on net monetary position	(80)[5]	(20)[5]

Notes

(1) Monetary item; not restated
(2) Restated for change in prices since acquisition until current reporting date: Historical cost x (200 / 100)
(3) Restated for change in prices since acquisition until comparative reporting date: Historical cost x (120 / 100)
(4) Balancing figure
(5) Loss recognised in profit or loss relates to changes in prices in the current reporting period and is calculated as follows:

Change in prices related to:		
Land	400 - 240 =	160
Capital	(600) - (360) =	(240)
Loss on net monetary position		(80)

2.4.100 Method 2: Comparatives are not restated

	2010	2009
Statement of financial position		
Cash	100[1]	100[2]
Land	400[3]	200[2]
	500	300
Capital	600[3]	300[2]
Retained earnings	(100)[4]	–[2]
	500	300
Statement of comprehensive income		
Loss on net monetary position	(80)[5]	–[2]

Notes

(1) Monetary item; not restated
(2) Comparatives; not restated
(3) Restated for change in prices since acquisition until current reporting date:
     Historical cost x (200 / 100)
(4) Balancing figure; including loss on net monetary position arising from changes in prices before current period recognised directly in equity
(5) Loss recognised in profit or loss is the same as under Method 1; relates to changes in prices in the current reporting period only

2.4.110 *Cessation of hyperinflationary accounting*

IAS 29.38 2.4.110.10 When an economy ceases to be hyperinflationary, an entity that discontinues preparing its financial statements in accordance with IAS 29 does so for annual periods ending on or after the date that the economy is identified as being non-hyperinflationary. Judgement is required in determining when the economy ceases to be hyperinflationary.

2.4.120 *Translation of comparative amounts in a presentation currency different from the functional currency*

IAS 21.42,
29.8

2.4.120.10 When the financial results or the position of an entity whose functional currency is that of a hyperinflationary economy are translated into a different presentation currency, this is done in accordance with IAS 21 (see 2.7.310). If the presentation currency is *not* the currency of a hyperinflationary economy, then the comparative amounts are not restated for either changes in the price level (i.e. as otherwise required by IAS 29), or changes in exchange rates. As such, the comparative amounts remain those amounts reported as current for the previous year. Conversely, when the presentation currency is that of a hyperinflationary economy, the comparative amounts will be restated in accordance with both IAS 29 and IAS 21.

2.4.130 *Supplementary historical cost information*

2.4.130.10 When restated financial statements are presented, in our view it is not appropriate to present additional supplementary financial information prepared on a historical cost basis.

2.4.130.20 Since money rapidly loses its purchasing power in a hyperinflationary economy, reporting an entity's financial position and operating results in the currency of a hyperinflationary economy without restatement would be meaningless to users; comparative figures also would have little or no value. Therefore the presentation of historical cost information in these cases may be misleading to users of the financial statements.

2.4.140 **Changing prices**

2.4.140.10 Entities whose functional currency is not hyperinflationary may choose to disclose certain information about the effects of changing prices on a current cost basis as supplementary information to its financial statements (see 5.8).

2.4.150 – 160 [not used]

2.4.170 **Judgement**

IAS 1.122

2.4.170.10 An entity should disclose judgements (other than estimates (see 2.4.180)) made by management in applying the entity's accounting policies. Disclosure is required of the judgements that have the most significant effect on the measurement of items recognised in the financial statements (e.g. whether risks and rewards have been transferred or whether a special purpose entity is controlled).

2.4.180 **Estimation**

IAS 1.125

2.4.180.10 An entity discloses the key assumptions about the future, and other major sources of estimation uncertainty at the reporting date, that have a significant risk of resulting in a material adjustment to the carrying amounts of assets and liabilities within the next financial year. The assumptions and other major sources of estimation uncertainty to be disclosed relate to the estimates that require management's most difficult, subjective or complex judgements. These disclosures are intended to help users understand these judgements.

2.4.190 **Future developments**

2.4.190.10 In May 2009 the IASB published ED/2009/5 *Fair Value Measurement* (the 2009 ED). The proposals in the 2009 ED are intended to replace the fair value measurement guidance contained in individual IFRSs with a single, unified definition of fair value, as well as provide further authoritative guidance on the application of fair value measurement in inactive markets. The 2009 ED proposes a framework for measuring fair value and disclosures about fair value measurements. The proposals in the 2009 ED explain how to measure fair value when it already is required or permitted by existing IFRSs; they do not introduce new fair value measurements, nor do they eliminate the practicability exceptions to fair value measurements that exist currently in certain standards.

2.4.190.20 In June 2010 the IASB published ED/2010/7 *Measurement Uncertainty Analysis Disclosure for Fair Value Measurements* (the 2010 ED). The 2010 ED expands on the proposal in the 2009 ED for an entity to disclose a measurement uncertainty analysis (or sensitivity analysis) for assets and liabilities measured at fair value categorised within Level 3 of the fair value hierarchy. The 2010 ED proposes that an entity consider the effect of correlation between unobservable inputs, if relevant.

2.4.190.30 A final standard on fair value measurement and disclosure, which is expected to be converged with a forthcoming amended standard under US GAAP, is scheduled for the first quarter of 2011.

2.5　Consolidation
(IAS 27, SIC-12)

2.5 Consolidation
(IAS 27, SIC-12)

Overview of currently effective requirements

- Consolidation is based on control, which is the power to govern, either directly or indirectly, the financial and operating policies of an entity so as to obtain benefits from its activities.

- The ability to control is considered separately from the exercise of that control.

- The assessment of control may be based on either a power-to-govern or a *de facto* control model.

- Potential voting rights that are currently exercisable are considered in assessing control.

- A special purpose entity (SPE) is an entity created to accomplish a narrow and well-defined objective. SPEs are consolidated based on control. The determination of control includes an analysis of the risks and benefits associated with an SPE.

- All subsidiaries are consolidated, including subsidiaries of venture capital organisations and unit trusts, and those acquired exclusively with a view to subsequent disposal.

- A parent and its subsidiaries generally use the same reporting date when consolidated financial statements are prepared. If this is impracticable, then the difference between the reporting date of a parent and its subsidiary cannot be more than three months. Adjustments are made for the effects of significant transactions and events between the two dates.

- Uniform accounting policies are used throughout the group.

- Non-controlling interests (NCI) are recognised initially at fair value or at their proportionate interest in the recognised amount of the identifiable net assets of the acquiree at the acquisition date.

- An entity recognises a liability for the present value of the (estimated) exercise price of put options held by NCI, but there is no detailed guidance on the accounting for such put options.

- Losses in a subsidiary may create a deficit balance in NCI.

- **NCI in the statement of financial position are classified as equity but are presented separately from the parent shareholders' equity.**

- **Profit or loss and comprehensive income for the period are allocated to NCI and owners of the parent.**

- **Intra-group transactions are eliminated in full.**

- **Upon the loss of control of a subsidiary, the assets and liabilities of the subsidiary and the carrying amount of the NCI are derecognised. The consideration received and any retained interest, measured at fair value, are recognised. Amounts recognised in other comprehensive income are reclassified as required by other IFRSs. Any resulting gain or loss is recognised in profit or loss.**

- **Changes in the parent's ownership interest in a subsidiary without a loss of control are accounted for as equity transactions and no gain or loss is recognised in profit or loss.**

Currently effective requirements

This publication reflects IFRSs in issue at 1 August 2010. The currently effective requirements cover annual periods beginning on 1 January 2010. The requirements related to this topic are derived mainly from IAS 27 *Consolidated and Separate Financial Statements* and SIC-12 *Consolidation – Special Purpose Entities*.

Forthcoming requirements and future developments

When a currently effective requirement will be changed by a new requirement that is issued but is not yet effective, it is marked with a # as a **forthcoming requirement** and the impact of the change is explained in the accompanying boxed text. The forthcoming requirements related to this topic are derived from the *Improvements to IFRSs 2010*. A brief outline of the impact of the *Improvements to IFRSs 2010* is given in 2.5.308.10, and a brief outline of the annual improvements process is given in 1.1.85.

When a significant change to the currently effective or forthcoming requirements is expected, it is marked with a * as an area that may be subject to **future developments** and a brief outline of the relevant project is given in 2.5.570.30. In addition, a brief outline is given in 2.5.570.10 – 20 of a project that may affect several aspects of consolidation accounting.

2.5.10 Entities included in the consolidated financial statements

IFRS 5.BC53-BC55, 2.5.10.10 Consolidated financial statements include all subsidiaries of the parent, without exception. See 2.1.50 for the requirement to prepare consolidated financial

IAS 27.12   statements. The guidance provided by IAS 27 also may be used for identifying an acquirer in a business combination (see 2.6.60).

2.5.10.20 The definition of a subsidiary focuses on the concept of control and has two parts, both of which need to be met in order to conclude that one entity controls another:

- the power to govern the financial and operating policies of an entity…
- …so as to obtain benefits from its activities.

IAS 27.4,   2.5.10.30 There is no requirement for the parent to have a shareholding in a subsidiary,
SIC-12.9   and this is not a necessary pre-condition for control.

IAS 27.13   2.5.10.40 Control is presumed to exist when the parent owns, directly or indirectly through subsidiaries, more than half of the voting power of an entity. This presumption of control may be rebutted in exceptional circumstances if it can be demonstrated clearly that such ownership does not constitute control (see 2.5.140).

IAS 27.13   2.5.10.50 Even if the parent owns half or less of the voting power of an entity, control exists in *any* of the following circumstances:

- the investor has power over more than half of the investee's voting power through an agreement with other investors;
- the investor has the power to govern the investee's financial and operating policies by virtue of a statute or agreement;
- the investor has the power to appoint or remove the majority of the investee's board of directors or governing body members, and control of the entity is exercised through that board or body; or
- the investor has the power to cast the majority of votes at meetings of the investee's board of directors or governing board, and control of the entity is exercised through that board or body.

AS 27.4, 12   2.5.10.60 An entity included in the consolidated financial statements could be a part of a legal entity, for example, a division of a company. However, in our view an approach in which only part of a legal entity is assessed for consolidation is appropriate only when the activities, assets and liabilities (i.e. the risks and rewards) of that part of the legal entity are "ring-fenced" from the risks and rewards of the other parts of the legal entity. On the other hand, if the activities and net assets are not ring-fenced, then the assessment of consolidation should be made in the context of the legal entity as a whole. See 2.5.200 for further discussion of this issue in the context of SPEs.

2.5.20 The power to govern the financial and operating policies of an entity

2.5.30 *Power to govern vs de facto control*

2.5.30.10 The assessment of whether one entity controls another entity depends on the application of the control concept in IAS 27.

IAS 27.4, 13   2.5.30.20 Under one view, consolidation is based on the *power* to govern. Under this view, in assessing control it is considered whether the ability to control has a legal or contractual basis rather than whether that control actually is exercised. For example, significant minority shareholder B has a 40 percent interest in an investee; the other holdings are dispersed such that no other individual shareholder has an interest of more than 5 percent. B does not have the *power* to govern the investee since the other shareholders could unite to oppose it. Therefore, B does not consolidate the investee. Rather, it would be accounted for using the equity method in accordance with IAS 28 *Investments in Associates* (see 3.5).

2.5.30.30 Another view is that, in addition to the power-to-govern analysis, the evaluation of consolidation requirements should take into account *de facto* circumstances. *De facto* control arises when an entity holding a significant minority interest can control another entity without legal arrangements that would give it majority voting power. In the example in 2.5.30.20, *de facto* control exists as the balance of holdings with other shareholders is dispersed and the other shareholders have not organised their interests in such a way that they commonly exercise more votes than the significant minority shareholder. Under a *de facto* control model the *power* to govern an entity through a majority of the voting rights or other legal means is not essential for consolidation. Rather, the *ability in practice* to control, e.g. by casting a majority of the votes actually cast, in the absence of legal control may be sufficient if no other party has the power to govern. Under this view, in *de facto* control circumstances, which is evaluated based on all evidence available, the significant minority shareholder is required to consolidate.

2.5.30.40 In our view, both interpretations are acceptable. Therefore, in our view an entity should choose an accounting policy, to be applied consistently, with respect to the application of the control principle in IAS 27, in particular whether the entity includes or excludes *de facto* control aspects in its analysis of control. We prefer consolidation to be based on the *power* to govern. If a policy of *de facto* control is selected and no other party has the *power* to govern an investee, then the entity that has *de facto* control should consolidate.

IAS 27.4, 13,   2.5.30.50 Determining whether control exists requires a careful analysis of all facts and
IG3   circumstances. The definition of control permits only one entity to have control of another entity. Furthermore, control should be assessed without regard of whether that power actually is exercised in practice. Instead, it is considered whether the ability to control has a legal or contractual basis, under the power-to-govern model, or is present as a result of practical circumstances, under the *de facto* control model.

2.5.30.60 For example, Company R applies the power-to-govern model in consolidating subsidiaries. R owns 60 percent of the voting power in Company B, but never attends or votes at shareholder meetings and takes no other interest in running B's operations. In our view, R has the *power* to govern B because it can step in and exercise its rights at any time, for example if it is not satisfied with how B's operations are being run. Accordingly, R should consolidate B. Consolidation is based on the ability of one entity to control another, regardless of whether that power is exercised in practice.

2.5.40 *Governance structures*

AS 27.13(c),
(d)

2.5.40.10 An entity controls its investment if it has the power to appoint or remove the majority of the investee's board of directors or other governing body members, and control of the entity is exercised through that board or body. Similarly, an entity will control its investment if it has the power to cast the majority of votes at a meeting of the governing body (board of directors or other governing body) through which control of the entity is exercised.

2.5.40.20 Therefore, when determining whether one entity controls another, a clear understanding of the investee's governance structure is necessary. In many countries the governing body is the board of directors; however, in other countries there are layers of governance. Although the law may provide for different bodies to have certain rights and obligations, in assessing control any shareholders' agreements that amend these "typical" rights and obligations should be considered.

2.5.40.30 For example, there might be a supervisory board and an executive board. The executive board in certain jurisdictions determines the detailed financial and operating policies, whereas the supervisory board has a more detached role in overseeing the actions of management on behalf of shareholders and employees. Under these circumstances, generally the executive board is the governing body for the purpose of identifying control under IFRSs.

2.5.40.40 However, before reaching any conclusion it would be necessary to consider the respective roles of the supervisory and executive boards in a particular case. In some cases the role of the supervisory board is altered to give it much more authority over the entity's financial and operating policies; this is becoming increasingly common as the focus on corporate governance increases. For example, the supervisory board might approve the annual budgets and operational planning; or it might have the power to appoint or dismiss members of the executive board. Depending on the circumstances it might be appropriate to conclude that the supervisory board is the key governing body for the purpose of determining control under IFRSs.

2.5.40.50 The role of any nominations committee also is relevant in considering who has the power to appoint or remove the majority of the governing body members. For example, a single shareholder might have the *power* to nominate governing body members, but the operation of a nominating committee might require those nominees to be approved unanimously by a number of parties, including certain shareholders and employee representatives. Whether the role of a nominating committee is relevant in a particular case will depend on the circumstances. In this example, if the nominating shareholder also has the power to alter the operations of the nominating committee so that it can appoint or remove governing body members unopposed, then notwithstanding the participation of the committee, that shareholder still has the power to appoint or remove the majority of the governing body members.

2.5.40.60 In certain jurisdictions some or all members of the governing board are independent and/or are required by law to "act in the best interest of the entity". Nevertheless, in our view a shareholder with the power to appoint or remove the majority of the investee's board members generally has the power to govern the financial and operating policies of the other entity in that situation, even though the shareholder may by law be precluded from directing the decisions of the management of the other entity.

2.5.50 *Shareholders' agreements*

IAS 27.13   2.5.50.10 Shareholders' agreements may be an important part of assessing control. For example, Company E owns 60 percent of the voting power in Company G, and Company F owns the other 40 percent. E therefore appears to have the power to govern G. However, E has entered into an agreement with F such that E defers to the wishes of F with respect to voting; E has done this because it has no expertise in the area of G's operations. Therefore, in accordance with this agreement, F has the power to govern G.

2.5.50.20 However, before concluding that a shareholders' agreement confers power on a particular party, the break-up terms in the agreement, as well as its duration, should be considered. Continuing the example in 2.5.50.10, suppose that E can discontinue the agreement at any time without penalty. In that case, in our view E has the power to govern G since it can step in and exercise its rights at any time.

2.5.50.30 If a shareholders' agreement has a fixed duration, then depending on the facts and circumstances, it might be appropriate to conclude that the agreement covers too short a period to have any real impact on the power of control.

2.5.50.40 While a shareholders' agreement generally will be in writing, this is not a requirement of IFRSs. In our view, an oral shareholders' agreement may be as important as a written agreement in assessing control.

2.5.60 *Management vs governance*

IAS 31.12   2.5.60.10 In assessing the power to govern it is necessary to distinguish between the management of the operations and their control. A manager does not have control of an entity simply by virtue of running the daily operations, when it does so only within the financial and operating policy framework established by another entity. Although IAS 27 is silent on this issue, this view is clarified in respect of the accounting for joint ventures.

2.5.60.20 For example, Company H owns 70 percent of the voting power in Company K, and Company J owns the other 30 percent. In addition, J runs the daily operations of K since it has expertise in that area. However, H actually has the power to govern the operations of K since it has the majority of voting power, and therefore has the power to remove J as manager.

2.5.70 *Economic power*

IAS 24.11 2.5.70.10 A party may be able to restrict the freedom of another entity by virtue of their
SIC-12.App trading or economic relationship. Examples of parties that may have such power include
financiers, trade unions, public utilities, government departments or agencies, and major
customers and suppliers. Such relationships do not give rise to the power to govern in
the sense of IAS 27 because the relationship is not one of investor-investee. This is
clarified in SIC-12, which notes that economic dependence, such as relations between
a supplier and a significant customer, does not by itself lead to control.

2.5.80 *The rights of minorities*

2.5.80.10 In many cases minorities have certain rights even if another party owns the
majority of the voting power in an entity; sometimes these rights are derived from law,
and other times from the entity's constitution.

2.5.80.20 IFRSs do not address the issue of minority rights. In our view, it is necessary
to consider the nature and extent of the rights of minorities in determining control,
including the distinction between participating rights that allow minorities to block
significant decisions that would be expected to be made in the ordinary course of business, and rights that are protective in nature. For example, approval of the minority may
be necessary for:

- amendments to the entity's constitution;
- the pricing of related party transactions;
- the liquidation of the entity or the commencement of bankruptcy proceedings; and
- share issues or repurchases.

2.5.80.30 In our view, these minority rights are protective and would not in isolation overcome a presumption of control by the majority holder of voting power (see also 2.5.80.80).

2.5.80.40 On the other hand, the approval of the minority may be necessary for:

- appointing and removing governing body members, including setting their remuneration; or
- making operating and capital decisions, including approving budgets, in the ordinary
  course of operations.

2.5.80.50 In our view, such rights are participating in nature and therefore granting
such rights to minorities may overcome the presumption of control by the majority
owner under IFRSs when considered together with all other facts and circumstances.
However, overcoming the presumption of control by the majority owner does not mean
that the minority shareholder has control. All facts and circumstances should be taken
into consideration in determining the degree of influence of each party involved. The
majority investor may have joint control (see 3.5.110 and 120) or significant influence
(see 3.5.20 and 30) over the entity.

2.5.80.60 In considering the significance of rights given to minorities, it also is important to consider what happens in the event of deadlock. For example, if the minority shareholders have the power to veto the investee's annual operating budget, then this may indicate that the majority shareholder does not have the power to govern the operations of the investee. However, if the constitution provides that the minority shareholders have the right to object to the annual budget, and the majority shareholder is obliged to listen and respond to those concerns, but is not obliged to change the budget or to enter into independent discussions to decide the outcome, then in our view the minority rights are likely to be more protective than participative and would not, in isolation, overcome the presumption of control by the majority holder of voting power.

2.5.80.70 Other rights that should be considered include, for example, minority shareholder approval of major asset acquisitions and disposals, distributions, financing, the ability of the minority shareholders to liquidate the entity, and any "kick-out rights" that could force the majority shareholder to sell its interest in the investee. Although kick-out rights most commonly occur in limited partnerships (see 2.5.90), they also can occur outside a partnership. In analysing kick-out rights, care should be taken to ensure that they are currently exercisable.

2.5.80.80 For example, Company X acquired 65 percent of the voting shares of Company Y on 1 January 2010 and nominates three of the five directors. There are two minority shareholders who each can nominate one director. A separate shareholders' agreement gives the minority shareholders the right as from 1 January 2012 to "kick out" X, after two formal disagreements between the majority and minority shareholders (whether those disagreements occur before or after 1 January 2012). Until 1 January 2012 the minority shareholders' kick-out rights should not be considered when determining which entity has control as such rights are not currently exercisable (see 2.5.130). However, from 1 January 2012, when the minority shareholders' kick-out rights become exercisable, this may lead to a reassessment of which company controls Y. This would depend on a further analysis of the specific facts and circumstances at that time.

2.5.80.90 An entity's constitution or a shareholders' agreement may give the minority shareholders the right to object to certain decisions related to the entity's financial and operating policies, to delay the decision-making process, and/or to require protracted discussions with the majority shareholder. If, after following the process set up in the constitution or shareholder agreement, including procedures in the event of deadlock, the majority shareholder is provided with an explicit power to make a decision unilaterally, i.e. without the agreement of the minority shareholders, then in our view the majority shareholder has control. In our view, this conclusion would not change if the minority shareholders have the right to put their shares to the majority shareholder (put option) if the majority shareholder takes such a decision against their will.

2.5.90 *Limited partnerships and certain rights of limited partners*

2.5.90.10 In some cases, an entity that is not an SPE is managed by an owner who is fully liable for the obligations of the entity and who also holds the majority of voting rights.

Other owners have a residual interest in the entity, but have limited liability and hold no voting rights. This structure commonly is referred to as a limited partnership, and the party that has unlimited liability for the obligations of such a partnership is referred to as a general partner. There is a presumption that the general partner has the power to govern the partnership, regardless of the general partner's voting interest in the limited partnership. These structures often are seen in the private equity and hedge fund industry (see 2.5.210).

2.5.90.20 In the case of a limited partnership, consideration should be given to the ability of the limited partners to remove the general partner ("kick-out rights") and to rights to dissolve or liquidate the partnership. In our view, if kick-out rights are substantive, then this will overcome the presumption that the general partner has the power to govern the partnership even when the general partner holds the majority of the voting rights. In analysing kick-out rights, care should be taken to ensure that they are currently exercisable (see 2.5.80.80). However, in our view, a limited partner's ability to withdraw funding from the partnership would not, on its own, overcome the presumption of the general partner's power to govern.

2.5.90.25 In some cases the voting required to exercise kick-out rights may mean that they vest in a single limited partner, e.g. if a single limited partner holds 67 percent of the voting rights of all limited partners and a simple majority is required to remove the general partner. In our view, the fact that in substance only one limited partner has the ability to exercise the kick-out rights does not prevent the rights from being substantive.

2.5.90.30 [Not used]

2.5.90.40 As a general principle, in our view the rights of the limited partners are regarded as substantive if there are no significant barriers to exercising those rights. The rights should be exercisable without cause, i.e. not only in the case of misconduct, such as negligence by the general partner, and there should be no other significant barriers to the exercisability of the rights. Such barriers would include the following, for example:

- The voting thresholds make it unlikely that the rights will be exercisable.
- The exercise of the rights is subject to other conditions, e.g. related to the partnership's performance, that make exercisability unlikely.
- Significant disincentives exist for the limited partners to exercise their rights as a result of financial penalties or operational barriers on exercise.
- There is an absence of an adequate number of qualified replacement general partners or a lack of opportunities to attract a qualified replacement.
- There is no mechanism to exercise the rights.
- The limited partners do not have the ability to obtain the information necessary to exercise the rights.

2.5.90.50 If the analysis set out in 2.5.90.40 leads to the conclusion that the liquidation and/or kick-out rights of the limited partners are substantive, then we believe that the presumption that the general partner has control over the limited partnership is overcome.

2.5.90.60 If it is concluded that the general partner does not control the partnership because the limited partners have substantive kick-out rights, then it follows that the general partner will not have the ability to exercise significant influence even if it holds more than 20 percent of the voting rights in the partnership (see 3.5.60.10).

2.5.100 *Indirect holdings*

2.5.100.10 Indirect holdings may or may not result in one entity having control over another. Although the total ownership interest may exceed 50 percent, this may not mean that the entity has control.

2.5.100.20 For example, Company L owns 35 percent of the voting power in Company N, and 40 percent of the voting power in Company M. M owns 60 percent of the voting power in N. Therefore, L has, directly and indirectly, a 59 percent (35% + (60% x 40%)) ownership interest in N. However, L does not control 59 percent of the vote because it does not have control over the votes exercised by M; rather, it is limited to significant influence (see 3.5.20). Therefore, in the absence of any contrary indicators, L does not control N.

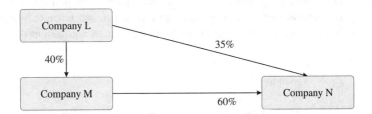

IAS 27.13   2.5.100.30 This issue is alluded to in IAS 27 when it refers to voting power held indirectly through *subsidiaries*, i.e. not through associates or lesser investments.

2.5.110 *Control vs fellow subsidiaries*

2.5.110.10 In some cases it is not clear whether one entity is controlled by another entity, or whether they are both under the control of a third entity. This issue sometimes arises in a closely held group of entities.

2.5.110.20 For example, individual P owns 100 percent of the voting power in Company Q, which owns 10 percent of the voting power in Company R. P owns 55 percent of the voting power in R indirectly through a number of other subsidiaries. The remaining 35 percent of R's voting power is widely held. The governing bodies of Q and R are identical, and include P. Initially it may appear that Q controls the operations of R since the governing body members are identical. However, in the absence of any contrary indicators, it is P who controls both Q and R in this case. Therefore, it would not be appropriate for Q to consolidate R; rather, they are fellow subsidiaries under the common control of P.

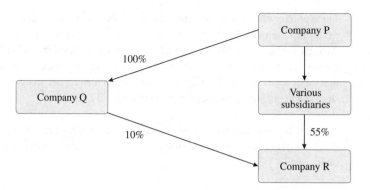

2.5.120 So as to obtain benefits from its activities

2.5.120.10 Although IFRSs are silent on the matter, in our view the benefits referred to in the definition of control are the benefits derived from having the power to govern the financial and operating policies of an entity, i.e. ownership benefits. We believe that the two dominant typical features of such ownership benefits are participation in future dividends and participation in future changes in the value of the entity, both positive and negative; these features together typically determine the total shareholder return. The right to participate in these economic benefits generally arises at the point of becoming an actual owner in the entity.

IC-12.9, 10   2.5.120.15 In our view, synergistic benefits such as revenue enhancements, cost savings or benefits from economies of scale are not in the nature of ownership benefits in the context of IAS 27. This is supported by the consensus reached in SIC-12 in respect of SPEs (see 2.5.150). Benefits received from ordinary business transactions are not benefits that lead to control as long as the terms of the transactions are established on an arm's length basis. For example, if a shareholder sells inventory to the investee, then the sales price of the goods is a normal trading benefit as long as the investee does not pay more or less than any of the shareholder's other customers under similar conditions. Similarly, a performance fee paid to an investment manager that is on market terms is not in the nature of ownership benefits (see 2.5.210.60). Conversely, ownership-type benefits may be present if the benefits received from "ordinary" business transactions are in excess of the benefits that would have been received had the transactions been on market terms, i.e. there are "hidden dividends".

IAS 27.4   2.5.120.20 Control does not require the parent to receive a *majority* of the benefits from the subsidiary. For example, a company issues A and B shares. They carry equal voting rights, but class A shares have far greater rights to dividends in the event of a distribution. As a result of holding a mixture of A and B shares, S owns 60 percent of the voting power in the entity, but receives only 10 percent of the dividends. In the absence of any contrary indicators, S controls the entity despite its share of benefits being disproportionately low compared with its power.

2.5.120.30 While the benefits of ownership normally are realised in the form of dividends, this is not necessary to establish control over an entity. This is consistent with the absence of a requirement for the parent to hold shares in a subsidiary (see 2.5.10.30). For example, Company T appoints the majority of Company W's governing body members through a long-term or non-cancellable agreement entered into with W's shareholders. T receives no dividends from W, but it receives a management fee based on W's profits that far exceeds the fee that might be expected in the market. In our view, such a benefit should be considered a benefit of control under IFRSs.

2.5.120.40 In summary, the key issue is assessing whether benefits may be obtained. No single aspect of benefits, i.e. magnitude, form or mechanism for receipt, is determinative on its own.

2.5.130 **Potential voting rights**

IAS 27.14   2.5.130.10 In assessing control, the impact of potential voting rights that currently are exercisable should be considered. All potential voting rights are taken into account, whether held by the entity or by other parties. Such potential voting rights may take many forms, including call options, warrants, convertible shares and contractual arrangements to acquire shares. Only those rights that either would give the entity voting power or that would reduce another party's voting rights are considered. Written put options are not considered potential voting rights as the writer of a put option does not have control over the exercise of that option and therefore cannot control the acquisition of the associated voting rights. Accordingly, the holder of a put option takes into consideration the voting rights associated with the underlying shares when considering whether it controls the entity.

2.5.130.20 For example, Company X owns 40 percent of the voting power in Company A, Company Y owns 25 percent, and Company Z owns the remaining 35 percent. Also, X holds a call option to acquire from Y an additional 20 percent of the voting power in A; the call option can be exercised at any time. Accordingly, it is X that has the power to govern A. Therefore, X consolidates A with 60 percent allocated to NCI.

2.5.130.30 In another example, Company P grants Company O a call option to acquire the share capital of company Q between June 2012 and December 2014 at a fixed price. The option cannot be exercised before June 2012 and therefore O does not have the power to control Q currently. However, once the option becomes exercisable consideration should be given to whether O controls Q. This would depend on a further analysis of the specific facts and circumstances at that time.

2.5.130.40 In another example, Company D acquires 51 percent of the shares and voting rights in Company E, which was a wholly-owned subsidiary of Company F. E is a legal entity in which F's IT function is located and, as part of the acquisition, E and F enter into an outsourcing contract in relation to future IT services. D and F also enter into a shareholder agreement that provides that if, over the term of the outsourcing contract, one of the parties to that contract, E or F, fails to comply with its key obligations as defined in the contract, then F has the right to reacquire D's 51 percent interest if E is the failing party, and D has the right to acquire F's 49 percent interest if F is the failing party. In our view, because F's call option to reacquire D's shares is contingent upon a future event, i.e. that one of the parties fails to comply with its obligations under the contract, the option is not currently exercisable. Therefore, the issue of the call option to F does not preclude D from controlling E. If, on the other hand, the "breach" of a condition that triggers the exercisability of an option is at the discretion of the holder of the option, then in our view the option is currently exercisable.

2.5.130.45 In another example, Company X has no shareholding in Company Z, but has a call option to acquire the share capital of Z at any time for a nominal amount; in our experience, the parties to such an arrangement are likely to be related (see 5.5). X has the power to govern Z by virtue of the call option that is currently exercisable. However, in this example X also has ownership benefits in Z by virtue of the pricing of the call option; the fixed price means that X has both the upside and downside risk of changes in the fair value of Z, which we believe are a form of ownership benefits (see 2.5.120.10).

IAS 27.15 2.5.130.50 Management's intentions with respect to the exercise of potential voting rights are ignored in assessing control because these intentions do not affect the existence of the *ability* to exercise power. Continuing the example of X in 2.5.130.20, even if X had no intention of exercising the call option it still would be deemed to have the power to govern A.

IAS 27.15 2.5.130.60 The exercise price of potential voting rights, and the financial capability of the holder to exercise them, also are ignored. However, the capability to exercise power does not exist when potential voting rights lack economic substance, e.g. when the price deliberately is set so high that the chance of the potential voting rights being exercised is remote.

IAS 27.15 2.5.130.70 In some cases the exercise of potential voting rights may be subject to regulatory approval. Only when regulatory approval is deemed a mere formality should the rights be considered currently exercisable. The nature of regulatory approval, together with all relevant facts and circumstances, is considered when making this assessment.

2.5.140 Rebutting the presumption of control

IAS 27.13, 14 2.5.140.10 It is possible for an entity that has less than a 50 percent interest in another entity to be considered its parent as long as it controls that other entity. Similarly, ownership of more than a 50 percent interest may not give rise to control. The determination of where control lies is a question of fact based on all relevant facts and circumstances, examples of which are discussed in 2.5.20 – 130.70.

IAS 27.13, IG3 2.5.140.20 A related issue is whether an entity could have two parents. For example, Company D holds 60 percent of the voting power in Company F, but Company E has the right to appoint and remove a majority of F's governing body members. The indicators in IAS 27 might lead to a conclusion that both D and E should consolidate F. However, control is a question of fact and therefore there can be only one parent because no more than one entity can have the current power to govern. In this example it would be necessary to consider how the financial and operating policies of F are set, and the rights of the shareholders in general meetings compared to the rights of the governing body members.

2.5.150 **Special purpose entities**

SIC-12.3, 9   2.5.150.10 An SPE is an entity created to accomplish a narrow and well-defined objective, e.g. a vehicle into which trade receivables are securitised. The principles discussed above for identifying control apply equally to an SPE. However, SIC-12 sets out additional guidance since many of the traditional indicators of control, e.g. power over more than half of the voting rights as a result of ownership or contractual agreement, are not present in an SPE; for example, the activities of the SPE may be predetermined so that there is no need for a governing body.

SIC-12.6,   2.5.150.20 SIC-12 does not apply to employee benefit plans, both post-employment
15A-E   benefit plans and other long-term employee benefit plans within the scope of IAS 19 *Employee Benefits*; however, it does apply to equity compensation plans (see 4.5.1060). See 4.4.1090 for a discussion of the treatment of entities that exist in relation to plans excluded from the scope of SIC-12, e.g. employee benefit trusts.

SIC-12.1, 3,   2.5.150.30 SIC-12 describes an SPE as an entity that:
14

- often is created with legal arrangements that impose strict limits on the decision-making powers of its governing body; in some cases these restrictions are permanent; or
- frequently operates in a predetermined way such that virtually all rights, obligations and aspects of activities are controlled through the legal/contractual provisions determined at inception, commonly referred to as "auto-pilot".

2.5.150.35 Typically an SPE has only one creator or sponsor.

2.5.150.40 In our view, an entity would be an SPE if the powers to direct its activities do not amount to powers of governance because they are limited or constrained and therefore an analysis of the power to govern is inappropriate. For example, retail investment funds typically are subject to regulations that can place significant restrictions on the activities and decision-making powers of the investment manager. Another example may be a tracker fund that is an investment fund that tracks a predetermined public index. In our view, a tracker fund is an example of an entity that would be considered to be an SPE, as the investment decisions are predetermined and the investment manager simply executes these decisions, i.e. it operates on auto-pilot. See 2.5.210 for further discussion of investment funds.

SIC-12.10,   2.5.150.50 The control concept in SIC-12 is based on the substance of the relationship
12, IU 11-06   between an entity and an SPE, and considers a number of indicators that are discussed in 2.5.160 – 180. Each factor is analysed independently. There is no requirement to meet all of the factors in order for control to exist and none of the factors is a conclusive indicator of control on its own. The party having control over an SPE is determined

through the exercise of judgement in each case, taking into account all relevant facts and circumstances. Also important to bear in mind when analysing an SPE is the requirement to account for the substance and economic reality of a transaction rather than only its legal form (see 1.2.100).

2.5.150.60 If, as a result of performing an analysis as outlined in 2.5.160 – 80, it is concluded that an entity does not have control over an SPE, then in our view the entity generally would account for its interest in the SPE as a financial asset in accordance with IAS 39 *Financial Instruments: Recognition and Measurement.* We believe that an analysis in accordance with SIC-12 generally will lead to a conclusion that the entity does not have significant influence (see 3.5.50.50) over an SPE's financial and operating policies when they are largely predetermined.

2.5.160 *Business needs*

SIC-12.10(a) 2.5.160.10 Determining whose business needs the SPE benefits requires an evaluation of the SPE's purpose, its activities and which entity benefits most from them. An example is when the SPE is engaged in an activity that supports one entity's ongoing major or central operations.

2.5.160.20 For example, Company G sells its main operating asset to an SPE and then leases it back (see 5.1.470); a bank provides the SPE's capital. In the absence of any contrary indicators, it appears that the SPE has been set up primarily to support the business needs of G.

2.5.170 *Decision-making powers*

IC-12.10(b) 2.5.170.10 Many SPEs run on auto-pilot because all key decisions have been made as part of the formation of the SPE and delegated to other parties (managers). In such cases it is necessary to identify the entity that made all the key decisions and delegated their execution as part of the process of identifying the party that obtains the majority of benefits from the SPE's activities.

2.5.170.20 For example, major decisions that relate to the operations of an SPE that holds securitised receivables include the profile of receivables eligible for securitisation, servicing arrangements, liquidity facility arrangements, the ranking of claims against the SPE's cash flows and the wind-up of the SPE. If it is determined that the transferor made these key decisions, then it is likely to be deemed to have control over the SPE. Even if the conclusion is that the transferor did not make these key decisions, the other indicators of control in respect of SPEs still may lead to a conclusion that the transferor should consolidate the SPE.

2.5.180 *The majority of risks and benefits, and ownership of the residual interests*

SIC-12.10 2.5.180.10 An evaluation of the majority of risks and benefits, and the ownership of the residual interests in an SPE, often is the most crucial element of determining whether

85

consolidation of an SPE is necessary. The benefits that should be analysed can take various forms; for example, the holder of a beneficial interest in an SPE may receive a fixed or stated rate of return in some cases and in other cases may have rights or access to other future economic benefits of the SPE's activities. In our view, the analysis of benefits and risks is focused on the residual-type benefits and risks rather than the gross cash flows of all of the assets and liabilities in the SPE. For example, if there are reserves or equity that would be distributed when the SPE is wound up, then the entity entitled to the majority of this potential upside may be required to consolidate the SPE.

2.5.180.20 Although risk is not part of the definition of control in IFRSs (see 2.5.10.20), in analysing an SPE often the risks are easier to identify than the benefits. Therefore, the focus often is on analysing the risks on the basis that an entity would not assume risks without obtaining equivalent benefits, which in turn may lead to a presumption of control. In evaluating the majority of risks, if for example there are senior and subordinated cash flows in an SPE, then the evaluation should focus on the exposure to subordinated cash flows and any residual equity. In this respect, both the proportion as well as the likelihood of the eventual existence of any residual interest should be considered. An entity with the majority of this exposure may be required to consolidate the SPE.

2.5.180.30 For example, an entity (transferor) transfers 110 of receivables into an SPE for proceeds of 100, with 10 being over-collateralisation for the transaction. If credit losses are greater than 10, then these excess losses are absorbed by the transferee, or in substance the beneficial interest holders in the SPE; if the losses are less than 10, then the transferor receives the difference as additional proceeds. Historically credit losses have amounted to 4 and this trend is expected to continue. The transferor's position could be analysed in one of two ways:

- The transferor does not bear the majority of the risk associated with the SPE since the 10 represents only 9 percent (10 / 110) of the maximum potential losses. Therefore, the transferor should not consolidate the SPE. In our view, this is not the appropriate interpretation of SIC-12.
- The transferor bears the majority of the risk associated with the SPE since the 10 is expected to cover all expected losses. Therefore, the transferor may be required to consolidate the SPE. In our view, this is the appropriate interpretation of SIC-12.

2.5.180.40 An entity may provide servicing to an SPE. As noted in 2.5.120.15, in our view an arm's length and market-based servicing fee for services performed would not be viewed as receiving benefits from the SPE. However, a servicing fee that varies based on the performance, or non-performance, of the SPE's assets, or that entitles the servicer to residual benefits, might be akin to the servicer having the ability to obtain benefits from, or being exposed to, the risks of the SPE, in which case the variability in those fees would be included in the analysis of risks and benefits under SIC-12.

2.5.180.50 Conversely, an entity might bear substantially all risks and benefits of an SPE if the entity assumes all of the risks and benefits from an SPE in an arm's length transaction. For example, Company J transfers some receivables to an SPE for 90 percent of their face value as the expected losses are 10 percent. At the same time the SPE enters into an agreement with Company K, a credit insurance company, to assume the residual credit risk associated with these receivables. Under this arrangement, any amounts collected in excess of the expected loss would flow to K. The SPE and K are not related and the consideration paid is based on a market price for similar types of arrangements. If the credit risk is assumed to be the sole risk of the SPE, then K bears all the risks and benefits and would be required to consolidate the SPE.

2.5.190 *Purchases of the residual interests of an SPE in the secondary market*

2.5.190.10 Some time after the formation of an SPE an entity, typically an investment company with no prior connection to the SPE, might purchase the residual interest in the SPE in the secondary market. The SPE may be a securitisation vehicle whose assets consist of mortgage loans, trade receivables etc., which refinances itself by issuing senior and junior notes, sometimes called equity and/or mezzanine tranche. The SPE usually is operated on auto-pilot and the sponsor of the SPE benefits from its activities by receiving funds from the SPE and transferring risks to it.

IC-12.10(a), (c), (d)   2.5.190.20 Assume that the residual interest acquired by the investment company contains substantially all of the risk in the underlying assets of the SPE. In this scenario, the application of the indicators in SIC-12 for consolidating an SPE points to different parties being the controlling party of the SPE. Whereas it is clear that the original purpose of the SPE was to benefit the sponsor, and therefore the sponsor of the SPE was required to consolidate the SPE from the date of formation, after the sale transaction substantially all the risk in the assets of the SPE and the corresponding benefits have been transferred to the acquiring entity.

SIC-12.10   2.5.190.30 In our view, when an entity acquires substantially all of the risks and benefits of an SPE operated on auto-pilot, and when the benefits received by the sponsor from the activities of the SPE are insignificant, the acquiring entity should be identified as the controlling party and consequently should consolidate the SPE. We believe that when considering whether consolidation of an SPE is required, the primary test should be to analyse which party is exposed to a majority of the risks and a majority of the benefits in respect of the SPE. Furthermore, in respect of the "business needs" indicator (see 2.5.160), we believe that the acquisition of the residual interests in an SPE should be analysed similarly to the origination of an SPE. In other words, by purchasing the residual interests and from the purchase date onwards, the activities of the SPE are conducted on behalf of the acquiring entity. Therefore, in substance this entity becomes the (new) sponsor of the SPE.

2.5.200 *Multi-seller SPEs*

2.5.200.10 Sometimes an SPE obtains assets from multiple, and often unrelated, entities. These SPEs sometimes are referred to as "multi-seller" SPEs, or "commercial paper conduits" if they issue notes backed by short-term financial assets obtained from other entities. Often these SPEs are sponsored by a financial institution that does not transfer any of its own assets into the SPE.

2.5.200.20 For multi-seller SPEs in which the transferor retains some risk with respect to the transferred assets, and those assets are *not* cross-collateralised with other assets in the SPE, in our view each transferor of assets should evaluate the risks and benefits only of those assets that it has transferred to the SPE. This sometimes is referred to as a "ring-fenced" approach as each transfer is evaluated as an individual "silo" within the SPE.

2.5.200.30 On the other hand, if all transfers of assets to a multi-seller SPE cross-collateralise all liabilities of the SPE, then the transferor should evaluate its risks and benefits in relation to all assets held by the entire SPE. In this case it becomes less likely that any one transferor will be viewed as having a majority of the residual risks or benefits of the multi-seller SPE.

2.5.200.40 If the structure is sponsored by a financial institution, then that financial institution should consider whether it should consolidate the SPE. For example, as shown in the diagram below, Companies A and B each create an SPE (SPE-A and SPE-B) and transfer trade receivables, including a credit enhancement, to their respective vehicles. Another SPE is created (SPE-R), which issues commercial paper, thereby acting as the refinancing vehicle for SPE-A and SPE-B. A bank facilitates the creation of this securitisation programme by providing an overall programme-wide credit enhancement to SPE-R as a second loss guarantee. In our view, the bank may be required to consolidate SPE-R if it bears the residual risk, without consideration of the likelihood of the credit enhancement being called upon; this is because SIC-12 requires an analysis of which party bears the majority of the residual risk even if the total residual risk is itself immaterial. If the bank was required to consolidate SPE-R, then it would consolidate the entire commercial paper liability of SPE-R and the loans provided to SPE-A and SPE-B.

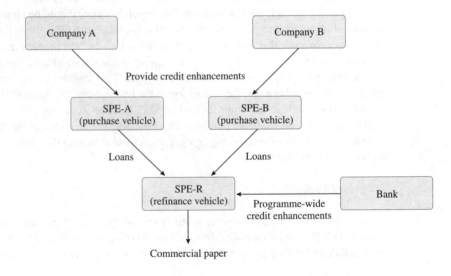

2.5.200.50 In our view, a similar result would occur in the case of a multi-seller SPE with no cross-collateralisation of the transferred assets. In this case each originator, e.g. Companies A and B in the example in 2.5.200.40, would consolidate its specific silo, which would include the receivables transferred as financial assets and its share of the loan from the refinancing part of the SPE as a financial liability, even though there is no corresponding loan agreement. The bank would consolidate the refinancing part of the SPE by presenting a collateralised loan to A and B, for which no corresponding agreement exists, as a financial asset and the entire commercial paper as a financial liability.

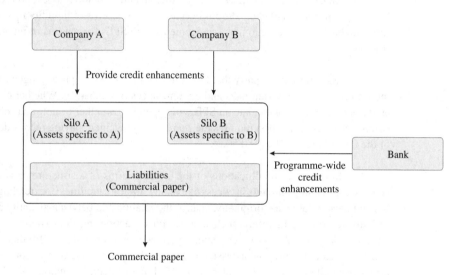

2.5.205 *Reassessment arising from unfavourable market conditions*

2.5.205.10 It is common for structured investment vehicles and other SPEs to have liquidity facilities in place with financial institutions, often the originating/sponsoring financial institution. The risks arising from such facilities form part of the analysis under SIC-12 as to whether the vehicle should be consolidated (see 2.5.150).

2.5.205.20 Under normal market conditions, such facilities rarely may have been drawn down for prolonged periods, and usually this will not have been a significant factor in determining control under SIC-12. However, if liquidity conditions change, then facilities may be drawn down more frequently and for periods longer than was expected when the initial assessment of consolidation was performed. An entity lending under such a liquidity facility may be exposed to credit losses through wind-down mechanisms that may require the entire structure to be liquidated in the event that replacement financing is not obtained within a stipulated period.

2.5.205.30 If market conditions change, then originators/sponsors also may make additional voluntary investments, lending amounts in excess of existing liquidity facilities or extending terms beyond those established originally, in part to avoid reputational risk from the forced liquidation of a sponsored vehicle.

2.5.205.40 The assessment of whether or not an entity has control over an SPE is carried out at inception and normally no further reassessment of control is carried out in the absence of changes in the structure or terms of the SPE, or additional transactions between the entity and the SPE. Day-to-day changes in market conditions normally do not lead to a reassessment of control.

2.5.205.50 An issue therefore arises as to whether an entity should reassess control of an SPE given changed market conditions because of draw-downs of liquidity facilities, or sponsors having entered into new arrangements with SPEs for reasons of reputational risk.

2.5.205.60 Determining the party that has control over an SPE requires judgement, taking into account all relevant facts and circumstances (see 2.5.150). Whether or not an entity is required to consolidate an SPE will depend on whether or not it has obtained control. Such an evaluation requires the exercise of judgement having reconsidered all of the factors in 2.5.160 – 180.50.

2.5.205.70 In our view, modifications of the original terms of a structure or voluntary actions, e.g. lending amounts in excess of existing liquidity facilities or extending terms beyond those established originally, change the relationship between an entity and the SPE that it sponsors; therefore, such modifications or actions result in a reassessment of control under SIC-12. In our view, entering into a transaction with an SPE that was not contemplated in the original assessment of control is similar to a transaction in which an entity purchases the residual interest in an SPE in the secondary market (see 2.5.190) and therefore should lead to a reassessment of control.

2.5.205.80 If other sponsors in the marketplace have stepped in to provide support to enable investment vehicles to continue conducting business, then in our view this should cause an entity to consider whether any SPE that it sponsors might require such support. The entity then should consider whether, if required, it would provide such support for reputational or other reasons. When an entity concludes that support might be required and that it would provide such support, in our view the entity should reassess the need to consolidate the vehicle under SIC-12. This is because new market conditions may have altered the substance of the relationship between the entity and the SPE. In our view, it is not the transaction with the SPE that causes reassessment, but the change in the substance of the relationship between the sponsor and the SPE.

2.5.205.90 A reassessment of control under SIC-12 may or may not lead to consolidation. In particular, an entity will need to re-evaluate, taking into consideration its overall relationship with the SPE and the market's long-term assessment of credit and liquidity risk, whether it is exposed to the majority of risks and benefits in the SPE. In making such a reassessment an entity may, following changing market events, need to change its assumptions with respect to loss probabilities, the likelihood of liquidity facilities being drawn down in the future, and the likelihood of future actions being taken for reputational reasons.

IAS 1.122, 2.5.205.100 An entity may conclude that there is no event that would cause it to *123, 125* reassess consolidation, or it may reassess and conclude that consolidation is not required. When an entity sponsors or is otherwise associated with investment vehicles that are not consolidated, there are no specific disclosure requirements in IFRSs that would apply. However, IAS 1 *Presentation of Financial Statements* requires an entity to disclose information about the assumptions concerning the future, and other major sources of estimation uncertainty at the reporting date (see 2.4.180.10). The assessment of control under SIC-12 relies on significant estimates and assumptions about the probabilities assigned to various potential cash flow outcomes, and therefore the sharing of risks and benefits between those parties that hold an interest in the SPE and its assets. In addition, IAS 1 requires the disclosure of judgements that management has made in the process of applying the entity's accounting policies and that have the most significant effect on the amounts recognised in the financial statements; one of the examples provided in IAS 1 is the judgement applied in determining whether the substance of the relationship between an entity and an SPE indicates that the SPE is controlled by the entity.

2.5.205.110 In our view, entities should consider providing disclosures about SPEs that it sponsors or is associated with, the reasons for non-consolidation and the factors that might cause consolidation to be reassessed in future periods. Under changing market conditions, in our view entities should consider such disclosure in both interim and annual financial statements.

2.5.210 **Investment funds**

2.5.210.10 Investment funds generally have many characteristics that are similar to SPEs. As there is specific guidance for determining whether to consolidate an SPE (see 2.5.150), the first question that should be addressed is whether the fund is an SPE.

2.5.210.20 In many cases retail investment funds are highly regulated and are created by legal arrangements that impose strict and sometimes permanent limits on the ability of the investment manager to make decisions. In our experience, in most jurisdictions hedge funds are less regulated than other investment funds. In our view, the following are examples of factors that may suggest that an investment fund is an SPE:

- the investment manager has no power to change the investment policy without approval/authorisation of a third party, e.g. investors' vote and/or custodian and/ or regulators;
- the investment manager cannot enter into a transaction on the fund's behalf that conflicts with the investment policy or statute of the fund;
- the trustee holds custody over all assets; or
- an independent party monitors compliance with the regulation.

SIC-12.1   2.5.210.30 In our view, a broad investment mandate, e.g. a mandate to invest in global equities, in itself does not preclude an entity from being an SPE. Therefore, another factor to consider in evaluating whether or not an investment fund is an SPE is the degree of influence that the fund has on its investments. If the investment vehicle can be involved actively in the investment, i.e. it is not precluded from obtaining significant influence or (joint) control over the investment, then generally we would assume that the vehicle does not have a "narrow and well-defined objective", which is one of the characteristics of an SPE (see 2.5.150.10). In this case normally we would conclude that the vehicle is an operating entity and not an SPE. If, however, the investment vehicle is restricted to act as a passive investor, i.e. it is not allowed to have significant influence over its investments, then in our view this may be an indicator that the vehicle's activities are designed to follow a narrow and well-defined objective. In such cases it might be concluded that the vehicle is an SPE.

2.5.210.40 Investment funds should be evaluated for consolidation by both the investment manager and investors; generally it is the role of the investment manager that requires the more careful analysis. If the fund is an SPE, then this evaluation should be carried out using SIC-12 (see 2.5.150). One of the triggers for consolidation under SIC-12 is when an entity has the right to obtain the majority of benefits and retains the majority of risks (see 2.5.180). In our view, a retail investment fund that is considered to be an SPE should be consolidated by the party holding an investment of over 50 percent, or holding an investment of less than 50 percent and obtaining a variable performance fee that together total the majority of benefits.

2.5.210.50 If the fund is not considered to be an SPE, then the general consolidation principles in IAS 27 apply (see 2.5.20). The fund manager should consider whether it has control over the fund, i.e. the power to govern the financial and operating policies of the fund so as to obtain benefits from its activities. When considering whether the fund manager has the power to govern the fund, the power of other investors also should be considered, including their substantive ability to remove the fund manager without cause (see 2.5.90 for kick-out rights). If the manager concludes that it possesses the power to govern, then in our view a meaningful level of ownership benefits, including performance related fees to the extent that they are not on market terms, will trigger consolidation.

2.5.210.60 In assessing the level of ownership benefits, in our view amounts to be received by the fund manager that are in substance compensation for the manager's performance should not be considered as ownership benefits if they are on market terms. For example, a manager may be provided with a separate class of shares, sometimes called "carried interest", that entitles it to receive a certain percentage of the fund's profits in excess of a defined hurdle. The arrangement is expected to result in payments to the fund manager that are equivalent to performance fees otherwise paid in the market-place. We believe that the benefits flowing from these shares are received by the fund manager in its capacity as an investment manager rather than as an owner; therefore, we would not consider these benefits to be ownership benefits.

2.5.210.65 In our view, compensation for the manager's performance includes both fixed and variable fees, as well as any fees that the fund manager earns directly, i.e. not from managing the fund, to the extent that such fees are on market terms.

2.5.210.67 For example, an investment property fund, which invests in real estate entities, is managed by a fund manager. The fund manager has an interest in the property fund and a direct interest in the entities owned by the fund. The fund manager receives an annual fixed fee of 100 and a variable performance fee of 15 percent of any fund returns in excess of 10 percent. The fund manager also receives a separate fee from the entities owned by the fund for managing their underlying assets. In our view, the compensation-type benefits that the manager obtains through its involvement in the arrangement include the 100 annual fixed fee, the 15 percent variable performance fee and the fees received directly for managing the underlying assets.

2.5.210.70 In determining whether the level of ownership benefits is meaningful, a manager, or general partner in a limited partnership structure, should consider the arrangement as a whole, including the relative importance of the ownership benefits and compensation-type benefits that the manager obtains through its involvement in the arrangement. In our view, if the manager can demonstrate that receiving at-market compensation, including performance fees, for its services, irrespective of their legal form, clearly is the dominant purpose of its involvement and that obtaining ownership benefits (see 2.5.120) clearly is secondary to that purpose, then this could lead to the conclusion that the fund manager does not control the fund. This is because the manager fails to meet the "so as to obtain benefits" criterion.

2.5.210.80 Determining whether receiving compensation for services clearly is the dominant purpose of the manager's involvement in the entity requires judgement, taking into account the specific arrangements. In our view, the higher the level of ownership benefits that the manager holds in relation to its compensation for services, the more difficult it will be to conclude that receiving compensation for services is the dominant purpose of the manager's involvement in the investment entity. Conversely, the higher the level of compensation for services in relation to the manager's ownership benefits, the easier it will be to conclude that receiving compensation for services is the dominant purpose of the manager's involvement in the investment entity. If it is demonstrated clearly that the manager's dominant purpose in relation to the investment entity is to maximise the compensation for its services, then in our view the manager does not have the power to govern so as to obtain benefits and hence does not have control of the investment fund.

2.5.210.90 In our view, the size of the ownership interest of the fund manager, including any indirect interests held, also should be taken into account in determining whether the fund manager should consolidate the fund.

2.5.210.100 The following flowchart summarises the decisions to be made in order to determine whether a fund manager consolidates the fund:

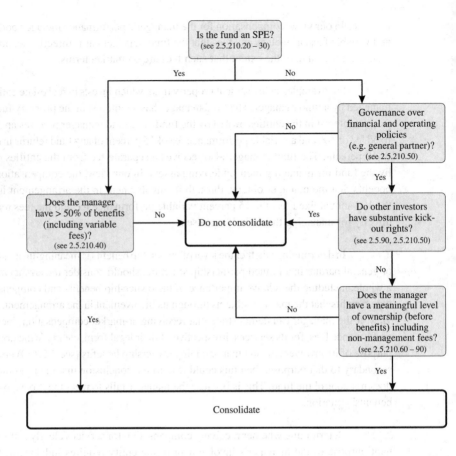

2.5.220 *Presentation*

2.5.220.10 Investment managers typically are required to consolidate investment funds if most of the investment is funded by seed money provided by the investment manager, i.e. the investment manager owns more than 50 percent of the ownership interests in the fund. In such cases the presentation requirements for disposal groups held for sale may apply if the manager plans to sell the fund to third-party investors within 12 months and the criteria are met for a disposal group to be classified as held for sale (see 5.4.20).

2.5.230 **Structured transactions**

2.5.230.10 There is no formal definition of a structured transaction. However, typically a structured transaction arises when parties undertake a series of actions to achieve a desired outcome. For example:

- assets are transferred into an SPE, which may or may not be controlled by the transferor (a securitisation of receivables often takes this form); and

- an entity obtains control of an investee with a view to increasing its shareholding at a later date.

2.5.230.20 The analysis of a vehicle that arises from a structured transaction takes into account all of the factors described above. However, often such transactions have characteristics that require careful consideration. It is important to bear in mind the substance of the transaction as a whole when the complete transaction comprises a series of smaller transactions that would be accounted for differently if each one were viewed in isolation.

2.5.230.30 In our experience, the use of derivatives, including potential voting rights, is much more common in structured transactions. The terms and conditions of the derivatives need to be considered to determine the impact that they may have on the rights of the parties involved. In derecognition transactions, an analysis of the derivatives involved may result in the conclusion that the underlying asset should not be derecognised (see 3.6.1070).

IAS 27.33 2.5.230.40 In the context of losing control of a subsidiary, IAS 27 contains specific requirements for determining whether two or more transactions should be accounted for (i.e. linked) as a single transaction (see 2.5.500).

2.5.240 Exclusions from consolidation

2.5.240.10 There are no exclusions from the requirement for an entity to consolidate all subsidiaries.

IAS 27.17 2.5.240.20 Subsidiaries cannot be excluded from consolidation on the basis that their activities are dissimilar from those of the parent; relevant information is provided by the consolidation of such subsidiaries and the resulting disclosure of additional information concerning the impact of those activities. For example, the disclosures required by IFRS 8 *Operating Segments* help to explain the significance of different business activities within the group (see 5.2).

2.5.250 *Severe long-term restrictions*

AS 27.BC20 2.5.250.10 An entity considers severe long-term restrictions that significantly impair its ability to transfer funds to the parent when assessing its ability to control an entity; however, such restrictions do not in themselves preclude control. In our view, the transfer of funds should be interpreted as funds related to the benefits of ownership (see 2.5.120).

2.5.260 *Disposal in the near future*

FRS 5.6, 11 2.5.260.10 An entity is required to consolidate a subsidiary even if it is acquired exclusively with a view to its subsequent disposal. However, the disposal group, comprising the assets that are to be disposed of and directly related liabilities, is classified in the consolidated financial statements as held for sale or distribution upon acquisition if certain criteria are met (see 5.4.20 and 35).

2.5.270 *Immaterial subsidiaries*

2.5.270.10 Although IFRSs do not address explicitly the treatment of immaterial subsidiaries, in our view subsidiaries do not need to be consolidated if, both alone and in aggregate, they are *immaterial* (see 1.2.80) to the financial position, performance and cash flows of the group, whether consolidated or accounted for at fair value.

IAS 1.7, 2.5.270.20 Materiality depends on both the size and nature of the omission or misstate-
29-31 ment, or a combination of the two, judged in the surrounding circumstances. In considering materiality, the nature of a subsidiary may be important, for example if it is an SPE. In our view, the non-consolidation of a subsidiary should be reconsidered in preparing financial statements at each reporting date.

2.5.280 *Venture capital organisations and investment entities**

IAS 27.16, 2.5.280.10 Venture capital organisations, investment funds, mutual funds, unit trusts and
38 similar entities are not exempt from the requirements for consolidation, and therefore their subsidiaries should be consolidated. See 3.5.160 for guidance on identifying a venture capital organisation. This is notwithstanding the view that the aggregation of modified historical cost statements of financial position and statements of comprehensive income may present less relevant information to investors who are concerned primarily with the fair value of each individual investment in a portfolio and the net asset value per share. If appropriate, information about the fair value of investments may be disclosed in the notes to the consolidated financial statements; alternatively, separate financial statements (see 2.1.70) in which investments are recognised at cost or fair value may be prepared.

2.5.290 Subsidiaries' accounting periods and policies

IAS 27.22, 2.5.290.10 The financial statements of the parent and its subsidiary are prepared as of
23 the same reporting date. When the reporting dates are different, additional financial statements of the subsidiary are prepared as of the parent's reporting date, unless it is impracticable to do so. In any case, the difference between the reporting dates of the parent and subsidiary should not be greater than three months and adjustments should be made for the effects of significant transactions and events in that period.

IAS 27.23 2.5.290.20 When there is a difference between the reporting dates of the parent and a subsidiary, the length of the reporting periods and the gap between them should be consistent from period to period. However, IFRSs are silent on the approach to take when a subsidiary changes its annual reporting date in order to align it with that of the parent.

2.5.290.30 For example, the parent has an annual reporting date of 31 December, and its subsidiary's annual reporting date is 31 October. Each year the consolidated financial statements are prepared using financial information for the subsidiary at 31 October, adjusted for any significant transactions in November and December. In 2010 the subsidiary changes its annual reporting date to 31 December. In our view, the 2010 consolidated financial statements should include the results of the parent for the

12 months to 31 December 2010, and the results of the subsidiary for the 14 months to 31 December 2010, unless the parent already has included the subsidiary's transactions in that time as adjustments made for significant transactions. In our view, this is more appropriate than an alternative approach of adjusting the group's opening retained earnings at 1 January 2010 in respect of the results of the subsidiary for the two months to 31 December 2009, an approach that would be necessary to limit the consolidated financial statements in the current period to 12 months of the subsidiary's results.

IAS 27.24, 25 2.5.290.40 For the purpose of consolidation, the financial information of all subsidiaries is prepared on the basis of IFRSs. Uniform accounting policies for like transactions and events are used throughout the group. Therefore, if a subsidiary uses different accounting policies from those applied in the consolidated financial statements, then appropriate consolidation adjustments to align accounting policies are made when preparing those consolidated financial statements. However, see 5.10.60 for an exception in relation to insurance contracts.

2.5.300 Non-controlling interests

IFRS 3.A, IAS 27.4 2.5.300.10 NCI represent the equity in a subsidiary not attributable directly or indirectly to the parent. For example, if a parent owns 80 percent of a subsidiary directly and the remaining 20 percent is owned by a third party, then in the parent's consolidated financial statements the 20 percent interest held by the third party is the NCI in that subsidiary.

2.5.300.20 NCI can be divided into following two components:

- Instruments that are present ownership interests and entitle their holders to a proportionate share of the entity's net assets in the event of liquidation (e.g. ordinary shares owned).
- Instruments that are not present ownership interests and do not entitle their holders to a proportionate share of the entity's net assets in the event of liquidation, e.g. equity components of convertible bonds and options under share-based payment arrangements. These instruments meet the definition of NCI because they represent equity not attributable to the parent.

2.5.305 *Initial measurement of NCI#*

IFRS 3.19 2.5.305.10 When less than 100 percent of a subsidiary's equity is acquired, the acquirer can elect on a transaction-by-transaction basis to measure the present ownership component of NCI at:

- fair value at the acquisition date, which means that goodwill, or the gain on a bargain purchase, includes a portion attributable to NCI; or
- its proportionate interest in the recognised amount of the identifiable net assets of the acquiree, which means that goodwill recognised, or the gain on a bargain purchase, relates only to the controlling interest acquired.

2.5.305.15 This accounting policy choice relates only to the initial measurement of NCI. After initial recognition the option of measuring NCI at fair value is not available.

2.5.305.20 The implication of recognising the present ownership component of NCI at its proportionate interest in the recognised amount of the identifiable assets and liabilities of the acquiree is that both the NCI and goodwill are lower because no goodwill is ascribed to the NCI. This "day one" difference between the measurement options will result in a smaller impairment loss under IFRSs if a cash-generating unit subsequently is found to be impaired (see 3.10.160).

2.5.308 *Forthcoming requirements*

2.5.308.10 The *Improvements to IFRSs 2010* clarified that the measurement choice between fair value and proportionate interest in identifiable net assets for NCI is only available upon initial recognition for NCI that are present ownership interests and entitle their holders to a proportionate share of the entity's net assets in the event of liquidation. Other components of NCI are measured at fair value or a measurement basis required by other IFRSs, e.g. IFRS 2 *Share-based Payment* (see 2.6.805).

2.5.310 *Percentage attributable to NCI*

2.5.310.10 NCI is the equity in a subsidiary not attributable directly or indirectly to the parent (see 2.5.300.10). Therefore, the NCI includes any equity interests in a subsidiary that are not held by the parent directly or indirectly through subsidiaries, associates or joint ventures.

2.5.310.20 For example, Company P prepares consolidated financial statements that include its two subsidiaries, Company S1 and Company S2, and the group's interest in an associate, Company Q. Company P's interests in the respective companies are shown in the following diagram:

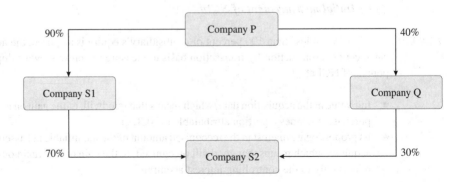

2.5.310.30 P owns 90 percent of S1 directly and has no indirect interest in S1. Therefore, the NCI in S1 is 10 percent. P recognises in its consolidated financial statements 100 percent of the results of S1, with 10 percent allocated to NCI.

2.5.310.40 P owns 63 percent of S2 indirectly through S1 (70% x 90%), and 12 percent of S2 indirectly through Q (30% x 40%). Therefore, P's total interest in S2 is 75 percent and the NCI is 25 percent. P recognises in its consolidated financial statements 100 percent of the results of S2, with 25 percent allocated to NCI. However, when accounting for Q using the equity method, P also would recognise 12 percent of the results of S2, resulting in double counting which should be eliminated. See 2.5.315 for a discussion of the elimination of the double counting in these cases.

IAS 27.IG5, IG6 2.5.310.50 In some cases the economic interests of investors will not equal their shareholding. For example, an entity may control 60 percent of the voting power in a subsidiary, but own only a 55 percent economic interest in the profits and net assets. In this case the NCI is measured based on economic interest, i.e. 45 percent.

2.5.310.60 An entity may transfer interests in a subsidiary to a defined benefit pension plan and the interests may then qualify as plan assets under IAS 19 (see 4.4.350). If the contributing entity retains control over the subsidiary but a plan asset nevertheless arises under IAS 19 (see 4.4.410.20), then in our view the entity recognises NCI for the interests held by the pension plan. In the event that no plan asset arises, e.g. the interest is not transferable (see 4.4.400.10), then no accounting entries result; the pension plan has no asset and therefore the entity continues to account for the interest in the subsidiary.

2.5.310.70 We believe that after a contribution that qualifies as a plan asset, the ownership benefits associated with the shareholdings (see 2.5.120) accrue to the pension plan rather than to the contributing entity. It might be argued that the contributing entity continues to have these ownership benefits indirectly because, as sponsor of the plan, the benefits help reduce its obligation in respect of any deficit in the plan. However, we believe that it is only the initial contribution of the equity interests that reduces the net obligation and that, once the contribution has been made, any benefits arising from those interests thereafter (either through a change in value of the asset or a distribution) accrue directly to the plan as a return on its plan asset and are accounted for by the sponsor in accordance with the requirements of IAS 19 (including the accounting for actuarial gains or losses); they do not represent further benefits accruing to the parent entity which then contributes them to the plan on an annual basis. Furthermore, the pension plan is a separate entity that is excluded from the requirements of IAS 27 (see 2.5.150.20), which is the basis upon which the NCI is recognised upon the contribution of the shares to the plan.

AS 27.30, 31, 32.33 2.5.310.80 Changes in a parent's ownership interest in a subsidiary that do not result in the loss of control are accounted for as equity transactions and no gain or loss is recognised (see 2.5.380). We believe that the transfer of interests in a subsidiary to become plan assets constitutes such a change in ownership interest. Therefore, net assets have to be reallocated to NCI in order to reflect such a change. As set out in 4.4.410.30, plan assets are measured at fair value upon contribution, which is the consideration received in accounting for the reduction in ownership of the subsidiary. Any resulting difference between the measurement of NCI and the fair value of the interest transferred is recognised directly in equity.

2.5.310.90 For example, Company P holds 100 percent of the shares in Subsidiary S, and no goodwill arose on the acquisition. The carrying amount of the net assets of S is 1,000. P transfers 20 percent of its interest in S to its pension plan, which qualifies as a plan asset under IAS 19. At the time of the transfer the fair value of that interest transferred is 300. P records the following entry:

	Debit	Credit
Defined benefit liability (plan assets)	300	
NCI		200
Parent equity		100
To recognise transfer of shares and resulting NCI		

2.5.315 *Indirect interests and the elimination of double counting*

2.5.315.10 The example in 2.5.310.40 highlights the double counting that arises when an interest in a subsidiary is held indirectly through associates or joint ventures.

2.5.315.20 In our view, the double counting highlighted in the example in respect of P's interest in S2 should be eliminated against the equity-accounted earnings of Q. Effectively this means that the equity-accounted earnings of S2 will be reduced to zero because the consolidated financial statements of the parent already include P's 12 percent interest in S2 (i.e. 100 percent of the assets, liabilities, income and expenses of the subsidiary S2 have already been included).

2.5.320 *Potential voting rights*

IAS 27.14, 15, IG5 2.5.320.10 Even though the determination of control of an entity takes into account potential voting rights, the calculation of NCI generally is based on current ownership interests because this corresponds with the economic interests of the parties (see 2.5.130).

2.5.325 **Attribution of profits and losses**

IAS 27.28 2.5.325.10 Profit or loss and each component of other comprehensive income generally are attributed to the owners of the parent and to NCI in proportion to their ownership interests in the subsidiary. For example, if Company P owns 80 percent of Company S, then 80 percent of the earnings are allocated to the owners of the parent and 20 percent to the NCI in S.

IAS 27.28 2.5.325.20 Losses applicable to the NCI in a subsidiary (including components of other comprehensive income) are allocated to the NCI even if doing so causes the NCI to have a deficit balance.

2.5.330 *Profit-sharing arrangement or parent has obligation to cover losses attributable to NCI*

AS 27.BC35 2.5.330.10 A parent and the NCI in a subsidiary may enter into an arrangement to share profits (losses) in a manner other than in proportion to their ownership interests (i.e. a profit-sharing arrangement) or to place the parent under an obligation to absorb losses attributable to NCI. In our view, in its consolidated financial statements the parent should choose an accounting policy, to be applied consistently, in accounting for such a profit-sharing arrangement or guarantee:

- take the profit-sharing arrangement/guarantee into account when doing the original attribution in the statement of comprehensive income; or
- use the following two-step approach:
  (1) The parent attributes to the NCI its portion of the profits/losses in the statement of comprehensive income in proportion to its present ownership interests in the subsidiary, i.e. unaffected by the existence of the profit-sharing arrangement/ guarantee.
  (2) The parent accounts for the profit-sharing arrangement/guarantee separately in the statement of changes in equity by attributing any additional profits/losses to the controlling interest or NCI based on the terms of the agreement.

2.5.330.20 A guarantee to absorb losses issued by the parent does not result in a liability from the point of view of the consolidated financial statements, i.e. the transaction is between the parent and the subsidiary, and no entries are recorded in the consolidated financial statements.

2.5.335 *Presentation of NCI*

IAS 1.54(q), 2.5.335.10 In the parent's consolidated statement of financial position NCI is presented
83, 27.27 within equity, separately from the equity of the owners of the parent. If there is NCI in more than one subsidiary, then those interests are presented in aggregate in the consolidated financial statements. In the parent's consolidated statement of comprehensive income the amount of profit or loss and total comprehensive income attributable to owners of the parent and NCI are shown separately; they are not presented as an item of income or expense.

IAS 27.20 2.5.335.20 Income, expenses, assets and liabilities are reported in the parent's consolidated financial statements at the consolidated amounts, which include the amounts attributable to the owners of the parent and NCI. In addition, the amounts of intra-group income, expenses and balances to be eliminated in the parent's consolidated financial statements are not affected by the existence of NCI (see 2.5.370).

2.5.335.30 In our view, the presentation of NCI does not change if part of NCI is associated with a disposal group classified as held for sale or distribution and/or a discontinued operation (see 5.4.20 and 5.4.120). For example, Group B has an 80 percent interest in Subsidiary C, which is classified as held for sale and is a discontinued operation. The net profit of the discontinued operation for the year is 200, the related disposal group comprises assets of 1,200, liabilities of 500 and the NCI is measured at 140:

- In the statement of comprehensive income the result of the discontinued operation is 200. The result is not presented net of NCI of 40 (200 x 20%) because NCI are not an item of income or expense, but instead are presented as an allocation of the entity's profit or loss.
- In the statement of financial position the assets of the disposal group of 1,200 are presented as a separate line item. Likewise, the liabilities of the disposal group of 500 are presented as a separate line item. The NCI of 140 continue to be presented as a component of equity.

2.5.335.40 Entities should consider whether the NCI related to a disposal group and/or a discontinued operation should be disclosed separately from the NCI related to the continuing operations of the entity.

2.5.340 – 350 [Not used]

2.5.360 *Non-controlling shareholders holding put options*

2.5.360.10 Sometimes non-controlling shareholders of an entity's subsidiary are granted put options that convey the right to those shareholders to sell their shares in that subsidiary for an exercise price (fixed or variable) specified in the option agreement. From the perspective of the entity, such written put options meet the definition of a financial liability in IAS 32 *Financial Instruments: Presentation* if the entity has an obligation to settle in cash or in another financial asset, and should be recognised as such. See 2.5.460 for the accounting for put options written to non-controlling shareholders.

2.5.370 **Intra-group transactions**

IAS 27.20, 21   2.5.370.10 Intra-group balances and transactions, and resulting profits, are eliminated in full regardless of whether the unearned profit is in the parent or the subsidiary. Intra-group losses are eliminated in full except to the extent that the underlying asset is impaired.

2.5.370.20 The following example illustrates the elimination in a "downstream" sale of inventory from the parent to an 80 percent subsidiary.

	Parent	Subsidiary
Cost of inventory	700	1,000
Selling price of inventory	1,000	Not yet sold
Net profit prior to elimination	15,000	8,000
Net assets prior to elimination	125,000	65,000

Elimination entry on consolidation	Debit	Credit
Revenue	1,000	
Cost of sales		700
Inventory		300
To eliminate downstream transaction		
NCI share of profit		1,600 = 8,000 x 20%

2.5.370.30 This example shows that the NCI are calculated without regard to the elimination entry because the unearned profit is in the parent's result. This is notwithstanding the fact that the unearned profit is included in the carrying amount of the inventory in the subsidiary's separate financial statements.

2.5.370.40 The following example is the same as in 2.5.370.20 except that the 80 percent subsidiary makes an "upstream" sale of inventory to the parent.

	Parent	Subsidiary
Cost of inventory	1,000	700
Selling price of inventory	Not yet sold	1,000
Net profit prior to elimination	15,000	8,000
Net assets prior to elimination	125,000	65,000

Elimination entry on consolidation	Debit	Credit
Revenue	1,000	
Cost of sales		700
Inventory		300
To eliminate upstream transaction		
NCI share of profit		1,540 = (8,000 - 300) x 20%

2.5.370.50 This example shows that NCI are calculated after eliminating the unearned profit that is included in its results. In addition, the NCI share of net assets also is calculated after the elimination even though the inventory that was overstated from the group's perspective is in the parent's separate statement of financial position.

IAS 27.18, 2.5.370.60 Similarly, a subsidiary's holding of shares in its parent raises the question of
.33, 33.IE2 whether the NCI in that subsidiary is calculated before or after the impact of treasury shares. For example, Parent X has a 60 percent interest in Subsidiary Y. Y holds 1,000 shares in X and accounts for those shares at fair value through profit or loss. On con-

solidation X eliminates the treasury shares in Y's financial statements, including any fair value changes. In our view, the NCI in Y should be calculated after the elimination; that is, the NCI should be calculated based on 40 percent of X's equity net of the elimination adjustment caused by the treasury shares and based on 40 percent of Y's profit or loss after elimination of the fair value adjustments related to the treasury shares. However, when X calculates its earnings per share (EPS), the number of shares used is reduced by 1,000, i.e. the number is not reduced by the portion attributable to NCI. This is because EPS is earnings per share attributable to ordinary shareholders of the parent (see 5.3.30).

2.5.380 Changes in ownership interests while retaining control

2.5.385 *General principle*

2.5.385.10 After a parent has obtained control of a subsidiary it may change its ownership interest in that subsidiary without losing control. This can happen, for example, through the parent buying shares from, or selling shares to, the NCI or through the subsidiary issuing new shares or reacquiring its shares.

IAS 27.30   2.5.385.20 Transactions that result in changes in ownership interests while retaining control are accounted for as transactions with equity holders in their capacity as equity holders. As a result, no gain or loss on such changes is recognised in profit or loss but rather in equity. Also, no change in the carrying amounts of assets (including goodwill) or liabilities is recognised as a result of such transactions. This approach is consistent with NCI being a component of equity.

IAS 27.31   2.5.385.30 The interests of the parent and NCI in the subsidiary are adjusted to reflect the relative change in their interests in the subsidiary's equity. Any difference between the amount by which NCI is adjusted and the fair value of the consideration paid or received is recognised directly in equity and attributed to the owners of the parent.

2.5.385.35 The principles set out in 2.5.385.30 also apply when a subsidiary issues new shares and the ownership interests change due to that issuance. For example, Company S has 100 ordinary shares outstanding and the carrying amount of its equity (net assets) is 300. Company P owns 90 percent of S, i.e. 90 shares. S has no other comprehensive income. S issues 20 new ordinary shares to a third party for 120 in cash, as a result of which:

- S's net assets increase to 420.
- P's ownership interest in S reduces from 90 percent to 75 percent (P now owns 90 shares out of 120 issued); and
- NCI in S increases from 30 (300 x 10%) to 105 (420 x 25%).

2.5.385.37 In P's consolidated financial statements the increase in NCI in S arising from the issue of shares is recorded as follows:

	Debit	Credit
Cash	120	
NCI (equity)		75
Other equity (or retained earnings)		45
To recognise overall change in equity as a result of		
partial disposal to NCI		

2.5.385.40 IFRSs do not provide guidance on the presentation of the resulting gain or loss within equity. Alternative approaches include establishing a separate category of equity (other equity) in which such amounts are recognised, or recognising those amounts in retained earnings. In our view, either treatment is acceptable.

AS 27.41(e) 2.5.385.50 If there is a change in the ownership interest in a subsidiary without the loss of control, then the parent discloses in its consolidated financial statements a schedule showing the effects of such changes on the equity attributable to the parent.

2.5.390 *Determination of the adjustment to NCI*

2.5.390.10 IFRSs do not provide guidance on the treatment of goodwill when the interests of the parent and NCI are adjusted to reflect the change in interests. Dependent on the initial measurement of NCI there are different approaches possible.

2.5.392 *NCI initially measured at proportionate interest in the identifiable net assets of acquiree*

2.5.392.10 When NCI were initially measured at their proportionate interest in the identifiable net assets of a subsidiary, because no goodwill was initially attributed to NCI, there are different approaches to the determination of the adjustment to NCI that are acceptable for purchases and sales of NCI when retaining control. In our view, each of the following approaches is acceptable (see 2.5.405 – 410 for examples):

- *Approach 1.* Attribute a proportionate amount of all the net assets of the subsidiary including recognised goodwill. This view interprets "interests in the subsidiary" in paragraph 31 of IAS 27 as related to all net assets, including goodwill, recognised in the parent's consolidated financial statements. Under this approach, recognised goodwill is treated as any other asset.
- *Approach 2.* Attribute a proportionate amount of the net assets of the subsidiary; however, in doing so there are two separate asset pools: one asset pool is in respect of the parent's interest (net assets including goodwill) and the other asset pool is in respect of the NCI (identifiable net assets but no goodwill). Under this approach, a purchase of equity interests from the non-controlling shareholders results in adjusting NCI for the proportionate amount of the NCI asset pool because the parent is buying a portion of that pool of assets. Conversely, a sale of equity interests to the

non-controlling shareholders results in adjusting NCI for a proportionate amount of the parent's assets-plus-goodwill pool because the parent is selling a portion of that asset pool to the NCI. In the examples in 2.5.405, we illustrate the first transaction with NCI after obtaining control of a subsidiary; the calculations would be more complicated when there are several transactions with NCI, e.g. a purchase of NCI and a subsequent sale of NCI.

- *Approach 3*. Attribute a proportionate amount of only the identifiable net assets of the subsidiary. This view interprets "interests in the subsidiary" in paragraph 31 of IAS 27 as related to identifiable assets only since NCI have been initially recognised only in respect of identifiable assets.

2.5.392.20 Other approaches also may be acceptable depending on the circumstances. An entity should choose an accounting policy, to be applied consistently, to both sales and purchases of equity interests in subsidiaries when control exists before and after the transaction when NCI are measured initially at their proportionate interest in the identifiable net assets of the acquiree.

2.5.395 *NCI measured initially at fair value*

2.5.395.10 In our view, when NCI were initially measured at fair value, the adjustment of NCI on purchases or sales of equity interests in the subsidiary when control of the subsidiary by the parent exists before and after the transaction includes a portion of goodwill (see 2.5.405 – 410 for examples). This view interprets "interests in the subsidiary" in paragraph 31 of IAS 27 as relating to all net assets, including goodwill, because goodwill is attributed to NCI when NCI were measured initially at fair value.

2.5.395.20 Likewise, when an entity initially acquires 100 percent of a subsidiary, the same approach would be taken in respect of subsequent sales or purchases of NCI because full goodwill was recognised in the acquisition accounting just as is the case when NCI are initially measured at fair value.

2.5.400 *Impact of a control premium*

2.5.400.10 If NCI initially are measured at fair value and there is a control premium in the consideration paid to obtain control of the acquiree, then a question arises as to the determination of the adjustment to NCI when the parent sells equity interests to the non-controlling shareholders. In this case, we believe that a rational method should be used, based for example on a proportionate amount of the goodwill recognised in the financial statements (similar to approach 1 in 2.5.390.30), or on a proportionate amount of the goodwill attributable to NCI (similar to approach 2 in 2.5.390.30).

2.5.405 *Example of a purchase of equity interests from non-controlling shareholders*

2.5.405.10 Company P acquired 80 percent of Company S in a business combination several years ago. P subsequently purchases an additional 10 percent interest in S.

2.5.405.20 The contribution of S to P's consolidated financial statements before the purchase of NCI is as follows:

	NCI measured initially at fair value	NCI measured at proportionate interest in identifiable net assets
Goodwill	100	80
Identifiable net assets	1,000	1,000
Total net assets	1,100	1,080
Equity (parent)	880	880
Equity (NCI)	220[1]	200
Total shareholders' equity	1,100	1,080

Notes
(1) Assuming no control premium

2.5.405.30 The contribution of S to P's consolidated financial statements after the purchase of the additional 10 percent interest (exclusive of the consideration paid) is as follows:

	NCI measured initially at fair value	NCI measured at proportionate interest in identifiable net assets		
		Approach 1	Approach 2	Approach 3
Goodwill	100	80	80	80
Identifiable net assets	1,000	1,000	1,000	1,000
Total net assets	1,100	1,080	1,080	1,080
Equity (parent)	990	988	980	980
	(880 + 110)	(880 + 108)	(880 + 100)	(880 + 100)
Equity (NCI)	110	92	100	100
	(220 - 110[1])	(200 - 108[2])	(200 - 100[3])	(200 - 100[4])
Total shareholders' equity	1,100	1,080	1,080	1,080

Notes
The decrease in NCI is calculated as follows:
(1) 110 = 10% x 1,100 (total net assets including goodwill) when NCI are initially measured at fair value
(2) 108 = 10% x 1,080 (total net assets including goodwill) under approach 1
(3) 100 = (10% / 20%) x 200 (NCI) under approach 2
(4) 100 = 10% x 1,000 (total identifiable net assets) under approach 3

2.5.410 *Example of a sale of equity interests to non-controlling shareholders*

2.5.410.10 Company P acquired 80 percent of Company S in a business combination several years ago. P subsequently sells a 20 percent interest in S but retains control of S.

2.5.410.20 The contribution of S to P's consolidated financial statements before the sale of NCI is as follows:

	NCI measured initially at fair value	NCI measured at proportionate interest in identifiable net assets
Goodwill	100	80
Identifiable net assets	1,000	1,000
Total net assets	1,100	1,080
Equity (parent)	880	880
Equity (NCI)	220[1]	200
Total shareholders' equity	1,100	1,080

Notes
(1) Assuming no control premium

2.5.410.30 The contribution of S to P's consolidated financial statements after the sale of equity interests to NCI (exclusive of the consideration received) is as follows:

	NCI measured initially at fair value	NCI measured at proportionate interest in identifiable net assets		
		Approach 1	Approach 2	Approach 3
Goodwill	100	80	80	80
Identifiable net assets	1,000	1,000	1,000	1,000
Total net assets	1,100	1,080	1,080	1,080
Equity (parent)	660	664	660	680
	(880 - 220)	*(880 - 216)*	*(880 - 220)*	*(880 - 200)*
Equity (NCI)	440	416	420	400
	(220 + 220[1])	*(200 + 216[2])*	*(200 + 220[3])*	*(200 + 200[4])*
Total shareholders' equity	1,100	1,080	1,080	1,080

Notes
The increase in NCI is calculated as follows:
(1) 220 = 20% x 1,100 (total net assets including goodwill) when NCI are initially measured at fair value
(2) 216 = 20% x 1,080 (total net assets including goodwill) under approach 1
(3) 220 = [20% / 80%] x 880 (parent equity) under approach 2
(4) 200 = 20% x 1,000 (total identifiable net assets) under approach 3

2.5.415 *Changes in ownership interests in a subsidiary that has other comprehensive income*

IAS 21.48C 2.5.415.10 When the relative interests of the parent and NCI change, in our view the balance of components of other comprehensive income should be reallocated between the parent and NCI in order to reflect the new interests; in respect of any foreign currency translation reserve, such reallocation is required explicitly following a partial disposal (see 2.7.320).

2.5.415.20 For example, Company P owns 80 percent of the shares in Company S. On 1 January 2010 P acquires an additional 10 percent of S for cash of 30. The carrying amount of the cumulative NCI in S before the acquisition is 48, which includes 4 in respect of the NCI's portion of gains recognised in other comprehensive income in relation to foreign exchange movements on translation of that subsidiary. In P's consolidated financial statements the decrease in NCI in S is recorded as follows:

	Debit	Credit
NCI (equity)	24	
Other equity (or retained earnings)	6	
Cash		30
To reflect overall change in equity as a result of		
acquisition of NCI		
Other equity (or retained earnings)	2	
Foreign currency translation reserve (4 x 10 / 20))		2
To recognise change in attribution of other comprehensive		
income following acquisition of NCI		

2.5.420 *Transaction costs*

[IAS 1.106(d) (iii), 109, 32.35, IU 07-09] 2.5.420.10 In our view, an entity recognises transaction costs related to transactions with NCI while retaining control directly in equity. This approach is consistent with treating transactions with NCI as equity transactions and the requirement in IAS 32 that transaction costs of an equity transaction are accounted for as a deduction from equity (see 3.11.350).

2.5.425 *Contingent consideration*

[IAS 32.AG8] 2.5.425.10 In our view, contingent consideration payable in relation to an acquisition of NCI is accounted for similarly to contingent consideration payable in a business combination (see 2.6.920). An obligation to pay contingent consideration is classified either as equity or as a financial liability based on the definitions in IAS 32 (see 3.11.67). Such an obligation initially is recognised at fair value as part of the transaction with NCI recognised in equity. If the obligation is classified as a financial liability, then subsequent changes in the value of the liability are recognised in profit or loss in accordance with IAS 39.

2.5.430 *Impairment considerations*

2.5.430.10 When the parent's ownership interest in a subsidiary changes but control is retained, the change in ownership does not result in any adjustment to the carrying amount of the subsidiary's assets or liabilities, including goodwill. However, in our view, if the price paid to acquire non-controlling interests is less than the carrying amount of those interests in the consolidated financial statements, then this might be an indication that certain assets of the subsidiary are impaired. In such cases, we believe that the entity should consider whether any of the underlying assets are impaired prior to accounting for the change in ownership interests.

2.5.440 – 450 [Not used]

2.5.460 *Written put option or forward*

IAS 32.23 2.5.460.10 An entity may write a put option or enter into a forward purchase agreement with the non-controlling shareholders in an existing subsidiary on their shares in that subsidiary. If the put option or forward purchase agreement granted to the non-controlling shareholders provides for settlement in cash or in another financial asset by the entity (see 3.11.45), then IAS 32 requires the entity to recognise a liability initially at fair value, which in a simple case may be measured at the present value of the exercise price of the option or of the forward price; this is consistent with the IFRS 3 requirement to measure contingent consideration at fair value in the acquisition accounting.

2.5.460.20 – 100 [Not used]

2.5.460.110 If the NCI still have present access to the economic benefits associated with the underlying ownership interests, then in our view the entity should choose an accounting policy, to be applied consistently, to recognise the debit side of the transaction using either:

IAS 32.DO1 • *The anticipated acquisition method*. Such agreements are accounted for as an anticipated acquisition of the underlying NCI, i.e. as if the put option had been exercised already or the forward contract had been satisfied by the non-controlling shareholders (see 2.5.461). This is independent of how the exercise price is determined, e.g. fixed or variable, and how likely the exercise of the option.

IAS 27.IG5 • *The present access method*. Under this method NCI continue to be recognised as the NCI still have present access to the economic benefits associated with the underlying ownership interests; therefore the debit entry is to "other equity" (see 2.5.463).

2.5.460.120 If the NCI do not have present access to the economic benefits associated with the underlying ownership interests, then in our view the entity should apply the anticipated acquisition method.

2.5.460.130 In our view, the economic benefits associated with the underlying ownership interests comprise participation in future dividends and participation in future changes in the value of the entity, both positive and negative; these features together determine the total shareholder return (see 2.5.120.10).

2.5.461 *Anticipated acquisition method*

IAS 1.83, 32.DO1

2.5.461.10 Under the anticipated acquisition method the interests of the non-controlling shareholders that hold such put options/forwards are derecognised when the financial liability is recognised. This is because the recognition of the financial liability implies that the interests subject to the put option are deemed to have been acquired already. Therefore the corresponding interests are presented as already owned by the entity, both in the statement of financial position and in the statement of comprehensive income, even though legally they still are NCI. In other words, profits and losses attributable to the holder of the puttable NCI are presented as attributable to the owners of the parent and not as attributable to those non-controlling shareholders.

2.5.461.20 If the put option or forward purchase agreement granted to the non-controlling shareholders provides for gross physical settlement in equity instruments, i.e. a fixed number of shares of the parent or a variable number of shares of the parent based on the fair value of the subsidiary, then the anticipated acquisition method does not apply (see 2.5.475).

IAS 39.55, AG8

2.5.461.25 In our view, subsequent to initial recognition, changes in the carrying amount of the liability are recognised in profit or loss.

2.5.461.28 If the put option expires unexercised, then the liability is derecognised and NCI are recognised. In our view, this should be treated as a disposal of the "anticipated interests" and should be treated consistently with a decrease in ownership interests in a subsidiary while retaining control.

2.5.463 *Present access method*

IAS 27.IG5

2.5.463.10 Under the present access method the interests of non-controlling shareholders that hold such put options/forwards are not derecognised when the financial liability is recognised. This is because the NCI have present access to the ownership benefits that are the subject of the put option. However, if the NCI do not have present access to those ownership benefits, then in our view this method is not appropriate; instead, the entity should follow the anticipated acquisition method (see 2.5.461).

2.5.463.20 Under this method the transaction is not treated as an anticipated acquisition; instead, upon initial recognition of the liability, the debit entry is to "other equity". Subsequently, remeasurement of the liability should be recognised in profit or loss. The application of this method has no impact on the "normal" accounting for NCI (see 2.5.300).

2.5.465 *Likelihood of exercise of put options*

2.5.465.10 In our view, the likelihood of a written put option being exercised is relevant only in assessing whether the terms of the put are genuine. If the terms affecting the exercisability of the option are genuine, then we believe that a liability for the put option should be recognised and that the anticipated acquisition method or present access method applies (see 2.5.460). This is the case even if the put option is exercisable only under uncertain future events that are outside the control of both the seller and acquirer.

2.5.465.20 For example, Company X sells 25 percent of its wholly-owned Subsidiary S to Company Y. A put option is written by X to Y that entitles Y to sell the 25 percent interest back to X. The put is exercisable only if a key patent held by S is revoked by the relevant regulatory authorities. In our view, if the condition related to the revoking of the patent is genuine, i.e. it could occur notwithstanding that it might not be probable, then the anticipated acquisition method or present access method applies.

2.5.470 *Dividends*

IAS 32.23   2.5.470.10 In accordance with the anticipated acquisition method set out in 2.5.461, any discretionary dividends paid to the non-controlling shareholders holding the put option are recognised as interest expense in profit or loss. This is because under an anticipated acquisition approach the put holder is not an equity holder, but rather is a debt instrument holder. Therefore, dividends should not be accounted for as a transaction with equity holders. If the payment of dividends is not at the discretion of the entity, then such payments should be incorporated into the measurement of the liability upon initial recognition (see also 3.11.80 and 170).

2.5.475 *Written put option to be settled in shares of the parent entity*

IAS 32.23   2.5.475.10 When a put option granted to the non-controlling shareholders provides for gross physical settlement in equity instruments, e.g. a fixed number of shares of the parent or a variable number of shares of the parent based on the fair value of the subsidiary, neither the anticipated acquisition method nor the present access method applies. This is because the relevant provision of IAS 32 to recognise a financial liability for the present value of the redemption amount applies only to obligations that will be settled in cash or in another financial asset by the entity (see 3.11.65.100), but not to obligations to settle in a fixed or variable number of the entity's own equity instruments. Accordingly, no financial liability in respect of the estimated redemption amount under the put option is recognised, and the NCI subject to the put option are not derecognised. Instead, the option is accounted for in accordance with IAS 39 (see 3.6.170 and 180.50).

2.5.475.20 The conclusion that no financial liability for the estimated redemption amount is recognised does not change if the parent, in addition to settling the put option in a fixed or variable number of own equity instruments, has an option to settle in cash. This is because the parent would have two settlement alternatives and there is no obligation to deliver cash. Nevertheless, the put option would still be accounted for under IAS 39, which may lead to the recognition of a financial liability for the fair value of the option.

2.5.480 *Written put option to be settled in shares of another subsidiary of the entity*

IAS 32.23   2.5.480.10 When the put option granted to the non-controlling shareholders provides for gross physical settlement in shares of another subsidiary of the entity, assuming that the settlement of this option does not lead to deconsolidation of the subsidiary, neither the anticipated acquisition method nor the present access method applies. This is because no financial liability arises since, from the perspective of the consolidated financial statements, no financial asset of the entity will be delivered upon settlement of the option. However, it could be questioned whether, by analogy to the requirements in IAS 32, the acquisition of the underlying NCI could be anticipated (see 2.5.461).

2.5.480.20 If the acquisition were to be anticipated in this case, then the calculation of NCI would not be based on their current interest in the entity's subsidiary, but based on their interest as if they had already exercised the put option. In our view, in current IFRSs there is no basis for such anticipation. Therefore we believe that the interests of the non-controlling shareholders that hold such put options should be computed based on their current shareholdings.

2.5.480.30 For example, Company P acquires control over Company S by purchasing a 70 percent interest in S. The NCI were recognised with an initial carrying amount of 1,200, which represented their 30 percent interest in S. The non-controlling shareholders were granted the option of exchanging their shares in S for a fixed number of shares in Company T, another subsidiary of P, at any time in the future if S failed to meet certain performance criteria. We believe that it should not be anticipated that the non-controlling shareholders of S might become shareholders of T in the future. Therefore, the NCI in P's consolidated financial statements in respect of S continue to be stated at 1,200.

2.5.490 Loss of control

IAS 27.32   2.5.490.10 A parent can lose control of a subsidiary in a variety of ways. The loss of control can occur without a change in absolute or relative ownership levels or in the absence of a transaction. Examples of events that may result in a loss of control include:

- a parent sells all or part of its ownership interest in its subsidiary such that it loses control;
- a contractual agreement that gave control of the subsidiary to the parent expires;
- the subsidiary issues shares to third parties, thereby reducing the parent's ownership interest in the subsidiary so that it no longer has control of the subsidiary;
- substantive participating rights are granted to other parties;
- the parent distributes its ownership interest in the subsidiary; or
- the subsidiary becomes subject to the control of a government, court, administrator, or regulator.

IAS 27.34   2.5.490.20 When a parent loses control of a subsidiary, it:

- ceases consolidation of the subsidiary by derecognising the assets (including goodwill), and liabilities of the subsidiary and NCI in the subsidiary, including any components of other comprehensive income attributable to them;
- recognises the fair value of the consideration received, if any;
- recognises the distribution of shares to the new owners of the subsidiary, i.e. the owners of the former parent, if the loss of control involves such a distribution (see also 2.5.510);
- recognises any non-controlling investment retained at fair value; and

- reclassifies to profit or loss, or transfers directly to retained earnings, amounts recognised in other comprehensive income in relation to the subsidiary on the same basis as would be required if the parent had disposed directly of the related assets or liabilities.

IAS 27.34(f) 2.5.490.30 As a consequence, the amount recognised in profit or loss upon the loss of control of a subsidiary is measured as the difference between (a) and (b), together with any profit or loss reclassifications:

(a) The sum of:
- the fair value of the consideration received, if any;
- the recognised amount of the distribution of shares, if applicable;
- the fair value of any retained non-controlling investment; and
- the carrying amount of the NCI in the former subsidiary, including the accumulated balance of each class other comprehensive income attributable to the NCI (see 2.5.490.50).

(b) The carrying amount of the former subsidiary's net assets.

IAS 27.35 2.5.490.40 From the group's perspective, the loss of control of a subsidiary results in derecognition of the individual assets and liabilities of the subsidiary. Upon disposal, components of other comprehensive income related to the subsidiary's assets and liabilities are accounted for on the same basis as would be required if the individual assets and liabilities had been disposed of directly. As a result, the following amounts are reclassified to profit or loss:

- exchange differences that were recognised in other comprehensive income in accordance with IAS 21 *The Effects of Changes in Foreign Exchange Rates*;
- changes in the fair value of available-for-sale financial assets recognised previously in other comprehensive income in accordance with IAS 39; and
- the effective portion of gains and losses on hedging instruments in a cash flow hedge recognised previously in other comprehensive income in accordance with IAS 39.

IAS 27.35 2.5.490.50 In our view, on loss of control of a non-wholly-owned subsidiary, the reserve to be reclassified to profit or loss or transferred to retained earnings, as the case may be, is the net amount, i.e. excluding the amount of reserve allocated to NCI. In the case of amounts reclassified to profit or loss, no amount of the reclassification is allocated to NCI because the reclassification of the reserve occurs as a consequence of the loss of control of the subsidiary, which results in the derecognition of the NCI through profit or loss at the same time (see 2.5.490.60).

IAS 27.35, 2.5.490.60 When a parent loses control of a subsidiary by contributing it to an associate
21.48C or a jointly controlled entity, there is some ambiguity in IFRSs as to how the gain or loss on the loss of control should be calculated (see 2.5.525). If the entity applies the IAS 27 approach and recognises the gain or loss in full in profit or loss, then the components of other comprehensive income of the former subsidiary also are reclassified in full as described in 2.5.490.40. If the entity applies the IAS 28/IAS 31 *Interests in Joint Ventures*

approach and eliminates a part of the gain or loss in respect of the continuing interest in the assets and liabilities contributed, then in our view the components of other comprehensive income of the former subsidiary are not reclassified in full, but instead are reclassified on a proportionate basis. See also 3.5.470 and 3.5.600 for further discussion.

AS 27.34(b)   2.5.490.70 The NCI's share of the carrying amount of the net assets of the former subsidiary immediately before control is lost, which includes the share of all profit or loss and other comprehensive income that was attributed to the NCI, is derecognised.

AS 27.34(d), 36   2.5.490.80 Any retained non-controlling equity investment in the former subsidiary is generally remeasured to its fair value at the date that control is lost; see 2.5.525 for a potential exception. The gain or loss on such remeasurement is included in determining the gain or loss on the loss of control. From the date that control is lost, any remaining investment is accounted for in accordance with IAS 39, IAS 28 or IAS 31, as appropriate.

2.5.490.90 For example, Company P owns 60 percent of the shares in Company S. On 1 January 2010 P disposes of a 20 percent interest in S for cash of 400 and loses control over S. The fair value of the remaining 40 percent investment is determined to be 800. At the date that P disposes of a 20 percent interest in S, the carrying amount of the net assets of S is 1,750. Other comprehensive income includes the following related to the subsidiary, which are net of amounts that were allocated to NCI:

- foreign currency translation reserve of 60; and
- available-for-sale revaluation reserve of 120.

2.5.490.100 The amount of NCI in the consolidated financial statements of P on 1 January 2010 is 700. The carrying amount of NCI includes the following amounts that were recognised in other comprehensive income before being allocated to NCI:

- foreign currency translation reserve of 40 (60 / 60% x 40%); and
- available-for-sale revaluation reserve of 80 (120 / 60% x 40%).

2.5.490.110 P records the following entry to reflect its loss of control over S at 1 January 2010:

	Debit	Credit
Cash	400	
Equity (NCI)	700	
Foreign currency translation reserve	60	
Available-for-sale revaluation reserve	120	
Investment in S	800	
Net assets of S (including goodwill)		1,750
Profit or loss		330
To recognise loss of control over S		

2.5.490.120 The 330 recognised in profit or loss represents the increase in the fair value of the retained 40 percent investment of 100 (800 - (1,750 x 40%)), plus the gain on the disposal of the 20 percent interest of 50 (400 - (1,750 x 20%)), plus the reclassification adjustments of 180 (60 + 120). Assuming that the remaining interest of 40 percent represents an associate, the fair value of 800 represents the cost on initial recognition and IAS 28 applies going forward (see 3.5.10 and 3.5.240).

2.5.500 Linkage of transactions

2.5.500.10 Because different accounting treatments apply depending on whether or not control is lost, the structure of transactions could affect the accounting result. As a consequence, IAS 27 contains provisions for determining whether two or more transactions or arrangements that result in the loss of control of a subsidiary should be treated as a single transaction.

IAS 27.33 2.5.500.20 In some instances it will be clear that a series of transactions are linked and should be accounted for as a single transaction. However, in other instances a careful analysis of the facts and circumstances and the exercise of judgement will be required in making the determination. If one or more of the following indicators is present, then this may indicate that the transactions or arrangements that result in a loss of control should be accounted for as a single transaction or arrangement:

- they are entered into at the same time or in contemplation of one another;
- they form a single arrangement that achieves, or is designed to achieve, an overall commercial effect;
- the occurrence of one transaction or arrangement is dependent on the other transaction(s) or arrangement(s) occurring; or
- one or more of the transactions or arrangements considered on their own is not economically justified, but are economically justified when considered together, e.g. when one disposal is priced below market, compensated by a subsequent disposal priced above market.

2.5.500.30 For example, Company P owns 70 percent of the shares in Subsidiary S. P intends to sell all of its 70 percent interest in S and is considering the following structures to effect the sale:

- sell all of its 70 percent interest in one transaction; or
- initially sell 19 percent of its interest in S without the loss of control and then afterwards sell the remaining 51 percent and lose control.

2.5.500.40 In the first case, the full amount of the gain or loss on the sale of the 70 percent interest would be recognised in profit or loss. In the second case, if the transactions are determined not to be linked, then the gain or loss on the sale of the 19 percent interest would be recognised in equity, whereas the gain or loss from the sale of the remaining 51 percent interest would be recognised in profit or loss. If they are determined to be linked, then the treatment would be the same as the first case.

2.5.500.50 In another example, Company P sells a subsidiary to Company Q. The purchase and sale agreement includes a manufacturing and supply agreement. According to the manufacturing and supply agreement, P agrees to supply specific products to Q. The selling price of the products covers all of P's manufacturing costs (direct and indirect), transportation costs, duties and other taxes, and insurance costs, but includes no profit margin to P. The manufacturing and supply agreement commences upon completion of the purchase and sale agreement and ends five years later. Other relevant facts include:

- P has no similar manufacturing and supply agreement with other customers.
- It is believed that P would not have received the same price for the sale of the subsidiary if the purchase and sale agreement had not been entered into simultaneously with the manufacturing and supply agreement.
- Each year Q provides P with a two-year non-binding forecast of the expected order quantities and a 12-month rolling forecast is provided on a monthly basis.

2.5.500.60 The agreement appears to include two transactions: (1) the disposal of a subsidiary; and (2) a manufacturing and supply agreement of goods. However, in our view the transactions are linked and should be accounted for together. Therefore, a portion of the proceeds on the sale of the subsidiary should be deferred and recognised as revenue as the goods are delivered. Any subsequent changes in the estimate of goods to be delivered are changes in estimates and should be accounted for as such in accordance with IAS 8 *Accounting Policies, Changes in Estimates and Errors* (see 2.8.60).

2.5.510 *Demergers/spin-offs*

2.5.510.10 If a parent distributes its ownership interest in a subsidiary and loses control as a result (demerger or spin-off), then consideration should be given as to whether the distribution is within the scope of IFRIC 17 *Distributions of Non-cash Assets to Owners*.

IFRIC 17.3, 4, 6, 7 2.5.510.20 IFRIC 17 applies to non-reciprocal distributions of non-cash assets to owners acting in their capacity as owners, in which all owners of the same class of equity instruments are treated equally. It also applies to distributions in which each owner may elect to receive either their share of the non-cash asset or a cash alternative. IFRIC 17 excludes from its scope:

- common control transactions; and
- distributions of part of the ownership interests in a subsidiary when control is retained.

IFRIC 17.6 2.5.510.30 A common control transaction in this context is a distribution in which the asset being distributed ultimately is controlled by the same party (or parties) both before and after the distribution (see 5.13.10).

2.5.510.40 For a demerger within the scope of IFRIC 17, the distribution is measured at the fair value of the assets to be distributed and any gain or loss on the distribution is recognised in profit or loss (see 3.11.452).

2.5.510.50 The accounting for demergers that are not within the scope of IFRIC 17 is not addressed specifically in IFRSs. Therefore, an entity should develop an accounting policy for such demergers using the hierarchy for the selection of accounting policies in IAS 8. In our view, for a demerger that is not within the scope of IFRIC 17, the distribution can be measured using either book values or fair value. See 5.13.90 for a discussion in the context of common control transactions.

2.5.515 *Non-current assets held for sale*

IFRS 5.6-8A 2.5.515.10 When an entity is committed to a sale plan involving the loss of control of a subsidiary, it classifies all of the assets and liabilities of that subsidiary as held for sale when the IFRS 5 criteria for such classification are met (see 5.4.20). This is regardless of whether the entity will retain a non-controlling interest in its former subsidiary.

IFRS 5.30- 2.5.515.20 If the subsidiary being sold meets the definition of a discontinued operation, *36A* then it is presented accordingly.

2.5.520 *Amount owed to or from a former subsidiary that remains outstanding after control is lost*

IAS 27.34, 2.5.520.10 Sometimes an amount owed to or from a former subsidiary prior to losing *36, 39.4* control will remain payable after control of that subsidiary is lost, and the question arises as to how that amount should be accounted for upon the loss of control. Since the receivable or payable is recognised for the first time, at the point of loss of control, it is required under IAS 39 to be recognised at fair value (and IAS 39 applies thereafter).

2.5.520.20 For example Company P sells to Company Q 100 percent of Subsidiary S, on 31 March 2010 for cash of 1,000. P has a receivable of 100 due from S immediately prior to losing control over S. This amount remains payable to P from S after the loss of control. The fair value of the receivable at 31 March 2010 also is 100. The receivable is part of the consideration received by P for S. Therefore, the total consideration is 1,100 (1,000 + 100). The receivable is subsequently accounted for in accordance with IAS 39.

2.5.525 *Contribution of a subsidiary to an associate or a jointly controlled entity*

IAS 28.22, 2.5.525.10 Sometimes a parent may contribute a subsidiary to an associate or a jointly *31.48,* controlled entity. The question arises as to how the gain or loss should be calculated as *SIC-13.5* there appears to be some ambiguity in IFRSs in this regard. IAS 27 requires that when control of a subsidiary is lost, any resulting gain or loss is recognised in full in profit or loss (see 2.5.490), i.e. no elimination is made in respect of a continuing interest in the assets and liabilities contributed. However, IAS 28, IAS 31 and SIC-13 *Jointly Controlled Entities – Non-Monetary Contributions by Venturers* require an elimination to be made in respect of a continuing interest in the assets and liabilities contributed. At this stage it is not clear which requirement should take precedence.

2.5.525.20 In our view, this conflict means that the entity should choose an accounting policy, to be applied consistently, to apply either the IAS 27 approach or the IAS 28/ IAS 31 (SIC-13) approach:

- *The IAS 27 approach.* Under this approach, no elimination of the gain or loss is performed and the fair value of the retained investment is its deemed cost for the purpose of subsequent accounting.
- *The IAS 28/IAS 31 (SIC-13) approach.* Under this approach, the gain or loss is eliminated to the extent of the retained interest in the former subsidiary.

2.5.525.30 See 3.5.470 and 3.5.600 for further discussion, and 2.5.490.60 for a discussion of the allocation of reserves.

2.5.530 *Written call option to sell shares in a subsidiary*

2.5.530.10 In some cases an entity will sell a portion of its shares in a subsidiary and at the same time write a call option for the potential sale of additional shares. In our view, the proceeds should be split between the call option and the shares by determining the fair value of the call option at inception, required to be recognised by IAS 39, and attributing the remaining proceeds to the sale of shares.

2.5.535 *Agreement to sell ownership interests in a subsidiary at a later date*

AS 27.IG5-8 2.5.535.10 In some cases an entity may enter into an agreement to sell some of its ownership interests in a subsidiary at a later date. The entity considers the derecognition criteria in IAS 39 to determine the percentage attributable to the NCI. If the derecognition criteria have not been met in respect of the remaining shares to be sold, then the NCI would be measured without taking the agreement to sell into account.

2.5.535.20 For example, Company P owns 100 percent of Company S. P enters into an agreement with Company Q to sell 40 percent of its shares in S at the reporting date and an additional 20 percent at the end of each year for the next three years. The price of the shares to be sold will be based on a fixed price determined at the agreement date. If P retains control of S, then P considers the derecognition criteria in IAS 39 to determine the percentage attributable to the NCI. If the derecognition criteria have not been met in respect of the remaining shares to be sold, then the NCI would be measured based on a 40 percent interest at the reporting date.

2.5.540 **Transitional issues upon the adoption of IAS 27 (2008)**

2.5.545 *Losses attributable to NCI*

IAS 27.35 2.5.545.10 IAS 27 (2003) required losses incurred in excess of minority interests
2003), 45(a) to be allocated against the parent's interest unless the minority had a binding obligation to fund the losses and was able to make an additional investment to cover the losses. If the subsidiary subsequently reported profits, then these profits were allocated to the

parent until the share of losses absorbed previously by the parent had been recovered. Under IAS 27, losses applicable to the NCI in a subsidiary, including components of other comprehensive income, are allocated to the NCI even if doing so causes the NCI to be in a deficit position (see 2.5.325). This amendment is applied prospectively.

2.5.545.20 The question arises as to what the accounting treatment should be upon the adoption of IAS 27 if prior to the adoption of IAS 27 the owners of the parent have absorbed losses that were attributable to the minority interests. In our view, upon transition to IAS 27 no adjustment should be made to reflect such a balance in the opening statement of financial position on the adoption of IAS 27. After adoption of IAS 27 in its consolidated financial statements, we believe that the parent should allocate total comprehensive income on the basis of the present interests of the owners of the parent and NCI. In our view, gains should not be first allocated to the parent until a deficit recognised in previous periods in the parent's equity is eliminated.

2.5.550 *Direct method used to allocate profits to the non-controlling/minority interest*

2.5.550.10 It is unclear as to whether NCI should be adjusted on transition to IAS 27 if an entity previously used the direct method to allocate profits of a subsidiary between the equity holders of the parent and minority interests. In our view, no adjustment should be made to NCI on transition as a result of the revised definition of NCI.

IAS 27.4   2.5.550.20 Under IAS 27 (2003), *minority interests* were the portion of profit or loss and net assets of a subsidiary attributable to equity interests that are not owned, directly or indirectly through subsidiaries, by the parent. Under IAS 27, *NCI* is the equity in a subsidiary not attributable, directly or indirectly, to the parent. The implication of the changed definition is that under IAS 27 interests in a subsidiary held by an associate or joint venture of the parent are no longer considered to be part of NCI.

2.5.550.30 Under IAS 27 (2003), in our view an entity had an accounting policy choice in respect of the allocation of profit between the equity holders of the parent and minority interests to use either the direct method or the indirect method.

2.5.560 *Written put with non-controlling shareholders*

2.5.560.10 In some cases a put with non-controlling shareholders may have been written while IFRS 3 (2004) and IAS 27 (2003) were in effect, and remain outstanding upon the adoption of IFRS 3 and IAS 27. It is unclear whether an entity may continue its existing accounting, or whether it needs to change its accounting policy in accordance with the new standards. In our view, an entity continues its existing accounting policy under IFRS 3 (2004) and IAS 27 (2003) in respect of that put.

2.5.560.20 In our view, an entity should choose an accounting policy, to be applied consistently, to subsequently account for the carrying amount of the non-controlling shareholder put liability in the context of IAS 27 (2003) using either:

- *The IAS 39 approach.* Under this approach, changes in the carrying amount of the liability are recognised in profit or loss.
- *The adjustment to initial accounting approach.* Under this approach, changes in the carrying amount of the liability are recognised by adjusting the carrying amount of the balancing item affected by the initial recognition of the transaction, e.g. goodwill; this excludes the effect of unwinding the discount, which is recognised in profit or loss.

2.5.560.30 The adjustment to initial accounting approach is supported by the fact that variability in the consideration payable is contingent consideration, even when it relates to the acquisition of non-controlling interests. In our view, contingent consideration arising under IFRS 3 (2004) is scoped out of IAS 39 even though the IAS 39 exemption for contingent consideration was removed for annual periods beginning on or after 1 January 2009 (see 2.6.1160).

2.5.570 Future developments

2.5.570.10 The IASB has a consolidation project on its agenda, the objective of which is to develop a basis for consolidation that will apply to all entities, including "structured entities". In December 2008 the IASB published ED 10 *Consolidated Financial Statements*, which proposed a single *de facto* control model for all entities, including structured entities. A final standard is scheduled for the fourth quarter of 2010.

2.5.570.20 As a result of its redeliberations following comments received on the ED, the IASB has decided to publish a separate comprehensive standard that is expected to require extensive disclosures in respect of an entity's involvement with consolidated and unconsolidated entities, including structured entities. A final standard is scheduled for the fourth quarter of 2010.

2.5.570.30 The IASB and the FASB have added a joint project in respect of investment entities to their agendas, the objective of which is to exempt investment companies (as defined) from the requirement to consolidate controlled entities. An ED is scheduled for the fourth quarter of 2010.

2.6 Business combinations
(IFRS 3)

2.6 Business combinations
(IFRS 3)

Overview of currently effective requirements

- All business combinations are accounted for using the acquisition method, with limited exceptions.

- A business combination is a transaction or other event in which an acquirer obtains control of one or more businesses.

- A business is an integrated set of activities and assets that is capable of being conducted and managed to provide a return to investors (or other owners, members or participants) by way of dividends, lower costs or other economic benefits.

- The acquirer in a business combination is the combining entity that obtains control of the other combining business or businesses.

- In some cases the legal acquiree is identified as the acquirer for accounting purposes ("reverse acquisition").

- The acquisition date is the date on which the acquirer obtains control of the acquiree.

- Consideration transferred by the acquirer, which generally is measured at fair value at the acquisition date, may include assets transferred, liabilities incurred by the acquirer to the previous owners of the acquiree and equity interests issued by the acquirer.

- Contingent consideration transferred is recognised initially at fair value. Contingent consideration classified as a liability generally is remeasured to fair value each period until settlement, with changes recognised in profit or loss. Contingent consideration classified as equity is not remeasured.

- Any items that are not part of the business combination transaction are accounted for outside of the acquisition accounting. Examples include:
  - the settlement of a pre-existing relationship between the acquirer and the acquiree;
  - remuneration to employees who are former owners of the acquiree; and
  - acquisition-related costs.

- The identifiable assets acquired and the liabilities assumed as part of a business combination are recognised separately from goodwill at the acquisition date if they meet the definition of assets and liabilities and are exchanged as part of the business combination.

- The identifiable assets acquired and liabilities assumed as part of a business combination are measured at the acquisition date at their fair values.

- There are limited exceptions to the recognition and/or measurement principles in respect of contingent liabilities, deferred tax assets and liabilities, indemnification assets, employee benefits, reacquired rights, share-based payment awards and assets held for sale.

- Goodwill or a gain on a bargain purchase is measured as a residual.

- Adjustments to the acquisition accounting during the "measurement period" reflect additional information about facts and circumstances that existed at the acquisition date. The measurement period ends when the acquirer obtains all information that is necessary to complete the acquisition accounting, or learns that more information is not available, and cannot exceed one year from the acquisition date.

- The acquirer in a business combination can elect, on a transaction-by-transaction basis, to measure non-controlling interests at fair value or at their proportionate interest in the recognised amount of the identifiable net assets of the acquiree at the acquisition date.

- When a business combination is achieved in stages (step acquisition), the acquirer's previously held non-controlling equity interest in the acquiree is remeasured to fair value at the acquisition date, with any resulting gain or loss recognised in profit or loss.

- In general, items recognised in the acquisition accounting are measured and accounted for in accordance with the relevant IFRS subsequent to the business combination. However, as an exception, IFRS 3 includes some specific guidance, for example in respect of contingent liabilities and indemnification assets.

Currently effective requirements

This publication reflects IFRSs in issue at 1 August 2010. The currently effective requirements cover annual periods beginning on 1 January 2010. The requirements related to this topic are derived mainly from IFRS 3 *Business Combinations*.

KPMG's publication *IFRS Handbook: Business combinations and non-controlling interests* provides a comprehensive analysis of IFRS 3 and the accounting for non-controlling interests (NCI) in accordance with IAS 27 *Consolidated and Separate Financial Statements*. In addition to including additional clarification of the requirements of IFRS 3 and of our interpretative guidance, the Handbook includes extensive illustrative examples to elaborate or clarify the practical application of IFRS 3, and as such is more in-depth than this chapter.

Forthcoming requirements and future developments

When a currently effective requirement will be changed by a new requirement that is issued but is not yet effective, it is marked with a # as a **forthcoming requirement** and the impact of the change is explained in the accompanying boxed text. The forthcoming requirements related to this chapter are derived from the *Improvements to IFRSs 2010*. A brief outline of the impact of the *Improvements to IFRSs 2010* on this topic is given in 2.6.510 and 2.6.850 – 890, and a brief outline of the annual improvements process is given in 1.1.85.

When a significant change to the currently effective or forthcoming requirements is expected, it is marked with a * as an area that may be subject to **future developments** and a brief outline of the relevant projects is given in 2.6.1180.

2.6.10 **Scope**

IFRS 3.2   2.6.10.10 IFRS 3 applies to a transaction or other event that meets the definition of a business combination. IFRS 3 does not apply to:

- the formation of a joint venture;
- the acquisition of an asset or a group of assets that does not meet the definition of a business; or
- a combination of entities or businesses under common control.

2.6.10.20 Transactions that give rise to the formation of a joint venture are outside the scope of IFRS 3 because they do not meet the definition of a business combination, i.e. none of the participants obtains control over the joint venture. However, IFRS 3 is applied to a business combination entered into by a joint venture after its formation.

IFRS 3.2(b)   2.6.10.30 If an entity acquires an asset or a group of assets, including any liabilities assumed, that does not constitute a business, then the transaction is outside the scope of IFRS 3 because it cannot meet the definition of a business combination. Such transactions are accounted for as asset acquisitions in which the cost of acquisition is allocated between the individual identifiable assets and liabilities in the group based on their relative fair values at the acquisition date.

2.6.10.40 A business combination in which all of the combining entities or businesses ultimately are controlled by the same party or parties both before and after the combination, and that control is not transitory, is outside the scope of IFRS 3. See 5.13 for a detailed discussion of common control transactions.

2.6.20 **Identifying a business combination**

IFRS 3.B5   2.6.20.10 A *business combination* is a transaction or other event in which an acquirer obtains control of one or more businesses. An acquirer may obtain control in a number of ways including, for example, by transferring cash or other assets, incurring liabilities, issuing equity instruments or without transferring consideration. The structure of a transaction or event does not affect the determination of whether it is a business combination; whether an acquirer obtains control of one or more businesses is determinative.

IFRS 3.A, B7   2.6.20.20 A *business* is an integrated set of activities and assets that is capable of being conducted and managed to provide a return to investors (or other owners, members or participants) by way of dividends, lower costs or other economic benefits. A business generally consists of inputs, processes applied to those inputs and the ability to create outputs.

2.6.20.30 For a transaction or event to be a business combination, the activities and assets over which the acquirer has obtained control *must* constitute a business.

2.6.30 *Inputs, processes and outputs*

IFRS 3.B7,   2.6.30.10 For an integrated set of activities and assets to be considered a business, the
B8   set needs to contain both inputs and processes. Outputs are not required to qualify as a business as long as there is the ability to create outputs. If the acquired set includes only inputs, then it is accounted for as an asset acquisition rather than as a business combination (see 2.6.10.30). The key terms are defined as follows:

- *Inputs* are economic resources that create (or have the ability to create) outputs when one or more processes are applied to them. Examples of inputs include non-current assets (including intangible assets or rights to use non-current assets), intellectual property, the ability to obtain access to necessary materials or rights, and employees.
- *Processes* are systems, standards, protocols, conventions or rules that create (or have the ability to create) outputs when they are applied to inputs. Examples of processes include strategic management processes, operational processes and resource management processes. These processes typically are documented, but an organised workforce with the necessary skills and experience following rules and conventions may provide the necessary processes that are capable of being applied to inputs to create outputs. Accounting, billing, payroll and other administrative systems typically are not processes used to create outputs.
- *Outputs* are the result of inputs and processes applied to those inputs that provide, or have the ability to provide, a return in the form of economic benefits.

IFRS 3.B8,   2.6.30.20 The acquisition of all of the inputs and processes used by the seller in operating
B11   a business is not necessary for the activities and assets acquired to meet the definition
of a business. What is important is that a market participant (see 2.6.1040.60 – 80 in the
context of fair value) would be capable of producing outputs by integrating what was
acquired with either its own inputs and processes or with inputs and processes that it
could obtain. Therefore, it is not relevant whether the seller operated the set as a business or whether the acquirer intends to operate it as a business.

2.6.30.30 In our view, a significant characteristic of a business is that the underlying
activities and assets are integrated. A group of assets without connecting activities is
unlikely to represent a business.

2.6.30.40 If the acquiree has employees and the related employment contracts are transferred to the acquirer, then this may be an indicator that a business has been acquired.
However, in our view a group of assets acquired still could be a business even if some
(or all) of the staff employed formerly by the acquiree are replaced by the acquirer's
own staff and those staff will carry out the acquiree's existing activities necessary to
generate economic benefits. Not taking over all of the employees might be a major part
of the synergies that the acquirer is seeking to achieve by the acquisition. The acquirer's
decision not to retain all employees does not mean that the acquired activities and assets
do not comprise a business.

2.6.30.50 If some of the acquiree's processes and activities were outsourced before the
acquisition and the related contracts are taken over by the acquirer, then this could
indicate that the processes and activities necessary to create outputs are in place,
and therefore that the group of assets acquired is a business. Conversely, if none
of the processes or activities are in place at the acquisition date, but instead would
be designed and established by a market participant (or a market participant would
already have similar processes), then this could indicate that what was acquired is
not a business.

IFRS 3.B8   2.6.30.60 The exclusion of some components of a business does not preclude classification of an acquisition as a business combination if a market participant could operate
the remaining activities and assets as a business. However, judgement is required in
making this determination.

2.6.30.70 For example, Company P owns and operates restaurant groups in various metropolitan areas. P acquires from Company S a group of 10 restaurants located in a major
city. The acquired group of assets includes land, buildings, leased assets and leasehold
improvements, equipment, and the rights to the trade name used by the restaurant group.
P also offers employment to the restaurants' employees, including management-level
employees, service staff and chefs. P acquires S's procurement system used to purchase
the food, drinks and other supplies necessary to operate the restaurants. P will integrate
the 10 restaurants into its existing accounting and human resource systems.

2.6.30.80 The elements in the acquired set include:

- *Inputs*. Non-current assets (land, buildings, leased assets, leasehold improvements and equipment); rights to the trade name; employees; and access to food, drinks and other supplies that when subjected to processes will create outputs.
- *Processes*. Management and operational processes necessary to create outputs through the retention of management and staff; and the procurement system.
- *Outputs*. The intended outputs include food, drinks and service.

2.6.30.90 The acquired set of restaurants is a business since it contains all of the inputs and processes necessary for it to be capable of creating outputs to provide a return to P. While the administrative systems (accounting and human resources) of S are not acquired by P, the acquired restaurants will be integrated into P's existing accounting and human resources systems. As the acquired group of assets is a business, the acquisition is accounted for as a business combination.

2.6.30.100 Assume the same facts as in 2.6.30.70 except that P does not acquire S's procurement system. The elements in the acquired set include:

- *Inputs*. Non-current assets (land, buildings, leased assets, leasehold improvements and equipment); rights to the trade name; and employees.
- *Processes*. Management and operational processes necessary to create outputs (through the retention of management and staff).
- *Outputs*. The intended outputs include food, drinks and service.

2.6.30.110 We believe that the acquired set of restaurants is a business, notwithstanding the fact that it does not contain all of the inputs and processes necessary for it to be capable of creating outputs to provide a return to P as S's procurement system was not acquired. The acquired activities and assets do not need to be "self-sustaining" in order to be a business. The fact that some elements of a business are not taken over does not mean that what is acquired is not a business. A market participant could integrate the procurement needs of the acquired restaurants into its own procurement process. In fact, not taking over the procurement system of the acquiree may be a part of the synergies that a market participant would intend to obtain by entering into the business combination. As the acquired group of assets is a business, the acquisition is accounted for as a business combination.

2.6.30.120 Assume the same facts as in 2.6.30.70 except that P acquires only the land, buildings, leased assets and leasehold improvements, and equipment. S closed the restaurants comprising the acquired set a significant period of time before the acquisition by P. P does not acquire employees, the rights to the trade name or the processes from S. The elements in the acquired set include:

- *Inputs*. Non-current assets (land, buildings, leased assets, leasehold improvements and equipment).
- *Processes*. No processes were acquired.
- *Outputs*. The intended outputs include food, drinks and service.

2.6.30.130 We believe that the acquired set of restaurants is not a business. A business consists of inputs and processes applied to those inputs that have the ability to create outputs. In this case no processes are acquired and some key inputs are missing. Therefore, we believe that there is no business and consequently no business combination; instead, the acquisition is accounted for as an asset acquisition. Even if a market participant would be capable of acquiring the land, buildings and equipment and integrating these into its own business to create outputs, the acquired set is not a business.

2.6.30.140 The seller may retain an option to repurchase key components of the business sold. In such cases it is necessary to consider the nature of those components to determine whether the assets and activities acquired would meet the definition of a business in their absence. The terms and substance of the option also are considered.

2.6.30.150 For example, Company P acquires Company S's research and development (R&D) business. However, at the same time the parties agree on an option for S to reacquire the service contracts of the key research personnel in the business, exercisable at any time over the next two years. The R&D activities acquired are extremely specialised and the research personnel have unique knowledge that is not readily available in the marketplace. Without the research personnel, one of the key elements necessary for the group of assets to comprise a business is missing. Therefore, in this example we believe that there is no business and consequently no business combination; instead, the acquisition is accounted for as an asset acquisition (see 2.6.10.30).

IFRS 3.B12 2.6.30.160 IFRS 3 contains a rebuttable presumption that a group of assets in which goodwill is present is a business. However, a business does not need to have goodwill. Therefore, the presence of goodwill implies that the acquired set is a business. However, the acquirer should consider whether all of the tangible and intangible assets acquired have been correctly identified, recognised and valued before concluding that goodwill is present.

IFRS 3.B10 2.6.30.170 IFRS 3 provides some example factors to consider when determining whether an integrated set of activities and assets in the development stage is a business, although not all of these factors need to be present for the set to be considered a business:

- Planned principal activities have commenced.
- There are employees, intellectual property and other inputs and there are processes that could be applied to those inputs.
- A plan to produce outputs is being pursued.
- There will be an ability to obtain access to customers who will purchase the outputs.

2.6.40 *Investment property*

2.6.40.10 When investment property is acquired, a careful analysis of what is acquired often is needed to determine whether it constitutes a business. In practice it can be difficult to decide whether the acquired set meets the definition of a business, and judgement will be required. Factors that may be relevant in making the determination include whether property management services are acquired and the nature of those services, and the level of ancillary services (e.g. security, cleaning and maintenance) acquired and the nature of those services.

2.6.40.20 For example, Company P purchases four investment properties (shopping malls) that are fully rented to tenants. P also takes over the contract with the property management company, which has unique knowledge related to investment properties in the area and makes all decisions, both of a strategic nature and related to the daily operations of the malls. Ancillary activities necessary to fulfil the obligations arising from these lease contracts also are in place, specifically activities related to maintaining the building and administering the tenants.

2.6.40.30 The elements in the acquired set include:

- *Inputs*. Non-current assets (land and buildings) and contracts.
- *Processes*. Management with unique knowledge related to investment properties in the area.
- *Outputs*. The intended outputs include rental income.

2.6.40.40 In our view, the acquired set is a business since it contains all of the inputs and processes necessary for it to be capable of creating outputs to provide a return to P.

2.6.40.50 In contrast, if the property management is not taken over, then the group of assets might not be a business. The acquired set might not represent an integrated set of activities and assets as the key element of the infrastructure of the business, property management, is not taken over. If so, P would account for the transaction as the purchase of individual investment properties, and not as the purchase of a business. It is necessary to consider all the relevant facts and circumstances and significant judgement may be required.

2.6.50 Overview of the acquisition method

IFRS 3.4,5   2.6.50.10 IFRS 3 requires that acquisition accounting be applied to all business combinations within its scope. There are a number of steps in applying acquisition accounting for a business combination, which are discussed in more detail throughout this chapter:

- Identify the acquirer (see 2.6.60).
- Determine the acquisition date (see 2.6.180).
- Identify the consideration transferred in the business combination, and elements of the transaction that should be accounted for separately from the business combination (see 2.6.260 and 340).
- Measure the consideration transferred (see 2.6.260).
- Identify the identifiable assets acquired and liabilities assumed in the business combination (see 2.6.560).
- Measure the identifiable assets acquired and liabilities assumed in the business combination (see 2.6.600 and 1050).

- Measure NCI (see 2.6.840).
- Determine the amount of goodwill or the gain on a bargain purchase (see 2.6.900).
- Recognise any measurement period adjustments (see 2.6.910).

2.6.60 Identifying the acquirer

IFRS 3.6, A, 2.6.60.10 An acquirer is identified for each business combination. The acquirer is the
IAS 27.4 combining entity that obtains control of the other combining business or businesses, where control is the power to govern the financial and operating policies of an entity so as to obtain benefits from its activities (see 2.5.20 and 2.5.120).

IFRS 3.7 2.6.60.20 In most business combinations identifying the acquirer is straightforward because it will be clear which one of the combining entities has obtained control. The acquirer is identified in the following steps:

AS 27.13-15 (1) Apply the guidance in IAS 27 to determine who has control.

IFRS 3.B13- (2) If an acquirer cannot be identified clearly from the guidance in IAS 27, then the
B18 additional factors identified in IFRS 3 are considered. These consist mainly of examining the form of the consideration transferred, the relative size of the combining entities, relative voting rights, and the composition of the board of directors and senior management.

2.6.60.30 In our view, the IAS 27 guidance discussed in 2.5 should not be the sole focus of identifying an acquirer even if it appears that an acquirer can be identified; the additional guidance in IFRS 3 also should be taken into account. Otherwise there is a risk that the analysis of which party is the acquirer may lead to an answer that conflicts with what we believe is the intention of IFRS 3. For example, only applying the IAS 27 guidance on control would mean that a reverse acquisition (see 2.6.170) could not arise as the entity that owns all of the share capital of another entity always will have the power to govern its financial and operating policies so as to gain benefits from that other entity's activities.

2.6.70 *Combinations effected primarily by transferring cash or other assets or by incurring liabilities*

IFRS 3.B14 2.6.70.10 In business combinations effected primarily by the transfer of cash or other assets or by incurring liabilities, the acquirer usually is the entity that transfers the cash or other assets or incurs the liabilities. For example, if Company P acquires Company S by transferring cash to the owners of S, then P usually would be identified as the acquirer in the business combination, assuming that S meets the definition of a business (see 2.6.20).

2.6.80 *Combinations effected primarily by exchanging equity interests*

IFRS 3.B15, 2.6.80.10 In most business combinations effected primarily through the exchange of
B18 equity interests, the acquirer is the entity that issues the new equity interests. One exception to this general principle is a reverse acquisition, in which case the issuing entity

is the acquiree (see 2.6.170). Another exception is situations in which a new entity is created to issue equity instruments to effect a business combination (see 2.6.160).

2.6.80.20 While not exhaustive, other factors to consider in identifying the acquirer are discussed in 2.6.90 – 140. The factors have no hierarchy, and some factors may be more relevant to identifying the acquirer in one combination and less relevant in others. Judgement is required when the various factors individually point to different entities as the acquirer.

2.6.90 *The relative voting rights in the combined entity after the business combination*

IFRS 3.B15(a)
IAS 27.14, 15
2.6.90.10 The acquirer usually is the combining entity whose owners, as a group, hold the largest portion of the voting rights in the combined entity. Typically the weight attached to this factor increases as the portion of the voting rights held by the majority increases; for example, a split of 80 percent to 20 percent is likely to be determinative in the absence of other factors. In making this determination, consideration is given to the existence of any unusual or special voting arrangements, and potential voting rights such as options, warrants or convertible securities.

IAS 27.15
2.6.90.20 The exercise price of potential voting rights and the financial capability of the holder to exercise them are ignored. However, the capability to exercise power does not exist when potential voting rights lack economic substance, e.g. when the price deliberately is set so high that the chance of the potential voting rights being exercised is remote.

2.6.90.30 In some cases the exercise of potential voting rights may be subject to regulatory approval. In our view, the rights are considered currently exercisable only when regulatory approval is deemed a mere formality. The nature of regulatory approval, together with all relevant facts and circumstances, is considered when making this assessment.

2.6.90.40 In some transactions the voting rights of one or more classes of shares automatically change at a future date or on the occurrence of specified events. For example, a class of shares may be designated as non-voting for a limited time period following the business combination. All of the facts and circumstances of the transaction are evaluated to determine how this affects the identification of the acquirer. The factors described in 2.6.110 also may be helpful in evaluating whether the period of time that the shares are non-voting is substantive.

2.6.100 *The existence of a large minority voting interest in the combined entity if no other owner or organised group of owners has a significant voting interest*

IFRS 3.B15(b)
2.6.100.10 When there is a large minority voting interest and no other owner or organised group of owners has a significant voting interest, the acquirer usually is the combining entity whose single owner or organised group of owners holds the largest minority voting interest in the combined entity. For example, if one investor owns 40 percent of the newly combined entity and the remaining 60 percent is shared equally by six other investors

who are not organised as a group, then the entity previously owned by the investor holding 40 percent of the combined entity is likely to be the acquirer. See 2.6.160.30 – 40 for an illustration of this principle.

2.6.110 *The composition of the governing body of the combined entity*

IFRS 3.B15(c)   2.6.110.10 The acquirer usually is the combining entity whose shareholders (owners) have the ability to appoint or remove a majority of the members of the governing body, e.g. board of directors, of the combined entity.

2.6.110.20 IFRS 3 is silent as to whether these rights need to exist only at the acquisition date, or for a period of time thereafter. However, if control of the governing body by a shareholder group is temporary, then consideration is given to whether that control is substantive. In making this determination, the period of time that each governing body member is entitled to hold their position also is considered, taking into account scheduled retirements and elections after the acquisition date.

2.6.110.30 While there is no minimum duration required for a shareholder group to be in control of the governing body for it to be deemed substantive, in our view control generally should extend for a sufficient duration to allow the governing body to consider and act on substantive matters following the acquisition. These may include matters related to corporate governance, the appointment and compensation of senior management, the issue of debt or equity securities, and substantive business integration, exit and disposal activities. When the period of control of the governing body is temporary, judgement will be required in determining whether that control is substantive.

2.6.120 *The composition of the senior management of the combined entity*

IFRS 3.B15(d)   2.6.120.10 The acquirer usually is the combining entity whose former management dominates the management of the combined entity.

IAS 24.9   2.6.120.20 IFRS 3 is silent on what is meant by "senior" management. In our view, it is consistent with "key management personnel" defined in IAS 24 *Related Party Disclosures* as being those persons having authority and responsibility for planning, directing and controlling the activities of the entity. The definition of key management personnel includes directors (both executive and non-executive) of an entity or any of the entity's parents (see 5.5.40 and 5.5A.40).

2.6.130 *The terms of the exchange of equity interests*

IFRS 3.B15(e)   2.6.130.10 The acquirer usually is the combining entity that pays a premium over the pre-combination fair value of the equity interests of the other combining entity or entities. This factor applies equally when the equity instruments exchanged are not publicly traded.

2.6.130.20 For example, Company P acquires 15 percent of the outstanding shares of Company S, a public company, for cash, paying a premium of 10 percent above the market price; and acquires the remaining outstanding shares of S in exchange for shares of P. After the acquisition, the former shareholders of S own 58 percent of the outstanding shares of the combined company. If exercised, warrants held by former shareholders of S would increase their interest to 71 percent; however, the warrants cannot be exercised for three years from the closing date.

2.6.130.30 The board of directors of the combined entity consists of five nominees of P and four nominees of S for a two-year term. The removal of board members requires a vote of at least two-thirds of the shareholders. The chairman and the CEO of P retain their positions in the combined company. No other relevant circumstances exist with respect to voting, ownership of significant blocks of shares, or management.

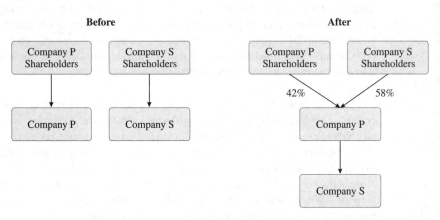

2.6.130.40 In this example we believe that P is the acquirer, notwithstanding the voting majority of the former shareholders of S. Although S's former shareholders will own the majority of the shares in the combined company, they will not own two-thirds of the shares for at least three years following the business combination; accordingly, they will not be able to vote out the board of directors in place immediately after the business combination. P paid partly in cash, including a premium above market price, and dominates the board of directors and senior management of the combined entity. Therefore, we would identify P as the acquirer as it has the most influence in the combined entity.

2.6.140 *The relative size of the combining entities*

IFRS 3.B16   2.6.140.10 The acquirer usually is the combining entity that is significantly larger than the other combining entity or entities. Size can be measured by reference to, for example, assets, revenue or profit. Other examples of relative size include operating cash flows and market capitalisation. If assets are being used to compare relative size, then in our view it is the fair value of the assets that should be used.

2.6.140.20 Judgement is required when comparing the combining entities based on their relative size. When each combining entity is involved in similar businesses, a comparison of relative size may be straightforward, although not necessarily so. However, when the combining entities are involved in different businesses, a comparison of relative size may not be straightforward and certain adjustments to reported amounts in the financial statements may be required. Information other than the reported amounts in the financial statements also is considered.

2.6.140.30 For example, two entities' principal revenue-generating assets are intangible. In one case the assets were internally developed and therefore are not recognised in the statement of financial position; in the other case the assets were acquired in a series of business combinations and therefore are recognised in the statement of financial position. Accordingly, comparing the reported assets of the two entities may not be appropriate. As noted in 2.6.140.10, we believe that the fair value of the assets should be used.

2.6.140.40 Similarly, comparing the amount of reported revenues without considering the nature and source of those revenues may not be appropriate. For example, comparing revenues generated by an entity with high volumes and low gross margins (e.g. a grocery store chain) with revenues generated by an entity with low volumes and high gross margins (e.g. a custom designer and manufacturer of specialised equipment) might not be meaningful.

2.6.150 *New entity formed to effect a business combination*

IFRS 3.B18 2.6.150.10 A new entity (Newco) formed to effect a business combination is not necessarily the acquirer. In such cases one of the combining entities that existed before the combination is identified as the acquirer by considering the additional factors provided in IFRS 3 (see 2.6.70 – 140).

IFRS 3.B18 2.6.150.20 A newly formed entity that pays cash rather than issuing shares in a business combination might be identified as the acquirer; however, it will not always be the acquirer. All facts and circumstances are considered in identifying the acquirer in a business combination and judgement is required.

IFRS 3.B18 2.6.150.30 A business combination in which two or more entities transfer net assets that constitute businesses to a newly formed entity, or the owners of those entities transfer their equity interests to a newly formed entity, is a business combination within the scope of IFRS 3; in some countries such a business combination is referred to as a "roll-up" or "put-together" transaction. See 2.6.160.30 also the example in 2.6.160.30.

2.6.160 *Combinations involving more than two entities*

IFRS 3.B17 2.6.160.10 There is only one acquirer in a business combination. In business combinations involving more than two entities, determining the acquirer includes consideration of, among other things, which of the combining entities initiated the combination and the relative size of the combining entities.

2.6.160.20 The guidance in respect of combinations involving the exchange of equity interests, which indicates that the acquirer usually is the combining entity whose single owner or organised group of owners holds the largest minority voting interest in the combined entity (see 2.6.100), may be particularly helpful in identifying the acquirer in some combinations involving more than two entities.

2.6.160.30 For example, Companies A, B, C and D each operate independent florist shops in the suburbs of Metro City. Company E operates four florist shops in Metro City. To capitalise on economies of scale and other synergies, the owners agree to form a single entity (Metro Florists) by contributing their businesses in return for shares in Metro Florists. The ownership of Metro Florists will be as follows:

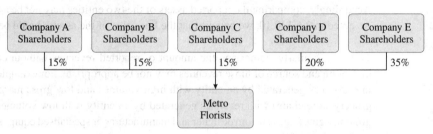

2.6.160.40 E's shareholders receive a greater interest in Metro Florists (35 percent) than the shareholders of any of the other combining companies. Because no other factors indicate to the contrary, E is identified as the acquirer. Metro Florists' financial statements will include the assets and liabilities of E at their pre-combination carrying amounts, and the assets and liabilities of A, B, C and D will be subject to acquisition accounting.

2.6.170 *Reverse acquisitions*

IFRS 3.B19   2.6.170.10 In business combinations effected through an exchange of equity interests, the entity that issues the equity interests usually is the acquirer. However, in some business combinations, referred to as reverse acquisitions, application of the guidance in IFRS 3 results in the identification of the legal acquirer (i.e. the entity that issues the securities) as the accounting acquiree and the legal acquiree as the accounting acquirer.

IFRS 3.IE1-   2.6.170.20 The accounting for reverse acquisitions is illustrated in the illustrative examples
IE15   that accompany IFRS 3.

2.6.180 **Determining the acquisition date**

IFRS 3.8   2.6.180.10 The acquisition date is the date on which the acquirer obtains control of the acquiree, i.e. the date from which the acquirer has the power to govern the financial and operating policies of the acquiree so as to obtain benefits from its activities (see 2.5.20 and 2.5.120).

IFRS 3.9   2.6.180.20 Determining the acquisition date usually will be straightforward. However, in certain business combinations it will require a careful analysis of the facts and circumstances, and judgement will be required. The acquisition date usually will be the closing date, i.e. the date on which the consideration legally is transferred and when the assets are acquired and liabilities are assumed, but this will depend on the facts and circumstances of each case.

2.6.180.30 Determining the acquisition date is important because it is the date on which the fair value of the consideration transferred and of the assets acquired and liabilities assumed is determined, and the date on which NCI and goodwill are measured and recognised. It also is only from this date that the results of the acquiree are included in the consolidated financial statements of the acquirer.

2.6.190 *Designating an effective acquisition date other than the actual date control is obtained*

2.6.190.10 It is not possible to designate an effective acquisition date other than the actual date on which control is obtained. However, in some cases it may be acceptable for an acquirer to consolidate a subsidiary from a reporting date close to the acquisition date for convenience, as long as the effect thereof is immaterial. For example, a subsidiary acquired on 13 October might be consolidated with effect from 30 September, provided that the effect of the 13 days is immaterial to the consolidated financial statements. For disclosure purposes the acquisition date would still be 13 October.

2.6.200 *Agreements with retroactive effect*

2.6.200.10 In some cases an agreement will provide that the acquisition is effective on a specified date. Irrespective of any date specified in an agreement, the acquisition date is the date on which the acquirer obtains the power to govern the financial and operating policies of the acquiree so as to obtain benefits from its activities, i.e. the date that control is obtained. This may or may not correspond to a specified date in an agreement.

2.6.200.20 For example, Companies P and S commence negotiations on 1 January 2010 for P to acquire all of the shares in S. On 1 March 2010 the agreement is finalised and P obtains the power to control S's operations on that date. However, the agreement states that the acquisition is effective as of 1 January 2010 and that P is entitled to all profits after that date. In addition, the purchase price is determined by reference to S's net asset position at 1 January 2010. In our view, notwithstanding that the price is based on the net assets at 1 January 2010 and S's shareholders do not receive any dividends after that date, the acquisition date for accounting purposes is 1 March 2010. This is because it is only on 1 March 2010 that P has the power to govern the financial and operating policies of S and obtain benefits from its activities.

2.6.210 *Shareholder approval*

2.6.210.10 In some cases management may agree on an acquisition subject to receiving shareholder approval, sometimes referred to as a "revocable" agreement. In our view, the acquisition date cannot be prior to shareholder approval if the passing of control is conditional upon their approval, e.g. the voting rights do not transfer or the board of directors remains unchanged until the acquisition is approved by the shareholders. However, it is necessary to consider the substance of the requirement of the shareholder approval to assess the impact that it has on obtaining the power to govern.

2.6.210.20 For example, Company P enters into an agreement with the shareholders of Company S on 1 March 2010 to acquire a controlling interest in S. The agreement provides that the effective date of transfer is 1 April 2010 and is subject to approval by the shareholders of P at a meeting scheduled for 1 May 2010. The voting rights are not transferred and the board of directors remains unchanged until the approval of P's shareholders. The board of directors of P does not control the majority of the voting interests in S. In our view, the acquisition date cannot be prior to P's shareholders approving the transaction as the passing of control is conditional upon their approval, i.e. the voting rights are not transferred and the board of directors remains unchanged until the approval of P's shareholders. However, if the board of directors of P also controlled the majority of the voting interests in S, then the acquisition date might be before the date that shareholder approval is obtained.

2.6.220 *Regulatory approval*

2.6.220.10 In some cases a business combination cannot be finalised prior to regulatory approval being obtained. Although at the acquisition date the acquirer is required to have the ability to govern the financial and operating policies of the acquiree, it is not necessary for the transaction to be finalised legally. It is necessary to consider the nature of the regulatory approval in each case and the impact that it has on the passing of control.

2.6.220.20 For example, Companies P and S are manufacturers of electronic components for a particular type of equipment. P makes a bid for S's business and the competition authority announces that the proposed transaction is to be scrutinised to ensure that competition laws will not be breached. P and S agree the terms of the acquisition and the purchase price before competition authority clearance is obtained, but the contracts are made subject to competition authority clearance. In this case the acquisition date cannot be earlier than the date that approval is obtained from the competition authority since this is a substantive hurdle to be overcome before P is able to control S's operations.

2.6.220.30 In another example, Company P acquires the shares in Company S on 1 April 2010. However, before the sale of shares becomes legally binding, the transaction needs to be registered, a process that takes up to six weeks. The registration of the shares is a formality and there is no risk that the sale could be rejected. In this case the acquisition date is 1 April 2010 since the registration of the sale does not prevent the passing of control. However, if the facts of this case were different and the registration was not a formality because the authorities were required to consider and accept or reject each transaction, then it is likely that the acquisition date could not be earlier than the date of registration.

2.6.230 **Public offers**

2.6.230.10 When a public offer is made for the acquisition of shares, it is necessary to consider the impact of the nature and terms of the offer and any other relevant laws or regulations when determining the acquisition date.

2.6.230.20 In some jurisdictions an offer, at a certain minimum price, to buy the shares of all other shareholders must be made once a shareholder owns a certain percentage of the voting rights in an entity (a "mandatory offer"). Typically the acquirer obtains the voting rights associated with each share as each individual shareholder accepts the offer.

2.6.230.30 For example, Company P makes an offer to acquire all of the shares in Company S and each shareholder can decide individually whether to accept or reject the offer; the offer is conditional on at least 75 percent acceptance. The offer is made on 15 September 2010 and closes on 15 November 2010, at which time ownership of the shares, and the rights associated with ownership, will be transferred. At 20 October 2010 enough offers have been accepted to give P its minimum 75 percent of the shares of S. Whether or not P has the power to control S at 20 October 2010 will depend on the local laws and regulations in respect of public offers. If P does not have the power to control S's operations until the public offer has closed and P is not able to make decisions and impose its will on S's operations, then the acquisition date could not be earlier than 15 November 2010.

2.6.230.40 In another example, Company P increases its shareholding in Company S to above 30 percent and in accordance with local law makes a mandatory offer on 15 March 2010 to acquire all of the shares in S. Each shareholder can decide individually whether to accept or reject the offer, and P obtains the voting rights and all other rights associated with each share as each individual shareholder accepts. The offer is not conditional on a minimum level of acceptance. The offer closes on 15 June 2010 but on 1 May 2010 enough shareholders have accepted the offer for P's interest in S to exceed 50 percent. In this case the acquisition date is 1 May 2010 as P obtains control of S on this date.

2.6.240 **Acquirer consulted on major decisions**

2.6.240.10 In some cases the seller in a business combination agrees to consult the acquirer on major business decisions prior to completion of the transaction. The requirement to consult with the acquirer does not mean necessarily that the power to govern the operations has passed to the acquirer from this time. It is necessary to consider all relevant facts and circumstances to determine the substance of the agreement between the parties. In any case the acquirer would need both *power* and *benefits* in order to have control.

2.6.240.20 For example, Company P makes an offer to buy all of the shares in Company S, which is wholly owned by Company Q. The offer is subject to the satisfactory completion of due diligence. In the meantime the parties agree that P should be consulted on any major business decisions. In our view, P does not have the power to govern S simply because it will be consulted on major decisions; P does not have the ability to impose its will on S's business and the due diligence is yet to be completed. Therefore, the offer date is not the acquisition date in this example.

2.6.250 *Acquisition date in a business combination achieved in stages*

IFRS 3.8, 41 2.6.250.10 Sometimes control is obtained in successive share purchases, i.e. the acquirer obtains control of an acquiree in which it held an equity interest immediately before the acquisition date. Such a business combination commonly is referred to as a "business combination achieved in stages" or a "step acquisition". Consistent with all other business combinations within the scope of IFRS 3, for a step acquisition the acquisition date is the date on which the acquirer obtains control of the acquiree.

2.6.250.20 See 2.6.1020 for a discussion of the accounting for a business combination achieved in stages.

2.6.260 **Consideration transferred**

2.6.260.10 Consideration transferred includes contingent consideration (see 2.6.280) and certain elements of share-based payment awards exchanged for awards held by the acquiree's employees (see 2.6.420). However, a number of items are excluded from consideration transferred (see 2.6.340). Consideration often is transferred directly to the former owners of the acquired business; however, consideration given in exchange for an acquired business may be transferred indirectly, for example when the acquirer contributes a business to an acquired subsidiary (see 2.6.530).

IFRS 3.51 2.6.260.20 In some cases the consideration transferred in a business combination will relate not just to the acquirer obtaining control over the acquiree, but also to other elements of the overall transaction. Amounts that are not part of the exchange for control over the acquiree are excluded from the accounting for the business combination; instead, they are accounted for as separate transactions in accordance with other relevant IFRSs.

IFRS 3.37 2.6.260.30 The consideration transferred in a business combination is measured at fair value except for any portion of the acquirer's share-based payment awards issued to replace awards held by the acquiree's employees, which are measured in accordance with IFRS 2 *Share-based Payment* (see 2.6.430).

2.6.270 *Deferred consideration*

2.6.270.10 Deferred consideration comprises obligations to pay specified amounts at future dates, i.e. there is no uncertainty about the amount to be paid. Deferred consideration is recognised and measured at fair value at the acquisition date and is included in the consideration transferred. In our view, fair value is determined by discounting the amount payable using a market rate of interest for a similar instrument of an issuer with a similar credit rating. The unwinding of any interest element of deferred consideration is recognised in profit or loss.

2.6.280 *Contingent consideration*

2.6.280.10 Contingent consideration is an obligation by the acquirer to transfer additional assets or equity interests to the former owners of an acquiree as part of the exchange for control of the acquiree if specified future events occur or conditions are met. Contingent consideration also may include an acquirer's right to the return of previously transferred consideration if certain conditions are met, for example a repayment to the acquirer of consideration transferred to the former owners of an acquired business if that business does not meet financial or operating targets that were specified in the acquisition agreements.

2.6.280.20 Contingent consideration may include the transfer of additional cash, the issue of additional debt or equity securities, or the distribution of other consideration on resolution of contingencies based on post-combination earnings, post-combination security prices or other factors. All contingent consideration is measured at fair value on the acquisition date and included in the consideration transferred in the acquisition.

IFRS 3.40 2.6.280.30 Obligations of an acquirer under contingent consideration arrangements are classified as equity or a liability in accordance with IAS 32 *Financial Instruments: Presentation* (see 3.11.10) or other applicable IFRSs, i.e. in the case of non-financial contingent consideration. See 2.6.1010 for a discussion of the subsequent measurement of contingent consideration, which depends on its classification upon initial recognition.

2.6.290 *Assets transferred or liabilities assumed by the acquirer*

IFRS 3.38 2.6.290.10 Assets transferred or liabilities assumed by the acquirer as part of the consideration transferred in a business combination generally are measured at their acquisition-date fair values; any gain or loss is recognised in profit or loss in accordance with the relevant IFRSs. However, this guidance applies only if the acquirer does not retain control of the assets or liabilities transferred after the acquisition (see 2.6.530).

2.6.300 *Business combinations in which no consideration is transferred*

IFRS 3.43 2.6.300.10 A business combination can occur without the acquirer transferring consideration. Examples of business combinations achieved without the transfer of consideration include:

FRS 3.43(a) • an acquiree repurchases a sufficient number of its own shares so that an existing shareholder obtains control of the acquiree;

FRS 3.43(b) • substantive participating rights held by another equity holder expire; and

FRS 3.43(c) • business combinations achieved by contract alone, e.g. "stapled" arrangements or the formation of a dual-listed entity. In these business combinations the acquirer transfers no consideration in exchange for control of an acquiree and obtains no equity interests in the acquiree on obtaining control.

IFRS 3.33 2.6.300.20 In business combinations in which no consideration is transferred, an acquirer uses the acquisition-date fair value of its interest in the acquiree, determined using a valuation technique, instead of the acquisition-date fair value of the consideration transferred to determine the amount of goodwill.

2.6.300.30 For example, Company P owns 45 percent of Company S. On 31 October 2010 S repurchases a number of its shares such that P's ownership interest increases to 65 percent. The repurchase transaction results in P obtaining control of S. Therefore, the transaction is a business combination accounted for by applying the acquisition method and P is the acquirer.

2.6.300.40 The carrying amount of P's 45 percent interest in S in P's financial statements immediately prior to the share repurchase is 40. At 31 October 2010, after the repurchase, the fair value of S is 100 and the fair value of the identifiable net assets of S is 80. The fair value of 65 percent of S is 65. P elects to measure NCI at fair value at the acquisition date (see 2.6.840), which is assumed to be 35 in this example.

2.6.300.50 P records the following entry in respect of the acquisition:

	Debit	Credit
Identifiable net assets of S	80	
Goodwill[1]	20	
Investment in associate S		40
NCI (equity)		35
Gain on previously held interest in S (profit or loss)[2]		25
To recognise acquisition of S		

Notes

(1) *Goodwill is calculated as follows:*

Fair value of equity interest in S after the share repurchase	65
Plus NCI	35
Less fair value of identifiable net assets acquired	(80)
Goodwill	20

As P elects to measure NCI at fair value at the acquisition date, goodwill includes 7 attributable to NCI, i.e. 35 - (80 x 35%). If P had elected to measure NCI at its proportionate interest in the fair value of the identifiable net assets of S, then NCI would be recognised at 28 (80 x 35%) and goodwill recognised would be 13.

(2) *The gain on previously held interest in S is calculated as follows:*

Fair value of interest in S immediately after the share repurchase	65
Carrying amount of interest in S before the share repurchase	(40)
Gain on previously held interest in S	25

2.6.300.60 In a business combination achieved by contract alone the acquirer receives no additional equity interests in the acquiree. Therefore, if the acquirer held no equity interest in the acquiree prior to the business combination, then 100 percent of the acquiree's equity would be attributed to the NCI. If in such circumstances the acquirer elects to measure NCI at fair value at the acquisition date, then in our view this does not include any control premium as it is a non-controlling interest.

2.6.310 Business combinations involving mutual entities

IFRS 3.33   2.6.310.10 When a business combination takes place between mutual entities, the acquisition method is applied. In a combination involving mutual entities, the acquirer and acquiree exchange only equity interests. If the fair value of the equity or member interests in the acquiree is more reliably measurable than the fair value of the member interests transferred by the acquirer, then the acquirer determines the amount of goodwill by using the acquisition-date fair value of the acquiree's equity interests instead of the acquirer's equity interests transferred as consideration.

2.6.320 Business combination effected through derivatives

IAS 39.2(g)   2.6.320.10 IAS 39 *Financial Instruments: Recognition and Measurement* does not apply to contracts between the acquirer and the seller in a business combination to buy an acquiree at a future date. Therefore, when an entity effects a business combination by entering into a forward contract, an issue arises as to whether the contract to acquire the target should be recognised as a derivative in accordance with IAS 39 or as an unrecognised executory contract (see 1.2.60) prior to the acquisition date (see 3.6.90).

IAS 39.2(g)   2.6.320.20 The scope exemption in IAS 39 is limited to situations in which the acquisition will occur subject only to the passage of time in order to allow administrative-type tasks to be completed, e.g. registration with the authorities, and any approval from a third party, e.g. regulatory approval. For example, Company F enters into a forward contract with Company H to acquire the shares of Company G in 60 days' time. In the industry in which G operates, 60 days generally is the time required to complete the administrative tasks associated with such a business combination. Therefore, in this example we believe that IAS 39 does not apply and that the forward contract to acquire G should be treated as an executory contract.

2.6.320.30 If a forward contract in respect of a business combination does not qualify for the scope exemption, then it is accounted for in accordance with IAS 39, i.e. as a derivative prior to the acquisition date. In such cases the derivative will be measured at fair value through profit or loss, and the consideration transferred should include the fair value of the derivative at the acquisition date.

IAS 39.BC 24C   2.6.320.40 An option to acquire a business is a derivative that falls within the scope of IAS 39 (see 3.6.60.30); the scope exemption discussed in 2.6.320.10 does not extend to options because in that case an acquisition is conditional on the option being exercised.

Therefore, the option will be measured at fair value through profit or loss, and the consideration transferred should include the fair value of the derivative at the acquisition date.

2.6.310.50 For example, on 1 January 2009 Company P purchased a European-style call option for 60 percent of the shares in Company S, which was exercisable on 1 January 2010. P paid a premium of 50 for the option, which had a strike price for the entire underlying of 1,000. The fair value of the call option at 31 December 2009 was 80, and therefore 30 (80 - 50) was recognised in profit or loss. On 1 January 2010 the option became exercisable and P became the parent of S because of these potential voting rights (see 2.5.130); P also exercised the call option at that date. In this case the consideration transferred at 1 January 2010 is 1,080 (cash of 1,000 plus the fair value of the derivative of 80).

2.6.330 *Hedging a future business combination*

IAS 39.AG98   2.6.330.10 A firm commitment to acquire a business in a business combination can be a hedged item only for foreign exchange risk because other risks cannot be specifically identified and measured. In our view, an entity also may hedge the foreign exchange risk of a highly probable forecast business combination. In our view, in the consolidated financial statements, a cash flow hedge of the foreign exchange risk of a firm commitment to acquire a business or a forecast business combination relates to the foreign currency equivalent of the consideration paid. In a cash flow hedge designation, the effective portion of the gain or loss arising from the hedging instrument is recognised in other comprehensive income.

2.6.330.20 See 3.7.610 for a discussion of when and how the amount recognised in other comprehensive income should be reclassified to profit or loss.

2.6.340 **Determining what is part of the business combination**

IFRS 3.B50   2.6.340.10 Determining what is part of the business combination transaction involves an analysis of the elements of an overall arrangement. Generally, a transaction entered into by or on behalf of the acquirer or primarily for its benefit or that of the combined entity, rather than being entered into before the combination primarily for the benefit of the acquiree or its former owners, is likely to be a separate transaction. IFRS 3 provides three examples of transactions that are not part of a business combination and which therefore are accounted for separately in accordance with other relevant IFRSs. However, this list is not intended to be exhaustive:

- a transaction that in effect settles a pre-existing relationship between the acquirer and the acquiree (see 2.6.350);
- a transaction that remunerates employees or former owners of the acquiree for future services (see 2.6.400); and
- a transaction that reimburses the acquiree or its former owners for paying the acquirer's acquisition-related costs (see 2.6.520).

146

IFRS 3.B50   2.6.340.20 The implementation guidance in IFRS 3 provides factors that entities should consider in assessing whether a transaction is part of a business combination or is a separate transaction that should be accounted for separately:

- the reasons for the transaction;
- who initiated the transaction; and
- the timing of the transaction.

IFRS 3.B50   2.6.340.30 These factors are not mutually exclusive or individually conclusive. An acquirer determines whether any portion of the amounts transferred by the acquirer relate to transactions other than the acquisition of a business that should be accounted for separately from the consideration exchanged for the acquiree and the assets acquired and liabilities assumed in the business combination.

2.6.340.40 For example, the acquirer in a business combination may have outstanding debt with terms that could result in an increase in the interest rate in the event of a merger or acquisition. If the interest rate on debt of the acquirer is increased as a result of a business combination, then in our view the additional interest costs are not part of the business combination transaction and therefore are not included in the consideration transferred. This is because changes in the acquirer's interest rate are not part of the exchange for control of the acquiree. The acquirer should account for the variable interest feature and any related additional interest expense in accordance with IAS 39, i.e. in profit or loss.

2.6.350 *Pre-existing relationships*

IFRS 3.B51   2.6.350.10 A "pre-existing relationship" is any relationship that existed between the acquirer and the acquiree before the business combination was contemplated. Such relationships may be contractual or non-contractual, and include defendant and plaintiff, customer and vendor, licensor and licensee, lender and borrower, and lessee and lessor relationships. In our view, the guidance in respect of pre-existing relationships also is applied to relationships entered into while the business combination is being contemplated but before the acquisition date.

IFRS 3.BC 122   2.6.350.20 Because the acquirer consolidates the acquiree following a business combination, pre-existing relationships effectively are settled as a result of the combination, i.e. following the business combination such transactions generally are eliminated in the consolidated financial statements. Therefore, such pre-existing relationships are accounted for separately from the business combination.

IFRS 3.B52   2.6.350.30 The settlement of a pre-existing relationship gives rise to a gain or loss that is recognised by the acquirer in profit or loss at the acquisition date. How the resulting gain or loss is calculated depends on whether the pre-existing relationship was contractual or non-contractual in nature. In general:

- settlement of a relationship that is favourable to the acquirer results in a gain being recognised by the acquirer, subject to adjustment in respect of any existing carrying amount in the financial statements of the acquirer; and

- settlement of a relationship that is unfavourable to the acquirer results in a loss being recognised by the acquirer, subject to adjustment in respect of any existing carrying amount in the financial statements of the acquirer.

2.6.350.40 See 3.13.780 for a discussion of the income tax effects of the effective settlement of a pre-existing relationship.

2.6.360 *Pre-existing non-contractual relationships*

2.6.360.10 An example of a pre-existing non-contractual relationship between the acquirer and acquiree is a lawsuit related to a non-contractual matter in which the two parties had a relationship as plaintiff and defendant.

IFRS 3.B 52(a) 2.6.360.20 The gain or loss on effective settlement of a non-contractual relationship is measured at fair value. The difference between the fair value of the lawsuit and any amounts recognised previously by the acquirer in accordance with applicable IFRSs is recognised as a gain or loss at the acquisition date.

2.6.360.30 For example, Company P is the defendant in a lawsuit in which Company S is the plaintiff. P has recognised a liability in the amount of 8,000 related to this lawsuit in accordance with IAS 37 *Provisions, Contingent Liabilities and Contingent Assets*. On 1 January 2010 P acquires S in a business combination, and pays cash consideration of 100,000 to S's shareholders. The acquisition effectively settles the lawsuit.

2.6.360.40 The fair value of the lawsuit at 1 January 2010 is determined to be 5,000. P recognises a 3,000 gain on the effective settlement of the lawsuit at the acquisition date in profit or loss, being the difference between the 8,000 liability recognised previously under IAS 37 less the 5,000 fair value of the lawsuit at the acquisition date:

	Debit	Credit
Liability for litigation	8,000	
Gain on settlement (profit or loss)		3,000
Consideration transferred		5,000
To recognise settlement of pre-existing relationship		

2.6.360.50 In accounting for the acquisition, the consideration transferred to acquire S is 95,000, being the total amount paid to the shareholders of 100,000 less the 5,000 recognised in connection with the effective settlement of the lawsuit.

2.6.370 *Pre-existing contractual relationships*

2.6.370.10 Examples of pre-existing contractual relationships between the acquirer and acquiree include a customer and vendor relationship, a licensor and licensee relationship, and a lender and borrower relationship.

IFRS 3.B 52(b)   2.6.370.20 The gain or loss on effective settlement of a contractual relationship is measured at the lesser of:

- the amount by which the contract is favourable or unfavourable compared to market ("off-market") from the perspective of the acquirer; and
- the amount of any stated settlement provisions in the contract available to the counterparty to whom the contract is unfavourable.

2.6.370.30 This valuation of the off-market component of a contract is the same as would be done for the valuation of a contract with a third party. However, instead of being included in the valuation of the contract recognised in the statement of financial position, the resulting value is included in the accounting for the settlement of the pre-existing relationship.

IFRS 3.B52   2.6.370.40 The difference between the amount calculated in 2.6.370.20 and any amounts recognised previously by the acquirer is recognised as a gain or loss at the acquisition date.

2.6.370.50 For example, Company P sells goods to Company S under a long-term, fixed-price supply agreement. The supply agreement commenced on 1 June 2008 and expires on 1 June 2013. A clause in the agreement states that either party has the right to cancel the agreement upon payment of a penalty of 5,000. P acquires S on 1 June 2010, when the supply agreement has three years left to run.

2.6.370.60 At the time of the acquisition, P determines that, while the contract currently remains profitable, the pricing under the contract is less than the current market price for the goods, i.e. the agreement is unfavourable to P. P values the off-market component of the contract at 3,000.

2.6.370.70 As the cancellation penalty is higher than the off-market value of the contract, the loss on settlement of the pre-existing relationship is measured based on the value of the off-market component of the contract from P's perspective, i.e. at the lower amount:

	Debit	Credit
Loss on settlement (profit or loss)	3,000	
Consideration transferred		3,000
To recognise settlement of pre-existing relationship		

2.6.380 *Prepaid contracts*

2.6.380.10 When the pre-existing relationship between the acquirer and acquiree is a prepaid contract, e.g. a prepaid licence or prepaid lease agreement, an issue arises as to how to determine the favourable or unfavourable aspect of the pre-existing relationship from the acquirer's perspective. Any amount paid or received by the acquiree or the acquirer prior to the business combination is not itself recognised in the acquisition accounting (see also 2.6.830.120 – 130). Instead, the favourable/unfavourable element at the acquisition date is determined by comparing the actual future payment stream under the contract with the market rate that would need to be paid to the counterparty based on the future periods in the contract if the contract were entered into anew for those remaining periods.

IFRS 3.B52   2.6.380.20 In the case of downstream prepaid transactions, applying the mechanical calculation (see 2.6.370.20) will indicate that the pre-existing relationship is unfavourable compared to market from the perspective of the acquirer, as the acquirer will not receive any future rental payment from the acquiree. However, in such transactions the acquirer also may have recognised deferred revenue in its financial statements prior to the business combination; the carrying amount of such deferred revenue will be derecognised at the acquisition date.

2.6.380.30 For example, Company P (lessor) entered into a five-year operating lease with Company S (lessee). The contractual rental payments of 10,000 were fully prepaid by S upon entering into the contract, and P recognised deferred revenue of 10,000 in its statement of financial position. The contract was concluded at market terms and there are no stated settlement provisions. P acquires S in a business combination two years later. At the acquisition date, P's balance of deferred revenue is 6,000 (10,000 / 5 x 3 remaining years).

2.6.380.40 At the acquisition date, a market participant granting a lease for a similar asset over a three-year period would expect to receive a present value of lease payments of, say, 6,600 (whether as an upfront payment or over three years with interest). As a result of the business combination, P will receive rental payments of zero. Therefore, the pre-existing relationship is unfavourable by 6,600 compared to market from P's perspective. This amount is recognised separately as a settlement loss after the derecognition of P's deferred revenue of 6,000.

	Debit	Credit
Deferred revenue	6,000	
Loss on settlement (profit or loss)	600	
Consideration transferred		6,600
To recognise settlement of pre-existing relationship		

IFRS 3.B52   2.6.380.50 In the case of upstream prepaid transactions, applying the mechanical calculation (see 2.6.370.20) will indicate that the pre-existing relationship is favourable compared to market from the perspective of the acquirer, as the acquirer will not make any future rental payment to the acquiree. However, in such transactions the acquirer also may have recognised an intangible asset (see 3.3.100) or prepaid rent (see 5.1.310.20)

in its financial statements prior to the business combination; the carrying amount of any such asset will be derecognised at the acquisition date.

2.6.380.60 For example, Company P (lessee) enters into a five-year operating lease with Company S (lessor). The contractual rental payments of 10,000 were fully prepaid by P on entering into the contract, and P recognised prepaid rent of 10,000 in its statement of financial position. The contract was concluded at market terms and there are no stated settlement provisions. P acquires S in a business combination two years later. At the acquisition date, P's balance of prepaid rent is 6,000 (10,000 / 5 x 3 remaining years).

2.6.380.70 At the acquisition date, a market participant entering into a lease contract for a similar asset over a three-year period would expect to pay a present value of lease payments of, say, 6,600 (whether as an upfront payment or over three years with interest). As a result of the business combination, P will pay zero for the right to use the asset. Therefore, the pre-existing relationship is favourable by 6,600 compared to market from P's perspective. This amount is recognised separately as a settlement gain after the derecognition of P's asset for prepaid rent of 6,000.

	Debit	Credit
Consideration transferred	6,600	
Prepaid rent		6,000
Gain on settlement (profit or loss)		600
To recognise settlement of pre-existing relationship		

2.6.380.80 Further complexity is likely to arise in practice as contracts between the acquirer and the acquiree may include prepayments as well as ongoing payments. Additionally, in downstream transactions the contractual relationship can also give rise to a reacquired right (see 2.6.390).

2.6.390 *Reacquired rights*

IFRS 3.29, 2.6.390.10 The pre-existing relationship may take the form of a right granted by the
B35, B36 acquirer to the acquiree prior to the business combination. For example, an acquirer may have previously granted the acquiree the right to use the acquirer's trade name under a franchise agreement. As a result of the business combination, effectively the acquirer reacquires that previously granted right. Rights of this kind reacquired by an acquirer in a business combination are identifiable intangible assets that the acquirer recognises separately from goodwill (see 2.6.690).

2.6.390.20 The following table summarises the accounting for the settlement of pre-existing "upstream" relationships (under which the acquiree previously has granted a right to the acquirer) and "downstream" relationships (under which the acquirer previously has granted a right to the acquiree) under which a right is granted by one party to another involved a business combination:

Favourable for	Upstream relationship	Downstream relationship
Licensee	• Licensee is the acquirer • Settlement gain arises	• Licensee is the acquiree • Settlement loss arises (see example in 2.6.390.20)
Licensor	• Licensor is the acquiree • Settlement loss arises	• Licensor is the acquirer • Settlement gain arises

2.6.390.30 For example, Franchisor P acquires the business of operating Franchisee S for 30,000. In connection with the acquisition, P reacquires previously granted franchise rights. The reacquired franchise right is valued at 3,000 in accordance with the measurement guidance in IFRS 3 (see 2.6.690).

2.6.390.40 The terms of the contract covering the rights are unfavourable for P, by 4,000 relative to the terms of current market transactions for similar items. The contract includes a cancellation penalty of 5,000. The value of the identifiable net assets of S, excluding the franchise right, which is measured in accordance with IFRS 3, is 17,000.

2.6.390.50 The cancellation penalty is higher than the off-market value of the contract; therefore, the loss on settlement of the pre-existing relationship is measured based on the value of the off-market component of the contract from P's perspective, i.e. at the lower amount (see 2.6.370.20). P records the settlement of the pre-existing relationship and the reacquisition of the franchise right as follows:

	Debit	Credit
Loss on settlement (profit or loss)	4,000	
Consideration transferred		4,000
To recognise settlement of pre-existing relationship		
Reacquired rights (intangible asset)	3,000	
Other identifiable net assets of S	17,000	
Goodwill	6,000	
Consideration transferred		26,000
To recognise reacquired right as part of acquisition accounting		

2.6.400 *Payments to employees who are former owners of the acquiree*

IFRS 3.B54   2.6.400.10 In a business combination an acquirer may enter into an arrangement for payments to employees or selling shareholders of the acquiree that are contingent upon a post-acquisition event. The accounting for such arrangements depends on whether such payments represent contingent consideration issued in the business combination

152

(which are included in the acquisition accounting), or are separate transactions (which are accounted for in accordance with other relevant IFRSs).

IFRS 3.A   2.6.400.20 Contingent consideration issued in a business combination is an obligation of the acquirer to transfer additional consideration to the former owners of an acquiree as part of the exchange for control of the acquiree if specified future events occur or conditions are met. Such additional consideration may be in the form of cash, other assets or equity interests. Contingent consideration also may give the acquirer the right to the return of previously transferred consideration if specified conditions are met or fail to be met.

IFRS 3.51   2.6.400.30 Arrangements for contingent payments to employees or selling shareholders that do not meet the definition of contingent consideration, i.e. that are not part of the exchange for control of the acquiree, are not part of the accounting for the business combination; such payments are accounted for separately in accordance with other relevant IFRSs.

IFRS 3.B55   2.6.400.40 The application guidance of IFRS 3 provides indicators to be evaluated when determining whether contingent payments to employees or selling shareholders comprise contingent consideration or are a transaction to be accounted for separately from the business combination. Judgement frequently will be required in this respect.

IFRS 3.B 55(a)   2.6.400.50 An arrangement under which contingent payments automatically are forfeited if employment terminates is compensation for post-combination services. Although this requirement is included within a group of indicators to assist in identifying amounts that are part of consideration transferred, the language in the standard is plain and rules out an alternative interpretation. Therefore, this is the case even if an evaluation of some, or even all, of the other indicators suggests that the payments otherwise would be considered to be additional consideration transferred in exchange for the acquiree; and even if the relevant employee is entitled to remuneration at rates comparable with those earned by people in similar roles.

2.6.400.60 In our view, contingent payments that are forfeited at the discretion of the acquirer if employment terminates also are compensation for post-combination services. In such arrangements, generally it is the fact that continuing employment is required to be provided by the recipient of the contingent payment that is relevant. However, in our view careful consideration is given to arrangements in which a related party of the beneficiary of such an award is required to provide continuing services. For example, a contingent payment arrangement may be structured so that the spouse of an employee will benefit from payments that are contingent on the employee's continued employment. Such arrangements may, in substance, be compensation for post-combination services.

2.6.400.70 If all or part of a contingent consideration arrangement is not affected by employment termination, then other indicators are considered in determining whether the arrangement is part of the business combination or a separate transaction.

2.6.410 *Forgiveness of full-recourse loans*

2.6.410.10 Full-recourse loans granted to employees of an acquiree may be forgiven in connection with a business combination. This could include loans granted to employees in connection with the exercise of share options, as well as loans granted for other purposes. If it is not clear whether the forgiveness of the loans is part of the exchange for the acquiree or is a transaction separate from the business combination, then all relevant facts and circumstances are considered in making the determination, paying particular attention to the factors in 2.6.480. For example:

- If the loans were entered into prior to the commencement of negotiations for the business combination, and the original terms of the loans require forgiveness in the event of a change in control, then in our view such forgiveness generally would be accounted for as part of the acquisition accounting. However, if such forgiveness includes any post-combination service requirements, or is tied to another agreement that includes post-combination service requirements, then in our view the forgiveness would be accounted for separately.

- If the acquisition agreement includes a clause requiring forgiveness of the loans, then a determination as to why the clause was included, as well as a review of other arrangements entered into with the participating employees, will be helpful in making a determination. For example, if the clause was included at the request of the acquirer, and a termination agreement was also entered into with the employee before the combination, then the forgiveness might in substance constitute a severance payment to the employee that should be accounted for as a transaction separate from the business combination. In our view, an acquirer cannot avoid the recognition of a severance cost that it would otherwise expect to incur immediately following a business combination by arranging for the acquiree to make the payment before the business combination, or by putting clauses in an acquisition agreement that effectively provide for the payments.

2.6.410.20 In reviewing arrangements such as those discussed in 2.6.410.10, all arrangements with the participating employees are considered. For example, if two arrangements are entered into at about the same time, such as an arrangement providing for the forgiveness of a loan with no service requirement and a second arrangement that includes a service requirement, then in our view consideration is given as to whether the service requirement included in the second arrangement should impact the determination of whether the first arrangement is part of the exchange for the acquiree or is a transaction separate from the business combination.

2.6.420 *Acquirer share-based payment awards exchanged for awards held by employees of the acquiree#*

IFRS 3.B56 2.6.420.10 In some circumstances the acquirer is obliged to issue share-based payment awards (replacement awards) to employees of an acquiree in exchange for share-based payment awards issued previously by the acquiree. Such exchanges are accounted for as modifications of share-based payment awards under IFRS 2, and all or a portion of the amount of the acquirer's replacement awards is included in measuring the consideration transferred in the business combination.

IFRS 3.B56   2.6.420.20 An acquirer is *obliged* to issue replacement awards if the acquiree or its employees are able to enforce replacement. Such obligations may arise from various sources, including:

- the terms of the acquisition agreement;
- the terms of the acquiree's awards; or
- applicable laws or regulations.

2.6.430 *Measurement*

IFRS 3.30   2.6.430.10 Share-based payment awards are an exception to the fair value measurement principle of IFRS 3 (see 2.6.600). This exception requires that such awards be measured at the acquisition date in accordance with IFRS 2 and refers to the amounts so determined as the "market-based measure" of the awards. This applies regardless of whether the market-based measurement of the replacement awards is included in measuring the consideration transferred in a business combination, or is recognised as remuneration cost in the post-combination financial statements.

2.6.440 *Attribution*

IFRS 3.B56   2.6.440.10 In some instances a portion of the value of the replacement awards is allocated to post-combination service and accounted for separately from the business combination. This is the case, for example, when post-combination service is required to be rendered by the employees of the acquiree in connection with the acquirer issuing replacement awards or when the market-based measure of the replacement awards exceeds the market-based measure of the acquiree awards.

2.6.440.20 The amount of the market-based measure of the replacement awards treated as consideration transferred is determined in the following manner:

IFRS 3.B57	(1) Determine at the acquisition date, in accordance with the market-based measurement method in IFRS 2: • the market-based measure of the acquiree's awards (FVa); and • the market-based measure of the replacement awards (FVr). (2) Determine: • the period for which services have been provided by the employees prior to the acquisition date, i.e. the pre-combination vesting period (see A in the following diagram); • the original vesting period of the acquiree's awards (see B in the following diagram);

- the post-combination vesting period, if any, for the replacement awards (see C in the following diagram); and
- the greater of the total vesting period (the sum of A plus C) and the original vesting period of the acquiree's awards (B).

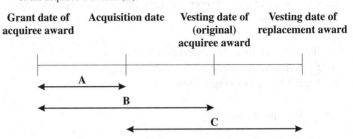

| **Grant date of acquiree award** | **Acquisition date** | **Vesting date of (original) acquiree award** | **Vesting date of replacement award** |

IFRS 3.B58

(3) Calculate the portion of the replacement awards attributable to pre-combination service as the product of:

- the market-based measure of the acquiree's awards at the acquisition date; and
- the ratio of the pre-combination vesting period to the greater of the total vesting period and the original vesting period of the acquiree's awards.

$$\text{Amount included in consideration transferred} = FVa \times \frac{A}{\text{Greater of } (A + C) \text{ and } B}$$

IFRS 3.B59

Any remaining amount of the market-based measure of the replacement awards after deducting the amount attributed to consideration transferred is treated as post-combination remuneration cost.

IFRS 3.B61 2.6.440.30 These requirements for determining the portions of a replacement award attributable to pre-combination and post-combination service apply equally regardless of whether the replacement award is classified as cash settled or as equity settled in accordance with IFRS 2.

2.6.440.40 The process in 2.6.440.20 demonstrates several points:

- The acquirer measures both the replacement awards given to employees by the acquirer and the acquiree awards at the acquisition date. The measurement and attribution of replacement awards issued in a business combination are independent of the original grant-date value of the acquiree awards.
- IFRS 3 sets two limits on the amount of the replacement awards' value that is included in the consideration transferred:
  - the amount cannot exceed the market-based measure at the acquisition date of the *acquiree* awards; and
  - the amount includes only the value attributed to *pre-combination* service.
- Any incremental value of the replacement awards over the value of the acquiree awards at the acquisition date is attributed to post-combination service and is not part of the consideration transferred, even if all service has been rendered as of the acquisition date. In this case, the excess value is recognised immediately as remuneration cost in the post-combination financial statements of the combined entity. If additional service is required, then the remuneration cost is recognised in

the post-combination financial statements by applying the requirements of IFRS 2 (see 4.5.1093).

- Even if acquiree awards are fully vested at the time of a business combination, a portion of the replacement award is allocated to post-combination service if the acquiree's employee is required to render service in the post-combination period in order for the replacement award to vest.

2.6.440.50 For example, Company P acquires Company S on 30 June 2011. At the acquisition date S's employees hold share options with a total acquisition-date value, measured under IFRS 2, of 3,000. All of the acquiree awards were granted on 1 July 2008, i.e. three years prior to the acquisition date. S's share option plan does not contain a change-in-control clause (see 2.6.480 – 490). The vesting period of the acquiree awards was four years. Accordingly, prior to the acquisition date, the acquiree awards have a remaining vesting period of one year.

2.6.440.60 Pursuant to a requirement in the acquisition agreement, P replaces the unvested acquiree awards with unvested awards with a value, measured under IFRS 2, of 3,000. Those awards require two years of service subsequent to the acquisition date, i.e. they will vest a year later than the acquiree awards would have vested under their original terms. In its consolidated financial statements, P records the following entries:

	Debit	Credit
Goodwill	1,800	
Equity		1,800
To recognise replacement awards attributed to		
pre-combination service as part of consideration transferred		
Remuneration cost	1,200	
Equity		1,200
To recognise replacement awards not attributed to		
pre-combination service as remuneration cost. This amount is		
recognised in accordance with IFRS 2 (see 4.5.1093.20 - 60)		

Amount attributed to pre-combination service

$3,000^1$ x 60% (3 years / 5 years)^2 = 1,800

(1) Market-based measure of acquiree awards at the acquisition date.

(2) Ratio of service rendered as of 30 June 2011 compared to the greater of the original vesting period (four years in this scenario) and the sum of the pre-combination vesting period plus the post-combination vesting period (five years in this scenario).

Amount attributed to post-combination service

$3,000^3$ - $1,800^4$ = 1,200

(3) Market-based measure of replacement awards.

(4) Amount attributed to pre-combination service (see above).

2.6 Business combinations

2.6.450 Replacement awards with expected failure to meet vesting conditions other than market conditions

IFRS 2.19-21, 30, 3.B60   2.6.450.10 Recognition of remuneration cost in respect of share-based payment awards is based on the best available estimate at the acquisition date of the total number of replacement awards expected to vest. Accordingly, the determination of the amount of replacement awards to be attributed to pre- and post-combination service takes into account the expected rate of forfeitures of the replacement awards due to expected failure to meet vesting conditions other than market conditions (see 2.6.460).

2.6.450.20 There are two types of vesting conditions that are not market conditions (see 4.5.380):

- Service conditions that require the counterparty to complete a specified period of service.
- Non-market performance conditions that require the counterparty, in addition to completing a specified period of service, to meet specified performance targets unrelated to the market price of the entity's equity instruments, e.g. a specified increase in profit or an earnings per share target.

IFRS 3.B60   2.6.450.30 Consistent with the guidance in IFRS 2, changes in the number of replacement awards for which the requisite service is expected to be rendered generally are reflected as an adjustment to post-combination remuneration cost in the period in which the change in estimate occurs. Therefore, the acquirer does not adjust consideration transferred in periods subsequent to the acquisition date if actual forfeitures differ from the forfeitures estimated at the acquisition date.

2.6.460 Replacement awards with market conditions

IFRS 2.A   2.6.460.10 A share-based payment may contain a market condition, i.e. a performance condition that determines whether a share-based payment vests that is related to the market price of the entity's equity instruments. Examples of market conditions include a specific share price target or total shareholder return, measured based on the share price of an entity's shares adjusted for the reinvestment of dividends, or based on the share price of an entity's shares relative to a stock-exchange index.

IFRS 2.21, 2.33, 3.30   2.6.460.20 Market conditions are reflected as an adjustment (discount) to the market-based measure of both the replacement and the acquiree's awards at the acquisition date. This applies regardless of the classification of the share-based payment as equity-settled or cash-settled.

IFRS 3.B61   2.6.460.30 The attribution of the acquisition-date market-based measure of the replacement awards to pre-combination service and post-combination service follows the general requirements set out in 2.6.440. This applies regardless of the classification of the share-based payment as equity settled or cash settled.

158

2.6.470 *Replacement awards with non-vesting conditions*

IFRS 3.B61   2.6.470.10 The attribution of the acquisition-date market-based measure of the replacement awards to pre-combination service and post-combination service follows the general requirements set out in 2.6.440. This applies regardless of the classification of the share-based payment.

FRS 2.21A,   2.6.470.20 For equity-settled share-based payments, non-vesting conditions, similar to
IG24   market conditions, are reflected in the market-based measurement of the share-based payments at the acquisition date.

2.6.470.30 For cash-settled share-based payments, in our view non-vesting conditions also should be taken into account when measuring the market-based measure of a cash-settled liability at the acquisition date, similar to market conditions.

2.6.480 *Share-based payment award includes change-in-control clauses*

2.6.480.10 Share options or other share-based payment plans often include a clause that provides for the acceleration of vesting in the event of a change in control of the issuer (a "change-in-control" clause). In other instances, existing awards sometimes are modified to add a change-in-control clause in contemplation of a change in control of an acquiree. The effect of the change-in-control clause that accelerates vesting on the attribution of an acquirer's replacement awards between pre-combination and post-combination service depends on how the change-in-control clause arose.

2.6.480.20 In some circumstances a change-in-control clause is included in the original terms of an acquiree award and the clause is triggered by an acquisition of the acquiree such that unvested awards immediately vest at the acquisition date. In such cases, the shortened vesting period resulting from the change in control was provided for by the terms of the acquiree award and is in our view regarded as the original vesting period for the purposes of determining the amount of a replacement award to be attributed to pre-combination service and to post-combination service.

2.6.480.30 Therefore, we believe that if an acquiree award that includes a change-in-control clause that provides for the acceleration of vesting in its terms is exchanged for a replacement award that does not require post-combination service to vest, then the sum of the pre-combination vesting period plus the post-combination vesting period and the original vesting period would be the same for purposes of attributing the replacement award to pre-combination and post-combination services. Accordingly, if in such situations the market-based measure of the replacement award is not in excess of that of the acquiree award, then we believe that the total market-based measure of the replacement award would be attributed to the consideration transferred in the business combination; no amount would be attributed to post-combination remuneration cost. Any market-based measure of the replacement award in excess of that of the acquiree award would be recognised as post-combination cost.

2.6.490 *Acquirer requests modification of acquiree award in contemplation of change in control*

2.6.490.10 If a change-in-control clause is added to an acquiree's share-based payment award at the request of an acquirer, then in our view the accounting would be the same as if the acquirer issued a fully-vested replacement award in exchange for an unvested acquiree award.

2.6.500 *Awards with graded vesting*

IFRS 2.IG11   2.6.500.10 In some cases share-based payment awards vest in instalments over the vesting period (graded-vesting awards). IFRS 2 requires each such instalment to be treated as a separate grant of share-based payment awards. Accordingly, an entity determines the portion of replacement awards to be attributed to pre- and post-combination service separately for each tranche of a graded-vesting award.

2.6.510 **Forthcoming requirements**

2.6.510.10 The *Improvements to IFRSs 2010* amended IFRS 3 to extend the guidance on the mandatory replacement of acquiree awards (see 2.6.500) to the voluntary replacements of unexpired awards.

2.6.510.20 In addition, the amendments introduce requirements in respect of the accounting for acquiree awards that the acquirer does not replace. If an acquiree award is not replaced in a business combination, then the amendments distinguish between two scenarios:

- If an equity-settled unreplaced acquiree award is vested at the acquisition date, then those acquiree awards are part of the NCI in the acquiree (see 2.5.300) and are measured at their market-based measure at the acquisition date in accordance with IFRS 2.
- If an equity-settled unreplaced acquiree award is not vested at the acquisition date, then it is measured at its market-based measure as if the acquisition date were the grant date under IFRS 2, and is allocated to the NCI on the basis of the ratio of the portion of the vesting period completed to the greater of the total vesting period and the original vesting period of the share-based payment.

2.6.510.30 The amendments, which are effective for annual periods beginning on or after 1 July 2010, are required to be applied prospectively from the date that an entity first applied IFRS 3 (2008) (see 2.6.1150).

2.6.520 **Acquisition-related costs**

IFRS 3.53   2.6.520.10 Acquisition-related costs incurred by an acquirer to effect a business combination are not part of the consideration transferred. They are accounted for as an expense in the period incurred, unless such costs are incurred to issue debt or equity securities, in which case they are recognised in accordance with IAS 32 (for equity) and IAS 39 (for debt).

RS 3.52(c) 2.6.520.20 If acquisition-related costs incurred by, or in substance on behalf of, an acquirer are paid by the acquiree or selling shareholders, those costs also are accounted for as a separate transaction and are not part of the accounting for the business combination.

IFRS 3.53, 2.6.520.30 An acquirer may incur costs related to equity securities issued to effect a
IAS 32.37 business combination. Such costs may include, for example, fees charged by underwriters, attorneys, accountants and printers. These costs effectively reduce the proceeds from the issue, and therefore the amount is recognised in equity. An entity recognises as an expense in profit or loss all costs that are not *incremental* to the issue of the securities, because such costs would have been incurred even without the issue of the equity securities.

IFRS 3.53, 2.6.520.40 An acquirer may incur costs in connection with the issue of debt associated
IAS 39.43 with a business combination. For example, such costs may include fees paid to creditors, attorneys and rating agencies. Debt issue costs reduce the proceeds from the debt issued and are an element of the effective interest cost of the debt; neither the source of the debt financing nor the use of the proceeds changes the nature of such costs. Only costs incurred in connection with a debt issue that are *directly attributable* to that debt issue are capitalised and amortised over the term of the debt as a component of interest cost. In our view, directly attributable costs comprise only those that are *incremental*. Costs that are not directly attributable to the issue of debt are recognised as an expense in profit or loss because such costs would have occurred even without the issue of debt.

2.6.520.50 An entity may incur fees in connection with the issue of debt and also pay fees to the same service provider/creditor in a related business combination. The fees allocated to the debt issue and the cost of the acquisition (which are expensed), in our view should be representative of the actual services provided. For example, if an entity pays fees to an investment bank in connection with a business combination plus additional financing, then those fees should be allocated between the costs of the acquisition and debt issue costs considering factors such as the fees charged by investment banks in connection with other similar recent transactions, e.g. fees charged by an investment bank solely for advisory services for an acquisition or fees charged by an investment bank solely for arranging financing.

2.6.520.60 In our view, costs incurred by the acquirer in respect of due diligence procedures, which may be internal or external costs, generally are acquisition-related costs rather than being related to financing. However, a final determination will depend on the facts and circumstances of each case.

2.6.520.70 In some circumstances a vendor may commission due diligence procedures. Some vendor due diligence engagements are commissioned by selling shareholders, before potential buyers for a business are identified, to facilitate a rapid sale or to obtain a better transaction price. In other circumstances an acquirer may be involved at some stage in setting the scope or procedures to be performed in such due diligence procedures. Factors to be taken into account in assessing whether the costs of such transactions borne by the vendor are in substance reimbursed by the acquirer include, but are not limited to:

- the extent to which the acquirer uses the vendor due diligence report;
- the extent to which the acquirer avoids paying for a due diligence process itself;
- the extent of the acquirer's involvement in the vendor due diligence process;
- the extent to which the vendor due diligence assists the former owners of the acquiree, e.g. by facilitating a quicker sale and/or a higher price; and
- who bears the cost of the due diligence if the business combination does not take place.

2.6.530 **Control maintained over assets transferred**

IFRS 3.38   2.6.530.10 An acquirer may transfer a business or a subsidiary to the acquiree as consideration in a business combination. Other forms of consideration transferred may include assets and liabilities of a subsidiary or other assets of the acquirer. Regardless of the structure of the transaction, if the acquirer retains control of the transferred assets or liabilities after the acquisition, then it recognises no gain or loss in profit or loss and measures those assets and liabilities at their carrying amounts immediately before the acquisition.

2.6.530.20 Additionally, if an acquirer transfers an equity interest in a subsidiary, but continues to hold a controlling interest in the subsidiary after the transfer, then the change in the parent's ownership interest in the subsidiary is accounted for as an equity transaction, and no gain or loss is recognised in profit or loss (see 2.5.380).

2.6.530.30 For example, Company P transfers its wholly-owned Subsidiary S1 to Company S2 in exchange for a 60 percent interest in S2. The fair value of the consideration transferred (the proportionate fair value of S1), is equal to the fair value of the consideration received (the proportionate investment in S2), i.e. there is no bargain purchase. It also is determined that there is no minority discount or control premium in this transaction.

The following values are relevant:	S1	S2
Book value	250	200
Fair value of identifiable assets and liabilities	500	350
Fair value	600	400

2.6.530.40 P controls the transferred asset (Subsidiary S1) directly before the transaction, and indirectly after the transaction through its control of S2. Therefore, P continues to measure the assets and liabilities of S1 following the acquisition at their carrying amounts immediately before the acquisition. However, as a result of the acquisition P has given up a 40 percent interest in S1. This decrease in interest is accounted for as an equity transaction.

Proof that the fair value of the consideration transferred is equal to the fair value of the consideration received:
Consideration transferred (40 percent of S1): 600 x 40% = 240
Consideration received (60 percent of S2): 400 x 60% = 240

2.6.540 *Scenario 1: NCI measured at fair value*

2.6.540.10 P records the following entry in respect of the acquisition:

	Debit	Credit
Identifiable net assets of S2	350	
Goodwill	50	
NCI (equity) (see 2.6.840)		260
Other equity		140
To recognise acquisition of S2		

2.6.540.20 The above amounts are calculated as follows:

- The fair value of the identifiable net assets of S2 was given in the fact pattern. S1 is already consolidated and therefore its net assets are excluded from the above entry.
- Goodwill of 50 is the consideration transferred (240) plus the amount attributed to NCI in respect of S2 (160), less the fair value of its identifiable net assets (350).
- The NCI in S2 comprises:
  - the NCI interest in S2 measured using the fair value of 160 (400 x 40%), based on the assumption that there was no minority discount or control premium in the transaction; and
  - the NCI interest in S1 measured using book values of 100 (250 x 40%).
- The entry to "other" equity comprises the difference between:
  - consideration transferred, P's interest in S1, measured at fair value of 240 (600 x 40%); and
  - P's interest in S1 given up measured using book value of 100 (250 x 40%).

2.6.540.30 There is no specific guidance in IFRSs about where this credit should be recognised within equity; alternatives might include additional paid-in capital (share premium) and retained earnings.

2.6.550 *Scenario 2: NCI measured at proportionate interest in identifiable net assets*

2.6.550.10 P records the following entry in respect of the acquisition:

	Debit	*Credit*
Identifiable net assets of S2	350	
Goodwill	30	
NCI (equity) (see 2.6.840)		240
Other equity		140
To recognise acquisition of S2		

2.6.550.20 The above entry differs from scenario 1 in 2.6.540 as follows:

- Goodwill of 30 is the consideration transferred (240) plus the amount attributed to NCI in respect of S2 (140), less the fair value of its identifiable net assets (350).
- The NCI in S2 comprises:
  - the NCI interest in S2 measured using the fair value of the identifiable net assets of 140 (350 x 40%); and
  - the NCI interest in S1 measured using book values of 100 (250 x 40%).

2.6.550.30 An economically similar result would occur if, in the fact pattern in 2.6.540 – 550, S1 had issued new shares representing a 40 percent interest to the shareholders of S2 in exchange for all the ordinary shares of S2. The same accounting treatments as those described above would apply in such a transaction.

2.6.560 Identifiable assets acquired and liabilities assumed

IFRS 3.23, 31 2.6.560.10 IFRS 3 contains general principles on the recognition and measurement of the identifiable assets acquired and the liabilities assumed as part of a business combination. There are limited exceptions to these recognition and measurement principles. For example, certain contingent liabilities assumed in a business combination are recognised separately as part of the acquisition accounting, and non-current assets (or disposal groups) classified as held for sale are measured at fair value less costs to sell.

2.6.560.20 Subsequent to the business combination, assets and liabilities generally are measured in accordance with applicable IFRSs; this subsequent measurement is outside the scope of this chapter other than for certain items in respect of which IFRS 3 does contain guidance (see 2.6.970).

2.6.570 *Recognition principle*

IFRS 3.11, 12 2.6.570.10 The recognition principle in IFRS 3 is that the identifiable assets acquired and the liabilities assumed as part of a business combination are recognised separately from goodwill at the acquisition date, if they:

- meet the definition of assets and liabilities in the *Framework for the Preparation and Presentation of Financial Statements* (see 1.2.30); and
- are exchanged as part of the business combination, instead of as a separate transaction (see 2.6.340).

164

IFRS 3.BC 126   2.6.570.20 As a result of the recognition principle, the usual recognition criteria for assets and liabilities acquired in a business combination always are considered satisfied, i.e. probable inflow or outflow of economic benefits and that their values can be measured reliably.

FRS 3.11, 12, 51-53   2.6.570.30 Costs incurred due to the acquisition because of planned or future actions of the acquirer are not recognised as liabilities by the acquirer because they are notliabilities of the acquiree at the acquisition date. For example, the cost of restructuring the acquiree is recognised as a liability as part of the acquisition accounting only if it is a liability of the acquiree at the acquisition date.

2.6.570.40 There are limited exceptions to the recognition principle (see 2.6.640).

2.6.580 *Classifying and designating assets acquired and liabilities assumed#*

IFRS 3.15   2.6.580.10 IFRS 3 provides a general principle that at the acquisition date the acquirer classifies and designates identifiable assets acquired and liabilities assumed as necessary to apply other IFRSs subsequently. Those classifications are made based on the contractual terms, economic conditions, the acquirer's operating or accounting policies and other pertinent conditions at the acquisition date.

IFRS 3.17   2.6.580.20 There are two exceptions to this general classification and designation principle: the classification by the acquiree of a lease as operating or finance in accordance with IAS 17 *Leases* and the classification of a contract as an insurance contract in accordance with IFRS 4 *Insurance Contracts* are retained, unless the acquiree's classification was made in error. The classification and designation of these contracts are based on the contractual terms at inception of the contract, or at the date of the latest modification that resulted in a change of classification.

2.6.590 *Financial instruments*

IFRS 3.16   2.6.590.10 The acquirer goes through the process of designating financial instruments as hedging instruments and designating any hedge relationships of the acquiree, and reassessing whether separation of an embedded derivative from its host is required at the acquisition date based on conditions as they exist at the acquisition date.

2.6.590.20 This means that in its consolidated financial statements the acquirer cannot automatically continue to apply the hedge accounting model to the hedge relationship designated previously by the acquiree. Rather, if it wishes to apply hedge accounting, then the acquirer has to designate a new hedge relationship. This might involve the same financial instruments and hedged items, but the inception of the hedge relationship can be no earlier than the acquisition date.

2.6.590.30 Designation can be made only if the hedging relationship meets all hedging requirements in IAS 39 at the acquisition date and can be made prospectively only from that date. This requires the acquirer to assess whether the hedge will be effective over the designated period. If the hedging instrument has a significant fair value at the acquisition date, then the hedge may fail the prospective effectiveness test in IAS 39, i.e. whether the hedge is expected to be highly effective in achieving offsetting changes in fair value or cash flows attributable to the hedged risk during the period for which the hedge is designated (see 3.7.460). Accordingly, in our view meeting the hedge accounting criteria for some hedges, in particular for cash flow hedges of interest risk, may be problematic.

2.6.600 **Measurement principle**

IFRS 3.18, A   2.6.600.10 The measurement principle in IFRS 3 is that the identifiable assets acquired and the liabilities assumed as part of a business combination are measured at the acquisition date at their fair values. *Fair value* is the amount for which an asset could be exchanged, or a liability settled, between knowledgeable, willing parties in an arm's length transaction. Fair value is based on the concept of a hypothetical market participant, rather than being specific to either the acquirer or the acquiree (see 2.6.1040.60 – 80).

2.6.600.20 There are limited exceptions to the measurement principle (see 2.6.640).

2.6.600.30 IFRS 3 provides specific guidance on applying the fair value measurement principle to the following assets:

- assets with uncertain cash flows (valuation allowances);
- assets subject to operating leases in which the acquiree is the lessor; and
- assets that the acquirer intends not to use or to use differently from the way in which other market participants would use them.

2.6.610 *Assets with uncertain cash flows (valuation allowances)*

IFRS 3.B41,   2.6.610.10 IFRS 3 prohibits recognition at the acquisition date of a separate valuation
B64(h)   allowance on assets acquired that are measured at fair value. The rationale is that the fair value incorporates uncertainties about cash flows. For example, because accounts receivable acquired in a business combination are recognised at fair value at the acquisition date, they cannot be recognised in the statement of financial position at their gross amounts (contractual amount of the receivable without taking into account credit risk) less a separate valuation allowance based on estimated uncollectable cash flows. The acquirer is required to disclose separately the fair value of the receivables acquired, as well as their gross contractual amounts and the best estimate of the amounts of the contractual cash flows that the acquirer does not expect to collect.

2.6.610.20 For example, Company P acquires Company S in a business combination on 31 October 2010. At the acquisition date the gross contractual amount of S's short-term trade receivables is 100. The fair value of the trade receivables at 31 October 2010 is 75 and the best estimate of the amount expected to be collected also is 75. P recognises trade receivables at their acquisition-date fair value of 75 in applying the acquisition accounting. In addition, P discloses the fair value of the receivables acquired of 75, as well as their gross contractual amounts of 100 and the best estimate of the amounts of the contractual cash flows that the acquirer does not expect to collect of 25.

2.6.620 *Assets subject to operating leases in which the acquiree is the lessor*

IFRS 3.B42   2.6.620.10 If the acquiree is the lessor in an operating lease, then the asset subject to the operating lease (e.g. a building) is recognised at fair value taking into account the terms of the related lease, i.e. the acquirer does not recognise a separate intangible asset or liability related to the favourable or unfavourable aspect of an operating lease relative to market terms or prices. See 2.6.830 for further guidance on leases acquired in a business combination.

2.6.630 *Assets that the acquirer intends not to use or to use in a way that is different from how market participants would use them*

2.6.630.10 Many assets have different uses and often the value of an asset to an entity may be highly dependent on its specific use. Sometimes the acquirer intends to use an asset in a manner different from the way in which market participants would use it. In an extreme scenario, the acquirer in a business combination may intend not to use one of the assets acquired, whereas market participants would use and generate economic benefits from the asset. There can be a variety of reasons for this. An example is defensive intangible assets acquired that the acquirer does not intend to use, but intends to hold and prevent others from gaining access to them, thereby increasing the value of the acquirer's existing (competing) assets. The question arises as to how such assets should be valued in the acquisition accounting.

2.6.630.20 The standards do not exempt an entity from recognising an asset acquired at the fair value based on market participants' use of the asset because the entity does not intend to use that asset, or intends to use it in a way that is not similar to how market participants would be expected to use it. Therefore, such assets are recognised at fair value rather than based on the way in which the acquirer intends to use them (see 2.6.1030). However, see 2.6.1060 for guidance on assets held for sale.

2.6.630.30 For example, Company P, a confectionary company, acquires one of its main competitors, Company S, in a business combination on 31 October 2010. While P intends to use S's production plant, distribution network and research facilities, it does not intend to use S's brand name for its confectionary. However, it is envisaged that other market participants would use that brand name. Even though P does not intend to use S's brand name that it acquired, it still is required to recognise and measure S's brand name at its fair value at the acquisition date based on its use by other market participants. Therefore, P estimates the likely plans of market participants for the brand.

2.6.630.40 See 3.3.235 for a discussion of the amortisation of an intangible asset that the acquirer intends not to use or to use in a way that is different from how market participants would use them.

2.6.640 *Exceptions to the recognition and measurement principles*

RS 3.24-31   2.6.640.10 IFRS 3 provides the following exceptions to the recognition and/or measurement principles:

2.6 Business combinations

Exception to the recognition principle	Exceptions to both the recognition and measurement principles	Exceptions to the measurement principle
• Contingent liabilities (see 2.6.650)	• Deferred tax assets and liabilities and tax uncertainties (see 2.6.660) • Indemnification assets (see 2.6.670) • Employee benefits (see 2.6.680)	• Reacquired rights (see 2.6.690) • Share-based payment awards (see 2.6.700) • Assets held for sale (see 2.6.710)

2.6.650 *Contingent liabilities*

IFRS 3.22,
IAS 37.10

2.6.650.10 A *contingent liability* is:

- a possible obligation that arises from past events whose existence will be confirmed only by the occurrence or non-occurrence of one or more uncertain future events not wholly within the control of the entity; or
- a present obligation that arises from past events but is not recognised because it is not probable that economic outflow will be required to settle the obligation or it cannot be measured with sufficient reliability.

2.6.650.20 The following flowchart outlines the application of IFRS 3 in respect of contingent liabilities.

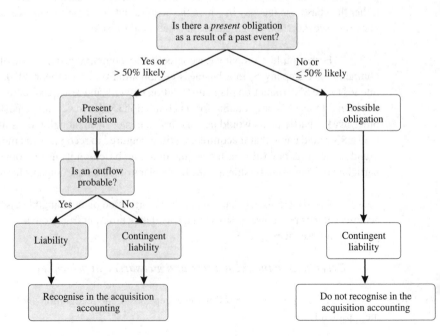

168

IFRS 3.23, BC274, BC275   2.6.650.30 A contingent liability acquired in a business combination is recognised in the acquisition accounting if it is a present obligation and its fair value can be measured reliably; this is because it meets the definition of a liability in that case. A contingent liability that is a possible obligation is not recognised because it does not meet the definition of a liability.

IAS 37.15   2.6.650.40 In some cases it will not be clear whether a present obligation exists, for example when the parties dispute facts and circumstances giving rise to the contingent liability. In that case IAS 37 clarifies that a past event is deemed to give rise to a present obligation if it is "more likely than not" that a present obligation exists. Although this is not stated explicitly in IFRS 3, in our view it is appropriate to extend this requirement of IAS 37 in applying the acquisition method since IFRS 3 does not deal with the issue itself.

IFRS 3.23   2.6.650.50 The probability of payment being required is not relevant in determining whether a contingent liability that is a present obligation should be recognised in a business combination, but this probability will impact its fair value.

2.6.650.60 Contingent liabilities may arise due to actual or intended post-acquisition actions of the acquirer. Such contingent liabilities are not recognised as part of the acquisition accounting since the intentions of the acquirer are not reflected in the acquisition accounting and the definition of a liability is not met at the acquisition date. For example, risks arising from transactions after the acquisition date to achieve tax optimisation for the acquirer would not be reflected as of the acquisition date.

2.6.650.70 See 2.6.990 for a discussion of the subsequent measurement of contingent liabilities recognised in the acquisition accounting.

IFRS 3.BC 276, IAS 37.10   2.6.650.80 Contingent assets are not recognised because a contingent asset is a "possible" asset that does not meet the definition of an asset. For example, Company P acquires Company S in a business combination on 31 October 2010. S leases a property to Company Q under an operating lease. The terms of the lease state that if Q cancels the contract, then Q would be required to pay 100 to S. P would not recognise this contingent asset in accounting for the business combination.

2.6.660 Deferred tax assets and liabilities

IFRS 3.24   2.6.660.10 Deferred tax assets and liabilities that arise from the assets acquired and liabilities assumed in a business combination are recognised and measured in accordance with IAS 12 *Income Taxes* rather than at fair value. Deductible temporary differences and unused tax losses of the acquiree also are accounted for in accordance with IAS 12.

2.6.660.20 See 3.13.670 for a discussion of the accounting for the income tax effects of business combinations.

2.6.670 *Indemnification assets*

2.6.670.10 Purchase agreements sometimes provide that the seller indemnifies the acquirer against a particular contingent liability outstanding at the acquisition date. For example, a contingent liability could relate to a legal case of the acquiree for environmental pollution or to specific tax uncertainties. The seller may agree to reimburse the acquirer if the outcome of the legal case or resolution of the tax uncertainty requires payment by the acquiree. As a result, the acquirer obtains an indemnification asset.

IFRS 3.27, 28 2.6.670.20 When the seller is obliged contractually to indemnify the acquirer for a specific liability, an asset is recognised at the same time and measured using the same measurement basis as the liability. This ensures that both the asset and the liability are measured on a consistent basis using similar assumptions, subject to management's assessment of collectibility of the asset.

2.6.670.30 This accounting applies to indemnities related to a specific liability or contingent liability of the acquiree. It does not apply in accounting for general representations and warranties provided by the seller to the acquirer that do not create a specific right of reimbursement.

IFRS 3.57 2.6.670.40 After initial recognition an indemnification asset continues to be measured based on the assumptions used to measure the related liability, subject to management's assessment of collectibility of the asset, and is limited to the amount of the liability to which it relates (see 2.6.1000).

2.6.670.50 For example, Company P acquires Company S in a business combination on 31 October 2010. S is being sued by one of its customers for breach of contract. The sellers of S provide an indemnification to P for the reimbursement of any losses greater than 500. There are no collectibility issues around this indemnification. At the acquisition date it is determined that there is a present obligation and therefore the fair value of the contingent liability of 530 is recognised by P in the acquisition accounting. In the acquisition accounting P also recognises an indemnification asset of 30 (530 - 500).

2.6.680 *Employee benefits*

IFRS 3.26 2.6.680.10 Employee benefit liabilities (and assets, if any) are recognised and measured in accordance with IAS 19 *Employee Benefits* (see 4.4) except those to which IFRS 2 applies (see 2.6.700). Defined benefit plan surpluses (to the extent recoverable) and deficits are recognised at the full present value of the obligation less the fair value of any plan assets, i.e. all actuarial gains and losses and past service costs of the acquiree effectively are recognised.

2.6.680.20 The measurement of the liability does not take into account plan amendments, terminations or curtailments that the acquirer has no obligation to make at the acquisition date; therefore, it does not take into account the acquirer's intentions or future actions, such as an intention to change the terms of the plan to conform to the acquirer's existing plan.

2.6.690 *Reacquired rights*

IFRS 3.B35 2.6.690.10 The acquisition of a right that had been granted previously to the acquiree to use one of the acquirer's assets (recognised or unrecognised) is a reacquired right, which is recognised as part of the acquisition accounting. The reacquired right represents an identifiable intangible asset that is recognised separately from goodwill.

2.6.690.20 Reacquired rights are measured by taking into account only the remaining contractual terms of the related contract. Any potential renewals are ignored even if a market participant would take these into account in its determination of fair value. This is to be consistent with the requirement that the amortisation period of reacquired rights cannot take into account expected renewals (see 2.6.980).

2.6.700 *Share-based payment awards*

2.6.700.10 In certain instances an acquirer's share-based payment awards (replacement awards) may be exchanged for awards held by the acquiree's employees (acquiree awards). Such payments are accounted for as modifications in accordance with IFRS 2. Any liability or equity instrument related to a share-based payment award is measured in accordance with IFRS 2, which is a market-based measurement principle rather than a fair value measurement principle. See 2.6.420 for a discussion of the accounting for share-based payment awards.

2.6.710 *Assets held for sale*

IFRS 3.31 2.6.710.10 Assets (or disposal groups) acquired solely with the intention of disposal in the short term are consolidated. However, they are classified separately as non-current assets (or disposal groups) held for sale if they meet the criteria for classification as held for sale, in IFRS 5 *Non-current Assets Held for Sale and Discontinued Operations* within a short period of time after the acquisition date, generally three months or less. Such assets (or disposal groups) classified as held for sale are measured at fair value less costs to sell in accordance with IFRS 5.

2.6.720 **Intangible assets**

2.6.720.10 All *identifiable* intangible assets acquired in a business combination are recognised separately from goodwill and are measured initially at their acquisition-date fair values. This often involves identifying and recognising intangible assets not recognised previously by the acquiree in its financial statements. Therefore, the identification, recognition and measurement of intangible assets is an important part of the acquisition accounting that often requires considerable time and attention.

IAS 38.21, 33 2.6.720.20 In general an intangible asset is recognised only if it meets the asset recognition criteria, i.e. it is *probable* that the expected future economic benefits attributable to the asset will flow to the entity, and its cost can be measured reliably. For identifiable intangible assets acquired in a business combination these recognition criteria always are considered to be satisfied. Therefore, all identifiable intangible assets acquired in a business combination are recognised separately from goodwill.

2.6.720.30 IAS 38 *Intangible Assets* provides guidance on the subsequent accounting for intangible assets acquired in a business combination (see 3.3.190 – 320).

IAS 38.12   2.6.720.40 An asset is identifiable if it either is separable or arises from contractual or other legal rights, regardless of whether those rights are transferable or separable from the entity or from other rights and obligations (see 3.3.40).

IFRS 3.IE16-   2.6.720.50 The implementation guidance to IFRS 3 provides examples of intangible assets
IE40   that meet the identifiability criteria for recognition as intangible assets separately from goodwill, i.e. either arise from contractual-legal rights or are separable. The intangible assets are grouped into the following categories:

- marketing-related
- customer-related
- artistic-related
- contract-based
- technology-based.

IFRS 3.B34,   2.6.720.60 Sometimes an intangible asset acquired is separable only together with a
IAS 38.36   related contract, identifiable asset or liability. In this case it is recognised separately from goodwill together with the related item.

IFRS 3.B   2.6.720.70 Examples of intangible assets that may be separable only together with a
32(b)   related item include:

- a trademark for a product may be separable only together with the recipe or documented but unpatented technical expertise used to manufacture that product;
- a trademark for natural spring water may relate to a particular spring and be separable only together with that spring;
- depositor relationship intangible assets may be separable only together with the related deposit liabilities; and
- a licence to operate an item may be separable only together with the related item, for example a licence to operate a nuclear power plant or an airport.

IAS 38.37   2.6.720.80 Sometimes a group of complementary identifiable intangible assets may be acquired, e.g. a trademark for a drug and its related trade name, formula, recipe and technological expertise. In this case the group of complementary assets may be recognised together as a single asset separate from goodwill provided that the individual assets have similar useful lives.

2.6.720.90 Many intangible assets arise from rights conveyed legally by contract, statute or similar means. An intangible asset that meets the contractual/legal criterion is identifiable, regardless of whether it meets the separability criterion. Examples of intangible assets that may meet the contractual-legal criterion include:

- franchises granted, for example in respect of fast-food outlets, restaurant chains or car dealers;
- trademarks;
- patents;
- contracts negotiated with customers or suppliers and related relationships;
- licence agreements;

IFRS 3.B 32(a)
- the favourable terms of an acquired operating lease compared with current market terms, regardless of whether the lease terms prohibit the acquirer from selling or otherwise transferring the lease; and

IFRS 3.B 32(b)
- licences to operate, regardless of whether the licence can be sold or otherwise transferred separately from the related item, for example licences to operate a nuclear power plant or an airport.

IFRS 3. IE30(c) 2.6.720.100 Contractual or other legal rights are not defined in IFRS 3, but it is clear from the examples in the standard that the definition is intended to be broad. For example, customer relationships may meet the contractual-legal criterion at the acquisition date even if there is no contract in place with the customer at the acquisition date, if the acquiree has a practice of establishing contracts with customers.

FRS 3.IE30 2.6.720.110 Sometimes a contract may be cancellable by the customer, but this does not affect it meeting the contractual-legal criterion.

FRS 3.IE26 2.6.720.120 Sometimes the terms of a contract may prohibit its sale or transfer separately from the acquiree. This does not affect it meeting the contractual-legal criterion, but it may in some cases affect its fair value (see 2.6.1040).

IFRS 3.A 2.6.720.130 *Goodwill* is an asset representing the future economic benefits arising from other assets acquired in a business combination that are not individually identified and recognised separately. An intangible asset acquired in a business combination that meets neither the separability criterion nor the contractual-legal criterion at the acquisition date is subsumed into goodwill. Similarly, any value attributable to items that do not qualify as assets at the acquisition date are subsumed into goodwill. See 2.6.900 for a discussion of the recognition and measurement of goodwill.

2.6.720.140 Examples of items that are not identifiable include:

FRS 3.B37, BC179
- assembled workforce of the acquiree, i.e. an existing collection of employees that permits the acquirer to continue to operate an acquired business from the acquisition date;

IFRS 3.B38
- potential future contracts at the acquisition date, although there may be a related customer relationship intangible asset (see 2.6.760);
- synergies from combining the acquiree's net assets with those of the acquirer; and
- market share.

IFRS 3.BC   2.6.720.150 While individual employees may have employment contracts that are
178   intangible assets, the assembled workforce as a whole does not have such a contract
and it is not separable.

2.6.720.160 A collective bargaining agreement typically dictates the terms of the employment (e.g. wage rates) but normally does not oblige the covered employees to remain
with the employer for a specified period. The assembled workforce of the acquiree is not
recognised as an intangible asset because it is not identifiable. In our view, the existence
of a collective bargaining agreement does not change this for the employees covered by
that agreement. However, in our view the underlying collective bargaining contract could
meet the criteria for recognition as a separate intangible asset (favourable contract terms)
or a liability (unfavourable contract terms). We would expect the separate recognition of
a collective bargaining agreement intangible asset to arise rarely in practice.

2.6.720.170 In our view, a group of individual employment contracts entered into by an
acquiree with a broad group of employees should not be viewed, collectively, as an assembled workforce. However, the facts and circumstances in each situation should be
evaluated. For example, non-compete clauses included in such contracts are evaluated
separately for possible recognition as identifiable intangible assets.

IFRS 3.45-50,   2.6.720.180 If an item acquired in a business combination is included in goodwill,
B38   for example because it is not identifiable at the acquisition date, then the acquirer does not
subsequently reclassify that value from goodwill for events that occur after the acquisition
date. See 2.6.910 for a discussion of subsequent adjustments to the acquisition accounting.

2.6.730 Customer-related intangible assets

IFRS 3.IE23   2.6.730.10 Customer-related intangible assets may meet the contractual-legal and/or the
separability criterion (see 2.6.720.40 and 3.3.40). Identifying, recognising and measuring customer-related intangible assets is an area that often requires careful analysis
and attention. The relationship that an acquiree has with its customers may encompass
a number of distinct intangible assets that need to be recognised separately from each
other, e.g. a specific contract with a customer may need to be recognised separately
from the relationship with that customer. This can pose challenges in the acquisition
accounting. Examples of customer-related intangible assets include:

- customer lists (non-contractual)
- order or production backlog (contractual)
- customer contracts and related customer relationships (contractual)
- non-contractual customer relationships.

2.6.740 Customer lists

IFRS 3.IE24   2.6.740.10 A customer list consists of information about customers, such as names and
contact information. It also may be a database that includes other information about
customers, such as order histories and demographic information. Customer lists gener-

ally do not arise from contractual or other legal rights, but frequently are sold, leased or exchanged. A customer list that is separable might meet the definition of an intangible asset even if the acquiree does not control the customer relationship. However, not all customer lists are separable. In some countries regulations exist that prevent an entity from selling, leasing or exchanging the information in such a list. Sometimes there are terms of confidentiality or other agreements that prohibit an entity from selling, leasing or otherwise exchanging information about its customers. The existence of such regulation or similar agreements prevents recognition as the list would not be separable in such cases.

2.6.740.20 It is important to distinguish between a customer list and a customer base. A customer list includes specific information about the customer, such as name, contact information, order history and demographic information. A customer base represents a group of customers that are neither known nor identifiable to the entity, e.g. the customers that visit a particular fast-food restaurant. A customer base does not meet the criteria for recognition separately from goodwill because a customer base meets neither the contractual-legal nor the separability criterion.

2.6.740.30 For example, Company P acquires Company S, a medical testing company, in a business combination on 31 October 2010. S provides testing services to patients, such as blood screening, based on referrals from their general practitioners (medical practitioners who provide primary care to patients). S maintains a database with each patient's information, such as name, address, telephone number, doctor's name, insurer's name and policy number. However, this patient information is protected by privacy laws and S cannot sell, licence, transfer or otherwise exchange it. The customer list does not meet the separability criterion because privacy laws and regulations over patient information prevent selling, transferring, licensing or exchanging patient information separately from the acquiree. Whether or not P could recognise a separate intangible asset for the relationship with the patients and the general practitioner would depend on the specific facts and circumstances of each case.

2.6.750 Order or production backlog

FRS 3.IE25   2.6.750.10 Order or production backlog arises from contracts such as purchase or sales orders. An order or production backlog acquired in a business combination meets the contractual-legal criterion even if the purchase or sales orders are cancellable by the customer (see 2.6.720.110).

2.6.760 Customer contracts and related customer relationships

FRS 3.IE28   2.6.760.10 Customer relationships are identifiable intangible assets if they arise from contractual or legal rights, or are separable. The following criteria must be met in order to conclude that a customer relationship exists:

- the acquiree should have information about the customer and regular contact with the customer; and

175

- the customer should have the ability to make direct contact with the acquiree.

IFRS 3.IE27   2.6.760.20 Care is taken to distinguish between a customer contract and the related customer relationship as they may represent two distinct intangible assets, which may need to be recognised separately from each other since they may have different useful lives.

IFRS 3.IE26,   2.6.760.30 If an entity establishes relationships with its customers through contracts,
IE30   then those customer relationships arise from contractual rights and therefore meet the contractual-legal criterion. This is unaffected by confidentiality or other contractual terms that prohibit the sale or transfer of a contract separately from the acquiree. The interpretation of what is a contractual customer relationship is broad.

IFRS 3.IE29,   2.6.760.40 For example, Company P acquires Company S in a business combination on
IE30(c)   31 October 2010. S has a practice of using purchase orders when entering into transactions with its customers. At the acquisition date S:

- has a backlog of open purchase orders with 75 percent of its recurring customers; and
- does not have open purchase orders, or other contracts, with the other 25 percent of its recurring customers.

2.6.760.50 Regardless of whether or not they are cancellable, the purchase orders from the 75 percent of S's recurring customers meet the contractual-legal criterion. The related relationships with those customers also meet the contractual-legal criterion. Therefore, both the contracts and the relationships are recognised as intangible assets separately from goodwill, and separately from each other as they represent two distinct intangible assets. Since S has a practice of establishing customer relationships with customers through purchase orders, the customer relationships with the 25 percent of recurring customers with whom S does not have open purchase orders also meet the contractual-legal criterion. Therefore, these customer relationship assets are recognised at fair value, separately from goodwill.

2.6.760.60 In another example, Company P acquires Company S, a department store, in a business combination on 31 October 2010. S runs a loyalty programme and has access to relevant customer information and the ability to contact customers participating in the loyalty programme. In addition, the customers have the ability to make direct contact with S. On the basis of the information presented in this example, in our view the customer relationship is recognised as an intangible asset separately from goodwill at its acquisition-date fair value.

2.6.770 Overlapping customer relationships

2.6.770.10 Sometimes both the acquirer and the acquiree can have relationships with the same customer. In our view, the acquirer still recognises the acquiree's relationship with that customer at its fair value at the acquisition date if that relationship is identifiable.

2.6.770.20 For example, Company P acquires Company S in a business combination on 31 October 2010. P and S operate in the same industry and both sell their products to Customer C. Assuming that the relationship meets the separability or contractual-legal criterion, an issue arises as to whether P should recognise an intangible asset for S's relationship with C separately from goodwill since P already has a relationship with C. In our view, P should recognise a customer relationship intangible asset for S's relationship with C. We believe that it meets the definition of an identifiable intangible asset. The relationship is measured at its fair value at the acquisition date from a market participant's perspective.

2.6.780 Acquiree has a pre-existing customer relationship with the acquirer

2.6.780.10 Sometimes the acquiree may have a pre-existing customer relationship with the acquirer, and the question arises as to whether the acquirer recognises this relationship in applying the acquisition accounting. In our view, the acquirer should not recognise an intangible asset separately from goodwill for a customer relationship that the acquiree has with the acquirer because, from the perspective of the consolidated group, the definition of an asset is not met because no future economic benefits will be derived from outside of the group; the asset cannot be disposed of and the contract is between members of the consolidated group.

FRS 3.B35   2.6.780.20 In contrast to this, a reacquired right granted previously by the acquirer to the acquiree to use an asset of the acquirer is recognised in the acquisition accounting (see 2.6.390). The reason for the difference is that in the case of a reacquired right, the acquirer regains the right to use one of its assets; however, in the case of a customer relationship that the acquiree has with the acquirer, the acquirer is not obtaining an identifiable asset because from the group's perspective the acquirer and acquiree are part of the same entity.

2.6.780.30 For example, Company P acquires Company S, one of its suppliers, in a business combination on 31 October 2010. The question arises as to whether P can recognise an intangible asset separately from goodwill for S's customer relationship with P. We believe that P should not include S's relationship with P in the measurement of the customer relationship intangible asset arising from the acquisition of S, because from the perspective of the consolidated group, the definition of an asset is not met. However, P should consider whether there are other related identifiable intangible assets acquired, e.g. reacquired rights.

2.6.790 Purchased legal relationships with customers

2.6.790.10 Sometimes an acquiree may have a purchased legal relationship with customers, but does not have direct contact with those customers. In our view, purchased legal relationships with customers may meet the criteria to be recognised as contract-based intangible assets even if the entity does not have a direct contract with its customers and only limited or no information about their identity, as long as the relationship nonetheless is established through contractual or other legal rights.

2.6.790.20 For example, Company P acquires Company S, a fund management company, in a business combination on 31 October 2010. S has a portfolio of customers (investors) who invest their money in the funds run by S and pay a management fee to S as the fund manager. There is no contact between S and its investors, and S does not have any information about its investors. Rather, several banks act as intermediaries by advertising S's funds to their customers and enabling them to invest in the funds. By doing so, the investors agree to the terms and conditions included in a prospectus that is issued by the fund, which includes all relevant provisions, including those applying to the management fee. In our view, in this situation P should recognise a contract-based intangible asset as part of the acquisition accounting, based on the terms and conditions contained in the prospectus. In this case the intangible asset effectively is the right of S to receive management fees.

2.6.800 Non-contractual customer relationships

IFRS 3.B33, B34, IE31   2.6.800.10 A customer relationship that does not meet the contractual-legal criterion can be identifiable if it meets the separability criterion. Separability is demonstrated if the entity has the ability to dispose of the asset, or for the asset to be disposed of as a package with a related asset, liability or related contract, but not as part of a business combination. Therefore, in our view, if an asset is capable of being divided from the entity, then separability is demonstrated by the following:

- There is a market for the same or similar assets to be exchanged in transactions that are not business combinations. There is a market if there are exchange transactions for similar assets.
- The entity has access to this market, i.e. the entity would be able to sell its customer relationship in that market.

2.6.810 *In-process research and development assets*

IAS 38.8   2.6.810.10 In-process research and development (IPR&D) may be acquired in a business combination:

- *Research* is original and planned investigation undertaken with the prospect of gaining new knowledge and understanding. Outside of a business combination, research costs are expensed as incurred.
- *Development* is the application of research findings or other knowledge to a plan or design for the production of new or substantially improved materials, products, processes etc. before the start of commercial production or use; it does not include the maintenance or enhancement of ongoing operations.

2.6.810.20 IFRS 3 does not contain an exception to the recognition or measurement principles for IPR&D. Therefore, IPR&D is recognised separately from goodwill and measured at its fair value at the acquisition date, if it is identifiable (see 2.6.720.40) and otherwise meets the definition of an intangible asset (see 3.3.30). This is irrespective of whether the acquiree had recognised the asset in its financial statements before the business combination. Similar to other intangible assets acquired in a business combination, the asset recognition criteria of probable future economic benefits and being able to measure its cost reliably are considered to be satisfied in all cases (see 2.6.720.20). If there is uncertainty about the outcome of a project, then this will be reflected in the measurement of its fair value.

2.6.810.30 At the acquisition date IPR&D is capitalised as an intangible asset not yet ready for use. The subsequent measurement of an acquired IPR&D project and the treatment of subsequent expenditure on it are in accordance with IAS 38.

2.6.810.40 For example, Company P acquires Company S, a pharmaceutical company, in a business combination on 31 October 2010. The identifiable net assets acquired by P include an IPR&D project for a new drug. S has capitalised 1,000 in accordance with IAS 38 in respect of this project. The fair value of the project at the acquisition date is 3,000. As part of its acquisition accounting P recognises separately from goodwill an intangible asset of 3,000 for the IPR&D project.

2.6.820 *Intangible assets that an acquirer intends to not use or to use in a way that is different from how other market participants would use them*

IFRS 3.B43 2.6.820.10 Sometimes the acquirer may intend not to use an acquired intangible asset, or it may intend to use it in a way that is not its highest and best use. There are a variety of reasons why an acquirer may intend not to use an acquired asset, e.g. competitive reasons, incidental asset acquired as part of the business acquired. Nevertheless, it is measured at its fair value at the acquisition date based on its use by other market participants (see 2.6.1040.60 – 80).

2.6.830 *Leases*

2.6.830.10 When the acquiree in a business combination is a party to lease agreements at the acquisition date, the acquirer needs to account for these leases assumed as part of the acquisition accounting. This may result in the recognition of assets and liabilities. The type of lease, i.e. operating or finance, and whether the acquiree is the lessee or the lessor will impact how the assets and liabilities are recognised. The terms of the lease compared to market terms at the acquisition date will impact the determination of the fair value of the asset or liability.

IFRS 3.B28, 2.6.830.20 When the acquiree is the lessee in an operating lease, the underlying
B29 asset that is the subject of the lease (e.g. a building) is not recognised by the acquiree or the acquirer. However, the acquirer recognises a separate intangible asset or liability in respect of operating leases of the acquiree that are acquired in a business combination; in respect of an asset, these lease agreements meet the contractual-legal criterion (see 2.6.720.40). The lease contract asset or liability is recognised at its fair value at the acquisition date. Factors that affect the fair value may include factors such as the lease not being priced at market rates at the acquisition date, the existence of renewal options and the difficulty in securing such a lease. Leasehold improvements of the acquiree are recognised as tangible assets at their fair values at the acquisition date.

2.6 Business combinations

IFRS 3.B42   2.6.830.30 If the acquiree is the lessor in an operating lease, then the asset subject to the operating lease (e.g. a building) is recognised at fair value taking into account the terms of the related lease, i.e. the acquirer does not recognise a separate intangible asset or liability related to the favourable or unfavourable aspect of an operating lease relative to market terms or prices.

IAS 16.44   2.6.830.40 If the asset that is the subject of the operating lease is measured subsequent to the acquisition using the cost model in accordance with IAS 16, then the off-market value of the lease, favourable or unfavourable, becomes a separate component of the asset for the purpose of calculating depreciation.

2.6.830.50 In addition to recognising the lease contract, an intangible asset may be recognised for the relationship that the lessor has with the lessee at its fair value at the acquisition date, since the contractual-legal criterion is satisfied (see 2.6.720.40).

2.6.830.60 When the acquiree is the lessee in a finance lease, the acquirer recognises the fair value of both the asset held under the finance lease and the related liability. Depending on the terms of the lease, the fair value of the leased asset may be less than the fair value of the asset itself. This is because the acquirer acquires as part of the business combination the right to use an asset over the remaining term of the lease, which could be shorter than the economic life of the asset. In other words, although the asset is accounted for according to its type, e.g. property, plant and equipment, the acquirer measures the fair value of the asset based on the fair value of the leasehold interest acquired rather than on the underlying asset itself.

2.6.830.70 When the acquiree is the lessor in a finance lease, the acquirer recognises a receivable for the net investment in the finance lease. This is measured at its acquisition-date fair value, determined based on the assumptions about discount rates and other factors market participants would use. In our view, an acquirer would not recognise separately an additional asset or liability related to favourable or unfavourable contracts, because measurement of the fair value of the lease receivables and the unguaranteed residual values at fair value would consider all of the terms of the lease contracts.

2.6.830.80 In addition, an intangible asset may be recognised for the relationship the lessor has with the lessee (see 2.6.760).

IAS 17.25   2.6.830.90 Outside of a business combination, contingent rent generally is not recognised until it becomes payable. However, in our view the existence of contingent rent in a lease contract acquired in a business combination will be incorporated into the fair value measurement of the asset or liability arising from the lease that is recognised as part of the acquisition accounting.

2.6.830.100 For example, Company P acquires Company S in a business combination on 31 October 2010. S is a retailer and leases its retail outlets under operating lease contracts. One of S's operating lease agreements, with a remaining lease period of eight

180

years, requires a fixed annual lease payment of 500 plus an additional contingent rental payment equal to 2.5 percent of annual sales in excess of 10,000.

2.6.830.110 At the acquisition date the market rate of an eight-year lease for a similar property is a fixed annual lease payment of 500 plus an additional contingent rental payment equal to 2 percent of annual sales in excess of 10,000. P has determined that all other terms of the lease contracts are consistent with market terms.

2.6.830.120 In applying the acquisition method, P recognises a liability for an unfavourable lease contract, due to the unfavourable contingent rental payments relative to market terms for the remaining eight years of the lease term, i.e. the contingent rental payments of 2.5 percent on annual sales in excess of 10,000 is unfavourable to the market rate of 2 percent on a comparable lease.

IAS 17.33   2.6.830.130 In accordance with IAS 17, lease payments under an operating lease usually are recognised on a straight-line basis over the lease term; when the timing of lease payments does not represent the time pattern of the lessee's benefits under the lease agreement, prepaid rent or accrued liabilities for rental payments is recognised (see 5.1.310.20). Such prepaid rent or accrued liability does not meet the definition of an asset acquired or a liability assumed (see 2.6.570). Therefore, prepaid or accrued rent recognised previously by an acquiree in order to recognise lease payments under an operating lease on a straight-line basis in accordance with the requirements of IAS 17 should not be recognised by the acquirer under the acquisition method; this is regardless of whether an acquiree is the lessee or lessor. Instead, the favourable/unfavourable element of the lease contract, which is recognised in the acquisition accounting, is determined by comparing the actual future payment stream under the operating lease with the market rate that would need to be paid based on the future periods in the contract as if a new contract were granted in respect of those periods. This either forms the basis of an acquiree asset or liability, or is included in the accounting for the settlement of a pre-existing relationship (see 2.6.370).

2.6.840 Measurement of NCI in acquisition accounting#

IFRS 3.19   2.6.840.10 When less than 100 percent of a subsidiary is acquired, the acquirer can elect on a transaction-by-transaction basis to measure the present ownership component of NCI at:

- fair value at the acquisition date, which means that goodwill, or the gain on a bargain purchase, includes a portion attributable to NCI; or
- their proportionate interest in the recognised amount of the identifiable net assets of the acquiree, which means that goodwill recognised, or the gain on a bargain purchase, relates only to the controlling interest acquired.

2.6.840.20 This accounting policy choice relates only to the initial measurement of NCI. After initial recognition the option of measuring NCI at fair value is not available.

2.6.840.30 The implication of recognising the present ownership component of NCI at their proportionate interest in the recognised amount of the identifiable assets and liabilities of the acquiree is that both the NCI and goodwill are lower because no goodwill is ascribed to the NCI.

2.6.840.40 For example, on 31 October 2010 Company P acquires 60 percent of Company S for cash of 1,000. The fair value of the identifiable net assets of S is 1,500 and their carrying amount is 1,200. The fair value of the NCI is 650 based on the market price of the shares that the acquirer does not obtain.

2.6.840.50 If P elects to measure the NCI in S at fair value, then in its consolidated financial statements P recognises the identifiable net assets of S at 1,500 (full fair value), NCI at 650 (full fair value), and the resulting goodwill at 150 (1,000 + 650 - 1,500); see 2.6.900 for the calculation of goodwill. In its consolidated financial statements, P records the following entry:

	Debit	Credit
Identifiable net assets of S	1,500	
Goodwill	150	
NCI (equity)		650
Cash		1,000
To recognise acquisition of S		

2.6.840.60 Assuming the same facts as in 2.6.840.40, if P elects to recognise the NCI in S at their proportionate interest in the fair value of the identifiable assets and liabilities, then in its consolidated financial statements P recognises the identifiable net assets of S at 1,500 (full fair value), NCI at 600 (1,500 x 40%), and the resulting goodwill at 100 (1,000 + 600 - 1,500); see 2.6.900 for the calculation of goodwill. In its consolidated financial statements, P records the following entry:

	Debit	Credit
Identifiable net assets of S	1,500	
Goodwill	100	
NCI (equity)		600
Cash		1,000
To recognise acquisition of S		

2.6.850 *Forthcoming requirements*

2.6.850.10 The *Improvements to IFRSs 2010* amended IFRS 3 to limit the accounting policy choice in respect of the measurement of NCI upon initial recognition to instruments that give rise to a present ownership interest and currently entitle the holder to a share of net assets in the event of liquidation.

2.6.850.20 Therefore, the accounting policy choice does not apply to other NCI instruments, such as equity components of convertible bonds or options under share-based payment arrangements. Such instruments are measured at fair value or in accordance with other relevant IFRSs, e.g. share-based payments that give rise to NCI are measured using the market-based measure in accordance with IFRS 2.

2.6.850.30 The amendment, which is effective for annual periods beginning on or after 1 July 2010, is required to be applied prospectively from the date that an entity first applied IFRS 3 (2008) (see 2.6.1150).

2.6.850.40 However, when different components of NCI are present in an acquisition and the acquirer intends to measure the NCI component eligible for the measurement choice ("ordinary NCI") at their proportionate interest in the identifiable net assets of the acquiree, an issue arises as to how that proportionate interest should be calculated.

2.6.850.50 The following fact pattern is used in the discussion in 2.6.860 - 890 to illustrate the different accounting approaches:

- Company P acquires 80 percent of the ordinary shares of Company S for 1,600.
- P elects to measure ordinary NCI at their proportionate interest in the identifiable net assets of S. The identifiable net assets are determined under IFRS 3 as 1,800.
- S also has outstanding 200 equity-classified preference shares that have a preference in liquidation and participate with a fixed amount of 1 per share in liquidation; none of these shares were acquired by P. As the preference shares do not entitle the holders to a proportionate share of net assets in the event of liquidation, they are not eligible for the measurement choice and are measured in the acquisition accounting at fair value, which is determined to be 240.

2.6.850.60 In our view, there are two possible approaches for determining the proportionate interest in identifiable net assets in measuring ordinary NCI (see 2.6.860 and 2.6.870); a third approach has been identified that we do not believe is appropriate (see 2.6.880). The chosen approach should be applied consistently for all business combinations in which NCI are measured at their proportionate interest in the identifiable net assets.

2.6.860 *Approach 1: Fair value of other components of NCI*

2.6.860.10 We prefer the proportionate interest in the identifiable net assets of ordinary NCI to be determined using the following steps:

(1) Start with the recognised amount of the identifiable net assets of the acquiree, measured in accordance with IFRS 3.

(2) Deduct the values assigned to the components of NCI other than ordinary NCI, e.g. the market-based measure of a share-based payment, from the identifiable net assets of the acquiree. This step is the key difference between the approaches.

(3) Multiply the determined subtotal by the percentage interest attributable to ordinary NCI.

2.6.860.20 Applying Approach 1 to the fact pattern in 2.6.850.50, ordinary NCI is measured as follows at the acquisition date:

Step 1. Identifiable net assets S	1,800
Step 2. Minus share of preference shareholders (fair value)	(240)
Residual identifiable net assets	1,560
Step 3. Measure ordinary NCI (1,560 x 20%)	312

2.6.860.30 Under Approach 1 it is argued that NCI for which the measurement option is not available also have a share in the identifiable net assets of the acquiree. Accordingly, ordinary NCI are measured after taking account of the value of the interests in the identifiable net assets attributable to other components of NCI. The value taken into account (deducted) for such other components of NCI is represented by the amount recognised under IFRS 3 (fair value in this example).

2.6.860.40 By way of contrast with Approach 2 in 2.6.870, Approach 1 assumes that a proportionate share in liquidation is the trigger for allowing the measurement option in IFRS 3. However, this trigger does not direct how ordinary NCI should be measured.

2.6.870 *Approach 2: Participation in liquidation*

2.6.870.10 Approach 2 is based on the idea that a proportionate share in liquidation should not only be the trigger for allowing the measurement option in IFRS 3, but also directs the measurement of ordinary NCI. Under Approach 2, step 2 in 2.6.860.10 comprises the amount that components of NCI other than ordinary NCI would receive in liquidation; this deduction is determined based on an assumed liquidation on the acquisition date.

2.6.870.20 Applying this approach to the fact pattern in 2.6.850.50, ordinary NCI is measured as follows at the acquisition date:

Step 1. Identifiable net assets S	1,800
Step 2. Minus share of preference shareholders (in liquidation)	(200)
Residual identifiable net assets	1,600
Step 3. Measure ordinary NCI (1,600 x 20%)	320

2.6.880 *Approach 3: No adjustment*

2.6.880.10 Another possible approach is to determine the proportionate share of identifiable net assets of ordinary NCI without any adjustment for other components of NCI, i.e. without step 2 illustrated in 2.6.860.20 and 870.20. We do not believe that Approach 3 is acceptable because it fails to take into account any value attributable to other stakeholders' interests in the acquiree and therefore overvalues ordinary NCI.

2.6.880.20 If this approach were applied to the fact pattern in 2.6.850.50, then ordinary NCI would measured as follows at the acquisition date:

Step 1. Identifiable net assets S	1,800
Step 2. Minus share of preference shareholders	0
Residual identifiable net assets	1,800
Step 3. Measure ordinary NCI (1,800 x 20%)	360

2.6.890 *Goodwill calculation*

2.6.890.10 Depending on the approach taken, there is a consequential effect on the calculation of goodwill. Applying the acceptable approaches in 2.6.860 and 870 to the fact pattern in 2.6.850.50, goodwill is determined as follows:

	Approach 1 (2.6.860)	Approach 2 (2.6.870)
Consideration transferred	1,600	1,600
NCI – preference shares	240	240
Ordinary NCI	312	320
Total NCI	552	560
Minus identifiable net assets	(1,800)	(1,800)
Goodwill	352	360

2.6.890.20 In the calculations in 2.6.890.10, the amount attributed to preference shareholder NCI is 240 in both cases, i.e. fair value. This is because the different approaches to measuring other components of NCI are solely for the purpose of measuring ordinary NCI. These calculations have no effect on the amount at which other components of NCI are stated in the statement of financial position at the acquisition date. Instead, it is the calculation of goodwill that is affected.

2.6.900 **Goodwill or a gain on a bargain purchase**

IFRS 3.32 2.6.900.10 Goodwill is recognised at the acquisition date, measured as a residual. Goodwill recorded previously by an acquiree is not recorded as a separate asset by the acquirer.

IFRS 3.32   2.6.900.20 The acquirer measures goodwill as the excess of (a) over (b):

(a) The aggregate of:

IFRS 3.37   • consideration transferred, which generally is measured at fair value at the acquisition date (see 2.6.260);

IFRS 3.19   • the amount of any NCI in the acquiree, which may be measured either at fair value or at their proportionate share in the fair value of the identifiable assets and liabilities of the acquiree at the acquisition date (see 2.6.840); and

IFRS 3.42   • in a business combination achieved in stages, the acquisition-date fair value of the acquirer's previously held equity interest in the acquiree (see 2.6.1020.30).

IFRS 3.18   (b) The net of the acquisition-date amounts of the identifiable assets acquired and the liabilities assumed measured in accordance with IFRS 3 (see 2.6.560).

IFRS 3.34   2.6.900.30 A gain on a bargain purchase arises when (b) is greater than (a).

IFRS 3.35   2.6.900.40 A bargain purchase may arise for a number of reasons, for example in the case of a forced liquidation or distressed sale or due to applying the measurement requirements of IFRS 3, which require in certain instances measurement of the identifiable assets acquired and liabilities assumed at amounts other than fair value (see 2.6.640). A business combination does not, however, need to exhibit any particular characteristics such as evidence of a forced or distressed sale in order for a bargain purchase to be recognised. Such a gain is the result of applying the formula described in 2.6.900.20, regardless of other factors, such as the economic rationale for the transaction.

IFRS 3.36   2.6.900.50 Before recognising a gain on a bargain purchase, the acquirer reassesses whether it has correctly *identified* all of the assets acquired and the liabilities assumed. In our view, the acquirer also should reassess whether it has correctly identified any NCI in the acquiree, any previously held equity interest in the acquiree, and the consideration transferred. Following that reassessment, the acquirer reviews the procedures used to *measure* the following amounts required to be recognised at the acquisition date to ensure that the measurements reflect consideration of all available information as of the acquisition date:

• the identifiable assets acquired and liabilities assumed;
• any NCI in the acquiree;
• for a business combination achieved in stages, the acquirer's previously held equity interest in the acquiree; and
• the consideration transferred.

2.6.900.60 In our view, an acquirer also should review the procedures used to identify amounts that are not part of what the acquirer and acquiree exchanged in the business combination. For example, a business combination may:

• result in the effective settlement of a pre-existing relationship between the acquirer and the acquiree, e.g. a supply agreement or an operating lease arrangement (see 2.6.350);

- include transactions that compensate employees or former owners of an acquiree for future services (see 2.6.400); or
- include transactions that reimburse the acquiree or its former owners for paying the acquirer's acquisition-related costs (see 2.6.520).

2.6.900.70 Such transactions are not part of the business combination transaction and therefore are accounted for as separate transactions. Accounting for such arrangements as separate transactions, rather than as part of the acquisition, affects the determination of goodwill or the gain from a bargain purchase that arises from the business combination.

IFRS 3.B 2.6.900.80 Any remaining gain from a bargain purchase after completing the re-
64(n), assessment is recognised in profit or loss at the acquisition date. Disclosure is required
IAS 1.87 of the amount of any recognised gain from a bargain purchase, the line items in profit or loss in which the gain is recognised, and a description of the reasons why the transaction resulted in a gain.

2.6.910 **Measurement after the initial accounting for the business combination**

2.6.920 *The measurement period*

2.6.920.10 The initial accounting for a business combination comprises a number of steps, including identifying and/or measuring:

- the identifiable assets acquired and liabilities assumed (see 2.6.560);
- any NCI (see 2.6.840);
- consideration transferred (see 2.6.260);
- any pre-existing equity interest in the acquiree (see 2.6.1020); and
- goodwill or the gain on a bargain purchase (see 2.6.900).

IFRS 3.45, 2.6.920.20 The measurement period cannot be longer than one year from the acquisition
BC392 date. However, the standard does not allow an "open" one-year period following the acquisition date. Instead, the measurement period ends when the acquirer receives the information that it was seeking about facts and circumstances existing at the acquisition date, or learns that more information is not available. While the final outcome of some items may not be known within a year, e.g. a liability for which the outcome was uncertain at the acquisition date, the purpose of the measurement period is to provide time to obtain the information necessary to measure items at the acquisition date; determining the ultimate outcome of, for example, provisions, is not part of the acquisition accounting.

IFRS 3.45 2.6.920.30 An entity reflects measurement period adjustments by revising its comparative financial statements as if the new information had been known when the business combination was accounted for initially.

2.6.930 *Reporting when the acquisition accounting is incomplete*

IFRS 3.45 2.6.930.10 If the acquisition accounting is not complete in any financial statements issued during the measurement period, then the acquirer reports provisional amounts for the assets, liabilities, equity interests, or items of consideration for which the accounting is incomplete.

2.6.930.20 IFRS 3 does not provide specific guidance on determining provisional amounts. Those amounts are determined based on the available information at the acquisition date, consistent with the recognition and measurement requirements of the standard. In our view, entities should make a reasonable effort to determine provisional amounts. Accordingly, we believe that it would not be appropriate to assign only nominal amounts, or no amounts, solely because the acquirer anticipates receiving additional information about facts and circumstances that existed at the acquisition date.

IFRS 3.B 67(a), IAS 34.16(i) 2.6.930.30 Until the accounting for a business combination is complete, the acquirer is required to disclose the following in its annual financial statements and in any interim financial statements:

- the reasons why the initial accounting for the business combination is incomplete;
- the assets, liabilities, equity interests, or items of consideration for which the initial accounting is incomplete; and
- the nature and amount of any measurement period adjustments recognised during the period.

2.6.940 *Adjustments to provisional amounts during the measurement period*

IFRS 3.BC 399 2.6.940.10 Measurement period adjustments are analogous to adjusting events after the reporting date under IAS 10 *Events after the Reporting Period* (see 2.9). Adjusting events are events that occur after the reporting date but before the financial statements are issued and that provide evidence of a condition that existed at the reporting date; such events are reflected in the financial statements. Similarly, the effects of information that first becomes available during the measurement period and that provides evidence of conditions or circumstances that existed at the acquisition date are reflected in the accounting at the acquisition date. All other changes to amounts included in the acquisition accounting that occur after the acquisition date, including those occurring within the measurement period, generally do not affect the acquisition accounting (see 2.6.960).

2.6.940.20 For example, Company P acquires Company S in a business combination on 30 April 2010. Provisional amounts are recognised for certain of the assets acquired and liabilities assumed, including a liability related to a contractual dispute between S and one of its customers. Shortly before the acquisition date S's customer claimed that certain amounts were due by S under penalty clauses for completion delays included in the contract.

2.6.940.30 P evaluates the dispute based on the information available at the acquisition date and concludes that S was responsible for at least some of the delays in completing the contract. P recognises a provisional amount for this liability of 1,000 in its acquisition accounting, which is its best estimate of the fair value of the liability to the customer based on the information available at the acquisition date:

	Debit	Credit
Goodwill	1,000	
Liability		1,000
To recognise liability at acquisition date based on		
provisional estimates		

2.6.940.40 The interim consolidated financial statements of P for the six months ending 30 June 2010 include appropriate disclosure in respect of the provisional accounting.

2.6.940.50 P obtains no new information about the possible outcome of the dispute until September 2010, when the customer presents additional information in support of its claim. Based on this information, P concludes that the fair value of the liability for the customer's claim at the acquisition date was 2,000. Accordingly, in its consolidated financial statements P records the following entry:

	Debit	Credit
Goodwill	1,000	
Liability		1,000
To increase liability within measurement period		

2.6.940.60 P continues to receive and evaluate information related to the claim after September 2010. Its evaluation does not change until May 2011, when it concludes, based on additional information and responses received from the customer to enquiries made by P, that the liability for the claim at the acquisition date was 1,900. P determines that the amount that would be recognised with respect to the claim under IAS 37 at May 2011 would be 2,200. Accordingly, in its consolidated financial statements P records the following entry:

	Debit	Credit
Profit or loss	200	
Liability		200
To increase liability after end of measurement period		

2.6.940.70 The decrease in the estimated fair value of the liability for the claim in May 2011 occurred after the measurement period, and therefore would not be recognised as an adjustment to the acquisition accounting. When the amount determined in accordance with IAS 37 subsequently exceeds the previous estimate of the fair value of the liability, P recognises an increase in the liability. Because the information resulting in this change was obtained after the end of the measurement period, the increase in the liability is recognised in profit or loss.

2.6.940.80 It is important to distinguish new information about conditions that existed at the acquisition date from information about changes in the value of acquired assets or liabilities that result from events that occur subsequent to the acquisition date. Only the former results in adjustments to the acquisition accounting.

2.6.940.90 A degree of tension exists between the general requirement in IFRS 3 to measure amounts recognised in the acquisition accounting at fair value and the requirement to amend acquisition accounting retrospectively for measurement period adjustments. In our view, additional information that becomes available during the measurement period that, if known, might have affected observable market data on which the measurement of an item included in the acquisition accounting is based should not give rise to a measurement period adjustment. This is because such information does not affect the basis of estimation of the fair value of an asset or liability at the acquisition date, that is, the amount at which an asset could be exchanged, or a liability settled, between knowledgeable, willing parties in an arm's length transaction at that date. In contrast, when fair values are estimated based on other than observable market data, the measurement of such values in the acquisition accounting is adjusted when new information obtained during the measurement period represents a basis for a better estimate of fair value at the acquisition date. See 2.9.70 for a discussion of the discovery of a fraud after the end of the reporting period.

2.6.950 *Changes in the recognition of assets and liabilities during the measurement period*

IFRS 3.45   2.6.950.10 Measurement period adjustments may affect not only the measurement of assets and liabilities but also their recognition. Therefore, during the measurement period the acquirer recognises additional assets or liabilities if new information is obtained about facts and circumstances that existed at the acquisition date that, if known, would have resulted in the recognition of those assets and liabilities at that date.

2.6.950.20 Generally it is expected that the possibility of subsequent adjustments to the acquisition accounting during the measurement period would have been identified in the disclosures in any financial statements of the acquirer issued subsequent to the business combination but prior to the adjustments being identified. Accordingly, unless an acquirer has a high level of confidence that it has identified all contingent liabilities assumed, it is advisable for the acquirer to disclose in financial statements that include the measurement period the status of its identification of such liabilities.

IFRS 3.45   2.6.950.30 Adjustments made during the measurement period are recognised retrospectively and comparative information is revised, i.e. as if the accounting for the business combination had been completed at the acquisition date. Such adjustments include adjustments to the assets acquired, liabilities assumed and goodwill or gain on a bargain purchase recognised at the acquisition date, and any change in depreciation, amortisation, or other effects on comprehensive income that arise as a result of the adjustments.

2.6.950.40 For example, Company P acquires Company S on 30 November 2010. As part of the acquisition accounting P recognises a provisional amount of 10,000 in respect of a patent developed by S, based on the historical earnings attributable to products developed using that patent. However, the technology covered by the patent is new and P expects the cash flows to be generated by the patent to increase beyond those currently being generated. Accordingly, P commissions an independent valuation report from a third-party consultant, which is not expected to be finalised for several months. P assesses the useful life of the patent to be ten years. Goodwill of 20,000 is recognised in the provisional accounting.

2.6.950.50 The consolidated financial statements of P at 31 December 2010 include appropriate disclosure in respect of the provisional accounting (see 2.6.930).

2.6.950.60 The valuation report is finalised subsequent to the issue of the 2010 financial statements but before the end of the measurement period. Based on the valuation, P concludes that the fair value of the patent was 15,000 at 30 November 2010. Management does not revise the estimated useful life of the patent, which remains at ten years. As a result of this measurement period adjustment, the comparative information presented in the 2011 financial statements is revised as follows:

	31 December 2010	
	As stated originally	*Revised*
Profit or loss (patent amortisation)[1,2]	83	125
Goodwill[3]	20,000	15,000
Patent[4,5]	9,917	14,875

Notes
(1) 83 = 10,000 x 1/10 x 1/12
(2) 125 = 15,000 x 1/10 x 1/12
(3) 15,000 = 20,000 - 5,000
(4) 9,917 = 10,000 - 83
(5) 14,875 = 15,000 - 125

2.6.960 Adjustments after the measurement period

IFRS 3.50   2.6.960.10 After the measurement period ends, the acquisition accounting is adjusted only to correct an error or, in our view, to reflect a change in accounting policy in certain circumstances. Other adjustments are accounted for in accordance with the relevant standards.

IFRS 3.50, *IAS 1.10, 39,* *8.41*   2.6.960.20 If an error in the acquisition accounting is discovered after the measurement period, then the acquisition accounting is adjusted in accordance with IAS 8 *Accounting Policies, Changes in Accounting Estimates and Errors* (see 2.8.40) and comparative amounts are restated. In addition, it also is likely that the entity will be required to present a statement of financial position as at the beginning of the earliest comparative period (see 2.8.80.10).

2.6.960.30 The measurement of certain identifiable assets acquired and liabilities assumed is an exception to the general fair value measurement principle (see 2.6.640). For example, deferred taxes and employee benefits are not measured at fair value in the acquisition accounting; instead, they are measured in accordance with IAS 12 and IAS 19 respectively (see 2.6.660 and 680). An issue therefore arises as to whether the acquisition accounting is adjusted when the accounting for those items changes. For example, IFRIC 14 *IAS 19 – Limit on a Defined Benefit Asset, Minimum Funding Requirements and their Interaction*, which became effective for annual periods beginning on or after 1 January 2008 and which provides guidance about the recognition of a net defined benefit pension asset when minimum funding requirement exist, applied retrospectively to a limited extent.

2.6.960.40 In our view, when changes in accounting policy affect items that initially were measured in accordance with a specific standard at other than fair value and those changes are effective retrospectively, the acquisition accounting is adjusted to reflect the change in accounting policy.

2.6.960.50 In some instances, particularly when a new standard is applicable fully retrospectively, retrospective adjustment of the acquisition accounting may present practical difficulties. In such cases, entities consider the requirements of IAS 8 to determine whether full retrospective adoption is impracticable (see 2.8.50).

2.6.970 Subsequent measurement and accounting

2.6.970.10 IFRS 3 provides specific guidance on the subsequent measurement of the following items, which are discussed in this chapter:

- reacquired rights
- contingent liabilities
- indemnification assets
- contingent consideration.

2.6.980 *Reacquired rights*

2.6.980.10 See 2.6.690 for a discussion of the concept of reacquired rights and their measurement at the acquisition date.

IFRS 3.29, 55 2.6.980.20 The acquirer amortises a reacquired right over the remaining contractual period of the related contract in which the right was granted, regardless of the likelihood of renewals. This is consistent with the exception to the fair value measurement principle for the initial measurement of a reacquired right, which does not take into account potential contract renewals.

2.6.990 *Contingent liabilities that are present obligations*

IFRS 3.56 2.6.990.10 A contingent liability assumed in a business combination is recognised and measured at fair value at the acquisition date if the contingent liability represents a present obligation that arises from past events and can be measured reliably (see 2.6.650). Subsequently such contingent liabilities are recognised at the higher of:

- the amount recognised initially less, if appropriate, cumulative amortisation recognised in accordance with IAS 18 *Revenue*; and
- the amount that would be recognised in accordance with IAS 37.

IFRS 3.56 2.6.990.20 These requirements do not apply to contracts accounted for under IAS 39.

2.6.990.30 Subsequent adjustments to the carrying amount of a contingent liability recognised in the acquisition accounting might be recognised as a change to the acquisition accounting or be recognised in profit or loss subsequent to the acquisition. In determining the appropriate accounting, an entity considers whether the events or conditions that result in such an adjustment existed at the acquisition date. If new information is discovered within the measurement period that relates to conditions that existed at the time of the business combination, then the acquisition accounting is adjusted (see 2.6.940 – 950). If such new information relates to events subsequent to the business combination or is discovered subsequent to the expiry of the measurement period, then the remeasurement of the contingent liability is recognised in profit or loss.

IFRS 3.56 2.6.990.40 A contingent liability initially recognised in a business combination is not derecognised until it is settled, cancelled or it expires. In our view, if a contingency for which a liability is recognised in the acquisition accounting is reassessed subsequently as "probable to occur", then the guidance in 2.6.990.10 in respect of subsequent measurement still applies even if the amount recognised exceeds what the entity expects to pay notwithstanding that a similar liability recognised initially, other than in a business combination, would be measured under IAS 37. This effectively establishes a "floor" on the amount recognised in respect of a contingent liability initially recognised in a business combination.

2.6.990.50 For example, Company P acquires Company S in November 2010. Prior to the acquisition date Company X filed a lawsuit against S. Based on the legal foundations of the lawsuit, P's management determines that a present obligation exists; however, based on previous experience, the likelihood of the case being decided against P is less than probable. Taking these factors into account, P recognises a liability of 5,000 in respect of the contingent liability as part of the acquisition accounting.

2.6.990.60 In December 2011 P reassesses the likelihood of the lawsuit being settled or determined in court and determines that settlement is now probable, although the amount at which the liability now is estimated to be settled is less than management previously considered possible. Management's best estimate of the amount of settlement is 4,000. We believe that the liability continues to be measured at 5,000 until it is settled, i.e. the fair value of the contingent liability at the acquisition date.

2.6.1000 *Indemnification assets*

IFRS 3.27 2.6.1000.10 Indemnification assets are an exception to the recognition and measurement principles of IFRS 3. An acquirer recognises indemnification assets at the same time and measures them on the same basis as the indemnified item, subject to contractual limitations and adjustments for collectibility, if applicable (see 2.6.670).

IFRS 3.57 2.6.1000.20 Subsequent to initial recognition, the acquirer continues to measure an indemnification asset on the same basis as the related indemnified asset or liability. For example, an indemnification asset related to an asset or liability measured at fair value, such as an indemnification related to a forward contract accounted for at fair value under IAS 39, is itself measured at fair value.

IFRS 3.57 2.6.1000.30 The initial and subsequent accounting for indemnification assets recognised at the acquisition date applies equally to indemnified assets and liabilities that are recognised and measured under the principles of IFRS 3 and those that are subject to exceptions to the recognition or measurement principles of IFRS 3 (see 2.6.640). For example, an acquirer would initially recognise and measure an indemnification asset related to a defined benefit pension obligation using assumptions consistent with those used to measure the indemnified item, i.e. assumptions consistent with IAS 19; this basis of measurement would continue subsequent to the business combination.

2.6.1000.40 An acquirer may hold an indemnification related to an item that is not recognised at the acquisition date. For example, an indemnification may relate to a contingent liability that is not recognised because it cannot be measured with sufficient reliability (see 2.6.650.30). In our view, notwithstanding that no amount was recognised in the acquisition accounting, in these circumstances the indemnification asset is recognised and measured at the same time and on the same basis as the indemnified item subsequent to the business combination, subject to any contractual limitations on the amount of the indemnification and subject to adjustments for collectibility.

2.6.1000.50 For example, Company P is fully indemnified for any obligation arising from a contingent liability assumed in the acquisition of Company S. The fair value of the contingent liability recognised at the acquisition date was 10,000. P also recognised an indemnification asset of 10,000 at the acquisition date, i.e. there were no concerns about the collectibility of the indemnification asset.

	Debit	*Credit*
Indemnification asset	10,000	
Contingent liability		10,000
To reflect contingent liability and associated		
indemnification asset as part of acquisition accounting		

2.6.1000.60 Following the acquisition P obtains new information about events subsequent to the acquisition date and, based on this new information, concludes that the contingent liability would be measured at an amount of 5,000 under IAS 37; this does not impact the measurement of the contingent liability at the acquisition date (see 2.6.650). P still has no concerns about the collectibility of the indemnification asset.

2.6.1000.70 Because the acquisition-date fair value of the contingent liability of 10,000 is higher than the IAS 37 amount of 5,000, the carrying amount of the liability remains at 10,000, notwithstanding that payment is now probable (see 2.6.990.10). Under IFRS 3, the measurement of the indemnification asset follows the measurement of the liability, subject to management's assessment of collectibility and contractual limitations. Because there are no concerns over the collectibility of the indemnification asset or contractual limitations on the amount of the indemnification, P continues to recognise the indemnification asset at 10,000.

IFRS 3.27   2.6.1000.80 Collectibility of the indemnification asset may affect its measurement. For indemnification assets measured at fair value, management's assessment of collectibility is considered in determining fair value. For items measured at other than fair value, the carrying amount of the indemnification asset is reduced to reflect management's assessment of any uncollectible amounts under the indemnity.

IFRS 3.28   2.6.1000.90 The measurement of an indemnification asset is subject to any contractual limitations on its amount.

IFRS 3.57   2.6.1000.100 The acquirer derecognises an indemnification asset only when it collects the asset, sells it, or otherwise loses the right to it.

2.6.1000.110 If the amounts recognised by an acquirer for an indemnified liability and a related indemnification asset recognised at the acquisition date do not change subsequent to the acquisition and ultimately are settled at the amounts recognised in the acquisition accounting, then there will be no net effect on profit or loss providing that those amounts are the same.

2.6.1010 *Contingent consideration*

IFRS 3.39   2.6.1010.10 The fair value of contingent consideration initially is recognised by an acquirer at the acquisition date as part of the consideration transferred, measured at its acquisition-date fair value (see 2.6.280).

2.6.1010.20 Subsequent changes in the fair value of contingent consideration that result from additional information about facts and circumstances that existed at the acquisition date that the acquirer obtains during the measurement period are measurement period adjustments; therefore, the acquisition accounting is adjusted (see 2.6.940 – 950).

2.6.1010.30 The accounting for changes in the fair value of contingent consideration after the acquisition date, other than measurement period adjustments, depends on whether the contingent consideration is classified as equity, an asset or a liability. Contingent consideration classified as equity is not remeasured and its subsequent settlement is accounted for within equity. See 2.6.280.30 for a discussion of the classification of contingent consideration.

IFRS 3.58(b)(i), BC355   2.6.1010.40 Contingent consideration that is liability classified (or in some instances asset classified) that falls within the scope of IAS 39 is remeasured to fair value at each reporting date until the contingency is resolved. Changes in the fair value of such contingent consideration subsequent to the acquisition date generally are recognised in profit or loss. Contingent consideration that is not within the scope of IAS 39 is accounted for under IAS 37 or other IFRSs as appropriate.

2.6.1010.50 An acquirer recognises changes in the fair value of liability-classified contingent consideration within the scope of IAS 39 in profit or loss as they occur, unless the changes result from measurement period adjustments.

2.6.1010.60 For example, Company P acquires Company S in June 2010 for cash. Additionally, P agrees to pay 5 percent of profits in excess of 5,000 generated over the next two years in cash in a lump sum at the end of the two years. P determines the fair value of the contingent consideration liability to be 45 at the acquisition date. In its consolidated financial statements, P records the following entry:

	Debit	Credit
Goodwill	45	
Liability for contingent consideration		45
To recognise contingent consideration at fair value as		
part of acquisition accounting		

2.6.1010.70 A year after acquisition S has performed better than projected initially by P, such that a significant payment is now expected to be made at the end of year two. The fair value of this financial liability is 185 at the end of the first year. Accordingly, P recognises the remeasurement of the liability in profit or loss. In its consolidated financial statements, P records the following entry:

	Debit	Credit
Profit or loss	140	
Liability for contingent consideration (185 - 45)		140
To remeasure contingent consideration		

2.6.1010.80 The adjustment to the financial liability to reflect the final settlement amount (final fair value) will also be recognised in profit or loss if the amount differs from the fair value estimate at the end of the first year.

2.6.1020 Business combinations achieved in stages

IFRS 3.41 2.6.1020.10 Sometimes control is obtained in successive share purchases, i.e. the acquirer obtains control of an acquiree in which it held a non-controlling equity interest immediately before the acquisition date. Such a business combination commonly is referred to as a "business combination achieved in stages" or a "step acquisition". For example,

Company P acquires a 10 percent interest in Company S, and an additional 60 percent interest some years later in order to gain control.

2.6.1020.20 The acquisition method is applied in the normal manner to a business combination achieved in stages, e.g. determining the acquisition date (see 2.6.180), recognising and measuring the consideration transferred (see 2.6.260 and 340) and recognising and measuring the assets acquired and liabilities assumed (see 2.6.560, 600 and 1050).

IFRS 3.32(a) (iii), 42   2.6.1020.30 In a step acquisition the fair value of any non-controlling equity interest in the acquiree that is held immediately prior to obtaining control is used in the determination of goodwill, i.e. it is remeasured to fair value at the acquisition date with any resulting gain or loss recognised in profit or loss. Care is taken to adjust for any control premium if the fair value of the previously held non-controlling interest is being calculated by reference to the controlling interest.

IFRS 3.BC 384   2.6.1020.40 This treatment effectively considers that any investment in the acquiree that was held prior to obtaining control is sold and subsequently repurchased at the acquisition date. Accordingly, in our view the disclosure of that gain or loss should be on the same basis as if the investment had been disposed of to a third party.

IFRS 3.42, BC384   2.6.1020.50 Upon obtaining control any amounts recognised in other comprehensive income related to the previously held equity interest are recognised on the same basis as would be required if the acquirer had disposed of the previously held equity interest directly.

IFRS 3.42, BC384   2.6.1020.60 For example, prior to obtaining control over Company S, Company P classified its investment in S as available for sale and recognised changes in its fair value in other comprehensive income. Upon obtaining control over S the amount that was recognised in other comprehensive income is reclassified and included in the calculation of any gain or loss recognised in profit or loss.

IFRS 3.42, IAS 16.41, 21.48A   2.6.1020.70 Also, for investments not classified as available for sale prior to obtaining control, unrealised gains or losses may have been recognised in other comprehensive income, e.g. foreign exchange gains or losses, and revaluation surpluses on property, plant and equipment. The treatment of these amounts upon obtaining control is consistent with how they would be treated if the previously held equity interest was disposed of to a third party. For example, foreign exchange gains or losses previously recognised in other comprehensive income are reclassified from equity to profit or loss on the date control is obtained, while revaluation surpluses on property, plant and equipment may be reclassified within equity to retained earnings.

2.6.1020.80 For example, on 1 January 2010 Company P acquired 30 percent of the voting ordinary shares of Company S for 80,000. P equity accounts its investment in S under IAS 28 *Investments in Associates*. At 31 December 2010 P recognised equity accounted earnings of 7,000 in profit or loss and unrealised gains in other comprehensive income of 1,000 related to exchange differences and 500 related to the revaluation of property, plant and equipment. The carrying amount of the investment in the associate on 31 December 2010 was therefore 88,500 (80,000 + 7,000 + 1,000 + 500).

2.6.1020.90 On 1 January 2011 P acquires the remaining 70 percent of S for cash of 250,000. At this date the fair value of the 30 percent interest owned already is 90,000 and the fair value of S's identifiable assets and liabilities is 300,000. In its consolidated financial statements, P records the following entry:

	Debit	Credit
Identifiable net assets of S	300,000	
Goodwill[1]	40,000	
Foreign currency translation reserve	1,000	
Property, plant and equipment revaluation reserve	500	
Cash		250,000
Investment in associate S		88,500
Retained earnings[2]		500
Gain on previously held interest in S recognised in profit or loss[3]		2,500
To record the acquisition of S		

Notes

(1) *Goodwill is calculated as follows:*

Cash consideration	250,000
Fair value of previously held equity interest in S	90,000
Total consideration	340,000
Fair value of identifiable net assets acquired	(300,000)
Goodwill	40,000

(2) The credit to retained earnings represents the reversal of the unrealised gain of 500 in other comprehensive income related to the revaluation of property, plant and equipment. In accordance with IAS 16, such amount is not reclassified to profit or loss (see 3.2.410).

(3) *The gain on the previously held equity interest in S is calculated as follows:*

Fair value of 30 percent interest in S at 1 January 2011	90,000
Carrying amount of interest in S at 1 January 2011	(88,500)
	1,500
Unrealised gain recognised previously in other comprehensive income	1,000
Gain on previously held interest in S recognised in profit or loss	2,500

IFRS 3.BC
384, 5.6-8,
BU 05-09

2.6.1020.100 Notwithstanding the fact that upon obtaining control amounts recognised in other comprehensive income are recognised on the same basis as would be required if the acquirer had disposed of the previously held equity interest directly, in our view classification as held for sale or as a discontinued operation is not appropriate because there is no actual sale of the investment.

2.6.1030 **Fair value measurement in a business combination***

2.6.1040 *General principles*

2.6.1040.10 The revised IFRS 3 includes more emphasis on fair value than the previous standard. However, there is almost no guidance in the standard on the determination of fair value; even the limited guidance that was included in the previous standard related to the fair value of identifiable assets and liabilities has been deleted. Instead, guidance on the determination of fair value will be included in a single standard (see 2.6.1180).

IFRS 3.A 2.6.1040.20 Consistent with other IFRSs, *fair value* is the amount for which an asset could be exchanged, or a liability settled, between knowledgeable, willing parties in an arm's length transaction. Fair value measurements are based on a hypothetical transaction at the acquisition date, considered from the perspective of market participants.

2.6.1040.30 Generally the measurement of fair value includes determining:

- the particular asset or liability that is the subject of the measurement, including its unit of account;
- the market participants who would engage in a transaction for the asset or liability, including the assumptions that such market participants would make regarding the asset or liability; and
- the valuation technique(s) appropriate for the measurement, considering the availability of data with which to develop inputs that represent the assumptions that market participants would make.

2.6.1040.40 A fair value measurement is for a particular asset or liability, considering various factors such as its condition and location at the measurement date. The asset or liability may be a stand-alone asset and/or liability (e.g. an individual security within the scope of IAS 39 that is traded in an active market) or a group of assets and/or liabilities (e.g. a group of complementary intangible assets). When measuring the fair value of an asset or liability, an entity first determines the item being measured based on its unit of account.

2.6.1040.50 The unit of account is particularly relevant for identifiable intangible assets because intangible assets are grouped with other assets or liabilities in certain circumstances (see 2.6.720).

2.6.1040.60 The definition of fair value does not refer to the actual buyer; rather, it refers to a hypothetical transaction with hypothetical, typical buyers, i.e. market participants. Therefore, the acquirer's intention with respect to an asset or liability is not relevant in determining fair value. Instead, fair value is determined by reference to market participants and their expectations. Many assets have different uses and often the value of an asset may be highly dependent upon its use.

2.6.1040.70 Therefore, for example, the fact that a particular acquirer plans to shelve a brand acquired in a business combination is ignored if market participants would continue to use the asset (see 2.6.630). In addition, future restructuring and enhancements are taken into account to the extent that they are actions that a typical market participant would take, even if the actual owner or buyer is not planning such action. Conversely, if the actual owner or buyer would restructure but the typical market participant would not, then the future restructuring and/or enhancements are excluded from the valuation.

2.6.1040.80 Fair value is based on assumptions that are consistent with those of market participants; such data includes market prices, capital market data, information obtained from market studies and analysts' reports. When such market data is not observable, an approach that sometimes is followed in practice is to start with the information and assumptions that the actual buyer has used, and then to look for indicators that would lead to the conclusion that other potential buyers would have based their valuation on different information and assumptions. If such indicators are not found, then the information and assumptions that the actual buyer has used are considered in determining fair value after removing any entity-specific synergies or expertise that would not be available to other market participants.

2.6.1050 *Identifiable assets acquired and liabilities assumed*

2.6.1060 *Assets (disposal groups) held for sale*

IFRS 3.31 2.6.1060.10 In an exception to the fair value measurement principle in IFRS 3, assets (or disposal groups) classified as held for sale in accordance with IFRS 5 (see 2.6.710) are measured at fair value less costs to sell. Therefore, while the general guidance in this chapter in respect of fair value applies, the estimated disposal costs are deducted as an additional step in determining the amount to be included in the acquisition accounting.

2.6.1060.20 See 5.4.60 for guidance on the valuation of assets (or disposal groups) held for sale or distribution.

2.6.1070 *Property, plant and equipment*

IAS 16.32, 33 2.6.1070.10 In our view, the guidance in IAS 16 should be used as a basis for determining the fair value of property, plant and equipment in the acquisition accounting. In accordance with IAS 16, the fair value of land and buildings usually is determined by reference to market-based evidence, while the fair value of plant and equipment usually is determined by appraisal. However, when there is no market-based evidence of fair value for a specialised item of property, plant and equipment that is rarely sold other than as part of a continuing business, fair value may be estimated using an income or cost approach. See 3.2.300 for more detailed guidance.

2.6.1080 *Investment property*

IAS 40.33-52 2.6.1080.10 In our view, the guidance in IAS 40 should be used as a basis for determining the fair value of investment property in the acquisition accounting. Determination of the fair value of investment property generally involves consideration of:

- the actual current market for that type of property in that type of location at the reporting date and current market expectations;
- rental income from leases and market expectations regarding possible future lease terms;
- hypothetical sellers and buyers, who are reasonably informed about the current market and who are motivated, but not compelled, to transact in that market on an arm's length basis; and
- investor expectations, for example investors' expectations of the potential for future enhancement of the rental income or market conditions etc.

2.6.1080.20 See 3.4.150 for guidance on the valuation of investment property.

2.6.1090 *Intangible assets*

IAS 38.41 2.6.1090.10 A number of specific valuation methods that fall under the income approach have been developed in practice to deal with the valuation of intangible assets for which there is no market evidence of fair value. IAS 38 itself refers to the following methods: discounted cash flows; the relief-from-royalty approach; and the cost approach. In our experience, the cost approach rarely is appropriate in practice for determining the fair value of intangible assets other than internal-use software.

2.6.1100 *Inventories*

2.6.1100.10 The technique used to arrive at fair value depends on the inventory's stage of development in the production cycle. Under the previous version of IFRS 3, the fair value of manufactured finished goods and work-in-process was measured based on the estimated selling price, less certain costs (and a margin thereon), that would be realised by a market participant. While this guidance was not carried forward into the revised standard, in our view this technique continues to be acceptable in the absence of other guidance.

2.6.1100.20 The fair value of finished goods inventory most frequently is estimated using the market approach or income approach, at the estimated selling price less the sum of the costs of disposal and a reasonable profit allowance for the selling effort of the acquirer ("selling profit"), both of which are estimated from the perspective of a market participant.

2.6.1100.30 Judgement is required in determining a reasonable amount of profit attributable to the effort incurred by the acquiree pre-acquisition, and the profit attributable to the effort that is likely to be incurred by the acquirer post-acquisition. In our view, the analysis should take into account the current profitability of the product at the acquisition date, even if conditions were different when the inventory was manufactured.

2.6.1100.40 For example, the acquiree has finished goods measured at a cost of 100; the expected selling price is 150. The inventory is specialised and there are very few potential customers; this inventory already has been earmarked for one of those customers.

Distribution costs are estimated at 20. In the absence of any additional factors indicating that market participants would arrive at a different estimate of the fair value of the inventory, in our view the fair value of the inventory would be close to 130 (150 - 20) because the selling effort to be incurred by the seller is minimal.

2.6.1100.50 Work-in-process inventory of the acquiree typically is valued in a similar manner as finished goods inventory, most frequently using the market approach or income approach, at estimated selling price of the work-in-process inventory, as if finished, less the sum of costs to complete, costs of disposal and a reasonable profit allowance for the completion and selling effort of the acquirer, all of which are estimated from the perspective of a market participant.

2.6.1100.60 The valuation approach used for recognising the acquisition-date fair value of raw materials is a market approach using observable market prices, if available, or a cost approach when market information is not available, both of which are estimated from the perspective of a market participant.

2.6.1110 *Financial instruments*

2.6.1110.10 In our view, the fair value of financial instruments should be determined following the valuation guidance in IAS 39 (see 3.6.920).

2.6.1110.20 In many cases financial instruments will be measured on a fair value basis by an acquiree already applying IFRSs; in these cases fair value may just need updating as of the acquisition date, e.g. derivatives, investments held for trading or available-for-sale financial instruments. However, other financial instruments will be measured on the basis of cost or amortised cost, and the acquirer will need to determine fair value.

2.6.1120 *Equity-accounted investees*

2.6.1120.10 In certain circumstances a premium might be paid to obtain significant influence rather than control over an entity's operations. In such cases, the unit of account is the holding rather than the individual security, as outlined in 3.10.190.60. An analysis of whether such a shareholding might be valued in excess of its *pro rata* share of a company's market capitalisation would consider similar factors to those outlined in 3.10.190.70 – 80, i.e. based on an evaluation of the potential of such a shareholder to increase cash flows or reduce risk. However, a non-controlling, influential shareholder generally receives the same *pro rata* cash flows as other non-controlling shareholders. Therefore, in practice it may be difficult to support a fair value significantly in excess of the listed share price.

2.6.1130 *Contingent liabilities*

2.6.1130.10 A contingent liability is recognised in a business combination if it is a present obligation that arises from past events and its fair value can be measured reliably (see 2.6.650). In our view, the fair value of a contingent liability should be estimated using expected cash flows, i.e. the valuation method should apply probabilities to different possible future outcomes to estimate an expected outcome. This is then discounted at an appropriate discount rate.

2.6.1140 **Disclosures**

2.6.1140.10 The overall objective of the disclosure requirements of IFRS 3 is for the acquirer to provide information that enables the users of its financial statements to evaluate:

RS 3.59, 60 ● the nature and financial effects of a business combination that occurs either during the current reporting period, or after the reporting date but before the financial statements are authorised for issue; and

RS 3.61, 62 ● the financial effects of adjustments recognised in the current reporting period that relate to business combinations that occurred in the current or previous reporting periods.

IFRS 3.63 2.6.1140.20 If the specific disclosures do not meet the overall disclosure objective, then the acquirer discloses whatever additional information is required to meet that objective.

FRS 3.B64- 2.6.1140.30 The disclosure requirements cover the following:
B67

  - general information on the business combination
  - consideration transferred
  - assets acquired and liabilities assumed
  - goodwill (or a gain on a bargain purchase)
  - transactions that are not part of the business combination
  - business combinations in which the acquirer holds less than 100 percent of the acquiree
  - business combinations achieved in stages, i.e. step acquisitions
  - *pro forma* information about revenue and profit or loss
  - adjustments, including measurement period adjustments and contingent consideration adjustments.

IFRS 3.B 2.6.1140.40 The disclosures are required for each material business combination, or in
64(q)(ii), aggregate for individually immaterial business combinations that are material collectively.
B65, B67 The exception to this is the requirement to disclose revenue and profit or loss of the combined entity for the current reporting period as though the acquisition date for all business combinations that occurred during the period had been at the beginning of the annual reporting period.

2.6.1140.50 The disclosures are as of the acquisition date even if the acquirer consolidates the subsidiary from a different date for convenience (see 2.6.190.10).

IFRS 3.B66 2.6.1140.60 Disclosures generally are required in respect of a business combination that occurs after the end of the reporting period but before the financial statements are authorised for issue. The only exception is if the initial accounting is incomplete when the financial statements are authorised, in which case the entity discloses why the disclosures cannot be given.

IFRS 3.61   2.6.1140.70 The IFRS 3 disclosures are provided in respect of business combinations occurring in the current and comparative periods.

IAS 34.16(i)   2.6.1140.80 The disclosure requirements also are applicable for interim financial statements prepared in accordance with IAS 34 *Interim Financial Reporting*.

2.6.1140.90 The disclosure requirements of IFRS 3 are illustrated in KPMG's illustrative financial statements for annual and interim financial reporting periods.

2.6.1150 **Transitional requirements**

IFRS 3.64   2.6.1150.10 IFRS 3 and IAS 27 are effective for annual periods beginning on or after 1 July 2009. IFRS 3 is applied prospectively, while the requirements of IAS 27 are applied retrospectively with certain exceptions (see 2.5.540). Early adoption of IFRS 3 and IAS 27 was permitted, but only for annual periods beginning on or after 30 June 2007 and only if both standards were adopted at the same time.

2.6.1160 *Acquisitions prior to adopting IFRS 3*

IFRS 3.65, 67   2.6.1160.10 The accounting for assets and liabilities that arose from business combinations occurring prior to the adoption of IFRS 3 is not changed by the adoption of the standard, except in respect of the subsequent recognition of deferred tax assets acquired in such business combinations that were not recognised at the acquisition date (see 3.13.710).

IFRS 3.45   2.6.1160.20 The measurement period for a business combination accounted for under IFRS 3 (2004) *Business Combinations* may not have ended as of the date of adoption of IFRS 3. Adjustments to the acquisition accounting during the remainder of the allocation period are accounted for in accordance with IFRS 3 (2004). Because of differences between the previous and revised versions of IFRS 3 in the initial recognition and measurement of the assets acquired and liabilities assumed in a business combination, the accounting for adjustments to the acquisition accounting during the measurement period under IFRS 3 (2004) sometimes will be different from the adjustments that would have resulted if IFRS 3 had applied, for example in relation to contingent liabilities. See 2.6.910 for a discussion of the measurement period.

IFRS 3.32   2.6.1160.30 Under IFRS 3 (2004) contingent consideration was included in the cost of
(2004)   a business combination when such consideration was probable and reliably measurable; subsequent adjustments to the amount payable were recognised by adjusting the purchase price, usually resulting in an adjustment to goodwill. Under IFRS 3, however, contingent consideration is recognised at fair value at the acquisition date and subsequent adjustments other than measurement period adjustments do not affect the acquisition accounting. See 2.6.1010 for a discussion of the subsequent measurement of contingent consideration.

2.6.1160.40 In our view, adjustments of contingent consideration payable in respect of a business combination with an acquisition date prior to the adoption of IFRS 3 should continue to be recognised in accordance with IFRS 3 (2004), which generally will result in an adjustment to goodwill. This is consistent with the transitional requirements of IFRS 3, which state that assets and liabilities from previous business combinations are not adjusted. We believe that it would not be appropriate to account for such contingent consideration in accordance with IAS 39, notwithstanding the deletion from that standard of the scope exemption in respect of contingent consideration related to a business combination.#

2.6.1170 *Forthcoming requirements*

2.6.1170.10 The *Improvements to IFRSs 2010* amended IFRS 7 *Financial Instruments: Disclosures*, IAS 32 and IAS 39 to clarify that those standards do not apply to contingent consideration amendments that relate to business combinations that occurred prior to the adoption of IFRS 3. This is consistent with the view expressed in 2.6.1160.40.

2.6.1180 **Future developments**

2.6.1180.10 In May 2009 the IASB published ED/2009/5 *Fair Value Measurement* (the 2009 ED). The proposals in the 2009 ED are intended to replace the fair value measurement guidance contained in individual IFRSs with a single, unified definition of fair value, as well as provide further authoritative guidance on the application of fair value measurement in inactive markets. The 2009 ED proposes a framework for measuring fair value and disclosures about fair value measurements. The proposals in the 2009 ED explain how to measure fair value when it already is required or permitted by existing IFRSs; they do not introduce new fair value measurements, nor do they eliminate the practicability exceptions to fair value measurements that exist currently in certain standards.

2.6.1180.20 In June 2010 the IASB published ED/2010/7 *Measurement Uncertainty Analysis Disclosure for Fair Value Measurements* (the 2010 ED). The 2010 ED expands on the proposal in the 2009 ED for an entity to disclose a measurement uncertainty analysis (or sensitivity analysis) for assets and liabilities measured at fair value categorised within Level 3 of the fair value hierarchy. The 2010 ED proposes that an entity consider the effect of correlation between unobservable inputs, if relevant.

2.6.1180.30 A final standard on fair value measurement and disclosure, which is expected to be converged with a forthcoming amended standard under US GAAP, is scheduled for the first quarter of 2011.

2.7 Foreign currency translation
(IAS 21, IAS 29)

2.7 Foreign currency translation
(IAS 21, IAS 29)

Overview of currently effective requirements

- An entity measures its assets, liabilities, income and expenses in its functional currency, which is the currency of the primary economic environment in which it operates.

- An entity may present its financial statements in a currency other than its functional currency.

- All transactions that are not denominated in an entity's functional currency are foreign currency transactions; exchange differences arising on translation generally are recognised in profit or loss.

- The financial statements of foreign operations are translated for the purpose of consolidation as follows: assets and liabilities are translated at the closing rate; income and expenses are translated at actual rates or appropriate averages; and equity components (excluding the current year movements, which are translated at actual rates) are translated at historical rates.

- Exchange differences arising on the translation of the financial statements of a foreign operation are recognised in other comprehensive income and accumulated in a separate component of equity. The amount attributable to any non-controlling interest (NCI) is allocated to and recognised as part of NCI.

- If the functional currency of a foreign operation is hyperinflationary, current purchasing power adjustments are made to its financial statements prior to translation and the financial statements are translated into a different presentation currency at the closing rate at the end of the current period. However, if the presentation currency is not hyperinflationary, comparative amounts are not restated.

- When an entity disposes of an interest in a foreign operation, which includes losing control over a foreign subsidiary, the cumulative exchange differences recognised in other comprehensive income and accumulated in a separate component of equity are reclassified to profit or loss. A partial disposal of a foreign subsidiary may lead to a reclassification to NCI, while other partial disposals result in a proportionate reclassification to profit or loss.

Currently effective requirements

This publication reflects IFRSs in issue at 1 August 2010. The currently effective requirements cover annual periods beginning on 1 January 2010. The requirements related to this topic are derived mainly from IAS 21 *The Effects of Changes in Foreign Exchange Rates* and IAS 29 *Financial Reporting in Hyperinflationary Economies.*

Forthcoming requirements and future developments

When a currently effective requirement will be changed by a new requirement that is issued but is not yet effective, it is marked with a # as a **forthcoming requirement** and the impact of the change is explained in the accompanying boxed text. In respect of this topic no forthcoming requirements are noted.

When a significant change to the currently effective or forthcoming requirements is expected, it is marked with a * as an area that may be subject to **future developments**. In respect of this topic no future developments are noted.

2.7.10 **Definitions**

2.7.20 *Reporting entity*

IAS 21.11   2.7.20.10 *Reporting entity*, as used in this chapter, refers to the parent entity of a consolidated group, which may include legal entities and foreign operations within each legal entity.

2.7.25 *Foreign operation*

IAS 21.8   2.7.25.10 A *foreign operation* is an entity that is a subsidiary, associate, joint venture or branch of a reporting entity, the activities of which are based or conducted in a country or currency other than those of the reporting entity.

2.7.30 *Functional currency*

IAS 21.8   2.7.30.10 An entity's *functional currency* is the currency of the primary economic environment in which it operates.

2.7.40 *Determining a functional currency*

IAS 21.1N7,   2.7.40.10 An entity measures its assets, liabilities, equity, income and expenses in its
20   functional currency. All transactions in currencies other than the functional currency are foreign currency transactions (see 2.7.80).

2.7.40.20 Each entity in a group has its own functional currency. There is no concept of a group-wide functional currency under IFRSs. See 2.7.180 for further discussion of this issue.

IAS 21.9 2.7.40.30 In determining its functional currency, an entity emphasises the currency that determines the pricing of the transactions that it undertakes, rather than focusing on the currency in which those transactions are denominated. The following factors are considered in determining an appropriate functional currency:

- the currency that mainly influences sales prices for goods and services; this often will be the currency in which sales prices are denominated;
- the currency of the country whose competitive forces and regulations mainly determine the sales prices of its goods and services; and
- the currency that mainly influences labour, material and other costs of providing goods and services; often this will be the currency in which these costs are denominated and settled.

IAS 21.10 2.7.40.40 The factors in 2.7.40.30 are the primary indicators of an entity's functional currency. While these factors are provided as an inclusive list, this should not be interpreted as meaning that *all* of these factors should indicate a certain currency in order for that currency to be the entity's functional currency. Additional, or "secondary", indicators may exist that provide supporting evidence to determine an entity's functional currency, namely:

- the currency in which funds from financing activities are generated; this would be the currency used for issuing debt and equity instruments; and
- the currency in which receipts from operating activities usually are retained.

IAS 21.11 2.7.40.50 Furthermore, when determining the functional currency of a foreign operation it is necessary to consider whether this should be the same as the functional currency of its parent (see 2.7.190).

IAS 21.12 2.7.40.60 Often in practice entities operate in a mixture of currencies and consideration of the factors in 2.7.40.30 does not result in an obvious conclusion as to the entity's functional currency. This will require management to exercise its judgement to determine the most appropriate functional currency. In doing so, priority should be given to the primary indicators before considering the secondary indicators.

2.7.40.70 In many cases an entity's functional currency is its local currency. For example, an entity in Russia produces goods that are exported throughout Europe. Sales prices are denominated in euro for the convenience of trade and consistency in pricing, and some of the entity's cash reserves are held in euro; however, all of the other factors, including the currency that mainly influences the costs of providing goods, indicate that the rouble is the entity's functional currency. In our view, the functional currency is the rouble because there is not enough evidence to indicate that the euro overcomes the presumption that the rouble *best* reflects the economic substance of the underlying events and circumstances relevant to the entity.

2.7.40.80 In another example, in which a manufacturer of steel products in Chile has analysed its operations as follows:

- The majority of products are sold into the local Chilean market using the international price for steel, quoted in US dollars, as a starting point for setting the local sales price. Competitive forces in Chile also influence the local sales price.
- The majority of raw material purchases are from local suppliers, denominated in Chilean pesos, based on the price of steel, quoted in US dollars, on the London Metal Exchange.
- These sales and raw material purchases are invoiced and settled in pesos; most other expenses are in pesos.
- A significant amount of financing is in US dollars to match the currency in which the sales are priced.
- Cash reserves are held in pesos.

2.7.40.90 In our view, despite the entity using the US dollar-denominated international spot price for steel as the starting point for pricing its domestic sales, and despite the fact that the US dollar-denominated steel price largely drives the cost of its raw materials, this does not result in the US dollar being the key influencer of the sales price of the entity's products or its raw material purchases. While the market price of steel is driven by international forces of supply and demand, the market price is quoted in US dollars because it is a stable and widely traded currency. The US economy does not determine the entity's sale price and raw material purchase prices. The local sales prices and most costs of the entity are determined by the competitive forces in the Chilean economy. As a result, the cash collection may be significantly different from the US dollar-equivalent sales value. In our view, the primary economic environment in which the entity operates is Chile, and therefore the functional currency of the entity is the peso.

2.7.40.100 However, it should not be assumed that the local currency always will be the functional currency. For example, an entity in the Philippines manufactures sports clothing that is exported to the United States. Sales prices are established having regard to prices in the United States, and are denominated in US dollars. Sales are settled in US dollars and the receipts are converted to Philippine pesos only when necessary to settle local expenses. The majority of the entity's borrowings are denominated in US dollars; the cost of the manufacturing equipment, which is the entity's major item of property, plant and equipment, is denominated in US dollars. Management's salaries, which represent the significant portion of labour costs, are denominated and paid in US dollars; other labour costs, as well as all material costs, are denominated and settled in pesos. In our view, the entity's functional currency is the US dollar.

2.7.40.110 In some cases an analysis of the underlying events and circumstances relevant to an entity may indicate that two (or more) currencies are equally relevant. For example, a Turkish entity has analysed its operations as follows:

- The majority of short- and long-term debt is financed in US dollars; the balance is financed in Turkish lira.
- The activities of the entity are financed mainly by its own capital (denominated in Turkish lira and currencies other than US dollars).
- The majority of cash reserves are held in US dollars.

- Export sales make up approximately 95 percent of total sales, which are priced and denominated largely in US dollars.
- The majority of operating expenses are priced and denominated in Turkish lira; the balance is denominated in US dollars.

2.7.40.120 In our view, both the Turkish lira and the US dollar are key to the entity's operations. However, since an entity can have only one functional currency, management will apply judgement to determine whether the Turkish lira or the US dollar should be the entity's functional currency. In doing so, greater weighting will be given to the primary indicators. In this example, further consideration would need to be given to the specific facts and circumstances and the environment in which the entity operates. For example, it would have to be considered whether the US dollar is used to achieve stability in the financial results and position of the entity rather than because the US economy is a determining factor for those results and position. However, in the absence of further evidence, it seems that in this example the US dollar might be considered the functional currency of the entity.

IAS 21.14 2.7.40.130 An entity may not choose to adopt a functional currency other than that determined under IAS 21. An entity whose functional currency is that of a hyperinflationary economy may not avoid applying hyperinflationary accounting by choosing a different stable currency as its functional currency.

2.7.50 *Changing the functional currency*

IAS 21.13, 35 2.7.50.10 Once an entity has determined its functional currency, it is not changed unless there is a change in the relevant underlying transactions, events and circumstances. If circumstances change and a change in functional currency is appropriate, the change is accounted for prospectively from the date of the change. However, a prospective change triggers an issue with respect to the comparative financial information.

2.7.50.20 For example, an entity incorporated in the United Kingdom with a 31 December reporting date had the euro as its functional and presentation currency until the end of 2009. From the beginning of 2010 the focus of the entity's operations changes and the appropriate functional currency is determined to be sterling going forward. Additionally, the entity changes its presentation currency to sterling. At 1 January 2010, the financial position should be translated from euro into sterling using the exchange rate at that date. From 2010 the financial statements will be prepared with any non-sterling transactions translated following the requirements for foreign currency transactions (see 2.7.80). In our view, the entity should choose an accounting policy, to be applied consistently, to present the 2009 comparative information using either of the following approaches:

- The 2009 comparatives should be translated from euro, which is the functional currency for that period, into sterling using the amounts determined under the new functional currency as at 1 January 2010. Therefore, all comparative information will be translated at the exchange rate as at 1 January 2010.
- The 2009 comparatives should be translated from the euro into sterling using the methodology specified in 2.7.290 in respect of translation of financial statements

from an entity's functional currency to its presentation currency (i.e. use of appropriate 2009 exchange rates).

2.7.50.25 If, in the example in 2.7.50.20, there is no change to the presentation currency (e.g. the entity's presentation currency is euro for both 2009 and 2010), then translation of comparative amounts into the new functional currency using the procedures that apply for translation into a different presentation currency (see 2.7.290) would allow the entity to avoid restatement of its comparatives (i.e. there would be no change in the 2009 comparatives presented in euro in this example).

2.7.50.30 In our view, these procedures would apply equally when the legal currency of a country is changed. For example, on 1 January 2009 the legal currency in Slovakia changed from the Slovak koruna to the euro.

2.7.60 *Presentation currency*

IAS 21.8, 38   2.7.60.10 Although an entity measures items in its financial statements in its functional currency, it may decide to present its financial statements in a currency or currencies other than its functional currency. For example, an entity with a euro functional currency may choose to present its financial statements in US dollars because its primary listing is in the United States.

IAS 1.39   2.7.60.15 The same presentation currency is used for all periods presented. The presentation of comparative information when there is a change in presentation currency connected with a change in functional currency is discussed in section 2.7.50. In our view, the translation of comparative information into a new presentation currency is a change that would require, in accordance with IAS 1, presentation of a third statement of financial position as at the beginning of the earliest period presented when such information is considered material (see 2.1.35).

2.7.60.20 When an entity presents its financial statements in a presentation currency that is not its functional currency, there is no requirement for it to present additional financial information in its functional currency.

2.7.70 Summary of approach to foreign currency translation

IAS 21.BC18,   2.7.70.10 The following is a summary of the approach under IFRSs to foreign currency
IFRIC 16.17   translation, which is explained in more detail in 2.7.80 – 310.20:

- An entity determines its functional currency. All transactions that are not denominated in its functional currency are foreign currency transactions. First these transactions are translated into the entity's functional currency at the transaction date.
- At the reporting date assets and liabilities denominated in a currency other than the entity's functional currency are translated as follows:
  - monetary items are translated at the exchange rate at the reporting date;

- non-monetary items measured at historical cost are not retranslated; they remain at the exchange rate at the date of the transaction; and
- non-monetary items measured at fair value are translated at the exchange rate when the fair value was determined.
- Next an entity determines the functional currency of each of its branches, subsidiaries, associates or joint ventures, including consideration of whether or not this is the same as the entity's own functional currency.
- The financial statements of the parent, branches, subsidiaries, associates and joint ventures are translated into the group presentation currency if their functional currencies are different from the group presentation currency. Two methods for such translation exist:
  - *The step-by-step method.* The financial statements of a foreign operation are translated into the functional currency of any intermediate parent and financial statements of the intermediate parent that include the foreign operation are then translated into the functional currency of the ultimate parent (or the presentation currency if different).
  - *The direct method.* The financial statements of the foreign operation are translated directly into the functional currency or presentation currency of the ultimate parent.
- The result of all of the above is that the entity will present its financial statements or consolidated financial statements in either the functional currency of the parent entity or another chosen presentation currency.

2.7.80 Translation of foreign currency transactions

2.7.90 *At the transaction date*

AS 21.21, 22 2.7.90.10 Each foreign currency transaction is recorded in the entity's functional currency at the rate of exchange at the date of the transaction, or at rates that approximate the actual exchange rates. An average exchange rate for a specific period may be a suitable approximate rate for transactions during that period, particularly when exchange rates do not fluctuate significantly.

IAS 39.98 2.7.90.20 Inventory purchased in a foreign currency is measured on initial recognition at the spot exchange rate. An entity may hedge its future inventory purchases to minimise its exposure to movements in exchange rates. For example, an entity plans to purchase inventory at a price of foreign currency (AC) 100. In anticipation of the transaction the entity enters into a forward exchange contract to purchase AC 100 for an amount of functional currency (FC) 180. The spot exchange rate at the date of purchase is AC 1 to FC 2. The inventory is measured on initial recognition at the spot exchange rate. If the forward contract was designated and determined effective as a cash flow hedge of the foreign currency exposure on the anticipated inventory purchase, then the effective portion of the gain or loss on the hedging instrument may, as a matter of accounting policy choice, be added to or deducted as a basis adjustment from the inventory amount initially recognised. Alternatively, this portion is retained in equity and reclassified to profit or loss usually when the inventory affects profit or loss. See 3.7.60 – 80 for a discussion of the accounting for cash flow hedges.

IAS 21.26 2.7.90.30 In some countries there are dual exchange rates: the official exchange rate and an unofficial parallel exchange rate. In our view, individual transactions should be translated using the exchange rate that will be used to determine the rate at which the transaction is settled. Normally this will be the official rate. However, use of an unofficial exchange rate may be more appropriate in very limited circumstances, for example, when it is:

- a legal rate (i.e. domestic and foreign entities can and do purchase and sell foreign currency on a local market at this rate legally); or
- the only rate at which the transaction can be settled because long-term lack of liquidity in the exchange market means that sufficient amounts of cash are not available at the official rate.

2.7.100 *At the reporting date*

2.7.110 *General requirements*

IAS 21.23 2.7.110.10 At the reporting date assets and liabilities denominated in a currency other than the entity's functional currency are translated as follows:

- monetary items are translated at the exchange rate at the reporting date;
- non-monetary items measured at historical cost are not retranslated; they remain at the exchange rate at the date of the transaction; and
- non-monetary items measured at fair value are translated at the exchange rate when the fair value was determined.

2.7.120 *Monetary vs non-monetary*

IAS 21.8, 16 2.7.120.10 *Monetary items* are units of currency held, and assets and liabilities to be received or paid, in a fixed or determinable number of units of currency. Conversely, non-monetary items lack such a feature. Examples of non-monetary items include:

- prepaid expenses and income received in advance, on the basis that no money will be paid or received in the future; and
- equity securities held and share capital, on the basis that any future payments are not fixed or determinable.

IAS 39.IG 2.7.120.20 Most debt securities are classified as monetary items because their contractual
E.3.4 cash flows are fixed or determinable. There is no exemption from this classification when the security is classified as available for sale if the future cash flows are fixed or determinable.

IFRIC 7.
BC21, 22 2.7.120.30 The appropriate classification of deferred taxes is not clear in IFRSs; they comprise both monetary and non-monetary components. Classification as a monetary item is based on the view that deferred tax represents future amounts of cash that will be paid to/received from the tax authorities. In our experience, normally deferred tax is classified as a monetary item, and this is our preferred approach. An entity that normally classifies deferred tax as a monetary item may nonetheless classify individual deferred tax items as non-monetary if an event that would result in realisation of the asset or liability is not expected to occur and not result in a cash flow, e.g. temporary differences arising on revaluation of a non-depreciable asset that an entity does not plan to sell. If this approach is taken, then a review to determine the appropriate classification should be performed for all deferred tax items, and consistent criteria should be applied. If a portion of a deferred tax item is likely to result in realisation of the asset or liability, then in our view that the item should be treated as a monetary item in its entirety.

2.7.120.35 [Not used]

2.7.120.40 When a non-monetary asset is stated at fair value (see 2.7.110.10), an issue arises as to how to distinguish the change in fair value from the related foreign exchange gain or loss.

2.7.120.50 For example, Company Y, whose functional currency is FC, acquires an investment property for AC 1,000 when the exchange rate is AC 1:FC 1.5. Therefore the property is recorded initially at FC 1,500. Y measures all investment property at fair value (see 3.4.150). At the reporting date the fair value of the property has increased to AC 1,200 and the exchange rate is now AC 1:FC 1.7.

IAS 1.35 2.7.120.60 In our view, the foreign exchange gain or loss is the difference between the carrying amount recorded initially at the spot rate at the acquisition date and the same carrying amount measured at the exchange rate at the reporting date, i.e. 200 ((1,000 x 1.7) - 1,500). Therefore the fair value gain excluding the impact of changes in foreign currency rates is 340 ((1,200 - 1,000) x 1.7). Although both the exchange gain and the change in the fair value of the investment property measured at fair value are recognised in profit or loss, they are disclosed separately, if they are material.

2.7.130 Intra-group transactions

IAS 21.45 2.7.130.10 Although intra-group balances are eliminated on consolidation (see 2.5.370), any related foreign exchange gains or losses will not be eliminated. This is because the group has a real exposure to a foreign currency since one of the entities will need to obtain or sell foreign currency in order to settle the obligation or realise the proceeds received.

2.7.130.20 For example, Parent P has a functional currency of AC, and Subsidiary S has a functional currency of FC. P, whose reporting date is 31 December, lends AC 100 to S on 1 June 2010. S converted the cash received into FC on receipt.

	AC		FC
Exchange rate at 1 June 2010	1	=	1.5
Exchange rate at 31 December 2010	1	=	2.0

Entries in S	Debit (FC)	Credit (FC)
Cash	150	
Intra-group payable		150
To recognise intra-group loan		
Exchange loss	50	
Intra-group payable		50
To recognise exchange loss on intra-group loan		

2.7.130.30 In S's second entry in 2.7.130.20, the liability is remeasured at 31 December 2010 and a translation loss is recorded. The entry in P is as follows:

Entry in P	Debit (AC)	Credit (AC)
Intra-group receivable	100	
Cash		100
To recognise intra-group loan on issue		

2.7.130.40 On consolidation the FC 200 will convert to AC 100 (see 2.7.220) and the receivable and payable will eliminate. However, an exchange loss equivalent to FC 50 will remain on consolidation. This is appropriate because S will need to obtain AC in order to repay the liability; therefore the group as a whole has a foreign currency exposure. It is not appropriate to transfer the exchange loss to equity on consolidation unless the loan forms part of P's net investment in S (see 2.7.150).

2.7.140 *Recognition of foreign exchange gains and losses*

IAS 21.28, 30, 32 2.7.140.10 Foreign exchange gains and losses generally are recognised in profit or loss; exceptions relate to monetary items that in substance form part of the reporting entity's net investment in a foreign operation and hedging instruments in a qualifying cash flow hedge or hedge of a net investment in a foreign operation (see 3.7). Also, when a gain or loss on a non-monetary item is recognised in other comprehensive income, the foreign exchange component is recognised in other comprehensive income. For example, as IAS 16 *Property, Plant and Equipment* requires gains and losses arising on a revaluation of property, plant and equipment to be recognised in other comprehensive income (see 3.2.300), the related exchange difference is recognised in other comprehensive income.

2.7.150 *Net investment in a foreign operation*

IAS 21.15,
15A, 32, 33,
BC25F

2.7.150.10 A monetary item receivable from or payable to a foreign operation may form part of the net investment in the foreign operation. In order to qualify, settlement of the monetary item should be neither planned nor likely to occur in the foreseeable future. To form part of the net investment in a foreign operation, the entity that has the monetary item receivable or payable may be the reporting entity or any subsidiary in the group. An investment in a foreign operation made by an associate of the reporting entity is not part of the reporting entity's net investment in that operation because an associate is not a group entity.

2.7.150.15 In the financial statements that include the reporting entity and its foreign operation (e.g. the consolidated financial statements), foreign exchange gains and losses arising from monetary items that in substance form part of the net investment in a foreign operation are recognised in other comprehensive income and are presented within equity in the foreign currency translation reserve (see 2.7.260).

IAS 21.32, 33

2.7.150.20 The exception in 2.7.150.15 applies only in the financial statements that include both the reporting entity and the foreign operation. In the separate financial statements of the reporting entity or subsidiary, and those of the foreign operation, the foreign exchange gains and losses are recognised in profit or loss.

2.7.150.30 For example, Parent P has a functional currency of AC, and Subsidiary S has a functional currency of FC. P sells inventory to S for FC 300. At the reporting date S has not yet paid the amount owing to P, but payment is expected to be made in the foreseeable future. Accordingly, the exchange gain or loss incurred by P should be recognised in profit or loss. Even if repayment was not due for three years (for example) or even longer, in our view if repayment still is planned, then the gain or loss should be recognised in profit or loss.

2.7.150.40 In addition to the trading balances between P and S, P lends an amount of FC 500 to S that is not expected to be repaid in the foreseeable future; P regards the amount as part of its permanent funding to S. In this case the exchange gain or loss incurred by P on the FC 500 loan should be recognised in profit or loss in P's separate financial statements, but recognised in other comprehensive income and presented within equity in the consolidated financial statements.

2.7.150.50 If the loan in this example was denominated in AC rather than in FC (i.e. in P's functional currency rather than S's functional currency), then S would incur an exchange gain or loss. In its separate financial statements S would recognise the gain or loss in profit or loss. On consolidation the gain or loss would be recognised in other comprehensive income.

2.7.150.60 When the exchange gain or loss incurred by either P or S is recognised in other comprehensive income on consolidation, any related deferred or current tax also is recognised in other comprehensive income (see 3.13.370, 530 and 570).

2.7.150.70 In the example in 2.7.150.30 and 40, P and/or S could avoid recognising an exchange gain or loss only if the funding did not meet the definition of a financial liability (see 3.6.150.60), which is unlikely to be the case in practice. If that were the case, then, in the example in 2.7.150.30 and 40, P's "contribution" of FC 500 that is not required to be repaid would be classified as a capital contribution in S's financial statements and would not be retranslated subsequent to initial recognition (see 2.7.100). Similarly, in P's separate financial statements the funding would be classified as part of P's investment in the equity instruments of S, which also would not be retranslated if P has a policy of measuring investments in subsidiaries at cost in its separate financial statements.

2.7.150.80 Modifying the example in 2.7.150.30 and 40, suppose that the "permanent" funding extended to S is made via another entity in the group, T, rather than from P directly; this is done for tax reasons.

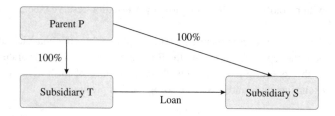

IAS 21.15A, 2.7.150.90 Any exchange difference in respect of the loan is recognised in other compre-
32, 33 hensive income in the consolidated financial statements because from the group's point of view the funding relates to an investment in a foreign operation. This is the case irrespective of the currency in which the loan is denominated. So if the loan is denominated in T's functional currency, and this is different from that of S, then exchange differences still should be recognised in other comprehensive income in the consolidated financial statements.

2.7.160 *Presentation of items in profit or loss*

IAS 21.52 2.7.160.10 Disclosure is required of the amount of exchange differences recognised in profit or loss for the period, except for those arising on financial instruments measured at fair value through profit or loss. However, the standard does not specify the line item in which such differences should be presented.

2.7.160.20 In our experience, the most common practice is for all such exchange differences related to monetary items to be included as part of finance costs (see 4.6.540.60). However, it also is acceptable to allocate the exchange differences to the various line items affected. For example, an entity might classify exchange differences on trade payables arising from the purchase of inventory as part of cost of sales, and exchange differences arising from loans as part of finance costs. If exchange differences are allocated in this way, then this should be done consistently from period to period having regard to the guidance in IAS 1 *Presentation of Financial Statements* on offsetting (see 4.1.170), and in our view it would be necessary, to disclose the entity's allocation policy if significant in the financial statements.

2.7.170 **Foreign operations**

IAS 21.8   2.7.170.10 A foreign operation of an entity is a subsidiary, associate, joint venture or branch whose activities are conducted in a country or currency other than those of the reporting entity (see 2.7.25.10). IFRSs define the terms subsidiary (see 2.5), associate (see 3.5.10) and joint venture (see 3.5.90). However a branch is not defined in IFRSs and issues arise regarding the level and nature of activities that can comprise a foreign operation (see 2.7.190).

2.7.180 *Functional currency of a foreign operation*

IAS 21.11   2.7.180.10 The guidance provided on determining an entity's functional currency also applies to determining the functional currency of a (potential) foreign operation of the entity (see 2.7.40). This guidance places greater emphasis on the currency that determines the pricing of transactions than on the currency in which transactions are denominated. Especially relevant in the case of a foreign operation is whether or not it has the same functional currency as the reporting entity. To determine this, the relationship between the foreign operation and the reporting entity should be considered. In considering the relationship between the foreign operation and the reporting entity, in addition to the primary and secondary indicators discussed in 2.7.40, the following factors are relevant:

- whether the activities of the foreign operation are conducted as an extension of the reporting entity rather than with a significant degree of autonomy;
- whether a high or low proportion of the foreign operation's activities comprise transactions with the reporting entity;
- whether cash flows from the foreign operation's activities directly affect the cash flows of the reporting entity and are readily available for remittance to it; and
- whether the foreign operation generates sufficient cash flows from its own activities to service existing and normally expected debt obligations without additional funds from the reporting entity.

AS 21.9, 12   2.7.180.20 The factors in 2.7.180.10 should be relied upon only to provide supporting evidence of an entity's determined functional currency. When the indicators are mixed and the functional currency is not obvious, priority still should be given to indicators that focus on the primary economic environment, i.e. which currency mainly influences sales prices for goods and services, the country whose competitive forces and regulations mainly determine the sales prices of entity's goods and services, and the currency that is the main influence on labour, material and other costs of providing goods or services.

2.7.180.30 In our view, the conclusion as to a foreign operation's functional currency should be the same irrespective of whether the analysis is performed on a stand-alone basis or with reference to the entity's relationship with the reporting entity. In other words, if an entity determines that its functional currency is the same as that of the reporting entity with reference to the factors noted in 2.7.180.10 in the consolidated financial statements of the reporting entity, then it should use the same functional currency to measure items in its separate financial statements.

2.7.190 *Issues in determining whether a foreign operation has the same functional currency as the reporting entity*

2.7.190.10 A significantly different accounting result may be achieved depending on whether the foreign operation is considered to have the same functional currency as the reporting entity or not. When the foreign operation has the same functional currency as the reporting entity, but undertakes a large number of transactions in a foreign currency, the effect of these transactions will be reflected in profit or loss. To reduce or eliminate volatility the reporting entity may choose to hedge its exposure and therefore may be able to apply hedge accounting. Conversely, if it is concluded that the foreign operation has a functional currency different from that of the reporting entity, then foreign exchange gains or losses on translation of the foreign operation into the group presentation currency will be recognised in other comprehensive income as it is part of a net investment in a foreign operation. This avoids profit or loss volatility. These issues are particularly significant when the activities are conducted through a special purpose entity (SPE) (see 2.7.210.10).

2.7.190.20 In 2.7.200 – 210, we discuss some of the issues that require particular attention when determining the functional currency of a foreign operation.

2.7.200 *Separate legal entity*

2.7.200.10 In our view, the analysis of whether a foreign subsidiary consists of more than one operation should be based on the substance of the activities of the foreign operation, rather than its legal structure. Accordingly, we believe that a single legal entity may comprise multiple foreign operations with different functional currencies in certain circumstances.

IAS 21.BC6   2.7.200.20 For example, Parent P is based in the United States and its functional currency is US dollars. Subsidiary S is based in the United Kingdom. S has three distinct operations (X, Y and Z), which are conducted from the United Kingdom but under different economic environments as a result of differences in the nature of their products and markets. Separate accounting records are kept for each of the operations. In our view, the functional currency of each of X, Y and Z should be determined separately.

IAS 21.BC6   2.7.200.30 Care should be taken in assessing whether X, Y and Z indeed could have different functional currencies. The fact that they are part of the same legal entity normally will make it more difficult to demonstrate that any of them is independent of the reporting entity. In particular, if separate accounting records for each operation are not kept or if their operations and cash flows are managed on a unified basis, then in our view it would not be appropriate to conclude that each is a foreign operation.

2.7.210 *An operation*

AS 21.9, 11 2.7.210.10 In our view, a foreign operation should carry out its own activities. We do not believe that an *ad hoc* collection of assets comprises an operation. Furthermore, when the foreign operation under consideration is an SPE, in our view in order for the foreign operation to have a functional currency that differs from the reporting entity, it is necessary that:

- there is a substantive business reason for establishing a separate entity to conduct these activities;
- there is a substantive business reason for choosing the currency in which that entity transacts; and
- both substantial cash inflows and substantial third-party funding are denominated in that currency.

2.7.210.20 In our view, an example of a substantive business reason would be providing security for an external borrowing. However, we believe that obtaining a natural hedge or avoiding the need for hedge accounting would not, on its own, be a sufficient business reason for the purpose of determining whether an SPE has its own functional currency.

2.7.210.30 For example, a reporting entity in New Zealand sets up an SPE to finance the acquisition of a cargo ship. The SPE obtains a loan from an external financier, buys the ship and then leases the ship to the reporting entity on normal commercial terms for a period of 7 years (compared to the 25 to 30 year life of the ship). The ship serves as security for the loan. The interest and capital repayments on the loan will be financed partly through the lease payments, with the outstanding balance to be settled with the proceeds from the sale of the ship after 7 years. All of these transactions are denominated in US dollars. The reporting entity's functional currency is New Zealand dollars.

2.7.210.40 In our view, the SPE can have a functional currency that differs from the functional currency of the reporting entity. By acquiring the ship as illustrated in 2.7.210.30, the reporting entity is able to isolate the ship as security in favour of the external financier and therefore it has a substantive business reason. Given that most ship purchase and sale transactions are denominated in US dollars it follows that the SPE's transacting currency would be the US dollar. Also, the loan from an external party is provided and settled in US dollars. While the lease payments mostly are internal, these would not be sufficient to settle the entire loan and the settlement is effected by using the proceeds from the sale of the ship to an external party. In such circumstances, in our view the functional currency of the SPE would be US dollars, in part because of the substantial residual US dollar value risk.

2.7.210.50 In a contrasting example, an SPE is established as a vehicle through which the reporting entity leases a production plant to a third party. The SPE obtains a loan from the reporting entity, buys the plant and then leases the plant to a third party. The lease payments are sufficient to finance the interest and capital repayments on the loan. All of these transactions are denominated in US dollars. The reporting entity's functional currency is euro.

2.7.210.60 In our view, in this case the SPE cannot have a functional currency that differs from that of the reporting entity because there is no substantive business purpose for establishing a separate entity through which to purchase the production plant and affect the lease agreement. The reporting entity also could have acquired the production plant and entered into the lease agreement itself. The SPE does not operate with a significant degree of autonomy from the reporting entity; the reporting entity determines the asset profile and future cash flows of the SPE because the reporting entity has written the lease agreement and also provided the funding for the purchase of the production plant. Also, there is no clear reason for choosing US dollars as the transacting currency. Any currency could have been chosen as the transacting currency, which means that it is not relevant that substantially all of the SPE's assets, liabilities, income and expenses are denominated in a currency different from that of the reporting entity. The US dollar cash flows of the SPE directly affect the cash flows of the reporting entity since these are remitted immediately to the reporting entity in the form of interest and principal payments.

2.7.210.70 We believe that the reporting entity and the SPE will have the same functional currency, which in this case will be determined by analysing the combined operations.

2.7.220 Translation of foreign currency financial statements

2.7.230 *Foreign operations*

IAS 7.26, 27, 21.39, 52   2.7.230.10 The financial statements of foreign operations are translated into the group presentation currency as follows:

- assets and liabilities are translated at the exchange rate at the reporting date;
- items of income and expense are translated at exchange rates at the dates of the relevant transactions, although appropriate average rates may be used;
- the resulting exchange differences are recognised in other comprehensive income and are presented within equity (generally referred to as the foreign currency translation reserve or currency translation adjustment); and
- cash flows are translated at exchange rates at the dates of the relevant transactions, although an appropriate average rate may be used (see 2.3.80).

2.7.230.20 In addition, although IFRSs are not explicit on these points, in our view:

- capital transactions (e.g. dividends) are translated at exchange rates at the dates of the relevant transactions; and

- components of equity are not retranslated, i.e. each component of equity is translated once, at the exchange rates at the dates of the relevant transactions.

2.7.230.30 In practice, capital transactions are translated using exchange rates at the dates of the relevant transactions. In our view, this may be approximated by use of an average rate, as used for translation of income and expenses, when appropriate (e.g. for the translation of gains and losses on available-for-sale financial assets).

IAS 21.47   2.7.230.40 Goodwill and fair value acquisition accounting adjustments related to a foreign operation should be treated as assets and liabilities of the foreign operation. In other words, they are considered to be expressed in the functional currency of the foreign operation and should be translated at the exchange rate at the reporting date as other assets and liabilities.

IAS 21.46   2.7.230.50 When the reporting date of a foreign operation that is a subsidiary, associate or joint venture is prior to that of the parent (see 2.5.290 and 3.5.270), adjustments should be made for significant movements in exchange rates up to the reporting date of the parent for group reporting purposes.

2.7.240 *Using average exchange rates*

IAS 21.22   2.7.240.10 In determining whether average rates may be used to translate income and expenses (and cash flows), in our view fluctuations in the exchange rate and the volume and size of transactions should be considered. For example, if the flow of transactions (by size and volume) is fairly stable over the period and exchange rates have not altered significantly, then it may be acceptable to update exchange rates only quarterly; in this case the translated amounts for each quarter would be combined to obtain the annual total. However, at the other extreme daily exchange rates might be used for an entity with complex operations in which there is an uneven flow of transactions, or when exchange rates are not stable.

2.7.250 *Dual exchange rates*

2.7.250.10 As noted in 2.7.90.30, in some countries there are dual exchange rates: the official exchange rate and an unofficial parallel exchange rate. In our view, when a foreign operation operates in a dual exchange rate environment, subject to the considerations highlighted above, its financial statements should be translated using the rate applicable to dividends and capital repatriation since this is how the investment in the foreign operation will be recovered.

2.7.250.15 In our view, the determination of which rate to use in these circumstances may be a matter of judgement and the conclusion may change over time. For example, although a company legally may apply to a government agency for foreign currency at the official rate for the purpose of paying dividends, it also may be able to effect dividends or capital repayments through parallel market transactions. In this case, an entity should consider all relevant facts and circumstances in determining what is the more appropriate rate to use for the purposes of translation, including:

- practical difficulties, uncertainties or delays associated with applying for foreign currency at the official rate;
- whether an entity would plan to remit a dividend or repayment of the net investment through an application for funds at the official rate or through parallel market transactions;
- past and current practice in relation to remittance of dividends or capital; and
- the ability to source funds for dividend or capital repayments through parallel market transactions.

2.7.250.20 In our view, the financial statements should disclose the reasons for not applying an official exchange rate as well as information about the rate used, if a rate other than the official rate has been used.

2.7.260 *Foreign currency translation reserve*

IAS 21.41 2.7.260.10 The net exchange difference that is recognised in the foreign currency translation reserve in each period represents the following:

- In respect of income, expenses and capital transactions, the difference between translating these items at actual or average exchange rates, and using the exchange rate at the reporting date.
- In respect of the opening balance of equity (excluding the foreign currency translation reserve), the difference between translating these items at the rate used at the reporting date at the end of the previous period, and using the rate at the reporting date at the end of the current period.

2.7.260.20 The proof of the foreign currency translation reserve is illustrated in the worked example in 2.7.280.

2.7.260.30 In addition, the foreign currency translation reserve may include exchange differences arising from loans that form part of the parent's net investment in the foreign operation (see 2.7.150) and gains and losses related to hedges of a net investment in a foreign operation (see 3.7.90).

2.7.260.40 In some cases the foreign currency translation reserve may have a debit balance. A debit balance on the reserve is acceptable under IFRSs and the balance should not be reclassified to profit or loss simply because it represents a "loss". It is reclassified to profit or loss only on disposal of the foreign operation (see 2.7.320).

IAS 21.41, 2.7.260.50 When there is a non-controlling interest in a foreign operation subsidiary,
27.28 the amount of accumulated exchange differences attributable to the NCI is allocated to and recognised as part of the NCI.

226

2.7.270 **Hyperinflation**

S 21.42, 43   2.7.270.10 When the functional currency of a foreign operation is hyperinflationary, the foreign operation's financial statements first should be restated into the measuring unit current at the reporting date, except for the comparative amounts when the group presentation currency is non-hyperinflationary. All amounts in the financial statements (excluding the comparatives noted above) then are translated using the exchange rate at the reporting date of the current reporting period.

IAS 21.42   2.7.270.20 When the financial statements of a hyperinflationary foreign operation are translated into the currency of a non-hyperinflationary economy, the comparative amounts are not adjusted for changes in the price level or exchange rate since the relevant earlier date. In other words, the comparatives are those presented previously.

2.7.270.30 For example, an entity has prepared financial statements as at and for the year ended 31 December 2010 with comparative information as at and for the year ended 31 December 2009. If the presentation currency is hyperinflationary, then the 2009 and 2010 financial statements are restated to be presented in the measuring unit current at 31 December 2010. Accordingly, the relevant exchange rate at 31 December 2010 is applied in translating both years of financial information. However, if the presentation currency was non-hyperinflationary but the functional currency was hyperinflationary, then the 2010 financial statements would be restated, and would be translated at the relevant (period end) exchange rate at 31 December 2010. The 2009 comparative amounts, on the other hand, would remain unchanged and would be presented as they were in 2009.

2.7.270.40 See 2.4.20 for a discussion of the accounting treatment of hyperinflation, including the presentation of exchange differences arising on translation into a non-hyperinflationary presentation currency.

2.7.280 **Worked example**

2.7.280.10 The following example illustrates the translation of the financial statements of a foreign operation. As a result of the translation process, the exchange difference recognised in the foreign currency translation reserve is a balancing figure; however, the amount can be proved, and this is illustrated in this example (see 2.7.280.30). In addition, an exchange difference will arise in reconciling the opening and closing balances of the various assets and liabilities; the proof of these exchange differences is illustrated in 2.7.280.60 using property, plant and equipment as an example.

2.7.280.20 The subsidiary was acquired on 1 January 2009. To simplify the example, assume that there were no goodwill or fair value adjustments that arose in the business combination. Income and expenses since acquisition have been translated using annual average exchange rates (see 2.7.240). No dividends have been paid since acquisition. The subsidiary's functional currency is FC; the group presentation currency is PC.

	FC	PC
Exchange rate at 1 January 2009	1.0	1.0
Average exchange rate during 2009	1.0	1.25
Exchange rate at 31 December 2009	1.0	1.5
Average exchange rate during 2010	1.0	2.0
Exchange rate at 31 December 2010	1.0	2.5

The above rates are illustrative only and are not intended to indicate hyperinflation.

Subsidiary statement of financial position – 2010

	FC	Rate	PC	
Share capital	400	1.0	400	
Retained earnings – at acquisition	2,200	1.0	2,200	
Earnings of 2009 that were retained	900	1.25	1,125	
Net profit for the year – 2010	1,300		2,600	See below
Foreign currency translation reserve	-		5,675	See 2.7.280.30
Equity	4,800		12,000	
Property, plant and equipment	2,800	2.5	7,000	
Other assets and liabilities	2,000	2.5	5,000	
Net assets	4,800		12,000	

Subsidiary statement of comprehensive income – 2010

	FC	Rate	PC	
Revenue	2,000	2.0	4,000	
Depreciation	(200)	2.0	(400)	
Other expenses	(500)	2.0	(1,000)	
Net profit for the year – 2010	1,300		2,600	
Other comprehensive income:				
Exchange difference on translating				
foreign operations – 2010			4,150	See 2.7.280.45
Total comprehensive income for				
the year	1,300		6,750	

2.7.280.30 The proof of the foreign currency translation reserve is determined by taking the difference between the actual exchange rate used to translate each component of equity (i.e. the amount in FC recognised in the statement of financial position) and the closing exchange rate, and multiplying this by the balance of the item in FC. This proof of translation reserve is a theoretical proof, and each equity component is not actually retranslated to the closing exchange rate when presented in the group financial statements.

Proof of foreign translation	Actual	Closing	Rate difference	Amount in FC	Difference in PC
Share capital	1.0	2.5	1.5	400	600
Retained earnings – at acquisition	1.0	2.5	1.5	2,200	3,300
Earnings of 2009 that were retained	1.25	2.5	1.25	900	1,125
Net profit for the year – 2010	2.0	2.5	0.5	1,300	650
Translation reserve (accumulated)					5,675

2.7.280.40 While this proof is cumulative for the period to the end of 2010 to match the example, in practice the proof would be done on an annual basis.

2.7.280.45 The proof of the change in the foreign currency translation during 2010 is provided as follows:

Proof of exchange difference (2010)	Opening	Closing	Rate difference	Amount in FC	Difference in PC
Share capital	1.5	2.5	1.0	400	400
Retained earnings – at acquisition	1.5	2.5	1.0	2,200	2,200
Earnings of 2009 that were retained	1.5	2.5	1.0	900	900
Net profit for the year – 2010	2.0	2.5	0.5	1,300	650
Translation reserve					4,150

IAS 16.73 2.7.280.50 The reconciliation of property, plant and equipment for 2010 will appear as follows in the notes to the consolidated financial statements (assuming no additions or disposals):

Property, plant and equipment – 2010	PC	
Opening balance	4,500	(FC 2,800 + FC 200) x 1.5
Depreciation	(400)	FC 200 x 2
Foreign exchange difference	2,900	See below
Closing balance	7,000	

2.7.280.60 The proof of the exchange difference in the reconciliation of property, plant and equipment is determined by taking the difference between the actual exchange rates used to translate each item and the closing exchange rate, and multiplying this by the amount of each item in FC.

Proof of exchange difference	*Actual*	*Closing difference*	*Rate in FC*	*Amount in FC*	*Difference in PC*
Opening balance	1.5	2.5	1.0	3,000	3,000
Current year depreciation	2.0	2.5	0.5	200	(100)
Exchange difference					2,900

2.7.290 **Translation from functional to presentation currency**

2.7.300 *General requirements*

IAS 21.39   2.7.300.10 When an entity presents its financial statements in a presentation currency that is different from its functional currency, the translation procedures are the same as those for translating foreign operations (see 2.7.230).

2.7.300.20 The standard does not provide specific guidance on the translation of components of equity, other than in respect of the current year's income and expense and the foreign currency translation reserve.

2.7.300.30 In our view, the method of translation to any presentation currency should be consistent with translation of a foreign operation for consolidation purposes. Therefore, after the initial translation into the presentation currency, components of equity at the reporting date should not be retranslated.

2.7.300.40 The following example is similar to the one used in 2.7.280.20 to illustrate the translation of foreign operations. The entity's functional currency is FC; however, the financial statements will be presented in presentation currency (PC). Income and expenses have been translated using an annual average exchange rate (see 2.7.240).

	FC		PC	
Exchange rate at 31 December 2009	1.0		1.5	
Average exchange rate during 2010	1.0		2.0	
Exchange rate at 31 December 2010	1.0		2.5	
Historical exchange rate used for opening retained earnings and share capital	1.0		1.0	

Statement of financial position – 2010				
	FC	Rate	PC	
Share capital	400	1.0	400	
Opening retained earnings	3,100	1.0	3,100	
Net profit for the year – 2010	1,300		2,600	See below
Foreign currency translation reserve	-		5,900	See 2.7.300.50
Equity	4,800		12,000	

Property, plant and equipment	2,800	2.5	7,000
Other assets and liabilities	2,000	2.5	5,000
Net assets	4,800		12,000

Statement of comprehensive income – 2010

	FC	Rate	PC
Revenue	2,000	2.0	4,000
Depreciation	(200)	2.0	(400)
Other expenses	(500)	2.0	(1,000)
Net profit for the year – 2010	1,300		2,600

Other comprehensive income:
Exchange differences on translation
– 2010   4,150   See 2.7.300.60

Total comprehensive income for the year	1,300		6,750

2.7.300.50 The proof of the foreign currency translation reserve is determined by taking the difference between the actual exchange rate used to translate an item and the closing exchange rate, and multiplying this by the balance of the item in FC.

Proof of foreign translation	Actual	Closing	Difference in rate	Amount in FC	Difference in PC
Share capital	1.0	2.5	1.5	400	600
Opening retained earnings	1.0	2.5	1.5	3,100	4,650
Net profit for the year – 2010	2.0	2.5	0.5	1,300	650
Translation reserve					5,900

2.7.300.60 The proof of exchange differences recognised in other comprehensive income and of the change in the foreign currency translation reserve during 2010 is provided as follows:

Proof of exchange difference (2010)	Opening or actual	Closing	Difference in rate	Amount in FC	Difference in PC
Share capital	1.5	2.5	1.0	400	400
Retained earnings – at acquisition	1.5	2.5	1.0	2,200	2,200
Earnings of 2009 that were retained	1.5	2.5	1.0	900	900
Net profit for the year – 2010	2.0	2.5	0.5	1,300	650
Translation reserve					4,150

2.7.310 *Hyperinflation*

21.42, 43   2.7.310.10 When both the entity's functional and presentation currencies are hyperinflationary, all items in the financial statements (current period and comparatives) are translated into the presentation currency at the closing rate at the end of the most recent period presented after being restated for the effects of inflation.

IAS 21.42 2.7.310.20 However, when the entity's functional currency is hyperinflationary and its financial statements are to be translated into a non-hyperinflationary presentation currency, only the current period's amounts are remeasured for the effects of inflation in the current period, and then translated at the exchange rate at the reporting date. In this case, comparative amounts are not adjusted for changes in the price level or exchange rate during the current period, i.e. the comparatives reported as current in prior year financial statements are presented as they were previously.

2.7.320 Sale or liquidation of a foreign operation

2.7.320.05 The following decision tree outlines the principles that apply to reclassification of the foreign currency translation reserve on disposal or partial disposal of a foreign operation.

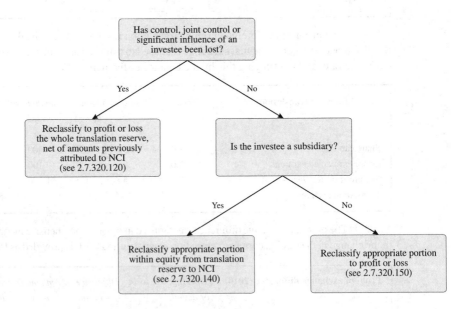

IAS 21.48, 49 2.7.320.10 The cumulative exchange differences related to a foreign operation that have been included in the foreign currency translation reserve are reclassified to profit or loss when the foreign operation is disposed of. A disposal may arise, for example, through sale, liquidation or repayment of share capital. The standard does not specify in which line item this amount is included. In our experience, typically it is included as part of the gain or loss on the disposal.

IFRIC 16.17 2.7.320.20 The cumulative exchange differences recorded and hence subject to reclassification in respect of an individual foreign operation is affected by whether the entity uses a direct or step-by-step method of consolidation (see 2.7.70.10). However, when an entity uses the step-by-step method of consolidation, it may adopt an accounting policy of determining the amount to be reclassified as that which would have arisen if the direct method of consolidation had been used to translate the financial statements of the foreign operation into the functional currency of the ultimate parent.

2.7.320.30 For example, a group consists of Parent P with a euro functional currency, Intermediate Subsidiary B with a sterling functional currency, and Subsidiary C with a US dollar functional currency. B has a net investment in C of USD 300. Assume that all gains and losses are distributed as they arise so that the amount of the net investment remains the same in US dollar terms throughout its life. P has borrowed USD 300 which is designated as a hedge of the group's US dollar net investment in C against euros. The hedge is based on spot rates and has been fully effective throughout.

2.7.320.40 C was purchased by B, and the USD borrowing was incurred by P, on 1 January 2010 when the three currencies were at par. C was sold on 31 December 2010 at which time the US dollar had strengthened and the sterling had weakened against the euro. Exchange rates at 31 December 2010 and the average rates for the year then ended were as follows:

USD 1 = EUR 1.25 = GBP 1.5 or GBP 1 = USD 0.67 = EUR 0.83

2.7.320.50 In its separate financial statements, P recognises a foreign exchange loss of EUR 75 on its US dollar liability. In P's consolidated financial statements this is reclassified from profit or loss to the foreign currency translation reserve.

2.7.320.60 If P had used the direct consolidation method, a corresponding foreign exchange gain of EUR 75 would have been recognised in the foreign currency translation reserve as a result of retranslating the USD 300 net investment into euro.

2.7.320.70 However, P has used the step-by-step consolidation method. B has first consolidated C, which recognises a foreign exchange gain in its foreign currency translation reserve of GBP 150. This is translated at the rate (see 2.7.230.40) of 0.83 into euro, so that P Group's foreign currency translation reserve with respect to its net investment in C consists of:

- EUR 75 loss on the hedging instrument; and
- EUR 125 gain on B's net investment in C.

2.7.320.80 When P then consolidates B, B's net assets, including the GBP 450 net assets of C, are translated at the closing exchange rate from sterling into euro. This gives rise to a foreign exchange loss of EUR 50 which, because of the consolidation method, is treated as part of the foreign currency translation reserve related to B Group.

2.7.320.90 On disposal of C, P may simply reclassify the net EUR 50 gain to profit or loss that is presented in its foreign currency translation reserve related to C. Alternatively, it may also reclassify the loss of EUR 50 that relates indirectly to the net assets of C but was treated as part of the foreign currency translation reserve for B, as if it had applied the direct consolidation method. The second method better reflects the economic effect of the hedge transaction, which was designed to eliminate the effect of the exchange differences on the group's USD net investment in Subsidiary C.

IAS 21.48A, 48B   2.7.320.100 In addition to the disposal of an entity's entire interest in a foreign operation, the following are accounted for as disposals even if the entity retains an interest in the former subsidiary, associate or jointly controlled entity:

- the loss of control of a subsidiary that includes a foreign operation;
- the loss of significant influence over an associate that includes a foreign operation; and
- the loss of joint control over a jointly controlled entity that includes a foreign operation.

2.7.320.110 For example, Parent P owns 100 percent of Subsidiary S. P sells 60 percent of its investment and loses control of S. The entire balance in the foreign currency translation reserve in respect of S is reclassified to profit or loss.

2.7.320.120 On disposal of a subsidiary that includes a foreign operation, the cumulative amount of the exchange differences related to that foreign operation that have been attributed to the NCI forms part of the NCI that is derecognised and is included in the calculation of the gain or loss on disposal, but it is not reclassified to profit or loss. For example, Parent P acquired 90 percent of Subsidiary S some years ago. P now sells its entire investment in S for 1,500. The net assets of S are 1,000 and the NCI in S is 100. The cumulative exchange differences that have arisen during P's ownership are gains of 200, resulting in P's foreign currency translation reserve in respect of S having a credit balance of 180 while the cumulative amount of exchange differences that have been attributed to the NCI is 20. P's gain on disposal would be calculated as:

Sale proceeds	1,500
Net assets of S	(1,000)
NCI derecognised	100
Foreign currency retranslation reserve	180
Gain on disposal	780

2.7.320.130 When a parent loses control of a subsidiary by contributing it to an associate or a jointly controlled entity, there is some ambiguity in IFRSs as to how the gain or loss on the loss of control should be calculated (see 2.5.525). If the entity applies the IAS 27 approach and recognises the gain or loss in full in profit or loss, then the components of other comprehensive income of the former subsidiary are also reclassified in full as described in 2.7.320.120. If the entity applies the IAS 28/IAS 31[1] approach

(1)   IAS 28 *Investments in Associates* and IAS 31 *Interests in Joint Ventures.*

and eliminates a part of the gain or loss in respect of the continuing interest in the assets and liabilities contributed, then in our view the components of other comprehensive income of the former subsidiary are not reclassified in full, but instead are reclassified on a proportionate basis.

IAS 21.48C, 48D 2.7.320.140 Reductions in an entity's ownership interest in a foreign operation, except for those reductions described in 2.7.320.100, are regarded as partial disposals. In the case of the partial disposal of a subsidiary that includes a foreign operation, the entity re-attributes the proportionate share of the cumulative amount of the exchange differences recognised in other comprehensive income to the NCI in that foreign operation. For example, Parent P owns 100 percent of Subsidiary S. P sells 20 percent of its investment and retains control over S. Therefore, 20 percent of the balance in the foreign currency translation reserve is reclassified to NCI.

IAS 21.48C 2.7.320.150 In any other partial disposal of a foreign operation, the entity reclassifies to profit or loss only the proportionate share of the cumulative amount of the exchange differences recognised in other comprehensive income. In another example, Parent P owns 30 percent of Associate B. P sells a 5 percent stake and retains significant influence over B. Therefore one-sixth of the balance in the foreign currency translation reserve is reclassified to profit or loss.

IAS 21.8, D, BC25D 2.7.320.160 A reporting entity may make a loan to a foreign operation that is classified as part of its net investment such that exchange differences on the loan are recognised in the foreign currency translation reserve (see 2.7.260). IFRSs are silent as to whether repayment of an intercompany loan forming part of the net investment is a partial disposal. In our view, an entity should choose an accounting policy, to be applied consistently, as to whether repayment of an intercompany loan forming part of the net investment in a foreign operation is considered a partial disposal. We prefer that such a repayment not be considered a partial disposal as it does not change the percentage share interest held by the reporting entity. However, given historical practice, the definition of "net investment" and its similarity to "ownership interest", and the IASB's view that such loans are treated similarly to equity investments, an accounting policy that treated such repayments as partial disposals also would be acceptable.

IAS 21.48C, 49 2.7.320.170 If an entity elects to treat repayment of a long-term intercompany loan forming part of the net investment as a partial disposal, then in our view the principles noted in 2.7.320.140 and 150 should be applied as follows:

- *Loan to a subsidiary.* There would be no reclassification to profit or loss, only a reat-tribution between the foreign currency translation reserve of the entity and NCI. If the subsidiary is wholly owned and there is no NCI, no amount would be reattributed.
- *Loan to an associate or jointly-controlled entity.* The proportionate share of the for-eign currency translation reserve of the entity would be reclassified to profit or loss.

IAS 21.49 2.7.320.180 In our view, it also would be necessary to consider whether the repayment of a loan results in substance in a liquidation of a subsidiary and a full disposal.

2.7.320.190 For example, Company P subscribed 1,000 in return for a 25 percent interest in Associate B, and extended "permanent" funding of a further 500 at the same time. If S repays the loan of 500 and P's accounting policy is to treat repayment of a loan forming part of the net investment as a partial disposal, then we believe that one-third of the balance in the foreign currency translation reserve should be reclassified to profit or loss.

2.7.320.200 If P had extended the permanent funding some time after the original investment, then we believe that the amount to be reclassified to profit or loss should be one-third of the change in the balance of the foreign currency translation reserve that arose while the funding was outstanding. Alternatively, if P had tracked the actual exchange differences arising on the permanent funding, then we consider that it would be acceptable for P to reclassify to profit or loss the actual exchange differences that previously had been recognised in other comprehensive income.

IAS 21.49 2.7.320.210 In the event of an impairment loss, the standard is clear that this does not constitute a partial disposal and no amount of the foreign currency translation reserve should be reclassified to profit or loss.

2.7.320.220 In our view, a major restructuring that results in reducing the scale of operations of a foreign operation does not in itself trigger any amount of the foreign currency translation reserve to be reclassified to profit or loss because the parent has not realised its investment in the foreign operation.

2.7.325 Disposal of non-foreign operations

2.7.325.10 IFRSs are silent on the accounting treatment for exchange differences on disposal of a non-foreign operation when the group presentation currency is not the same as the parent's functional currency. For example, a parent that presents its consolidated financial statements in US dollar but whose functional currency is euro disposes of its entire interest in a directly-owned subsidiary whose functional currency also is euro.

IAS 21.8, 2.7.325.20 When the step-by-step method of consolidation is used (see 2.7.70.10), no
BC18-20 exchange difference in respect of the subsidiary would exist in the parent's consolidated financial statements. However, if the direct method is applied such that the financial statements of the subsidiary had been directly translated into the presentation currency, then the exchange differences would have been separately accumulated in respect of the subsidiary. In our view, no reclassification of these differences in respect of the subsidiary is required or permitted in the parent's consolidated financial statements as the subsidiary did not meet the definition of a foreign operation.

2.7.330 Convenience translations

IAS 21.BC14 2.7.330.10 A convenience translation occurs when an entity decides to present financial statements in addition to the financial statements required to be presented in accordance with IFRSs. For example, an entity has a functional currency of Danish krone and a presentation currency of euro; in addition it wishes to show US dollar figures for the most recent year's primary financial statements, but it will not publish a full set of US dollar financial statements.

IAS 21.39,   2.7.330.20 There is a difference between a convenience translation and translation to
42, 55, 57   presentation currency. An entity that presents its financial statements in a currency or currencies that are different from its functional currency should describe the financial statements as complying with IFRSs only if they comply with the translation method as set out in IAS 21. If an entity displays its financial statements or other financial information in a currency that is different from either its functional currency or its presentation currency and does not comply with the translation method set out under IAS 21, then it needs to provide disclosures, e.g. that the information in the convenience translation is supplementary, what the convenience currency is and the functional currency and method of translation used. The convenience translation may be used only for selected information and can be provided only as supplemental information (see 5.8).

2.8 Accounting policies, errors and estimates
(IAS 1, IAS 8)

2.8 Accounting policies, errors and estimates
(IAS 1, IAS 8)

> **Overview of currently effective requirements**
>
> - Accounting policies are the specific principles, bases, conventions, rules and practices that an entity applies in preparing and presenting financial statements.
>
> - A hierarchy of alternative sources is specified when IFRSs do not cover a particular issue.
>
> - Unless otherwise permitted specifically by an IFRS, the accounting policies adopted by an entity are applied consistently to all similar items.
>
> - An accounting policy is changed in response to a new or revised IFRS, or on a voluntary basis if the new policy is more appropriate.
>
> - Generally accounting policy changes and corrections of prior period errors are made by adjusting opening equity and restating comparatives unless this is impracticable.
>
> - Changes in accounting estimates are accounted for prospectively.
>
> - When it is difficult to determine whether a change is a change in accounting policy or a change in estimate, it is treated as a change in estimate.
>
> - Comparatives are restated unless impracticable if the classification or presentation of items in the financial statements is changed.
>
> - A statement of financial position as at the beginning of the earliest comparative period is presented when an entity restates comparative information following a change in accounting policy, correction of an error, or reclassification of items in the financial statements.

Currently effective requirements

This publication reflects IFRSs in issue at 1 August 2010. The currently effective requirements cover annual periods beginning on 1 January 2010. The requirements related to this topic are derived mainly from IAS 1 *Presentation of Financial Statements* and IAS 8 *Accounting Policies, Changes in Accounting Estimates and Errors*.

IAS 1.7, 8.5   IAS 1 (2007) introduced some changes in terminology. As a result the terms "a stand-ard or an interpretation" and "standards or interpretations" replace in IFRSs the terms "IFRS" and "IFRSs" respectively. Throughout this publication generally we use the terms "IFRS" and "IFRSs" (see 1.1.80).

Forthcoming requirements and future developments

When a currently effective requirement will be changed by a new requirement that is issued but is not yet effective, it is marked with a # as a **forthcoming requirement** and the impact of the change is explained in the accompanying boxed text. In respect of this topic no forthcoming requirements are noted.

When a significant change to the currently effective or forthcoming requirement is expected, it is marked with a * as an area that may be subject to **future developments**. In respect of this topic no future developments are noted.

2.8.5 Selection of accounting policies

IAS 8.5   2.8.5.10 Accounting policies are the specific principles, bases, conventions, rules and practices that an entity applies in preparing and presenting financial statements.

2.8.5.20 See 6.1.170 for a discussion of the selection of accounting policies by an entity applying IFRSs for the first time.

2.8.6 *Hierarchy*

IAS 8.7   2.8.6.10 When specifically addressed by an IFRS, an entity applies the accounting policy or policies required by that IFRS to a transaction.

IAS 8.10, 11   2.8.6.20 When IFRSs do not cover a particular issue, management uses its judgement in developing and applying an accounting policy that results in information that is relevant to the economic decisions of users and is reliable. There is a hierarchy of accounting literature to be used in arriving at the policy selected, which provides entities with a basic structure for resolving issues in the absence of specific guidance.

IAS 8.11   2.8.6.30 When IFRSs do not cover a particular issue, the entity considers:

● the guidance and requirements in standards and interpretations dealing with similar and related issues; and
● the Framework (see 1.2).

IAS 8.12   2.8.6.40 The entity also may consider the pronouncements of other standard-setting bodies (e.g. the FASB) and accepted industry practice, to the extent that they do not conflict with the standards, interpretations and the Framework (see 1.2).

2.8.7 *Consistency*

IAS 8.13 2.8.7.10 Unless otherwise permitted specifically by an IFRS, the accounting policies adopted by an entity are applied consistently to all similar items. For example, if an entity chooses to account for jointly controlled entities using the equity method (see 3.5.550), then it uses that method consistently for all jointly controlled entities; it cannot use the equity method for some jointly controlled entities and proportionate consolidation for others.

AS 2.25, 26 2.8.7.20 Certain IFRSs permit the application of different methods of accounting to different categories of items. For example, IAS 2 *Inventories* requires the same cost formula to be used for all inventories having a similar nature and use to the entity, but recognises also that different cost formulae may be justified for inventories with a different nature or use. However, IAS 2 recognises that a difference in geographical location of inventories, by itself, is not sufficient to justify the use of different cost formulae. For example, an oil company could not use a weighted average costing formula for crude oil supplies in the United States and use a FIFO (first-in, first-out) costing formula at other non-United States locations. However, a manufacturer may have computer chips that are used in industrial machinery, and computer chips that are used in domestic appliances; in our view the cost of the computer chips for each end-product could be measured differently. However, in our view a difference in customer demographic (e.g. end-user vs retailer) does not meet the IAS 2 criteria of inventories with a different nature or use to justify a difference in costing formula.

IAS 27.24 2.8.7.30 Accounting policies within a group are applied consistently, including those which are established for the purpose of consolidation (see 2.5.290.40). An exception is that insurance contracts accounted for under IFRS 4 *Insurance Contracts* need not be accounted for consistently on a group-wide basis (see 5.10.60).

2.8.7.40 See 5.9.230 for a discussion of the accounting policies followed in an interim reporting period.

2.8.10 **Changes in accounting policy**

2.8.10.05 [Not used]

IAS 8.14, 15 2.8.10.10 A change in accounting policy is made when required to adopt a new or revised IFRS. A voluntary change may be made if it will result in a reliable and more relevant presentation (see 2.8.30). In applying an IFRS that contains more than one acceptable accounting policy, generally in our view an entity may change its accounting policy from one acceptable accounting policy to another, since both methods are considered acceptable in providing a fair presentation.

IAS 8.14 2.8.10.20 Notwithstanding our general view in 2.8.10.10, we do not believe that it is appropriate for an entity to change an accounting policy multiple times without considering carefully the requirement to qualify for a voluntary change in accounting policy. For example, in 2008 Company B changed its accounting policy for property, plant and equipment from the cost model to the revaluation model. During 2010 B reassesses its accounting policy and decides to change its accounting policy back to the cost model. In our view, since B demonstrated previously that the revaluation model was more appropriate, B would need to demonstrate that the need for a reversal of its previous change in accounting policy is due to a change in circumstances. Such a circumstance could occur as a result of the acquisition of B by a new parent if the new parent instructs B to change its accounting policy for property, plant and equipment to the cost model in order to align B's policy with the rest of the group.

IAS 8.14(b),   2.8.10.30 In addition, IFRSs provide specifically that in respect of investment
40.31   property (see 3.4.140) it is "highly unlikely" that a change in accounting policy from a fair value to a cost basis will result in a more appropriate presentation in the financial statements. Similarly, in our view an entity that has an existing accounting policy of immediate recognition of actuarial gains and losses in profit or loss or other comprehensive income cannot, in the future, adopt an accounting policy of recognising actuarial gains and losses under the "corridor" approach as this does not provide "reliable and more relevant information" about the effects of transactions (see 4.4.560.30).

IFRS 4.22,   2.8.10.40 The following changes in accounting policy are subject to special requirements:
6.13, IAS 8.17

- *First-time adoption.* Changes in accounting policy that arise upon the first-time adoption of IFRSs are the subject of a separate standard, IFRS 1 *First-time Adoption of International Financial Reporting Standards*. In our view, this includes changes in policies between interim and annual financial statements in the year of first-time adoption of IFRSs (see 6.1.170).
- *Property, plant and equipment and intangible assets.* A change in accounting policy to revalue items of property, plant and equipment (see 3.2.300) or intangible assets (see 3.3.280) is accounted for as a revaluation in accordance with the relevant IFRSs.
- *Insurance contracts.* An entity is permitted to change its existing IFRS accounting policy for insurance contracts only if the change improves either the relevance or the reliability of its financial statements without reducing either (see 5.10.90).
- *Exploration and evaluation activities.* An entity is permitted to change its existing IFRS accounting policy for exploration and evaluation activities only if the change makes the financial statements more relevant and no less reliable, or more reliable and no less relevant, to the needs of the users (see 5.11.350).

2.8.10.50 In addition, individual IFRSs may contain specific requirements for accounting policy changes that result from their adoption (see 2.8.20).

IAS 8.16   2.8.10.60 Neither the adoption of an accounting policy for new transactions or events, nor the application of an accounting policy to previously immaterial items, is a change in accounting policy. When a functional currency becomes hyperinflationary and the restatement requirements of IFRSs are applied (see 2.4.20), in our view this is not a change in accounting policy because restatement could not have been applied prior to the functional currency being judged hyperinflationary, which is similar to accounting for a new transaction or event. This is notwithstanding the fact that purchasing power adjustments should be computed from the date that non-monetary assets (liabilities) are acquired (incurred).

2.8.10.70 See 2.8.7 for a discussion of the consistency of accounting policies within an entity and in the consolidated financial statements.

AS 8.28, 29   2.8.10.80 Disclosures required in respect of changes in accounting policy include the reasons for the change and the amount of the adjustment for the current period and for each period presented. In our view, such disclosures should be made separately for each such change.

IAS 8.26   2.8.10.90 In addition, any accompanying financial information presented in respect of prior periods (e.g. historical summaries) also is restated as far back as is practicable to reflect the change in accounting policy (see 2.8.50.60).

2.8.10.100 See 3.13.380 for a discussion of the accounting for income taxes as a result of a change in accounting policy.

2.8.20 *Accounting policy change upon adoption of a new IFRS*

IAS 8.19   2.8.20.10 When a change in accounting policy arises from the adoption of a new, revised or amended IFRS, an entity follows the specific transitional requirements in that IFRS, which take precedence over the general requirements for changes in accounting policies.

IFRS 8.36   2.8.20.20 For example, the transitional requirements in IFRS 8 *Operating Segments*, which are applicable for financial statements for periods beginning on or after 1 January 2009 (see 5.2), state that comparative segment information in the first year of application is restated to conform to the requirements of IFRS 8, unless the necessary information is not available and the cost to develop it would be excessive (see 5.2.250.10).

AS 8.28, 29   2.8.20.30 When an entity follows the specific transitional requirements of an IFRS, in our view it nonetheless should comply with the disclosure requirements of IAS 8 in respect of a change in accounting policy to the extent that the transitional requirements do not include disclosure requirements. Even though it could be argued that the disclosures are not required because they are set out in the requirements for *voluntary* changes in accounting policy, we believe that they are necessary in order to give a fair presentation.

2.8.30 *Voluntary change*

IAS 8.14, 20   2.8.30.10 An entity may change an accounting policy voluntarily if the new policy provides reliable and more relevant information. The early adoption of a new IFRS is not a voluntary change in accounting policy.

IAS 8.21   2.8.30.15 If in the absence of IFRSs specifically addressing an accounting issue, an entity adopted an accounting policy based on the pronouncements of other standard-setting bodies (see 2.8.6.40) and chooses to change that accounting policy as a result of an amendment to the underlying pronouncement, the change is accounted for and disclosed as a voluntary change in accounting policy.

IAS 8.22   2.8.30.20 Generally an entity applies a change in accounting policy retrospectively (i.e. as if the new accounting policy always had been applied), including any income tax effect. This is done by adjusting the opening balance of each affected component of equity for the earliest prior period presented and the other comparative amounts disclosed for each prior period presented.

IAS 8.24   2.8.30.30 If it is impracticable to determine the period-specific effects for one or more prior periods presented (see 2.8.50), then the entity restates the opening balances of assets, liabilities and equity for the earliest period for which retrospective restatement is practicable.

IAS 8.25, 27   2.8.30.40 If it is impracticable to determine the cumulative effect at the beginning of the current period of a change in accounting policy (see 2.8.50), then the entity restates the comparative information prospectively from the earliest date practicable. Nevertheless, a change in accounting policy is permitted even if it is impracticable to apply the policy prospectively for any prior period.

IAS 8.29   2.8.30.50 The financial statements include disclosure regarding the change in accounting policy, including the reasons why applying a voluntary change in accounting policy provides reliable and more relevant information.

2.8.40 **Errors**

IAS 8.5   2.8.40.10 Errors result from the misapplication of policies or the misinterpretation of facts and circumstances that exist at the reporting date. Examples include mathematical mistakes, fraud (see 2.9.70) and oversight.

IAS 8.41   2.8.40.20 Financial statements containing material errors do not comply with IFRSs. Potential current year errors are corrected before the financial statements are authorised for issue. Material prior period errors are corrected by restating the comparative information presented in the financial statements for that subsequent period.

IAS 8.42   2.8.40.30 The correction of a material prior period error is made by either:

- restating the comparative amounts for the prior period(s) presented in which the error occurred; or
- if the error occurred before the earliest prior period presented, by restating the opening balances of assets, liabilities and equity for the earliest prior period presented.

IAS 8.43 2.8.40.40 IAS 8 requires that material errors be corrected by restating the opening balance of equity and comparatives unless this is impracticable.

IAS 8.44 2.8.40.50 If it is impracticable to determine the period-specific effects for one or more prior periods presented (see 2.8.50), then the entity restates the opening balances of assets, liabilities and equity for the earliest period for which retrospective restatement is practicable.

IAS 8.45 2.8.40.60 If it is impracticable to determine the cumulative effect at the beginning of the current period of an error on all prior periods (see 2.8.50), then the entity restates the comparative information to correct the error prospectively from the earliest date practicable.

2.8.40.70 The following example illustrates the correction of an error.

2.8.40.80 During 2010 Company X discovered that prepayments of 400 made during 2008 had not been recognised in profit or loss as the related expenses were incurred. The prepayments should have been recognised as an expense of 100 in 2008; 250 in 2009; and 50 in 2010. The misstatement is material.

Extract from draft 2010 financial statements before correction of the error		
	Draft	
	2010	*2009*
Extract from statement of comprehensive income		
Revenue	6,000	4,000
Expenses	(5,500)	(3,600)
Net profit	500	400
	Draft	
	2010	*2009*
Extract from statement of changes in equity		
Opening retained earnings	14,400	14,000
Current year net profit	500	400
Closing retained earnings	14,900	14,400

2.8.40.90 The opening balance of retained earnings is adjusted and comparatives are restated when practicable to reflect the correction of the error. The restatement should reflect any tax effects, which are ignored for the purposes of this example.

	2010	2009 Restated
Extract from statement of comprehensive income		
Revenue	6,000	4,000
Expenses	(5,550)	(3,850)
Net profit	450	150
Extract from statement of changes in equity		
Opening retained earnings as reported previously	-	14,000
Correction of an error related to previous years (note reference)	-	(100)
Opening retained earnings (restated)	14,050	13,900
Current year net profit	450	150
Closing retained earnings	14,500	14,050

IAS 8.49 2.8.40.100 In restating the comparatives the adjustment will be included in the appropriate line item of the statement of comprehensive income in the usual way (see 4.1). For example, if the expense in this case was insurance of X's head office and X classified its expenses by function, then the expense normally would be included in administrative expenses. In addition, the financial statements will include full disclosure regarding the error and the adjustments made to correct it.

IAS 8.IG 2.8.40.110 Although not mentioned specifically in the standard, the standard's implementation guidance shows the restated comparative financial statements with the heading "restated". In our view, this is necessary in order to highlight for users the fact that the comparative financial statements are not the same as the financial statements published previously.

IAS 1.106(b) 2.8.40.120 In this example the component of equity affected by the error was retained earnings. If the error affects more components of equity, then the effect on each component of equity is disclosed separately.

2.8.50 Impracticability of retrospective application

IAS 8.5, 50 2.8.50.10 The retrospective application of changes in accounting policies (see 2.8.10) and the restatement of material errors (see 2.8.40) is required, unless impracticable. Guidance is given on when restatement will be impracticable.

IAS 8.52 2.8.50.20 Retrospective application or restatement is done using only information that:

- would have been available in preparing the financial statements for that earlier period; and
- provides evidence of circumstances that existed on the date(s) that the transaction or event occurred.

IAS 8.53 2.8.50.30 Other information, for example, information that uses the benefit of hindsight, may not be used.

2.8.50.40 Retrospective application or restatement is impracticable when restatement requires:

IAS 8.52 • significant estimates to be made that cannot, after making every reasonable effort, distinguish information that may be used from that which may not; or

IAS 8.50 • information regarding transactions or events that is not available to the entity after making every reasonable effort to retrieve the necessary information.

2.8.50.50 In such cases the financial statements are adjusted as at the beginning of the earliest period from which retrospective adjustment is practicable.

IAS 8.23 2.8.50.60 If an entity presents any accompanying financial information in respect of prior periods (e.g. historical summaries), then in our view an inability to restate all of the periods presented in the historical summaries or other prior period information is not a reason to conclude that none of the comparative information required by IFRSs would be restated. For example, Company X prepares a 10-year historical summary as accompanying financial information to its annual report. As a result of a change in accounting policy, X attempts to adjust the historical summary for the entire 10-year period, but concludes that it is impracticable to restate beyond the last four years. X therefore restates the affected financial information as far back as practicable, being the last four years of the financial summary.

2.8.60 Changes in accounting estimates

S 8.32, 33, 2.8.60.10 Estimates are an essential part of financial reporting and changes therein are
39, 40 accounted for in the period in which the change occurs. For example, a change in the estimate of recoverable receivables is accounted for in the period in which the change in estimate is made. Disclosure of the nature and amount of such changes is required (see 4.1.150).

IAS 8.35 2.8.60.20 In some cases it can be difficult to determine whether a change represents a change in accounting policy or a change in estimate. In such cases the change is treated as a change in estimate and appropriate disclosure is given. In our view, when an entity changes its method of measuring the cost of inventory (see 3.8.280), for example, from FIFO to weighted average, this is a change in accounting policy notwithstanding the fact that both methods measure cost.

IAS 8.32, 2.8.60.30 A change in the estimate of the useful life or method of recognising the depre-
16.51, 61, ciation or amortisation of property, plant and equipment (see 3.2.140) or an intangible
38.104 asset (see 3.3.210) is accounted for prospectively as a change in estimate by adjusting depreciation or amortisation in the current and future periods.

2.8.60.40 For example, Company C acquired a printing machine at the beginning of 2006 and its useful life was estimated to be 10 years. At the end of 2009 the carrying amount of the machine was 240. At the beginning of 2010 C revised the estimated useful life downwards to a further two years from that date. Therefore the carrying amount of 240 is depreciated over the next two years. In addition, the decrease in useful life may indicate that the carrying amount of the machine is impaired (see 3.10.110).

IAS 8.5, 34, 2.8.60.50 A change in estimate is different from the correction of an error because an
48 error results from the misapplication of policy or misinterpretation of existing facts and circumstances. Changes in accounting estimates result from new information or new developments. An estimate takes into account all existing facts and circumstances, but changes over time as those facts and circumstances change or the entity obtains more experience and/or knowledge. If an objective determination cannot be made of whether a change is a change in estimate or the correction of an error, then in our view it should be accounted for as a change in estimate; this is consistent with the approach taken to distinguishing between changes in estimates and changes in accounting policy.

IAS 34.26 2.8.60.60 Any significant change in estimate made during the last interim period in a financial year is disclosed in a note to the annual financial statements, unless separate interim financial statements are published for this period.

2.8.70 **Change in classification or presentation**

IAS 1.41, 45, 2.8.70.10 In some cases it may be appropriate to change the classification or presentation
46 of items in the financial statements even though there has been no change in accounting policy in order to achieve a more appropriate presentation. In such cases the comparatives are restated unless impracticable and appropriate explanatory disclosures are included in the financial statements.

IAS 1.39, 2.8.70.20 For example, in 2009 Company D presents its entire obligation for post-
19.118 employment benefits as non-current as allowed by IFRSs (see 4.4.1100). In 2010 D decides to split the obligation into current and non-current components in the statement of financial position. We believe that the 2009 comparatives should be restated if D has the information necessary to do so and a third statement of financial position as at the beginning of the earliest comparative period should be presented (see 2.1.35.30).

2.8.80 **Presentation of a third statement of financial position**

IAS 1.10(f) 2.8.80.10 IAS 1 requires an additional statement of financial position to be presented as at the beginning of the earliest comparative period following a retrospective change in accounting policy, the correction of an error or the reclassification of items in the financial statements.

2.8.80.20 In our view, this requirement should be interpreted having regard to materiality based on the particular facts and circumstances (see 2.1.35).

2.9 Events after the reporting period
(IAS 1, IAS 10)

2.9 Events after the reporting period
(IAS 1, IAS 10)

Overview of currently effective requirements

- The financial statements are adjusted to reflect events that occur after the end of the reporting period, but before the financial statements are authorised for issue, if those events provide evidence of conditions that existed at the end of the reporting period.

- Financial statements are not adjusted for events that are indicative of conditions that arose after the end of the reporting period, except when the going concern assumption no longer is appropriate.

- Dividends declared after the end of the reporting period are not recognised as a liability in the financial statements.

- Liabilities generally are classified as current or non-current based on circumstances at the end of the reporting period.

Currently effective requirements

This publication reflects IFRSs in issue at 1 August 2010. The currently effective requirements cover annual periods beginning on 1 January 2010. The requirements related to this topic are derived mainly from IAS 1 *Presentation of Financial Statements* and IAS 10 *Events after the Reporting Period*.

Forthcoming requirements and future developments

When a currently effective requirement will be changed by a new requirement that is issued but is not yet effective, it is marked with a # as a **forthcoming requirement** and the impact of the change is explained in the accompanying boxed text. In respect of this topic no forthcoming requirements are noted.

When a significant change to the currently effective or forthcoming requirements is expected, it is marked with a * as an area that may be subject to **future developments**. In respect of this topic no future developments are noted.

2.9.10 Overall approach

IAS 10.3   2.9.10.10 The following diagram illustrates the scope of IAS 10, which deals with events that occur after the end of the reporting period but before the financial statements are authorised for issue.

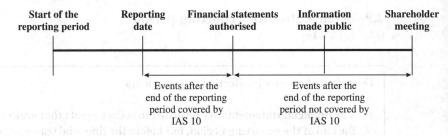

2.9.15 *Date that the financial statements were authorised for issue*

IAS 10.17 2.9.15.10 Disclosure is required in the financial statements of the date that the financial statements were authorised for issue and who gave such authorisation, in order to inform users of the date to which events have been considered. If the shareholders have the power to amend the financial statements after issue, then the entity discloses that fact.

IAS 10.5, 6 2.9.15.20 The date that the financial statements are authorised for issue generally is the date that the financial statements are authorised and issued by management, either to the supervisory board or to the shareholders. Even if the shareholders are required to approve the financial statements, the date that the financial statements are authorised for issue is the date of issue, not the date when shareholders approve the financial statements.

IAS 10.4-7 2.9.15.22 Identification of the date that the financial statements are authorised for issue is a key area in the application of IAS 10. This is because any event that occurs after this date is not disclosed or reflected in the financial statements of the current period. However, the date that the financial statements are authorised for issue is not always easily identifiable. In our view, the determination of this date should be assessed based on all facts and circumstances, including the rights and responsibilities of the governing body and local governance rules in respect of authorisation protocols.

2.9.15.25 In our view, two different dates of authorisation for issue of the financial statements (dual dating of financial statements) should not be disclosed, because we believe that only a single date of authorisation for issue of the financial statements is in compliance with IAS 10.

2.9.15.30 Sometimes financial statements of a subsidiary are prepared after the financial statements of a group that includes the subsidiary. In our view, when financial statements of a subsidiary are authorised for issue after the publication of the consolidated financial statements of the group that includes this subsidiary, the date that the subsidiary's financial statements are authorised for issue is the date through which events after the end of the reporting period should be considered. Therefore, when preparing the financial statements of the subsidiary management should consider events that occurred after the consolidated financial statements of the group are authorised but before the subsidiary's financial statements are authorised for issue.

2.9.15.40 In our view, the term "authorised for issue" in IAS 8 *Accounting Policies, Changes in Accounting Estimates and Errors* refers only to the most recent reporting period and does not include comparative information if that comparative information (annual or interim) previously was authorised for issue.

2.9.20 Adjusting events

IAS 10.3, 8, 14 2.9.20.10 The financial statements are adjusted to reflect events that occur after the end of the reporting period, but before the financial statements are authorised for issue, if either they provide evidence of conditions that existed at the end of the reporting period (adjusting events) or they indicate that the going concern basis of preparation is inappropriate (see 2.9.55).

2.9.20.20 For example, Company T is being sued for breach of contract. At the end of the reporting period T asserted that it had not breached the contract and had legal opinions supporting this as the most likely outcome. Therefore, T had not recognised any provision in its draft financial statements (see 3.12 and 3.14). Prior to the financial statements being authorised by the directors, the judge in the case delivered a preliminary ruling that T was guilty and liable for damages of 1,000. A final judgement was made after the financial statements had been authorised for issue. In our view, the financial statements should be adjusted and a provision of 1,000 recognised because the preliminary ruling provides sufficient evidence that an obligation existed at the end of the reporting period, in the absence of any evidence to the contrary, notwithstanding the fact that a final judgement had not yet been reached.

2.9.20.30 See paragraph 9 of IAS 10 for other examples of adjusting events.

2.9.30 Non-adjusting events

IAS 10.3, 10, 14 2.9.30.10 Financial statement amounts are not adjusted for non-adjusting events. Non-adjusting events are events that are a result of conditions that arose after the end of the reporting period. An exception is when events after the end of the reporting period indicate that the financial statements should not be prepared on a going concern basis (see 2.9.55).

IAS 37.33, 35 2.9.30.15 Continuing the example in 2.9.20.20 from the point of view of Company V, which is suing Company T for breach of the contract, V is uncertain about the outcome of the legal proceeding at the end of the reporting period. V's financial statements are authorised for issue after the final court judgement. V considers whether the favourable court ruling is an adjusting or non-adjusting event in respect of its claim, which has been treated as a contingent asset (see 3.14.40) because its realisation was probable but not virtually certain. In our view, the change in probability of realisation of income and the recovery of the related asset due to the court ruling is an event that should be reflected in the financial statements of the period in which the change occurs and should not be treated as an adjusting event in the prior period financial statements. This is because the recognition of an asset for an item that is a contingent asset is specified as "recognised in the period in which the change occurs". We believe that the phrase "in which the change occurs" is the change in probability of the related inflows of economic benefits, which provides sufficient evidence that from that point in time the item meets the definition of and the recognition requirements for an asset. We believe that this specific guidance should be applied rather than considering the change in probability to be an event that provides additional information regarding circumstances at the end of the reporting period, even though this is not symmetrical with the accounting by the counterparty (T).

IAS 10.12, 2.9.30.20 Dividends declared (i.e. the dividends are authorised and no longer at the
13, BC4 discretion of the entity) after the end of the reporting period are non-adjusting events that are not recognised as a liability in the financial statements, but are disclosed in the notes to the financial statements. This is because no obligation exists at the end of the reporting period. See 3.11.450 for further discussion of the timing of the recognition of dividends.

IAS 10.22(h) 2.9.30.25 A change in tax rate or tax law enacted or substantively enacted after the end of the reporting period is a non-adjusting event that generally would result in disclosure (see 3.13.310.30).

2.9.30.28 Market conditions that arise after the reporting date should be considered to determine whether they are an adjusting or non-adjusting event. If the post-reporting date market conditions are a change that could not reasonably have been foreseen at the reporting date, then it follows that the cash flow projections used in impairment testing should not be adjusted. However, the entity should consider whether disclosure would be appropriate (see 2.9.30.30). While the inability to forecast significant unforeseen changes in market conditions does not call into question the reasonableness of prior forecasts, such conditions should be considered in the forecasts in future impairment testing (see 3.10.315.10).

IFRS 3.59- 2.9.30.30 For significant non-adjusting events, an entity discloses the nature of the event
63, and an estimate of its financial effect, or a statement that an estimate cannot be made.
IAS 10.21 A non-adjusting event is considered to be significant when it is of such importance that non-disclosure would affect the ability of users of the financial statements to make proper evaluations and decisions. In all cases, when a business combination occurs after the end of the annual reporting period but before the financial statements are authorised for issue, an entity discloses information as prescribed by IFRS 3.

2.9.30.40 See paragraph 22 of IAS 10 for other examples of non-adjusting events.

2.9.40 Current vs non-current classification

IAS 1.72-76 2.9.40.10 Generally, the classification of long-term debt as current or non-current reflects circumstances at the end of the reporting period. Refinancings, amendments, waivers etc. signed after the reporting date are not considered in determining the classification of debt. However, if an entity expects, and has the discretion, at the end of the reporting period to refinance or to reschedule payments on a long-term basis, then the debt is classified as non-current (see 3.1.40).

2.9.50 **Earnings per share**

IAS 33.64 2.9.50.10 Earnings per share is restated to include the effect on the number of shares of certain share transactions that occur after the end of the reporting period even though the transactions themselves are non-adjusting events (see 5.3.360).

2.9.55 **Going concern**

IAS 10.14 2.9.55.10 An entity does not prepare its financial statements on a going concern basis if management determines, after the end of the reporting period but before the financial statements are authorised for issue, that it intends, or has no alternative other than to liquidate the entity or stop trading (see 2.4.15.10).

2.9.60 **Identifying the key event**

2.9.60.10 In some cases an event after the end of the reporting period actually may have been triggered by an event that occurred prior to the end of the reporting period. In such cases it is necessary to determine the underlying causes of the event and its timing in order to determine the appropriate accounting.

IAS 10.9 2.9.60.20 For example, Company B receives notice after the end of the reporting period that one of its major customers has gone into liquidation. In this case the standard states that the bankruptcy of a customer after the end of the reporting period usually confirms that a loss existed at the end of the reporting period. Therefore, B should assume that the bankruptcy is an adjusting event unless evidence to the contrary exists (e.g. the customer became bankrupt because its main operating plant was destroyed in a fire that occurred after the end of the reporting period).

IAS 10.9, 37.16 2.9.60.30 An entity considers whether adjusting events impact not only recognised items but also previously unrecognised items. For example, a financier extends a loan to Company C before the end of its reporting period. Company D provides a financial guarantee to the financier so D has the credit risk of non-repayment of the loan by C to the financier. After the end of its reporting period, D receives notice that C has gone into administration (bankruptcy). D should assume that the administration is an adjusting event (subject to evidence to the contrary (see previous example in 2.9.60.20)) and should recognise a provision for its estimate of the amount that it will pay under the guarantee (see 3.12), despite not having recognised the loan as an asset in its own accounting records.

2.9.60.40 In other cases multiple events may occur, some before and some after the end of the reporting period, and it is necessary to determine which of the events should trigger the recognition of the event in the financial statements.

2.9.70 **Discovery of a fraud after the end of the reporting period**

IAS 8.5 2.9.70.10 A fraud may be discovered after the financial statements have been authorised for issue. In our view, if information about the fraud could not reasonably be expected to have been obtained and taken into account by an entity preparing financial statements when those financial statements were authorised for issue, then subsequent discovery of such information is not evidence of a prior period error in those financial statements. This is because the definition of a prior period error focuses on whether information was available or reasonably could have been obtained and taken into account.

2.9.70.20 In other circumstances a fraud may be discovered after the end of the reporting period but before the financial statements are authorised for issue. In our view, in concluding whether the discovery of the fraud should be treated as an adjusting or non-adjusting event related to reporting the fair value of financial assets under IAS 39 *Financial Instruments: Recognition and Measurement* in financial statements that have not yet been authorised for issue, management first identifies whether there is a question of existence, valuation or both.

2.9.70.30 In our view, if the discovery of a fraud raises issues related to the existence of financial assets involved, then it should be treated as an adjusting event for financial statements that have not yet been authorised for issue. This is because the discovery of the fraud provides additional information regarding the existence of financial assets at the reporting date. If, however, the fraud raises issues related only to the valuation of financial assets that do exist, then in our view it should be treated as a non-adjusting event for reporting the fair values of financial assets within the scope of IAS 39. This is because of the following fair value measurement requirements of IAS 39:

IAS 39.AG
71-AG73
- *Quoted instruments.* Fair value is determined based on the price at which a transaction would occur at the *end of the reporting period* in the most advantageous active market to which the entity has immediate access. In our view, while the market may have been mispricing the underlying value of traded securities due to inaccurate or incomplete information, a quoted price for a financial instrument in an active market should not be overridden.

IAS 39.48A
- *Unquoted instruments.* If there is no quoted price for a financial instrument in an active market then its fair value is determined using a valuation technique that incorporates all factors that knowledgeable market participants would consider in setting a price at the end of the reporting period. The measurement objective for an unquoted instrument measured at fair value is the same as the measurement objective for a quoted instrument measured at fair value – what the price was or would have been at the reporting date. Therefore, in our view a valuation that has as its objective the fair value at the reporting date should not reflect information that both was not and would not have been reasonably available to market participants at that date.

2.9.70.40 In some cases it may be difficult to separate the existence and the valuation issues. In our view, if it is impracticable to separate the existence and the valuation issues, then the entire effect should be treated as an issue related to the existence of assets. For example, Fund Q reports an investment in government bonds and had its investment adviser, K, act as a custodian; Fund Q discovers in March 2011 that K has been charged with fraud. In this case, K is alleged to have reported these government bonds as assets of multiple investors and their owner of record is an affiliate of K. While these government bonds were in existence, the existence of Fund Q's claim to those assets is uncertain.

IAS 10.21 2.9.70.50 If an entity concludes that the subsequent discovery of a fraud is a valuation issue, and therefore it is treated as a non-adjusting event, then such a non-adjusting event should be disclosed if it is material.

3.1 General
(IAS 1)

Chapter 3

3. Specific statement of financial position items

3.1 General
(IAS 1)

Overview of currently effective requirements

- Generally an entity presents its statement of financial position classified between current and non-current assets and liabilities. An unclassified statement of financial position based on the order of liquidity is acceptable only when it provides reliable and more relevant information.

- While IFRSs require certain items to be presented in the statement of financial position, there is no prescribed format.

- A liability that is payable on demand because certain conditions are breached is classified as current even if the lender has agreed, after the end of the reporting period but before the financial statements are authorised for issue, not to demand repayment.

- Some assets and liabilities that are part of working capital are classified as current even if they are due to be settled more than 12 months after the end of the reporting period.

Currently effective requirements

This publication reflects IFRSs in issue at 1 August 2010. The currently effective requirements cover annual periods beginning on 1 January 2010. The requirements related to this topic are derived mainly from IAS 1 *Presentation of Financial Statements*.

Forthcoming requirements and future developments

When a currently effective requirement will be changed by a new requirement that is issued but is not yet effective, it is marked with a # as a **forthcoming requirement** and the impact of the change is explained in the accompanying boxed text.

When a significant change to the currently effective or forthcoming requirements is expected, it is marked with a * as an area that may be subject to **future developments** and a brief outline of the relevant project is given in 3.1.60.

3.1.10 **Format of the statement of financial position***

IAS 1.10   3.1.10.05 The revised version of IAS 1, effective for annual periods beginning on or after 1 January 2009, replaced the term "balance sheet" with the term "statement of financial position". However, use of the new title is not mandatory (see 2.1.10.20).

IAS 1.60   3.1.10.10 IFRSs generally require an entity to present a classified statement of financial position, which distinguishes current from non-current assets and liabilities. However, entities may present assets and liabilities broadly in order of liquidity when such a presentation provides information that is reliable and more relevant.

IAS 1.64   3.1.10.20 An entity may present some of its assets and liabilities using a current/non-current classification and others in order of liquidity if such a mixed presentation provides information that is reliable and more relevant. In our experience, presentation based on the order of liquidity is used most commonly by financial institutions and insurance companies.

IAS 1.30-31,   3.1.10.30 When relevant to an understanding of the entity's financial position, the state-
55 ment of financial position includes line items, headings and subtotals in addition to the minimum items specified. Additional items may be presented because of their size or nature or to distinguish them from other items with different timing, liquidity or function. For example, an entity with significant trademarks may decide to present these separately in the statement of financial position, rather than combine them with other intangible assets.

3.1.20 **Current vs non-current***

3.1.30 *Assets*

IAS 1.66   3.1.30.10 An asset is classified as current if it meets any of the following conditions:

- it is expected to be realised in, or is held for sale or consumption in, the entity's normal operating cycle;
- it is held primarily for trading purposes;
- it is expected to be realised within 12 months of the end of the reporting period; or
- it is cash or a cash equivalent (see 2.3.10) that is not restricted from being exchanged or used to settle a liability for at least 12 months after the end of the reporting period.

3.1.30.20 For example, an entity constructs office buildings for third parties; often construction takes two to three years to complete. The entity's construction work in progress would be classified as a current asset because construction over two to three years is the entity's normal operating cycle.

3.1.30.30 If an entity has different operating cycles for different parts of the business (e.g. retail and construction), then the classification of an asset as current is based on the normal operating cycle that is relevant to that particular asset. In our view, the entity need not identify a single operating cycle.

IAS 1.61 3.1.30.40 If a line item in the statement of financial position includes a combination of assets that are expected to be realised both before and after 12 months of the end of the reporting period, then an entity discloses the amount expected to be realised after more than 12 months. For example, all trade receivables are classified as current assets (assuming that they are expected to be realised in their respective operating cycles), but an entity discloses in the notes the amount expected to be realised more than 12 months after the end of the reporting period.

IAS 1.68, 3.1.30.45 Financial assets, including derivatives, that are classified as held for trading
BC38A- and that are expected to be realised more than 12 months after the end of the reporting
BC38D period or outside of the entity's normal operating cycle are classified as non-current assets; this is despite their classification as held for trading (see 5.6.460.50).

IFRS 5.3, 3.1.30.50 A non-current asset is not classified as current unless it is classified as held for
IAS 1.66 sale (see 5.4.110).

IAS 1.68 3.1.30.60 The current portion of a non-current financial asset is classified as a current asset.

IAS 1.66 3.1.30.70 All assets that do not meet the definition of current assets are classified as non-current.

3.1.40 *Liabilities*

IAS 1.69 3.1.40.10 A liability is classified as current if it meets any of the following conditions:

- it is expected to be settled in the entity's normal operating cycle;
- it is held primarily for trading purposes;
- it is due to be settled within 12 months of the end of the reporting period; or
- it is not subject to an unconditional right of the entity to defer settlement of the liability for at least 12 months after the end of the reporting period.

3.1.40.15 Terms of a liability that could, at the option of the counterparty, result in its settlement by the issue of equity instruments, do not affect its classification.

AS 1.70, 71 3.1.40.20 Usually debt is classified as current or non-current based on whether it is due to be settled within 12 months of the end of the reporting period. However, if a liability is part of the working capital used in the entity's normal operating cycle, then it is classified as current even if it is due to be settled more than 12 months after the end of the reporting period. For example, an entity develops software for third parties that takes two years to complete and receives payment for this service upfront. Deferred revenue recognised as a result of the upfront payment is classified as current even if the related service is not expected to be performed within 12 months of the end of the reporting period.

IAS 1.61   3.1.40.30 As in the case of assets, if a line item in the statement of financial position includes a combination of liabilities that are expected to be settled both before and after 12 months of the end of the reporting period, then an entity discloses the amount expected to be settled after more than 12 months.

IAS 1.71,   3.1.40.35 Financial liabilities, as in the case of assets, including derivatives, that are
BC38A-   classified as held for trading and that are expected to be realised more than 12 months
BC38D   after the end of the reporting period or outside of the entity's normal operating cycle are classified as non-current liabilities; this is despite their classification as held for trading (see 5.6.460.50) and is consistent with the treatment of financial assets classified as held for trading (see 3.1.30.45).

3.1.40.37 In our view, liabilities of a disposal group classified as held for sale also are classified as current in the statement of financial position as they are expected to be realised within 12 months of the date of classification as held for sale (see 5.4.110.30).

IAS 1.71   3.1.40.40 If an entity presents a classified statement of financial position and has a long-term interest-bearing liability that includes a portion due within 12 months of the end of the reporting period and a portion due in later periods, then the liability is split into its current and non-current components.

IAS 1.72, 73   3.1.40.50 The current portion of long-term debt is classified as current even if an agreement to refinance or reschedule payments on a long-term basis is completed after the end of the reporting period but before the financial statements are authorised for issue. However, if an entity expects and is able, solely at its own discretion, to refinance or roll over an obligation for at least 12 months after the end of the reporting period under an existing loan facility, then it classifies the obligation as non-current even if the loan otherwise would be current.

3.1.40.55 For example, during the reporting period Company D borrowed from a bank under a five-year revolving facility. Under the terms of the facility, D can borrow 1,000 in fixed tranches that must be repaid twelve months after withdrawal. D expects and has the discretion to immediately redraw that same 1,000 for a further twelve months. In our view, the borrowings under the facility are presented as non-current liabilities as the entity has the intention and the discretion to refinance, i.e. immediately re-draw an equivalent amount.

IAS 1.74   3.1.40.57 A liability that is payable on demand because loan conditions have been breached is classified as current even if the lender has agreed, after the end of the reporting period but before the financial statements are authorised for issue, not to demand repayment as a result of the breach.

IAS 1.74-76,   3.1.40.60 A lending agreement may include covenants that if breached render the related
BC47   debt repayable before its contractual maturity date. Such an acceleration of required payments may be automatic or may be at the discretion of the lender. The debt is classified as current even if the lender agrees, subsequent to the reporting date, not to demand

payment as a consequence of the breach. However, the debt is classified as non-current if the lender agrees by the end of the reporting period to provide a period of grace ending at least 12 months after the end of the reporting period.

3.1.40.70 Under some circumstances compliance with a loan covenant is assessed after the end of the reporting period but the related tests for covenant compliance are based on financial information as at or before the end of the reporting period. In our view, any breach of such a covenant that renders the related debt payable within 12 months after the end of the reporting period is treated as an adjusting subsequent event (see 2.9.20) and the related liability is classified as current at the end of the reporting period.

3.1.40.80 In our view, covenant tests that are based on information as of a date after the end of the reporting period are disregarded when assessing the classification of the liability at the end of the reporting period, even when the entity assesses the likelihood of a breach at such future date as probable.

3.1.40.90 In some circumstances, an entity may, prior to the end of the reporting period, obtain from a lender an agreement to amend a lending arrangement. Such amendments may defer the date as of which information is assessed for testing covenant compliance from a date at or prior to the end of the reporting period to a later date. In our view, tests for covenant compliance based on information as of a date after the end of the reporting period are disregarded when assessing the classification of the liability at the end of the reporting period (see 3.1.40.80). Accordingly, we believe that in such situations whether or not the entity would have breached the related covenant had the agreement not been amended does not affect the classification of the liability at the end of the reporting period.

3.1.50 Offsetting

IAS 32.42   3.1.50.10 A financial asset and a financial liability are offset and reported net only when the entity has a legally enforceable right to offset and it intends to settle the asset and the liability either simultaneously or on a net basis (see 5.6.490).

3.1.50.20 Specific offsetting rules exist for deferred tax assets and liabilities (see 3.13.460) and defined benefit plan assets and obligations (see 4.4.420).

3.1.50.30 Non-financial assets and liabilities cannot be offset under IFRSs.

3.1.60 Future developments

3.1.60.10 The overall objective of the comprehensive financial statement presentation project is to establish a global standard that prescribes the basis for presentation of financial statements of an entity that are consistent over time, and that promote comparability between entities. The financial statement presentation project is conducted in three phases:

- Phase A was completed in September 2007 with the release of a revised IAS 1;
- Phase B is in progress and addresses the more fundamental issues related to financial statement presentation; and
- Phase C has not been initiated, but is expected to address issues related to interim financial statements.

3.1.60.20 In July 2010 the IASB posted a staff draft of a proposed ED reflecting tentative decisions made to date in respect of phase B to obtain further stakeholder feedback. An ED is scheduled for the first quarter of 2011.

3.2 Property, plant and equipment
(IAS 16, IFRIC 1, IFRIC 18)

3.2 Property, plant and equipment
(IAS 16, IFRIC 1, IFRIC 18)

Overview of currently effective requirements

- Property, plant and equipment is recognised initially at cost.

- Cost includes all expenditure directly attributable to bringing the asset to the location and working condition for its intended use.

- Cost includes the estimated cost of dismantling and removing the asset and restoring the site.

- Changes to an existing decommissioning or restoration obligation generally are added to or deducted from the cost of the related asset and depreciated prospectively over the remaining useful life of the asset.

- Borrowing costs that are directly attributable to the acquisition, construction or production of a qualifying asset form part of the cost of that asset.

- Property, plant and equipment is depreciated over its useful life.

- An item of property, plant and equipment is depreciated even if it is idle, but not if it is held for sale.

- Estimates of useful life and residual value, and the method of depreciation, are reviewed at least at each annual reporting date. Any changes are accounted for prospectively as a change in estimate.

- When an item of property, plant and equipment comprises individual components for which different depreciation methods or rates are appropriate, each component is depreciated separately.

- Subsequent expenditure is capitalised only when it is probable that it will give rise to future economic benefits.

- Property, plant and equipment may be revalued to fair value if fair value can be measured reliably. All items in the same class are revalued at the same time and the revaluations are kept up to date.

- Compensation for the loss or impairment of property, plant and equipment is recognised in profit or loss when receivable.

- The gain or loss on disposal is the difference between the net proceeds received and the carrying amount of the asset.

Currently effective requirements

This publication reflects IFRSs in issue at 1 August 2010. The currently effective requirements cover annual periods beginning on 1 January 2010. The requirements related to this topic are derived mainly from IAS 16 *Property, Plant and Equipment* and IFRIC 18 *Transfers of Assets from Customers*.

Forthcoming requirements and future developments

When a currently effective requirement will be changed by a new requirement that is issued but is not yet effective, it is marked with a # as a **forthcoming requirement** and the impact of the change is explained in the accompanying boxed text. In respect of this topic no forthcoming requirements are noted.

When a significant change to the currently effective or forthcoming requirements is expected, it is marked with a * as an area that may be subject to **future developments** and a brief outline of the relevant project is given in 3.2.470.

3.2.10 **Definition**

IAS 16.6 3.2.10.10 Property, plant and equipment comprises tangible assets held by an entity for use in the production or supply of goods or services, for rental to others or for administrative purposes, that are expected to be used for more than one period.

IAS 16.8 3.2.10.20 Spare parts and stand-by and servicing equipment held by an entity generally are classified as inventories (see 3.8.30). However, if major spare parts and stand-by equipment are expected to be used for more than one period or can be used only in connection with an item of property, plant and equipment, then they are classified as property, plant and equipment.

IAS 16.9, 37 3.2.10.25 IAS 16 does not prescribe what constitutes an item of property, plant and equipment. Therefore, judgement is required in determining the unit of account to which the recognition and measurement requirements of IAS 16 should be applied. For example, individually insignificant items, such as tools and dies, may be combined into a single unit of account in some circumstances. However, in our view generally an item that is separately identifiable and individually significant will constitute a unit of account under IAS 16. The assessment of whether an item is significant requires an entity to consider all facts and circumstances. For example, an entity might compare the total cost of the aggregated items to the cost of the item under review. Items of a dissimilar nature and use in an entity's operations constitute separate classes of property, plant and equipment (see 3.2.370) and may not be aggregated.

3.2.10.30 A long-term leasehold interest in a property classified as an operating lease may be classified as an investment property (see 5.1.235.20). In our view, any payment made to acquire such a leasehold interest is classified as a lease prepayment rather than as property, plant and equipment.

3.2.20 **Initial recognition**

IAS 16.7   3.2.20.10 Property, plant and equipment is recognised if, and only if, it is probable that future economic benefits associated with the item will flow to the entity and its cost can be measured reliably.

IAS 16.15   3.2.20.20 Property, plant and equipment is recognised initially at cost.

AS 16.7, 24,   3.2.20.30 An entity that has received a customer contribution within the scope of IFRIC 18
IFRIC 18.9,   recognises an asset if it determines that the transferred item meets the definition of an
11   asset and the recognition criteria for property, plant and equipment. In this regard it is not essential that the entity has legal ownership of the item of property, plant and equipment.

FRIC 18.10   3.2.20.40 The interpretation applies to transfers of property, plant and equipment that the recipient is required to use to connect the customer to a network or to provide the customer with ongoing access to a supply of goods or services, or both. Generally the receiving entity is not able to use that asset for purposes other than the provision of services to the contributor and, in certain circumstances, to other parties; nor is the receiving entity able to exchange the asset, to distribute it to its owners or to use it to settle liabilities. However, the restrictions imposed on the use of the asset by the terms of the arrangement do not preclude the receiving entity from assessing that it controls the asset.

IAS 16.24,   3.2.20.50 The cost of an item of property, plant and equipment received in exchange
RIC 18.11,   for services to be provided is determined by reference to its fair value when
BC14   it is received. Depending on the circumstances and the nature of the asset, the determination of fair value may be a difficult exercise. When determining the fair value of the asset received, an entity takes into account all of its characteristics at the date of initial recognition, such as covenants and restrictions attached, including those arising from rate regulation.

3.2.30 *Directly attributable expenditure*

AS 16.16(b)   3.2.30.10 Cost includes all expenditure directly attributable to bringing the asset to the location and condition necessary for its intended use. "Intended use" means being capable of operating in the manner intended by management.

   3.2.30.20 Borrowing costs that are directly attributable to the acquisition, construction or production of a qualifying asset form part of the cost of that asset (see 4.6.350).

S 16.16(c),   3.2.30.30 The cost of an item of property, plant and equipment includes the estimated
RIC 1.5(a)   cost of its dismantlement, removal or restoration. This includes not only the initial estimate of such costs made at the time of installing the item, but also changes in that initial estimate and costs incurred through operations (use) for purposes other than producing inventory. For example, changes in the original estimate of dismantlement, removal or restoration costs are recognised as changes in the cost of the item (see 3.2.90).

3.2 Property, plant and equipment

IAS 16.17(a) 3.2.30.40 The cost of employee benefits, including share-based payment transactions, that are incurred for employees working directly on the construction or acquisition of the asset are directly attributable costs of that item.

3.2.30.50 The costs incurred need not be external or incremental in order to be directly attributable. For example, Company G is installing a major piece of equipment at one of its factories. One of G's existing engineers is assigned to manage the installation on a full-time basis; installation is expected to take six weeks. In our view, the cost of the engineer, including all employee benefits, during the period of installation should be included in the cost of the equipment even though those costs would have been incurred in any event.

3.2.30.60 In some cases an entity will incur expenditure in carrying out a feasibility study prior to deciding whether to invest in an asset or in deciding which asset to acquire. In our view, expenses incurred for feasibility assessment should be expensed as incurred because they are not linked to a specific item of property, plant and equipment. This is consistent with the approach taken under IFRSs for the development of a website (see 3.3.130). However, in our view the cost of property, plant and equipment does include expenditure that is incurred only if an asset is acquired. For example, a fee may be payable to a broker or agent only if a suitable property is identified and purchased. We believe that such a fee is directly attributable to the acquisition of the property acquired and therefore should be included in the cost of the property.

IAS 16.19(c) 3.2.30.70 Often staff need to be trained in the use of a new item of property, plant and equipment. Training costs are not recognised as part of the cost of an item of property, plant and equipment. If the asset is installed by a third party and training is part of the total contract price, then in our view some part of the total price should be allocated to training and expensed as incurred.

IAS 16.19(a) 3.2.30.80 The costs of opening a new facility, as well as general overhead and administrative costs, are not part of the cost of an item of property, plant and equipment. For example, Company B rents a retail store under an operating lease. The store could be opened immediately but B will first re-brand the store so that it conforms with the design of its other stores. B cannot commence the renovations until it takes possession of the store. In our view, lease payments incurred during the renovation period should be expensed as incurred, regardless of whether the renovations are avoidable or unavoidable. Therefore, we believe that B would expense the lease payments as incurred even if the store were incapable of being opened prior to renovation.

IAS 16.19(a), 23.10 3.2.30.85 In another example, if a building is constructed on land that is leased under an operating lease, then in our view the land operating lease costs incurred during the construction period may be capitalised as part of the cost of the building provided that these costs are directly attributable to bringing the asset to the location and condition necessary for it to be capable of operating in the manner intended by management. The approach should be applied consistently. In our view, land operating lease costs incurred during the construction period do not constitute the costs of opening a new facility, and are analogous to borrowing costs that are directly attributable to the construction of a qualifying asset.

AS 16.20(b) 3.2.30.90 Initial operating losses such as those incurred while demand for the item's output builds up are not part of the cost of an item of property, plant and equipment.

3.2.30.100 An entity may purchase land with the intention of constructing a new building on the site. In our view, the cost of demolishing any existing building on the site should be capitalised as part of the cost of the property. However, it is not clear whether the cost should be capitalised to the cost of the land or to the cost of the building; this distinction is important because land and buildings generally are depreciated differently (see 3.2.140). In our view, the amount should be capitalised to the cost of the building because the demolition is a direct result of the decision to construct a new building.

3.2.30.110 A similar but less common example is when an entity relocates a community (or part thereof) in order to construct an asset. For example, Company D plans to construct a golf course on a site occupied currently by a small town. D agrees to pay the cost of relocating the residents to another site. In our view, the relocation costs should be capitalised as they are directly attributable to the construction of the golf course.

3.2.30.120 While it is common for the design of a complex asset to be modified and improved during construction, care should be taken to avoid double counting costs. For example, Company E is constructing a hotel; the cost of designing the hotel has been capitalised as part of the cost of the asset. During construction the directors of E reassess their plans and decide that a hotel is no longer viable in the current economic environment. Instead, the directors decide to develop the site into a retirement village, which requires a complete redesign of the site. In our view, although it is appropriate to capitalise the cost of designing the retirement village, the original hotel design costs should be written off since they are not part of the eventual asset. A similar approach should be adopted for any other costs (e.g. construction costs) that do not form part of the eventual asset because of changes made in the course of construction.

AS 16.16(b) 3.2.30.130 In our view, cancellation costs incurred in order to acquire an item of property, plant and equipment are not directly attributable costs as they are not directly related to the acquisition of that item and are not required to bring the item to the location and condition necessary for it to be capable of operating in the manner intended by management. For example, Company T has signed a contract with Company S to purchase several machines over the next five years. T can cancel the contract in relation to undelivered machines, but only if it pays a cancellation fee. One year after signing the contract, T receives an offer from Company Q to supply the remaining machines at a significantly lower cost. T cancels the contract with S and incurs the cancellation fee. In our view, the cancellation fee should not be capitalised as part of the cost of the machines purchased from Q; instead it should be expensed as incurred.

3.2.40 *Abnormal waste*

IAS 16.22 3.2.40.10 Similar to determining the cost of inventory (see 3.8.120), when an item of property, plant and equipment is constructed by an entity, the standard requires abnormal amounts of wasted material, labour and other resources to be expensed as incurred instead of being capitalised. A determination of what should be considered "abnormal" is subjective, but in our view the factors to consider include the level of technical difficulty involved with the construction, the scale of the project, the estimates and timelines included in the project planning, and the usual construction process for that type of asset.

3.2.40.20 For example, Company F is constructing a plant that produces plastic building blocks for children. During the commissioning phase, which should take two weeks, sample building blocks are produced to ensure that the plant is operating correctly; the engineers use the test results to finalise the calibration of the machines. Most of the building blocks produced during testing are unfit for sale and are disposed of. The commissioning phase lasts two weeks as scheduled. In this example the costs incurred as part of the testing are a normal part of the construction process and the related costs should be capitalised.

3.2.40.30 Continuing the example in 3.2.40.20, if commissioning was due to take two weeks but actually took four weeks (e.g. because a trainee engineer had installed a machine incorrectly or because site management forgot to schedule machine operators for the testing phase), then in our view any additional costs incurred as a result of such events should be considered abnormal and expensed as incurred. The additional costs could be measured by reference to the amount of testing that was planned.

3.2.40.40 Staying with the same example, if testing took four weeks instead of two because F was introducing a new and previously untested technology into its production process and unforeseen technical difficulties were experienced, then in our view the additional costs incurred should be capitalised because the costs are not abnormal.

IAS 16.22 3.2.40.50 Abnormal waste is discussed in the context of assets that are constructed by the entity. In our view, these principles apply equally when the asset is not constructed by the entity, but the installation process nonetheless is necessary to bring the asset to its working condition.

3.2.50 *Pre-operating costs and losses*

IAS 16.19 3.2.50.10 Start-up and pre-operating costs are not capitalised as part of the cost of property, plant and equipment unless those costs are necessary to bring the asset to its working condition. For example, Company G is opening a new plant in a town where it has not operated previously. In addition to obtaining a certificate to confirm that the plant meets environmental specifications, G is required to obtain general permits that allow it to conduct business in the town. In our view, the cost of these permits should not be capitalised because it is a general business cost that does not relate specifically to the asset.

IAS 16.20   3.2.50.20 An entity may incur losses prior to the asset reaching its planned performance level; such losses are not capitalised. Continuing the example in 3.2.40.20 – 40 of F and its building blocks, if after installation F runs the new plant at half capacity for a month while staff are trained in how to use it correctly, then any loss incurred during that period would be recognised in profit or loss.

3.2.60 *Interruptions*

IAS 23.21   3.2.60.10 In some cases construction will not be continuous and interruptions will occur during which time costs still may be incurred. For example, the entity may have to continue paying site insurance costs. IFRSs are silent as to whether such costs may be capitalised, but in our view the guidance in IAS 23 *Borrowing Costs* regarding the capitalisation of borrowing costs is relevant (see 4.6.350).

3.2.60.20 Accordingly, we believe that costs incurred during an interruption should be capitalised only if:

- the interruption is temporary and is a necessary part of getting the asset into its working condition, e.g. the construction of a bridge is suspended while water levels are high, provided that such costs are not abnormal waste (see 3.2.40); or
- the costs are an integral part of getting the asset into its working condition even though physical construction has been suspended, e.g. the cost of delays for obtaining permits for the eventual operation of the asset.

3.2.70 *Decommissioning*

AS 16.16(c)   3.2.70.10 The cost of property, plant and equipment includes the estimated cost of dismantling and removing the asset and restoring the site to the extent that such cost is recognised as a provision (see 3.12.420).

IAS 37.IE.   3.2.70.20 For example, Company H constructs a chemical plant that has a useful life of
C.Ex3   30 years. Environmental laws require H to dismantle the plant at the end of its useful life. H recognises a provision for removal costs, which is capitalised as part of the cost of the asset. No provision is made, and no amount capitalised, in respect of damage that has yet to occur, i.e. damage caused by future operations rather than by the construction of the asset.

S 16.16(c),   3.2.70.30 The cost of an item of property, plant and equipment includes not only the
18,   initial estimate of the costs related to the dismantlement, removal or restoration of
'RIC 1.5(a)   property, plant or equipment at the time of installing the item, but also costs incurred during the period of use for purposes other than producing inventory. Decommissioning and restoration costs incurred through the production of inventory are included as part of inventory costs (see 3.8.180). For example, the installation and testing of H's new chemical plant results in contamination of the ground at the plant. H will be required to clean up the contamination caused by the installation when the plant is dismantled. H recognises a provision for restoration, which is capitalised as part of the cost of the

asset. If the contamination had occurred as a consequence of the production of inventory, then the cost would be included in the cost of inventory or expensed in the period (e.g. if the costs were abnormal) as appropriate.

3.2.80 *Changes to existing provisions*

IFRIC 1.3 3.2.80.10 Subsequent to initial recognition the amount of a decommissioning provision generally will change due to the following:

- changes in the estimate of the amount or timing of expenditures required to dismantle the plant;
- changes in the discount rate; and
- the unwinding of the discount.

IFRIC 1.4, 5 3.2.80.20 The accounting for changes to an existing obligation due to changes in the estimated timing or amount of expenditures or a discount rate is consistent with the accounting treatment for changes in estimates (see 2.8.60). This treatment is discussed further in 3.2.90 – 100.

IAS 21.23(a), 28, IFRIC 1 3.2.80.25 IFRSs are not clear on how an entity should account for foreign exchange gains and losses arising on the retranslation of a decommissioning provision. Foreign currency denominated obligations are translated at current exchange rates when the obligation is a monetary liability. Non-monetary liabilities denominated in a foreign currency are not retranslated (see 2.7.110.10). In our view, a decommissioning liability is monetary if it is expected to be settled by payment of a fixed or determinable number of units of currency, or non-monetary if it will be settled by providing services (i.e. by the entity carrying out the remedial works itself or by paying another party to do so) or a non-monetary asset. Generally, foreign exchange gains and losses arising on the retranslation of monetary items are recognised immediately in profit or loss (see 2.7.140.10). However, IFRIC 1 *Changes in Existing Decommissioning, Restoration and Similar Liabilities* requires changes in a decommissioning provision resulting from changes in estimated cash flows to be added to or deducted from the cost of the related asset. In our view, an entity should choose an accounting policy, to be applied consistently, either to recognise foreign exchange gains and losses arising on the retranslation of decommissioning provisions in profit or loss, or to recognise them as adjustments to the cost of the related asset (see 3.12.475).

3.2.90 Cost model

IFRIC 1.5(a), (b) 3.2.90.10 Under the cost model all changes in the liability, other than changes resulting from the unwinding of the discount (see 3.2.80.10), are added to or deducted from the cost of the related asset in the current period. However, the amount deducted from the cost of the asset cannot exceed its carrying amount. Any excess is recognised immediately in profit or loss since an asset cannot have a negative carrying amount.

IFRIC 1.5(c) 3.2.90.20 An increase in the cost of an asset may require consideration of whether there is an indication of impairment (see 3.10.110).

3.2.90.30 For example, Company X built a new plant that was brought into use on 1 January 2010. The cost to construct the plant was 1,500. The estimated useful life of the plant is 20 years and X accounts for plant using the cost model.

3.2.90.40 The initial carrying amount of the plant included an amount of 100 for decommissioning, which was determined using a discount rate of 10 percent. At the end of 2010, X remeasures the provision for decommissioning to 130. Accordingly, X records the following entries in the year ending 31 December 2010:

	Debit	Credit
Depreciation (profit or loss)	75	
Accumulated depreciation (plant)		75
To recognise depreciation of plant (1,500 x 5%)		
Interest expense (profit or loss)	10	
Provision for decommissioning		10
To recognise unwinding of discount on provision (100 x 10%) (see 3.12.840)		
Plant	20	
Provision for decommissioning		20
To recognise increase in provision (130 - (100 + 10))		

3.2.100 Revaluation model

IAS 16.34 3.2.100.10 Under the revaluation model, valuations should be kept sufficiently up to date such that the carrying amount does not differ materially from its fair value at the reporting date. A change in the liability does not, of itself, affect the valuation of the asset, since the value of the liability should be excluded from the asset valuation.

RIC 1.6(a), (b) 3.2.100.20 The change in the liability affects the difference between the valuation and what would have been recognised under the cost model. Therefore, changes in the liability other than changes resulting from the unwinding of the discount (see 3.2.80.10) affect the revaluation surplus or deficit recognised previously in respect of that asset:

- A decrease in the liability is recognised in other comprehensive income, except to the extent that it reverses a revaluation deficit recognised previously in profit or loss, or when it would result in the depreciated cost of the asset being negative (see 3.2.100.30).
- An increase in the liability is recognised in profit or loss, except to the extent that any credit balance remains in the revaluation surplus in equity.

IFRIC 1.6(b) 3.2.100.30 The depreciated cost of the asset cannot be negative. For example, suppose that the depreciated cost of an unimpaired asset is 25 and its revalued amount is 100, giving a revaluation surplus of 75. If the decommissioning liability is reduced by 30, then 25 is recognised in other comprehensive income, which notionally reduces the depreciated cost to zero, and the remaining 5 is recognised in profit or loss.

IAS 16.36,
IFRIC 1.6(c) 3.2.100.40 A change in the liability is an indicator that the market value of the asset also may have changed and an entity should consider whether a revaluation is required. If a revaluation of the impacted asset is required, then all other assets in the same asset class are revalued.

3.2.100.50 For example, Company X built a new plant that was brought into use on 1 January 2010. The cost to construct the plant was 1,500. The estimated useful life of the plant is 20 years and X accounts for plant using the revaluation model.

3.2.100.60 The initial carrying amount of the plant included an amount of 100 for decommissioning, which was determined using a discount rate of 10 percent. At the end of 2010, X remeasures the provision for decommissioning to 130. X also revalues the plant at the end of 2010 to an amount of 1,800. Accordingly, X records the following entries in the year ending 31 December 2010:

	Debit	Credit
Depreciation (profit or loss)	75	
Accumulated depreciation (plant)		75
To recognise depreciation of plant (1,500 x 5%)		
Interest expense (profit or loss)	10	
Provision for decommissioning		10
To recognise unwinding of discount on provision		
(100 x 10%) (see 3.12.840)		
Plant	375	
Revaluation surplus (other comprehensive income)		375
To recognise revaluation of plant		
(1,800 - (1,500 - 75)) (see 3.2.380)		
Revaluation surplus (other comprehensive income)	20	
Provision for decommissioning		20
To recognise increase in provision (130 - (100 + 10))		

3.2.100.70 Assume the same facts as in 3.2.100.50 – 60 except that X revalues the plant at the end of 2010 to an amount of 1,440. Accordingly, X records the following entries in the year ending 31 December 2010:

	Debit	Credit
Depreciation (profit or loss)	75	
Accumulated depreciation (plant)		75
To recognise depreciation of plant (1,500 x 5%)		
Interest expense (profit or loss)	10	
Provision for decommissioning		10
To recognise unwinding of discount on provision		
(100 x 10%) (see 3.12.840)		
Plant	15	
Revaluation surplus (other comprehensive income)		15
To recognise revaluation of plant (1,440 - (1,500 - 75))		
(see 3.2.380)		
Revaluation surplus (other comprehensive income)	15	
Profit or loss	5	
Provision for decommissioning		20
To recognise increase in provision (130 - (100 + 10))		

3.2.105 Fully depreciated property, plant and equipment

IFRIC 1.7 3.2.105.10 Once an item of property, plant and equipment has been fully depreciated and the asset has a net carrying amount (gross carrying amount less accumulated depreciation) of zero in the statement of financial position, further changes in any related provision for decommissioning are recognised in profit or loss. This applies under both the cost model and the revaluation model, i.e. regardless of whether any revaluation surplus remains recognised in equity.

3.2.110 *New obligations*

IAS 37.IE. 3.2.110.10 IFRSs contain no explicit guidance for a new obligation that arises subsequent
C.Ex2A to the initial recognition of the asset. Continuing the example in 3.2.70.20 – 30, when H first constructs its chemical plant there are no applicable environmental laws. However, two years later the government introduces a new law requiring the plant to be dismantled at the end of its useful life. In our view, the principles that apply to changes in estimates of existing obligations should be applied and the amount of the provision should be recognised as part of the cost of the asset. The capitalisation of these costs should not result in the carrying amount of the asset exceeding its recoverable amount (see 3.10.180).

3.2.120 *Incidental operations*

3.2.120.10 Generally there are two types of incidental income:

- Income earned from the operation of the asset. For example, referring back to the example in 3.2.40.20 – 40, Company F earns income from the sale of imperfect samples of building blocks produced during testing.
- Income incidental to the construction of the asset, but not generated by the asset itself. For example, Company K acquires a sports hall with the intention of constructing a supermarket on the site. While K waits to receive permits for the construction, it rents out the sports facilities to a local school.

IAS 16.17(e) 3.2.120.20 Incidental income from operating (including testing) a new asset is part of the directly attributable cost of the asset. Therefore income earned in the example in 3.2.120.10 from selling the building blocks produced during testing is deducted from the cost of testing the asset. The cost of testing the asset (less the income) is recognised as part of the cost of the item of property, plant and equipment. If the income from the testing activity is higher than the cost of testing the asset, then the net effect will be a deduction from the cost of the asset.

IAS 16.21 3.2.120.30 Other incidental operations (e.g. the rental of the sports facilities in 3.2.120.10) are not considered necessary to bring the item to the location and condition necessary for it to be capable of operating in the manner intended by management. Therefore income and expenses from incidental operations are recognised in profit or loss, included in their respective classifications of income and expense.

3.2.130 *Deferred payment*

IAS 16.23 3.2.130.10 When payment is deferred beyond normal credit terms, the cost of the asset is the cash price equivalent (i.e. current cash price) at the recognition date. This calculation is different from the calculation of the financial liability (the amount due in respect of the acquisition) that otherwise would be made under IAS 39 *Financial Instruments: Recognition and Measurement*, which would require the cash flows to be discounted using a market rate of interest (see 3.6.740). However, in our view the requirements of IAS 16 should apply because the standard addresses specifically deferred payment for property, plant and equipment.

3.2.130.20 The difference between the cash price equivalent and the amount payable is recognised as interest expense over the period until payment, unless it is capitalised in accordance with IAS 23. In our view, the effective interest method should be applied as it would for other financial instrument liabilities (see 4.6.40) since there is nothing to the contrary in IAS 16.

3.2.140 **Depreciation**

IAS 16.43, 51 3.2.140.10 Subsequent to initial recognition, property, plant and equipment is depreciated on a systematic basis over its useful life. Each part of an item of property, plant and equipment with a cost that is significant in relation to the total cost of the item is depreciated separately.

IAS 16.51, 61   3.2.140.20 The useful life of an asset and the depreciation method applied is reviewed at least at each annual reporting date. A change in the useful life or depreciation method is accounted for prospectively as a change in accounting estimate (see 2.8.60).

3.2.140.30 For example, Company L acquired a printing machine at the beginning of 2007 and its useful life was estimated to be 10 years. At the end of 2009 the carrying amount of the machine was 240. At the beginning of 2010 L revises the estimated useful life downwards to a further two years from that date. Therefore the carrying amount of 240 should be depreciated over the next two years (2010 and 2011). In addition, the decrease in useful life may indicate that the carrying amount of the machine is impaired (see 3.10.120).

IAS 16.6, 50, 60   3.2.140.40 The purpose of depreciation is not the recognition of decreases in the value of property, plant and equipment; rather, the purpose is to allocate the cost or revalued amount of an asset over its useful life on a systematic basis. Therefore, depreciation is recognised even if the value of the asset (e.g. a hotel) is being maintained by regular repairs and maintenance.

IAS 16.48   3.2.140.50 The depreciation charge for each period is recognised as an expense in profit or loss, unless it is included in the carrying amount of another asset. For example, the depreciation of manufacturing plant and equipment is included in the cost of inventories.

3.2.150 *Residual value*

IAS 16.6   3.2.150.10 An asset's depreciable amount is its cost less its residual value. Residual value is the amount that an entity could receive for the asset at the reporting date if the asset were already of the age and in the condition that it will be in when the entity expects to dispose of it. Residual value does not include expected future inflation.

IAS 16.6, 53   3.2.150.20 The estimated residual value is based on similar assets that have reached the end of their useful lives at the date that the estimate is made. In many cases the residual value will be zero because the asset will be scrapped at the end of its useful life.

3.2.150.30 For example, Company M buys a machine costing 400. M plans to use the machine for three years before selling it on the second-hand market. At the acquisition date similar machines that are three years old are traded for 150 on the second-hand market. Therefore, residual value is 150 and the depreciable amount is 250.

IAS 16.51   3.2.150.40 The residual value of an asset is reviewed at least at each annual reporting date and changes in the residual value are accounted as a change in accounting estimate (see 2.8.60).

IAS 16.54   3.2.150.50 If the residual value of an asset increases to an amount equal to or more than the asset's carrying amount, then the asset's depreciation charge will be zero. The entity would resume charging depreciation when the residual value falls below the asset's carrying amount.

3.2 Property, plant and equipment

3.2.160 **Methods of depreciation**

IAS 16.60, 61   3.2.160.10 The method of depreciation reflects the pattern in which the benefits associated with the asset are consumed, and is reviewed at least at each annual reporting date.

IAS 16.61   3.2.160.20 A change in the depreciation method is accounted for prospectively as a change in accounting estimate (see 2.8.60).

IAS 16.62   3.2.160.30 IFRSs do not require a specific method of depreciation to be used, and mention the straight-line method, the diminishing (or reducing balance) method and the sum-of-the-units (or unit-of-production) method. Other methods of depreciation that are not mentioned in the standard include the annuity method and renewals accounting.

3.2.170 *Straight-line method*

3.2.170.10 In our experience, the straight-line method is used most commonly, and in our view it is the most appropriate method when the level of consumption of an asset over the years is uncertain.

3.2.170.20 For example, a machine cost 150, has a residual value of 30 and a useful life of eight years. Therefore, the annual depreciation charge is:

Yr 1	Yr 2	Yr 3	Yr 4	Yr 5	Yr 6	Yr 7	Yr 8
15	15	15	15	15	15	15	15

3.2.180 *Reducing balance method*

3.2.180.10 Under the reducing balance method, depreciation is measured as a percentage of the current carrying amount of the asset (i.e. cost or revalued amount less accumulated depreciation to date). Using the same example as before, the machine would be depreciated at 18.25[1] percent per annum in order to reduce the carrying amount to the residual value of 30 at the end of eight years. Therefore the annual depreciation charge would be:

Yr 1	Yr 2	Yr 3	Yr 4	Yr 5	Yr 6	Yr 7	Yr 8
27	22	18	15	12	10	8	7

---

(1)   Calculated using the following formula: $R = 1 - n\sqrt{\dfrac{RV}{C}}$, with
     R – depreciation rate
     n – useful life in years
     RV – residual value of the asset
     C – cost of the asset

3.2.180.20 Using this method the depreciation charge declines over the years, which is appropriate when the machine provides greater benefits to the entity in its earlier years, for example because it will be less capable of producing a high-quality product in later years, or because the machine will be less technologically advanced in later years.

3.2.190 *Unit-of-production method*

3.2.190.10 Under the unit-of-production method, depreciation is based on the level of output or usage expected to be achieved. While this method may provide a more accurate picture of the consumption of an asset, it may be difficult to estimate the expected output over the life of the asset.

3.2.190.20 Continuing the example in 3.2.170.20, assume that the expected output over the life of the asset is 8,600 units and that the estimated annual output is as follows:

Yr 1	Yr 2	Yr 3	Yr 4	Yr 5	Yr 6	Yr 7	Yr 8
1,500	1,200	1,200	1,100	1,100	1,000	1,000	500

3.2.190.30 Therefore, the annual depreciation charge would be:

Yr 1	Yr 2	Yr 3	Yr 4	Yr 5	Yr 6	Yr 7	Yr 8
21	17	17	15	15	14	14	7

IAS 16.51 3.2.190.40 If this method of depreciation is used, then the estimates of future production would be reviewed and revised if necessary at each annual reporting date in accordance with the requirement to review the expected useful life. The impact on depreciation expense of a revision to estimates of future production would be treated as a change in estimate (see 2.8.60) and previous depreciation would not be restated.

3.2.200 *Annuity depreciation*

3.2.200.10 "Annuity depreciation" refers to depreciation methods under which the depreciation charge is adjusted to reflect the time value of money. Such depreciation methods result in lower depreciation charges in initial periods and larger depreciation charges in later periods. These methods are used under some national accounting practices, for example by operating lessors in order to recognise a level profit after considering financing costs related to the leased asset over the lease term. In our view, the financing costs of an asset should not impact the selection of a depreciation policy. IFRSs require depreciation to reflect the consumption of the economic benefits of an asset. We believe that this does not extend to consideration of financing costs or inflation adjustments.

3.2.210 *Renewals accounting*

3.2.210.10 In some countries it has been common in certain industries (e.g. utilities) not to recognise depreciation on the basis that the assets are maintained at a certain performance or service level and all maintenance costs, including costs incurred to replace components of the asset, are expensed immediately. It has been argued that the amount recognised in profit or loss in respect of the upkeep of the assets is similar to the depreciation charge that would have been recognised.

3.2.210.20 A variation on renewals accounting is condition-based depreciation whereby the condition of the asset is assessed and depreciation is measured as the increased cost required to restore the asset to a predetermined performance or service level.

3.2.210.30 In our view, these methods of depreciation are not acceptable under IFRSs unless the impact on the financial statements is immaterial.

3.2.220 **Commencement of depreciation**

IAS 16.55   3.2.220.10 Depreciation of an asset begins when it is available or ready for use (i.e. when it is in the location and condition necessary for it to be capable of operating in the manner intended by management). In some cases depreciation may commence before the asset actually is brought into use.

3.2.220.20 For example, Company N buys computer equipment that it knows will be technologically obsolete after two years. The equipment is ready for use when acquired, but N does not bring it into use until six months after the acquisition. In our view, depreciation should commence when the asset is ready for use.

3.2.220.30 In addition, when an item of property, plant and equipment is substantially complete, but is not yet in use, an entity should ensure that the asset is reviewed for potential indicators of impairment (see 3.10.120).

3.2.230 **Component accounting**

IAS 16.43-49   3.2.230.10 When an item of property, plant and equipment comprises individual components for which different depreciation methods or rates are appropriate, each component is depreciated separately. A separate component may be either a physical component or a non-physical component that represents a major inspection or overhaul. An item of property, plant and equipment is separated into parts ("components") when those parts are significant in relation to the total cost of the item.

IAS 16.46   3.2.230.20 Component accounting is compulsory when it would be applicable. However, this does not mean that an entity should split its assets into an infinite number of components if the effect on the financial statements would be immaterial.

IAS 16.46   3.2.230.30 When an entity depreciates some parts of an item of property, plant and equipment separately, it depreciates the remainder of the item separately. The remainder consists of the parts of the item that are not significant individually. If an entity has varying expectations for these parts, then it uses approximation techniques to estimate an appropriate depreciation pattern for the remainder to reflect the consumption pattern and/or usefulness of its parts.

3.2.230.40 For example, Company Q buys a machine for 100. The machine consists of four components, of which two components comprise 80 of the total cost of 100. The remaining two components have a cost of 10 each, which is considered insignificant, and they have useful lives of 4 and 6 years respectively. In our view, in this situation these two components could be combined to give a cost of 20 and a useful life of 5 years.

3.2.230.50 Although individual components are accounted for separately, the financial statements continue to disclose a single asset. For example, an airline generally would disclose aircraft as a class of assets, rather than disclosing separate information in respect of the aircraft body, hydraulics, engines, seating etc.

3.2.240 *Physical components*

3.2.240.10 When the component is a physical component (e.g. the motor in an engine) the carrying amount of the component is determined by reference to its cost. For example, Company O constructs a sports stadium that has an overall useful life of 50 years; one of the components of the stadium is the seating, which has an expected useful life of 10 years. The cost of the stadium in total is 500, which included 50 in respect of the seating. Therefore, the seating component is measured at 50 and has a useful life of 10 years.

3.2.240.20 In many cases an entity acquires an asset for a fixed sum without knowing the cost of the individual components. In our view, the cost of individual components should be estimated either by reference to current market prices (if possible), in consultation with the seller or contractor, or using some other reasonable method of approximation (e.g. relative values).

3.2.250 *Major inspection or overhaul costs*

IAS 16.14   3.2.250.10 Major inspections and overhauls are identified and accounted for as a separate component if that component is used over more than one period.

S 16.13, 14   3.2.250.20 When a major inspection or overhaul cost is embedded in the cost of an item of property, plant and equipment, it is necessary to estimate the carrying amount of the component. The carrying amount of the component is determined by reference to the *current* market price of such overhauls and not the expected future price.

3.2.250.30 For example, Company P runs a merchant shipping business and has just acquired a new ship for 400. The useful life of the ship is 15 years, but it will be dry-docked every three years and a major overhaul carried out. At the acquisition date the dry-docking costs for similar ships that are three years old are approximately 80. Therefore, the cost of the dry-docking component for accounting purposes is 80 and this amount would be depreciated over the three years to the next dry-docking. The remaining carrying amount, which may need to be split into further components, is 320. Any additional components will be depreciated over their own estimated useful lives.

IAS 16.12 3.2.250.40 Component accounting for inspection or overhaul costs is intended to be used only for major expenditure that occurs at regular intervals over the life of an asset. Costs associated with routine repairs and maintenance are expensed as incurred.

3.2.260 Costs to be included

3.2.260.10 IFRSs are silent with regard to the specific costs that should be included in measuring the component attributable to major inspection or overhaul costs (i.e. whether they should be incremental and/or external costs).

3.2.260.20 Continuing the example in 3.2.250.30 of P and its ship, the current market price of a dry-docking service is 80. However, P's currently-employed technicians will carry out most of the work of future dry-dockings and the external costs incurred are likely to be only 30. In our view, the entity should attribute the entire 80 to the component on the basis that the cost of an item of property, plant and equipment includes internal as well as external costs, and there is no requirement for the costs to be incremental (see 3.2.30.50).

3.2.270 Relationship with physical components

3.2.270.10 IFRSs do not address the allocation of costs to a major inspection or overhaul when the underlying asset comprises a number of physical components. Continuing the example in 3.2.260.20, P's ship comprises two physical components: the ship's body of 250 and the engines of 150. The dry-docking will involve servicing both of these components. In reality the ship would comprise a number of other components; however, the example has been simplified for illustrative purposes.

3.2.270.20 In our view, one acceptable method of allocating the cost of the dry-docking component between the ship's body and the engines is on the basis of their relative carrying amounts. On this basis, the components of the ship would be:

•	dry-docking costs	80	
•	body	200	(250 - (250 / 400) x 80)
•	engines	120	(150 - (150 / 400) x 80)

3.2.270.30 This issue arises only prior to the first major inspection or overhaul being carried out because the component cost is assumed rather than actual.

3.2.280 *Replacing a component*

IAS 16.14 3.2.280.10 The remaining portion of a component that is replaced by a new component is derecognised. Continuing the example in 3.2.260.20, P carries out the dry-docking of its ship after two years instead of three as originally envisaged. The carrying amount of the overhaul at that date is 27 (80 / 3). The actual dry-docking costs are 100.

3.2.280.20 The remaining carrying amount of the component that has been replaced is written off immediately because the component effectively has been disposed of. However, in our view the amount written off should be included in depreciation instead of being classified as a loss on disposal because the requirement is to depreciate each asset separately. We believe that the extra depreciation of 27 is in effect a revision of the estimated useful life of the dry-docking.

3.2.280.30 The actual dry-docking costs of 100 will be capitalised to the cost of the ship and depreciated over the expected period until the next dry-docking.

3.2.290 Subsequent expenditure

IAS 16.7, 12   3.2.290.10 Subsequent expenditure on an item of property, plant and equipment is recognised as part of its cost only if it meets the general recognition criteria, i.e. it is probable that future economic benefits associated with the item will flow to the entity and the cost of the item can be measured reliably.

IAS 16.12   3.2.290.20 Costs of the day-to-day servicing of property, plant and equipment are recognised in profit or loss as incurred.

IAS 16.20   3.2.290.30 In some cases an entity may incur costs in relocating assets. The standard requires that the recognition of costs as part of the carrying amount of an item of property, plant and equipment ceases when the item is in the location and condition necessary for it to be capable of operating in the manner intended by management. Therefore, costs of relocating or reorganising part or all of an entity's operations are not included in the carrying amount of an item of property, plant and equipment.

IAS 16.11   3.2.290.40 Expenditure incurred to acquire safety or environmental equipment may be recognised as a separate item of property, plant and equipment if it enables the future economic benefits of other assets to be realised, even though the expenditure itself does not give rise directly to future economic benefits.

IAS 16.11   3.2.290.50 For example, the government introduces new emissions laws that require aluminium smelters to be fitted with a new grade of filter; unless the new filters are fitted, smelters are no longer permitted to operate. The cost of the new filters is capitalised as property, plant and equipment as long as the total carrying amount of the smelter plus the new filters does not exceed its recoverable amount (see 3.10.140).

3.2.300 Revaluations

IAS 16.36, 39, 40   3.2.300.10 An entity may elect to measure a class of property, plant and equipment at fair value, if fair value can be measured reliably. If this accounting policy is chosen, then revaluations should be kept up to date, such that the carrying amount of an asset at the reporting date does not differ materially from its fair value. Any surplus arising on the revaluation is recognised in other comprehensive income except to the extent that the surplus reverses a previous revaluation deficit on the same asset recognised in profit or loss, in which case the credit to that extent is recognised in profit or loss. Any deficit on revaluation is recognised in profit or loss except to the extent that it reverses a previous revaluation surplus on the same asset, in which case the debit to that extent is recognised in other comprehensive income. Therefore, revaluation increases and decreases cannot be offset, even within a class of assets.

IAS 16.58   3.2.300.20 Land and any asset situated on the land (e.g. a building or specialised plant) are separate assets. Accordingly, increases and decreases in the fair value attributed to the land and to the building are recognised separately (see 3.2.360).

3.2.310 *Fair value**

3.2.320 *Market value*

IAS 16.32   3.2.320.10 The fair value of property, plant and equipment is its market value, which has a similar meaning to fair value. Disposal costs are not deducted in determining market value.

3.2.320.20 In addition, market value is the highest possible price that could be obtained for the item of property, plant and equipment, without regard to its existing use. For example, Company S owns offices situated in a prime residential location. The value of the property as residential real estate exceeds its value as an office building. Accordingly, market value is determined based on its value as residential real estate.

3.2.330 *Depreciated replacement cost*

IAS 16.33   3.2.330.10 Plant and equipment is valued using depreciated replacement cost (DRC) only when there is no evidence of market value. This might occur when the asset is specialised and rarely sold except as part of a continuing business. A DRC valuation considers how much it would cost to reproduce an asset after adjusting for depreciation and optimisation, i.e. it estimates the replacement cost of the required capacity rather than the actual capacity of the asset. The adjustment for depreciation takes into account the age of the asset in relation to its useful life and its residual value. The adjustment for optimisation takes into account situations in which the asset is obsolete, over-engineered or has capacity greater than that required.

3.2.330.20 For example, Company T operates a network of water pipes; the diameter of the pipes is greater than that required currently, and greater than is expected to be required even for necessary stand-by or safety purposes. The DRC valuation would be optimised to eliminate the cost of replacing the surplus capacity in T's network.

3.2.330.30 When an asset is obsolete, the DRC valuation is optimised by reducing the reproduction cost of the entity's specific asset so that it is not greater than the cost of a modern equivalent asset that provides an equivalent standard of performance or service capacity.

3.2.330.40 When an asset has surplus capacity, in our view the optimisation adjustment for the DRC valuation should consider whether the surplus capacity has an alternative use. When there is no alternative use, no cost should be reflected for reproducing this surplus capacity. However, when there is an alternative use that is physically possible and financially feasible, in our view the surplus capacity should be included in the valuation, either using fair value (if determinable) or replacement cost. However, surplus capacity is unlikely to have an alternative use unless it is physically and operationally separable from the required capacity.

3.2.330.50 Continuing the example in 3.2.330.20, in addition to the surplus diameter of the pipes, T's network includes an additional discrete segment of pipes that is surplus to requirements, but which could be closed off and used for other purposes such as a liquid storage facility. While the surplus diameter would be excluded, in our view the surplus segment should be included in the valuation.

3.2.340 Possible impairment

3.2.340.10 In valuing plant and equipment using a DRC valuation, there is a risk that the value of the asset will exceed its recoverable amount (see 3.10.140). This is because DRC is based on reproduction cost, whereas impairment losses are measured by reference to future cash flows and selling prices.

AS 36.5(b), 9   3.2.340.20 In our view, a DRC valuation should be accompanied by a review of the recoverable amount of the cash-generating unit(s) to which the assets being valued relate. When this review indicates a possible impairment, full impairment testing is required (see 3.10.110). If the determined recoverable amount is less than the fair value of the asset as determined by the DRC calculation, then the impairment loss should be recognised against the gross DRC recognised as the revalued amount.

3.2.340.30 For example, Company R determines the cost to reproduce an asset, after adjustment for depreciation and optimisation, to be 1,000. However, the recoverable amount (determined in accordance with IAS 36 *Impairment of Assets* (see 3.10)) of the asset is 800 based on the value in use of the related cash-generating unit. In this situation R should revalue the asset to 1,000 (gross DRC) and subsequently recognise an impairment loss of 200, resulting in a carrying amount of 800. The fair value is not the net figure of 800. While this distinction between fair value and impairment testing may not impact the accounting at the date of the revaluation, it is important for the subsequent accounting and determining the amount of impairment losses that can be reversed. In our experience, based on this example, R would carefully reassess the calculations and assumptions made in determining the DRC of 1,000 before recognising the difference of 200 as an impairment loss. In this case, care should be taken to test the economic obsolescence factor in the DRC calculation.

3.2.350 *Income approach*

IAS 16.33   3.2.350.10 Fair value may be estimated using an income approach if there is no market-based evidence of fair value because of the specialised nature of the item of property, plant and equipment and the item rarely is sold, except as part of a continuing business.

3.2.360 *Apportioning values between land, buildings and specialised plant*

IAS 16.32   3.2.360.10 In many cases the valuation of specialised plant and equipment is linked to the valuation of the land on which it is situated. The land should be measured at fair value at the date of the revaluation, but an issue arises as to how the valuation of a site should be allocated between the land itself and the specialised plant and equipment on that land.

3.2.360.20 For example, Company V runs a brewery that is located in a prime residential location. The fair value of the site as a whole is 400; this represents its value for housing development, which would require demolishing the brewery. The DRC valuation of the brewery is 150. V cannot value the land at 400 and the brewery at 150 because the total of 550 is more than the fair value of the site as a whole. In our view, an entity should choose an accounting policy, to be applied consistently, either to:

- value the land as the difference between the total site value and the DRC valuation of the related plant – in this example 250; or
- apportion the value of the site to the land and the related plant proportionate to their fair values – in this example the land would be valued at 291 ((400 / 550) x 400) and the brewery would be valued at 109 ((150 / 550) x 400).

3.2.360.30 A third alternative, which we do not recommend, would be to attribute the entire value of the site to the land because this is where the value lies. In that case the related plant would be valued at zero.

3.2.370 *All assets in a class*

IAS 16.31,   3.2.370.10 If an asset is revalued, then all property, plant and equipment of the
36-38   same class is revalued at the same time and these revaluations should be kept up to date. A class of assets is a grouping of items that have a similar nature and use in an entity's operations. The following are examples of classes of property, plant and equipment:

- land
- land and buildings
- machinery
- ships
- aircraft
- motor vehicles

- furniture and fittings
- office equipment.

3.2.370.20 In our view, different geographical locations do not justify concluding that the assets are in different classes. For example, Company T has office buildings in Europe and Asia; the buildings in both regions are used for administrative purposes. We believe that the buildings belong to the same class of property, plant and equipment. Accordingly, the buildings in Europe should not be revalued without the buildings in Asia also being revalued.

3.2.380 *Accumulated depreciation*

3.2.380.10 When property, plant and equipment is revalued, an entity should choose an accounting policy, to be applied consistently, either to:

IAS 16.35
- restate both the gross carrying amount of the asset and the related accumulated depreciation proportionately; or
- eliminate the accumulated depreciation against the gross carrying amount of the asset.

3.2.380.15 An entity should follow the same approach when fully depreciated assets are revalued.

3.2.380.20 The following example illustrates both of these methods; in our experience, the second method is more common.

3.2.380.30 Company V revalues all of its land and buildings at the beginning of 2009. The following information relates to one of the buildings:

Gross carrying amount	200
Accumulated depreciation	(80)
Carrying amount	120
Fair value	150

3.2.390 *Restate the gross carrying amount and accumulated depreciation*

3.2.390.10 If both the gross carrying amount and the accumulated depreciation are restated, then the revised carrying amount of the building will be:

Gross carrying amount	250	(200 / 120) x 150
Accumulated depreciation	(100)	(80 / 120) x 150
Carrying amount	150	

3.2.400 *Eliminate accumulated depreciation*

3.2.400.10 If the balance of accumulated depreciation is eliminated, then the revised carrying amount of the building will be:

Gross carrying amount	150
Accumulated depreciation	-
Carrying amount	150

3.2.410 *Transferring the revaluation surplus to retained earnings*

IAS 16.6, 48 3.2.410.10 The depreciable amount of a revalued asset is based on its revalued amount and not its cost. The depreciation charge for each period is recognised as an expense in profit or loss unless it is included in the carrying amount of another asset (see 3.2.140.50).

IAS 16.41 3.2.410.20 However, the revaluation surplus may be transferred directly to retained earnings as the surplus is realised. Realisation of the surplus may occur through the use (and depreciation) of the asset or upon its disposal. The wording of the standard is not entirely clear, but in our view an entity should choose an accounting policy, to be applied consistently, to:

(1) not transfer any part of revaluation reserve to retained earnings;
(2) transfer all of the revaluation reserve to retained earnings upon ultimate disposal; or
(3) transfer a relevant portion of the revaluation reserve to retained earnings as the asset is depreciated, with the balance being transferred upon ultimate disposal.

3.2.410.30 Continuing the example in 3.2.380.30 – 400, at the date of the revaluation the building has a remaining useful life of 15 years and is depreciated on a straight-line basis; the revaluation reserve is 30. Regarding the third option in 3.2.410.20, each year an amount of 2 will be transferred from the revaluation reserve to retained earnings to match the additional depreciation of 2 that relates to the revalued portion of the asset (30 / 15).

3.2.420 *Change in accounting policy*

IAS 8.17 3.2.420.10 If an entity changes its accounting policy from the cost to the fair value model of accounting for property, plant and equipment, then the effect of the change is recognised as a revaluation (see 3.2.300.10); the opening balance of equity is not adjusted and comparatives are not restated.

IAS 8.19 3.2.420.20 When an entity changes its accounting policy from the fair value to the cost model of accounting for property, plant and equipment, all previous revaluations, including subsequent depreciation charges, should be reversed. In this case the usual procedures for a change in accounting policy apply, i.e. the effect of the change is calculated retrospectively and the adjustment generally is recognised by adjusting the opening balance of retained earnings for the earliest prior period presented and restating comparative amounts presented (see 2.8.10).

3.2.420.30 In our view, since IAS 16 allows two accounting treatments for the subsequent measurement of property, plant and equipment, an entity may change its accounting policy from one to the other accounting treatment since both treatments are considered acceptable in providing a fair presentation. However, care should be taken if an accounting policy is changed more than once to ensure that the requirement to qualify for a voluntary change in accounting policy is met (see 2.8.10.10).

3.2.430 Compensation received

IAS 16.65, 66 3.2.430.10 Compensation for the loss or impairment of property, plant and equipment is recognised in profit or loss when receivable (see 3.2.430.40). The loss or impairment of the property, plant and equipment is recognised in profit or loss as an expense when it occurs.

3.2.430.20 For example, Company W's main operating plant is destroyed in a fire. The carrying amount of the plant was 600. W's insurers pay out an amount of 1,000, which comprises 800 for the rebuilding of the plant and 200 for loss of profits. The actual cost of rebuilding the plant is 900.

3.2.430.30 The following entries will be recorded by W:

	Debit	Credit
At the time of the fire:		
Loss (profit or loss)	600	
Property, plant and equipment		600
To recognise write-off of carrying amount of plant		
When the insurance proceeds are receivable:		
Insurance claim receivable	1,000	
Income (profit or loss)		1,000
To recognise insurance claim receivable		
When the plant is reconstructed:		
Property, plant and equipment	900	
Cash		900
To recognise cost of rebuilding plant		

3.2.430.40 Recognition of the loss or impairment may occur at a different point, and even in a different period, from the recognition of the compensation. In our view, income related to the compensation for damaged assets should be recognised when the damage giving rise to any loss or impairment has occurred and the entity has an unconditional contractual right to receive the compensation.

3.2.440 Retirements, disposals and changes in use

3.2.440.10 When an item of property, plant and equipment is disposed of or permanently withdrawn from use, a gain or loss is recognised for the difference between any net proceeds received and the carrying amount of the asset.

IAS 16.70 3.2.440.20 When part of an asset is disposed of or permanently withdrawn from use, the carrying amount of that part is derecognised. For example, when subsequent expenditure is recognised in the carrying amount of an item in respect of a replacement part, the carrying amount of the replaced part is derecognised, even if it had not been depreciated separately.

IAS 16.67, 3.2.440.30 The gain or loss on derecognition generally is included in profit or
68, 71 loss unless the transaction is a sale and leaseback and deferral is required (see 5.1.470), and is not classified as revenue.

3.2.440.32 – 35 [Not used]

IAS 16.68A 3.2.440.37 If an entity in the normal course of its business routinely sells items of property, plant and equipment that it previously held for rental to others, then it transfers such items to inventory when they cease to be rented and become held for sale. Such assets are outside the scope of IFRS 5 *Non-current Assets Held for Sale and Discontinued Operations*. The items are transferred at their carrying amounts at the date of transfer, and the entity recognises the proceeds from the sale of such assets as revenue in accordance with IAS 18 *Revenue*. For example, Company Z operates a car rental business and also sells second-hand cars as part of its business model. Z acquires new cars with the intention of renting the cars for three years and then selling them. Z should recognise the cars as property, plant and equipment during the rental period and transfer the cars to inventory at their carrying amount when they cease to be rented and become held for sale. Z should recognise the proceeds from the sale of cars as revenue.

IAS 16.41 3.2.440.40 Any attributable revaluation surplus may be transferred to retained earnings (see 3.2.410), but is not recognised in profit or loss.

3.2.440.50 In determining the *net* proceeds received, generally all directly attributable incremental costs of disposal, such as advertising, legal fees, stamp duty, agency fees and removal costs, are deducted. In our view, it also is appropriate to deduct any amounts recognised as liabilities (see 3.12) in relation to the disposal of the asset, such as provisions made for probable claims under warranties in the sales agreement, or for an agreed schedule of repairs to be done at the current owner's expense.

IAS 16.68, 69, 18.14   3.2.440.60 The date of disposal of an asset is determined by applying the revenue recognition criteria (see 4.2.130) unless the disposal is by sale and leaseback. In our view, sale and leaseback accounting will apply even if some of the general revenue recognition criteria have not been met (see 5.1.470).

IFRS 5.6, 15, 15A   3.2.440.70 When an asset's carrying amount is to be recovered principally through a sale transaction or distribution rather than through continuing use, the asset is classified as a non-current asset (or disposal group) held for sale or distribution if certain criteria are met (see 5.4.30 and 37). Depreciation of that asset ceases at the earlier of the date that the asset (or disposal group) is classified as held for sale and the date that the asset (or disposal group) is derecognised. An entity measures such a non-current asset (or disposal group) at the lower of its carrying amount and fair value less costs to sell (see 5.4.40).

IAS 16.55   3.2.440.80 Depreciation is recognised even when an asset is idle and retired from active use unless the asset is held for sale. However, under usage methods of depreciation, the depreciation charge can be zero while there is no production.

3.2.440.90 See 5.7 for a discussion of exchanges of non-monetary assets.

3.2.450 Government grants

IAS 20.23-28   3.2.450.10 A government grant may be related to an item of property, plant or equipment whether it is received in cash or is an asset received by way of non-monetary grant. See 4.3 for a discussion of the treatment of a government grant that relates to property, plant or equipment.

3.2.460 Disclosure

IAS 16.73   3.2.460.10 The disclosure requirements for property, plant and equipment, examples of which are included in KPMG's series of illustrative financial statements, include a reconciliation between the carrying amount of property, plant and equipment at the beginning and end of the current reporting period and also the beginning and end of the comparative reporting period.

IAS 16.73   3.2.460.20 The reconciliation includes separate line items for additions and acquisitions through business combinations. Therefore acquisitions should be split between property, plant and equipment acquired in a business combination and other acquisitions. However, all disposals are presented in a single line item in the reconciliation.

3.2.470 Future developments

3.2.470.10 In May 2009 the IASB published ED/2009/5 *Fair Value Measurement* (the 2009 ED). The proposals in the 2009 ED are intended to replace the fair value measurement guidance contained in individual IFRSs with a single, unified definition of fair value, as well as provide further authoritative guidance on the application of fair value measurement in inactive markets. The 2009 ED proposes a framework for measuring fair value and disclosures about fair value measurements. The proposals in the 2009 ED explain how to measure fair value when it already is required or permitted by existing IFRSs; they do not introduce new fair value measurements, nor do they eliminate the practicability exceptions to fair value measurements that exist currently in certain standards.

3.2.470.20 In June 2010 the IASB published ED/2010/7 *Measurement Uncertainty Analysis Disclosure for Fair Value Measurements* (the 2010 ED). The 2010 ED expands on the proposal in the 2009 ED for an entity to disclose a measurement uncertainty analysis (or sensitivity analysis) for assets and liabilities measured at fair value categorised within Level 3 of the fair value hierarchy. The 2010 ED proposes that an entity consider the effect of correlation between unobservable inputs, if relevant.

3.2.470.30 A final standard on fair value measurement and disclosure, which is expected to be converged with a forthcoming amended standard under US GAAP, is scheduled for the first quarter of 2011.

3.3 Intangible assets and goodwill
(IFRS 3, IAS 38, SIC-32)

3.3 Intangible assets and goodwill

(IFRS 3, IAS 38, SIC-32)

Overview of currently effective requirements

- An intangible asset is an identifiable non-monetary asset without physical substance.

- An intangible asset is identifiable if it is separable or arises from contractual or legal rights.

- Intangible assets generally are recognised initially at cost.

- The initial measurement of an intangible asset depends on whether it has been acquired separately, as part of a business combination, or was generated internally.

- Goodwill is recognised only in a business combination and is measured as a residual.

- Acquired goodwill and other intangible assets with indefinite useful lives are not amortised, but instead are subject to impairment testing at least annually.

- Intangible assets with finite useful lives are amortised over their expected useful lives.

- Subsequent expenditure on an intangible asset is capitalised only if the definition of an intangible asset and the recognition criteria are met.

- Intangible assets may be revalued to fair value only if there is an active market.

- Internal research expenditure is expensed as incurred. Internal development expenditure is capitalised if specific criteria are met. These capitalisation criteria are applied to all internally developed intangible assets.

- Advertising and promotional expenditure is expensed as incurred.

- Expenditure on relocation or a reorganisation is expensed as incurred.

- The following are not capitalised as intangible assets: internally generated goodwill, costs to develop customer lists, start-up costs and training costs.

Currently effective requirements

This publication reflects IFRSs in issue at 1 August 2010. The currently effective requirements cover annual periods beginning on 1 January 2010. The requirements related to this topic are derived mainly from IAS 38 *Intangible Assets*.

Forthcoming requirements and future developments

When a currently effective requirement will be changed by a new requirement that is issued but is not yet effective, it is marked with a # as a **forthcoming requirement** and the impact of the change is explained in the accompanying boxed text. In respect of this topic there are no forthcoming requirements.

When a significant change to the currently effective or forthcoming requirements is expected, it is marked with a * as an area that may be subject to **future developments** and a brief outline of the relevant projects is given in 3.3.330.

3.3.10 **Definition**

3.3.20 *Goodwill*

IFRS 3.32 3.3.20.10 Goodwill arising in a business combination, which is measured as a residual, is recognised in the statement of financial position. Goodwill recognised previously by an acquiree is not recognised as a separate asset by the acquirer.

IFRS 3.32 3.3.20.20 The acquirer recognises goodwill at the acquisition date, measured as the excess of (a) over (b):

(a) The aggregate of:

IFRS 3.37 • consideration transferred, which generally is measured at fair value at the acquisition date (see 2.6.260);

IFRS 3.19 • the amount of any non-controlling interests in the acquiree, which may be measured either at fair value or at their proportionate share in the fair value of the identifiable assets and liabilities of the acquiree at the acquisition date (see 2.6.840); and

IFRS 3.42 • in a business combination achieved in stages, the acquisition-date fair value of the acquirer's previously held equity interest in the acquiree (see 2.6.1020.30).

IFRS 3.18 (b) The net of the acquisition-date amounts of the identifiable assets acquired and the liabilities assumed measured in accordance with IFRS 3 *Business Combinations* (see 2.6.560).

3.3.30 *Intangible assets*

IAS 38.8 3.3.30.10 An intangible asset is an identifiable non-monetary asset without physical substance. The asset can be held for any purpose, i.e. unlike property, plant and equipment, the asset need not be held for use in the production or supply of goods or services, for rental to others or for administrative purposes.

IAS 17.2(b), 38.6   3.3.30.15 Licences are one example of an intangible resource that may meet the definition of an intangible asset. However, since licences grant a right of use and because IAS 17 *Leases* does not state clearly that all licence arrangements are excluded from its scope, it can be difficult to determine whether a licence is within the scope of IAS 17 or IAS 38. In our experience, generally licences are accounted for in accordance with IAS 38.

IAS 38.4   3.3.30.20 There may be instances in which an intangible asset is incorporated within a physical asset, for example knowledge contained within a book. In such circumstances an assessment is made as to what aspect of the asset, tangible or intangible, is more significant and the asset is accounted for accordingly. In the example of the book, in our view it should be accounted for as an intangible asset as the knowledge within the book dominates the nature of the asset (and its value) as opposed to the tangible nature of the medium (the paper).

IAS 38.4   3.3.30.25 In another example, the operating system on a computer typically is treated as part of the computer itself and the entire asset is accounted for in accordance with IAS 16 *Property, Plant and Equipment*. However, additional software acquired or developed for the computer typically will be treated as an intangible asset separate from the tangible asset (computer) on which it is installed.

IAS 38.8-17   3.3.30.30 To meet the definition of an intangible asset, an item should lack physical substance and should be:

- identifiable;
- non-monetary; and
- controlled by the entity and expected to provide future economic benefits to the entity, i.e. it should meet the definition of an asset.

3.3.30.40 These criteria apply to all intangible assets, whether acquired separately, acquired in a business combination or generated internally.

3.3.40 *Identifiability*

IAS 38.12   3.3.40.10 In order for an intangible asset to be recognised it should be *identifiable*. An item is identifiable if it:

- is separable, i.e. is capable of being separated or divided from the entity and sold, transferred, licensed, rented or exchanged either individually or together with a related contract, asset or liability; or
- arises from contractual or other legal rights, regardless of whether those rights are transferable or separable from the entity or from other rights and obligations.

IAS 38.12 3.3.40.20 Therefore, separability is not a necessary condition for an item to be identifiable. For example, a business licence of a radio station that the station needs to operate is identifiable because it arises from legal rights, even though the licence usually is not separable from the station operator.

3.3.40.30 In our experience, the decision of whether the identifiability criterion is met often is the critical factor in determining whether the definition of an intangible asset is met, and therefore whether an intangible asset qualifies for recognition.

3.3.40.40 For example, Company P is a successful engineering business. In past years P has achieved a market share for its products of 25 percent and contemplates recognising an intangible asset for this market share. In our view, market share does not meet the definition of an intangible asset because it is not separable and it does not arise from legal rights.

3.3.50 *Non-monetary*

3.3.50.10 Intangible assets are non-monetary. Monetary assets are subject to the requirements of other standards, e.g. financial instruments (see 3.6.150.40) and income tax receivables (see 3.13.15.10).

3.3.60 *Control*

IAS 38.13-16 3.3.60.10 In order to demonstrate control an entity should have the power to obtain the future economic benefits arising from the item *and* be able to restrict the access of others to those benefits.

IAS 38.15 3.3.60.20 For example, Company C has two key resources: customised software that it developed internally and for which a patent is registered; and the know-how of the staff that operate the software. Staff are required to give one month's notice of their resignation. It is clear that C controls the software. However, although it obtains economic benefits from the work performed by the staff, C does not have control over their know-how because staff could choose to resign at any time. Therefore, the know-how does not meet the definition of an intangible asset.

IAS 38.15 3.3.60.30 In another example, Company D is a football club. D has acquired contracts with individual players that entitle it to receive that player's services and prevent that player from leaving the club or providing services to another club for a specified period of time. Unlike the example in 3.3.60.20, these contracts each meet the definition of an intangible asset because they give D control over any future economic benefits that may arise from the player's services, and restrict the access of others to those benefits.

3.3.70 Exchange transactions

IAS 38.13-16 3.3.70.10 Normally control stems from legal rights that are enforceable in a court of law, which is equivalent to "contractual or other legal rights" – a criterion for identifiability (see 3.3.40.10). Control may be demonstrated by means other than legally enforceable rights, and therefore legal enforceability is not a necessary condition for control. In our view, the demonstration of separability through exchange transactions for the same or similar intangible assets generally provides evidence of control.

3.3.80 Intangible assets in a business combination

3.3.80.10 The identification of intangible assets as part of a business combination can be a challenging exercise and IFRS 3 includes specific guidance to assist in understanding the types of intangible assets in a business combination that are likely to meet the definition of intangible assets; see 2.6.720 – 820 for a discussion in this regard.

3.3.90 Initial recognition and measurement

3.3.100 *General requirements*

38.21, 24 3.3.100.10 An intangible asset that meets the following criteria is recognised initially at cost:

- it is probable that future economic benefits that are attributable to the asset will flow to the entity; and
- the cost of the asset can be measured reliably.

38.25, 26, 33 3.3.100.20 These criteria are most important in assessing the recognition of internally generated intangible assets (see 3.3.120.40). When an intangible asset is acquired in a business combination, these criteria are assumed to be met (see 2.6.720). When an intangible asset is acquired in a separate acquisition (i.e. outside of a business combination), the "probability" criterion is assumed to be met; additionally, IAS 38 notes that the "reliable measurement" criterion *usually* is met.

S 38.8, 26 3.3.100.30 The cost of an intangible asset acquired in a separate acquisition is the cash paid or the fair value of any other consideration given. If the intangible asset acquired is exchanged for non-cash consideration or the intangible asset is one of a group of items acquired, then the cost is estimated based on the fair value of the consideration exchanged (see 5.7.20). Intangible assets also may be purchased through the settlement of a derivative, e.g. a forward or call option, or an executory contract; the determination of cost in these circumstances is discussed in 3.6.90.30.

IAS 38.30, 66, 67 3.3.100.40 The cost of an internally generated intangible asset includes the directly attributable expenditure of preparing the asset for its intended use, and the principles discussed in respect of property, plant and equipment (see 3.2.30) apply equally to the recognition of intangible assets. Expenditure on training activities, clearly identified inefficiencies and initial operating losses are expensed as incurred.

IAS 38.32 3.3.100.50 When payment is deferred, the cost of the asset is the cash price equivalent. The issues that arise in accounting for deferred payment are similar to those in respect of property, plant and equipment (see 3.2.130).

3.3.100.55 The determination of cost is more complicated when the consideration paid in exchange for receiving an intangible asset is wholly or partly variable. For example, Company Y purchases a five-year licence to use technology owned by Company Z. Y agrees to pay a minimum amount of 200, 25 percent of which is due at the outset of the licence arrangement, with the remaining 75 percent due one year later. In addition to this minimum payment, Y also agrees to pay to Z 10 percent of the future revenues that will be generated with the licensed technology. Y's current best estimate of the revenues expected to be generated with the technology is 1,000 for each of the following five years. In our view, the cost of Y's intangible asset (the licence) should be determined on the basis of the agreed minimum payments, i.e. 50 plus the present value of 150. The revenue-based payments are not a present obligation of Y and therefore do not form part of the cost of the licence. Instead, we believe that any additional payments generally are expensed as the related sales occur.

3.3.100.56 If the minimum unconditional payments change due to a contract renegotiation, then in our view any changes to the carrying amount of the liability, other than in respect of finance costs, should be accounted for as an adjustment to the carrying amount of the intangible asset. This assumes that the recognition criteria for an intangible asset still are met (see also 3.12.150.60).

IAS 38.33-41 3.3.100.60 The cost of an intangible asset acquired in a business combination is its fair value. See 2.6.1040 for a discussion of the general principles of determining fair value in a business combination.*

3.3.110 *Specific application*

3.3.120 *Research and development*

IAS 38.8, 54 3.3.120.10 Research is original and planned investigation undertaken with the prospect of gaining new scientific or technical knowledge and understanding. Research costs are expensed as incurred.

IAS 38.8 3.3.120.20 Development is the application of research findings or other knowledge to a plan or design for the production of new or substantially improved materials, devices, products, processes, systems or services before the start of commercial production or use. Development does not include the maintenance or enhancement of ongoing operations.

3.3.120.30 Development does not need to be in relation to an entirely new innovation, but rather should be new to the specific entity. For example, Company K is developing a new IT system for processing its customer orders. The project meets the definition of development notwithstanding the fact that most of K's competitors use similar systems already.

IAS 38.57 3.3.120.40 If an internally generated intangible asset arises from the development phase of a project, then directly attributable expenditure is capitalised from the date that the entity is able to demonstrate:

- the technical feasibility of completing the intangible asset so that it will be available for use or sale;
- its intention to complete the intangible asset and use or sell it;
- its ability to use or sell the intangible asset;
- how the intangible asset will generate probable future economic benefits;
- the availability of adequate technical, financial and other resources to complete the development and to use or sell the intangible asset; and
- its ability to measure reliably the expenditure attributable to the intangible asset during its development.

IAS 38.57, 60   3.3.120.50 In assessing how the intangible asset will generate probable future economic benefits, the entity needs to demonstrate the existence of a market for the output of the intangible asset or the intangible asset itself; or, if it is to be used internally, then the usefulness of the intangible asset. In carrying out this assessment an entity uses the principles of IAS 36 *Impairment of Assets*. If the asset will generate economic benefits only in combination with other assets, then the entity applies the concept of cash-generating units (see 3.10.60).

3.3.120.60 Although "probable" is not defined in relation to intangible assets, it does not mean that a project should be certain to succeed prior to capitalising any development costs. For example, in our view, a pharmaceutical company should not expense all development costs as incurred simply because there is a possibility that new medicines will not be approved for sale by the relevant authorities. Rather, an assessment should be made of the likelihood of success in each individual case. If a positive outcome is determined to be probable, then the company should capitalise the related development costs incurred after success is determined to be probable.

IAS 38.61   3.3.120.70 Financial and other resources needed to complete the development are not required to be secured at the start of the project. Entities may be able to demonstrate their ability to secure these resources through business plans and external financing plans in which potential customers, investors or lenders have expressed interest.

IAS 38.63, 64   3.3.120.80 IFRSs specifically prohibit the capitalisation of expenditure on internally generated intangible assets such as brands, mastheads, publishing titles, customer lists and similar items. This is because the expenditure cannot be distinguished from developing the business as a whole. As a result, expenditure on these assets is viewed as not being reliably measurable.

3.3.120.90 For example, Company B has developed a successful business based on products that have a distinct house style and design. B uses its unique house style to develop a standard format for product development. In our view, the standard format does not meet the definition of an intangible asset because the asset is an integral part of the goodwill of the business and cannot be identified separately.

IAS 38.25, 34, 35, 43   3.3.120.100 If an entity acquires in-process research and development in a business combination, then it is recognised as an intangible asset (see 2.6.810); typically in-process research and development acquired separately but outside of a business combination also will meet the criteria to be recognised (see 3.3100.10 – 3.3.100.20). However, any subsequent expenditure on the in-process research and development projects may be added to the carrying amount of the intangible asset only if they meet the recognition criteria for internally generated intangible assets (see 3.3.270).

3.3.130 *Website development costs*

SIC-32.14   3.3.130.10 Costs associated with websites developed for advertising or promotional purposes are expensed as incurred.

SIC-32.9, 16   3.3.130.20 In respect of other websites, expenditure incurred during the application and infrastructure development stage, the graphical design stage and the content development stage is capitalised if the criteria for capitalising development costs (see 3.3.120.40) are met; this applies equally to internal and external costs. The costs of developing content for advertising or promotional purposes are expensed as incurred.

3.3.140 *Goodwill*

IFRS 3.32   3.3.140.10 Goodwill arising in a business combination is capitalised (see 3.3.20).

IAS 38.48   3.3.140.20 Internally generated goodwill is never recognised as an asset.

3.3.150 *Items that should be expensed as incurred*

IAS 38.48, 69   3.3.150.10 Expenditure associated with the following is expensed as incurred regardless of whether the general criteria for recognition appear to be met:

- internally generated goodwill;
- start-up costs, unless they qualify for recognition as part of the cost of property, plant and equipment (see 3.2.20);
- training activities;
- advertising and promotional activities; and
- expenditure on relocating or reorganising part, or all, of an entity.

3.3.150.20 Except as noted in 3.3.150.10 in relation to start-up costs, these costs are not allowed to be capitalised either as stand-alone intangible assets or as a part of the cost of another intangible asset. In respect of advertising and other promotional costs, in our view it does not matter whether the activities relate to a specific product or to the business as a whole; the related expenditure should be expensed as incurred in either case.

3.3.150.30 [Not used]

IAS 38.69, 70   3.3.150.40 Expenditure in respect of advertising and promotional activities is expensed when the benefit of those goods or services is available to the entity. In respect of the acquisition of goods, an expense is recognised when the entity has the right to access those goods. In respect of the acquisition of services, an expense is recognised when the services are received. This requirement does not prevent the recognition of an asset for prepaid expenses, but a prepayment is recognised only for payments made in advance of the receipt of the corresponding goods or services.

S 38.69, 70, BC46G 3.3.150.50 Catalogues are considered to be a form of advertising and promotional material, and not inventory, as the primary objective of catalogues is to advertise to customers.

3.3.160 Subscriber acquisition costs*

3.3.160.10 An entity may incur costs in entering into supply or sales contracts with new customers, for example commissions paid to internal or external sales personnel. These costs commonly are referred to as subscriber acquisition costs, which are costs incurred with parties other than the customer itself. Although supply or sales contracts may have different features, broadly they can be considered as either fixed-term contracts (i.e. contracts that require a minimum purchase) or open-ended contracts (i.e. contracts that do not include any such restrictions).

3.3.160.20 In our view, generally intangible assets can be recognised only if they arise from fixed-term contracts that require a minimum consideration. The contracts should meet the definition and recognition criteria of an intangible asset. When these criteria are met, internal or external subscriber acquisition costs should be recognised as intangible assets provided that they are incremental to the contracts, i.e. they would not have been incurred had the contracts not been entered into, and they can be measured reliably.

3.3.160.30 For example, Company W pays its sales personnel a salary. They also are paid a commission for each new customer that signs a minimum purchase contract. We believe that the incremental costs include only the commissions paid and do not include a portion of the salary.

3.3.160.40 When an entity enters into an open-ended contract that gives the customer the right to cancel at any time, no obligation exists for the customer to purchase a minimum quantity from the entity. However, a contract may require the customer to pay a penalty for cancelling the contract during its term. The existence of an enforceable penalty is in substance similar to a minimum purchase quantity because it gives rise to economic benefits under the contract, either in the form of cash flows from the supply of goods or services, payment of the penalty, or a combination thereof. In our view, if the contract meets the other definition and recognition criteria of an intangible asset, then the intangible asset is recognised and measured initially at its cost, i.e. the subscriber acquisition costs are capitalised up to the amount of the penalty.

3.3.160.45 If the open-ended contract does not include a penalty for cancellation, then we believe that the entity does not control the future economic benefits expected to arise from a specific contract. This is because there is no means of compelling the customer to make future purchases and the entity does not receive economic benefits in the form of a penalty if the customer changes to another supplier. Consequently, the definition of an intangible asset is not met. The history of past customer relationships should not be taken into account in determining whether an asset exists, as historical experience for a portfolio of such contracts does not mean that a specific customer can be compelled to make a purchase in the future. Therefore, in our view subscriber acquisition and other incremental costs related to obtaining open-ended contracts without a cancellation penalty generally should be expensed as incurred.

3.3.160.50 However, in our view deferred acquisition costs on investment management contracts are not within the scope of IAS 38 because such costs are accounted for in accordance with IAS 18 *Revenue* (see 4.2.590).

3.3.160.60 In our view, payments (in cash or in kind) that an entity makes directly to a customer on entering into a contract are not subscriber acquisition costs, which are transactions with parties other than the customer itself. We believe that normally such payments represent incentives to motivate the customer to enter into a contract and should be accounted for as a reduction in the consideration received or receivable under IAS 18, i.e. like other sales incentives such as discounts (see 4.2.340). However, to the extent that the payments are in kind rather than in cash, e.g. free installation, it first should be analysed whether these payments represent a separate deliverable within the overall arrangement with the customer that should be accounted for as a separate element for revenue recognition purposes (see 4.2.340).

3.3.170 *Emissions allowances**

3.3.170.10 IFRSs do not have any specific guidance on accounting for emissions allowances. In our view, emissions allowances received by a participant in a "cap and trade" scheme, whether purchased or issued by the government, are intangible assets. For emissions allowances that are government grants, non-monetary government grants may be recognised either at fair value or at a nominal amount (see 4.3.50). Recognition of a non-monetary government grant at the amount paid (often zero) would result in no liability being recognised if the liability is measured at the carrying amount (zero) of the related assets. Therefore, we prefer allowances to be measured initially at fair value.

3.3.170.20 Cap and trade schemes typically grant a number of certificates in relation to a specified period over which emissions will be measured ("compliance period"). Under some schemes the relevant government may have identified a date by which it will determine and announce the allocation of the allowances for the next compliance period. This date may be prior to the date from which entities are entitled to their allowances and the date on which they actually are issued. For example, a national government announced that it would determine by 15 December 2009 the allocation of the allowances to be issued on 28 February 2010. The grant is conditional on the entity being in business on

1 January 2010 to receive its allowances. In our view, provided that there are no other conditions attached to the grant, the entity should recognise the government grant and the intangible asset on 1 January 2010 as this is the date on which there is reasonable assurance that the entity will comply with the condition attached to the grant and that the grants will be received.

3.3.170.30 Subsequently, the general requirements for intangible assets apply (see 3.3.190 – 310). If the allowances are accounted for using the revaluation model for intangible assets (see 3.3.280), then any balance on the revaluation reserve in respect of the allowances that is derecognised when the entity settles its obligation under the scheme may be transferred directly to retained earnings within equity (see 3.3.310). This accounting treatment precludes any reclassification of fair value increments related to the allowances to profit or loss when the entity settles its obligations under the scheme. Conversely, if the entity accounts for its allowances under the cost method, then any difference between the carrying amount of the asset and the liability will be recognised in profit or loss upon settlement of the obligation.

3.3.170.40 For most allowances traded in an active market, no amortisation will be required as the condition of the asset does not change over time, and therefore the residual value will be the same as cost. As a result, the depreciable amount will be zero (see 3.3.220).

3.3.170.50 If the market value of the allowances falls below its cost, or other indications of impairment exist, then the general impairment guidance should be followed to determine whether the assets are impaired (see 3.10.120).

3.3.170.60 IFRSs are silent on how an entity should determine the carrying amount of an allowance for the purposes of calculating a gain or loss on disposal. Therefore, the hierarchy for selecting accounting policies should be applied (see 2.8.6). In our view, the guidance for determining the cost of inventories should be applied by analogy (see 3.8.280). In some cases the certificates will have unique identification numbers, and therefore it will be possible to apply the specific identification method if the holder tracks cost on an individual certificate basis. Otherwise, any reasonable cost allocation method, e.g. average cost or first-in first-out (FIFO), may be used. The method used should be applied consistently.

3.3.170.70 See 3.12.510 for further discussion of the accounting for obligations arising from schemes for emissions allowances.

3.3.170.80 An entity may receive emissions allowances in a cap and trade scheme that are surplus to its expected usage requirements. In our view, the income from the sale of such allowances should be recognised as other income. We believe that it should not be recognised as revenue unless it arises in the ordinary course of the activities of the entity (see 4.2.10.30).

3.3.175 *REACH costs*

3.3.175.10 REACH is a regulation for the Registration, Evaluation and Authorisation of CHemicals in the European Union (EU). The REACH regulation requires manufacturers and importers to register all chemical substances not covered by other specific regulations (e.g. regulations regarding medicinal products) that they produce or import in quantities over a specified amount. The registration consists of submitting a technical report about the substance and paying a registration fee.

3.3.175.20 Once a chemical substance has been registered, another manufacturer has the right, and in certain cases the obligation, to use the registration documentation of the original registrant, who is obliged to grant the potential additional registrant access to all information, documentation and analyses. The potential additional registrant is required to reimburse the original registrant for a portion of the costs incurred in its original registration, and the regulation specifies a protocol for the sharing of data and costs. Claims are enforceable in the national courts.

3.3.175.30 An entity might incur significant costs in obtaining a REACH registration. In addition to the registration fee itself, costs incurred might relate to preparing the technical report, performing the chemical safety assessment, e.g. internal and external laboratory tests, and preparing the chemical safety report. Additional registrants instead incur costs for reimbursing previous registrants.

3.3.175.40 In our view, the registration costs under the REACH regulation fall within the scope of IAS 38. We believe that generally the definition of an intangible asset and the general recognition criteria of IAS 38 will be met (see 3.3.30.30 and 3.3.100.10). However, an analysis specific to each registration should be performed in order to demonstrate the recovery of the actual costs by the specific entity.

IAS 38.27, 29 3.3.175.50 In our view, REACH costs are a separately acquired intangible asset, similar to a product-specific licence. IAS 38 requires separately acquired intangible assets to be measured initially at cost, which comprises the purchase price and any directly attributable cost of preparing the asset for its intended use (see 3.3.100.40). For example, in our view the labour costs for an employee while preparing the registration should be included if such costs are directly attributable. In contrast, administrative and other general overhead costs should not be included in the cost, e.g. the labour costs for an employee or external contractor administering the registration of substances to be registered.

3.3.175.60 Normally the probability test is considered to be met automatically for separately acquired intangible assets (see 3.3.100.20). However, in our view entities should consider explicitly the probability test for registration costs for REACH. We believe that this is appropriate because the acquisition of this intangible asset is mandated rather than being an unconstrained choice.

3.3.175.70 In our view, the costs that are directly attributable to a REACH registration are likely to include the preparation of a technical report, costs incurred for performing the chemical safety assessment, if any, and for documenting those results in the chemical safety report. Both internal and external costs may qualify for recognition, which may include internal and external laboratory costs.

3.3.175.80 However, in our view costs incurred in the following activities usually would not be directly attributable to a REACH registration and therefore should be expensed as incurred: evaluating the REACH requirements, assessing business impacts, database maintenance, and ongoing analyses after registration. We believe that these costs are feasibility and operating costs that are not directly attributable to a specific registration.

3.3.175.90 For registration based on a third party's previous registration, in our view the cost of the intangible asset will include the registration fee and the reimbursement to the original registrant.

IAS 38.78 3.3.175.100 Subsequent to initial measurement, in our view the intangible asset should be measured using the cost model; since there is no active market for REACH registrations, the intangible asset would not qualify to be measured at fair value (see 3.3.280.10).

3.3.175.110 An entity assesses whether the useful life of the intangible asset is finite or indefinite in the usual way (see 3.3.190). While generally a registration itself has no time limit, an entity should consider the technological and commercial life cycles of the chemical substance and the related products (i.e. preparations and/or articles) in which it is to be used. Therefore, generally an intangible asset in respect of REACH registration would have a finite useful life. The most appropriate method of amortisation is determined by applying the general guidance in IAS 38, i.e. it should reflect the pattern of consumption of the economic benefits (see 3.3.230).

3.3.175.120 In our view, the reimbursement of costs by a potential additional registrant is an *incidental operation* of the original registrant, i.e. an operation that is not necessary to bring the asset (registration) to the location and condition necessary for it to be capable of operating in the manner intended by management. The fact that a potential additional registrant can purchase (at cost) work carried out by the original registrant does not affect whether the original registrant can obtain registration or how that registration is utilised in the pursuit of economic benefits.

IAS 18.7, 3.3.175.130 Therefore, we believe that it is not appropriate to credit any reimbursement
38.31 to the cost of the registration. In our view, the reimbursement should be recognised as income. It should not be recognised as revenue since it does not arise in the ordinary course of the activities of an entity (see 4.2.10.30).

IAS 37.14, 3.3.175.140 In our view, the REACH regulation does not give rise to a present obligation
IE.C.Ex6 because an entity makes its own decision as to whether or not it will apply for registration. Since the cost of registration can be avoided by ceasing to use the chemical substance, we believe that a provision should not be recognised for estimated future registration costs in accordance with IAS 37 *Provisions, Contingent Liabilities and*

Contingent Assets (see 3.12.90). We believe that the REACH registration requirement is similar to example 6 of appendix C to IAS 37 in respect of a legal requirement to fit smoke filters.

3.3.180 *Regulatory assets*

3.3.180.10 In many countries utility companies (or other entities operating in regulated industries) have contractual arrangements with the local regulator to charge a price based on a cost-plus model. Some arrangements will allow the entity to recover excess costs incurred through future price increases. Typically under such arrangements the regulator approves the costs to be recovered based on conditions set out in the contractual arrangement. In our view, any excess cost that is incurred that may be recovered through future price increases does not qualify for recognition as an asset as it does not meet the definition of an intangible asset and there is no contractual right to receive cash or other financial assets. The legal right to increase prices in the future is not sufficient to satisfy the definition of an intangible asset because the entity does not control the customers. The customers might decide not to buy or buy less and thereby leave the entity with uncovered costs. See 3.12.720 for a discussion of regulatory liabilities.

3.3.185 *Service concession arrangements*

3.3.185.10 IFRIC 12 *Service Concession Arrangements* provides guidance to private sector entities on certain recognition and measurement issues that arise in accounting for public-to-private service concession arrangements.

3.3.185.20 IFRIC 12 addresses how service concession operators should apply existing IFRSs in accounting for the obligations that they undertake and the rights that they receive in service concession arrangements. IFRIC 12 focuses on arrangements in which the private sector entity (the operator) incurs expenditure in the early years of the arrangement as it constructs or upgrades public service infrastructure.

3.3.185.30 Under IFRIC 12 the operator recognises consideration receivable from the grantor for construction services, including upgrades of existing infrastructure, as a financial asset and/or an intangible asset. If an intangible asset is recognised, then the guidance provided in this chapter is relevant for recognition and measurement. See 5.12 for a more detailed discussion of the key requirements of IFRIC 12.

3.3.190 **Classification of intangible assets**

IAS 38.88 3.3.190.10 The classification of an intangible asset depends on whether its useful life is finite or indefinite. An intangible asset has an indefinite useful life when, based on an analysis of all relevant factors, there is no foreseeable limit to the period over which the asset is expected to generate net cash inflows for the entity.

3.3.190.20 Various external and internal factors need to be considered when assessing the useful life of an intangible asset.

3.3.190.30 External factors include:

- the term of any agreements and other legal or contractual restrictions on the use of the asset;
- the stability of the industry, changes in market demand and expected actions by competitors; and
- technological, commercial and other types of obsolescence.

IAS 38.90 3.3.190.40 Internal factors include:

- the expected use of the asset and required maintenance;
- dependency on other assets; and
- typical product life cycles.

IAS 38.94 3.3.190.50 When control of an intangible asset is based on legal rights that have been granted for a finite period, the useful life cannot exceed that period unless:

- the legal rights are renewable; and
- there is evidence to support that they will be renewed.

IAS 38.94-96 3.3.190.60 In addition, the cost of renewal should not be significant. If the cost of renewing such rights is significant when compared with the future economic benefits expected to flow to the entity from renewal, then the renewal costs represent the cost to acquire a new intangible asset at the renewal date.

IAS 38.91 3.3.190.70 Determining that an intangible asset has an indefinite useful life does not mean that its life is infinite. Conversely, an intangible asset that has no legal or contractual restrictions on its use does not mean necessarily that it has an indefinite useful life. For example, Company B is a fishery operating in various jurisdictions. One of the local governments wants to restrict fishing activities in its waters to preserve and ultimately rebuild its fish stocks. Accordingly, the local government introduces a temporary programme whereby each fishery should purchase a permanent licence (i.e. it has no expiry date). This licence restricts the number of fish that it can catch for a particular species of fish (the "catch quota"). The catch quota changes each year. In our view, B cannot conclude automatically that the licence has an indefinite useful life simply because the licence is permanent. All facts and circumstances should be considered, including in this case an estimate of the duration of the programme and its effectiveness at maintaining the fish stock.

3.3.190.80 Difficulties in determining useful life do not mean that an intangible asset has an indefinite useful life; nor does it mean that its useful life is unrealistically short. For example, Telecom T purchases a wireless spectrum licence that covers various regions and frequencies. Although the licence has an unlimited life, it is expected that a new technology eventually will be developed that will require different frequencies and therefore render the licence obsolete. Although the timing of such obsolescence may be difficult to determine, T expects that at some point in the future the licence will cease to generate net cash inflows. Accordingly, T concludes that the licence has a finite useful life. However, T should not assign an unrealistically short useful life to the licence, e.g. one year, to avoid ongoing amortisation charges. In our view, the estimate of useful life should be consistent with management's assumptions used in its budgeting process to forecast cash flows from operations supported by the licence.

3.3.190.85 In our view, in assessing whether the useful life of a brand is finite or indefinite, an entity should include the following factors in addition to the general factors outlined in 3.3.190.20 – 40, which are not exhaustive or necessarily in order of importance, in its assessment:

- How well and for how long has the brand been established in the market? And what has been the brand's resilience to economic and social changes since its creation? If the brand is mature and contributes significant value to the business and therefore its abandonment would represent an unrealistic decision, then this might be an indication of an indefinite useful life.
- How stable is the industry in which the brand is used? In rapidly changing industries it is less likely that a brand will be identified as having an indefinite useful life.
- Is the brand expected to become obsolete at some point in the future, e.g. through a decline in market demand for the products sold under the brand, or because of the technological obsolescence of these products? Can the brand be deployed in more than one industry or with more than one technology? If a brand is dependent on factors applying to a particular industry or technology, then it is less likely that it will be identified as having an indefinite useful life.
- Is the brand used in a market that is subject to significant, enduring entry barriers? If yes, then it is more likely that it will be identified as having an indefinite useful life.
- Is sufficient ongoing marketing effort to support the brand included in the entity's financial forecasts, such that benefits arising from the use of the brand are expected to be maintained beyond the foreseeable future, and is this level of marketing effort economically reasonable?
- Is the useful life of the brand dependent on the useful lives of other assets of the entity? If so, what are the useful lives of those assets?

IAS 38.IE 3.3.190.90 Further examples of determining whether an intangible asset has a finite or indefinite useful life are provided in the illustrative examples to IAS 38.

IAS 38.109 3.3.190.100 The events and circumstances relevant to the classification of an intangible asset as having either a finite or indefinite useful life may change over time. Therefore, an entity reviews the classification in each annual reporting period to decide whether the classification made in the past still is appropriate.

3.3.200 Goodwill and intangible assets with indefinite useful lives

IFRS 3.54, 55, 3.3.200.10 Subsequent to initial recognition, goodwill and intangible assets with indefinite
IAS 38.107, useful lives are measured at cost, or in some cases at a revalued amount (see 3.3.280),
108 less accumulated impairment charges. Goodwill and intangible assets with indefinite useful lives are not amortised, but instead are subject to impairment testing at least annually (see 3.10.130).

IAS 38.109,
110
3.3.200.20 The useful life of an intangible asset that is not being amortised is reviewed in each annual reporting period to determine whether events and circumstances continue to support an indefinite useful life for that asset. Reassessing the useful life of an intangible asset from indefinite to finite is an indication that the asset may be impaired and the entity performs an impairment test when the change is identified (see 3.10.120).

3.3.210 Intangible assets with finite useful lives

IAS 38.97,
104
3.3.210.10 Subsequent to initial recognition, an intangible asset with a finite useful life is amortised on a systematic basis over its useful life, which is reviewed at least at each annual reporting date.

3.3.210.20 A change in the useful life is accounted for prospectively as a change in estimate (see 2.8.60).

IAS 38.105
3.3.210.30 For example, Company M acquired software, an intangible asset with a finite useful life, on 1 January 2003 and its useful life was estimated to be 10 years. On 31 December 2009 the carrying amount of the software is 240. On 1 January 2010 M revises the estimated remaining useful life downwards to a further two years from that date. Therefore, the carrying amount of 240 should be amortised over the next two years. In addition, the decrease in useful life may indicate that the carrying amount of the software is impaired (see 3.10.120).

3.3.220 *Residual value*

IAS 38.8, 102
3.3.220.10 The depreciable amount of an intangible asset with a finite useful life is determined after deducting its residual value. The residual value of an intangible asset is the estimated amount that an entity would obtain currently from disposal of the asset, after deducting the estimated costs of disposal, if the asset were in the condition expected at the end of its useful life.

IAS 38.100
3.3.220.20 However, unlike property, plant and equipment, the residual value of an intangible asset with a finite useful life is assumed to be zero unless:

- a third party has committed to buy the asset at the end of its useful life; or
- there is an active market (see 3.3.280) from which a residual value can be obtained, and it is probable that such a market will exist at the end of the asset's useful life.

IAS 38.101
3.3.220.30 The effect of these criteria is that generally the residual value of an intangible asset with a finite useful life is assumed to be zero. A residual value other than zero implies that an entity expects to dispose of the intangible asset before the end of its economic life.

IAS 38.102,
103
3.3.220.40 The residual value of an intangible asset with a finite useful life is reviewed at least at each annual reporting date. A change in the asset's residual value is accounted for prospectively as a change in estimate (see 2.8.60). If the residual value of an intangible

asset increases to an amount equal to or greater than the asset's carrying amount, then amortisation stops until its residual value subsequently decreases to an amount below the asset's carrying amount.

3.3.230 *Methods of amortisation*

3.3.230.10 The method of amortisation of an intangible asset with a finite useful life reflects the pattern of consumption of the economic benefits embodied in the asset. The method used is reviewed at least at each annual reporting date and a change in the method applied is accounted for prospectively as a change in estimate (see 2.8.60).

3.3.230.20 No specific method of amortisation is required to be used, and the straight-line method, the diminishing (or reducing balance) method and the unit-of-production method are cited as possible approaches; these methods are illustrated in 3.2.160. If the pattern in which the asset's economic benefits are consumed cannot be determined reliably, then the straight-line method is used.

3.3.230.30 [Not used]

3.3.230.40 In some circumstances a revenue-based method of amortisation may be appropriate. In our view, such a method of amortisation should be applied only when both the related revenues can be estimated reliably and when use of such a method reflects the pattern in which the economic benefits of the asset are expected to be consumed.

3.3.230.50 In our experience, it is difficult in many circumstances to estimate reliably the expected revenues to be generated by an intangible asset over its useful life. For example, the amount and timing of revenues expected to be generated from a licence to produce and sell a new pharmaceutical product may be subject to significant uncertainties even though the costs incurred in obtaining that licence are expected to be recovered. Additionally, in our view the economic benefits of some intangible assets are not best reflected by the use of such a method.

3.3.230.60 Under a revenue-based method, amortisation of an intangible asset is based on the revenues expected to be generated from use of that asset. For example, a company expects to sell 100 units of a product in each of the three years of its product lifecycle but expects to reduce selling prices in the third year to maintain that level of sales. The related intangible asset costs 200 and initially is expected to generate revenues of 500 over its estimated three-year life as follows:

	Yr 1	Yr 2	Yr 3
Unit sales	100	100	100
Unit price	2	2	1
Revenue	200	200	100

3.3.230.70 If actual revenues are equal to those expected initially, then the amortisation charge for each year will be as follows:

	Yr 1	Yr 2	Yr 3
	80	80	40

IAS 38.104   3.3.230.80 The estimates of the timing and amount of future revenues are reviewed and revised if necessary at each annual reporting date in accordance with the requirement in IAS 38 to review the expected useful life. The impact on amortisation expense of a revision to estimates of future revenues is treated as a change in estimate and recognised in the current and future periods over which revenues are expected to occur. Previous amortisation is not restated.

3.3.230.90 Continuing the example in 3.3.230.60 and 70, during year 2 the company revises its estimates of future revenues as follows:

	Yr 1	Yr 2	Yr 3
Unit sales	100	175	200
Unit price	2	2	1.25
Revenue	200	350	250

3.3.230.100 Accordingly, the amortisation charge in year 2 is calculated as follows:

Net carrying amount (200 - 80) x (revenues in year 2 (350) / expected current and future revenues (350 + 250)) = 70.

3.3.235 *Intangible assets that an acquirer intends not to use or to use in a way that is different from how other market participants would use them*

3.3.235.10 As discussed in 2.6.820.10, an acquirer may intend not to use an acquired intangible asset, or it may intend to use it in a way that is not its highest and best use; determining the fair value of such an intangible asset is discussed in 2.6.1040.50 – 80. However, an issue arises as to the appropriate amortisation method to be applied to such an intangible asset. In our view, the guidance in 3.3.230 applies in the usual way, and it is not appropriate to recognise an immediate impairment loss for the carrying amount of the asset simply because it will not be actively used.

3.3.235.20 For example, Company P acquires Company S in a business combination. Both companies are involved in the manufacture of chocolate and other confectionary; while P's brands are dominant in the global marketplace, S's chocolate brand is a major competitor in certain markets. P does not plan to use S's brand after the acquisition, which will benefit P's brands by removing competition.

3.3.235.30 In this example P concludes that it is likely to benefit from S's brand being removed from the marketplace for a period of five years. P further determines that it is appropriate to use the straight-line method of amortisation because it cannot measure the pattern in which the economic benefits associated with S's brand are consumed reliably (see 3.3.230.20). Accordingly, P amortises the carrying amount of S's brand on a straight-line basis over five years.

3.3.235.40 In some cases it may be possible to use the decline in fair value of the unused intangible asset (S's chocolate brand in the example in 3.3.235.20 – 30) at consecutive reporting dates as a proxy for measuring the consumption of economic benefits. However, whether such a method is indeed an appropriate proxy will depend on the specific facts and circumstances of a case.

3.3.235.50 See 3.10.120.60 – 110 for a discussion of the level at which impairment testing is carried out. In particular, since an intangible asset acquired for "defensive" purposes does not generate independent cash inflows, it will be tested as part of the larger cash-generating unit that it benefits.

3.3.240 *Commencement and cessation of amortisation*

IAS 38.97 3.3.240.10 The amortisation of intangible assets with a finite useful life begins when the asset is available for use, i.e. when it is in the location and condition necessary for it to be capable of operating in the manner intended by management.

IAS 38.97 3.3.240.20 Except as discussed in 3.3.220.40, amortisation ceases at the earlier of the date that the asset is:

- classified as held for sale (see 5.4.20); or
- derecognised.

3.3.240.30 For example, Company P develops new software for its human resources department. The software is completed in October 2010 and could be implemented at that date. However, management decides not to implement the software until early in 2011. In our view, the software should be amortised from October 2010 as the software is available for use from this date.

IAS 38.BC74, 3.3.240.40 In contrast to the example in 3.3.240.30, in some cases an intangible asset
36.10 is to be used only in conjunction with other assets that are not yet available for use. In such cases judgement is required in determining when the consumption of the future economic benefits embodied in that asset commences in order to determine the commencement of amortisation. For example, telecoms frequently acquire wireless spectrum licences prior to constructing the related infrastructure that is required in

order to realise the future economic benefits embodied in the licence (the intangible asset).

3.3.240.50 In our view, there are two acceptable approaches to determining when amortisation should commence:

- The first approach is to commence amortisation of the licence once the network as a whole is ready to commence operations, since in effect it is from this point that the entity will realise the future economic benefits embodied in the licence. Applying this approach will require the entity to perform annual impairment testing as the asset is not yet available for use (see 3.10.130).
- The second approach considers the intangible asset's availability for use on a stand-alone basis, i.e. not as an integral part of a group of assets. Applying this approach to the example in 3.3.240.40, the licence would be amortised from its acquisition date since on a stand-alone basis it is available for use.

3.3.250 *Classification of amortisation expense*

IAS 38.99   3.3.250.10 When an intangible asset with a finite useful life is used in the production of another asset (e.g. inventory), the amortisation charge is included in the cost of that asset. Otherwise, amortisation is recognised in profit or loss. When an entity classifies its expenses by function (see 4.1.30), care should be taken in allocating the amortisation of intangible assets.

3.3.250.20 For example, continuing the example in 3.3.240.30, Company P's human resources department is part of the administrative function of the business. Therefore, amortisation of the department's software should be included in administrative expenses.

3.3.260 *Impairment*

IAS 38.111   3.3.260.10 Intangible assets with finite useful lives are tested for impairment when there is an indication of impairment (see 3.10.120). Goodwill, intangible assets with indefinite useful lives and intangible assets not yet available for use are tested for impairment annually *and* when there is an indication of impairment (see 3.10.130).

3.3.270 **Subsequent expenditure**

IAS 38.18   3.3.270.10 Subsequent expenditure to add to, replace part of, or service an intangible asset is recognised as part of the cost of an intangible asset if an entity can demonstrate that the item meets:

- the definition of an intangible asset (see 3.3.10); and
- the general recognition criteria for intangible assets (see 3.3.100).

S 38.20, 43   3.3.270.20 It will be rare for subsequent expenditure to be recognised in the carrying amount of an intangible asset except in the case of acquired in-process research and development projects (see 3.3.120). Often it is difficult to attribute subsequent expenditure directly to a particular intangible asset rather than to the business as a whole. In addition, most subsequent expenditure is likely to be the cost to maintain the expected future economic benefits embodied in an existing intangible asset rather than an expenditure that meets the definition of an intangible asset (see 3.3.10) and the initial recognition criteria (see 3.3.100).

IAS 38.42, 3.3.270.30 The general recognition criteria for internally generated intangible assets are
54-62 applied to subsequent expenditure on in-process research and development projects acquired separately or in a business combination. Therefore, capitalisation after initial recognition is limited to development costs that meet the recognition criteria.

IAS 38.20, 63 3.3.270.40 Consistent with the requirements in respect of initial recognition (see 3.3.100), subsequent expenditure on items such as brands, mastheads, publishing titles and customer lists, and items similar in substance, is not capitalised. This is on the basis that the expenditure cannot be distinguished from developing the business as a whole, and therefore it cannot be identified separately from goodwill.

3.3.280 **Revaluations**

IAS 38.8, 75 3.3.280.10 Intangible assets for which there is an active market may be revalued to fair value. An active market exists when:*

- the items traded are homogeneous;
- willing buyers and sellers normally can be found at any time; and
- prices are available to the public.

IAS 38.78 3.3.280.20 Many intangible assets do not qualify for the revaluation model as they are considered unique, and therefore there is no active market for them; examples include customised software, brands, mastheads, publishing rights, patents and trademarks. An example of an intangible asset for which an active market may exist, thereby allowing such assets to be revalued, is an emissions allowance (see 3.3.170).

IAS 38.72, 3.3.280.30 If an intangible asset is revalued, then all intangible assets in that class are
85, 86 revalued to the extent that there is an active market for these assets. Revaluations should be made with sufficient regularity such that at the reporting date the carrying amount does not differ materially from its fair value. Any surplus arising on the revaluation is recognised in other comprehensive income (and presented in the revaluation reserve within equity) except to the extent that the surplus reverses a previous revaluation deficit on the same asset recognised in profit or loss, in which case a credit up to the amount of the deficit charged previously to profit or loss is recognised in profit or loss. Any deficit on revaluation is recognised in profit or loss except to the extent of any balance in the revaluation reserve on the same asset, in which case it is recognised in other comprehensive income (and deducted from the revaluation reserve in equity). Therefore, under IFRSs, revaluation increases and decreases within a class of assets cannot be offset.

3.3.290 **Retirements and disposals**

3.3.300 *Goodwill*

IAS 36.86 3.3.300.10 When an operation to which goodwill relates is disposed of, the part of the carrying amount of goodwill that has been allocated to the respective cash-generating units is included in calculating the gain or loss on disposal (see 3.10.490).

FRS 1.C4(i), 3.3.300.20 Goodwill recognised previously as a deduction from equity is not recognised
3.80 in profit or loss when the entity disposes of all or part of the business to which that goodwill relates.

3.3.310 *Intangible assets*

IAS 38.87, 3.3.310.10 When an intangible asset is disposed of or when no further economic benefits
112, 113 are expected from it, i.e. neither from its future use nor from its future disposal, the asset is derecognised and the resulting gain or loss is the difference between any proceeds received and the carrying amount of the intangible asset. Any attributable revaluation surplus (see 3.3.280) may be transferred to retained earnings, but is not recognised in profit or loss.

IAS 38.115 3.3.310.20 If an entity recognises the cost of replacing a part of an intangible asset in the carrying amount of an intangible asset, then it derecognises the carrying amount of the replaced part. If it is impracticable for an entity to determine the carrying amount of the replaced part, then it may use the cost of the replacement as an indication of what the cost of the replaced part was at the time that it was acquired or generated internally.

IAS 38.11, 3.3.310.30 The consideration receivable on disposal of an intangible asset is recognised
18, 116 initially at its fair value. If payment for the intangible asset is deferred, then the consideration received is recognised initially at its cash price equivalent. The difference between the nominal amount of the consideration and the cash price equivalent is recognised as interest revenue in accordance with IAS 18 (see 4.6.20).

IAS 38.112, 3.3.310.40 The amortisation of an intangible asset with a finite useful life does not cease
117 when the intangible asset is no longer used, unless the asset has been fully amortised, has been derecognised or is classified as held for sale. Non-current assets held for sale or distribution are presented separately from other assets in the statement of financial position and are not amortised or depreciated (see 5.4.20 and 35).

3.3.310.50 See 5.7 for a discussion of exchanges of non-monetary assets.

3.3.320 **Disclosure**

IAS 38.118 3.3.320.10 The disclosure requirements for intangible assets, which are illustrated in KPMG's series of illustrative financial statements, include a reconciliation between the carrying amount of intangible assets at the beginning and end of the period. The reconciliation is required for both the current and the comparative period.

IAS 38.118   3.3.320.20 The reconciliation for intangible assets other than goodwill includes separate line items for additions and acquisitions through business combinations. Therefore, acquisitions should be split between intangible assets acquired in a business combination and other acquisitions. However, all disposals are presented in a single line item in the reconciliation.

IAS 38.118   3.3.320.30 The calculation of the net exchange difference in respect of foreign operations, which is part of the reconciliation, is illustrated in 2.7.280.

3.3.330 Future developments

3.3.330.10 In May 2009 the IASB published ED/2009/5 *Fair Value Measurement* (the 2009 ED). The proposals in the 2009 ED are intended to replace the fair value measurement guidance contained in individual IFRSs with a single, unified definition of fair value, as well as provide further authoritative guidance on the application of fair value measurement in inactive markets. The 2009 ED proposes a framework for measuring fair value and disclosures about fair value measurements. The proposals in the 2009 ED explain how to measure fair value when it already is required or permitted by existing IFRSs; they do not introduce new fair value measurements, nor do they eliminate the practicability exceptions to fair value measurements that exist currently in certain standards.

3.3.330.20 In June 2010 the IASB published ED/2010/7 *Measurement Uncertainty Analysis Disclosure for Fair Value Measurements* (the 2010 ED). The 2010 ED expands on the proposal in the 2009 ED for an entity to disclose a measurement uncertainty analysis (or sensitivity analysis) for assets and liabilities measured at fair value categorised within Level 3 of the fair value hierarchy. The 2010 ED proposes that an entity consider the effect of correlation between unobservable inputs, if relevant.

3.3.330.30 A final standard on fair value measurement and disclosure, which is expected to be converged with a forthcoming amended standard under US GAAP, is scheduled for the first quarter of 2011.

3.3.330.40 In June 2010 the IASB published ED/2010/6 *Revenue from Contracts with Customers*, which provides guidance on the accounting for costs incurred to fulfil a contract. If finalised as proposed, then there is some doubt as to whether any subscriber acquisition costs could continue to be capitalised. A final standard is scheduled for the second quarter of 2011.

3.3.330.50 In December 2007 the IASB activated a joint project with the FASB to address the underlying accounting for emissions trading schemes. An ED is scheduled no earlier than the second half of 2011.

3.3.330.60 A group of national standard-setters is carrying out research for a possible future IASB project on intangible assets. No decisions have yet been made as to whether this work will develop into an active project of the IASB.

3.4 Investment property
(IAS 17, IAS 40)

Overview of currently effective requirements

- Investment property is property held to earn rentals or for capital appreciation, or both.

- Property held by a lessee under an operating lease may be classified as investment property if the rest of the definition of investment property is met and the lessee measures all its investment property at fair value.

- A portion of a dual-use property is classified as investment property only if the portion could be sold or leased out under a finance lease. Otherwise the entire property is classified as property, plant and equipment, unless the portion of the property used for own use is insignificant.

- When a lessor provides ancillary services, a property is classified as investment property if such services are a relatively insignificant component of the arrangement as a whole.

- Investment property is recognised initially at cost.

- Subsequent to initial recognition, all investment property is measured using either the fair value model (subject to limited exceptions) or the cost model. When the fair value model is chosen, changes in fair value are recognised in profit or loss.

- Disclosure of the fair value of all investment property is required, regardless of the measurement model used.

- Subsequent expenditure is capitalised only when it is probable that it will give rise to future economic benefits.

- Transfers to or from investment property can be made only when there has been a change in the use of the property. The intention to sell an investment property without redevelopment does not justify reclassification from investment property into inventory.

- The property continues to be classified as investment property until the time of disposal unless it is classified as held for sale.

Currently effective requirements

This publication reflects IFRSs in issue at 1 August 2010. The currently effective requirements cover annual periods beginning on 1 January 2010. The requirements related to this topic are derived mainly from IAS 40 *Investment Property* and IAS 17 *Leases*.

Forthcoming requirements and future developments

When a currently effective requirement will be changed by a new requirement that is issued but is not yet effective, it is marked with a # as a **forthcoming requirement** and the impact of the change is explained in the accompanying boxed text. In respect of this topic no forthcoming requirements are noted.

When a significant change to the currently effective or forthcoming requirements is expected, it is marked with a * as an area that may be subject to **future developments** and a brief outline of the relevant project is given in 3.4.280.30 – 50. In addition, an outline of a further project is given in 3.4.280.10 and 20 that affects several aspects of accounting for investment property.

3.4.10 **Definition**

IAS 16.2, 40.2   3.4.10.10 IAS 40 is not a specialised industry standard. Therefore, determining whether a property is investment property depends on the use of the property rather than the type of entity that holds the property. Classification as investment property is mandatory if the criteria of IAS 40 are met, although there is a choice regarding how investment properties are measured subsequent to initial recognition (see 3.4.140).

IAS 40.5   3.4.10.20 Investment property is property held to earn rental income or for capital appreciation, or both, rather than for:

- use in the production or supply of goods or services or for administrative purposes; or
- sale in the ordinary course of business.

3.4.10.30 For example, a retail site owned by Company G, but leased out to third parties in return for rental income, is an investment property. However, a factory owned and used by Company H is not an investment property because it is used in the production of goods.

IAS 40.14   3.4.10.40 Although the definition in 3.4.10.20 appears relatively straightforward, determining what is or is not investment property raises some difficult practical issues. Some of these issues are discussed in 3.4.20 – 120.

3.4.20 *Property*

IAS 40.5   3.4.20.10 An investment property may comprise:

- land;
- a building or part of a building; or
- both.

3.4.20.20 – 30 [Not used]

IAS 16.58   3.4.20.40 Land and assets situated on that land generally are separate assets. However, in some cases a structure that is not a building in its own right may be regarded as an integral part of the related land, and therefore still might meet the definition of investment property; e.g. golf courses and car parks. If the investment property is being accounted for under the cost model (see 3.4.180), then it is necessary to assess whether or not these structures are separately depreciable as components.

IAS 40.4   3.4.20.50 The following items are excluded specifically from the scope of the investment property standard because they are subject to requirements contained in other IFRSs:

- biological assets on land related to agricultural activities (see 3.9); and
- mineral rights and reserves such as oil, natural gas and similar non-regenerative resources (see 5.11).

3.4.30 *Equipment and furnishings*

IAS 40.50   3.4.30.10 Equipment and furnishings physically attached to a building are considered to be part of the investment property. So, for example, lifts, escalators, air conditioning units, decorations and installed furniture, such as built-in cabinetry, would be included as part of the cost and fair value of the investment property and would not be classified separately as property, plant and equipment.

IAS 40.50   3.4.30.20 When investment property is leased on a furnished basis, generally its fair value also includes the value of the related movable furniture. In such cases the furniture would not be accounted for as a separate asset if the investment property is accounted for at fair value (see 3.4.150). If the investment property is accounted for using the cost model (see 3.4.180), then the related movable furniture are accounted for under IAS 16 *Property, Plant and Equipment* as separate components. This is consistent with the components approach required by IFRSs (see 3.2.230). However, in our view care should be taken to ensure that the disclosure of fair value of the investment property is not misleading when the fair value of the property includes the fair value of the furniture.

3.4.40 *Leased property*

3.4.40.10 IAS 17, rather than IAS 40, applies to property leased out under a finance lease in the financial statements of a lessor (see 5.1).

IAS 40.6   3.4.40.20 A lessee under an operating lease may elect to classify its leasehold interest as an investment property, provided that the leasehold interest meets the rest of the definition of an investment property. In such cases the lessee accounts for the lease as if it were a finance lease (see 5.1.250). This election is available on a property-by-property basis. If a lessee follows this election for one such property, then it is required to apply the fair value model to all its investment property. In a lease of land and buildings, when the building is held under a finance lease, the land may qualify as investment property even if it is held under an operating lease.

3.4.40.30 [Not used]

3.4.40.35 When a lease includes both land and building elements, an entity determines the classification of each element based on the classification criteria of IAS 17 (see 5.1.230 and 240).

3.4.40.40 [Not used]

3.4.40.45 It may occur that a building is treated as being owned outright by the lessee of the land, even if the underlying land is held under an operating lease. This might be the case if, for example, during the lease term the lessee is entitled to build or remove any structures on the leased land and if the lease were to terminate, then the lessee would have both the right to remove the building and the obligation to do so if the lessor so required. In this case the building may be an investment property, even if the land, separately classified as held under an operating lease, is not treated as an investment property.

3.4.40.50 For example, Company D acquires a 30-year leasehold interest in a piece of empty land. D constructs and owns a retail building on the land, and assesses that the lease of the land is an operating lease. D can choose to classify the operating lease of the land as investment property if the fair value model is applied.

3.4.40.60 IAS 17 applies to property held by a lessee under an operating lease that is not classified as investment property (see 3.4.40.20). See 5.1 for guidance on the accounting for leases, and 5.1.240 for specific guidance on the classification of leases that cover both land and buildings.

3.4.50 *Investment property under construction/development*

3.4.50.10 – 40 [Not used]

IAS 40.8(e), 65   3.4.50.50 Property under construction or development for future use as an investment property (investment property under construction) is accounted for under the requirements of IAS 40, using the measurement model elected for investment property (see 3.4.140).

3.4.60 *Inventory vs investment property*

IAS 40.9   3.4.60.10 Property that is held for sale in the ordinary course of business, or that is in the process of construction or development for such sale, is classified as inventory (see 3.8) rather than as investment property.

IAS 40.8, 9   3.4.60.20 In some cases it may be difficult to distinguish between property held for sale in the ordinary course of business (inventory) and property held for capital appreciation (investment property). The standard gives examples of land held for *long-term* capital appreciation (investment property), land held for *short-term* sale (inventory) and property acquired exclusively with a view to subsequent disposal in the *near future* (inventory). "Short-term", "long-term" and "near future" are not defined in IFRSs and various interpretations are possible.

IAS 1.68   3.4.60.30 In our view, the business model of an entity (i.e. the entity's intentions regarding that property) is the primary criterion for classification of a property. The holding period (short- or long-term) is considered in the context of the business model rather than as a "bright line". Therefore, an entity that trades in properties would classify its property as inventory if it intends to dispose of the property in the course of its normal operating cycle.

3.4.60.40 For example, Building Company F acquires bare land with the intention of building residential homes that will be sold upon completion. In our view, property under construction and/or land held for future development by a developer generally would be classified as inventory because it is an asset held in the process of production for a sale. Therefore, we believe that F should classify the land and subsequently the property construction as inventory.

IAS 40.3, 8(b), 57   3.4.60.50 However, if the land is held for an undetermined future use, then it is classified as investment property. For example, Company E pays 400 to acquire an interest in a piece of empty land. E has not yet decided what it will do with the land, but it acquired the interest because it considered the asking price to be a bargain. E classifies the land as an investment property, as the land is held for an undetermined future use; it is transferred to inventory if and when development for sale commences.

3.4.60.60 Generally property investors classify their properties as investment property. However, in our view a property investor should classify properties as inventory when, at the acquisition date, the properties are "marked" as trading properties, i.e. the investor has the intention of selling them in the ordinary course of business. For example, Company H, an investor in commercial buildings, buys portfolios of properties including commercial and residential buildings on a regular basis; historically residential buildings generally have been sold shortly after acquisition. If at the acquisition date H has the intention of selling the residential buildings in its ordinary course of business, then they should be classified as inventory, irrespective of whether they are occupied by tenants.

3.4.60.70 Classification requires more judgement when, for example, an entity decides to hold a residential property until a tenant moves out and plans to sell the property only when it is unoccupied. Depending on particular circumstances and the entity's intentions, the waiting period may be viewed as part of preparing the property for sale at its best price, or it may be more appropriate to classify the residential property as investment property.

IAS 40.9   3.4.60.80 Completed developments held for sale in the ordinary course of business are classified as inventory. However, if the intention of the developer entity is to hold a completed development for a certain period and the developer rents the property out during that holding period, then in our view the developer should consider whether continuing to classify the property as inventory is appropriate or whether the property is reclassified to investment property.

IAS 40.8, 9, 58 3.4.60.90 Similarly, if an entity decides to redevelop an existing investment property with the intention of selling the property upon completion, then the investment property is transferred to inventories at the date that the redevelopment of the site commences. However, a decision to dispose of an investment property without redevelopment does not result in a reclassification to inventory. In this case the property continues to be classified as investment property until the time of disposal or earlier classification as held for sale (see 5.4.20).

IAS 40.58 3.4.60.95 Property classified previously as investment property that is being redeveloped for continued use as investment property is treated as investment property during its redevelopment (see 3.4.250).

3.4.60.100 See 3.4.200 for further guidance on transfers to or from investment property.

3.4.70 *Property as collateral*

IFRS 5.IGE3 3.4.70.10 Financial institutions sometimes take possession of property that originally was pledged as security in full and final settlement of the mortgage for loans (see 3.6.1490.20). When a financial institution acquires a property in this way, the property is classified in the normal way, for example, as investment property or property, plant and equipment (see 3.2), or classified as held for sale if appropriate (see 5.4.20).

IAS 40.8 3.4.70.20 When a financial institution is uncertain of its intentions with respect to land and buildings that it has repossessed, in our view those properties should be classified as investment property. This is consistent with the treatment of land held for an undetermined future use (see 3.4.60.50).

3.4.80 *Consolidated and separate financial statements*

IAS 27.4, 40.15 3.4.80.10 In determining the classification of a property in consolidated financial statements, the assessment is made from the point of view of the group as a single reporting entity. While this is consistent with the requirement for the consolidated financial statements to be presented as those of a single reporting entity (see 2.1.50), it means that a property might be classified differently in consolidated financial statements than in any separate financial statements (see 2.1.70).

3.4.80.20 For example, Company G leases an office block to its Subsidiary H, which uses the offices as its administrative head office. In G's separate financial statements the property is classified as investment property (assuming that the lease is an operating lease). However, in the consolidated financial statements the property is classified as property, plant and equipment because the property is owner-occupied (see 3.4.10).

IAS 27.4   3.4.80.30 In our view, the principles in 3.4.80.10 do not apply to property leased to an associate or a joint venture, because they are not part of the group. Changing the example in 3.4.80.20, if G leased the office block to Associate J, then the property would be classified as investment property in both G's individual or separate financial statements as well as in the consolidated financial statements.

IAS 40.15   3.4.80.40 When assessing the classification of a property leased to, or occupied by, another group entity in the entity's own financial statements, an issue arises as to whether transactions that are not conducted on an arm's length basis should impact the classification. For example, a subsidiary may be instructed to lease a property to another group entity at a price other than market rent.

IAS 40.8,   3.4.80.50 In our view, property leased to related parties, other than own employees,
9(c), 15 should be regarded as investment property, provided that the asset meets the definition of an investment property. This is irrespective of whether the rents charged are on an arm's length basis. The existence of related party relationships and the disclosure of transactions with related parties also would have to be addressed (see 5.5). Property leased to own employees is considered owner-occupied and also may trigger related party disclosures if the employees are key management personnel.

3.4.90 Dual-use property

IAS 40.10   3.4.90.10 Property often has dual purposes whereby part of the property is used for own use activities that would result in the property being considered property, plant and equipment and part of the property is used as an investment property. A portion of a dual-use property is classified as an investment property only if the portion could be sold or leased out separately under a finance lease; in some countries the ability to sell a portion of a property is referred to as strata title or condominiumisation.

3.4.90.20 For example, Company M owns an office block and uses two floors as its own office; the remaining 10 floors are leased out to tenants under operating leases. Under the laws in M's country, M could sell legal title to the 10 floors while retaining legal title to the other two floors. In this case the 10 floors would be classified as investment property.

3.4.90.30 In some countries the right to sell legal title to a portion of a property is not an automatic right and it is necessary first to apply to the relevant local authority for permission. In our view, the entity should be regarded as having the ability to sell legal title to a portion of a property if the process to obtain that right is relatively straightforward and procedural, rather than being subject to a review process in which the chance of rejection is more than remote (see also 3.4.130.40).

IAS 40.10   3.4.90.40 When a portion of the property could not be sold or leased out under a finance lease separately, the entire property is classified as investment property only if the portion of the property held for own use is insignificant. "Insignificant" is not defined, but in our view should be assessed on a property-by-property basis by reference to value and/or usable floor space. We believe that an own use portion below 5 percent of the measure used generally will be insignificant.

3.4.90.50 For example, Company N uses 10 percent of the office floor space of a building as its head office. N leases the remaining 90 percent to tenants, but is unable to sell the tenants' space or to enter into finance leases related solely to it. In our view, N should not classify the property as an investment property because the 10 percent of floor space used by N is more than an insignificant portion.

3.4.90.60 The following are examples of dual-use properties owned by an investor that also operates the properties. The examples illustrate:

- portions of the property that generally would be classified as investment property assuming that they could be sold or leased out under finance leases separately, subject to ancillary services being relatively insignificant (see 3.4.100); and
- portions of the property that often cannot be classified as investment property because they cannot be sold or leased out under finance leases separately.

Examples of dual-use properties	Examples of portions that might be classified as investment property	Examples of portions that often cannot be classified as investment property
Hotel complex	Separate retail premises Office block	Hotel bedrooms Restaurant facilities within the hotel complex Kiosks in the reception hall
Retail area	Separate retail premises with their own separate entrances or a retail area within another building (e.g. a shopping mall or a hotel)	Retail concessions or franchises within a department store
Airports	Separate buildings within the airport perimeter, such as hotels, warehousing, airline office blocks or courier facilities	Retail concessions in the airport terminal

3.4.100 *Ancillary services*

IAS 40.11, 12 3.4.100.10 In many cases the owner of a property provides ancillary services to tenants. In such cases the key to identifying investment property is to decide whether the services provided are a "relatively insignificant component of the arrangement as a whole". The standard gives two examples of properties for which ancillary services are provided:

- an owner-managed hotel is not an investment property because ancillary services provided are a significant component of the arrangement; and

- an office building for which security and maintenance services are provided by the owner is an investment property because these ancillary services generally are an insignificant component of the arrangement.

IAS 40.13   3.4.100.20 Classification difficulties arise in respect of properties that fall between these two extreme examples (e.g. serviced apartments and business centres). The standard acknowledges that judgement is required in assessing whether the definition of investment property is met and requires an entity to develop criteria that are applied consistently in making that assessment. In our view, an entity should make a decision in each case as to whether the substance of the arrangement is more like the example of the owner-managed hotel (not investment property) or the example of the office building with security and maintenance services provided by the owner (investment property). For example:

- Company P owns serviced apartments that are located within one of its hotel complexes; tenants have full access to the hotel facilities and P provides a full daily cleaning service and room service menu. The only significant difference between these accommodations and a hotel suite is a lower price per night, based on a weekly rather than a daily rate. We believe these serviced apartments are not investment property because they are similar to an owner-managed hotel.
- Company Q owns serviced apartments that are located within an apartment block. Q provides security and maintenance services and offers an optional weekly cleaning and laundry service. The leases have a minimum term of three months and references generally are required. The arrangement may be similar to an office building with security and maintenance services. We believe these serviced apartments qualify as investment property.

3.4.100.30 A similar approach applies when classifying business centres. Some business centres provide a high level of services (such as secretarial support, teleconferencing and other computer facilities) and tenants sign relatively short-term leases or service agreements; we believe these facilities are more like an owner-managed hotel (and not an investment property). Other business centres require the user to sign up to a minimum period and may provide only basic furnishings in addition to services such as security and maintenance; we believe these additional services are relatively insignificant and the property would be an investment property.

S 40.13, 14   3.4.100.40 When a property is operated by a third party under a management contract, it is necessary to apply judgement in assessing whether the definition of investment property is met. The standard acknowledges that the terms of management contracts vary widely and requires an entity to develop criteria that are applied consistently in making an assessment.

IAS 40.13   3.4.100.50 The standard gives two examples of hotels managed by others:

- at the one extreme, the entity's position is that of a passive property investor and thus the property is an investment property; and
- at the other extreme, the entity simply has outsourced certain day-to-day functions to a property manager and retains significant exposure to the variation in cash flows from operating the property, and so the property is not an investment property.

3.4.100.60 In our view, in order to classify properties that fall between these two extremes, the relevant factors to be considered include the following:

- under the management contract, which party has the power to make the significant operating and financing decisions regarding the operations of the property. For example, which party has the power to decide:
  - hiring, firing and remuneration of staff and setting staffing levels;
  - opening hours (if applicable);
  - terms and conditions offered to customers; and
  - products on offer;
- the calculation of the owner's return, for example:
  - a fixed or variable return based on property values is more indicative of investment property; and
  - a direct percentage of turnover or net revenue accruing to the owner as earned from the operations of the property is more indicative that the property is not investment property;
- the power of intervention that the owner has under the management contract; for example, whether it is greater or less than might be expected from a normal landlord/tenant relationship; and
- the duration of the contract; for example, whether it is on an annual renewal basis with early cancellation clauses or for a much longer fixed period of time.

3.4.100.70 In our view, when a property owner is sharing substantial operating risks with the property manager, the owner is in effect participating in the delivery of goods and services. This may still be the case even when the day-to-day running of a hotel has been entrusted to a third party hotel management company, as such arrangements still may leave the owner of the hotel significantly exposed to the variations in cash flows of the hotel's operations. In such cases the property is not investment property.

3.4.110 [Not used]

3.4.120 Recognition

3.4.120.10 [Not used]

IAS 40.16, 17 3.4.120.20 Investment property is recognised as an asset when, and only when:

- it is probable that the future economic benefits that are associated with the investment property will flow to the entity; and
- the cost of the investment property can be measured reliably.

3.4.120.30 These recognition criteria are applied to all investment property costs (initial costs to acquire an investment property and subsequent costs to add to or replace a part of an investment property (see 3.4.190)) when the costs are incurred.

3.4.130 **Initial measurement**

3.4.130.05 When investment property acquired constitutes a business, e.g. a property management contract is taken over together with the acquisition of investment property, it is accounted for as a business combination (see 2.6.30 and 2.6.40.20).

IAS 40.20   3.4.130.10 Investment property is measured initially at cost except when the asset is:

- transferred from another category in the statement of financial position (see 3.4.220);
- received as a government grant (see 4.3.40.60 and 4.3.70);
- acquired in a share-based payment arrangement granted by the acquiring entity (see 4.5.1100); or
- acquired in a business combination (see 2.6.560).

IAS 40.5   3.4.130.15 The cost of investment property is the amount of cash or cash equivalents paid or the fair value of other consideration given to acquire the investment property at the time of its acquisition.

S 40.20-23   3.4.130.20 The cost of investment property includes transaction costs and directly attributable expenditure on preparing the asset for its intended use. The principles discussed in respect of attributing cost to property, plant and equipment (see 3.2.20) apply equally to the recognition of investment property. In addition, clearly identified inefficiencies and initial operating losses are expensed as incurred, which is similar to the accounting for property, plant and equipment (see 3.2.40 and 50).

AS 23.4(a), 8, 9   3.4.130.25 Under IAS 23 *Borrowing Costs* an entity capitalises borrowing costs directly attributable to the acquisition, construction or development of an investment property that is a qualifying asset. However, an entity is not required to capitalise borrowing costs in this way if it measures the investment property at fair value.

IAS 40.24   3.4.130.30 When payment is deferred, the cost of the investment property is the cash price equivalent. The issues that arise in accounting for the deferred payment are similar to those in respect of property, plant and equipment (see 3.2.130).

3.4.130.40 In some cases determining the time of acquisition, and hence determining cost, is not straightforward. For example, on 15 February 2010 Company D enters into a contract to purchase a shopping centre for 500 in cash. D and the seller will be bound by the contract only when the competition authority approves the transaction. If such approval is obtained, then the contract stipulates that the sale is effective from 1 January 2010 and D is entitled to the returns made from that date (i.e. the purchase price is adjusted for those returns). On 10 June 2010 the approval is obtained. If the approval from the competition authority is considered to be a substantive hurdle to be overcome (see also 2.6.220.20 and 3.4.90.30), then in our view control of the shopping centre passes only when such approval is obtained, i.e. on 10 June 2010. Assuming that the returns made between 1 January 2010 and 10 June 2010 are 30, we believe the cost of investment property recognised at 30 June 2010 is 470 (500 - 30).

3.4.140 **Subsequent measurement**

IAS 40.30,
32A
3.4.140.10 Subsequent to initial recognition an entity chooses an accounting policy, to be applied consistently, either to:

- measure all investment property using the fair value model, subject to limited exceptions that are discussed in 3.4.170; or
- measure all investment property using the cost model (see 3.4.180).

IAS 40.32A
3.4.140.20 If the entity has issued liabilities that pay a return linked to a group of assets that includes investment property, then the entity may make a separate election for the investment properties that back the linked liabilities.

IAS 40.31,
79(e)
3.4.140.30 The standard implies a preference for measuring investment property at fair value, noting that it will be very difficult to justify a voluntary change in accounting policy from the fair value model to the cost basis of measurement. Entities adopting the cost model are required to disclose the fair value on the same basis as those adopting the fair value model.

IAS 40.6, 34
3.4.140.40 If an entity elects to classify one of its properties that is held under an operating lease as investment property, then the entity is required to use the fair value model for all its investment property (see 3.4.40.20).

3.4.150 *Fair value model**

3.4.160 *General requirements*

IAS 40.33-52
3.4.160.10 If an entity chooses to measure investment property using the fair value model, then it measures the property at fair value at each reporting date, with changes in fair value recognised in profit or loss. Determination of the fair value of investment property generally involves consideration of:

- the actual current market for that type of property in that type of location at the reporting date and current market expectations;
- rental income from existing leases and market expectations regarding possible future lease terms;
- hypothetical sellers and buyers, who are reasonably informed about the current market and who are motivated, but not compelled, to transact in that market on an arm's length basis; and
- investor expectations, e.g. investors' expectations of the potential for future enhancement of the rental income or market conditions etc.

IAS 40.20, 37
3.4.160.20 An entity includes transaction costs incurred on acquisition in the initial measurement of investment property, but does not deduct its estimated selling costs when subsequently measuring fair value. This means that when the property market remains flat or declines between the acquisition date and the date of revaluation, the capitalised

transaction costs included in the initial cost of a property measured at fair value will be recognised as a loss in profit or loss.

3.4.160.30 For example, Company R acquires an investment property for 300 and incurs transaction costs of 5. R elects to measure its investment property at fair value. The initial carrying amount of the property is 305. At the reporting date there has been no movement in the market and the fair value of the property is 300. The loss of 5, which is equivalent to the transaction costs on acquisition, is recognised in profit or loss. Conversely, if the fair value of the property at the reporting date is 310, then the gain recognised in profit or loss is 5, i.e. the difference between the initial carrying amount of 305 and the fair value.

3.4.160.33 Typically, the change in the carrying amount of investment property under construction in any given period will include additions recognised at cost and changes in the fair value of the property. Generally, the amount to be recorded in profit or loss is the change in carrying amount after accounting for additions at cost.

3.4.160.37 For example, Company D is constructing a property for future use as investment property. D applies the fair value model and capitalises attributable borrowing costs (see 4.6.350). On 1 July 2009, the fair value and hence the carrying amount of the property is 1,000. In the year ended 30 June 2010, D capitalises construction costs of 400 and attributable borrowing costs of 100. The fair value of the property at 30 June 2010 is 1,700. In this case, D will record a fair value gain of 200 in profit or loss.

IAS 40.32   3.4.160.40 An entity is encouraged, but is not required, to have valuations carried out by an independent valuer who holds a recognised and relevant professional qualification, and who has recent experience in the location and category of investment property being valued. In our experience, entities take into account the following factors when deciding whether or not to engage an independent valuer:

- the materiality of the assets to the statement of financial position;
- the degree of fluctuation in the market;
- the ease with which a non-expert can make a reasonable estimate of fair value from publicly available information (e.g. information on recent transactions involving comparable properties); and
- whether the entity has its own staff with relevant qualifications.

3.4.160.50 For example, when the property market is reasonably stable and there are frequent transactions in comparable properties for which information is readily available, the entity may adopt a practice of engaging independent property experts only every three years and estimating changes in fair value by other methods in the intervening periods. Such an approach is not, in itself, an accounting policy but rather an estimation method. If, for example, the market has been unusually volatile in the last accounting period, or has become less liquid, then the estimation method may not be appropriate and it may be necessary to obtain additional valuation information from professional valuers.

IAS 40.45, 3.4.160.60 When there is no freely available information on an active market in
46(c) comparable properties in similar locations, it may be possible to apply discounted cash
flow techniques to estimate fair value, if reliable estimates of future cash flows are
available.

IAS 40.46(c), 3.4.160.70 The fair value is estimated using discounted cash flow techniques based on
51 contracted and expected cash inflows and outflows arising from the investment property. Generally, the expected cash flows from planned improvements of the investment
property is not taken into consideration when estimating the fair value of investment
property. However, in some cases it may be clear that a buyer would seek to acquire
a given investment property with the intention of undertaking refurbishment work or
redeveloping the property, for example, if the building is dilapidated or the site has
received planning permission for a more valuable use. If this is the case, then in our
view the fair value should reflect the basis on which market participants would value the
investment property in practice (see also 3.4.165 that addresses fair value measurement
for investment property under construction).

3.4.160.75 For example, Company D acquires land for which planning permission has
been granted for the development of a large commercial and residential complex.
The principal reason that a market participant would acquire the land is to undertake this development project. Assuming that reliable estimates of future cash flows
associated with the project are available, D can estimate the fair value of the land
acquired taking into account the expected cash inflows and outflows arising from
the project.

IAS 40.50 3.4.160.80 When determining the carrying amount of investment property under the fair
value model, an entity does not double count assets or liabilities that are recognised as
separate assets or liabilities.

3.4.160.90 Rather, an entity ensures that the net amount of all the assets and liabilities
it recognises related to the investment property equals the fair value of the investment
property.

3.4.160.95 For example, Company S owns an investment property that it leases out to
Company A for a five-year period. According to the lease agreement no rent is payable
in year one and rent for years two to five equals 100 per annum. At the end of year
one S has accrued rental income of 80 in accordance with IAS 17 and the fair value of
the investment property is 1,000. The cash flows of 400 from the lease are included in
the estimation of the fair value. In our view, S should record the investment property
in the statement of financial position at the end of year one without double counting
the accrued rental income of 80. As the accrued rental income of 80 is included in the
investment property's fair value of 1,000, S may present in its statement of financial
position either:

- two assets with an aggregate carrying amount of 1,000, being accrued income of 80
  and an investment property of 920; or

- a single asset, being an investment property with a carrying amount of 1,000.

3.4.160.100 The chosen presentation method should be applied consistently.

3.4.160.110 See 4.3.70 for guidance about investment property measured at fair value for which a government grant has been received.

3.4.165 *Determining the fair value of investment property under construction*

3.4.165.10 IAS 40 contains no specific guidance on how to determine the fair value of investment property under construction. That is, an entity applies the guidance in IAS 40 applicable to all investment property (see 3.4.160).

3.4.165.20 In our experience, valuers typically determine the fair value of investment property under construction by estimating the fair value of the completed investment property, and then deducting from that amount the estimated costs to complete construction, financing costs and a reasonable profit margin. However, when IAS 40 was amended to bring investment property under construction within the scope of the standard, paragraph 51 of IAS 40, which states that "the fair value of investment property does not reflect future capital expenditure that will improve or enhance the property and does not reflect the related future benefits from this future expenditure", remained unchanged.

3.4.165.30 In our view, fair value should reflect the basis on which market participants would value the investment property in practice. If it is clear that a market participant would acquire a property in the course of construction in order to complete the construction, then we believe that fair value should be determined on this basis.

3.4.170 *Exemption from fair value*

IAS 40.53   3.4.170.10 In exceptional cases there will be clear evidence on initial recognition of a particular investment property that its fair value cannot be determined reliably on a continuing basis. In such cases the property in question is measured using the cost model as if it were property, plant and equipment (see 3.4.180), except that the residual value is deemed to be zero in all cases. The exemption applies only when comparable market transactions are infrequent and alternative estimates of fair value (e.g. based on discounted cash flow projections) are not available.

IAS 40.55   3.4.170.20 An assessment of whether the exemption applies is made only once, when the investment property is recognised initially (following either acquisition or transfer from another category in the statement of financial position). The exemption cannot be used after initial recognition if it was not invoked at the time of initial recognition, even if comparable market transactions become less frequent and alternative estimates of fair value become less readily available.

IAS 40.53   3.4.170.30 Once the exemption is applied, the property continues to be measured in accordance with IAS 16 until its disposal.

IAS
40.53-53B

3.4.170.40 However, if the fair value of an investment property under construction cannot be determined reliably but the entity expects the fair value of the completed property to be determinable reliably, then such investment property under construction is accounted for using the cost model until the earlier of the date when the fair value of the property can be determined reliably or the date when the construction is completed.

3.4.180 *Cost model*

IAS 40.56

3.4.180.10 If an entity chooses to measure investment property using the cost model, then the property is accounted for in accordance with the cost model for property, plant and equipment (i.e. at cost less accumulated depreciation (see 3.2.140) and less any accumulated impairment losses (see 3.10.380)). However, the property continues to be classified as investment property in the statement of financial position.

IAS 40.79(e)

3.4.180.20 If an entity adopts the cost model for measuring investment property, then it also is required to disclose the fair value of the investment property measured on the same basis as under the fair value model. In this regard the guidance in 3.4.150 in respect of the determination of fair value applies, including the exemptions from fair value measurement.

IFRS 5.2, 15,
25, IAS 40.56

3.4.180.30 If a property accounted for using the cost model is classified as held for sale (see 5.4.20), then the measurement requirements of IFRS 5 *Non-current Assets Held for Sale and Discontinued Operations* apply from the date that the criteria are met. In particular, such property is not depreciated when classified as held for sale.

3.4.190 Subsequent expenditure

IAS 40.16

3.4.190.10 Expenditure incurred subsequent to the completion or acquisition of an investment property is capitalised only if it meets the general asset recognition criteria (i.e. it is probable that future economic benefits associated with the item will flow to the entity and the cost of the item can be measured reliably). The standard is explicit that under this recognition principle an entity does not recognise in the carrying amount of investment property the cost of the day-to-day servicing of such a property. Instead, such costs are expensed as incurred. An example of such maintenance activity is the repair of a leaking roof.

IAS 40.16-19

3.4.190.20 Parts of investment property acquired through replacement are capitalised and included in the carrying amount of the investment property if the general asset recognition criteria are met. The carrying amount of the part replaced is derecognised. These requirements are consistent with the requirements in respect of property, plant and equipment (see 3.2.280).

3.4.190.30 The issues that arise in accounting for subsequent expenditure are similar to those in respect of property, plant and equipment (see 3.2.290).

3.4.200 **Transfers to or from investment property**

3.4.210 *Timing of transfers*

S 40.57, 58   3.4.210.10 Although an entity's business model plays a key role in the initial classification of property (see 3.4.60.30), the subsequent reclassification of property is based on an actual change in use rather than on changes in an entity's intentions.

IFRS 5.2,   3.4.210.20 For example, Company S owns a retail site that is an investment property. S
5(d),   decides to modernise the site and then to sell it. The investment property is transferred
S 40.56, 58   to inventory at the date that the redevelopment of the site commences as this evidences the change in use. However, a decision to dispose of an investment property without redevelopment does not result in it being reclassified as inventory. The property continues to be classified as investment property until the time of disposal unless it is classified as held for sale (see 5.4.20).

3.4.210.30 [Not used]

IAS 40.57   3.4.210.40 In order to reclassify inventories to investment property, the change in use is evidenced by the commencement of an operating lease to another party. In some cases a property (or a part of a property) classified as inventory (see 3.8) is leased out temporarily while the entity searches for a buyer. In our view, the commencement of such an operating lease, solely by itself, does not require the entity to transfer the property to investment property provided that the property continues to be held for sale in the ordinary course of business. Any rental income is incidental to such sale (see 3.2.120.10 and 30).

IAS 40.57   3.4.210.50 A reclassification of an investment property to inventory or property, plant and equipment is performed only when an entity's use of the property has changed. In our view, the commencement of construction for sale or own use usually would mean that the property is no longer available for rent to third parties. Hence, a change in use occurs on commencement of redevelopment and reclassification is appropriate at that point.

3.4.210.60 For example, Company G previously has classified a property as an investment property. G has decided to use the property as its administrative headquarters due to an expansion of its business, and commences redevelopment for own use in February 2010 (e.g. builders are on site carrying out the construction work on G's behalf). In our view, the redevelopment of the property for future use for administrative purposes effectively constitutes owner occupation, and therefore G should reclassify the property upon commencement of the redevelopment in February 2010.

3.4.220 *Measurement of transfers*

3.4.230 *Cost model*

IAS 40.59   3.4.230.10 If an entity chooses to measure investment property using the cost model, then transfers to and from investment property do not alter the carrying amount of the property. Therefore, revaluations recognised for property, plant and equipment carried at fair value (see 3.2.300) are not reversed when the property is transferred to investment property.

3.4.230.20 The standard does not state specifically whether the property's carrying amount should be brought up to date under its current policy immediately before the transfer. In our view, a restatement to bring the property's carrying amount up to date is required if the effect would be material to the way in which the results for the period are presented in the statement of comprehensive income.

3.4.230.30 For example, Company T has a property classified as inventory. Some time after acquisition, management decides to hold the property indefinitely because the market currently is depressed, and has leased out the property to another party under an operating lease. At the time that the lease is entered into, the net realisable value of the property is 450, which is lower than its cost of 480. In our view, T should write down the property to 450 prior to transferring it to investment property and the loss of 30 should be presented in the statement of comprehensive income in the same line as other inventory write-downs.

IAS 16.41, 40.62   3.4.230.40 IAS 40 is silent on the treatment of an existing revaluation reserve when revalued property is transferred from property, plant and equipment to investment property, where it will be measured under the cost model. In our view, any revaluation reserve accumulated while the property was accounted for as property, plant and equipment should be accounted for in accordance with IAS 16 (i.e. the reserve may be transferred to retained earnings when the amount is realised either through higher depreciation charges while the asset is being used or on disposal). Alternatively, none of the reserve is transferred to retained earnings. See 3.2.410 for further guidance on issues that arise in respect of this treatment.

3.4.240 *Fair value model*

IAS 40.61-65   3.4.240.10 If an entity chooses to measure investment property using the fair value model, then investment property transferred from another category in the statement of financial position is recognised at fair value upon transfer. The treatment of the gain or loss on revaluation at the date of transfer depends on whether or not the property previously was held for own use.

IAS 40.61, 62(b)(ii)   3.4.240.20 When the property previously was held for own use, the property is accounted for as property, plant and equipment up to the date of the change in use. Any difference at the date of the change in use between the carrying amount of the property and its fair value is recognised as a revaluation of property, plant and equipment in accordance with IAS 16, even if the property was measured previously using the cost model under IAS 16. Any existing or arising revaluation surplus previously recognised in other comprehensive income is not transferred to profit or loss at the date of transfer or on subsequent disposal of the investment property. However, on subsequent disposal of the investment property, any existing revaluation surplus that was recognised when the entity applied the IAS 16 revaluation model to the property may be transferred to retained earnings.

IAS 40.63, 64   3.4.240.30 When the property is inventory that is being transferred to investment property, the gain or loss on revaluation, based on the asset's carrying amount at the date of transfer, is recognised in profit or loss.

3.4.240.40 IFRSs are silent on where any gain or loss arising at the point of transfer should be recognised. In our view, any gain or loss on property previously classified as inventory should be included in the same line as other gains or losses on inventory.

3.4.240.50 The gain or loss should be identified separately if material (see 4.1.80).

IAS 40.65   3.4.240.55 If an entity measures investment property at fair value but cannot determine reliably the fair value of investment property under construction, and as a result of which it measures such investment property at cost until construction is completed (see 3.4.170.40), then typically there will be a difference between the carrying amount and fair value of investment property upon completion of construction. Any difference between the fair value of the property at that date and its previous carrying amount is recognised in profit or loss.

IAS 40.60   3.4.240.60 When a property is transferred from investment property measured at fair value (whether to own use properties or to inventories), the transfer is accounted for at fair value. The fair value at the date of transfer then is deemed to be the property's cost for subsequent accounting under IAS 2 *Inventories* or IAS 16 (see 3.8 and 3.2 respectively). Any difference between the carrying amount of the property prior to transfer and its fair value on the date of transfer is recognised in profit or loss in the same way as any other change in the fair value of investment property.

IFRS 5.2, 5,   3.4.240.70 If an investment property measured using the fair value model is classified as IAS 40.33-52   held for sale in accordance with IFRS 5 (see 5.4.20), then the measurement requirements of IAS 40 still apply (see 5.4.20.20).

3.4.250 Redevelopment

IAS 40.58   3.4.250.10 When an entity redevelops an existing investment property, the property is not transferred out of investment property during redevelopment. This means that an investment property undergoing redevelopment would continue to be measured under the cost model or at fair value (depending on the entity's accounting policy).

3.4.250.20 However, consideration is given to whether any of the property has been disposed of during the course of redevelopment. For example, significant items of equipment installed in the building, or even the building itself, may have been scrapped. In our view, any such disposals should be accounted for as follows:

- When investment property is measured under the cost model, components of the property should be accounted for as separate items of property, plant and equipment (see 3.2.230). Accordingly, such components should be written off as disposals.
- When an investment property is measured at fair value, information may not exist to enable the entity to account for the disposals separately. We believe it is acceptable to include the disposals as part of the change in fair value.

IAS 23.4(a)   3.4.250.30 When an entity obtains a loan for the redevelopment of existing investment property that is a qualifying asset under IAS 23 (see 4.6.350 and 360), the interest expenditure on the loan used for the incremental cost of redevelopment incurred during the period of construction is capitalised in accordance with IAS 23. If the redevelopment involves a complete redevelopment of a site, then in our view an entity also could capitalise interest expenditure on the historical cost of the land if a loan that was obtained to fund its initial acquisition is still outstanding. However, an entity is not required to capitalise borrowing costs in this way if it measures the investment property at fair value.

3.4.260 Disposals

IAS 40.69   3.4.260.10 The gain or loss on disposal of investment property is measured as the difference between the net disposal proceeds and the carrying amount of the property (unless the transaction is a sale and leaseback (see 5.1.470)). The standard gives no guidance on the meaning of "net" in this context. In our view, it should be determined in the same manner as for property, plant and equipment (see 3.2.440.50).

3.4.260.20 The standard does not state explicitly how to determine the carrying amount on disposal of investment property that is measured at fair value. In our view, one approach is to consider the carrying amount at the date of the last published statement of financial position (whether annual or interim), because paragraph 5 of IAS 40 defines carrying amount as the amount at which an asset is recognised in the statement of financial position, and paragraph 38 of IAS 40 requires the fair value of investment property to reflect market conditions at the end of the reporting period.

3.4.260.30 For example, Company V measures investment property at fair value. V's last published statement of financial position was as at the end of its half-year interim period, 30 September 2009. The carrying amount of one particular retail site was 500 at that date. On 28 February 2010 V obtained an independent valuer's report that stated that the fair value of the retail site had dropped to 470, and this was recognised in V's management accounts. On 31 March 2010 the property was sold for 490. A loss on disposal of 10 would be recognised in profit or loss.

3.4.260.33 An alternative approach is to update the fair value measurement immediately before the sale and then to compare that updated fair value to the sale proceeds when calculating the gain or loss on disposal. Continuing the example in 3.4.260.30, in that case the statement of comprehensive income includes a loss of 30 as part of the line including all investment property fair value changes, and a profit of 20 on disposal presented separately. However, if V assesses at 31 March 2010 that the sale price of

490 provides the best evidence of the fair value of the retail site at that date, then the gain or loss on disposal would be zero and an amount of 10 is presented as fair value changes.

3.4.260.37 An entity should choose an accounting policy, to be applied consistently, to apply one of the approaches outlined in 3.4.260.20 and 33.

IAS 40.70 3.4.260.40 When payment is deferred, the selling price of the investment property is the cash price equivalent for the property (i.e. the amount that the entity would be prepared to accept if settlement were immediate). In almost all cases the cash price equivalent will not differ significantly from the measurement of the receivable as a financial asset, which would require the gross cash flows receivable from the buyer to be discounted using a market rate of interest (see 3.6.710). When a significant difference does exist in a transaction, in our view the requirements of IAS 40 should apply because the standard addresses deferred consideration specifically. Under IAS 40 the difference between the cash price equivalent and the gross cash flows is recognised as interest income over the period until payment, using the effective interest method in accordance with IAS 18 *Revenue*.

3.4.270 Presentation and disclosure

IAS 1.54 3.4.270.10 Investment property is presented separately in the statement of financial position.

IAS 1.77, 40.74-79 3.4.270.20 Since IAS 40 makes no reference to making disclosures on a class-by-class basis, it could be assumed that the minimum requirement is to make the disclosures on an aggregate basis for the whole investment property portfolio. When investment property represents a significant portion of the assets we prefer entities to disclose additional analysis, for example:

- analysing the portfolio into different types of investment property, such as retail, offices, manufacturing and residential; and
- identifying separately any properties currently under redevelopment, vacant, whose use is undetermined and/or that are intended for sale.

3.4.280 Future developments

3.4.280.10 In July 2006 the IASB announced a project to reconsider the accounting requirement for leasing arrangements. The project is being conducted jointly with the FASB. In March 2009 the IASB and FASB published a DP *Leases – Preliminary Views* (the DP). The DP proposes, for lessees, to eliminate the requirement to classify a lease contract as an operating or finance lease, and to require a single accounting model to be applied to all leases. The DP proposes that a lessee recognise in its financial statements a "right-of-use" asset representing its right to use the leased asset, and a liability representing its obligation to pay lease rentals. The DP includes a high-level discussion of lessor accounting issues but expresses no preliminary views on lessor accounting.

3.4.280.20 An ED is scheduled for the third quarter of 2010. Unlike the DP, the ED is expected to address both lessee and lessor accounting. The proposals for lessee accounting will reflect the "right-of-use" model described in the DP. The proposals for lessor accounting will feature a "hybrid" approach under which a lessor will account for leases using either the performance obligation model or the partial derecognition model, depending on the nature of the lease. Under the performance obligation model, the lessor will continue to recognise the leased asset and will also recognise an asset for its right to receive lease rentals and a liability for its obligation to allow the lessee to use the leased asset. Under the derecognition model, the lessor will derecognise the leased asset and recognise an asset for its right to receive lease rentals and a residual value asset representing its interest in the leased asset at the end of the lease term. The IASB proposed an exemption from these requirements for lessors of investment property measured at fair value.

3.4.280.30 In May 2009 the IASB published ED/2009/5 *Fair Value Measurement* (the 2009 ED). The proposals in the 2009 ED are intended to replace the fair value measurement guidance contained in individual IFRSs with a single, unified definition of fair value, as well as provide further authoritative guidance on the application of fair value measurement in inactive markets. The 2009 ED proposes a framework for measuring fair value and disclosures about fair value measurements. The proposals in the 2009 ED explain how to measure fair value when it already is required or permitted by existing IFRSs; they do not introduce new fair value measurements, nor do they eliminate the practicability exceptions to fair value measurements that exist currently in certain standards.

3.4.280.40 In June 2010 the IASB published ED/2010/7 *Measurement Uncertainty Analysis Disclosure for Fair Value Measurements* (the 2010 ED). The 2010 ED expands on the proposal in the 2009 ED for an entity to disclose a measurement uncertainty analysis (or sensitivity analysis) for assets and liabilities measured at fair value categorised within Level 3 of the fair value hierarchy. The 2010 ED proposes that an entity consider the effect of correlation between unobservable inputs, if relevant.

3.4.280.50 A final standard on fair value measurement and disclosure, which is expected to be converged with a forthcoming amended standard under US GAAP, is scheduled for the first quarter of 2011.

3.5 Investments in associates and joint ventures
(IAS 28, IAS 31, SIC-13)

3.5 Investments in associates and joint ventures
(IAS 28, IAS 31, SIC-13)

Overview of currently effective requirements

- The definition of an associate is based on significant influence, which is the power to participate in the financial and operating policies of an entity.

- There is a rebuttable presumption of significant influence if an entity holds 20 to 50 percent of the voting rights of another entity.

- Potential voting rights that are currently exercisable are considered in assessing significant influence.

- A joint venture is an entity, asset or operation that is subject to contractually established joint control.

- Associates are accounted for using the equity method in the consolidated financial statements.

- Jointly controlled entities may be accounted for either by proportionate consolidation or using the equity method in the consolidated financial statements.

- In applying the equity method or proportionate consolidation, an associate's or jointly controlled entity's accounting policies should be consistent with those of the investor.

- The reporting date of an associate or jointly controlled entity may not differ from the investor's by more than three months, and should be consistent from period to period. Adjustments are made for the effects of significant events and transactions between the two dates.

- When an equity-accounted investee incurs losses, the carrying amount of the investor's interest is reduced to zero. Further losses are recognised by the investor only to the extent that the investor has an obligation to fund losses or has made payments on behalf of the investee.

- Unrealised profits and losses on transactions with associates or jointly controlled entities are eliminated to the extent of the investor's interest in the investee.

- Gains and losses on non-monetary contributions in return for an equity interest in a jointly controlled entity generally are eliminated to the extent of the investor's interest in the investee.

- For jointly controlled assets, the investor accounts for its share of the jointly controlled assets, the liabilities and expenses it incurs, and its share of any income or output.

- For jointly controlled operations, the investor accounts for the assets it controls, the liabilities and expenses it incurs, and its share of the income from the joint operation.

- Equity accounting or proportionate consolidation is not applied to an investee that is acquired with a view to its subsequent disposal if the criteria are met for classification as held for sale.

- Venture capital organisations, mutual funds, unit trusts and similar entities may elect to account for investments in associates and jointly controlled entities as financial assets.

- A loss of significant influence or joint control is an economic event that changes the nature of the investment. The fair value of any retained investment is taken into account to calculate the gain or loss on the transaction, as if the investment was fully disposed of. This gain or loss is recognised in profit or loss. Amounts recognised in other comprehensive income are reclassified or transferred as required by other IFRSs.

Currently effective requirements

This publication reflects IFRSs in issue at 1 August 2010. The currently effective requirements cover annual periods beginning on 1 January 2010. The requirements related to this topic are derived mainly from IAS 28 *Investments in Associates* and IAS 31 *Interests in Joint Ventures*.

Forthcoming requirements and future developments

When a currently effective requirement will be changed by a new requirement that is issued but is not yet effective, it is marked with a # as a **forthcoming requirement** and the impact of the change is explained in the accompanying boxed text. The forthcoming requirements related to this topic are derived from:

- *Improvements to IFRSs 2010*. A brief outline of the impact of the *Improvements to IFRSs 2010* on this topic is given in 3.5.875, and a brief outline of the annual improvements process is given in 1.1.85.
- IFRS 9 *Financial Instruments*. A brief outline of the impact of IFRS 9 on this topic is given in 3.5.715 and 3.5.815. See 3.6A for a full discussion of the forthcoming requirements of IFRS 9.

When a significant change to the currently effective or forthcoming requirements is expected, it is marked with a * as an area that may be subject to **future developments** and a brief outline of the relevant project is given in 3.5.880.

3.5.10 **Associates**

IAS 28.2 3.5.10.10 An associate is an entity, including an unincorporated entity such as a partnership, over which an investor has significant influence.

3.5.20 *Significant influence*

IAS 28.2 3.5.20.10 Significant influence is the *power* to participate in an entity's financial and operating policy decisions.

IAS 28.6 3.5.20.20 Significant influence may exist over an entity that is controlled by another party. More than one party may have significant influence over a single entity.

3.5.30 *Assessing significant influence*

3.5.40 *Voting rights*

IAS 27.13, 3.5.40.10 Significant influence is presumed to exist when an investor holds between
28.6 20 and 50 percent of the voting power of another entity. Conversely, it is presumed that significant influence does not exist with a holding of less than 20 percent. These presumptions may be overcome in circumstances when an ability, or lack of ability, to exercise significant influence is demonstrated clearly.

3.5.50 *Qualitative factors*

IAS 28.7 3.5.50.10 IAS 28 states that significant influence is usually evidenced in one or more of the following ways:

- representation on the board of directors or equivalent governing body of the investee;
- participation in the policy-making processes;
- material transactions between the investor and the investee;
- interchange of managerial personnel; or
- providing essential technical information.

3.5.50.20 In our view, additional factors that may indicate significant influence include:

- existence of a right of veto over significant decisions;
- influence over decisions concerning dividend or reinvestment policy;
- guarantees of indebtedness, extensions of credit, ownership of warrants, debt obligations or other securities; or
- lack of concentration of other shareholdings.

3.5.50.30 The first three factors in the list in 3.5.50.20 are considered as indicators of significant influence because they have the nature of participative rights (see 2.5.80) even if they are not sufficient to give the investor control over the investee.

3.5.50.40 In our view "one or more" in paragraph 7 of IAS 28 does not mean that a single factor in isolation necessarily indicates significant influence. For example, providing management services to an entity does not in itself result in the entity being an associate. Similarly, entering into material transactions with an entity does not necessarily give rise to significant influence over that entity. On the other hand, meaningful representation on the governing body of an entity generally indicates significant influence. Therefore, the analysis requires judgement considering all facts and circumstances.

3.5.50.50 In our view, an SPE as defined by SIC-12 *Consolidation – Special Purpose Entities* generally will not be an associate. When the financial and operating policies of an entity are largely pre-determined, most of the factors described in 3.5.50.10 to assess significant influence are not relevant. Therefore, if it is concluded that an entity does not have control over an SPE, then we believe that the entity generally would account for its interest in the SPE as a financial asset in accordance with IAS 39 *Financial instruments: Recognition and Measurement* (see 2.5.150.60).

3.5.60 Ability to exercise vs actual exercise of significant influence

IAS 28.8, 9   3.5.60.10 In determining whether an entity has significant influence over another entity, the focus is on the *ability* to exercise significant influence. It does not matter whether or not significant influence actually is exercised. In this respect assessing whether the investor has the ability to exercise significant influence is similar to the assessment of whether an investor has the power to control an entity. See 2.5.20 for additional guidance and examples illustrating this assessment process, and 2.5.90.60 for a discussion of the effect of kick-out rights.

3.5.70 Indirect holdings

IAS 28.6   3.5.70.10 In assessing whether voting rights give rise to significant influence, it is necessary to consider both direct holdings of the investor and holdings of the investor's subsidiaries. Holdings of the investor's joint ventures and other associates are not included in this evaluation.

3.5.80 Potential voting rights

IAS 28.8, 9   3.5.80.10 In assessing significant influence, the effect of potential voting rights that are currently exercisable, both those held by the entity and by other parties, are taken into account. Potential voting rights include warrants, call options, debt or equity instruments that are convertible into ordinary shares, or other similar instruments that have the potential, if exercised or converted, to give the entity voting power. They also include call options that currently are out of the money. See 2.5.130 for more guidance on this assessment process.

3.5.90 **Joint ventures**

IAS 31.3   3.5.90.10 The definition of a joint venture has two aspects, both of which should be present in order to conclude that an entity is a joint venture rather than an associate or subsidiary:

- a *contractual arrangement* whereby two or more parties undertake an economic activity…
- …that is subject to *joint control.*

3.5.100 *Contractual arrangement*

IAS 31.9   3.5.100.10 The existence of a *contractual* arrangement is a key aspect of the definition of a joint venture. An entity that has its shares split evenly among its shareholders, for example with two shareholders each having a 50 percent interest, or with four shareholders each having a 25 percent interest, is not a joint venture unless there is a contractual arrangement that establishes joint control.

IAS 31.10   3.5.100.20 The contractual arrangement between the venturers can take many forms. It could be a contract signed by the venturers, minutes of discussions between the venturers, or the joint venture arrangement could be incorporated into the articles or by-laws of a jointly controlled entity. The form of the contractual arrangement also may depend on the requirements of the local laws and regulations. However, in the event that the agreement is not in writing, it nonetheless should be a valid means of evidencing a contract in the relevant jurisdiction(s).

3.5.100.30 In our experience, it is uncommon for an entity whose shares are publicly traded to be subject to contractually established joint control.

3.5.100.40 For example, Company K is a public entity. The shares of K are held 50 percent by Company L and 50 percent by members of the public. L appoints four of the eight directors of the board of K. Decisions are made based on a majority vote. Therefore, the public shareholders as a group have the ability to block any decisions made by L. However, this does not make K a joint venture, as there is no contract between L and any other shareholder to share control.

3.5.110 *Joint control*

IAS 31.3   3.5.110.10 Joint control is the contractually agreed sharing of control over an economic activity, and exists only when the strategic financial and operating decisions essential to the accomplishment of the goals of the joint venture require the unanimous consent of the venturers. However, this does not preclude a joint venture from existing when *some* decisions do not require the consent of all the venturers, provided that significant decisions require consent by all parties.

3.5.110.20 Joint control does not require a 50:50 economic interest. Joint control has its origin in the contractual agreement and therefore can be created between more than two venturers and with various proportionate holdings. For example, three parties with holdings in the ratio of 40:30:30 may exercise joint control if there is a contractual agreement that requires unanimous consent for all key decisions. However, in our view if the holdings are significantly different, for example if one party holds 75 percent and another party holds 25 percent, then it may indicate that joint control does not exist, as it is unlikely that a party holding 75 percent of an entity would accept the sharing of control of the entity.

IAS 31.3   3.5.110.30 Joint control also exists between two or more venturers even when another entity has an interest that does not give that entity joint control, for example when the respective interests are 45:45:10, as long as the two venturers with a 45 percent holding share control contractually. The holder of the 10 percent interest would be considered an investor in the venture as opposed to a venturer.

3.5.120 *Assessing joint control*

3.5.120.10 In our view, factors that may be relevant in assessing joint control include the following:

- *The rights of each of the parties.* To convey joint control, rights should be over sub-stantive operating decisions, for example to approve annual business plans; to select, terminate, and set the compensation of management responsible for implementing the investee's policies and procedures; or to establish operating and capital decisions of the investee, including budgets, in the ordinary course of business. A right that is protective, for example to approve decisions to issue shares, is not an indication that joint control exists.
- *The terms of shareholder agreements.* If there are clauses in the shareholder agreements or financial arrangements that give additional rights to one of the parties, then this may indicate that joint control does not exist (see 2.5.20).
- *How disputes between the parties are resolved.* For joint control to exist, dispute resolution procedures should be neutral and not favour one of the parties; for example, a mutually agreed upon independent arbitrator should be used.
- *The termination provisions.* Consider how termination is initiated and whether any party has an advantage.
- *Subsequent transactions.* Consider a transaction that is contemplated when the joint venture is set up, for example a sell-off by one of the parties.
- *The governance structures.* Consider the roles and responsibilities of any sharehold-ers' committees, including the role of the supervisory board, executive board and/ or steering committees (see 2.5.40).
- *The terms of any profit-sharing arrangements.* For example, the parties may have a 50:50 economic interest in the net assets of a venture, but uneven profit sharing

may indicate the existence of other factors that should be considered in assessing whether there is joint control.

3.5.120.20 As an intermediate step in a business combination, the acquirer and seller may exercise joint control over an entity. In our view, in these cases it is necessary to consider the overall economic effect of all the transactions related to the business combination as a whole. If these facts and circumstances indicate that the joint control is not substantive, for example because the joint control is for too short a period to have any real economic effect, then the entity should not be treated as a joint venture. See 2.6 for a discussion of the accounting for business combinations.

3.5.120.30 Agreeing to act in the best interests of another party does not in itself establish joint control. For example, Companies R and S enter into an arrangement to develop and market a new product. R and S each have a 50 percent interest in new Company T. R knows the local market and therefore is responsible for the operation and management of T. R agrees to act in the best interests of both parties when determining the financial and operating policies to be adopted by T. Profits will be distributed equally to both parties after deducting a fee paid to R for the operational management work. Unless S has other rights that enable it to block policy decisions made by R, R has sole governance over the financial and operating policies of T. Therefore, T is a subsidiary of R and not a joint venture. T will be a joint venture only if the strategic financial and operating decisions require the unanimous consent of R and S.

IAS 31.24   3.5.120.40 In our view, an SPE as defined by SIC-12 generally will not be a jointly controlled entity. When the financial and operating policies of an entity largely are predetermined, no ongoing decisions can be taken by unanimous consent of the venturers after set-up. Therefore, the factors described in 3.5.50.50 to assess joint control are not relevant. If it is concluded that an entity does not have control over an SPE, then we believe that the entity generally would account for its interest in the SPE as a financial asset in accordance with IAS 39 (see 2.5.150.60).

3.5.130 *Management control*

IAS 31.12   3.5.130.10 Joint control is assessed in terms of the ability to control the key financial and operating policies. One party may be the operator or manager of a joint venture, as long as all parties agree on key operating and financial policies collectively and the non-managing parties have the power to ensure that these are followed.

3.5.140 **Jointly controlled entities***

IAS 31.24   3.5.140.10 When a joint venture activity is carried on through a separate entity, e.g. a corporation or partnership, it is known as a "jointly controlled entity". In our experience, this is the most common form of joint venture.

3.5.150 **Jointly controlled assets and operations***

IAS 31.18, 19   3.5.150.10 *Jointly controlled assets* arise from an arrangement that is a joint venture carried on with assets that are controlled jointly, whether or not owned jointly, but not through a separate entity. Examples of jointly controlled assets include:

- Two oil producers sharing the use of a pipeline to transport oil; both parties bear an agreed proportion of the operating expenses.
- Four parties entering into an arrangement to jointly control an investment portfolio; the joint venture is evidenced by a contract, but no separate entity is formed.

IAS 31.13, 14   3.5.150.20 A *jointly controlled operation* is a joint venture carried on by each venturer using its own assets in pursuit of the joint operation. For example:

- Three aircraft charter companies agree to operate a charter route jointly, using their own aircraft and sharing sales revenue.
- Four construction companies agree to act as a consortium to construct a hotel for a customer. One contract is signed between the customer and the members of the consortium. All four companies are party to the contract as the consortium is not a legal entity.

3.5.160 **Venture capital organisations**

IAS 28.1,   3.5.160.10 IFRSs contain an exemption from the requirement to apply equity accounting
31.1   or proportionate consolidation for investments in associates and in jointly controlled entities held by venture capital organisations, investment funds or mutual funds, unit trusts and similar entities, including investment-linked insurance funds provided that such investments are designated upon initial recognition as at fair value through profit or loss, or are classified as held for trading with changes in fair value recognised in profit or loss (see 3.6.460).

3.5.170 *Qualification as a venture capital organisation*

3.5.170.10 IAS 28 and IAS 31 do not provide criteria for determining whether an investor qualifies as a venture capital organisation. In our view, it is necessary to consider the nature and extent of an entity's investment activities as well as the entity's organisation and its relationship to the investees when determining whether it meets the definition of a venture capital organisation. We believe that entities that apply the exemption for venture capital organisations generally should meet the following criteria:

- the investor's *primary business activity* is investing for current income, capital appreciation or both;
- the investor's investment activities are *clearly and objectively distinct* from any other activities of the entity; and
- the investees are separate *autonomous businesses* from the investor.

3.5.170.20 Guidance on determining whether an entity meets these criteria is provided in 3.5.180 – 200.

3.5.180 *Primary business activity*

3.5.180.10 In our view, evidence that the investor's primary business activity is investing for current income, capital appreciation or both includes but is not limited to:

- the investor's expressed business purpose is to be a venture capital organisation;
- the investor holds multiple investments or has an investment plan to acquire multiple investments;
- the investor has no activities other than investment activities and has no significant assets or liabilities other than those related to its investment activities; or
- the investor has an exit strategy for each investment.

3.5.190 *Clearly and objectively distinct*

3.5.190.10 In our view, the investor is either a separate legal entity or is part of a legal entity conducting investment activities that are clearly and objectively distinct from the other activities of that legal entity. Further, the legal structure of an entity or a group should not determine whether an investor (or a clearly and objectively distinguished part of an entity) whose primary activity is investing in separate autonomous businesses, meets the definition of a venture capital organisation.

3.5.190.20 For the purpose of assessing whether an entity's investment activities are clearly and objectively distinct from its other activities, we believe that the investor should consider organisational and financial factors such as, but not limited to:

- whether the investment activity is carried out as an extension of the other activities, rather than being carried out with a significant degree of autonomy/separation from other activities;
- whether there is management that has been identified separately that has specific responsibility for the investment activities;
- whether the investment activity has its own control and reporting systems, including separate reporting to management and/or the board; and
- whether the investment activity is identified as a separate business segment, although materiality considerations may mean that it is not reported separately.

3.5.190.30 Some of these factors may be demonstrated more readily when the investor's activities are performed in a separate legal entity.

3.5.200 *Autonomous businesses*

3.5.200.10 In our view, investees are not separate autonomous businesses from the investor if, for example:

- the investor obtains benefits, or has the objective of obtaining benefits, that extend beyond the benefits generally afforded to the residual interest holders. Relationships or activities that would fall into this category include, for example: (1) the acquisition, use, exchange, or exploitation of the processes, intangible assets or technology of investees by the investor; (2) significant purchases or sales of assets between the investee and the investor; or (3) other transactions that are on terms that are not considered to be at arm's length;
- the investor provides significant administrative or support services to investees;
- investees provide financing guarantees or collateral for borrowing arrangements of the investor;
- compensation of management or employees of investees is dependent upon the financial results of the investor; or
- the investor directs the integration of operations of investees or the establishment of business relationships between investees.

3.5.210 *Partial use of the venture capital exemption*

IAS 28.1   3.5.210.10 In our view, if an investor has significant influence over an entity and a portion of the investor's interest in this entity is held by a subsidiary that qualifies as a venture capital organisation (as defined in 3.5.170), then the investor can, in its consolidated financial statements, apply the scope exemption in IAS 28 to the venture capital subsidiary's interest in the associate.

3.5.210.20 For example, Parent P has two wholly-owned subsidiaries, S and V. V is a venture capital organisation. S owns 10 percent in Company C and V owns 20 percent in C. V assesses that it has significant influence over C and applies the venture capital exemption in its consolidated financial statements. P assesses that it has significant influence over C as a result of its indirect 30 percent shareholding in C.

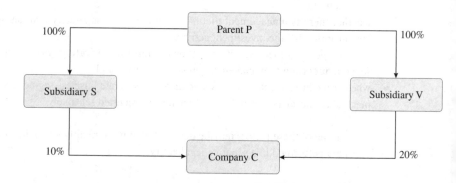

3.5.210.30 We believe that in its consolidated financial statements, P may account for the 10 percent of C held by S using the equity method and for the 20 percent held by V as a financial asset measured at fair value through profit or loss.

3.5.210.40 However, if the parent has control over an entity and a portion of the parent's interest in this entity is held by a subsidiary that qualifies as a venture capital organisation, then IAS 27 *Consolidated and Separate Financial Statements* does not provide any exemption that would allow the non-controlling interests (NCI) held via a subholding to be exempted from consolidation (see 2.5.310.10).

3.5.210.50 For example, Parent P has two wholly-owned subsidiaries, S and V. V is a venture capital organisation. S and V both own 40 percent of Company C. S and V both conclude that they have significant influence over C. S applies equity accounting in its consolidated financial statements and V applies the venture capital exemption in its consolidated financial statements. P assesses that it has control over C as a result of its indirect 80 percent shareholding in C.

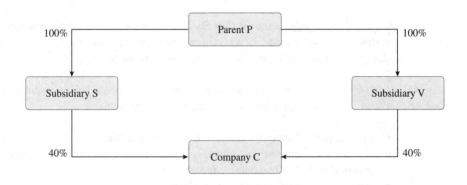

3.5.210.60 In its consolidated financial statements, P consolidates C with 20 percent NCI. The scope exemption applied in V's consolidated financial statements is not available at the group level.

3.5.220 Accounting for investments in associates and jointly controlled entities

3.5.220.10 In our view, the common control exemption in respect of business combinations under IFRS 3 *Business Combinations* applies equally to acquisitions of investments in associates and joint ventures among entities under common control (see 5.13.20.20). See 5.13.10 for a discussion of the accounting for common control transactions.

3.5.230 *Consolidated and individual financial statements*

IAS 28.1, 13, 31.1, 2, 30   3.5.230.10 In the investor's consolidated financial statements, or, if the investor has no subsidiaries, in its individual financial statements, use of the equity method for investments in associates, and either the equity method or proportionate consolidation for jointly controlled entities, is mandatory unless the investment is held for sale (see 3.5.660) or is held by a venture capital organisation (see 3.5.160).

3.5.240 **The equity method**

3.5.240.10 *Unless otherwise noted, all discussion regarding associates applies also to equity-accounted jointly controlled entities.*

3.5.250 *Commencement of the equity method*

IAS 28.23 3.5.250.10 An investment in an associate is accounted for using the equity method from the date on which the investor obtains significant influence over the associate.

3.5.260 *Overview of the equity method*

IAS 28.13 3.5.260.10 Associates are accounted for in the consolidated financial statements using the equity method.

IAS 28.2 3.5.260.20 The equity method is described as a method of accounting whereby the investment is initially recognised at cost and adjusted thereafter for the post-acquisition change in the investor's share of net assets of the investee.

IAS 28.11 3.5.260.30 The investment in the associate is further described as being recognised initially at cost and subsequently increased or decreased to recognise:

- the investor's share of the profit or loss of the investee;
- the investor's proportionate interest in the investee arising from changes in the investee's other comprehensive income; and
- the dividends received from the investee.

3.5.260.40 The descriptions of the equity method in the two paragraphs of IAS 28 (in 3.5.260.20 and 30) are not entirely consistent. In particular, a question arises as to how the investor should account for changes in the net assets of an associate that are recognised directly in the associate's equity, as paragraph 2 of IAS 28 seems to imply that the investor would adjust the investment by its share in these changes in equity whereas paragraph 11 of IAS 28 could be read as precluding recognition of an increase or decrease in the investment in the associate for such changes. In our view, the description in paragraph 2 of IAS 28 is more authoritative and takes precedence over paragraph 11. See 3.5.370 for a further discussion of this issue.

3.5.270 *Accounting periods and policies*

IAS 28.24, 25 3.5.270.10 Unless it is impracticable, associates' financial statements used for the purposes of applying the equity method are prepared for the same accounting period as that of the investor. When different periods are used, the length of reporting periods and the gap between reporting periods are consistent from period to period.

IAS 28.25 3.5.270.20 The difference between the reporting date and the date of the financial statements of an associate used when applying the equity method may not exceed three months.

IAS 28.25 3.5.270.30 When different reporting periods are used for the purpose of applying the equity method, adjustments are made for the effects of any significant events or transactions that occur between the two reporting dates. When an associate changes its reporting date to align with that of the investor, in our view the same accounting applies as when a subsidiary aligns its reporting date with that of the parent; see 2.5.290.20 for a discussion of the position in respect of subsidiaries.

S 28.26, 27 3.5.270.40 For the purpose of applying the equity method, the financial information of all associates is prepared on the basis of IFRSs. Uniform accounting policies are used in preparing the investor's financial statements, with one exception in relation to insurance contracts (see 5.10.60). Accordingly, when an associate applies different policies in its own financial statements, adjustments are required to conform to the investor's accounting policies.

3.5.280 *Availability of information*

3.5.280.10 It is acceptable to use either the most recently published information, which includes both audited financial statements and unaudited interim financial statements published by the associate, or the most recent management accounts of an associate for the purpose of applying equity accounting. Difficulty in obtaining financial information needed to apply the equity method is not grounds for exemption from equity accounting. It is presumed that the investor, by virtue of its ability to exercise significant influence, is able to obtain the necessary information from associates.

3.5.290 *The link between equity accounting and consolidation*

IAS 28.20, 3.5.290.10 It is not clear whether equity accounting should be understood as a one-line
39.BC24D consolidation or as a measurement approach. On the one hand, paragraph 20 of IAS 28 states that the procedures applicable to consolidation and the concepts underlying the procedures accounting for an acquisition apply to equity accounting. On the other hand, in the context of an amendment to IAS 39 in 2009, the Board noted that the linkage between acquisition accounting and equity accounting is only in respect of accounting "methodology" and not in respect of "principles".

3.5.290.20 In our view, the following are examples of accounting methodology in IAS 27 and IFRS 3 that should be extended in the context of equity accounting (see 2.5 and 2.6 respectively):

- determining the acquisition date and the fair value of identifiable net assets in the acquisition of an associate; and
- accounting for initial and subsequent measurement of contingent consideration (see 3.5.320.20).

3.5.290.30 In contrast, we believe that the following are examples of accounting "principles" in IAS 27 and IFRS 3 that should not be extended in the context of equity accounting:

- accounting for an equity-settled share-based payment issued by an associate (see 3.5.410); and
- accounting for a change in ownership interest in an associate while maintaining significant influence (see 3.5.720 and 730).

3.5.290.40 In some situations, it is not clear whether the treatments in IAS 27 or IFRS 3 should be extended to equity accounting. These include:

- accounting by the investor of sales or purchases of NCI by an associate (see 3.5.370);
- elimination of interest income or expense (see 3.5.460); and
- transactions between associates (see 3.5.480).

3.5.300 *Obligation or potential obligation to purchase equity instruments*

3.5.300.10 An entity may write a put option or enter into a (synthetic) forward purchase agreement with the non-controlling shareholders in an existing subsidiary on their shares in that subsidiary. If the put option or (synthetic) forward purchase agreement granted to the non-controlling shareholders provides for settlement in cash or in another financial asset by the entity, then the entity recognises a liability for the present value of the strike price of the option, and in our view accounts for such agreement under the anticipated acquisition method or the present access method (see 2.5.460 – 463).

3.5.300.20 It could be questioned whether, by analogy, the exercise of a put option to purchase an associate's or a jointly controlled entity's equity instruments, in other words the purchase of the underlying interests, should be anticipated. However, in our view, an obligation or potential obligation to purchase an associate's or a jointly controlled entity's equity instruments should not generally be anticipated. We believe that the recognition of a liability in relation to subsidiaries arises because of the specific requirement in paragraph 23 of IAS 32 *Financial Instruments: Presentation* to recognise a financial liability for an obligation or potential obligation to purchase group equity instruments, whereas associates and joint ventures are not part of the group. Therefore, the obligation or potential obligation to purchase the equity instruments in an associate or jointly controlled entity does not give rise to a financial liability. We believe that such an obligation or potential obligation therefore generally is within the scope of IAS 39 (see 3.11.65.130). Therefore, if the obligation meets the definition of a derivative (see 3.6.170), then it will be measured at fair value with changes therein recognised in profit or loss.

3.5.310 *Initial carrying amount of an associate*

3.5.320 *Cost of an investment in an associate*

IU 07-09 3.5.320.10 In our view, the cost of an investment in an associate determined in accordance with IAS 28 comprises the purchase price and other costs directly attributable to the acquisition of the investment such as professional fees for legal services, transfer taxes and other transaction costs.

RS 3.58(b), 3.5.320.20 In our view, contingent consideration arising from the acquisition of an
IAS 28.20 associate is recognised initially at fair value as part of the cost of acquisition. If the
contingent consideration is classified as a financial liability, then in our view any subsequent fair value adjustments to the liability, and its ultimate settlement, are accounted
for through profit or loss. We believe that the IFRS 3 (2008) treatment in respect of
contingent consideration arising on acquisition of subsidiaries should be applied to
contingent consideration arising on acquisition of associates (see 3.5.290.20). We also
believe that the approach of adjusting the purchase price, which applied when IFRS 3
(2004) was in effect, is now precluded.

3.5.320.30 For example, on acquisition of Associate C, Investor I agrees to pay 100
upfront, plus 5 percent of profits over 5,000 generated in the two years following the
acquisition, in cash as a lump sum at the end of the two years. The fair value of the
obligation is estimated at 45 at the acquisition date. A contingent consideration liability
of 45 is recognised as part of the cost of acquisition of C. A year after acquisition, C
has performed better than initially projected by I such that a significant payment is now
expected to be made at the end of year two. The fair value of this financial liability is
185 at the end of year one. The difference between initial fair value at acquisition and
the fair value at the end of year one is recognised as an additional liability with a charge
to profit or loss of 140 (185 current fair value - 45 original fair value). The adjustment
to the liability to reflect the final settlement amount (final fair value) will be recognised
in profit or loss in the same way if the amount differs from the fair value estimate at the
end of the previous period.

FRS 3.58(a), 3.5.320.40 In our view, equity-classified contingent consideration arising from the
IAS 28.20, acquisition of an associate is recorded at fair value at acquisition date with no subsequent
32.16 adjustments, as is the case for a contingent consideration arising from the acquisition
of a subsidiary.

IAS 3.5.320.50 A forward contract to acquire an investment in an associate is a derivative in
39.BC24D the scope of IAS 39. The scope exemption in paragraph 2(g) of IAS 39 for business
combinations cannot be applied by analogy to an acquisition of an interest in an associate as the latter represents the acquisition of a financial instrument. Therefore, the
derivative is measured at fair value through profit or loss, and the cost of investment
includes the fair value of the derivative at the acquisition date (see 2.6.320).

3.5.330 *Goodwill*

IAS 28.23, 33 3.5.330.10 On the acquisition date of an associate, fair values are attributed to the associate's identifiable assets and liabilities as explained in 2.6.600. Any positive difference
between the cost of the investment and the investor's share of the fair values of the
identifiable net assets acquired is goodwill.

IFRS 3.55, 3.5.330.20 Goodwill is included in the carrying amount of the investment in the
IAS 28.23 associate and is not shown separately. Goodwill is not amortised and therefore amortisa-

tion is not included in the determination of the investor's share of the associate's profit or loss. Goodwill attributable to an investment in an associate is not tested annually for impairment (see 3.10.580).

IAS 28.23   3.5.330.30 Any excess in the investor's share in the fair value of identifiable net assets over cost is included in the investor's share of the associate's profit or loss in the period in which the investment is acquired.

IAS 28.23   3.5.330.40 The investor's share of depreciation charges to be included with the share of the associate's profit or loss in the investor's financial statements reflects any fair value adjustments for depreciable assets at the acquisition date of the investment in the associate. The fair value adjustment is made only for the proportion of net assets acquired.

3.5.340 *Percentage attributable to the investor*

IAS 28.2, 11   3.5.340.10 In some cases the economic interests of investors will not equal their shareholding (voting interest). For example, an entity may control 30 percent of the voting power of an associate, but have only a 20 percent interest in the profits and net assets of the entity. In our view, in these cases the investor should account for the 20 percent interest, as equity accounting is described by reference to the investor's share in net assets and profit or loss (see 3.5.260.20).

3.5.350 *Indirect holdings*

IAS 28.21   3.5.350.10 Shareholdings of the parent and all of its subsidiaries are taken into account in applying the equity method. However, shareholdings of other associates and joint ventures are not considered.

3.5.350.20 For example, in addition to several subsidiaries, Company H has a 50 percent shareholding in Jointly Controlled Entity J and a 25 percent holding in Associate B. J also holds 10 percent of the share capital of B.

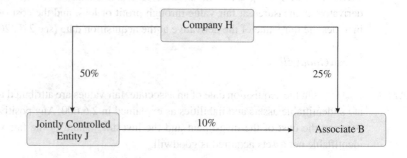

3.5.350.30 B reports a loss of 40, but pays a dividend of 200 from accumulated profits. In its consolidated financial statements H will apply the equity method for its 25 percent interest in B and will not apply the equity method to the additional interest, effectively 5 percent, held through J. Therefore, assuming no impairment, H will include its share of B's loss of 10 (40 x 25%). H also will reduce the carrying amount of its investment in B by the dividends received of 50 (200 x 25%). J has classified its investment in B as available for sale, and therefore recognises dividends received of 20 in profit or loss (see 4.6.260). Accordingly, in accounting for its interest in J, H will include J's share of the dividend received from B of 10 (200 x 50% x 10%).

3.5.350.40 This is different from the treatment that would result if H had taken into account J's 10 percent holding and therefore treated B as a 30 percent associate (25% + (50% x 10%)). Under that method, the share of losses would have been 12 (40 x 30%) and the amount applied against the carrying amount of B in respect of the dividends received, assuming that J passes the dividend onto H, would have been 60 (200 x 30%). This approach is not appropriate because H does not control J.

In H's consolidated financial statements	IAS 28 method[1]	If all equity accounted
Share of loss of B	(10)	(12)
Dividends received from B	(50)	(60)
Decrease in carrying amount of investment in B	(60)	(72)
Share of dividend received by J from B recognised in the statement of comprehensive income	10	-

Notes
(1) Ignoring any available-for-sale adjustment recognised by J.

IAS 28.21 3.5.350.50 An issue may arise when an entity acquires shares in an associate for strategic and potentially for trading purposes. For example, Company N is a wholly-owned subsidiary of Company M. M has a 30 percent interest in Associate O. N has significant investing activities and as part of these activities acquires a 3 percent interest in O. The issue is whether M's 3 percent indirect holding may be treated as an investment in a financial asset rather than being accounted for under the equity method in its consolidated financial statements. In our view, because an entity is required to evaluate both direct and indirect holdings in classifying an investment as an associate and in accounting for the investment, it would not be acceptable to account for N's investment in O as a financial asset in the consolidated financial statements of M. Accordingly, M's 3 percent indirect interest in O should be accounted for using the equity method. This situation differs from that in 3.5.210, which describes the partial use of the venture capital organisation, as neither N nor M are venture capital organisations and therefore the exemption from applying the equity method is not available.

3.5.360 *Interest in an associate held via a subsidiary*

3.5.360.10 An interest in an associate may be held via a subsidiary. A question arises as to how the equity method should be applied for such an associate in the consolidated financial statements of the investor.

3.5.360.20 For example, Company P owns 70 percent of Subsidiary S, which in turn has an investment of 40 percent in Associate R. S applies equity accounting to its 40 percent investment in R. Subsequently, P consolidates S. Assume that R's profit for the year is 100. Therefore, in the consolidated financial statements of P, the equity accounted profit of R is 40. Of this amount, 70 percent is allocated to the equity holders of P, i.e. effectively 28 percent of R's profit, and 30 percent to the NCI, i.e. effectively 12 percent of R's profit.

3.5.370 *Interest in an entity held via an associate*

IAS 28.21 3.5.370.10 An investor's associate may have non-wholly-owned subsidiaries. In the investor's consolidated financial statements, the NCI in the associate's subsidiary are not reflected. This is because the investor only takes into account its share in the comprehensive income and net assets of the associate's subsidiaries, joint ventures and associates. The investor's interest or entitlement is determined only after the associate's non-controlling shareholders have been attributed their interest in the associate.

3.5.370.20 The associate may sell or purchase NCI in its subsidiaries and account for these transactions as equity transactions in its consolidated financial statements. In our view, the investor should account for these transactions since they change the net assets of the associate, and changes in the associate's net assets are required to be reflected in the investor's accounting. However, a question arises as to how such transactions should be reflected in the investor's consolidated financial statements.

IAS 28.11 3.5.370.30 In our view, there are two possible approaches to account for such transactions, and an investor should choose an accounting policy, to be applied consistently to all transactions with NCI at the associate level. In the first approach, such transactions are not considered as equity transactions from the investor's perspective, as the NCI of the associate do not meet the definition of NCI at the investor's level. Therefore, the transaction is a transaction with third parties from the perspective of the investor and is accounted for accordingly. When the associate sells equity interests in its subsidiaries to its non-controlling shareholders in an equity transaction, it transfers its group equity instruments (equity interests in a member of the associate's own group) to third parties (the associate's non-controlling shareholders), which represents a dilution of the investor's indirect interest in the subsidiary of the associate, and gives rise to the recognition of a gain or loss in the investor's consolidated financial statements. The nature of the transaction changes at the investor level so that the investor recognises a dilution gain or loss. Similarly, when the associate purchases equity interests from its NCI, the investor recognises an increase in its interest in the associate and follows the guidance in 3.5.720.

368

3.5.370.40 For example, Company P owns 40 percent of Associate M, which has several subsidiaries. On 1 January 2010 M sells 30 percent of S, one of its wholly-owned subsidiaries, for 80 but retains control over S.

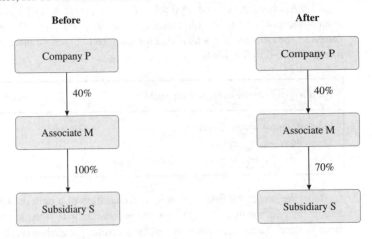

3.5.370.50 The carrying amount of S in M's consolidated financial statements is 200. As a result, M records the following entry:

In M's financial statements	Debit	Credit
Cash	80	
NCI (200 x 30%)		60
Shareholders' equity (parent)		20
To recognise increase in NCI		

3.5.370.60 At P's level, that increase in equity becomes a dilution gain and P records a gain of 8 (20 x 40%) in profit or loss. This amount would be adjusted at P's level if necessary due, for instance, to any purchase price allocation adjustments allocated to S at P's level.

In P's financial statements (first approach)	Debit	Credit
Investment in associate (20 x 40%)	8	
Dilution gain (profit or loss) (20 x 40%)		8
To recognise dilution of P's interest in S		

IAS 28.2, 20 3.5.370.70 In the second approach, such a transaction is reflected directly in equity at the investor level, based on the fact that it reflects the post-acquisition change in the net assets of the investee (see 3.5.260.20). Maintaining the entry in equity at the investor's level is consistent with the guidance in IAS 28 stating that many of the procedures appropriate for the application of the equity method are similar to consolidation pro-

cedures described in IAS 27, in which case the investor would replicate the associate's accounting by reflecting the investor's share of the associate's adjustment to its equity.

3.5.370.80 Applying the second approach to the example set out in 3.5.370.40 would result in an amount of 8 being recorded directly in equity at P's level. This amount would, if necessary, be adjusted at P's level due for instance to purchase price allocation adjustments allocated to S at P's level.

In P's financial statements (second approach)	*Debit*	*Credit*
Investment in associate (20 x 40%)	8	
Shareholders' equity (parent)		8
To recognise P's share in associate's increase in NCI		

3.5.370.90 We prefer the first approach, as recognition of a gain in profit or loss is the default entry for net asset changes that are not transactions with parent's equity instruments' holders. However, we believe that the second approach is an acceptable alternative in accordance with the guidance in IAS 28.

3.5.380 *Treasury shares held by associates*

3.5.380.10 An associate may have an investment in its investor. This means that the carrying amount of the associate under the equity method would include the investor's share of the associate's investment in the investor's own shares. In our view, the investor is not required to make any adjustment in respect of treasury shares held by an associate. See 3.11.300.20 for further discussion of this issue.

3.5.390 *Crossholdings*

3.5.390.10 Two entities may have an ownership interest in each other that results in mutual significant influence. In other words, an entity could be an investor in an associate and that associate could be an investor in the entity and have significant influence over it. A question arises regarding the accounting for such a crossholding in applying the equity method.

3.5.390.20 For example, Company C owns 30 percent in Company B, and B owns 25 percent in Company C. Each company has significant influence over the other and therefore applies the equity method.

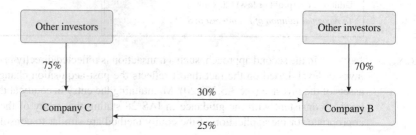

3.5.390.30 Effectively C has acquired 7.5 percent of its own shares (30% x 25%), and B has acquired 7.5 percent of its own shares (25% x 30%). Accordingly, an investor in either C or B effectively would have increased its share in each of these entities by a factor of 1.081 (1 / (100% - 7.5%)). From an investor's perspective, an investee's holding of own shares through a crossholding structure has the same effect on the investor's effective share of the interest of the investee as other share buy-backs. However, an investor is not required to make any adjustment in respect of treasury shares held by an associate (see 3.11.300.20).

3.5.390.40 Under the equity method, the investment is recognised initially at cost and adjusted thereafter for the post-acquisition change in the investor's share of the net assets of the investee. The comprehensive income of the investor includes the investor's share of the comprehensive income of the investee, i.e. the comprehensive income of C includes C's share of post-acquisition comprehensive income of B, and the comprehensive income of B includes B's share of post-acquisition comprehensive income of C. In the absence of specific guidance, in our view the term "the investor's share" in IAS 28 may be interpreted as the investor's effective share and therefore the approach described in 3.5.390.50 – 120 may be used in accounting for the crossholding.

3.5.390.50 Under the effective ownership interest approach, an investor, for example C, determines its share of comprehensive income of an investee (B) on the basis of the investor's effective interest in the investee, i.e. C's *effective* interest in B. The effect of the reciprocal interests is incorporated into the investee's (B's) financial statements through the investee's own equity accounting, i.e. the investee's (B's) comprehensive income already would include the equity pick-up for its (B's) own equity interest in the investor (C).

3.5.390.60 Assume that C and B both have a profit of 1,000 before taking into account their reciprocal investments. C's effective share of B's profit is 32.43 percent (30% / (1 - 25% x 30%)). Thus C's effective interest takes into consideration that B in fact holds 7.5 percent of its own equity. Therefore, the shares that are outstanding represent 92.5 percent of all shares (100 percent of shares minus 7.5 percent of shares held by B via its investment in C). As a result C's interest in B is in effect higher than 30 percent; it equals 30 percent in 92.5 percent of shares "outstanding". Therefore, the effective interest is calculated by dividing 30 percent by 92.5 percent. The resulting effective ownership interest of 32.43 percent is used to recognise C's share of profit of B. The profit or loss of B already includes B's share of profit or loss of C of 250 (1,000 x 25%). Therefore, C's equity-accounted profit of B is 405 ((1,000 + 250) x 32.43%).

3.5.390.70 Similarly, B's effective share of C's profit is 27.03 percent (25% / (1 - 25% x 30%) or 25 percent divided by 92.5 percent). B's effective ownership interest is applied to the profit of C, which includes the share of C in B of 300 (1,000 x 30%). Therefore, B's equity-accounted profit of C is calculated is 351 ((1,000 + 300) x 27.03%).

3.5.390.80 This is summarised as follows:

	Company C	Company B
Ownership interest in associate	30% in B	25% in C
Effective ownership interest in an associate	32.43% in B (30% / 92.5%)	27.03% in C (25% / 92.5%)
Profit or loss for the period *before* equity pick-up	1,000	1,000
Calculation of profit or loss of C and B including the equity pick-up for their respective interests in each other based on ownership interest (without taking into consideration the crossholding)	300 (1,000 x 30%)	250 (1,000 x 25%)
Profit or loss for the period *after* equity pick-up (without taking into consideration the crossholding)	1,300	1,250
Equity pick-up based on the effective ownership interest (taking into consideration crossholding)	405 (1,250 x 32.43%)	351 (1,300 x 27.03%)
Total including equity pick-up based on effective interest	1,405	1,351

3.5.390.90 As a result C's total profit would be 1,405, of which 1,054 (1,405 x 75% or 1,405 - 351) is attributable to shareholders other than B. B's total profit would be 1,351 of which 946 (1,351 x 70% or 1,351 - 405) is attributable to shareholders other than C. The total allocation to "external" shareholders is 2,000 (1,054 + 946), which equals the total profit of C and B (1,000 + 1,000).

3.5.390.100 A proof of the allocation in 3.5.390.90 to C's external shareholders (75% = 100% - 25%) can be determined on the basis of their effective share of B's profit as follows:

$(75\% / (1 - (25\% \times 30\%))) \times (1,000 + 300) = 1,054$

3.5.390.110 As an alternative to the effective interest approach outlined in 3.5.390.50 – 100, the same amounts for C's and B's total profits also can be determined using the following simultaneous equation approach, whereby pC = profit of C, and pB = profit of B:

I: $p^C = 1,000 + (30\% \times p^B)$
II: $p^B = 1,000 + (25\% \times p^C)$

II in I: $p^C = 1,000 + 30\% \times (1,000 + (25\% \times p^C)) = 1,405$, and including this result in II gives:
II: $p^B = 1,000 + (25\% \times 1,405) = 1,351$

These figures then are multiplied by the nominal share that C and B own in each other (i.e. 25 percent and 30 percent respectively) in order to determine the profit that should be considered in applying the equity method in respect of both investments. Consequently, C recognises income of 405 (1,351 x 30%) in respect of its investment in B, and B recognises income of 351 (1,405 x 25%) in respect of its investment in C.

3.5.390.120 It could be argued that there is an element of double counting under the effective interest approach. However, in our view, this effect is similar to not adjusting for treasury shares held by associates. This approach has the advantage that C would determine its share of the investment in B as investors in B would determine their share of their investment in B. In other words, the accounting method in C would be consistent with the accounting by B's other investors.

3.5.400 *Potential voting rights*

IAS 27.IG5-IG7, 28.12 3.5.400.10 Although an investor may have taken into account potential voting rights when considering whether it has significant influence (see 3.5.80), the share of comprehensive income recognised under the equity method is based on current ownership interests, unless the potential voting rights in substance give access at present to the economic benefits associated with an ownership interest; see 2.5.120.10 for the definition of ownership interests. For example, assume that Company G has significant influence over Company H as a result of a 15 percent shareholding in H and currently exercisable options to acquire a further 20 percent at fair value. G would account for 15 percent of H using the equity method. G would account for a 35 percent interest in H only if and when it exercises the options.

3.5.410 *Equity-settled share-based payment issued by an associate*

3.5.410.10 When an equity-settled share-based payment is issued by an associate to its own employees, in our view the investor records its share of the associate's share-based remuneration expense, as part of its share of the associate profit or loss. However, in our view the investor does not account for a share in the credit to shareholders' equity recognised by the associate. Instead, the offsetting credit entry reduces the investment in the associate as we believe that equity instruments of the investee that have been granted to third parties represent a dilution of the investor's interest in the associate.

3.5.410.20 For example, Company C issues stock options to its employees. The options entitle the employees to acquire shares of C. The grant date fair value of the options issued is 1,000. The options will vest over 5 years. C recognises a share-based remuneration expense of 200 in profit or loss and an offsetting credit to equity in the current year. Company B holds a 30 percent interest in C and has significant influence over C. B recognises its share of the remuneration expense (i.e. 60) in profit or loss as part of income from equity method investments but records the offsetting credit as a reduction of its investment in C.

3.5.410.30 The following entries are recorded:

In C's financial statements	Debit	Credit
Share-based payment remuneration	200	
Shareholders' equity (parent)		200
To recognise share-based payment at associate level		

In B's financial statements	*Debit*	*Credit*
Share-based payment remuneration (200 x 30%)	60	
Investment in associate		60
To recognise share-based payment at investor level		

3.5.420 **Losses**

IAS 28.29   3.5.420.10 The investor's share of losses of an associate is recognised only until the carrying amount of the investor's equity interest in the associate is reduced to zero.

IAS 28.30   3.5.420.20 After the investor's interest is reduced to zero, a liability is recognised only to the extent that the investor has an obligation to fund the associate's operations, or has made payments on behalf of the associate.

IAS 28.29,   3.5.420.30 The equity interest in an associate includes the carrying amount of the
39.2(a)   investment under the equity method and other long-term interests, e.g. loans that are in substance part of the investment. However, an entity accounts for these long-term interests that, in substance, form part of the investor's net investment in the associate in accordance with applicable IFRSs, e.g. IAS 39. These investments are not part of the scope exclusion of IAS 39. However, the measurement requirements in IAS 39 are in effect overruled by the requirement in IAS 28 to recognise an associate's losses against the investor's other long-term interests that in substance form part of the investment; when losses recognised under the equity method exceed the investor's investment in ordinary shares, the excess is applied to other components of the investor's interest in an associate. Other long-term interests do not include trade receivables, trade payables or any long-term receivables for which adequate collateral exists, e.g. secured loans.

IAS 28.29   3.5.420.40 In our view, the share of losses of an associate corresponds to the investor's share of the total comprehensive income, i.e. includes the profit or loss component and the other comprehensive income component. When total comprehensive income is a loss and comprises a loss component and a profit component, in our view the profit component is fully recognised and the loss component is recognised only until the carrying amount of the investor's equity interest is reduced to zero. This is because the loss component is the one that is the subject of the limitation.

3.5.420.50 For example, Company P owns 40 percent of the shares in Company B. B has negative equity of 200 in applying the equity method in P's consolidated financial statements, i.e. the equity of B after making adjustments necessary in applying the equity method, such as fair value adjustments upon initial recognition. Therefore, P's share of the equity of B is -80 (-200 x 40%). However, P is not committed to finance the losses of B and has not provided any guarantees of B's obligations. Therefore, once P reduces its interest in B to zero, it does not absorb any further losses of B. If B earns a profit in subsequent periods, then P recognises profits only after all unrecognised losses have been eliminated.

3.5.420.60 Changing the facts of the example in 3.5.420.50, assume that the carrying amount of P's interest in B was 5 at the beginning of the period. During the year B has a profit of 50, but total comprehensive income of -25 resulting from a net change of -75 in its cash flow hedging reserve. Therefore, P's share of the equity of B at the end of the period is -5 (5 + (-25 x 40%)). Assuming that P is not committed to finance the losses of B and has not provided any guarantees of B's obligations, once again P reduces its interest in B to zero but does not absorb any further losses of B. In our view, in its statement of comprehensive income P should recognise its share of the profit of B of 20 (50 x 40%), and limit its share of B's other comprehensive income to -25 (-75 x 40%, capped at the carrying amount of 5 + 20).

3.5.430 *Transactions with associates*

AS 28.20, 22 3.5.430.10 Unrealised profits on transactions with associates are eliminated to the extent of the investor's interest in the associate, regardless of whether that unrealised profit is in the investor, a subsidiary in the same group as the investor, or the associate. Losses on transactions with associates are eliminated in the same way, except to the extent that the underlying asset is impaired.

3.5.430.20 The following example illustrates the elimination in a "downstream" sale of inventory by the investor during 2010 to a 20 percent associate. The inventory has not been sold by the associate at the end of the 2010 financial year.

	Investor	Associate
Cost of inventory	50	150
Selling price of inventory	150	Not yet sold
Profit related to the transaction	100	

3.5.430.30 The entry required in 2010 to eliminate the investor's 20 percent interest in the profit from this transaction is as follows:

	Debit	Credit
Revenue (150 x 20%)	30	
Cost of sales (50 x 20%)		10
Investment in associate (100 x 20%)		20
To eliminate unrealised profit on downstream transaction		

3.5.430.40 The credit is recognised against the carrying amount of the investment in the associate and not against inventory because the inventory is an asset of the associate, and is included in the investment in associate line item in the statement of financial position.

3.5.430.50 The associate sells the inventory during the course of 2011. The following entry is required in 2011 to recognise the profit from the transaction in the investor's consolidated financial statements:

	Debit	Credit
Cost of sales (50 x 20%)	10	
Investment in associate (100 x 20%)	20	
Revenue (150 x 20%)		30
To recognise realised profit on downstream transaction		

3.5.430.60 In the example set out in 3.5.430.20 and 30, a portion of the whole transaction is eliminated against both revenue and cost of sales. Alternative approaches are possible, for example eliminating only the unrealised profit (i.e. the net 20) against revenue, with the 20 flowing through later as part of the associate income share in the year of sale by the associate. We prefer the elimination to be performed as illustrated in 3.5.430.30.

3.5.430.70 The following example is the same as the example at 3.5.430.20 except that the 20 percent associate makes an "upstream" sale of inventory to the investor.

	Investor	Associate
Cost of inventory	150	50
Selling price of inventory	Not yet sold	150
Profit related to the transaction	100 x 20% = 20	100

3.5.430.80 The investor's share of earnings from the associate will include 20 that represents the investor's share of the associate's profit on the transaction with the investor. This share of profit is eliminated. However, IFRSs do not specify whether the elimination should be presented as a reduction in the investment in the associate or as a reduction in the underlying asset, e.g. inventory. In our view, either approach is acceptable. The entry is as follows:

	Debit	Credit
Share of profit or loss of associate	20	
Investment in associate *or* inventory		20
To eliminate unrealised profit on upstream transaction		

3.5.430.90 This entry will be reversed when the inventory is sold by the investor to a third party.

3.5.440 *Elimination of gains on downstream transactions in excess of the associate's carrying amount*

3.5.440.10 An investor may enter into a downstream transaction with an associate for which its share of the gain arising from the transaction exceeds its interest in the associate. In our view, there are two possible approaches in respect of such an excess, and an entity should choose an accounting policy, to be applied consistently to all downstream transactions with associates. The same issue arises when dividends are paid by the associate in excess of the carrying amount of the investment and the chosen accounting policy for downstream transactions also should be applied for such dividend distributions.

3.5.440.20 In our view, the accounting policy also should be consistent with any policy chosen in respect of the sale of a subsidiary to an existing or newly created associate when the investor applies the "IAS 28/IAS 31 (SIC-13 *Jointly Controlled Entities – Non-Monetary Contributions by Venturers*) approach" (see 3.5.470).

IAS 28.29 3.5.440.30 Under the first approach, once the investor's interest in the associate (see 3.5.420.30) has been reduced to zero, any remaining portion of the investor's share of the gain should not be eliminated as the resulting credit in the statement of financial position does not meet the definition of a liability. Therefore, it is possible that the investor's share of the gain will not be eliminated fully in the investor's financial statements. If the associate earns a profit in subsequent periods, then the investor should recognise its share of such profits only after adjusting for the excess gain that was not eliminated previously.

3.5.440.40 The discussion in 3.5.440.30 assumes that the associate has the related goods in its statement of financial position. If the goods purchased were sold by the associate or used in production and therefore recognised as an expense, then no elimination entry would be necessary.

3.5.440.50 The following example illustrates the capped elimination in a downstream sale of inventory by the investor during 2010 to a 50 percent associate. The inventory is not yet sold by the associate at the end of 2011.

2010	*Investor*	*Associate*
Cost of inventory	600	900
Selling price of inventory	900	Not yet sold
Profit related to the transaction	300	
Carrying amount of associate	100	
2011		
Net profit		1,000

3.5.440.60 The investor's entry required to eliminate its 50 percent interest in the profit from this transaction, limited to the carrying amount of the investment in the associate, can be presented as follows; see 3.5.430.60 for an alternative presentation of the elimination entry:

	Debit	Credit
Revenue ((900 x 50%) x (100 / 150))	300	
Cost of sales ((600 x 50%) x (100 / 150))		200
Investment in associate ((300 x 50%) limited to 100)		100
To eliminate unrealised profit on downstream transaction		
subject to zero net investment limitation		

3.5.440.70 The investor's entry in 2011, in which the share of profits is adjusted for the previously unrecognised elimination, is as follows:

	Debit	Credit
Investment in associate	450	
Share of profit or loss of associate ((1,000 x 50%) - 50)		450
To adjust equity-accounted earnings in 2011 for		
limitation of elimination applied in 2010		

IAS 28.22 3.5.440.80 Under the second approach, the investor eliminates in full its share of the gain. The amount of the elimination in excess of the carrying amount of the investor's interest in the associate is presented as deferred income. If the associate earns a profit in subsequent periods and the carrying amount of the investment in the associate becomes positive, then the investor should change its presentation of the deferred income so that it is offset against the investment in the associate in the usual way. This approach is based on the view that the requirement to eliminate the investor's share of gains on downstream transactions with associates is not subject to a "floor" of a zero net investment.

3.5.440.90 Using the facts presented in 3.5.440.50, the following entries illustrate the full elimination of the investor's share of the profit from the transaction and the corresponding presentation of deferred income in a downstream sale of inventory. The following entry by the investor is required in 2010:

	Debit	Credit
Revenue (900 x 50%)	450	
Costs of sale (600 x 50%)	300	
Investment in associate ((300 x 50%) limited to 100)		100
Deferred income ((300 x 50%) - 100)		50
To eliminate fully unrealised profit on downstream		
transaction		

3.5.440.100 The following entries are recorded by the investor in 2011:

	Debit	Credit
Investment in associate	500	
Share of profit or loss of associate (1,000 x 50%)		500
To recognise equity-accounted earnings of associate		
Deferred income	50	
Investment in associate		50
To offset deferred income as associate earns profits		

3.5.450 *Elimination of balances*

IAS 28.22 3.5.450.10 IFRSs require the elimination of the investor's share of profits or losses on transactions with associates when applying the equity method. Balances such as receivables or payables and deposits or loans to or from associates are not eliminated.

3.5.460 *Elimination of interest income or expense*

AS 28.20, 22 3.5.460.10 The elimination of interest income or expense arising on balances with associates is not addressed specifically in IFRSs. The fact that many of the procedures appropriate for equity accounting are similar to consolidation procedures suggests that elimination should be performed (see 3.5.290.20). However, the examples of upstream and downstream transactions in the standard are sales of assets, which suggests that transactions that do not involve assets should not be eliminated. This is consistent with the fact that balances with associates are not eliminated (see 3.5.450). In our view, an entity should choose an accounting policy, to be applied consistently, as to whether to eliminate such transactions provided that none of the parties has capitalised the interest. The option selected by the entity affects only the presentation of the comprehensive income as it affects the split between finance costs and equity accounted earnings.

IAS 28.22 3.5.460.20 If one of the parties has capitalised the interest (see 4.6.350), then in our view the transaction should be eliminated. In such case, the transaction is viewed as an upstream or downstream transaction as it gives rise to an asset in the entity that has been charged the interest expense.

3.5.470 *Contribution of a subsidiary to an existing or newly created associate*

IAS 27.34, 3.5.470.10 Sometimes a parent may contribute a subsidiary to an existing associate
28.22, or jointly controlled entity (see 3.5.600). Significant influence or joint control
SIC-13.5 (see 3.5.600) in a former subsidiary may also be retained via an interest in the acquirer. In such cases, a question arises as to how the gain or loss should be calculated as there appears to be some ambiguity in IFRSs in this regard. IAS 27 requires that when control

of a subsidiary is lost, any resulting gain or loss is recognised in full in profit or loss (see 2.5.490), i.e. no elimination is made in respect of a continuing interest in the assets and liabilities contributed. However, IAS 28 and SIC-13 (applying IAS 31) require an elimination to be made in respect of a continuing interest in the assets and liabilities contributed.

3.5.470.20 In our view, this conflict means that the entity should choose an accounting policy, to be applied consistently, to apply either the IAS 27 approach or the IAS 28/IAS 31 (SIC-13) approach:

- *The IAS 27 approach.* Under this approach, no elimination of the gain or loss is performed and the fair value of the retained investment is its deemed cost for the purpose of subsequent accounting.
- *The IAS 28/IAS 31 (SIC-13) approach.* Under this approach, the gain or loss is eliminated to the extent of the retained interest in the former subsidiary.

3.5.470.30 For example, Company P sells its wholly-owned Subsidiary S to its 30 percent Associate M. The carrying amount of the net assets of S in P's consolidated financial statements at the date of the sale is 5,500 and S has no accumulated balance of other comprehensive income. The selling price is 9,000, which also is the fair value of S. Therefore, in the first instance P recognises a profit of 3,500 on the disposal of S.

3.5.470.40 If P applies the IAS 27 approach, then it recognises the full profit on the disposal of S. The amount included in the carrying amount of M in respect of the net assets of S in P's consolidated financial statements is 2,700 (9,000 x 30%).

3.5.470.50 If P applies the IAS 28/IAS 31 (SIC-13) approach, then it eliminates 30 percent of the profit recognised on the disposal of S against the carrying amount of the investment in M.

3.5.470.60 The following shows the accounting entries necessary for P to record the transaction and the subsequent elimination if P applies the IAS 28/IAS 31 (SIC-13) approach:

	Debit	Credit
Cash	9,000	
Net assets of S		5,500
Gain on disposal (profit or loss)		3,500
To recognise disposal of S		
Gain on disposal (profit or loss) (3,500 x 30%)	1,050	
Investment in M		1,050
To recognise elimination of 30 percent of profit on		
disposal of S		

3.5.470.70 The amount included in the carrying amount of M in respect of the net assets of S in P's consolidated financial statements, following the elimination, is 1,650 (9,000 x 30% - 1,050). This corresponds to the carrying amount of the net assets of S in P's financial statements before the disposal (1,650, or 5,500 x 30%).

IAS 21.48C   3.5.470.80 The election by the entity of one of these approaches has consequences on the treatment of reserves of the former subsidiary. In effect, if the entity applies the IAS 28/ IAS 31 (SIC-13) approach, then in our view the components of other comprehensive income of the former subsidiary are not reclassified in full, but instead are reclassified on a proportionate basis (see 2.7.320). This is because we believe that the requirement in IAS 21 *The Effects of Changes in Foreign Exchange Rates* to reclassify in profit or loss a proportionate share of the cumulative amount of the exchange differences recognised in other comprehensive income apply in such circumstances. We also believe that a similar approach should be applied to other components of other comprehensive income.

3.5.470.90 Changing the facts in 3.5.470.30, consider that S has a foreign currency translation reserve of 300 and an available-for-sale revaluation reserve of 200 on the date that it is sold to M.

3.5.470.100 If P applies the IAS 28/IAS 31 (SIC-13) approach, then the profit on disposal of 2,450 calculated in 3.5.470.60 is adjusted for the reclassification of amounts previously recognised in other comprehensive income by 350 ((300 + 200) x 70%).

3.5.470.110 An issue arises when an entity applies the IAS 28/IAS 31 (SIC-13) approach and the carrying amount of the entity's interest in the associate is insufficient to support the elimination of part or all of the gain attributable to the retained interest.

3.5.470.120 For example, Company X owns 100 percent of Company X1, and Company Y owns 100 percent of Company Y1. X, Y and Z incorporate a new entity (Newco) and invest cash of 875, 875 and 750 respectively, giving an interest of 35, 35 and 30 percent respectively. X, Y and Z each have significant influence over Newco. Newco obtains a loan of 7,500 and uses its cash of 10,000 (7,500 plus the 2,500 contributed on formation) to acquire X1 and Y1. In effect X and Y have each disposed of a subsidiary with significant influence retained.

3.5.470.130 The carrying amounts and fair values of X1 and Y1 are as follows:

	X1	Y1
Carrying amount	1,000	2,500
Fair value	7,000	3,000

3.5.470.140 The shareholdings in Newco, X1 and Y1 after the transaction are as follows:

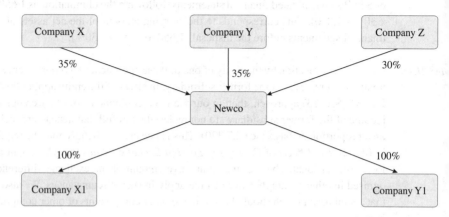

3.5.470.150 The statement of financial position of Newco after the transaction is as follows:

Investment in X1	7,000
Investment in Y1	3,000
	10,000
Non-current liability	7,500
Equity	2,500
	10,000

3.5.470.160 Considering the accounting for the disposal in X's consolidated financial statements, the carrying amount of X's investment in Newco is less than the profit elimination required in order to eliminate the gain attributable to X's retained interest in X1 if X applies the IAS 28/IAS 31 (SIC-13) approach. In our view, there are two possible approaches in respect of the excess profit elimination, and an entity should choose an accounting policy, to be applied consistently, consistent with the approach taken to the elimination of gains on downstream transactions in excess of the associate's carrying amount (see 3.5.440).

3.5.470.170 Under the first approach, once X's interest in the associate has been reduced to zero, any remaining portion of X's share of the gain should not be eliminated. If the associate earns a profit in subsequent periods, then X should recognise its share of such profits only after adjusting for the excess gain that was not eliminated previously (see also 3.5.440.30).

3.5.470.180 Under the second approach, X eliminates in full its share of the gain. The amount of the elimination in excess of the carrying amount of X's interest in the associate is presented in the statement of financial position as deferred income. If the associate earns a profit in subsequent periods and the carrying amount of the investment becomes positive, then X should change its presentation of the deferred income so that it is offset against the investment in the associate in the usual way (see also 3.5.440.80).

3.5.470.190 The entry in X to recognise its disposal of X1 is as follows:

	Debit	Credit
Cash	7,000	
Net assets of X1 (carrying amount)		1,000
Gain (profit or loss)		6,000
To recognise disposal of X1		

3.5.470.200 X would record the following entry to recognise its investment in Newco:

	Debit	Credit
Investment in Newco	875	
Cash		875
To recognise investment in Newco		

3.5.470.210 Under the first approach with a capped elimination (see 3.5.470.170), X would record the following entry to eliminate the effect of its continued 35 percent interest in X1 via Newco, limited to the carrying amount of the investment in Newco:

	Debit	Credit
Gain (profit or loss) (6,000 x 35% limited to investment)	875	
Investment in Newco		875
To eliminate gain on contribution to Newco subject to zero		
net investment limitation		

3.5.470.220 Under the second approach with full elimination (see 3.5.470.180), X would record the following entry to eliminate the effect of its continued 35 percent interest in X1 via Newco:

	Debit	Credit
Gain (profit or loss) (6,000 x 35%)	2,100	
Investment in Newco (limited to investment)		875
Deferred income		1,225
To eliminate fully gain on contribution to Newco		

3.5.480 **Transactions between associates**

IAS 28.20, 22   3.5.480.10 IFRSs are silent on whether unrealised profits or losses on a transaction between two associates should be eliminated. There is a conceptual argument to suggest that some of the profit should be eliminated, determined by multiplying the investor's interest in the first associate by its interest in the second associate applying the requirements for downstream and upstream transactions (see 3.5.430) by analogy, but in our view this is not clear whether a transaction between two associates is analogous to an inter-company transaction between subsidiaries.

3.5.490 **Preference shares**

IAS 28.28   3.5.490.10 If an associate has issued cumulative preference shares that are classified as equity, then before applying the equity method the investor adjusts the profit or loss of the associate by the amount of any dividends payable on the preference shares, whether or not these dividends have been declared.

3.5.500 **Presentation and disclosure**

IAS 1.82(c), (h)   3.5.500.10 An entity presents separately the following items in respect of equity-accounted investees in the statement of comprehensive income:

- a single amount for the investor's share of the post-tax profit or loss which may result in a reconciling item in the tax rate reconciliation (see 3.13.1000.20); and
- a single amount for the investor's share of other comprehensive income.

3.5.500.20 If an entity chooses to present a separate income statement, then the investor's share of the post-tax profit or loss of the equity-accounted investment will be included in that statement.

3.5.500.30 We prefer the investor's share of the comprehensive income of the equity-accounted investments to be allocated to the appropriate components of equity in the statement of changes in equity. In that case, for example, profit or loss would be allocated to retained earnings, and exchange differences recognised in other comprehensive income would be allocated to the foreign currency translation reserve (see 2.7.230.10).

3.5.510 *Gain or loss on disposal and impairment losses on loans to equity-accounted investees*

3.5.510.10 In our view, gains or losses arising on disposal of an associate or jointly controlled entity, or the impairment of a loan to an associate or jointly controlled entity, are not part of the investor's share of the equity-accounted earnings. We believe that it would be most appropriate for these items to be recognised in the same line item as other gains and losses on financial assets or sales of subsidiaries.

IFRS 3.
BC384 3.5.510.20 In our view, the gain or loss arising on the step acquisition of an associate is presented on the same basis as if the investment had been disposed of to a third party.

3.5.520 Goodwill

IAS 28.37 3.5.520.10 IFRSs are silent on disclosures related to goodwill on acquisition of investments in equity-accounted investees. In our view, it is not necessary to provide the disclosures for goodwill arising in a business combination in respect of goodwill on equity-accounted investees.

3.5.530 Accounting policies

3.5.530.10 Uniform accounting policies for like transactions and events in similar circumstances are used in preparing the investor's financial statements, with one exception in relation to insurance contracts (see 5.10.60). An associate may have accounting policies for items that are not applicable to the investor, for example when the investor's financial statements do not include line items in respect of an associate's financial statement items. If disclosure of the accounting policies of an associate is considered necessary for an understanding of income from associates, or the carrying amount of investments in associates in the statement of financial position, then in our view this information should be included in the accounting policy note regarding investments in associates.

3.5.540 Proportionate consolidation of jointly controlled entities*

31.30, 38 3.5.540.10 Either the equity method or proportionate consolidation is used to account for jointly controlled entities.

3.5.540.20 Generally the key difference between full consolidation and proportionate consolidation is that under proportionate consolidation only the investor's share of the assets and liabilities is accounted for and therefore there are no NCI recognised. However, when a jointly controlled entity has a controlling interest in a non-wholly-owned subsidiary, thereby resulting in NCI in the jointly controlled entity's consolidated financial statements, the venturer would reflect its proportionate share of that NCI if it elects to proportionately consolidate using the gross method (see 3.5.580).

IAS 31.33 3.5.540.30 In performing proportionate consolidation, the usual consolidation procedures apply. For example, inter-entity eliminations are made to the extent of the investor's interest. See 2.5 for guidance on the application of consolidation principles. Only specific issues that arise in the application of these principles to jointly controlled entities are addressed in this chapter.

3.5.540.40 When jointly controlled entities are accounted for using the equity method, the guidance provided in 3.5.240 – 530 for accounting for associates applies.

3.5.550 *Consistency and change in accounting method*

IAS 8.13   3.5.550.10 The chosen accounting policy, i.e. proportionate consolidation or the equity method, is applied consistently to all jointly controlled entities from period to period.

3.5.550.20 For example, Company W has investments in jointly controlled entities in Country B, which it has proportionately consolidated. During the reporting period, W invests in a jointly controlled entity in Country C. W believes that the nature of the jointly controlled entity in Country C is different in substance from those in Country B and wishes to use the equity method to account for the jointly controlled entity in Country C. IFRSs do not permit this approach. If a policy of proportionate consolidation is adopted, then it is applied consistently to all jointly controlled entities, regardless of the nature of the jointly controlled entities.

IAS 8.14   3.5.550.30 As with other voluntary changes in accounting policy, a change in accounting policy with respect to jointly controlled entities is justified only if the change results in more relevant and reliable information (see 2.8.30).

3.5.560 *Proportionate consolidation*

IAS 31.34   3.5.560.10 Proportionate consolidation may be done by:

- including the investor's share of each line item in the jointly controlled entity's financial statements with each relevant line item of the investor, in the same way as a normal consolidation; or
- presenting separate line items for the investor's share of each of the investee's assets, liabilities, income and expenses.

3.5.560.20 The following example illustrates the different approaches permitted for presentation of the statement of comprehensive income by presenting either a combined statement of comprehensive income, with additional disclosure in the notes to the financial statements, or by presenting the jointly controlled entity's amounts separately in the statement of comprehensive income. Other items in the financial statements would be dealt with in the same way.

Extract from the statement of comprehensive income – combined presentation	
Revenue	107,403
Cost of sales	(61,076)
Gross profit	46,327
Other income	1,571
Distribution costs	(18,090)
Administrative expenses	(15,635)
Other expenses	(3,284)
etc.	

Note: Included in the primary financial statements are the following amounts related to jointly controlled entities:

Revenue	12,657
Cost of sales	(7,341)
Gross profit	5,316
Other income	-
Distribution costs	(1,473)
Administrative expenses	(1,685)
Other expenses	(438)
etc.	

Extract from the statement of comprehensive income – separate presentation

	Group	Joint venture	Total consolidated
Revenue	94,746	12,657	107,403
Cost of sales	(53,735)	(7,341)	(61,076)
Gross profit	41,011	5,316	46,327
Other income	1,571	-	1,571
Distribution costs	(16,617)	(1,473)	(18,090)
Administrative expenses	(13,950)	(1,685)	(15,635)
Other expenses	(2,846)	(438)	(3,284)
etc.			

3.5.560.30 This second method significantly increases the information contained in the primary financial statements. We prefer this presentation if, due to the nature or significance of jointly controlled entities, this level of detail is considered helpful for an understanding of the financial statements.

3.5.570 *Losses*

3.5.570.10 There is no ceiling on the amount of losses to be recognised under proportionate consolidation. This differs from the approach to accounting for losses under the equity method, whereby the net investment normally is not reduced below zero (see 3.5.420).

3.5.580 *Interests in an entity held via a jointly controlled entity*

3.5.580.10 A jointly controlled entity may have a controlling interest in a subsidiary in which there are NCI. An issue arises of how to proportionately consolidate the jointly controlled entity's subsidiary in the consolidated financial statements of the venturers.

3.5.580.20 For example, Venturer E owns 50 percent of Joint Venture V, which in turn has an investment of 80 percent in Subsidiary S. The remaining 20 percent in S is held by non-controlling shareholders. E proportionately consolidates its interest in V. The issue is whether E should proportionately consolidate all line items in V's consolidated financial statements, i.e. including the NCI that V will recognise in respect of S (gross method); or whether E should proportionately consolidate its effective interest in S, i.e. 40 percent (50% x 80%) of all line items in S's financial statements, thereby excluding the NCI (net method).

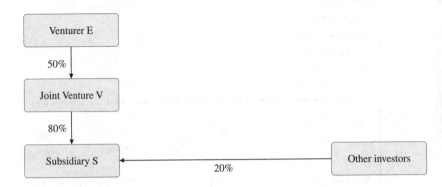

3.5.580.30 The gross method is supported by the view that a venturer should apply proportionate consolidation to the consolidated financial statements of the jointly controlled entity. The net method is supported by the view an entity should not recognise NCI that do not relate to its own subsidiary (S is a subsidiary of V, but not of E), and therefore do not meet the definition of NCI in IAS 27 (see 3.5.360).

3.5.580.40 While we prefer the gross method described in 3.5.580.20, in our view an entity should choose either the gross or net method as its accounting policy, to be applied consistently.

3.5.590 *Transactions with jointly controlled entities*

IAS 31.48, 49   3.5.590.10 Profits on transactions with jointly controlled entities are eliminated to the extent of the investor's interest in the jointly controlled entity. If an asset is sold at a loss and the loss provides evidence of impairment, then the full amount of the loss is recognised.

IAS 31.48, 49   3.5.590.20 Otherwise, when a venturer sells an asset to a jointly controlled entity, the venturer recognises only the share of any gain or loss attributable to the interests of the other venturers. When a jointly controlled entity sells assets to a venturer, the venturer eliminates its share of any gain or loss until the asset is sold to a third party. In our view, this elimination is presented as a reduction of the transferred asset (in the same way as for subsidiaries). As a result, when the asset is sold the gain on sale is automatically increased by the amount of the gain that had been previously eliminated.

3.5.590.30 Proportionate elimination also applies to loans and receivables between a venturer and the jointly controlled entity. For example, Companies D and B are both investors in Company C, a jointly controlled entity. D and B hold 60 percent and 40 percent respectively. D and B each grant a loan to C in proportion to their interest, i.e. 600 and 400.

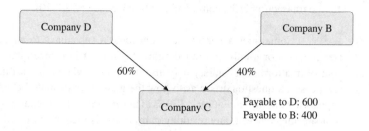

3.5.590.40 When D proportionately consolidates C, D's share of C's loan from D of 360 (600 x 60%) is eliminated against the receivable of 600 recognised in D's statement of financial position. Consequently, in D's consolidated or individual financial statements, there is a liability of 240 that corresponds to the share of C's loan from B and a receivable of 240 that corresponds to B's share in D's loan to C.

3.5.590.50 The following shows the accounting entry necessary for D to record the elimination:

	Debit	Credit
Payable to D (600 x 60%)	360	
Receivable due from C (600 x 60%)		360
To recognise elimination		

3.5.590.60 The following shows the remaining balances in D's statement of financial position:

	Debit	Credit
Non-eliminated part of D's receivable from C (600 x 40%)	240	
C's payable to B (400 x 60%)		240

3.5.590.70 In our view, the debtor and creditor cannot be eliminated against each other because although the 240 receivable corresponds to B's share it is not actually a receivable from B. Similar elimination techniques apply to any interests recognised in profit or loss.

3.5.600 *Non-monetary contributions to jointly controlled entities*

IAS 31.48, 3.5.600.10 When an entity contributes non-monetary assets in exchange for an equity
SIC-13.5 interest in a jointly controlled entity, the entity recognises a gain or loss to the extent that the assets have been sold to the other venturers. No gain or loss is recognised if:

- the significant risks and rewards of ownership of the contributed assets have not been transferred;
- the gain or loss cannot be measured reliably; or
- the transaction lacks commercial substance (see 5.7.20.20).

IAS 27.34, 3.5.600.20 Sometimes a parent may contribute a subsidiary to an existing associate
31.48, (see 3.5.470) or jointly controlled entity. Significant influence (see 3.5.470) or joint-
SIC-13.5 control in a former subsidiary may also be retained via an interest in the acquirer. In such cases, a question arises as to how the gain or loss should be calculated as there appears to be some ambiguity in IFRSs in this regard. IAS 27 requires that when control of a subsidiary is lost, any resulting gain or loss is recognised in full in profit or loss (see 2.5.490), i.e. no elimination is made in respect of a continuing interest in the assets and liabilities contributed. However, IAS 28 and SIC-13 (applying IAS 31) require an elimination to be made in respect of a continuing interest in the assets and liabilities contributed.

3.5.600.30 In our view, this means that the entity should choose an accounting policy, to be applied consistently, either to apply the IAS 27 approach or the IAS 28/IAS 31 (SIC-13) approach:

- *The IAS 27 approach.* Under this approach, no elimination of the gain or loss is performed and the fair value of the retained investment is its deemed cost for the purpose of subsequent accounting.
- *The IAS 28/IAS 31 (SIC-13) approach.* Under this approach, the gain or loss is eliminated to the extent of the retained interest in the former subsidiary.

3.5.600.40 The election by the entity of one of these approaches has consequences on the treatment of reserves of the former subsidiary (see 3.5.470.80).

3.5.610 *Elimination of gains on non-monetary contributions*

3.5.610.10 All discussion regarding the elimination of gains on non-monetary contributions applies to cases other than contributions of subsidiaries (except when an elimination policy is adopted in accordance with 3.5.600.30).

SIC-13.7 3.5.610.20 Gains or losses on non-monetary contributions to jointly controlled entities attributable to the share retained by the venturer in the contributed assets are eliminated against the contributed assets. This means that a venturer will recognise its share of the non-monetary assets of a jointly controlled entity using the previously recorded carrying amount of the underlying assets at the date of the transfer.

3.5.610.30 As a result, the venturer will recognise its share of the assets it contributed at their carrying amounts at the date of the transfer and its share of the assets contributed by the other venturers at fair value. The gain on disposal of the non-monetary asset is recognised to the extent of the interest of other venturers in the jointly controlled entity, i.e. to the extent of the interest in the asset given up. The gain will be determined as the difference between the fair value of the asset disposed of and its carrying amount, multiplied by the other venturer's percentage interest.

3.5.610.40 The following example illustrates the application of this approach. Entities P and Q form a jointly controlled entity in which they each own 50 percent. The transaction has commercial substance (see 3.5.600.10). As part of the formation of the joint venture they contribute non-monetary assets.

	P	Q
Carrying amount of non-monetary assets contributed	100	130
Fair value of non-monetary assets contributed	250	250
Share in jointly controlled entity	50%	50%

3.5.610.50 The entry in P to record the contribution is as follows:

	Debit	Credit
Assets of jointly controlled entity (500 x 50%)	250	
Assets contributed		100
Gain (profit or loss)		150
To recognise contribution of assets to jointly controlled entity		

SIC-13.5 3.5.610.60 50 percent of the gain is eliminated:

	Debit	Credit
Gain (profit or loss)	75	
Assets of jointly controlled entity		75
To eliminate 50% of gain on contribution to jointly controlled entity		

3.5.620 Allocation of the elimination to the individual assets contributed

3.5.620.10 There is no specific guidance as to how the profit that is attributable to the share in the contributed operations retained by the venturer, that should be eliminated, should be allocated to the individual assets of the jointly controlled entity. However, IFRSs indirectly establish the mechanics of proportionate consolidation, e.g. if the contribution of assets has commercial substance, then a gain or loss is recognised on the interest in the assets transferred to other venturers.

3.5.620.20 The retained interest is accounted for at its carrying amount before the transfer, i.e. on a book value (carry-over) basis. Therefore, in our view for the retained interest in the contributed operations to be measured on a book value basis, the profit attributable to the venturer's share in the contributed assets should be eliminated against any goodwill and fair value adjustments on the transaction. Continuing the example in 3.5.610.40:

	P	Q
Carrying amount of contributed operations	100	130
Fair value of identifiable assets contributed	230	220
Fair value of operations contributed	250	250
Goodwill arising	20	30
Share in jointly controlled entity	50%	50%

3.5.620.30 In the financial statements of P the elimination results in the following carrying amounts for the assets related to the jointly controlled entity:

Retained share of contributed assets at carrying amount	(100 x 50%)	50
Share of acquired assets at fair value, including goodwill	(250 x 50%)	125
		175

3.5.620.40 The remaining profit of 75 corresponds to the difference between the investor's share of the other venturer's contribution in the jointly controlled entity (250 x 50%) and the investor's interest in its former assets that now belongs to the joint venture partner (50).

3.5.630 Cash and monetary contributions

3.5.630.10 A contribution of cash to the jointly controlled entity that is not distributed to a venturer does not result in realisation of a gain or change the principles shown in 3.5.610.20. The cash would gross up the contribution to and assets of the jointly controlled entity. The profit elimination would not change.

3.5.630.20 Assume that the example in 3.5.610.40 is modified so that P contributes cash to the jointly controlled entity in addition to contributing non-monetary assets. The respective contributions of P and Q are as follows:

	P	Q
Carrying amount of non-monetary assets contributed	100	130
Fair value of non-monetary assets contributed	250	300
Cash contributed	50	-
Share in jointly controlled entity	50%	50%

3.5.630.30 The entry in P to record the contribution is as follows:

	Debit	Credit
Assets of jointly controlled entity (600 x 50%)	300	
Non-monetary assets contributed		100
Cash contributed		50
Gain (profit or loss)		150
To recognise contribution to jointly controlled entity		

SIC-13.5   3.5.630.40 Provided that the criteria in paragraph 5 of SIC-13 are met, then 50 percent of the profit will be eliminated:

	Debit	Credit
Gain (profit or loss)	75	
Assets of jointly controlled entity		75
To eliminate 50% of gain on contribution to jointly		
controlled entity		

3.5.630.50 As a result, P's share in the jointly controlled entity's assets amounts to 225, and is detailed as follows:

Non-monetary assets contributed by P	(100 x 50%)	50
Cash contributed by P	(50 x 50%)	25
Non-monetary assets contributed by Q	(300 x 50%)	150
Total		225

3.5.640 *Losses on non-monetary contributions*

IAS 31.49   3.5.640.10 If the transaction results in a loss, then no portion of the loss is eliminated to the extent that it provides evidence of an impairment of a contributed asset.

IAS 31.50   3.5.640.20 In the unusual situation that the loss on the transaction does not provide evidence of impairment, it is eliminated to the extent that it is attributable to the share in the contributed assets retained by the venturer, and is allocated in the same way as any profit arising from contributions (see 3.5.620).

3.5.650 **Impairment**

3.5.650.10 An investment in an associate or jointly controlled entity may be impaired, even if the investee already has accounted for any impairment of the underlying assets. Therefore, investments in associates and jointly controlled entities are subject to impairment testing requirements.

IAS 28.31-33 3.5.650.20 Fair value adjustments and goodwill recognised on acquisitions of equity-accounted investees are not recognised separately. Goodwill recognised upon the acquisition of an associate is not subject to an annual impairment test. Instead, after applying equity accounting, the investment is tested for impairment when there is an indication of a possible impairment. The guidance in IAS 39 for financial asset impairment is used to determine whether it is necessary to perform an impairment test for investments in associates (see 3.6.1370). However, the impairment test applied if there is an indication of impairment follows the principles in IAS 36 *Impairment of Assets* (described in 3.10) rather than the IAS 39 financial asset impairment recognition and measurement requirements.

3.5.650.30 In contrast, if an investment in a jointly controlled entity is accounted for using proportionate consolidation, then goodwill is tested for impairment annually (see 3.3.200). This is because under the proportionate consolidation method the investor accounts for the underlying assets, including goodwill, and liabilities of the investee as opposed to the investment in equity instruments of the investee (see 3.10.590).

IAS 28.33 3.5.650.40 The *Improvements to IFRSs 2008* amended IAS 28 to specify that the requirements of IAS 36 are applied to the entire carrying amount of an investment in an associate without "looking through" the investment to the investor's carrying amount of individual assets within the investee. Therefore, after applying the equity method, any impairment loss on an investment in an associate is not allocated to the underlying assets that make up the carrying amount of the investment, including goodwill. Accordingly, any such impairment loss is reversed if the recoverable amount increases subsequently. The amendment was effective for annual periods beginning on or after 1 January 2009. For entities that were required to change their accounting policy as a result of the amendment, the transitional requirements allowed, but did not require, prospective application, which has consequences on their accounting for impairment losses related to associates after 2009, as discussed in 3.5.650.50 – 100.

IAS 28.41C 3.5.650.50 In our view, if an entity elected to apply the amendment *prospectively* in 2009, then it had the following choice in applying the transitional requirements of the amendment:

- not to reverse any impairment loss recognised and allocated to goodwill prior to the application of the amendment. This was on the basis that the purpose of effecting a change in accounting policy prospectively was to draw a line under the previous accounting policy and to move forward with the new policy;
- to reverse any impairment loss recognised and allocated to goodwill prior to the application of the amendment only to the extent that recovery occurred after the application date of the amendment. This was on the basis that IAS 8 *Accounting Policies, Changes in Accounting Estimates and Errors* defines *prospective application* as applying the new accounting policy to transactions, other events and

conditions occurring after the date as at which the policy is changed, i.e. after 1 January 2009 for calendar-year entities.

3.5.650.60 An entity that wished to reverse all impairments previously allocated to goodwill could elect to apply the amendment retrospectively in accordance with the general requirements of IAS 8.

3.5.650.70 For example, Company X has a 20 percent investment in Associate Y. In the year ended 31 December 2005, after applying the equity method X recognised an impairment loss of 20 in Y, resulting in a carrying amount for Y of 80 in X's consolidated financial statements. The impairment loss was allocated to the goodwill embedded in the carrying amount of Y, and therefore was not eligible for reversal (see 3.10.420.30). Assume that the carrying amount of Y remained at 80 at 31 December 2008. On 1 January 2009 X adopted the amendment to IAS 28. At that date 5 of the previously recognised impairment loss had been "recovered" but this recovery had not been recognised in the financial statements of X. By 31 December 2009 the situation was unchanged compared to 1 January 2009. By 31 December 2010 the full amount of the impairment loss is now recovered.

3.5.650.80 If the amendment has been applied prospectively and X has elected not to reverse any impairment loss recognised and allocated to goodwill prior to the application of the amendment, then none of the impairment loss recognised in 2005 will be reversed. The practical implication of this option is that the carrying amount of Y will never be the same as if X always had applied an accounting policy consistent with the amendment; the difference will be the full amount of the previously recognised impairment loss (20 in this example).

3.5.650.90 If the amendment has been applied prospectively and X has elected to reverse any impairment loss recognised and allocated to goodwill prior to the application of the amendment only to the extent that recovery occurs after the application date of the amendment, then the reversal of 15 that occurs during 2010 will be recognised in 2010, but the reversal of 5 that occurred prior to 1 January 2009 will never be reversed. As in 3.5.650.80, the practical implication of this option is that the carrying amount of Y will never be the same as if X always had applied an accounting policy consistent with the amendment; the difference will be the amount of any increase in the recoverable amount occurring prior to the application of the amendment (5 in this example).

3.5.650.100 If the amendment has been applied retrospectively in 2009 in the example in 3.5.650.80, then the reversal of 5 that occurred prior to 1 January 2009 would have been recognised in the comparatives, or in the opening balance of retained earnings if the reversal occurred prior to the earliest comparative period presented, and during 2010 the reversal of 15 that occurs during 2010 would be recognised, i.e. the entire 20 would be reversed. Consequently, the carrying amount of the associate would be the same as if the entity had always applied an accounting policy consistent with the 2009 amendment.

3.5.660 **Associates and jointly controlled entities classified as held for sale**

IAS 28.14,
31.2
3.5.660.10 Associates or jointly controlled entities that meet the criteria to be classified as held for sale (see 5.4.20 and 5.4.260) are measured at the lower of their existing carrying amount and fair value less costs to sell. Equity accounting or proportionate consolidation ceases at the time of reclassification.

3.5.660.20 In our view, the requirements of IFRS 5 *Non-current Assets Held for Sale and Discontinued Operations* should not be applied when an entity plans to obtain control over an existing associate or jointly controlled entity because there is no actual sale of the investment (see 2.6.1020.100).

IFRIC 17.11
3.5.660.30 See 3.11.452 for a discussion of the intended distributions of investments in associates or jointly controlled entities.

IAS 28.15,
31.43
3.5.660.40 If the classification of an investment in an associate or jointly controlled entity as held for sale ceases, then the investor reverts to applying the equity method or proportionately consolidates the investment. The comparative amounts disclosed for the periods since the classification as held for sale are restated (see 5.4.100.10).

3.5.670 **Changes in the status of jointly controlled entities and associates**

3.5.680 *Overview of the changes in status of equity-accounted investees*

From: / To:	Financial assets	Associates	Equity-accounted jointly controlled entities
Financial assets	N/A	Gain or loss for the difference between (a) sum of the fair value of any retained investment and any proceeds on disposal; and (b) the carrying amount of the investment (see 3.5.750.30). Retained investment initially measured at fair value for the purpose of applying IAS 39 (see 3.5.750.60). All reserves reclassified or transferred (see 3.5.750.40).	Gain or loss for the difference between (a) sum of the fair value of any retained investment and any proceeds on disposal; and (b) the carrying amount of the investment (see 3.5.750.30). Retained investment initially measured at fair value for the purpose of applying IAS 39 (see 3.5.750.60). All reserves reclassified or transferred (see 3.5.750.40).

From: To:	Financial assets	Associates	Equity-accounted joint-ly controlled entities
Associates	Preferred view: remeasurement of previously held interest through profit or loss. Available-for-sale revaluation reserve reclassified to profit or loss (see 3.5.700). Acceptable alternative: cost method. Available-for-sale revaluation reserve transferred to retained earnings (see 3.5.710).	Additional interest purchased: partial step-up approach (see 3.5.720). No reclassification of reserves. Sale of interest: gain or loss on proportion of investment sold (see 3.5.730). A portion of reserves reclassified or transferred (see 3.5.730.30).	Gain or loss for the difference between (a) the sum of the fair value of any retained investment and any proceeds on disposal and (b) the carrying amount of the investment (see 3.5.750.30). Retained investment initially measured at fair value for the purpose of applying IAS 28 (see 3.5.750.70). All reserves reclassified or transferred (see 3.5.750.40).
Equity-accounted jointly controlled entities	Preferred view: remeasurement of previously held interest through profit or loss. Available-for-sale revaluation reserve reclassified to profit or loss (see 3.5.700). Acceptable alternative: cost method. Available-for-sale revaluation reserve transferred to retained earnings (see 3.5.710).	Remeasurement of previously held investment at fair value through profit or loss (see 3.5.755.30). All reserves reclassified or transferred (see 3.5.750.40).	Additional interest purchased: partial step-up approach (see 3.5.720). No reclassification of reserves. Sale of interest: gain or loss on proportion of investment sold (see 3.5.730). A portion of reserves reclassified or transferred (see 3.5.730.30).

3.5.680.10 See 3.5.850 for transitional issues related to changes in status of associates and jointly controlled entities.

3.5.690 *Investment becomes an equity-accounted investee#*

3.5.690.10 An investment may become an associate or jointly controlled entity when:

- the investor acquires an additional holding; or

- there is a change in circumstances that results in significant influence or joint control being obtained.

IAS 28.20-23, 31.33   3.5.690.20 In our view, there are two possible approaches to account for a step acquisition to achieve significant influence:

IAS 28.20   • *The remeasurement approach.* Under this approach, the previously held interest is remeasured to fair value through profit or loss for the period. This approach is consistent with the approach in IFRS 3 (2008) in respect of step acquisitions to achieve control (see 2.6.1020). Obtaining significant influence is seen as a significant economic event in this approach, which also is consistent with the loss of significant influence being a significant economic event (see 3.5.750.20). This method is detailed in 3.5.700.

IAS 28.11   • *The cost approach.* Under this approach, the newly incurred additional cost is
IU 07-09   added to the carrying amount of the previously held financial instrument. The support for a cost accumulation approach stems from the definition of the equity method as a cost model, as emphasised by the Interpretations Committee in July 2009. See 3.5.710 for further discussion of this approach.

3.5.690.30 While we prefer the remeasurement approach, we believe that the cost approach is an acceptable alternative.

3.5.700 *The remeasurement approach*

IFRS 3.42,   3.5.700.10 Previously held interests will in almost all cases have been available-for-
IAS 28.20-23, sale investments and therefore already at fair value under IAS 39. As a result, no
31.33   remeasurement in the statement of financial position arises in practice, but since the investment is treated as sold there is reclassification to profit or loss of the available-for-sale revaluation reserve. If the previously held interests were financial instruments carried at cost under paragraph 46(c) of IAS 39, then they are adjusted to fair value through profit or loss and the fair value of the prior investment is added to the consideration paid for the additional interest.

3.5.700.20 For example, Company P acquired 10 percent of Company M for 200 on 30 January 2010. M is a listed entity and on 31 December 2010 the quoted price of the investment is 300. On 1 January 2011 P acquires an additional 20 percent of M for 600, ignoring directly attributable costs. The fair value of the identifiable net assets of M is 2,500 on 1 January 2011.

3.5.700.30 In this example, P's original investment is accounted for as a financial asset under IAS 39. Assuming that on initial recognition P designated the investment as available for sale, P will recognise a fair value gain of 100 (300 - 200) in its 2010 other comprehensive income (available-for-sale revaluation reserve).

3.5.700.40 On 1 January 2011 P obtains significant influence and records the following entry:

	Debit	Credit
Investment in associate	900	
Available-for-sale revaluation reserve	100	
Cash		600
Investment in financial asset		300
Profit or loss (gain)		100
To recognise acquisition of M		

3.5.700.50 Goodwill included in the investment in associate is calculated by adding the consideration paid for the new acquisition to the fair value of the previously held investment as follows:

Fair value of investment in financial asset at 1 January 2011		300	
Additional consideration		600	
Total investment in associate at 1 January 2011			900
Fair value of net assets at 1 January 2011	(at 100% level)	2,500	
30% share of fair value of net assets	(2,500 x 30%)		(750)
Goodwill			150

3.5.710 *The cost approach*

3.5.710.10 Under this approach, the available-for-sale revaluation reserve is transferred to retained earnings rather than being reclassified to profit or loss as in the remeasurement approach in 3.5.700. In the example in 3.5.700.20, all entries and computations illustrated would be the same apart from the transfer of the 100 available-for-sale revaluation reserve directly to retained earnings rather than to profit or loss.

3.5.710.20 If the previously held interests were financial instruments carried at cost under paragraph 46(c) of IAS 39, then they are not adjusted to fair value in the cost approach. The cost of the prior investment is added to the consideration paid for the additional interest. In such a case, following the example in 3.5.700.20, the goodwill calculation is as follows:

Cost of investment in financial asset at 1 January 2011		200	
Additional consideration		600	
Total investment in associate at 1 January 2011			800
Fair value of net assets at 1 January 2011	(at 100% level)	2,500	
30% share of fair value of net assets	(2,500 x 30%)		(750)
Goodwill			50

3.5.715 *Forthcoming requirements*

3.5.715.10 Upon the adoption of IFRS 9, all equity investments discussed in 3.5.700 – 710 are measured at fair value, including retrospectively by restatement if the investments were held at cost under paragraph 46(c) of IAS 39 prior to adoption of IFRS 9. Therefore, the preferred and cost approaches for step acquisitions presented in 3.5.700 – 710 are the same subsequent to adoption except that the cumulative gain or loss in other comprehensive income may be transferred within equity but will not be reclassified to profit or loss.

3.5.720 *Acquisition of additional interests in an associate (while maintaining significant influence) or equity-accounted jointly controlled entity (while maintaining joint control)*

3.5.720.10 IFRSs are silent as to how an entity accounts for additional investments while still maintaining significant influence, or additional investments while still maintaining joint control, i.e. without a change in the relationship for accounting purposes.

3.5.720.20 In our view, an entity should apply a "partial step-up" approach, whereby goodwill is calculated on the incremental interest acquired as a residual after valuing the incremental share of identifiable net assets at fair value. This results in identifiable net assets being valued on a mixed measurement basis. Under this approach, reserves are not reclassified to profit or loss or transferred to retained earnings.

3.5.720.30 The following illustrates the application of the partial step-up approach. Company P owns 25 percent of Associate C. On 1 October 2010 P acquires an additional 10 percent in C for 250 (including directly attributable costs); C remains an associate. The investment in C as at 1 October 2010 is 633 which includes goodwill of 100. The fair value of identifiable net assets as at 1 October 2010 is 2,300. Goodwill arising on the additional 10 percent interest is 20 (250 - 2,300 x 10%).

3.5.720.40 The investment in C as at 1 October 2010 can be detailed as follows:

	Goodwill	Identifiable net assets	Total investment in C
Tranche 1 (25%)	100	533	633
Tranche 2 (10%)	20	230	250
Total	120	763	883

3.5.730 *Decrease in interest in an associate (while maintaining significant influence) or equity-accounted jointly controlled entity (while maintaining joint control)*

IAS 28.19A   3.5.730.10 In our view, the partial disposal of the investor's ownership interest in an associate (while maintaining significant influence) or jointly controlled entity (while maintaining joint-control) is recognised in profit or loss for the difference between the proceeds from the sale and the cost of the investment sold. However, IFRSs are silent as to how to determine the cost of the investment sold. In our view, the guidance regarding cost formulas for inventories should be applied to determine the cost of financial assets sold when the financial assets are part of a homogeneous portfolio (see 3.6.1280.50). Therefore, any reasonable cost allocation method (e.g. average cost or first-in, first-out) may be used, although we prefer use of the average cost method. However, the use of specific identification is not precluded if the entity is able to identify the specific items sold and their costs. The selected method should be applied consistently.

AS 28.19A,
IU 07-09

3.5.730.20 A decrease in interest (while maintaining significant influence or joint control) can also result from a dilution. A dilution of an interest in an associate or jointly controlled entity may occur, for example, when the investee issues shares to other parties. The dilution gain or loss is the difference between the carrying amounts of the investment in the associate or jointly controlled entity, immediately before and after the transaction that resulted in the dilution. The carrying amount of the investment in the associate or jointly controlled entity after the transaction is determined by multiplying the new (reduced) ownership interest in the investee by the amount of net assets after the transaction. The gain or loss on the dilution of an interest in an associate or jointly controlled entity is recognised in profit or loss; the amount of profit or loss arises from the new (reduced) ownership interest in the assets subscribed for the new shares (e.g. the cash paid by the other party) compared with the reduction in ownership interest in the pre-existing investee's net assets. Such a transaction is not a transaction with equity holders in their capacity as equity holders, and therefore any resulting gain or loss should be recognised in profit or loss. See 3.5.750 if the dilution results in a loss of significant influence or joint control.

AS 21.48C,
28.19A,
IU 07-09

3.5.730.30 A decrease in the investor's ownership interest in an associate while maintaining significant influence results in the reclassification of a portion of reserves to profit or loss (e.g. available-for-sale revaluation reserve, foreign currency translation reserve) or in their transfer to retained earnings (e.g. revaluation reserve). In our view, the portion of reserves reclassified or transferred is calculated in proportion to the interest disposed of, so that it is calculated on a consistent basis with the gain or loss calculated on the partial disposal. If the cost of investment sold is determined using a first-in, first-out method (see 3.5.730.10), then the determination of the amounts to be reclassified or transferred would require detailed analysis.

3.5.730.40 The following illustrates the decrease in the investor's ownership interest in an associate when the average cost method is applied to account for decreases in interests in associates. For example, Company P owns 30 percent of Associate D. The contribution of D to P's consolidated statement of financial position before the decrease in ownership interest is as follows:

Investment in associate (D)	120
Net assets	120
Foreign currency translation reserve	24
Available-for-sale revaluation reserve	18
Revaluation reserve	15
Equity	63
Total shareholder's equity	120

3.5.730.50 On 1 January 2010 P sells 10 percent of D for 50 and maintains significant influence in D. D records the following entry:

	Debit	Credit
Cash	50	
Foreign currency translation reserve (24 x 10% / 30%)	8	
Available-for-sale revaluation reserve (18 x 10% / 30%)	6	
Revaluation reserve (15 x 10% / 30%)	5	
Retained earnings		5
Gain (50 - 40 + 8 + 6)		24
Investment in associate (D) (10% / 30% x 120)		40
To recognise decrease in interest in D while maintaining *significant influence*		

3.5.740 *Loss of significant influence or joint control*

IAS 28.10, 18, 3.5.740.10 The equity method or proportionate consolidation continues to apply until
31.36, 41 joint control or significant influence ceases, or until the investment is classified as held for sale (see 3.5.660). This may occur when:

- the investment or a portion of the investment is sold;
- there is a dilution in shareholding;
- there is a change in facts and circumstances; or
- the investor obtains control of an associate or jointly controlled entity or obtains joint control of an associate.

3.5.740.20 In our view, once an investment has been classified as an associate or jointly controlled entity, the investor will be regarded as continuing to have significant influence or joint control until a specific, identifiable event or transaction occurs that changes the circumstances. Insignificant or temporary changes in the relationship between the investor and the investee normally would not result in cessation of joint control or significant influence.

3.5.750 *Accounting for the loss of significant influence or joint control*

3.5.750.10 *All discussion regarding the accounting for the loss of significant influence or joint control deals with "step down" situations, i.e. with the loss of significant influence through disposal or partial disposal with a non-controlling interest retained, and with the loss of joint control through disposal or partial disposal with significant influence or a non-controlling interest retained. See 3.5.755 for a description of "step-up" situations.*

AS 28.BC21,
31.BC16   **3.5.750.20** A loss of significant influence or joint control is an economic event that changes the nature of the investment. Such an event is economically similar to a loss of control of a subsidiary and is accounted for similarly.

IAS 28.18,
28.19A,
31.45, 45B   **3.5.750.30** When an investor loses significant influence or joint control over an associate or jointly controlled entity, it recognises a gain or loss in profit or loss calculated as the difference between:

(a) the sum of:
- the fair value of any proceeds from the interests disposed of;
- the fair value of any retained investment; and
- the amount reclassified from other comprehensive income (see 3.5.750.40); and

(b) the carrying amount of the investment at the date that significant influence is lost.

IAS 28.19A,
31.45B   **3.5.750.40** Amounts recognised in other comprehensive income in relation to the associate or jointly controlled entity are accounted for on the same basis as would be required if the associate or jointly controlled entity had disposed directly of the related assets and liabilities. As a result, the investor's share of the following amounts is reclassified to profit or loss:

- exchange differences that were recognised in other comprehensive income in accordance with IAS 21;
- changes in the fair value of available-for-sale financial assets recognised previously in other comprehensive income in accordance with IAS 39; and
- the effective portion of gains and losses on hedging instruments in a cash flow hedge recognised previously in other comprehensive income in accordance with IAS 39.

3.5.750.50 The investor's share in any revaluation reserve may be transferred to retained earnings (see 3.2.410.20).

IAS 28.19,
31.45A   **3.5.750.60** When an investment ceases to be an associate or a jointly controlled entity and is accounted for in accordance with IAS 39, the fair value of the investment at the date when it ceases to be an associate or a jointly controlled entity is regarded as its fair value on initial recognition as a financial asset in accordance with IAS 39.

IAS 31.45   **3.5.750.70** If a jointly controlled entity becomes an associate, then the fair value of the retained investment is the deemed cost of the associate for the purpose of applying the equity method (see 3.5.320).

3.5.755 *Accounting for the gain of control or joint control of an existing associate or the gain of control of an existing jointly controlled entity*

IFRS 3.
BC384,
IAS 28.BC21,
31.BC16

3.5.755.10 Loss of significant influence or joint control are economic events that change the nature of the investment. It is as if any investment in the acquiree that was held prior to obtaining control was sold and subsequently repurchased at the acquisition date.

3.5.755.20 See 2.6.1020 for a discussion of the accounting when the investor obtains control over an existing associate or a jointly controlled entity.

3.5.755.30 If the investor obtains joint control over an existing associate, then there is a loss of significant influence resulting in a remeasurement of the investment in the associate at fair value through profit or loss and a reclassification of reserves (see 3.5.750.40).

3.5.760 *Investor's elimination of profits on previous downstream transactions*

3.5.760.10 The investor's elimination of profits on previous downstream sales to associates or jointly controlled entities is effectively reversed upon a loss of significant influence or joint control. For example, Company F previously was a 20 percent associate of Company P. On 1 April 2010 P sells half of its investment in F and no longer has significant influence over F. Therefore, P discontinues the use of the equity method. In a previous period, P sold land to F at a profit of 100. P eliminated the portion of the profit attributable to its interest in F of 20 against the equity-accounted carrying amount of its investment in F. As the former carrying amount, that was reduced by the elimination, is replaced with the sale proceeds and the fair value of the retained interest, the elimination is automatically reversed, resulting in a correspondingly larger profit.

3.5.770 *Dividends received after a loss of significant influence or joint control*

IAS 18.30(c)

3.5.770.10 There is no specific guidance when an investee that previously was an associate or jointly controlled entity declares dividends from earnings that accrued in a period when it was accounted for as an associate or jointly controlled entity. As the loss of significant influence or joint control is a major economic event that changes the nature of investment, in our view the dividends received are accounted for in accordance with IAS 18 *Revenue* with no specific adjustment needed.

3.5.780 **Retained investment in an associate or a jointly controlled entity following the loss of control of a subsidiary**

IAS 27.37

3.5.780.10 Any retained investment in a former subsidiary that represents an associate or a jointly controlled entity is remeasured to its fair value at the date that control is lost (see 2.5.490). An exception arises when the subsidiary is contributed to an associate or a jointly controlled entity and an elimination approach has been selected (see 3.5.470.50 and 600.30). The remaining investment is accounted for in accordance with IAS 28 or IAS 31 from the date that control is lost, and the fair value at the date that control is lost is the deemed cost of the associate for the purposes of applying the equity method (see 3.5.320).

3.5.790 Accounting for jointly controlled assets

IAS 31.21 3.5.790.10 The investor includes in its financial statements its share of the jointly controlled assets, the liabilities and expenses that it incurs and any income from the sale or use of its share of the output of the joint venture. In addition, it recognises any owned assets or liabilities that it controls alone.

3.5.790.20 For example, Companies S and T enter into a 50:50 joint venture arrangement to develop and market a new software product. The total software development costs that qualify for capitalisation as an intangible asset under IFRSs are 200; costs of 80 do not meet the criteria for capitalisation (see 3.3.120). Assuming that S and T each incurred 50 percent of the related costs, then S and T each should recognise software development costs of 100 as an asset in the statement of financial position and costs of 40 in profit or loss. In future periods S and T amortise the software over its estimated useful life and account for their share of any revenues or costs associated with marketing the software.

3.5.800 Accounting for jointly controlled operations

IAS 31.15 3.5.800.10 For jointly controlled operations the venturer includes in its financial statements the assets that it controls and the liabilities and expenses that it incurs in the course of pursuing the joint operation, plus its share of the income from the joint operation.

IAS 31.15, 16 3.5.800.20 The recognition by the venturer of the expenses that it incurs and of its share of the income that it earns from the sale of goods or services by the joint venture in a jointly controlled operation differs from proportionate consolidation (see 3.5.540). For instance, no adjustments or consolidation procedures such as eliminations are necessary in the consolidated financial statements of the venturer.

3.5.800.30 For example, Companies E and B each have a 50 percent interest in a jointly controlled operation. During the period B, on behalf of the jointly controlled operation, enters into sales contracts with customers and earns revenue of 100, and also incurs operating expenses of 40; E incurs operating expenses of 30 in relation to the jointly controlled operation's activities. Therefore, the profit generated by the jointly controlled operation is 30 (100 - 70). In order to share this income equally between E and B (15 for each venturer), B recognises a reduction in revenue and a payable to E of 45 (100 - 40 - 15), and E recognises an increase in revenue and a receivable from B of 45 (30 + 15).

3.5.810 Separate financial statements#

IAS 28.35,
31.46,
27.38-43 3.5.810.10 In separate financial statements (see 2.1.70), investments are accounted for on the basis of an investor's direct equity interest, rather than on the basis of the reported comprehensive income and net assets of its investees. Separate financial statements may be, but are not required to be, presented in addition to consolidated or individual financial statements.

IAS 27.38   3.5.810.20 Use of the equity method, or proportionate consolidation, for a subsidiary, associate or jointly controlled entity by an investor in its separate financial statements is prohibited.

IAS 27.38   3.5.810.30 Unless investments in associates and jointly controlled entities are classified as held for sale, in separate financial statements they should be accounted for either:

- at cost; or
- in accordance with IAS 39 (see 3.6.460).

3.5.810.40 The same accounting policies are applied for each category of investments, i.e. subsidiaries, jointly controlled entities and associates. In our view, those categories can be further divided into sub-categories only if a sub-category can be defined clearly and objectively, and results in information that is relevant and reliable. This is because IAS 8 requires that consistent accounting policies be applied to similar transactions, other events and conditions unless another IFRS specifically permits categorisation of items for which different policies may be appropriate. We believe that whether these latter tests are met should be judged similarly to choosing an accounting policy under the hierarchy for the selection of accounting policies (see 2.8.6). For example, venture capital investments that meet the scope exclusion criteria (see 3.5.160) may be a sub-category of associates.

3.5.810.50 All dividends from an associate or a jointly controlled entity are recognised in profit or loss in the separate financial statements of the investor when the right to receive the dividend is established (see 4.6.260). The recognition in profit or loss in the separate financial statements of the investor is independent of any consideration of whether the distribution is out of profit from the point of view of the investee. In addition, the receipt of dividend income may be an indicator of impairment (see 3.10.600.30).

3.5.815 *Forthcoming requirements*

3.5.815.10 Upon the adoption of IFRS 9, investments in associates and jointly controlled entities in separate financial statements (unless classified as held for sale) will be accounted for either:

- at cost; or
- in accordance with IFRS 9 and IAS 39.

3.5.820 Accounting by jointly controlled entities for contributions received

IAS 31,   3.5.820.10 IFRSs address the accounting for jointly controlled entities from the point
SIC-13   of view of the venturers. They are silent as to what treatment should be applied by the jointly controlled entity itself. When a jointly controlled entity prepares its own financial statements an issue arises as to whether it should account for the contributions received at their carrying amounts in the venturers' accounts before the transfer (a book value basis) or based on their fair values.

3.5.820.20 The accounting treatment applied by the venturers is independent of the treatment applied by the jointly controlled entity itself, i.e. the venturers will reverse the accounting applied by the jointly controlled entity when they account for their interest in the jointly controlled entity, so this issue is relevant only to the financial statements of the jointly controlled entity.

3.5.830 *The contributed assets do not comprise a business*

IFRS 2.5   3.5.830.10 When assets not comprising a business are contributed to a jointly controlled entity in exchange for equity instruments, the jointly controlled entity applies IFRS 2 *Share-based Payment* and measures the contributed assets at fair value (see 4.5.10.20). The contribution of assets falls within the scope of IFRS 2 as the joint venture has received goods and paid for these goods in shares (see 4.5.20.15). If the contributed assets represent a business, then the contribution is specifically excluded from the scope of IFRS 2.

3.5.840 *The contributed assets comprise a business*

3.5.840.10 In the absence of specific guidance on accounting by jointly controlled entities, some entities use fair values, and others use a book value basis, to record the contributions received from venturers.

IFRS 3.36   3.5.840.20 Although the formation of a jointly controlled entity is outside the scope of IFRS 3, if contributed assets meet the definition of a business, we prefer the jointly controlled entity to recognise the contribution at fair value. If the contribution is measured at fair value, then we believe the jointly controlled entity should apply the principles in accounting for business combinations (see 2.6.600) by analogy in measuring the fair values of the contributed assets, including the requirements for recognition and fair value measurement of contributed contingent liabilities.

3.5.840.30 However, in our view this applies only to a contribution received by a jointly controlled entity. We believe that the step-up to fair value cannot be applied when the jointly controlled entity is itself a former subsidiary, in relation to its own assets. This is because there is no contribution received and the change of control of an entity is not an occasion for this entity to step-up its own assets.

3.5.840.40 A jointly controlled entity should account for similar contributions from venturers consistently.

3.5.850 Transitional issues upon the adoption of IAS 27 (2008)#

FRS 3.64-65,   3.5.850.10 Both IFRS 3 (2008) and the paragraphs in IAS 28 revised by IAS 27 (2008)
IAS 28.41B   contain grandfathering (i.e. carry forward) provisions for transactions accounted for prior to the adoption of these standards.

3.5.860 *Contingent consideration arising on the acquisition of an associate*

3.5.860.10 In our view, adjustments of contingent consideration payable in respect of an acquisition of an associate that was first accounted for prior to the adoption of IFRS 3 (2008) should continue to be recognised in accordance with the old standards, i.e. by adjusting the purchase price, which will generally result in an adjustment to goodwill. However, subsequent to the adoption of IFRS 3 (2008) any contingent consideration in respect of newly acquired associates should be recognised at fair value at the acquisition date and, for financial liabilities, subsequent adjustments recognised in profit or loss (see 3.5.320.20). This is consistent with the transitional requirements for contingent considerations on acquisition of subsidiaries (see 2.6.1160.30).

3.5.870 *Changes in the status of associates and jointly controlled entities*

3.5.870.10 The guidance on changes in the status of equity-accounted investees in 3.5.670 is derived from the 2008 versions of the standards. In our view, prior transactions accounted for under the equivalent guidance derived from IFRS 3 (2004) and IAS 28 (2003) are grandfathered. Therefore, there is no need to restate past changes in the status equity-accounted investees. However, in the first set of financial statements in which an entity applies IFRS 3 (2008) and subsequently, any such new change in the status of equity-accounted investees should be accounted for in accordance with the guidance in 3.5.670.

3.5.875 *Forthcoming requirements*

3.5.875.10 The *Improvements to IFRSs 2010* amended the transitional requirements in IAS 28 and IAS 31 for amendments arising as a result of IAS 27 (2008) to clarify that the new requirements related to the loss of significant influence and joint control are applied prospectively. These amendments to transitional requirements are applicable for annual periods beginning on or after 1 July 2010; earlier application is permitted.

3.5.880 **Future developments**

3.5.880.10 The IASB is working on a short-term convergence project, partly to reduce the main differences between IAS 31 and US GAAP in the investor's accounting for an interest in a joint arrangement. In September 2007 the IASB published ED 9 *Joint Arrangements*, which proposed accounting for joint arrangements based on the contractual rights and obligations agreed to by the parties to joint arrangements; the legal form of the arrangement would no longer be the most significant consideration in determining the accounting for joint arrangements. The ED proposed that an entity recognise an interest in a joint venture, previously a "jointly controlled entity", using the equity method. Unlike IAS 31, proportionate consolidation would not be permitted. A final standard is scheduled for the third quarter of 2010.

3.6 Financial instruments

(IAS 21, IAS 32, IAS 39, IFRIC 9)

3.6 Financial instruments
(IAS 21, IAS 32, IAS 39, IFRIC 9)

Overview of currently effective requirements

- Financial assets and financial liabilities, including derivative instruments, are recognised in the statement of financial position at trade date. However, "regular way" purchases and sales of financial assets are recognised either at trade date or at settlement date.

- An embedded derivative is one or more implicit or explicit terms in a host contract that affect the cash flows of the contract in a manner similar to a stand-alone derivative instrument.

- A host contract may be a financial or a non-financial contract.

- An embedded derivative is not accounted for separately from the host contract when it is closely related to the host contract, or when the entire contract is measured at fair value through profit or loss.

- Financial assets are classified into one of four categories: at fair value through profit or loss; loans and receivables; held to maturity; or available for sale. Financial liabilities are categorised as either at fair value through profit or loss, or other liabilities. The categorisation determines whether and where any remeasurement to fair value is recognised.

- Financial assets and financial liabilities classified at fair value through profit or loss are further subcategorised as held for trading or designated as such on initial recognition.

- Financial assets are measured at fair value except for loans and receivables, held-to-maturity investments, and unlisted equity instruments in the rare circumstances that fair value cannot be measured reliably.

- All derivatives (including separated embedded derivatives) are measured at fair value. Fair value gains and losses on derivatives are recognised immediately in profit or loss unless they qualify as hedging instruments in a cash flow hedge or in a net investment hedge.

- An entity may reclassify a non-derivative financial asset out of the held-for-trading category in certain circumstances if it is no longer held for the purpose of being sold or repurchased in the near term. An entity also may reclassify, if certain conditions are met, a non-derivative financial asset from the available-for-sale category to loans and receivables.

- A financial asset is derecognised only when the contractual rights to the cash flows from the financial asset expire or when the financial asset is transferred and the transfer meets certain specified conditions.

- A financial asset is considered to have been transferred if an entity transfers the contractual rights to receive the cash flows from the financial asset, or enters into a qualifying "pass-through" arrangement. If a transfer meets the conditions, then an entity evaluates whether or not it has retained the risks and rewards of ownership of the transferred financial asset.

- An entity derecognises a transferred financial asset if it has transferred substantially all of the risks and rewards of ownership, or if it has not retained substantially all of the risks and rewards of ownership and it has not retained control of the financial asset; otherwise it continues to recognise the asset.

- An entity continues to recognise a financial asset to the extent of its continuing involvement if it has neither retained nor transferred substantially all of the risks and rewards of ownership, and it has retained control of the financial asset.

- A financial liability is derecognised when it is extinguished or when its terms are modified substantially.

- When there is objective evidence that a financial asset measured at amortised cost, or at fair value with changes recognised in other comprehensive income, may be impaired, the amount of any impairment loss is recognised in profit or loss.

Currently effective requirements

This publication reflects IFRSs in issue at 1 August 2010. The currently effective requirements cover annual periods beginning on 1 January 2010. The requirements related to this topic are derived mainly from IAS 21 *The Effects of Changes in Foreign Exchange Rates*, IAS 32 *Financial Instruments: Presentation* and IAS 39 *Financial Instruments: Recognition and Measurement*.

Forthcoming requirements and future developments

When a currently effective requirement will be changed by a new requirement that is issued but is not yet effective, it is marked with a # as a forthcoming requirement and the impact of the change is explained in the accompanying boxed text. The forthcoming requirements related to this topic are derived from IFRS 9 *Financial Instruments* which will replace the currently effective requirements in IAS 39 with respect to classification and measurement of financial assets. IFRS 9 is the subject of chapter 3.6A and therefore, these forthcoming requirements are not added to each section of this chapter.

When a significant change to the currently effective or forthcoming requirements is expected, it is marked with a * as an area that may be subject to **future developments** and a brief outline of the relevant project is given in 3.6.1630.70 – 90. In addition, a brief outline on further projects is given in 3.6.1630.10 – 60 that may affect all aspects of accounting for financial instruments.

3.6.10 Scope

IAS 32.4-10 3.6.10.10 IAS 32 addresses the presentation of financial instruments (see 5.6); generally it does not address recognition or measurement issues, but it does contain accounting principles for own equity instruments.

IAS 39.2-7 3.6.10.20 IAS 39 provides recognition and measurement requirements covering most financial instruments, other than assets and liabilities arising from employee benefit plans, own equity instruments, certain guarantees and other exceptions discussed in more detail below.

3.6.10.30 The scopes of the two standards are not identical, and consequently a scope exclusion in one standard should not be assumed to apply equally in the context of the other standard.

3.6.10.40 Certain instruments and contracts are excluded from the scope of IAS 32, IAS 39 and IFRS 7 *Financial Instruments: Disclosures* even though they possess all of the required characteristics of a financial instrument. For the financial assets and liabilities listed in 3.6.20, entities should refer to other existing standards, if applicable.

3.6.20 *Items excluded from the financial instruments standards*

	IAS 32	IAS 39	IFRS 7	Applicable standard[1]
Interests in subsidiaries[2]	X	X	X	IAS 27
Interests in associates[2]	X	X	X	IAS 28
Interests in joint ventures[2]	X	X	X	IAS 31
Employers' rights and obligations under employee benefit plans	X	X	X	IAS 19
Financial instruments, contracts and obligations under share-based payment transactions	X	X	X	IFRS 2
Rights and obligations under insurance contracts (except embedded derivatives and certain financial guarantees)	X	X	X	IFRS 4[3]
Financial instruments with a discretionary participation feature (except embedded derivatives)	X	X	–	IFRS 4[4]
Rights and obligations under leases	–	X	–	IAS 17[5]

Equity instruments issued by the entity, including warrants and options that meet the definition of an equity instrument (for the issuer)	–	X	–	IAS 32
Financial instruments issued by the entity that are classified as equity instruments in accordance with paragraphs 16A and 16B or paragraphs 16C and 16D of IAS 32 (for the issuer)	–	X	X	IAS 32
Forward contracts between an acquirer and a selling shareholder for the sale/acquisition of an acquiree that will result in a business combination at a future acquisition date	–	X	–	IFRS 3
Loan commitments that cannot be settled net in cash or another financial instrument	–	X	–	IAS 37
Rights to reimbursement payments in relation to provisions	–	X	–	IAS 37

("X" indicates a specific exclusion from the standard)

Notes

(1) In our view, if an item which is otherwise excluded from the scope of IAS 39 contains an embedded derivative, then the entity should evaluate whether the particular IFRS that addresses the accounting for the scoped-out item also addresses the accounting for the embedded derivative. If that IFRS addresses the accounting for the embedded derivative, then the entire hybrid instrument is accounted for in accordance with that IFRS. In our view, if the IFRS does not address the accounting for the embedded derivative, then the principles in IAS 39 should be applied to evaluate whether the embedded derivative is to be separated. If the embedded derivative is required to be separated, then the host contract is accounted for under the relevant IFRS and the embedded derivative is accounted for under IAS 39 (see 3.6.270.33).

(2) However, an entity applies the requirements of IAS 39 and IFRS 7 when, as permitted by IAS 27 *Consolidated and Separate Financial Statements*, IAS 28 *Investments in Associates* or IAS 31 *Interests in Joint Ventures*, it has chosen to account for an interest in a subsidiary, associate or joint venture using IAS 39. An entity also applies IAS 39 and IFRS 7 to derivatives linked to interests in subsidiaries, associates or joint ventures, unless the derivative is an equity instrument of the entity to which IAS 32 applies.

(3) IAS 39 applies to an insurance contract that is a financial guarantee entered into, or retained, on transferring to another party financial assets or financial liabilities within the scope of IAS 39 and issued financial guarantee contracts not accounted for under IFRS 4 *Insurance Contracts*. Financial guarantee contracts held are not within the scope of IAS 39. See 3.6.38.10 for guidance on accounting for financial guarantee contracts from the perspective of the holder.

(4) The issuer of such instruments is exempted from applying the financial liability/equity classification principles to the discretionary participation feature.

(5) However, the following are subject to the specified provisions of IAS 39 and to the requirements of IFRS 7: (1) lease receivables recognised by a lessor – derecognition and impairment provisions; (2) finance lease payables recognised by a lessee – derecognition provisions; and (3) derivatives embedded in leases – embedded derivative provisions.

3.6.30 *Insurance contracts*

3.6.30.10 There is a dividing line in IFRSs between financial risk and insurance risk that is especially relevant when it comes to counterparty risk because it determines the nature of the contract as being either an insurance contract to which IFRS 4 applies, or a financial instrument in respect of which IAS 32 and IAS 39 apply.

IFRS 4.A   3.6.30.20 An *insurance contract* is a contract under which the insurer accepts significant insurance risk from the policyholder by agreeing to compensate the policyholder if a specified uncertain future event affects the policyholder (see 5.10.30).

IAS 39.2(e)   3.6.30.30 Although IAS 32 and IAS 39 do not address accounting for insurance contracts, they do not scope out insurance entities. Insurance entities apply IAS 32 and IAS 39 to all financial instruments other than those that meet the definition of an insurance contract or a contract with a discretionary participation feature. Therefore, financial instruments that meet the definition of an insurance contract and that are within the scope of IFRS 4 are not subject to IAS 39. However, IAS 39 applies to a derivative that is embedded in a contract that is an insurance contract, unless the derivative also is an insurance contract (see 5.10.40).

3.6.35 *Financial guarantee contracts**

IAS 39.2(e)   3.6.35.10 The scope paragraphs of IAS 39 include specific requirements in respect of financial guarantee contracts issued by an entity. Such contracts fall within the scope of IAS 39 from the issuer's perspective except as discussed below. In our view, a financial guarantee contract held by an entity that is not an integral element of another financial instrument is not within the scope of IAS 39 (see 3.6.38.10).

3.6.36 *Definition*

IAS 39.9   3.6.36.10 A *financial guarantee contract* is a contract that requires the issuer to make specified payments to reimburse the holder for a loss it incurs because a specified debtor fails to make payment when due in accordance with the original or modified terms of a debt instrument.

IAS 39.9   3.6.36.20 Credit-related contracts that require payment in circumstances other than mentioned in 3.6.36.10, e.g. if there is no failure to make payment when due by a specified debtor or if the holder would not incur a loss, are credit derivatives that are measured at fair value under IAS 39.

IAS 39.9   3.6.36.30 The first key condition in the definition of a financial guarantee contract is that the contract should compensate the holder only for losses it incurs on debt instruments, i.e. the "reference obligation" in a contract should be a debt instrument. However, in our view this does not preclude a contract that contains a revolving portfolio as the reference obligation from being classified as a financial guarantee contract under IAS 39.

3.6.36.40 IAS 39 requires that a financial guarantee contract compensate the holder for losses it incurs because of failure to make payment when due by "specified debtors". Consequently, in our view such a revolving portfolio structure does not violate the requirements of a financial guarantee contract if the following criteria are met:

- The portfolio of debt instruments is specified, i.e. the contract includes a list of debtors included in the reference portfolio at all times.
- All replacements to the portfolio are documented and contain restrictions, so that the replacement mechanism does not compensate indirectly the holder for any form of fair value loss on the reference portfolio.

3.6.36.50 However, in our view the inclusion of a derivative instrument in the reference portfolio will violate the requirement that a financial guarantee contract compensate the holder only for losses it incurs on debt instruments. Consequently, we do not believe that contracts on reference portfolios that include derivative instruments will meet the definition of a financial guarantee contract.

IAS 39.9   3.6.36.60 The second condition that has to be met for a contract to be classified as a financial guarantee contract under IAS 39 is that it should compensate the holder only for a loss it *incurs* on the debt instrument. In our view, such a loss cannot be an opportunity loss or a fair value loss on a debt instrument but should be an actual loss that the entity incurs as a result of failure to make payment when due by a specified debtor. Consequently, contracts compensating the holder for losses arising from the restructuring of an entity do not lead automatically to a loss for the holder of the debt instrument other than a fair value loss, and it is possible that the holder will recover from the restructuring event. Therefore, we do not believe that a contract that compensates the holder for such losses will meet the definition of a financial guarantee contract.

3.6.36.70 However, IAS 39 is silent as to when the cash flows for compensation of a loss an entity incurs should occur. In our view, a contract still may meet the definition of a financial guarantee contract if the issuer makes payment to the holder for a past due amount provided the contract requires that any subsequent recovery of that amount from the specified debtor be reimbursed to the issuer (see 3.6.36.100).

3.6.36.80 Generally, a contract does not qualify as a financial guarantee contract if it provides for payments by the issuer in respect of amounts that are not past due. However, in many debt agreements non-payment of an amount that is due contractually would be an event of default that would trigger the entire remaining amount (principal and accrued interest) on the debt instrument to fall due. For example, a contract between a guarantor and the holder of a loan with a maturity of five years allows for physical settlement, i.e. the guarantor is required to purchase the entire outstanding debt amount at par plus accrued interest in the event of any non-payment by the debtor (e.g. a missed interest payment) that persists for 30 days beyond its due date. Under the terms of the loan, such a non-payment is an event of default. In our view, the contract would meet the definition of a financial guarantee contract if the non-payment condition that requires settlement of the guarantee also causes the entire outstanding debt amount to become immediately repayable. The issue of whether immediate repayment of the full amount of the debt instrument actually is requested by the creditor following the default does not affect the analysis.

IAS 39.AG4   3.6.36.90 Guarantee contracts that require payments to be made in response to changes in another specified variable, e.g. an interest rate, credit rating or credit index, are accounted for as derivatives within the scope of IAS 39 provided that, in the case of a non-financial variable, the variable is not specific to a party to the contract (see 3.6.30).

IAS 39.9   3.6.36.100 The third condition that needs to be satisfied is that the contract should not compensate the holder for an amount greater than the loss it incurs on the debt instrument. Consequently, contracts that are based on levered compensation of greater than one do not meet the definition of a financial guarantee contract. For example, a contract such as a credit default swap (CDS) that pays out to the protection buyer even if the holder does not own or have any other exposure to the specified debt instrument does not meet the definition.

IAS 39.9 3.6.36.110 In order to be classified as a financial guarantee contract, a contract should comply with all of the conditions as described in 3.6.36.10. In all other circumstances the contract will be classified as a derivative under IAS 39 (see 3.6.160).

IS 39.AG4 3.6.36.120 Financial guarantee contracts can have various legal forms, including certain letters of credit, credit default contracts and insurance contracts. However, the legal form of such contracts does not affect their accounting treatment.

3.6.36.130 For example, a bank makes a loan to Company D and Company B issues a guarantee to the bank that if D fails to make a payment within 30 days after the payment falls due, then B will make the payment on behalf of D. The agreement states that if the bank recovers subsequently the payment from D, then the bank is required immediately to reimburse B for the amount received from D (i.e. the bank cannot retain an amount in excess of the loss it ultimately incurs on the loan). In this example, the contract would meet the definition of, and accounted for as a financial guarantee contract in B's financial statements. This is because the three conditions for classification as a financial guarantee contract have been met:

- The reference obligation is a debt instrument.
- The holder of the financial guarantee contract is compensated only for a loss it incurs. In the example, the bank actually may or may not have incurred a loss when payment was not made within 30 days of the due date. However, as described in 3.6.36.70 and 80, if payment is made prior to a loss actually being incurred, then the instrument still can qualify as a financial guarantee contract if the contract includes a provision that any subsequent recoveries of the overdue amount be repaid to the guarantor as the inclusion of this provision ensures that the holder of the financial guarantee can be compensated only for its actual losses incurred.
- The financial guarantee contract does not compensate the holder for more than its actual losses incurred. In the example, this is achieved by the inclusion of the provision that any subsequent repayments of the overdue amount be repaid to the guarantor.

3.6.36.140 Modifying the example in 3.6.36.130, assume the same structure except that B will make payments to the bank based on changes in the credit rating of D. In this case the contract would not meet the definition of a financial guarantee contract and hence it should be accounted for as a derivative in the financial statements of both B and the bank.

3.6.37 *Accounting by the issuer*

IFRS 4.4, 3.6.37.10 Financial guarantee contracts, although they meet the definition of an insurance
B18, contract, generally are outside the scope of IFRS 4 and are accounted for under IAS 39.

IAS 39. BC23A However, if an entity issuing financial guarantee contracts has previously asserted explicitly that it regards them as insurance contracts and has accounted for them as such, then the issuer has an accounting policy choice on a contract-by-contract basis to apply either IAS 39 or IFRS 4 to each such contract. The election for each contract is irrevocable.

IAS 39.AG4 3.6.37.20 If a financial guarantee contract meets the definition of an insurance contract in IFRS 4, but the issuer applies IAS 39, then the issuer of the contract would measure it:

- initially at fair value; if the financial guarantee contract was issued in a stand-alone arm's length transaction to an unrelated party, then its fair value at inception is likely to equal the premium received unless there is evidence to the contrary; and
- subsequently at the higher of the amount determined in accordance with IAS 37 *Provisions, Contingent Liabilities and Contingent Assets*, and the amount recognised initially less, when appropriate, cumulative amortisation recognised in accordance with IAS 18 *Revenue*.

IAS 39. AG4(a) 3.6.37.30 If there is no upfront payment, then the fair value of a financial guarantee contract between unrelated parties at inception is likely to be zero under IFRSs. An exception would be a guarantee provided by a parent over the liability of a subsidiary. Even if no consideration is received by the parent, the parent is required to recognise a liability in its separate financial statements for the fair value of the guarantee. In our view, if no payments from the subsidiary to the parent are agreed for such a guarantee, then the parent has provided the guarantee in its capacity as a shareholder and accounts for this guarantee as a capital contribution (see 3.11.230).

3.6.37.40 An exception to the general measurement principles is provided for financial guarantee contracts that were entered into or retained upon transferring financial assets or financial liabilities to another party. Such contracts are measured in accordance with the provisions in IAS 39 related to the accounting for transfers that do not qualify for derecognition if the financial guarantee contract prevents derecognition or results in continuing involvement (see 3.6.1290.20).

IAS 39.2(e) 3.6.37.50 As stated in 3.6.37.10, if the issuer has previously asserted explicitly that it regards such contracts as insurance contracts and has used the accounting applicable to insurance contracts, then the issuer may apply either IAS 39 or IFRS 4 to such contracts (see 5.10.20.40).

IAS 39.AG4A 3.6.37.60 For an entity whose business includes the writing of financial guarantee contracts, generally it will be clear from contract documentation, previously published financial statements etc. whether it regards, and has accounted for, such contracts as insurance contracts previously.

3.6.37.70 In other cases it may be less clear. For example, an entity might provide financial guarantees from time to time that are incidental to its main business, perhaps to support borrowings of its subsidiaries or major customers. In such cases, in our view judgement is required in determining whether previous assertions in financial statements or elsewhere are sufficiently explicit to continue to apply insurance accounting.

3.6.38 *Accounting by the holder*

3.6.38.10 In our view, the criteria for identification of a contract as a financial guarantee contract are the same for both the holder and the issuer. In our view, a financial guarantee contract held by an entity that is not an integral part of another financial instrument is not within the scope of IAS 39. In our view, the holder accounts for such a financial guarantee contract as a prepayment measured at an amount equal to the guarantee premium and a compensation right accounted for by analogy to the guidance for reimbursements in IAS 37 (see 3.12.195).

3.6.38.20 An entity may purchase a debt instrument whose terms include, or which is accompanied by, a guarantee of payments on the debt instrument, which is issued by a party other than the issuer of the debt instrument and which has the features of a financial guarantee contract. In determining its accounting for such a guarantee, the holder determines whether the guarantee is an integral element of the debt instrument that is accounted for as a component of that instrument, or is a contract that is accounted for separately. If the holder determines that the guarantee is an integral element of the debt instrument, then the guarantee would not be accounted for separately but the holder would consider the effect of the protection on the fair value of the debt instrument and in estimating the expected cash receipts, and any impairment losses in respect of the debt instrument.

3.6.40 **Share-based payments**

3.6.40.10 A separate standard provides guidance on the accounting for share-based payments. Accordingly, the initial classification, measurement and subsequent measurement of financial instruments arising from share-based payment transactions within the scope of IFRS 2 *Share-based Payment* are subject to the requirements of that standard (see 4.5.220). Without this scope exclusion, financial instruments arising from these transactions generally would fall within the scope of IAS 32 and IAS 39.

3.6.50 **Lease rights and obligations**

IAS 39.2(b) 3.6.50.10 Rights and obligations under leases are recognised and measured under IAS 17 *Leases* (see 5.1), and consequently are not subject to the general recognition and measurement requirements of IAS 39. However, lease receivables recognised by a lessor are subject to the derecognition and impairment requirements of IAS 39. Also, finance lease payables recognised by a lessee are subject to the derecognition principles of IAS 39.

IAS 39.2(b) 3.6.50.20 Derivatives embedded in leases (both finance and operating leases) are within the scope of IAS 39 (see 3.6.270.40).

IAS 32.AG9 3.6.50.30 A finance lease is a financial instrument. IFRS 7 applies to all financial instruments, and rights and obligations under leases are not excluded specifically from its scope. Consequently, recognised financial assets and liabilities arising from finance leases are subject to the financial instrument disclosure requirements (see 5.6).

3.6.60 *Investments in subsidiaries, associates and joint ventures*

IAS 32.4(a),
39.2(a)

3.6.60.10 Investments in subsidiaries, associates and joint ventures that are consolidated, equity accounted or proportionately consolidated (see 2.5 and 3.5) are excluded from the scope of IAS 32 and IAS 39.

IAS 27.37(b)

3.6.60.20 However, IAS 39 does apply to such investments in the separate financial statements of the parent or investor if it elects to account for those instruments in accordance with IAS 39.

IAS 32.4(a),
39.2(a)

3.6.60.30 IAS 39 does apply to derivatives written on an interest in a subsidiary, associate or joint venture unless the derivative meets the definition of an equity instrument of the reporting entity (see 3.11.65.110). Essentially, the scope exclusion would apply to forward purchases and sales and to written and purchased options that can be settled only by exchanging a fixed amount of cash for a fixed number of shares (see 3.11.65.40). Similarly, IAS 32 and IAS 39 apply to derivatives held by the entity on interests in subsidiaries, associates and joint ventures that are owned by other parties.

3.6.60.40 A parent may invest in a convertible instrument issued by a subsidiary. In our view, if the convertible instrument is classified as equity by the subsidiary (e.g. because it is mandatorily convertible into a fixed number of ordinary shares (see 3.11.65)), then, in the separate financial statements of the parent, its investment should be considered to be an investment in a subsidiary and therefore would be excluded from the scope of IAS 39. However, we believe if the subsidiary classifies the instrument wholly or partly as debt, then the parent's investment in the subsidiary's liability would be subject to IAS 39. The conversion feature would be either an embedded derivative or an investment in an equity instrument, depending on whether the conversion feature is classified by the subsidiary as liability or equity (see 3.11.65).

3.6.60.50 [Not used]

3.6.60.60 However, IFRSs do not otherwise mandate symmetrical accounting between the holder and the issuer of an instrument. This is especially the case if a subsidiary classifies a financial instrument issued to its parent as a financial liability only because the subsidiary has a fixed life, i.e. all other conditions for equity classification are met. In our view, the parent should classify the acquired financial instrument based on its characteristics, including whether or not the instrument represents a residual interest in the subsidiary, and in this instance no symmetry in classification is required between the subsidiary and the parent (see 3.11.10).

3.6.65 *Forward contracts between an acquirer and a selling shareholder in a business combination*

IAS 27.IG7,
39.2(g),

3.6.65.10 IAS 39 excludes from its scope forward contracts between an acquirer and a selling shareholder to buy or sell an acquiree in a business combination at a future

9.BC24C-D acquisition date. The term of such a forward contract should not exceed a reasonable period normally necessary to obtain any required approvals and to complete the transaction. The scope exclusion does not apply to option contracts, whether or not currently exercisable, that on exercise will result in control of an entity (see 2.6.320 for a discussion of business combinations effected through derivatives). The scope exemption also does not apply by analogy to contracts to acquire investments in associates and similar transactions such as investments in joint ventures.

3.6.70 *Venture capital and similar entities*

IAS 28.1, 3.6.70.10 Venture capitalists, mutual funds, unit trusts and similar entities may choose
1.1, 39.AG3 to account for investments in associates and joint ventures at fair value under IAS 39, with all changes in fair value recognised in profit or loss, rather than apply the equity method or proportionate consolidation. However, there is no exemption for these entities from the requirement to consolidate all entities that they control.

3.6.70.20 In our view, an entity that has substantive and separately managed venture capital operations may use the exemption from applying the equity method and proportionate consolidation, even if the entity also has other operations. However, this exemption may be applied only to the investments held as part of the venture capital portion of the entity's operations.

3.6.70.30 See 3.5.170 and 180 for a discussion of whether an investor qualifies as a venture capital organisation.

3.6.70.40 [Not used]

IAS 39.50 3.6.70.50 If a venture capital organisation meets the exemption in IAS 28 to accounting for an investment at fair value through profit or loss, then ordinarily it would not be able to reclassify that investment out of fair value through profit or loss. A very limited exemption does, in our view exist if an investment has been transferred from a venture capital division within a group and the following conditions have been met:

- The group has different activities and one of the activities is a venture capital activity which is clearly ring-fenced from the business activity of the rest of the group. In order for this condition to be met the venture capital division should have its own strategy, objectives and management reporting system.
- The investment has been transferred from the venture capital division to another business in the group.
- The investment after the transfer is no longer managed as part of the venture capital division.

3.6.70.60 If the conditions in 3.6.70.50 are met, then the investment may be reclassified out of fair value through profit or loss.

3.6.80 *Reimbursements*

IAS 39.2(j)   3.6.80.10 Rights to reimbursement for expenditure that an entity is required to make to settle a liability recognised as provision, are outside the scope of IAS 39. They are recognised and measured in accordance with IAS 37 (see 3.12).

3.6.90 *Purchases and sales of non-financial items*

IAS 39.5,   3.6.90.10 A contract to buy or sell a non-financial item may be required to be accounted
32.8   for as a derivative, even though the non-financial item itself falls outside the scope of the financial instruments standards. Non-financial items include commodities such as gold, oil, wheat and soya beans, as well as motor vehicles, aircraft and real estate. If contracts to buy or sell non-financial items can be settled net in cash or another financial instrument, or if the non-financial item is readily convertible to cash, then they are included in the scope of the financial instruments standards.

IAS 39.5   3.6.90.20 There is an exception to this scope inclusion for contracts that are entered into and continue to be held for the receipt or delivery of a non-financial item in accordance with the entity's expected purchase, sale or usage requirements (the "normal sales and purchases" or "own use" exemption).

3.6.90.30 The accounting for a contract to purchase non-financial items (e.g. commodities, property, plant and equipment, intangible assets and investment properties) differs depending on whether or not the purchase contract is regarded as a derivative. When the purchase contract is considered to be a derivative, the purchase contract and the initial recognition of the non-financial item on settlement of the derivative are treated as separate transactions. The derivative is measured at fair value through profit or loss under IAS 39 (see 3.6.800.10), and the consideration paid for the non-financial item is the cash paid plus the fair value of the derivative on settlement. When the purchase contract is not regarded as a derivative it is treated as an executory contract (see 1.2.60). Under this approach there is only one transaction, being the purchase of a non-financial item under the contract, and the consideration paid for that non-financial item is the agreed price under the purchase contract.

3.6.90.40 For example, Company J enters into a contract to purchase 100 tonnes of cocoa beans at 1,000 per tonne for delivery in 12 months. On the settlement date the market price for cocoa beans is 1,500 per tonne. If the contract cannot be settled net in cash, or if the own use exemption applies, then the contract is considered to be an executory contract outside the scope of IAS 39. Under IFRSs only one transaction is recognised, being the purchase of inventory under IAS 2 *Inventories* (see 3.8) and the consideration paid is 100,000. However, if the contract can be settled net in cash and the own use exemption does not apply, then two transactions are recognised. The purchase contract is accounted for as a derivative under IAS 39. The purchase of inventory is a separate transaction and the consideration paid under IAS 2 is cash of 100,000 plus the fair value of the derivative on settlement of 50,000, hence bringing the total cost of inventory to 150,000. See 3.7.410 for a discussion of the hedging of non-financial items.

3.6.100 *Settlement net in cash*

IAS 39.6   3.6.100.10 A commitment to buy or sell a non-financial item will be considered settled net in cash if:

- the terms of the contract permit either party to settle in cash or another financial instrument or by exchanging financial instruments (e.g. a written option that permits cash settlement);
- the entity has a past practice of settling similar contracts net in cash or other financial instruments or by exchanging financial instruments;
- the entity has a past practice of taking delivery of the underlying and selling it within a short period after delivery for trading purposes; or
- the non-financial item that is subject to the contract is readily convertible into cash.

3.6.100.20 A contract that can be settled net in cash or one with the underlying item readily convertible to cash may qualify as a contract entered into and held in accordance with the entity's expected purchase, sale or usage requirements as long as the entity has no past practice of settling similar contracts net or trading the underlying.

3.6.100.30 However, a contract cannot be considered entered into in accordance with the entity's expected purchase, sale or usage requirements if the entity has a past practice of settling similar contracts net in cash or other financial instruments or by exchanging financial instruments, or taking delivery of the underlying and selling it within a short period after delivery for trading purposes. Such contracts are within the scope of IAS 39.

3.6.100.40 In our view, "past practice" should be interpreted narrowly. Infrequent historical incidences of net settlement in response to events that could not have been foreseen at inception of a contract would not taint an entity's ability to apply the own use exemption to other contracts. An example is an unplanned and unforeseeable break-down (outage) in a power plant. However, any regular or foreseeable events leading to net settlements or closing out of contracts would taint the ability to apply the own use exemption to similar contracts.

3.6.100.50 In our view, the concept of "similar contracts" includes all contracts held for a similar purpose. For example, Power Generating Company P, has sales contracts on electricity, each of which is held for one of the following purposes:

(1) held for trading (i.e. P has entered or intends to enter into offsetting purchase contracts);
(2) may result in delivery of the underlying power (commodity) but are available to be closed out from time to time as required (i.e. net cash settlement with the counterparty before or at the delivery date);
(3) intended to be settled by delivery of the underlying power but may be closed out only in the case of *force majeure* or other similar unforeseen events; or
(4) always will be settled by delivery of the underlying power.

3.6.100.55 Only contracts of types (3) and (4) qualify as own use. However, in our view P should designate contract types (3) and (4) into an "own use" category at inception in order to qualify for the exemption. Transfers out of these categories (e.g. closing out a contract other than because of an unforeseen one-off event) would taint P's ability to use the own use exemption in the future. Furthermore, P should be able to distinguish between contracts that qualify for the own use exemption and other contracts.

3.6.100.60 In another example, a chocolate manufacturer enters into a combination of physical contracts for the purchase of cocoa beans and cash-settled futures contracts. The physical contracts and the derivatives are managed together in order to hedge fixed price sales contracts from an economic point of view. In our view, the physical contracts and the derivatives would be regarded as similar in purpose and therefore the physical contracts would not qualify for the own use exemption.

3.6.100.70 A contract for differences is a contract wherein two parties agree to pay or receive in cash the difference between the spot price and the fixed price on an underlying item, without actual delivery or receipt of that underlying item.

3.6.100.71 Sometimes the market structure in some countries or industries may preclude a supplier and customer from entering into a direct transaction for the purchase/sale of a non-financial item. In such situations, the supplier may enter into a contract with a market intermediary to sell the non-financial item at the spot price, and the customer separately may enter into a contract with a market intermediary (possibly the same intermediary as that for the supplier) to purchase the non-financial item at the spot price. Depending on the structure of the market, the market intermediary may act as a principal in its separate contracts with the customer and the supplier or, alternatively, it may act as an agent on behalf of the customer and the supplier. In order to fix the price for the non-financial item, the supplier and the customer separately may enter into a direct contract for differences between themselves, and agree to pay/receive the difference between the spot price and a fixed price for that non-financial item.

3.6.100.72 When the market intermediary is acting as a principal in its separate contracts with the customer and the supplier, although the customer and supplier may be permitted to apply the own use exemption to their respective contracts with the market intermediary to purchase or sell the non-financial item, in our view the own use exemption cannot be applied to the separate contract for differences between the customer and the supplier, as the contract for differences is not a contract to buy or sell a non-financial item that will be settled by the delivery or receipt of that non-financial item.

3.6.100.75 For example, market regulations in the electricity market established by law may preclude an electricity generator and a customer from contracting directly for the delivery and purchase of electricity, i.e. the generator must deliver electricity to, and a customer (retailer) only can buy electricity from, a central "grid", whereby the grid acts as a principal in its separate contracts with the customer and the generator. The generator and the customer manage their exposure to the risk of fluctuations in electricity spot prices by entering into a bilateral contractual arrangement (contract for differences) that is settled outside the spot market, whereby the two parties agree to exchange in cash the difference between the contractually-agreed fixed price and the variable spot price that the customer pays in the market. The notional volume in such a contract for differences generally is determined either by the physical energy flow under the customer's contract with the grid to purchase electricity or the generator's contract with the grid to deliver electricity.

3.6.100.80 In our view, the transactions comprising the customer's contract with the grid to purchase electricity and the customer's contract for differences with the generator, or the generator's contract with the grid to deliver electricity and the generator's contract for differences with the customer, do not form a single arrangement because:

- these transactions have two distinct, separate purposes; and
- each contract is with different parties.

3.6.100.85 Since the structure is not considered as a single accounting unit, the contract for differences and the customer's contract to purchase electricity (or the generator's contract to deliver electricity) are analysed separately under IAS 39. Since the contract for differences is settled in cash, it is precluded from qualifying for the own use exemption, despite the linkage of the notional volume of the contract for differences to the physical energy flow under the customer's contract with the grid to purchase electricity (or the generator's contract with the grid to deliver electricity). However, the customer's contract with the grid to purchase electricity or the generator's contract with the grid to deliver electricity may qualify for the own use exemption.

3.6.100.90 The customer/generator would, however, be able to designate a contract for differences derivative in a hedge of the variability in cash flows arising from the forecast purchases/sales of electricity at spot rate if it satisfies the hedge designation and effectiveness criteria in IAS 39 (see 3.7.120).

3.6.110 *Readily convertible to cash*

IAS 39.AG71 3.6.110.10 In our view, the following indicators are useful in determining whether a non-financial item is readily convertible to cash:

- There is an active market for the non-financial item. This refers to the spot market rather than the forward market, if any. The relevant spot market is the market where the entity sells its products based on its business model. An entity assesses whether this specific market is active, according to the guidance provided in IAS 39. With respect to non-financial items it is important that willing buyers and sellers are present at any time (indicated, for example, by daily trading frequency (traded contracts) and daily trading volumes). Other indicators that might be considered are:
  - binding prices for the instrument are readily obtainable;
  - transfers of the instrument involve standardised documentation;
  - individual contract sales do not require significant negotiation and unique struc-

turing (normal time taken to close a transaction);
- the period required until the contract finally is closed is not extensive because of the need to permit legal consultation and document review; and
- the difference between the transaction price and the entity's assessment of the value of the contract is insignificant, as a significant difference would indicate low liquidity.
- The non-financial item is fungible.
- Transaction costs, including commission, distribution and transport costs, are insignificant compared to gross sale proceeds.

3.6.120 *Written options*

IAS 39.7 3.6.120.10 A written option, under which an entity might be required to purchase or sell a commodity or other non-financial asset that can be settled net in cash or another financial instrument, never can qualify for the own use exemption because the entity cannot control whether or not the purchase or sale will take place. Therefore, such a contract cannot be entered into to meet an entity's expected purchase, sale or usage requirements. However, written options for commodities that cannot be settled net in cash (see 3.6.100) are not within the scope of IAS 39.

3.6.120.20 Sometimes forward contracts, which may qualify for the own use exemption, are combined with written options in one contract. For example, an agreement to sell a fixed amount of a product at a fixed price may be combined with a written option under which a customer may purchase additional amounts. In our view, in such cases the contract may be split so that the forward element may qualify as own use even though the written option component will not.

3.6.120.30 In the energy sector it is common for a power company to provide "whole of meter" contracts, under which the customer pays a fixed price per unit for the number of units of power it uses in a particular period. In our view, such contracts generally are not written options because the customer does not have the right to buy more or less of the product depending on the market price nor does the customer have the ability to net settle such contracts in cash. In the case of electricity, the product cannot be stored or resold by customers and therefore from the perspective of the customer the power obtained under such contracts is not readily convertible into cash.

3.6.130 *Embedded derivatives*

3.6.130.10 When a contract contains an embedded derivative, an entity first determines whether the embedded derivative should be separated from the host contract and accounted for separately (see 3.6.280). When the embedded derivative is accounted for separately, in our view the host contract might still qualify for the own use exemption.

IAS 39.AG54 3.6.130.20 A purchase or sale contract for a non-financial item that is required to be treated as a derivative is measured at fair value through profit or loss in the period between trade and settlement date.

3.6.130.30 For contracts to purchase or sell non-financial items that are not treated as derivatives, the underlying purchase or sale transaction is accounted for in accordance with the relevant standard. Generally such contracts will be executory contracts (see 1.2.60) to purchase or sell the underlying commodity. However, if such contracts contain a "price adjustment" clause, then an assessment is made as to whether such a clause is an embedded derivative that requires separation under IAS 39 (see 3.6.280). In our view, whether or not a contract to purchase or sell a non-financial item has an embedded derivative that requires separation (e.g. in the form of a price adjustment clause) does not affect the conclusion regarding the host contract meeting the own use exemption under IAS 39 (see 3.6.90.20).

3.6.130.40 For example, an airline operator purchases an aircraft directly from the manufacturer. In order to protect prices of aircraft in the secondary market, the manufacturer writes an option under which it may be required to repurchase the aircraft from the airline operator at a specified price after a specified period, which is consistent with the useful life of the aircraft for the particular airline operator. Assuming that the repurchase option cannot be settled net in cash, from the perspective of the airline operator the repurchase option is not treated as a derivative. The repurchase option is an executory contract, which would not be recognised in the financial statements of the airline operator. If the option is exercised, then the airline operator will treat the exercise of the option as the sale of an asset. The proceeds from the sale of the asset is the amount received (i.e. the option exercise price). From the perspective of the manufacturer, the option generally will be treated as a derivative unless it contains an underlying that is specific to a party to the contract, such as the condition of the aircraft on its return (see 3.6.180.60).

3.6.140 *Loan commitments*

3.6.140.10 A loan commitment, in terms of which both the lender and the borrower are committed to a future loan transaction, can be regarded as a forward contract to grant/ receive a loan. A loan arrangement whereby the lender is obliged contractually to grant a loan, but the borrower is not required to take the loan (i.e. lender's written option), also is a loan commitment.

3.6.140.20 Generally, loan commitments that cannot be settled net in cash or another financial instrument are excluded from the scope of IAS 39 but are subject to the derecognition provisions of the standard. However, there are two circumstances in which a loan commitment falls entirely within the scope of IAS 39, namely:

- when the entity designates the loan commitment as a financial liability at fair value through profit or loss; or
- when the entity has a past practice of selling the assets resulting from its loan commitments shortly after their origination, in which case IAS 39 applies to all loan commitments in the same class, and they should be treated as derivatives.

3.6.140.30 A loan commitment that is a hedged item in a fair value or cash flow hedge will fall partially under the requirements of IAS 39. Generally only loan commitments that are scoped out of IAS 39 could qualify as a hedged item; loan commitments within the scope of IAS 39 generally are accounted for as derivatives and hence do not qualify as hedged items.

IAS 39.47(d)   3.6.140.40 Notwithstanding their exclusion from IAS 39, the standard includes specific provisions regarding the measurement of loan commitments. When an entity commits itself to providing a loan at a below-market interest rate, the loan commitment should be measured initially at fair value and subsequently at the higher of (1) the amount recognised under IAS 37; and (2) the amount recognised initially less cumulative amortisation recognised under IAS 18. All other loan commitments that are not within the scope of IAS 39 should be accounted for under IAS 37.

3.6.140.50 In our view, under IAS 37 it is likely that a provision for a loan commitment would be recognised either if an entity is committed to make a loan which would be considered to be impaired, or otherwise only when the contract becomes onerous.

3.6.150 Definitions*

3.6.150.10 Financial instruments embrace a broad range of financial assets and liabilities. They include both primary financial instruments (such as cash, receivables, debt, and shares in another entity) and derivative financial instruments (e.g. options, forwards, futures, interest rate swaps and currency swaps).

IAS 32.AG11   3.6.150.20 Deferred revenue and prepaid expenses are not financial instruments.

IAS 32.11   3.6.150.30 A *financial instrument* is any contract that gives rise to both a financial asset of one entity and a financial liability or equity instrument of another entity.

IAS 32.11   3.6.150.40 A *financial asset* is any asset that is:

- cash;
- a contractual right:
  - to receive cash or another financial asset; or
  - to exchange financial assets or financial liabilities under potentially favourable conditions;
- an equity instrument of another entity; or
- a contract that will or may be settled in the entity's own equity instruments and is:
  - a non-derivative for which the entity is or may be obliged to receive a variable number of the entity's own equity instruments; or
  - a derivative that will or may be settled other than by the exchange of a fixed amount of cash or another financial asset for a fixed number of the entity's own equity instruments. For this purpose, the entity's own equity instruments do not include: puttable financial instruments or instruments that impose on the entity an obligation to deliver to another party a pro rata share of the net assets of the entity only on liquidation that do not meet the definition of equity instruments even if they are classified as equity instruments (see 3.11.48); or instruments

that are contracts for the future receipt or delivery of the entity's own equity instruments.

IAS 39.IGB.1   3.6.150.50 Gold bullion is a commodity and not a financial asset; therefore it is not within the scope of IAS 32 or IAS 39. Physical holdings of other commodities also are outside the scope of the financial instruments standards. However, contracts to buy or sell commodities and other financial assets in the future are accounted for as derivatives unless certain criteria are met (see 3.6.90).

IAS 32.11   3.6.150.60 A *financial liability* is defined as:

- a contractual obligation:
  - to deliver cash or another financial asset to another entity; or
  - to exchange financial instruments under potentially unfavourable conditions; or
- a contract that will or may be settled in the entity's own equity instruments and is:
  - a non-derivative for which the entity is or may be obliged to deliver a variable number of the entity's own equity instruments; or
  - a derivative that will or may be settled other than by the exchange of a fixed amount of cash or another financial asset for a fixed number of the entity's own equity instruments. For this purpose the entity's own equity instruments are limited as described in 3.6.150.40.

IAS 32.11   3.6.150.70 An *equity instrument* is any contract that evidences a residual interest in the assets of an entity after deducting all of its liabilities.

IAS 32.16,   3.6.150.75 The following two categories of financial instruments issued by an entity are
16A-D   exempt from liability classification even if they contain an obligation for the entity to deliver cash or another financial asset:

- puttable financial instruments that meet certain conditions; and
- an instrument, or components of instruments, that contain an obligation for the issuing entity to deliver to the holder a *pro rata* share of the net assets of the issuing entity only on its liquidation.

3.6.150.77 These instruments are classified as equity instruments provided both the financial instrument and the issuing entity meet certain conditions (see 3.11.48).

IAS 32.21-24,   3.6.150.80 IAS 32 provides a comprehensive framework on the accounting for transac-
33, AG27,   tions in an entity's own equity instruments, including derivatives whose underlying is
AG36   an entity's own equity instruments. IAS 32 also addresses the accounting treatment of treasury shares. See 3.11 for further discussion of these issues.

IAS 32.13   3.6.150.90 The terms *contract* and *contractual* in the definitions in 3.6.150.40 and 60 refer to an agreement between two or more parties that has clear economic consequences and that the parties have little, if any, discretion to avoid, usually because the agreement is enforceable by law. Contracts defining financial instruments may take a variety of forms and do not need to be in writing. An example of an item not meeting the definition of a financial instrument would be a tax liability, as it is not based on a contract between two or more parties; rather, it arises as a result of tax law.

3.6.160 **Derivatives**

3.6.170 *Definition*

IAS 39.9   3.6.170.10 A derivative is a financial instrument or other contract within the scope of IAS 39, the value of which changes in response to some underlying variable (e.g. an interest rate), that has an initial net investment smaller than would be required for other instruments that have a similar response to the variable, and that will be settled at a future date.

IAS 39.IGB.3   3.6.170.20 The definition of a derivative does not require specific settlement features. As such, a contract that allows either net or gross settlement may be a derivative.

3.6.170.30 In our view, a derivative should not be split into its component parts. For example, an interest rate collar should not be separated into an interest rate cap and an interest rate floor that are accounted for separately.

3.6.180 *Change in value based on an underlying*

IAS 39.IGB.8   3.6.180.10 A derivative financial instrument is a financial instrument that provides the holder (or writer) with the right (or obligation) to receive (or pay) cash or another financial instrument in amounts determined by reference to price changes in an underlying price or index, or changes in foreign exchange or interest rates, at a future date. A derivative may have more than one underlying variable.

IAS 39.AG9   3.6.180.20 A derivative usually has a notional amount, which can be an amount of currency, a number of shares, a number of units of weight or volume or other units specified in the contract. However, in our view contracts without notional amounts or with variable notional amounts also meet the definition of a derivative. In addition the holder or writer is not required to invest in or receive the notional amount at inception of the contract.

3.6.180.30 A contract to pay or receive a fixed amount on the occurrence or non-occurrence of a future event meets the definition of a derivative, provided that this future event depends on a financial variable or a non-financial variable not specific to a party to the contract. For example, an entity may enter into a contract under which it will receive a fixed payment of 1,000 if a specified index increases by a determined number of points in the next month. The settlement amount is not based on and does not need to change proportionally with an underlying.

IAS 39.IGB.2   3.6.180.40 The underlying price change upon which a derivative instrument is based may be that of a primary financial instrument (such as a bond or equity security) or a commodity (such as gold, oil or wheat), a rate (such as an interest rate), an index of prices (such as a stock exchange index) or some other indicator that has a measurable value.

IAS 39.9   3.6.180.50 An option, forward or swap that is exercisable at the fair value of the underlying always has a fair value of zero. Therefore, it does not meet the definition of a derivative because its value does not depend on an underlying variable.

3.6.180.60 The definition of a derivative excludes instruments with a non-financial underlying variable that is specific to a party to the contract.

3.6.180.70 IFRSs do not provide guidance on how to determine whether a non-financial variable is specific to a party. In our view, the analysis comprises two successive steps:

(1) Is the variable non-financial or financial?
(2) Is it specific to a party?

3.6.180.80 In our view, this exclusion is intended primarily to exclude insurance contracts. For example, a residual value guarantee on a motor vehicle, where the holder is compensated not only for declines in the market value of the vehicle but also for the condition of the vehicle, would not meet the definition of a derivative.

3.6.180.83 However, in our view items such as earnings before interest, tax, depreciation and amortisation (EBITDA), profit, sales volume (e.g. revenue) or the cash flows of one counterparty may be considered to be non-financial variables that are specific to a party to the contract even though such contracts do not meet the definition of an insurance contract (see 3.6.1630). In our view, an entity should choose an accounting policy, to be applied consistently, as to whether such items are considered to be non-financial variables that are specific to a party to the contract.

3.6.180.85 In our view, if an instrument has more than one underlying variable (i.e. dual-indexed), with one underlying being a non-financial variable specific to one of the parties, then whether such an instrument is a derivative or not depends on its predominant characteristics. We believe a dual-indexed instrument is normally a derivative if it behaves in a manner that is highly correlated with the behaviour of the financial underlying variables.

3.6.190 No or a "smaller" initial net investment

IAS 39.AG11   3.6.190.10 There is no quantified guidance as to how much smaller the initial net investment should be compared to the investment required for other contracts that would be expected to have a similar response to changes in market factors, in order for the contract to meet the definition of a derivative. The standard requires that the initial net investment be less than the investment needed to acquire the underlying financial instrument to which the derivative is linked. However, "less than" does not necessarily mean "insignificant" in relation to the overall investment and needs to be interpreted on a relative basis.

3.6.190.20 Debt and equity securities generally are not derivatives, although their fair values have similar responses to changes in the underlying (e.g. interest rates or a share price) as derivatives on these instruments.

3.6.190.30 Many derivatives, such as at-market forward contracts, do not have any initial net investment.

IAS 39.IGB.9   3.6.190.40 Purchased options normally require payment of an upfront premium, but the amount paid normally is small in relation to the amount that would be paid to acquire the underlying instrument. However, certain call options may have a very low exercise price so that the amount paid to acquire the option is likely to be equivalent to the amount that would be paid to acquire the underlying asset outright at inception of the option. In our view, such options should be treated as a purchase of the underlying asset and not as derivatives. In other words, if an option is so deep in the money, at the date of issue or acquisition, that the cost of the option almost is equal to the value of the underlying asset at that date, then it should be accounted for as an investment in the underlying asset and not as a derivative.

IAS 39.AG11   3.6.190.50 A cross-currency swap meets the definition of a derivative, even though there is an exchange of currencies at inception of the contract, because there is zero initial net investment.

IAS 39.IG   3.6.190.60 Any required deposits or minimum balance requirement held in margin
B.10   accounts as security for derivatives are not considered part of the initial investment. For example, the variation margin required in respect of exchange-traded futures comprises cash collateral for the particular trade rather than being either part of the initial investment in the underlying commodity or an amount paid in settlement of the instrument.

IAS 39.IGB.4,   3.6.190.70 Sometimes part of a derivative is prepaid. The question then arises as to
IGB.5   whether the remaining part still constitutes a derivative. This depends on whether all of the criteria of the definition still are met.

3.6.190.80 If a party to an interest rate swap prepays its pay-fixed obligation at inception but will continue to receive the floating rate leg over the life of the swap, then the floating rate leg of the swap still is a derivative instrument. In this circumstance all of the criteria for a derivative are met: the initial net investment (i.e. the amount prepaid by the entity) is less than investing in a similar primary financial instrument that responds equally to changes in the underlying interest rate; the instrument's fair value changes in response to changes in interest rates; and the instrument is settled at a future date. If the party prepays the pay-fixed obligation at a subsequent date, then this would be regarded as a termination of the old swap and an origination of a new instrument that is evaluated under IAS 39.

3.6.190.90 In the reverse situation, if a party to an interest rate swap prepays its pay-variable obligation at inception using current market rates, then the swap is no longer a derivative instrument because the prepaid amount now provides a return that is the same as that of an amortising fixed rate debt instrument in the amount of the prepayment. Therefore, the initial net investment equals that of other financial instruments with fixed annuities.

3.6.200 *Settlement at a future date*

AS 39.IGB.7   3.6.200.10 Derivatives require settlement at a future date. A forward contract is settled on a specified future date, an option has a future exercise date, and interest rate swaps have several dates on which interest is settled. An option is considered settled upon exercise or at its maturity. Therefore, even though the option may not be expected to be exercised when it is out of the money, the option still meets the criterion of settlement at a future date. Any contract in which there is a delay between the trade date and the settlement date would be a derivative if the other criteria also are met.

3.6.200.20 A key element of a derivative within the scope of IAS 39 is that the transaction should allow for settlement in the form of cash or the right to another financial instrument.

3.6.200.30 Settlement of a derivative, such as an interest rate swap, may be either a gross or net exchange of cash or other financial instruments.

3.6.210 **Exemptions from derivative treatment**

3.6.220 *Regular way contracts*

AS 39.9, 38,   3.6.220.10 Regular way contracts are contracts to buy or sell financial assets that will
AG53-AG56   be settled within the time frame established by regulation or convention in the market concerned, not necessarily an organised market. Regular way contracts are not treated as derivatives between trade date and settlement date.

3.6.220.20 For example, a commitment for three-day settlement of a security is not treated as a derivative if three days is the normal settlement period for this type of transaction in the environment in which the transaction takes place. However, in a market with three-day settlement, if a contract specifies that settlement will take place only in three months, then the exception does not apply and the contract is treated as a derivative between trade date and settlement date.

3.6.220.30 IFRSs do not offer any specific guidance on how to treat a delay in the settlement of a regular way contract. In our view, a delay would not preclude the use of the regular way exemption if the contract requires delivery within the time frame established by the convention in the market, and the delay is caused by a factor that is outside the control of the entity.

3.6.230 *Derivatives on own equity*

IAS 39.2(d)   3.6.230.10 Derivatives on own equity are excluded from the scope of IAS 39 if they meet the definition of an equity instrument. See 3.11.45 and 65 for further guidance.

3.6.240 [Not used]

3.6.245 *Gaming contracts*

3.6.245.10 A gaming institution may enter into different transactions with its customers. For example:

- transactions in which the gaming institution administers a scheme amongst its customers and receives a commission based upon the amount wagered; in such transactions the gaming institution will receive its commission regardless of the outcome of the wager; or
- transactions in which the gaming institution takes a position against its customers; in these transactions the value of the individual contract is contingent on the outcome of a specified event and the gaming institution therefore normally is not guaranteed a specific commission or return.

3.6.245.20 In our view, the first type of transaction in 3.6.245.10 does not meet the definition of a derivative, as the value of such contracts does not fluctuate based on an underlying variable. These transactions should be accounted for under IAS 18. Conversely, the second type of transaction in 3.6.245.10 normally will meet the definition of a derivative, as the value of such contracts varies depending upon the likelihood of the occurrence of a specified event. Therefore, such transactions should be accounted for under IAS 39.

3.6.250 *Other*

IAS 39.AG49   3.6.250.10 Rights and obligations arising on the transfer of a financial asset that does not qualify for derecognition are not treated as derivatives under IAS 39, if recognising the derivative would result in recognising the same rights or obligations twice.

3.6.260 **Embedded derivatives**

3.6.270 *Definition*

IAS 39.11   3.6.270.10 IAS 39 requires an embedded derivative to be separated from the host contract and accounted for as a stand-alone derivative if the following conditions are met:

- the economic characteristics and risks of the embedded derivative are not closely related to those of the host contract;
- a separate instrument with the same terms as the embedded derivative would meet the definition of a derivative; and
- the hybrid instrument is not measured at fair value with changes in fair value recognised in profit or loss.

IAS 39.10   3.6.270.20 A derivative contract attached to a host contract that is transferable separately from the host contract, or that is added by a third party, is a stand-alone derivative and not an embedded derivative. For example, a finance lease or loan may have an associated interest rate swap. If the swap can be sold separately, then it is a stand-alone derivative and not an embedded derivative, even if both the derivative and the host contract have the same counterparty.

IAS 39.IGC.6   3.6.270.30 Generally, each component of a "synthetic instrument" is accounted for separately. A synthetic instrument is a combination of separate instruments that, viewed together, "create" a different instrument. For example, Company D holds a five-year floating rate debt instrument and a five-year pay-floating, receive-fixed interest rate swap; together these two instruments create, for D, a synthetic five-year fixed rate investment. The individual components of synthetic instruments are not embedded derivatives; rather they are stand-alone instruments, which are accounted for separately.

3.6.270.33 In our view, if an item that is otherwise excluded from the scope of IAS 39 contains an embedded derivative, then the entity evaluates whether the particular IFRS that addresses the accounting for the scoped-out item also addresses the accounting for the embedded derivative. If that IFRS addresses the accounting for the embedded derivative, then the entire hybrid instrument should be accounted for in accordance with that particular IFRS. If the IFRS does not address the accounting for the embedded derivative, then we believe the principles in IAS 39 should be used for evaluating whether the embedded derivative is to be separated. If the embedded derivative is required to be separated, then the host contract is accounted for under the relevant IFRS and the embedded derivative is accounted for under IAS 39.

3.6.270.37 In our view, the entity should evaluate whether the nature of the embedded derivative is such that the hybrid instrument in its entirety does not qualify for the IAS39 scope exemption. For example, we believe a commitment to enter into a loan in the future under which the principal advanced is fixed but the principal repayable is indexed to the price of a commodity would be regarded at inception as a freestanding derivative rather than a loan commitment.

IAS 39.2(b),   3.6.270.40 Although lease contracts and insurance contracts generally are excluded from
(e)   the scope of IAS 39, derivatives embedded in these contracts are subject to the requirements for separation of embedded derivatives. However, an embedded purchase option for a leased asset included in a lease contract is not separated since such an option is accounted for as part of the lease (see 5.1). All other derivatives embedded in lease contracts (e.g. foreign currency derivatives, leveraged escalation clauses etc.) should be considered for separation.

IAS 39.11   3.6.270.50 If an embedded derivative is separated, then the host contract is accounted for under IAS 39 if it is itself a financial instrument within the scope of IAS 39, or otherwise in accordance with other appropriate IFRSs if it is not a financial instrument.

IAS 39.AG29   3.6.270.55 If a single host contract has more than one embedded derivative with different underlying risk exposures that are readily separable and are independent of each other, then they are accounted for separately. For example, a debt instrument may contain an option to choose the interest rate index on which interest is determined and the currency in which the principal is repaid. These are two distinct embedded derivative features with different underlying risk exposures, which are accounted for separately.

IAS 39.11,
11A
3.6.270.60 If the hybrid (combined) instrument (i.e. the host contract plus the embedded derivative) is measured at fair value with changes in fair value recognised in profit or loss, then separate accounting is not permitted.

3.6.270.70 In particular, if a contract is a financial instrument and contains one or more embedded derivatives, then an entity can designate the entire combined contract as a financial asset or financial liability at fair value through profit or loss unless:

- the embedded derivative does not modify significantly the cash flows that would otherwise arise on the contract; or
- it is clear with little or no analysis when a similar hybrid instrument is first considered that separation would be prohibited.

3.6.270.80 For example, if an investment in convertible bonds is classified as an available-for-sale asset, then changes in its fair value would be recognised in other comprehensive income. Therefore, an entity would be required to account for and measure the embedded derivative (equity conversion option) separately. However, it may be simpler for an entity to designate the entire investment as at fair value through profit or loss and measure it at its fair value, and thereby avoid the need to separately value and account for the embedded conversion option.

3.6.270.90 Another example may be a complex investment product that comprises a host bond contract and a number of embedded derivatives based on interest rates, equity prices etc. It may be simpler for an entity to determine a fair value for the instrument as a whole than separately for the embedded derivative components.

IAS 39.12
3.6.270.100 If an embedded derivative cannot be measured reliably, although the characteristics are such that separation is required, then the entire combined contract (i.e. host contract and embedded derivative) is designated as at fair value through profit or loss. In our experience, this situation will be encountered only in rare circumstances, for example when the embedded derivative is based on an unquoted equity instrument.

3.6.270.110 If an embedded derivative is not required to be separated, then IAS 39 does not permit an entity to separate the hybrid instrument, i.e. separation is not optional.

3.6.280 **When to separate**

3.6.280.10 Determining whether an embedded derivative is closely related to the host contract requires the nature (i.e. the economic characteristics and risks) of the host contract and the nature of the underlying of the derivative to be considered. If the nature of both the underlying and the host contract are similar, then they generally are closely related.

S 39.AG30,   3.6.280.20 However, a derivative with economic characteristics and risk factors similar
AG33   to the host contract is not necessarily closely related to the host contract. This is the
case in the following situations, for example:

- An equity host contract and an embedded equity index-linked derivative are not closely related unless they are both exposed to the equity characteristics of the same entity.
- The derivative embedded in an inflation-indexed lease contract is closely related to the lease only if the inflation index relates to the same economic environment as the lease contract.
- A leverage feature that is not insignificant usually causes an embedded derivative feature not to be closely related. Leverage in this context (for contracts other than options) means that the value of the hybrid instrument changes in proportion to changes in the fair value of the underlying by a factor that is other than 100 percent.

3.6.280.25 [Not used]

IAS 39.11,   3.6.280.26 An option or automatic provision to extend the remaining term to maturity
AG30(c)   of a debt instrument is not closely related to the host debt instrument unless there is a
concurrent adjustment to the approximate current market rate of interest at the time of
the extension. However, depending on its terms, an entity may consider an extension
feature in a debt host contract to be equivalent to a loan commitment that would not
be within the scope of IAS 39, and consequently would not meet the definition of a
derivative (see 3.6.140.20). In our view, when an entity adopts this approach it would
not separate such an extension feature from the host debt contract.

IAS 39.11,   3.6.280.27 A call, put or prepayment option embedded in a host debt contract or host
AG30(g)   insurance contract is closely related to the host contract in either of the following scenarios:

- The exercise price of the option is approximately equal on each exercise date to the amortised cost of the host debt instrument or the carrying amount of the host insurance contract.
- The exercise price of the prepayment option reimburses the lender for an amount up to the approximate present value of lost interest for the remaining term of the host contract. Lost interest is the product of the principal amount prepaid, multiplied by the interest rate differential. The interest rate differential is the excess of the effective interest rate of the host contract over the effective interest rate the entity would receive at the prepayment date if it reinvested the principal amount prepaid in a similar contract for the remaining term of the host contract. This exception is conditional on the exercise price compensating the lender for loss of interest by reducing the economic loss from reinvestment risk.

3.6.280.28 Although generally it is presumed that a call, put or prepayment option is
closely related to the host contract when the exercise price is approximately equal to
the amortised cost of the host contract at each exercise date, in our view, this presump-

tion is relevant only when the assessment relates to a call, put or prepayment option that otherwise shares similar economic characteristics and risks to those of the host contract. For example, a five-year bond contains an early redemption option that allows the issuer to redeem it at any time after the second anniversary of the issue date if the volume weighted average price of the shares of the issuer, for at least 20 consecutive trading days, is not less than 30 percent of the entity's share price at the issue date of the bond. As the redemption option's underlying risk exposure is the share price of the entity rather than interest rate and credit risk of the host contract, in our view the call option should be separated from the host contract and measured at fair value through profit or loss (see 3.6.800.10).

IAS 39.AG27,   3.6.280.30 Evaluating whether an embedded derivative is closely related to its host con-
IGC.5   tract requires identifying the nature of the host contract. The nature of a host financial instrument (e.g. debt or equity) sometimes is not obvious. A debt host contract usually is characterised by a fixed or determinable maturity and fixed or determinable payments, while an equity host contract gives the holder a residual interest in the net assets of the entity. For example, consider a five-year instrument with a principal of 100,000 that will be redeemed on a specified date at an amount equal to the principal plus the change in the fair value of 10,000 shares in a listed entity over the term of the instrument. Even though the redemption amount is linked to a listed entity's share price, the instrument has a stated maturity and the host contract therefore has the nature of a debt instrument.

3.6.280.40 [Not used]

IFRIC 9.7   3.6.280.50 The assessment of whether an embedded derivative is required to be separated from the host contract and accounted for as a derivative is made at inception of the contract, i.e. when the entity first becomes a party to the contract. Subsequent reassessment is prohibited unless there is a change in the terms of the contract that significantly modifies the cash flows that otherwise would be required under the contract, in which case it is required.

3.6.280.55 For example, a foreign currency derivative embedded in a host sales contract would not be separated when it is not leveraged, does not contain an option, and the payments are denominated in the functional currency of any substantial party to the contract. Although the functional currency of a substantial party to the contract may change during the life of the contract, this does not result in reassessment of the derivative embedded in the contract as there have been no changes to the terms of the contract that significantly modify the cash flows that otherwise would be required under the contract. However, if there are changes to the terms of the contract that significantly modify the cash flows that otherwise would be required under the contract, then an entity would be required to make a subsequent reassessment for embedded derivative separation.

IFRIC 9.7,   3.6.280.56 When an entity reclassifies a hybrid financial asset out of the fair value through
7A   profit or loss category (see 3.6.860.11), it also is required to assess whether an embedded derivative is required to be separated from the host contract. The assessment is to be made on the basis of the circumstances that existed on the later date of:

- when the entity first became a party to the contract; and
- when there was a change in the terms of the contract that significantly modified the cash flows that otherwise would have been required under the contract.

3.6.280.57 If an entity is unable to measure separately the fair value of an embedded derivative that would have to be separated on reclassification out of the fair value through profit or loss category, then reclassification is prohibited and the entire hybrid financial asset remains in the fair value through profit or loss category.

3.6.280.58 For example, on 1 January 2010 Company X purchases a 10-year debt instrument for 100 (par), which is redeemable at any time at the issuer's option, for 100. X classifies the debt instrument as held for trading and it is accounted for at fair value with changes in fair value recognised in profit or loss. On 1 October 2010 the conditions for reclassification from the fair value through profit or loss category loans and receivables are met and the entity reclassifies the debt instrument to the loans and receivables (see 3.6.860.11). At this date, the fair value of the debt instrument is 70 and this becomes the new amortised cost of the debt instrument (see 3.6.860.15).

3.6.280.59 Upon reclassification, X evaluates the embedded call option to determine whether it is an embedded derivative that requires separation from the host debt instrument. As there have been no changes in the terms of the host debt instrument between the date of purchase and the date of reclassification, X performs the embedded derivatives assessment based on the circumstances that existed on the date of purchase, i.e. 1 January 2010 (see 3.6.280.57). On 1 January 2010, given the amortised cost of the host debt instrument of 100, X likely would have concluded that the embedded call option is closely related to the host debt instrument as the exercise price of the call option would be approximately equal to the amortised cost of the host debt instrument at each exercise date. Hence, X does not separate the embedded call option upon reclassification. In contrast, if the embedded derivatives assessment was to be based on circumstances that existed on the reclassification date, then X likely would have to separate the call option since, given the new amortised cost of the host debt instrument of 70, the exercise price of the call option of 100 would not be approximately equal to the amortised cost of the host debt instrument on each exercise date.

IAS 39. 3.6.280.60 An exception to the requirement that all derivatives with leverage require
AG33(a) separation is provided for embedded interest rate derivatives. For embedded interest rate derivatives leverage does not result automatically in separation as long as the following conditions are met:

- the embedded interest rate feature could not result in the holder of such a hybrid instrument not recovering substantially all of its investment at settlement date; or
- the embedded interest rate feature could not result in the holder receiving a rate of return on the hybrid instrument that is at least double its initial rate of return on the host instrument, and could not result in a rate of return that is at least twice the market return of an instrument with the same terms as the host instrument.

3.6.280.70 In our view, this analysis should not be based on the likelihood of these limits being exceeded in practice, but rather on whether the contractual terms make it *possible* that the limits will be exceeded.

3.6.290 [Not used]

3.6.300 *Foreign currency embedded derivatives*

IAS 39.
AG33(d)

3.6.300.10 A host contract may be denominated in a foreign currency, for example the premiums on an insurance contract or the price of non-financial items in a purchase or sales transaction. In these circumstances, the foreign currency embedded derivative is accounted for separately from the host contract, unless it is not leveraged and does not contain an option feature, and the payments required under the contract are denominated in one of the following currencies:

- the functional currency of one of the substantial parties to the contract;
- the currency in which the price of the related goods or service being delivered under the contract is routinely denominated in commercial transactions around the world; or
- the currency that is commonly used in contracts to purchase or sell non-financial items in the economic environment in which the transaction takes place.

3.6.300.12 In our view, if the conditions in 3.6.300.10 are not met, then a foreign currency embedded derivative should be separated from the host contract. For example, Company E enters into a contract to provide goods and services to Company B. E and B have the same functional currency. The settlement of the host contract is to be made in that currency. However, certain of the goods and services that E will purchase from unrelated third parties in order to fulfil its obligations will be denominated in a foreign currency. Accordingly, E and B agree that the final contract settlement price will be adjusted based on the movement in the foreign currency. In this case, because the embedded derivative is a foreign currency embedded derivative and does not meet the conditions in 3.6.300.10, we believe that it should be separated from the host contract even though it may have some economic relationship to the cost and value of the goods and services supplied.

3.6.300.15 IAS 39 does not provide guidance on how to identify "substantial parties to the contract". In our view, the legal parties to a contract are not necessarily also the substantial parties to that contract. In our view, the entity that will provide the majority of the resources required under a contract is a substantial party to that contract. When determining who is a substantial party to a contract, an entity needs to consider all facts and circumstances related to that contract including whether a legally contracting party possesses the requisite knowledge, resources, and technology to fulfil the contract without relying on related parties. To make this assessment, an entity should look through the legal form of the contract to evaluate the substance of the underlying relationships. In our view, only one entity within a consolidated group can be deemed a substantial party with respect to a particular contract. Identifying the entity that will provide the majority of the resources is subjective, and should be based on an analysis of both quantitative and qualitative factors. Certain resources, for example, employees and material costs specifically used to fulfil the contract, can be quantified. Qualitative factors that may not be measured easily include developed technology, knowledge, experience and infrastructure.

IAS 39.IGC.9 3.6.300.20 "Routinely denominated", as noted under the second bullet in 3.6.300.10, should in our view be interpreted narrowly, so that only a few transactions qualify for this exemption, including:

- an oil transaction denominated in US dollars;
- transactions related to large passenger aircraft, which routinely are denominated in US dollars; and
- transactions in certain precious metals, such as gold, silver and diamonds, may be considered to be routinely denominated in US dollars in commercial transactions around the world.

3.6.300.21 To qualify, the currency would have to be used in similar transactions around the world, not just in one local area. For example, if cross-border transactions in natural gas are denominated in US dollars in North America and in euros in Europe, then neither the US dollar nor the euro would be the currency in which natural gas routinely is denominated.

3.6.300.23 In our view, routinely denominated in commercial transactions around the world means that a large majority of transactions should be traded in international commerce around the world in that currency. This implies that in respect to each commodity, transactions cannot be routinely denominated in more than one currency.

3.6.300.25 In our view, if transactions on a local or regional exchange are denominated in local currency but are priced using the international price (e.g. US dollar per barrel of oil) at the spot exchange rate, then those transactions are, in effect, denominated in the international currency.

3.6.300.27 In addition, we believe the existence of a relatively small proportion of transactions denominated in a local currency in one or two markets, or particular jurisdictions, does not preclude a commodity from meeting the definition of routinely denominated in commercial transactions around the world.

3.6.300.30 The third exemption noted in 3.6.300.10 usually refers to the situation in which the local currency of a country is not stable, causing businesses in that environment generally to adopt a more stable and liquid currency for internal and cross-border trade. Before concluding that a currency, other than the local currency of a country, is commonly used in contracts to purchase or sell non-financial items in that country, careful consideration should be given to the state of the economy and business practices in that country. In our view, the assessment of "commonly used currency" in a specified environment requires judgement and needs to be evaluated in the context of the particular facts and circumstances in the national jurisdiction, but not in the context of a specific industry. We believe that the following parameters can provide evidence as to whether or not a currency is commonly used in a particular jurisdiction:

- for a cross-border transaction analysing the level of foreign trade transactions in that currency;
- for a domestic transaction analysing the level of domestic commercial transactions; or
- for either a cross-border or domestic transaction, analysing the level of both foreign trade transactions and domestic commercial transactions.

3.6.300.40 In our view, the analysis of foreign trade transactions in 3.6.300.40 needs to exclude transactions with entities whose functional currency is the currency being evaluated. For example, in order to conclude that the euro is a currency commonly used by Norwegian entities with Norwegian kroner as their functional currency, the cross-border transactions that require consideration are those entered into by such entities with other entities that do not have euro as their functional currency; this would exclude the majority of cross-border transactions between entities in the European Union.

3.6.300.50 Furthermore, in our view the analysis of a commonly used currency should be performed on a country-by-country basis, and not by reference to specific goods and services. For example, it is not appropriate to conclude that a particular currency is commonly used for cross-border leasing transactions and therefore that the foreign exchange embedded derivatives in all cross-border leases denominated in that currency do not require separation.

3.6.300.60 In our view, if a group entity has a separable foreign currency derivative, then the derivative is separable both in its financial statements and in the consolidated financial statements even if the transaction is denominated in the functional currency of the parent, which may be chosen as the presentation currency of the consolidated financial statements (see 2.7.30 and 60). The consolidated entity does not have a functional currency and as such cannot be viewed as having a definable foreign currency exposure that would remove, on consolidation, the need for separation.

3.6.300.70 For an embedded derivative to exist, the host contract should represent a contractual commitment. For example, forecast but uncommitted sales in a foreign currency, no matter how likely, would not give rise to an embedded derivative. Similarly, in our view a lease contract gives rise to an embedded derivative only for the period for which the contract is not cancellable. For example, Company X leases a coffee machine from Company Y under an operating lease that contains an embedded derivative requiring separation. X can cancel the lease at any time by giving three months' notice. In our view, at each reporting date, X has an embedded derivative only for the three months of committed, non-cancellable lease payments.

3.6.310 *Inflation-indexed embedded derivatives*

IAS 39.
AG33(f) 3.6.310.10 Inflation-indexed lease payments are considered to be closely related to the host lease contract provided that there is no leverage feature (e.g. a multiple that would

be applied to the inflation rate such that the lease payments would increase by *x* times inflation) and the index relates to inflation in the entity's economic environment (e.g. the consumer price index of the country in which the leased asset is operated). If the index is based on inflation rates in a different economic environment, then the embedded derivative is not closely related.

3.6.310.20 In our view, inflation-indexed embedded derivatives in loans are considered to be closely related to the host debt instrument when the inflation index is one commonly used for this purpose in the economic environment of the currency in which the debt is denominated and it is not leveraged.

3.6.320 *Examples of hybrid financial instruments*

3.6.320.10 Discussed below are specific examples of hybrid financial instruments that may be encountered in practice, particularly in the financial services sector. The names of these instruments may vary from one country to another, but their accounting treatment should be similar.

3.6.330 *Bond with a constant maturity yield*

3.6.330.10 Bonds with a constant maturity yield have a floating rate of interest that resets periodically on the basis of a market rate that has a duration extending beyond that of the reset period. For example, the interest rate on a 10-year bond resets semi-annually to the then current weighted average yield on identified treasury bonds with a 10-year maturity. The effect of this feature is that the interest rate always is equivalent to the market return on an instrument with 10 years' remaining maturity, even when the instrument itself has a maturity of less than 10 years.

IAS 39. AG33(a)
3.6.330.20 In our view, this constant maturity feature comprises an embedded derivative – a constant maturity swap. This embedded derivative is not closely related to the host debt instrument as potentially it could double the holder's initial rate of return and result in a rate of return that is at least twice what the market return would be for a contract with the same terms as the host contract, unless it has a cap at an appropriate level to prevent the doubling effect. In this example, after seven years the bond still would be yielding a return that is the same as an instrument with a 10-year maturity. It is possible that this would be twice the market rate on an instrument similar to the host contract without the constant maturity feature and with three years left to maturity. In our view, when assessing whether separation of the embedded derivative is required, the host debt instrument can be assumed to be either a fixed rate or a variable rate instrument.

3.6.340 *Cash or share bonds*

3.6.340.10 In a cash or share bond the principal is determined by reference to movements in fair value of a single equity instrument or an equity index. If the fair value of the equity index or share price falls below a certain level, then it is the fair value of this equity index or share price that will be the basis for repayment (rather than the nominal value of the bond itself) or the bond will be settled by delivering the underlying shares. Therefore, the holder of the instrument might not recover substantially all of their initial investment. The bond will pay a higher coupon to compensate the holder for this increased level of risk.

IAS 39. **3.6.340.20** The holder of such a bond has in effect written a put option. In the example
AG30(d)   in 3.6.340.10 the underlying of the written option is either the single equity instrument or the equity index. The option premium is embedded in the interest rate of the bond, which therefore will exceed the current market rate at the date of issuing the bond. This derivative embedded in the bond is not closely related to the host contract and should be separated.

3.6.350 *Bonds with interest payments linked to an equity index*

IAS 39.   **3.6.350.10** If the interest payment on a bond is linked to movements in an equity index,
AG30(d),   then the fixed interest on the debt instrument is swapped against a variable return
IGB.13,   based on the movement in the equity index. The interest payments are not dependent on
IGB.14   interest rate risk but on equity risk. Therefore, this swap is not closely related to the host contract and should be separated.

3.6.350.20 Typically an equity index would comprise a number of equity instruments of different entities, and therefore its movements would arise from the changes in the fair value of numerous underlying equity instruments. In order to be considered closely related to the host contract, the embedded derivative would have to possess equity characteristics related to the issuer of the bond (host contract). Consequently, even if the host contract (bond) were to meet the definition of an equity instrument, it is unlikely that the embedded derivative could be considered closely related, and therefore most likely should be separated.

3.6.360 *Step-down bonds*

3.6.360.10 Step-down bonds contain an interest feature such that the fixed interest rate declines over the life of the bond. For example, the first coupon is fixed at 10 percent whereas the last coupon is fixed at 5 percent.

IAS 39.IG   **3.6.360.20** The interest step-down feature alone would not be an embedded derivative
B.27   that needs to be separated from the host contract. Instead, the step-down feature is taken into account in determining the amortised cost and the effective interest rate on the bond. Thus at inception part of the interest received is deferred and released when the interest rate coupon falls below the effective interest rate of the bond.

3.6.370 *Reverse (inverse) floating notes*

3.6.370.10 Reverse (inverse) floating notes are bonds that have a coupon that varies inversely with changes in specified general interest rate levels or indexes (e.g. Euribor). Typically for such bonds coupon payments are made as per a pre-set formula such as:

> X% - (Y x three-month Euribor on a specified date)
> where X = a fixed interest rate; Y = a leverage factor.

IAS 39.   3.6.370.20 Such instruments can be viewed as a combination of a fixed rate debt instrument
AG33(a)   with a fixed-for-floating interest rate swap that is referenced to an interest rate index. Therefore, the instrument contains an embedded derivative. If the embedded derivative potentially could result in the investor not recovering substantially all of its initial recorded net investment in the bond (if the inverse floater contains no floor to prevent erosion of principal due to a negative interest rate), or if the embedded derivative could increase the investor's rate of return on the host contract to an amount that is at least twice the initial rate of return on the host contract and could result in a rate of return that is at least twice what the market rate would be for a similar instrument, then the embedded derivative is not closely related to the host contract and should be separated. If such an instrument is capped at less than twice the market rate at the date of issue and floored at zero, then the embedded interest rate swap is considered closely related and is not separated.

3.6.380 *Callable zero-coupon bonds*

IAS 39.   3.6.380.10 Callable zero-coupon bonds typically have long maturities, e.g. 30 years.
AG30(g)   The issuer of the bond has the right to redeem the bond at predetermined dates prior to the bond's contractual maturity at the accreted amount. In this case, the embedded derivative (call option) is closely related to the host contract if the bond is callable at an amount that is approximately equal to the amortised cost of the host debt instrument at each predetermined date, and is not separated.

IAS 39.11,   3.6.380.20 In our view, if the embedded call, put or prepayment option has underlying
AG30(g)   risks that are other than those of the host contract, e.g. equity price risk, then the economic characteristics and risks of the embedded call, put or prepayment option is not closely related to the host contract and should be separated (see 3.6.280.27).

3.6.390 *Perpetual reset bonds*

3.6.390.10 Perpetual reset bonds do not have a stated maturity although the issuer may have the right to redeem the bond at specified dates. If the issuer does not exercise this right, then the interest rate on the bond will be reset to a new level (based on a predetermined formula) on these dates.

IAS 39.   3.6.390.20 The embedded derivative, which is an automatic provision to extend the term
AG30(c)   of the debt, is not closely related to the host contract unless there is a concurrent adjustment to the market rate of interest at the date of the extension. Because the resetting of the interest rate is based on a predetermined formula, this may or may not reflect current market rates, and consequently such a feature generally would not be considered to be closely related and should be separated (see 3.6.280.26).

3.6.400 Credit linked notes and cash collateralised debt obligations

3.6.400.10 Credit linked notes are debt instruments that are bundled with an embedded credit derivative or a financial guarantee. In exchange for a higher yield on the note, investors accept exposure to a specified credit risk that is not the credit risk of the issuer of the note. Coupon payments and/or repayment of the principal are made only if no default occurs in the specified debt portfolio that may or may not be held by the issuer.

3.6.400.20 One form of credit linked notes is collateralised debt obligations (CDOs), which are securitised interests in pools of financial assets. The assets usually comprise loans or debt instruments. Multiple tranches of securities normally are issued by the CDO vehicle, offering investors various maturities and credit risk characteristics. Senior and mezzanine tranches typically are rated, with the ratings reflecting both the credit quality of underlying collateral as well as how much protection a given tranche is afforded by the more junior tranches.

3.6.400.30 In evaluating whether the holder of an investment in a CDO needs to separate an embedded derivative, it is important to distinguish between cash and synthetic CDOs. Cash CDOs expose investors to credit risk through the CDO vehicle holding the reference assets.

3.6.400.40 In our view, generally the holder of an investment in a credit linked note is required to separate the embedded CDS because the credit risk inherent in the embedded derivative is not closely related to the credit risk of the issuer. However, we believe the holder of an investment in a cash CDO is not required to separate an embedded credit derivative if the exposure is structured such that the embedded credit feature meets the definition of a financial guarantee and not a derivative. The terms of the cash CDO need to be evaluated to determine whether or not the embedded feature meets the definition of a financial guarantee contract (see 3.6.35).

3.6.400.50 On the other hand, a synthetic CDO represents a pool of credit derivatives together with government bonds. In other words, rather than the debt obligation being collateralised through an actual pool of mortgages or loans (cash instruments), it is backed by government bonds together with a pool of credit derivatives including CDS and credit default options. In such structures the issuer of the synthetic CDO is the protection buyer, and the holders of the synthetic CDO the protection sellers, as the credit risk inherent in the credit derivatives is passed to the bond holder. These instruments have all the characteristics of normal debt obligations, i.e. fixed or determinable payments and a fixed maturity; however, holders of such instruments share a credit risk inherent in the pool of credit derivatives that is different from the credit risk of the issuing entity.

IAS 39.
AG30(h) 3.6.400.60 In our view, the credit derivative embedded in such a synthetic CDO should be accounted for separately by the holder. This embedded derivative should be valued by reference to the credit risk inherent in the pool of credit derivatives that back the obligation. In some cases the underlying credit derivatives may be packaged into a

special purpose entity (SPE), which in turn issues the obligation. The credit risk of the embedded derivative still is the credit risk of the underlying pool of credit derivatives, and not the credit risk of the SPE. The fact that junior and senior tranches are issued does not change the fact that each tranche of bonds contains a separate embedded derivative, although the value of the embedded derivatives in senior tranches may be small.

IAS 39.   3.6.400.70 Distinguishing between a cash or synthetic CDO can become complex when,
AG30(h)   for example, an entity invests in a CDO whose reference portfolio includes CDOs issued by another entity (generally termed "CDO squared" or "CDO2"). In our view, the holder of a CDO2 should account for it based on the reference portfolio of the first CDO (a "look-through" approach). In this circumstance, the accounting treatment reflects the true risks of the investment, i.e. the holder's risk exposure in the referenced portfolio is impacted by the underlying risks of the CDOs contained within the portfolio.

3.6.410 *Examples of hybrid non-financial contracts*

AS 39.10, 11   3.6.410.10 Often embedded derivatives are associated with financial instruments. However, embedded derivatives may arise in non-financial contracts, e.g. contracts for the delivery of goods and services. These embedded derivatives also should be subjected to the analysis described in 3.6.270 – 310 and accounted for separately, when appropriate. In such cases the host contract will not be a financial instrument, but will be accounted for under other appropriate standards. The examples in 3.6.420 – 430.30 illustrate circumstances in which embedded derivatives exist in non-financial contracts.

3.6.420 *Price-indexation of a non-financial item*

3.6.420.10 For example, manufacturing entity enters into a contract for the purchase of three specialised machines that will be delivered and installed at the end of 2008, 2009 and 2010 respectively. The price of each of the machines is determined by reference to a formula that uses the market price of such a machine at the end of 2007 as the base price. This base price is adjusted for twice the change in an employment cost index, as well as an index that reflects cost increases associated with the industry.

3.6.420.20 The indexation as described in 3.6.420.10 incorporates leverage into the pricing mechanism and therefore should be considered an embedded derivative that requires separate accounting. However, if the manufacturing entity is able to demonstrate that the market prices of similar machines ordinarily move in tandem with the indexation (i.e. there is a high degree of correlation between the two), then separation would be avoided.

3.6.430 *Maintenance cost guarantee*

3.6.430.10 For example, a logistics company purchases its entire fleet of delivery vehicles from one vehicle manufacturer. The vehicle manufacturer provides a guarantee to the logistics company under which it agrees to reimburse the logistics company for vehicle maintenance costs in excess of a specified level.

3.6.430.20 Whether or not this arrangement comprises an embedded derivative in the sales contract depends on the terms of the guarantee. If the fair value of a derivative instrument changes in response to the change in a specified non-financial variable that is not specific to a party to the contract, then such an instrument meets the definition of a derivative under IAS 39.

3.6.430.30 In our view, the variation in maintenance charges comprises a non-financial variable. Furthermore, this non-financial variable is specific to the fleet held by the logistics company as it is dependent on the condition of the company's own vehicles. Consequently, this feature of the contract does not meet the definition of a derivative and does not require separate accounting under IAS 39.

3.6.440 *Accounting for separable embedded derivatives*

IAS 39.46, 55   3.6.440.10 Separable embedded derivatives are required to be measured at fair value with all changes in fair value recognised in profit or loss unless they form part of a qualifying cash flow or net investment hedging relationship.

IAS 39.AG28,   3.6.440.20 The initial bifurcation of a separable embedded derivative does not result in *IGC.1, IGC.2*   any gain or loss being recognised.

IAS 32.31,   3.6.440.30 As the embedded derivative component is measured at fair value on initial *39.13, AG28*   recognition, the carrying amount of the host contract at initial recognition is the difference between the carrying amount of the hybrid instrument and the fair value of the embedded derivative. If the fair values of the hybrid instrument and host contract are more reliably measurable than that of the derivative component, e.g. due to quoted market prices being available, then it may be acceptable to use those values to determine the fair value of the derivative upon initial recognition indirectly, i.e. as a residual amount.

IAS 39.AG28,   3.6.440.40 When separating an embedded derivative that is a forward contract, the forward *IGC.1, IGC.2*   price is set such that the fair value of the embedded forward contract is zero at inception. The same applies if the embedded derivative is a swap. Consequently, the forward price should be at market on initial recognition. When separating an embedded derivative that is an option, the separation is based on the stated terms of the option feature documented in the hybrid instrument. As a result, the embedded derivative would have a fair value of other than zero at initial recognition of the hybrid instrument. However, the embedded derivative is valued based on terms that are clearly present in the hybrid instrument.

3.6.440.43 For example, Company G, whose functional currency is sterling (GBP), enters into a contract on 1 March 2010 to purchase goods from Company B whose functional currency is euro. The purchase contract stipulates the payment in US dollars and requires G to pay USD 380,000 on delivery of the goods in six months' time. The applicable exchange rates on 1 March 2010 are:

- Spot rate (1 USD = GBP 0.556)

- Six-month forward rate (1 USD = GBP 0.526)

3.6.440.45 The contract between G and B contains a foreign currency derivative that requires separation under IAS 39 as it does not fall under any of the exemptions for non-separation of embedded foreign currency derivatives (see 3.6.300).

3.6.440.47 The host contract is a purchase contract denominated in the functional currency of G, i.e. GBP. The embedded derivative is a foreign currency forward contract to sell USD 380,000 for GBP at 0.526 at 1 March 2010 (i.e. GBP 200,000). Since the forward exchange rate is the market rate on the date of the transaction, the embedded forward contract has a fair value of zero on initial recognition.

3.6.440.49 The embedded foreign currency forward contract is accounted for as a free-standing derivative (see 3.6.805), and the host instrument as an executory contract (see 1.2.60.20).

3.6.440.50 When the contract in which a separable derivative financial instrument is embedded is settled or extinguished, the embedded derivative also is settled or extinguished. For example, a foreign currency derivative embedded in a contract to deliver goods or services is settled when the goods or services are paid for.

3.6.440.60 [Not used]

3.6.440.70 Embedded derivatives accounted for separately may be designated as hedging instruments. The normal hedge accounting criteria outlined in section 3.7.120 apply to embedded derivatives used as hedging instruments.

3.6.450 *Presentation and disclosure*

IAS 39.11   3.6.450.10 IAS 39 does not require separate presentation of embedded derivatives in the statement of financial position. In our view, under certain circumstances embedded derivatives should be presented together with the host contract (see 5.6.200). However, an entity is required to disclose separately financial instruments carried at cost and those carried at fair value. Therefore, as a minimum, embedded derivatives that are not presented separately in the statement of financial position should be disclosed in the notes.

3.6.460 **Classification**

IAS 39.45   3.6.460.10 IAS 39 establishes specific categories into which all financial assets and liabilities are classified. The classification of financial instruments dictates how these assets and liabilities are measured subsequently in the financial statements of an entity. There are four categories of financial assets: financial assets at fair value through profit or loss; held-to-maturity investments; loans and receivables; and available-for-sale financial assets; and two categories of financial liabilities: financial liabilities at fair value through profit or loss; and other financial liabilities.

3.6.460.20 In our view, if an entity acquires financial instruments as part of a business combination, then the entity should classify the acquired financial instruments at the acquisition date applying the normal classification rules, without regard to how the instruments were classified by the acquiree before the acquisition. If these classifications differ from the classifications made by the acquiree, then the reclassifications are not treated as transfers between portfolios, i.e. they would not raise issues of "tainting" with respect to items classified as held to maturity (see 2.6.560).

3.6.460.30 The classification rules for each of the categories are discussed below.

3.6.470 *Financial assets or financial liabilities at fair value through profit or loss, including derivatives*

<table>
<tr><td>IFRS 3.58,
IAS 39.9</td><td>3.6.470.10 This category includes:</td></tr>
</table>

- financial assets or liabilities held for trading (i.e. any financial asset or liability acquired or incurred to generate short-term profits, or that is part of a portfolio of financial instruments that are managed together for that purpose);
- all derivatives other than hedging instruments (see 3.7.310);
- contingent consideration as defined in IFRS 3 *Business Combinations* classified as a financial liability that is within the scope of IAS 39; and
- financial assets or liabilities that are designated by the entity at the time of initial recognition as measured at fair value through profit or loss.

<table>
<tr><td>IAS 39.9</td><td>3.6.470.20 Under IFRSs the designation of financial instruments as at fair value through profit or loss is permitted, provided that certain specified criteria are met, for any financial instrument other than equity instruments that do not have a quoted market price in an active market and whose fair value cannot be measured reliably. This designation is available only upon initial recognition of the instrument and is irrevocable.</td></tr>
</table>

3.6.480 *Financial assets and liabilities held for trading*

<table>
<tr><td>IAS 39.9</td><td>3.6.480.10 A financial asset or financial liability is classified as held for trading if it is:</td></tr>
</table>

- acquired or incurred principally for the purpose of selling or repurchasing it in the near term;
- on initial recognition, part of a portfolio of identified financial instruments that are managed together and for which there is evidence of a recent actual pattern of short-term profit taking; and
- a derivative, except for a derivative that is a designated and effective hedging instrument.

<table>
<tr><td>IAS 39.AG14</td><td>3.6.480.20 Trading generally refers to the active and frequent buying and selling of an item. Financial assets and financial liabilities classified as held for trading generally are held with the objective of generating a profit from short-term fluctuations in price or dealer's margin. However, in our view these general characteristics are not a pre-</td></tr>
</table>

requisite for all financial instruments that the standard requires to be classified as held for trading.

IAS 39.9   3.6.480.25 For example, a bank originates a loan with the intention of syndication but fails to find sufficient commitments from other participants. The bank intends to sell all or part of the loan in the near term rather than hold it for the foreseeable future. The definition of loans and receivables in IAS 39 requires a loan or a portion of a loan that is intended to be sold immediately or in the near term to be classified as held for trading on initial recognition. In our view, notwithstanding the general characteristics of trading activity (see 3.6.480.20), the loan or the portion that the bank intends to sell in the near term should be classified as held for trading in accordance with the specific guidance in the standard. If subsequent to initial recognition the bank changes its intention with respect to the loan and demonstrates the intention and ability to hold the loan for the foreseeable future or until maturity, then the bank may, at such subsequent date, reclassify the loan from the fair value through profit or loss category to either loans and receivables or the available-for-sale category (see 3.6.860.11 – 13).

IAS 39.9,   3.6.480.30 The definition of held for trading refers to an asset or liability being part of a
IGB.11   portfolio of financial instruments. While IAS 39 does not define portfolio explicitly, in this context it is possible to consider a portfolio to be a collection of financial assets or financial liabilities that are managed as part of the same group. For example, the takings and placings of a money market desk may be viewed as comprising one portfolio that qualifies for classification as held for trading.

IAS 39.9,   3.6.480.40 The intention to profit from short-term fluctuations in price or dealer's margin
IGB.11   need not be stated explicitly by the entity. Other evidence may indicate that a financial asset is being held for trading purposes. Evidence of trading may be inferred based on the turnover and the average holding period of financial assets included in the portfolio. For instance, an entity may buy and sell shares for a specific portfolio, based on movements in those entities' share prices. When this is done on a frequent basis, the entity has established a pattern of trading for the purpose of generating profits from short-term fluctuations in price. Additional purchases of shares into this portfolio also would be designated as held for trading.

IAS 39.9,   3.6.480.50 In our view, if an entity makes an investment in a fund that is managed
IGB.12   independently by a third party, then the classification of the entity's investment in that fund should not be influenced by the fact that the underlying assets within the fund are traded actively. Therefore, the entity's investment in that fund would not meet the definition of an asset held for trading unless the entity actively trades in the investments it holds in such funds. This situation may be contrasted with one in which an entity holds a portfolio of investments that are managed by a portfolio manager on the entity's behalf. In such cases the entity determines the investment policies and procedures and, consequently, if the portfolio manager actively buys and sells instruments within the portfolio to generate short-term profits, then the instruments in the portfolio are considered held for trading and are classified as at fair value through profit or loss.

IAS 39.IG 3.6.480.60 On the other hand, a manager of an investment portfolio might buy and sell
B.12 investments in order to rebalance the portfolio in line with an investment mandate. This
activity generally would not result in the investments being classified as held for trading
because the activity may not be aimed at generating profits from short-term fluctuations
in prices. Furthermore, if an entity acquires a non-derivative financial asset with the
intention to hold it for a period irrespective of short-term fluctuations in price, then such
an instrument cannot be classified as held for trading.

IAS 39.AG15 3.6.480.70 Liabilities held for trading include derivatives with a negative fair value, except
those that are hedging instruments, and obligations to deliver financial assets borrowed
by a short seller. This category further includes financial liabilities that are incurred with
an intention to repurchase them in the near term and those that are part of a portfolio of
financial liabilities for which there is evidence of a recent pattern of short-term profit
taking.

3.6.480.80 In our view, a liability should not be considered as held for trading simply
because it funds trading activities. However, liabilities that fund trading activities could
be designated as instruments at fair value through profit or loss if the criteria for designation are met (see 3.6.490).

3.6.480.90 The standard does not define "near term". In our view, an entity should adopt
a definition and apply a consistent approach to the definition used. When there is the
intention of generating a profit from short-term fluctuations in price or dealer's margin,
the financial asset is classified appropriately as trading, even if the asset is not sold
subsequently within a short period of time.

3.6.480.100 [Not used]

IAS 39.AG15 3.6.480.110 To generate short-term profits, traders may actively trade an asset's risks
rather than the asset itself. For example, a bank may invest in a 30-day money market
instrument for the purpose of generating profit from short-term fluctuations in the interest rate. When the favourable movement in the interest rate occurs, instead of selling
the instrument the bank will issue an offsetting liability instrument. The 30-day money
market instrument is classified as held for trading despite the fact that there is no intention
to sell the instrument physically. The offsetting liability instrument also is classified as
trading because it was issued for trading purposes and will be managed together with
the related asset.

3.6.490 *Financial assets and liabilities designated as at fair value through profit or loss*

IAS 39.9, 11A 3.6.490.10 In addition to financial assets and liabilities held for trading, financial assets
and liabilities are classified in the fair value through profit or loss category when an
entity chooses, upon initial recognition, to designate such instruments as at fair value
through profit or loss using the fair value option. An entity may use this designation
only:

- when doing so results in more relevant information because either:
  - it eliminates or significantly reduces a measurement or recognition inconsistency that would result from measuring assets or liabilities or recognising gains or losses on them on different bases (an "accounting mismatch"); or
  - a group of financial assets or financial liabilities (or both) is managed and its performance is evaluated on a fair value basis in accordance with the entity's documented risk management or investment strategy, and information is provided to key management personnel on this basis; or
- in respect of an entire hybrid contract, when such contract contains one or more embedded derivatives, unless those embedded derivatives either:
  - do not significantly modify the cash flows that otherwise would be required by the contract; or
  - are ones for which it is clear with little or no analysis when first considering a similar hybrid instrument that separation is prohibited.

IAS 39.9   3.6.490.20 Investments in equity securities that do not have a quoted market price in an active market, and whose fair value cannot be measured reliably, cannot be designated as at fair value through profit or loss.

3.6.490.30 The designation of an instrument as at fair value through profit or loss may be used only upon initial recognition and is not reversible. Therefore, this alternative to hedge accounting cannot be used if an entity buys or issues an instrument and later wishes to put a hedge in place. Applying the fair value option also may result in excessive earnings volatility if the hedge is put in place for only part of the life of the instrument.

AS 39.AG4C   3.6.490.40 There is no requirement for consistency in the use of the fair value through profit or loss designation, meaning that an entity can choose which, if any, of its financial assets and liabilities are to be designated into this category.

3.6.500 *Reducing a mismatch**

AS 39.AG4E   3.6.500.10 The following examples illustrate the circumstances in which an accounting mismatch arises, which may cause the relevant financial assets and financial liabilities to qualify for designation as at fair value through profit or loss:

- An entity has liabilities whose cash flows are linked contractually to the performance of certain assets that otherwise would have been classified as available for sale; for example, liabilities with a discretionary participation feature that pay benefits based on realised investment returns of a specified pool of the insurer's assets.
- An entity has liabilities under insurance contracts that are measured using current information as allowed under IFRS 4, and related financial assets that otherwise would be classified as available for sale or measured at amortised cost.
- An entity has financial assets and financial liabilities that share a particular risk, such that their fair values change in opposite directions, tending to offset each other.

However, either:
- only some of the instruments are measured at fair value through profit or loss, notably derivatives and those that are held for trading;
- hedge accounting cannot be applied because the hedge criteria for example, the effectiveness requirements, are not met;
- hedge accounting cannot be applied because none of the instruments is a derivative, and without hedge accounting there is a significant inconsistency in the recognition of gains or losses; or
- even though hedge accounting is applicable, hedge documentation or effectiveness testing, for example, is too onerous.

IAS 39.AG4F 3.6.500.20 In practice there may be a delay between acquiring or incurring one related financial asset or financial liability and another that would create an accounting mismatch. In the event of a reasonable delay, designation of the respective financial asset and financial liability as at fair value through profit or loss is not precluded provided that the designation is made upon initial recognition, and at the time that the first of the instruments is so designated, the acquisition or incurrence of the other is expected in the very near future in accordance with a documented strategy.

IAS 39.BC75 3.6.500.30 One of the main benefits of this category is that it may allow an entity to avoid the cost and complexity of meeting the criteria for hedge accounting in some cases. For example, an entity that purchases (or issues) a fixed rate bond and immediately enters into an interest rate swap to convert the interest to a floating rate might, instead of claiming hedge accounting, designate the bond as at fair value through profit or loss. Since both the bond and the swap will be measured at fair value through profit or loss, the offsetting effects of changes in market interest rates on the fair value of each instrument will be recognised in profit or loss without the need for hedge accounting.

3.6.500.40 However, the fair value changes of an item designated into this category will be affected by more than one risk such that using this designation may not achieve the exact results that hedge accounting for a particular risk would. Continuing the example in 3.6.500.30 when applying hedge accounting for interest rate risk, the fixed rate bond would be adjusted for changes in its fair value attributable to interest rate risk only. However, designating the bond as at fair value through profit or loss means that it will be remeasured to fair value in respect of all risks, including, for a bond issued by the entity, the entity's own credit risk, or, for a bond purchased by the entity, the counterparty's credit risk; and this may result in a greater difference between the fair value gains and losses on the interest rate swap and those on the bond than when hedge accounting is applied.

3.6.510 *Assets and liabilities managed on a fair value basis*

IAS 39.AG4I 3.6.510.10 The following examples indicate the circumstances in which an entity could be considered to be managing and evaluating the performance of a group of financial assets, financial liabilities or both on a fair value basis, such that those financial assets and financial liabilities may qualify for designation as at fair value through profit or loss:

- The entity is a venture capital organisation, mutual fund, unit trust or similar entity that invests in financial assets with the objective of profiting from their total return in the form of interest or dividends and changes in fair value.
- An entity has financial assets and financial liabilities that share one or more risks, which are managed and evaluated on a fair value basis according to a documented asset and liability management policy; for example, a portfolio of structured products that contain multiple embedded derivatives and that are managed on a fair value basis using a mixture of derivatives and non-derivatives.
- The entity is an insurer that holds a portfolio of financial assets and manages that portfolio to maximise its total return from interest or dividends and changes in fair value, and evaluates its performance on that basis.

3.6.520 *Assets and liabilities containing an embedded derivative*

IAS 39.13   3.6.520.10 A financial asset or financial liability may not be designated into the fair value through profit or loss category simply because it includes an embedded derivative that cannot be measured separately either at acquisition or at a subsequent reporting date. Such cases are expected to arise very rarely, for example, when the embedded derivative has an underlying that is the fair value of an unquoted equity instrument. In such cases, it is necessary first to consider whether the fair value of the embedded derivative can be measured reliably by deducting the fair value of the host contract from the fair value of the entire hybrid instrument. If that is not possible, then the entire contract is designated as at fair value through profit or loss.

3.6.520.20 An example of an embedded derivative for which it is clear that separation would be prohibited is a mortgage loan that is prepayable at an amount approximating its amortised cost (see 3.6.280.28). Another example would be an instrument containing a non-leveraged cap that is out of the money at inception.

IAS 39.11A   3.6.520.30 An entity can apply the fair value option to contractual arrangements that contain one or more embedded derivatives only when the host contract meets the definition of a financial instrument under IAS 39.

3.6.530 *Held-to-maturity investments*

IAS 39.9   3.6.530.10 Held-to-maturity investments are non-derivative financial assets with fixed or determinable payments and a fixed maturity that an entity has the positive intention and ability to hold to maturity, other than:

- those that the entity upon initial recognition designates as at fair value through profit or loss;
- those that the entity designates as available for sale; and
- those that meet the definition of loans and receivables.

IAS 39.9,   3.6.530.20 Types of instruments that may meet the held-to-maturity definition include:
G17, AG18

- a fixed maturity debt security that bears interest at a fixed or variable rate;
- a fixed maturity debt security even if there is a high risk of non-payment, provided that the security's contractual payments are fixed or determinable and the other criteria for classification are met;
- a debt instrument that is callable by the issuer, as long as substantially all of the carrying amount would be recovered if the call were exercised; and
- shares with a fixed maturity (or callable by the issuer) that are classified as liabilities by the issuer (see 3.11).

IAS 39.9,
AG16-AG19,
AG23

3.6.530.30 The following instruments cannot be classified as held to maturity:

- equity securities;
- an investment that the investor intends to hold for an undefined period or that does not have fixed or determinable payments;
- an investment that the investor stands ready to sell in response to changes in market conditions;
- a perpetual debt instrument that will pay interest in perpetuity;
- an instrument that is redeemable at the option of the issuer at an amount significantly below amortised cost;
- an instrument that is puttable by the holder, because paying for the put feature is inconsistent with an intention to hold the instrument to maturity, i.e. it is questionable whether the holder has the intent to hold the instrument to its maturity if the holder simultaneously acquires the right to require the issuer to redeem the instrument before its maturity date;
- an asset that the entity does not have adequate resources to hold to maturity; and
- an asset that is subject to legal constraints that mean that the entity may be unable to hold it to maturity.

3.6.530.40 The effect of using the held-to-maturity classification is that the investments will be measured at amortised cost. Therefore, the category generally is used for fixed interest debt instruments quoted in an active market that are exposed to significant fair value risk. Debt instruments that are not quoted in an active market meet the definition of loans and receivables, and would not be classified as held to maturity.

3.6.530.50 An entity is not permitted to classify any investments as held to maturity if the entity has, during the current financial year or during the two preceding financial years, sold or reclassified more than an insignificant amount in relation to the total amount of held-to-maturity investments before maturity, other than sales or reclassifications that:

- are so close to maturity or the investments call date, e.g. less than three months before maturity, that changes in the market rate of interest would not have a significant effect on its fair value;
- occur after the entity has collected substantially all of the investments original principal through scheduled payments or prepayments; or

- are attributable to an isolated event that is beyond the entity's control, is non-recurring and could not have been reasonably anticipated by the entity.

AS 39.AG25   3.6.530.60 A prerequisite for the classification of an investment as held to maturity is the entity's intent and ability to actually hold that investment until maturity. An entity should assess its intent and ability to hold its held-to-maturity investments not only at initial acquisition, but again at each reporting date.

3.6.530.70 Circumstances may arise in which the entity disposes of a significant amount of its held-to-maturity investments after the reporting date, but prior to the financial statements being authorised for issue. In our view, this calls into question the entity's intent and ability at the reporting date to hold those investments to maturity and may require the classification of these investments to be revised as at the reporting date. If a reclassification is required, this would result in tainting the entire held-to-maturity portfolio. Such a case requires further consideration of the other evidence available at the reporting date to support the entity's intent and ability.

3.6.530.80 There is no requirement to use the held-to-maturity classification. An instrument with fixed and determinable payments may be designated as available for sale even if the entity might hold the instrument until its maturity. In our view, this applies even if there are legal restrictions that require an instrument to be held until its maturity.

IAS 39.79   3.6.530.90 Hedge accounting is not allowed for hedges of the interest rate risk on held-to-maturity investments (see 3.7.170.40).

3.6.540 *Fixed maturity and determinable payments*

IAS 39.9,   3.6.540.10 Investments classified as held to maturity should have a fixed maturity and
AG17   fixed or determinable payments, meaning a contractual arrangement that defines both the amounts and dates of payments to the holder, such as interest and principal payments on debt. A significant risk of non-payment does not preclude an investment from being classified as held to maturity automatically.

AS 39.AG17   3.6.540.20 Since held-to-maturity investments should have a fixed maturity, mainly debt contracts are classified as held to maturity. Nevertheless, even certain debt instruments have an unlimited or unspecified maturity. For example, perpetual bonds that provide for interest payments for an indefinite period would not qualify as held-to-maturity investments.

3.6.540.30 In our view, investments that have an equity nature because payments are dependent on residual cash flows (e.g. subordinated notes for which the amount of interest or principal paid to the holder will be determined based on the residual remaining after interest and principal amounts in respect of other creditors are paid) should not be classified as held-to-maturity investments.

3.6.540.40 Similarly, in our view investments in funds for which the amount to be paid out as distributions or on liquidation is not fixed or determinable because it is based upon the performance of the fund generally should not be classified as held to maturity, even if the fund has a final liquidation date (e.g. ten years after the fund closes to additional investments).

IAS 39.IG   3.6.540.50 For example, Bank Q wants to categorise a bond issued by an oil company as
B.13, IGB.14   held to maturity. The interest on the bond is indexed to the price of oil. The fact that the return is dependent on the price of oil means that the bond includes an embedded derivative that is not closely related to the host contract (see 3.6.280). The embedded derivative and host contract should be separated, resulting in an embedded commodity contract to be measured at fair value and a host debt instrument. If Q has the intent and ability to hold the host contract to maturity, then it may categorise the host contract as held to maturity.

3.6.550 Intent to hold to maturity

IAS 39.AG16,   3.6.550.10 If an entity only has the intent to hold an investment for some period, but
AG18, AG19   has not actually defined that period to be to maturity, then the positive intent to hold to maturity does not exist. Likewise, if the issuer has the right to settle the investment at an amount that is significantly below the carrying amount, and therefore is expected to exercise that right, then the entity cannot demonstrate a positive intent to hold the investment until maturity. Also, an embedded option that may shorten the stated maturity of a debt instrument casts doubt on an entity's intent to hold an investment until maturity. Therefore, the purchase of an instrument with a put feature is inconsistent with the positive intent to hold the asset until maturity. However, if the issuer may call the instrument at or above its carrying amount, then this does not affect the investor's intent to hold the instrument until maturity. The issuer's call option, if exercised, simply accelerates the instrument's maturity.

IAS 39.AG21   3.6.550.20 The demonstration of positive intent to hold an investment to maturity would not be negated by a highly unusual and unlikely occurrence, such as a run on a bank, that could not be anticipated by the entity when deciding whether it has the positive intent (and ability) to hold an investment until maturity.

3.6.550.30 A debt instrument that is convertible at the option of the holder generally cannot be classified as held to maturity. This applies in particular when there is no specified date for exercising the conversion option. Paying for an early conversion right is inconsistent with an intention to hold the investment to its maturity. However, in our view an investment that is convertible at the option of the holder at the maturity date may be classified as held to maturity.

IAS 39.AG17,   3.6.550.40 Also, the risk profile of a particular financial investment may raise similar
IGB.15   questions about the entity's intention. For example, the high risk and volatility of a mortgage-backed interest-only certificate makes active management of such strips more likely than holding them to maturity. The same reasoning may apply to debt in-

struments with high credit risk, for example high yield (junk) bonds and subordinated bonds. A significant risk of non-payment of interest and principal on a bond is not in itself a consideration in qualifying for the held-to-maturity category as long as there is an intent and ability to hold the bond until maturity. However, an entity would taint its held-to-maturity portfolio if it subsequently sold such a bond as a result of a rating downgrade that could have been foreseen.

3.6.560 *Ability to hold to maturity*

AS 39.AG23   3.6.560.10 An entity cannot demonstrate an ability to hold an investment to maturity if:

- financial resources are not available to the entity to finance the investment to maturity (e.g. if it is expected or likely that an entity will acquire another business and will need all of its funding for this investment, then the resources may not be available to continue to hold certain debt instruments); or
- legal or other constraints could frustrate the intention of the entity to hold the investment to maturity (e.g. there might be an expectation that a regulator will exercise its right in certain industries, such as the banking and insurance industries, to force an entity to sell certain investments in the event of a credit risk change of the entity).

3.6.570 *Tainting of the held-to-maturity portfolio*

IAS 39.9   3.6.570.10 If an entity sells or transfers more than an insignificant amount of the portfolio of held-to-maturity investments, then it may not classify any investment as held to maturity for the remainder of the current financial year plus two financial years after the financial year in which the event occurred.

IAS 39.9   3.6.570.20 While "more than an insignificant amount" is interpreted in relation to the total amount of held-to-maturity investments, the standard does not provide more detailed guidance; rather, this is assessed by an entity based on the facts and circumstances when a potential tainting situation arises. It also is important to consider the reasons for an entity's actions when determining if the portfolio has been tainted.

3.6.570.30 For example, Company T sells 1,000 bonds from its held-to-maturity portfolio on 15 April 2010. The fair value of the bonds had appreciated significantly over the carrying amount and management decided that T should realise the gains through a sale. In these circumstances selling investments from the held-to-maturity portfolio taints the entire portfolio and all remaining investments in that category are reclassified. T will be prohibited from classifying any investments as held to maturity for two full financial years. Assuming that T's annual reporting date is 31 December, it cannot use the held-to-maturity classification for its assets until at least 1 January 2013.

IAS 39.IG   3.6.570.40 The tainting rules are intended to test an entity's assertion that it intends and *3.19-IGB.21*   is able to hold an investment until maturity. Tainting requires a reclassification of the total remaining held-to-maturity portfolio in the financial statements into the available-for-sale category.

3.6 Financial instruments

IAS 39.IG B.20, IGB.21 3.6.570.50 The tainting requirements apply group-wide, so that a subsidiary that sells more than an insignificant amount from its held-to-maturity portfolio can preclude the entire group from using the held-to-maturity category in its consolidated financial statements. If an entity has various portfolios of held-to-maturity investments, for example by industry or by country of issue, then the sale or transfer of instruments from one of the portfolios taints all the other held-to-maturity portfolios of the entity.

IAS 39.IG B.18 3.6.570.60 Selling securities classified as held to maturity under repurchase agreements does not constrain the entity's intent and ability to hold those investments until maturity, unless the entity does not expect to be able to maintain or recover access to those investments. For example, if an entity is expected to receive back other comparable securities, but not the securities lent, then classification as held to maturity is not appropriate.

3.6.580 Exceptions to tainting

IAS 39.9 3.6.580.10 There is a limited number of exceptions to the tainting rules. Firstly, the tainting rules do not apply if only an insignificant amount of held-to-maturity investments is sold or reclassified. Any sale or reclassification should be a one-off event. If an entity sells or transfers insignificant portions periodically, then this may cast a doubt on the entity's intent and ability with regard to its held-to-maturity portfolio. In cases when the sales are not isolated, the amount sold or reclassified is assessed on a cumulative basis in assessing whether the sales are insignificant.

IAS 39.9 3.6.580.20 Another exception is when almost the entire principal has been collected through scheduled payments or through prepayments; the remaining part would not be affected materially by changes in the interest rate, and therefore the sale would not result in a significant gain or loss. IAS 39 does not define the phrase substantially all of the principal investment; however, in our view the main question is whether the remaining fair value exposure is significant.

IAS 39.9, IGB.16 3.6.580.30 In very rare instances, circumstances may arise that the entity could not reasonably have foreseen or anticipated. If, in such a situation, an entity has to sell held-to-maturity investments, then the remaining portfolio is not tainted if the event leading to the sale of investments is isolated and non-recurring. If the event is not isolated or is potentially recurring, and the entity anticipates further sales of held-to-maturity investments, then this inevitably casts doubt on its ability to hold the remaining portfolio until maturity. Also, if the event reasonably could have been anticipated at the date that the held-to-maturity classification was made, then the investment should not have been classified as such initially. If an entity has control over or initiated the isolated or non-recurring event, for example sales made after a change in senior management, then this also calls into question the entity's intent to hold the remaining portfolio until maturity.

IAS 39.AG22, IGB.15, IGB.17 3.6.580.40 Situations that may not have been anticipated when investments were included in the held-to-maturity category and would not call into question the entity's intent and ability to hold investments to maturity may result, for example, from any of the following:

- a significant deterioration in the creditworthiness of the issuer of the investment that could not have been anticipated when the investment was acquired;
- significant changes in tax laws, affecting specific investments in the portfolio;
- major business combinations or disposals with consequences for the interest rate risk position and credit risk policies of an entity; and
- significant changes in statutory or regulatory requirements.

3.6.590 Deterioration in creditworthiness

IAS 39.AG22, IGB.15   3.6.590.10 Although IAS 39 does not provide a definition of a significant deterioration in an issuer's creditworthiness, an example of this would be a significant downgrade by a credit rating agency. Downgrades as reflected in an entity's proprietary internal credit rating system also may support the demonstration of significant deterioration. However, the initial quality of the investment should have been such that the deterioration could not reasonably have been foreseen. A credit downgrade of a notch within a class or from one rating class to an immediately lower rating class often could be considered reasonably anticipated. Therefore, a sale triggered by such a minor downgrading would result in tainting.

3.6.600 Changes in tax laws

IAS 39.AG22   3.6.600.10 A significant change in tax laws, such as the elimination or the significant reduction of the tax-exempt status of an investment, might not cast doubt on the intention or ability of the entity with respect to the held-to-maturity category.

3.6.600.20 For example, an entity may have a captive finance company in a tax haven and, due to changes in tax laws that affect the whole group, needs to relocate its treasury activities and in that process liquidates the held-to-maturity portfolio in the finance company. In our view, the classification as held-to-maturity in other group entities would not be violated, since the entity could not have foreseen the change in tax laws.

3.6.600.30 However, in our view a change in the applicable marginal tax rate for interest income is not sufficient justification for sales of held-to-maturity investments, since this change impacts all debt instruments held by the entity.

3.6.600.40 In our view, if an entity holds a put option that it intends to use only in the event of a change in laws, then a voluntary exercise of that option by the entity nevertheless would result in tainting. However, if the exercise of an option is conditional upon a change in laws, or the option comes into existence only as a result of a change in laws, then a sale through exercise of such an option would not give rise to tainting.

3.6.610 Major business combination or disposition

IAS 39.AG22   3.6.610.10 Although a major business combination or the sale of a significant segment of the entity is a controllable event, it may have a consequence on the entity's interest rate risk and credit risk positions. In such situations, sales that are necessary to maintain the entity's existing risk positions and that support proper risk management do not taint the held-to-maturity portfolio.

IAS 39.IG
B.19
3.6.610.20 Although sales subsequent to business combinations and segment disposals might not taint the held-to-maturity portfolio, sales of held-to-maturity investments prior to a business combination or disposal, or in response to an unsolicited tender offer, will cast doubt on the entity's intent to hold its remaining investments until maturity.

3.6.610.30 In our view, if investments acquired in a business combination were classified as held to maturity by the acquiree, but the acquirer does not have the intent or ability to hold these securities until maturity, then the instruments should be reclassified and the tainting rules would not apply in the consolidated financial statements. However, transferring investments held by the acquirer before the acquisition from the held-to-maturity portfolio would result in tainting.

3.6.610.40 In our view, a sale following a group reorganisation, including a common control transaction, that is not a major business combination or disposition would result in tainting. We do not believe that a sale of a held-to-maturity asset between group entities would result in tainting in the consolidated financial statements, as long as the investment remains classified as held to maturity in the consolidated financial statements. However, in the separate financial statements of the individual entities within the group, such intra-group transactions may give rise to tainting.

3.6.620 Changes in statutory or regulatory requirements

IAS 39.AG22
3.6.620.10 Examples of changes in statutory or regulatory requirements that do not have tainting implications for the held-to-maturity portfolio are:

- changes either in the applicable laws or in regulations affecting the entity that modify what constitutes a permissible investment or the maximum level of certain types of investments, as a result of which the entity has to sell (part of) these investments; and
- significant increases in the industry's capital requirements or in the risk weightings of held-to-maturity investments used for risk-based capital purposes, as a result of which the size of the held-to-maturity portfolio has to be decreased.

IAS 39.IG
B.17
3.6.620.20 The exceptions are intended to shield entities operating in regulated industries from potential tainting situations resulting from actions taken by the industry's regulator. These are actions applicable to the industry as a whole, and not to a specific entity. However, sales could occur in response to an entity-specific increase in capital requirements set by the industry's regulator. In that case it will be difficult to demonstrate that the regulator's action could not reasonably have been anticipated by the entity, unless the increase in entity-specific capital requirements represents a significant change in the regulator's policy for setting entity-specific capital requirements.

3.6.630 *Loans and receivables*

IAS 39.9
3.6.630.10 Loans and receivables are non-derivative financial assets with fixed or determinable payments that are not quoted in an active market, other than those:

- that the entity intends to sell immediately or in the near term, which are classified as held for trading, and those that the entity upon initial recognition designates as at fair value through profit or loss;
- that the entity upon initial recognition designates as available for sale; or
- for which the holder may not recover substantially all of its initial investment, other than because of credit deterioration, which are classified as available for sale.

3.6.630.20 An interest acquired in a pool of assets that are not loans and receivables (e.g. an interest in a mutual fund or similar fund) is not a loan or receivable. Cash CDOs (see 3.6.400) are securitised interests in a pool of financial assets that expose investors to credit risk on reference assets through the vehicle holding the reference assets. In our view, the holder of a cash CDO may be able to classify the financial asset as loans and receivables if the reference assets in the pool meet the criteria as set out in 3.6.630.10.

3.6.630.30 In our view, fixed or determinable payments generally means that the cash flows are either fixed or determined by a formula.

IAS 39.AG26 3.6.630.40 The main requirement for a financial asset to be classified as a loan or receivable is that it has fixed or determinable payments and is not a derivative. However, the definition also excludes any instrument that is quoted in an active market. This means that a listed debt security that is actively traded in a market cannot be classified within loans and receivables, even if it is acquired at the date of its original issue by providing funds directly to the issuer.

IAS 39.BC28 3.6.630.50 Both originated loans and purchased loans are included in this category. This ensures, as far as possible, a consistent accounting treatment across all loan portfolios. Also, as many entities manage purchased loans and originated loans together, this prevents system problems arising from having to separate purchased loans from originated loans purely for financial reporting purposes.

3.6.630.60 In addition, an entity has a free choice of classifying any loan or receivable as available for sale at initial recognition.

3.6.630.70 Reclassifications and sales of loans and receivables are possible without any of the tainting issues applicable to the held-to-maturity category (see 3.6.570). However, in our view, if financial assets classified as loans and receivables are subsequently sold within a short period after origination or purchase, then this may cast doubt on whether other assets classified as loans and receivables are not held for the purpose of selling in the near term.

3.6.640 *Available-for-sale financial assets*

IAS 39.9 3.6.640.10 Available-for-sale financial assets are non-derivative financial assets that are designated as available for sale, or that are not classified as loans and receivables, held-to-maturity investments, or financial assets at fair value through profit or loss.

IAS 39.9 3.6.640.20 A financial asset that the entity intends to hold to maturity, or a loan and receivable, also may be designated as available for sale on initial recognition. This category normally includes all debt securities quoted in an active market other than those classified as held to maturity and all equity securities that are not classified as at fair value through profit or loss.

3.6.640.30 Any financial asset that does not fall into any of the three categories in 3.6.640.10 is classified as available for sale.

3.6.650 *Other liabilities*

3.6.650.10 Other liabilities constitute the residual category similar to the available-for-sale category of financial assets. All liabilities other than trading liabilities, liabilities designated as at fair value through profit or loss, and derivatives that are hedging instruments fall automatically into this category. Common examples are an entity's trade payables, borrowings and customer deposit accounts.

3.6.660 **Initial recognition**

IAS 39.14 3.6.660.10 An instrument is recognised in the statement of financial position when the entity becomes party to a contract that is a financial instrument.

IAS 39.AG35 3.6.660.20 Situations in which an entity has become a party to the contractual provisions include committing to a purchase of securities or agreeing to enter into a derivative. In contrast, planned but not committed future transactions, no matter how likely, are not financial assets or liabilities as they do not represent situations in which the entity becomes a party to a contract requiring the future receipt or delivery of assets. For example, an entity's expected but uncommitted issue of commercial paper does not qualify as a financial liability.

3.6.660.30 Similarly, if an entity makes an offer to enter into a contract to purchase or sell a financial instrument, then the entity has not become party to a contract requiring the future receipt or delivery of a financial instrument. In our view, the entity should not account for such an offer until the counterparty accepts the offer and the entity becomes a party to a contractual arrangement.

3.6.670 *Trade and settlement date accounting*

3.6.670.10 An application of the general recognition principle in IAS 39 would result in all transactions that occur in regulated markets being accounted for on trade date, which is when an entity becomes party to the contract. However, the standard recognises that practice by many financial institutions and other entities is to use settlement date accounting for financial assets, and that it would be cumbersome to account for such transactions as derivatives between the trade and settlement dates.

IAS 39.AG12   3.6.670.20 Because of the short duration between the trade date and the settlement date in these types of regulated market situations, such regular way contracts are not recognised as derivative contracts under IAS 39.

IAS 39.AG55,   3.6.670.30 A non-derivative financial asset that will be delivered within the time frame
AG56 generally established by regulation or convention in the market concerned (e.g. a regular way transaction (see 3.6.220)) may be recognised on the date that the entity commits to the transaction (trade date) or on the date that the instrument actually is transferred (settlement date).

IAS 39.38,   3.6.670.40 An entity should choose a method to be applied consistently to all purchases and
AG53-AG56 all sales of financial assets in the same category.

IAS 39.IG   3.6.670.50 There are no specific requirements for trade date and settlement date account-
B.32 ing in respect of financial liabilities, and therefore financial liabilities are recognised on the date that the entity becomes a party to the contractual provisions of the instrument, i.e. trade date accounting applies. Such contracts generally are not recognised unless one of the parties has performed or the contract is a derivative contract not exempted from the scope of IAS 39. In our view, the regular way exemption (see 3.6.670.20) is applicable to short sales of a security. Therefore, a liability arising from a short trading position is not accounted for as a derivative as it represents a transaction in a financial asset for which either trade date or settlement date accounting may be applied in accordance with the entity's policy choice.

IAS 39.AG55,   3.6.670.60 Changes in the fair value of an asset between trade date and settlement date
AG56, are attributable to the buyer. Therefore, if the item purchased is measured at fair
IGD.2.2 value, then ultimately the buyer recognises changes in value of the instrument between the trade date and the settlement date, regardless of the method applied. Under settlement date accounting, while the underlying asset is not recognised until settlement date, changes in value on the underlying asset are recognised. Therefore the fair value adjustment is shown as a receivable or payable until the settlement date, at which date the receivable or payable adjusts the amount recognised initially for the asset. This results in the asset being measured at its fair value on settlement date. Fair value changes between trade date and settlement date will be recognised in profit or loss for financial assets classified as at fair value through profit or loss, or in other comprehensive income for financial assets classified as available for sale.

IAS 39.AG56   3.6.670.70 When the item purchased is measured at cost or amortised cost, any change in the fair value of the asset between trade date and settlement date is not recognised.

IAS 39.IG   3.6.670.80 The difference between trade date and settlement date accounting for a sale
D.2.2 of financial instruments is in the timing of derecognition of the transferred instruments and of recognition of any profit or loss on disposal. Changes in the value of an asset between trade date and settlement date are attributable to the buyer. Therefore, if the instrument is carried at fair value, then the seller stops recognising changes in value from the trade date regardless of the method applied.

IAS 39.AG55   3.6.670.90 If trade date accounting is applied, then the asset is derecognised and the profit or loss on disposal and a receivable for the sales proceeds are recognised on trade date.

IAS 39.AG56   3.6.670.100 If settlement date accounting is applied, then the asset continues to be recognised until settlement date, although no changes in its fair value are recognised. On the settlement date, the asset is derecognised and a profit or loss on the disposal is recognised. The proceeds are the contract amount; the carrying amount of the asset sold will not reflect gains and losses between the trade and settlement date.

3.6.670.110 In our view, a change from settlement date to trade date accounting (or vice versa) is a voluntary change in accounting policy (see 2.8.30).

3.6.670.120 A commitment to grant a loan at a predetermined interest rate at a future date is, in our view, a loan commitment that is excluded from the scope of IAS 39 and consequently from the requirements in respect of trade date and settlement date accounting.

3.6.680 Normal purchases and sales

IAS 39.   3.6.680.10 Normal purchases and sales are contracts for purchases and sales of non-
AG35(b)   financial instruments, other than certain commodity contracts that are within the scope of IAS 39. Normal purchases and sales that are not considered derivatives (see 3.6.90) are outside the scope of IAS 39. Therefore, IAS 39 does not impact the timing of recognition of these contracts. For example, a binding purchase order is not recognised until the risks and rewards of ownership of the underlying goods are transferred (see 3.8.90).

3.6.690 Linked transactions

3.6.690.10 Generally the terms of each contract determine the appropriate accounting, and two financial instruments, even if entered into simultaneously, are accounted for separately. However, two financial instruments are accounted for as a single combined instrument if:

- they are entered into at the same time and in contemplation of each other;
- they have the same counterparty;
- they relate to the same risk; and
- there is no economic need or substantive business purpose for structuring the transactions separately that could not also have been accomplished in a single transaction.

IAS 39.IGB.6   3.6.690.20 In our view, structuring transactions separately may be regarded as a substantive business purpose when separate transactions are necessary to achieve a direct tax benefit. However, when such a tax benefit is derived primarily from an accounting result, for example when the purpose for structuring transactions separately is to achieve an accounting result that produces a tax advantage, then we believe the substantive business purpose requirement is not met. Similarly, if an entity structures transactions separately in order to achieve an accounting result that produces a regulatory advantage, then in our view the substantive business purpose requirement is not met.

3.6.700 *Agency relationships*

3.6.700.10 When an entity enters into what might described as an agency relationship, an analysis is required of whether the entity is acting as an agent or as a principal with respect to any transaction entered into as a result of that relationship. Determining whether an entity is acting as a principal or as an agent may require judgement and consideration of all relevant facts and circumstances.

3.6.700.20 For example, Company S is operating as a securities and derivatives broker at a stock exchange. S is acting on behalf of one party, entering the order (buy or sell of the customer) into the system of the stock exchange. The order will be executed on the stock exchange when/if there is a corresponding counterparty offer available. The offers at the stock exchange are all given by authorised brokers acting at the exchange. It is possible that the counterparty of the deal executed at the stock exchange is the same broker party, i.e. S acting on behalf of another customer.

3.6.700.30 The settlement term in the market in which S is the broker is trade date plus three days. After this term the broker is obliged to settle the open deal in case the buyer or the seller does not fulfil their part of the trade. At settlement date the money will be paid by the broker acting on behalf of the buyer through the central depository and the broker acting on behalf of the seller will receive the money through the central depository. The only party known to the stock exchange is the broker.

3.6.700.40 In our view, despite the fact that the broker is acting as an agent (on behalf) of a client, the broker is entering into two separate transactions: one with the stock exchange and one with the client. With respect to the transaction with the stock exchange, the broker is responsible for the delivery, clearing and settlement and therefore is acting as a principal in the trade. Each transaction results in a financial instrument and therefore should be recognised separately in the statement of financial position of S.

3.6.710 **Measurement at initial recognition**

IAS 39.43,
AG64   3.6.710.10 At initial recognition a financial instrument is measured at fair value plus directly attributable transaction costs, except when the instrument is classified as at fair value through profit or loss. Normally, the fair value at initial recognition is the transaction price, i.e. the amount of consideration given or received. However, if the transaction is not based on market terms and no market prices are observable for such a transaction, then the consideration may include compensation for something in addition to the financial instrument. In these cases it is necessary to use a valuation technique to determine the appropriate fair value for initial recognition of the financial instrument, e.g. an estimate of future cash payments or receipts, discounted using the current market interest rate for a similar financial instrument.

IAS 39.AG76,
AG76A   3.6.710.20 IAS 39 presumes that the transaction price is the best evidence of fair value upon the initial recognition of a financial instrument. When an entity believes otherwise, it should prove its assertion by comparison with other observable current market trans-

actions or by using a valuation technique that uses data only from observable markets. If a gain or loss would arise on initial recognition of a transaction, but the fair value is derived from a valuation technique that includes non-observable data, then the model is adjusted such that no gain or loss is recognised. A gain or loss arising from the use of such a valuation technique is not recognised until observable market data indicates that there has been a change in a factor that market participants would consider in setting the price of that financial asset or liability. A change in such a factor may include the passage of time, such that in practice some entities are able to release the unrecognised gain or loss over the life of the transaction.

3.6.720 *Transaction costs*

IAS 39.9, 43, AG13   3.6.720.10 Transaction costs are included in the initial measurement of financial assets and liabilities, except for those classified as at fair value through profit or loss. These costs may be incurred when an entity enters into a contractual arrangement. Transaction costs include only those costs that are directly attributable to the acquisition of a financial asset or issue of a financial liability. They are incremental costs that would not have been incurred if the instrument had not been acquired or issued. In practice few internal costs are likely to meet this requirement. The requirement is applied on an instrument-by-instrument basis. Transaction costs do not include the internal costs associated with developing a new investment product.

IAS 39.IG E.1.1   3.6.720.20 In the case of financial assets, transaction costs are added to the amount recognised initially, while for financial liabilities transaction costs are deducted from the amount recognised initially. Transaction costs on financial instruments at fair value through profit or loss are not included in the amount at which the instrument is measured initially; instead they are recognised immediately in profit or loss.

3.6.720.25 In our view, transaction costs that are related directly to the probable issuance of a security that is classified as a financial liability should be recognised as a prepayment (asset) in the statement of financial position. Such transaction costs are deducted from the amount of the financial liability when it initially is recognised, or recognised in profit or loss when the issuance is no longer expected to be completed.

3.6.720.30 See 4.6.150 for additional guidance on transaction costs.

3.6.730 *Low-interest and interest-free loans*

IAS 39.AG64, AG65   3.6.730.10 In most cases the fair value of a financial instrument on initial recognition will be equal to its cost. However, sometimes interest-free or low-interest loans are given (e.g. by a shareholder or government) to attract customers, or as a means of passing on tax benefits.

3.6.730.20 In our view, in assessing whether the interest charged on a loan is at a below-market rate, consideration should be given to the terms and conditions of the loan, local industry practice and local market circumstances. Evidence that a loan is at market rates might include the interest rates currently charged by the entity or by others for loans with similar remaining maturities, cash flow patterns, currency, credit risk, collateral and interest basis. For example, very low interest rates on current accounts would be viewed as market rates if they are given in arm's length transactions.

3.6.740 *Determining fair value*

AS 39.AG64   3.6.740.10 The fair value of below-market loans is the present value of the expected future cash flows, discounted using a market-related rate.

IAS 39.49   3.6.740.15 In our view, the fair value of an interest-free loan of which the lender can demand repayment at any time (i.e. a loan repayable on demand) is not less than its face value, and therefore discounting is not required by the borrower.

3.6.740.20 If a loan has no fixed maturity date and is available in perpetuity, then in our view discounting should reflect this assumption. In our view, loans that have no specified repayment dates and that are not repayable on demand generally should be discounted based on expected future cash flows.

3.6.750 *Short-term receivables and payables*

AS 39.AG79   3.6.750.10 Interest is required to be imputed when the impact of discounting would be significant. Therefore, in our view receivables and payables with maturities of up to six months generally are not required to be discounted. However, in high-interest environments, the impact of discounting may be significant even for maturities of less than six months.

3.6.760 *Accounting for differences between fair value and the loan amount*

AS 39.AG64   3.6.760.10 Any difference between the cost and the fair value of the instrument upon initial recognition is recognised as a gain or a loss unless it qualifies to be recognised as an asset or liability.

3.6.760.20 For example, if a low-interest loan is given in anticipation of a right to receive goods or services at favourable prices, then the right may be recognised as an asset if it qualifies for recognition as an intangible asset (see 3.3.30) or other asset (e.g. prepaid expenses).

3.6.760.30 In our view, if the loan is from a shareholder acting in the capacity of a shareholder, then the resulting credit normally should be reflected in equity as the substance of the favourable terms typically is a contribution by a shareholder (see 3.11.230).

IAS 20.10A   3.6.760.40 If the loan is from a government, then the credit is treated as a government grant (see 4.3.100).

3.6.760.50 For example, the shareholders of Company C provide C with financing in the form of loan notes to enable it to acquire investments in subsidiaries. The loan notes will be redeemed solely out of dividends received from these subsidiaries, and only become redeemable when C has sufficient funds to do so. In this context, "sufficient funds" refers only to dividend receipts from subsidiaries. Therefore, C could not be forced to obtain additional external financing or to liquidate its investments in order to redeem the shareholder loans. Consequently, the loans could not be considered payable on demand.

3.6.760.60 Accordingly, the loans should be measured initially at their fair value (plus transaction costs), being the present value of the expected future cash flows, discounted using a market-related rate. The amount and timing of the expected future cash flows should be determined on the basis of the expected dividend flow from the subsidiaries. Also, the valuation would need to take into account possible early repayments of principal and corresponding reductions in interest expense.

3.6.760.70 Given that the loan notes are interest-free or bear lower than market interest, there will be a difference between the nominal value of the loan notes (i.e. the amount granted) and their fair value upon initial recognition. As the financing is provided by shareholders, acting in the capacity of shareholders, we believe that the resulting credit should be reflected in equity as a shareholder contribution in the statement of financial position of C.

3.6.770 *Intra-group low-interest and interest-free loans*

3.6.770.10 When low-interest or interest-free loans are granted to subsidiaries, the effect of discounting is eliminated on consolidation. Therefore, the discounting will be reflected only in the financial statements of the subsidiary and any separate financial statements of the parent. In our view, in the separate financial statements of the investor the discount should be recognised as an additional investment in the subsidiary.

3.6.770.20 Similar principles apply in the case of low-interest or interest-free loans to associates, except that since the equity method is applied, the discounting effect on profit or loss will be eliminated only to the extent of the investor's interest in the associate (see 3.5.430).

3.6.770.30 Particularly in the case of loans between entities in a group, in addition to the possibility of these being granted on an interest-free basis, there may be no stated terms of repayment. This complicates the measurement of the loan as it is not clear when repayments will take place, what the value of such repayments will be and what the term of the loan is. In such cases, consideration first should be given to whether:

- classification as a liability is appropriate;
- there is no agreed means of repayment, either directly in the agreement or via a side agreement; and
- it is possible to estimate when the loan repayments will take place.

3.6.770.40 In our view, having considered these factors and concluded that no alternative treatment is available, such a loan may be considered to be payable on demand. This means that it should be measured at its face value.

3.6.780 *Related party transactions*

3.6.780.10 In our view, the requirement to recognise all financial assets and liabilities at fair value applies to all low-interest or interest-free loans, including those to or from related parties. In addition, if the counterparty is a related party, then related party disclosures will be required (see 5.5).

3.6.790 **Subsequent measurement**

3.6.800 *General considerations*

IS 39.43, 46, 47   3.6.800.10 Subsequent to initial measurement:

- Derivatives always are measured at fair value.
- Loans and receivables and held-to-maturity investments are measured at amortised cost. Financial assets at fair value through profit or loss and available-for-sale financial assets are measured at fair value with changes therein included in profit or loss or, for available-for-sale financial assets, in other comprehensive income.
- Other financial liabilities are measured at amortised cost, and financial liabilities at fair value through profit or loss are measured at fair value with changes therein included in profit or loss.

IS 39.46, 47   3.6.800.20 Financial assets and financial liabilities that are designated as hedged items may require further adjustment in accordance with the hedge accounting requirements (see 3.7.50).

3.6.805 *Derivatives*

IS 39.46(c),   3.6.805.10 Derivatives are measured at fair value except for those contracts that are linked G80, AG81   to and must be settled using unquoted equity instruments whose fair value cannot be measured reliably. Such derivatives are measured at cost. In our view, this exemption cannot be extended to cover other underlying variables with no available market data (see 3.6.980).

3.6.810 *Held-to-maturity investments*

IAS 39.46(b)   3.6.810.10 Held-to-maturity investments, like quoted bonds with a fixed maturity, are measured at amortised cost using the effective interest method (see 4.6.20).

3.6.820 *Loans and receivables*

IAS 39.46(a)   3.6.820.10 Loans and receivables are measured at amortised cost using the effective interest method.

IAS 39.IG   3.6.820.20 Loans and receivables that do not have a fixed maturity and that have either a B.24   fixed or a market-based variable rate of interest are measured at cost. For example, in the case of perpetual floating rate loans with no repayments of principal and when fixed or market-based interest payments will be paid in perpetuity, the amortised cost always will equal the fair value of the proceeds given, plus transaction costs. Consequently, there is no amortisation of a difference between the initial amount and a maturity amount.

IAS 39.AG79 3.6.820.30 Short-duration receivables with no stated interest rate may be measured at original invoice amount unless the effect of imputing interest would be significant, e.g. in high-inflation countries.

3.6.830 *Available-for-sale financial assets*

IAS 39.46, 3.6.830.10 Available-for-sale financial assets are measured at fair value. There is an
AG80, AG81 exemption from measurement at fair value if the available-for-sale asset's fair value cannot be measured reliably. This exemption applies only to unquoted equity instruments or derivative contracts linked to and settled by delivery of those instruments when there is significant variability in the range of reasonable fair value estimates and the probabilities of the various estimates within the range cannot be assessed reasonably. IAS 39 assumes that normally it is possible to estimate the fair value of a financial asset that has been acquired from a third party. Consequently, in our view the exemption would apply mainly to start-up entities. In rare cases, even though it may be possible to measure the fair value at initial recognition reliably, it may become more difficult over time to measure the fair value of an available-for-sale instrument reliably. In our view, in such cases the financial asset subsequently is measured at its cost, subject to impairment testing, based on the carrying amount determined at the last date that the fair value could be determined reliably.

IAS 39.27, 3.6.830.20 Fair value changes are recognised in other comprehensive income. When the
55(b), 67 relevant asset is derecognised, upon sale or other disposal, or is impaired, the cumulative fair value changes recognised in other comprehensive income are reclassified from equity to profit or loss as a reclassification adjustment. For a partial disposal, a proportionate share of the fair value gains and losses recognised previously in other comprehensive income are reclassified from equity to profit or loss. Such gains and losses include all fair value changes until the date of disposal (see 3.6.1280.50).

3.6.830.30 In our view, when financial assets classified as available for sale are distributed as dividends in kind to shareholders, the accumulated gains or losses in other comprehensive income are reclassified from equity to profit or loss upon derecognition of the financial assets, even if the transaction with the shareholders is accounted for in equity.

IAS 39.55(b) 3.6.830.40 Interest income is recognised using the effective interest method, with the effective interest rate being calculated upon the instrument's initial recognition. Therefore, even though a debt instrument is measured at fair value, the holder applies the effective interest method and calculates the amortised cost of the instrument to determine interest income. Impairment losses and foreign exchange gains and losses on available-for-sale debt instruments are excluded from the fair value gains and losses recognised in other comprehensive income. Rather, such gains and losses are recognised in profit or loss as they arise.

3.6.840 *Liabilities*

IAS 39.47   3.6.840.10 Subsequent to initial recognition, other financial liabilities are measured at amortised cost calculated using the effective interest method except for liabilities:

- measured at fair value through profit or loss (see 3.6.800); or
- that arise when a transfer of a financial asset that does not qualify for derecognition and therefore is accounted for using the continuing involvement approach (see 3.6.1240).

3.6.850 *Reclassification of financial assets*

IAS 39.9,   3.6.850.10 An entity may wish or need to reclassify a financial asset from one category
50-54   to another subsequent to its initial recognition. However, reclassifications are permitted/ required only if certain criteria are met and may not be allowed at all without tainting implications. In our view, an asset is required to meet the definition of the category of asset into which it is proposed to be reclassified at the time of reclassification in order for the reclassification to be permissible.

IAS 39.9,   3.6.850.20 The following table summarises the possible reclassifications of financial
50-54   assets. The criteria for reclassification and the circumstances under which reclassification is permitted or required are discussed in further detail below.

To: / From:	Fair value through profit or loss	Available for sale	Held to maturity	Loans and receivables	Measured at cost
Fair value through profit or loss (non-derivatives held for trading)	N/A	P	P	P	R
Fair value through profit or loss (derivatives or designated)	N/A	X	X	X	R
Available for sale	X	N/A	P	P	R
Held to maturity	X	R	N/A	X	X
Loans and receivables	X	P	X	N/A	X
Measured at cost	R	R	X	X	N/A

P – permitted in certain circumstances
R – required in certain circumstances
X – not allowed

473

3.6.860 *To or from the fair value through profit or loss category*

IAS 39.50 (a)-(c) 3.6.860.10 An entity may not reclassify any financial asset into the fair value through profit or loss category after initial recognition. An entity may not reclassify out of the fair value through profit or loss category any derivative financial asset or any financial asset designated as at fair value through profit or loss on initial recognition. When a financial asset is held for trading, it is included in this category based on the objective for which it was acquired initially, which was for trading purposes. Reclassifying such an asset out of this category generally would be inconsistent with this initial objective.

IAS 39.50(c) 3.6.860.11 However, an entity may be permitted to reclassify a non-derivative financial asset out of the held-for-trading category if it is no longer held for the purpose of being sold or repurchased in the near term. There are different criteria for reclassifications of loans and receivables, and of other qualifying assets:

IAS 39.50D ● If the financial asset would have met the definition of loans and receivables (see 3.6.630) if the financial asset had not been required to be classified as held for trading at initial recognition, then it may be reclassified if the entity has the intention and ability to hold the financial asset for the foreseeable future or until maturity.

IAS 39.50B, 39.BC104D ● If the financial asset is not of the type described in the previous bullet, then it may be reclassified only in rare circumstances. IAS 39 does not provide a definition of "rare circumstances" but rare circumstances arise from a single event that is unusual and highly unlikely to recur in the near term. In our view, it is not a necessary feature of rare circumstances that the market for the asset has ceased to be active or become highly illiquid.

3.6.860.12 The reclassification criteria do not refer directly to financial assets that are classified as held for trading because they are or were part of a portfolio of financial instruments that are managed together and for which there is evidence of a recent pattern of short-term profit taking. In our view, if an asset was classified as held for trading because previously it was managed as part of such a portfolio but it is no longer managed as part of such a portfolio, then it may be eligible for reclassification out of trading, provided that at the date of reclassification the entity did not hold the financial asset for the purposes of selling it in the near term. However, if the asset continues to be managed as part of a portfolio for which there is evidence of a recent pattern of short-term profit taking, then it is unlikely that the entity would be able to assert credibly that the asset is no longer held for the purpose of selling it in the short term. If the entity is not able to demonstrate this intent, then the financial asset would not be eligible to be reclassified.

3.6.860.13 In order to be eligible for reclassification, the financial asset should meet the definition of loans and receivables, except for it having been classified as held for trading. In our view, a financial asset would meet this criterion if it would have met the definition of loans and receivables immediately prior to, and at the time of, reclassification, except for it previously having been classified as held for trading, and it is not necessary for the financial asset to have met the definition of loans and receivables at initial recognition. Furthermore, notwithstanding that the asset meets the definition of loans and receivables at the time of reclassification, it is not precluded from being reclassified to the available-for-sale category.

3.6.860.14 Financial assets previously classified as at fair value through profit or loss, which are reclassified out of this category, may contain embedded derivatives. Prior to the reclassification, the embedded derivative would not have been accounted for separately as a derivative as the entire instrument was classified as at fair value through profit or loss (see 3.6.270.60). If an asset is classified out of trading and is no longer accounted for at fair value through profit or loss, then upon reclassification, an entity assesses whether the financial asset contains an embedded derivative that requires separate accounting (see 3.6.280.56). If an entity is unable to measure separately the fair value of an embedded derivative that would have to be separated on reclassification out of the fair value through profit or loss category, then reclassification is prohibited and the entire hybrid financial instrument remains in the fair value through profit or loss category.

IS 39.50C, F 3.6.860.15 If an entity reclassifies a financial asset out of the fair value through profit or loss category, then the financial asset is reclassified at its fair value on the date of reclassification and this fair value becomes the new cost or amortised cost, as applicable. Any gain or loss previously recognised in profit or loss is not reversed. On the same date, a new original effective interest rate is calculated based on the expected future cash flows as of the reclassification date.

IS 39.103H 3.6.860.16 Reclassifications from the held-for-trading category could be applied retrospectively to dates on or after, but not before, 1 July 2008 provided the reclassification was made prior to 1 November 2008. Any reclassification made on or after 1 November 2008 takes effect prospectively from the date it is made and therefore cannot be applied retrospectively. A reclassification may not be effected prior to the date that the entity has met all the criteria for reclassification, including as applicable: a change in management intent; the occurrence of a rare circumstance; or the date on which the financial asset would have met the definition of loans and receivables.

3.6.860.17 If an entity reclassifies a financial asset out of the held-for-trading category on the basis that it is no longer held for the purpose of selling in the near term, or that the entity has the intention and ability to hold the asset for the foreseeable future or until maturity, there is no automatic consequence of subsequent sales of such assets similar to the tainting rules for sales of held-to-maturity assets. However, in our view if reclassified financial assets are sold subsequently, then this may cast doubt on whether the entity has the intention and ability to hold those or other reclassified financial assets for the foreseeable future or until maturity or, more generally, whether other assets are not held for the purpose of selling in the near term.

3.6.860.20 Entities within the same group may undertake transactions in instruments classified in the fair value through profit or loss category. From a consolidated perspective such instruments may not be reclassified out of the fair value through profit or loss category purely as a result of intra-group transactions, unless the instrument was a financial asset held for trading and the criteria for reclassification out of the held-for-trading category were met (see 3.6.860.10), even if the instruments are not classified into this category by the acquiring group entity in its own financial statements. For example, Subsidiary A sells a debt instrument that it designated upon initial recognition as at fair value through profit or loss to Subsidiary B; however, B classifies that instrument as available for sale;

the consolidated financial statements should continue to reflect that debt instrument as at fair value through profit or loss.

3.6.860.30 In some circumstances an entity's trading desk may be responsible for the acquisition of financial assets for the investment purposes of other divisions within the entity. In our view, when the trading desk clearly acts on behalf of the investing division, such that an investment is acquired and passed directly to that division, the entity is not precluded from classifying such investment into the available-for-sale or held-to-maturity category on initial recognition. This applies even if, for operational reasons only, the investment is recognised initially in the trading book. However, should the trading desk have an existing portfolio of financial assets, which were classified for accounting purposes as held for trading, such assets would retain their classification even if an investing division of the entity subsequently acquired some of the assets for its investment purposes unless the criteria for reclassification out of the held-for-trading category were met (see 3.6.860.10).

3.6.860.40 [Not used]

3.6.860.50 Movements of derivatives out of or into the fair value through profit or loss category when they become designated and effective hedging instruments in cash flow or net investment hedges or when they no longer qualify as designated and effective hedging instruments in such hedges, are not "reclassifications".

3.6.870 *From held to maturity to available for sale*

IAS 39.51, 52 3.6.870.10 All held-to-maturity investments are required to be reclassified to the available-for-sale category if there is tainting of the held-to-maturity portfolio (see 3.6.570).

IAS 39.52 3.6.870.20 A reclassification of an instrument out of the held-to-maturity category (e.g. because the entity no longer has the positive intent or ability to hold it to maturity) generally will trigger the tainting rules (see 3.6.570).

IAS 39.55(b) 3.6.870.30 Any adjustment on remeasurement from amortised cost to fair value on the date of the reclassification is recognised in other comprehensive income.

3.6.875 *From the available-for-sale category to measurement at cost or amortised cost*

3.6.880 From available-for-sale to loans and receivables

IAS 39.50E 3.6.880.05 A financial asset that is classified as available for sale that would have met the definition of loans and receivables (see 3.6.630) if it had not been designated as available for sale may be reclassified out of the available-for-sale category to loans and receivables if the entity has the intention and ability to hold the financial asset for the foreseeable future or until maturity. In our view, such an asset should meet the definition of loans and receivables at the date of reclassification in order to qualify for reclassification into that category, but it is not necessary for the financial asset to have met the definition at initial recognition. See 3.6.860.35 for a discussion of the consequence of subsequent sales of such assets.

IAS 39.50F 3.6.880.06 If an entity reclassifies a financial asset from the available-for-sale category to loans and receivables, then the financial asset is reclassified at its fair value on the date of reclassification and this fair value becomes its new cost or amortised cost, as applicable. Any gain or loss previously recognised in other comprehensive income is accounted for in accordance with 3.6.885.40. On the same date, a new original effective interest rate is calculated based on the expected future cash flows as of the reclassification date.

AS 39.103H 3.6.880.07 Reclassifications from the available-for-sale category to loans and receivables can be applied retrospectively to dates on or after, but not before, 1 July 2008 provided the reclassification was made prior to 1 November 2008. Any reclassification made on or after 1 November 2008 takes effect prospectively from the date it is made and therefore cannot be applied retrospectively. A reclassification cannot be effected prior to the date that the entity met all the criteria for reclassification, i.e. management has the intent and ability to hold the financial asset for the foreseeable future or until maturity, and the financial asset would have met the definition of loans and receivables.

3.6.880.08 If an available-for-sale asset is impaired, it still may be reclassified provided it meets the definition of loans and receivables and the entity has the intention and ability to hold the asset for the foreseeable future or until maturity.

3.6.885 From available for sale to held to maturity

IAS 39.54 3.6.885.10 A reclassification from the available-for-sale category to the held-to-maturity category is permitted once any tainting period has lapsed, or if there is a change in intent or ability.

3.6.885.20 [Not used]

IAS 39.54 3.6.885.30 The fair value immediately prior to the reclassification to the held-to-maturity category becomes the new cost or amortised cost, as applicable.

IAS 39.54 3.6.885.40 Following reclassification of a financial asset with a fixed maturity, any gain or loss previously recognised in other comprehensive income, and the difference between the newly established cost and the maturity amount are both amortised over the remaining term of the financial asset using the effective interest method (see 4.6.30). However, any gain or loss previously recognised in other comprehensive income is immediately reclassified from equity to profit or loss if the asset subsequently is impaired. For a financial asset with no stated maturity, any gain or loss previously recognised in other comprehensive income is reclassified from equity to profit or loss when the financial asset is disposed of or impaired.

3.6.887 *To or from financial instruments measured at cost*

IAS 39.54 3.6.887.10 For certain unquoted equity instruments and derivatives linked to such instruments (see 3.6.980), a reclassification to measure a financial instrument at cost that was measured previously at fair value is permitted only in the rare case that a reliable

477

measure of the fair value no longer is available. The reason for any such reclassifications is disclosed.

IAS 39.53   3.6.887.20 If a reliable measure becomes available for a financial instrument for which such a measure was previously not available, and the financial instrument is required to be measured at fair value if a reliable measure is available, then the financial instrument is remeasured at fair value. The difference between the carrying amount and fair value at the date of such remeasurement is recognised in profit or loss if the financial instrument is classified as held for trading or is recognised in other comprehensive income if the financial instrument is classified as available for sale.

3.6.890 *From loans and receivables to at fair value through profit or loss*

IAS 39.9, 50   3.6.890.10 Loans and receivables are classified as at fair value through profit or loss upon initial recognition if the intent is to sell such loans immediately or in the short term (see 3.6.480.25), or if they are part of a portfolio of loans for which there is an actual pattern of short-term profit taking. An entity further may decide to designate specific loans and receivables into the fair value through profit or loss category upon initial recognition. A subsequent reclassification from loans and receivables to the fair value through profit or loss category is prohibited.

3.6.900 *From loans and receivables to available for sale*

IAS 39.9   3.6.900.10 The definition of loans and receivables excludes financial assets that are quoted in an active market. If subsequently a market becomes active, then in our view generally that would not permit a reclassification from loans and receivables to the available-for-sale category unless the market is expected to remain active for the foreseeable future.

3.6.910 *Internal transfers of financial instruments*

3.6.910.10 While internal transactions are eliminated upon consolidation, an internal transfer might be an indication that there has been a change in the group's intent for holding the portfolios concerned.

3.6.915 **Reclassification of financial liabilities**

3.6.915.10 IAS 39 prohibits reclassifications of financial liabilities out of or into the fair value through profit or loss category after initial recognition.

3.6.917 *Loan commitments*

3.6.917.10 Loan commitments measured at fair value through profit or loss on the basis that they were so designated on initial recognition or because they are derivatives, may not be reclassified. However, in our view if the loan commitment is drawn down and a financial asset representing the advance is recognised, then that financial asset would be eligible for reclassification if it satisfied all eligibility criteria (see 3.6.860).

3.6.920 **Fair value***

3.6.930 *General considerations*

IAS 32.11,
9.9, IGE.1.1

3.6.930.10 *Fair value* is the amount for which an asset could be exchanged, or a liability settled, between knowledgeable and willing parties in an arm's length transaction. Fair value does not take into consideration transaction costs expected to be incurred on transfer or disposal of a financial instrument.

IAS 39.AG69

3.6.930.20 Underlying the concept of fair value is the presumption that the entity is a going concern, and does not have an intention or a need to liquidate instruments nor undertake a transaction on adverse terms. Therefore, normally fair value is not an amount that an entity would receive or pay in a forced transaction, involuntary liquidation or distress sale.

3.6.930.25 The objective of determining fair value is to arrive at a price at which an orderly transaction would take place between market participants at the measurement date. In our view, an orderly transaction is one that involves market participants that are willing to transact, and allows for adequate exposure to the market. If a transaction is determined to be forced, then it is not used for measuring fair value. Whether a transaction is forced or not requires analysis of the facts and circumstances and use of judgement. In our view, all transactions in an inactive market cannot automatically be assumed to be forced. Also, in our view, transactions initiated during bankruptcy should not automatically be assumed to be forced. Further, in our view, an imbalance between supply and demand, for example fewer buyers than sellers, is not always a determinant of a forced transaction.

3.6.930.26 In our view, indicators of a forced transaction may include, for example:

● a legal requirement to transact, for example a regulatory mandate;
● a necessity to dispose of an asset immediately with insufficient time to market the asset to be sold; and
● the existence of a single potential buyer as a result of legal or time restrictions imposed.

3.6.930.28 However, in our view, if an entity sells assets to market participants to meet regulatory requirements, the regulator does not establish the transaction price, and the entity has a reasonable amount of time to market the assets, then the transaction price provides evidence of fair value.

IAS 39.AG80,
AG81

3.6.930.30 The fair value of a financial instrument should be reliably measurable. The fair value of investments in equity instruments that do not have a quoted price in an active market and of related derivatives is reliably measurable if (a) the variability in the range of reasonable fair value estimates is not significant for that instrument; and (b) the probabilities of various estimates within the range can be reasonably assessed (see 3.6.980).

IAS 39.49

3.6.930.40 The fair value of a financial liability with a demand feature is not less than the amount payable on demand, discounted from the first date that the amount could be required to be repaid. For example, a bank offers a fixed rate savings deposit product whereby individuals deposit an amount of 10,000 at 1 January 2010 for a minimum period of two years. This product provides a fixed return of 5 percent per annum giving a payment of 11,025 after two years. The individuals are able to withdraw their money after one year, but in this case the amount paid would be only 10,400.

3.6.930.50 Assume that the market interest rate is 8 percent one year after inception of the deposit. In this case the bank calculates the fair value of its liability at 31 December 2010, considering the minimum period of two years, at an amount of 10,208 (11,025 discounted for one year by 8 percent). However, the fair value of the financial liability at 31 December 2010 is not less than the amount payable on demand, which is 10,400. Therefore, the liability is measured at 10,400.

IAS 39.48   3.6.930.60 IAS 39 provides detailed guidance on how an entity should measure the fair value of a financial asset or a financial liability. In particular, it requires a hierarchical approach to fair value measurement, which aims to clarify that an entity should use the fair value that is closest to a market transaction in the specific financial asset or financial liability. In other words, the use of valuation techniques and models is not used to override an observable market price.

IAS 39.AG72,   3.6.930.70 Generally, fair value is determined on an instrument-by-instrument basis. In
AG86-AG93   our view, a portfolio valuation approach could be applied when it is impracticable to determine the fair value of each individual item in that portfolio. For example, an entity may purchase a portfolio of non-performing loans. It is possible for the entity to reliably estimate the future cash flows for the portfolio as a whole, but not for each individual loan. If the entity were required to determine the fair value per loan, then at best this would involve an arbitrary allocation of the fair value of the portfolio; consequently, whether the loans are valued individually or as a portfolio would not impact the overall accounting result.

3.6.935 *Immediate profit*

3.6.935.10 Sometimes an entity acquires a financial instrument in one market and intends to sell it or to issue an offsetting instrument in a different market. An issue arises as to whether the instrument initially may be measured at its fair value in the selling market and therefore a gain recognised on initial recognition ("day one profit").

3.6.935.20 Similarly, an entity may believe that the initial fair value of an instrument exceeds the consideration paid or received, due to the entity's repackaging of the instrument or a built-in "fee". An issue arises as to whether this fee may be recognised immediately (similar to a day one profit).

IAS 39.AG76   3.6.935.30 The best evidence of the fair value of a financial instrument at initial recognition is deemed to be the transaction price (i.e. the consideration paid or received), unless the fair value can be evidenced by comparison to other observable current market transactions in the same financial instrument, or is based on a valuation technique that uses only observable market data as inputs. Therefore, a gain may be recognised on the initial recognition of a financial instrument only if a fair value for that same financial instrument higher than the transaction price is calculated by reference only to market data.

3.6.935.40 In a simplified example, Company M acquires a portfolio of impaired loans for 30 from Company N that recognised the loans at 29 (a face value of 100 less impairment losses of 71). M has superior cash collection processes in place and expects to recover 50 of the principal amount of the loans. Based on a discounted cash flow analysis, M values the loan portfolio at 36. In our view, it would not be appropriate to conclude that the transaction price of 30 does not represent the fair value of the loan portfolio acquired. The valuation technique used to arrive at the value of 36 takes into account M's specific cash collection processes, which is not appropriate as only current observable market data should be considered. Also, a subsequent sale transaction with an independent counterparty on the market would take into account only current observable market data in valuing the position and would ignore the seller-specific cash collection processes. Furthermore, it is unlikely that data for observable current market transactions in the same instrument is available. Consequently, M should recognise the portfolio of loans acquired at the transaction price. M's estimates in respect of the amounts and timing of cash flows rather should be used to determine the effective interest rate of the loan, which should be used in subsequent periods to measure the loan.

IAS 39. AG76A   3.6.935.50 Following from the assessment in 3.6.935.40, when a gain or loss is not recognised upon initial recognition of a financial instrument, it is not appropriate to recognise a gain or loss subsequently unless the market factors relevant to determining the fair value of the instrument at initial recognition have changed.

3.6.940 *An active market – quoted price*

IAS 39.AG71   3.6.940.10 A published price quotation in an active market is the best indicator of the fair value of a financial asset or financial liability and, if available, should be used as a preference to other fair values. A financial instrument is regarded as quoted in an active market if quoted prices are readily and regularly available from an exchange, dealer, broker, industry group, pricing service or regulatory agency, and those prices represent actual and regularly occurring market transactions on an arm's length basis.

IAS 39.AG71   3.6.940.20 There is no further detailed guidance in IAS 39 on how to determine whether there is an active market for a financial instrument. In our view, characteristics of an inactive market include:

- when there has been a significant decline in trading volume and level of trading activity;
- when available prices vary significantly over time or between market participants;
- when available prices are not current; or
- if significant trading volume is between related parties.

3.6.940.25 Also, if there are restrictions on trading, then the market could, depending on facts and circumstances, be considered inactive. However, these factors alone may not necessarily mean that a market is no longer active and determining that a market is not active requires judgement. An active market is one in which transactions are taking place regularly on an arm's length basis. In our view, whether transactions are taking place "regularly" is a matter of judgement and depends upon the facts and circumstances of the market for the instrument.

3.6.940.30 In our view, it is not necessary for there to be a large number of dealers or brokers in order for an active market to exist. As long as an entity is able to dispose of or acquire a reasonable quantity of a particular financial instrument at a price that is not discounted significantly or does not include a significant premium, then it may be concluded that such financial instrument is traded in an active market. In some cases information about pricing and volumes traded may be available from only one independent source, e.g. a broker. In determining whether that one source is providing an active market in the instrument, in our view an entity should take into account its past experience, knowledge of the local market and professional judgement.

IAS 39.AG72 3.6.940.40 The fair value of financial assets *to be acquired* is determined using the current ask price; and for financial liabilities *to be issued*, the current market bid price. For purposes of the subsequent measurement of recognised financial assets and financial liabilities, the current market bid price is used for financial assets held, and the current ask price is used for liabilities held. An exception to this occurs when an entity has assets and liabilities with offsetting market risks, in which case the mid prices can be used for the offsetting risk positions, while bid and ask prices are applied to the net open position as appropriate. It is presumed that such offsetting positions would be settled within a similar time period. When current bid and asking prices are not available, an entity may use the price of the most recent transaction in the particular financial instrument, provided that there has not been a significant change in economic circumstances since that transaction. Adjustments are made when significant changes have occurred since.

IAS 39.IG
E.2.1 3.6.940.50 An entity may not depart from using bid and ask prices in order to comply with regulatory requirements. For example, some investment funds are required to report their net asset values to investors using mid-market prices; this would be a departure from IAS 39. However, the difference between the fair values recognised and the prices used for the net asset value calculation may be explained by means of a reconciliation in the notes to the financial statements.

3.6.940.60 Problems often are encountered in the reporting by investment funds that offer linked investment products (i.e. when the fund's obligation to unit holders is linked to the value of the underlying investments). The investments held by the fund are valued at bid prices while, in the absence of a contractual agreement, the liability to unit holders is measured at the market ask price. If there is a contractual agreement between the entity and the unit holders, then the liability is valued in accordance with that agreement (e.g. mid-market price). Owing to differences in the valuation bases of the investments and the unit liability, a mismatch results in the statement of financial position. This in turn causes a presentation issue. In our view, one solution may be to present the unit liability in a two-line format. The first line would be the amount of the net assets attributable to holders of redeemable shares measured in accordance with the prospectus, which reflects the actual redemption amount at which the redeemable shares would be redeemed at the reporting date, and the next line would include an adjustment for the difference between this and the amount recognised in the statement of financial position. This reflects the fact that, for a fund with no equity, all recognised income and expense should be attributed to unit holders, which also means that, if all units were redeemed, then a dilution levy of such amount would be required. This presentation is illustrated in KPMG's series of illustrative financial statements.

3.6.940.70 The problem in 3.6.940.60 also may be encountered by other entities, such as insurance companies, offering linked investment products. We believe that the approach discussed in 3.6.940.60 also could be applied in these circumstances.

AS 39.AG74, AG79, IGE.2.2   3.6.940.80 Quoted market prices may not be indicative of the fair value of an instrument if the activity in the market is infrequent, the market is not well-established or only small volumes are traded relative to the number of units of the financial instrument outstanding. In such cases it may be appropriate for the entity to use a valuation technique, which comprises making adjustments to the quoted price, but only if the entity can present objective, reliable evidence validating a higher or lower amount. For example, if an entity entered into a contract with a third party to sell shares at a fixed price in the immediate future, then that might justify an adjustment to the quoted price which is, for example, based on infrequent transactions. However, generally it would be inappropriate to make adjustments when valuing large holdings. For example, an entity cannot depart from the quoted market price solely because independent estimates indicate that the entity would obtain a higher or lower price by selling the holding as a block. Therefore, market prices are not adjusted for control premiums or discounts that may exist when an entity has a large holding of a particular instrument.

3.6.940.90 In our view, adjustments to a quoted market price may be justified when conditions are attached to a financial instrument that are not reflected in the quoted market price. For example, assume that an investor contractually is bound by lock-up provisions that prohibit or restrict the sale of the instrument for a specified period. In our view, it can be argued that the instrument held by the investor is not the same as the one with the quoted market price due to the contractual lock-up provisions. In those circumstances, we believe it is appropriate to use a valuation model to make adjustments to the quoted market price. See 4.5.590 for a discussion of post-vesting restrictions in the context of a share-based payment.

3.6.940.100 After the end of the reporting period but before the financial statements are authorised for issue, an entity may become aware of a fraud committed by a third party, which affects a financial asset at the reporting date. In our view, if the entity concludes that the fraud does not call into question the existence of that financial asset as at the reporting date, then, in determining fair value, the entity would not make any adjustment to the quoted market price at the reporting date on account of the fraud (see 2.9.70).

3.6.950 *No active market – valuation techniques**

AS 39.AG74   3.6.950.10 When a financial instrument is not traded in an active market, its fair value is determined using a valuation technique. The entity should use a valuation technique that is commonly used by market participants to price the financial instrument concerned, when that technique has been demonstrated to provide reliable estimates of prices obtained in actual market transactions. Examples of valuation techniques include using recent market transactions in the same instrument, adjusted for changes in market factors between the date of such recent transactions and the measurement date; current or recent market transactions in another financial instrument that is substantially the same as the instrument being valued, adjusted for factors unique to the instrument being valued; discounted cash flow analyses; or option pricing models.

3.6.950.15 Regardless of the level of activity, transaction prices that do not represent distressed transactions cannot be ignored when measuring fair value using a valuation technique, although they might require significant adjustment based on unobservable data.

IAS 39.AG75 3.6.950.20 The objective when choosing and developing an appropriate valuation technique is to establish what a transaction price would have been on the measurement date in an arm's length exchange motivated by normal business conditions. In our view, the valuation technique used should reflect current market conditions and appropriate risk adjustments that market participants would make for credit and liquidity risks on the measurement date.

IAS 39.AG75, 3.6.950.30 The chosen valuation technique makes use of observable market data
AG76, AG82 about the market conditions and other factors that are likely to affect the instrument's fair value. The technique should be consistent with accepted economic methodologies, and its inputs include factors that market participants usually would take into account when pricing an instrument, relying as little as possible on entity-specific factors. Also, it is necessary for the validity of the results of the technique to be tested regularly so that the technique can be recalibrated as required.

3.6.950.33 After the end of the reporting period but before the financial statements are authorised for issue, an entity may become aware of a fraud committed by a third party, which affects a financial asset at the reporting date. In our view, if the entity concludes that the fraud does not call into question the existence of that financial asset as at the reporting date, then the fair value at the reporting date determined using a valuation technique would not reflect knowledge of this fraud if this knowledge both was not and would not have been reasonably available to market participants at that date (see 2.9.70).

IAS 39.AG69 3.6.950.35 Fair value reflects the credit quality of the financial instrument. Accordingly, valuation techniques for derivative instruments reflects the credit risk of the counterparty and the credit risk of the reporting entity (own credit risk) as appropriate, including consideration of collateral and margining requirements, and the effect of master netting arrangements.

IAS 39.AG82 3.6.950.40 In our view, it would not be appropriate to adjust the results of a model-based valuation for entity-specific factors such as uncertainty in estimated cash flows, liquidity or administration costs. We believe such factors should be incorporated into a valuation model based on the amounts that market participants as a whole would consider in setting a price. Furthermore, it is not appropriate to adjust the result of a valuation technique to reflect the model risk of the model used unless other market participants would make similar adjustments.

AS 39.AG81   3.6.950.50 When the outcome of the valuation model is a range of estimates, the probabilities of the estimates within the range are determined and applied to arrive at a single estimate of fair value. In our view, if different models are used and each model gives a different outcome, then judgement should be used in determining which outcome is likely to be the most reliable. We do not believe it is appropriate simply to average the outcomes of the various valuations.

3.6.960 *Valuation assumptions*

3.6.960.10 IAS 39 does not prescribe whether the discount rate or the cash flows should be adjusted to reflect risk. In our experience, an approach of adjusting the discount rate for risks inherent in the cash flows usually is the more common method. However, in some cases it may be possible to incorporate all risks into the expected cash flows. These risk adjusted expected cash flows represent a "certainty-equivalent" cash flow, which is discounted at a risk-free interest rate. A certainty-equivalent cash flow refers to an expected cash flow, adjusted for risk such that one is indifferent to trading a certain cash flow for an expected cash flow.

AS 39.AG82   3.6.960.20 In determining the inputs to valuation models, market information is considered whenever possible. For example:

- A risk-free discount rate may be derived from government bond prices, which often are quoted. However, in some countries government bonds may carry significant credit risk and may not provide a stable benchmark rate for instruments denominated in that currency. Some entities in that country may have a better credit standing. In such cases basic interest rates may be determined by reference to the highest rated corporate bonds issued in the currency of that jurisdiction. Well-accepted and readily observable general rates such as LIBOR also may be used as a benchmark rate.
- An appropriate credit spread may be derived from quoted prices for corporate bonds of similar credit quality to the instrument being valued, or rates charged to borrowers of a similar credit rating.
- Foreign currency rates usually are quoted in daily financial publications and electronic financial databases.
- Observable market prices are available for most commodities.
- Quoted market prices often are available for equity securities. For unquoted equity securities, valuation techniques based on discounted projected earnings may be used to estimate fair value.
- Measures of the volatility of actively traded items normally can be estimated on the basis of historical market data or by using volatilities implied in current market prices.
- Expected prepayment patterns for financial assets and surrender patterns for financial liabilities can be estimated on the basis of historical data.

3.6.970 [Not used]

3.6.980 *No active market – equity instruments: fair value exemption*

IAS 39.46 3.6.980.10 As noted earlier (see 3.6.930.30), it is presumed that the fair value of all financial instruments is reliably measurable. This presumption can be overcome only for an investment in an equity instrument that does not have a quoted price in an active market and whose fair value cannot be reliably measured, and for derivatives that are linked to and are settled by the delivery of such instruments. This exemption applies to both instruments classified as trading and those classified as available for sale.

3.6.980.20 This exemption is very limited. It is unlikely that an investment would be purchased if its fair value could not be estimated. In particular, venture capitalists and other entities that undertake significant investing activities use some form of valuation technique for the purpose of evaluating investment decisions. In our view, in these circumstances the same techniques used to make investment decisions should be used subsequently to determine the fair value of investments. The exemption may be used only in rare cases when it can be demonstrated that the valuation technique generates a wide range of possible fair values, and when the probability of the various outcomes cannot be estimated.

IAS 39.AG80 3.6.980.30 When determining the fair value of these instruments, an entity uses a supportable methodology rather than simply choose a fair value from the range of reasonable estimates obtained.

3.6.980.40 If an embedded derivative that is required to be separated cannot be measured reliably because it will be settled using an unquoted equity instrument whose fair value cannot be reliably measured, then the entire combined contract should be designated as a financial instrument at fair value through profit or loss. The entity might conclude, however, that the equity component of the combined instrument may be sufficiently significant to preclude it from obtaining a reliable estimate of fair value for the entire instrument. In that case the combined instrument is measured at cost less impairment.

3.6.990 *Valuation of investment funds*

3.6.990.10 Many venture capital entities use industry valuation guidelines. In our view, although the valuation determined using these methods may be used as a starting point in determining fair value, adjustments may be required to the valuation derived in order to determine a fair value measurement that is IFRS-compliant. This is because valuations using these models often result in a more conservative measure of value than current market-based fair value; the objective of fair value measurement under IFRSs.

3.6.990.20 An issue sometimes arises as to whether an investment in a fund can be valued reliably. In our view, if the fund invests in marketable securities, then the investment in the fund can be valued. In most cases, even if the fund invests in unlisted entities, it should be possible to determine a valuation of the investment in the fund. In our view, if the valuation reported by the fund (e.g. based on the net asset value of the fund) represents the amount at which the interest in the fund could be exchanged in an arm's length transaction, then this value should be used for the valuation of the investment.

3.6.990.30 If the valuation reported by the fund does not represent the amount at which an arm's length transaction would occur, then the value of the investment in the fund should be determined by applying a valuation technique to the investment in the fund, including consideration of the fund's underlying investments.

3.6.990.40 In some cases a fund invests in another fund. In our view, in this case the same principles apply. Therefore, if a fair value is not available for the investment in the fund directly, then an attempt should be made to value the underlying investments in the underlying fund. Only in the rare circumstances that the value of these underlying investments cannot be estimated reliably would it be acceptable to measure the interest in the fund at cost.

3.6.1000 Amortised cost

3.6.1000.10 Amortised cost applies to both financial assets and financial liabilities. The effective interest method is used for amortising premiums, discounts and transaction costs for both financial assets and liabilities.

3.6.1000.20 When applying the amortised cost method, interest is recognised in profit or loss in the period to which it relates, regardless of when it is to be paid. Therefore, interest is recognised in the period in which it accrues, even if payment is deferred.

IAS 39.9, AG5-AG8 3.6.1000.30 See 4.6.30 for guidance on applying the effective interest method.

3.6.1010 Financial instruments denominated in a foreign currency

3.6.1020 *General considerations*

3.6.1020.10 Entities may have exposure to foreign currency risk, either from transactions in foreign currencies or from investments in foreign operations. The principles for foreign currency transactions explained in 2.7 apply equally to financial instruments. The application of these principles to various foreign currency denominated financial instruments is explained below.

IAS 21.8 3.6.1020.20 Monetary items are units of currency held and assets and liabilities to be received or paid in a fixed or determinable number of units of a currency. This definition is narrower than the definition of a financial instrument, which means that not all financial instruments are monetary. Consequently, contractual rights/obligations to receive/pay cash when the amount of money is neither fixed nor determinable are non-monetary financial instruments. This is the case, for example, with equity securities and other instruments when the holder has no right to a determinable amount of money.

IAS 21.16, 39.AG83 3.6.1020.30 Derivative contracts are settled at amounts that are determinable at the settlement date in accordance with the terms of the contract and the price of the underlying. Derivatives that are settled in cash are monetary items, even if the underlying is a non-monetary item.

3.6.1020.40 In our view, the liability component of a convertible bond should be considered to be a monetary item.

3.6.1030 *Monetary items carried at amortised cost*

3.6.1030.10 Monetary items denominated in a foreign currency and carried at amortised cost (i.e. loans and receivables, held-to-maturity investments and other liabilities) are measured as follows:

- The functional currency carrying amount at the beginning of the period (i.e. the amount reported in the functional currency of the entity at the previous reporting date) is the starting point.
- The interest income or expense to be recognised in the period is the amount calculated in the foreign currency using the effective interest method, multiplied by the average spot exchange rate for the period. This accrual adjusts the functional currency carrying amount at the beginning of the period.
- Then the foreign currency amortised cost of the monetary item is calculated as at the end of the period.
- The functional currency carrying amount at the end of the period is the above foreign currency amortised cost multiplied by the spot exchange rate at the reporting date.
- Then the functional currency carrying amount as calculated above is compared to the functional currency carrying amount at the beginning of the period adjusted for the interest accrual and any payments during the period. Any difference between these two amounts is an exchange gain or loss, which is recognised in profit or loss.

3.6.1040 *Available-for-sale monetary items*

3.6.1040.10 For the purpose of recognising foreign exchange differences, available-for-sale monetary items, such as debt securities, are treated as if they were measured at amortised cost in the foreign currency. Accordingly, the foreign exchange differences arising from changes in amortised cost are recognised in profit or loss and not in other comprehensive income.

3.6.1040.20 The foreign currency differences on these instruments are measured as follows:

- The functional currency amortised cost at the beginning of the period (i.e. the amount calculated (but not reported) in the functional currency of the entity at the previous reporting date) is the starting point.
- The interest income to be recognised in the period is the amount calculated in the foreign currency using the effective interest method, multiplied by the average spot exchange rate for the period. This accrual adjusts the functional currency amortised cost at the beginning of the period. For such available-for-sale monetary items, interest calculated using the effective interest method is required to be recognised in profit or loss (see 3.6.830.40).
- Then the foreign currency amortised cost of the monetary item is calculated as at the end of the period.

- The functional currency amortised cost at the end of the period is the above foreign currency amortised cost multiplied by the spot exchange rate at the reporting date.
- Then the functional currency amortised cost at the end of the period is compared to the functional currency amortised cost at the beginning of the period adjusted for the interest accrual and any payments during the period. Any difference between these two amounts is an exchange gain or loss, which is recognised in profit or loss.

3.6.1040.30 The reported carrying amount of such available-for-sale monetary items is calculated as follows:

- The fair value of the monetary item at the end of the period should be calculated in the foreign currency.
- The functional currency carrying amount at the end of the period is determined by multiplying the fair value in the foreign currency by the exchange rate at the reporting date.
- The difference between the functional currency carrying amount at the end of the period (i.e. fair value), and the functional currency amortised cost at the end of the period, is the cumulative gain or loss to be recognised in other comprehensive income at the end of the year.

3.6.1040.40 For example, on 31 December 2009 Company H, which has a euro functional currency, acquires a bond denominated in US dollars for its fair value of USD 1,000. The bond has five years remaining to maturity, the principal amount of USD 1,250, carries fixed interest of 4.7 percent that is paid annually of 59 (USD 1,250 x 4.7%), and has an effective interest rate of 10 percent. H classifies the bond as available for sale, and consequently recognises gains and losses in other comprehensive income. The exchange rate is USD 1 to EUR 1.5 and the carrying amount of the bond is EUR 1,500 (USD 1,000 x 1.5). H recognises the bond initially as follows:

	Debit (EUR)	Credit (EUR)
Bond	1,500	
Cash		1,500
To recognise initial acquisition of bond		

3.6.1040.50 On 31 December 2010 the foreign currency has appreciated and the exchange rate is USD 1 to EUR 2. The fair value of the bond is USD 1,060 and therefore the carrying amount is EUR 2,120 (USD 1,060 x 2). The amortised cost is USD 1,041 (EUR 2,082). In this case the cumulative gain or loss to be recognised in other comprehensive income is the difference between the fair value and the amortised cost on 31 December 2010, i.e. a gain of EUR 38 (EUR 2,120 - EUR 2,082). Interest received on the bond on 31 December 2010 is USD 59 (EUR 118). Interest income determined in accordance with the effective interest method is USD 100 (USD 1,000 x 10%).

IAS 39. 3.6.1040.60 The average exchange rate during the year is USD 1 to EUR 1.75. Therefore,
IGE3.2 reported interest income is EUR 175 (USD 100 x 1.75), including interest accrued but

not yet settled of EUR 72 ((USD 100 - USD 59) x 1.75). Accordingly, the exchange difference on the bond that is recognised in profit or loss is: (1) a gain of EUR 500 (1,000 x (2 - 1.5)) arising from changes in the carrying amount since initial recognition; and (2) a gain of EUR 25 (100 x (2 - 1.75)) arising from the interest income.

	Debit (EUR)	Credit (EUR)
Bond	620	
Cash	118	
Interest income		175
Exchange gain		525
Fair value change in other comprehensive income		38
To recognise changes in fair value and foreign exchange on bond		

3.6.1050 *Non-monetary items measured at fair value*

IAS 21.30, 3.6.1050.10 There is no distinction between fair value adjustments and exchange differ-
39.AG83 ences on non-monetary items, such as investments in equity securities.

IAS 39.AG83 3.6.1050.20 Non-monetary items measured at cost are not translated subsequent to initial recognition. However, some non-monetary financial instruments, such as equity securities, are measured at fair value. Such instruments should be reported using the exchange rates that existed when the fair values were determined. Thus the fair value first is determined in the foreign currency, which is translated into the functional currency. Foreign exchange gains and losses are not separated from the total fair value changes. Therefore, for available-for-sale equity instruments, the entire change in fair value, including any related foreign exchange component, is recognised in other comprehensive income.

3.6.1060 *Dual currency loans*

IAS 39. 3.6.1060.10 A dual currency loan is an instrument with the principal and interest denomi-
AG33(c) nated in different currencies. A dual currency loan with principal denominated in the functional currency, and interest payments denominated in a foreign currency, contains an embedded foreign currency derivative. However, the embedded derivative is not separated because changes in the spot rate on the foreign currency denominated element (the accrued interest or the principal) are measured under IAS 21 at the closing rate with any resulting foreign exchange gains or losses recognised in profit or loss. However, IAS 21 does not provide guidance on how to account for a dual currency bond.

3.6.1060.20 For example, Company G issues a bond with the principal denominated in euro and the interest denominated in US dollars. The functional currency of G is sterling. In our view, in order to reflect the foreign currency exposure, the dual currency bond consists of two components for measurement purposes:

- a zero-coupon bond denominated in euro; and

- an instalment bond with annual payments denominated in US dollars.

3.6.1060.30 On initial recognition the two components are recognised at fair value. Subsequently, assuming that the instrument is not classified as at fair value through profit or loss, each component is measured separately at amortised cost using the effective interest method. The interest expense related to each component is calculated separately in the relevant foreign currency (i.e. in euro for the zero-coupon bond and in US dollars for the instalment bond) and translated into sterling at the average rate for the period. The carrying amount of both elements is translated to sterling at each reporting date using the closing exchange rate with movements recognised in profit or loss (see 2.7.140.10).

3.6.1070 Derecognition of financial assets

IAS 39.15-37   3.6.1070.10 IAS 39 contains specific provisions for derecognition of financial assets and liabilities.

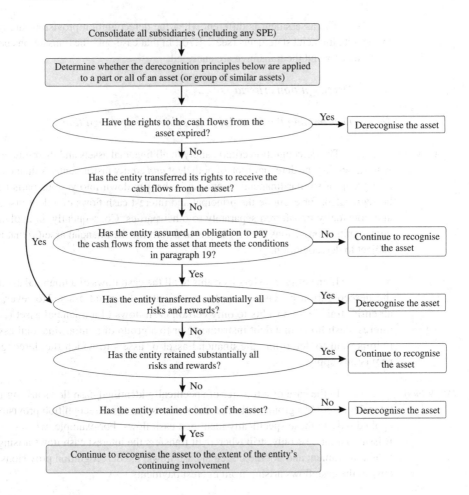

491

IAS 39.15 3.6.1070.20 In consolidated financial statements the derecognition criteria are applied at a consolidated level. This avoids the unnecessary consideration of transactions between individual entities in a group, the effect of which is eliminated on consolidation. Therefore, if financial instruments are transferred within a group, then the consolidated financial statements will not reflect derecognition for intra-group transfers, including transfers to consolidated SPEs (see 2.5.150), even if such transfers qualify for derecognition in the individual financial statements of the entity that is the transferor.

3.6.1070.30 When derecognition is assessed at the consolidated level, the issue of whether or not the transferee consolidates the transferor or vice versa has a significant impact on the accounting. For example, if an SPE is consolidated by the transferring entity (the transferor), then in consolidated financial statements the transaction to be considered for the purposes of applying the derecognition provisions is that between the group (including the SPE) and any external beneficial holders in the SPE. On the other hand, if the SPE is not consolidated, then the transaction to be considered is the transfer between the transferor and the SPE.

3.6.1070.40 The assessment is different when the derecognition provisions are applied to separate financial statements (see 2.1.70). In that case only the transactions between the transferor and the transferee are analysed.

3.6.1080 *Derecognition criteria*

3.6.1090 *Determining the financial asset subject to derecognition*

IAS 39.16 3.6.1090.10 The derecognition criteria apply to all financial assets and therefore are used when assessing the derecognition of both debt *and* equity instruments. A financial asset or a group of similar financial assets can be broken down into various parts that can be segregated, for example the principal and interest cash flows of a debt instrument, and potentially transferred separately to other parties. Consequently, in applying the derecognition provisions the first step is to determine the financial asset(s) that is (are) subject to derecognition.

3.6.1090.20 If an entity transfers its rights to all the cash flows of a financial asset, then the derecognition provisions apply to the entire financial asset. However, when an entity transfers its rights to only certain cash flows of a financial asset (e.g. the interest cash flows in a debt instrument) or to a group of similar financial assets, it is important to determine the financial asset or assets to which the derecognition provisions apply.

IAS 39.16(a) 3.6.1090.30 In the case of a transfer of specifically identified cash flows arising from a financial asset (or a group of similar financial assets), the derecognition provisions are applied only to those specifically identified cash flows. For example, when Company B issues an interest-only strip whereby it transfers the interest cash flows arising from a debt instrument and not the principal cash flows, the derecognition provisions apply only to the cash flows arising from interest payments.

3.6.1090.40 When a fully proportionate share of the cash flows of a financial asset is transferred, in order to consider only the proportion transferred for derecognition it is important to ensure that the transferring entity also retains only a fully proportionate share of the cash flows. The derecognition provisions do not require that there be only one counterparty to whom such cash flows are transferred or that such counterparties obtain a proportionate right to the cash flows being transferred. For example, Company J may decide to transfer 80 percent of the interest cash flows on an existing investment to various counterparties; each counterparty takes up a different proportion of the 80 percent, with the interests of some counterparties subordinated to those of others. J still subjects the 80 percent to a derecognition assessment as it retains a fully proportionate share (20 percent) of the interest cash flows for itself, irrespective of the actual distribution of the 80 percent among the various counterparties.

3.6.1090.50 In all other cases the derecognition assessment should be applied to a financial asset in its entirety. For example, if an entity transfers the rights to the first or last 80 percent of cash receipts on a debt instrument, or 80 percent of the cash collections on a group of trade receivables but provides a guarantee to compensate the buyer for any credit losses up to 9 percent of the principal amount of the receivables, then the derecognition assessment is applied to the financial asset in its entirety and not only to the part that the entity has transferred. This is because the entity has not transferred a fully proportionate share of the cash flows, but rather a portion of the cash flows.

3.6.1090.60 IAS 39 indicates that the derecognition assessment may be applied either to an individual financial asset or to a portfolio of similar financial assets. However, the standard does not specify the circumstances in which a portfolio assessment would be appropriate.

3.6.1090.70 In our view, if in a transfer there are contractual terms that have an effect on the risks and rewards of a group of financial assets, then the group of financial assets rather than each individual financial asset should be assessed for derecognition. Generally, the existence of such contractual terms is evidence that the financial assets are similar and share similar risks and rewards. For example, a financial guarantee issued by the transferor covering a percentage of credit losses in a portfolio of financial assets would link the risks and rewards associated with the individual financial assets in that portfolio. Consequently, the financial asset that is considered as having been transferred is the group rather than individual financial assets. However, the financial guarantee is not considered to be part of the group that is being transferred. Such a situation often is encountered in securitisations when credit-enhancement is provided by the transferor over a portfolio of financial assets in the form of financial guarantees, subordinated loans and reserve funds.

3.6.1090.80 In our view, it would be inappropriate to consider debt and equity instruments as a group of similar financial assets.

3.6.1090.90 All subsequent references to "the financial asset" in this section refer to either a financial asset, a part of a financial asset, a portfolio of financial assets or a part of a portfolio of financial assets, determined in accordance with the discussion in 3.6.1090.

3.6 Financial instruments

3.6.1095 *Evaluating whether the contractual rights to the cash flows have expired*

IAS 39.17   3.6.1095.10 When the contractual rights to cash flows from the asset have expired, that asset is derecognised and no further analysis is required.

3.6.1095.20 If a financial asset has been replaced with a new financial asset, then in our view the holder should perform a quantitative and a qualitative evaluation of whether the cash flows of the two instruments are substantially different. If the cash flows from the two financial assets are substantially different, then the contractual rights to cash flows from the original financial asset should be deemed as having expired. In our view, in making this analysis, an entity may analogise to the guidance on derecognition of financial liabilities (see 3.6.1330).

IAS 39.AG84   3.6.1095.30 If the terms of a financial asset carried at amortised cost are renegotiated or otherwise modified because of financial difficulties of the borrower or issuer, then impairment is measured using the effective interest rate before the modification of terms. In other words, even if the asset is derecognised, an impairment assessment is made, and an impairment loss is recognised if necessary, before derecognising the asset. In our view, this requirement to assess impairment applies irrespective of whether the modification of the existing asset leads to its derecognition.

3.6.1100 *Evaluating whether there is a transfer*

IAS 39.17   3.6.1100.10 To achieve derecognition under IAS 39 either the contractual rights to the cash flows from a financial asset expire or the entity transfers a financial asset in a transfer that meets the criteria specified in the standard.

3.6.1110 *Transfer of contractual rights*

IAS 39.18   3.6.1110.10 In our view, the transfer of legal title should result in a transfer of all existing rights associated with the financial asset without any additional restrictions being imposed as a result of the transfer. A right to demand payment or to obtain legal title that is conditional on the transferor defaulting under a servicing agreement does not constitute a transfer of contractual rights. In this case, the transfer should be evaluated using the pass-through requirements (see 3.6.1160).

3.6.1110.15 A transferor may continue to administer or provide servicing on assets that it previously transferred to another entity. For example, a transferor may transfer all rights to receivables but then continue to collect the cash flows of those receivables as a servicer in the capacity of an agent of the transferee. The determination of whether the contractual rights to cash flows have been transferred is not affected by the transferor retaining the role as agent to collect the cash flows of the receivables in this case. Therefore, retention of the servicing rights by the entity transferring the financial asset does not in itself cause the transfer to fail the requirements of paragraph 18(a) of IAS 39.

3.6.1110.20 However, depending on the legal environment in which an entity operates and the contractually agreed terms, there may be circumstances in which it is not clear whether the contractual rights to receive the cash flows of the financial asset have been transferred. For example, the beneficial interests in a receivable could be sold without legal title to that financial asset being transferred; the seller avoids having to notify the debtor of the sale, thus retaining its relationship with the debtor, and the debtor continues to make payments directly to the seller. In the event of breach, the buyer has the right to "perfect" the sale by acquiring legal title to the receivables. In such circumstances, whether or not transfer has taken place is a question of fact, viewed together with the relevant legal environment in which the entity operates, and requires the use of judgement.

3.6.1110.30 In our view, in order for a transfer of contractual rights to take place, the transferee should have an unconditional right to demand payment from the original debtor in case of default by the original debtor (see 3.6.1110.10). A right that is conditional on the transferor failing to pass on payments under a servicing contract is not sufficient. Consequently, in the example in 3.6.1110.20, the fact that the buyer is able to perfect a sale only in the event of default means that there is no transfer of contractual rights. Therefore, the transaction would need to be assessed under the pass-through requirements (see 3.6.1160).

3.6.1110.40 In addition, because of the transfer requirements discussed in 3.6.1110.10 – 30, we believe that it is not possible to achieve derecognition of a financial asset by synthetic means.

3.6.1110.50 For example, a bank has a portfolio of customer loans, which yield various fixed rate returns. In an effort to improve its advances-to-deposits ratio, the bank enters into a synthetic securitisation structure, comprising the following underlying transactions:

3.6.1120 Credit default swap

3.6.1120.10 The bank enters into a CDS with an SPE, under which it transfers to the SPE the default risk on a referenced portfolio of loans (originated customer loans) in exchange for a fixed premium.

3.6.1130 Deposit

3.6.1130.10 The SPE provides a cash deposit to the bank, which serves as cash collateral against default by the underlying obligors (note holders in the SPE). The bank pays interest at LIBOR on the deposit, which is passed on to the underlying obligors.

3.6.1130.20 The combination of the CDS and the deposit effectively provides the SPE with a return equal to that earned by the bank on the referenced financial assets. In return the SPE compensates the bank for any default on the referenced financial assets.

3.6.1140 Notes

3.6.1140.10 The SPE issues credit linked notes to external parties to fund its ability to take exposure to credit risk in the referenced financial assets. These notes pay interest at LIBOR plus a fixed margin, which is the margin earned by the SPE on the written CDS less any amount needed by the SPE to cover its operating costs. The principal on the notes equals the notional amount on the CDS and the deposit with the bank, which in turn is equal to the principal amount of the referenced financial assets. Any defaults on the referenced financial assets result in an equivalent reduction to the principal of the notes and the deposit with the bank.

3.6.1150 Analysis

3.6.1150.10 Assuming that the SPE is consolidated by the bank (due to the bank holding the equity tranche (see 2.5.150)), the transaction subject to the derecognition assessment is the one that takes place between the consolidated entity and the credit linked note holders.

3.6.1150.20 While the cash flows in the structure, related to the CDS, deposit and notes, are determined based on the portfolio of referenced financial assets, in our view the concurrent working of these three instruments is not sufficient to conclude that the consolidated entity has transferred the referenced financial assets to the note holders as the entity has not transferred the contractual cash flows arising from the referenced assets.

3.6.1160 *Pass-through arrangements*

IAS 39.19 3.6.1160.10 When an entity retains the contractual right to the cash flows of a financial asset, but also assumes a contractual obligation to pay the cash flows to the transferee (sometimes called a "pass-through arrangement"), the transaction is considered as a transfer if and only if:

- there is no obligation to pay amounts to the transferee unless the entity collects equivalent amounts from the original financial asset;
- the entity is prohibited from selling or pledging the original financial asset under the terms of the pass-through arrangement; and
- the entity is obliged to remit all cash flows it collects without material delay.

3.6.1160.20 For example, Company N enters into an agreement with Company B in respect of a security it owns. Physical custody of and legal title to the security is retained by N, but N agrees to pass any cash flows generated by the security to B immediately. There is no obligation for N to pay any amount to B other than the cash it receives on the security (i.e. neither the principal nor any interest in case of late payment). The agreement prohibits N from selling the security. The transaction qualifies as a transfer and should be evaluated under the derecognition provisions.

3.6.1163 Pass-through arrangements involving SPEs

IAS 39.AG37 3.6.1163.10 A typical situation in which a pass-through arrangement may exist is in a securitisation involving SPEs. See 3.6.1310 for further discussion of practical issues.

3.6.1165 Pass-through arrangements involving total return swaps on equity instruments

3.6.1165.10 A holder of an equity instrument may enter into a total return swap (TRS) under which the holder remits all the cash flows (i.e. dividends) from the equity instrument and receives a stream of fixed or floating rate cash flows. If the terms of such a TRS or any other arrangements that are part of the transfer require that the equity instrument be transferred at the expiry of the TRS, then in our view such a transfer may meet the pass-through requirements in IAS 39. For example, on 1 July 2009 Company S forward sells an equity instrument to Company T, with physical delivery to T on 30 June 2010. On the same date, S and T enter into a TRS with expiry on 30 June 2010, under which S remits all the cash flows (i.e. dividends) from the equity instrument and receives a stream of floating rate cash flows. Under the terms of the arrangement S cannot pledge or sell the equity instrument and has no obligation to pay any dividends to T unless it receives an equivalent amount as dividends from the equity instrument. We believe the transaction meets the pass-through conditions and assuming that S has transferred substantially all risks and rewards, it should derecognise the equity instrument.

3.6.1165.20 Conversely, if a TRS or the transfer arrangement does not require the equity instrument to be transferred at expiry but only requires the transfer of all dividends during the period of the TRS, then in our view the holder of the equity instrument would only have transferred a dividend strip until the expiry of the TRS. As the dividend strip constitutes separately identifiable cash flows it can be considered separately for derecognition. In our view, the dividend strip, until the expiry of the TRS, meets the pass-through conditions assuming the entity cannot separately pledge or sell the dividend strip arising from the equity instrument and it has no obligation to pay any dividends under the arrangement unless it receives an equivalent amount from the equity instrument and the agreement provides for remittance of the cash flows without any material delay. Consequently, assuming that the entity has transferred substantially all risks and rewards, the dividend strip until expiry of the TRS should be derecognised and the remaining part of the equity instrument continues to be recognised.

3.6.1170 *Risks and rewards evaluation*

3.6.1170.10 For all transactions that meet the transfer requirements, the entity next evaluates whether it has transferred or retained the risks and rewards of ownership of the financial asset.

IAS 39.21, 22   3.6.1170.20 The risks and rewards analysis is performed by comparing the entity's exposure, before and after the transfer, to the variability in the present value of the future net cash flows from the financial asset. This evaluation can be done either separately for each type of risk that the financial asset under consideration is exposed to or for all the risks arising from the financial asset. Thus, for each type or types of risk transferred and retained, an entity should determine its exposure to the variability in the amounts and timing of the net cash flows of the transferred asset arising from that type of risk or risks. Even if individual risk types are considered in isolation, the evaluation of whether or not an entity has transferred or retained substantially all risks and rewards is based on the aggregate exposure arising from each risk type.

3.6.1180 *Risk types*

3.6.1180.10 The different types of risk can be summarised briefly as follows:

3.6.1180.20 Price risk, which is an inherent risk in equity instruments.

3.6.1180.30 Risks inherent in debt instruments:

- credit risk, also called default risk or risk of default;
- interest rate risk, comprising fair value interest rate risk and cash flow interest rate risk; and
- late payment risk (i.e. the risk that payments received from the underlying financial assets occur on a different date than expected, sometimes called slow payment risk); late payment risk is not defined in IFRSs.

3.6.1180.40 Risks inherent in both equity and debt instruments:

- currency risk; and
- other risks – this category covers any risks that may occur in a particular fact pattern in practice that is not covered explicitly by the above risk categories (e.g. dispute and legal risks).

3.6.1190 Dispute and legal risk

3.6.1190.10 Dispute risk (also known as warranty or dilution risk) is the risk that there is or will be a dispute over a financial asset, e.g. a receivable, because of a claim from the customer that the quality of goods delivered or services performed varied from what was agreed contractually. Therefore, the debtor is not obliged legally to pay the stated amount of the receivable. Therefore, the originator has sold a financial asset that does not legally exist or that does not exist to the extent of its stated amount.

3.6.1190.20 Typically the transferee will not accept liability for any such dispute risk, i.e. the transferor remains liable for any deductions arising from disputes and has to reimburse the transferee for losses incurred, or the transferee has a right to put the disputed financial asset(s) back to the transferor. Since there is no (legally existing) financial asset, there is no risk that could be transferred unless the transferee accepts this risk without the possibility of recourse; in our experience, the chance of this is remote.

3.6.1190.30 Therefore, in our view dispute risk should not be included in the risk and rewards analysis, because it relates to the existence of a financial asset rather than to the risk and rewards inherent in an existing financial asset.

3.6.1190.40 Similar considerations apply to other legal risks, i.e. normally they should not be included in the risk and rewards analysis, because again they relate to the existence of a financial asset rather than to the risk and rewards inherent in a financial asset. In addition, the transferee usually will not accept this risk without a right of recourse.

3.6.1200 Structural/liquidity risk

3.6.1200.10 Structural/liquidity risk arises primarily in securitisations when there is a mismatch between the cash inflows from financial assets and cash outflows on financial liabilities. It is important to differentiate structural/liquidity risk from late payment and default risk. For example, in a securitisation structural/liquidity risk may arise because of variability in the timing of defaults on the assets whereby the SPE does not have enough cash to meet its obligations. Such variability can arise without altering the cumulative expectation of defaults on the portfolio. In our view, such a risk is not inherent in the financial asset transferred, but arises as a result of the structure of the transaction. Consequently, we believe such a risk should not be included in the risks and rewards analysis. However, structural liquidity risk should be included in the assessment of benefits and risks under SIC-12 *Consolidation — Special Purpose Entities* (see 2.5.150).

3.6.1200.20 In certain structures a transferor also provides a liquidity facility to a structure that represents the most senior debt component in the structure. In such circumstances the provision of the liquidity facility does not generally impact the analysis of risks and rewards for derecognition purposes. On the other hand, if such a facility does not represent the most senior debt component in the structure, then it is possible that the transferor is absorbing credit risk through the provision of such a facility. In such circumstances the granting of such a liquidity facility will have an impact on the risks and rewards analysis as it absorbs credit risk. Consequently, the terms of any liquidity facility need careful evaluation to determine whether or not it plays a part in the risks and rewards analysis.

3.6.1210 *Substantially all*

IAS 39.21   3.6.1210.10 No specific quantitative guidance is provided on what constitutes "substantially all" risks and rewards of a financial asset. In our view, the analysis should be based on all of the facts and circumstances, considering all of the risks (except for dispute and other legal risks) associated with the financial asset on a probability-weighted basis. The analysis should not consider each risk in isolation. If substantially all of the total variability in the present value of the future cash flows associated with the financial asset is retained, then we believe the entity would be considered to have retained substantially all risks and rewards.

3.6.1210.13 For example, Company X holds an equity investment in Company W, an unquoted company, which has been classified as available for sale. W's parent company is a listed entity. X's shareholders have agreed to exchange their shares in W for shares in W's parent. Subsequent to the transfer, W is merged into its parent and X receives shares in the parent (i.e. a new financial asset). In our view, as long as, subsequent to the transfer, the equity instruments received by X have cash flows that are significantly different from the cash flows of the original equity instrument (i.e. X has received a new financial asset and not the existing asset only with a repackaging), the derecognition criteria are met, and consequently X should derecognise the original asset and recognise the new financial asset at fair value.

3.6.1210.17 In our view, the fact that a transferor may have a reimbursement right from another entity (i.e. an insurance company), and thereby economically hedges its risk exposure arising from the transferred financial assets, is irrelevant in an analysis of risks and rewards. Only the risks and rewards between the transferor and the transferee are included in the analysis. Hence, the analysis of risks and rewards does not consider whether and how the transferor has entered into other contracts with third parties that reimburse the transferor for losses incurred in connection with the transferred assets.

3.6.1210.20 In our view, generally it is not necessary to use cash flow and/or similar models in performing a risks and rewards analysis. In most cases evaluation of the terms and conditions of the transaction should be sufficient to determine whether, and to what extent, an entity's exposure to variability in the amounts and timing of the net cash flows has changed as a result of the transfer.

3.6.1210.30 However, under certain circumstances a degree of statistical analysis might be required. For example, in transactions in which the transferor and the transferee share the exposure to the variability in cash flows arising from credit risk it might be difficult to determine whether or not substantially all the risks and rewards have been transferred.

3.6.1210.40 The example in 3.6.1210.50 – 90 illustrates how in such circumstances an analysis of the transfer of risks and rewards might be performed. In the example the expected loss is the difference between the notional amount and fair value at the date that the risk is transferred and the unexpected loss is the maximum exposure within a given confidence interval.

3.6.1210.50 For example, Company R transfers short-term receivables of 100,000 to Company S for 95,000. Assume that there is no risk other than credit risk inherent in the receivables and that the default rates are as follows:

- expected credit losses are 5 percent of the notional amount; and
- the likely range of losses is between 4.5 percent and 6.5 percent of the notional amount with a 99.9 percent confidence interval.

3.6.1210.60 R provides a guarantee to reimburse S for losses exceeding 6.5 percent. The risk is that actual credit losses will exceed expected credit losses of 5 percent. The rewards, which remain with S, are that actual credit losses will be less than expected credit losses of 5 percent. R has transferred substantially all risks and rewards associated with the receivables, because R is not exposed to the variability in cash flows within the range of reasonably possible outcomes.

3.6.1210.70 In some cases it is possible that a third party instead of the transferor provides credit enhancement. In our view, if the transferor is the beneficiary to the credit enhancement contract, but agrees to compensate the transferee for credit losses, then this is an indication that the transferor has retained credit risk. In this case, in evaluating whether or not the financial assets qualify for derecognition, the credit enhancement contract should be disregarded and it should be assumed that the transferor continues to bear the credit risk. In order to transfer the credit risk inherent in the financial assets, in our view the transferee needs to be the beneficiary under the credit enhancement contract and not the transferor.

3.6.1210.80 For financial assets with relatively short maturities, such as most trade receivables, generally the only substantial risk to consider is credit risk. If the transferor retains credit risk on short-term financial assets, then in our view it would not be appropriate to conclude that it has transferred substantially all the risks and rewards.

3.6.1210.90 Also, in evaluating risks and rewards it is important that the entity not only transfers substantial rewards but also that it transfers its exposure to a significant loss arising from a substantial risk. A risk of loss could be considered as significant, for example, when based on historical loss experience for the type of financial asset transferred. For example, if a transfer of credit risk, which generally is considered to be a substantial risk of the financial assets transferred, will occur only in a catastrophe or similar situation because historical losses are covered through a guarantee by the transferor, then this is considered to be outside the range of likely loss outcomes. This would not be considered a transfer of a significant exposure to loss from credit risk.

3.6.1230 *Control evaluation*

AS 39.20(c) 3.6.1230.10 If an entity neither transfers nor retains substantially all of the risks and rewards of ownership of a financial asset, then it evaluates whether or not it has retained control of the financial asset.

3.6.1230.20 For example, Company V transfers long-term mortgage receivables to entity W such that it retains credit risk while transferring prepayment/late payment risk and interest rate risk. Assuming that both credit and the combined prepayment and interest rate risk are considered to be significant, V has neither retained nor transferred substantially all risks and rewards and therefore should determine if it has retained control of the receivables.

IAS 39.23 3.6.1230.30 An entity is considered to have lost control if the transferee has the practical ability to unilaterally sell the transferred financial asset in its entirety to an unrelated third party without needing to impose additional restrictions on the sale. If there is a market for the financial asset (i.e. if the financial asset is readily obtainable), then the transferee often has the practical ability to sell the financial asset, even if the contractual arrangements between the transferor and the transferee restrict such a sale.

IAS 39.23, 3.6.1230.40 Conversely, the transferee usually does not have the practical ability to sell
G43, AG44 the financial asset if there is no market for the financial asset, even if the contractual arrangements between the transferor and transferee permit such a sale. The transferee

also will not have this practical ability when a call option or a guarantee constrains the transferee from selling the financial asset. As a result, the transferor would not be considered to have lost control. In the example in 3.6.1230.20, if V attaches conditions to the transfer that prevent the transferee from selling the mortgage receivables to a third party, for example to maintain customer relationships, then V has retained control over the transferred financial assets.

3.6.1230.50 In another example, Company P sells financial assets, e.g. a portfolio of corporate loans, to Company B. P simultaneously enters into a call option with B under which it has the right to repurchase the financial assets after five years. While B has the legal right to sell the financial assets, it does not have the practical ability to do so as it could be required to return the financial assets to P at the end of five years. Should B attempt to sell the financial assets to another party, it would have to attach a similar call option so as to be able to repurchase the financial assets in the event of P exercising its option. It also is unlikely that there is an active market for such financial assets that would allow B to sell the financial assets without attaching the aforementioned call option on the financial assets. Consequently, due to the call option held by P, it has in our view retained control over the financial assets and will have to consider accounting under continuing involvement.

3.6.1230.60 In another example, a transfer of trade receivables includes an option that allows the transferor to acquire overdue receivables at face value. Although the option has no economic substance, the transferor has retained control to be able to protect its customer relationships.

3.6.1230.70 In our view, no distinction should be made in the separate financial statements between a derecognition transaction between a parent entity and one of its operating subsidiaries and an independent third party. Therefore, a parent entity normally should not include indirect control through the ownership of an operating subsidiary in the evaluation of control, as this control is not related to the financial asset.

3.6.1240 Continuing involvement

IAS 39.20(c)
(ii)
3.6.1240.10 If an entity retains control of a financial asset for which some but not substantially all risks and rewards have been transferred, then the entity should continue to recognise the financial asset to the extent of its continuing involvement in the financial asset.

IAS 39.AG48
3.6.1240.20 For example, Company P transfers short-term receivables of 100,000 to Company Q. P provides a credit loss guarantee of 2,000. Expected credit losses are 4,000, and historically have varied between 1,000 and 5,000. Q is not permitted to sell or pledge the receivables. In our view, P has retained some, but not substantially all, of the risks and rewards of ownership associated with the receivables. In addition, Q is not permitted to sell or pledge the receivables and there is no market for such receivables. Therefore, P has not given up control and should continue to recognise the receivables to the extent of its continuing involvement. The maximum extent of P's continuing

involvement is 2,000 (the amount of the guarantee). Therefore, P should derecognise 98,000 and continue to recognise 2,000, which is the lower of (1) the carrying amount of the financial asset; and (2) the maximum amount received in the transfer that P could be required to repay.

IAS 32.42, 3.6.1240.30 Generally, measurement under continuing involvement requires that the net
39.36 carrying amount of the financial asset and the associated financial liability reflect, depending on the measurement basis of the financial asset, either the amortised cost or fair value of the rights and obligations retained by the entity. However, notwithstanding the requirement to arrive at a particular net carrying amount, the financial asset and associated financial liability may not be offset. To achieve offset, generally an entity would have to demonstrate the existence of a legally enforceable right of offset, i.e. a cash flow received on the transferred financial asset would have to result in the elimination of a proportion of the financial liability of the transferor to the transferee. This would imply that the risks associated with the transferred financial asset lie with the transferee, which in turn implies that derecognition should have taken place; a conclusion that is contrary to that reached in the derecognition analysis. Consequently, when a transaction does not result in derecognition, generally it is not possible to meet the offset requirements. Similarly, an entity is, in our view, prohibited from offsetting any income arising on the transferred financial asset or expenses arising on the associated financial liability, which follows from the more general prohibition on offsetting in IAS 1 *Presentation of Financial Statements* (see 5.6.90).

3.6.1250 *Assessment of derecognition in separate financial statements*

3.6.1250.10 In our view, the derecognition requirements in IAS 39, other than the requirement in the standard to start by consolidating all subsidiaries, apply equally to separate financial statements.

3.6.1250.20 However, the transfer that needs evaluation in the separate financial statements is different from that at the consolidated level. Consequently, depending upon the fact pattern, it is possible to achieve derecognition in separate financial statements while failing to do so in consolidated financial statements. In our experience, this situation arises primarily with transactions involving SPEs.

3.6.1260 *Assessment of control*

3.6.1260.10 From the perspective of the separate financial statements, in most instances the transferee will be the SPE. In such circumstances an evaluation of whether or not control of the transferred assets has been passed by the transferor raises certain practical considerations. In order to assess whether or not control has been transferred, we believe that the following need to be addressed:

- Is there any contractual restriction preventing the SPE from selling or pledging the financial assets? It is common practice to have such restrictions in place, as when an SPE is set up for a securitisation transaction the financial assets also are used as collateral. In our view, in order to meet the control criterion in the standard and therefore achieve derecognition of the transferred assets, the SPE cannot be prevented from selling the financial assets by means of any "pre-determined" autopilot rules/ pre-agreements.

- Can the SPE unilaterally sell the financial assets, or is this decision controlled directly by the transferor?

3.6.1270 *Accounting for a sale*

3.6.1280 *Transfers that qualify for derecognition*

IAS 39.27 3.6.1280.10 Sometimes only part of a financial asset qualifies for derecognition (e.g. if an interest-only strip is retained). In these cases the carrying amount of the entire financial asset before the transfer is allocated between the sold and retained portions based on their relative fair values on the date of the transfer.

IAS 39.24, 25 3.6.1280.20 Sometimes new financial assets or financial liabilities are created in the transfer (e.g. a servicing financial liability on transferred loans, or a credit guarantee). New financial assets or financial liabilities created as a result of the transfer are recognised separately and measured at fair value.

IAS 39.26, 27 3.6.1280.30 A gain or loss is recognised based on the difference between (1) the carrying amount of the financial asset or portion of the financial asset transferred; and (2) the sum of the proceeds received, including the fair value of any new financial assets acquired or financial liabilities assumed in the transfer, and the cumulative gain or loss previously recognised in other comprehensive income in respect of the transferred financial asset, or the portion of the transferred financial asset.

3.6.1280.40 If financial instruments are exchanged in a transaction that meets the criteria for derecognition, then the financial assets received are measured at fair value and the profit or loss on disposal should be calculated based on the fair value of the financial assets received.

3.6.1280.50 IFRSs are silent on how to determine the cost of financial assets sold when the financial assets are part of a homogenous portfolio. Therefore, the application of the hierarchy for the selection of accounting policies (see 2.8.6) should be applied. In our view, the guidance regarding cost formulas for inventories should be applied (see 3.8.280). Therefore, any reasonable cost allocation method (e.g. average cost or first-in, first-out) may be used, although we prefer the average cost method. However, the use of specific identification is not precluded if the entity is able to identify the specific items sold and their costs. An entity should choose a reasonable cost allocation method, to be applied consistently, to determine the cost of financial assets sold when the financial assets are part of a homogeneous portfolio. In addition, in our view the approach used to determine the cost of financial assets sold should be applied consistently when assessing impairment and accounting for the resulting impairment losses (see 3.6.1370).

3.6.1290 *Transfers not qualifying for derecognition*

IAS 39.29,   3.6.1290.10 If a transfer does not qualify for derecognition, then the financial asset, or
AG47   the retained portion of the financial asset, remains in the statement of financial position
and a corresponding financial liability is recognised for any consideration received.
Disclosure of the fact that the financial asset is pledged as collateral for the financial
liability is required (see 5.6.560.10).

AS 39.AG49   3.6.1290.20 When contractual rights and obligations (e.g. derivatives) related to a transfer
prevent the transferor from derecognising the financial assets, these rights and obligations
are not accounted for separately. For example, a call option retained by the transferor
may prevent derecognition of certain financial assets, but recognising the financial assets
as well as the call option would result in the entity double counting its rights to such
financial assets.

IAS 39.   3.6.1290.30 It is important to contrast the situation in 3.6.1290.20 with one in which the
AG51(p)   derivative requires separate recognition. For example, Company F transfers fixed rate
financial assets to Company B. F simultaneously enters into an interest rate swap with
B under which it receives fixed rate interest (equal to the rate on the transferred financial
assets) and pays floating rate interest (equal to the rate on the notes issued by the SPE
to fund the acquisition of the financial assets); the payments are based on a notional
amount equal to the principal amount of the transferred financial assets, but are not
conditional upon B receiving any cash flows from the underlying financial assets. In
this case the interest rate swap would not cause the transaction to fail derecognition and
therefore would require separate recognition and subsequent accounting as a derivative
instrument.

3.6.1300 Receivables sold with full recourse

3.6.1300.10 Receivables sold with full recourse generally would not qualify for derecgo-
nition. For example, Company F sells receivables due in six months with a carrying
amount of 100,000 for a cash payment of 95,000, subject to full recourse. Under the
right of recourse, the transferor is obligated to compensate the transferee for the failure
of any debtor to pay when due. In addition to the recourse, the transferee is entitled to
sell the receivables back to the transferor in the event of unfavourable changes in interest
rates or credit ratings of the underlying debtors.

3.6.1300.20 The transaction is accounted for by the transferor as a collateralised borrowing as it does not qualify for derecognition. Assuming that the rights to all of the cash
flows on the receivables legally are transferred, this transaction fails the derecognition requirements because the transferor has retained substantially all of the risks and
rewards associated with the financial assets. The transferor is obliged to compensate
the transferee for the failure of the debtors to pay when due. In addition, the transferor
has granted the transferee a put option on the transferred financial assets allowing the
transferee to sell the receivables back to the transferor in the event of actual credit
losses and/or changes in underlying credit ratings or interest rates. Consequently,

the transferor is regarded as having retained substantially all the risks and rewards of ownership of the receivables.

3.6.1300.30 The transferor recognises 95,000 as a financial liability. The financial liability is measured at amortised cost with an interest expense of 5,000 being recognised over the six-month period until maturity. The transferor continues to recognise the receivables as financial assets. Cash received on the receivables by either the transferor or transferee reduces both the receivables and the financial liability. If uncollected receivables are returned to the transferor for cash, then the financial liability is reduced and an impairment loss is recognised if not recognised previously by the transferor.

3.6.1310 *Securitisations*

3.6.1310.10 Entities commonly use securitisations to monetise financial assets, such as homogeneous consumer loans, credit card receivables, trade receivables or mortgage loans, by selling newly created securities collateralised by these financial assets to investors. Such securitisation transactions often use SPEs for various reasons. Generally an SPE will be a legal entity with limited activities whose purpose is to hold the beneficial interests in the securitised financial assets and to pass-through monies earned on these financial assets to the investors in the securities issued by the SPE. In a typical securitisation the transferring entity assigns financial assets to the SPE in return for cash proceeds. All of these steps usually will occur simultaneously, i.e. the transfer of financial assets, issue of securities to investors and payment of proceeds to the transferor.

3.6.1310.20 When financial instruments are transferred using an SPE, additional considerations arise with respect to the evaluation of derecognition of such financial assets.

IAS 39.15 3.6.1310.30 The first step in the derecognition assessment is to assess whether or not the SPE should be consolidated under SIC-12. If the SPE is consolidated, then the transaction to evaluate for derecognition at the group level is the transfer of financial assets by the group, including the SPE, to the investors in the securities issued by the SPE. If on the other hand the SPE does not require consolidation under SIC-12, then the transaction to evaluate for derecognition at the group level is the transfer of financial assets by the group (excluding the SPE) to the SPE.

3.6.1310.35 In our experience with current securitisation structures, in the majority of cases it is unlikely that consolidation by the originator can be avoided.

3.6.1310.40 An SPE is unlikely to transfer legal rights to the cash flows from its financial assets to its investors. Therefore, in many cases the critical issue may be whether or not all the cash flows from the financial assets, and only the cash flows from the financial assets, are passed through without material delay in an arrangement that meets the pass-through requirements.

3.6.1310.50 In many securitisation transactions involving SPEs, the pass-through requirements will be difficult to achieve and certain arrangements may need to be restructured, e.g. those in which the transferring entity has other than a fully proportionate share in the cash flows. Specific practical issues are identified and discussed in 3.6.1310.60 – 1317.30.

3.6.1310.60 Often the purpose of a securitisation transaction is the raising of highly-rated, low cost finance. To this end, the originator of financial assets that are securitised and transferred into an SPE typically provides some form of credit enhancement to the SPE, for example, the originator guarantees an agreed rate of return to the investors in the SPE. By doing so the originator reduces the risk that is transferred to the SPE and consequently also reduces the risk that the investors are exposed to. When the securitisation SPE is not consolidated, the provision of such a guarantee will influence whether or not a qualifying pass-through arrangement between the originator and the SPE is considered to be in place. Such a guarantee can be a credit enhancement provided in connection with the transferred financial assets (e.g. a portfolio of loans) and can be provided by means of a cash collateralised financial guarantee, a subordinated loan or a reserve fund that is built up from the cash collected from the underlying loans that have been transferred to the SPE. In our view, such a funded credit enhancement arrangement does not violate the pass-through requirements of IAS 39.

3.6.1310.70 In a securitisation structure in which credit enhancement is provided by the transferor and the SPE is consolidated, the contractual arrangements between the consolidated entity and the beneficial interest holders should be analysed to determine whether the requirements for a qualifying pass-through arrangement are met.

3.6.1310.71 The underlying financial asset may or may not have been transferred to the SPE. Assuming that the SPE is consolidated by the entity, a transaction transferring the underlying financial assets from the entity (the originator) to the SPE is not considered for derecognition in the consolidated financial statements of the transferor. Rather, the transaction between the SPE and the holders of the debt instruments is considered. Typically the SPE, and therefore the group, will not transfer the contractual rights to the cash flows on the underlying financial assets to the holders of the debt instruments. However, the terms of the debt instruments may provide for payments to be made to the holders based on cash received on the underlying financial assets in such a manner that the entity's only role is acting as an agent on behalf of the note holders. Therefore, it is possible that such a transaction could meet the pass-through conditions listed in 3.6.1160.10. Such an analysis raises a number of practical issues, especially concerning transactions involving SPEs.

AS 39.19(c) 3.6.1310.72 Below are our views on some specific application issues for determining whether a pass-through arrangement involving an SPE qualifies for a transfer.

3.6.1312 *Without material delay*

3.6.1312.10 In order to meet the pass-through conditions an entity is required to remit all cash flows it collects on behalf of the eventual recipients without material delay. In our view, the entity can invest the cash flows for periods of up to three months without violating this requirement provided that: the investments are only in cash and cash equivalents (see 2.3.10); and all cash flows, both amounts collected and any income earned on investments in cash or cash equivalents, are remitted to the bondholders on the next payment date. Conversely, we believe refinancing terms exceeding three months will not meet this criterion; neither will investments in cash and cash equivalents on a revolving basis over periods exceeding three months.

3.6.1315 *Credit enhancements*

3.6.1315.10 In situations in which the nature of credit enhancements (whether provided in the form of financial guarantees or other non-funded transactions) is such that additional amounts will be paid to the transferee or investors in an SPE in the event of default (i.e. the entity will make additional payments in excess of the amounts collected from the original financial assets), in our view such credit enhancements provided by the transferor will violate the pass-through requirements in the standard.

3.6.1317 *Revolving transactions*

IAS 39.19   3.6.1317.10 When cash flows collected from the underlying financial assets are reinvested by the SPE in new financial assets, other than cash or cash equivalents, under a revolving structure, problems may be encountered in meeting the condition that all cash flows should be remitted to the eventual recipients without material delay. Further analysis of the terms and conditions governing this reinvestment is required in order to determine whether or not the conditions for a qualifying pass-through arrangement are met.

3.6.1317.20 In our experience, there are four general scenarios that may be encountered, each having an effect on the pass-through requirement:

- The SPE automatically reinvests the cash flows to purchase additional receivables in accordance with predetermined contractual arrangements embedded in the structure; in our view the pass-through requirements are violated as the investments are not in cash or cash equivalents and derecognition is precluded.
- The SPE remits the cash flows to the bondholders without material delay, at which time the bondholders may decide whether or not to reinvest the cash flows with the SPE for purposes of acquiring further financial assets; in our view the pass-through requirements are met and the transaction should be considered further for derecognition.
- The SPE automatically will reinvest the cash flows to purchase additional financial assets, unless the bond holders indicate at that stage that they do not want to reinvest in the SPE, i.e. the cash flows are remitted to the bond holders only if they decide not to reinvest; in our view, the pass-through requirements are not violated as the SPE is obliged to remit the cash flows to the bond holders if so notified. The lack of a physical flow of cash from the SPE to the bond holder and back to the SPE does not impact the derecognition analysis and the transaction should be considered further for derecognition.
- The SPE remits the cash flows to the bond holders, but the bond holders agree contractually upfront that all cash flows will be reinvested immediately by the

SPE; in our view despite the physical flow of cash, the pass-through requirements are violated as the bond holders contractually are obliged to reinvest the cash flows immediately in order for the SPE to acquire additional financial assets. Therefore derecognition is precluded.

3.6.1317.30 Even when the pass-through requirements are met and it is concluded that some but not substantially all of the risks and rewards of the financial assets are transferred to the beneficial interest holders, it is likely that the SPE will have retained control of the transferred financial assets. This is because in a typical structure the SPE will be precluded from selling the financial assets, and consequently the beneficial interest holders also will be unable to sell the financial assets. In such circumstances partial derecognition may be appropriate under continuing involvement accounting (see 3.6.1240).

3.6.1320 *Repurchase agreements and securities lending*

IAS 39.
AG51(a)

3.6.1320.10 If a sale of a financial asset is subject to a repurchase agreement at a fixed price, or at the initial selling price plus interest, or if the asset is lent to a third party who agrees to return it, then the seller retains substantially all risks and rewards of ownership of the asset. Therefore, the seller does not derecognise the financial asset. If the transferee obtains the right to sell or pledge the financial asset that does not qualify for derecognition, then the seller reclassifies the financial asset in its statement of financial position, for example as a loaned financial asset or repurchase receivable.

IAS 39.
G51(b), (c)

3.6.1320.20 This treatment applies regardless of whether the financial asset subject to the agreement is readily obtainable in the market, such that the transferee could repurchase the financial asset in the market in order to meet its return obligation to the seller, or the returned financial asset is required to be the same or substantially the same, when the terms of the repurchase agreement provide as such.

S 39.AG50

3.6.1320.30 Similarly, the transferee does not recognise the financial asset received under a repurchase or securities lending arrangement. If the transferee sells the financial asset, then it recognises a financial liability to return the financial asset based on the fair value of the financial asset.

3.6.1320.40 If there is an event of default by the seller, then the seller derecognises the financial asset and the transferee recognises the financial asset at fair value, or, if it has sold the financial asset already, derecognises the financial liability to return the financial asset.

3.6.1330 Derecognition of financial liabilities#*

IAS 39.39,
40, AG57,
AG59

3.6.1330.10 A financial liability is derecognised when it is extinguished (i.e. it is discharged, cancelled or expires). This may happen when:

- payment is made to the lender, for example when the issuer of a debt instrument redeems the instrument;

- the borrower legally is released from primary responsibility for the financial liability – this condition can be satisfied even if the borrower has given a guarantee, as long as the borrower is released from primary responsibility; or
- there is an exchange of debt instruments with substantially different terms or a substantial modification of the terms of an existing debt instrument (together referred to as "modification of terms" hereinafter).

IAS 39.AG58 3.6.1330.20 The derecognition conditions also are satisfied and a financial liability is derecognised when an entity repurchases its own debt instruments issued previously, irrespective of whether the entity intends to resell those instruments to other parties in the near term or is itself a market-maker in those instruments. This is consistent with the treatment of own equity instruments acquired by an entity, except that in the case of an extinguishment of a financial liability, a gain or loss may be recognised in profit or loss.

IAS 39.AG59, 3.6.1330.30 It is not possible for an entity to extinguish a financial liability through an
AG60 in-substance defeasance of its debt. An in-substance defeasance occurs when an entity transfers financial assets covering its obligations to a third party (typically into a trust or similar vehicle), that then makes payments to the lender from principal and interest on the transferred financial assets, without the third party having legally assumed the responsibility for the financial liability and without the lender being part of the contractual arrangements related to the third party. The entity is not legally released from the obligation, and therefore derecognition of the financial liability would be inappropriate. An entity may arrange for a third party to assume the primary responsibility for the obligation for a fee while continuing to make the contractual payments on behalf of the third party. In order for the entity to derecognise the financial liability, it should obtain legal release from the creditor whereby the creditor agrees to accept the third party as the new primary obligor.

3.6.1330.40 Similar to a financial asset, when transferring a financial liability, parts of the financial liability could be retained and new financial instruments (either financial assets or financial liabilities) could be created. The accounting is similar to the accounting for derecognition of parts of financial assets with the creation of new instruments.

3.6.1330.50 Any gain or loss arising from the extinguishment of the financial liability is recognised in profit or loss.

3.6.1335 *Forthcoming requirements*

3.6.1335.10 In November 2009 the IASB issued IFRIC 19 *Extinguishing Financial Liabilities with Equity Instruments*. The interpretation addresses the following issues in respect of the accounting by the debtor in a debt for equity swap transaction:

- Equity instruments issued to a creditor to extinguish all or part of a financial liability in a debt for equity swap are consideration paid in accordance with paragraph 41 of IAS 39.

- Equity instruments are measured at fair value, unless that fair value cannot be measured reliably, in which case the equity instruments are measured to reflect the fair value of the financial liability extinguished. The equity instruments are measured initially when the financial liability (or part of that liability) is extinguished.
- The difference between the carrying amount of the financial liability (or part of the financial liability) extinguished and the initial measurement amount of the equity instruments issued is recognised in profit or loss (see 3.6.1330).
- If only part of the financial liability is extinguished by the issue of equity instruments, an assessment is made of whether some of the consideration paid relates to a modification of the part of the liability that remains outstanding. If it does, then the consideration paid is allocated between the part of the liability extinguished and the part of the liability that remains outstanding. The consideration allocated to the part of the liability that remains outstanding forms part of the assessment of whether there has been a substantial modification of the terms of that remaining liability. Any gain or loss arising from the extinguishment of a financial liability (or a part of a financial liability) in accordance with the interpretation is disclosed as a separate line item in profit or loss or in the notes.

3.6.1335.15 The interpretation does not address the accounting by the creditor and does not apply when:

- the creditor also is an existing direct or indirect shareholder and is acting in its capacity as such;
- the creditor and the entity are controlled by the same party or parties before and after the transaction and its substance includes an equity distribution from, or contribution to, the entity; and
- the extinguishment of the financial liability by issuing equity shares is in accordance with the original terms of the financial liability.

3.6.1335.20 The interpretation is applicable for annual periods beginning on or after 1 July 2010; early application is permitted.

3.6.1340 *Modification of terms*

3.6.1340.10 Issues surrounding whether it is appropriate to derecognise a financial liability often arise when the terms of such an instrument are renegotiated, including an exchange between an existing borrower and lender of debt instruments.

IAS 39.40 3.6.1340.20 When a debt instrument is restructured or refinanced and the terms have been modified substantially, the transaction is accounted for as an extinguishment of the old debt instrument, with a gain or loss. The new debt instrument is recognised at fair value (see 3.6.920). In our view, it is not appropriate simply to assume that the nominal amount of the new loan is the fair value. In the absence of an available quoted price in an active market for the new debt instrument, fair value is established using a valuation technique. In our view, if the valuation technique does not use only data from observable markets, this does not preclude the recognition of a gain or loss as the estimate of fair value is used as the estimate of the transaction price.

3.6.1340.25 In our view, the requirements in relation to modifications and exchanges of debt instruments do not extend to the usual repayment of a loan at maturity and its replacement by a new loan at arm's length terms, even if the new loan is with the same lender, since the original loan is not modified or exchanged but is settled in accordance with its original terms. Also, we believe they do not apply to changes in the amounts or timing of payments required under a loan that arise from existing features included in the original debt agreement, e.g. interest rate step-ups or acceleration of maturity contingent on a credit downgrade, since these are not modifications of terms. However, changes in estimated cash flows attributable to such features may result in the recognition of a gain or loss (see 4.6.60).

IAS 39.AG62　3.6.1340.30 Terms are considered to have been modified substantially when the net present value of the cash flows under the new terms, including any fees paid net of any fees received and discounted using the original effective interest rate (i.e. of the original debt instrument), differs by at least 10 percent from the present value of the remaining cash flows under the original terms (the so-called "10 percent test" or "quantitative assessment").

3.6.1340.32 IAS 39 does not define the term fees in this context. In our view, fees include any payments made to or on behalf of the lender or the borrower, whether or not described as a fee, as part of the exchange or modification but do not include any payments made by the borrower or lender to its own advisers or agents, or other transaction costs incurred by the borrower or lender.

3.6.1340.34 When the terms of a debt instrument are modified and the cash flows under the new or original terms of the instruments are not fixed, IAS 39 does not contain any further guidance on how to determine the cash flows for the purpose of the 10 percent test. In our view, if either the original or new financial terms include an early prepayment, call or put feature or a term extension feature that is not separately accounted for as a derivative, then the effect of the feature should be included in determining the cash flows under the quantitative assessment. In our view, any of the following approaches would be a reasonable application of this principle:

- Calculate probability-weighted cash flows taking into account different scenarios including exercise or non-exercise of the features, and use these cash flows as the basis for the 10 percent test.
- Calculate the present value for each of the different scenarios, i.e. exercise and non-exercise. The cash flow scenario that results in the smaller difference between the present values of the cash flows under the original terms and the cash flows under the revised terms would be the basis for the 10 percent test.
- Use the outcome of the most likely scenario to determine cash flows.

3.6.1340.35 In our view, if the original terms of the debt instrument provide for a higher rate of interest in the event of default, acceleration of maturity in the event of default, or a higher credit spread in the event of credit deterioration or other contingent payment terms or unusual interest terms, then an entity should use judgement in determining the appropriate cash flows to be included in performing the 10 percent test. We believe similar judgement would apply in determining the cash flows under the new terms for the purpose of the 10 percent test. This might be reflected by using the most likely scenario or probability-weighted outcomes in performing the 10 percent test.

3.6.1340.37 For a floating rate instrument there is no explicit guidance in IAS 39 on how to determine the cash flows under the new terms or the remaining cash flows under the original terms of the debt instrument. In our view, any of the following approaches may be acceptable, as long as it is applied consistently, for determining the variable benchmark components of the cash flows under the new terms and of the remaining cash flows under the original terms to ensure a like-for-like comparison for purposes of the 10 percent test:

- the relevant benchmark interest rate determined for the current interest accrual period according to the original terms of the debt instrument;
- the relevant benchmark interest rate at the date of modification, other than any remaining coupon of the original liability for which the interest rate has been determined, in which case the contractual rate should be used; or
- the relevant benchmark interest rates for the original remaining term based on the relevant forward interest rate curve, other than any remaining coupon of the original liability for which the interest rate has been determined for which the contractual rate should be used, and the relevant benchmark interest rates for the new term of the instrument based on the relevant forward interest rate curve.

3.6.1340.38 For example, on 30 June 2010 Company S modifies the terms of a bond that was paying interest based on six month LIBOR that resets on 1 April and 1 October. On 1 April 2010, six month LIBOR was reset to 3.5 percent and as at 30 June 2010 six month LIBOR is 4 percent. Under the modified terms, the bond will bear interest at a fixed rate of 4.5 percent. We believe, for determining the cash flows under the original terms of the bond for purposes of the 10 percent test, the entity may determine the remaining future interest cash flows under the original terms of the bond by using:

- The six month LIBOR applicable to the current reset period (i.e. 3.5 percent);
- the six month LIBOR on the date of modification (i.e. 4 percent); however, the entity should use 3.5 percent for the period 1 July 2010 to 30 September 2010 as the interest rate for this period has been fixed already; or
- interest rates from the six month LIBOR forward curve; however, the entity should use 3.5 percent for the period 1 July 2010 to 30 September 2010 as the interest rate for this period has been fixed already.

3.6.1340.40 The original effective interest rate to be applied to discount the cash flows is the effective interest rate of the original unmodified instrument that is being used to calculate its amortised cost and interest expense under IAS 39. However, in our view the original effective interest rate excludes adjustments made to the effective interest rate of a debt instrument as a result of having applied fair value hedge accounting as these adjustments do not reflect changes in the amount or timing of cash flows payable on the hedged debt instruments.

3.6.1340.45 For floating rate liabilities, in our view the original effective interest rate is the current effective interest rate based on the re-pricing of the instrument's coupon to reflect movements in market rates of interest, determined according to the unmodified terms of the contract. Such an effective yield might be a variable benchmark interest rate plus/minus a margin, e.g. three-month LIBOR plus 40 basis points. In other words, the original effective interest rate should consider adjustments to the benchmark interest rate, but the original credit risk spread is held constant and is not adjusted to reflect changes in credit risk spread.

3.6.1340.50 – 70 [Not used]

3.6.1340.80 The circumstances under which a modification of the terms of a financial liability is negotiated (such as due to financial difficulties of the borrower) are not relevant in determining whether or not the modification is an extinguishment of debt.

3.6.1340.90 In our view, the derecognition assessment generally should be performed on an instrument-by-instrument basis, and not by grouping together similar financial liabilities. For example, an entity may have issued 100 individual bonds that are held by different parties, of which it intends to replace 60 with new debt instruments and redeem the other 40 bonds. The bonds should be considered individually for derecognition, i.e. the unit of account is each bond. Hence, the assessment should be made for each of the 60 bonds replaced and not for all the outstanding bonds in total. In this way the entity would derecognise 40 of the bonds that are redeemed, while the remaining 60 bonds may or may not qualify for derecognition, depending on the extent to which the terms of the original and new instruments differ. However, if an entity has issued one bond with a nominal amount of 100 held by a single party and intends to pay an amount of 40 and replace the bond with a debt instrument with modified terms and a nominal amount of 60, then the assessment is made for the bond as a whole. In our view, the agreement to make a payment of 40 is an element of the modification and accordingly that payment is taken into account in calculating the present value of cash flows under the new arrangement in the quantitative assessment. In contrast, in some cases an entity may amend or settle a proportion of a single instrument, that is a fully *pro rata* share in the cash flows of the instrument, while there is no amendment to the remaining proportion or to any other instrument entered into with the creditor; in this case, in our view, the unit of account is the part amended or settled since this is the only part whose terms are modified.

3.6.1340.92 In our view, if an entity has issued multiple instruments held by a single party and the different instruments are modified together in what in substance is a single agreement, then the entity should assess the impact of the modification by reference to the group of instruments that together is the subject of the single modification agreement. In determining whether the modification of the different instruments in substance is a single agreement, an entity should consider the indicators discussed in 3.6.690.

3.6.1340.100 In our view, if the difference in the present value of the cash flows under the quantitative assessment is at least 10 percent, then a modification should be accounted for as an extinguishment in all cases. However, if the 10 percent limit is not breached (i.e. the difference in the present values of the cash flows is less than 10 percent), then in our view an entity should perform a qualitative assessment to determine whether the terms of the two instruments are substantially different. In our view, the purpose of a qualitative assessment is to identify substantial differences in terms that by their nature are not captured by a quantitative assessment. Accordingly, we believe modifications whose effect is included in the quantitative assessment, and are not considered substantial based on that assessment, cannot be considered substantial on their own from a qualitative perspective. Such modifications may include changes in principal amounts, maturities, interest rates, prepayment options and other contingent payment terms. However, a combination of cash flow changes captured by the quantitative test, but not on their own considered substantial, and other changes not captured by the quantitative test together may be considered to constitute a substantial modification. Performance of the qualitative assessment may require a high degree of judgement based on the facts and circumstances of each individual case.

3.6.1340.101 In our view, changes in terms of the following types are of a formal or incidental nature rather than related to the substance of the liability, and accordingly we believe that they carry no weight in the assessment of whether the modification of terms is substantial:

- legal form of the instrument;
- tax treatment; and
- whether the instrument is listed.

3.6.1340.102 In our view, a substantial change in the currency of a debt instrument, or a deletion or addition of a substantial equity conversion feature to a debt instrument is a substantial modification of the terms. A change in currency is considered substantial unless the exchange rate between the old and new currencies is fixed or managed within narrow bounds by law or relevant monetary authorities. For example, a debt instrument might be modified such that the new instrument is in a different currency, and a different maturity to the existing financial liability. We believe the terms of the new debt instrument in this case would be substantially different even if the present values of the cash flows were almost identical using the quantitative test. Other modifications may require a higher degree of judgement as to whether they represent a substantial change in terms, e.g. a change in the seniority or subordination of a financial liability.

3.6.1340.103 In our view, an equity conversion option is substantial unless it is not reasonably possible that it will be exercised over its term, e.g. a call option that is deeply out-of-the money and expected to remain so. When an equity conversion option included in the original liability is modified as part of a restructuring of the debt, judgement should be applied in assessing whether the modification of the conversion option is substantial. This might include consideration of the change in fair value of the conversion option and its likelihood of exercise. When debt with detachable equity options is exchanged for convertible debt that includes non-detachable equity conversion options, this should be considered a modification of an equity conversion feature rather than its addition or deletion.

3.6.1340.104 If the terms of a financial liability are amended such that the financial liability subsequent to the amendment of the terms meets the definition of an equity instrument, then such a transaction should be accounted for as an extinguishment of a financial liability. For example, Company G issues preference shares which meet the definition of a financial liability. Subsequently, G and the holders of the preference shares agree to amend the terms of the preference shares so that they meet the criteria for equity classification (see 3.11.20.40). In our view, such a transaction involves two steps:

- an extinguishment of a financial liability; and
- the issuance of new equity instruments at fair value.

3.6.1340.105 [Not used]

3.6.1340.110 The standard does not provide guidance on the accounting treatment for the difference in the present value arising as a result of a modification in terms of a debt instrument that does not result in derecognition, i.e. because the terms are not substantially different.

3.6.1340.120 The standard states that a gain or loss can be recognised only when a debt instrument is derecognised. Consequently, when there has been a modification in the terms of a debt instrument that does not meet the derecognition conditions the carrying amount of the liability is adjusted for fees and transaction costs incurred, and no gain or loss should be recognised. In our view, any difference in present value arising as a result of the modification should be recognised as an adjustment to the effective interest rate and amortised over the remaining new life of the financial liability.

3.6.1350 *Troubled debt restructurings*

3.6.1350.10 There are no special requirements for troubled debt restructurings under IFRSs. The guidance on modifications of financial liabilities applies whether or not the borrower is experiencing financial difficulties.

3.6.1360 *Accounting for modification of terms*

IAS 39.41 3.6.1360.10 If a modification of the terms of a debt instrument meets the derecognition conditions in IAS 39, then any difference between the carrying amount of the original liability and the consideration paid is recognised in profit or loss. The consideration paid includes non-financial assets transferred and the assumption of liabilities, including the new modified financial liability. Any new financial liability recognised is measured initially at fair value. If a modification of terms is accounted for as an extinguishment, then any costs or fees incurred are recognised as part of the gain or loss on extinguishment and do not adjust the carrying amount of the new liability. Accordingly, in our view no transaction costs are included in the initial measurement of the new liability unless it can be demonstrated incontrovertibly that they relate solely to the new liability instrument and in no way to the modification of the old liability. This usually would not be possible but might apply to taxes and registration fees payable on execution of the new liability instrument.

3.6.1360.20 In our view, in the case of the forgiveness of debt, the accounting treatment should be based on an analysis of the nature of the transaction. If a shareholder forgives the debt, then it is likely that the shareholder is acting in the capacity of a shareholder and that the forgiveness of debt should be treated as a capital transaction. The outstanding financial liability should be reclassified to equity and no gain or loss should be recognised (see 3.11.230). When there is clear evidence that the shareholder is acting as a lender, i.e. in the same way as an unrelated lender, a gain or loss should be recognised in profit or loss (with related party disclosures (see 5.5)). If a government forgives a loan, then the forgiveness should be treated as a government grant (see 4.3) unless the government also is a shareholder and is acting in that capacity.

3.6.1360.30 IFRSs do not specify where in the statement of comprehensive income a gain or loss on the extinguishment of debt should be presented. In our view, it should be included within finance income or finance costs (see 4.6.230).

3.6.1370 Impairment of financial assets*

IAS 39.58 3.6.1370.10 Addressing the impairment of financial assets is a two-step process. First the entity assesses whether there is objective evidence that impairment exists for a financial asset or a group of financial assets. This assessment is done at least at each reporting date. If there is no objective evidence of impairment, then generally no further action needs to be taken at that time for that instrument. However, if there is objective evidence of impairment, then the entity calculates the amount of any impairment loss and recognises it during that reporting period.

3.6.1370.20 The assessment of whether or not objective evidence of an incurred impairment loss on a financial asset exists is based on all available information at the reporting date. However, in our view this does not imply that a full loan review in accordance with the entity's normal operating procedures should be carried out at the reporting date as long as the entity has procedures, processes and systems that provide the relevant information required for such an assessment for the purposes of financial reporting.

3.6.1370.30 As discussed in 3.6.1380, there is different guidance on impairment of investments in equity instruments compared to investments in debt instruments. IFRSs do not define a debt instrument or an equity instrument from the holder's perspective. In our view, determining whether the holder has an investment in a debt instrument or in an equity instrument requires use of judgement and consideration of facts and circumstances. A debt instrument usually is characterised by a fixed or determinable maturity and fixed or determinable payments, while an equity instrument gives the holder a residual interest in the net assets of the entity. The determination of the nature of the investment may impact impairment assessments, including identification of objective evidence of impairment and recording reversals of impairment losses. Once determined, the nature of the holder's investment should be applied consistently for purposes of other requirements of the standard that distinguish between debt and equity instruments, such as identification of the host contract for assessing embedded derivatives and reference asset for financial guarantee contracts.

3.6.1380 *Impairment of individual financial assets*

3.6.1390 *Objective evidence of impairment*

IAS 39.59 3.6.1390.10 A financial asset is considered to be impaired only if objective evidence indicates that one or more events ("loss events"), occurring after its initial recognition, have an effect on the estimated future cash flows of that asset. It may not be possible to pinpoint one specific event that caused the impairment because it may have been caused by the combined effect of a number of events.

IAS 39.59 3.6.1390.20 Indicators that a financial asset may be impaired include:

- significant financial difficulty of the issuer;
- payment defaults;
- renegotiation of the terms of an asset due to financial difficulty of the borrower;
- significant restructuring due to financial difficulty or expected bankruptcy;
- disappearance of an active market for an asset due to financial difficulties; and
- observable data indicating that there is a measurable decrease in the estimated future cash flows from a group of financial assets since their initial recognition, although the decrease cannot yet be identified with the individual assets in the group.

IAS 39.60,
IGE.4.1 3.6.1390.30 A change in credit rating is not of itself evidence of impairment. However, it may be evidence of impairment when considered with other available information, such as one of the indicators noted in 3.6.1390.20. In addition, an entity should take into account information about the debtor's/issuer's liquidity and solvency, trends for similar financial assets, and local economic trends and conditions when evaluating evidence of impairment.

3.6.1390.40 Similarly, in our view a commitment to sell a financial asset measured at amortised cost at an amount below its amortised cost is not of itself evidence of impairment, but may be evidence of impairment when considered with other available information. We believe that whether such an asset is impaired and the measurement of impairment would be based on the general impairment guidance discussed in this section focussing on the cash flows that the asset will generate. It would not be appropriate simply to write the asset down to the expected sales price or recognise a gain or loss on sale prior to derecognition of the asset. In addition, an entity should assess whether a contractual agreement to sell a financial asset at a future date should be accounted for as a derivative within the scope of IAS 39 (see 3.6.160) or is a regular way sale (see 3.6.220).

3.6.1400 Debt instruments

IS 39.59, 60   3.6.1400.10 A debt instrument is impaired if there is an indication that a loss event, that has occurred since initial recognition has a negative impact on the estimated future cash flows. Therefore, a decline in the fair value of a debt instrument due to changes in market interest rates is not in itself an indication of impairment. For example, the fair value of a fixed rate debt security would decrease if market interest rates increased. This is not evidence of impairment if the future contractual cash flows associated with the debt security still are expected to be received.

IAS 39.AG8   3.6.1400.20 A debt instrument may be acquired at a deep discount that reflects incurred credit losses (see also 5.6.170.20). Complications may arise when the carrying amount of the debt instrument is subsequently adjusted upwards due to improved recoverability, and then adjusted downwards again due to reduced recoverability. For example, an impaired debt instrument with a nominal principal of 100 initially was recognised at its fair value of 70 on acquisition, and its carrying amount (amortised cost) subsequently was increased to 80 using the effective interest method to reflect revised estimated cash flows due to increased recoverability (see 4.6.60). If the carrying amount of the debt instrument subsequently was then reduced to 75 due to further revisions to estimated cash flows as a result of reduced recoverability, a question arises as to whether the downward adjustment of 5 is an impairment loss or an adjustment to interest or other income (see 4.6.60). In our view, two approaches are possible:

- Recognise an adjustment of 5 to interest or other income (see 4.6.60) on the basis that the reduced recoverability was not below that expected on initial recognition of the debt instrument and therefore it can be argued that such a decline does not represent a loss event that has occurred since initial recognition. This analysis is based on the premise that for a loss event to occur subsequent to initial recognition, it has to reduce the expected cash flows below those expected on initial recognition.
- Recognise an impairment loss of 5 on the basis that a loss event has occurred in the period since the initial recognition of the debt instrument.

3.6.1410 Equity instruments

IAS 39.61,   3.6.1410.10 For equity instruments, impairment cannot be identified based on analys-
IGE.4.10,   ing cash flows as it can with debt instruments. Instead, if there has been a significant
IU 07-09   or prolonged decline in the fair value of an equity instrument below its cost, then this should be considered objective evidence of impairment. In our view, there is no basis for overriding this evidence in the light of qualitative factors.

IU 07-09   3.6.1410.15 For an equity instrument denominated in a foreign currency, the assessment of significant or prolonged decline in fair value is made in the functional currency of the holder of the instrument as this is consistent with how any impairment loss is determined.

IAS 39.61,   3.6.1410.20 In our view, in evaluating whether a decline in fair value is significant in
IGE.4.9   periods after an impairment loss has been recognised, the extent of the decline should be evaluated in relation to the original cost of the instrument, not its carrying amount at the date

that the last impairment loss was recognised. Similarly, in our view in evaluating whether the period of a subsequent decline in the fair value of equity instruments is prolonged, the period of the decline is the entire period for which fair value has been below cost, and not just the period since the last impairment loss was recognised. Therefore, we believe that once a decline in fair value below cost has been recognised as an impairment, any subsequent further decline below the carrying amount at the date when that impairment loss was recognised also is an impairment, even if the fair value had recovered since the original decline and regardless of whether the "new" decline is significant or prolonged.

3.6.1410.30 In our view, an entity should establish criteria that it applies consistently to determine whether a decline in a quoted market price is significant or prolonged. IFRSs do not contain any specific quantitative thresholds for "significant" or "prolonged". In our view, for equity securities that are quoted in an active market, the general concepts of significance and materiality should apply. We believe:

- a decline in excess of 20 percent generally should be regarded as significant; and
- a decline in a quoted market price that persists for nine months generally should be considered to be prolonged; however, it may be appropriate to consider a shorter period.

3.6.1410.40 In our view, apart from significant or prolonged thresholds, an entity can establish additional events triggering impairment. These can include, among other things, a combination of significant and prolonged thresholds based on the particular circumstances and nature of that entity's portfolio. For example, a decline in the fair value in excess of 15 percent persisting for six months could be determined by an entity to be an impairment trigger.

3.6.1410.50 However, in our view the combination of thresholds applied should result in a decline that is either significant or prolonged, under the guidance set out in 3.6.1410.30, being recognised as impairment.

3.6.1410.60 In our view, if a decline in fair value is significant or prolonged, then there is objective evidence of impairment and an impairment loss should be recognised, regardless of how long management intends to hold the investment. Therefore, if there has been a significant or prolonged decline in the market price at the reporting date, then an impairment loss should be recognised, even if the prospects of recovery are good.

IU 07-09 3.6.1410.65 A significant or prolonged decline in the fair value of an equity instrument below its cost which is in line with the overall level of decline in the relevant market does not mean that an entity can conclude the equity instrument is not impaired.

3.6.1410.70 A subsequent change in market value normally reflects circumstances that have arisen subsequently and, once it has been concluded that there has been a significant or prolonged decline, an impairment may not be reversed.

3.6.1410.75 In the case of shares in an investment fund, it is likely that a decrease in the fair value of an investment fund is due to an impairment of at least some of the underlying assets held by the fund. However, in our view an interest in an investment fund should be evaluated based on the fair value of the investment fund itself rather than on the underlying investments held by the fund, because there are some risks that can be evaluated only by considering the investment fund as a whole.

IAS 39.61 3.6.1410.80 Even if a decline in fair value is neither significant nor prolonged it still is necessary to consider other objective evidence that may indicate impairment. This requires an assessment of the indicators described in 3.6.1410.40, as well as significant changes in the technological, market, economic or legal environment in which the issuer operates that may affect the fair value of an investment in the equity instruments of that issuer negatively. In practice additional indicators and sources of evidence of impairment of equity securities may include:

- a decline in the fair value of the equity instrument that seems to be related to issuer conditions rather than to general market or industry conditions;
- market and industry conditions, to the extent that they influence the recoverable amount of the financial asset (e.g. if the fair value at the acquisition date had been extremely high due to a market level that is unlikely to be recovered in the future, this may be an impairment indicator due to pure market and/or industry conditions);
- a declining relationship of market price per share to net asset value per share at the date of evaluation compared to the relationship at acquisition;
- a declining price/earnings ratio at the time of evaluation compared to at the acquisition date;
- financial conditions and near-term prospects of the issuer, including any specific adverse events that may influence the issuer's operations;
- recent losses of the issuer;
- a qualified independent auditor's report on the issuer's most recent financial statements;
- negative changes in the dividend policy of the issuer, such as a decision to suspend or decrease dividend payments; and
- realisation of a loss on subsequent disposal of the investment.

IAS 39.61 3.6.1410.90 In our view, this assessment should be performed for all equity securities whose fair value is below cost, but for which the decline in fair value is not considered significant or prolonged. In our view, the higher or longer the entity's thresholds for determining whether a decline is significant or prolonged, the more comprehensive the qualitative evaluation needs to be.

3.6.1410.100 Generally, we would expect an equity security to become impaired earlier than a debt security issued by the same counterparty due to the nature of each instrument and the rights each conveys to its holder.

3.6.1420 Portfolios of assets

IAS 39.59(f) 3.6.1420.10 A decrease in the estimated future cash flows from a group of financial assets usually indicates impairment of that group of assets. Evidence of a decrease in estimated cash flows from a group of assets includes:

- an adverse change in the payment status of borrowers in the group (e.g. an increased number of customers exceeding their credit limit or not making payments on time); or
- a change in national or local economic conditions that is likely to cause higher defaults on payments.

3.6.1430 *Impairment loss calculations*

IAS 39.58 3.6.1430.10 If there is objective evidence that a financial asset is impaired, then the entity determines the amount of any impairment loss. The measurement of the impairment loss differs for assets carried at amortised cost or cost, and available-for-sale financial assets. For assets carried at amortised cost, impairment is measured based on incurred credit losses using the instrument's original effective interest rate (see 3.6.1430.15). However, for available-for-sale financial assets an impairment loss is calculated based on fair value, which reflects market interest rates and market expectations of expected future, as well as incurred, credit losses. These differences are summarised below.

IAS 39.AG8, 3.6.1430.15 In calculating an impairment loss for a financial asset (or a group of financial
AG84 assets) carried at amortised cost, an entity uses the financial asset's *original* effective interest rate to discount the estimated future cash flows. In computing the original effective interest rate an entity takes into account the following:

- For a variable rate financial asset measured at amortised cost, the discount rate used is the current effective interest rate(s) determined under the contract. Such an effective yield might be a variable benchmark interest rate plus/minus a margin, e.g. three-month LIBOR plus 40 basis points. In other words the appropriate current effective interest rate should consider adjustments for the variable benchmark interest rate, but the original credit risk spread should be held constant and not be adjusted to reflect changes in credit risk spread.
- When a financial asset has been reclassified out of the available-for-sale category to loans and receivables (see 3.6.880.06) or out of the fair value through profit or loss category (see 3.6.860.15), a new original effective interest rate is calculated based on the expected future cash flows as of the reclassification date. This effective interest rate would be adjusted if the entity, subsequent to reclassification, increases its estimates of future cash receipts as a result of increased recoverability of those cash receipts (see 4.6.60.15).
- When the financial asset is the hedged item in a fair value hedge, the original effective interest rate is adjusted to take account of recognised changes in fair value attributable to the hedged risk (see 3.6.1480.40).
- In the event that the terms of a loan, receivable or held-to-maturity investment are renegotiated or modified due to financial difficulties of the borrower or issuer, impairment is measured using the original effective interest rate before the modification of the terms.

IAS 12.58, 3.6.1430.20 An impairment loss may be recognised by writing down the asset or
39.63 recording an allowance to be deducted from the carrying amount of the asset. If the impairment loss relates to an available-for-sale asset and a deferred tax liability or deferred

tax asset was recognised previously for an unrealised gain or loss on the instrument, then the deferred tax amount also is recognised in profit or loss (see 3.13.370).

3.6.1440 Loans and receivables and held-to-maturity investments

IAS 39.59, 63   3.6.1440.10 An impairment loss for financial assets measured at amortised cost is the difference between the asset's carrying amount and the present value of the estimated future cash flows discounted at the asset's original effective interest rate (see 3.6.1430.15). The estimated future cash flows include only those credit losses that have been incurred at the time of the impairment loss calculation, i.e. an "incurred loss model". Losses expected as a result of future events, no matter how likely, are not taken into account. This is particularly relevant when financial assets are evaluated for impairment collectively.

IAS 39.63,   3.6.1440.20 The asset's original effective interest rate (see 3.6.1430.15) is used in cal-
AG84   culating the impairment loss because discounting at the current market rate of interest would, in effect, impose fair value measurement on the financial asset. This would not be appropriate as such assets are measured at amortised cost. The aim of this requirement is to recognise losses due to changes in expected cash flows as a result of loss events occurring after initial recognition, not to reflect changes in the value of the asset due to changes in credit spreads or market interest rates.

3.6.1450 Available-for-sale financial assets

IAS 39.67,   3.6.1450.10 For financial assets measured at fair value, impairment is an issue only for
IGE.4.9   those classified as available for sale since changes in fair value are recognised in other comprehensive income rather than in profit or loss. For such assets, when there is objective evidence of impairment, the cumulative loss that had been recognised in other comprehensive income is reclassified from equity to profit or loss. Furthermore, once an investment in equity instruments has been impaired, all subsequent losses are recognised in profit or loss until the asset is derecognised.

IAS 39.68   3.6.1450.20 In the case of an equity instrument included in the available-for-sale category, the cumulative loss referred to in 3.6.1450.10 is the difference between the acquisition cost (see 3.6.1280.50) and the current fair value of the instrument, less any impairment loss on that equity instrument previously recognised in profit or loss. In the case of a debt instrument included in the available-for-sale category, the cumulative loss is the difference between the amortised cost, i.e. the acquisition cost net of principal repayments and amortisation, and the current fair value of the instrument, less any impairment loss on that debt instrument previously recognised in profit or loss.

IAS 39.68   3.6.1450.30 Any previous net upward revaluation recognised in other comprehensive income in respect of the asset is reversed first. Any additional write-down below the initial amount recognised for the asset is recorded as an impairment loss in profit or loss.

IAS 39.68   3.6.1450.40 If the asset previously was revalued through other comprehensive income to an amount below the carrying amount at initial recognition, then the cumulative loss that had been recognised in other comprehensive income in respect of that asset is re-classified from equity and recognised as an impairment loss in profit or loss. The entire amount of the revaluation below original cost is recognised as an impairment loss even if the estimated cash flows indicate that some of that decline is reversible.

IAS 39.IG   3.6.1450.50 The implementation guidance to IAS 39 acknowledges that the available-
E4.10   for-sale revaluation reserve in equity may become negative. This may occur naturally through the remeasurement to fair value of available-for-sale assets and is not necessarily an indication that the available-for-sale asset is impaired and that the cumulative net loss that has been recognised in other comprehensive income should be reclassified to profit or loss. There is detailed guidance on indicators of impairment, and the decline in the fair value as evidence of impairment.

3.6.1455 Subsequent impairment of available-for-sale debt instruments

3.6.1455.10 When an available-for-sale debt instrument is impaired, IAS 39 does not address explicitly the accounting treatment of a subsequent further decline in the fair value when there is no objective evidence of any further credit-related loss event. In our view, an entity should choose an accounting policy, to be applied consistently, as to whether to recognise such further declines either in other comprehensive income or in profit or loss. See 3.6.1520.60 for a discussion of the possible interrelationship with the entity's accounting policy for reversals of impairment losses on available-for-sale debt instruments. Before applying an accounting policy to recognise such a further decline in other comprehensive income, an entity should first consider all available evidence to determine whether the further decline in fair value is objective evidence of a further credit-related loss event, including consideration of the magnitude and duration of the subsequent loss. If there is objective evidence of a further credit-related loss event, the further decline in fair value is recognised in profit or loss.

3.6.1460 Impairment examples

3.6.1460.10 For example, Bank Y granted a loan (classified as loans and receivables) in 2007 to Company Z. The interest rate on the loan was 10 percent and the loan was issued at 98 percent of its face value. The maturity date is 31 December 2011. The effective interest rate at the date of origination was 10.53 percent.

3.6.1460.20 At 31 December 2009 it becomes clear that Z is experiencing severe financial difficulties and Y determines that this represents objective evidence that the loan is impaired. At that date the carrying amount of the loan at amortised cost is 49,539.

3.6.1460.30 Y expects that it will receive the contractual interest payment of 10 percent due at 31 December 2010. However, on maturity of the loan, Y expects to recover only 25,000 of the 50,000 principal due and does not expect to receive the interest payment due at 31 December 2011.

3.6.1460.40 The impairment loss is measured as the difference between the carrying amount of the loan and the present value of the estimated future cash flows on the loan, using as a discount rate the original effective interest rate of 10.53 percent. Given that only 25,000 of the principal and the 31 December 2010 interest payment are expected to be received, the present value using the original effective interest rate is 24,985. Assume that accrued interest is paid at 31 December 2009 and therefore is not included in the calculation. The discounted remaining cash flows are calculated as follows:

$$24,985 = \frac{5,000}{1.1053} + \frac{25,000}{(1.1053)^2}$$

3.6.1460.50 An impairment loss of 24,554 (49,539 - 24,985) should be recognised in profit or loss. Y should reassess the impairment loss at each reporting date.

3.6.1460.60 If this loan had been classified as available for sale, then the amount of the impairment loss would be measured as the difference between the acquisition cost of the loan, net of principal repayments and amortisation, and the current fair value of the loan.

3.6.1460.70 Y calculates the fair value of the loan by obtaining the current market interest rate for loans similar to the loan under consideration and uses this to discount the estimated future cash flows of the loan. Assume for loans to entities with similar credit risk profiles as Z, and that have terms and structures similar to Z's loan, an effective interest rate of 12.5 percent would apply. Y uses this rate to determine the fair value of the loan as follows:

$$24,198 = \frac{5,000}{1.125} + \frac{25,000}{(1.125)^2}$$

3.6.1460.80 The calculated fair value of 24,198 results in an impairment loss of 25,341 (49,539 - 24,198). This represents the amount that should be reclassified from equity to profit or loss. It is adjusted for any amount reclassified from equity to profit or loss previously.

3.6.1460.90 Assume the same information as in 3.6.1460.10 – 60, except that the loan (classified as available for sale) is collateralised by liquid securities. Y expects that it will be able to recover only the amount owed on the loan by taking legal possession of the securities.

3.6.1460.100 The fair value of the loan would not exceed the fair value of the securities less any costs expected to obtain and sell the securities (see 3.6.1490.25). The cumulative loss to be reclassified from equity to profit or loss is calculated as the difference between the loan's acquisition cost, net of principal repayments and amortisation, and the fair value calculated by reference to the collateral. However, the collateral itself should not be recognised in Y's statement of financial position until the securities meet the recognition criteria for financial assets.

3.6.1470 Assets measured at cost because fair value is not reliably measurable

IAS 39.66   3.6.1470.10 For financial assets measured at cost because their fair value is not reliably measurable (i.e. certain unquoted equity instruments and derivatives linked to such instruments (see 3.6.980)), the impairment loss is measured as the difference between the carrying amount and the present value of estimated future cash flows discounted at the current market rate of return for a similar financial asset.

3.6.1480 Hedged assets

IAS 36.58   3.6.1480.10 The principles for hedge accounting do not override the accounting treatment under IAS 36 *Impairment of Assets* or IAS 39 if there is impairment of the hedged item. Therefore, if a hedged item is impaired, then this impairment is recognised even if the risk that causes the impairment is being hedged and hedge accounting is being applied. However, the hedge accounting principles may require that a gain on a hedging instrument used to hedge the risk that gave rise to the impairment be recognised simultaneously in profit or loss and offset (partly) against the recognised impairment.

IAS 39.59, 61   3.6.1480.20 For example, Company T holds a portfolio of securities that are classified as available for sale. The fair value of the portfolio is 300. T has an option to put the securities to a third party for a fixed price of 250. T may apply hedge accounting to this transaction provided that the hedge relationship meets the relevant criteria (see 3.7.120). T designates the option as a hedge of the cash flows from an expected future sale of the securities, with the hedged risk being the elimination of the variability in cash flows arising from the price of the securities going below 250. Assume that the fair value of the portfolio subsequently decreases by 120 and that there is objective evidence of impairment. The amount of the impairment, which should be recognised in profit or loss, is the difference between the original fair value of the securities (300) and the new fair value (180), irrespective of whether or not the entity has hedged the downside risk using an option. However, since at this point the impairment on the hedged item affects profit or loss, the related gain on the put option also would be recognised in profit or loss. This means that a gain of 70 (250 - 180), ignoring time value, will be recognised in profit or loss and will partly offset the loss on the securities.

IAS 39.97, 98   3.6.1480.30 For cash flow hedges of highly probable acquisitions of financial and non-financial assets, amounts previously recognised in other comprehensive income may be reclassified from equity to profit or loss when the asset affects profit or loss. For non-financial assets this is only possible if the accounting policy is not to apply a basis adjustment for such items. In the event that such an asset is impaired, an appropriate amount of the gain or loss previously recognised in other comprehensive income should be reclassified from equity to profit or loss.

IAS 39.IG   3.6.1480.40 In a fair value hedge, both the original effective interest rate (see 3.6.1430.15)
E.4.4   and the amortised cost of the hedged item are adjusted to take account of recognised changes in fair value attributable to the hedged risk. The adjusted effective interest rate is calculated using the adjusted carrying amount of the loan. The impairment assessment

is based on the carrying amount of the asset after any adjustments as a result of applying hedge accounting, which is compared to the estimated future cash flows of the hedged item discounted at the original effective interest rate adjusted for changes in fair value attributable to the hedged risk.

3.6.1490 *Collateral*

AS 39.AG84,   3.6.1490.10 If the entity holds collateral for a financial asset, and the collateral does not
IGE.4.8   qualify for recognition as a separate asset under other standards, then the collateral is not recognised as an asset separate from the impaired financial asset before foreclosure as this would result in double counting.

3.6.1490.20 In our view, the accounting treatment of collateral after foreclosure is dependent upon the legal environment in which the entity operates and the terms on which the collateral is provided. For example, in the case of a mortgage loan collateralised by a property two distinct sets of circumstances could apply:

- The bank (lender) could repossess the property as a result of the borrower's default with the intention of recovering the amounts owing on the understanding that: any amounts received in excess of the mortgage balance will be refunded to the borrower; and any shortfall remains the obligation of the borrower. The bank may continue to charge interest on the outstanding balance. The bank remains exposed to interest rate risk on the mortgage and is not exposed to property price risk. We believe repossession is used only to reinforce the bank's contractual right to cash flows from the loan, and consequently the bank should continue to recognise the loan and should not recognise the property.
- The bank could repossess the property, which in terms of the contract comprises the full and final settlement of the mortgage, i.e. the bank retains any excess proceeds over the outstanding balance on the mortgage and the borrower is released of its obligation in the event of a shortfall. Therefore, the bank is exposed to property price risk rather than to interest rate risk on the loan, and we believe the bank should derecognise the loan and recognise the property.

AS 39.AG84   3.6.1490.25 If the entity holds collateral for a financial asset carried at amortised cost that is not accounted for separately from that financial asset, then in calculating the impairment loss in respect of that financial asset, an entity could choose to use either of the following approaches whether or not foreclosure is probable:

- *Approach 1.* Use the fair value of the collateral at the reporting date less costs for obtaining and selling the collateral; or
- *Approach 2.* Use the cash flows that may result from foreclosure less the costs for obtaining and selling the collateral.

3.6.1490.27 Under approach 1 in 3.6.1490.25, in determining the cash flows from the collateral, an entity uses the current fair value of the collateral on the reporting date assuming that this current fair value will be realised in future, and then discounts this current fair value back to the reporting date using the financial asset's original effective interest rate (see 3.6.1430.15). Under approach 2 in 3.6.1490.25, in determining the cash flows from the collateral, an entity estimates the fair value of the collateral at the expected future date of realisation of the collateral and then discounts this value back to the reporting date using the financial asset's original effective interest rate (see 3.6.1430.15).

3.6.1490.30 For example, Bank S issues a mortgage loan of 10,000, which is collateralised by the financed residential property. At the reporting date S identified objective evidence of impairment and estimated that the only cash flows to be received will arise from the foreclosure of the collateral. The current fair value of the collateral is estimated at 10,000. It will take S two years to foreclose the collateral and during this period no other cash flows are expected. In our view, when computing the impairment loss, if S elects to use the current fair value of the collateral in determining cash flows from the collateral for computing the impairment loss, then S should discount the current fair value of the collateral (i.e. 10,000) using the loan's original effective interest rate (see 3.6.1430.15). The impairment loss recognised would be the difference between the loan's carrying amount and the net present value of the estimated future cash flows.

3.6.1490.40 When measuring an impairment loss incurred on a financial asset originated in the entity's functional currency but collateralised by an asset denominated in foreign currency, in our view the estimated foreign currency future cash flows resulting from the foreclosure of the collateral should be translated into the functional currency of the reporting entity using the appropriate forward rates and then discounted together with the estimated cash flows in the functional currency, if any, using the instrument's original effective interest rate (see 3.6.1430.15).

3.6.1490.50 When an entity is calculating the impairment loss for a collateralised financial asset, in our view a gain should not be recognised, even if the collateral is expected to have a higher value than the carrying amount of the loan, if any surplus will be returned to the borrower.

3.6.1490.60 On the date of foreclosure, in our view any collateral received initially should be measured based on the carrying amount of the defaulted loan. Thereafter it should be accounted for under the relevant standard and classified as held for sale if appropriate (see 5.4.20).

3.6.1500 *Reversals of impairment losses*

3.6.1510 Loans and receivables and held-to-maturity investments

IAS 39.65 3.6.1510.10 If in a subsequent period, the amount of any impairment loss of a loan or receivable or held-to-maturity investment decreases due to an event occurring subsequent to the write-down, then the previously recognised impairment loss is reversed through profit or loss with a corresponding increase in the carrying amount of the underlying asset. The reversal is limited to an amount that does not state the asset at more than what its amortised cost would have been in the absence of impairment.

3.6.1520 Available-for-sale financial assets

IAS 39.69 3.6.1520.10 Impairment losses on an available-for-sale equity instrument may not be reversed through profit or loss. Any increase in the fair value of such an instrument after an impairment loss has been recognised is treated as a revaluation and is recognised in other comprehensive income.

3.6.1520.20 [Not used]

IAS 39.70 3.6.1520.30 If, in a subsequent period, the fair value of an available-for-sale debt instrument increases and the increase can be objectively related to an event occurring after the impairment loss was recognised, then the impairment loss is reversed, with the amount of the reversal recognised in profit or loss. IAS 39 does not further describe the nature of an "event" that gives rise to reversal of an impairment loss through profit or loss, nor does it discuss situations in which there continues to be some objective evidence of impairment but in which the amount of the impairment may be reduced. This raises two questions: what types of events trigger reversal; and how to measure the amount of any reversal.

3.6.1520.40 In our view, entities should choose an accounting policy, to be applied consistently, with regard to the nature of an event that would trigger reversal. In particular:

- An entity may limit reversals to reversals of credit events that gave rise to the impairment and that have a positive impact on the estimated future cash flows of the asset (option 1).
- An entity may interpret reversal events as also including subsequent improvements in the credit standing of the issuer that do not affect the estimate of expected future cash flows from the asset, and then should specify criteria for identifying such events (option 2).
- Alternatively, an entity may interpret reversal events to include also any event that reverses an amount that was included in the measurement of the original impairment (see 3.6.1430.10). For example, to the extent that the original impairment loss included a decline in the fair value of the asset related to an increase in benchmark interest rates, a subsequent increase in the fair value related to a subsequent decline in benchmark interest rates would represent a reversal event (option 3).

3.6.1520.50 In developing their accounting policies, entities also should consider how to measure the amount of the impairment loss that is reversed through profit or loss when there is an increase in fair value and a reversal event has been identified. In our view:

- If there is no longer objective evidence that the asset is impaired at the reporting date, then, depending on its accounting policy under 3.6.1520.40, the entity reverses through profit or loss either (1) the full original impairment loss previously recognised in profit or loss; or (2) the lesser of the full original impairment loss previously recognised in profit or loss and the subsequent increase in fair value.

- If there continues to be objective evidence of impairment at the reporting date but the amount of the original impairment loss was reduced, then the cumulative loss that continues to be recognised in profit or loss is not less than any excess of the original cost over the current fair value of the asset. When option 3 as described in 3.6.1520.40 is applied and there is no improvement in the credit standing of the issuer, the amount of reversal is limited to the portion of the original impairment loss which actually has been reversed as a result of a subsequent decrease in benchmark interest rates (or other relevant factor).
- For purposes of measuring the amount of impairment loss to be reversed, the original impairment loss as well as the subsequent increase in fair value are reduced for any increase in the amortised cost of the debt instrument due to interest accretion recognised in profit or loss subsequent to recognition of original impairment.

3.6.1520.60 The scenarios in 3.6.1520.61 – 67 illustrate the application of these principles.

3.6.1520.61 *Scenario 1.* An entity purchases an available-for-sale debt instrument for 100. The fair value of the instrument decreases to 70, and an impairment loss of 30 is recognised in profit or loss. Subsequently the fair value of the instrument increases to 95, the amortised cost is 74 and the entity determines that there is no longer any objective evidence of impairment.

3.6.1520.62 Depending on its chosen accounting policy, an entity would either (1) recognise in profit or loss the reversal of 26 comprising the full amount of the original impairment loss of 30 less the subsequent increase of 4 in the amortised cost of the instrument and record the current cumulative loss (the amount by which fair value is below original cost) of 5 in other comprehensive income; or (2) recognise in profit or loss only 21 as a reversal of original impairment, being the subsequent increase in fair value of 25 less the subsequent increase of 4 in the amortised cost of the instrument.

3.6.1520.63 *Scenario 2.* An entity purchases an available-for-sale debt instrument for 100. The fair value of the instrument decreases to 70 and an impairment loss of 30 is recognised in profit or loss. The entity determines that this loss comprises the effect of a credit-related decrease in estimated future cash flows of 20 and the effect of an increase in the liquidity/risk premium of 10. Subsequently the fair value of the instrument increases to 75 and the amortised cost to 72; there is no change in the estimated future cash flows and the entity determines that the entire subsequent net increase in the fair value of 3, net of interest accretion of 2 recognised in profit or loss, relates to a subsequent reduction in the liquidity/risk premium.

3.6.1520.64 Under option 1 as described in 3.6.1520.40, the entity would recognise the subsequent net increase in fair value of 3 in other comprehensive income as there is no credit-related increase in expected future cash flows. Under option 3, the entity would recognise the net increase in fair value of 3 in profit or loss as there was a partial reversal of the increase in liquidity/risk premium that was included in the measurement of the original impairment loss. Under option 2, the answer would depend on the entity's policy for identifying improvements in the credit standing of the issuer.

3.6.1520.65 *Scenario 3*. An entity purchases an available-for-sale debt instrument for 100. The fair value of the instrument decreases to 70 and an impairment loss of 30 is recognised in profit or loss. The entity determines that this loss comprises the effect of a credit-related decrease in future cash flows of 20 and the effect of an increase in the risk-free interest rate of 10. Subsequently the fair value of the instrument increases to 85; there is no change in the estimated future cash flows and the entity determines that the entire subsequent increase in the fair value of 15 relates to a reduction in the risk-free interest rate. Assume that there is no interest accretion in the intervening period.

3.6.1520.66 Under options 1 and 2 as described in 3.6.1520.40, the entity would record the subsequent increase in fair value in other comprehensive income as there is no credit-related increase in future cash flows and no other improvement in the credit standing of the issuer.

3.6.1520.67 Under option 3, the entity would record 10 of the increase in fair value in profit or loss as there was a reversal of the increase in the risk-free interest rate that was one of the events that was incorporated in the original impairment loss. The entity would not record the entire fair value increase of 15 related to the reduction in the risk-free rate in profit or loss as the amount of reversal is limited to the portion of the original impairment loss, which actually has been reversed as a result of the subsequent decrease in the risk-free rate.

3.6.1520.70 In our view, the accounting policy choices adopted in respect of reversals of impairments do not necessitate the selection of particular accounting policies in respect of subsequent impairments, or *vice versa* (see 3.6.1450.65). However, IAS 8 *Accounting Policies, Changes in Accounting Estimates and Errors* requires that management use its judgement in developing accounting policies that result in information that is, *inter alia*, neutral and prudent. Accordingly, entities should consider whether selection of policies that would lead to both (a) subsequent declines (losses) in the fair value of an impaired debt instrument arising from changes in interest rates and risk premiums being recognised in other comprehensive income; and (b) subsequent increases (gains) arising from the same cause, without any improvement in expected cash recoveries, being recognised in profit or loss would be consistent with these criteria.

3.6.1530 Assets carried at cost because fair value is not reliably measurable

IAS 39.66   3.6.1530.10 For an investment in unquoted equity instruments and a derivative asset that is linked to and should be settled by delivery of such an instrument, both of which are carried at cost because their fair value cannot be measured reliably, impairment losses may not be reversed.

IFRIC 10.8   3.6.1530.20 Under IFRSs an entity is prohibited from reversing an impairment loss, recognised in a previous interim period, in respect of an available-for-sale equity instrument or a financial instrument carried at cost (not amortised cost).

3.6.1540 [Not used]

3.6.1550 *Measuring impairment of financial assets denominated in a foreign currency*

3.6.1550.10 For monetary financial assets denominated in a foreign currency, there is no specific guidance on how to measure impairment losses. In our view, the present value of estimated future cash flows or fair value of the asset first is determined in the foreign currency. This amount should be translated into the functional currency using the exchange rate at the date that the impairment is recognised. The difference between the translated amount and the carrying amount in the functional currency is recognised in profit or loss. In certain circumstances, this may lead to an impairment loss determined in the foreign currency, and a foreign exchange gain on translation of the carrying amount of the financial asset into the functional currency.

IAS 39.65 3.6.1550.20 Foreign exchange gains and losses on an impaired monetary financial asset measured at amortised cost continue to be recognised in profit or loss. If, through a subsequent improvement in circumstances, an entity is able to reverse the impairment loss, in part or entirely, then in our view such reversal should be recognised at the spot exchange rate at the date that the reversal is recognised.

IAS 21.23, 3.6.1550.30 For non-monetary financial assets classified as available for sale, the amount
39.68, of loss to be removed from equity and included in profit or loss is the cumulative net
IGE.4.9 difference between the asset's acquisition cost and current fair value in the functional currency. This will include all foreign currency changes on the asset that had been recognised in other comprehensive income.

IAS 39.69, 70 3.6.1550.40 We prefer that an entity records any subsequent reversal of impairment of a debt instrument classified as available for sale at the spot rate in effect on the date that the reversal is recognised. Any subsequent reversal is limited to the amount of loss, denominated in foreign currency, previously recognised. In our view, until the previously recognised loss denominated in foreign currency is reversed fully, the related exchange differences should be recognised in profit or loss. As a minimum, the accounting treatment applied should be disclosed along with the nature and the amount of any impairment loss or reversal.

3.6.1550.50 Generally, changes in foreign exchange rates would not trigger an assessment of impairment for an investment in a debt instrument. However, there may be situations when the fair value of an asset in its currency of denomination is affected by exchange rates. This may occur if there is a sudden and severe devaluation of a foreign currency. The devaluation of the currency may influence the credit risk and country risk associated with entities operating in that environment. In our view, an entity that has foreign currency loans or receivables or that holds debt securities denominated in a foreign currency that becomes devalued should consider whether the decline should be treated as an impairment loss rather than as a normal foreign exchange translation loss.

3.6.1560 *Collective impairment assessment*

3.6.1570 *Determining whether an individual or collective assessment is appropriate*

IAS 39.64,
AG88,
IGE.4.7

3.6.1570.10 An entity starts the impairment assessment by considering whether objective evidence of impairment exists for financial assets that are individually significant. For financial assets that are not individually significant, the assessment can be performed on an individual or collective (portfolio) basis. If an asset is assessed individually for impairment and found to be impaired, then it is not included in a collective assessment for impairment.

IAS 39.
BC114

3.6.1570.20 IAS 39 does not provide specific guidance on determining whether or not a loan is individually significant. Rather, the standard indicates that the assessment of significance differs from one entity to another such that identical exposures will be evaluated on different bases, individually or collectively, depending on their significance to the entity holding them. In our view, an entity may use its normal loan review policies and procedures in determining what is considered a significant exposure.

3.6.1570.25 An entity may reclassify a financial asset from the available-for-sale category to loans and receivables (see 3.6.880). If such a financial asset is subsequently impaired, then the gain or loss that was recognised previously in other comprehensive income is reclassified to profit or loss (see 3.6.1570.10). In our view, this requires the entity to assess whether each individual reclassified financial asset is impaired at the end of each reporting period following reclassification.

3.6.1570.27 If the entity does not identify an impairment of an individual reclassified asset, then the entity includes, if appropriate, that reclassified asset in a collective assessment of impairment (see 3.6.1570.40 and 50). If the entity identifies impairment on a collective basis, then in our view it is not necessary for the entity to reclassify from equity to profit or loss the full amount of loss recognised in other comprehensive income in respect of the asset prior to reclassification.

IAS 39.64

3.6.1570.30 A collective evaluation of impairment is performed for:

- assets that have not been assessed individually for impairment; and
- assets that are tested individually but for which no impairment is identified.

3.6.1570.33 In our view, a collective evaluation of impairment for available-for-sale financial assets is not required.

IAS 39.AG88

3.6.1570.35 Impairment losses recognised on a collective basis represent an interim step pending the identification of impairment losses on individual assets in the group of financial assets that are collectively assessed for impairment. As soon as information is available that specifically identifies losses on individually impaired assets in a group, those assets are no longer included in the collective evaluation for impairment.

3.6.1570.40 In the case of assets tested individually but not impaired, an entity might conclude that no collective provision is required, either because no portfolio of similar items can be identified, or because all possible risks have been considered in the individual impairment tests.

IAS 39.64,   3.6.1570.50 A collective assessment of impairment is required for financial assets that
AG87,   have been assessed individually for impairment and found not to be impaired, e.g.
IGE.4.7   impairment triggers have been identified but no impairment loss is recognised, for example due to sufficient collateral. However, loss probabilities and other loss statistics differ at a group level between assets that have been evaluated individually for impairment and found not to be impaired and assets that have not been assessed individually for impairment, with the result that a different amount of impairment loss may be required. Therefore, in our view financial assets that have been assessed individually for impairment and found not to be impaired generally should be treated as one or more separate portfolios for the purpose of the collective assessment of impairment based on the principle that financial assets should be grouped into homogenous portfolios, i.e. based on similar credit risk characteristics. For example, if the underlying reason for not recording an impairment loss is sufficient collateral for some of those financial assets, and a change in the expected cash flow structure for the other financial assets, then normally those financial assets are not homogenous as they do not share the same credit risk characteristics and hence should be treated as two separate portfolios.

IAS 39.AG87   3.6.1570.60 Assets are grouped for collective assessment for impairment only if the assets share similar credit risk characteristics. Groups of assets that share similar credit risk characteristics may be identified based on:

- credit risk grades
- types of loan
- geographic location of the borrower
- type of collateral
- type of counterparty
- aging profile
- maturity.

3.6.1570.70 In our view, a portfolio approach to impairment is not appropriate for individual equity instruments because equity instruments of different issuers do not have similar risk characteristics, and therefore their equity price risk differs.

3.6.1570.80 Impairment recognised with respect to non-performing loans differs from that in respect of performing loans. With respect to performing loans the approach used in assessing impairment is aimed at minimising detection risk (i.e. the risk that a loss, which has been incurred but not yet reported, will not be detected). In contrast, the assessment of non-performing loans for impairment is not subject to detection risk since these loans already have been identified as possibly being impaired.

3.6.1580 *Recognition of impairment losses incurred but not reported*

AS 39.AG89 3.6.1580.10 IAS 39 requires the recognition of impairment in respect of losses that have been "incurred but not reported". The objective of the collective assessment for impairment is to identify losses that have been incurred, but not yet identified, on an individual basis.

AS 39.AG90 3.6.1580.20 Of particular relevance to a collective assessment of impairment is the example of deaths of cardholders in a credit card portfolio, which is identified as the major cause of defaults. This example assumes that while the death rate may not change from year to year, it is reasonable to assume that some deaths have occurred, and therefore that the portfolio contains assets that are impaired even if the impaired loans have not been identified individually. It is clear from IAS 39 that an unchanged death rate represents observable data supporting the estimate that one or more borrowers have died and that, based on experience, this will result in the loss of one or more cash flows. Because observable data includes unchanged data, normally there will be observable data that, through the passage of time, can be used to support estimates based on historical loss experience.

3.6.1580.30 For a portfolio of loans it has been suggested that it may be more appropriate to refer to "risk conditions" being in place as indicators of impairment, rather than "impairment triggers", since triggers may not be specifically or individually identified or captured. Risk conditions represent a set of market and economic events or variables which are associated, based on historical evidence, with the impairment of financial assets.

3.6.1580.40 In our view, the approach of considering risk conditions rather than impairment triggers is consistent with the requirements in IAS 39 as long as each risk condition is associated with a combination of observable data that is relevant to losses in that portfolio and that has been observed in practice. In our view, it is not necessary to establish statistical cause-and-effect relationships between a change in a risk condition and an estimate of incurred losses. However, we believe that the number of risk conditions identified should be sufficient that it is possible to find a set of historical data that approximates closely the actual data that is observed at the reporting date. Over time an entity should develop its database of observed risk conditions to improve and update its ability to match risk conditions with an estimate of incurred losses.

3.6.1580.50 An entity not having its own specific historical data is not a sufficient rationale for not performing the collective impairment assessment. Relevant and reliable information available in the market should be obtained to perform the assessment. However, the historical data used, whether internal or external, should be consistent with the characteristics of the group of financial assets being tested.

3.6.1580.60 The historical data used in the analysis should support the assessment of losses incurred but not reported and should:

- reflect the relationship between a change in the factor and impairment loss; these may be social drivers or economic factors; and

- be updated to reflect current economic conditions resulting in impairment losses recognised being directionally consistent with changes in related observable data from period to period.

3.6.1580.70 In our view, the practical implementation of the requirements to recognise impairment losses incurred but not reported on loans and receivables can be based on the analysis of historical loss data, together with the analysis of the underlying factors causing loss, and the emergence periods.

3.6.1590 *Emergence period*

3.6.1590.10 One of the possible methodologies for quantifying the collective allowance, or component thereof, is the "emergence period" approach. This approach recognises that there will be a period between the occurrence of a specific impairment event and objective evidence of impairment becoming apparent on an individual basis. In other words, it is the time it takes an entity to identify that the loss event actually occurred or a time period that lapses between the date that the loss event occurred and the date that an entity identified that it had occurred. This period is referred to as the emergence period.

3.6.1590.20 In our view, an emergence period should be established individually for each entity, each portfolio and/or possibly for each risk condition or combination thereof. Emergence periods may vary across entities, portfolios and according to the risk conditions.

IAS 39.AG89   3.6.1590.30 As a result, entities can use historical loss experience as indicators of impairment provided it can be linked to the factors (risk conditions) causing impairment loss, e.g. interest rates, unemployment rates, GDP growth rate etc. Consequently, entities should recognise an impairment loss subsequent to the loan origination date if historical loss experience indicates that X percent of loans have become impaired as a result of the risk conditions in place, and it takes an entity Y months (emergence period) to identify which individual exposures became impaired. In our view, the emergence period generally should be relatively short, but this will depend on the entity's credit risk management policies and procedures, the nature of the portfolio being considered (e.g. consumer or commercial loans, credit card balances or mortgage loans), and the relevant risk conditions. We believe that it is unlikely that an emergence period will exceed 12 months.

3.6.1590.40 In the retail business, the emergence period potentially might be the time period between the occurrence of a loss event and the default date (breach of contract), as the actual default of customers may be the only or most reliable way to identify a loss event.

3.6.1590.50 In our view, entities should justify and support their assessment of the emergence periods by back-testing them. However, this back-testing does not need to identify an exact time period elapsing between a loss event occurring and loss event being identified as this would require individual (specific) identification of loss events, which is impracticable in many circumstances. Instead, back-testing should test the reasonableness of the estimate made by management based on the identified loss factors. This should be reassessed when there is evidence that the loss events or customer behaviour or the entity's processes have changed. In our view, emergence periods should remain relatively stable, subject to the changes mentioned above, and any changes should be justified and disclosed.

3.6.1600 *Measuring the collective impairment*

IAS 39.63, AG92 3.6.1600.10 The estimated future cash flows determined for assets carried at amortised cost assessed for impairment on a collective basis are discounted at a rate that approximates the original effective interest rate (see 3.6.1430.15). For portfolios of similar assets, these assets will have a range of interest rates, and therefore judgement is necessary to determine a discounting methodology appropriate to that portfolio, which may result in using the average effective yield if it is a homogeneous portfolio.

IAS 39.60 3.6.1600.20 The methodology used may include a "risk migration" approach. Entities may use their historical risk migration data together with observable market data to support their assessment of losses incurred but not reported. However, a downgrade of an entity's credit rating is not in itself evidence of impairment, although it may be evidence of impairment when considered with other available information. Therefore, if a risk migration methodology is used, then it should distinguish between migration data that evidences incurred losses and data that evidences expected future losses.

IAS 39.59, AG92, IGE.4.2 3.6.1600.30 Although impairment losses can be determined using a portfolio methodology for groups of similar assets, this does not mean that an entity is allowed to take an immediate write-down upon recognising a new financial asset.

3.6.1610 *Bad debts and loan losses*

IAS 39.63, AG90-AG93, IGE.4.2, IGE.4.5, IGE.4.6 3.6.1610.10 The following practices related to bad debt losses are not acceptable under IFRSs:

- Recognising a provision for losses based on a set percentage of receivable balances having certain characteristics (e.g. according to the number of days overdue) rather than actual incurred losses, unless these percentages are validated using historical data.
- Recognising a loss for the gross expected shortfall on non-performing assets, and suspending interest accrual. This sometimes is referred to as putting a loan on non-accrual status.
- Recognising an impairment loss in excess of incurred losses calculated based on estimated cash flows, even if local regulations require a specific amount to be set aside ("general risk provisions"). In our view, if an entity wishes to identify reserves in addition to the impairment losses calculated under IFRSs, then it may do so by transferring amounts from retained earnings to a separate category of equity, for example a loan loss reserve (see 3.11.410). It is not acceptable to recognise any

amounts in profit or loss or to reduce the carrying amount of the assets by more than the estimated actual loss.

3.6.1620 *Interest recognised after impairment*

IAS 39.AG93   3.6.1620.10 Once a financial asset or a group of similar financial assets has been written down as a result of an impairment loss, interest income thereafter is recognised using the rate of interest used to discount the future cash flows for the purpose of measuring impairment loss. For assets measured at amortised cost this interest rate would be the original effective interest rate (see 3.6.1430.15). In our view for an available-for-sale financial asset, an entity may use a new effective interest rate computed based on the fair value at the date of impairment.

3.6.1630 **Future developments**

3.6.1630.10 In March 2008 the IASB published a DP *Reducing Complexity in Reporting Financial Instruments*, seeking constituents' views on all the issues addressed in the DP. The objectives of the DP were to gather information to assist the IASB in its decision on how to proceed with developing a less complex and principles-based standard on the accounting for financial instruments, which is consistent with the IASB and FASB's long-term objective of measuring all financial instruments at fair value; and to simplify or eliminate the need for special hedge accounting requirements.

3.6.1630.20 Following the comment period and recommendations from various stake-holders, including the Financial Crisis Advisory Group (FCAG) and the Group of Twenty (G20), the IASB and the FASB subsequently added projects to replace the current financial instruments standards to their agendas.

3.6.1630.30 The IASB's project to replace IAS 39 includes the following phases:

- classification and measurement (see 3.6A and 3.6.1630.50);
- impairment (see 3.6.1630.40); and
- hedging (see 3.7.900.20).

3.6.1630.40 In November 2009 the IASB published ED/2009/12 *Financial Instruments: Amortised Cost and Impairment*, which proposes to replace the incurred loss method for impairment of financial assets with a method based on expected losses (i.e. expected cash flow or ECF approach) and to provide a more principles-based approach to measuring amortised cost. The proposals in the ED would apply to all financial instruments within the scope of IAS 39 that are measured at amortised cost. A final standard is scheduled for the second quarter of 2011.

3.6.1630.50 Except for the presentation of changes in the fair value of financial liabilities due to own credit risk (see 5.6.530.20), the IASB has decided generally to retain the current requirements in IAS 39 in respect of the classification and measurement of financial liabilities. A final standard is scheduled for the second quarter of 2011.

3.6.1630.60 In March 2009 the IASB published ED/2009/3 *Derecognition*. The proposals in the ED aimed to simplify the derecognition model for financial assets. However, except for the proposed disclosure requirements, the IASB has decided not to proceed with the ED at this point in time (see 5.6.530.20).

3.6.1630.70 In May 2009 the IASB published ED/2009/5 *Fair Value Measurement* (the 2009 ED). The proposals in the 2009 ED are intended to replace the fair value measurement guidance contained in individual IFRSs with a single, unified definition of fair value, as well as provide further authoritative guidance on the application of fair value measurement in inactive markets. The 2009 ED proposes a framework for measuring fair value and disclosures about fair value measurements. The proposals in the 2009 ED explain how to measure fair value when it already is required or permitted by existing IFRSs; they do not introduce new fair value measurements, nor do they eliminate the practicability exceptions to fair value measurements that exist currently in certain standards.

3.6.1630.80 In June 2010 the IASB published ED/2010/7 *Measurement Uncertainty Analysis Disclosure for Fair Value Measurements* (the 2010 ED). The 2010 ED expands on the proposal in the 2009 ED for an entity to disclose a measurement uncertainty analysis (or sensitivity analysis) for assets and liabilities measured at fair value categorised within Level 3 of the fair value hierarchy. The 2010 ED proposes that an entity consider the effect of correlation between unobservable inputs, if relevant.

3.6.1630.90 A final standard on fair value measurement and disclosure, which is expected to be converged with a forthcoming amended standard under US GAAP, is scheduled for the first quarter of 2011.

3.6.1630.100 In July 2010 the IASB issued ED/2010/8 *Insurance Contracts*. The ED addresses accounting for insurance contracts issued by insurers and reinsurance contracts held by insurers; it does not address policyholder accounting. The ED proposes significant changes from current practice in the accounting for insurance contracts. It may also impact current practice in accounting for financial guarantee contracts. A final standard is scheduled for the second quarter of 2011.

3.6A Financial instruments
(IFRS 9)

3.6A Financial instruments
(IFRS 9)

Overview of forthcoming requirements

- The first chapters of IFRS 9 apply only to financial assets, and not to financial liabilities, within the scope of IAS 39.

- There are two primary measurement categories for financial assets: amortised cost and fair value. The IAS 39 categories of held to maturity, loans and receivables and available for sale are eliminated and so are the existing tainting provisions for disposals before maturity of certain financial assets.

- A financial asset is measured at amortised cost if both of the following conditions are met:
  - the asset is held within a business model whose objective is to hold assets in order to collect contractual cash flows; and
  - the contractual terms of the financial asset give rise, on specified dates, to cash flows that are solely payments of principal and interest.

- All other financial assets are measured at fair value.

- There is specific guidance on classifying non-recourse financial assets and contractually linked instruments that create concentrations of credit risk (e.g. securitisation tranches). Financial assets acquired at a discount that may include incurred credit losses are not precluded automatically from being classified at amortised cost.

- Entities have an option to classify financial assets that meet the amortised cost criteria as at fair value through profit or loss if doing so eliminates or significantly reduces an accounting mismatch.

- Embedded derivatives with host contracts that are financial assets within the scope of IAS 39 are not separated; instead the hybrid financial instrument is assessed as a whole for classification under IFRS 9. Hybrid instruments with host contracts that are not financial assets within the scope of IAS 39 (e.g. financial liabilities and non-financial host contracts) are outside the scope of IFRS 9 and continue to be accounted for in accordance with IAS 39.

- If a financial asset is measured at fair value, then all changes in fair value are recognised in profit or loss. However, for investments in equity

---

instruments which are not held for trading, an entity has the option, on an instrument-by-instrument basis, to recognise gains and losses in other comprehensive income with no reclassification of gains and losses into profit or loss and no impairments recognised in profit or loss. If an equity investment is so designated, then dividend income generally is recognised in profit or loss.

- There is no exemption allowing some unquoted equity investments and related derivative assets to be measured at cost. However, guidance is provided as to the limited circumstances in which the cost of such an instrument may be an appropriate approximation of fair value.

- The classification of a financial instrument is determined on initial recognition. Reclassifications are made only upon a change in an entity's business model that is significant to its operations. These are expected to be very infrequent. No other reclassifications are permitted.

Forthcoming requirements and future developments

In November 2009 the IASB published the first chapters of IFRS 9 *Financial Instruments* which will supersede the provisions of IAS 39 *Financial Instruments: Recognition and Measurement* on classification and measurement of financial assets. IFRS 9 does not change substantively the existing guidance in IAS 39 on impairment, derecognition or hedge accounting for financial assets.

IFRS 9.8.1.1 IFRS 9 is effective for annual periods beginning on or after 1 January 2013; earlier application is permitted. Entities that adopt the standard early are required to disclose that fact and apply all the consequential amendments to other standards at the same time.

IFRS 9.BC93 There is a possibility that the effective date of IFRS 9 may be delayed if the impairment phase of the IASB's financial instruments replacement project makes it necessary or if the expected new IFRS on insurance contracts has a mandatory effective date later than 2013. See 3.6A.500.10 – 50 for further discussion of the IASB's financial instruments replacement project.

IFRS 9.8.2.1 The standard is applied retrospectively in accordance with IAS 8 *Accounting Policies, Changes in Accounting Estimates and Errors* with certain exemptions (see 3.6A.490).

See 3.6A.360 for a discussion of the transitional issues related to the date of initial application.

The forthcoming requirements may be subject to future developments and a brief outline of the relevant project is given in 3.6A.500.60 – 80.

3.6A.5 **Overview**

3.6A.5.10 The flowchart below provides an overview of the classification and measurement model in IFRS 9. Each element of the model is explained further in the succeeding paragraphs.

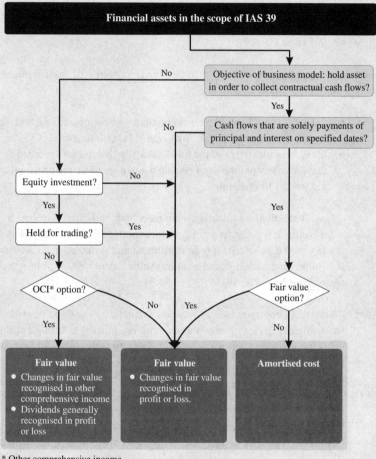

* Other comprehensive income

3.6A.10 **Scope**

IFRS 9.2.1 3.6A.10.10 IFRS 9 applies to financial assets within the scope of IAS 39, but not to financial liabilities.

3.6A.20 **Initial recognition**

RS 9.3.1.1,
IAS 39.14,
G34, AG35 3.6A.20.10 A financial asset is recognised when and only when the entity becomes a party to the contractual provisions of the instrument. IFRS 9 does not amend substantively the initial recognition requirements of IAS 39 (see 3.6.660).

3.6A.30 **Classification**

3.6A.40 *Basic principles*

IFRS 9.4.1 3.6A.40.10 Upon initial recognition, a financial asset is classified into one of two primary measurement categories:

- amortised cost; or
- fair value.

IFRS 9.4.2 3.6A.40.20 A financial asset qualifies for amortised cost measurement only if it meets both of the following conditions:

- the asset is held within a business model whose objective is to hold assets in order to collect contractual cash flows (the HTC criterion or HTC business model); and
- the contractual terms of the financial asset give rise on specified dates to cash flows that are solely payments of principal and interest on the principal amount outstanding (the SPPI criterion).

3.6A.40.30 If a financial asset does not meet both of these conditions, then it is measured at fair value. If a financial asset does meet both of these conditions, then it is measured at amortised cost, even if it is an instrument that is quoted in an active market, unless it is eligible for and designated as at fair value through profit or loss under the fair value option (see 3.6A.200.10).

IAS 39.9 3.6A.40.40 In contrast, IAS 39 requires financial assets to be classified into one of the following categories upon initial recognition: fair value through profit or loss, held to maturity, loans and receivables, or available for sale. IFRS 9 eliminates the last three categories.

IAS 39.31 3.6A.40.50 There is no change to the measurement guidance in IAS 39 related to a transferred asset that continues to be recognised to the extent of the entity's continuing involvement in the asset. Accordingly, such assets and associated liabilities continue to be measured on a basis that reflects the rights and obligations retained by the entity.

3.6A.50 *Business model*

IFRS 9.4.1, 3.6A.50.10 In order to determine whether a financial asset that meets the cash flow
B4.2 characteristics test in 3.6A.40.20 should be classified as measured at amortised cost or fair value, an entity needs to identify and assess the objective of the entity's business model in which the asset is held. The objective of the entity's business model is not based on management's intentions with respect to an individual instrument, but rather is determined at a higher level of aggregation. The assessment of the objective of the entity's business model should reflect the way an entity manages its business or businesses. For example, a single reporting entity may have more than one business model for managing its financial instruments and the standard provides an example of different

portfolios being managed on different bases. In this case, the objective of the business model is assessed for each portfolio rather than determining classification based on a single assessment at the reporting entity level. For example, an entity holding a portfolio of investments that it manages in order to collect contractual cash flows may have a different classification for financial assets in that portfolio from those in another portfolio of investments that the entity manages in order to trade to realise fair value changes.

IFRS 9.B4.3   3.6A.50.20 If an entity's business model for a portfolio is to hold the assets in the portfolio in order to collect contractual cash flows then the portfolio may qualify for measurement at amortised cost. However, not all assets in such a portfolio have to be held to maturity in order for the objective of the business model to meet the HTC criterion as there are few business models which entail holding all instruments in the portfolio until maturity. The following are examples in which sales of financial assets may be regarded as being consistent with an HTC business model:

- a financial asset no longer meets the entity's investment policy (e.g. the credit rating of the asset declines below that required by the entity's investment policy);
- an insurer adjusts its investment portfolio to reflect a change in expected duration (i.e. the expected timing of payouts); or
- an entity needs to fund capital expenditures.

3.6A.50.30 Some sales out of such a portfolio may be possible but if there is more than an infrequent number, then an entity assesses whether and how those sales are consistent with the objective of an HTC business model. Although frequent buying and selling of assets is not consistent with an HTC business model, there is no quantitative bright-line measure as to what frequency of anticipated sales would preclude a single business model from meeting the HTC criterion. In many cases, entities will need to exercise significant judgement to determine the appropriate classification of financial assets.

FRS 9.BC26,   3.6A.50.40 An entity should consider at what level of its business activities different *BC27* business models and their objectives should be identified and assessed. Generally, an entity's business model is a matter of fact which can be observed from the way an entity is managed and the information provided to management. However, there may be circumstances in which it is not clear whether a particular activity involves one business model with some infrequent sales of assets or whether these anticipated sales indicate that in fact an entity has two different business models, only one of which would meet the HTC criterion.

IFRS 9.1.1   3.6A.50.50 In our view, in making this assessment, an entity should consider the stated objective of IFRS 9 to provide relevant and useful information to users of the financial statements for their assessment of the amounts, timing and uncertainty of the entity's future cash flows. The more that a business model envisages holding financial assets for an extended period or until maturity in order to collect contractual cash flows, the more relevant and useful amortised cost information is. Conversely, the more that a business model envisages sales of assets significantly prior to maturity, the less relevant and useful amortised cost information becomes and the more relevant and useful is fair value information. We believe that the following are among the factors that an entity may consider in making such an assessment for a portfolio of assets:

- management's stated policies and objectives for the portfolio and the operation of those policies in practice;
- how management evaluates the performance of the portfolio;
- whether management's strategy focuses on earning contractual interest revenues;
- the degree of frequency of expected sales of assets;
- the reasons for sales of assets; and
- whether assets that are sold are held for an extended period of time relative to their contractual maturity or are sold shortly after acquisition or an extended time before maturity.

IFRS 9 A,   3.6A.50.60 The following are not consistent with an HTC business model:
B4.5, B4.6

- a portfolio that is actively managed in order to realise fair value changes;
- a portfolio that is managed and whose performance is evaluated on a fair value basis; or
- a portfolio of financial assets that meets the definition of held for trading.

3.6A.50.70 IFRS 9 retains the definition of held for trading in IAS 39 in so far as an asset is considered held for trading if it was acquired for sale in the near term, on initial recognition was part of a portfolio for which there is evidence of a recent actual pattern of short-term profit taking, or is a derivative.

3.6A.50.80 It is unclear what the consequences are of an entity concluding that the management of a portfolio that was previously held to collect contractual cash flows is no longer consistent with an HTC business model following a change to an ongoing frequent level of sales of financial assets from that portfolio, but the reclassification criteria (see 3.6A.310) have not been met. For example, an entity may conclude that it no longer holds a particular portfolio of financial assets for collection of contractual cash flows but the change is not sufficiently significant to the entity's operations to trigger reassessment of the classification of the existing items in the portfolio. However, when new financial assets are acquired subsequent to the change in business model, the HTC criterion would not be met and so the new assets would not meet the amortised cost criteria. This may lead to some financial assets in the portfolio being measured at amortised cost and others, acquired after the change, being measured at fair value; effectively, following the new assessment, the entity would have two portfolios rather than one.

3.6A.60 *Interaction with consolidation and derecognition standards*

IFRS 9.B4.4   3.6A.60.10 A portfolio of financial assets acquired with the objective of selling to a securitisation vehicle may be consistent with an HTC business model depending on the circumstances. For example, an entity originates loans for the purpose of selling them to a securitisation vehicle and the entity controls and consolidates the vehicle. The loans are derecognised from the entity's statement of financial position and recognised by the securitisation vehicle. On consolidation, the loans remain within the consolidated group. In the consolidated financial statements, the HTC criterion is met as the consolidated group originated the loans with the objective of collecting the contractual cash flows. However, in the entity's separate financial statements, the HTC criterion is not met as the individual entity has originated the loans with the objective of selling them to the securitisation vehicle rather than holding them to collect the contractual cash flows.

3.6A.60.20 An entity may hold a portfolio of financial assets for which its objectives include selling some of those financial assets to third parties in transactions that do not qualify for derecognition of the sold assets. For example, an entity holds financial assets to collect the contractual cash flows through to maturity but its objectives include selling some of those financial assets as part of sale and repurchase transactions (repos) in which the entity agrees to repurchase the financial assets at a later date prior to their maturity. During the term of the repos, the transferee is required to remit immediately to the entity an amount equal to any payments the transferee receives from the transferred assets. In our view, this scenario is consistent with an HTC business model, based both on the entity's continuing recognition of the assets for accounting purposes and the terms of the repo transactions in regards to the remittance of income payments and the reconveyance of the transferred assets back to the entity prior to their maturity.

3.6A.60.30 In another example, an entity originates trade receivables and immediately sells some to a factor. The factor obtains outright legal ownership of the receivables and the trade debtors are required to remit funds directly to the factor. However, under the factoring agreement, the entity retains substantially all the credit risk of the receivables through a guarantee given to the factor. Because of the guarantee, the entity continues to recognise the trade receivables in its statement of financial position. In our view, the entity should choose an accounting policy, to be applied consistently, as to whether such receivables are held within an HTC business model. The entity may conclude that the assets are held within an HTC business model consistent with its continuing recognition of the receivables. Alternatively, given that it immediately sells the assets and has no right to collect any of the contractual cash flows, it may conclude that the HTC criterion is not met.

3.6A.70 *Acquiring distressed assets*

IFRS 9.B4.4 3.6A.70.10 Acquiring financial assets with incurred losses is not in itself inconsistent with an HTC business model. For example, an entity may have a business model to acquire impaired loans and then collect the contractual cash flows by chasing the debtors for payment.

3.6A.80 **Cash flow characteristics**

IFRS 9.4.2, 3.6A.80.10 The second criterion an entity assesses in order to determine whether a
B4.8 financial asset should be classified as measured at amortised cost or fair value is whether the cash flows from the financial asset represent, on specified dates, solely payments of principal and interest on the principal amount outstanding.

3.6A.90 *Interest*

IFRS 9.4.3, 3.6A.90.10 *Interest* is consideration for the time value of money and for the credit risk
B4.8 associated with the principal amount outstanding during a particular period of time. The assessment as to whether cash flows meet this definition is made in the currency in which the financial asset is denominated.

IFRS 9.B4.12 3.6A.90.20 Interest rates that are fixed or variable may be consistent with the SPPI criterion. IFRS 9 states that the component of a variable interest rate that represents compensation for credit risk may be fixed at initial recognition. However, in practice compensation for credit risk is not always fixed at inception and can vary in response to perceived changes in the creditworthiness of the borrower (e.g. if covenants are breached). If there are variations in the contractual cash flows of an instrument related to credit risk, then entities consider whether the variation can be regarded as compensation for credit risk and therefore whether the instrument may meet the SPPI criterion. In our view, it is not necessary for such a feature to reset to a current market credit spread in order to meet the SPPI criterion; however, the feature should not be leveraged and should be designed reasonably to reflect an estimate of the additional credit premium that a lender would require in response to the apparent deterioration in the creditworthiness of the borrower. For example, a term that required an increase in contractual interest of 1 percent per annum if the debtor's credit rating falls below a specified level might be consistent with the SPPI criterion.

3.6A.90.30 Although interest that is indexed to a debtor's performance is not consistent with the SPPI criterion, in our view this would not preclude amortised cost classification of a financial asset when the performance based term (e.g. interest coverage ratio or gearing ratio) that varies the interest rate is a reasonably proxy for the variation in credit risk of the financial asset, even though it is linked to a quantitative measure specific to the debtor. For example, a term that required an increase in contractual interest of 1 percent per annum if the debtor's interest coverage ratio fell below a specified threshold may be consistent with the SPPI criterion if the term represents consideration (i.e. higher interest) for higher credit risk. Conversely, a term that required interest payments equal to a percentage of the debtor's earnings could not qualify for amortised cost accounting because the lender would be sharing in a portion of the borrower's results and any additional receipts would not be solely consideration for the time value of money and credit risk.

3.6A.90.40 An equity investment does not give rise to cash flows that are solely principal and interest. In addition, the dates of cash flows usually are not specified.

3.6A.100 *Leverage*

IFRS 9.B4.9 3.6A.100.10 Leverage is described as increasing the variability of the contractual cash flows such that they do not have the economic characteristics of interest. Leverage is not consistent with the SPPI criterion. Examples of instruments that contain leverage are derivatives such as freestanding swaps, options and forward contracts.

3.6A.110 *Prepayment options, term extension options and puttable instruments*

FRS 9.B4.10,   3.6A.110.10 Contractual terms that permit the issuer to prepay before maturity, the holder
   B4.11   to put the financial asset back to the issuer before maturity or either party to extend the
term of a financial asset meet the SPPI criterion only if:

- the feature is not contingent on future events or, if contingent, it protects:
  - the holder against a credit deterioration or change in control of the issuer; or
  - the holder or the issuer against changes in relevant taxation or law;
- in the case of a prepayment or put feature, the prepayment amount substantially
  represents unpaid principal and interest, but may include reasonable additional
  compensation for early termination; or
- in the case of a term extension option, it results only in contractual cash flows
  during the extension period that are solely payments of principal and interest
  on the principal amount outstanding.

3.6A.120 *Changes in contractual payments*

FRS 9.B4.12   3.6A.120.10 Any contractual term that changes the timing or amount of payments does not
meet the SPPI criterion unless it is a variable interest rate that represents consideration
for the time value of money and credit risk (see 3.6.A.90) or is a qualifying prepayment,
term extension or put feature (see 3.6.A.110).

3.6A.130 *Contractual term that is not genuine*

IFRS 9.B4.18,   3.6A.130.10 A contractual term that is not genuine is not considered in the assessment
 BC31, BC32   of whether a financial asset meets the SPPI criterion. A characteristic is not genuine if
it affects the instrument's contractual cash flows only on the occurrence of an event that
is extremely rare, highly abnormal and very unlikely to occur.

3.6A.130.20 Demonstrating that a term in not genuine may be difficult in practice as it
would be unusual for parties to an agreement to negotiate a term that they considered
to be of no significance. For example, a term may fail the SPPI criterion if it gives rise
to cash flows in circumstances that are rare (but not extremely rare) or unlikely (but not
very unlikely) to occur.

IFRS 9.B4.13   3.6A.130.30 Examples when the SPPI criterion may be met:

- An instrument with a stated maturity and variable interest rate for which the borrower can choose a market interest rate that corresponds to the reset period on an
  ongoing basis. The fact that the interest rate is reset during the life of the instrument
  does not disqualify the instrument from meeting the SPPI criterion. However, if the
  borrower was able to choose to pay the one-month LIBOR rate for a three-month
  term without reset each month, the SPPI test would be failed.
- A bond with a stated maturity and payments of principal and interest linked to an
  unleveraged inflation index of the currency in which the instrument is issued, subject

to protection of the principal amount. This linkage resets the time value of money to the current level and therefore the bond's cash flows may be solely payments of principal and interest on the principal outstanding.

- In our view, the same conclusion would apply even when there is no principal protection clause (i.e. the principal amount repayable is reduced in line with any cumulative reduction in the inflation index) since this would merely indicate that a component of the time value of money could be negative.
- Usually with inflation-linked instruments there is a time lag between the period over which the change in the relevant inflation index is measured and the period during which the instrument is outstanding and over which coupon payments and changes in principal amounts contractually accrue. This time lag usually is a result of the delay between the date at which an inflation index is measured and the date of publication, as well as difficulties associated with accrual or payment dates on the instrument that do not coincide with dates for which the index is published. In our view, a reasonable time lag that is applicable consistently through the life of the instrument and is necessary for administrative purposes or consistent with usual market conventions does not preclude an inflation-linked instrument from meeting the SPPI criterion.

- A bond with variable interest and an interest cap. The instrument is like a combination of a fixed and floating rate bond, as the cap reduces the variability of cash flows.
- A full recourse loan secured by collateral. The fact that a full recourse loan is secured by collateral does not affect the analysis.

3.6A.130.40 The fact that an instrument is perpetual does not preclude it from meeting the SPPI criterion.

IFRS 9.B4.13, B4.14 3.6A.130.50 Examples when the SPPI criterion is not met include:

- A bond convertible into equity of the issuer. The SPPI criterion is not met as the return on the bond is not just consideration for the time value of money and credit risk but also reflects the value of the issuer's equity.
- An inverse floating interest rate loan, e.g. the interest rate on the loan increases if an interest rate index decreases. The SPPI criterion is not met as interest has an inverse relationship to market rates and so does not represent consideration for the time value of money and credit risk.
- A perpetual instrument that is callable at any time by the issuer at par plus accrued interest but for which interest is only payable if the issuer remains solvent after payment and any deferred interest does not accrue additional interest. The SPPI criterion is not met as the issuer may defer payments and additional interest does not accrue on the amounts deferred. As a result, the holder is not entitled to the consideration for the time value of money and credit risk.
- An instrument with interest payments indexed to the debtor's performance, e.g. the debtor's net income or an equity index. The SPPI criterion is not met as a return linked to performance or an equity index is not consideration for the time value of money and credit risk (see also 3.6A.90.20 and 30).

3.6A.140 *Non-recourse and limited recourse assets*

IFRS 9.4.5, B4.17   3.6A.140.10 A financial asset may have contractual cash flows that are described as principal and interest, but those cash flows do not represent the payment of principal and interest. This may be the case if the instrument represents an investment in particular assets or cash flows, or when a creditor's claims are limited to specified assets, which may be financial or non-financial assets. A possible example is a non-recourse financial asset.

IFRS 9.B4.16   3.6A.140.20 The fact that a financial asset is non-recourse does not in itself necessarily mean that the SPPI criterion is not met. The holder is required to assess the underlying assets or cash flows. If the terms of the financial asset being evaluated give rise to cash flows other than principal and interest on the principal amount outstanding, or if they limit the cash flows in a manner inconsistent with them representing principal and interest, then the SPPI criterion is not met.

3.6A.140.30 In our view, if the contractual payments due under a financial asset are determined contractually by the cash flows received on specified assets, then unless the criteria described in 3.6A.150 are met, the financial asset generally cannot meet the SPPI criterion. An example of where the SPPI criterion is not met might be a loan to a property developer where interest is payable only if specified rental income is received. However, in our view a financial asset that represents a full or a *pro rata* share in the contractual cash flows of an underlying financial asset that meets the SPPI criterion could itself meet the SPPI criterion.

IFRS 9.B4.19   3.6A.140.40 In most lending transactions an instrument is ranked relative to other instruments and the SPPI criterion would not fail just because of such relative ranking. For example, a creditor may have issued collateralised debt which, in the event of bankruptcy, would give the holder priority over other creditors in respect of the collateral, but this arrangement would not affect the contractual rights of other creditors to the amounts due to them.

3.6A.150 *Contractually linked instruments*

IFRS 9.B4. 20-26   3.6A.150.10 The standard provides specific guidance for circumstances in which an entity prioritises payments to holders of multiple contractually linked instruments that create concentrations of credit risk, i.e. tranches. The right to payments on more junior tranches (i.e. exposed to more credit risk) depends on the issuer's generation of sufficient cash flows to pay more senior tranches. A look-through approach is required to determine whether the SPPI criterion is met (see 3.6A.150.40).

IFRS 9.B4.21, 23-25   3.6A.150.20 A tranche meets the SPPI criterion only if all the following conditions are met:

    (a) the contractual terms of the tranche itself gives rise to cash flows that are solely payments of principal and interest on the principal amount outstanding;

(b) the underlying pool of financial instruments:

    (i) contains one or more instruments that gives rise to cash flows that are solely payments of principal and interest on the principal amount outstanding;

    (ii) also may contain instruments that:

- reduce the cash flow variability of the instruments under (i) and the combined cash flows give rise to cash flows that are solely payments of principal and interest on the principal amount outstanding (e.g. interest rate caps and floors, credit protection); or

- align the cash flows of the tranches with the cash flows of the instruments under (i) arising as a result of differences in whether interest rates are fixed or floating or the currency or timing of cash flows; and

(c) the exposure to credit risk inherent in the tranche is equal to or less than the exposure to credit risk of the underlying pool of financial instruments.

3.6A.150.30 If any instrument in the underlying pool does not meet the conditions under (b) as described in 3.6A.150.20, or if the pool can change later in a way that would not meet those conditions, then the tranche does not meet the SPPI criterion.

IFRS 9.B4.22   3.6A.150.40 The look-through approach is carried through to the underlying pool of instruments that create, rather than pass through, the cash flows. For example, if an entity invests in contractually linked notes issued by SPE 1 whose only asset is an investment in contractually linked notes issued by SPE 2, then the entity looks through to the assets of SPE 2 in performing the assessment.

IFRS 9.B4.26   3.6A.150.50 If an entity is not able to make an assessment based on the criteria in 3.6A.150.20, then it measures its investment in the tranche at fair value.

3.6A.160 *Derivatives*

3.6A.160.10 A pool may include derivative instruments which align the cash flows of a tranche with the cash flows of the underlying instruments. In our view, when determining whether the exposure to credit risk inherent in the tranche is equal to or less than the exposure to credit risk of the underlying pool of financial instruments, any losses due to changes in the fair value of the derivative instruments should be excluded from the test to the extent that they do not represent credit losses on the derivative instruments.

3.6A.160.20 In addition, when a pool includes more than one derivative instrument, in our view an entity is able to combine derivatives when performing the assessment described in condition (b) in 3.6A.150.20 if the combined derivative would give the same result as if a single derivative had been included in the portfolio. For example, an SPE has a portfolio of variable interest rate financial assets denominated in euro and issues fixed-rate contractually linked notes denominated in US dollars. If the entity enters into two derivatives: (1) a pay variable euro, receive variable US dollar swap; and (2) a pay variable US dollar, receive fixed US dollar swap then the combination of these two swaps would be the same as if the entity had entered into one cross-currency interest rate swap to pay variable euro and receive fixed US dollars. In such a situation, the holder of an investment in the notes could combine the two derivatives and assess them in combination rather than performing an individual assessment for each derivative.

3.6A.160.30 In order for the SPPI criterion to be met the guidance on contractually linked instruments requires that any derivatives reduce the cash flow variability of other instruments in the pool so that the combined cash flows meet the SPPI criterion or align the cash flows of tranches with the cash flows of other instruments in the pool. The guidance also states that, if the underlying pool of instruments can change in such a way that the pool may not meet these conditions, then the tranche does not meet the SPPI criterion. The pool of underlying instruments and their cash flows may change as a result of prepayments or credit losses and by any permitted extinguishments or transfers. In our view, for the SPPI criterion to be met, the terms of the contractually linked structure should include a mechanism that is designed to ensure that the amount of any derivatives is reduced in response to any such events so that they do not fail to meet the cash flow variability or alignment tests, e.g. a clause in an interest-rate swap under which the notional amount is automatically reduced to match any declines in the principal amount of performing assets within an underlying pool.

3.6A.170 – 180 [Not used]

3.6A.190 *Exposure to credit risk*

3.6A.190.10 In order for the SPPI criterion to be met, the exposure to credit risk inherent in the tranche should be equal to or less than the exposure to credit risk of the underlying pool of financial instruments. The term credit risk is not defined in IFRS 9 although under IFRS 7 it is the risk that one party to a financial instrument will cause a financial loss for the other party by failing to discharge an obligation (see 5.6.740.10). In a tranched structure, the issuer usually is obliged to make payments to an investor only if and to the extent that the underlying pool of assets generates sufficient cash flows. Therefore, shortfalls in cash flows and associated losses for investors arising from defaults on the underlying pool of assets result in a reduction in the issuer's obligations, rather than the issuer failing to discharge its obligations. In our view, in assessing the exposure to credit risk in the underlying pool of financial assets inherent in a tranche, an entity considers losses that may result from contractual adjustments to the cash flows on the tranche arising from credit losses in the underlying pool of assets as well as losses that may result from the issuer failing to discharge its obligations because of credit losses in the underlying pool of assets. Consistent with this analysis, the presence of such adjustment features does not imply that the contractual terms of the tranche itself do not give rise to cash flows that are solely payments of principal and interest on the principal amount outstanding, i.e. failure of condition (a) in 3.6A.150.20.

IFRS 9.B4.
21C 3.6A.190.20 The condition that the exposure to credit risk in the underlying pool of financial instruments inherent in the tranche is equal to or lower than the exposure to credit risk of the underlying pool of financial instruments would be met if the underlying pool of instruments were to lose 50 percent as a result of credit losses and under all circumstances

the tranche would lose 50 percent or less. In such a case, an investor in the tranche would always lose a lower proportionate share of its investment in the tranche as a result of credit losses than would a *pari passu* investment in the total underlying pool.

3.6A.190.30 For example, Company B, an SPE, has issued two tranches of debt that are contractually linked: a Class I tranche of 15 and a Class II tranche of 10. Class II is subordinated to Class I and receives distributions only after payments have been made to the holders of Class I instruments.

3.6A.190.40 B's assets should consist of loans of 25 all of which meet the SPPI criterion.

3.6A.190.50 Investor X has invested in Class I instruments. X determines that the contractual terms of the tranche give rise solely to payments of principal and interest on the principal. X then needs to look through to the underlying pool of investments of B. Since B has invested in loans that meet the SPPI criterion, the pool contains at least one instrument with cash flows that are solely payments of principal and interest on the principal amount outstanding. B has no other financial instruments. Therefore, B's underlying pool of financial instruments does not have features that would prohibit the tranche from meeting the SPPI criterion. The last step in the analysis is for X to assess whether the exposure to credit risk inherent in the tranche is equal to or lower than the exposure to credit risk of the underlying pool of financial instruments. If the underlying pool of loans were to lose 50 percent, then a total loss of 12.5 (25 x 50%) would arise. Of that loss, 10 would be absorbed by Class II investors, leaving 2.5 to be absorbed by Class I investors. This indicates that the ratio of loss suffered by the holders of Class I instruments would be 17 percent (2.5 / 15). The ratio of 17 percent is less than 50 percent which indicates that the credit risk of Class I instruments is lower than the credit risk of the underlying pool. Accordingly, X concludes that the Class I instruments meet the SPPI criterion.

3.6A.190.60 Investor Y has invested in Class II instruments. This tranche does not meet the credit risk test because whenever the underlying pool suffers a loss, investors in Class II instruments always suffer a proportionately greater loss. Therefore, Y should measure any investment in Class II instruments at fair value.

IFRS 9.BC 42(f) 3.6A.190.70 However, the standard does not mandate a single method to determine whether the credit risk condition is satisfied and, in our view it is not necessary to demonstrate that the 50 percent test in the example is passed in all circumstances in order to conclude that the credit risk condition is satisfied. We believe that an entity also may adopt an approach that models probability-weighted expectations of credit losses to derive a weighted average range of expected losses within the pool and their allocation to each tranche in order to determine whether the exposure of a tranche is proportionately more or less than the average exposure of the pool. If the range of expected losses on the issued instrument is greater than the weighted average range of expected losses on the underlying pool of financial instruments, then the issued instrument should be measured at fair value.

3.6A.190.80 As in the example in 3.6A.190.30, in some cases a fundamental analysis of the tranching structure may lead to an answer for some tranches without detailed scenario modelling. For example, an underlying pool consists of financial assets of 100 and credit losses are allocated to three tranches of contractually linked notes in the following order: up to 10, allocated to Tranche C; 10 – 20, allocated to Tranche B; and 20 – 100, allocated to Tranche A. In this case, it is apparent that Tranche C would fail the credit risk condition whereas Tranche A would pass. However, further analysis would be required in respect of Tranche B. If, for example, the range of expected losses in the underlying pool did not exceed 10, then Tranche B also would pass the credit risk condition. However, if that range did exceed 10, then completing the assessment would require more detailed modelling.

IFRS 9.3.1.1, 4.9   3.6A.190.90 As with other elements of the classification assessment, the assessment of whether the credit risk condition is met is assessed at initial recognition of the contractually linked instrument and would therefore reflect circumstances and expectations at that date. This might result in a different conclusion from performing the test based on circumstances and expectations at the date the contractually linked instruments were created. For example, a structure may be established that includes a most junior Tranche C, which provides credit protection to Tranche B (next most junior) and Tranche A (most senior). At establishment of the structure, an original investor in Tranche B may have concluded that the protection provided by Tranche C relative to the level of expected credit losses is sufficient for the credit risk test to be passed and that its investment should be classified as measured at amortised cost. However, over time, credit losses are greater than expected and the credit protection provided by Tranche A is exhausted. A subsequent investor in Tranche B would likely therefore conclude that the credit risk condition was failed. However, in our view it would not be appropriate for the original investor to reclassify its investment based on the change in circumstances.

3.6A.200 *Option to designate financial assets as at fair value through profit or loss*

IFRS 9.4.5, BC61-64   3.6A.200.10 On initial recognition, an entity may choose to designate a financial asset which otherwise would qualify for amortised cost accounting as measured as at fair value through profit or loss. This optional designation is permitted only if it eliminates or significantly reduces a measurement or recognition inconsistency (an "accounting mismatch") that otherwise would arise from measuring assets or liabilities, or recognising gains or losses on them, on different bases. The election is available only on initial recognition and is irrevocable. This option is retained from IAS 39 and the relevant application guidance in IAS 39 continues to apply (see 3.6.490). However, the other two fair value designation conditions available currently in IAS 39 (i.e. for instruments managed on a fair value basis and for certain hybrid instruments) are not retained in IFRS 9 as the requirements of IFRS 9 rendered them redundant for financial assets.

3.6A.210 *Embedded derivatives*

IFRS 9.4.6, IAS 39.10   3.6A.210.10 An *embedded derivative* is a component of a hybrid contract that includes also a non-derivative host with the effect that some of the cash flows of the combined instrument vary in a way similar to a stand-alone derivative. An embedded derivative causes some or all of the cash flows that otherwise would be required by the contract to be modified according to a specified interest rate, financial instrument price, commodity price, foreign exchange rate, index of prices or rates, credit rating or credit index, or other variable, provided in the case of a non-financial variable that the variable is not specific to a party to the contract. A derivative that is attached to a financial instrument but is contractually transferable independently of that instrument, or has a different counterparty, is not an embedded derivative, but a separate financial instrument.

IFRS 9.4.7   3.6A.210.20 When a hybrid contract contains a host that is a financial asset within the scope of IAS 39, the entire hybrid contract, including all embedded features, is assessed for classification under IFRS 9.

IFRS 9.4.8   3.6A.210.30 IFRS 9 does not impact the accounting for derivative features with host contracts that are not financial assets (e.g. financial liabilities) or host contracts that are financial assets not within the scope of IAS 39, such as rights under leases or insurance contracts. When a hybrid contract contains a host that is not a financial asset or not within the scope of IAS 39, the hybrid contract is assessed to determine whether the embedded derivative(s) required to be separated from the host contract in accordance with IAS 39 (see 3.6.260).

3.6A.210.40 The diagram below illustrates the accounting for hybrid contracts.

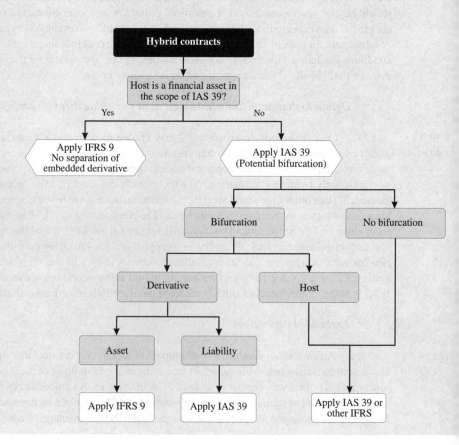

3.6A.210.50 The existence of a derivative feature in a hybrid contract may not preclude amortised cost classification of the entire contract when the feature meets the SPPI criterion. For example, a prepayment or term extension option that satisfies the requirements for amortised cost classification may allow the entire hybrid contract to be classified at amortised cost.

3.6A.210.60 However, many embedded derivative features may cause the entire hybrid instrument to fail the SPPI criterion and result in the entire hybrid contract being classified as at fair value through profit or loss.

3.6A.210.70 For example, Company B has an investment in a convertible bond. Under the terms of the bond, the holder has the option to convert it into a fixed number of equity shares of the issuer. The convertible bond should be analysed for classification in its entirety. The presence of the conversion option causes the instrument to fail the SPPI criterion because the contractual terms of the convertible bond do not give rise solely to payments of principal and interest on the principal amount outstanding on the bond. Therefore, the convertible bond in its entirety should be classified as at fair value through profit or loss.

3.6A.220 Measurement

FRS 9.3.1.1, 3.6A.220.10 A financial asset is recognised when and only when the entity becomes
5.1.1 party to its contractual terms. The financial asset initially is measured at fair value. If the financial asset is not accounted for subsequently as at fair value through profit or loss, then the initial measurement also includes transaction costs that are directly attributable to its acquisition.

IFRS 9.5.2.1- 3.6A.220.20 After initial recognition, financial assets are measured either at fair
5.2.3 value or amortised cost depending on their classification (see 3.6A.30). IFRS 9 refers to the guidance in IAS 39 with respect to the following items that impact measurement:

- fair value measurement (see 3.6.920)
- effective interest method (see 4.6.30)
- impairment of financial assets measured at amortised cost (see 3.6.1370)
- derecognition (see 3.6.1070)
- hedge accounting (see 3.7).

3.6A.230 *Gains or losses*

IFRS 9.5.4.1 3.6A.230.10 Gains or losses on the remeasurement of financial assets to fair value, assuming they are not hedging instruments in a hedging relationship, generally are recognised in profit or loss. The only exception is for gains and losses on equity investments designated as at fair value through other comprehensive income (see 3.6A.250).

IFRS 9.5.4.2 3.6A.230.20 Gains or losses on financial assets accounted for at amortised cost, assuming they are not part of a hedging relationship, are recognised in profit or loss upon derecognition, impairment, reclassification or through amortisation under the effective interest method.

IFRS 9.5.4.3 3.6A.230.30 If a financial asset is designated as the hedged item in a fair value hedge, or is designated as a hedging instrument, then the hedge accounting requirements of IAS 39 apply to such financial assets (see 3.7).

3.6A.240 *Investments in equity instruments*

IFRS 9.B5.5 3.6A.240.10 All investments in equity instruments and contracts on those instruments are measured at fair value. Any changes in fair value are to be recognised in profit or loss unless the exception described in 3.6A.250 is elected.

IFRS 9.B5.5, 3.6A.240.20 In limited circumstances, cost may be used as an approximation of fair value
B5.6 for unquoted equity instruments and contracts linked to them that are settled by delivery of such instruments. That may be the case if insufficient recent information is available to determine fair value, or if there is a wide range of possible fair value measurements and cost represents the best estimate of fair value within that range. Examples of indicators of the circumstances in which cost may not be the best estimate of fair value include:

- a significant change in the performance of the investee compared with budgets, plans or milestones;
- changes in expectation that the investee's technical product milestones will be achieved;
- a significant change in the market for the investee's equity or its products or potential products;
- a significant change in the global economy or the economic environment in which the investee operates;
- a significant change in the performance of comparable entities, or in the valuations implied by the overall market;
- internal matters of the investee such as fraud, commercial disputes, litigation, changes in management or strategy; or
- evidence from external transactions in the investee's equity, either by the investee (such as a fresh issue of equity), or by transfers of equity instruments between third parties.

IFRS 9.BC80 3.6A.240.30 The circumstances described in 3.6A.240.20 are not applicable to equity investments held by particular entities such as financial institutions and investment funds.

3.6A.240.40 Application of the guidance in 3.6A.240.20 will require careful consideration of all facts and circumstances. For example, one of the indicators given is if there is a significant change in performance of the investee in comparison with budgets, plans or milestones or significant changes in expectations whether the investee's technical product milestones will be achieved. In some cases, for example start up companies, even performance in accordance with original plans, or the launch of a new product as expected, may lead to a significant increase in the fair value of the investment as uncertainty over those events is removed. This may mean that even if there are no significant changes in performance against plan, then cost may not be an appropriate estimate of fair value.

IAS 39.46, 47 3.6A.240.50 Unlike IAS 39, IFRS 9 does not have an exception for investments in equity instruments that do not have a quoted market price in an active market to be measured at cost if their fair value cannot be measured reliably. Similarly, it has no exception for derivative assets that are linked to and settled by delivery of such unquoted equity instruments.

3.6A.250 *Designation exception for investments in equity instruments*

IFRS 9.5.4.4, B5.12 3.6A.250.10 At initial recognition only, an entity may elect to present changes in the fair value of an investment in an equity instrument that is not held for trading in other comprehensive income. The election is irrevocable and can be made on an instrument-by-instrument (e.g. individual share) basis.

3.6A.260 *Definition of an equity instrument*

IFRS 9.BC82, IAS 32.11, 16A-D 3.6A.260.10 Equity instruments are defined consistently with IAS 32. This means that a holder of an investment assesses whether the instrument meets the definition of equity from the perspective of the issuer. IAS 32 both defines an equity instrument and provides guidance on what other instruments are classified as equity (see 3.11). However, in our view the fair value through other comprehensive income option refers only to equity instruments defined as such by IAS 32 and not to instruments defined as liabilities but classified as equity by the issuer, e.g. not to puttable instruments classified as equity by the issuer.

IAS 32.11, 39.9 3.6A.260.20 An entity may invest in a derivative instrument that meets the definition of an equity instrument of the issuer because it satisfies the fixed-for-fixed criterion in IAS 32 (see 3.11.20.40). However, the entity could not classify its investment as at fair value through other comprehensive income because derivative instruments are within the definition of held for trading (see 3.6.480.10) in IAS 39 and the election only pertains to investments that are not held for trading as defined by IAS 39.

IFRIC 2.9 3.6A.260.30 In some cases, it may not be possible for a holder to determine whether the particular instrument it holds meets the definition of an equity instrument of the issuer. For example, an entity may hold an investment in members' shares of a co-operative entity. The co-operative may be obliged to redeem members' shares subject to a right to refuse redemptions in excess of a certain amount, meaning that it might treat a proportion of the total shares in issue as equity and the remaining proportion as liabilities. In this case, the holder would not be able to determine that the instruments it holds meet the definition of an equity instrument and therefore, in our view it would be precluded from applying the fair value through other comprehensive income election to its investment.

3.6A.270 Exercise of a conversion feature in a convertible bond

3.6A.270.10 In our view, if an entity exercises a conversion feature in a convertible bond and converts the bond to equity instruments of the issuer, then the equity instruments should be accounted for as new assets which the entity may be able to classify as at fair value through other comprehensive income at the time of their initial recognition if all conditions for such classification are met.

3.6A.280 Amounts recognised in other comprehensive income

IFRS 9.B5.12 3.6A.280.10 For investments classified at fair value through other comprehensive income, the fair value that are recognised in other comprehensive income are not transferred to profit or loss on disposal of the investment or in any other circumstances, although they may be reclassified within equity. Accordingly, there is no need for impairment testing for these assets.

3.6A.290 Dividend income

IFRS 9.B5.12 3.6A.290.10 Dividend income on investments classified as at fair value through other comprehensive income is recognised in profit or loss in accordance with IAS 18 *Revenue* unless the dividend clearly represents a repayment of part of the cost of the investment. In this case, the dividend is recognised in other comprehensive income.

3.6A.300 Associates and joint ventures

IFRS 9.C21, 3.6A.300.10 IFRS 9 modifies the scope exemptions in IAS 28 and IAS 31 for venture
C22 capital organisations, mutual funds, unit trusts and similar entities, which allows investments in associates and joint ventures held by those entities to be accounted for under IAS 39. Prior to adoption of IFRS 9, this exemption is available if the eligible entity upon initial recognition designates the investments as at fair value through profit or loss or classifies the investments as trading. However, the consequential amendments make the exemption available in respect of all equity investments held by eligible entities, as under IFRS 9, all equity investments may be accounted for as at fair value through profit or loss.

3.6A.300.20 The consequential amendments to IAS 28 and IAS 31 potentially widen the scope exemption for some entities upon adoption of IFRS 9 as all equity investments may be accounted for as at fair value through profit or loss, not just those meeting the definition of held for trading or meeting the criteria for designation under the fair value option. However, the amendments do not permit such an investor to elect the fair value through other comprehensive income option in lieu of equity accounting or proportionate consolidation.

3.6A.310 ***Reclassifications***

IFRS 9.4.9, 3.6A.310.10 Classification of financial assets is determined on initial recognition
B5.9 (see 3.6A.40.10). Subsequent reclassification between categories generally is prohibited. However, when, and only when, an entity changes it business model in a way that is

significant to its operations, a reassessment is required as to whether the initial determination remains appropriate. If it is not, a reclassification of financial assets in accordance with the guidance on initial classification is required. Such changes to business models are expected to be very infrequent. They are determined by senior management of the entity as a result of internal or external changes and are demonstrable to external parties.

IFRS 9.B5.9   3.6A.310.20 The following are examples of a change in business model:

- An entity holds a portfolio of commercial loans for sale. Subsequently it acquires an entity whose business model is to hold similar loans in order to collect contractual cash flows and the commercial loans originally held for sale are transferred to the acquired entity to be managed together with the entity's other loans.
- An entity decides to shut down part of its business.

IFRS 9.B5.11   3.6A.310.30 The following changes do not represent a change in business model:

- a change in intention related to particular financial assets, even in circumstances of significant changes in market conditions;
- a temporary disappearance of a particular market for financial assets; or
- a transfer of financial assets between parts of the entity with different business models.

IFRS 9.5.3.1,   3.6A.310.40 If an entity determines that its business model has changed in a way that is
B5.10   significant to its operations, then all affected assets are reclassified from the first day of the next reporting period (the reclassification date). The change in business model must be effected before the reclassification date. In order for reclassification to be appropriate, the entity must not engage in activities consistent with its former business model after the date of change in business model. No prior periods are restated.

3.6A.310.50 IFRS 9 does not define the term reporting period. In our view, the reclassification date is dependent on the frequency of the entity's reporting, i.e. quarterly, semi-annually etc. For example, a company with an annual reporting period ending 31 December that reports quarterly determines that its business model has changed on 15 March 2010. Its reclassification date would be 1 April 2010.

IFRS 9.BC73   3.6A.310.60 In some cases there may be a long time period between the change in an entity's business model and the reclassification date. During this time period the financial assets existing at the date of change in business model continue to be accounted for as if the business model had not changed, although this no longer reflects the actual business model in operation. However, in our view the classification of any new assets initially recognised after the date of change in business model would be based on the new business model in effect at the date of their initial recognition.

3.6A.320 Accounting for a reclassification

IFRS 9.5.3.2,   3.6A.320.10 If a financial asset is reclassified from being measured at amortised cost
5.3.3   to being measured at fair value, then it is measured at fair value at the reclassification date

and any gain or loss arising from the difference between amortised cost and fair value is recognised in profit or loss. If a financial asset is reclassified from being measured at fair value to being measured at amortised cost, then the fair value at the reclassification date becomes the new carrying amount.

3.6A.330 **Lapse of a contractual term**

3.6A.330.10 Financial assets may contain a feature which is significant in determining the classification of a financial asset but this feature may expire before maturity of the financial asset. In our view, an entity should not reclassify the financial asset upon the expiration of the feature. For example, a bond convertible into equity of the issuer does not meet the SPPI criterion (see 3.6A.130.50) and therefore the entire instrument should be classified as at fair value through profit or loss. Assume however that the bond has a ten-year maturity but the conversion feature is only exercisable for the first five years. If at the end of five years the conversion feature has not been exercised, then the bond should remain classified as at fair value through profit or loss until its maturity.

3.6A.340 [Not used]

3.6A.350 **Transitional issues**

3.6A.360 *Date of initial application*

IFRS 9.8.2.2   3.6A.360.10 The transition requirements refer to the date of initial application which is the date on which an entity initially applies IFRS 9. The date of initial application can be:

- for initial application before 1 January 2011, any date between 12 November 2009 (issue date of IFRS 9) and 31 December 2010; or
- for initial application on or after 1 January 2011, the beginning of the first reporting period in which an entity adopts IFRS 9.

3.6A.360.20 The diagram below illustrates how different dates of initial application of IFRS 9 impact the date of initial application.

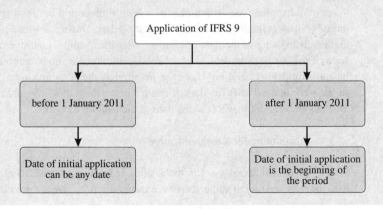

3.6A.360.30 IFRS 9 does not define date of initial application beyond stating that it is the date when an entity first applies the requirements of this IFRS. Therefore, entities will have to exercise judgement to determine what the date is when they first apply the standard, in particular if the date is not the beginning of a reporting period but a date during the reporting period. Identification of the date of initial application is relevant to several assessments necessary to apply IFRS 9 and may have important implications.

IFRS 9.8.2.3 3.6A.360.40 If the date of initial application is not the beginning of a period, then this fact and the reasons for using a different date are disclosed.

IFRS 9.8.2.1 3.6A.360.50 In calculating the transition adjustments, the general requirements of IAS 8 for changes in accounting policy apply, unless IFRS 9 contains more specific provisions for a particular aspect of the transition.

IFRS 9.8.2.1 3.6A.360.60 In particular, IFRS 9 is not applied to financial assets that already have been derecognised at the date of initial application. Accordingly, even when comparative information is restated to reflect the adoption of the IFRS 9, information related to financial assets derecognised before the date of initial application would continue to be reported in accordance with IAS 39 and the classification and measurement categories of that standard.

3.6A.360.70 For example, Company C adopts IFRS 9 in the annual period ending 31 December 2010. As C applies IFRS 9 before 1 January 2011, the date of initial application does not have to be the beginning of the reporting period. C determines that its date of initial application is 1 December 2010.

3.6A.360.80 In November 2010 C sold an investment in a debt security that was classified as available for sale under IAS 39. As IFRS 9 does not apply to financial assets that have been derecognised prior to the date of initial application, the debt security will be measured in accordance with the requirements of IAS 39 related to available-for-sale assets both in 2010 and in all comparative periods presented.

3.6A.360.90 However, if the date of initial application was determined to be the beginning of the accounting period (i.e. 1 January 2010), then the exemption would not apply as the asset would not have been derecognised prior to the date of initial application. Accordingly, the debt security would be accounted for in accordance with the requirements of IFRS 9 throughout the year ended 31 December 2010 and in any comparative period to which C applies IFRS 9 (see 3.6A.460 regarding comparative information).

3.6A.370 *Classification*

IFRS 9.8.2.1, 3.6A.370.10 On adoption of IFRS 9, an entity determines which of its financial assets
IAS 8.19, 22 meet the criteria to be measured at amortised cost. As a general rule, retrospective

application in accordance with IAS 8 is required, except where IFRS 9 sets out specific requirements. Retrospective application requires adjustment to the opening balance of equity for the earliest period presented and the other comparative amounts disclosed for each prior period presented as if the new accounting policy had always been applied. However, IFRS 9 contains significant exemptions from this principle (see 3.6A.460).

IFRS 9.8.2.4 3.6A.370.20 The assessment of whether the objective of an entity's business model is to hold an asset in order to collect the contractual cash flows is based on facts and circumstances at the date of initial application. The resulting classification is applied retrospectively irrespective of the entity's business model in prior reporting periods.

3.6A.370.30 Continuing the example in 3.6A.360.70, the assessment of whether the HTC criterion is met for financial assets recognised by C at 1 December 2010 would be made as at that date.

3.6A.370.40 There are no specific transition requirements as to the date at which an entity should assess whether the SPPI criterion is met. Therefore, the general provisions are applicable and an entity makes this assessment on the basis of facts and circumstances existing at the time of initial recognition of the financial asset.

3.6A.380 *Contractually linked instruments*

3.6A.380.10 Based on 3.6A.190.10, in our view the assessment of whether or not the exposure to credit risk in the underlying pool of financial instruments inherent in a contractually linked instrument is equal to or lower than the exposure to credit risk of the underlying pool should be based on the facts and circumstances that existed as at the date the entity initially recognised its investment in the instrument rather than at the date of initial application.

3.6A.390 *Investments in equity instruments*

IFRS 9.8.2.7 3.6A.390.10 At the date of initial application, an entity may designate an equity investment as at fair value through other comprehensive income.

IFRS 9.5.4.4, 3.6A.390.20 Designation of equity investments as at fair value through other comprehensive
B8.1, C27.9, income at the date of initial application is made on the basis of facts and circumstances
IAS 39.9 that exist at the date of initial application. This election is available only for equity investments that are not held for trading. IFRS 9 retains the definition of held for trading in IAS 39 in so far as an asset is considered held for trading if it was acquired for sale in the near term or on initial recognition was part of a portfolio for which there is evidence of a recent actual pattern of short-term profit taking. However, for the purpose of determining eligibility for the fair value through other comprehensive income election on transition, an entity determines whether an asset is held for trading as if it had

acquired the asset on the date of initial application. Therefore, in our view it is possible to designate as at fair value through other comprehensive income an investment in an equity instrument that was classified as held for trading at the investment's original acquisition date if it does not meet the held for trading definition at the date of initial application.

3.6A.400 *Option to designate financial assets as at fair value through profit or loss*

FRS 9.8.2.7-9 3.6A.400.10 The fair value option is reopened based on facts and circumstances at the date of initial application for financial assets and, partially, for financial liabilities. At that date, an entity:

- may choose to designate any financial asset or liability as at fair value through profit or loss if the accounting mismatch criterion in the standard is met;
- revokes an existing designation of a financial asset if the accounting mismatch criterion in the standard is not met;
- revokes an existing designation of a financial liability if it was originally designated on the basis of the accounting mismatch criterion but that criterion is no longer met; and
- may choose to revoke any existing designation of a financial asset or of a financial liability (but only if the liability was originally designated on the basis of the accounting mismatch criterion) even if the accounting mismatch criterion continues to be met.

3.6A.400.20 Although financial liabilities generally are excluded from the scope of IFRS 9, its transitional provisions allow limited re-opening of the designation of financial liabilities as at fair value through profit or loss, but only in relation to the accounting mismatch criterion. If an entity had an existing financial liability that had been designated as at fair value through profit or loss on the basis of the accounting mismatch criterion in IAS 39 but the criterion is no longer met at the date of initial application, then the designation is revoked; if the criterion is still met revocation of the designation is optional. Additionally, an entity may choose to designate an existing financial liability as at fair value through profit or loss if the accounting mismatch criterion is met based on facts and circumstances at the date of initial application.

3.6A.400.30 For example, Company D has a financial asset that was accounted for as a loan and receivable under IAS 39 but is required to be reclassified as at fair value through profit or loss on transition to IFRS 9. D manages the asset in conjunction with an existing financial liability that has been accounted for at amortised cost. If, at the date of initial application, D determines that designating the liability as at fair value through profit or loss would reduce an accounting mismatch compared to measuring the financial liability at amortised cost and the financial asset as at fair value through profit or loss, then D may so designate the financial liability as at fair value through profit or loss at the date of initial application.

Hybrid instruments

IFRS 9.8.2.5,   3.6A.410.10 If under IFRS 9 a hybrid instrument is required to be measured at fair
6   value in its entirety but its fair value has not been determined in previous periods,
then the sum of the fair values of the components at the end of each comparative
period is deemed to be the fair value of the entire instrument at those dates. These
circumstances might arise when a hybrid instrument was required to be separated
into a non-derivative host contract and an embedded derivative under IAS 39. At the
date of initial application any difference between the fair value of the entire hybrid
contract and the sum of the fair values of the components of the hybrid contract is
recognised:

- in opening retained earnings if IFRS 9 is applied at the beginning of the reporting
  period; or
- in profit or loss if IFRS 9 is applied initially during a reporting period; this is only
  applicable if an entity applies IFRS 9 before 1 January 2011 since after that date the
  date of initial application is always the beginning of a reporting period.

3.6A.410.20 For example, Company C has determined that its date of initial application
is 1 December 2010, which is not the beginning of a reporting period and restates its
comparatives in accordance with IFRS 9. Assume that C has a hybrid instrument with
a financial asset host. Under IAS 39, the host was accounted for at amortised cost and
the embedded derivative was separated and accounted for as at fair value through profit
or loss. In accordance with IFRS 7, C has disclosed previously the fair value of the host
at each reporting date. C determines that under IFRS 9 the entire hybrid instrument
will be accounted for as at fair value through profit or loss. The fair value of the hybrid
instrument in its entirety had not been determined in previous periods. Relevant amounts
related to the hybrid instrument are as follows:

Date	Fair value - embedded derivative	Fair value - host contract	Fair value - hybrid instrument
1 January 2009	5	87	N/A
31 December 2009	8	90	N/A
1 December 2010	6	91	95
31 December 2010	N/A	N/A	94

3.6A.410.30 The amortised cost of the host contract at 1 January 2009 is 88.

3.6A.410.40 C recognises the following amounts in its statement of financial position
under IFRS 9:

Date	Amount recognised for the hybrid contract	
1 January 2009	92	(5 + 87)
31 December 2009	98	(8 + 90)
1 December 2010	95	
31 December 2010	94	

3.6A.410.50 C recognises the following amounts in profit or loss:

Period	Amount recognised in profit or loss	
1 January 2009 – 31 December 2009	gain of 6	(98 - 92)
1 January 2010 – 1 December 2010	loss of 3	(95 - 98)
1 December 2010 – 31 December 2010	loss of 1	(94 - 95)

3.6A.410.60 C would record a transition adjustment in opening retained earnings as at 1 January 2009 of 1 (debit) being the difference between the amortised cost of the host of 88 and its fair value of 87. The difference between the sum of the fair values of the host and the embedded derivative at 1 December 2010 and the fair value of the hybrid instrument at that date of 2 ((91 + 6) - 95) is included in profit for the year ended 2010. By contrast, if C's date of initial application was 1 January 2010, then the difference between the sum of the fair values of the host and the embedded derivative at 1 January 2010 would be included in opening retained earnings at 1 January 2010 and not in profit or loss for the period.

3.6A.410.70 If, under IAS 39, the economic characteristics and risks of the embedded derivative in a financial asset had been considered closely related to those of the host contract and the embedded derivative was not separated from the host contract, the fair value of the hybrid instrument in its entirety should have been determined in previous annual periods, either because the entire instrument would have been measured at fair value under IAS 39 or for the purpose of disclosure under IFRS 7. In this case, the specific transitional provision outlined in 3.6A.400.10 would not be applicable.

3.6A.420 *Effective interest method and impairment*

FRS 9.8.2.10, IAS 8.5 3.6A.420.10 If retrospective application of the effective interest method and impairment requirements for financial instruments reclassified to the amortised cost category is impracticable (see 2.8.50), then the fair value at the end of each comparative period is treated as amortised cost. The fair value at the date of initial application is treated as the new amortised cost at that date.

3.6A.420.20 When the impracticable exemption has been used, IFRS 9 does not provide guidance on how the profit or loss impact should be presented, i.e. whether the difference between the opening and closing period values should be presented as interest or impairment. If an entity held a debt investment that was classified as available for sale in prior periods, then the effective interest method would have been applied under IAS 39 to determine the recognition of interest income. However, if the investment was impaired, the amortised cost under IAS 39 could have been reset to fair value at the date of impairment, giving an amortised cost under IAS 39 that is different from the amortised cost that would have been calculated if the investment had been measured on an amortised cost basis (see 3.6.1430.15).

3.6A.430 *Previously reclassified financial assets*

3.6A.430.10 An entity may have reclassified previously under IAS 39 a financial asset from the held-for-trading or available-for-sale categories, measured at fair value, to loans and receivables, measured at amortised cost. Under IAS 39, the entity would have reclassified the financial asset at its fair value and this fair value would have become the new amortised cost (see 3.6.860.15 and 880.06). Upon transition to IFRS 9, entities generally are required to retrospectively apply its classification and measurement requirements as if the new classification under IFRS 9 had always been applied (see 3.6A.370.10). Therefore, in our view if such a previously reclassified financial asset is classified as measured at amortised cost under IFRS 9 then the amortised cost should be recalculated as if the asset had always been measured at amortised cost rather than by carrying forward the amortised cost measurement under IAS 39.

3.6A.440 *Unquoted equity investments measured at cost*

IFRS 9.8.2.11 3.6A.440.10 If unquoted equity investments or related derivatives previously were measured at cost, then those investments are measured at fair value at the date of initial application with any difference between the carrying amount and fair value recognised in opening retained earnings in the reporting period of initial application.

3.6A.440.20 As the difference between the fair value and the carrying amount of the instrument at the date of initial application is recorded as an adjustment to opening retained earnings of the reporting period of initial application, only fair value changes after the date of initial application are recognised in profit or loss or other comprehensive income. This means that the impact on profits in the first period of reporting in accordance with IFRS 9 may depend on the choice of the date of initial application.

3.6A.440.30 Continuing the example in 3.6A.360.70, assume that Company C had an equity investment that was measured at cost less impairment under IAS 39. The carrying amount of the investment was 450. Under IFRS 9, C determines the fair value of the investment at the date of initial application is 630. The difference between the carrying amount of 450 and the fair value on the date of initial application of 1 December 2010 of 630 is recognised in opening retained earnings of the reporting period of initial application, which for C is 1 January 2010. Any fair value changes arising between

1 December 2010 and 31 December 2010 are recognised in profit or loss unless C designates the investment as at fair value through other comprehensive income.

3.6A.450 *Hedge accounting*

3.6A.450.10 IFRS 9 does not contain specific transitional guidance in respect of hedge accounting.

3.6A.450.20 If fair value hedge accounting was applied to an asset that was measured at amortised cost or at fair value through other comprehensive income (i.e. available for sale) under IAS 39, but is measured as at fair value through profit or loss under IFRS 9, then hedge accounting will be discontinued and the hedged item will be subject to full fair value measurement through profit or loss rather than re-measurement only in respect of the risk being hedged. No adjustment to periods before the date of initial application will be required in respect of the derivative hedging instrument as gains and losses would have been already reflected in profit or loss.

3.6A.460 *Comparatives*

FRS 9.8.2.12   3.6A.460.10 If an entity adopts IFRS 9 for reporting periods beginning before 1 January 2012, then the entity can elect not to restate prior periods. If such an election is made, any difference between the carrying amount of a financial asset prior to the adoption of IFRS 9 and the new carrying amount calculated in accordance with the standard at the beginning of the annual reporting period that includes the date of initial application is recognised in opening retained earnings (or another component of equity if appropriate) of the reporting period that includes the date of initial application.

3.6A.460.20 The diagram below illustrates how different dates of adoption of IFRS 9 impact the presentation of comparatives.

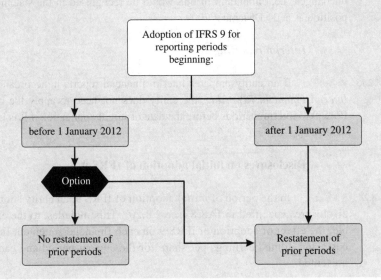

3.6A.460.30 Continuing the example in 3.6A.360.70, as Company C adopts IFRS 9 prior to 1 January 2012 i.e. its date of initial application is 1 December 2010), it may elect not to restate comparative information. If so, the comparatives would be unchanged and would reflect previous accounting for financial assets under IAS 39. The impact of the retrospective application according to IAS 8 will be recognised in opening equity as of 1 January 2010.

3.6A.460.40 For example, assume that C has an investment in a financial asset that was measured at amortised cost under IAS 39 and it has determined that under IFRS 9 the asset will be measured as at fair value through profit or loss. The carrying amount of the asset was 350 on 31 December 2008 and 368 on 31 December 2009. The fair value of the asset was 355 on 31 December 2008 and 370 on 31 December 2009. C presents one year of comparative information.

3.6A.460.50 Under the general rules of retrospective application of IAS 8 in the December 2010 financial statements, the difference between the fair value and the previous carrying amount at the beginning of the earliest period presented is recognised in opening retained earnings as of 1 January 2009. This would mean that 5, being the difference between the fair value at 31 December 2008 of 355 and the previous carrying amount at the date of 350, would be recognised as a credit adjustment to opening retained earnings at 1 January 2009. The change in fair value between 31 December 2008 of 355 and at 31 December 2009 of 370, a gain of 15, would be recognised in profit or loss for the year ended 31 December 2009.

3.6A.460.60 However, if C decided to take the exemption from restatement of comparative information, then 2, being the difference between fair value at 31 December 2009 of 370 and the carrying amount at that date of 368, would be recognised in opening retained earnings as of 1 January 2010. The comparative figures for 2009 would remain unchanged, i.e. an amount of 368 would be recognised in the statement of financial position as at 31 December 2009.

3.6A.470 *Interim reporting*

IFRS 9.8.2.13   3.6A.470.10 If an entity prepares interim financial reports in accordance with IAS 34 *Interim Financial Reporting*, the entity does not need to apply the requirements of IFRS 9 to interim periods before the date of initial application if it is impracticable as defined by IAS 8.

3.6A.480 Disclosures on initial adoption of IFRS 9

IAS 8.28   3.6A.480.10 In the period of initial adoption of IFRS 9, an entity should provide the disclosures specified in IAS 8 (see 2.8.20). This includes, to the extent practicable, the effect of adoption of IFRS 9 on each financial statement line item and on basic and diluted earnings per share for the current period and each prior period presented.

IFRS 9.C8.
44I

3.6A.480.20 The following disclosures in tabular format (unless another format is more appropriate) are required for each class of financial assets at the date of initial application:

- the original measurement category and carrying amount under IAS 39;
- the new measurement category and carrying amount under IFRS 9; and
- the amount of any financial assets that were previously designated as at fair value through profit or loss, but for which the designation has been revoked, distinguishing between mandatory and elective de-designations.

IFRS 9.C8.
44J

3.6A.480.30 Entities also should provide qualitative disclosures to enable users to understand:

- how the entity applied the classification requirements of IFRS 9 to those financial assets whose classification has changed as a result of applying IFRS 9; and
- the reasons for any designation or de-designation of financial assets or financial liabilities as measured as at fair value through profit or loss.

3.6A.490 First-time adoption

IFRS 9.C2

3.6A.490.10 Generally IFRS 1 *First-time Adoption of International Financial Reporting Standards* requires full retrospective application of IFRSs that are effective at the end of the entity's first IFRS reporting period. However, the consequential amendments introduced by IFRS 9 prohibit retrospective application. Instead, the assessment whether a financial asset meets the criteria for amortised cost classification (the HTC and SPPI criteria) is made on the basis of facts and circumstances that exist at the date of transition to IFRSs, i.e. the beginning of the earliest period for which an entity presents full comparative information under IFRSs. This is in contrast to the transitional provisions of IFRS 9 for entities that already report under IFRSs, which require an assessment of the business model based on facts and circumstances as at the date of initial application and an assessment of the SPPI criterion as at the inception of the instrument.

IFRS 9.C3

3.6A.490.20 The amendments to IFRS 1 includes some exemptions that may be applied voluntarily:

- A financial asset may be designated as at fair value through profit or loss to avoid an accounting mismatch based on facts and circumstances at the date of transition. A similar rule is retained for financial liabilities.
- An equity investment may be designated as at fair value through other comprehensive income based on facts and circumstances at the date of transition.

3.6A.490.30 Additionally, if it is impracticable to apply the effective interest method or the impairment requirements of IAS 39 retrospectively, the fair value at the date of transition is the new amortised cost.

3.6A.490.40 The diagram below illustrates application of the requirements described in 3.6A.490.20, assuming one year of comparative information is provided.

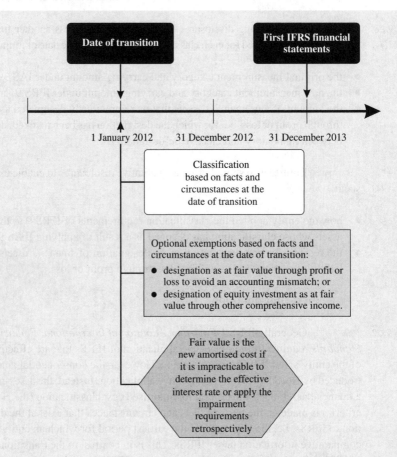

IFRS 9.C3 3.6A.490.50 If a first-time adopter adopts IFRSs for an annual period beginning before 1 January 2012 and chooses to apply IFRS 9, then comparative information in the first IFRS financial statements does not have to be restated in accordance with IFRS 9. This exemption includes also IFRS 7 disclosures related to assets in the scope of IAS 39. If this option is taken:

- with respect to the application of IFRS 9, the *date of transition* is the beginning of the first IFRS reporting period;
- for assets in the scope of IAS 39, previous GAAP is applied in comparative periods (rather than IFRS 9 or IAS 39);
- the fact that the exemption is applied, as well as the basis of preparation of the comparative information, is disclosed; and
- the differences arising on adoption of IFRS 9 are treated as a change in accounting policy; all adjustments resulting from applying IFRS 9 are recognised in the statement of financial position at the beginning of the first IFRS reporting period and certain disclosures required by IAS 8 are given.

3.6A.490.60 Accordingly, on transition to IFRS, a first-time adopter of IFRSs with an adoption date before 1 January 2012 may take advantage of this exemption from restating comparative information in accordance with IFRS 9. This means that, in comparative periods, information related to financial assets will be presented on the basis of previous GAAP. However, as there is no similar relief for financial liabilities, they would have to be fully restated in comparative periods in accordance with IAS 39.

3.6A.490.70 The diagram below illustrates the application by a first-time adopter in 2010 who has elected not to provide comparative information in accordance with IFRS 9.

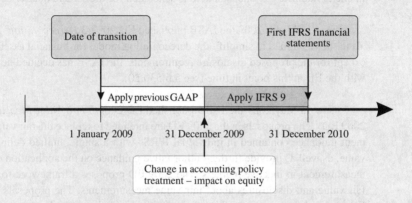

3.6A.500 **Future developments**

3.6A.500.10 In March 2008 the IASB published a DP *Reducing Complexity in Reporting Financial Instruments*, seeking constituents' views on all the issues addressed in the DP. The objectives of the DP were to gather information to assist the IASB in its decision on how to proceed with developing a less complex and principles-based standard on the accounting for financial instruments, which is consistent with the IASB and FASB's long-term objective of measuring all financial instruments at fair value; and to simplify or eliminate the need for special hedge accounting requirements.

3.6A.500.15 Following the comment period and recommendations from various stakeholders, including the Financial Crisis Advisory Group (FCAG) and the Group of Twenty (G20), the IASB and the FASB subsequently added projects to replace the current financial instruments standards to their agendas.

3.6A.500.20 The IASB's project to replace IAS 39 includes the following phases:

* classification and measurement (see 3.6A.500.40);
* impairment (see 3.6A.500.30); and
* hedging (see 3.7.900.20).

3.6A.500.30 In November 2009 the IASB published ED/2009/12 *Financial Instruments: Amortised Cost and Impairment*, which proposes to replace the incurred loss method for impairment of financial assets with a method based on expected losses (i.e. expected cash flow or ECF approach) and to provide a more principles-based approach to measuring amortised cost. The proposals in the ED would apply to all financial instruments within the scope of IAS 39 that are measured at amortised cost. A final standard is scheduled for the second quarter of 2011.

3.6A.500.40 Except for the presentation of changes in the fair value of financial liabilities due to own credit risk (see 5.6.530.20), the IASB has decided generally to retain the current requirements in IAS 39 in respect of the classification and measurement of financial liabilities. A final standard is scheduled for the second quarter of 2011.

3.6A.500.50 In March 2009 the IASB published ED/2009/3 *Derecognition*. The proposals in the ED aimed to simplify the derecognition model for financial assets. However, except for the proposed disclosure requirements, the IASB has decided not to proceed with the ED at this point in time (see 5.6.530.20).

3.6A.500.60 In May 2009 the IASB published ED/2009/5 *Fair Value Measurement* (the 2009 ED). The proposals in the 2009 ED are intended to replace the fair value measurement guidance contained in individual IFRSs with a single, unified definition of fair value, as well as provide further authoritative guidance on the application of fair value measurement in inactive markets. The 2009 ED proposes a framework for measuring fair value and disclosures about fair value measurements. The proposals in the 2009 ED explain how to measure fair value when it already is required or permitted by existing IFRSs; they do not introduce new fair value measurements, nor do they eliminate the practicability exceptions to fair value measurements that exist currently in certain standards.

3.6A.500.70 In June 2010 the IASB published ED/2010/7 *Measurement Uncertainty Analysis Disclosure for Fair Value Measurements* (the 2010 ED). The 2010 ED expands on the proposal in the 2009 ED for an entity to disclose a measurement uncertainty analysis (or sensitivity analysis) for assets and liabilities measured at fair value categorised within Level 3 of the fair value hierarchy. The 2010 ED proposes that an entity consider the effect of correlation between unobservable inputs, if relevant.

3.6A.500.80 A final standard on fair value measurement and disclosure, which is expected to be converged with a forthcoming amended standard under US GAAP, is scheduled for the first quarter of 2011.

3.6A.510 *FASB exposure draft*

3.6A.510.10 The FASB published its proposals on financial instruments accounting on 26 May 2010 in a comprehensive ED that addresses classification and measurement, impairment and hedge accounting.

3.6A.510.20 This ED contains the following proposals:

- Most financial instruments would be measured at fair value.

- For derivatives and financial instruments for which an entity's strategy is to trade the instruments, fair value would continue to be required, with all changes in fair value recognised in profit or loss.
- Changes in the fair value of equity instruments, certain hybrid instruments and financial instruments that can be contractually prepaid in such a way that the holder would not recover substantially all of its investment would be recognised in profit or loss regardless of the entity's business strategy with respect to those instruments.
- For financial instruments held under a business model which is to collect contractual cash flows an entity may provide a reconciliation from amortised cost to fair value on the face of the statement of financial position.
- The existing "probable" threshold for recognising impairments on loans has been removed.
- In relation to hedge accounting:
  - Quantitative based hedging requirements have been replaced with more qualitative based requirements with the anticipated effect of making it easier to qualify for hedge accounting and better reflecting the economics of the hedging relationship.
  - The short-cut method is eliminated and replaced with the critical terms match method similar to IFRS.
  - The ability to voluntarily discontinue hedge accounting has been eliminated. It is proposed that hedge accounting would be discontinued only if the criteria for hedge accounting are no longer met or the hedging instrument expires, is sold, terminated, or exercised.

3.7 Hedge accounting
(IAS 39, IFRIC 16)

3.7 Hedge accounting

(IAS 39, IFRIC 16)

Overview of currently effective requirements

- Hedge accounting allows an entity to selectively measure assets, liabilities and firm commitments on a basis different from that otherwise stipulated in IFRSs, or to defer the recognition in profit or loss of gains or losses on derivatives.

- Hedge accounting is voluntary; however, it is permitted only when strict documentation and effectiveness requirements are met.

- There are three hedge accounting models: fair value hedges of fair value exposures, cash flow hedges of cash flow exposures, and net investment hedges of currency exposure on a net investment in a foreign operation.

- Qualifying hedged items can be recognised assets, liabilities, unrecognised firm commitments, highly probable forecast transactions or net investments in foreign operations.

- Only derivative instruments, and for hedges of foreign exchange risk only, non-derivative financial instruments, entered into with an external party qualify as hedging instruments.

- Effectiveness testing is conducted on both a prospective and retrospective basis. In order for a hedge to be effective, changes in the fair value or cash flows of the hedged item attributable to the hedged risk should be offset by changes in the fair value or cash flows of the hedging instrument within a range of 80 – 125 percent.

Currently effective requirements

This publication reflects IFRSs in issue at 1 August 2010. The currently effective requirements cover annual periods beginning on 1 January 2010. The requirements related to this topic are derived mainly from IAS 39 *Financial Instruments: Recognition and Measurement* and IFRIC 16 *Hedges of a Net Investment in a Foreign Operation*.

Forthcoming requirements and future developments

When a currently effective requirement will be changed by a new requirement that is issued but is not yet effective, it is marked with a # as a **forthcoming requirement** and the impact of the change is explained in the accompanying boxed text. The forthcoming requirements related to this topic are derived from IFRS 9 *Financial Instruments*. IFRS 9 will replace the currently effective requirements in IAS 39 with respect to classification and measurement of financial assets. A brief outline of the impact of IFRS 9 on this topic is given in 3.6A.450.

When a significant change to the currently effective or forthcoming requirements is expected, it is marked with a * as an area that may be subject to **future developments** and a brief outline of the relevant project is given in 3.7.900.

3.7.10 **Introduction**

3.7.10.10 IAS 39 uses a mixed measurement model that requires the measurement of financial assets and liabilities on different bases; for example, certain financial assets and liabilities are measured at amortised cost while, in principle, all derivatives are measured at fair value through profit or loss (see 3.6.790). This results in an accounting mismatch in profit or loss, which results in volatility in reported results.

3.7.10.12 Similarly, other IFRSs require or permit assets and liabilities to be measured on bases other than fair value through profit or loss, and certain contracts are recognised in financial statements only to the extent of performance (see 1.2.60). When an entity offsets the risks arising from these recognised assets and liabilities or unrecognised contracts by entering into hedging instruments, there is a resulting accounting mismatch in profit or loss.

3.7.10.14 Consequently, an entity could measure selectively assets, liabilities and firm commitments on a basis different from that stipulated under other requirements of IFRSs, or to defer the recognition in profit or loss of gains or losses on derivatives, using hedge accounting. Since hedge accounting results in an entity deviating from the normal measurement or presentation requirements under IFRSs, it is permitted only when strict documentation and effectiveness testing requirements are met.

3.7.10.20 There are three hedge accounting models, and the type of model applied depends on whether the hedged exposure is a fair value exposure, a cash flow exposure or a currency exposure on a net investment in a foreign operation.

3.7.10.30 Hedge accounting is voluntary and the decision to apply hedge accounting is made on a transaction-by-transaction basis or for a group of similar transactions. If an economic hedge does not qualify for hedge accounting, then any derivative used is measured at fair value with all changes in fair value recognised in profit or loss. Often these changes will not be matched by offsetting gains or losses on the items being hedged when changes in the fair value of the hedged item that do occur are not permitted under IFRSs to be recognised in profit or loss without hedge accounting being applied. In our view, an entity's risk management disclosures should contain appropriate explanation of economic hedges that do not qualify for hedge accounting.

3.7.10.40 When entering into a derivative transaction to reduce or eliminate a fair value risk exposure, an entity may find it easier to designate a potential hedged item that is

582

a non-derivative financial asset or liability as at fair value through profit or loss, rather than apply hedge accounting. Such a designation does not require the entity to perform an assessment of effectiveness; nor does it require rigorous documentation. However, the entity needs to comply with the conditions for applying the fair value option, which is irrevocable (see 3.6.490).

3.7.20 Hedge accounting models

3.7.30 *Fair value hedges*

3.7.40 *Definition*

IAS 39.86(a)   3.7.40.10 A fair value hedge is a hedge of changes in the fair value of a recognised asset or liability, an unrecognised firm commitment, or an identified portion of such an asset, liability or firm commitment, that is attributable to a particular risk and could affect profit or loss.

IAS 39.78,   3.7.40.20 The following are examples of fair value hedges:
AG102

- a hedge of interest rate risk associated with a fixed rate interest-bearing asset or liability (e.g. converting a fixed rate instrument to a floating rate instrument using an interest rate swap);
- a hedge of a firm commitment to purchase an asset or to incur a liability; or
- a hedge of interest rate risk on a portfolio basis (portfolio fair value hedge (see 3.7.210)).

IAS 39.87   3.7.40.30 A hedge of the foreign currency risk of a firm commitment may be accounted for as either a fair value hedge or a cash flow hedge, although in our experience cash flow hedging is applied more commonly in practice. Fair value hedge accounting can be applied only if there is a firm commitment. Consequently, if a highly probable forecast transaction exists prior to an entity entering into a firm commitment, then the hedge would have to be accounted for as a cash flow hedge until the entity enters into a firm commitment, from which time it could be accounted for as a fair value hedge. Generally it is simpler to implement a single model for hedge accounting purposes, rather than having to switch models during the life of the hedge.

3.7.50 *Accounting*

IAS 39.89   3.7.50.10 If the hedging instrument is a derivative, then it is measured at fair value with changes in fair value recognised in profit or loss. The hedged item is remeasured to fair value in respect of the hedged risk, even if normally it is measured at amortised cost, e.g. a fixed rate borrowing. Any resulting adjustment to the carrying amount of the hedged item related to the hedged risk is recognised in profit or loss, even if such a change normally would be recognised in other comprehensive income, e.g. for an available-for-sale financial asset (see 5.6.620). In our view, the categorisation of the fair value hedge adjustment as either a monetary or non-monetary item, under IAS 21 *The Effects of Changes in Foreign Exchange Rates*, should be consistent with the categorisation of the hedged item under IAS 21 (see 2.7.120).

IAS 39.93, 94 3.7.50.20 Upon entering into a firm commitment, an entity typically would not recognise the firm commitment in the statement of financial position. However, for a hedge of a firm commitment, fair value hedge accounting results in the change in the fair value of the firm commitment attributable to the hedged risk during the period of the hedge relationship being recognised as an asset or a liability in the statement of financial position. When the firm commitment is settled the amount recognised previously in the statement of financial position in respect of the fair value of the firm commitment is transferred to adjust the initial measurement of the asset or liability recognised.

IAS 39.90 3.7.50.30 The adjustment to the carrying amount of the hedged item in a fair value hedge often results in the item being measured neither at cost nor fair value. This is because the adjustment:

- is made only for changes attributable to the risk being hedged — not for all risks;
- only occurs during the period in which hedge accounting is applied; and
- is limited to the extent that the item is hedged.

3.7.50.40 For example, Company Z has a fixed interest liability denominated in its functional currency and measured at amortised cost. Z enters into a pay-LIBOR receive-fixed interest rate swap to hedge half of the notional amount of the liability in respect of its benchmark interest exposure. The swap qualifies for hedge accounting. Half of the liability (i.e. the proportion that is hedged) will be remeasured with respect to changes in fair value due to changes in benchmark interest rates from the beginning of the hedge relationship. The liability will not be remeasured for any changes in its fair value due to changes in credit spread, liquidity spread or other factors.

3.7.50.50 [Not used]

3.7.50.60 All changes in the fair value of the hedging instrument are recognised in profit or loss immediately. In a fair value hedge any ineffectiveness automatically is reported in profit or loss through the accounting process, unlike in a cash flow hedge when the ineffectiveness has to be calculated and recognised separately.

3.7.60 *Cash flow hedges*

3.7.70 *Definition*

IAS 39.86(b) 3.7.70.10 A cash flow hedge is a hedge of the exposure to variability in cash flows that is attributable to a particular risk associated with a recognised asset or liability, or a highly probable forecast transaction, that could affect profit or loss.

IAS 39.AG103 3.7.70.20 Examples of cash flow hedges are:

- hedges of floating rate interest-bearing instruments using an interest rate swap;
- hedges of floating rate interest-bearing instruments using an interest rate cap, floor or collar;
- hedges of the currency exposure on foreign currency denominated future operating lease or payroll payments; and
- hedges of highly probable forecast purchase or sale transactions.

3.7.80 *Accounting*

IAS 39.95 3.7.80.10 If the hedging instrument is a derivative, then the hedging instrument is measured at fair value with the effective portion of changes in its fair value recognised in other comprehensive income and presented within equity, normally in a hedging reserve. The ineffective portion of the gain or loss on the hedging instrument is recognised immediately in profit or loss.

3.7.80.20 If the hedging instrument is a non-derivative monetary item, which is permitted only for hedges of foreign currency risk, then the effective portion of the foreign exchange gains and losses on the hedging instrument are recognised in other comprehensive income.

IS 39.97-100 3.7.80.30 The change in fair value of the hedging instrument that is recognised in other comprehensive income is reclassified to profit or loss when the hedged item affects profit or loss. Consequently, if the impact of the hedged risk on profit or loss arising from the hedged item is deferred, then the amount recognised in the cash flow hedge reserve may remain in equity until the hedged item affects profit or loss.

3.7.80.40 The standard provides some flexibility in the accounting for such reclassifications, which are:

- If the future transaction results in the recognition of a non-financial asset or a non-financial liability, then an entity may either include the cumulative amount in equity in the initial carrying amount of that asset or liability (basis adjustment), or retain the amount in equity and reclassify it to profit or loss in the same period(s) during which the asset or liability affects profit or loss (e.g. when the asset is sold or as it is depreciated). The same choice applies to a forecast transaction of a non-financial asset or a non-financial liability that becomes a firm commitment for which fair value hedge accounting subsequently is applied. An entity should choose an accounting policy, to be applied consistently, to all cash flow hedges of transactions that lead to the recognition of non-financial assets or liabilities.
- If the future transaction results in the acquisition of a financial instrument, then the cumulative amount remains in equity and is reclassified to profit or loss in the same period(s) during which the financial instrument's hedged forecast cash flows affect profit or loss (e.g. as it is amortised or when it is impaired or sold). For example, Company V has a highly probable forecast purchase of a listed equity security which it designates as the hedged item in a cash flow hedge. On 30 November 2010 V

purchases the equity security, and classifies it as available for sale; subsequently, changes in the fair value of the equity instrument are recognised in other comprehensive income until either an impairment event or a disposal occurs. In our view, the gain or loss on the hedging instrument should remain in equity until the equity instrument is either impaired or sold.

3.7.80.50 The accounting in 3.7.80.40 applies also when cash flow hedge accounting is used to hedge the exposure to the foreign currency risk of firm commitments. See 3.7.610 for hedges of foreign currency risk of firm commitments to acquire a business and forecast business combinations.

3.7.90 *Net investment hedges*

3.7.90.10 While IAS 39 does not override the principles of IAS 21 (see 2.7), it does introduce the hedge accounting model for hedging an entity's foreign exchange exposure arising from net investments in foreign operations.

3.7.100 *Definition*

IAS 39.86(c)   3.7.100.10 A net investment hedge is a hedge of the foreign currency exposure arising from a net investment in a foreign operation using a derivative, and/or a non-derivative monetary item, as the hedging instrument.

3.7.100.20 The hedged risk is the foreign currency exposure arising from a net investment in a foreign operation when the net assets of that foreign operation are included in the financial statements (see 3.7.630.10).

3.7.100.30 Often the exposure to changes in the value of a net investment due to movements in foreign exchange rates is hedged through borrowings denominated in the foreign operation's functional currency or, in more limited circumstances, derivative currency contracts.

3.7.110 *Accounting*

IAS 39.102, 3.7.110.10 If the hedging instrument in a net investment hedge is a derivative, then it is
IFRIC 16.3, measured at fair value. The effective portion of the change in fair value of the hedging
15 instrument, computed by reference to the functional currency of the parent entity against whose functional currency the hedged risk is measured, is recognised in other comprehensive income and presented within equity in the foreign currency translation reserve (see 2.7.260). The ineffective portion of the gain or loss on the hedging instrument is recognised immediately in profit or loss.

IFRIC 16.15 3.7.110.20 If the hedging instrument is a non-derivative, e.g. a foreign currency borrowing, then the effective portion of the foreign exchange gain or loss arising on translation of the hedging instrument under IAS 21 into the functional currency of the hedging entity is recognised in other comprehensive income. The effective portion is computed by reference to the functional currency of the parent entity against whose functional currency the hedged risk is measured.

AS 21.48-49,
39.102,
IFRIC 16.6,
16, 17 3.7.110.30 When a net investment in a foreign operation is disposed of, the cumulative amounts related to both the foreign exchange differences arising on translation of the results and the financial position of the foreign operation, and the effective portion of the gain or loss on the hedging instrument recognised in other comprehensive income and presented within equity in the foreign currency translation reserve (the "cumulative amounts") are treated as follows:

- Upon disposal of the entire interest in a foreign operation, including a reduction in an ownership interest that results in the entity losing control, joint control or significant influence over the other entity that includes the foreign operation (see 2.7.320.14), the cumulative amounts recognised previously in other comprehensive income are reclassified to profit or loss and no amount of the reclassification is allocated to non-controlling interests (see 2.5.490.40).

  As an exception, when a parent loses control of a subsidiary by contributing it to an associate or a jointly controlled entity and elects to eliminate the part of the gain or loss in respect of the continuing interest in the assets and liabilities contributed, then in our view only a proportionate share of the cumulative amounts recognised previously in other comprehensive income is reclassified to profit or loss (see 3.5.470).

- When an entity partially disposes of a subsidiary that includes a foreign operation, but retains control, the entity reattributes a proportionate share of the cumulative amounts recognised previously in other comprehensive income to non-controlling interests (see 2.7.320.22).

- In any other partial disposal of a foreign operation, the entity reclassifies to profit or loss only a proportionate share of the cumulative amounts recognised previously in other comprehensive income (see 2.7.320.30).

3.7.110.35 Therefore, it is necessary for an entity to keep track of the amount recognised in other comprehensive income separately in respect of each foreign operation, in order to identify the amounts to be reclassified to profit or loss on disposal or partial disposal.

FRIC 16.17 3.7.110.40 The method of consolidation, i.e. step-by-step or direct method, may affect the amount that is included in the foreign currency translation reserve for an individual foreign operation. When the step-by-step method of consolidation is applied, it may lead to the reclassification to profit or loss of an amount that is different from the amount used to assess hedge effectiveness. An entity may eliminate this difference by retrospectively determining the amount that would have resulted from using the direct method of consolidation. The amount so determined would then be reclassified from equity to profit or loss upon disposal or partial disposal as discussed in the preceding paragraph. This adjustment is not required by IAS 21. However, an entity should choose an accounting policy, to be applied consistently, for all net investments (see 2.7.320.12).

3.7.120 *Hedge accounting criteria*

IAS 39.88   3.7.120.10 Hedge accounting is permitted only if all of the following conditions are met:

- There is formal designation and written documentation at the inception of the hedge (see 3.7.120.30).
- The effectiveness of the hedging relationship can be measured reliably. This requires the fair value of the hedging instrument, and the fair value (or cash flows) of the hedged item with respect to the risk being hedged, to be reliably measurable.
- The hedge is expected to be highly effective in achieving fair value or cash flow offsets in accordance with the original documented risk management strategy.
- The hedge is assessed and determined to be highly effective on an ongoing basis throughout the hedge relationship. A hedge is highly effective if changes in the fair value of the hedging instrument, and changes in the fair value or expected cash flows of the hedged item attributable to the hedged risk, offset within the range of 80 – 125 percent.
- For a cash flow hedge of a forecast transaction, the transaction is highly probable and creates an exposure to variability in cash flows that ultimately could affect profit or loss.

3.7.120.20 In our view, the key challenges in implementing hedge accounting are identifying a specific asset or liability, or portfolio of similar assets or liabilities, to designate as the hedged item and demonstrating that the hedge is highly effective (both prospectively and retrospectively).

IAS 39.88   3.7.120.30 At inception of the hedge, formal documentation of the hedge relationship should be established. The hedge documentation prepared at inception includes a description of the following:

- the entity's risk management objective and strategy for undertaking the hedge;
- the nature of the risk being hedged;
- clear identification of the hedged item (asset, liability, firm commitment or cash flows arising from a forecast transaction) and the hedging instrument; and
- how hedge effectiveness will be assessed both prospectively and retrospectively. The method and procedures should be described in sufficient detail to establish a firm and consistent basis for measurement in subsequent periods for the particular hedge.

3.7.120.40 IAS 39 does not mandate a specific format for the documentation and, in practice, hedge documentation may vary in terms of layout, methodology and processes used. Various formats are acceptable as long as the documentation includes the content from 3.7.120.30.

3.7.130 *Risk reduction*

IAS 39.IG
F.2.6

3.7.130.10 Risk exposure is assessed on a transaction basis, and entity-wide risk reduction is not a condition for hedge accounting. For example, an entity may have fixed rate assets and liabilities that provide a natural economic hedge that leaves the entity with no exposure to interest rate risk. The entity may decide to enter into a pay-fixed receive-floating swap and to designate this as a hedge of the fixed rate assets. Although this would increase the entity's overall exposure to interest rate risk, hedge accounting may be applied to this transaction provided that the relevant hedge accounting criteria are met.

3.7.140 *Flexibility in the type of hedge accounting*

IAS 39.87,
IGF.3.3,
IGF.3.6

3.7.140.10 In some cases a hedge can be designated either as a cash flow hedge or as a fair value hedge. For example:

- A hedge of the foreign currency risk of a firm commitment may be designated as a fair value hedge or as a cash flow hedge.
- A forward contract to buy foreign currency may be designated as the hedging instrument in a fair value hedge of a foreign currency financial liability or alternatively in a cash flow hedge of the forecast settlement of that liability.
- A receive-fixed pay-floating interest rate swap may be designated as a fair value hedge of a fixed interest liability or as a cash flow hedge of a variable interest asset. However, the interest rate swap cannot be designated as a cash flow hedge of a fixed interest liability because it converts known (fixed) interest cash outflows, for which there is no exposure to variability in cash flows, into unknown (variable) interest cash outflows. Similarly, the swap cannot be designated as a fair value hedge of a variable interest asset because a variable interest instrument is not exposed to changes in fair value due to changes in market interest rates.
- A purchased put option on a commodity may be designated as the hedging instrument in a fair value hedge of the commodity inventory or alternatively, in a cash flow hedge of a forecast sale of the commodity inventory when such a sale is highly probable to occur.

IAS 39.88 3.7.140.15 The designation should be done at inception of the hedge.

3.7.140.20 Although the net profit or loss effect of a hedging relationship ultimately will be the same regardless of the type of hedge accounting applied, the timing of recognition in the statement of financial position and in profit or loss, effectiveness testing, and the nature of the accounting adjustments made, will differ. Therefore, it is important to choose the model and the method of effectiveness testing at inception of the hedge and to designate and document the hedge accordingly.

3.7.140.30 The decision regarding which hedge accounting model to use also may be influenced by the entity's information systems. The entity should assess whether its existing information systems are best set up to manage and track the information required under a fair value hedge model or a cash flow hedge model. This decision also may depend upon the characteristics of the hedged items and whether hedge accounting criteria can be met.

IAS 39.IG
F.6.2
3.7.140.40 Under a fair value hedge model, an asset or liability designated as a hedged item is remeasured for fair value changes attributable to the hedged risk. For interest sensitive assets and liabilities the original effective yield is modified through the amortisation of this "hedge adjustment". Usually this requires a system that is able to track changes in the hedged risk, and that can calculate associated changes in the fair value of the hedged item. Also, the system should be able to recompute the effective yield of the hedged item and amortise the changes to profit or loss over the remaining life of the hedged item.

IAS 39.95-100
3.7.140.50 Under a cash flow hedge model, the effective portion of the fair value changes of the hedging instrument is recognised in other comprehensive income and is reclassified to profit or loss only when the hedged forecast cash flows (see 3.7.80.40) affect profit or loss. Moreover, the ineffective portion of such hedges is calculated separately. In addition, it is necessary to demonstrate that forecast transactions are highly probable. This requires a system that enables an entity to track the timing of the cash flows of the hedged item, as well as the timing of the reclassification of the hedging gains and losses from equity. Although this may prove a challenge, for many entities such information can be based on the cash flow information captured already in its risk management systems.

3.7.140.60 In our experience, for hedges of interest rate risk generally it is easier to meet the hedge criteria and to apply hedge accounting if the cash flow hedge model is used. This is because complex systems are necessary to make partial fair value adjustments to the carrying amount of interest-bearing hedged items and often it is difficult to demonstrate hedge effectiveness, particularly if there is a risk of prepayments (see 3.7.260).

3.7.150 *Situations in which hedge accounting is not necessary*

IAS 39.IG
F.1.1
3.7.150.10 In some cases there is no accounting mismatch and therefore hedge accounting is not necessary. Examples of situations in which hedge accounting is not necessary are:

- hedges of recognised foreign currency monetary items with offsetting monetary items; the remeasurement of both items with respect to changes in foreign exchange rates is required to be recognised in profit or loss; and
- hedges of changes in the fair value of instruments measured at fair value through profit or loss; both the hedged item and derivative hedging instruments are remeasured to fair value through profit or loss.

3.7.160 *Income taxes*

IAS 12.61A
3.7.160.10 For transactions recognised directly in equity or in other comprehensive income, all current and deferred tax also are recognised in equity or in other comprehensive

income. In respect of hedge accounting this means that current and deferred taxes on gains or losses on hedging instruments recognised in other comprehensive income in a cash flow or net investment hedge also are recognised in other comprehensive income until such time as the gain or loss is reclassified to profit or loss.

3.7.170 Qualifying hedged items

3.7.170.10 The hedged item is the item that is exposed to the specific risk that an entity has chosen to hedge.

IAS 39.78   3.7.170.20 The hedged item can be:

- a single recognised asset or liability, unrecognised firm commitment, highly probable forecast transaction or a net investment in a foreign operation;
- a group of recognised assets or liabilities, unrecognised firm commitments, highly probable forecast transactions or net investments in foreign operations, if they share the same hedged risk; or
- in a portfolio hedge of interest rate risk, a portion (i.e. an amount of currency) of a portfolio of financial assets or financial liabilities that share the risk being hedged.

IAS 39.80   3.7.170.22 In order to qualify for hedge accounting the hedged item should involve a party external to the entity. Hedge accounting can be applied to transactions between entities in the same group only in the individual or separate financial statements of those entities and not in the consolidated financial statements of the group. However, as an exception, the foreign currency risk of an intra-group monetary item (for example, a foreign currency denominated payable or receivable between two subsidiaries) may qualify as a hedged item in the consolidated financial statements if it results in an exposure to foreign exchange rate gains or losses that are not fully eliminated on consolidation (see 3.7.750).

IAS 39.78,   3.7.170.25 In our view, a synthetic instrument that combines non-derivative and derivative
IGF.2.1   instruments cannot qualify as a hedged item, because a derivative instrument normally cannot be designated as the hedged item (see 3.7.280.10).

IAS 39.IG   3.7.170.26 Since hedge accounting is assessed on a transaction-by-transaction basis, in
F.2.6   our view a non-derivative hedging instrument in one hedging relationship can be designated as a hedged item in a different hedging relationship.

3.7.170.27 For example, a sterling functional currency entity may have in place two hedges. The first hedge is a net investment hedge of yen net assets of a foreign operation whereby the hedging instrument is a yen denominated floating rate bond issued by the entity. The second hedge is a cash flow hedge of the variability in the interest cash flows on the yen denominated floating rate bond due to changes in benchmark interest rates whereby the hedging instrument is a yen pay-fixed receive-floating interest rate swap. In this scenario, the issued bond is the hedging instrument of foreign currency risk while it is simultaneously designated as the hedged item in a cash flow hedge of interest rate risk.

IAS 39.80, 86 3.7.170.30 In order to qualify for hedge accounting, the hedged risk ultimately should be capable of affecting profit or loss.

IAS 39.79 3.7.170.40 An exception is that a held-to-maturity investment may never be the hedged item in a hedge of interest rate or prepayment risk. The designation of an investment as held to maturity requires an intention to hold the investment until maturity without regard to changes in the fair value or cash flows of the investment due to changes in interest rates. In addition, because prepayment risk on interest-bearing instruments primarily is a function of interest rates, this risk is like interest rate risk and therefore also cannot be the hedged risk when the hedged item is a held-to-maturity investment. This is an important factor to consider before classifying an investment as held to maturity (see 3.6.530).

IAS 39.79, 3.7.170.50 Although a held-to-maturity investment may not be hedged for interest rate
IGF.2.10, risk, the reinvestment of cash flows generated by such an asset may be hedged. Ad-
IGF.2.11 ditionally, a held-to-maturity investment can be hedged with respect to credit risk and/ or foreign currency risk. Also, the forecast purchase of an asset to be classified as held to maturity may be hedged for the period until the asset is recognised in the statement of financial position.

IAS 39.IG 3.7.170.60 While IAS 39 specifically prohibits the designation of a hedging instrument
F.2.17 for only a portion of the time that it remains outstanding, it permits a financial instrument to be designated as hedged for only a portion of its period to maturity (see 3.7.360.10). It is possible to designate a hedging relationship after initial recognition of the hedged item, hedging instrument or both.

3.7.170.65 If the hedged item is a non-financial asset or non-financial liability, the standard requires the item to be designated as a hedged item (a) for foreign currency risks, or (b) in its entirety for all risks. However, in our view an entity may hedge, in a fair value hedging relationship, a recognised non-financial item for a specified period. A recognised non-financial item such as inventory does not have a fixed tenure and hence, can be hedged up to a specific date as long as the item is hedged for all changes in fair value and the other conditions in the standard for hedge accounting are met.

IAS 39.86, 3.7.170.70 An entity's own equity instruments under IAS 32 *Financial Instruments:*
IGF.2.7 *Presentation* may not be designated as the hedged item in either a fair value or a cash flow hedge because changes in fair value or cash flows arising from such an instrument do not affect profit or loss (see 3.7.290.10).

IAS 39.IG 3.7.170.80 Non-monetary items, such as an investment in equity securities quoted on
F.2.19 an exchange (or other recognised marketplace) in which trades are denominated in a foreign currency and classified as available for sale, also may be the hedged item.

3.7.170.90 For example, Company Q acquires equity securities in Company B on a foreign stock exchange in which trades are denominated in a foreign currency. Q classifies its investment as available for sale. To hedge against foreign currency risk, Q enters into a forward currency contract to sell foreign currency. The forward contract may be designated as a hedging instrument for the fair value changes of the securities related to foreign currency risk provided that:

- the acquired securities are not traded on a stock exchange on which trades are denominated in the same currency as Q's functional currency. This might be the case if B's equity securities are dual-listed and one of the listings is on an exchange where trades are denominated in Q's functional currency; and
- dividends to Q are not denominated in Q's functional currency.

IAS 39.IG   3.7.170.100 If an equity security is traded in multiple currencies and one of those curren-
F.2.19   cies is the functional currency of the investor, then designation of the foreign exchange risk of the equity security is not permitted. However, in our view a forecast sale or purchase of a foreign currency denominated equity security may qualify for cash flow hedge accounting. In our view, a highly probable purchase of additional foreign currency denominated shares in a subsidiary, i.e. buying additional shares in a controlled entity, may qualify as the hedged item as the acquisition of additional shares will impact profit or loss when the shares are disposed of. Also, a net investment in a foreign operation in the consolidated financial statements may qualify as the hedged item for foreign exchange risk.

3.7.180 *Hedging a portion*

IAS 39.81,   3.7.180.10 In addition to hedging all changes in the fair value or cash flows of a financial
AG99E   instrument, IAS 39 allows designating as the hedged item:

- all of the cash flows of the financial instrument for cash flow or fair value changes attributable to some, but not all, risks; or
- some, but not all, of the cash flows of the financial instrument for cash flow or fair value changes attributable to all or certain risks; i.e. a portion of the cash flows of the financial instrument may be designated for changes attributable to all or certain risks.

IAS 39.81   3.7.180.12 For example, in respect of a financial item IAS 39 permits the following:

- Hedging all cash flows for a specific risk, e.g. hedging only the foreign exchange risk on the principal and interest cash flows on a foreign currency borrowing.
- Hedging specifically identified cash flows for all risks, e.g. hedging the coupon payments on financial liabilities for all risks.
- Hedging a portion of specifically identified cash flows for a specific risk, e.g. hedging the interest rate risk for the first five years of a ten-year fixed rate bond with a five-year pay-fixed receive-floating interest rate swap. In this situation the bond is hedged for less than its full term. However, the hedging instrument is designated for its entire term to maturity.
- Hedging a portion of specifically identified cash flows for a specific risk, e.g. hedging the interest rate risk on only the risk-free component of coupon payments on financial liabilities, excluding the credit risk premium.

- Hedging specifically identified cash flows for a specific risk, e.g. hedging the currency risk on interest cash flows, but not the currency risk on the principal cash flows of a foreign currency borrowing.

3.7.180.13 In addition it is possible to designate a portion of a net investment as the hedged item (see 3.7.640.10).

IAS 39.AG 99F   3.7.180.15 As described in 3.7.180.10, there are numerous options available when identifying portions of cash flows as the hedged item in relation to the specific risk(s) being hedged. An entity may hedge a portion of cash flows due to all risks or specifically identifiable risks inherent in the hedged item, or it may hedge all or a portion of cash flows due to specific risks inherent in the hedged item. However, to be eligible for hedge accounting, the designated risks and portions should be separately identifiable components of the financial instrument, and changes in the cash flows or fair value of the entire financial instrument arising from changes in the designated risks and portions should be reliably measurable. For example, when designating a fixed rate bond for fair value changes arising from changes in the risk-free or benchmark interest rate, the risk-free or benchmark interest rate normally is regarded as being both a separately identifiable component and being reliably measurable.

IAS 39.AG 99C   3.7.180.20 If a portion of the cash flows of a financial asset or liability is designated, then that portion should be less than the total cash flows of the asset or liability. However, the entity may designate all of the cash flows of the entire financial asset or financial liability as the hedged item and hedge them for only one particular risk. For example, a financial liability bearing interest at LIBOR less 100 basis points could be hedged in its entirety, i.e. principal plus interest at LIBOR less 100 basis points, for the change in its cash flows attributable to changes in LIBOR, but could not be hedged for changes in value of the LIBOR component of the total cash flows.

3.7.180.25 The entity may choose a hedge ratio other than one-to-one in order to improve the effectiveness of the hedge. Generally this involves identifying whether there is a statistical relationship between the hedging instrument and the hedged item, and if there is such a relationship, using the correlation between the items as the hedge ratio.

3.7.180.30 In our view, it is possible for an entity to designate a portion of the variable interest payments or receipts on a financial asset or liability as the hedged item, if, in addition to the conditions outlined in 3.7.120.10, the following conditions are met:

- The actual interest payments or receipts on the hedged item are expected, based on historical evidence, to exceed the hedged cash flows during the entire hedging relationship.
- There is a reasonable economic relationship between the component of cash flows designated as the hedged item and the variable rate on which the contractual cash flows are based.

3.7.180.40 For example, Company X will issue three variable rate notes (liabilities) with a notional of 1,000 each, which reset on the basis of the following rates:

594

- 90-day LIBOR;
- 90-day LIBOR minus 100 basis points; and
- 90-day LIBOR plus 100 basis points.

3.7.180.50 X simultaneously enters into three swaps with the same notional as the notes, receiving LIBOR and paying fixed, to hedge its exposure to variability in interest rates.

3.7.180.60 In each case in 3.7.180.40 the margin above or below LIBOR is fixed, and consequently any change in the cash flows of the swaps will perfectly offset the change in cash flows of the liabilities. Therefore, in our view it is not necessary to designate a portion of cash flows as the hedged item when the margin above or below the benchmark rate is fixed.

3.7.180.70 However, in certain instances the margin above or below the benchmark rate may not be fixed. For example, consider a bank that raises 90-day deposits at three-month Euribor minus 50 basis points. Upon maturity it is highly probable that customers will roll over the deposits and the interest rate on the deposits will be reset to market which may not be based on three-month Euribor minus 50 basis points. In accordance with its hedging strategy, the bank enters into a swap paying fixed and receiving three-month Euribor flat.

3.7.180.80 We believe that in this specific scenario it is not possible to designate a Euribor portion of the variable cash flows as the hedged item because there is no clear economic relationship between the rate on which the contractual cash flows are based and the benchmark rate identified as the hedged item. The entire cash flow variability should be taken into consideration in designating the hedge relationship.

3.7.180.90 In our view, it is possible to reduce ineffectiveness in certain circumstances by designating a portion of the cash flows as the hedged item. Consider an entity that issues a five-year bond in 2008 with notional of 1,000 and bearing interest at a fixed rate of 5 percent. In 2010 the entity acquires a three-year interest rate swap, receiving fixed at 3 percent and paying variable. Apart from interest rate, the other terms of the hedged item and hedging instrument match. The mismatch between the interest rate on the bond and the interest rate on the fixed leg of the swap arises entirely from a decrease in benchmark rates over the two-year period.

3.7.180.100 We believe that in this example it is possible to designate the hedge relationship with the hedged item as a portion of the interest coupons, i.e. 3 percent of the 5 percent contractual interest cash flows, so as to minimise hedge ineffectiveness. We believe that in this scenario the hedged item can be defined in such a way that no ineffectiveness arises (assuming no change in fair values due to credit and liquidity risk). The hedged item is a clearly identifiable and measurable portion of the coupon cash flows, i.e. the 3 percent portion of the 5 percent cash flows, and therefore can be designated as a valid portion under IAS 39.

IAS 39.AG   3.7.180.110 Inflation cannot be designated as a risk or a portion of a financial instru-
99F   ment, as it is not separately identifiable or reliably measurable, unless:

- it is a contractually specified portion of the cash flows of a recognised inflation-linked bond (assuming there is no embedded derivative required to be separately accounted); and
- the other cash flows of the instrument are not affected by the inflation portion.

3.7.180.120 For example, in a bond that contractually specifies the interest payments as comprising a fixed rate plus inflation, inflation could be designated as the hedged risk or portion. However, in an ordinary variable rate bond that does not contractually specify an inflation indexation, an entity cannot impute an inflation indexation and then designate it as the hedged risk or portion.

IAS 39.AG   3.7.180.130 An entity may designate all changes in the cash flows or fair value of a hedged
99BA   item in a hedging relationship. An entity also may designate only changes in the cash flows or fair value of a hedged item above or below a specified price or other variable, i.e. a one-sided risk. The intrinsic value of a purchased option hedging instrument (assuming that it has the same principal terms as the designated risk), but not its time value, reflects a one-sided risk in a hedged item.

3.7.180.140 For example, an entity forecasts a future purchase of a commodity and it purchases a commodity call option to hedge against future increases in commodity prices above the strike price specified in the purchased option. The entity designates the variability of future cash flow outcomes arising from the forecast commodity purchase as a result of a price increase above the strike price. In such a situation, only cash flow losses that result from an increase in the price above the specified level are designated. The hedged risk does not include the time value of a purchased option because the time value is not a component of the forecast transaction that affects profit or loss.

3.7.190 *Hedging a proportion*

3.7.190.10 The term "portion" (see 3.7.180.10) should be distinguished from the term "proportion", the latter being used in IAS 39 to indicate a certain percentage only.

IAS 39.81,   3.7.190.20 It is possible to designate a proportion of the cash flows, fair value or net
AG107A   investment as a hedged item, for example, 85 percent of the exposure. However, once a partial designation is made, hedge effectiveness is measured on the basis of the hedged exposure. Considering effectiveness on the basis of changes in the fair value or cash flows associated with the full underlying, or a proportion different from that designated as the hedged item, in order to maximise effectiveness is not permitted.

3.7.190.30 If a proportion of the cash flows or fair value of a financial asset or financial liability is designated as the hedged item, then that designated proportion should be less than the total cash flows of the asset or liability.

3.7.200 *Hedging a group of items*

IAS 39.83,   3.7.200.10 The hedged item can be a portfolio of similar assets, liabilities, highly prob-
BC176   able forecast transactions or net investments in foreign operations. Consequently, the

standard allows only "similar" items to be grouped together in a portfolio. Items are considered to be similar if they:

- share the hedged risk; and
- the change in fair value attributable to the hedged risk for each individual item is expected to be approximately proportional to the overall change in the fair value of the portfolio attributable to the hedged risk.

IAS 39.83, 3.7.200.20 However, it is not necessary that each item in the portfolio share all of the same *IGF.6.2* risks and be correlated with respect to all risks, as long as the hedged risk is a common risk characteristic. For example, in our view a portfolio of interest-bearing receivables may be hedged for benchmark interest rate exposure because, although each receivable in the portfolio has a different credit risk exposure, the receivables all carry a similar exposure to benchmark interest rates.

3.7.200.30 An entity can group more than one net investment in foreign operations together as the hedged item, provided that such investments are denominated in the same currency (see 3.7.90).

IAS 39.IG 3.7.200.40 An example of a portfolio that would not qualify as a hedged item is a portfolio *F.2.20* of different securities that replicates a particular share index. An entity may hold such a portfolio and economically hedge this with a put option on the share index. However, in this scenario the fair value changes of individual items in the portfolio would not be approximately proportional to the fair value change of the entire group. Therefore, the portfolio does *not* qualify for hedge accounting. However, as an alternative to hedge accounting, the financial instruments comprising the portfolio could be designated as at fair value through profit or loss (see 3.6.490).

IAS 39.78, 3.7.200.50 Generally, when items are grouped together and designated as a portfolio in *81A* a hedging relationship, the portfolio in its entirety comprises the hedged item, i.e. all of the financial assets or financial liabilities included in the portfolio are included in the hedging relationship in their entirety for the risk being hedged. However, in the case of a portfolio hedge of interest rate risk, the hedged item may comprise a portion of the portfolio of financial assets or financial liabilities that share the risk being hedged (see 3.7.210).

3.7.200.60 The following are examples of items that may be designated as a portfolio for hedge accounting:

- A portfolio of short-term non-callable corporate bonds may be hedged as one portfolio with respect to a shared risk-free interest rate. To achieve the required correlation, the bonds would need to have the same or very similar maturity or repricing date and exposure to the same underlying interest rate.
- A group of expected future sales may be hedged as one portfolio with respect to foreign currency risk. Usually such a designation requires that the individual sales be denominated in the same currency and be expected to take place in the same time period (see 3.7.600.50).

3.7.200.70 In order to identify a group of transactions, an entity is required to identify the hedged transactions with sufficient specificity so that it is possible to determine which transactions are the hedged transactions when they occur. This can be done either by specifying the number of units expected to be purchased/sold, e.g. the first 500 units out of expected purchases/sales of 800 units, or by specifying the monetary value of the purchases or sales, e.g. the first 25 (see 3.7.605). It is not permitted to designate the first 50 percent of sales as the hedged item as this designation would not lead to an identifiable amount being hedged, i.e. the first 50 percent of sales would depend on the total amount of sales in the period, which is not known until after the fact.

3.7.210 *Portfolio fair value hedges of interest rate risk*

IAS 39.78, 3.7.210.10 Entities, banks in particular, often manage interest rate risk on a portfolio
81A, basis, for example for a portfolio of mortgage loans or vehicle financing arrangements.
AG114(c), Such hedging practices, whereby an entity hedges its net exposures, generally do not
AG116, qualify for hedge accounting under IFRSs. However, an entity is permitted to designate
AG118 the *interest rate* exposure of a portfolio of financial assets or financial liabilities as the hedged item in a portfolio fair value hedge. The hedged item is designated in terms of an amount of currency rather than as individual assets or liabilities. Although the portfolio may, for risk management purposes, include only assets, only liabilities or both assets and liabilities, the amount designated is an amount of assets or an amount of liabilities. Designation of a net amount, comprising both assets and liabilities, is not permitted. The entity may hedge a portion of the interest rate risk associated with the designated amount.

IAS 39.81A, 3.7.210.20 The portfolio fair value hedge model accommodates prepayment risk more
AG114(b) readily than the normal fair value hedge model for individual assets or liabilities. However, the model can be applied only for hedges of interest rate risk and cannot be used for other risk types, for example foreign currency risk. Under the portfolio fair value hedge model, prepayable items are scheduled into repricing time periods based on expected, rather than contractual, repricing dates. This captures the effect of prepayments, and consequently there is no need to assess separately the impact of prepayment risk on the fair value of the portfolio.

IAS 39.49, 3.7.210.25 Since under this hedging model the hedged item is designated as an amount
BC187(d), of currency, IAS 39 requires that all the assets or liabilities from which the hedged item
AG118 is derived are items whose fair value changes in response to changes in the interest rate being hedged, and items that could have qualified for fair value hedge accounting if they had been designated as hedged items individually. In particular, because IAS 39 specifies that the fair value of a financial liability with a demand feature (such as demand deposits and some types of time deposits) is not less than the amount payable on demand, discounted from the first date that the amount could be required to be paid (see 3.6.930.40), such an item cannot qualify for hedge accounting for any time period beyond the shortest period in which the holder can demand payment. For example, since the fair value of a liability that is repayable immediately on demand usually is equal

to the amount payable on demand, there is no fair value exposure to hedge as the fair value of such a deposit is unaffected by interest rates and does not change when interest rates change.

IAS 39.AG 126, AG127 3.7.210.30 The standard provides specific guidance on the measurement of effectiveness for such a hedging relationship, as well as the presentation of the fair value adjustment and its subsequent amortisation to profit or loss. However, since IAS 39 does not specify a single method for assessing hedge effectiveness (see 3.7.480), in our view such specific guidance does not preclude the use of regression analysis for testing the effectiveness (see 3.7.505) of such macro fair value hedges.

3.7.210.40 In the event that the hedged prepayable items are subject to a prepayment penalty that represents the difference between the fair value of the hedged item and its carrying amount, in our view it is acceptable to schedule the hedged items based on contractual repricing dates. The penalty has the effect of eliminating all fair value exposures arising from prepayment risk.

IAS 39.89A 3.7.210.50 For a fair value hedge of the interest rate exposure arising from a portion of a portfolio of financial assets or financial liabilities, the gain or loss attributable to the hedged item may be presented as a single separate line item within assets or liabilities depending on whether the hedged item is an asset or a liability for that particular repricing time period. If amortising this gain or loss using a recalculated effective interest rate is impracticable, then it is amortised using a straight-line method (see 3.7.570.50).

3.7.220 *Net positions*

3.7.220.10 Many entities use net position hedging strategies under which a centralised treasury function accumulates risk originated in the operational subsidiaries or divisions. The treasury function hedges the net exposure in accordance with the group's risk policies by entering into a hedging transaction with a party external to the group.

IAS 39.84 3.7.220.20 Net position hedging does not by itself qualify for hedge accounting treatment because of the inability to:

- associate hedging gains and losses with a specific item being hedged when measuring effectiveness; and
- determine the period in which such gains and losses should be recognised in profit or loss.

IAS 39.AG 101 3.7.220.30 However, an entity is not necessarily precluded from hedge accounting by hedging net positions. That is, an entity may choose to manage and (economically) hedge risk on a net basis, but for hedge accounting purposes designate a specific item within the net position as the hedged item. For example, if an entity has 100 of assets and 90 of liabilities with risks and terms of a similar nature, it can designate 10 of assets as the hedged item.

3.7.230 *Highly probable forecast transactions*

IAS 39.88(c)   3.7.230.10 Forecast transactions should be highly probable and should present an exposure to variations in cash flows that could ultimately affect profit or loss.

IAS 39.88(c),   3.7.230.20 In our view, for a forecast transaction to be considered highly probable, there
IGF.2.4, should be at least a 90 percent probability of the transaction occurring. In assessing
IGF.3.7 whether a transaction is highly probable, consideration should be given to:

- the quality of the budgeting processes;
- the extent and frequency of similar transactions in the past;
- whether previous similar expected cash flows actually occurred;
- the availability of adequate resources to complete the transaction;
- the impact on operations if the transaction does not occur;
- the possibility of different transactions being used to achieve the same purpose;
- how far into the future the transaction is expected to occur; and
- the quantity of anticipated transactions.

IAS 39.IG   3.7.230.30 Normally it is possible to meet the highly probable criterion if significant
F.3.7 similar transactions are expected and hedge accounting is limited to a percentage of these forecast transactions. For example, the hedged item may be designated as the first 80 of anticipated sales of approximately 100 expected in March 2010, since it is highly probable that 80 percent of the anticipated sales will be made. However, if the hedged item is designated as 100 of anticipated sales of 100 in March 2010, then it is unlikely that the highly probable criterion will be met.

3.7.230.40 In our view, the highly probable criterion might not be met when an entity purchases an option as a hedge of a particular foreign currency because it has made a bid for a large contract in that foreign currency. For example, if it is not highly probable that the entity will win the bid for the contract, then the foreign currency cash flows would not be highly probable since they are dependent on the probability of the entity winning the bid for the contract.

3.7.230.50 In our view, it is more likely that a large number of homogenous forecast transactions will meet the highly probable criterion than a single forecast transaction. When determining whether a single forecast transaction meets this criterion, an entity considers the facts and circumstances that influence the probability of occurrence of the transaction. Indicators that may suggest that a forecast transaction is not highly probable may be an illiquid market in which the forecast transaction takes place, a low number of transactions, no past experience of the entity with such transactions or historical experience that such transactions do not occur often.

3.7.230.60 For example, a bank enters into fixed rate mortgage loan commitments with potential customers. Such commitments give the customer 90 days to lock in a mortgage at a discounted variable rate. To reduce the interest rate risk inherent in the anticipated mortgage transactions, the bank enters into forward-starting interest rate swaps based on the expected acceptances. When evaluating the probability of acceptance by only a single customer, a high probability would be difficult to demonstrate. On the other hand, when evaluating the probability of a group of commitments, it is possible that the bank can estimate with high probability the amount of mortgages that eventually will be closed. Therefore, the bank could use cash flow hedge accounting for the hedge of interest rate risk on the amount of mortgages that are highly probable of being entered into.

3.7.230.70 Similarly, when designating assets or liabilities with prepayment risk in a cash flow hedge, assessing the probability of interest cash flows arising from the entire portfolio rather than for a single instrument could result in identifying a bottom layer of interest cash flows that then could be considered as highly probable.

IAS 39.IG
F.3.7
3.7.230.80 An entity should be careful in its designation of forecast transactions as hedged items, as a history of such forecast transactions not occurring when expected could jeopardise its ability to continue to designate these types of hedges in future.

3.7.240 *Defining the time period in which the forecast transaction is expected to occur*

IAS 39.IG
F.3.11
3.7.240.10 The standard does not specify a time frame in which the forecast transaction should occur, although it should be expected to occur within a "reasonable, specific and generally narrow range of time". IAS 39 requires that the forecast transaction be identified and documented with sufficient specificity so that when the transaction occurs it is clear whether or not the transaction is the hedged transaction. An entity is not required to predict and document the exact date that a forecast transaction is expected to occur, but the documentation should identify a time period in which the forecast transaction is expected to occur within a reasonably specific and narrow range, as a basis for assessing hedge effectiveness.

3.7.240.20 In determining appropriate time periods for hedge accounting purposes an entity may look to the following:

- *Forecasts and budgets.* An entity generally would not identify longer time periods for hedge accounting purposes than those used for forecasting and budgeting.
- *The nature of the business or industry.* The forecasting and budgeting periods used by an entity are influenced by its ability to forecast reliably the timing of its transactions. Generally the forecast periods for manufacturers of ships or aircraft would be longer than those of retail stores; usually retailers sell smaller items in large quantities and can forecast more easily the timing of sales over shorter periods of time.

IAS 39.IG
F.3.7
3.7.240.30 Although the factors in 3.7.240.20 provide an indication of what may be the appropriate time period in which the transaction is expected to occur, the actual time period always should be determined on a case-by-case basis and will involve some degree of judgement. Generally, the sooner that the anticipated transaction is expected to occur, the easier it will be to demonstrate that the highly probable criterion is met.

3.7.240.40 In our view, some delay in the occurrence of a highly probable forecast trans-action is acceptable as long as the transaction is considered to be the *same* forecast transaction, i.e. the transaction that happens subsequently is clearly identifiable as the original forecast transaction. Therefore, the subsequent transaction should have the same specifications as the originally forecast transaction. It would not be appropriate, for example, for a retailer to designate as the hedged item the first 50 of foreign cur-rency sales in January and when this does not happen to argue that it is highly probable that there will be 50 of additional foreign currency sales in February to replace the lost sales in January. In such a case, there would be a forecast error regarding the 50 sales in January i.e. these sales would be considered "no longer expected to occur", which means that hedge accounting would be terminated (see 3.7.570). On the other hand, if a shipbuilder has a highly probable forecast sale of a specified ship to a particular customer but the expected delivery date moves from January to February, then it may be possible to continue hedge accounting because of the specific nature of the hedged forecast cash flow (see 3.7.580).

IAS 39.IG
F.3.10 3.7.240.50 If the hedged item is a series of forecast transactions, then the hedged item should be identified and documented with sufficient specificity so that when the transac-tion occurs, it is clear that it is the hedged transaction. For this reason the documentation should specify that the hedged item is an identifiable portion of a series of transactions that will occur in a specified period. It is not acceptable to designate a set percentage of transactions in a period, or the last in a series of transactions, as the hedged item because these cannot be identified specifically when they occur. For example, the hedged item may be designated as the *first* 20,000 of anticipated foreign currency sales in March 2010, but not 20,000 of anticipated foreign currency sales in March 2010. As another example, the hedged item is not permitted to be designated as 20 percent of anticipated foreign currency sales over the 2010 financial year.

3.7.250 *Expected interest cash flows*

3.7.250.10 To meet the hedge accounting criteria a forecast debt issue should be highly probable. This could be the case once the entity enters into an agreement to issue the debt, but may be evidenced at an earlier stage when management decides upon a debt issue as part of its funding strategy.

3.7.250.20 An entity may apply cash flow hedge accounting to an anticipated debt is-sue, as changes in interest rates between the date of deciding on the debt issue and the actual issue date will influence the rate at which the debt will be issued, or the discount or premium that will apply to the proceeds. For example, if the long-term interest rate were to increase, the debt would be issued at a higher rate or for lower proceeds than anticipated originally.

3.7.250.30 Normally a gain or loss on an appropriate hedging instrument will offset the higher/lower interest rate or the decrease/increase in proceeds. Using the cash flow hedge model, the effective portion of the gains or losses resulting from the hedging instrument until the debt is issued will be recognised in other comprehensive income.

Upon issuance of the debt, such gains and losses will remain in equity and be reclassi-fied to profit or loss in the same periods in which the hedged forecast cash flows affect profit or loss, i.e. when the interest expense is recognised. This will require the entity to track the amount of gains or losses recognised in other comprehensive income to ensure that the correct amounts are reclassified to profit or loss at the correct times.

3.7.250.40 For example, an entity in the process of issuing a bond may wish to hedge the risk of changes in interest rates between the time that it decides to issue the bond and the date of issue. This could be done using an interest future or other derivative instruments. To the extent that the hedge is effective, the gain or loss on the deriva-tive will be recognised in other comprehensive income. This gain or loss will remain in equity and will be reclassified to profit or loss as interest payments on the bond affect profit or loss and will effectively adjust the interest expense recognised on the bond.

3.7.250.50 Another example of a hedge of forecast interest payments is an entity that plans to issue two tranches of floating rate notes, each with a maturity of three years. The entity intends to issue the second tranche upon maturity of the first. In this situation the entity may enter into a six-year swap to hedge the variability in expected interest cash flows on both note issues. For hedge accounting purposes the hedge could be designated as a hedge of the expected interest payments in different periods, including interest payments arising from the forecast refinancing of the debt. To qualify for hedge accounting, at inception of the hedge the criteria for hedge accounting should be met, including the criteria that the hedge will be highly effective, and that the second issue after three years is highly probable.

3.7.250.60 In our view, in order for a forecast issue of debt to qualify for hedge accounting, all of its critical terms should be highly probable. For example, an entity with a euro functional currency may have a highly probable bond issue, but the currency of issue may not have been determined. If the entity issues the bond in US dollars, then it will enter into a currency swap to convert the cash flows to euros; however, regardless of the currency in which the bond is issued, the entity wishes to hedge its euro interest rate exposure using an interest rate swap. In our view, since the currency denomination of the forecast bond is not highly probable, the forecast bond issue cannot qualify for hedge accounting. Similarly, it will not be possible to achieve hedge accounting for forecast issues of commercial paper unless the currency and maturity (including rollovers) of the future issues can be determined reliably.

3.7.260 *Prepayment risk*

3.7.260.10 Prepayment risk also may affect whether a forecast transaction designated in a cash flow hedge is considered to be highly probable of occurring. However, when the hedged item is designated as the first cash flows of a portfolio occurring in a given period, the effect of a prepayment is less likely to cause the hedged forecast transac-tions to not be highly probable as long as there are sufficient cash flows in the period. This could be demonstrated by the entity preparing a cash flow maturity schedule that shows sufficient levels of expected cash flows in each period to support a highly probable assertion. For example, a bank may be able to determine accurately what levels of prepayments are expected for a particular class of its originated loans. The bank might hedge only a portion of the contractual cash flows from that portfolio of loans as it expects a number of borrowers to repay their loans early.

3.7.270 Items that do not qualify as hedged items

3.7.270.10 There are a number of items that for different reasons do not qualify for hedge accounting. In these cases the normal recognition and measurement principles of IAS 39 or other relevant IFRSs are applied.

3.7.280 *Derivatives*

IAS 39.IG
F.2.1, AG94

3.7.280.10 IAS 39 generally precludes derivatives from being the hedged item; therefore, generally derivatives can only serve as hedging instruments. An exception to this is a purchased option that is embedded in another financial instrument and which is closely related to the host contract (see 3.6.280) such that it is not separately accounted for as a derivative. In this case it is possible to designate the embedded derivative as the hedged item in a fair value hedge, with a written option as the hedging instrument.

3.7.290 *Own equity instruments*

IAS 39.86,
IGF.2.7

3.7.290.10 An entity's own equity instruments cannot be the hedged item since there is no risk exposure that affects profit or loss because transactions in own shares are recognised directly in equity. Likewise forecast transactions in an entity's own equity cannot be a hedged item, and neither can distributions to holders of the entity's equity instruments. However, a dividend that has been declared but not yet paid and is recognised as a financial liability may qualify as a hedged item, for example for foreign currency risk if it is denominated in a foreign currency.

3.7.300 *Dividends*

3.7.300.10 Entities also might wish to hedge anticipated dividends from foreign operations. However, expected dividends do not give rise to an exposure that will be recognised in profit or loss in the consolidated financial statements. Therefore, these cannot be hedged in a cash flow hedge or a net investment hedge in the consolidated financial statements. It is only once dividends are declared and become a receivable that hedge accounting may be applied in consolidated financial statements. For example, dividends declared and receivable from a foreign subsidiary may be hedged for foreign currency risk as changes in foreign exchange rates would affect the consolidated profit or loss.

3.7.310 Qualifying hedging instruments

IAS 39.72, 74,
75, AG94

3.7.310.10 All derivatives, including separable embedded derivatives, can qualify as hedging instruments, with the following limitations:

- Written options may be designated as hedging instruments only of purchased options (see 3.7.330).
- A derivative may not be designated as a hedging instrument for only a portion of its remaining period to maturity.
- Derivatives generally should be designated as hedging instruments in their entirety. Except as noted in 3.7.310.20, it is not permitted to designate only certain components of a derivative as a hedging instrument. For example, the foreign currency component of a cross-currency swap may not be designated as the hedging instrument without the interest rate component of the swap also being designated in the same or another qualifying hedge relationship. However, a *proportion* of the entire hedging instrument may be designated as the hedging instrument (see 3.7.350).

IAS 39.74   3.7.310.20 There are two exceptions from the requirement not to split the components of derivative hedging instruments:

- separating the intrinsic value and time value of an option; and
- separating the interest element and the spot price element in a forward.

AS 39.74-77,   3.7.310.30 The following uses of hedging instruments are permitted:
IGF.1.12-
IGF.1.14,   • designating a derivative as a hedging instrument subsequent to its initial recognition;
IGF.3.9,   • designating two or more derivatives in combination as the hedging instrument, as long
IGF.5.4   as none of the derivatives is a written option (see 3.7.330.40);
- designating two or more non-derivatives, or a combination of derivatives and non-derivatives (see 3.7.710.40), as a hedge of foreign currency risk;
- replacing or rolling over a hedging instrument at its maturity, if the replacement or rollover is planned and documented at inception of the hedge relationship;
- designating a derivative with an external party that offsets an internal derivative as a hedging instrument (see 3.7.730);
- applying hedge accounting in the consolidated financial statements to a derivative entered into by a group entity different from the one that has the risk exposure (see 3.7.720); and
- applying hedge accounting to a derivative, even though that derivative is fully offset by another derivative with equal but opposite terms, as long as the second instrument was not entered into in contemplation of the first or there is a substantive business purpose for entering into both instruments in separate transactions (see 3.7.740.40).

IAS 39.72   3.7.310.40 Non-derivatives may be designated as hedging instruments for hedges of foreign currency risk only.

3.7.320 *Purchased options*

AS 39.AG94   3.7.320.10 Purchased options may be used as hedging instruments provided that the hedge accounting criteria are met. Options, in contrast to forward and futures contracts, contain both an intrinsic value and a time value.

IAS 39.AG
99BA

3.7.320.20 For example, a forecast transaction in a foreign currency may be hedged with an option. In this situation the cash flows of the forecast transaction do not include a time value component while the option does. If the option is designated in its entirety (including time value), then effectiveness testing should be based on comparing the full fair value change of the option and the present value of the change in cash flows of the forecast transaction (see 3.7.530). The change in fair value of the option and the change in the present value of the cash flows of the forecast transaction will not be the same since the change in the time value element of the option is not offset by an equal and opposite change in the cash flows of the forecast transaction.

IAS 39.74,
AG99BA

3.7.320.30 IAS 39 allows the time value of an option to be excluded from the hedging relationship. In this case the option is more likely to be an effective hedge if the hedged relationship excludes time value and effectiveness is measured based on changes in intrinsic value alone. Designating only the changes in the intrinsic value of an option as a hedging instrument in the hedge of a one-sided risk in a hedged item may achieve perfect hedge effectiveness if the principal terms of the hedged item (i.e. amount, maturity etc.) and the hedging instrument are the same. However, this results in changes in the time value of the option being recognised directly in profit or loss regardless of the hedging model used (see 3.7.530.20).

3.7.320.40 In our view, either the spot or the forward price/rate can be used in determining the intrinsic value of an option; however, the approach should be specified as part of the hedge documentation and applied consistently during the term of the hedge. Furthermore, if the forward rate is used for determining the fair value of an American style option, then the rate should be determined using the option's maturity date.

3.7.325 *Dynamic hedging strategies*

IAS 39.74,
75, 91(a),
101(a),
IGF.1.9

3.7.325.10 IAS 39 allows an entity to apply dynamic hedging strategies such as "delta-neutral" hedging strategies and other dynamic strategies under which the quantity of the hedging instrument is constantly adjusted in order to maintain a desired hedge ratio. This may include a dynamic hedging strategy that assesses both the intrinsic value and time value of an option contract. To qualify for hedge accounting, the entity documents how it will monitor and update the hedge and measure hedge effectiveness, be able to track properly all terminations and re-designations of the hedging instruments, and demonstrate that all other hedge accounting criteria are met (see 3.7.120), including the requirement that the hedging instruments are designated as such for the whole time period during which they remain outstanding. An entity also is required to be able to demonstrate an expectation that the hedge will be highly effective for a specified short period of time during which the hedge is not expected to be adjusted and, accordingly, an entity documents that under such dynamic strategies both prospective and retrospective effectiveness are assessed over these short periods as if each of these short periods is a separate hedging relationship. In our view, when the quantity of the hedging instrument is adjusted, such as a change in the proportion of the derivative instrument designated as the hedging instrument or the addition of or deletion from a group of hedging derivatives (other than documented rollovers and replacements (see 3.7.570.40)), then generally the existing hedging relationship should be discontinued prospectively.

3.7.325.20 In our view, IAS 39 does not preclude a dynamic hedging strategy under which, in order to maintain a desired hedge ratio, the quantity of the designated hedged item rather than the quantity of the hedging instruments is adjusted. For example, an entity has designated a forecast foreign currency transaction as the hedged item in a cash flow hedge relationship. The hedged risk is the variability in the cash flows arising from movements in the spot foreign exchange rate and the hedging instrument is a foreign currency option. The entity designates a dynamic hedging relationship under which the designated amount of the hedged item is adjusted each week based on weekly changes in the delta of the foreign currency option. Each time that the hedged item is adjusted, generally the existing hedge relationship is terminated and a new hedge relationship is designated. Under this approach, effectiveness is assessed separately for each weekly period and ineffectiveness would be recognised to the extent that the change in the fair value of the option over this period is greater than the change in present value of the hedged cash flows. The present value of the hedged cash flows would be based on their expected settlement dates.

3.7.330 *Written options*

IAS 39.AG94   3.7.330.10 The potential loss on an option that an entity writes could be significantly greater than the potential gain in the fair value of the related hedged item. In other words, a written option is not effective in reducing the profit or loss exposure of a hedged item and therefore does not qualify as a hedging instrument unless it is designated as an offset of a closely related purchased option that is embedded in, and not separated from, a host contract. If the embedded purchased option is separated, then hedge accounting would be unnecessary as both the separated purchased option and the written option would be measured at fair value through profit or loss.

IAS 39.77,   3.7.330.20 In our view, a combined hedging instrument that is created in a single transac-
IGF.1.3   tion with the same counterparty and that is made up of a number of components that are not separately transferable may be designated as a hedging instrument, even if one of the components is a written option (e.g. a zero-cost collar created in a single transaction with the same counterparty) as long as the combination of derivative components does not result in a net written option.

IAS 39.IG   3.7.330.30 Consequently, an interest rate collar or other single derivative instrument that
F.1.3   includes a written option component and a purchased option component can be designated as a hedging instrument as long as the instrument is a net purchased option or zero-cost collar, as opposed to a net written option. The following should be considered in determining whether a combination of derivatives constitutes a net written option:

- No net premium is received either at inception or over the life of the combination. If a premium is received, then it would be evidence that the instrument is a net written option as it serves to compensate the writer of the option for the risk incurred.

- The option components have similar critical terms and conditions and, with the exception of strike prices, the same underlying variable or variables, currency, denomination and maturity.
- The notional amount of the written option component is not greater than the notional amount of the purchased option component.

IAS 39.77 3.7.330.40 An entity is not permitted to designate as the hedging instrument a combination of derivatives, concluded in *separate transactions*, that includes a written option or a net written option even if the result of such a grouping is economically equivalent to entering into a net purchased option or a zero-cost collar. For example, a zero-cost collar that is created synthetically by entering into a cap in one transaction and a floor in a separate transaction would not qualify as a hedging instrument.

3.7.340 *Non-derivatives*

IAS 39.AG95, 3.7.340.10 Only for foreign currency hedges, the hedging instrument may be a loan or
IGF.1.2 receivable, a held-to-maturity investment, an available-for-sale monetary asset, a financial liability or a cash balance. However, a foreign currency firm commitment or forecast transaction does not qualify as a hedging instrument as it is neither a derivative nor a non-derivative monetary asset or liability.

IAS 39.IG 3.7.340.20 For example, Company J has the yen as its functional currency and has a fixed
F.1.1, IGF.1.2 interest rate US dollar borrowing. The borrowing may be designated as a hedge of the foreign exchange exposure on a net investment in a US dollar foreign operation or a US dollar sales commitment. However, the US dollar borrowing may not be designated as a hedge of the interest and currency exposure on a fixed rate US dollar debt security or the entire fair value exposure on a US dollar sales commitment. This is because non-derivatives qualify as hedges of foreign currency risk only.

3.7.340.30 In a foreign currency hedge the currency of the hedging instrument and the currency of the hedged item should be the same, or it should be possible to demonstrate a high degree of correlation between the two currencies. Therefore, extending the example in 3.7.340.20, the US dollar borrowing may not be designated as a hedge of a euro sales commitment unless a very strong correlation between the US dollar and the euro can be demonstrated.

IAS 39.77 3.7.340.40 A combination of derivatives and non-derivatives, or proportions thereof, may be used as the hedging instrument in a hedge of foreign currency risk (see 3.7.710.40).

3.7.340.50 In our view, an operating lease cannot be designated as a hedging instrument for a hedge of foreign currency risk. This is because payments due or receivable under an operating lease are not recognised financial liabilities or assets that could qualify as a hedging instrument for a hedge of foreign currency risk. However, if the operating lease payments are denominated in a foreign currency, then the foreign exchange exposure of these lease payments could qualify as a hedged item (rather than as a hedging instrument) in a cash flow hedge (see 3.7.405.30).

3.7.340.60 Conversely, in our view a recognised finance lease receivable can qualify as a hedging instrument of foreign currency risk even though finance lease receivables otherwise are outside the scope of IAS 39, provided that all hedge accounting requirements are met (see 3.7.405.10).

IAS 39.72,
BC144,
BC145

3.7.340.70 In our view, a financial liability arising from an entity's obligation to repurchase its own equity instruments does not qualify as a hedging instrument. The ability to use non-derivative items as hedging instruments is restricted to cash instruments. In this case even though the repurchase obligation is measured at amortised cost as if it were a non-derivative financial liability, the instrument is in fact a derivative instrument and not a cash instrument.

3.7.350 *Proportion of an instrument*

IAS 39.75

3.7.350.10 A proportion of a financial instrument may be designated as the hedging instrument. For example, 50 percent of the notional amount of a forward contract may be designated as the hedging instrument in a cash flow hedge of a highly probable forecast sale. Gains or losses on the proportion of the derivative financial instrument not designated as the hedging instrument are recognised immediately in profit or loss.

3.7.360 *Designation for the entire period*

IAS 39.74, 75

3.7.360.10 Derivatives and non-derivatives should be designated as hedging instruments for the entire period for which they are outstanding, as the entire fair value of the hedging instrument should be considered when assessing the effectiveness of the hedge. For instance, a pay-fixed receive-floating interest rate swap with a maturity of ten years cannot be designated as a hedging instrument of a floating rate bond for just the first eight years by using the eight-year yield curve to measure the changes in the fair value of the swap when assessing hedge effectiveness. Such a method would allow an entity to exclude part of the hedging instrument's fair value, which is not allowed. Hedge designation would, however, be permitted in this case if the derivative is designated as the hedging instrument in its entirety; i.e. the changes in the fair value of the swap are computed using all of its cash flows based on the ten-year yield curve when assessing hedge effectiveness. However, such a strategy would lead to ineffectiveness and also may result in hedge accounting being precluded if the hedging relationship is not expected to be highly effective.

3.7.360.20 It is possible to designate a derivative or non-derivative as the hedging instrument subsequent to initial recognition provided that the fair value for the entire remaining period for which the derivative or non-derivative remains outstanding is included when assessing hedge effectiveness. For example, if a derivative is designated as a hedging instrument at inception, but hedge accounting ceases due to the hedge criteria not being met or the designation being revoked at a later date, then it is possible to designate the derivative as the hedging instrument in another hedging relationship at a later stage as long as the designation and assessment of hedge effectiveness includes the fair value for the entire period for which it remains outstanding.

3.7.360.30 A derivative may be designated as the hedging instrument in a hedge of a forecast transaction that has a maturity shorter than the remaining maturity of the hedging derivative. Since the derivative is required to be designated for its entire remaining term to maturity, in such a hedge there will be some ineffectiveness due to the differences in maturity dates of the hedged item and hedging derivative. Also, sometimes the ineffectiveness may be significant so as to preclude application of hedge accounting altogether if the hedge is assessed as not being highly effective.

3.7.370 *Basis swaps*

3.7.370.10 An entity may swap one floating rate exposure into another using basis swaps. Basis swaps are interest rate swaps that exchange one base rate for another. For example, an entity that issues a bond paying 12-month Euribor enters into a basis swap whereby it receives 12-month Euribor and pays 3-month Euribor with the notional and maturity of the swap matching those of the bond. The question arises as to whether such a basis swap can be designated as a hedge of the floating rate bond.

3.7.370.20 While swapping one base rate for another with a different repricing period may eliminate some of the cash flow variation or some of the fair value variation, there is no model in IAS 39 that allows explicitly for hedge accounting when one floating rate is swapped into another. As the bond in 3.7.370.10 has a floating rate of interest it may be eligible for cash flow hedge accounting. However, as the interest rate swap exchanges one floating cash flow stream into another, some variability in cash flows remains.

3.7.370.30 Therefore, in our view generally a basis swap does not qualify as a hedging instrument in a cash flow hedge except in very specific circumstances as discussed in 3.7.370.40.

IAS 39.IG 3.7.370.40 If an entity has both an asset and a liability on which it receives interest at
F.2.18 a rate indexed to the base rate on the pay leg (e.g. LIBOR) of the basis swap, and pays interest at a rate equal to the base rate on the receive leg (e.g. Euribor) of the basis swap, then in our view hedge accounting would be appropriate assuming that the other hedge criteria are satisfied. Both the existing asset and the liability should be designated as hedged items in the same hedging relationship, and both positions should be considered in effectiveness testing. If the hedge fails to be highly effective in offsetting the exposure to variability in cash flows in response to changes in the designated interest rates on either or both of the designated asset or liability, then hedge accounting is terminated for the entire relationship. In this case the combined variability in cash flows due to movements in base rates arising from both the asset and the liability is eliminated by the basis swap. Consequently, we believe that it is possible to designate the basis swap in a cash flow hedge relationship in this limited circumstance.

3.7.380 *Liability bearing a constant maturity interest rate*

3.7.380.10 An entity may issue instruments that have a floating rate of interest that resets periodically according to the fixed maturity market rate based on an instrument that has a duration extending beyond that of the reset period (a "constant maturity" interest rate); for example, a ten-year bond on which the interest rate resets semi-annually to the current weighted average yield on treasury bonds with a ten-year maturity. The effect of this feature is that the interest rate always is equal to the market return on an instrument with ten years left to maturity, even as the instrument paying the coupon itself nears maturity. In order to hedge its exposure to the constant maturity interest rate, an entity may enter into an interest rate swap that pays LIBOR or a similar rate and receives the constant maturity rate.

3.7.380.20 A question arises as to whether such an interest rate swap can be designated as the hedging instrument in a hedge of the liability (i.e. issued floating rate instrument). First, it is necessary to consider whether the constant maturity feature in the liability comprises a separable embedded derivative. Only after this analysis can the appropriateness of hedge accounting for the proposed transaction be considered.

3.7.380.30 In our view, the constant maturity feature comprises an embedded derivative (a constant maturity swap). This embedded derivative is not closely related to the host debt instrument as it could potentially double the holder's initial rate of return and could result in a rate of return that is at least twice what the market return would be for a contract with the same terms as the host contract, unless it has a cap at an appropriate level to prevent the doubling effect (see 3.6.260).

IAS 39.IG
F.2.1 3.7.380.40 In the absence of an appropriate cap, the entity separately accounts for a fixed rate host debt instrument and a constant maturity swap. As the constant maturity swap is a non-option embedded derivative, its terms would have to be determined so as to result in a fair value of zero at inception (see 3.6.440.40). Both the embedded derivative and the interest rate swap will be measured at fair value with gains and losses recognised in profit or loss. Hedge accounting would not be permitted in these circumstances as the interest rate swap would have to be designated as the hedging instrument in a hedge of the separately accounted for embedded derivative, which is not allowed under IAS 39.

3.7.380.50 However, if the terms of the liability include an appropriate cap, then the embedded derivative is not accounted for separately and the issue arises as to whether such a loan can be hedged with an interest rate basis swap that pays LIBOR and receives the same constant maturity rate. Although the bond issued is a variable rate bond, the variable rate it pays is a constant maturity rate. Consequently, the bond has a fair value exposure arising from the difference between the discounting rate used to value the bond (the repricing basis) and the ten-year constant maturity rate (the interest-rate basis). For a "plain vanilla" floating rate bond there is no such difference and consequently no fair value exposure due to interest rate changes. Similarly, the basis swap in this example being a basis swap that has a repricing basis different from its interest rate basis also has a fair value exposure for its entire life.

3.7.380.60 Consequently, in our view, the constant maturity bond with an appropriate interest rate cap in 3.7.380.50 can be designated as the hedged item in a fair value hedge of interest rate risk with the hedging instrument being a constant maturity basis swap that also has a matching interest rate cap, assuming that the other hedge accounting criteria are met. In such a hedging relationship the hedge is of the fair value exposure for the life of the hedged item and hedging instrument, rather than of an exposure that exists only between repricing dates. Conversely, in our view it is not possible to designate a plain vanilla floating rate bond in a fair value hedging relationship using a plain vanilla basis swap as the hedging instrument, as neither the bond nor the swap has a fair value exposure over its entire life. This designation is possible only when a fair value exposure exists for the entire life of the hedged item and the instrument.

3.7.390 *Hedging a zero-coupon bond with a plain vanilla interest rate swap*

3.7.390.10 Zero-coupon debt instruments in the form of bonds, bills of exchange and commercial paper are exposed to, among other risks, fair value interest rate risk; entities may seek to hedge this risk using plain vanilla interest rate swaps.

3.7.390.20 For example, Company V acquires a one-year zero-coupon bond at 95 with a face value (redemption amount) of 100. At the same date V enters into a one-year interest rate swap. The swap reprices on a quarterly basis and the interest rate on the fixed leg of the swap is equal to the bond's yield. Swap settlements are made quarterly. V wishes to designate the interest rate swap as the hedging instrument in a fair value hedge of interest rate risk arising from the bond.

3.7.390.30 Such a designation is unlikely to be effective as there are significant differences between the instruments and the way in which their fair values respond to changes in market interest rates. In particular, there are only two cash flows on the bond (an acquisition outflow of 95 and a redemption inflow of 100), while there are four cash flows on the interest rate swap since interest coupons are exchanged on a quarterly basis. Therefore the hedge is unlikely to meet the prospective effectiveness requirements of IAS 39; at any time after the first period the fair value change of a single cash flow of 100 at the bond's redemption date will not correspond to the fair value change of the three remaining interest cash flows on the swap.

IAS 39.AG 107 3.7.390.40 In our view, in order to achieve hedge accounting in these circumstances an entity would need to adopt a dynamic hedging strategy. At each payment date of the swap, it would need to adjust the hedging instrument, e.g. by designating an additional swap into the hedging relationship. Using this strategy the entity would need to prove that the hedge remains effective for the period until the hedging instrument is next adjusted. This hedging strategy would have to be documented clearly at inception of the hedging relationship.

3.7.395 *Derivatives with knock-in or knock-out features*

IAS 39.72 3.7.395.10 IAS 39 does not prohibit the use of derivatives as hedging instruments, except for some written options, if the other requirements for hedge accounting are met (see 3.7.120). Therefore, if an entity intends to designate a derivative with a knock-in or knock-out feature as a hedging instrument, then in our view the entity should assess whether the knock-in or knock-out feature indicates that the instrument is a net written option for which hedge accounting is precluded (see 3.7.330). In our view, knock-in or knock-out features should be considered a net written option if a net premium is received by the entity in the form of a favourable rate or other term in exchange for these features.

3.7.395.15 For example, an entity enters into an arm's length pay-6 percent receive-LIBOR interest rate swap under which the rights and obligations of both the entity and the counterparty are extinguished if a contingent event occurs. If the entity had entered into an otherwise identical interest rate swap without the knock-out feature, then the swap would have been priced at pay-8 percent receive-LIBOR. In our view, unless the hedged item contains an offsetting and closely related embedded net purchased option, the entity is not permitted to designate the instrument since the favourable difference between the fixed payment legs represents a net premium that the entity receives over the life of the instrument in return for writing the option (see 3.7.330).

IAS 39.88,
IGF.5.5　　3.7.395.20 Even if a derivative with a knock-in or a knock-out feature is not considered a net written option and therefore not precluded from being designated as a hedging instrument, it is unlikely that such an instrument will be highly effective in offsetting changes in the fair value or the cash flows arising from the hedged risk unless the hedged item contains a similar offsetting knock-in or knock-out feature.

3.7.400 Qualifying hedged risks

3.7.400.05 The hedged risk is the specific financial risk of the qualifying hedged item (see 3.7.170) that the entity is exposed to and has chosen to hedge.

IAS 39.86,
AG110　　3.7.400.10 The hedged risk should be one that could affect profit or loss. For example, a hedge of the purchase price of treasury shares could not qualify for hedge accounting because all treasury share transactions are recognised in equity (see 3.11.260).

IAS 39.81,
IGF.3.5　　3.7.400.20 A financial asset or liability can be hedged against exposure to any one or more of its individual risk types that is identifiable and measurable, including market prices, interest rates or a component of interest rates, foreign currency rates or credit risk. Conversely, a non-financial item may be hedged with respect to either all of its risks or currency risk only (see 3.7.410).

3.7.405 *Lease payments and receipts*

IAS 32.AG9　　3.7.405.10 In our view, whether cash flows payable or receivable under a lease arrangement should be financial items or non-financial items with respect to their designation as a hedged item depends on whether the lease is classified as a finance lease or an operating lease. In our view, a recognised finance lease payable or receivable is a financial item even though such an item is not generally within the scope of IAS 39.

3.7.405.20 However, an operating lease arrangement is an executory contract. Under an operating lease arrangement the lessor performs when, and only when, the asset is made available for the lessee in the agreed time period, i.e. the lessor does not fully perform under the contract by initially providing the lessee with the access to the leased asset. Accordingly, in our view an operating lease is not regarded as a financial item, although individual payments currently due and payable with respect to the elapsed period of the lease term for which performance has occurred are financial items.

3.7.405.30 For example, a lessor or lessee may wish to designate the future cash flows in an operating lease arrangement as the hedged item in a hedge of the variability in cash flows due to movements in a benchmark interest rate or the inflation rate, when rentals are indexed to such a rate. Although the variability in the cash flows due to the interest or inflation rate may be separately identifiable and reliably measurable, the entity is not permitted to designate the interest rate or inflation rate as the hedged risk, nor designate a portion of the cash flows corresponding thereto (see 3.7.410.10). However, an entity may be able to designate the entire variability in cash flows arising from the operating lease arrangement if it can demonstrate high effectiveness. In a situation in which operating lease rentals are denominated in a foreign currency, the entity may be able to designate the variability in those cash flows due to currency risk as the hedged risk (see 3.7.420).

3.7.410 *Non-financial items*

IAS 39.82, AG100 3.7.410.10 A non-financial item is hedged with respect to either all of its risks or currency risk only; this is because currency risk is the only risk associated with a non-financial item that is considered to be separately measurable. This is an outright prohibition in IAS 39. Consequently, even if an entity is able to isolate and measure the appropriate portion of the cash flows or fair value changes attributable to a specific risk component, it is not allowed to designate these cash flows or fair value changes as the hedged item.

3.7.410.20 For example, Company C is a producer of chocolate bars. C wishes to hedge the fair value of its inventory in respect of changes in the sugar price by taking out a sugar forward in the commodity market. It would not be permissible in this situation to designate as the hedged risk the price risk only related to the price of sugar since the hedged item is a non-financial item and the risk of changes in sugar prices is a risk component other than foreign currency risk. As an alternative, C may designate the sugar forward as a hedge of all fair value changes of the entire chocolate bar inventory. However, generally it is not possible to predict or measure reliably the effect that a change in the price of an ingredient or component will have on the price of an entire non-financial asset or liability. Consequently, it is unlikely that a direct and consistent relationship exists between changes in the sugar price and changes in the fair value of C's chocolate bar inventory. As chocolate bars consist of ingredients other than sugar (cocoa, milk etc.), the hedge is unlikely to be highly effective, and in that case hedge accounting would not be possible unless the other ingredients also are hedged. However, it may be possible to achieve hedge accounting if all of the main ingredients are hedged and the ineffectiveness arising from changes in fair value of the unhedged ingredients is not significant.

3.7.410.30 However, in our view it is acceptable to hedge a non-financial item with respect to all of its risks *other than* currency risk. For example, an entity with euro as its functional currency may wish to hedge its forecast purchases of jet oil. The forecast purchase exposes the entity to two risks, both of which are reliably measurable: price risk of jet oil denominated in US dollars; and foreign exchange risk of US dollars against the euro. Under IAS 39 the entity would be able to designate the foreign currency component of jet oil purchases as the hedged item. Moreover, we believe that as the price risk of the jet oil denominated in US dollars represents the risk of the underlying purchases in their entirety, except for retranslation to euro, it also is acceptable to designate this as the hedged risk.

3.7.410.40 Certain commodity exchange-traded derivatives are based on a standard quality or grade. Entities often enter into derivatives for a standard commodity prior to determining the actual quality of product that they require for production. Examples of commodities that are traded in a standardised form are wheat, corn, coffee beans and metals.

3.7.410.50 For example, a producer of commodities uses traded commodity futures to hedge committed future sales of commodities. The contract price for the physical sale of the commodities is split into two components, which are specified in the contract terms: the standard commodity price based on the index underlying the futures contract; and a discount or premium for the specific quality, delivery location, timing and payment terms for the specific delivery. This clearly enables the separation of the appropriate portion of the cash flows of the physical contract attributable to changes in the price of the standard commodity. However, given the outright prohibition in IAS 39, the entity would not be allowed to designate as the hedged item only the portion of cash flows under the sales contract that are linked to the standard commodity price or designate all the cash flows in the contract but for the risk of the changes in standard commodity price only.

3.7.410.60 Instead, the actual sales price should be designated as the hedged item. However, because of the difference between the hedging instrument (futures contract based on the standard commodity) and the hedged item (actual fair value/price of the product to be sold), hedge ineffectiveness may arise. Additionally, it may be difficult to demonstrate on a prospective basis that the hedge relationship is expected to be highly effective in achieving offsetting changes in fair value or cash flows attributable to the hedged risk throughout the hedging period.

IAS 39.AG 3.7.410.70 The problem of ineffectiveness can be addressed partly by designating the
100 hedging instrument and hedged item in a relationship using a hedge ratio of other than one. While the futures contract based on a standard commodity and the actual purchase or sale differ in some respects, it may be possible to identify a correlation between the price of the standardised commodity and the actual commodity. This may be done using statistical models such as regression analysis. The slope of the resulting regression line can be used to establish a hedge ratio that maximises hedge effectiveness. For example, an entity might hedge its future purchase of Brazilian coffee with a commodity future whose underlying is the price of Colombian coffee. Assuming that there is a valid sta-

tistical relationship between the two prices, which is expressed through a regression analysis giving a slope of 1.02 of the regression line, a derivative with a notional amount of 1.02 tonnes of Colombian coffee could be designated as a hedge of the purchase of one tonne of Brazilian coffee. While some ineffectiveness inevitably will result, using a hedge ratio of other than one may help to keep this within an acceptable range such that hedge accounting can be continued.

3.7.410.80 A similar issue arises when an entity hedges an ingredient of a non-financial item. For example, when hedging the purchase of jet fuel an entity may want to hedge its entire jet fuel price exposure or a component of this price exposure. The price of jet fuel is derived from the prices of the various components that make up jet fuel. Each of the components is traded independently with market prices available for each component. Although the quantity of each of the components in a metric tonne of jet fuel always is fixed, the relative value of each of the components differs as the prices of these components change more or less independently. Various strategies are possible when hedging a transaction such as jet fuel purchases. However, not all would qualify for hedge accounting:

- *Hedge the components of jet fuel price.* An entity may choose to hedge its price exposure to only certain components of jet fuel (e.g. brent or gas oil) and to retain its price exposure to the other components. This may be due to:
  - the costs of hedging;
  - the relatively more liquid nature of these components;
  - the fact that these components represent the most significant components of jet fuel prices; or
  - the independent nature of the pricing of the various components.

  For example, brent and gas oil swaps could be economic hedges of the corresponding brent or gas oil components of jet fuel purchases. This may result in perfect effectiveness for these components, as the critical terms of the derivative and the component match, their prices move in tandem and the notional amount of the derivative equals the quantity of the component in the jet fuel that will be purchased. However, as noted in 3.7.410.10, IAS 39 prohibits hedge accounting for components of risk for non-financial items such as jet fuel. Therefore, in order for this hedging strategy to qualify for hedge accounting, the entire price risk of the jet fuel purchase should be designated as the hedged item, and a high degree of correlation should be demonstrated between the price of the hedged ingredient and the jet fuel price. Alternatively, if there is some degree of correlation the entity may use a hedge ratio of other than one to maximise hedge effectiveness. However, if the prices of the individual components move more or less independently, then it may not be possible to demonstrate any correlation. This also would make it difficult to demonstrate on a prospective basis that the hedge relationship is expected to be highly effective throughout the hedging period even within the prescribed range of 80 – 125 percent (see 3.7.460).
- *Hedge the entire price of jet fuel.* In order to meet the requirements of IAS 39 regarding the hedging of commodity price risk, an entity may use a jet fuel deriva-

tive to hedge the entire price risk exposure arising from the purchase of jet fuel. This hedging strategy would qualify for hedge accounting assuming that all other criteria have been met.

IAS 39.IG   3.7.410.90 Commodity price exposure on inventory qualifies as a hedged risk even if the
F.3.6   inventory is measured at cost; the profit or loss impact arises when the inventory is sold. However, as noted in 3.7.410.80, the hedged item is the entire change in the fair value of the inventory, and not just a component of the fair value changes. For example, it is not possible to hedge only the rubber component in an inventory of tyres.

3.7.420 *Foreign currency exposures*

3.7.420.10 Hedge accounting is not permitted for hedges that convert one currency exposure to another currency exposure, unless the entity has a corresponding position in the second foreign currency, or that second currency is closely correlated to the entity's functional currency.

IAS 39.IG   3.7.420.20 For example, Company S has the rand as its functional currency. S has
F.2.18   issued a yen denominated bond and has a US dollar receivable; both instruments have the equivalent notional amount and the same maturity. To hedge both the US dollar and the yen exposures, S enters into a forward contract to convert yen to US dollars. This relationship between the bond and the receivable (the hedged items) and the yen to US dollar forward (the hedging instrument) would qualify for hedge accounting. In our view, the hedge documentation should identify both foreign currency positions in designating the hedged risk, and in measuring effectiveness both positions should be considered. If the hedge fails to be highly effective in offsetting the exposure to changes in the designated foreign currency exposures on either or both of the designated US dollar receivable or the yen denominated bond, then hedge accounting is terminated for the entire relationship. However, if S had issued only the bond and did not have a US dollar receivable, then the forward contract would not qualify for hedge accounting because it merely changes one currency exposure for another.

IAS 39.IG   3.7.420.30 The currency risk on foreign currency non-financial items (e.g. property, plant
F.3.6, IGF.5.6, and equipment and intangible assets) will affect profit or loss only if the owner has
IGF.6.5   a forecast sale that will be denominated in a foreign currency. The asset itself has no separately measurable foreign currency risk. Therefore, in our view this risk qualifies to be hedged in a cash flow hedge only if the forecast sale is highly probable.

3.7.420.35 In addition, in our view when the transaction date, i.e. delivery date of the non-financial asset, precedes the cash settlement date of the related receivable or payable in a highly probable forecast sale or purchase, the variability in cash flows arising from movements in the foreign exchange rates may be hedged until the transaction date or the cash settlement date. For example, an entity forecasts a highly probable future sale denominated in a foreign currency to occur on 30 September 2010, in respect of which the cash settlement is expected to occur on 31 October 2010. In our view, the entity may hedge the forecast sale in respect of the risk of changes in foreign exchange rates either to 30 September 2010 or to 31 October 2010. In the former case, a cash inflow from the sale and a simultaneous cash outflow for the financing of the sale would be deemed to occur on 30 September 2010; financing of the sale is a different transaction from the forecast sale transaction and thus the timing of the settlement of the financing does not result in ineffectiveness for the hedging relationship.

3.7.420.40 In our view, an entity may designate its exposure to changes in either the spot or the forward rate as the hedged risk. If exposure to changes in the forward rate is designated as the hedged risk, then the interest component included in the forward rate is part of the hedged foreign currency risk. Changes in the fair value or cash flows of the hedged item then are measured based on changes in the applicable forward rate.

3.7.420.45 If, in a cash flow hedge of a recognised foreign currency financial asset or liability, an entity designates the variability in cash flows arising from movements in the forward exchange rates as the hedged risk, then the effective portion of the changes in the fair value of the hedging instrument (e.g. forward contract) is recognised in other comprehensive income. The amount recognised in other comprehensive income includes also the effective portion of the change in fair value of the forward points included in the forward contract. At each reporting date during the term of the hedge, the entity reclassifies from equity an amount equal to the remeasurement of the hedged item under IAS 21 based on the spot exchange rates. In addition, in our view in order to ensure that the forward points recognised in other comprehensive income are reclassified fully to profit or loss over the life of the hedge, the entity reclassifies from equity an amount equal to the cumulative change in the forward points recognised in other comprehensive income amortised over the life of the hedging relationship using the interest rate implicit in the forward contract.

3.7.420.46 If, in a cash flow hedge of a highly probable forecast sale or purchase of a non-financial item, an entity uses a forward contract to hedge the forward exchange rate through to the transaction's cash settlement date, then in our view cash flow hedge accounting may be applied as follows:

- The effective portion of the gain or loss on the hedging instrument computed by reference to the hedged forward rate is recognised in other comprehensive income during the period prior to the occurrence of the forecast purchase or sale.
- The functional currency interest rate implicit in the hedging relationship as a result of entering into the forward contract (i.e. forward points) is used to determine the amount of cost or income to be ascribed to each period of the hedging relationship. The period of the hedging relationship in this case includes the period from the date of the hedge designation to the date of cash settlement of the forecast transaction.
- For a highly probable forecast sale, the amount of cost or income ascribed to the forecast period until the date the sale occurs is reclassified from equity to profit or loss on that date. For a highly probable forecast purchase, the amount of cost or

income ascribed to the forecast period until the date of purchase is either reclassified from equity as a basis adjustment to the initial cost or other carrying amount of the purchased non-financial item on the date of purchase, or is reclassified from equity to profit or loss in the same period or periods during which the item acquired affects profit or loss.

- Upon occurrence of the forecast sale (i.e. the transaction date), the difference between the spot foreign exchange rates at the inception of the hedge and on the transaction date is reclassified from equity to profit or loss. In a hedge of a forecast purchase, a similar amount may be reclassified from equity as a basis adjustment to the initial cost or other carrying amount of the purchased non-financial item on the date of purchase; alternatively, the entity may choose not to adjust the cost or the carrying amount of the purchased non-financial item and instead reclassify the deferred gain or loss from equity to profit or loss in the same period or periods during which the item acquired affects profit or loss.

- At each reporting date during the life of the recognised foreign currency receivable or payable, the entity reclassifies from equity to profit or loss an amount equal to the remeasurement of the receivable or payable under IAS 21 based on the spot exchange rates.

- The cost or income ascribed to each period during the life of the recognised foreign currency receivable or payable is reclassified from equity to profit or loss at the end of each reporting period.

IAS 39.IG 3.7.420.47 As an alternative to the cash flow hedge accounting described in 3.7.420.46,
F.5.6 an entity may apply cash flow hedge accounting as follows:

- The effective portion of the gain or loss on the hedging instrument computed by reference to the hedged forward exchange rate is recognised in other comprehensive income during the period prior to the occurrence of the forecast purchase or sale.

- For a highly probable forecast sale, this cumulative amount recognised in other comprehensive income for the effective portion of the gain or loss on the hedging instrument is reclassified from equity to profit or loss on the date the sale occurs. For a highly probable forecast purchase, this cumulative amount is either reclassified from equity as a basis adjustment to the initial cost or other carrying amount of the purchased non-financial item on the date of purchase, or is reclassified from equity to profit or loss in the same period or periods during which the item acquired affects profit or loss.

- At each reporting date during the life of the recognised foreign currency receivable or payable, the effective portion of the gain or loss on the hedging instrument, computed with respect to the forward exchange rate and recognised in other comprehensive income is reclassified to profit or loss.

IAS 39.AG98 3.7.420.50 A firm commitment to acquire a business in a business combination can qualify as the hedged item only in a hedge of foreign currency risk. In our view, the same applies to a forecast business combination, assuming that the transaction is highly probable and meets the other hedge accounting criteria (see 3.7.610).

3.7.430 *General business risks*

IAS 39.AG 98, AG110, IGF.2.8 3.7.430.10 To qualify for hedge accounting, the hedged risk should be specific and identifiable. A hedge against general business risks, such as physical damage of an asset, an increase in the price payable in a business combination or the risk that a transaction will not occur, does not qualify for hedge accounting.

3.7.440 *Hedges of more than one risk type*

IAS 39.74, 75 3.7.440.10 A hedging instrument, or a proportion thereof, is designated in its entirety, since normally there is a single fair value measure for a hedging instrument and the factors (risk components) that cause changes in fair value are co-dependent. While using an entire instrument or a proportion of an instrument is acceptable for hedge accounting, using only a portion, e.g. a single risk component, generally is not allowed. For example, a cross currency interest rate swap is designated with respect to all changes in its fair value, including those arising from foreign currency risk and interest rate risk.

IAS 39.76 3.7.440.20 However, it is possible to designate a single derivative (e.g. a cross-currency swap) as a hedge of more than one risk type if the following conditions are met:

- the risks being hedged can be identified clearly;
- the effectiveness of the hedge can be demonstrated; and
- it is possible to ensure that there is specific designation of the hedging instrument and the different risk positions.

3.7.440.30 Consequently, a derivative hedging instrument may be designated for a particular risk provided that the other parts of the hedging instrument are designated as hedging other risks of the hedged item (or other hedged items) and all other hedge accounting criteria are met. However, practical difficulties in separating fair values between interrelated risks could present difficulties in meeting the conditions under which such a designation is permissible.

IAS 39.IG F.2.18 3.7.440.40 For example, Company W with euro as its functional currency issues a floating rate sterling denominated bond. W also has a fixed rate US dollar financial asset with the same maturity and payment dates as the bond. In order to offset the currency and interest rate risk on the financial asset and liability, W enters into a pay-US dollar fixed receive-sterling floating interest rate swap.

3.7.440.50 The swap may be designated as a hedging instrument of the US dollar financial asset against the fair value exposure arising from changes in US interest rates and the foreign currency risk between US dollar and sterling. Alternatively, it could be designated as a cash flow hedge of the cash flow exposure arising from the variable cash outflows of the sterling bond and the foreign currency risk arising from movements in the US dollar/sterling exchange rate.

3.7.440.60 Both of these designations would be permissible under IAS 39 even though the hedge does not convert the currency exposure to the entity's functional currency of euro. In our view, this type of hedge is appropriate only as long as the entity has foreign currency exposures to both US dollar and sterling, and is not creating a new foreign currency position but rather is decreasing its risk exposure compared to its functional currency. Both currency exposures should be referred to in the hedge documentation and the hedge is a single hedging relationship (see 3.7.120.30). It should be clear in the documentation that the relationship between the swap and the US dollar financial asset qualifies for hedge accounting only due to the existence of both a US dollar financial asset and a sterling financial liability, i.e. both are hedged items in a single hedging relationship.

3.7.450 Hedging other market price risks

3.7.450.10 Entities that hold equity securities as investments are exposed to market price risk. Hedge accounting for the price risk of such securities is relevant only for securities classified as available for sale since fair value changes are recognised as a component of equity. For financial assets and liabilities measured at fair value through profit or loss, gains and losses are recognised directly in profit or loss, making hedge accounting unnecessary. The issues related to hedge accounting for equity price risk are similar to those for commodity price risk (see 3.7.410).

3.7.455 Hedging credit risk

AS 39.79, 81   3.7.455.10 IAS 39 indicates that a financial item may be hedged with respect to credit risk. In order for a hedge relationship to be eligible for hedge accounting, the designated risk should be separately identifiable, and changes in the cash flows or fair value of the entire hedged item arising from changes in the designated risk should be reliably measurable such that effectiveness can be measured. This provides a practical barrier to hedging credit risk to the extent that it may not be possible to measure changes in the fair value of a hedged debt instrument due to changes in credit risk separately from those arising from changes in liquidity risk.

3.7.455.20 A credit default swap (CDS) is a derivative financial instrument that provides protection against the risk of default by an obligor with respect to a reference debt instrument of the obligor. Under a typical CDS, if a specified credit event occurs, the seller of protection would either purchase the reference debt instrument from the buyer of protection for a fixed amount, usually par or par plus accrued interest, or pay the difference between that fixed amount and the fair value of the reference debt instrument at that time. The buyer of protection would pay fixed periodic premiums to the seller until the end of the term of the CDS or a credit event occurs. A holder of a debt instrument may purchase a CDS referenced to that debt instrument, or a similar debt instrument of the same obligor, to provide protection against the risk of a fair value loss arising on the occurrence of a credit event as specified in the CDS contract. In our view, an entity may designate this risk as the hedged risk in a hedging relationship provided that the entity can measure reliably changes in the fair value of the debt instrument attributable to this risk and can demonstrate high effectiveness. This approach may be acceptable in the following circumstances, assuming that the relevant testing demonstrated high effectiveness:

- the hedging CDS is referenced to the hedged asset and there is an active market (see 3.6.940.10) for such CDSs, in which case there is likely to be high effectiveness; or
- the hedging CDS is referenced to a similar but not identical obligation issued by the same issuer as the hedged asset and there is an active market both for: CDSs of the same type as the hedging CDS and CDSs referenced to the hedged asset.

3.7.456 *All-in-one cash flow hedges*

IAS 39.IG
F.2.5

3.7.456.10 An entity may enter into a contract to purchase or sell a non-financial item or a financial asset and such contract may be required to be accounted for as a derivative under IAS 39. For example, a fixed price contract to purchase a commodity would not be eligible for the own-use scope exemption when the entity has a past practice of taking delivery of the underlying and selling it within a short period after delivery for trading purposes (see 3.6.100.10). In such a scenario, if the derivative will be settled gross, then the entity may designate this derivative as the hedging instrument in a cash flow hedge of the variability of the consideration to be paid or received in the future transaction that will occur on gross settlement of the derivative contract itself (i.e. hedge of the forecast transaction that is implicit in the derivative itself), assuming that the other cash flow hedging criteria are met.

3.7.456.20 This hedging strategy is referred to as an all-in-one cash flow hedge and applies to all fixed price contracts that are accounted for as derivatives under IAS 39. By designating an all-in-one cash flow hedge, the entity avoids recognising in profit or loss the changes in the fair value of the purchase/sale contract that would otherwise be so recognised because the contract is accounted for as a derivative under IAS 39.

3.7.456.30 An all-in-one hedge also may be designated in a forecast purchase or sale involving a financial asset. For example, a financial institution manages the price risk associated with forecast sales of loans that it originates by entering into forward loan sale agreements to sell mortgage loans at a fixed price. This forward contract to sell loans meets the definition of a derivative and is required to be accounted for at fair value through profit or loss. However, the forward loan sale agreement may be designated as a cash flow hedge of the forecast sale of loans, i.e. as an all-in-one hedge of price risk, provided the contract will be settled gross.

3.7.460 **Effectiveness testing**

IAS 39.88(b),

3.7.460.10 To qualify for hedge accounting, a hedge should be "expected to be" (prospectively) and "actually have been" (retrospectively) highly effective. In other words, a hedge is regarded at inception and at subsequent assessment dates as highly effective only if the following conditions are met:

- the hedge is expected to be highly effective in achieving offsetting changes in fair value or cash flows attributable to the hedged risk during the period for which the hedge is designated or for the period until the amount of the hedging instrument is adjusted next (see 3.7.480.10) (prospective effectiveness); and
- the actual results of the hedge are within the range of 80 – 125 percent (retrospective effectiveness).

AS 39.95(b), 3.7.460.20 If either one of these tests fails, then hedge accounting may not be applied
102(b) at all. Even when a hedge relationship is expected to be highly effective and meets the retrospective effectiveness criterion (i.e. actual effectiveness is in the range of 80 – 125 percent), ineffectiveness still may arise from the relationship. Such ineffectiveness should be recognised immediately in profit or loss even if it is within the 80 – 125 percent range.

3.7.470 *Frequency of effectiveness tests*

IAS 39.AG 3.7.470.10 IFRSs do not specify how often effectiveness should be measured, beyond
106 noting that it should be done at a minimum at each reporting date, including interim reporting dates.

IAS 39.AG 3.7.470.20 If a hedge no longer is effective, then hedge accounting is discontinued pro-
113 spectively from the last date that the hedge was proven to be effective (see 3.7.570). Therefore, the more frequently that effectiveness is tested, the sooner the entity will identify the opportunity to rebalance its hedges to minimise the impact of ineffectiveness. This provides an incentive to perform hedge effectiveness testing frequently for hedges that may fail the effectiveness tests.

3.7.480 *Methods for measuring effectiveness*

AS 39.88(a), 3.7.480.10 IFRSs do not prescribe the methods that should be used in measuring effective-
AG107 ness. The method an entity adopts depends on its risk management strategy and hedge accounting systems and practices. For example, if the entity's risk management strategy is to adjust the amount of the hedging instrument periodically to reflect changes in the hedged position, then the entity needs to demonstrate that the hedge is expected to be highly effective only for the period until the amount of the hedging instrument next is adjusted.

IAS 39.88(a) 3.7.480.20 The method that will be used in measuring hedge effectiveness is specified in the hedge documentation.

3.7.480.30 Different methods may be used to measure prospective effectiveness and retrospective effectiveness for a single hedge relationship, as well as for different hedging relationships.

IAS 39.88(a) 3.7.480.40 Also, the method that will be used to measure effectiveness is determined on a hedge-by-hedge basis. There is no requirement to adopt a consistent method for all hedge relationships. However, in our view an entity should adopt a method for assessing hedge effectiveness that is applied consistently for similar types of hedges unless different methods are justified explicitly. For example, an entity should use the same methods for assessing effectiveness prospectively, as well as the same methods for measuring actual hedge effectiveness for forecast sales to the same export market undertaken on a regular basis.

IAS 39.AG 107A 3.7.480.50 If an entity hedges less than 100 percent of the exposure on an item, for example 85 percent, then it should designate the hedged item as that 85 percent and should measure ineffectiveness based on the change in that designated exposure only.

IAS 39.IG F.4.1 3.7.480.60 Effectiveness calculations may be done on a pre-tax or post-tax basis. Whichever method is used, the basis of calculating the change in fair value or cash flows of the hedged item and the change in fair value of the hedging instrument should be consistent.

3.7.490 *Prospective effectiveness*

IAS 39.AG 105, IGF.4.4 3.7.490.10 Prospective effectiveness may be demonstrated in several ways, for example by:

- demonstrating a high statistical correlation between the fair value or cash flows of the hedged item and those of the hedging instrument using, for example a statistical model such as regression analysis to analyse this correlation for a given period; or
- comparing past changes in the fair value or cash flows of the hedged item that are attributable to the hedged risk with past changes in the fair value or cash flows of the hedging instrument (offset method); or
- demonstrating that a "critical terms match" (see 3.7.520) exists at inception and in subsequent periods.

3.7.490.20 There is no specific guidance on what is meant by "highly effective in achieving offsetting changes" in the context of prospective effectiveness. In our view, this should be interpreted as correlation within a range of 80 – 125 percent, in line with the requirement for retrospective effectiveness testing.

3.7.490.30 A prospective effectiveness test that is based on an 80 – 125 percent range provides some latitude for hedging non-financial assets and liabilities. For example, transactions for the sale or purchase of commodities that practically can only be hedged using exchange-traded commodity contracts that refer to standardised quantities and grades of the particular quantity (see 3.7.410.40). The primary concern is that such hedging relationships will not qualify for hedge accounting as a result of ineffectiveness that arises due to the terms of the hedging instrument being different from those of the hedged item. However, if the fair values or cash flows of the hedging instrument and hedged item respectively are expected to generate an 80 – 125 percent offset, then there is a chance that such a hedging relationship will qualify for hedge accounting.

3.7.490.40 Also, such a prospective effectiveness test would accommodate interest rate hedges using swaps when, for example, ineffectiveness arises due to differences between the fixed rate in the swap and that on the hedged item, or in the timing of cash flows on the hedged item and those on the swap. Although ineffectiveness will be recognised in profit or loss, the hedge relationship will not necessarily fail to qualify for hedge accounting on the basis of there not being an almost perfect offset of fair values or cash flows at inception.

3.7.490.50 [Not used]

IAS 39.IG F.5.5   3.7.490.60 IAS 39 prohibits an effectiveness assessment approach that considers only the cash flows generated by a derivative hedging instrument as they are paid or received. The expectations of cash flows in subsequent periods and any resulting ineffectiveness are taken into account in assessing effectiveness.

IAS 39.IG F.5.5   3.7.490.70 It is common for entities to hedge their exposure to interest rate variability by entering into a pay-fixed receive-variable interest rate swap. If such a hedge is designated in a cash flow hedge relationship it would be inappropriate for the entity to measure retrospective effectiveness by comparing the actual cash flows on the swap with the actual cash flows on the hedged item. Such an effectiveness test would ignore the impact of past interest rate movements on the future cash flows of both the hedged item and the hedging instrument, i.e. it would ignore the impact of the movements in past rates on forward rates. While the actual cash flows on the hedged item and hedging instrument may offset perfectly, the future cash flows may not. Such a situation may arise when the cash flows on the hedged item and hedging instrument are based on different yield curves or when the maturities of the hedged item and hedging instrument are different.

IAS 39.AG 109   3.7.490.80 When the critical terms of the hedged item and the hedging instruments are not exactly the same prospective hedge effectiveness should be assessed and documented other than by a "critical terms match" (see 3.7.520). When a statistical model is used, the hedge documentation should specify how the results of the analysis are to be interpreted.

3.7.500 *Retrospective or ongoing assessment of effectiveness*

IAS 39.88(e)   3.7.500.10 Effectiveness is measured on an ongoing basis and the hedge relationship should be shown to have been actually highly effective throughout the reporting period.

IAS 39.89, 95(b)   3.7.500.20 The gain or loss on the hedged item is measured independently from that on the hedging instrument, i.e. it cannot be assumed that the change in fair value or cash flows of the hedged item in respect of the hedged risk equals the fair value change of the hedging instrument. The reason for this is that any ineffectiveness of the hedging instrument is recognised in profit or loss.

IAS 39.AG 107A   3.7.500.30 An entity may decide to designate less than 100 percent of the exposure on an item, e.g. the changes in fair value attributable to interest rate risk on 85 percent of the notional amount of a fixed rate debt instrument. In such circumstances the hedged item comprises the actual percentage being hedged, 85 percent in this case, and ineffectiveness should be measured based on the changes in fair value of that exposure.

3.7.500.40 The standard does not require a single method for prospective and retrospective assessment of effectiveness and the method applied may be different for different types of hedges. In practice, the periodic measurement of hedge effectiveness usually involves a method that compares the actual change in fair value of the hedged asset or liability or in cash flows with respect to the hedged risk to the change in the fair value of the hedging instrument (an offset method). However, in our view when assessing both prospective and retrospective effectiveness and when measuring actual effectiveness, the creditworthiness of the counterparty to the hedging instrument and of the entity itself, and the likelihood of default should be considered. For example, the value of a swap could be affected by changes in the credit rating of the swap counterparty or in the entity's credit rating.

3.7.500.50 Although IAS 39 does not specify any particular method for retrospective effectiveness testing, the offset method normally is used in practice. The offset method expresses the degree of offset between changes in the fair value of the hedging instrument and changes in the fair value or cash flows of the hedged item, as a percentage.

3.7.500.60 Retrospective effectiveness may be measured on a cumulative or period-by-period basis. Normally it is advantageous to measure effectiveness on a cumulative basis. For example, if the hedging instrument is an interest rate swap that resets at different times to the interest rate on the underlying, then the hedge is more likely to meet the effectiveness tests if effectiveness is measured on a cumulative basis.

3.7.500.70 In our view, when statistical methods such as regression analysis are used to demonstrate the effectiveness of a hedge relationship, it is permitted to use data originated prior to the date that the hedge relationship was designated to demonstrate retrospective effectiveness.

3.7.500.72 For example, Company T is assessing retrospective hedge effectiveness at the first reporting period after inception of a fair value hedge (e.g. one quarter after inception) and the changes in the fair value of the hedging instrument did not offset the changes in the fair value of the hedged item attributable to the hedged risk as anticipated. If T had chosen initially to use an offset approach, which is based only on the hedge period, then it would conclude that the retrospective hedge effectiveness test is failed. However, if T had chosen initially to use a statistical analysis based on a trailing twelve-month average, which includes three months of the hedge period and nine months prior to the hedge period, then it may be able to conclude that the retrospective effectiveness test was met. This is because the results of the earlier nine months may negate the unfavourable hedge results of the last three months. Moreover, by using data originated prior to the inception of the hedge, an entity may use the same regression test for assessing both prospective and retrospective effectiveness.

3.7.500.75 In our view, the use of a statistical method such as regression analysis requires that the quality of the output from the statistical method be evaluated on an ongoing basis to ensure that the results are statistically valid. If a statistical method does not provide valid results, then this method cannot be used to demonstrate hedge effectiveness. For example, an entity concludes that a hedge is effective using regression analysis as it meets the 80 – 125 percent requirement (see 3.7.460.10). However, had the offset method been applied then the hedge would have consistently failed the 80 – 125 percent requirement. In our view, the fact that the hedge relationship, on a consistent basis, would not have been highly effective had the offset method been applied indicates that the data used for the regression analysis may not be statistically valid.

3.7.500.80 See 3.7.540.90 for further discussion of a cash flow hedge of interest rate risk using interest rate swaps.

3.7.505 *Regression analysis*

3.7.505.10 Linear regression techniques are used for determining *whether* and by *how much* a change in one variable will result in a change in another variable. Consequently, through the use of regression analysis it is possible to demonstrate the effectiveness of a hedge relationship by determining how much of the change in the fair value or cash flows of the dependent variable is caused by a change in the fair value or cash flows of the independent variable. In our view, the hedging instrument or the hedged item may be assigned as the dependent variable and likewise either can be assigned as the independent variable.

3.7.505.20 In reviewing the regression model, in our view as a minimum the following parameters should be assessed:

- R squared (coefficient of determination), which measures the proportion of the variability in the dependent variable that can be explained by the variation in the independent variable.
- Slope of the regression line, which indicates the change in the dependent variable for every change in the independent variable. The slope should be within a 0.8 – 1.25 range, which indicates that the hedging relationship is within the 80 – 125 percent effectiveness requirement.
- Confidence interval of the slope being within the 80 – 125 percentage range; in our view a minimum 95 percent confidence level should be used when assessing the effectiveness of the hedge relationship.

3.7.510 **Actual ineffectiveness**

IAS 39.IG 3.7.510.10 In a cash flow hedge, regardless of the methods that are used to assess
F.5.5 prospective and retrospective effectiveness, the actual ineffectiveness recognised in profit or loss is calculated using the offset method on a cumulative basis to ensure that all ineffectiveness is recognised in profit or loss immediately.

AS 39.95, 96 3.7.510.20 In a cash flow hedge, if the cumulative gain or loss on the hedging instrument is more than the cumulative change in the fair value of the expected future cash flows on the hedged item attributable to the hedged risk, then the difference is recognised in profit or loss as ineffectiveness. However, if the reverse is true then the full cumulative gain or loss on the hedging instrument is recognised in other comprehensive income.

Consequently, in a cash flow hedge ineffectiveness is recognised in profit or loss only when the cumulative change in fair value of the hedging instrument is greater than the cumulative change in fair value of the expected future cash flows on the hedged item attributable to the hedged risk.

3.7.510.30 In other words, ineffectiveness arising from over-hedging is recognised in profit or loss, but ineffectiveness arising from under-hedging is not recognised because the hedged item is not recognised.

3.7.510.40 In a fair value hedge, ineffectiveness is recognised automatically in profit or loss as a result of separately remeasuring the hedging instrument and the hedged item. No separate calculation is required of the amount of ineffectiveness to be recognised in profit or loss.

3.7.515 *Effect of credit risk on effectiveness testing and ineffectiveness measurement**

IAS 39.AG 109, IGF.4.3   3.7.515.10 In our view, entities should consider the effect of both changes in counterparty credit risk and own credit risk on the assessment of hedge effectiveness and the measurement of hedge ineffectiveness.

IAS 39.IG F.4.3   3.7.515.20 For all hedges, an entity considers the risk that the counterparty to the hedging instrument will default by failing to make any contractual payments to the entity. For cash flow hedges, if it becomes probable that a counterparty will default by failing to make any contractual payments to the entity, then the entity would be unable to conclude that the hedging relationship will be highly effective.

IAS 39.AG 107, IGF.5.2   3.7.515.30 For all hedges, changes in both counterparty credit risk and own credit risk impact the measurement of changes in the fair value of a derivative hedging instrument. These changes will likely have no offsetting effect on the measurement of the changes in the value of the hedged item attributable to the hedged risk. Such differences in measurement resulting from changes in counterparty and own credit risk will impact assessments of effectiveness and may lead to a conclusion that the hedging relationship has not been and/or is not expected to be highly effective (see 3.7.570). Even when it is concluded that a hedge has been highly effective, such differences will result in ineffectiveness being recognised in profit or loss for fair value hedges. Such differences also would require the recognition of ineffectiveness in profit or loss for cash flow hedges if the cumulative gain or loss on the hedging instrument is greater than the cumulative change in fair or present value of the expected future cash flows on the hedged item. Similarly, for net investment hedges in which the hedging instrument is a derivative, ineffectiveness is recognised in profit or loss if the gain or loss on the hedging instrument exceeds the foreign exchange differences arising on the designated net investment.

3.7.515.40 When an entity has a number of derivative instruments with a counterparty that are subject to a master netting agreement, margining or collateralisation, the entity may calculate the effect of changes in counterparty and own credit risk by means of a valuation adjustment at the portfolio level. However, for assessing hedge effectiveness and recognising ineffectiveness an entity needs to determine the individual credit risk adjustments to arrive at the fair values of the individual hedging derivatives or the appropriate credit adjustment for a group of derivatives that have been designated together as the hedging instrument in a single hedging relationship. In our view, the entity should adopt a reasonable and consistently applied methodology for allocating credit risk adjustments determined at a portfolio level to individual derivative instruments for the purpose of measuring the fair values of individual hedging instruments that are used in assessing effectiveness and measuring hedge ineffectiveness.

3.7.520 *Matching critical terms*

IAS 39.AG 08, IGF.4.7 3.7.520.10 If the critical terms of the hedging instrument and the hedged item exactly match, then prospective hedge effectiveness can be assumed, but there is no exemption from the requirement to demonstrate retrospective effectiveness.

3.7.520.20 In our view, applying a qualitative approach for assessing prospective effectiveness is not precluded and may be appropriate, but only when *all* critical terms exactly match, which as a minimum includes notional, maturity, repricing dates, and underlying (e.g. the index on which the asset or liability's variable rate is based), and the hedging instrument has a fair value of zero at inception. Applying a qualitative approach does not mean applying the "short-cut method" as allowed under US GAAP, whereby an entity compares the critical terms of the hedging instrument and the hedged item at inception and is not required to perform any reassessment in the subsequent periods. This is not permitted under IFRSs. A qualitative approach requires that all critical terms be reviewed and compared at inception and in subsequent periods. If it is concluded that there is no change in any critical term, then such a test would be sufficient to satisfy the prospective effectiveness testing requirements. However, the effect of credit risk should be considered (see 3.7.515). Also, retrospective effectiveness can never be assumed and always should be measured numerically.

IAS 39.AG 08, IGF.4.7 3.7.520.30 Examples of situations in which the critical terms exactly match are:

- a hedge of a foreign currency sales commitment with a futures contract to sell the same amount of the same foreign currency on the same date, if the fair value of the future at inception of the hedge is zero;
- a hedge of benchmark interest rate risk associated with a recognised asset or liability using a swap with a zero fair value at inception of the hedge and the same notional amount as the asset or liability and with the same key terms;
- a hedge of a forecast commodity sale with a forward contract to purchase the same quantity of the same commodity on the same date, if the fair value of the forward at inception of the hedge is zero, and either the change in the discount or premium on the forward contract is excluded from the assessment of effectiveness and recognised directly in profit or loss, or the change in expected cash flows on the forecast transaction is based on the forward price of the commodity; and

- a hedge of a specific bond held with a forward contract to sell an equivalent bond with the same notional amount, currency and maturity, if the forward contract has at designation date a fair value of zero.

3.7.530 *Time value and interest element*

IAS 39.74 3.7.530.10 If appropriately documented at inception of the hedge relationship, the time value of an option may be excluded from the effectiveness tests and effectiveness may be tested based solely on the intrinsic value of the option. Similarly, the interest element of a forward contract may be excluded and effectiveness may be measured based solely on the spot component of the forward contract. This choice is available on a hedge-by-hedge basis, and there is no requirement to have a consistently applied policy. However, an entity is not permitted to exclude the credit risk (or any other risk) associated with a derivative from the measurement of hedge effectiveness.

IAS 39.96(c) 3.7.530.20 Changes in the fair value of components of the hedging instrument that are excluded from effectiveness measurement (i.e. the time value or interest component) are recognised immediately in profit or loss.

3.7.530.30 If the hedging instrument is an option, then we recommend that effectiveness be measured based only on the intrinsic value of the option. This is because the hedged transaction is unlikely to have an equivalent time value effect and therefore, if the time value component of the option is included, it will give rise to ineffectiveness. When intrinsic value designation is used and the option remains out of the money during the period for which effectiveness is being assessed (on period-by-period basis or cumulative basis depending on the method used by the entity; see 3.7.500.60), then quantitative retrospective effectiveness assessment is not necessary; however, prospective assessment still is required.

3.7.530.40 If the time value or the interest element is included in the measurement of hedge effectiveness, then the full fair value of the option or forward contract, respectively, is used in the effectiveness calculation.

IAS 39.IG 3.7.530.50 Whichever method is used to deal with the time value or interest elements of
F.5.5 hedged items and hedging instruments, the basis of calculating the change in fair value or cash flows of the hedged item and the change in fair value of the hedging instrument is consistent. For example, if the interest element is excluded from the measurement of changes in the fair value of the hedging instrument, then the change in the cash flows or fair value of the hedged item attributable to the hedged risk should be measured based on spot rates. However, if the interest element is included in the effectiveness measurement, then the change in fair value or cash flows of the hedged item attributable to the hedged risk should be based on forward rates.

3.7.530.60 It is possible to apply a dynamic hedging strategy, including both the intrinsic and time value of an option, although there is little elaboration in IAS 39 about how this should be performed. A delta-neutral hedging strategy, whereby the hedging instrument is adjusted constantly in order to maintain a desired hedge ratio, may qualify for hedge accounting under IAS 39 if the other hedge accounting criteria are met (see 3.7.325).

3.7.540 *Interest rate risk*

3.7.540.10 To maximise effectiveness, when hedging interest rate risk, the hedged risk normally is designated as the benchmark interest rate only and the credit risk spread on the hedged item is excluded from the hedged risk. This is because credit risk normally will not affect the fair value or cash flows of the hedged item and the hedging instrument in the same way.

IAS 39.IG 3.7.540.20 Similarly, if the interest exposure on an interest-bearing instrument is hedged
F.2.17 for only a portion of the instrument's remaining period to maturity, then it is easier to meet the effectiveness rules if the hedged risk is documented as being based on the same yield curve as the derivative. For example, Company D hedges the interest rate risk on a ten-year bond for the first five years using a five-year interest rate swap. Effectiveness could be maximised by designating the swap as a hedge of the fair value of the interest payments on the bond for the first five years, and of the change in the value of the principal amount of the bond due to changes in the yield curve related to the five years of the swap. If the hedged risk is simply designated as the change in fair value of the bond, then the hedge is likely to be ineffective because the value of the bond will be affected by changes in the ten-year yield curve whereas the value of the derivative will be affected by changes in the five-year yield curve.

3.7.540.30 – 40 [Not used]

3.7.540.50 It is quite common for financial instruments having an exposure to interest rate risk also to be exposed to prepayment risk. For a prepayable asset or liability, changes in interest rates will have an effect on the fair value of the asset or liability by changing the expectations about the timing of future cash flows. This has an impact on effectiveness assessment and measurement.

3.7.540.60 Prepayment risk affects the timing as well as the amount of cash flows. Consequently, this may impact the effectiveness of fair value hedges as well as the highly probable requirement for forecast cash flows. A prepayable hedged item generally will experience smaller fair value changes when interest rates fall than a non-prepayable hedged item, while fair value changes as interest rates rise will be closer to those of a non-prepayable item. When hedging a portfolio of such instruments effectiveness is likely to be more difficult to demonstrate for a fair value hedge than for a cash flow hedge. In a static fair value hedge, it may be difficult to group a portfolio of fixed rate assets subject to prepayment risk, since it may be difficult to prove that the changes in fair value of the individual assets are approximately proportional to the overall change in fair value of the portfolio, unless each item contains identical prepayment options. As a result, fixed rate assets subject to prepayment risk may have to be hedged on a one-to-one basis. In this case ineffectiveness will arise unless the hedging instrument also contains a prepayment option.

3.7.540.70 Therefore, the risk of prepayment or changes to the timing of future cash flows should be considered when an entity designates its hedge relationships. In our view, prepayment is not a risk that is capable of separate designation; rather, it is a component of interest rate risk and is designated as such. This is because it is difficult to measure and isolate the change in fair value due to a change in prepayments separately from the overall change arising from a change in interest rates.

3.7.540.80 In a portfolio fair value hedge of interest rate risk the assessment of hedge effectiveness can be performed using a maturity schedule. Such a schedule usually determines the net position for each maturity period by aggregating assets and liabilities maturing or repricing in that maturity period. However, the net exposure should be associated with a specific asset, liability, cash inflow or outflow in order to apply hedge accounting, such that the correlation of the changes of the hedging instrument and the designated hedged item can be assessed.

3.7.540.90 In our view, the following are some of the methods that could be used for measuring hedge ineffectiveness in a cash flow hedge of interest rate risk using an interest rate swap.

3.7.543 *Change in fair value method*

3.7.543.10 Ineffectiveness is measured by considering movements in the present value of the cumulative expected/contractual future interest cash flows that are designated as the hedged item and the cumulative change in the fair value of the designated hedging instrument, for example a pay-fixed receive-floating interest rate swap. Although this approach is permitted and simple to apply, it will lead to ineffectiveness because the overall change in the fair value of the hedging instrument will be influenced by the change in value of the pay-fixed leg of the interest rate swap as this pay-fixed leg does not reprice to the current fixed market rate at each testing date. As a result, ineffectiveness arises as there is no such change in the present value of the hedged item since it does not include a fixed leg.

3.7.545 *Hypothetical derivative method*

3.7.545.10 Ineffectiveness is measured by comparing the change in the fair value of the actual derivative designated as the hedging instrument and the change in the fair value of a hypothetical derivative representing the hedged item. The hypothetical derivative is defined so that it matches the critical terms of the hedged item, e.g. notional, repricing dates, index on which the asset or liability's variable rate is based, mirror image caps and floors etc. The hypothetical derivative should have a zero fair value at inception of the hedge. The hypothetical derivative would be expected to perfectly offset the hedged cash flows, and the change in fair value of the hypothetical derivative is regarded as a proxy for the present value of the cumulative change in the expected future cash flows on the hedged item.

3.7.545.20 The hypothetical derivative method is likely to be more difficult to apply in practice as a separate hypothetical derivative needs to be identified for each hedging relationship. However, this method does result in lower ineffectiveness in most instances compared to the change in fair value method. Only one hypothetical derivative should be identified for each hedged item based on the terms of the hedged item; without such a restriction entities could design a perfect hypothetical derivative to match exactly the terms of the hedging instrument, thereby reporting no ineffectiveness.

3.7.547 *Measuring hedge ineffectiveness*

3.7.547.10 In most circumstances the effectiveness of both the variable and the fixed legs of the swap needs to be considered when using one of the methods described in 3.7.543 and 545. Considering only the change in fair value of the floating leg of the swap would, in our view be appropriate for effectiveness testing purposes when using the hypothetical derivative only when the fixed rate on the swap is equal to the fixed rate that would have been obtained on the hedged item at its designation date (i.e. when the fixed leg of the hedging swap equals the fixed leg on a hypothetical derivative that, had such hypothetical derivative been created on the hedge designation date, would perfectly offset the hedged cash flows). In other words if the fixed leg of the swap is the market rate at inception of the hedge relationship such that the swap has a fair value of zero or close to zero, and there are no differences in the principal terms (notional, repricing dates, basis) and credit risk (or credit risk is not designated in the hedging relationship), then such a method for testing effectiveness may be appropriate. In such circumstances the changes in fair value arising on the fixed leg of the hedging instrument and on the fixed leg of the perfectly effectively hypothetical derivative offset each other perfectly and consequently do not contribute to any ineffectiveness in the relationship.

3.7.547.20 If the hedge is designated subsequent to entering into the hedging swap, then it is unlikely that the fixed leg of the hedging swap will be equal to the fixed rate on the perfectly effective hypothetical derivative, and hence, a method that compares only the changes in the fair values of the floating legs of the hedging swap and the hedged item is not appropriate to use in this case.

3.7.547.30 In our view, IFRSs do not permit what has been termed as "terminal value" hedging under US GAAP. Additionally, it is not appropriate to identify and designate as the hedged item a portion containing a risk exposure similar to that of a written option (e.g. designating a written option as the hypothetical derivative in highly probable forecast cash flows). For example, if an entity purchases an option to hedge the downside currency risk in a highly probable foreign currency revenue stream, then it is not appropriate to designate as the hedged item a portion of the forecast cash flows such that it represents an exposure to losses in a way that this portion is a written option, including time value, which then perfectly offsets the purchased option.

3.7.547.40 It is not possible, in the absence of actual optionality in the hedged item, to designate the hedged risk in a manner such that it has a time value component. Therefore, in most cases hedge effectiveness can be achieved only by excluding the time value from the hedging relationship (see 3.7.530).

3.7.547.50 Forecast transactions create a cash flow exposure to interest rate changes because interest payments will be based on the actual market rate when the transaction occurs. In these circumstances hedge effectiveness is based on the highly probable expected interest payments calculated using the forward interest rate based on the applicable yield curve. For forecast transactions such as anticipated debt issues, it is not possible to determine what the actual market interest rate will be for the debt issue. In these situations, retrospective hedge effectiveness may be measured based on changes in the interest rates that have occurred between the designation of the hedge and the date that effectiveness testing is performed. The forward interest rates that should be used are those that correspond with the term of the expected transaction at inception and at the date of the effectiveness testing. The implementation guidance to IAS 39 provides an example of how hedge effectiveness may be measured for a forecast transaction in a debt instrument.

3.7.550 *"Clean" vs "dirty" prices*

3.7.550.10 In hedging interest rate risk arising from fixed rate financial assets or liabilities using interest rate swaps, a highly effective hedge relationship usually can be achieved by ensuring that the principal terms of the hedged item and hedging instrument match. However, when the interest rate on the swap reprices at a date other than the reporting date (at which date effectiveness should be assessed), ineffectiveness may arise from the variable leg of the swap due to interest rate movements between these two dates. For example, an interest rate swap reprices every three months and the last repricing date is 30 November, which is before the reporting date. On 30 November the interest on the variable leg of the swap is fixed for the next three months. Consequently, changes in market interest rates between this date and the reporting date of 31 December will cause the fair value of the floating leg of the swap to change, giving rise to ineffectiveness (this is reflected in the "dirty" price of the swap). During initial periods and periods near the end of a hedge relationship, this ineffectiveness may be substantial enough, in relative terms, to preclude hedge accounting.

3.7.550.20 In our view, an entity could indicate that in assessing hedge effectiveness it will disregard the accrued interest on the hedging instrument and the hedged item (this is referred to as the "clean" price of the swap). In this case it may be possible to prove that the relationship was effective on a retrospective basis, i.e. within the 80 – 125 percent range, and therefore to continue hedge accounting, assuming that the other conditions continue to be met. Disregarding accrued interest implies that the entity will, for the purposes of assessing hedge effectiveness only, determine the fair value of the swap as the clean price. By considering clean prices, while the entire ineffectiveness from the floating leg of the swap would not be eliminated, the resulting ineffectiveness would then be limited to fair value changes on the unaccrued portion of the interest coupon to the next swap settlement date.

3.7.550.30 In our view, such a methodology should improve both the retrospective and prospective effectiveness of the hedge relationship. However, this does not mean that there will be no ineffectiveness. The entity still is required to calculate the extent to which the hedge was ineffective and this amount should be recognised in profit or loss. So while the continuation of hedge accounting should be possible, the actual ineffectiveness should be recognised in profit or loss using the offset method (see 3.7.510).

3.7.560 *Ineffectiveness in a fair value hedge due to different fixed rates*

3.7.560.10 Entities may designate fixed rate financial assets or financial liabilities as hedged items in a fair value hedge, with the hedged risk being changes in fair value due to changes in interest rates. The hedged cash flows in this case would include all coupons and principal payments arising from the instruments. In such a hedge relationship it may be possible to demonstrate prospective effectiveness, but an issue may arise in respect of retrospective effectiveness due to mismatches between the fixed rate on the hedged item and the fixed interest rate on the hedging instrument. Such a mismatch could arise in the following circumstances:

- The hedged item bears interest at a fixed rate calculated as the benchmark rate on issue plus 100 basis points for credit spread, while the fixed leg of the hedging instrument is based on the benchmark interest rate at inception plus 50 basis points.
- The interest rate on the hedged item is based on the benchmark interest rate at the date of issue, while the fixed leg of the hedging instrument is based on the benchmark interest rate at a later date. This difference is due to movements in the benchmark rate between these two dates.

3.7.560.20 In the first case in 3.7.560.10 in which the difference arises due to a credit spread, the question is whether it is possible to define the hedged item as the fair value changes due to changes in only the benchmark interest rate on the principal and the risk-free element of the interest payments.

3.7.560.30 If the hedged item is a financial asset or liability, then it may be a hedged item with respect to the risks associated with only a portion of its cash flows or fair value, such as one or more selected contractual cash flows or portions thereof, if effectiveness can be measured reliably. The hedged portion should be less than or equal to the total cash flows of the asset or liability.

3.7.560.40 In the case described in 3.7.560.20 effectiveness can be measured clearly and reliably. Therefore, in our view designating as the hedged item the fair value changes due to changes in a benchmark interest rate on the principal and the interest payments is possible. Such a designation appropriately reflects the economics of the hedge relationship and avoids accounting for ineffectiveness that does not exist; the benchmark risk is a portion that has a strong economic relationship with the cash flows of the hedged item.

3.7.560.50 In the second case described in 3.7.560.10, ineffectiveness is likely to arise given the difference in benchmark interest rates.

3.7.570 **Discontinuing hedge accounting**

IAS 39.91,
101, AG113,
IGF.6.2(i)

3.7.570.10 Hedge accounting should be discontinued prospectively if the hedged transaction no longer is highly probable, the hedging instrument expires, is sold, terminated or exercised, the hedged item is sold, settled or otherwise disposed of, the hedge no longer is highly effective or the entity revokes the designation. If an entity does not meet all hedge effectiveness criteria, then hedge accounting is terminated as of the date that the hedge was last proved effective, which may be the previous interim or annual reporting date, or from the date that the hedged item or hedging instrument is derecognised. For this reason testing hedge effectiveness more frequently is a way of reducing the impact of the unexpected termination of a hedge relationship. If the entity can identify the event or change in circumstances that caused the hedge to fail the effectiveness criteria, and can prove that the hedge was effective before the date on which this occurred, then the entity can cease hedge accounting from the date of such event or change in circumstances. If there is a retrospective hedge effectiveness test failure, then even if prospective effectiveness can be demonstrated for the existing hedge relationship, hedge accounting based on the previous designation is discontinued, although it may be possible to designate prospectively a new hedging relationship. Also, since the retrospective effectiveness criterion is not met, hedge accounting cannot be applied for the period just ended. In contrast, if a hedge relationship is demonstrated to be highly effective for the period just ended, but the prospective effectiveness criterion is not met, then hedge accounting is discontinued prospectively from the date of such assessment. Also, in this case it is necessary to report any ineffectiveness in profit or loss on the date that hedge accounting is discontinued.

3.7.570.11 Hedge accounting would be discontinued also if the recognised asset, liability, firm commitment or forecast transaction no longer is eligible for designation as a hedged item. This would occur, for example, when an entity acquires, or otherwise begins to consolidate, the counterparty to a hedged forecast transaction or firm commitment resulting in that transaction no longer involving a party external to the reporting entity. Another example is when an entity sells, or otherwise is required to deconsolidate, a subsidiary (see 2.5.490) resulting in a hedged item of that subsidiary becoming derecognised. Also, when there is a change in the functional currency of an entity, currency exposures denominated in the new functional currency will no longer qualify for hedge accounting for foreign currency risk.

3.7.570.12 When an entity voluntarily terminates a hedge relationship in-between two regular effectiveness assessment dates, then, in our view the hedge relationship should be assessed for effectiveness on the date of voluntary termination to determine whether it was retrospectively effective. If the hedge is determined to be retrospectively effective, then hedge accounting should be applied up to the date of voluntary termination, including recognising any ineffectiveness up to that date in profit or loss. If, however, the retrospective test is failed, then hedge accounting cannot be applied after the last date on which the effectiveness criteria were met.

3.7.570.15 A hedging relationship is discontinued when the hedging instrument is sold or terminated. In our experience, certain events of default, such as a filing for bankruptcy by the counterparty would, under standard International Swaps and Derivatives Association (ISDA) terms for some derivatives, either result automatically in termination of the derivative, or permit the entity to terminate the derivative in exchange for a net cash settlement and to replace it with another instrument having similar terms with another counterparty. Whether this is the case is likely to depend on the legal and contractual arrangements in each country. In our view, unless it is a replacement of a hedging instrument as part of the entity's existing documented hedging strategy, the termination of a hedging derivative and its replacement by another derivative with another counterparty would result in the termination of the existing hedge relationship and, if appropriately designated, the establishment of a new one.

3.7.570.17 Beginning a new replacement hedging relationship using a derivative that has a fair value other than zero may result in hedge ineffectiveness in the future. This is because the initial fair value of the derivative is, itself, subject to change with changes in market interest rates. Unless an offsetting fair value effect also is present in the hedged item, ineffectiveness may result.

3.7.570.20 If the hedged item is partially repaid (determination depends on how the hedged item has been defined in the hedge designation) prior to its expected repayment date, then this will cause the entity to be over-hedged as the notional amount of the hedging instrument may be more than the remaining outstanding amount of the hedged item. In this case the entity would be required to terminate the existing hedge relationship unless the existing hedge relationship continues to be highly effective with the reduced hedged item; i.e. if the originally designated hedging instrument continues to be highly effective in offsetting the changes in fair value or cash flows of the now reduced hedged item. If, as a result of the partial repayment of the hedged item, the over-hedge is such that the 80 – 125 percent effectiveness test no longer is met, then the original hedge relationship should be discontinued in its entirety. The entity may re-designate the remaining hedged item in a new hedge relationship, which may include a proportion of the original hedging instrument, if all the criteria for hedge accounting are met. The adverse effect of a partial repayment of the hedged item on continuity of the entire hedge relationship may be mitigated by use of a layering hedge strategy as discussed in 3.7.605.

IAS 39.75   3.7.570.30 If a hedging instrument ceases to be part of a hedge relationship, then it may be re-designated in a new hedge relationship, as long as the re-designation is for the entire remaining term of the instrument. For example, a forward contract of 100 that initially was designated as the hedging instrument to hedge forecast transactions of 100 would no longer be expected to be highly effective if revisions to forecasts subsequent to the hedge designation date indicate that that only 70 of the forecast transactions are now highly probable of occurrence. In this situation the original hedge designation would be discontinued as it would no longer meet the highly effective criteria. A new hedging relationship under which a proportion (e.g. 70 percent) of the original forward is designated to hedge the highly probable forecast transactions of 70 is permissible. The new hedging relationship may not be fully effective, as the forward contract normally would have a fair value other than zero at the date of re-designation. Changes in fair value of the remaining proportion of the forward (i.e. 30 percent), if not designated in another hedging relationship, would be recognised in profit or loss.

IAS 39.91,
101   3.7.570.40 A replacement or rollover of a hedging instrument is not deemed to be a termination if the new instrument has the same characteristics as the instrument being replaced, it continues to meet the hedge criteria, and the rollover strategy was documented properly at inception of the initial hedge. In our view, using a rollover hedge strategy, the entity may continue to perform hedge effectiveness testing on a cumulative basis from the beginning of the period in which the first hedging instrument was rolled over. The amortisation of any fair value adjustment made to the hedged item under a fair value hedge may continue to be deferred until the rollover hedge strategy is discontinued.

3.7.570.45 For example, Company X forecasts a highly probable purchase of a commodity in one year. As part of its risk management strategy, X wants to fix the cash flow variability that would arise from changes in market prices of the commodity from now until the date of purchase. However, the market to which X has access does not offer commodity future contracts for a duration longer than three months. Hence, X decides to hedge its exposure to changes in commodity prices by entering into four successive commodity futures. If X documents this hedging strategy, including the expected rollovers of the hedging futures, at inception of the hedge, then the expiry of one future contract and its replacement with a successive future contract with the same characteristics would not be deemed to be a termination of the hedge.

IAS 39.92   3.7.570.50 When an effective hedge relationship no longer exists, the accounting for the hedging instrument and the hedged item revert to accounting under the usual principles of IAS 39 and other applicable IFRSs. All derivatives within the scope of IAS 39 are accounted for at fair value with changes in fair value recognised in profit or loss. When fair value hedge accounting is prospectively discontinued, any hedging adjustment made previously to a hedged financial instrument for which the effective interest method is used is amortised to profit or loss by adjusting the effective interest rate of the hedged item from the date that amortisation begins. Amortisation may begin as soon as an adjustment exists (i.e. while the hedging relationship still exists) but should not begin later than the date on which the hedged item ceases to be adjusted for changes in fair value attributable to the hedged risk. If, in the case of a portfolio hedge of interest rate risk, amortising using a recalculated effective interest rate is impracticable, then the adjustment is amortised using a straight-line method. The adjustment should be amortised fully by maturity of the financial instrument or, in the case of a portfolio hedge of interest rate risk, by the expiry of the relevant repricing time period. In the event that the hedged item is derecognised, the adjustment is recognised immediately in profit or loss when the item is derecognised.

IAS 39.102   3.7.570.60 For a *hedge of a net investment* in a foreign operation, the cumulative amount previously recognised in other comprehensive income remains in the foreign currency translation reserve until there is a disposal or partial disposal of the investment (see 3.7.110.30 – 35). A partial disposal of a net investment in a foreign operation may require the existing hedge to be terminated if the hedging instrument no longer is highly effective in offsetting the foreign currency risk on the reduced net investment.

3.7.580 *Effect of delays and other changes in the forecast transaction*

AS 39.101(b) 3.7.580.10 The notion of a highly probable forecast transaction implies a higher degree of probability than one that is merely expected to occur. If a forecast transaction no longer is highly probable but still is expected to occur, then this means that the criteria for hedge accounting no longer are met and, prospectively, the entity should cease applying hedge accounting. However, the net cumulative gain or loss that was recognised in other comprehensive income during the effective period of the hedge remains in equity until the expected transaction actually occurs. The same treatment applies in any other case when hedge accounting is terminated due to the hedging criteria no longer being met.

IAS 39.101 3.7.580.20 If a hedged forecast transaction no longer is expected to occur within the original time period or a relatively short period thereafter, then hedge accounting is terminated. The related cumulative gain or loss on the hedging instrument that was recognised in other comprehensive income should be reclassified to profit or loss immediately. An entity cannot continue to defer the cumulative gains or loss in equity on the basis that the original hedged transaction has been replaced by a new forecast transaction that has features similar to the original hedged transaction. In our view, if the extension of the time period is relatively short, then the hedge still may qualify for hedge accounting if the effectiveness criteria continue to be met (see 3.7.460).

3.7.580.30 In determining the appropriate accounting treatment for delayed transactions, it is important to distinguish between hedged cash flows related to:

- a firm commitment;
- a highly probable forecast transaction with an identified counterparty; and
- forecast transactions with unidentified counterparties.

3.7.590 *Firm commitments and forecast transactions with identified counterparties*

IAS 39.91, 3.7.590.10 When the timing of delivery, payments or other terms under a firm commit-
101 ment are changed, an entity evaluates whether the original firm commitment still exists or whether a new firm commitment has been created. The latter situation would result in the original hedge relationship being terminated and hedge accounting being discontinued prospectively (see 3.7.570).

3.7.590.20 If a firm commitment is delayed but still will occur, then it is important to determine the cause and extent of the delay. In our view, when delays occur in the cash flows associated with a firm commitment, hedge accounting may be continued under the following circumstances:

- the firm commitment still can be uniquely identified; and

- a binding agreement still exists and the cash flows are still expected to occur within a *relatively short period of time* after the original delivery/payment date.

3.7.590.30 The contract supporting a firm commitment should specify a date or range of dates within which the cash flows are expected to occur. If a date, such as a delivery or completion date, is not specified, then the transaction is unlikely to meet the definition of a firm commitment; rather, it can be hedged only as a forecast transaction with an identified counterparty.

IAS 39.IG F.3.11 3.7.590.40 For a highly probable forecast transaction with an identified counterparty, there may be a little more flexibility in what could be regarded as a *relatively short period of time* if a delivery date has not yet been established.

3.7.590.50 The key issue, when taking into account all the facts and circumstances surrounding the delay, is whether the entity can demonstrate that the delayed transaction is the *same transaction* as the one that was hedged originally.

IAS 39.IG F.5.4 3.7.590.60 When the timing of a firm commitment or a highly probable forecast transaction is delayed, some degree of ineffectiveness is likely to occur, if the timing of the hedged item and the timing of the hedging instrument no longer are the same. When the hedging instrument originally had a duration longer than the original expected time frame for the firm commitment or forecast transaction, then the effectiveness could, in fact, improve as a result of the delay in the hedged transaction. In other cases the hedged cash flow may arise earlier than originally expected. Since the hedging instrument will expire later than the hedged cash flows, some ineffectiveness is likely to occur in this situation as well. However, the hedging instrument may not be re-designated for a shorter period.

3.7.600 *Forecast transactions with unidentified counterparties*

3.7.600.10 An example of a forecast transaction with an unidentified counterparty is the sale of mobile telephone handsets. Typically the hedged cash flow would be the first x amount of sales revenue to be received on the sale of handsets in a particular month or quarter (see 3.7.605). Exactly which retailer or end-user will purchase the handsets is not specified in the hedge documentation.

IAS 39.IG F.3.7 3.7.600.20 Cash flows from forecast transactions with unidentified counterparties are designated by reference to the time period in which the transactions are expected to occur.

3.7.600.30 When forecast cash flows in a particular period do not occur, it is possible that such a shortfall will be offset by increased cash flows in a later period. For example, an entity initially forecasts sale of summer clothing amounting to 100 in each of the first two quarters of the coming year. Subsequently the entity revises its forecast to sales of 75 in the first quarter and 125 in the second quarter. The total amount of sales in the two quarters remains unchanged at 200.

IAS 39.88, 3.7.600.40 For hedge accounting to be continued the original forecast transaction still
101 should exist and be highly probable. If the hedged item is a forecast transaction (e.g. forecast sales) with unidentified counterparties within a certain time period, then it is unlikely that an entity will be able to demonstrate that sales in later periods replace a shortfall in an earlier period. Consequently, hedge accounting should be discontinued. In addition, a history of designating hedges of forecast transactions and then determining that they no longer are expected to occur may call into question the entity's ability to predict forecast transactions accurately, as well as the propriety of using hedge accounting in the future for similar transactions.

3.7.600.50 In our view, the transactions should be grouped into relatively narrow bands of time within which the forecast transactions are expected to occur. In determining the length of such a period, the industry and environment in which the entity operates should be considered. In our view, for forecast transactions with unidentified counterparties, this narrow range of time should be interpreted more strictly (i.e. a shorter time period used) than for forecast transactions with identified counterparties.

3.7.605 *Use of layering with first-payments-received (paid) approach*

3.7.605.10 In hedging groups of forecast transactions in a cash flow hedge using a first-payments-received/paid approach (see 3.7.200.70), an entity may choose to enter into multiple derivative contracts and layer these contracts such that each derivative will be designated in a separate hedging relationship. For example, on 1 January 2010 Company J whose functional currency is sterling, forecasts euro 1,000 sales to occur during the month of June 2010 and, on the same date it enters into four separate forward contracts, each to sell euro 250, that expire in June 2010. Instead of combining the four forward contracts and designating them as the hedging instrument in a single hedge (3.7.310.30), J may designate four separate cash flow hedging relationships in which the first forward contract hedges the cash flows from the first euro 250 of forecast sales, the second forward hedges the next euro 250 of sales that have not been identified as hedged forecast sales in a previously designated hedging relationship etc.

3.7.605.20 Using this layering approach meets the requirements in the standard to identify, for each of the individual hedging relationships, the hedged forecast transactions with sufficient specificity so that the entity can determine which transactions are the hedged transactions when they occur. The layering approach provides an entity with the flexibility to add additional hedging relationships (i.e. add layers) and to remove existing relationships (i.e. delete layers), without affecting the other hedging relationships via termination and re-designation because no change to the identification of the hedged forecast transactions associated with those other relationships is required. This approach is possible because the designation of each relationship will always identify the hedged forecast transactions as the first payments received after (a) those cash flows that have already been identified as hedged forecast transactions in a previously designated hedging relationship that continues to be active, and (b) those cash flows that were previously identified in a hedging relationship that has been terminated (i.e. is inactive) but are still at least expected to occur such that some portion of the gain or loss on the terminated hedging relationship remains in other comprehensive income.

3.7.605.30 Continuing the example in 3.7.605.10, if subsequent to designation, J revises its sales forecasts and determines that only euro 725 of future sales remain highly probable to occur, then under the layered hedge designation:

- the first two hedge relationships in respect of the first euro 500 of forecast sales will continue unaffected;
- the third hedge relationship will likely continue, albeit with higher ineffectiveness, if the third euro 250 forward contract remains highly effective in offsetting the foreign currency risk on future cash flows of euro 225; and
- the fourth hedge relationship will be terminated.

3.7.605.40 In contrast, if the entity had designated all the four forward contracts as the combined hedging instrument in a single hedging relationship, then hedge accounting would be required to be terminated for all forecast sales as the combined hedging instrument to sell euro 1,000 would not be effective in offsetting the foreign currency risk arising from only euro 725 of highly probable sales.

3.7.605.50 Adding a derivative to the existing layers will put that relationship at the end of the priority chain such that it will be designated as hedging the first forecast transactions occurring after (a) and (b), as discussed in 3.7.605.20, without impacting the designation of those earlier relationships. Furthermore, if a derivative matures such that a relationship early in the priority chain terminates, the identification of the forecast transactions for the relationships later in the priority chain are not impacted because they will continue to hedge the first payments received after (a) those that are already hedged in active hedging relationships, and (b) those that were previously identified in a hedging relationship that has been terminated (i.e. inactive) for which amounts remain in equity. If no amounts remain in equity related to the derivative that matured, the forecast transactions that are identified with the (i) active relationships, and (ii) those inactive relationships that continue to have amounts in equity, are the forecast transactions occurring earlier in the priority chain than before. This is because those relationships will have moved up in priority due to the disappearance of the earlier layer as a result of the derivative's maturity and the reclassification of its related amounts from equity to profit or loss. When a relationship moves up in the priority chain, then the perfectly effective hypothetical derivative (assuming that the entity employs the hypothetical derivative method discussed in 3.7.545) associated with that relationship will be adjusted to reflect the most recent best estimate of the forecast transactions that are identified with that relationship; the terms of the adjusted perfectly effective hypothetical derivative would be so determined that if constructed at hedge inception it would have a fair value of zero.

3.7.605.60 While we believe that the layering approach is a simple and effective methodology for identifying the hedged forecast transactions for many hedging programs, entities cannot lose sight of the fact that each hedging relationship stands on its own;

that is, entities cannot apply a hedge documentation approach that ignores the priority chain designation of forecast transactions. Thus, complexities arise, and the level of documentation may be higher in certain hedging programs, particularly those in which an entity is actively managing groups of existing hedging relationships (e.g. terminating or dedesignating derivatives prior to maturity) and is experiencing shortfalls of forecast transactions.

3.7.610 *Cash flow hedges of firm commitments to acquire a business and forecast business combinations*

IAS 39.AG98   3.7.610.10 A firm commitment to acquire a business in a business combination can be a hedged item only for foreign exchange risk because other risks cannot be specifically identified and measured. In our view, an entity also may hedge the foreign exchange risk of a highly probable forecast business combination. In our view, in the consolidated financial statements, a cash flow hedge of the foreign exchange risk of a firm commitment to acquire a business or a forecast business combination relates to the foreign currency equivalent of the consideration paid.

3.7.610.20 In a cash flow hedge designation, the effective portion of the gain or loss arising from the hedging instrument is recognised in other comprehensive income. However, an issue arises as to when and how this amount accumulated in equity is reclassified to profit or loss. The answer depends on whether the hedge represents a hedge of a non-financial item or a financial item.

3.7.610.30 In our view, a hedge of a firm commitment to acquire a business or a forecast business combination that will be effected through the acquisition of the assets and liabilities that comprise the business rather than the acquisition of an equity interest in the entity should be accounted for as a hedge of a non-financial item because the legal form of the transaction does not involve the acquisition of a financial asset.

3.7.610.40 In our view, since a hedge of a firm commitment to acquire a business or forecast business combination relates to the foreign currency equivalent of the consideration paid, the acquisition of an equity interest in the entity may be viewed as either a hedge of the purchase of shares of an entity or a hedge of the purchase of a business. A hedge of the purchase of shares represents a hedge of a financial item whereas a hedge of the purchase of a business represents a hedge of a non-financial item. Therefore, we believe that an entity should choose an accounting policy, to be applied consistently, as to whether such hedges are considered hedges of a financial item or non-financial item.

3.7.610.50 For hedges of a financial item, the accounting for the reclassification from equity to profit or loss is complicated by the fact that the shares acquired are not recognised in the consolidated financial statements and therefore will never directly impact profit or loss. However, for hedges of financial and non-financial items, the effective portion of the gain or loss arising from the hedging instrument relates to the foreign currency equivalent of the consideration paid. Therefore, reclassification of the effective portion of the gain or loss arising from the hedging instrument from equity to profit or loss should occur when the residual (i.e. goodwill) arising from the business combination affects profit or loss.

3.7.610.60 In our view, if the hedge is a hedge of a financial item, then the entity should retain the gain or loss from the hedging instrument recognised in other comprehensive income as a separate component of equity until the goodwill from the hedged business combination in part or in full affects profit or loss, for example, through transactions such as impairment of goodwill or sale of the business acquired. When the goodwill from the hedged business combination affects profit or loss, all or a portion of the gain or loss recognised in other comprehensive income should be reclassified to profit or loss.

3.7.610.70 In our view, if the hedge is a hedge of a non-financial item, then the entity should choose an accounting policy, to be applied consistently, to apply a basis adjustment (see 3.7.80.40) in respect of a transaction that results in the acquisition of a non-financial item. Therefore, the entity may either apply 3.7.610.60 similar to the accounting for a financial item or recognise the gain or loss from the hedging instrument recognised in other comprehensive income as an adjustment to goodwill when the business combination occurs.

3.7.620 Net investment hedge

3.7.630 *Net assets of the foreign operation*

IFRIC 16.2, 7 3.7.630.10 The hedged item in a net investment hedge is the foreign currency exposure on the carrying amount of the net assets of the foreign operation, but only if they are included in the financial statements. This includes consolidated subsidiaries in consolidated financial statements, and also includes financial statements that include investments accounted for using the equity method or interests in joint ventures that are proportionately consolidated, as well as financial statements that include a foreign branch. Hence, if an entity has an investment in an associate, or a foreign operation that is conducted through a branch, then such an investment would qualify as the hedged item in a net investment hedge in the individual financial statements (see 2.1.60).

IFRIC 16.14 3.7.630.12 In a hedge of a net investment in a foreign operation, a derivative instrument, a non-derivative instrument or a combination of both (see 3.7.710.40) may be used as the hedging instrument. The hedging instrument can be held by any entity within the group.

IFRIC 16.10, 3.7.630.14 The hedged risk is the foreign currency exposure arising from the functional
12, 13, BC14, currency of the foreign operation and the functional currency of any parent, i.e. im-
AG2 mediate, intermediate or ultimate parent of the foreign operation. The foreign exchange differences arising between the functional currency of the foreign operation and the presentation currency of any parent cannot be designated as the hedged risk (see 3.7.660). The foreign currency risk arising from the net investment in the consolidated financial statements can be hedged only once.

IFRIC 16.
AG2   3.7.630.15 When the hedging instrument is a forward contract, the entity may hedge the spot foreign exchange rate or the forward rate. If exposure to changes in the forward rate is designated as the hedged risk, then the interest component included in the forward rate is part of the hedged foreign currency risk. Hence, exchange differences on the net investment in the foreign operation that are recognised in other comprehensive income and accumulated in the separate component of equity are then measured based on changes in the applicable forward rate. However, when the entity hedges the spot foreign exchange rate, then the change in the interest element of the hedging derivative contract (i.e. the spot-forward premium or forward points) is recognised immediately in profit or loss, and only the changes in the fair value of the hedging derivative that are attributable to changes in spot foreign exchange differences are recognised in other comprehensive income. When the hedging instrument is a non-derivative financial instrument, IFRIC 16 suggests designating the spot foreign exchange risk as the hedged risk.

IFRIC 16.
AG2, AG9   3.7.630.16 For example, Parent Y, whose functional currency is sterling has the following net investments in each of its subsidiaries:

- Subsidiary D's functional currency is the euro. Y directly owns D and has a euro 500 net investment in the subsidiary;
- Subsidiary B's functional currency is the US dollar. Y directly owns B and has a US dollar 300 net investment in the subsidiary; and
- Subsidiary C's functional currency is the Australian dollar. B directly owns C and has an Australian dollar 100 net investment in the subsidiary. Therefore, assuming an Australian dollar/US dollar exchange rate of 1.25, Y's total US dollar 300 net investment in B includes US dollar 80 in respect of B's Australian dollar 100 net investment in C. In other words, B's net assets other than its investment in C are US dollar 220.

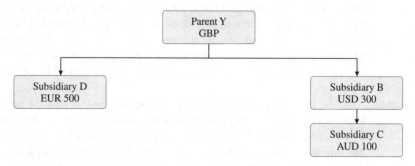

3.7.630.18 In this situation, the following are examples of alternative net investment hedge designations that may be possible in the consolidated financial statements of Y:

- Y can hedge its net investment in each of subsidiaries B, C and D for the foreign exchange risk between their respective functional currencies and sterling. The maximum amounts that can be designated as effective hedges in Y's consolidated financial statements are:
  - euro 500 net investment in D for sterling/euro risk;

- – US dollar 220 net investment in B for sterling/US dollar risk; and
- – Australian dollar 100 net investment in C for sterling/Australian dollar risk.
- Y can hedge its net investment only in B and D for the foreign exchange risk between their respective functional currencies and sterling. In this case, up to the full US dollar 300 investment in B could be designated. Note, however, that Y could not designate both the full US dollar 300 of its net investment in B with respect to the sterling/US dollar risk and its Australian dollar 100 net investment in C with respect to the sterling/Australian dollar risk as this would involve hedging the net investment in C with respect to the sterling twice.
- Y can hedge, in its consolidated financial statements, its Australian dollar 100 net investment in C for the US dollar/Australian dollar risk between the functional currencies of B and C, and also designate a hedge of the entire US dollar 300 of its net investment in B with respect to sterling/US dollar risk, since the designation of the US dollar/Australian dollar risk between B and C does not include any sterling/US dollar risk.

IAS 39.AG99 3.7.630.20 The hedged risk cannot be designated as the fair value of the underlying shares, or the currency exposure on the fair value of the shares, because the consolidation process recognises the subsidiary's profit or loss, rather than changes in the investment's fair value. The same is true of a net investment in an associate, because equity accounting recognises the investor's share of the associate's profit or loss (see 3.5.270).

3.7.630.30 Groups with foreign operations may wish to hedge the foreign currency exposure arising from the expected profits from the foreign operations by using derivatives or other financial instruments. In our view, a forecast transaction in the foreign operation's own functional currency does not create an exposure to variability in cash flows that could affect profit or loss at the consolidated level; therefore, at the consolidated level, hedge accounting cannot be applied. From a foreign operation's own perspective, cash flows generated from its operations are in its own functional currency and hence do not give rise to a foreign currency risk exposure; such cash flows therefore cannot be hedged. However, a foreign operation may hedge its foreign currency exposure in respect of transactions denominated in currencies other than its functional currency.

IAS 39.81 3.7.630.40 Hedging an amount of net assets equal to or less than the carrying amount of the net assets of a foreign operation is permitted. Effectiveness would be measured based on the amount of the net assets hedged. However, if the notional amount of the hedging instrument exceeds the carrying amount of the underlying net assets, e.g. due to losses incurred by the foreign operation that reduce its net assets, then changes in fair value on the excess portion of the hedging instrument are recognised in profit or loss immediately.

IFRIC 16.15 3.7.630.50 In testing hedge effectiveness, the change in value of the hedging instrument is determined by reference to the functional currency of the parent against which the hedged risk is measured. Depending on where the hedging instrument is held, in the absence of hedge accounting the total change in value of the hedging instrument may be recognised in profit or loss, other comprehensive income, or both. However, the assessment of hedge effectiveness is not affected by whether the change in value of the hedging instrument is recognised in profit or loss or other comprehensive income. The assessment of hedge effectiveness also is not affected by the method of consolidation, i.e. direct or step-by-step method, or whether the hedging instrument is a derivative or non-derivative instrument.

3.7.640 *Expected net profit or loss of a net investment in a foreign operation*

IAS 39.81,   3.7.640.10 The hedged item may be an amount of net assets equal to or less than the
AG3-AG6,   carrying amount of the net assets of the foreign operation at the beginning of any given
IFRIC 16.2,   period.
11

IAS 39.81,   3.7.640.15 Consequently, the expected profits from the foreign operation in that period
IFRIC 16.2,   cannot be designated as the hedged item in a net investment hedge. Translation risk
11   arises once the net profit is recognised as an increase in net assets of the foreign opera-
tion. The additional net assets can be designated as a hedged item in a net investment hedge as they arise, although in practice most groups will revisit their net investment hedges only quarterly or semi-annually.

AS 21.39, 40   3.7.640.20 Expected net profits from a foreign operation expose a group to potential volatility in consolidated profit or loss as transactions in the foreign operation are translated into the group's presentation currency at spot rates at the transaction dates, or at appropriate average rates (see 2.7.240). However, since expected net profits in future reporting periods do not constitute recognised assets, liabilities or forecast trans-actions that ultimately will affect profit or loss at the consolidated level, they cannot be designated in a hedging relationship under either a fair value or a cash flow hedge model.

3.7.640.30 Expected net losses in a foreign operation will reduce the net investment bal-ance, which could result in an over-hedged position. Therefore, if a group expects its foreign operation to make losses, then it may decide to hedge less than the full carrying amount of the net assets. Otherwise it will not be able to satisfy the hedge accounting criterion that the hedge relationship is expected to be highly effective on an ongoing basis. In our view, an entity should take into account expected losses in a foreign opera-tion when assessing hedge effectiveness if they are highly probable.

3.7.650 *Monetary items*

3.7.650.10 An investor's net investment also may include monetary items that are receivable from or payable to the foreign operation, and settlement is neither planned nor likely to occur in the foreseeable future. Loans provided by a subsidiary to a fellow subsidiary may form part of the group's net investment in a foreign operation, even when the loan is in neither the parent's nor the borrowing subsidiary's functional currency. Consequently, the net investment may include an intra-group loan in any currency when settlement is neither planned nor likely in the foreseeable future.

3.7.650.20 For example, in 2009 Company T, whose functional currency is the euro bought Company B for sterling 100. The carrying amount of B's net assets was sterling 60 and T recognised fair value adjustments to specific assets and liabilities of sterling 30 and goodwill of sterling 10. During 2009 T extended a loan to B of sterling 20.

3.7.650.30 In 2010 the carrying amount (excluding fair value adjustments from the acquisition) of B's assets and liabilities is sterling 70. The remaining fair value adjustments are sterling 25 and goodwill remains at sterling 10. The loan has not been repaid nor is it intended to be repaid. The carrying amount of the net investment that T may designate as the hedged item is equal to the amount of T's net investment in B, including goodwill. This amount would be sterling 125 (70 + 25 + 10 + 20).

3.7.660 *Presentation currency*

IFRIC 16.
BC13, BC14 3.7.660.10 The group's presentation currency is not relevant to net investment hedging. Translation of the financial statements of an entity into the group presentation currency under IAS 21 is an accounting exercise that does not create an exposure to foreign exchange risk, hence hedge accounting for such translation risk is not permitted. An economic exchange risk arises only from an exposure between two or more functional currencies, not from translation into a presentation currency.

3.7.660.20 For example, when a group's presentation currency differs from the parent's functional currency, then the appropriate hedged risk to be designated in a net investment hedge still is the exposure to changes in the exchange rate between the foreign operation's functional currency and the parent's functional currency. Therefore, net investment hedging may be applied only to hedge the exchange rate risk that exists between the functional currency of a parent entity and the functional currency of the foreign operation.

3.7.670 *Cross-currency interest rate swaps*

3.7.670.10 Net investments in foreign operations commonly are hedged with forward contracts or non-derivative monetary items such as foreign currency loans. Some entities may want to use, as hedging instruments, cross-currency interest rate swaps (CCIRSs) or a synthetic borrowing that is a combination of a borrowing and an interest rate swap and/or a CCIRS (see 3.7.710). In our view, while more complex, these hedging strategies may qualify for hedge accounting if particular care is taken in identifying and designating the hedging instrument and the hedged item.

3.7.680 *Fixed-for-fixed cross-currency interest rate swap*

3.7.680.05 In our view, a fixed-for-fixed CCIRS can be designated as the hedging instrument in a net investment hedge of the foreign currency exposure in relation to the carrying amount of the net assets of an entity's foreign operations. In our view, there are two possible approaches that can be applied.

3.7.680.10 The first approach takes the view that economically, a fixed-for-fixed CCIRS with initial and final exchanges of notional amounts is the same as a foreign currency

spot transaction representing the initial exchange and a series of foreign currency forward contracts representing the interest payments and the final exchange at specified
rates. Although the total fair value of such a series may be zero, each individual foreign
currency forward is off-market. Under this view, such an instrument may qualify as
the hedging instrument in a net investment hedge. However, the amount of the CCIRS
should be designated in a manner to avoid over-hedging.

3.7.680.20 For example, an entity with a euro functional currency wishes to hedge its net
investment of US dollar 100 using a fixed-for-fixed CCIRS. The CCIRS has notional
amounts of US dollar 100 and euro 80 respectively, and four interest coupon payments of
US dollar 2 and euro 1.6 each. The total amount of cash flows arising from the US dollar
leg of the CCIRS, after settlement of the foreign currency spot transaction, is US dollar 108.
Consequently, the CCIRS can be viewed as a series of foreign currency forward contracts
with a total notional amount of US dollar 108, which exceeds the net investment of US
dollar 100. Under this view, the entity should designate only a proportion of the CCIRS
as the hedging instrument, US dollar 100 or approximately 92 percent of the notional
amount, in order to avoid over-hedging. As payments are made under the CCIRS, the total
notional amount will reduce. Consequently, the entity may wish to adjust the designated
proportion of the hedging instrument over time in order to avoid ineffectiveness.

3.7.680.30 Given that the series of forwards comprising the CCIRS are off-market, under
this view, ineffectiveness will arise. To avoid being precluded from hedge accounting
as a result of this ineffectiveness, an entity could choose to hedge the foreign currency
spot risk rather than the foreign currency forward risk.

3.7.680.40 The second approach takes the view that a fixed-for-fixed CCIRS can be analysed as a foreign currency spot transaction, which represents the initial exchange, and
a single foreign currency forward contract. Economically, a foreign currency forward
contract and a fixed-for-fixed CCIRS are similar. The primary difference between the
two is that the interest component of the fixed-for-fixed CCIRS is identified explicitly
instead of being implicit as in the case of a foreign currency forward contract.

3.7.680.50 Based on this approach, excluding the interest payments on the CCIRS from
the designated hedging instrument is akin to ignoring the interest element in a foreign
currency forward contract, which is permitted under IAS 39 (see 3.7.310.20).

3.7.680.60 Consequently, in our view an entity could choose to designate only the foreign
currency notional of the fixed-for-fixed CCIRS, i.e. US dollar 100 in the example in
3.7.680.20 as the amount designated as the hedging instrument to hedge the foreign
currency spot risk in the net investment.

3.7.690 *Floating-for-floating cross-currency interest rate swap*

3.7.690.10 In our view, a floating-for-floating CCIRS with initial and final exchanges of
notional amounts potentially could be designated as a hedging instrument in a net investment hedge. Continuing the example in 3.7.680.20, the final exchange of US dollar 100

for euro 80 can be viewed as a single foreign currency forward contract to exchange US dollar 100 for euro 80. Such a contract will achieve a high degree of effectiveness. However, between repricing dates an additional foreign currency forward exists representing the floating interest payment fixed for the current period. This will give rise to some ineffectiveness due to movements in interest rate curves between repricing dates. Provided that the hedge is expected to be highly effective throughout the hedging relationship and the other hedge criteria are met, this hedging strategy should qualify for hedge accounting.

3.7.700 *Fixed-for-floating cross-currency interest rate swap*

3.7.700.10 A fixed-for-floating CCIRS is exposed to both interest rate risk and foreign currency risk. In our view, generally a fixed-for-floating CCIRS cannot be designated as a hedging instrument in a net investment hedge because the interest rate risk inherent in the instrument gives rises to ineffectiveness that precludes hedge accounting.

3.7.700.20 However, it may be possible to designate such an instrument in its entirety in more than one hedging relationship simultaneously and achieve hedge accounting. For example, a pay-fixed US dollar receive-floating euro CCIRS can be viewed as comprising a pay-fixed US dollar receive-fixed euro CCIRS and a pay-fixed euro receive-floating euro interest rate swap. The pay-fixed US dollar receive-fixed euro CCIRS can be designated as a hedging instrument of a US dollar net investment, while the pay-fixed euro receive-floating euro interest rate swap can be designated as either a fair value hedge of a fixed rate asset, or a cash flow hedge of a floating rate liability.

3.7.700.30 When such an approach is adopted, the hedge documentation should identify clearly the various hedged items for which the CCIRS is designated as the hedging instrument. Only in measuring effectiveness is the CCIRS separated into a fixed-for-fixed CCIRS and a fixed-for-floating interest rate swap. In the event that any of the hedges becomes ineffective, in our view hedge accounting would be terminated for all the hedge relationships in which the CCIRS is the designated hedging instrument.

3.7.710 *Synthetic borrowing*

3.7.710.10 A synthetic borrowing is created through the combination of a borrowing in one currency with a CCIRS that effectively changes the interest and principal payments of the original borrowing into a different currency. While such an instrument may seem to be similar to a plain vanilla borrowing, there are significant differences between the synthetic position and the plain vanilla position.

3.7.710.20 For example, Company T has a euro functional currency. T has a net investment in a sterling functional currency subsidiary and a bond in issue that is denominated in US dollars. T wishes to enter into a pay-floating sterling receive-fixed US dollar CCIRS and to designate the bond and the CCIRS together as the hedging instrument in a hedge of a net investment.

3.7.710.30 For a plain vanilla borrowing only the fair value movements on the amortised cost (mainly the principal amount) and accrued interest arising from foreign currency spot risk are recognised in accordance with IAS 21. The IAS 21 translation of the borrowing will offset the equivalent IAS 21 translation of the net investment and both are recognised in other comprehensive income. However, for a synthetic borrowing the bond and the CCIRS are not measured on a consistent basis. The carrying amount of the US dollar bond is translated into euro under IAS 21, but is not remeasured to fair value for changes in interest rates. On the other hand, the CCIRS is measured at fair value with respect to both currency and interest rate risk.

IAS 39.77 3.7.710.40 Under IAS 39 a combination of derivatives and non-derivatives can be used as the hedging instrument only in respect of foreign currency risk. As the synthetic borrowing, i.e. the plain vanilla bond combined with the CCIRS, has an exposure to both interest rate and currency risk, in our view such a combined designation generally would not be appropriate as the interest rate exposure on the hedging instrument would likely cause the hedge not to be highly effective. One solution that would reduce volatility in profit or loss would be to measure both the bond and the CCIRS at fair value. However, in our view there is no possibility under IFRSs to measure the bond at fair value and then to include these fair value changes in a net investment hedging relationship.

3.7.720 Hedging on a group basis

3.7.720.10 For a foreign currency hedge transacted on a group basis, it is important that the currency exposure of the hedging instrument and the hedged transaction is the same. For example, Company E has euro as its functional currency and Company F, a subsidiary of E, has Swiss francs as its functional currency. F has a foreign currency exposure arising from a highly probable forecast transaction denominated in US dollar. If E hedges this exposure through its central treasury by entering into a Swiss francs to US dollar forward contract, then the transaction may qualify for hedge accounting in E's consolidated financial statements. However, if E enters into a euro to US dollar forward contract, then the contract does not qualify as a hedging instrument because the currency of the forward contract does not match the underlying exposure that the entity wishes to hedge unless it can be demonstrated that the euro and Swiss francs are highly correlated.

3.7.730 *Internal derivatives*

3.7.730.10 One of the key issues that arise in applying hedge accounting at the group level is the need to eliminate internal derivatives for purposes of consolidation.

IAS 39.73, 3.7.730.20 An entity may use internal derivatives to transfer risk from individual opera-
IGF.1.4 tions within the group to a centralised treasury. Derivatives between entities within the same reporting group also can be used to control and monitor risks through the central treasury function in order to benefit from pricing advantages and also to offset equal and opposite exposures arising from different parts of the group. However, all such internal derivatives eliminate on consolidation and therefore are not eligible for hedge accounting in the consolidated financial statements, even if at a group level the overall net position is hedged externally. Therefore, only derivatives involving external third parties can be designated as hedging instruments in consolidated financial statements. However, it is

possible for the centralised treasury to enter into one or more derivatives with external counterparties in order to offset the internal derivatives. Such external derivatives may qualify as hedging instruments in the consolidated financial statements provided that they are legally separate contracts and serve a valid business purpose (e.g. laying off risk exposures on a gross basis). In our view, a relationship should exist between the internal transactions and one or multiple related external transactions and this relationship should be documented at inception of the hedging relationship.

3.7.740 *Externalisation and "round-tripping"*

IAS 39.IG   3.7.740.10 In consolidated financial statements, hedge accounting may be applied to an
F.1.4,   external hedge even if the group entity that is subject to the risk being hedged is not a
IGF.2.14   direct party to the hedging instrument.

IAS 39.IG   3.7.740.20 For example, Subsidiary B has a financial asset (with a counterparty outside
F.1.4   the group) on which it receives a fixed rate of interest. For purposes of hedging its individual exposure to the fixed interest rate, B enters into a pay-fixed receive-floating interest rate swap with the group's central treasury. The swap is an internal derivative, which does not qualify as a hedging instrument in the consolidated financial statements. To achieve hedge accounting at the group level, the central treasury enters into a matching pay-fixed receive-floating interest rate swap with an external counterparty and documents this link. The fixed interest financial asset and the external derivative then can be designated in a hedging relationship that qualifies for hedge accounting in the consolidated financial statements.

3.7.740.30 In these circumstances, by entering into an external derivative the group "externalises" the transaction in order to achieve hedge accounting in the consolidated financial statements. However, there may be circumstances in which the entity concurrently would enter into two offsetting external derivatives. The first of these derivatives would be designated as the hedging instrument in the consolidated financial statements, while the offsetting swap would be included in the entity's trading book. Normally the reason for the offsetting transaction is to "create" an external hedging instrument for hedge accounting purposes without changing the risk position of the central treasury. Continuing the example in 3.7.740.20, at the same time as entering into an external derivative that would qualify as a hedging instrument, the central treasury would enter into an exactly offsetting swap with the same counterparty. This is known as "round-tripping".

IAS 39.IG   3.7.740.40 The guidance in IAS 39 is clear that when offsetting derivatives are entered
F.1.14   into concurrently, an entity is prohibited from viewing the derivatives separately and therefore designating one of them in a hedging relationship, unless the derivatives were not entered into in contemplation of one another, or there is a substantive business purpose for structuring the transactions separately. Therefore, in order to qualify for hedge accounting when following the round-tripping approach, it is necessary for an entity to demonstrate compliance with one of these two conditions.

3.7.740.50 In our view, generally a substantive business purpose exists when group risk management is undertaken by a central treasury function, which gives separate consideration to whether and how much of an offsetting position is required. Since the cheapest form of risk mitigation usually is entering into offsetting transactions with the same derivative counterparty, it is plausible that a facility may exist to enter into an offsetting transaction. However, such an offset should not be put in place by an entity automatically, but should be based on an evaluation as to whether or not such an offsetting position is required. For example, consider the following two situations:

- Company H performs a day-end review of its risk exposures, documents this review and enters into offsetting derivatives as part of its risk balancing procedures.
- Company B immediately enters into an offsetting derivative for each transaction and undertakes no further formal risk management procedures.

3.7.740.60 H is likely to be able to prove that it has a substantive business purpose for entering into offsetting derivatives. B, on the other hand, has a practice of entering into offsetting derivatives automatically, without giving further consideration to its actual risk exposures. Accordingly, B would have difficulty in meeting the "substantive business purpose" condition.

IAS 39.IG F.1.4, IGF.2.16 3.7.740.70 In addition, in our view entering into a derivative with a non-substantive counterparty does not validate an internal hedge. For example, an SPE established to act as a dedicated counterparty to validate internal hedges might not be regarded as a substantive third-party counterparty even if consolidation of the SPE is not required.

3.7.740.80 An entity may designate a hedging relationship at the consolidated level that differs from the hedging relationship designated at the level of an individual entity within the group, provided that the hedge criteria are met.

3.7.750 *Intra-group balances or transactions as the hedged item*

3.7.750.10 Intra-group balances and transactions eliminate on consolidation and therefore these balances and transactions are not permitted to be designated as hedged items at the group level. However, foreign currency exposures on intra-group monetary items give rise to foreign currency exchange gains and losses that do not eliminate in the consolidated financial statements (see 2.7.130). Intra-group monetary items lead to an exposure that affects group profit or loss in the following instances:

- items have been transacted between group entities with different functional currencies; and
- the item is denominated in a currency other than the functional currency of the entity entering into the transaction.

3.7.750.20 For example, an intra-group payable/receivable between a parent with a euro functional currency and its foreign subsidiary denominated in USD (the subsidiary's functional currency) creates such a foreign currency exposure at the group level. Consequently, the foreign currency risk on recognised intra-group monetary items qualifies for hedge accounting in the consolidated financial statements.

IAS 39.73   3.7.750.30 In our view, it is not possible to extend this rationale to the designation of intra-group monetary items as hedging instruments in a hedge of foreign currency risk. This is because IAS 39 explicitly requires that only instruments involving external parties be designated as hedging instruments. Therefore, intra-group monetary items cannot be designated as hedging instruments in the consolidated financial statements.

3.7.750.40 The foreign currency risk of a highly probable forecast intra-group transaction may qualify as the hedged item in the consolidated financial statements provided that the transaction is denominated in a currency other than the currency of the entity entering into the transaction and the foreign currency risk will affect consolidated profit or loss. Examples of forecast intra-group transactions that will affect consolidated profit or loss include:

- forecast purchases or sales of inventory between group members, provided that there is an onward sale to a party outside the group; and
- a forecast sale of equipment by one group entity to another because the depreciation charge recognised on the equipment will differ if the transaction is denominated in a currency other than the buying entity's functional currency.

3.7.750.50 However, royalties, head office charges and similar items would not affect profit or loss in the consolidated financial statements as these transactions are eliminated completely; therefore such items do not qualify as hedged items.

3.7.760 [Not used]

3.7.770 **Worked examples**

3.7.770.10 The following examples demonstrate a number of the issues that have been discussed in this chapter.

3.7.780 *Cash flow hedge of a variable rate liability*

3.7.780.10 On 1 January 2010 Company P issues non-callable five-year floating rate bonds of 100 million denominated in its functional currency. The floating interest of six-month LIBOR plus 50 basis points (0.5 percent) is payable semi-annually. The bonds are issued at par.

3.7.780.20 As part of P's risk management policy, it determines that it does not wish to expose itself to cash flow fluctuations from changes in market interest rates. After the issue of the bonds, P immediately enters into a five-year interest rate swap with a notional of 100 million. Under the terms of the swap P pays 6 percent fixed and receives floating cash flows based on six-month LIBOR (set at 5.7 percent for the period 1 January to 30 June 2010). The timing of the swap's cash flows match those of the bond. The fair value of the swap at inception is zero.

3.7.780.30 The swap is designated and documented as the hedging instrument in a cash flow hedge of the variability of future interest payments on the bond attributable to movements in the benchmark interest rate, i.e. six-month LIBOR only, excluding the credit spread on the bond of 50 basis points. The hedge relationship is expected to be highly effective.

3.7.780.40 P indicates in its hedge documentation that it will use the hypothetical derivative method for assessing the effectiveness of the hedge relationship. P identifies a hypothetical swap in the bond under which it receives 6 percent fixed, i.e. the fixed market rate of interest at the time of issuing the bond, and pays six-month LIBOR. While the interest rate on the bond is LIBOR plus 50 basis points, P has designated as the hedged risk only the benchmark interest component of the total interest rate risk exposure of the bond. Thus the hypothetical swap has a floating leg equal to LIBOR, rather than LIBOR plus 50 basis points.

3.7.780.50 Considering the combined effect of the bond and the swap, the interest that effectively is payable is fixed at 6.5 percent (6 percent fixed on the swap plus the additional actual 0.5 percent on the bond). P records the following entries:

	Debit	Credit
1 January 2010		
Cash	100,000,000	
Bonds payable		100,000,000
To recognise proceeds from bond issue		

3.7.780.60 No entry is necessary for the swap, as its fair value is zero at inception.

3.7.780.70 At 30 June 2010 interest rates have increased. The fixed rate for the remaining term of the swap and bond has increased from 6 percent to 7 percent. Six-month LIBOR increases to 6.7 percent. The fair value of the swap is determined to be 3,803,843 after the settlement of interest due on 30 June 2010. The fair value of the hypothetical swap also is 3,803,843 at this date. Therefore the hedge is considered to be 100 percent effective. The full change in the fair value of the swap should be recognised in other comprehensive income.

	Debit	Credit
30 June 2010		
Interest expense	3,100,000	
Cash		3,100,000
To recognise payment of 6.2 percent floating interest		
(LIBOR 5.7 percent plus premium of 0.5 percent)		
Interest expense	150,000	
Cash		150,000
To recognise net settlement of swap from		
1 January to 30 June 2010 (pay 6 percent fixed		
3,000,000; receive 5.7 percent floating 2,850,000)		

	Debit	Credit
Swap (asset)	3,803,843	
Hedging reserve (other comprehensive income)		3,803,843
To recognise change in fair value of swap after settlement		
of interest		

3.7.780.80 At 31 December 2010 interest rates have not changed; however, the credit risk associated with the counterparty to the swap has worsened and is now higher than the general market rate. The increased credit risk of the counterparty results in a specific credit spread of 0.4 percent. Consequently, the rate used to determine the fair value of the swap will be 0.4 percent higher than that used to value the hypothetical swap, since the hypothetical swap is not affected by counterparty credit risk (see 3.7.515.40).

3.7.780.90 The fair value of the swap is 3,414,177 at 31 December 2010. The fair value of the hypothetical swap is 3,436,978 at the same date. Based on the offsetting of the change in the fair value of the swap and the change in the fair value of the hypothetical swap (99 percent offset), the hedge is still effective within the acceptable range of 80 – 125 percent; actual ineffectiveness of 22,801 results. This amount is recognised in other comprehensive income because the hedging reserve is adjusted to the lesser of the cumulative gain or loss on the hedging instrument and the cumulative change in fair value of the expected future cash flows on the hedged item attributable to the hedged risk, both from inception of the hedge (see 3.7.510.20).

	Debit	Credit
31 December 2010		
Interest expense	3,600,000	
Cash		3,600,000
To recognise payment of 7.2 percent floating interest		
(LIBOR of 6.7 percent plus a premium of 0.5 percent)		
Cash	350,000	
Interest income		350,000
To recognise net settlement of swap from 1 July to		
31 December 2010 (pay 6 percent fixed 3,000,000;		
receive 6.7 percent floating 3,350,000)		
Hedging reserve (other comprehensive income)	389,666	
Swap (asset)		389,666
To recognise fair value of change in swap		

3.7.780.100 The statement of financial position at 31 December 2010 will be as follows:

Assets		Liabilities and equity	
Cash	93,500,000	Retained earnings	(6,500,000)
Swap	3,414,177	Hedging reserve	3,414,177
		Bonds payable	100,000,000
	96,914,177		96,914,177

3.7.790 *Cash flow hedge using an interest rate cap*

3.7.790.10 At 1 January 2010 Company R obtains a three-year loan of 10 million. The interest rate on the loan is variable at LIBOR plus 2 percent. R is concerned that interest rates may rise during the three years, but wants to retain the ability to benefit from LIBOR rates below 8 percent. In order to hedge itself R purchases for 300,000 an out-of-the-money interest rate cap from a bank. Under the cap, when LIBOR exceeds 8 percent for a particular year R receives from the bank an amount calculated as 10 million x (LIBOR - 8 percent).

3.7.790.20 The combination of the cap and the loan results in R paying interest at a variable rate (LIBOR plus 2 percent) not exceeding 10 percent. On both the variable rate loan and the interest rate cap, rates are reset on 1 January and interest is settled on 31 December.

3.7.790.30 R designates and documents the intrinsic value of the purchased interest rate cap as the hedging instrument in a cash flow hedge of the interest rate risk attributable to the future interest payments on the loan for changes in LIBOR above 8 percent. Changes in the time value of the option are excluded from the assessment of hedge effectiveness and are recognised in profit or loss as they arise.

3.7.790.40 The critical terms of the cap are identical to those of the loan and R concludes that, both at inception of the hedge and on an ongoing basis, the hedge relationship is expected to be highly effective in achieving offsetting cash flows attributable to changes in LIBOR when LIBOR is greater than 8 percent. As the cap is being used to purchase one-way protection against any increase in LIBOR, R does not need to assess effectiveness in instances when LIBOR is less than 8 percent. The cumulative gains or losses on the interest rate cap, adjusted to remove time value gains and losses, can reasonably be expected to equal the present value of the cumulative change in expected future cash flows on the debt obligation when LIBOR is greater than 8 percent. This should be reassessed each reporting period.

3.7.790.50 During the three-year period LIBOR rates and related amounts are as follows:

Date	Rate	Receivable under cap	Interest payable on loan	Net interest payable	Net interest payable
2010	7%	-	900,000	900,000	9%
2011	9%	(100,000)	1,100,000	1,000,000	10%
2012	10%	(200,000)	1,200,000	1,000,000	10%

3.7.790.60 The fair value, intrinsic value and time value of the interest rate cap and changes therein at the end of each accounting period, but before the settlement of interest, are as follows:

Date	Fair value	Intrinsic value	Time value	Change in fair value gain/(loss)	Change in time value gain/(loss)
1 January 2010	300,000	-	300,000	-	-
31 December 2010	280,000	-	280,000	(20,000)	(20,000)
31 December 2011	350,000	200,000	150,000	70,000	(130,000)
31 December 2012	200,000	200,000	-	(150,000)	(150,000)

3.7.790.70 IAS 39 does not specify how to compute the intrinsic value of a cap option when the option involves a series of payments. In this example the intrinsic value of the cap is calculated based on simplified assumptions. Alternatively and more precisely, the intrinsic value of the cap (in the case of a long position) can be calculated for each single period by subtracting the forward LIBOR of the respective period from the cap rate, multiplying the result with the notional amount of the cap contract and then discounting the result to the date under consideration. The sum of the discounted values yields the intrinsic value of the cap.

3.7.790.80 Assuming that all criteria for hedge accounting have been met, the following entries are required:

	Debit	Credit
1 January 2010		
Cash	10,000,000	
Loan payable		10,000,000
To recognise proceeds from loan		
Interest rate cap (asset)	300,000	
Cash		300,000
To recognise purchase of interest rate cap		

	Debit	Credit
31 December 2010		
Interest expense	900,000	
Cash		900,000
To recognise interest expense on loan		
(LIBOR + 2 percent)		
Hedge expense (profit or loss)	20,000	
Interest rate cap (asset)		20,000
To recognise change in fair value of cap (time value		
change)		
31 December 2011		
Interest expense	1,100,000	
Cash		1,100,000
To recognise interest expense on loan		
(LIBOR + 2 percent)		
Hedge expense (profit or loss)	130,000	
Interest rate cap (asset)	70,000	
Hedging reserve (other comprehensive income)		200,000
To recognise change in fair value of cap (130,000		
represents the change in time value, which is excluded		
from the assessment of hedge effectiveness, and 200,000		
represents the increase in the interest rate cap's intrinsic		
value)		
Hedging reserve (other comprehensive income)	100,000	
Hedge income/interest income (profit or loss)		100,000
To reclassify proportion of increase in intrinsic		
value of cap related to realised cash flow		
through interest expense incurred in 2011		
Cash	100,000	
Interest rate cap (asset)		100,000
To recognise cash received upon settlement of interest		
rate cap		
31 December 2012		
Interest expense (profit or loss)	1,200,000	
Cash		1,200,000
To recognise interest expense on loan		
(LIBOR + 2 percent)		

	Debit	Credit
Hedge expense (profit or loss)	150,000	
Interest rate cap (asset)		50,000
Hedging reserve (other comprehensive income)		100,000
To recognise change in fair value of cap (150,000		
represents the change in time value, which is excluded		
from the assessment of hedge effectiveness, and 100,000		
represents the increase in the interest rate cap's		
intrinsic value)		
Hedging reserve (other comprehensive income)	200,000	
Hedge income/interest income (profit or loss)		200,000
To reclassify proportion of increased intrinsic value		
of cap related to realised cash flow through interest		
expense incurred in 2012		
Cash	200,000	
Interest rate cap (asset)		200,000
To recognise cash received upon final settlement of		
interest rate cap		

3.7.790.90 As a result of the hedge, effectively R has capped its interest expense on the three-year loan at 10 percent. Specifically, during those periods when the contractual terms of this loan would result in an interest expense greater than 10 percent or 1 million, i.e. in instances when LIBOR exceeded 8 percent, the payments received from the interest rate cap effectively reduce interest expense to 10 percent as illustrated below. However, the recognition in profit or loss of changes in the fair value of the cap due to changes in time value results in variability of total interest expense.

	2010	2011	2012
Interest on LIBOR plus 2 percent debt	900,000	1,100,000	1,200,000
Reclassified from other comprehensive income (effect of cap)	-	(100,000)	(200,000)
Interest expense adjusted by effect of hedge	900,000	1,000,000	1,000,000
Change in time value of cap	20,000	130,000	150,000
Total expense	920,000	1,130,000	1,150,000

3.7.800 *Cash flow hedge of foreign currency sales transactions*

3.7.800.10 Company M produces components that are sold to domestic (UK) and foreign customers (US). Company M's functional currency is sterling. Export sales to customers in the United States are denominated in the customers' functional currency (US dollar). In order to reduce the currency risk from the export sales, M has the following hedging policy:

- A transaction is committed when the pricing, quantity and timing are fixed.
- Committed transactions are hedged 100 percent.
- Anticipated transactions that are highly probable are hedged 50 percent.
- Only transactions anticipated to occur within six months are hedged.

3.7.800.20 For export sales, cash payment falls due one month after the invoice date. M projects sales to its foreign customers during April 2010 of 100,000 units, amounting to sales revenue of US dollar 10 million.

3.7.800.30 At 28 February 2010, all of the US dollar 10,000,000 of sales in April 2010 still are anticipated but uncommitted. Therefore, only 50 percent of the total anticipated sales are hedged. The hedge is transacted by entering into a foreign currency forward contract (forward 1) to sell US dollar 5 million and receive sterling at 0.6829 on 15 May 2010 and is documented as a cash flow hedge of the cash receipts pertaining to the first US dollar 5 million of forecast sales. The hedge is expected to be highly effective. Hedge effectiveness will be assessed by comparing the changes in the discounted cash flows of the incoming amounts of US dollar to the changes in the fair value of the forward contract. M includes the interest element of the foreign currency forward contract when measuring hedge effectiveness. This is expected to result in a highly effective cash flow hedge as the fair value of the sales transactions during the period of the hedge will be affected by US dollar interest rates as well as by the spot exchange rates.

3.7.800.40 A review of the sales order book at 31 March 2010 shows that all of the anticipated sale contracts for invoicing in April are now signed. In accordance with the hedging policy, a further foreign currency forward contract (forward 2) is entered into to sell US dollar 5 million and receive sterling at 0.7100 on 15 May 2010 in order to hedge the cash receipts pertaining to the next US dollar 5 million of forecast sales.

3.7.800.50 The spot and forward exchange rates and the fair value of the forward contracts are as follows:

Date	Spot rate (1 US dollar = sterling)	Forward rate (1 US dollar = sterling)	Fair value of forward sale of US dollar 5,000,000 (forward 1) (in sterling)	Fair value of forward sale of US dollar 5,000,000 (forward 2) (in sterling)
28 February	0.6860	0.6829	-	N/A
31 March	0.7120	0.7100	(134,491)	-
30 April	0.7117	0.7108	(139,152)	(3,990)
15 May	0.7208	N/A	(189,500)	(54,000)

3.7.800.60 The fair value of the foreign currency forward contracts at each measurement date is computed as the present value of the expected settlement amount, which is the difference between the contractually set forward rate and the actual forward rate on the date of measurement multiplied by the notional foreign currency amount. The discount rate used is 6 percent.

3.7.800.70 During April export sales of US dollar 10 million are invoiced and recognised in profit or loss. The deferred gain or loss on the hedging forward contracts that was recognised in other comprehensive income up to the date of sale is reclassified from equity to profit or loss. The cash flows being hedged are recognised in the statement of financial position as receivables of US dollar 10 million. M determines that hedge accounting no longer is necessary because foreign currency gains and losses on the amounts receivable are recognised in profit or loss and will mostly be offset by the revaluation gains and losses on the forwards.

3.7.800.80 Assuming that all criteria for hedge accounting have been met, the journal entries recorded by M are as follows (amounts in sterling):

	Debit	Credit
28 February 2010 *No entries in profit or loss or statement of financial* *position required; fair value of forward contract is zero.*		
31 March 2010 Hedging reserve (other comprehensive income) Derivatives (liabilities) *To recognise change in fair value of forward 1*	134,491	134,491
1 to 30 April 2010 Trade receivables Export sales *To recognise US dollar 10,000,000 sales transactions* *at exchange rates on dates of transactions (on average* *assumed to be 0.7115)*	7,115,000	7,115,000
30 April 2010 Trade receivables Foreign exchange gain on trade receivables (profit or loss) *To remeasure trade receivables at closing spot rate;* *US dollars 10,000,000 x (0.7117 - 0.7115)*	2,000	2,000

	Debit	Credit
Hedging reserve (other comprehensive income) Derivatives (liabilities) *To recognise change in fair value of forward 1 from* *31 March to 30 April*	4,661	4,661
Hedging reserve (other comprehensive income) Derivatives (liabilities) *To recognise change in fair value of forward 2*	3,990	3,990
Export sales (profit or loss) Hedging reserve (other comprehensive income) *To reclassify deferred hedge results upon recording* *sales (sterling 139,152 + sterling 3,990)*	143,142	143,142
1 to 15 May 2010 Cash Trade receivables *To recognise receipts from receivables from first* *US dollar 5,000,000 of sale at spot rate at date of* *payment (on average 0.7150)*	3,575,000	3,575,000
Trade receivables Foreign exchange gain on trade receivables (profit or loss) *To recognise gain on trade receivables;* *US dollar 5,000,000 x (0.7150 - 0.7117)*	16,500	16,500
15 May 2010 Cash Foreign exchange gain on cash (profit or loss) *To remeasure bank balance at spot rate;* *US dollar 5,000,000 x (0.7208 - 0.7150)*	29,000	29,000
Trade receivables Foreign exchange gain on trade receivables (profit or loss) *To recognise foreign exchange gain on trade receivables;* *US dollar 5,000,000 x (0.7208 - 0.7117)*	45,500	45,500
Foreign exchange loss on forward (profit or loss) Derivatives (liabilities) *To recognise change in fair value of forward 1 for* *period*	50,348	50,348

	Debit	Credit
Foreign exchange loss on forward (profit or loss)	50,010	
Derivatives (liabilities)		50,010
To recognise change in fair value of forward 2 for period		
Derivatives (liabilities)	189,500	
Cash		189,500
To recognise settlement of forward 1		
Derivatives (liabilities)	54,000	
Cash		54,000
To recognise settlement of forward 2		
15 to 31 May 2010		
Cash	3,655,000	
Trade receivables		3,655,000
To recognise payments of receivables at spot rate at date of payment (on average 0.7310)		
Foreign exchange loss on cash (profit or loss)	51,000	
Cash		51,000
To recognise foreign exchange loss on forwards settled before all receivables settled; US dollars bank account was overdrawn for a period;		
US dollar 5,000,000 x (0.7310 - 0.7208)		
Trade receivables	51,000	
Foreign exchange gain on trade receivables (profit or loss)		51,000
To recognise foreign exchange gain on settlement of receivables; US dollar 5,000,000 x (0.7310 - 0.7208)		

3.7.800.90 After all transactions have been settled, the statement of financial position, including the profit or loss impact, is as follows (amounts in sterling):

Assets		Equity	
Cash	6,964,500	Export sales (retained earnings)	6,971,858
		Foreign exchange loss	
		(retained earnings)	(7,358)
Total assets	6,964,500	Total equity	6,964,500

3.7.800.100 The bank balance reflects the settlement of the two forward contracts (amounts in sterling):

Forward 1: US dollar 5,000,000 at 0.6829	3,414,500
Forward 2: US dollar 5,000,000 at 0.7100	3,550,000
Total	6,964,500

3.7.800.110 The foreign exchange loss in this example is caused by:

- *Timing mismatches.* Receivables and sales are recognised at the spot exchange rate at the date of the transaction (on average 0.7115) during April, whereas the release from the hedging reserve is recognised at the end of April (for practical reasons) when the rate was 0.7117. Furthermore, receivables are collected during the month of May and recognised at the relevant spot rates, whereas the forward contracts are settled on 15 May.
- *Interest element on the forward contracts for the period in which hedge accounting is not applied* (1 to 15 May). From 30 April the cash flow hedge is de-designated, but the forward contracts remain as an economic hedge of the receivables to be collected during May. The foreign exchange results on the receivables are recognised in profit or loss, as are changes in the fair value of the forward contracts. However, a perfect offset is not achieved due to the interest element included in the changes in fair value of the forward contracts.

3.7.800.120 As an alternative to the cash flow hedge accounting described in 3.7.800, M could have applied the approach suggested in 3.7.420.46, with the following results:

- Upon occurrence of the forecast sales (i.e. the transaction date), the difference between the spot foreign exchange rates at the inception of each of the two hedges and spot foreign exchange rates on the sale dates would have been reclassified from equity to profit or loss.
- The forward points (interest cost in this case) in each hedge relationship that are ascribed to the period until sale would have been recognised in profit or loss upon sale. For example, in the hedge of the cash receipts pertaining to the first US dollar 5 million of forecast sales using the first forward contract, the forward points of sterling 15,500 (US dollar 5,000,000 x (0.6860 - 0.6829)) would be allocated to sales in the ratio of the period from hedge inception to date of sale and period from date of sale till estimated date of cash collection.
- The net effect of these steps would be that the sales under each of the two hedging relationships would be recognised in sterling in profit or loss at the respective spot exchange rates at hedge inception, less an allocation of the interest cost represented by the forward point ascribed to the sale under each hedge.
- Subsequent to recognition of the accounts receivables arising from the US dollar sales, the entire change in the fair value of the hedging forward contracts would be recognised in other comprehensive income, and the forward points (other than

those allocated to period up to sale as discussed above) would be amortised and reclassified from equity to profit or loss. If there was a reporting date between the dates when the receivables are recognised and when they are collected, M would reclassify from equity to profit or loss an amount equal to the remeasurement of the receivable or payable under IAS 21 based on the spot exchange rates.

3.7.810 *Termination of hedge accounting*

3.7.810.10 Altering the example in 3.7.800 slightly, assume that on 31 March 2010 the committed transactions actually are only US dollar 3 million and that no more transactions for April are anticipated. It is now unlikely that the original forward contract to sell US dollar 5 million would be highly effective in hedging the cash flows pertaining to the now expected future sales of US dollar 3 million. Hence, the original hedge relationship should be discontinued. However, M may designate the remaining US dollar 3 million of committed sales as the hedged item in a new hedging relationship.

3.7.810.20 The unrealised foreign exchange loss deferred in equity related to the forecast sales of US dollar 2 million that no longer are expected to occur should be recognised immediately in profit or loss as the cash flow no longer is expected to occur. The unrealised foreign exchange loss related to the US dollar 3 million of sales that still are expected to occur remains in equity.

3.7.810.30 [Not used]

3.7.810.40 The following entry is required (amounts in sterling):

	Debit	Credit
31 March 2010		
Foreign exchange losses (profit or loss)	53,796	
Hedging reserve (other comprehensive income)		53,796
To reclassify portion of deferred losses that reflects		
cash flows that no longer are expected to occur		
(134,491 x 2 / 5)		

3.7.820 *Fair value hedge of foreign currency risk on available-for-sale equities*

3.7.820.10 Company S is a large pension fund set up for the employees of a brewery. In recent years the pension fund assets have grown and management is finding it increasingly difficult to achieve a sufficient diversification in the domestic equity market. Also, management believes that it is possible to earn a higher return on equity shares in certain foreign markets. Consequently, management decides to invest in a large foreign equity market. However, all of S's pension obligations are denominated in sterling, its functional currency, and as part of the investment strategy S seeks to hedge all significant exposure to foreign currency risk beyond certain limits.

3.7.820.20 On 1 April 2010 S buys a portfolio of equity shares of Company T on a foreign stock exchange in which transactions are denominated in US dollars. T's shares are traded on only one stock exchange. T's shares are acquired for US dollars 30 million and are classified as available-for-sale financial assets.

3.7.820.30 Although a steady growth in the value of the shares is expected in the medium to long term, creating an increased foreign currency exposure, S decides to hedge only the foreign exchange exposure on a portion of the market value of the portfolio in foreign currency. This is because of the uncertainty about the short-term development in the market value, and therefore, the exposure. S enters into a foreign currency forward contract to sell US dollars 25.5 million and receive sterling on 15 October 2010. This contract will then be rolled for as long as the position is outstanding (see 3.7.570.40).

3.7.820.40 The forward contract is designated as a fair value hedge of the currency risk associated with the US dollar 25.5 million portion of the fair value of the shares. The time value of the forward contract is excluded from the assessment of hedge effectiveness. The hedge is expected to be highly effective and hedge effectiveness will be assessed by comparing the changes in the fair value of the US dollar 25.5 million portion of shares due to changes in spot exchange rates to the changes in the value of the forward contract also due to changes in spot rates (since the time value is excluded from the hedge relationship).

3.7.820.50 The terms of the forward contract are as follows:

- sell US dollars 25,500,000;
- buy sterling 64,359,915; and
- maturity of 15 October 2010.

3.7.820.60 The terms imply a forward rate of 2.5239.

3.7.820.70 During the period of the hedge the value of the forward is as follows (amounts in sterling):

Date	Spot rate (1 US dollar = sterling)	Value of contract forward	Value change	Spot element	Forward element
1 April	2.55	-	-	-	-
30 June	2.41	3,031,769	3,031,769	3,570,000	(538,231)
30 September	2.39	3,406,748	374,979	510,000	(135,021)
15 October	2.45	1,884,915	(1,521,833)	(1,530,000)	8,167
		1,884,915	2,550,000	(665,085)	

3.7.820.80 The value of the foreign equity portfolio changes as follows, as a result of changes in equity prices and changes in the exchange rate:

667

Date	Value (in US dollar)	Value (sterling)	Value change (in sterling)
1 April	30,000,000	76,500,000	-
30 June	35,000,000	84,350,000	7,850,000
30 September	28,000,000	66,920,000	(17,430,000)
15 October	32,000,000	78,400,000	11,480,000

3.7.820.90 Assuming that all the criteria for hedge accounting have been met, the required entries are as follows:

	Debit	Credit
1 April 2010 *No entries in profit or loss or statement of financial position required; fair value of forward contract is zero.*		
Available-for-sale financial assets Cash *To recognise purchase of securities;* *US dollars 30 million at 2.55*	76,500,000	76,500,000
30 June 2010 Available-for-sale financial assets Available-for-sale revaluation reserve (other comprehensive income) *To recognise change in fair value of securities*	7,850,000	7,850,000
Derivatives (assets) Derivative revaluation gain (profit or loss) *To recognise change in fair value of forward*	3,031,769	3,031,769
Hedge revaluation loss (profit or loss) Available-for-sale revaluation reserve (other comprehensive income) *To reclassify fair value change of securities in respect* *of the hedged risk to profit or loss;* *US dollars 25.5 million x (2.41 - 2.55)*	3,570,000	3,570,000
30 September 2010 Available-for-sale revaluation reserve (other comprehensive income) Available-for-sale financial assets *To recognise change in fair value of securities*	17,430,000	17,430,000

	Debit	Credit
Derivatives (assets)	374,979	
Derivative revaluation gain (profit or loss)		374,979
To recognise change in fair value of forward		
Hedge revaluation loss (profit or loss)	510,000	
Available-for-sale revaluation reserve		
(other comprehensive income)		510,000
To reclassify fair value change of securities in		
respect of the hedged risk to profit or loss;		
US dollars 25.5 million x (2.39 - 2.41)		
15 October 2010		
Available-for-sale securities	11,480,000	
Available-for-sale revaluation reserve		
(other comprehensive income)		11,480,000
To recognise change in fair value of securities		
Derivative revaluation loss (profit or loss)	1,521,833	
Derivatives (assets)		1,521,833
To recognise change in fair value of forward		
Available-for-sale revaluation reserve		
(other comprehensive income)	1,530,000	
Hedge revaluation gain (profit or loss)		1,530,000
To reclassify fair value change of securities in respect		
of the hedged risk to profit or loss;		
US dollars 25.5 million x (2.45 - 2.39)		
Cash	1,884,915	
Derivatives (assets)		1,884,915
To recognise settlement of forward		

3.7.820.100 The hedge stays effective for the full period as changes in the fair value of the forward contract, due to changes in spot rates, offset perfectly changes in the value of US dollars 25.5 million of the equity portfolio due to the same spot exchange rates.

3.7.820.110 Variability in the fair value of the shares in foreign currency would not affect the assessment of hedge effectiveness unless the fair value of the shares in foreign currency declined below US dollars 25.5 million.

3.7.820.120 In order for fair value hedge accounting to be applied, the portfolio of shares that was designated as the hedged item at 1 April 2010 should continue to be the hedged item for the entire period of the hedge. This means that active management of the portfolio may preclude fair value hedge accounting.

3.7.820.130 As an alternative approach, management may designate the hedge as a hedge of the anticipated disposal of the shares providing that the timing of such disposal is highly probable, and apply cash flow hedge accounting. Cash flow hedge accounting requires specifying the size and timing of the cash flow being hedged. The model that is more appropriate may depend also on the entity's ability to collect the relevant information required under each model.

3.7.825 *Cash flow hedge of foreign currency risk of a recognised financial liability*

3.7.825.10 On 1 January 2010 Company G issues a non-callable three-year 5.5 percent fixed rate bond of US dollar 15 million at par. G's functional currency (see 2.7.30) is sterling.

3.7.825.20 As part of its risk management policy, G decides to eliminate the exposure arising from movements in the US dollar/sterling exchange rates on the principal amount of the bond for three years. G enters into a foreign currency forward contract to buy USD 15 million and sell sterling 9,835,389 at 31 December 2012.

3.7.825.30 G designates and documents the forward contract as the hedging instrument in a cash flow hedge of the variability in cash flows arising from the repayment of the principal amount of the bond due to movements in forward US dollar/sterling exchange rates.

3.7.825.40 G states in its hedge documentation (see 3.7.120.300) that it will use the hypothetical derivative method to assess hedge effectiveness. G identifies the hypothetical derivative as a forward contract under which it sells USD 15 million and purchases sterling 9,835,389 at 31 December 2012 (the repayment date of the bond). The hypothetical foreign currency forward contract has a fair value of zero at 1 January 2010.

3.7.825.50 The spot and the forward exchange rates and the fair value of the foreign currency forward contract are as follows:

Date	Spot rate 1 USD = GBP	Forward rate 1 USD = GBP	Fair value of forward contract GBP
1 January 2010	0.6213	0.6557	–
31 December 2010	0.5585	0.5858	(957,205)
31 December 2011	0.5209	0.5280	(1,833,457)
31 December 2012	0.5825	0.5825	(1,097,889)

3.7.825.60 For the purpose of this example, it is assumed that the average exchange rates approximate the exchanges rates at the end of the respective years.

3.7.825.70 The hedge remains effective for the entire period, with changes in the fair value of the hypothetical forward contract and the hedging instrument being perfectly offset. As G has designated the variability in cash flows arising from movements in the forward rates as the hedged risk, the entire change in the fair value of the forward contract is recognised in other comprehensive income. At each reporting date, G reclassifies from equity an amount equal to the movement in the spot rate on the principal amount of the bond. In addition, in order to ensure that the forward points recognised in other comprehensive income are reclassified fully to profit or loss over the life of the hedge, G reclassifies from equity an amount equal to the cumulative change in the forward points recognised in other comprehensive income amortised over the life of the hedging relationship using the interest rate implicit in the forward contract.

3.7.825.80 Assuming that all criteria for hedge accounting have been met, the journal entries recorded by G are as follows (amounts in sterling):

	Debit	*Credit*
1 January 2010 *No entries in profit or loss or statement of financial position required; fair value of forward contract is zero.*		
Cash Bond (financial liability) *To recognise issue of bond:* *USD 15 million at 0.6213*	9,319,500	9,319,500
31 December 2010 Hedging reserve (other comprehensive income) Derivative (liability) *To recognise change in fair value of forward* *contract (100 percent effective)*	957,205	957,205
Bond (financial liability) Foreign currency translation (profit or loss) *To recognise foreign exchange gain on issued bond*	942,000	942,000
Foreign currency translation (profit or loss) Hedging reserve (other comprehensive income) *To reclassify movement in spot rate*	942,000	942,000

	Debit	Credit
Foreign currency translation (profit or loss) Hedging reserve (other comprehensive income) *To reclassify forward points using interest rate* *implicit in forward contract*	168,884	168,884
Interest expense (profit or loss) Cash *Interest: 5.5 percent of USD 15 million at 0.5585*	460,763	460,763
31 December 2011 Hedging reserve (other comprehensive income) Derivative (liability) *To recognise change in fair value of forward contract* *(100 percent effective)*	876,252	876,252
Bond (financial liability) Foreign currency translation (profit or loss) *To recognise foreign exchange gain on issued bond*	564,000	564,000
Foreign currency translation (profit or loss) Hedging reserve (other comprehensive income) *To reclassify movement in spot rate*	564,000	564,000
Foreign currency translation (profit or loss) Hedging reserve (other comprehensive income) *To reclassify forward points using the interest rate* *implicit in forward contract*	171,945	171,945
Interest expense (profit or loss) Cash *To recognise interest:* *5.5 percent of USD 15 million at 0.5209*	429,743	429,743
31 December 2012 Derivative (liability) Hedging reserve (other comprehensive income) *To recognise change in fair value of forward contract* *(100 percent effective)*	735,568	735,568

	Debit	Credit
Foreign currency translation (profit or loss)	924,000	
Bond (financial liability)		924,000
To recognise foreign exchange loss on issued bond		
Hedging reserve (other comprehensive income)	924,000	
Foreign currency translation (profit or loss)		924,000
To reclassify movement in spot rate		
Foreign currency translation (profit or loss)	175,060	
Hedging reserve (other comprehensive income)		175,060
To reclassify forward points using interest rate implicit in forward contract		
Bond (financial liability)	8,737,500	
Cash		8,737,500
To recognise settlement of bond:		
USD 15 million at 0.5825		
Derivative (liability)	1,097,889	
Cash		1,097,889
To recognise settlement of forward contract		
Interest expense (profit or loss)	480,563	
Cash		480,563
To recognise interest:		
5.5 percent of USD 15 million at 0.5825		

3.7.830 *Hedging on a group basis – foreign currency risk*

3.7.830.10 A group consists of a parent entity (including corporate treasury) and its subsidiaries, Company J and Company B, all of which have a euro functional currency. J has highly probable cash inflows from future revenues of US dollar 200 that it expects to receive in 60 days. To hedge this exposure, J enters into a forward contract with the corporate treasury to pay US dollar 200 in 60 days.

3.7.830.20 B has highly probable forecast purchases of US dollar 500 that it expects to pay in 60 days. B hedges this exposure by entering into a forward contract with the corporate treasury to receive US dollar 500 in 60 days.

3.7.830.30 The parent entity itself has no expected exposure to that foreign currency during this period.

673

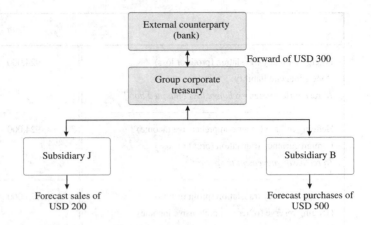

3.7.830.40 The effect of the internal derivatives with the subsidiaries is to transfer the foreign currency risk to the corporate treasury. The net currency exposure from US dollar in the next time period is a US dollar 300 outflow. The corporate treasury hedges this exposure by entering into a forward contract with an external third party.

3.7.830.50 In order to apply hedge accounting to this transaction the group designates the external forward contract as a hedge of a gross exposure in one of the subsidiaries rather than the net exposure. The group does this by designating the first US dollar 300 of cash outflows from purchases in B as the hedged item and the external forward contract as the hedging instrument. Whether or not adjustments are required on consolidation to the hedge accounting entries made by J and B depends on whether the forecast transactions of J and B are recognised in profit or loss at the same time. Two possibilities are considered in 3.7.840 and 850.

3.7.840 *Transactions recognised concurrently in income*

3.7.840.10 The forecast sales and forecast purchases of J and B respectively are recognised in profit or loss at the same time and both subsidiaries applied cash flow hedge accounting for their respective internal derivatives. On consolidation the internal transactions offset, leaving only the external derivative and its associated gain or loss to be accounted for. The group can apply hedge accounting to the relationship between this external derivative and the first US dollar 300 of outflows representing B's purchases without making any adjustments to the hedge accounting entries made at the subsidiary level. The internal derivatives are used as an indicator of the external transaction that qualifies for hedge accounting.

3.7.850 *Transactions recognised in different periods*

3.7.850.10 The forecast sales of J are recognised in profit or loss in July, while B's purchases are recognised in June. Both subsidiaries applied cash flow hedge accounting for their respective internal derivatives. On consolidation the internal transactions will not offset completely as they are recognised in profit or loss in different periods. Consequently, the group cannot apply hedge accounting automatically to the relationship between the external derivative and the first US dollar 300 of outflows representing B's purchases; some adjustments will have to be made to the subsidiaries' accounting. In this case, the internal derivatives cannot be used as an indicator of the external transaction that qualifies for hedge accounting. An alternative approach would be to:

- enter into external derivatives to hedge aggregate long positions and short positions in each currency and each time period separately (i.e. by aggregating and not netting internal derivatives at corporate treasury) and then designating the external derivatives as hedging instruments at the group level; and
- put in place additional documentation at the group level to link each external derivative to its associated group of internal derivatives such that the chain of hedge documentation is completed, via the internal contracts, between each hedged cash flow within the group and a portion of the related external derivative.

3.7.860 *Hedge of a net investment in a foreign operation*

3.7.860.10 Company G, whose functional currency is the euro, has a net investment in a foreign subsidiary of sterling 50 million. On 1 October 2010, G enters into a foreign exchange forward contract to sell sterling 50 million and receive euro on 1 April 2011. G will review the net investment balance on a quarterly basis and adjust the hedge to the value of the net investment. The time value of the forward contract is excluded from the assessment of hedge effectiveness.

3.7.860.20 The exchange rate and fair value of the forward contract move as follows:

Date	Spot rate 1 sterling = euro	Forward rate 1 sterling = euro	Fair value of forward contract
1 October 2010	1.71	1.70	-
31 December 2010	1.64	1.63	3,430,000
31 March 2011	1.60	N/A	5,000,000

3.7.860.30 Assuming that all criteria for hedge accounting have been met, the required entries are as follows (amounts in euro):

	Debit	Credit
1 October 2010 *No entries in profit or loss or statement of financial position required; fair value of forward contract is zero.*		

675

	Debit	Credit
31 December 2010		
Derivatives (asset)	3,430,000	
Foreign exchange losses (profit or loss)	70,000	
Foreign currency translation reserve (other comprehensive income)		3,500,000
To recognise change in fair value of forward		
Foreign currency translation reserve (other comprehensive income)	3,500,000	
Net investment in subsidiary (asset)		3,500,000
To recognise foreign exchange loss on net investment in the subsidiary (the adjustment to the net investment would be derived by translating the subsidiary's statement of financial position at the spot rate at the reporting date)		
31 March 2010		
Derivatives (asset)	1,570,000	
Foreign exchange losses (profit or loss)	430,000	
Foreign currency translation reserve (other comprehensive income)		2,000,000
To recognise change in fair value of forward		
Foreign currency translation reserve (other comprehensive income)	2,000,000	
Net investment in subsidiary (asset)		2,000,000
To recognise change in foreign exchange losses on net investment		
Cash	5,000,000	
Derivatives (assets)		5,000,000
To recognise settlement of the forward		

3.7.860.40 The gain on the hedging transaction will remain in equity until the subsidiary is disposed of (see 3.7.110.30 – 35).

3.7.870 Hedging other market price risks

3.7.870.10 For example, Company X owns equity securities in an entity listed on a domestic stock exchange. The securities are classified as available for sale. At 1 January 2010 the fair value of the securities is 120 million; the fair value at initial recognition was 115 million. The revaluation gain of 5 million is recognised in other comprehensive income.

676

3.7.870.20 At 30 June 2010 the value of the securities has increased from 120 million to 130 million. The securities are remeasured at fair value with the cumulative change of 15 million recognised in other comprehensive income.

3.7.870.30 At 30 June 2010, due to volatility in the price risk of the securities and to comply with internal risk management policies, management decides to purchase a European put option on the securities with a strike price equal to the current market price of 130 million and a maturity date of 30 June 2010. The option premium paid is 12 million.

3.7.870.40 Management has documented and assessed the purchased put option as an effective hedge in offsetting decreases in the fair value of the equity securities below 130 million. The time value component will not be included in determining the effectiveness of the hedge. The fair value of the securities and the put option during the period are as follows:

Date	Value of securities	Total option value	Intrinsic value	Time value
1 January 2010	120,000,000	-	-	-
30 June 2010	130,000,000	12,000,000	-	12,000,000
30 September 2010	136,000,000	7,000,000	-	7,000,000
31 December 2010	126,000,000	9,000,000	4,000,000	5,000,000

3.7.870.50 The following entries are made to record the remeasurement of the securities and the payment of the option premium:

	Debit	Credit
30 June 2010		
Available-for-sale securities	10,000,000	
Available-for-sale revaluation reserve (other comprehensive income)		10,000,000
To recognise remeasurement gain on available-for-sale securities		
Hedging derivatives (assets)	12,000,000	
Cash		12,000,000
To recognise payment of the option premium		
30 September 2009		
Available-for-sale securities	6,000,000	
Available-for-sale revaluation reserve (other comprehensive income)		6,000,000
To recognise remeasurement gain on available-for-sale securities		

	Debit	Credit
Hedging costs (profit or loss)	5,000,000	
Hedging derivatives (assets)		5,000,000
To recognise remeasurement loss on option due to change		
in time value (not part of the hedge relationship)		

3.7.870.60 The option still is expected to be effective as a hedge of decreases in the fair value of the available-for-sale securities below the strike price of the option.

3.7.870.70 At 31 December 2010 the value of the hedged securities decreases to 126 million. The value of the put option increases to 9 million; of that amount, 4 million represents intrinsic value and 5 million represents time value. As such, the following entries are made to recognise the change in the fair value of the available-for-sale securities and the changes in the fair value of the option.

3.7.870.80 For illustrative purposes, these entries have been separated into two parts to demonstrate the accounting for the changes in the value of the securities that are not being hedged (decrease to 130 million) and the changes in value that are being hedged (decrease below 130 million). Likewise, changes in the fair value of the option are separated to demonstrate changes in the time value, which have been excluded from the hedge relationship, and changes in the option's intrinsic value.

	Debit	Credit
31 December 2010		
Available-for-sale revaluation reserve (other		
comprehensive income)	6,000,000	
Available-for-sale securities		6,000,000
To recognise unhedged decrease in fair value of securities		
(from 136 million to 130 million)		
Hedge results (profit or loss)	4,000,000	
Available-for-sale securities		4,000,000
To recognise hedged decrease in fair value of securities		
(from 130 million to 126 million)		
Hedging costs (profit or loss)	2,000,000	
Hedging derivatives (assets)		2,000,000
To recognise changes in time value of option		
(excluded from hedge relationship)		
Hedging derivatives (assets)	4,000,000	
Hedge results (profit or loss)		4,000,000
To recognise change in intrinsic value of option		
(effective part of the hedge)		

3.7.870.90 At 31 December 2010 the equity securities are recognised at a fair value of 126 million compared to an original cost of 115 million. As a result of the hedging strategy designated by X in 3.7.870.10, a gain of 15 million has been included in the available-for-sale revaluation reserve, while a loss of 4 million, i.e. the decline in the value from 130 million to 126 million, has been included in profit or loss.

3.7.900 **Future developments**

3.7.900.10 The IASB is working on a project that will ultimately replace IAS 39 (see 3.6.1360.10). The IASB's project includes the following phases:

- classification and measurement (see 3.6A and 5.6.530.20);
- impairment (see 4.6.560.20); and
- hedging (see 3.7.900.20).

3.7.900.20 The IASB and FASB are working jointly on a project to replace the current accounting requirements for hedge accounting with the goal of substantially simplifying the existing requirements. An ED is scheduled for the third quarter of 2010.

3.8   Inventories

(IAS 2)

3.8 Inventories
(IAS 2)

Overview of currently effective requirements

- Generally inventories are measured at the lower of cost and net realisable value.

- Cost includes all direct expenditure to get inventory ready for sale, including attributable overheads.

- The cost of inventory generally is determined using the FIFO (first-in, first-out) or weighted average method. The use of the LIFO (last-in, first-out) method is prohibited.

- Other cost formulas, such as the standard cost or retail method, may be used when the results approximate actual cost.

- The cost of inventory is recognised as an expense when the inventory is sold.

- Inventory is written down to net realisable value when net realisable value is less than cost.

- If the net realisable value of an item that has been written down subsequently increases, then the write-down is reversed.

Currently effective requirements

This publication reflects IFRSs in issue at 1 August 2010. The currently effective requirements cover annual periods beginning on 1 January 2010. The requirements related to this topic are derived mainly from IAS 2 *Inventories*.

Forthcoming requirements and future developments

When a currently effective requirement will be changed by a new requirement that is issued but is not yet effective, it is marked with a # as a **forthcoming requirement** and the impact of the change is explained in the accompanying boxed text. In respect of this topic no forthcoming requirements are noted.

When a significant change to the currently effective or forthcoming requirements is expected, it is marked with a * as an area that may be subject to **future development** and a brief outline of the relevant project is given in 3.8.450.

3.8.10 **Definition**

IAS 2.6 3.8.10.10 Inventories are assets:

- held for sale in the ordinary course of business (finished goods);
- in the process of production for sale (work in progress); or
- in the form of materials or supplies to be consumed in the production process or in the rendering of services (raw materials and consumables).

IAS 2.8, 38.2, 3.8.10.20 Inventory may include intangible assets that are being produced for resale,
3, 40.5, 9 e.g. software. Inventory also includes properties that have been purchased or are being developed for resale in the ordinary course of business (see 3.4.60).

3.8.10.30 Financial assets, such as investments held for sale, are not inventory (see 3.6.150).

3.8.20 *Property, plant and equipment held for sale*

IAS 2.6, 8 3.8.20.10 Inventories encompass assets purchased or constructed with the intention of resale in the ordinary course of business. This includes items that would meet the definition of property, plant and equipment, for example, buildings, had they been purchased or constructed with the intention of use in the production or supply of goods or services, for rental to others or for administrative purposes.

IFRS 5.3, 3.8.20.20 However, it is not appropriate to reclassify an existing item of property, plant
IAS 1.66 and equipment, for example, a building, as inventory when the entity decides to sell it. In our view, this also is the case when management, during construction of a building, changes its intention in such a way that the building will be sold once construction is completed, unless the entity sells buildings in the ordinary course of business. See 5.4 for further information on the accounting treatment of non-current assets held for sale.

IAS 16.68A 3.8.20.30 Items of property, plant and equipment that are rented and then subsequently sold on a routine basis (e.g. rental cars) are transferred to inventories at their carrying amount when they cease to be rented and become held for sale (see 3.2.440.37).

3.8.25 *Investment property*

3.8.25.10 The classification of property as held for sale in the ordinary course of business (inventory) or as held for capital appreciation (investment property) can be difficult (see 3.4.60).

3.8.30 *Spare parts*

IAS 16.8 3.8.30.10 Spare parts, stand-by and servicing equipment (e.g. tools and consumable lubricants) are classified as inventory unless they are expected to be used during more than one period or can be used only in connection with an item of property, plant and equipment, in which case they are classified as property, plant and equipment (see 3.2.10.20). This applies to assets held for use within the entity and to those held to provide maintenance services to others.

IAS 16.8 3.8.30.20 For example, Company F, an aircraft charter company that offers aircraft maintenance services, has spare parts. Some of the spare parts will be used during less than one period in the day-to-day repair and maintenance of aircraft on behalf of customers. Others will be used only in connection with F's own aircraft. The spare parts to be used in the servicing business are accounted for as inventory as they are consumed during less than one period in the rendering of maintenance services. Those that will be used in F's own aircraft are accounted for as property, plant and equipment (see 3.2). Therefore, F needs to distinguish between spare parts to be used for its own aircraft and those to be used in servicing because the accounting treatment of these items is different. When it is difficult to distinguish those items to be used in servicing aircraft on behalf of customers from those to be used for its own aircraft, an allocation should be made based upon how the business is managed. If it is not possible to allocate these items, then in our view all items should be included as inventory.

3.8.40 *Reusable and returnable packaging or parts*

3.8.40.10 Packaging or parts that are sold to a customer, but will be returned to the seller to be reused, are not inventory if the items will be used during more than one period.

3.8.40.20 For example, Company C produces and distributes bottled drinks. C receives a deposit for the bottles when drinks are sold. C is required to buy back empty bottles, which are used again in future periods. Bottles are used for more than one period and are not bought for the purpose of resale. Therefore the bottles are not inventory; they are an item of equipment (see 3.2).

3.8.40.30 See 3.12.370.30 and 40 for a discussion of the accounting for deposits from customers.

3.8.50 *Samples*

AS 38.69, 70 3.8.50.10 For advertising and promotional purposes, some entities may manufacture samples that they intend to hand out free of charge, e.g. beauty products. The costs of manufacturing such samples are expensed as incurred; they are not recognised as inventory. Other entities may purchase such samples that they intend to hand out free of charge. The costs of purchasing those samples are expensed when the entity receives, or otherwise has the right to access, the samples; they are not recognised as inventory. A prepayment (asset) for such samples can be recognised in the statement of financial position only for payments made in advance of the receipt of the samples (see 3.3.150). However, if a producer sells products to a retailer and the retailer then gives samples to customers free of charge, then the samples would be treated as inventory of the producer.

3.8.60 *Catalogues*

AS 38.69, 70, 3.8.60.10 Catalogues describing the entity's products and services that are distributed
BC46G free of charge to prospective customers are not inventory or property, plant and equip-

ment. Instead catalogues are considered to be a form of advertising and promotional material as the primary objective of catalogues is to advertise to customers. Therefore, the cost of catalogues is recognised as an expense when the entity receives, or otherwise has the right to access, the catalogues. A prepayment (asset) can be recognised in the statement of financial position only for payments made in advance of the receipt of the catalogues (see also 3.3.150).

3.8.70 *Commodities*

IAS 2.3   3.8.70.10 The measurement requirements of IAS 2 do not apply to minerals and mineral products held by producers that are measured at net realisable value in accordance with well established practices in certain industries. When such inventories are measured at net realisable value, changes in value are recognised in profit or loss. This exemption applies only to producers of these inventories. There is no exemption for entities that process or convert these products.

IAS 2.3, 5   3.8.70.20 The measurement requirements of IAS 2 also do not apply to inventories held by commodity broker-traders who measure their inventories at fair value less costs to sell. All changes in the fair value less costs to sell of such inventories are recognised in profit or loss. Such inventories normally are acquired with the purpose of selling them in the near future and generating a profit from fluctuations in price or broker-traders' margin. In assessing whether an entity acts as a commodity broker-trader, the term "near future" needs to be interpreted. In our view, such an assessment may vary from entity to entity and factors considered in this assessment include the business model of the entity. The entity should consider the extent to which it provides additional services related to the underlying commodities, such as distribution, storage or repackaging services, as well as the fact that entities that sell goods in the near future after receipt do not have significant storage capacity. When an entity acts as a commodity broker-trader, generally the "own use exemption" under IAS 39 *Financial Instruments: Recognition and Measurement* will not be available (see 3.6.90).

3.8.70.30 For example, Wholesaler C buys coffee and resells the commodity in the same condition a short period after physical delivery. The commodity received under such a contract is accounted for under IAS 2, except for the measurement requirements of inventories when the commodity is measured at fair value less costs to sell. In another example, Company L performs significant services for Company M by repackaging coffee into small retail units and then selling it. In this case the transaction should be accounted for in accordance with IAS 2, including measurement, unless L is acting as an agent (see 4.2.660).

3.8.70.33 Another factor to consider in determining whether an entity acts as a broker-trader is whether the entity is exposed to risk of fluctuation in prices. If the entity has hedged most or all of its price risk, then it is unlikely to be acting as a trader.

IAS 38.3(a)   3.8.70.37 In general, emissions allowances (or carbon credits) are accounted for as intangible assets (see 3.3.170). However, if such allowances are held for sale in the ordinary course of business, then in our view they may be inventories (see 3.8.10.20). Notwithstanding the fact that they do not have physical substance they may, in our view be classified as commodities. The term "commodities" is not defined in IFRSs and an emissions allowance is not a financial asset (see 3.6.150), which means that there is no definitional restriction on classifying emissions allowances as commodities. In our view, if such allowances are held by a commodity broker-trader for the purpose of selling them in the near future and generating a profit from fluctuations in price or broker-traders' margin, and the broker-trader measures its inventories at fair value less costs to sell, then the measurement requirements of IAS 2 do not apply to those emissions allowances.*

3.8.70.40 The presentation and disclosure requirements of IAS 2 apply to items of inventory held by producers or commodity broker-traders.

3.8.80 *Agricultural produce*

IAS 41.3 3.8.80.10 IAS 2 applies to agricultural produce from the point of harvest. See 3.9 for a discussion of the accounting for biological assets prior to harvest.

IAS 2.3 3.8.80.20 However, the measurement requirements of IAS 2 do not apply to *producers'* inventories of agricultural and forest products and to agricultural produce after harvest that are measured at net realisable value in accordance with well established industry practices. The presentation and disclosure requirements of IAS 2 do apply to such items.

3.8.90 Recognition and derecognition

3.8.90.10 Inventory is recognised on the date that the entity obtains the significant risks and rewards of ownership of the inventory (see also 4.2.120).

3.8.90.20 In some cases ownership passes on delivery. In other cases a legal principle establishes when the significant risks and rewards of ownership transfer. For example, when goods are shipped "free on board" (FOB), this generally means that the significant risks and rewards of ownership pass to the buyer when the goods are loaded onto the ship at the port of the seller; although the terms and conditions of an FOB arrangement should be assessed to determine whether this is the case. Therefore, inventory generally includes items purchased FOB that are in transit at the reporting date.

IAS 2.35 3.8.90.30 The carrying amount of inventories is recognised as an expense when the inventories are sold unless they form part of the cost of another asset, for example, property, plant and equipment under construction. Therefore derecognition depends on the timing of revenue recognition (see 4.2). As such, inventory does not include:

- items sold, even if a normal level of returns is expected (4.2.150); or
- items shipped to customers on or before the reporting date unless the risks and rewards of ownership have not transferred to the buyer, for example, prior to goods being loaded onto the ship in an FOB arrangement they would be included in inventory of the seller.

687

3.8.100 *Consignment stock*

3.8.100.10 The principles in 3.8.90 apply also in respect of consignment inventory. Therefore, items owned by an entity that are held on consignment at another entity's premises are included as inventory of the consignor. Items held on consignment on behalf of another entity are not included as inventory of the consignee. See 4.2.160 in respect of the recognition of revenue.

3.8.110 **Measurement**

IAS 2.9   3.8.110.10 Inventory is measured at the lower of cost and net realisable value (see 3.8.330).

IAS 2.3   3.8.110.20 As an exception to this general rule, producers' inventories of agricultural and forest products and mineral ores may be stated at net realisable value when this is accepted industry practice. Also, inventory held by commodity broker-traders may be measured at fair value less cost to sell (see 3.8.70.20). In those cases changes in value are recognised in profit or loss.

3.8.110.30 A group with diverse operating activities could measure the inventories held by commodity broker-traders within the group at fair value less costs to sell (see 3.8.70.20) and other inventories at the lower of cost and net realisable value.

3.8.120 **Cost**

IAS 2.10, 15   3.8.120.10 The cost of inventories comprises:

- purchase costs (see 3.8.130);
- production or conversion costs (see 3.8.170); and
- other costs incurred in bringing inventory to its present location and condition, including attributable non-production overheads (see 3.8.220).

3.8.130 *Purchase costs*

IAS 2.11   3.8.130.10 Purchase costs include the purchase price, transport and handling costs, taxes that are not recoverable and other costs directly attributable to the purchase.

3.8.130.20 A purchase price may be attributable to several assets, for example, if an entity purchases all of its inventories from a particular supplier. In our view, the purchase price should be allocated to the individual assets based on their relative fair values.

3.8.140 *Sales tax*

3.8.140.10 Sales tax paid, for example, value added tax (VAT), is not included in the cost recorded as inventory if the tax is recoverable. For items on which the sales tax is not recoverable, or for entities that are not entitled to a full refund, the sales tax paid that is not refundable is included as part of the cost of the inventory.

3.8.150 *Deferred payment*

IAS 2.18 3.8.150.10 When payment for inventory is deferred beyond normal credit terms, the arrangement contains a financing element and interest should be imputed if the impact is material.

IAS 2.18 3.8.150.20 When interest is imputed, the cost of the inventory should be based on a cash price equivalent. In practice the cash price equivalent is the price for normal credit terms. In our view, if a cash price equivalent is not available, then cost should be determined by discounting the future cash flows at an interest rate determined by reference to market rates. The difference between the total cost and the deemed cost should be recognised as interest expense over the period of financing using the effective interest method (see 4.6.30).

3.8.150.30 In our view, the length of normal credit terms will depend on the entity, the industry and the economic environment. Periods of high interest rates or high inflation levels also may affect the length of normal credit terms.

3.8.160 *Discounts and rebates on purchases*

IAS 2.11 3.8.160.10 Cash, trade or volume discounts and rebates are deducted from the cost of purchase.

3.8.160.20 There is no specific guidance on the timing of recognition of rebates or volume discounts. In our view, if it is probable that the rebate or volume discount will be earned and the amount can be estimated reliably, then the discount or rebate should be recognised as a reduction in the purchase price when the inventory is purchased. This assessment should be reviewed on an ongoing basis.

3.8.160.30 For example, Company Z is a furniture retailer. Z buys beds from Company Y at a cost of 100 each. Y has agreed to grant Z a 10 percent refund on all purchases if Z purchases at least 10,000 beds in a 12-month period. Based on past experience, it is probable that Z will purchase 10,000 beds from Y. Therefore, in our view Z should record the beds at the expected cost of 90 per unit, and recognise a receivable for the anticipated rebate.

3.8.160.40 On the other hand, if it is not probable that the required criteria will be met, or if the amount of the rebate cannot be estimated reliably, then the rebate should not be recognised until the receipt is probable and the amount can be estimated reliably.

3.8.160.50 If items have been sold when the discount or rebate is recognised, then in our view the proportion of the discount attributable to the sold items should be recognised immediately as an adjustment to cost of sales in the current period.

3.8.160.60 Extending the example in 3.8.160.30, assume it is not considered probable that Z will purchase the required 10,000 beds. After nine months Z reaches the target and receives a rebate of 100,000 (10 x 10,000). At that date 4,000 beds are still on hand. The other 6,000 beds have been sold. In our view, Z should reduce the cost of each of the remaining beds by 10, i.e. 40,000 (10 x 4,000) of the rebate should be allocated to reduce the cost of inventory. The remaining 60,000 should be recognised in profit or loss immediately as a reduction of cost of sales.

3.8.160.70 In our view, incentives for early payment (settlement discounts) should be treated as a reduction in the purchase price. In practice, when such discounts are not taken, the cost of inventory is the higher amount payable before discount, provided that payment is not deferred beyond normal credit terms (see 3.8.150). This approach is consistent with the assumption that there is no financing element when payment is within normal credit terms.

3.8.170 *Costs of production or conversion*

IAS 2.12   3.8.170.10 Costs of production or conversion include all direct costs such as labour, material and direct overheads and an allocation of fixed and variable production overheads. These include the depreciation and maintenance of factory buildings and equipment; amortisation of intangible assets such as software used in the production process; and the cost of factory management and administration. Labour costs include taxes and employee benefit costs associated with labour that is involved directly in the production process. The costs do not need to be external or incremental.

3.8.170.20 The following should be recognised as an expense and not allocated to the cost of inventory in the statement of financial position:

- impairment losses (including goodwill impairment losses);
- abnormal amounts of wasted material, labour or other production costs (see 3.8.200); and
- general administration costs unrelated to the production of inventory (e.g. costs of operating a finance department).

3.8.180 *Decommissioning and restoration costs*

IAS 16.16(c),   3.8.180.10 Decommissioning and restoration costs incurred as a consequence of the
18, IFRIC 1.4   production of inventory in a particular period are part of the cost of that inventory (see 3.2.70.30). Accordingly, the effect of any changes to an existing obligation for decommissioning and restoration costs related to items that have been sold should be recognised in profit or loss.

3.8.190 *Emissions allowances**

3.8.190.10 IFRSs do not contain specific guidance on accounting for emissions allowances. In general, emissions allowances are accounted for as intangible assets (see 3.3.170). However, in our view if such allowances are held for sale in the ordinary course of business, then they may be inventories (see 3.8.70.37). See 3.3.170 and 3.12.510 for a discussion of the accounting for emissions allowances received by a participant in a "cap and trade" scheme and the accounting for obligations arising from such schemes, respectively.

3.8.200 *Allocation of fixed production overheads*

IAS 2.13 3.8.200.10 The allocation of fixed production overheads is based on the normal capacity of production facilities. Any inefficiencies should be recognised in profit or loss, classified as other expenses, or, if an entity classifies expenses based on function, allocated to the appropriate function.

3.8.200.20 In determining what constitutes normal capacity, the following factors should be considered:

- the nature of the business, economic factors, the status of product life cycles and the reliability of forecasts;
- the capacity and expected utilisation of production facilities, including planned maintenance and shut-downs; and
- the expected levels of activity to be achieved on average over a number of periods, adjusted for unusual fluctuations or circumstances.

3.8.200.30 For example, assume that under normal operating conditions Company J expects to produce 100 coffee machines a year. Budgeted and actual fixed production overheads for 2010 are 800. Therefore the fixed overhead cost per machine based on normal production levels is 8.

3.8.200.40 During 2010, due to problems with the production machinery and decreased demand, J produced only 80 coffee machines. The production overheads should be allocated based on the normal production levels of 100 (i.e. 8 per unit). Therefore, of the total production overheads of 800, only 640 (8 x 80) is allocated to inventory. The other 160 is recognised as an expense as incurred.

3.8.200.50 On the other hand, if during 2010 in response to increased demand for coffee machines J increased production shifts and produced 130 machines, then the amount allocated to the inventory is limited to the actual expenditure. Therefore if the total production overheads remain constant at 800, a cost of 6.15 (800 / 130) is allocated to each machine.

3.8.200.60 If actual production differs substantially from the normal capacity over a period of time, then consideration should be given to revising the normal capacity.

3.8.200.70 Issues may arise when entities have a planned plant shut-down. For example, Company F is involved in freezing and canning fresh fruit. Production takes place during the first six months of the financial year when the fresh fruit is picked. During the second six months of the financial year the production plant is closed and maintenance is performed. No inventory is on hand during the shut-down period. The maintenance costs do not comprise a separate component of the plant (see 3.2.250). In determining the normal capacity over which production costs will be allocated, F should take into account the annual scheduled plant shut-down.

3.8.200.80 However, in our view the maintenance cost in the second half of the year cannot be accrued over the production in the first six months because:

- a provision cannot be recognised during the first half of the year for the maintenance costs to be incurred in the second half of the financial year (see 3.12.540); and
- the maintenance incurred in the second half of the year is a cost of producing the inventory in the following financial year, as it is not necessary to prepare the fruit produced in the first six months for sale.

3.8.200.90 In our view, the maintenance costs also cannot be capitalised and allocated to the following period's production. If F were to attribute the maintenance cost to the following period's production, then this would result in the maintenance expenditure being recognised as an asset in the statement of financial position. We believe that the maintenance costs do not give rise to an asset as defined in the Framework and therefore they should be expensed as incurred.

3.8.204 Common costs as part of inventory

IAS 40.9(a)   3.8.204.10 Properties for sale in the ordinary course of business or in the process of construction or development for such sale are accounted for under IAS 2 rather than IAS 40 *Investment Property* (see 3.4.60.10 and 3.8.20). If an entity is constructing individual units as part of a single complex with the objective to sell them, then the entity would need to identify and distinguish between costs specifically attributable to each unit (e.g. flooring) and common costs attributable to the complex as a whole (e.g. land). In our view, the common costs should be allocated to each unit on a systematic and rational basis that provides a reasonable approximation of the cost attributable to the individual items of inventory. The allocation method applied should reflect the construction efforts as well as the cost of a unit.

3.8.204.15 Common costs should be allocated by reference to the relative fair values of individual items of inventory only if fair value is a reasonable approximation of cost.

3.8.208 Capitalisation of operating lease expense as part of inventory

IAS 40.6   3.8.208.10 For example, Company P leases land under an operating lease that is not classified as investment property because it does not meet the conditions under IAS 40 (see 3.4.40). The lease payments are required to be paid in advance. P develops a multi-unit condominium complex on the land and the condominiums will be sold in the ordinary course of business (see also 3.8.204). The question arises whether the operating lease cost should be capitalised as part of the inventory cost of each unit or kept in the statement of financial position as a prepayment until sale. In our view, P should include the cost of the operating lease in the cost of inventory by recording the lease payment in inventory, preferably by recording the lease cost in inventory directly (see 3.2.30.85). Alternatively, the cost of inventory is determined by recording the lease premium as a prepayment initially, amortising it in accordance with IAS 17 *Leases* (see 5.1.310) and capitalising the operating lease expense as inventory.

3.8.210 *Interruptions*

IAS 23.24 3.8.210.10 Interruptions in production may occur while costs still are being incurred. For example, an entity may continue to pay rent on a factory during an unplanned plant shut-down or labour strike. IAS 2 does not deal specifically with such circumstances, but in our view guidance from IAS 23 *Borrowing Costs* should be used by analogy (see 4.6.350), as this standard deals specifically with a similar issue.

3.8.210.20 Accordingly, we believe that costs incurred during an interruption should be capitalised to inventory only if:

- the interruption is planned, is temporary and is a necessary part of getting the inventory ready for sale (e.g. the inventory requires time to mature); or
- the costs are costs of purchase, for example, purchases of additional raw materials during the shut-down period.

3.8.210.30 Therefore, in our view rent costs during a strike would not be recognised as part of inventory, but rent costs during scheduled maintenance shut-downs might be.

3.8.215 *Learning curve costs*

3.8.215.10 In certain industries learning curve costs are incurred on the early units produced, for example, in producing multiple units of complex goods for sale under IAS 18 *Revenue*. Learning curve costs are costs that are expected to be incurred on early units as production issues are resolved and are expected to decrease each time a unit is produced. This is based on the observation that repetition of the same operation results in less time or effort expended on that operation.

3.8.215.20 As a result of these learning curve costs, actual production costs on the earlier units produced may exceed the net realisable value of these units and therefore result in losses on initial production. On the other hand, profits may be made on later individual units. Losses on the earlier units may be incurred even if all these units are sold subject to one contract and that contract overall is profitable (see 4.2.520).

3.8.215.30 In our view, abnormal additional costs should be expensed as incurred (see 3.8.170.20). However, learning curve costs incurred in the production process should be included in the cost of inventory (subject to recoverability (see 3.8.335.10)) when there is clear objective evidence that these costs are not abnormal costs. In our view, such costs are not abnormal when they are planned and anticipated as part of the production process, and when they can be measured reliably.

3.8.220 *Other costs*

IAS 2.15,
38.97
3.8.220.10 Any other costs that are related directly to bringing inventories to the point of sale and getting them ready for sale also should be allocated. These may include non-production overheads or the costs of designing products for specific customers including, for example, the amortisation of development costs related to a specific product or process.

3.8.220.20 Selling and advertising costs should not be included in the cost of inventory.

3.8.230 *Distribution, packaging and transport costs*

3.8.230.10 Distribution costs and costs of transporting goods to customers are recognised as an expense as incurred; they are not allocated to inventory. However, transport and distribution costs that are necessary to get the inventory to a present location or condition for sale form part of the cost of inventory. The following are examples of costs that should be allocated to inventory:

- the cost of transporting goods from the *supplier*;
- transport or distribution costs that are incurred at an intermediate stage in the production process; and
- transport or distribution costs to get the inventory from a storage location (e.g. warehouse) to the point of sale.

3.8.230.20 Similarly, packaging costs incurred to prepare inventory for sale are part of the cost of inventory.

3.8.240 *Storage or holding costs*

IAS 2.16(b)
3.8.240.10 Storage or holding costs generally are expensed as incurred unless:

- storage is necessary before a further stage in the production process;
- the inventory is produced as a discrete project, for example, custom-built furnishings when the storage cost will be charged to the customer; or
- the inventory requires a maturation process in order to bring it into a saleable condition, for example, whisky, wine or cheese.

3.8.250 **Joint products and by-products**

3.8.250.10 A production process may result in more than one output being produced. For example, in the wine-making process, grappa is produced from the liquid distilled from the fermented residue of grapes after they have been pressed.

IAS 2.14
3.8.250.20 If the cost related to the individual products cannot be identified, then the total production costs are allocated between the products on a rational and consistent basis. One possible method is to allocate the total production costs based on the relative selling prices of each product. If this method is used, then it is reasonable to assume the

same profit margin for each product unless there is a more accurate method of making the allocation.

IAS 2.14 3.8.250.30 If a production process results in products that are incidental to the primary product, then the cost allocated to these by-products may be based on their net realisable value, which then is deducted from the cost of the main product.

3.8.260 *Borrowing costs*

IAS 2.17, 3.8.260.10 Borrowing costs are capitalised as part of the cost of inventories if the in-
23.4, 7, BC6 ventories are "qualifying assets". Inventories that are manufactured routinely in large quantities or that are produced on a repetitive basis in a short time are not qualifying assets (see 4.6.350).

3.8.270 *Agricultural produce*

IAS 2.20 3.8.270.10 The fair value less costs to sell of agricultural produce at the date of harvest is the deemed cost of the produce for the purpose of applying IAS 2 (see 3.9.100).

3.8.280 *Cost formulas*

IAS 2.23 3.8.280.10 When items of inventory are not interchangeable, cost is determined on an individual item basis. This is appropriate for unique items, such as custom-built furnishings, property developments, antiques and works of art.

IAS 2.25 3.8.280.20 A cost formula may be used when there are many interchangeable items. The cost formula used should be FIFO or weighted average cost.

3.8.280.30 The LIFO method is prohibited.

IAS 2.27 3.8.280.40 Under the weighted average cost formula, the cost of each item is determined from the weighted average of the cost of similar items at the beginning of a period and the cost of similar items purchased or produced during the period. The average may be calculated on a periodic basis or as each additional shipment is received.

3.8.280.50 The example below illustrates the application of each of the methods in an entity that uses a periodic inventory system. The following information pertains to December 2010.

	Units	Unit cost	Total cost
Inventory at 1 December	200	10	2,000
Purchases	50	11	550
Purchases	400	12	4,800
Purchases	350	14	4,900
	1,000		12,250

At 31 December 2010 there are 400 units in stock.

FIFO method

Inventory at 31 December 2010	350 units @ 14	4,900
	50 units @ 12	600
		5,500
Cost of sales December 2010	12,250 - 5,500	6,750

Weighted average cost method

Weighted average unit cost	12,250 / 1,000	12.25
Inventory at 31 December 2010	400 x 12.25	4,900
Cost of sales December 2010	12,250 - 4,900	7,350

3.8.290 *Standard cost method*

IAS 2.21   3.8.290.10 The standard cost method may be used for convenience if the results approximate actual cost. Under a standard costing system, the cost of a product is determined using predetermined rates for the material, labour and overhead expenses based on manufacturing specifications.

3.8.290.20 To be acceptable as a basis for measuring cost, standard costs should take into account normal levels of materials and supplies, labour efficiency and capacity utilisation, or should be adjusted for variances. Standard costs should be reviewed regularly, in our view at least at each reporting date, and adjusted to take into account changes in circumstances.

3.8.290.30 When standard costs are not updated to approximate actual costs, it is necessary to analyse the variance accounts and to apportion part of the variances to inventory. If the standard unit cost was 10 in the example in 3.8.280.50, then the closing standard cost of inventory of 4,000 (400 x 10) would be increased by 1,500. This adjustment would result in a closing inventory balance of 5,500, the same value obtained under the FIFO method. The adjustment of 1,500 is computed by allocating the purchase price variance applicable to the 400 units of inventory calculated as 350 x (14 - 10) + 50 x (12 - 10). Under the weighted average cost method, an increase of 900, calculated as 400 x (12.25 - 10), should be accounted for resulting in a closing balance as at 31 December of 4,900.

3.8.300 *Retail method*

IAS 2.21, 22   3.8.300.10 The retail method may be used if the result approximates actual cost. This assessment should be reviewed regularly, in our view at least at each reporting date. Under the retail method, inventory is recorded based on its selling price. The cost of the inventory is derived by deducting the profit margin from the selling price. Adjustments should be made when inventory has been marked down to below its original selling price. An average percentage for each retail department may be used if the margins on all the products within that department are similar.

3.8.300.20 The following example illustrates the retail method:

	Cost	Retail price
Opening inventory	6,250	8,000
Purchases	19,500	34,000
Inventory on hand		(23,000)
Sales for the period		19,000
Using the retail method, closing inventory and cost of sales are calculated as follows:		
Cost	6,250 + 19,500	25,750
Retail price	8,000 + 34,000	42,000
Cost percentage of retail price	25,750 / 42,000	61%
Closing inventory	23,000 x 61%	14,030
Cost of sales	6,250 + 19,500 - 14,030	11,720

3.8.300.30 The example does not consider the impact of mark-ups or mark-downs on the selling price, which would add to the complexity of the calculation under the retail method.

3.8.310 *Base stock method*

3.8.310.10 The base stock method often is used in the hospitality industry, for example, by hotels and restaurants in accounting for linen or silver and glassware. Under the base stock method, the cost of initial purchases of equipment to be used in operations is recognised as inventory and carried unamortised as base stock. The cost of replacement items is expensed when they are acquired.

3.8.310.20 IFRSs do not specifically allow for the base stock method. In our view, the base stock method may be used for practical reasons if the result obtained approximates the result that would be obtained by applying IFRSs. This assessment should be reviewed regularly, in our view at least at each reporting date.

3.8.310.30 The treatment that should be applied under IFRSs depends on whether the equipment will be used for more than one period. If it will be used for more than one period, then it is property, plant and equipment, and should be recognised at cost and depreciated over its estimated useful life (see 3.2). Otherwise it is inventory. If it is inventory, then it should be measured at the lower of cost and net realisable value and items should be expensed as they are consumed (replaced).

3.8.315 *Minimum inventory levels*

IAS 2.24, 25, 3.8.315.10 Sometimes entities maintain minimum inventory levels. In our view, this does
BC15-19 not by itself justify a different cost formula for the minimum level of inventory compared with inventory above the minimum level. In our view, a different cost formula for the minimum inventory level may be acceptable if, and only if, it reflects the inventory flows in the entity.

3.8.320 *Consistency*

IAS 2.25 3.8.320.10 The same type of cost formula need not be used for all inventory. However, the same cost formula is applied to all inventories having a similar nature and use to the entity.

IAS 2.26 3.8.320.20 A difference in geographic locations does not, by itself, justify different cost formulas. However, raw materials used by one segment may have a different use from the same raw materials used in another segment and this may justify a different treatment.

3.8.320.30 For example, Company J purchases gold and refines it. Some of the refined gold is sold by the wholesale segment. The remainder is used by a segment that manufactures jewellery. The wholesale and jewellery segments may use different cost formulas to account for the refined gold.

3.8.320.40 A change in cost formulas is justified only if the change results in more meaningful information (see 2.8.30).

3.8.320.50 However, if an entity purchases inventory items that it did not have in a previous period, then a new method may be used for the new inventories if they have a different nature and use from other items of inventory.

3.8.330 **Net realisable value**

IAS 2.6 3.8.330.10 Net realisable value is the estimated selling price in the ordinary course of business less the estimated costs of completion and sale. The costs of sale include relevant marketing and distribution costs. Net realisable value is an entity-specific value.

3.8.335 *Write-downs of inventories and reversals of write-downs*

IAS 2.34 3.8.335.10 Any write-down of inventories to net realisable value is recognised as an expense in the period in which the write-down occurs.

IAS 2.33, 34   3.8.335.20 A previous write-down of inventories to net realisable value is reversed if the net realisable value subsequently increases. The amount of the reversal is limited to the amount of the original write-down such that the new carrying amount is the lower of cost and the revised net realisable value. Reversals of previous write-downs are recognised in profit or loss in the period in which the reversal occurs as a reduction in the amount of inventories recognised as an expense in the period. For example, at 31 December 2010 Company P writes down its inventory from a carrying amount of 100 to its net realisable value of 95. During 2011 the inventory is still on hand and its net realisable value increases to 103. P recognises a reversal of 5 such that the new carrying amount of the inventory is the lower of its cost of 100 and its net realisable value of 103.

3.8.340 *Groups of items*

IAS 2.29   3.8.340.10 Net realisable value write-downs normally are determined on an individual item basis. However, in some cases it may be appropriate to evaluate similar products in groups. That may be the case for items of inventory related to the same product line that have similar purposes or end uses, are produced and marketed in the same geographical area, and cannot be practicably evaluated separately from other items in that product line.

3.8.340.20 For example, in the clothing textile industry it may not be possible to determine selling prices for each textile individually, and therefore it may be necessary to perform the net realisable value assessment on all textiles that will be used to produce clothing for a particular season.

3.8.340.30 However, retailers generally should not determine net realisable value write-downs on the basis of whole department stores as different departments usually have different margins.

3.8.350 *Intended use*

IAS 2.31   3.8.350.10 The estimated selling price takes into account the intended use of the items.

3.8.350.20 For example, if an entity has excess inventories of materials that it will not be able to use in production and it has made the decision to sell the excess materials, then the net realisable value of the excess materials should be based on their anticipated sale.

IAS 2.32   3.8.350.25 When materials and other supplies are held for use in the production of inventories, net realisable value is based on the estimated selling price of the finished products in which they will be incorporated (less the estimated costs of completion and sale). Therefore, such materials and supplies are not written down below cost if the finished products in which they will be incorporated are expected to be sold at or above cost. If, on the other hand, an entity intends to sell materials in their current form rather than incorporate them into finished products, then net realisable value is based on the estimated selling price of the materials in their current form.

3.8.350.27 For example, Company P, a cabinet manufacturer, has raw material timber inventory on hand at 31 December 2010 with a carrying amount of 100. The current market value of that timber is 95. P intends to use the timber to manufacture cabinets. Therefore, the net realisable value is based on the completed cabinets and not on the timber in its raw material form. P estimates costs to completion and sale of 50 and a selling price for the cabinets of 160. P does not write down inventory at 31 December 2010 because the net realisable value of the timber of 110 (160 - 50) is higher than its carrying amount of 100. If, on the other hand, P intended to sell the timber in its current raw material form, then it would be written down by 5 plus the estimated costs of sale.

3.8.350.28 In another example, Company Q, a property developer, has undeveloped land inventory at 31 December 2010 with a carrying amount of 1,000. The current market value of that undeveloped land is 950. Q intends to develop houses on the land. In this case, the net realisable value of the land is based on the estimated selling prices of the completed houses less the estimated costs of completion and sale. Therefore, the land will not be written down at 31 December 2010 if Q estimates that the finished houses will be sold above cost. If, on the other hand, Q intended to sell the land in its current form, then it would be written down by 50 plus the estimated costs of sale.

3.8.350.30 Operating losses do not result in an automatic write-down of inventory. For example, Company T is a tractor producer. T also has a servicing division that is operating at a loss. T has some parts that will be used in the servicing business and others that will be used in the production of tractors. The net realisable value of the parts to be used in tractors should be evaluated separately from the net realisable value of the parts to be used in the servicing business. The losses in the servicing division may result in a write-down of the parts that will be used by that division, but not of those that will be used in production.

3.8.360 *Events after the reporting period*

IAS 2.30   3.8.360.10 Estimates of net realisable value take into consideration fluctuations in price or cost to the extent that they provide evidence of conditions existing at the end of the reporting period (see 2.9.20). Events after the end of the reporting period may provide evidence that the cost of inventory exceeds its net realisable value at the reporting date. In these cases the inventory is written down to its net realisable value at the reporting date. For example, the carrying amount of Company P's inventory at the end of its 31 December 2010 reporting period is 100. At that date P estimates that the net realisable value of the inventory is 110. Events in January 2011 provide evidence that the net realisable value of the inventory at 31 December 2010 was 95. Therefore, P writes down its inventory to 95 in its 31 December 2010 financial statements.

3.8.370 *Replacement cost*

3.8.370.10 Lower replacement costs do not lead automatically to a net realisable value write-down. However, a write-down would be recognised if the fall in prices means that the finished products will be sold for less than production cost.

3.8.380 *Changes in exchange rates*

3.8.380.10 Changes in exchange rates may require a net realisable value write-down.

3.8.380.20 For example, Company Z is a book dealer. On 1 December Z orders 20 books at a cost of foreign currency (AC) 110 each. The expected selling price of the books is functional currency (FC) 120. The exchange rate AC:FC on 1 December was 1:0.9. On 20 December when the books are received, the exchange rate is 1:1.5. Assuming that Z had not hedged the foreign exchange risk on its order, the recorded unit cost of the books would be FC 165, because the inventory is measured based on exchange rates at the purchase date. The anticipated selling price of FC 120 has not changed. Therefore Z should recognise a net realisable value write-down of FC 45 on each book, assuming no further costs of sale.

3.8.390 *Sales contracts*

3.8.390.05 The determination of net realisable value should take into account firm sales contracts that have been entered into. The net realisable value of inventory held to satisfy firm sales contracts is based on the selling price under those contracts. The net realisable value of inventory held in excess of firm sales contracts is based on general selling prices without regard to the firm sales contracts. For example, Company P has 100 units of inventory on hand at the end of its financial year recorded at a carrying amount of 10 per unit. The current market price is 8 per unit. P has a firm sales contract with Company Q to sell Q 60 units at 11 per unit, which cannot be settled net (see 3.6.90). When P is performing its net realisable value test the net realisable value of the 60 units that will be sold to Q is 11 per unit less estimated selling costs. The net realisable value of the remaining 40 units is 8 per unit less estimated selling costs. Therefore P will write down those 40 units by 80 (40 x 2) plus estimated selling costs.

3.8.390.07 In another example, Company E manufactures semi-finished copper and copper alloy products. E enters into forward contracts to manage its copper inventory level and those forward contracts fall within the scope of IAS 39 and should be accounted for under its guidance. In our view, the net realisable value of the inventory held to satisfy firm sales contracts should be based on the contract price including the fair value of the related sales commitment derivatives (see 3.6.90.30). However, the net realisable value of inventory held in excess of firm sales contracts should be based on the general selling prices without regard to the specific sales contracts.

IAS 2.31   3.8.390.10 When an entity has a contract to sell inventory for less than the cost of fulfilling the obligations under the contract, then the inventory held to satisfy that contract is written down by the amount that the cost of fulfilling the obligations exceeds the selling price. If that excess is greater than the carrying amount of the inventory, then an onerous contract provision is recognised (see 3.12.630).

3.8.400 *Service providers*

3.8.400.10 The inventory of service providers consists of the accumulated costs of providing services to clients.

IAS 18.20   3.8.400.20 The inventories of service providers are accounted for in accordance with the general principles for inventories as discussed in this chapter. Inventory is recognised as revenue as services are provided, either as a specific significant act is performed or on a percentage of completion method as appropriate (see 4.2).

3.8.400.30 For example, Company L is a law firm. L's inventory will include unbilled time at the reporting date in respect of contracts that include a significant act that has yet to be performed.

3.8.410 *Cost*

IAS 2.19   3.8.410.10 The cost of inventory of service providers includes all costs directly related to rendering the services including, for example, labour, materials and supplies. The portion of rental premises and other overhead costs that are directly related to the rendering of services also should be included in the cost of inventory. Service providers do not include a profit element or non-production costs in inventory.

3.8.410.20 Extending the example of the law firm in 3.8.400.30, assume that lawyers have spent 325 hours on a job. No revenues have been recognised in respect of this job because the percentage of completion method is not appropriate for the services provided. The anticipated average hourly billing rate on the job is 200. The average hourly cost price (based on the lawyers' salaries and other direct costs) is 80. L's inventory should reflect work in progress related to this job of 26,000 (325 x 80).

3.8.420 *Net realisable value*

IAS 2.29   3.8.420.10 In determining net realisable value, each service for which a separate selling price will be charged is assessed individually.

3.8.430 **Construction contracts**

3.8.430.10 See 4.2.230 for a discussion of construction contracts.

3.8.440 **Presentation and disclosure**

IAS 1.61,   3.8.440.10 Inventories are current assets. However, an entity discloses the amount of
66-68   inventories that are expected to be recovered after more than 12 months from the reporting date.

3.8.440.20 Advance payments made in respect of purchases of inventories are not classified as inventory. Generally, such payments are either a right to receive inventory or a refund of cash.

3.8.440.30 For agreements other than construction contracts (see 4.2.260.40), advance payments received from customers are not netted against inventories. Advance payments received are presented in the liability section of the statement of financial position, for example, as other liabilities.

IAS 2.36, 37   3.8.440.40 The carrying amount of each class of inventory is disclosed separately. Classes of inventories include raw materials, work in progress and finished goods. The inventories of a service provider normally are described as work in progress.

IAS 2.36(d), (e)   3.8.440.50 The amount of inventories recognised as an expense during the period and the amount of any write-down of inventories recognised as an expense is disclosed.

IAS 2.36, 39   3.8.440.60 If an entity chooses to allocate expenses by function, then the cost of inventories sold during the period is disclosed. If an entity chooses an allocation of expenses by nature, then the costs recognised as an expense for raw materials and consumables, labour costs and other costs together with the amount of the net change in inventories for the period are disclosed. See 4.1 for additional guidance on presentation in the statement of comprehensive income.

3.8.440.70 In our view, write-downs of inventory to net realisable value as well as any reversals of such write-downs should be presented in cost of sales.

IAS 2.36(f)   3.8.440.80 The amount of a reversal of a write-down to net realisable value is disclosed separately. A gain on the sale of inventory previously written down is viewed as evidence of an increase in net realisable value, triggering this disclosure requirement in the period of sale. For example, assume that inventory with an original cost of 100 was written down to its net realisable value of 80. In the following period that item is sold for 120. This gain is viewed as evidence of an increase in net realisable value at the subsequent reporting date; therefore a reversal of the write-down of 20 should be disclosed in the period in which the inventory is sold.

3.8.450 Future developments

3.8.450.10 In December 2007 the IASB activated a joint project with the FASB to address the accounting for emissions trading schemes. An ED is expected no earlier than the second half of 2011.

3.9 Biological assets
(IAS 41)

3.9 Biological assets

(IAS 41)

Overview of currently effective requirements

- Biological assets are measured at fair value less costs to sell unless it is not possible to measure fair value reliably, in which case they are measured at cost.

- All gains and losses from changes in fair value are recognised in profit or loss.

- Agricultural produce harvested from a biological asset is measured at fair value less costs to sell at the point of harvest.

Currently effective requirements

This publication reflects IFRSs in issue at 1 August 2010. The currently effective requirements cover annual periods beginning on 1 January 2010. The requirements related to this topic are derived mainly from IAS 41 *Agriculture*.

Forthcoming requirements and future developments

When a currently effective requirement will be changed by a new requirement that is issued but is not yet effective, it is marked with a # as a **forthcoming requirement** and the impact of the change is explained in the accompanying boxed text. In respect of this topic no forthcoming requirements are noted.

When a significant change to the currently effective or forthcoming requirements is expected, it is marked with a * as an area that may be subject to **future developments** and a brief outline of the relevant project is given in 3.9.120.

3.9.10 Definition and scope

IAS 41.5   3.9.10.10 Biological assets are living animals and plants. Biological assets fall within the scope of IAS 41 if they are transformed by a process of management (i.e. agricultural activity) and are capable of biological transformation into either agricultural produce (thereafter accounted for as inventory (see 3.8) or under other applicable IFRSs) or even into additional biological assets. Biological transformation comprises the processes of growth, degeneration, production and procreation that cause qualitative or quantitative change in a biological asset. IAS 41 applies, for example, to the following activities: raising livestock, forestry, growing annual or perennial crops, cultivating orchards and plantations, floriculture and aquaculture (fish farming).

3.9.10.20 Determining whether an asset is a biological asset or inventory sometimes depends on the purpose for which the asset is held. For example, fertilised eggs held for hatching chicks are biological assets, whereas eggs held for sale are inventory.

3.9.10.30 [Not used]

3.9.10.40 Animals or plants that are not subject to a process of management of biological transformation are not within the scope of IAS 41. Such management of biological transformation distinguishes agricultural activity from other activities. For example, Company P is a pet shop. P buys baby animals from breeders and then sells them. The pets are accounted for as inventory and not as biological assets because P does not manage the biological transformation of the animals.

3.9.10.45 Harvesting from unmanaged sources, such as in the case of ocean fishing and deforestation, is another activity that does not involve a process of management of biological transformation, and therefore is outside the scope of IAS 41.

3.9.10.50 Similarly, animals or plants that are used primarily in activities in which there is no management of biological transformation, such as recreational parks or game parks, are outside the scope of IAS 41. In another example, Company G owns horses that it trains and uses for racing. The racehorses are owned primarily for activities that do not involve biological transformation (i.e. racing) and therefore are not accounted for as biological assets. Instead, the horses should be recognised as assets and depreciated over their estimated useful lives applying the principles for property, plant and equipment (see 3.2.140). On the other hand, if G uses the racehorses primarily for breeding purposes, then those horses would be within the scope of IAS 41.

IAS 41.3 3.9.10.60 IAS 41 applies to agricultural produce only at the point of harvest. IAS 2 *Inventories* or other applicable IFRSs apply after the agricultural produce is harvested (see 3.9.100). The following table provides examples of biological assets, agricultural produce and products that are the result of processing after harvesting:

IAS 41.4

Biological assets	Agricultural produce	Products that are the result of processing after harvest
Sheep	Wool	Yarn, carpet
Trees in a plantation forest	Felled trees	Logs, lumber
Plants	Cotton	Thread, clothing
	Harvested cane	Sugar
Dairy cattle	Milk	Cheese
Pigs	Carcass	Sausages, cured hams
Bushes	Leaf	Tea, cured tobacco
Vines	Grapes	Wine
Fruit trees	Picked fruit	Processed fruit

IAS 41.B54 3.9.10.70 IAS 41 does not deal with the measurement of contracts for the future sale of biological assets or agricultural products. Such contracts may fall within the scope of IAS 39 *Financial Instruments: Recognition and Measurement* if the contract can be settled net in cash or by another financial instrument, as if the contract were a financial instrument (see 3.6.90). A contract that is not in the scope of IAS 39 may be an onerous contract, in which case a provision would be recognised in accordance with IAS 37 *Provisions, Contingent Liabilities and Contingent Assets* (see 3.12.630).

3.9.20 Recognition

IAS 41.10 3.9.20.10 Biological assets are recognised when the asset is controlled by the entity, its cost or fair value can be measured reliably and it is probable that future economic benefits associated with the asset will flow to the entity.

3.9.30 Measurement

IAS 41.12, 30 3.9.30.10 Biological assets are measured at fair value less costs to sell. The presumption that a biological asset can be measured at fair value less cost to sell can be rebutted only on initial recognition when market-determined prices or values are not available and alternative estimates of fair value are determined to be clearly unreliable (see 3.9.40 and 110.30). When the fair value of a biological asset cannot be determined reliably at the date of initial recognition, the asset is stated at cost less any accumulated depreciation and impairment losses (see 3.9.110.30). If fair value subsequently becomes reliably determinable, then the asset is measured at fair value less costs to sell.

IAS 41.31 3.9.30.20 Once a biological asset has been measured at fair value less costs to sell, it continues to be measured on that basis until disposal.

IAS 41.26-29 3.9.30.25 A gain may arise upon initial recognition of a biological asset, such as when a calf is born or on initial recognition of agricultural produce as a result of harvesting. Losses also may arise in such circumstances due to the deduction of costs to sell in determining fair value. Gains or losses arising on initial recognition are recognised in profit or loss in the period in which they arise.

IAS 41.26 3.9.30.30 Changes in fair value less costs to sell are recognised in profit or loss.

3.9.30.40 [Not used]

IFRS 5.5, 3.9.30.50 Biological assets measured at fair value less cost to sell are excluded from
IAS 41.30 the measurement scope of IFRS 5 *Non-current Assets Held for Sale and Discontinued Operations*. However, once a biological asset meets the criteria to be classified as held for sale, or is included in a disposal group that is classified as held for sale, in accordance with IFRS 5, it is presumed that fair value can be measured reliably.

3.9.40 *Cost model*

IAS 41.33 3.9.40.10 There is no specific guidance on determining cost for biological assets. The general guidance on determining cost, as described in 3.2.20 and 3.8.120, applies. The general depreciation and impairment considerations described in 3.2.140 and 3.10 also are relevant.

3.9.40.20 IAS 23 *Borrowing Costs* requires the capitalisation of certain borrowing costs as part of the cost of qualifying assets (see 4.6.350 – 360).

3.9.50 [Not used]

3.9.60 *Fair value model**

IAS 41.9, 17 3.9.60.10 If a market price in an active market is available for a biological asset in its present location and condition, then the market price is used as the basis for the fair value of the asset. The fair value of the asset is based on its present location and condition. The costs of transportation of the asset to market are deducted from the market price in order to determine fair value. If an entity has access to different active markets, then the entity uses the most relevant one.

IAS 41.17 3.9.60.20 Active markets normally exist for agricultural produce. For example, there are active markets for different grades of green leaf (from which tea is manufactured) and for coffee and cocoa beans.

IAS 41.18-21 3.9.60.30 If there is no active market, then an entity uses one or more of the following as a basis for measuring fair value:

- prices of recent market transactions
- market prices for similar assets
- sector benchmarks
- present value technique (3.9.60.50).

3.9.60.35 In using prices of recent market transactions, market prices for similar assets or sector benchmarks, these prices are adjusted to reflect differences in characteristics and/or stages of growth of the assets. These methods would be appropriate when there are recent transactions or when markets exist for similar assets. For example, Company V owns a vineyard in a top wine-growing region in Australia. There is no active market for vineyards in this part of Australia. However, another vineyard recently was sold in another wine-growing region in which V operates. V should use the price of the transaction, adjusted for significant differences in characteristics of the vineyards, to determine a fair value. The price of the transaction also should be allocated between the biological asset and any other assets (e.g. land, irrigation equipment etc.) in order to estimate the fair value of the biological asset itself.

IAS 41.16 3.9.60.40 Owners of biological assets may enter into contracts to sell forward the assets or related produce. These contracts may not provide evidence of current fair value, because the fair value should reflect the current market in which a willing buyer and seller would enter into a spot transaction to sell the assets. If there is such a contract, then the asset to be sold still is measured at fair value less costs to sell.

3.9.60.45 [Not used]

AS 41.20, 21   3.9.60.50 If market-determined prices or values are not available for a biological asset in its present condition, then the value is estimated by discounting expected net cash flows for the asset at a current market-determined rate. The objective is to measure the fair value of the biological asset in its present condition and location. In determining the present value of expected net cash flows, an entity includes the net cash flows that market participants would expect the asset to generate in its most relevant market. The fair value of a biological asset (i.e. the price a buyer is willing to pay) therefore may include not only the asset's harvest value, but also a value for potential additional biological transformation that a market participant would include. The potential for future additional biological transformation should be included by reflecting the related risks associated with the period until the cash flows occur. This will require a number of factors to be considered, for example:

- risks associated with the asset, such as weather and disease
- estimated yields
- estimated costs of bringing the asset to its intended condition.

IAS 41.23   3.9.60.60 These risks address the uncertainty related to future cash flows (i.e. the possibility of variations in cash flows) and should be reflected in either the discount rate or the estimate of expected cash flows, or some combination of the two.

3.9.60.70 In our view, when estimating the future selling price for the purposes of discounting expected net cash flows, current market conditions generally will provide the best evidence on which to base estimates. Alternatively, forward prices may be quoted, reliable statistical models may exist or annual price increases may have been set if the market is regulated.

IAS 41.22   3.9.60.75 When determining the fair value of a biological asset using the expected net cash flows, an entity does not include cash flows for financing the assets, taxation or re-establishing the biological assets after harvest.

3.9.60.80 The following example illustrates the application of the fair value measurement hierarchy: Company F farms salmon. At the reporting date the average weight of the salmon is 0.2 kg. The average weight of salmon when they are sold is 4 kg. It is expected that the salmon will be ready for sale three years after the reporting date. F expects to sell the salmon for 12 per kg. The per kg value of a 0.2 kg salmon is unlikely to be the same as that of a fully grown salmon. Therefore, it would not be correct to value the salmon at 2.4 each (12 x 0.2). Instead, in our view the salmon should be valued as follows:

- If there is an active market for salmon of 0.2 kg, then F should use the market price to value the salmon.

- If an active market does not exist, then F should consider recent market transactions to sell 0.2 kg salmon, market prices for similar fish, or sector benchmarks.
- If market-based prices are not available, then F should determine the present value of the expected net cash flows from the salmon. In this case F will need to estimate an appropriate discount rate, the number of salmon expected to reach maturity, the estimated selling price, the time to maturity and the anticipated costs of cultivating the salmon until they are sold. Effectively, the potential growth of the salmon should be included in this fair value measurement. The risk that may impact on the potential growth (e.g. sickness and death of salmon) should be included, either in the discount rate or in the estimate of expected cash flows.

3.9.60.85 If an entity uses expected net cash flows to determine the fair value less costs to sell of biological assets, then generally the calculations include a contributory asset charge in respect of assets that are owned by the entity and used in the agricultural activity. For example, Company X owns the land on which its agricultural activities are carried out; in determining the fair value less costs to sell of the related biological assets, X deducts an amount (contributory asset charge) that reflects a charge for usage of the land in the agricultural activities.

IAS 41.B33   3.9.60.86 When measuring fair value, there is no requirement under IAS 41 to involve an independent valuer.

IAS 41.30   3.9.60.90 If fair value cannot be estimated reliably, then the cost model is used instead. IAS 41 clarifies that fair value measurement is rebutted only if estimates of fair value are determined to be "clearly unreliable". In our view, clearly unreliable should be understood as a threshold of unacceptably high variance. For biological assets that have short transformation cycles, in most cases it will be possible to estimate reliably a fair value.

3.9.60.100 For example, if F (the salmon farmer in 3.9.60.80) estimates fair value using a discounted cash flow model, then it considers the main indicators that determine the biological transformation of immature salmon; for example, mortality, growth performance and feeding costs, as well as future expected market prices of salmon. These factors often are subject to a high volatility and as a result the statistical variance on the estimated fair value can be high. If based on statistical analyses F cannot estimate fair value reliably, then we believe that the use of cost model is justified.

3.9.60.110 In some cases, a biological asset is purchased and held until maturity for breeding purposes and no active market exists, for example, salmon may be purchased for breeding purposes. There is no active market because mature breeding salmon are rarely sold. If it is not possible to determine fair value reliably using a discounted cash flow model, then the cost model would apply.

IAS 41.24   3.9.60.120 In some circumstances cost may be similar to fair value. This may be the case when, for example, there has been little biological transformation since purchase at fair value and costs to sell are immaterial.

3.9.60.130 As mentioned above, biological assets are measured at their fair value based on their present location and condition. Under this approach, costs involved in developing biological assets are expensed as incurred. Essentially, the entity's profit for the period is the difference between the increase in fair value of the biological asset and the costs incurred in that period.

3.9.60.140 Future agricultural produce that is still attached to the biological assets is not recognised separately before harvest. Until harvest the future agricultural produce forms part of the biological asset and the fair value measurement is determined based on the asset as a whole (e.g. trees and fruit).

3.9.70 *Costs to sell*

IAS 41.5,
BC22 3.9.70.10 Costs to sell are incremental costs directly attributable to the disposal of an asset, excluding finance costs and income taxes. Transportation costs are not part of costs to sell (see 3.9.6.10).

3.9.80 *Groupings of assets*

IAS 41.15 3.9.80.10 In measuring fair value, assets may be grouped according to their significant attributes. In deciding on the appropriate attributes to use in determining the groupings, an entity considers the attributes used in the market as a basis for pricing. For example, livestock or fish may be grouped according to age or weight, crops may be grouped according to quality, and trees in a forest may be grouped according to age and type. For assets that are unique, for example horses held for breeding, each asset may need to be valued individually.

3.9.90 *Land*

IAS 41.25 3.9.90.10 Biological assets often are attached physically to land, e.g. trees in a forest, and it may be possible to value the land and the biological assets only as a package. However, the accounting treatment for land and biological assets differs. For example, the land may be carried at cost (see 3.2) while the trees represent biological assets and are measured at fair value less costs to sell. Therefore, the value of the package should be allocated. An entity uses information regarding the fair value of the land and the biological assets as a basis to determine the fair value of the biological assets. For example, in some cases it may be appropriate to deduct the fair value of the land from the fair value of the combined assets to arrive at the fair value of the biological assets.

3.9.95 **Government grants**

IAS 41.37 3.9.95.10 IAS 20 *Accounting for Government Grant and Disclosure of Government Assistance* applies to government grants related to biological assets to which the cost exemption applies (see 3.9.30.10 and 4.3.40.10).

IAS 41.34, 35   3.9.95.20 An unconditional government grant related to biological assets that are measured at fair value less costs to sell is recognised in profit or loss when it becomes receivable. However, if the government grant is conditional, then it is recognised in profit or loss only when the conditions are met.

IAS 41.36   3.9.95.30 For example, Company X receives 100 as a government grant under the condition that it grow and harvest fruit trees in a certain location for at the least the next ten years. If X ceases these activities at any time during the 10 years, then the full amount of the grant is repayable to the government. Accordingly, the 100 is deferred in the statement of financial position and will be recognised in profit or loss once the 10-year period has expired. If the facts were different and X became entitled to retain the grant on a *pro rata* basis as time passed, on a straight-line basis over the ten years, then X would recognise 10 in profit or loss as each year of activity is completed.

IAS 41.B66   3.9.95.40 IAS 41 is different from IAS 20 in order to avoid government grants related to biological assets measured at fair value less costs to sell being recognised in profit or loss immediately when conditions are attached. In such circumstances, if an entity were to deduct the government grant from the carrying amount of the asset, and subsequently measures the related biological asset at fair value, then in effect the government grant would be recognised in profit or loss immediately.

3.9.96 Leased assets

IAS 41.B82(n)   3.9.96.10 A lease of a biological asset is classified as a finance lease or operating lease under IAS 17 *Leases* (see 5.1.100). IAS 41 applies to the presentation and measurement of lease contracts of biological assets in the statement of financial position of the lessee (finance lease) or lessor (operating lease).

3.9.100 Agricultural produce

IAS 41.3, 13, 32   3.9.100.10 Agricultural produce, which is the harvested product of an entity's biological assets, is measured at fair value less costs to sell at the point of harvest. Normally market prices are available for agricultural produce. After harvest, agricultural produce is treated as inventory (see 3.8).

IAS 41.IN2   3.9.100.20 Some harvested produce may be subject to processing that may be a logical and natural extension of biological activity. For example, the processing of grapes into wine or making cheese from milk may include an element of biological transformation. However, these assets are subject to the principles of accounting for inventory, rather than the requirements for biological assets, as IAS 41 does not deal with processing of agricultural produce after harvest.

3.9.110 Presentation and disclosure

IAS 41.40-56   3.9.110.05 Detailed disclosures regarding biological assets are required by IAS 41. Examples of such disclosures are included in KPMG's series of illustrative financial

714

statements and include a reconciliation of changes in the carrying amount of the biological asset.

IAS 41.40   3.9.110.10 Although changes in the fair value of biological assets are disclosed separately, there are no specific requirements about where in the statement of comprehensive income they should be presented. In our view, the appropriate presentation depends on the relative significance of agricultural activities. If agricultural activities are part of the primary operations of the entity, then we believe that changes in the fair value of biological assets should be presented as revenue in a separate line item (see 4.1.80 and 4.2.10.30). Otherwise, fair value changes may be presented as part of other income and disclosed separately in the notes.

IAS 41.47   3.9.110.20 When biological assets are measured at fair value, details about the fair value measurement techniques and assumptions are disclosed.

AS 41.54, 55   3.9.110.30 When biological assets are measured at cost because fair value cannot be estimated reliably, detailed additional disclosures are required.

3.9.120 Future developments

3.9.120.10 In May 2009 the IASB published ED/2009/5 *Fair Value Measurement* (the 2009 ED). The proposals in the 2009 ED are intended to replace the fair value measurement guidance contained in individual IFRSs with a single, unified definition of fair value, as well as provide further authoritative guidance on the application of fair value measurement in inactive markets. The 2009 ED proposes a framework for measuring fair value and disclosures about fair value measurements. The proposals in the 2009 ED explain how to measure fair value when it already is required or permitted by existing IFRSs; they do not introduce new fair value measurements, nor do they eliminate the practicability exceptions to fair value measurements that exist currently in certain standards.

3.9.120.20 In June 2010 the IASB published ED/2010/7 *Measurement Uncertainty Analysis Disclosure for Fair Value Measurements* (the 2010 ED). The 2010 ED expands on the proposal in the 2009 ED for an entity to disclose a measurement uncertainty analysis (or sensitivity analysis) for assets and liabilities measured at fair value categorised within Level 3 of the fair value hierarchy. The 2010 ED proposes that an entity consider the effect of correlation between unobservable inputs, if relevant.

3.9.120.30 A final standard on fair value measurement and disclosure, which is expected to be converged with a forthcoming amended standard under US GAAP, is scheduled for the first quarter of 2011.

3.10 Impairment of non-financial assets
(IAS 36, IFRIC 10)

3.10 Impairment of non-financial assets
(IAS 36, IFRIC 10)

Overview of currently effective requirements

- IAS 36 covers the impairment of a variety of non-financial assets, including property, plant and equipment, intangible assets and goodwill; investment property and biological assets carried at cost less accumulated depreciation; and investments in subsidiaries, joint ventures and associates.

- Impairment testing is required when there is an indication of impairment.

- Annual impairment testing is required for goodwill and intangible assets that either are not yet available for use or have an indefinite useful life. This impairment test may be performed at any time during the year provided that it is performed at the same time each year.

- Goodwill is allocated to cash-generating units (CGUs) or groups of CGUs that are expected to benefit from the synergies of the business combination from which it arose. The allocation is based on the level at which goodwill is monitored internally, restricted by the size of the entity's operating segments.

- Whenever possible an impairment test is performed for an individual asset. Otherwise, assets are tested for impairment in CGUs. Goodwill always is tested for impairment at the level of a CGU or a group of CGUs.

- A CGU is the smallest group of assets that generates cash inflows from continuing use that are largely independent of the cash inflows of other assets or groups thereof.

- The carrying amount of goodwill is grossed up for impairment testing if the goodwill arose in a transaction in which non-controlling interests were initially measured based on their proportionate share of identifiable net assets.

- An impairment loss is recognised if an asset's or CGU's carrying amount exceeds the greater of its fair value less costs to sell and value in use, which is based on the net present value of future cash flows.

- Estimates of future cash flows used in the value in use calculation are specific to the entity, and need not be the same as those of market participants.

- **The discount rate used in the value in use calculation reflects the market's assessment of the risks specific to the asset or CGU.**

- **An impairment loss for a CGU is allocated first to any goodwill and then *pro rata* to other assets in the CGU.**

- **An impairment loss generally is recognised in profit or loss. However, an impairment loss on a revalued asset is recognised in other comprehensive income, and presented in the revaluation reserve within equity, to the extent that it reverses a previous revaluation surplus related to the same asset. Any excess is recognised in profit or loss.**

- **Reversals of impairment are recognised, other than for impairments of goodwill.**

- **A reversal of an impairment loss generally is recognised in profit or loss. However, a reversal of an impairment loss on a revalued asset is recognised in profit or loss only to the extent that it reverses a previous impairment loss recognised in profit or loss related to the same asset. Any excess is recognised in other comprehensive income and presented in the revaluation reserve.**

Currently effective requirements

This publication reflects IFRSs in issue at 1 August 2010. The currently effective requirements cover annual periods beginning on 1 January 2010. The requirements related to this topic are derived mainly from IAS 36 *Impairment of Assets* and IFRIC 10 *Interim Financial Reporting and Impairment*.

Forthcoming requirements and future developments

When a currently effective requirement will be changed by a new requirement that is issued but is not yet effective, it is marked with a # as a **forthcoming requirement** and the impact of the change is explained in the accompanying boxed text. In respect of this topic no forthcoming requirements are noted.

When a significant change to the currently effective or forthcoming requirements is expected, it is marked with a * as an area that may be subject to **future developments** and a brief outline of the relevant project is given in 3.10.610.

3.10.10 Steps in impairment testing

3.10.10.10 There are a number of steps in performing impairment testing, which are discussed in more detail throughout this chapter:

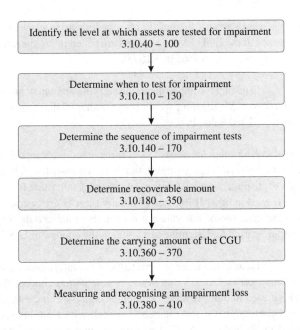

Identify the level at which assets are tested for impairment
3.10.40 – 100

Determine when to test for impairment
3.10.110 – 130

Determine the sequence of impairment tests
3.10.140 – 170

Determine recoverable amount
3.10.180 – 350

Determine the carrying amount of the CGU
3.10.360 – 370

Measuring and recognising an impairment loss
3.10.380 – 410

3.10.20 Scope

IAS 36.2-5   3.10.20.10 IAS 36 covers the impairment of all non-financial assets except for investment property that is measured at fair value (see 3.4); inventories (see 3.8); biological assets that are measured at fair value less estimated costs to sell (see 3.9); deferred tax assets (see 3.13); assets arising from construction contracts (see 4.2.230); assets arising from employee benefits (see 4.4); non-current assets (or disposal groups) classified as held for sale (see 5.4.20); and deferred acquisition costs and intangible assets arising from an insurer's contractual rights under insurance contracts (see 5.10). The standard does not cover financial assets (see 3.6) other than investments in subsidiaries, jointly controlled entities and associates.

IAS 36.3   3.10.20.20 The above assets are excluded from the scope of IAS 36 because other standards deal with their measurement. However, that does not mean that the assets are ignored entirely in the impairment testing process (see 3.10.360 – 370).

3.10.20.30 There is no scope exemption for assets that are not ready for use or sale, e.g. a building under construction (see 3.10.250.60).

3.10.30 Key definitions and objective

3.10.30.10 There are certain key definitions in IAS 36 that are used repeatedly in this chapter. Here we give a general description as an aid to understanding the concepts in IAS 36 as the chapter progresses.

IAS 36.6   3.10.30.20 A *cash-generating unit* (CGU) is the smallest group of assets that generates cash inflows from continuing use that are largely independent of the cash inflows of other assets or groups thereof. In our experience, in most cases impairment testing is performed at the CGU level, i.e. assets are tested in groups rather than on a stand-alone basis. CGUs are discussed in 3.10.60.

IAS 36.6 3.10.30.30 In testing for impairment, the carrying amount of an asset or CGU is compared to its *recoverable amount*, which is the higher of the asset's or CGU's fair value less costs to sell and value in use.

IAS 36.6 3.10.30.40 *Fair value less costs to sell* is the amount obtainable from the sale of an asset or CGU in an arm's length transaction between knowledgeable, willing parties, less the costs of disposal. In general, the definition of fair value is no different from how the term is used in other IFRSs and generally there is no "special" guidance in IAS 36 on the determination of fair value; however, there are certain restrictions on the method that can be used to determine fair value in the context of IAS 36 (see 3.10.190).

IAS 36.6 3.10.30.50 *Value in use* is the present value of the future cash flows expected to be derived from an asset or CGU. Value in use is a valuation concept that is specific to IAS 36 and not used in other IFRSs. It combines entity-specific estimates of future cash flows (from continuing use and eventual disposal) with a market participant-based discount rate. IAS 36 includes detailed rule-based requirements on the determination of value in use (see 3.10.220 – 350).

IAS 36.6 3.10.30.60 *Corporate assets* are assets other than goodwill that contribute to the future cash flows of both the CGU under review and other CGUs. IAS 36 includes specific requirements on how to test corporate assets for impairment because they benefit multiple CGUs. See 3.10.150 and 170 for a discussion of the general requirements related to corporate assets and 3.10.500 for application issues.

3.10.40 Identifying the level at which assets are tested for impairment

3.10.50 *Individual assets*

IAS 36.22, 3.10.50.10 Whenever possible IAS 36 is applied to the individual asset. However, a
66, 67 single asset generally is not tested for impairment on a stand-alone basis when it generates cash inflows only in combination with other assets as part of a larger CGU. There are exceptions to this basic rule, which are explored in 3.10.120.80 – 110.

3.10.50.20 In our experience, most single assets do not qualify to be tested alone, which means that most assets are tested for impairment in CGUs (see 3.10.120.60 – 100). An example of a single asset that might be tested individually is an investment property measured under the cost model (see 3.4.180).

3.10.60 *Cash-generating units*

IAS 36.68, 72 3.10.60.10 Assets are grouped together into the smallest group of assets that generates cash inflows from continuing use that are largely independent of the cash inflows of other assets or groups thereof (e.g. a plant or division of a larger entity). Such a group is known as a cash-generating unit (CGU). A CGU is identified consistently from period to period for the same asset or types of assets, unless a change is justified.

IAS 36.68, 69 3.10.60.20 The identification of CGUs requires judgement and can be one of the most difficult areas of impairment accounting. In identifying whether cash inflows from assets or CGUs are largely independent of the cash inflows from other assets or CGUs, various factors, including the manner in which management monitors operations and makes decisions about continuing or disposing of assets and/or operations, should be considered. However, the identification of independent cash inflows is the key consideration.

3.10.70 *Independent cash inflows*

IAS 36.68, 69, 3.10.70.10 When an individual operation generates cash inflows that are largely independ-
IE1-IE4 ent of other operations within a group, the operation is a separate CGU. This applies even if the operation is set up as part of an overall strategy within a region, for example based on management's objective of increasing overall market share or presence in the region. For example, in a retail store chain, the fact that stores have different customer bases (and therefore appear to be separate CGUs) is given more emphasis than the fact that the retail store chain is managed at a corporate level (implying that the stores form one CGU).

IU 03-07 3.10.70.20 In determining whether a group of assets is a CGU, in our view emphasis is placed on independent cash *in*flows, rather than net cash flows; therefore cash *out*flows are not relevant. For example, an individual store location with largely independent sales is a CGU. The fact that the store may share infrastructure, human resources, marketing and other operating expenses with other stores is not relevant in making this determination.

3.10.70.30 In assessing whether the cash inflows of an operation are generated largely independently, consideration is given to the extent to which revenues are generated through an operation's own customer base vs through referred business. In a multinational group that has significant referred sales, in our view cash inflows are independent, i.e. generated through the operation's own customer base, if individual units have at least some degree of autonomy to negotiate prices, quality and other features and to terminate contracts independently.

3.10.70.40 For example, Telecom T is a small subsidiary of a large telecom, catering to the residential customers in a particular region. It offers a "value-pack" to its customers, which is a bundle of three products and services: fixed line, broadband and television. Although customers can elect to purchase elements of the package, 75 percent of customers choose the value-pack. Accordingly, T concludes that its business as a whole comprises a single CGU since the cash inflows of each operation are not generated largely independently.

3.10.70.50 Changing the facts of the example in 3.10.70.40, only 45 percent of customers chooses the value-pack. In this case T concludes that it has three CGUs: fixed line, broadband and television.

IAS 36.IE1-
IE4 **3.10.70.60** In our view, if the recoverable amount of an operation is capable of being determined independently, for example because internal management reporting is organised to measure performance on an operation-by-operation basis (see 3.10.60), then normally that operation should be treated as a separate CGU. However, if various operations are interdependent, then in our view the interdependent operations together are likely to form a CGU, even if the recoverable amount of an operation is capable of being determined independently.

3.10.70.70 For example, Company P has been granted a contract by the government to provide services on a country-wide basis. P does not have discretion to choose the areas in which it will operate because the contract requires it to supply the entire country with services. Therefore, in our view all of the assets dedicated to the contract form a single CGU, even if cash flows are capable of being determined at a lower level (e.g. for each plant or region).

3.10.80 *Vertically integrated businesses*

3.10.80.10 In vertically integrated businesses (i.e. when one unit produces a product and transfers it to another unit within the same reporting entity for further processing or sale) an issue arises as to whether the business as a whole is a CGU, because the individual units do not generate cash inflows from outside the reporting entity.

IAS 36.70 **3.10.80.20** If an active market exists for the output from a group of assets, then that group of assets is a separate CGU, even if the output is sold only to other divisions of the same entity. This is because that group of assets *could* generate independent cash inflows.

3.10.90 **Corporate assets**

IAS 36.100,
101 **3.10.90.10** By definition (see 3.10.30.60), corporate assets contribute to the future cash inflows of two or more CGUs, without generating their own cash inflows that are largely independent. Therefore, a corporate asset is not tested for impairment as an individual asset on a stand-alone basis unless management has decided to dispose of the asset (see 3.10.50). Instead, IAS 36 includes specific requirements about how a corporate asset is tested for impairment as part of the testing of CGUs. See 3.10.150 for a discussion of the general requirements related to corporate assets and 3.10.500 for application issues.

IAS 36.100 **3.10.90.20** IAS 36 notes that examples of corporate assets include headquarter buildings, computer equipment and research centres. Other examples of corporate assets might be a warehouse shared by retail units, or plant and machinery shared by production lines. In practice such assets sometimes are referred to as "shared" rather than "corporate" assets, but they fall under the definition of a corporate asset in IAS 36 if they contribute to the cash flows of more than one CGU.

724

3.10.100 *Goodwill*

3.10.100.10 Similar to corporate assets, goodwill does not generate cash inflows independently of other assets or groups of assets and therefore is not tested for impairment separately. Instead, IAS 36 includes specific requirements about how goodwill is tested for impairment as part of the testing of CGUs. See 3.10.160 and 3.10.170 for a discussion of the general requirements related to goodwill and 3.10.450 for a discussion of application issues.

3.10.110 **Determining when to test for impairment**

IAS 36.9, 10   3.10.110.10 Impairment testing is required:

- at each reporting date for an asset or CGU when there is an indication of possible impairment (a triggering event); and
- annually for the following assets, regardless of whether there is a triggering event:
    - intangible assets with an indefinite useful life (see 3.3.200);
    - intangible assets not yet available for use; and
    - CGUs to which goodwill has been allocated (see 3.10.450).

IAS 36.10   3.10.110.20 The annual impairment test is required *in addition* to any impairment tests performed by the entity as a result of a triggering event.

3.10.120 *Indicator-based impairment testing*

IAS 36.9   3.10.120.10 An entity assesses at each reporting date whether there is an indication, based on either internal or external sources of information, that an asset or a CGU may be impaired.

3.10.120.20 The following are examples of internal indications of impairment that are considered in assessing whether indicator-based impairment testing is necessary:

IAS 36.12(e)
IAS 36.12(f)

- the obsolescence or physical damage of an asset;
- significant changes in the extent or manner in which an asset is (or is expected to be) used that have (or will have) an adverse effect on the entity;
- a plan to dispose of an asset before the previously expected date of disposal;

IAS 36.12(g)
IAS 36.14(a)
IAS 36.14(b)
AS 36.14(d)

- indications that the performance of an asset is, or will be, worse than expected;
- cash flows for acquiring the asset, operating or maintaining it are significantly higher than originally budgeted;
- net cash flows or operating profits are lower than originally budgeted; and
- net cash outflows or operating losses.

3.10.120.30 The following are examples of external indications of impairment that are considered in assessing whether indicator-based impairment testing is necessary:

IAS 36.12(a)

- a significant and unexpected decline in market value;

IAS 36.12(b) • significant adverse effects in the technological, market, economic or legal environment;

IAS 36.12(c) • an increase in market interest rates that will increase the discount rate used to determine an asset's value in use (see 3.10.300); and

IAS 36.12(d) • the carrying amount of the net assets of an entity exceeding its market capitalisation.

3.10.120.40 In our view, if the price paid to acquire non-controlling interests is less than the carrying amount of those interests in the consolidated financial statements, then this might be an indication that certain assets of the subsidiary are impaired. In such cases, we believe that the entity should consider whether any of the underlying assets are impaired prior to accounting for the change in ownership interests.

IAS 36.12, 16 3.10.120.50 The examples in 3.10.20 – 40 are indications of possible impairment that are considered in assessing whether impairment testing is required; they do not automatically lead to mandatory impairment testing. For example, an entity assesses whether the magnitude or effect of a change in interest rates or the gap between its net assets and market capitalisation requires the determination of recoverable amounts.

3.10.120.60 The nature of the indication of impairment and the nature of the asset determines the level at which impairment testing is carried out. For example, Company C's business comprises three CGUs, X, Y and Z. CGUs X and Y are profitable, but a downturn in the market for the product sold by CGU Z has resulted in operating losses for that CGU, which management concludes is an indication of possible impairment. Accordingly, C tests CGU Z for impairment, but does not test CGUs X and Y unless such testing is required because of the allocation of corporate assets (see 3.10.150) and/ or goodwill (see 3.10.160).

3.10.120.70 In another example, Company B is a listed multinational with various manufacturing operations. While all CGUs that make up the company continue to be profitable despite downward pressure on margins, the company's market capitalisation has fallen significantly below the carrying amount of B's recognised net assets. B is not able to identify a specific area of operations that is the driver for the fall in market capitalisation, and accordingly B concludes that all CGUs should be tested for impairment.

3.10.120.80 Another example illustrates the relationship between an indication of impairment of a single asset and the level at which impairment testing is carried out. Company Z comprises a single CGU engaged in the retail industry. Z acquired a new office building in 2008, from which it runs its operations. A property slump in the commercial building market causes Z to conclude that the carrying amount of the building may be impaired.

IAS 36.22, 3.10.120.90 Z performs the following analysis to determine the level at which the building
105 should be tested for impairment:

• Does the building generate cash inflows that are largely independent of those from other assets in the CGU? Answer: no.
• Is the building's fair value less costs to sell higher than its carrying amount?

- If the answer is yes, then no further testing is required. This is because an asset is not written down to below its known recoverable amount, and there is no further indication of impairment in this example.
- If the answer is no, then the next question is relevant.
- Can the building's value in use be estimated to be close to its fair value less costs to sell? Answer: no, because value in use cannot be determined for the building on its own. Accordingly, the building is tested for impairment as part of the CGU.

3.10.120.100 In a further example, Company Z has two CGUs, A and B, each of which operates under its own brand name. CGU B has been incurring losses and Z concludes that it should be tested for impairment. Within CGU B, the brand is the most significant asset and management is already aware from a recent preliminary report prepared by a valuation specialist that the fair value of the brand is lower than its carrying amount.

IAS 36.67   3.10.120.110 Having determined that the fair value of the brand (a single asset) is less than its carrying amount, Z concludes that the brand should *not* be tested for impairment as a stand-alone asset separate from the CGU as a whole (i.e. it should be tested for impairment as part of the CGU) based on the following analysis:

- Does the brand generate cash inflows that are largely independent of those from other assets in CGU B? Answer: no.
- Can the brand's value in use be estimated to be close to its fair value less costs to sell? Answer: no, because value in use cannot be determined for the brand on its own and there is no plan to sell the brand in the near future.

3.10.130 *Mandatory annual impairment testing*

IAS 36.10   3.10.130.10 Impairment testing is required annually for intangible assets with indefinite useful lives and intangible assets not yet available for use, irrespective of whether there is an indication that the related assets may be impaired, as well as whenever there is an indication that they may be impaired. Similarly, CGUs to which goodwill has been allocated are tested for impairment annually and whenever there is any indication of impairment.

IAS 36.10, 96   3.10.130.20 The annual impairment test for a CGU (or group of CGUs) to which goodwill has been allocated, intangible assets not yet available for use, and intangible assets with indefinite useful lives, may be performed at any time within an annual reporting period, provided that the test is performed at the same time every year. Different assets (and CGUs) can be tested for impairment at different times.

IAS 36.10   3.10.130.30 Intangible assets with an indefinite useful life or not yet available for use also are tested for impairment in the period in which they were recognised initially. For example, if in-process research and development (see 3.3.120.100) is acquired in April 2010 by a company with an annual reporting date of 31 December 2010, then the first impairment test is performed not later than 31 December 2010. See 3.10.480 for a discussion of the testing of goodwill for the first time.

3.10.140 **Determining the sequence of impairment tests**

3.10.140.10 The sequence of impairment tests becomes complicated when there are corporate assets or goodwill that relate to more than one CGU.

3.10.150 *Corporate assets*

IAS 36.102(a)   3.10.150.10 A portion of a corporate asset is allocated to a CGU when the allocation can be done on a "reasonable and consistent" basis.

IAS 36.102(b)   3.10.150.20 When a portion of a corporate asset cannot be allocated to a CGU on a reasonable and consistent basis, two levels of impairment tests are carried out:

- The first test is performed at the individual CGU level without the corporate asset (bottom-up test), and any impairment loss is recognised (see 3.10.380).
- The second test is applied to the minimum collection of CGUs to which the corporate asset can be allocated reasonably and consistently (top-down test).

3.10.150.30 For example, Company S and Company T both have two CGUs, A and B, and there is no goodwill attributable to any of the CGUs. Both CGUs in each company benefit from the use of an IT system (corporate asset) that is administered by their respective head offices. In each company there is an indication that CGU B is impaired:

- S concludes that a portion of the IT system can be allocated to CGU B's carrying amount on a reasonable and consistent basis. Accordingly, S carries out one impairment test: CGU B, including a portion of the IT system.
- T concludes that a portion of the IT system cannot be allocated to CGU B on a reasonable and consistent basis. Accordingly, T carries out two impairment tests:
  - CGU B, excluding any portion of the IT system from its carrying amount.
  - CGU A plus CGU B plus the IT system.

3.10.150.40 There is no guidance in IAS 36 as to what a *reasonable and consistent* basis means, and therefore judgement is required in this regard; depending on the nature of the asset, potential bases for allocation may include square metres occupied, headcount or transactions processed. However, in many cases it is likely that the basis of an inter-company charge will provide a reasonable and consistent basis for allocating a corporate asset to CGUs.

IAS 36.101   3.10.150.50 In some cases the indication of impairment may be specific to a corporate asset rather than to the CGUs to which the corporate asset relates. Continuing the example in 3.10.150.30, the IT system of S has become technically obsolete, but otherwise there is no indication of impairment in any of the CGUs in general. Because the corporate asset contributes exclusively to the cash flows of the S as a whole, S is identified as the relevant group of CGUs.

3.10.150.60 See 3.10.500 – 520 for specific guidance on determining value in use when there are corporate assets.

3.10.160 *Goodwill*

3.10.160.10 There are two scenarios in which goodwill is tested for impairment:

(1) a CGU or a group of CGUs to which goodwill has been allocated is being tested for impairment when there is an indication of possible impairment (see 3.10.120); or
(2) goodwill is being tested for impairment in the annual mandatory impairment testing, without there being an indication of impairment in the underlying CGUs.

IAS 36.97   3.10.160.20 In the first scenario in 3.10.160.10 (indicator-based impairment test), the way impairment testing is carried out depends on whether goodwill has been allocated to individual CGUs or to a group of CGUs. If goodwill has been allocated to a group of CGUs, then impairment testing is performed in the following steps:

- The first impairment test is performed at the individual CGU level without goodwill (bottom-up test), and any impairment loss is recognised (see 3.10.380).
- The second impairment test is applied to the collection of CGUs to which the goodwill relates (top-down test).

3.10.160.30 However, if the goodwill has been allocated to an individual CGU, then there is no need for a two-step approach and the entire CGU (including goodwill) is tested for impairment.

3.10.160.40 In the second scenario in 3.10.160.10 (annual impairment test), the collection of CGUs to which the goodwill relates is tested for impairment and there is no requirement for two-stage (bottom-up and top-down testing).

3.10.160.50 For example, Company P has determined that there is an indication of impairment in CGU R (carrying amount of 100). Goodwill (carrying amount of 50) relates not only to CGU R but also to two other CGUs, S and T (carrying amounts of 60 and 40, respectively). Company P performs impairment testing as follows:

(1) *Bottom-up test.* The carrying amount of CGU R is 100 and its recoverable amount is determined to be 80. An impairment loss of 20 is recognised.
(2) *Top-down test.* The carrying amount of CGU R + S + T, including goodwill, is 230 (80 + 60 + 40 + 50), i.e. the carrying amount of CGU R is after recognising the impairment loss in the bottom-up testing. This carrying amount is used in determining the impairment loss, if any, in the top-down test.

3.10.160.60 See 3.10.530 for discussion of the impairment testing of goodwill when there are non-controlling interests in a subsidiary.

3.10.170 *Corporate assets and goodwill*

3.10.170.10 Although IAS 36 has guidance on the testing of each of corporate assets (see 3.10.150) and goodwill (see 3.10.160), there is no guidance on how the testing interacts when there are corporate assets *and* goodwill present. In our view, the testing requirements overlap rather than being done in consecutive steps.

3.10.170.20 For example, Company Z allocates goodwill to the group of CGUs A, B and C. Z uses the same IT system (corporate asset) for all its CGUs, A, B, C and D. Management concludes that the corporate asset's carrying amount cannot be allocated to each CGU on a reasonable and consistent basis (see 3.10.150.20). There is an indication of impairment for CGU B.

3.10.170.30 Therefore, Z carries out impairment testing in the following sequence:

(1) CGU B is tested for impairment without goodwill and without any allocation of the corporate asset to its carrying amount.
(2) The group of CGUs A + B + C is tested for impairment with goodwill but without any allocation of the corporate asset to its carrying amount.
(3) The group of CGUs A + B + C and CGU D are tested together for impairment with goodwill and with the corporate asset included in its carrying amount.

3.10.170.40 If the facts in example 3.10.170.20 were different and Z concluded that it could allocate the corporate asset's carrying amount to CGUs on a reasonable and consistent basis, then Z would carry out impairment testing in the following sequence:

(1) CGU B would be tested for impairment without goodwill but with an allocation of the corporate asset included in its carrying amount.
(2) CGU A + B + C would be tested for impairment with goodwill and with an allocation of the corporate asset (an allocation relevant to all three CGUs) to its carrying amount.

3.10.170.50 The example in 3.10.170.20 – 40 illustrates the additional burden in impairment testing if corporate assets are not allocated to CGUs. See 3.10.450 for additional discussion of the allocation of goodwill to CGUs or groups of CGUs.

3.10.180 **Determining recoverable amount**

IAS 36.6 3.10.180.10 The recoverable amount of an asset or CGU is the higher of its fair value less costs to sell and value in use.

3.10.180.20 The purpose of impairment testing is to determine whether recoverable amount is greater than carrying amount. If it is greater (based on *either* fair value less costs to sell or value in use), then there is no requirement to refine the determination of recoverable amount to a single number. However, if it is not greater, then more detailed work is required to determine the number that is recoverable amount in order to calculate the impairment loss.

IAS 36.19-22 3.10.180.30 Therefore, it is not always necessary to determine both an asset's or CGU's fair value less costs to sell and value in use. For example, if fair value less costs to sell exceeds the carrying amount of an asset or a CGU, or if there is no reason to believe that the asset's or CGU's value in use materially exceeds its fair value less costs to sell, then it is not necessary to calculate value in use. However, if it is not possible to determine fair value less costs to sell because there is no basis for making a reliable estimate of fair value, then value in use is used as the recoverable amount.

IAS 36.105   3.10.180.40 Notwithstanding these general requirements, if the impairment testing of another asset, e.g. goodwill, causes the CGU to be tested for impairment, then all assets within that CGU are included in the impairment test. However, in allocating any impairment loss an individual asset is not written down to below its known recoverable amount (see 3.10.410).

IAS 36.23   3.10.180.50 As acknowledged in IAS 36, in some cases forms of short-cut testing may be appropriate. Therefore, in estimating recoverable amount conservative assumptions (i.e. assumptions that would understate recoverable amount) can be used initially. Only if the resulting recoverable amount is less than the carrying amount of the asset or CGU will it be necessary to refine the assumptions, either to show that recoverable amount does exceed carrying amount or to calculate an actual recoverable amount in order to determine the impairment loss.

AS 36.BC69, BC70   3.10.180.60 Sometimes a CGU (with or without goodwill) that has been acquired recently is tested for impairment. In these situations the consideration paid to acquire that CGU in an arm's length transaction, adjusted for disposal costs and any changes in value arising from factors since acquisition, may provide the best evidence of the CGU's fair value less costs to sell (and therefore the recoverable amount if value in use is lower). Consequently, in our view impairment losses on recently acquired CGUs should occur infrequently in practice.

IAS 10.3, 8, 10   3.10.180.70 Market conditions that arise after the reporting date should be considered to determine whether they are an adjusting or non-adjusting event (see 2.9). If the post-reporting date market conditions are a change that could not reasonably have been foreseen at the reporting date, then it follows that the cash flow projections used in the impairment test should not be adjusted; this applies to cash flow projections used in determining either fair value less costs to sell or value in use. However, the entity should consider whether disclosure would be appropriate in accordance with IAS 10 *Events after the Reporting Period*. While the inability to forecast significant unforeseen changes in market conditions does not call into question the reasonableness of prior forecasts, such conditions should be considered in the forecasts in future impairment testing.

AS 36.24, 99   3.10.180.80 For the impairment testing of goodwill and intangible assets with indefinite useful lives, an entity may use the most recent determination of recoverable amounts (made in a preceding reporting period), provided that the following criteria are met:

- the assets and liabilities making up the CGU (when the asset is tested as part of a CGU) have not changed significantly since the last determination of recoverable amount;
- the last determination of recoverable amount resulted in the asset's or CGU's carrying amount being exceeded by a substantial margin; and
- management assesses, based on an analysis of the facts and circumstances, that the likelihood of an impairment loss is remote.

3.10.190 Fair value less costs to sell*

IAS 36.25 3.10.190.10 A binding sale agreement in an arm's length transaction provides the best evidence of fair value.

IAS 36.26 3.10.190.20 If there is no binding sale agreement but there is an active market for the asset, then the current market bid price provides the best evidence of fair value.

IAS 36.27, 3.10.190.30 If there is no binding sale agreement and no active market, then the fair value
BC69 is determined based on the best information available to reflect the amount that an entity could obtain at the reporting date from the disposal of the asset in an arm's length transaction between knowledgeable, willing parties. The fair value also reflects the market assessment of expected net benefits to be derived from restructuring the unit or from future capital expenditure. Recent transactions for similar assets in the same industry are considered in determining fair value.

3.10.190.40 In our experience, the most common technique used in determining fair value less costs to sell is discounted cash flows. In that case the assumptions used in determining fair value are consistent with those that a market participant would make (see 2.6.1040.60) and the special rules in IAS 36 for estimating the cash flows used in a value in use calculation are not applicable. For example, in determining value in use there are strict criteria as to when a restructuring may be taken into account (see 3.10.260); in determining fair value, a restructuring would be taken into account to the extent that a market participant acquiring the CGU would restructure.

IAS 36.BC 3.10.190.50 Depreciated replacement cost is not used to estimate the recoverable
Z29 amount of an asset because it does not consider the future economic benefits recoverable from its use and/or disposal.

IFRS 3.B45 3.10.190.60 In our view, in determining the fair value less costs to sell of a listed subsidiary that constitutes a CGU, a control premium may be taken into account since the quoted market price is for a minority interest in the CGU. Fair value less costs to sell assumes a hypothetical sales transaction to a market participant (see 2.6.1040.60). We believe that the unit of account in determining fair value less costs to sell under IAS 36 is the CGU rather than the individual security. Therefore, the addition of a control premium to the market price may be appropriate because the purpose of the impairment test is to assess the recoverability of the carrying amount of the CGU as a whole. The fair value less costs to sell element of the recoverable amount of a CGU reflects what a market participant would pay to acquire control of the CGU. This is consistent with the inclusion of a control premium in determining the fair value of a controlling stake in a business in accordance with IFRS 3 *Business Combinations*.

3.10.190.70 In understanding the reasons for a control premium arising, theoretically the value of an asset or CGU is the present value of the expected future benefits, measured by discounting expected future cash flows at a discount rate that reflects the time value of money and the risks associated with the cash flows. On that basis, an acquirer may value a business above its market capitalisation and be willing to pay a price that reflects a control premium if it believes that it can create value by increasing cash flows and/or reducing risk. There are three broad ways in which this may be achieved:

- An acquirer may believe that it can change the stand-alone cash flows of the business through better management. In our experience, it is uncommon for management to assert that a new owner would be able to better manage the stand-alone operations of the business.
- An acquirer may believe that as a controlling shareholder it would have a lower risk, and therefore a lower required rate of return than a minority shareholder in a public company. In our experience, this is likely to be less important in markets with strong corporate governance and minority shareholder protections.
- An acquirer may expect to create synergies through combining the acquired business with existing operations to increase the aggregate cash flow of the combining units. In our experience, typically this factor is the most significant factor contributing to the existence of a control premium.

3.10.190.80 The amount of a control premium is best corroborated by specific, comparable and current transactions in the entity's industry. The factors giving rise to such premiums in industry transactions are considered and their potential existence in a hypothetical acquisition of the CGU being tested for impairment assessed. For example, control premiums in industry transactions may reflect specific synergies that were anticipated to be available to the combining entities based on the nature of their operations, including the degree of overlap therein, anticipated tax benefits from the transaction etc. These benefits might not be available to a market participant acquirer of the CGU and therefore would not be included in the fair value less costs to sell. If there is no (or limited) current market activity to support the amount of the control premium, then historical transactions may need to be considered. However, control premiums based on arbitrary "rule of thumb" percentages or an amount selected in order to avoid an impairment loss are not appropriate. Changes in control premiums from prior periods should be supported by objective evidence.

3.10.200 *Costs to sell*

IAS 36.6, 28   3.10.200.10 Costs to sell are *incremental* costs directly attributable to the disposal of an asset. These costs include, for example, legal costs necessary to effect the sale, transaction taxes and other costs to prepare the asset or CGU for its sale. Finance costs and income tax expense are excluded, as are costs recognised already as a liability.

3.10.210 *Reasonableness tests of fair value less costs to sell*

3.10.210.10 When the recoverable amount of a CGU is determined on the basis of fair value less costs to sell and substantial parts of an entity are tested for impairment, a high-level comparison between market capitalisation and the recoverable amount generally is performed. In our view, in that case it may be appropriate to add a control premium to market capitalisation in performing the comparison (see 3.10.190.60 – 80). This approach differs from that when recoverable amount is based on value in use (see 3.10.220).

3.10.210.20 Earnings multiples resulting from the fair value less costs to sell calculation also can be compared to market multiples for the entity and comparable quoted companies to check for reasonableness. Comparable transactions also may provide some support. Multiples to consider include price/earnings (P/E) ratios, as well as EBIT and EBITDA multiples (see 3.10.350.30).

3.10.210.30 For example, the value in use of CGU X is estimated to be 100. In arriving at this estimate, some of the assumptions include current EBITDA of 8, terminal year EBITDA of 15 and a terminal value of 170. These figures can be used to calculate implied earnings multiples that can be compared to market multiples for reasonableness:

Implied current Enterprise Value/EBITDA multiple (100 / 8):	12.5
Implied terminal Enterprise Value/EBITDA multiple (170 / 15):	11.3
Market multiples of Enterprise Value/EBITDA:	5 – 7

3.10.210.40 The difference between the implied and market multiples suggests that the value in use estimate is inconsistent with market pricing because the implied multiples are significantly higher than those of comparable businesses. Such differences may be justified in terms of lower risk, higher growth rates etc. between the CGU and comparable entities. However, this might also indicate that the value in use estimate may be too high. For example, there may be increased uncertainty about the achievement of forecast growth, which may need to be reflected, for example, through the addition of a forecasting risk premium in the discount rate (see 3.10.300.170).

3.10.220 Value in use

3.10.220.10 Value in use is the present value of the future cash flows expected to be derived from an asset or CGU, both from its continuing use and ultimate disposal.

IAS 36.30   3.10.220.20 The determination of an asset's value in use reflects considerations such as:

(1) the estimated future cash flows that the entity expects the asset to earn;
(2) possible variations in the amount or timing of those future cash flows;

(3) the time value of money, which is reflected by using a discount rate that reflects the current market risk-free rate of interest;

(4) the price for the uncertainty inherent in the asset; and

(5) other factors, such as illiquidity, that would be reflected in valuing the expected future cash flows from the asset.

IAS 36.32   3.10.220.30 The second, fourth and fifth of these elements can be reflected either as adjustments to the future cash flows or as adjustments to the discount rate.

IAS 36.   3.10.220.40 Appendix A of IAS 36 discusses two approaches to projecting cash flows in
A4-A15   order to calculate present value:

- the traditional approach, which uses a single cash flow projection, or most likely cash flow; and
- the expected cash flow approach, which uses multiple, probability-weighted cash flow projections.

3.10.220.50 Whichever approach an entity adopts for measuring the value in use of an asset, interest rates used to discount cash flows should not reflect risks for which the estimated cash flows have been adjusted. Otherwise, the effect of some assumptions will be double counted.

3.10.220.60 The traditional approach does not involve adjustments to the cash flows relative to their risk, given that the single most likely cash flow projection is used; therefore, all adjustments for risk are considered as part of determining an appropriate discount rate. The discount rate used in the traditional approach is considered to be "the rate commensurate with the risk" inherent in the cash flows.

3.10.220.70 In contrast, the expected cash flow approach uses a range of different outcomes (cash flows) and the estimated probability associated with each outcome to address some of the risk inherent in the projection of future cash flows. Since some risk assessment is incorporated into the cash flows, the discount rate used under an expected cash flow approach typically is lower than under a traditional approach because a portion of the risk is captured through the probability-weighting of all expected future outcomes (cash flows). However, in our view even under the expected cash flow approach not all risk is incorporated into the cash flows, and therefore it would not be appropriate to use a risk-free discount rate.

3.10.220.80 In order to justify the use of a risk-free rate, the cash flows would need to be certain ("certainty-equivalent" cash flows) so that the investor (i.e. market participant) is indifferent between investing in the cash flows of the asset or CGU and investing in risk-free investments. In our view, while it is theoretically possible that cash flows could be adjusted to incorporate all relevant risks to ensure that the investor was indifferent, the practical application of this approach would be very difficult for a CGU with operating cash inflows and outflows. Therefore, risk should be incorporated into the discount rate in the value in use calculation and while there are judgements required, we do not believe that it is practically feasible to determine certainty-equivalent cash flows.

3.10.230 *Forecast period*

IAS 36.33, 35   3.10.230.10 The value in use calculation is based on reasonable and supportable assumptions concerning projections of cash flows approved by management (as part of the budget) and adjusted to the requirements of IFRSs. These cash flow forecasts should cover a maximum of five years unless a longer period can be justified. The cash flows after the forecast period are extrapolated into the future over the useful life of the asset or CGU using a steady or declining growth rate that is consistent with that of the product, industry or country, unless there is clear evidence to suggest another basis; these cash flows form the basis of what is referred to as the terminal value.

3.10.230.20 When economies enter a difficult period, in our view it may be necessary to determine the terminal value in two stages in order to reflect the impact of economic contraction and a subsequent return to maintainable earnings:

- In the first stage growth rates (potentially on a year-by-year basis) are applied to take the cash flows to a level at which they can be regarded as reflecting maintainable earnings and to the period in a mid-point of the cycle (i.e. not at the peak or trough of the cycle).

IAS 36.33(c) - The second stage is an extrapolation of those maintainable earnings until the end of the asset's life. In accordance with IAS 36 this growth rate should not exceed the long-term average growth rate appropriate to the asset or CGU unless a higher rate can be justified.

3.10.230.30 For example, a company has detailed forecasts for the next two years. It envisages recessionary conditions continuing for the year after that (the third year), with a slow recovery in the fourth and fifth years; the projection for the third to fifth years reflects that assumption (first stage). Believing that the position expected at the end of the fifth year represents the stable long-term position, those cash flows are extrapolated into the future using a steady growth rate (second stage).

IAS 36.34   3.10.230.40 In order to assess the reasonableness and supportability of the assumptions underlying current cash flow projections, management analyses the causes of differences between past cash flow projections and actual cash flows. Management also should ensure that changes in circumstances are reflected in its most current projections. This includes considering whether the effects of subsequent events or circumstances that did not exist when those actual cash flows were generated make the current projections inappropriate without adjustment.

3.10.230.50 In our view, the final year of management projections should be used to extrapolate cash flows into the future only if the final year represents a steady state in the development of the business. If a steady state has not been reached, then we believe that adjustments are necessary to reflect the expected development of the business. Using an average of the projections over the forecast period would be misleading if the estimated cash flows are increasing or decreasing over the forecast period. For a CGU that is in the start-up phase, cash flow projections should reflect realistic assumptions regarding revenue growth.

736

IAS 36.49 3.10.230.60 If a CGU consists of several assets that are essential to the ongoing business, then the impairment test is determined based on the essential asset with the longest useful life, and the replacement of assets with shorter lives is considered to be part of the day-to-day servicing of that CGU. For example, if a CGU includes a specialised factory that has a 50-year useful life and machinery with a 10-year useful life, then the cash flow projections are based on the 50-year useful life of the factory.

3.10.230.70 In some cases a CGU may contain an intangible asset with an indefinite useful life or goodwill. In our view, an entity cannot conclude automatically that the intangible asset with an indefinite useful life or goodwill is the essential asset. All facts and circumstances are considered to determine which asset is essential to the operations of the CGU. In our view, in the case of a service business, it is likely that intangible assets with indefinite useful lives or acquired goodwill will be the assets with the longest useful life that are essential to the ongoing operations of the CGU. However, in the case of a nuclear power plant, we believe that it is likely that the plant itself, which has a finite life, will be the asset essential to its ongoing operations.

3.10.230.80 After analysing all relevant facts and circumstances, if it is determined that an intangible asset with an indefinite useful life or allocated goodwill is essential to the ongoing operations of the CGU, then cash flow projections should be prepared for an indefinite period. In our view, entities could, as an approximation, project cash flows for a limited period and then estimate a terminal value at the end of the projection period; the limited period is subject to the rebuttable five-year maximum forecast period (see 3.10.230.10).

3.10.230.90 In our view, an essential asset need not be an asset recognised in the statement of financial position. For example, depending on the facts and circumstances of the CGU, it might be appropriate to conclude that a right to use land and other properties under a long-term operating lease, or an unrecognised brand, is the essential asset.

3.10.240 *Composition of cash flows*

3.10.240.10 The cash flows used in the determination of value in use are those specific to the entity.

AS 36.39, 41 3.10.240.20 Cash flows include cash inflows from continuing use, cash outflows necessary to generate the cash inflows (including overheads that can be attributed directly or allocated on a reasonable and consistent basis to the use of the asset), and net cash flows from the ultimate disposal of the asset or CGU. Particular care is required when considering the cash flows related to corporate assets (see 3.10.500 – 520).

IAS 36.39, 3.10.240.30 The net cash flow from the disposal of an asset at the end of its useful life is
52, 53 the amount that an entity expects to obtain from the disposal in an arm's length transaction after deducting the estimated costs of disposal. An entity uses current prices at the date of the estimate for similar assets that have reached the end of their useful life and have been used in conditions similar to those in which the asset will be used. These prices are adjusted for the effect of future price increases or decreases specific to the

asset. If the effect of inflation is not taken into consideration in estimating those prices, then the discount rate also does not take into consideration the effect of inflation.

IAS 36.42   3.10.240.40 In our view, in the case of an asset or CGU that is in the start-up phase, the cash flow projections should reflect outflows to be incurred in making the asset or CGU fully operational.

IAS 36.43, 78   3.10.240.50 Estimates of future cash flows do not include cash outflows that will be required to settle obligations that have been recognised as liabilities in the carrying amount of the CGU, e.g. provisions (see 3.12) or liabilities for post-employment benefits (see 4.4). For example, decommissioning costs should not be included in the determination of value in use if a provision for these costs is recognised, unless the recognised provision is included as part of the CGU being tested for impairment. Similarly, inflows from assets that generate inflows that largely are independent of the cash inflows from the asset or CGU under review (e.g. surplus property) should not be included; the carrying amount of such assets also should be excluded from the carrying amount of the CGU.

IAS 36.50, 51   3.10.240.60 Cash flows exclude those arising from financing activities and tax (but see 3.10.310).

3.10.240.70 In some cases an entity may wish to determine cash flows based on historic or projected net profits for the asset or CGU. However, net profits generally do not equate to net cash flows. Therefore, in our view this approach may be acceptable only if the net profit is adjusted to exclude the effects of non-cash items (including depreciation, amortisation, and accounting revaluations), and to include gross cash flows from the ultimate disposal of the asset or CGU and other cash flows that are not recognised as income or expenses in the respective future periods of the cash flow forecast, e.g. the replacement of assets with shorter useful lives in a CGU, or the replacement of the components of an asset with shorter useful lives.

3.10.250 *Capital expenditure*

IAS 36.44, 47   3.10.250.10 Cash flow estimates reflect the asset in its current condition. Therefore, they exclude future capital expenditure that will improve or enhance the asset's performance, or restructurings to which the entity is not yet committed and the related benefits (see 3.12.230).

IAS 36.48   3.10.250.20 The benefits from capital expenditure to improve or enhance an asset's performance are taken into account in the future net cash flow estimation only once the expenditure is incurred. In our view, capital expenditure is considered incurred once the project has substantively commenced, rather than it being necessary for the project to have been completed.

3.10.250.30 For example, Company S commences a capital expenditure project related to CGU A in 2010, which is forecasted to take three years to complete at a cost of 80. Once the project is completed, CGU A expects its annual cash inflows to increase by 35. At the end of 2010, costs of 20 have been incurred and capitalised, i.e. the project is

25 percent complete based on a cost measure. In determining the cash flow forecasts for the value in use calculation, management includes the benefit of the additional annual cash inflows of 35 resulting from completion of the project as the project has substantively commenced. The cash flow forecast also includes the remaining cash outflows of 60 to complete the project.

IAS 36.49 3.10.250.40 However, capital expenditure necessary to maintain the performance of an asset and maintenance expenditure are taken into account when estimating the future net cash flows, and therefore are treated like day-to-day servicing costs. If a CGU consists of assets with different useful lives, all of which are essential to the ongoing operation of the unit, then the replacement of assets and components with shorter lives is considered to be part of the day-to-day servicing of the unit when estimating the cash flows of the CGU.

3.10.250.50 For example, a company has a CGU that includes a factory with a useful life of 30 years and some equipment with a useful life of 10 years. The roof of the factory requires replacement after 15 years. If the factory is the essential asset of the CGU that determines the forecast period (see 3.10.230.60 – 90), then the maintenance of an asset or components of assets with shorter useful lives (e.g. the equipment and the roof) is considered to be part of the day-to-day servicing of the CGU.

IAS 36.42 3.10.250.60 When an asset that is not in use requires future expenditure to prepare it for use (e.g. a building under construction), these expected cash outflows are incorporated into the estimated cash flows when performing impairment testing.

3.10.260 *Restructuring*

3.10.260.10 For accounting purposes, an entity is committed to a restructuring only when it meets the criteria to recognise a restructuring provision (see 3.12.230).

IAS 36.46, 47 3.10.260.20 Typically management includes planned cash flows related to a restructuring in its internal budgets and forecasts. For the purposes of impairment testing, budgets are adjusted to exclude these amounts until the entity is committed to the restructuring.

3.10.270 *Relocation costs*

3.10.270.10 Relocation costs are not included in any restructuring provision recognised because they relate to the ongoing activities of the entity (see 3.12.330). However, in our view if assets that will be relocated are tested for impairment, then the relocation costs should be included in the estimation of future cash outflows.

3.10.280 *Transfer pricing*

IAS 36.70 3.10.280.10 If the cash inflows generated by an asset or CGU are affected by internal transfer pricing, then an entity uses management's best estimate of future prices that could be achieved in arm's length transactions, rather than internal transfer prices (if different), in estimating the future cash inflows used to determine the asset's or CGU's value in use; and the future cash outflows used to determine the value in use of other assets or CGUs affected by the internal transfer pricing.

IAS 24.17   3.10.280.20 If the two CGUs are in separate legal entities, then in our view the actual transaction price should be used when determining the value in use and calculating any impairment loss for the purposes of the separate or individual financial statements (see 2.1.60 and 70) of the individual entities. If such transactions take place, then IFRSs require related party disclosures in the separate or individual financial statements, including their nature and amounts (see 5.5).

3.10.290 *Foreign currency cash flows*

IAS 36.54   3.10.290.10 When an asset or a CGU generates cash flows in a foreign currency, those cash flows are estimated in the foreign currency and discounted using a discount rate appropriate for the currency in which the cash flows are generated.

IAS 21.25   3.10.290.20 When an asset being tested for impairment is non-monetary and is measured in a foreign currency, the following are compared: (1) the carrying amount in the functional currency (see 2.7.30), determined in accordance with IAS 21 *The Effects of Changes in Foreign Exchange Rates* (see 2.7.110); and (2) the recoverable amount determined in the foreign currency and translated into the functional currency at the exchange rate when the recoverable amount is determined.

3.10.290.30 The recoverable amount of a foreign operation, and any resulting impairment loss, is calculated in the functional currency of the foreign operation. This is consistent with the principle that the functional currency is the currency in which the transactions of an entity are *measured*. An impairment loss arises only if the recoverable amount in the functional currency of the foreign operation is less than its carrying amount in the functional currency. Any impairment loss determined in the functional currency then is translated into the presentation currency, which is the currency in which transactions are presented to users of the financial statements. To the extent that a decline in the recoverable amount of a CGU that is a foreign operation is due only to changes in the exchange rate from the functional currency of the foreign operation to the presentation currency of the group, this decline is recognised in the translation reserve in equity as a consequence of applying the requirements of IAS 21 (see 2.7.230).

3.10.290.40 For example, Group D's presentation currency is US dollars. D has an investment in Associate C whose functional currency is the euro. At the reporting date management of D determines that the carrying amount of its investment in C may be impaired (see 3.10.580). The fair value less costs to sell of C is lower than its carrying amount, and therefore value in use is calculated. The value in use of C is calculated entirely in euro, and then is translated into US dollars at the reporting date.

3.10.300 *Discount rate*

IAS 36.55,   3.10.300.10 In determining value in use, projected future cash flows are discounted us-
A15, BCZ53   ing a pre-tax discount rate that reflects current market assessments of the time value

of money and the risks specific to the asset or CGU. The discount rate is based on the return that investors would require if they were to choose an investment that would generate cash flows of amounts, timing and risk profile equivalent to those of the asset or CGU. In other words, the discount rate is based on a market participant's view of the asset or CGU as at the current date. Therefore, while the cash flows in the value in use calculation are entity-specific, the discount rate is not.

IAS 36.A17,   3.10.300.20 In our experience, it is rare that a discount rate can be observed directly from
A18   the market. Therefore, generally it will be necessary to build up a market participant discount rate that appropriately reflects the risks associated with the cash flows of the CGU being valued. In the absence of a discount rate that can be observed directly from the market, IAS 36 refers to other starting points in determining an appropriate discount rate: the entity's weighted average cost of capital (WACC), the entity's incremental borrowing rate, and other market borrowing rates.

3.10.300.30 In practice the most common approach is to estimate an appropriate rate using the WACC formula. Because a CGU-related rate is required, it is unlikely that the WACC of the entity as a whole can be used without adjustment. However, it may provide a useful reference point when determining the components of the appropriate WACC for the CGU. Adjustments to the entity's WACC should be made with the objective of developing a market participant discount rate.

3.10.300.40 WACC, which is a post-tax discount rate (see 3.10.310), incorporates the market's view of how an entity would structure its financing using both debt and equity, with each having a different rate of return. The formula for WACC is as follows:

$$WACC = \left(\frac{E}{K} \times r_e\right) + \left(\frac{D}{K} \times b\,(1 - t)\right)$$

E	=	fair value of equity as a component of total capital
D	=	fair value of debt as a component of total capital
K	=	$D + E$ = total capital
r_e	=	cost of equity (see 3.10.300.60)
b	=	cost of debt; the rate at which the entity could obtain financing for its operations, before any effects of interest reducing taxable income
t	=	corporate tax rate; used to reduce the debt rate to a post-tax rate as debt typically results in a reduction in taxable income

3.10.300.50 The relative weights of debt and equity in a WACC calculation are based on the fair value rather than the carrying amount of debt and equity. In addition, the weights generally are based on the estimated optimal long-term capital structure and therefore the entity's actual debt/equity ratio is not determinative in the calculation.

3.10.300.60 In determining the cost of equity as an input to the determination of WACC, it is common to use the capital asset pricing model (CAPM), which estimates the cost of equity by adding risk premiums to the risk-free rate. The formula for the CAPM is as follows:

$$r_e = r_f + \beta \times (r_m - r_f) + a$$

r_e = cost of equity

r_f = risk-free rate

β = beta, which is a measure of the correlation between a share's return in relation to the market return (or the return of a fully-diversified portfolio of investments)

$(r_m - r_f)$ = market return less the risk-free rate or the equity risk premium. This risk premium reflects systematic or market risk, i.e. the overall risk premium of a fully-diversified portfolio of investments above the risk-free rate

α = alpha, or unsystematic (entity-specific) risk premium

IAS 36.A19 3.10.300.70 The gearing (i.e. the proportion of asset or CGU financing that is funded by debt) and the cost of debt used in the WACC for the purpose of determining value in use are not entity-specific. IAS 36 notes that the discount rate should be independent of the entity's capital structure and the way in which the entity financed the acquisition of the asset or CGU. Therefore, the gearing and cost of debt are those that the market participant would expect in relation to the asset or CGU being tested for impairment. In other words, the actual funding of the asset or CGU, which often will include intra-group debt, is not relevant in determining gearing for the purposes of the market participant's WACC. Instead, the WACC for the value in use calculation is based on the cost and amount of debt of a market participant investing in the cash flows of the asset or CGU.

3.10.300.80 The cost of debt is based on long-term rates being incurred at the date of valuation for new borrowings, rather than the rates negotiated historically in the debt market for existing borrowings. The determination of appropriate rates includes consideration of the entity's incremental borrowing rate.

3.10.300.90 A key assumption underpinning WACC is a constant level of gearing throughout the cash flow period, including in the terminal value. If this assumption does not apply, then it will be necessary to calculate WACC separately each year using different gearing levels as applicable, or to use alternative methods.

3.10.300.100 In considering gearing and the cost of debt, the following are possible sources of information, none of which is likely to be determinative in isolation:

- the cost of debt incurred by the entity at present, taking into account any need to refinance, as a proxy for the cost of debt of a market participant;
- the current market borrowings of comparable entities, considering both levels of debt and interest rates;
- recent industry acquisitions and refinancing; and
- information available from the entity's bank or other financial advisors.

3.10.300.110 The components of the cost of equity are defined in the CAPM formula (see 3.10.300.40, which also shows how they are used in the determination of WACC). The discussion in 3.10.300.120 – 170 describes each component.

3.10.300.120 The *risk-free rate* generally is obtained from the yield on government bonds that are in the same currency and that have the same or a similar duration as the cash flows of the asset or CGU, often leading to 10- or 20-year government bonds being considered. Typically this information is readily available within a country, e.g. in newspapers, but the best sources for this data should be considered on a country-by-country basis.

3.10.300.130 Consideration should be given to whether the government bond yield selected represents a risk-free rate. For example, in a currency area that uses a common currency, zero coupon bonds from the government in the currency area with the lowest yield should be used as these are a better measure of the risk-free rate than bonds issued by other governments in the same currency with a higher yield, reflecting greater default risk. Similarly, when questions arise about the credit-worthiness of government bonds, credit default swap pricing on reference instruments in the same currency issued by the same government as the bonds from which the rate is derived may give an indication of default risk and may suggest that the government bonds do not reflect a risk-free rate. Consideration also should be given to the liquidity of the bonds used to estimate the risk-free rate.

3.10.300.140 *Beta factors* reflect the risk of a particular sector or industry relative to the market as a whole, and are a long-term rather than a short-term measure. Beta typically is calculated for individual listed companies using a regression analysis against an appropriate share index. When developing the cost of equity from a market participant's perspective, the selected beta generally is based on comparable companies' betas, even if the subject entity is a listed company.

3.10.300.150 Careful consideration is given to the period over which the beta is measured because any significant market volatility may have distorted the beta. In our experience, typically betas measured by reference to two-year or five-year historical data are used, with the five-year beta typically being favoured in volatile markets.

3.10.300.160 *Equity risk premium* is a measure of the long-term required rate of return on equities above the risk-free rate, and therefore should not be impacted significantly by short-term volatility. Various studies of equity risk premium based on historical data are available and these give a range of results depending on the exact period of the data included in the study and the method of calculation.

3.10.300.170 *The alpha factor* represents an asset- or CGU-specific risk premium, and may need to be added to the cost of equity when a CGU is determined to carry additional risk that may not be reflected in the beta, i.e. risk that cannot be attributed to market risk. An alpha factor may include some or all of the following elements:

- *Size risk.* An additional premium that takes into account that smaller businesses are more risky than larger organisations. Size premiums generally are based on long-term information that is not impacted significantly by short-term volatility.

- *Financing risk.* An additional premium that takes into account the difficulty of funding working capital or maintainable capital expenditure in the short to medium term, based on the market's view of the asset or CGU rather than the entity's specific financing.
- *Country risk.* An additional premium that takes into account the additional risk associated with generating and incurring cash flows in a particular country. In some cases country risk is incorporated into the equity risk premium and care should be taken to avoid double counting.
- *Forecasting risk.* An additional premium that takes into account the additional risk associated with achieving forecasts. In practice the need for such an additional risk factor often is identified when the value in use calculation is cross-checked to other indications of value (see 3.10.350).
- *Illiquidity risk.* An additional premium that takes into account the difficulty of being able to sell an investment.

3.10.310 **Pre- or post-tax**

IAS 36.50(b), 55 3.10.310.10 IAS 36 *prima facie* requires value in use to be determined using pre-tax cash flows and a pre-tax discount rate. However, in practice it is more common to use post-tax cash flows and a post-tax discount rate such as WACC (see 3.10.300.40). Challenges arise in following a post-tax approach appropriately so that the resulting value in use is consistent with the pre-tax principle.

IAS 36.130, A20, BCZ85 3.10.310.20 The pre-tax discount rate normally is not the post-tax rate grossed up by the standard tax rate. Differences arise because of the timing of future tax cash flows and discrepancies between the cost of an asset and its tax base. Therefore, it is possible to estimate reliably a pre-tax discount rate using a post-tax rate as a starting point only if information about post-tax cash flows is available. Adjusting projections of cash flows to a post-tax basis requires the allocation of tax cash flows to CGUs (as the actual tax return normally is calculated on the basis of legal entities) and the timing of tax cash flows to be determined. Additional adjustments may be required in some circumstances. Post-tax cash flows cannot be determined by applying the tax rate to the pre-tax cash flows. Whichever rate is used (pre- or post-tax), the pre-tax discount rate needs to be disclosed. An iterative method may be used to calculate the pre-tax rate from post-tax calculations.

3.10.310.30 In the following simplified example, the effect of discounting is ignored and it is assumed that deferred taxes are recognised in respect of all temporary differences:

Carrying amount of asset before impairment	500
Tax base of asset	400
Tax rate	30%
Deferred tax liability before impairment (100 x 30%)	(30)
Estimated future pre-tax net cash flows from use of asset	300

3.10.310.40 Based on this information, value in use is calculated as follows:

Future pre-tax net cash flows from use of asset	300
Less income tax on those cash flows at tax rate (300 x 30%)	(90)
Plus tax amortisation benefits (TAB) on VIU (VIU x 30%)	to be determined
= VIU	to be determined

3.10.310.50 In order to calculate the VIU, including the tax amortisation benefits, the following two equations are resolved simultaneously:

I:	TAB = 30% x VIU
II:	VIU = 300 - 90 + TAB

3.10.310.60 If equation II is inserted into equation I, the resulting TAB amounts to 90 and therefore VIU is 300:

TAB = 30% x (300 - 90 + TAB)
TAB = 63 + 30% TAB
70% TAB = 63
TAB = 63 / 70% = 90

3.10.310.70 Consequently, there is an impairment loss of 200 (500 - 300) to be recognised. The post-impairment carrying amount of the asset is 300 and assuming that the tax base of 400 remains unchanged, a deferred tax asset of 30 ((400 - 300) x 30%) is recognised. The resulting statement of financial position figures both before and after the impairment test are as follows:

	Before	*After*
Asset's carrying amount	500	300
Deferred tax asset (liability)	(30)	30
	470	330

3.10.310.80 If in 3.10.310.40 the actual tax base of 400 had been used to determine a tax amortisation benefit of 120 (400 x 30%), then part of this tax amortisation benefit would have been double counted as it also would have been taken into account when determining the resulting deferred tax asset.

3.10.310.90 This is a simplified example that ignores discounting. In practice the calculation is more complex as it involves discounting in determining the value in use while deferred taxes are not on a discounted basis in accordance with IAS 12 *Income Taxes*.

3.10.320 *Tax losses*

3.10.320.10 In our view, the best approach to ensuring that tax losses carried forward at the date of the impairment test do not distort the determination of value in use is to exclude them from both the carrying amount of the CGU and the cash flow forecasts. Instead, tax losses are accounted for in accordance with IAS 12 (see 3.13.210). This approach avoids the potential for double counting the tax: once in the deferred tax asset and again in the value in use calculation. This approach also avoids the potential for a measurement mismatch because the cash flows in the value in use are discounted, whereas any asset related to tax losses is not.

3.10.320.20 However, when unrecognised deferred tax assets related to tax losses are subsumed within goodwill in a business combination (see 2.6.660.10), the future tax benefit that was recognised in goodwill should be excluded from the carrying amount of the CGU when testing for impairment.

3.10.330 *Tonnage tax*

3.10.330.10 Some entities, e.g. shipping companies, may elect to be taxed based on tonnage capacity, in which case they are not subject to income tax. Tonnage tax is outside the scope of IAS 12 as this is not based on taxable profits (see 3.13.10.55). Therefore, in our view the cash flows in a value in use calculation should be determined net of the tonnage tax cash outflows.

3.10.340 *Inflation*

IAS 36.40   3.10.340.10 The cash flows and the discount rate applied to them should be determined on a consistent basis. If the cash flows include the effect of general inflation (i.e. they are expressed in nominal terms), then the discount rate also should include the effects of inflation. Conversely, if the cash flows exclude the effects of inflation, then the discount rate also should exclude the effects of inflation.

3.10.350 *Reasonableness tests of value in use*

IAS 36.33   3.10.350.10 Having calculated value in use, in our experience it is important to perform a sensitivity analysis on key cash flow assumptions, terminal value growth rates and the discount rate generally. In addition to sensitivity analysis, cross-checking to possible external evidence also provides support for the reasonableness of the discount rate and the cash flows used in determining value in use.

3.10.350.20 When the recoverable amount of a CGU is determined on the basis of value in use and substantial parts of an entity are tested for impairment, a high-level comparison between market capitalisation, adjusted for the market value of debt and any surplus assets, and the total value in use for all CGUs provides some support that the assumptions and discount rate used are appropriate for the cash flows. In doing this comparison, in our view a control premium should not be added to the market price since a value in use calculation incorporates all existing entity-specific synergies that are realisable for the use of the CGUs together. The addition of a control premium would assume a hypothetical acquisition, which is inconsistent with the concept of value in use. This approach differs from that when recoverable amount is based on fair value less costs to sell (see 3.10.210).

There may be circumstances in which it is supportable that an entity's value in use estimates exceed its debt-adjusted its market capitalisation. However, as an entity's market capitalisation can be viewed as the equity market's estimate of the value of the entity's operations, differences should be carefully considered. When such differences exist, an entity should carefully assess the reasonableness of the assumptions in its value in use calculations.

3.10.350.30 Earnings multiples implicit in the value in use calculation also can be compared to market multiples for the entity and comparable quoted companies to check for reasonableness. Comparable transactions also may provide some support that the assumptions and discount rate used are appropriate for the cash flows. Multiples to consider include P/E ratios, as well as EBIT and EBITDA multiples. See 3.10.210.30 – 40 for an example.

3.10.360 Determining the carrying amount of the CGU

IAS 36.6, 75, 78, 79   3.10.360.10 The carrying amount of a CGU should be determined in a way that is consistent with how the recoverable amount of the CGU is determined. For example, if the cash flow projections include outflows in respect of recognised liabilities, or inflows in respect of assets that generate cash flows independently, then the carrying amount of the CGU that is used to determine the impairment loss should include the related assets and liabilities.

3.10.370 *Working capital*

3.10.370.10 In our view, it is acceptable to include cash flows resulting from the realisation of working capital balances in cash flow projections and in the carrying amount of the CGU, even when such assets are excluded from the scope of IAS 36 (see 3.10.20). If realised in the short-term and the effects of discounting are not material, then in our view the working capital need not be discounted.

IAS 36.75   3.10.370.20 Alternatively, the cash flow projections may be adjusted to exclude the realisation of working capital balances. In this case the carrying amount of the CGU also should exclude working capital. However, even if working capital balances are not included in the carrying amount of a CGU, working capital cash flows related to amounts arising after the valuation date need to be reflected in the valuation analysis. Therefore, the cash flows related to the changes in working capital would be the assumed gross build-up in working capital.

3.10.370.30 For example, if working capital balances are included in the carrying amount of the CGU as net current assets of 100, then the cash flow movement in working capital in year 1 would be the net change in working capital levels over the assumed working capital of 100. Accordingly, if the working capital at the end of year 1 is 120, then the cash flows for year 1 include a cash outflow of 20. In a contrasting example, if the working capital balances of 100 are not included in the carrying amount of the CGU, then the cash flows shown in the impairment analysis for year 1 are an assumed gross build-up in working capital, meaning a cash outflow of 120.

3.10.370.40 These examples illustrate that the inclusion or exclusion of opening working capital balances will have limited or no effect on whether an asset's value in use exceeds its carrying amount, e.g. the benefit of a lower carrying amount from excluding working capital is offset by increased cash outflows or, if the alternative approach is followed, then the effect of including working capital is offset by lower cash outflows. The cash flows for future periods in both cases will include subsequent working capital movements.

3.10.380 Measuring and recognising an impairment loss

IAS 36.6, 59 3.10.380.10 An impairment loss is recognised to the extent that the carrying amount of an asset or CGU exceeds its recoverable amount.

IAS 36.60 3.10.380.20 Impairment losses generally are recognised in profit or loss unless the asset is carried at a revalued amount (see 3.10.390).

3.10.380.30 In our view, after an entity has tested an asset for impairment, it should consider whether changes are required to the useful life, depreciation method and residual value of the asset. Any such changes are accounted for prospectively as a change in accounting estimate (see 3.2.140.20 and 3.2.150.40).

3.10.390 *Revalued assets*

IAS 36.5 3.10.390.10 Property, plant and equipment and intangible assets that are measured at a revalued amount (see 3.2.300 and 3.3.280) first are revalued applying the principles in the relevant standard. Any impairment loss is calculated on the basis of the resulting carrying amount. As the recoverable amount used in impairment testing is the higher of the asset's fair value less costs to sell and its value in use, any impairment loss to be recognised generally would be limited to the costs to sell when fair value is determined on the basis of market values. However, when fair value is determined by reference to depreciated replacement cost, a subsequent impairment loss might arise (see 3.2.340).

IAS 36.60 3.10.390.20 Any impairment loss is recognised in other comprehensive income and presented in the revaluation reserve within equity, to the extent that it reverses a previous revaluation surplus related to the same asset.

3.10.400 *Foreign operations*

IAS 21.49 3.10.400.10 Impairment losses related to foreign operations are calculated based on the carrying amounts of the assets in the consolidated financial statements. When an entity prepares separate financial statements (see 2.1.70), the impairment loss is calculated based on the carrying amounts in the separate financial statements. No part of the accumulated translation gain or loss that is recognised in the foreign currency translation reserve in equity is transferred to profit or loss at the time of an impairment loss. The translation gain or loss remains in equity until disposal of the foreign operation (see 2.7.320).

3.10.410 *Allocation of impairment losses*

IAS 36.104-
108 3.10.410.10 Any impairment loss is allocated first by writing down the goodwill that is allocated to the CGU (if any) and then *pro rata*, based on the respective carrying amounts, against the CGU's other assets (including intangible assets) that are within the scope of IAS 36. However, no asset is written down to below its recoverable amount (if determinable) or zero; therefore, an entity should determine the recoverable amount of any of the individual assets or lower level CGU in the CGU being tested, if possible. Any excess impairment loss in respect of an asset is allocated *pro rata* to the other assets in the CGU to the extent possible. A liability is recognised for any unallocated impairment loss only if it is required by another standard.

3.10.410.20 See 3.10.530 for a discussion of the allocation of impairment losses related to goodwill when there are non-controlling interests in a subsidiary.

3.10.420 **Reversal of impairment**

IAS 36.110 3.10.420.10 At each reporting date an entity assesses whether there is an indication that a previously recognised impairment loss has reversed. If there is such an indication and the recoverable amount of the impaired asset or CGU subsequently increases, then the impairment loss generally is reversed.

IAS 36.116 3.10.420.20 An impairment loss is not reversed when the increase in recoverable amount is caused only by the unwinding of the discount used in determining the value in use.

IAS 36.122,
124,
IFRIC 10.8 3.10.420.30 An impairment loss recognised for goodwill is not reversed in subsequent periods, even if it was recognised in an interim period of the same financial year. Apart from this requirement, when testing a CGU for a reversal of an impairment loss, the allocation of the amount to be reversed follows the same principles as for the allocation of an impairment loss (see 3.10.410).

IAS 36.117,
123 3.10.420.40 In all cases the maximum amount of the reversal is the lower of (1) the amount necessary to bring the carrying amount of the asset to its recoverable amount; and (2) the amount necessary to restore the assets of the CGU to their pre-impairment carrying amounts less subsequent depreciation or amortisation that would have been recognised.

IAS 36.119 3.10.420.50 A reversal of an impairment loss for an asset generally is recognised in profit or loss. A reversal of an impairment loss on a revalued asset is recognised in profit or loss to the extent that it reverses an impairment loss on the same asset that was recognised previously as an expense in profit or loss. Any additional increase in the carrying amount of the asset is treated as a revaluation increase.

3.10.430 **Presentation**

IAS 36.126 3.10.430.10 IAS 36 does not specify the line item in profit or loss in which an impairment loss should be recognised, but does require disclosure of the line items in which impairment losses are included.

3.10.430.20 If an entity classifies expenses based on their function (see 4.1.30), then any loss is allocated to the appropriate function. In our view, in the rare case that an impairment loss cannot be allocated to a function, then it should be included in other expenses as a separate line item if significant, e.g. impairment of goodwill, (see 4.1.30.10), with additional information given in a note.

3.10.430.30 In our view, an impairment loss that is recognised in published interim financial statements should be presented in the same line item in the annual financial statements, even if the asset subsequently is sold and the gain or loss on disposal is included in a line item different from impairment losses in the annual financial statements.

3.10.440 Specific application issues

3.10.450 *Allocating goodwill to CGUs*

3.10.450.10 The guidance in 3.10.160 discusses the impairment testing of goodwill. However, prior to the actual impairment testing, it is necessary to understand how goodwill is allocated to CGUs or groups of CGUs and how that allocation may change over time.

3.10.460 *Level at which to allocate goodwill*

IAS 36.80-84 3.10.460.10 Each unit or group of units to which goodwill is allocated should:

- represent the lowest level within the entity for which information about goodwill is available and monitored for internal management purposes; and
- not be larger than an operating segment, determined in accordance with IFRS 8 *Operating Segments* before applying the aggregation criteria of IFRS 8 (see 5.2.50).

3.10.460.20 Prior to annual periods beginning on or after 1 January 2010, IAS 36 was not clear as to whether the operating segments referred to were before or after applying the aggregation criteria in IFRS 8. The clarification in IAS 36 was made as part of the *Improvements to IFRSs 2009* (see 1.1.85) to be applied prospectively.

3.10.460.30 In our view, an entity that changes its accounting policy as a result of the amendment has the following choices in applying the amendment prospectively:

- perform impairment testing as of the date of adoption of the amendment (e.g. on 1 January 2010 for an entity with an annual reporting date of 31 December), and recognise any impairment loss in profit or loss; or
- apply the amendment the next time that impairment testing is carried out in accordance with the requirements of IAS 36 (i.e. in the next annual impairment test of goodwill, or at an earlier reporting date when there is an indication of impairment).

3.10.460.40 The allocation test related to operating segments in IFRS 8 applies regardless of whether the entity is required to present segment information (see 5.2.10).

3.10.460.50 To avoid the need to develop additional reporting systems to support goodwill impairment testing, goodwill is allocated to the lowest level at which it is monitored for internal management purposes. However, this does not mean that entities can avoid testing goodwill at a level lower than an operating segment by simply not monitoring goodwill explicitly.

3.10.460.60 For example, Company Z has three operating segments under IFRS 8, each with two product-oriented sub-units. Z believes that the goodwill acquired reflects the synergies created in four of its six sub-units. However, these sub-units do not include goodwill in their internal performance reports to senior management. Instead, the target internal rate of return on the net assets of the sub-units (which do not include goodwill) was increased by senior management after the acquisition. These targets have been set to generate a desirable return on investment to shareholders. Although goodwill is not included explicitly in the management information delivered by the sub-units' management, in order to generate the expected return on investment, senior management takes into account goodwill by allocating it to the four sub-units. Consequently, in our view goodwill should be allocated to the four sub-units as it is monitored by management indirectly.

3.10.470 *Method of allocating goodwill to CGUs*

IAS 36.80   3.10.470.10 Goodwill arising in a business combination is allocated to the acquirer's CGUs that are expected to benefit from the synergies of the business combination in which goodwill arose. This is irrespective of whether other assets or liabilities of the acquiree are assigned to those units.

3.10.470.20 For example, Company M is a producer of specialised electronic equipment. It acquires one of its main competitors, Company N, which operates in another geographical area. As part of its acquisition strategy M gradually will shift N's customers onto M's products. M does not plan to support N's brand or product lines. In the absence of any factors to the contrary, in our view M will allocate the majority of goodwill acquired to its existing CGUs that are expected to benefit from the acquisition of N's customers and the related synergies.

3.10.470.30 In our view, the allocation of goodwill should take into account not only the expected synergies, but also the goodwill of the acquiree on a stand-alone basis ("core" goodwill).

3.10.470.40 For example, Company P acquires Company S for 100, having estimated the stand-alone value of S to be 80. P expects to realise potential synergies from the transaction with two of its existing CGUs, C and D. Assuming that S comprises a single CGU and has identifiable net assets of 60, we believe that of the 40 of goodwill (100 - 60), 20 should be allocated to S in respect of its stand-alone goodwill absent the acquisition (80 - 60), with the remaining goodwill of 20 related to synergies between S and CGUs C and D.

3.10.470.50 The pre-acquisition analysis of the acquirer may be useful in allocating the goodwill to CGUs. This analysis may indicate the drivers behind the synergies that are expected to arise from the acquisition, e.g. incremental profits arising from cost savings such as reduced administration costs and/or revenue synergies such as cross-selling opportunities, the deployment of a skilled workforce or access to new markets.

3.10.470.60 IAS 36 does not prescribe any specific method of allocating goodwill to CGUs. If the pre-acquisition analysis did not identify where synergies were expected to arise, another allocation method might be to use a "with or without" calculation, i.e. based on the difference between the fair value of a CGU before and after the acquisition. Continuing the example in 3.10.470.40, goodwill would then be allocated to each CGU based on the difference between the fair value of each of S, CGU C and CGU D before the acquisition and after the acquisition.

3.10.480 *Impact of the measurement period on the allocation of goodwill*

IFRS 3.45   3.10.480.10 In accordance with IFRS 3, an entity is allowed up to a maximum of one year from the acquisition date to finalise the acquisition accounting, and thereby determine the amount of goodwill (see 2.6.930); until that time, the acquisition accounting is regarded as "provisional".

IAS 36.84,   3.10.480.20 When goodwill allocated to a CGU arose in a business combination in the
85, 96, 133   reporting period, then that goodwill is tested for impairment before the end of that reporting period. However, when the acquisition accounting can be determined only provisionally, it also may not be possible to complete the allocation of goodwill to CGUs before the end of the annual period in which the business combination occurred. In such cases an entity discloses the amount of unallocated goodwill, together with the reason for not allocating the goodwill to CGUs. However, the allocation of goodwill to CGUs should be completed before the end of the first annual reporting period beginning after the acquisition date.

3.10.480.30 Judgement may be required when the allocation process is not yet complete, but there is an indication of impairment in a CGU to which goodwill is expected to be allocated. In that case it may be appropriate to test the goodwill for impairment based on a provisional allocation.

3.10.480.40 For example, Company P acquires Company S on September 2010. P is not able to complete the allocation of goodwill to CGUs before the end of the annual period in which the business combination occurred, 31 December 2010, because the acquisition accounting is not yet complete. In that case the allocation of goodwill to CGUs should be completed before 31 December 2011.

3.10.490 *Impact of disposals and reorganisations on the allocation of goodwill*

IAS 36.86   3.10.490.10 If an entity disposes of an operation within a CGU or group of CGUs to which goodwill has been allocated, then a portion of the goodwill is included in the carrying amount of the operation when determining the gain or loss on disposal. In other words, part of the goodwill is derecognised when disposing of an operation. The portion of the goodwill allocated is measured based on the relative values of the operation disposed of and the portion of the CGU retained at the date of partial disposal, unless the entity can demonstrate that another method better reflects the goodwill associated with the operation disposed of.

IAS 36.87 3.10.490.20 When the entity changes its composition of CGUs, reallocation is performed using a relative value approach at the date of reorganisation similar to that used when an entity disposes of an operation within a CGU, unless the entity can demonstrate that some other method provides a better allocation of goodwill to the reorganised units.

3.10.500 *Corporate assets*

3.10.500.10 The guidance in 3.10.150 discusses the impairment testing of corporate assets. However, complications may arise in respect of inter-company charges related to corporate assets in a value in use calculation.

3.10.510 *Corporate assets allocated to CGUs*

3.10.510.10 When a corporate asset is allocated to the underlying CGUs or to the group of CGUs that requires testing (see 3.10.150), care is required to ensure that the cash outflows attributable to the corporate asset are not double counted.

3.10.510.20 In order to avoid double counting, in our view the treatment of the recharge when a corporate asset(s) is allocated to a CGU follows these steps:

(1) Allocate the asset(s) to the CGU.
(2) Eliminate inter-company charges in respect of that asset(s) from the CGU's cash flows.
(3) Push down the corporate asset cash outflows incurred at the higher level to the CGU level.

3.10.510.30 For example, Company U owns and operates an IT system with a carrying amount of 100 that is used exclusively by CGU V and CGU W. Both CGU V's and CGU W's cash flows are dependent upon the corporate asset. U charges each CGU an annual amount of 30 for use of the IT system. The actual running costs incurred by U in respect of the IT system are cash outflows of 20 a year.

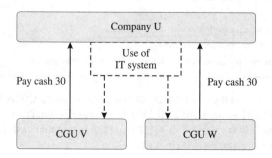

3.10.510.40 U performs the three-step process outlined in 3.10.510.20 as follows:

(1) U allocates the carrying amount of the IT system (100) to each CGU on the same basis used to allocate the inter-company charges (see 3.10.150.40). As both CGUs are charged the same amount of 30, the allocation to each CGU is 50.
(2) U reverses the inter-company charges allocated to each CGU, thereby decreasing their cash outflows by 30.
(3) The cash outflows for the corporate asset are pushed down to the CGU level, adding an amount of 10 to the outflows of each CGU.

	CGU V	CGU W
CGU carrying amount before adjustment	500	300
(1) Allocate portion of corporate asset	50	50
Adjusted carrying amount used in impairment testing	550	350
Net annual cash inflows before adjustment	60	80
(2) Eliminate inter-company charge	30	30
(3) Push down actual cash outflows	(10)	(10)
Adjusted net annual cash inflows used in impairment testing	80	100

3.10.520 Corporate assets not allocated to CGUs

3.10.520.10 When a corporate asset is not allocated to the underlying CGUs, then no cash outflows associated with the corporate assets are included in the testing of the CGU. As outlined in 3.10.150.20, the CGUs are first tested without the corporate asset, and then grouped together to test the corporate assets and the related cash flows.

3.10.520.20 Continuing the example in 3.10.510.30, if the IT system were only tested at the CGU V+W level, then in the first stage of the testing (bottom-up) the carrying amount of each CGU would not be adjusted, but the inter-company charges incurred would be reversed.

	CGU V	CGU W
CGU carrying amount	500	300
Net annual cash inflows before adjustment	60	80
Eliminate inter-company charge	30	30
Adjusted net annual cash inflows used in impairment testing	90	110

3.10.520.30 In the second stage of testing (top-down), CGUs V and W are tested together with the IT system (see 3.10.150). In that case the total carrying amount of the combined assets is 900 (500 + 300 + 100) and the net annual cash inflows used in impairment testing are 180 (90 + 110 - 20).

3.10.530 **Non-controlling interests**

3.10.530.10 Non-controlling interests may be measured at either fair value or at their proportionate share of the acquiree's identifiable net assets at the acquisition date. The choice is available on a transaction-by-transaction basis. See 2.6.840.

IAS 36.C4 3.10.530.20 When non-controlling interests were measured at acquisition date at their proportionate interest in the identifiable net assets of the subsidiary (that is a CGU or group of CGUs), goodwill attributable to non-controlling interests is included in the recoverable amount of the related CGU or group of CGUs but is not recognised in the parent's consolidated financial statements.

3.10.540 *Determining the amount of goodwill in the carrying amount of CGUs*

IAS 36.C4 3.10.540.10 When non-controlling interests are measured initially based on their proportionate interest in the identifiable net assets of the subsidiary, the carrying amount of goodwill allocated to such a CGU or group of CGUs is grossed up to include the unrecognised goodwill attributable to the non-controlling interests. For impairment testing purposes, it is this adjusted carrying amount that is compared with the recoverable amount (see 3.10.360). This gross-up is not required when non-controlling interests were measured initially at fair value.

IAS 36.C4, 3.10.540.20 IAS 36 illustrates the gross-up of the carrying amount of goodwill allocated
IE7A to a CGU or group of CGUs on the same basis as profit or loss is allocated to the parent and the non-controlling interests. However, in our view the standard does not preclude using another rational basis of gross-up, e.g. one that takes into account any control premium paid in the acquisition.

3.10.540.30 For example, Company P acquired 80 percent of Company S in a business combination several years ago and paid a control premium of 15. Non-controlling interests were measured at their proportionate interest in the identifiable net assets at the acquisition date. The contribution of S to P's consolidated financial statements at the acquisition date was as follows:

Goodwill		80
Identifiable net assets		1,000
Total net assets		1,080
Equity (parent)		880
Equity (non-controlling interests)		200
Goodwill share	-	
Identifiable share of net assets	200	
Total shareholders' equity		1,080

3.10 Impairment of non-financial assets

3.10.540.40 S is a CGU and goodwill arising on the acquisition is tested at this level. The recoverable amount of the CGU is determined to be 1,050.

3.10.540.50 A gross-up of goodwill on the same basis as the allocation of profit or loss (a "mechanical" gross-up) would be calculated as 100 (80 / 80%). In that case the impairment loss is 50 (1,050 - 1,100).

3.10.540.60 A rational way to gross up the goodwill would be to adjust the goodwill by the control premium before the gross-up. This would result in a grossed-up goodwill of 96 ((80 - 15) / 80% + 15). In that case the impairment loss would be 46 (1,050 - 1,096).

3.10.550 *Allocating the impairment loss to the parent and non-controlling interests*

IAS 36.C6 3.10.550.10 If a non-wholly-owned CGU is impaired, then any impairment losses are allocated between the amount attributable to the parent and to the non-controlling interests. IAS 36 refers to allocating the impairment loss on the same basis as profit or loss is allocated to the parent and the non-controlling interests (i.e. a mechanical allocation). However, in our view the standard does not preclude using another rational basis of allocation, e.g. one that takes account of any control premium paid in the acquisition.

IAS 36.C6, 3.10.550.20 If a non-wholly-owned CGU is impaired, then to the extent that the impair-
C8, IE7A-7C ment loss is allocated to non-controlling interests that were measured initially at their proportionate interest in the identifiable net assets of the subsidiary, that impairment is not recognised in the financial statements.

3.10.550.30 Continuing the example in 3.10.540.30 – 60:

- *Mechanical gross-up of goodwill and mechanical allocation.* The impairment loss allocated to the parent would be 40 (50 x 80%).
- *Rational gross-up of goodwill and rational allocation.* The impairment loss allocated to the parent would be 38 (46 - (46 / 96 x 20%) x (96 - 15)).
- *Rational gross-up of goodwill and mechanical allocation.* In our view, it would also be permitted to apply a rational gross-up of goodwill followed by a mechanical allocation of the impairment loss, in which case the part of the impairment loss allocated to the parent would be 37 (46 x 80%). We believe that this mixed method of rational gross-up and mechanical allocation is acceptable because the rational gross-up results in total goodwill that is broadly similar to the position if non-controlling interests were measured initially at fair value; therefore, there is consistency. However, we do not believe that it would be appropriate to apply a mechanical gross-up followed by a rational allocation.

3.10.550.40 Since no share of goodwill has been allocated to NCI and only the parent's share of the impairment loss is recognised in the consolidated financial statements, the outcome under each of the approaches is as follows:

	Mechanical gross-up and allocation	Rational gross-up and allocation	Rational gross-up and mechanical allocation
Calculated impairment loss	50	46	46
Recognised impairment loss	40	38	37
Parent's share	40	38	37
Non-controlling interests' share	-	-	-

3.10.560 *Choosing a rational basis of gross-up and allocation*

3.10.560.10 If a non-wholly-owned CGU is impaired, then as noted in 3.10.540.10 and 3.10.540.20, IAS 36 illustrates/refers to a simple basis of gross-up and allocation on the basis of how profits are shared between the parent and non-controlling interests. This approach has the benefit of simplicity even though it may not reflect the true goodwill allocation between the parent and non-controlling interests.

3.10.560.20 Applying a different method of gross-up and allocation on a rational basis has the benefit of better reflecting the true goodwill allocation between the parent and non-controlling interests. However, depending on the way in which the subsidiary's identifiable net assets were allocated to different CGUs and the allocation of the goodwill to the other CGUs of the acquirer upon acquisition of the subsidiary, and other transactions between the parent and non-controlling interests, the gross-up and allocation process could be more complex and sophisticated records may need to be maintained in order to track the allocation of goodwill.

3.10.570 **Recoverable amount of investments in associates and jointly controlled entities**

3.10.580 *Associates*

IAS 28.31-34, 39.59-62 3.10.580.10 Goodwill resulting from the acquisition of an associate is included in the carrying amount of the investment (see 3.5.330). Goodwill recognised upon the acquisition of an associate is not subject to an annual impairment test. Instead, after applying equity accounting, the investment is tested for impairment when there is an indication of a possible impairment. The guidance in IAS 39 *Financial Instruments: Recognition and Measurement* for financial asset impairment is used to determine whether it is necessary to perform an impairment test for investments in associates (see 3.6.1370). However, the impairment test applied if there is an indication of impairment follows the principles in IAS 36 and described in this chapter rather than the IAS 39 financial asset impairment recognition and measurement requirements.

IAS 28.33 3.10.580.20 The value in use of an investment in an associate may be calculated by estimating the cash flows from the investment (i.e. future dividends and estimated cash flows from disposal of the shares), or by measuring the cash flows of the underlying operations of the entity as a whole.

IAS 36.22

3.10.580.30 The forecast period should be over the useful life of the associate. In our view, as these assets relate to a portion of the net assets of an underlying business, the forecast period should be to perpetuity unless there is a planned disposal in the future or an expected termination of the business. If there is a planned disposal in the future but the asset is not classified as held for sale or distribution (see 5.4.20 and 35), then in our view cash flows should be forecast over the holding period and a disposal value should be estimated when determining value in use.

IAS 36.22 3.10.580.40 When the associate is a publicly traded, in our view the investor should carefully consider impairment analyses that suggest that value in use exceeds fair value less costs to sell (see 3.10.350).

3.10.580.50 When recoverable amount is based on fair value less costs to sell, a premium may be paid to obtain significant influence rather than control over an entity's operations. In such cases, the unit of account is the holding rather than the individual security, as outlined in 3.10.190.60. An analysis of whether such a shareholding might be valued in excess of its *pro rata* share of a company's market capitalisation would consider similar factors to those outlined in 3.10.190.70 – 80, i.e. based on an evaluation of the potential of such a shareholder to increase cash flows or reduce risk. However, a non-controlling influential shareholder generally receives the same *pro rata* cash flows as other minority shareholders. Therefore, in practice it may be difficult to support a fair value significantly in excess of the quoted share price.

IAS 28.33 3.10.580.60 Any impairment loss recognised by the investor with respect to its investment in an associate is allocated to the carrying amount of the investment as a whole, i.e. it is not allocated to any assets, including goodwill, that constitute the carrying amount of the investment. Accordingly, the impairment loss is reversed subsequently to the extent that the recoverable amount of the investment increases (see 3.10.420).

3.10.590 *Jointly controlled entities*

3.10.590.10 If an interest in a jointly controlled entity is accounted for using proportionate consolidation, then goodwill is tested for impairment annually in the same way as goodwill arising in a business combination. This is because under the proportionate consolidation method the investor accounts for its share of the underlying assets (including goodwill) and liabilities of the jointly controlled entity, as opposed to the investment in equity instruments of the associate.

3.10.590.20 When an interest in a jointly controlled entity is equity accounted, the guidance for associates in 3.10.580 applies.

3.10.600 **Separate financial statements**

IAS 27.38(b) 3.10.600.10 Investments in subsidiaries and associates, and interests in jointly controlled entities, that an entity elects to account for in accordance with IAS 39 are outside the scope of IAS 36. Instead, all of the requirements of IAS 39 apply, including impairment requirements (see 3.6.370).

IAS 27.38(a)   3.10.600.20 When an entity elects to account for investments in subsidiaries and associates, and interests in jointly controlled entities, at cost in its separate financial statements, the following applies:

- In our view, IAS 39 is applied in determining if there is an indication of impairment (see 3.6.370).
- If there is an indication of impairment, then the measurement and recognition of the impairment loss are in accordance with IAS 36 and the guidance included in this chapter.

IAS 36.12(h)   3.10.600.30 In respect of separate financial statements the receipt of dividend income from a subsidiary, associate or jointly controlled entity is considered as a possible indication of impairment when:

- the carrying amount of the investment in the separate financial statements exceeds the carrying amount in the consolidated financial statements of the investee's net assets (including any goodwill); or
- the dividend exceeds the total comprehensive income of the investee.

3.10.600.40 The guidance in 3.10.580 and 3.10.590.20 in respect of associates and jointly controlled entities in the consolidated financial statements of the investor applies equally to such investments in the separate financial statements, as well as to an investment in a subsidiary in the separate financial statements.

3.10.610 Future developments

3.10.610.10 In May 2009 the IASB published ED/2009/5 *Fair Value Measurement* (the 2009 ED). The proposals in the 2009 ED are intended to replace the fair value measurement guidance contained in individual IFRSs with a single, unified definition of fair value, as well as provide further authoritative guidance on the application of fair value measurement in inactive markets. The 2009 ED proposes a framework for measuring fair value and disclosures about fair value measurements. The proposals in the 2009 ED explain how to measure fair value when it already is required or permitted by existing IFRSs; they do not introduce new fair value measurements, nor do they eliminate the practicability exceptions to fair value measurements that exist currently in certain standards.

3.10.610.20 In June 2010 the IASB published ED/2010/7 *Measurement Uncertainty Analysis Disclosure for Fair Value Measurements* (the 2010 ED). The 2010 ED expands on the proposal in the 2009 ED for an entity to disclose a measurement uncertainty analysis (or sensitivity analysis) for assets and liabilities measured at fair value categorised within Level 3 of the fair value hierarchy. The 2010 ED proposes that an entity consider the effect of correlation between unobservable inputs, if relevant.

3.10.610.30 A final standard on fair value measurement and disclosure, which is expected to be converged with a forthcoming amended standard under US GAAP, is scheduled for the first quarter of 2011.

3.11 Equity and financial liabilities
(IAS 32, IAS 39, IFRIC 2, IFRIC 17)

3.11 Equity and financial liabilities
(IAS 32, IAS 39, IFRIC 2, IFRIC 17)

Overview of currently effective requirements

- An instrument, or its components, is classified on initial recognition as a financial liability, a financial asset or an equity instrument in accordance with the substance of the contractual arrangement and the definitions of a financial liability, a financial asset or an equity instrument.

- A financial instrument is a financial liability if the issuer can be obliged to settle it in cash or by delivering another financial asset.

- A financial instrument also is a financial liability if it will or may be settled in a variable number of the entity's own equity instruments.

- An obligation for an entity to acquire its own equity instruments gives rise to a financial liability.

- As an exception to the general principle, certain puttable instruments and instruments, or components of instruments, that impose on the entity an obligation to deliver to another party a *pro rata* share of the net assets of the entity only on liquidation are classified as equity instruments if certain conditions are met.

- The contractual terms of preference shares and similar instruments are evaluated to determine whether they have the characteristics of a financial liability. Such characteristics will lead to the classification of these instruments, or a component of them, as financial liabilities.

- The components of compound financial instruments, which have both liability and equity characteristics, are accounted for separately.

- A non-derivative contract that will be settled by an entity delivering its own equity instruments is an equity instrument if, and only if, it is settleable by delivering a fixed number of its own equity instruments. A derivative contract that will be settled by the entity delivering a fixed number of own equity instruments for a fixed amount of cash is an equity instrument. If it contains settlement options, it is an equity instrument only if all settlement alternatives lead to equity classification.

- Incremental costs that are directly attributable to issuing or buying back own equity instruments are recognised directly in equity.

> - **Treasury shares are presented as a deduction from equity.**
>
> - **Gains and losses on transactions in an entity's own equity instruments are reported directly in equity, not in profit or loss.**
>
> - **Dividends and other distributions to the holders of equity instruments (in their capacity as owners) are recognised directly in equity.**
>
> - **Non-controlling interests (NCI) are classified within equity, but separately from equity attributable to shareholders of the parent.**

Currently effective requirements

This publication reflects IFRSs in issue at 1 August 2010. The currently effective requirements cover annual periods beginning on 1 January 2010. The requirements related to this topic are derived mainly from IAS 32 *Financial Instruments: Presentation* and IAS 39 *Financial Instruments: Recognition and Measurement*.

Forthcoming requirements and future developments

When a currently effective requirement will be changed by a new requirement that is issued but is not yet effective, it is marked with a # as a **forthcoming requirement** and the impact of the change is explained in the accompanying boxed text. The forthcoming requirements related to this topic are derived from IFRIC 19 *Extinguishing Financial Liabilities with Equity* and the Amendment to IAS 32 *Classification of Rights Issues*. A brief outline of the interpretation, the amendment and their impact on this topic is given in 3.11.455.

When a significant change to the currently effective or forthcoming requirements is expected, it is marked with a * as an area that may be subject to **future developments** and a brief overview of the relevant projects is given in 3.11.460.

3.11.10 Classification

3.11.20 *Basic principles**

IAS 32.15   3.11.20.05 An instrument, or its components, is classified on initial recognition as a financial liability, a financial asset or an equity instrument in accordance with the substance of the contractual arrangement and the definitions of a financial liability, a financial asset or an equity instrument.

IAS 32.11,   3.11.20.10 An instrument is classified as a financial liability if it contains a contractual
15-20   obligation to transfer cash or other financial assets, or if it will or may be settled in a variable number of the entity's own equity instruments. An obligation to transfer cash may arise from a requirement to repay principal or to pay interest or dividends. However

puttable instruments and instruments that impose on the entity an obligation to deliver to another party a *pro rata* share of the net assets only on liquidation require separate consideration (see 3.11.20.100 and 3.11.48).

IAS 32.19, 3.11.20.20 Any financial instrument that an issuer could be obliged to settle in cash,
IU 11-06 or by delivering other financial assets, is a financial liability regardless of the financial ability of the issuer to settle the contractual obligation or the probability of settlement. In our view, such a contractual obligation could be established explicitly or indirectly, but it must be established through the terms and conditions of the instrument.

3.11.20.25 For example, an entity issues an non-redeemable, callable financial instrument (the "base" instrument) with dividends payable if interest is paid on another instrument (the "linked" instrument). The issuer is required to pay the interest on the linked instrument. We believe, the linkage to the linked instrument, on which interest is contractually payable, creates a contractual obligation to pay dividends on the base instrument; the base instrument therefore should be classified as a liability.

3.11.20.30 [Not used]

AS 32.11, 16, 3.11.20.40 In general, an equity instrument is any contract that evidences a residual
IFRIC 2 interest in the assets of an entity after deducting all of its liabilities. An *equity instrument* is an instrument that meets both of the following conditions:

- There is *no contractual obligation* to deliver cash or another financial asset to another party, or to exchange financial assets or financial liabilities with another party under potentially unfavourable conditions (for the issuer of the instrument).
- If the instrument will or may be settled in the issuer's own equity instruments, then it is:
  - a non-derivative that comprises an obligation for the issuer to deliver a fixed number of its own equity instruments; or
  - a derivative that will be settled only by the issuer exchanging a fixed amount of cash or other financial assets for a fixed number of its own equity instruments.

AS 32.16A, C 3.11.20.50 As an exception to the general principles, puttable instruments and instruments, or components of instruments, that impose on the entity an obligation to deliver to another party a *pro rata* share of the net assets of the entity only on liquidation are classified as equity instruments if certain conditions are met. Each of these conditions is discussed in more detail in 3.11.50 and 51.

IAS 32.35 3.11.20.60 The classification of an instrument as either liability or equity determines whether any distributions on the instrument will be treated as interest or dividends. If an instrument is classified as a liability, then coupon payments and any amortisation of discounts or premiums on the instrument are recognised as part of finance costs in profit or loss, using the effective interest method. If on the other hand the instrument is classified as equity, then dividends are accounted for directly in equity.

IAS 32.15, 3.11.20.70 The classification of an instrument, or its component parts, as either equity or
AG29 liability is made at initial recognition and, with the exception of puttable instruments and
instruments that impose on the entity an obligation only on liquidation (see 3.11.48),
generally is not revised as a result of subsequent changes in circumstances. However, a
reclassification between equity and liability or *vice versa* may be required (see 3.11.240)
if an entity amends the contractual terms of an instrument, if the effective terms of an
instrument change without any amendment of the contractual terms, or if there is a
relevant change in the composition of the reporting entity.

3.11.20.72 In our view, the effective terms of an instrument would be considered to have
changed if relevant contractual provisions of an instrument become effective or cease to
be effective as a result of the passage of time, the action of a party, or other contingent
events that are anticipated in the contractual terms of the instrument. The following are
examples of when the effective terms of an instrument have changed:

- The exercise price of a derivative that is settled in the entity's own equity instruments
  becomes fixed as a result of the passage of time. For example, the conversion ratio
  of certain convertible debt based on the lower of a fixed amount and an amount
  indexed to the entity's share price one year after the date of issuance would become
  fixed at the end of that year.
- A put option expires as a result of non-exercise. For example, a put option in an
  instrument that allows the holder to put the instrument back to the entity for a fixed
  amount of cash during only the first three years of the instrument's life would expire
  unexercised at the end of the three years.
- When the linked instrument in the example in 3.11.20.25 is redeemed, absent any
  other changes in terms and conditions of the instrument, the effective terms of the
  base instrument have changed because it no longer contains a contractual obligation
  to make payments.

3.11.20.75 A change in the composition of the reporting entity may arise in consolidated
financial statements from acquisitions or disposals of subsidiaries. In our view, such a
change in group structure may trigger a reassessment of the terms and conditions agreed
between members of the group and the holder of an instrument and reassessment of
whether the group as a whole has an obligation to pay cash or other financial assets to
the instrument holder. For example, Company A writes a call option under which it has
an obligation to deliver a fixed amount of equity shares in an unrelated party, Company
X, in exchange for a fixed amount of cash. Since equity shares in X are financial assets
from the perspective of A, A classifies the option as a financial liability on initial recognition. However, if A subsequently obtains control over and consolidates X, then A
would reclassify the option from financial liability to equity in its consolidated financial
statements as the option would now represent an obligation to deliver a fixed number
of equity instruments in A's group in exchange for a fixed amount of cash.

IAS 32.18, 3.11.20.80 The substance of a contractual arrangement rather than its legal form is
IU 11-06 assessed when determining the classification of a financial instrument as equity or a
financial liability. Therefore it is possible that instruments that qualify as equity for legal

or regulatory purposes will be classified as liabilities for the purposes of financial reporting. In our view, in assessing the substance of a contractual arrangement, factors not contained within the contractual arrangement should be excluded from the assessment. Furthermore, economic compulsion should not be used as the basis for classification. Instruments commonly affected by this requirement include preference shares, classes of shares that have special terms and conditions, and subordinated instruments, as well as convertible and perpetual instruments.

3.11.20.90 Equity instruments include shares, options and warrants, and any other instrument that evidences a residual interest in an entity and meets the relevant conditions in 3.11.20.40 – 80.

AS 32.AG29 3.11.20.100 The classification of financial instruments as equity or liabilities in the consolidated financial statements may differ from their classification in any separate or individual financial statements of entities within a group. For example, Subsidiary G issues non-redeemable preference shares to a party outside the group. Subsidiary B of the same group writes a put option on the preference shares issued by G. The put option, if exercised, will require B to purchase the preference shares from the holder. In its separate financial statements G classifies the preference shares as equity as it does not have a contractual obligation to redeem the shares or to pay dividends. However, the group as a whole has a contractual obligation to redeem the preference shares (through the put option written by B) and therefore classifies the preference shares as a financial liability in the consolidated financial statements.

3.11.20.110 See 2.2 for guidance on the presentation of movements in equity.

3.11.30 *Contractual obligation to deliver cash or another financial asset*

IAS 32.17 3.11.30.10 The primary factor determining classification is whether or not the instrument establishes a contractual obligation for the issuer to make payments (principal, interest/dividends or both). A right on the part of the holder does not necessarily translate to a contractual obligation on the part of the issuer. For example, while the holder of an equity instrument might have the *right* to receive dividends if they are paid, the issuer does not have a *contractual obligation* to make payments until the dividend is appropriately authorised *and* no longer at the discretion of the entity. The holder has a financial asset, while the issuer has an equity instrument rather than a financial liability.

IAS 32.19 3.11.30.20 IAS 32 further clarifies that an instrument that creates an obligation is a financial liability if the entity does not have the unconditional right to avoid delivering cash or another financial asset in settlement of that obligation. A contractual obligation is not negated merely because of a lack of funds, statutory restrictions or insufficient profits or reserves. For example, the terms of a loan might stipulate that it is repayable as long as its repayment does not violate certain covenants imposed by local law. In this case the entity does not have the unconditional right to avoid making payments; the breach of local covenants that prevent repayment at a specific point in time defers rather than negates the obligation. Consequently, the loan is classified as a financial liability. Also, an obligation that will be settled only if a holder exercises its right to redeem is a financial liability, irrespective of how likely or unlikely it is that the holder will actually exercise its right.

3.11.30.30 When the terms of a financial instrument provide for cash settlement at the option of the holder, entities may obtain a letter of undertaking from the holder indicating that this option will not be called upon. In our view, such an undertaking, unless legally enforceable and irrevocable, is not sufficient to warrant classification of the instrument as equity rather than as a financial liability.

IAS 32.20,   3.11.30.40 In most cases the terms and conditions of an instrument will establish a con-
BC9   tractual obligation explicitly. However, such an obligation also may arise indirectly. For example, an instrument that includes a non-financial obligation that is required to be settled if the entity fails to make distributions or redeem the instrument is a financial liability because the entity can avoid payment only by settling the non-financial obligation. Examples are:

- Company G issues an instrument that includes a term under which G is required to deliver a property in settlement if the instrument is not redeemed after ten years. Such an instrument is a financial liability because G can avoid settling the financial obligation only by settling the non-financial obligation.
- Company B issues an instrument that is required to be settled either in cash or in B's own shares, the value of which will substantially exceed the amount of cash. Such an instrument is a financial liability because, although B does not have an explicit contractual obligation to settle in cash, the value of the share settlement option is so high that B always will settle in cash.

3.11.30.50 Instruments classified as financial liabilities generally include the following:

- instruments that are redeemable at the option of the holder (e.g. redeemable preference shares);
- non-redeemable preference shares with dividends that are not discretionary (see 3.11.80);
- instruments that are redeemable or become redeemable at the option of the holder or on the occurrence of an uncertain future event that is beyond the control of both the holder and the issuer of the instrument (see 3.11.40); and
- subordinated liabilities.

IAS 32.16A, C   3.11.30.55 However, as an exception to the general principles, some instruments that are redeemable, either at the option of the holder or on liquidation, which either is certain to occur and outside the control of the entity or is uncertain to occur but is at the option of the instrument holder, are classified as equity instruments of the entity if certain conditions are met (see 3.11.50 and 51).

IAS 32.AG12   3.11.30.60 Distinction also should be made between a contractual obligation to deliver cash or another financial asset, which gives rise to a financial liability, and a statutory obligation, which does not necessarily result in a financial liability. For example, local law might require an entity to pay a minimum specified amount as dividends in each period for a particular instrument. In our view, such an obligation does not represent a contractual obligation and consequently the obligation is not classified as a financial liability under IAS 32. However, when an entity voluntarily incorporates a minimum specified amount of dividends into the terms of an instrument, for example, to achieve a desired tax outcome or to achieve a certain regulatory status, in our view the payment of such dividends represents a contractual obligation of the entity and consequently the obligation is classified as a financial liability.

3.11.40 *Contingent settlement provisions*

IAS 32.25   3.11.40.10 An instrument may contain a contractual obligation to deliver cash or another financial asset depending on the outcome of an uncertain future event that is beyond the control of both the issuer and the holder of the instrument. Examples of such uncertain events are changes in a stock market index, interest rate, taxation requirements and the issuer's future revenues or debt-to-equity ratio.

3.11.40.20 Since the issuer does not have the unconditional right to avoid making payments, an instrument that contains such contingent settlement provisions is a financial liability unless one of the following applies:

- the part of the contingent settlement provision that could require settlement in cash or another financial asset is not genuine; or
- the issuer can be required to settle in cash or another financial asset only in the event of its own liquidation.

3.11.40.30 For example, Company Y issues a bond that is convertible automatically into a fixed number of ordinary shares when an initial public offering (IPO) takes place. The offering is planned for two years' time, but is subject to the approval of a regulator. The bond is redeemable in cash only if the initial public offering does not take place. Y cannot avoid the obligation as it cannot ensure that regulatory approval will be received; nor can it ensure that the IPO will actually occur. Because the bond potentially is redeemable in cash and the contingency is beyond the control of both parties, the bond is classified as a liability regardless of the likelihood of cash settlement.

3.11.40.35 In a contrasting example to 3.11.40.30, if the bond were redeemable in cash only if the IPO takes place, then in our view the instrument would be classified as equity. In this situation, we believe that the issuer has the unconditional ability to avoid the obligation if it can decide whether or not to launch an IPO.

3.11.40.36 If, for example, Company Y issues an instrument that becomes immediately redeemable in cash on the occurrence of a change in control of Y, such as when a majority of the shareholders of Y choose to sell their shares to an acquiring party in a takeover, then in our view this feature would result in the instrument being classified as a financial liability. That is because we believe that such a change in control event is an uncertain future event that is not within the control of the entity, and therefore the entity does not have an unconditional right to avoid delivering cash. This would apply even if such a takeover required formal approval by a majority of shareholders at a general meeting since shareholders would in substance be acting in their capacity as individual investors rather than as a body as part of the company's internal corporate governance processes (see 3.11.40.40).

3.11.40.40 In our view, the shareholders of an entity should not be regarded as part of the entity (issuer) except when they act as a body under the entity's governing charter. For example, perpetual bonds with interest payments linked to dividends on ordinary shares should be classified as equity because the payment of dividends is at the discretion of the entity. The entity's shareholders, acting as a body on behalf of the entity, approve or disapprove the payment of dividends on ordinary shares. Therefore, we believe that the approval of dividends is not outside the control of the entity and in such cases paragraph 25 of IAS 32 is not applicable. In this case the term "issuer" incorporates both the entity and its shareholders, and the shareholders have discretion. On the other hand, shareholders are not acting as a body under the entity's governing charter when they are acting as individual investors on matters pertaining to their individual shareholding, for example, voting to dispose of their individual shareholding.

IAS 32.AG28   3.11.40.50 In our view, only in rare circumstances will a contingent settlement feature be considered non-genuine. We believe that a contingent settlement feature should be considered non-genuine only when it has no economic substance and could be removed by the parties to the contract without any compensation, either in the form of payment or by altering the other terms and conditions of the contract. In our view, in all other cases such provisions should be considered genuine and therefore should affect classification. For example, an instrument may provide for cash settlement in the event of a change in tax law because the terms of the instrument were structured so that the holder and/ or issuer could enjoy a specific tax benefit. However remote the chances of the tax law changing, such an instrument should be classified as a financial liability. A contingent settlement event such as a tax change or a takeover of the issuer always would be regarded as genuine unless it is inserted into the contract only to achieve liability classification.

3.11.40.55 In our view, subsequent changes in circumstances that lead to a genuine contingent settlement feature becoming extremely rare, highly abnormal and very unlikely to occur (i.e. a change in probability) do not change the initial assessment that the contingent settlement feature is considered genuine, and hence do not result in reclassification of the instrument from liability to equity; likewise, subsequent changes in circumstances that lead to a non-genuine contingent settlement feature becoming likely to occur do not result in a reclassification of an instrument from equity to liability notwithstanding that appropriate disclosure may be required.

IAS 32.16A,   3.11.40.60 A contractual provision that requires settlement of a financial instrument only *C, 25(b)*   in the event of liquidation of the issuer does not result in liability classification for that instrument. However, if the entity's liquidation date is predetermined or if the holder of such an instrument has the unconditional right to liquidate the issuer of the instrument and the instrument does not meet the conditions for classification as equity under the exceptions to the general principles described in 3.11.51, then in our view the exemption does not apply. Such an instrument should be classified as a financial liability as the issuer does not have the unconditional ability to avoid payment.

3.11.40.70 A contract that would otherwise be settled by delivery of a fixed number of the entity's own equity instruments in exchange for a fixed amount of cash may provide for net cash settlement in the event of the counterparty's involuntary liquidation or bankruptcy. In our view, the existence of such a clause does not preclude the entity from classifying the contract as equity.

3.11.45 *Obligation to acquire own equity instruments*

IAS 32.16A,
18(b)

3.11.45.10 Financial instruments that give the holder the right to "put" them back to the issuer for cash or other financial assets ("puttable instruments") are financial liabilities of the issuer, unless certain conditions are met, in which case they would be classified as equity (see 3.11.50). The put option creates a contractual obligation that the issuer does not have the unconditional ability to avoid. In our view, the fact that the instrument may not be puttable immediately does not affect its classification as a financial liability, although that fact may affect its classification as a current or non-current liability.

IAS 32.18(b)

3.11.45.20 This principle applies even when the amount of cash or other financial assets is determined on the basis of an index or other variable that has the potential to increase or decrease (e.g. a share index) or when the legal form of the puttable instrument gives the holder a right to a residual interest in the assets of the issuer.

3.11.45.30 If the amount payable to the holder of a puttable instrument varies in response to an index or another variable whose economic characteristics are not closely related to those of the host contract, then the instrument may contain an embedded derivative that requires separation (see 3.6.260). As a result, either the entire puttable instrument (hybrid) is measured at fair value through profit or loss, or the embedded derivative is separated and accounted for at fair value through profit or loss (see 3.6.790).

IAS 32.18(b)

3.11.45.40 Investors in many mutual funds, unit trusts and similar entities have the right to redeem their interests in exchange for cash that is equivalent to their share of the net asset value of the entity. This gives the issuer (the fund) a contractual obligation, and therefore these instruments are classified as liabilities unless they meet the conditions to be classified as equity instruments (see 3.11.50 and 51). These financial instruments are financial liabilities independent of considerations such as when the right is exercisable, how the amount payable on exercise is determined and whether the instrument has a fixed maturity, although these considerations may affect whether the instruments qualify for equity classification under the exceptions in 3.11.50 or 51.

IAS 32.IE32

3.11.45.50 The requirement addressed in 3.11.45.40 means that some entities do not show any equity; however IAS 32 does not preclude such instruments from being included in the statement of financial position within a "total members' interests" subtotal.

IFRIC 2.2, 3.11.45.60 The principles in 3.11.45.40 apply equally to shares issued to members of a
6-8 co-operative entity that give the holder the right to request redemption. Members' shares
and similar instruments that would be classified as equity if they did not convey the
right to request redemption to the holder are classified as equity only if:

- the entity has an unconditional right to refuse redemption; or
- redemption is unconditionally prohibited by local law, regulation or the entity's
  governing charter.

3.11.45.70 A distinction is made between unconditional and conditional prohibitions on
redemption. Only an unconditional prohibition on redemption can lead to the classification of members' shares and similar instruments as equity.

IFRIC 2.BC 3.11.45.80 An unconditional prohibition prevents an entity from incurring a liability for
14 redemption regardless of whether or not the entity will be able to satisfy the obligation.
However, a conditional prohibition prevents *payments* from being made unless certain
conditions are met (e.g. liquidity constraints). A conditional prohibition may only defer
payment of a liability that has already been incurred, e.g. redemption of members' shares
is possible as soon as the local liquidity or reserve requirements are met.

IFRIC 2.9 3.11.45.90 An unconditional prohibition may be partial in that it allows redemption but requires that a stated minimum amount of members' shares or paid-in capital is maintained
at all times. In that case, the proportion of members' shares subject to the unconditional
prohibition on redemption is classified as equity even though each individual instrument
may be redeemed.

3.11.45.100 For example, local law governing co-operative entities may prohibit a co-
operative from redeeming members' shares if it would cause the amount of paid-in
capital from members' shares to reduce below 75 percent of the highest amount of
paid-in capital from members' shares ever reported. If the highest amount of paid-in
capital from members' shares ever reported was 100, then 75 always would be classified as equity even though each member could, individually, request redemption of
their share.

IFRIC 2.9 3.11.45.110 An unconditional prohibition may be based on a factor that can change over
a period of time. For example, a co-operative's governing charter states that 25 percent
of the highest number of members' shares ever in issue should be maintained as equity.
If the entity decides to amend its governing charter by reducing this percentage to 20
percent, assuming that all other factors remain the same, then the number of members'
shares subject to the unconditional prohibition would reduce. Consequently, the entity
should increase its financial liability to redeem members' shares, while simultaneously
decreasing the amount of members' shares classified as equity. This and other such
changes to the amount of members' shares or paid-in capital subject to an unconditional
prohibition on redemption should be treated as transfers between financial liabilities
and equity. See 3.11.20.70 for a discussion of changes in the effective terms of an
instrument.

3.11.45.120 In our view, an unconditional prohibition also may result in equity classification when it prohibits a contingent event from taking place. For example, Company C has issued a put option on specified equity instruments that is exercisable in the event that there is change in control of C. C is controlled by the government and, due to public interest considerations, the law unconditionally prohibits a change in control. In our view, no liability should be recognised for the potential obligation to redeem the equity instruments unless there is a change in the law to remove the prohibition.

IFRIC 2.10 3.11.45.130 Upon initial recognition, an entity measures its financial liability at fair value. In the case of members' shares with a redemption feature, the entity measures the fair value of the financial liability for redemption at no less than the maximum amount payable under the redemption provisions of its governing charter or applicable law, discounted from the first date that the amount could be required to be paid. IFRSs do not provide guidance regarding the subsequent measurement of the liability for the redemption of members' shares.

3.11.48 *Puttable instruments and obligations arising on liquidation classified as equity by exception*

3.11.48.10 As exceptions to the general principles for liability and equity classification, a puttable instrument or an instrument (or a component of an instrument) that imposes on the entity an obligation only on liquidation is classified as equity if the conditions discussed in 3.11.50 or 51 are met.

IAS 32.AG 3.11.48.20 Puttable instruments and instruments that impose on the entity an obligation
29A, BC68 only on liquidation that are classified as equity in the separate or individual financial statements of the issuing entity and represent NCI should, however, be classified as financial liabilities in the consolidated financial statements of the group.

3.11.50 *Puttable instruments*

3.11.50.10 A *puttable instrument* is a financial instrument that gives the holder the right to put the instrument back to the issuer for cash or another financial asset or is automatically put back to the issuer on the occurrence of an uncertain future event or the death or retirement of the instrument holder.

IAS 32.16A 3.11.50.20 Even though a puttable instrument contains an obligation for the entity to deliver cash or another financial asset, it is classified as an equity instrument if all of the following conditions are met:

- The instrument entitles the holder to a *pro rata* share of the entity's net assets in the event of the entity's liquidation.
- The instrument belongs to a class of instruments that is subordinate to all other classes of instruments issued by the entity. When determining whether an instrument is in the most subordinate class, an entity should evaluate the instrument's claim on liquidation as if it were to liquidate on the date when it classifies the instrument.

- All financial instruments in this most subordinate class of instruments should have identical features, i.e. no instrument holder in that class can have preferential terms or conditions.
- Apart from the contractual obligation to repurchase or redeem the instrument, the instrument does not include any other contractual obligation to deliver cash or another financial asset to another entity, or to exchange financial assets or financial liabilities with another entity under conditions that are potentially unfavourable to the entity.
- The total expected cash flows attributable to the instrument over its life should be based substantially on the profit or loss, the change in the recognised net assets or the change in the fair value of the recognised and unrecognised net assets of the entity. Profit or loss and the change in recognised net assets are measured in accordance with IFRSs for this purpose.

IAS 32.16B 3.11.50.30 In addition to the conditions to be met by the instrument (see 3.11.50.20), the issuer has no other financial instrument or contract that has:

- total cash flows based substantially on the profit or loss, the change in the recognised net assets or the change in the fair value of the recognised and unrecognised net assets of the entity; and
- the effect of substantially restricting or fixing the residual return to the puttable instrument holders.

3.11.50.40 For this purpose, an entity does not consider a non-financial contract with the holder of the puttable instrument if it can determine that the non-financial contract has terms and conditions that are similar to those of an equivalent contract that might occur with a non-instrument holder.

IAS 32.11, 3.11.50.50 The issuer of a puttable instrument first evaluates the terms of the financial
16A, 28 instrument to determine whether it is a financial liability or equity instrument in its entirety, or is a compound instrument that contains both a liability and an equity component, in accordance with the general definitions of equity and liabilities in IAS 32. If the puttable instrument initially is determined to be a financial liability, or to contain a financial liability component, then the whole instrument is tested for equity classification under the exception in 3.11.48.10. If the instrument meets all the conditions for equity classification under the exception, then the whole instrument is classified as equity. If the whole instrument does not meet the conditions for equity classification under the exception, then the instrument is classified wholly as a liability or is split into its equity and liability components in accordance with the initial determination under the general requirements related to equity and liability classification in IAS 32.

3.11.51 *Instruments, or components of instruments, that impose on the entity an obligation to deliver to another party a pro rata share of the net assets of the entity only on liquidation*

IAS 32.16C 3.11.51.10 An entity may issue financial instruments that contain a contractual obligation for the entity to deliver to the holder a *pro rata* share of its net assets only on liquidation. In this case the obligation arises because liquidation either is certain to occur and is outside of the control of the entity (e.g. a limited life entity) or is uncertain to occur but is at the option of the instrument holder (e.g. some partnership interests). In order for such an instrument *or component* to qualify for equity classification by exception, the instrument is required to meet all of the following conditions:

- The instrument entitles the holder to a *pro rata* share of the entity's net assets in the event of the entity's liquidation.
- The instrument belongs to a class of instruments that is subordinate to all other classes of instruments issued by the entity. When determining whether an instrument is in the most subordinate class, an entity should evaluate the instrument's claim on liquidation as if it were to liquidate on the date when it classifies the instrument.
- All financial instruments in this most subordinate class of instruments should have an identical contractual obligation for the issuing entity to deliver a *pro rata* share of its net assets on liquidation.

IAS 32.16D 3.11.51.20 In addition to the conditions to be met by the instrument (see 3.11.53.10), the issuer has no other financial instrument or contract that has:

- total cash flows based substantially on the profit or loss, the change in the recognised net assets or the change in the fair value of the recognised and unrecognised net assets of the entity (see 3.11.53.30); and
- the effect of substantially restricting or fixing the residual return to the instrument holders.

3.11.51.30 For the purpose of 3.11.51.20, an entity does not consider a non-financial contract with the holder of the instrument if it can determine that the non-financial contract has terms and conditions that are similar to those of an equivalent contract that might occur with a non-instrument holder.

3.11.51.40 The conditions in 3.11.51.10 and 20 are similar to those for a puttable instrument (see 3.11.50.20 and 30), except that:

- there is no requirement that the instrument contains no other contractual obligation to deliver cash or other financial assets;
- there is no requirement to consider the total expected cash flows over the life of the instrument; and
- the only feature that must be identical among the instruments in the most subordinate class is the obligation for the issuing entity to deliver to the holder a *pro rata* share of its net assets on liquidation.

IAS 32.BC67 3.11.51.50 The reason for this distinction between a puttable instrument and an instrument that imposes on the entity an obligation only on liquidation is due to the difference in the timing of settlement of the obligations under both instruments. A puttable instrument can be exercised before liquidation of the entity. Therefore it is important to identify all contractual obligations that exist throughout its entire life to ensure that it always represents the most residual interest. However, for an instrument that imposes on the entity an obligation only on liquidation of the entity, it is appropriate to focus only on the obligations that exist at liquidation.

3.11.53 Components of instruments

3.11.53.10 If the instrument contains other contractual obligations, then those other obligations may need to be accounted for separately as liabilities in accordance with the requirements of IAS 32 (hence the term "components of").

3.11.53.20 An example of such an instrument would be a unit holder's interest in a limited-life entity which is not puttable and which includes only a right to fixed non-discretionary dividends each period and to a *pro rata* share of the entity's net assets on its liquidation. The obligation to pay fixed non-discretionary dividends represents a contractual obligation which is classified as a financial liability, while the obligation to deliver a *pro rata* share of the entity's net assets on its liquidation is classified as equity provided all other criteria are met. However, if there is no mandatory dividend requirement and dividends are entirely at the discretion of the entity, then the units are classified wholly as equity provided all other criteria are met.

3.11.53.30 In our view, in applying the condition set out in 3.11.51.20 when evaluating a component of an instrument for equity classification, an entity should choose an accounting policy, to be applied consistently, as to whether the term "other financial instrument" encompasses other components of that same financial instrument or relates only to financial instruments apart from the one that contains the component being evaluated. For example, an instrument includes an obligation to distribute mandatory dividends based on profits of the entity and an obligation to distribute a *pro rata* share of net assets on a fixed liquidation date. If the entity's policy is to regard the mandatory dividend feature like another financial instrument for the purpose of applying the condition in 3.11.51.20 to the component of the instrument that comprises the obligation arising only on liquidation, then equity classification of the obligation arising only on liquidation would be precluded since the mandatory dividends are based on profits and the condition for equity treatment in paragraph 16D of IAS 32 is not met. However, if the entity's policy is to restrict the analysis under 3.11.51.20 to consider only contracts other than the instrument that contains the obligation arising on liquidation, then the mandatory dividend feature in itself would not preclude equity classification of the obligation arising on liquidation since this feature is part of the same instrument and the condition for equity treatment in paragraph 16D of IAS 32 could be met.

3.11.53.40 For example, Company C, which has a limited life, issued a nonredeemable instrument X which requires payment of a dividend equalling 90 percent of profits of C. The holders of instrument X will also participate in liquidation of C on a *pro rata* basis. The instrument was issued for its fair value of 1,000. The fair value of the mandatory dividend feature is 800 upon issuance. This component of the instrument is classified as a liability. In making the assessment described in 3.11.51.20 in respect of the component that provides a *pro rata* participation in liquidation, C can elect to make it on a component basis in which case the component that provides a *pro rata* participation in liquidation could not be classified as equity since the cash flows for the mandatory dividend component are substantially based on profits and therefore the condition in paragraph 16D of IAS 32 is not met. On the other hand, it is possible to make the assessment considering instrument X in its entirety. In this case, the mandatory dividend feature of instrument X does not preclude the classification of the other component as equity since it is part of the same financial instrument.

3.11.54 Consideration of the "entity" for umbrella fund financial statements

3.11.54.10 In certain jurisdictions a collective investment scheme may be structured as an umbrella fund that operates one or more sub-funds, whereby investors purchase instruments that entitle the holder to a share of the net assets of a particular sub-fund. The umbrella fund and sub-funds together form a legal entity although the assets and the obligations of individual funds are fully or partially segregated.

3.11.54.20 If the umbrella fund presents separate financial statements that include the assets and liabilities of the sub-funds, which together with the umbrella fund form a single legal entity, then the sub-fund instruments should be assessed for equity classification in those financial statements from the perspective of the umbrella fund as a whole. Therefore, these instruments cannot qualify for equity classification under the conditions in 3.11.50 or 51 as they could not meet the "*pro rata* share of the entity's net assets on liquidation" test and, if puttable instruments, the "identical features" test, as discussed in 3.11.55 and 57.

IAS 32.AG
29A 3.11.54.30 If the umbrella fund presents consolidated financial statements in accordance with IAS 27 *Consolidated and Separate Financial Statements* that consolidate the sub-funds as subsidiaries, then sub-fund instruments that qualified for equity classification under the conditions in 3.11.50 or 51 in the individual financial statements of each sub-fund and that represent NCI are classified as liabilities in the consolidated financial statements.

3.11.54.40 If the umbrella fund presents combined financial statements, then, to the extent that they are expressed as being prepared in accordance with IFRS, in our view puttable sub-fund instruments would not qualify for equity classification in the combined financial statements for the reasons described in 3.11.54.30 in respect of both separate and consolidated financial statements.

3.11.55 *Pro rata* share of the entity's net assets on liquidation

IAS 32.16A 3.11.55.10 A *pro rata* share of the entity's net assets on liquidation is determined by:
(a)

- dividing the entity's net assets on liquidation into units of equal amount; and
- multiplying that amount by the number of the units held by the financial instrument holder.

3.11.55.20 In our view, the requirement in 3.11.55.10 means that each instrument holder has an entitlement to an identical monetary amount per unit on liquidation. For example, an instrument that entitles the holder to a fixed dividend on liquidation, in addition to a share of the entity's net assets, would not qualify under this requirement. Similarly, if payments to instrument holders on liquidation are subject to fees that are not computed on an identical per-unit basis, for example a fixed fee per holder rather than per unit, then the instrument would not satisfy this criterion. Furthermore, instruments that entitle the holder to a pro rata share of only a specific portion or component of the net assets of an entity would not satisfy this criterion.

3.11.56 The class of instruments that is subordinate to all other classes

IU 03-09 **3.11.56.10** IAS 32 does not preclude the existence of several types or classes of equity. A financial instrument first is classified as a liability or equity instrument in accordance with the general requirements of IAS 32. That classification is not affected by the existence of puttable instruments or instruments that impose an obligation only on liquidation. As a second step, if a financial instrument meets the definition of a financial liability because it is puttable to the issuer, or because it imposes on the issuer an obligation on liquidation because liquidation either is certain to occur and outside of the control of the entity or is uncertain to occur but is at the option of the instrument holder, then the entity considers the exceptions in paragraphs 16A and 16B, or 16C and 16D of IAS 32 (see 3.11.50 and 51), to determine whether it should be classified as equity.

3.11.56.20 For example, Company X issues two types of instruments. Instrument A is a perpetual instrument with no put rights; Instrument B is a puttable instrument. Both instruments could qualify as equity provided that all applicable criteria in IAS 32 are met. The existence of the puttable feature in Instrument B does not in itself imply that the instrument is less subordinate than Instrument A as the level of an instrument's subordination is determined by its priority in liquidation. If Instrument A and Instrument B are equally subordinate, then together they form the most subordinate class for the purpose of the identical features test discussed in more detail in 3.11.57. However, in this case, Instrument B would fail equity classification due to the existence of the puttable feature which does not exist in Instrument A. If Instrument B is more subordinate than Instrument A, e.g. if Instrument A is entitled to a fixed claim on liquidation and Instrument B is entitled to the residual net assets, then Instrument B may qualify for equity classification provided all other conditions in the exceptions are met.

3.11.56.30 Many investment funds have a nominal amount of founder shares that are issued to the fund manager. These shares typically are non-redeemable and have no entitlements to dividends. In our view, even a small amount of founder shares would disqualify investors' shares that are puttable from equity classification if the founder shares are subordinate to the puttable investors' shares. This is due to the puttable investors' shares not being in the most subordinate class of instruments.

3.11.56.40 If an investment fund issues redeemable participating shares and redeemable founder shares that rank *pari passu* in respect of their respective nominal amounts in liquidation and the management shares have no further payment rights, then in our view the management shares and participating shares together form the most subordinate class. However, because the redeemable participating shares have other payment rights, we believe that the participating shares would be classified as liabilities as they do not have identical features to the management shares.

3.11.57 Identical features test

IAS 32.AG 14F, G, I 3.11.57.10 In respect of puttable instruments, all financial instruments in the class of instruments that is subordinate to all other classes of instruments must have identical features to qualify for equity classification. In our view, this should be interpreted strictly to mean identical contractual terms and conditions, including non-financial features such as governance rights, related to the holders of the instruments in their roles as owners of the entity. Differences in cash flows and contractual terms and conditions of an instrument attributable to an instrument holder in its role as non-owner therefore are not considered to violate the identical features test, provided that the transaction is on similar terms to an equivalent transaction that might occur between a non-instrument holder and the issuing entity.

3.11.57.20 For example, some general partners in a limited partnership that has limited partners and general partners may provide a guarantee to the entity, and may be remunerated for providing that guarantee. In such situations, if the guarantee and the associated cash flows relate to the general partner in its role as a guarantor and not in its role as owner of the entity, then such a guarantee and the associated cash flows would be disregarded when assessing whether the contractual terms of the limited partnership instruments held by the general partners and limited partners are identical.

3.11.57.30 In another example, a fund manager who holds units in an investment fund may have access to certain information rights which are not granted to other unit holders. If these information rights are granted to the fund manager in its role as manager of the fund, then these rights similarly are not considered to violate the identical features test.

3.11.57.40 As discussed in 3.11.54, we expect units issued by umbrella investment funds, which consist of several sub-funds, to fail equity classification in the separate financial statements of the umbrella fund. In our view, different contractual features that would violate the identical features test include different rates of management fees, choice *on issuance* by holders whether to receive income or additional units as distributions (such that the distributive or accumulative feature differs for each instrument after they are issued), different lock-up periods, different reference assets on which *pro rata* share of net assets is calculated or different currencies in which payments are denominated.

3.11.57.50 However, in our view the following features are not considered to violate the identical features test as there are no inherent differences in the features of each instrument within the most subordinate class:

- administrative charges based on the volume of units redeemed prior to liquidation as long as all unit holders in the most subordinate class are subject to the same fee structure;
- different subscription fees payable upon initial subscription, as long as all other features become identical once the subscription fees are paid;
- choice by holders *on each distribution date* to receive income or additional units as distributions, as long as the same ability to choose distributions or reinvestment is afforded to all the unit holders in the most subordinate class, i.e. the "choice" is an identical feature for all the instruments in this most subordinate class; and
- a term contained in identical instruments that carry equal voting rights which caps the maximum amount of voting rights that any individual holder may exercise.

3.11.58 No other contractual obligation to deliver cash or another financial asset

IAS 32.16A(d)   3.11.58.10 In respect of puttable instruments, one of the conditions for equity classification is that the instrument does not include any other contractual obligation to deliver cash other than the put feature.

3.11.58.20 For example, an unlisted unit trust issues instruments that enable the holder to put the instrument back to the trust at any time. The trust is contractually required to distribute its net accounting profit on an annual basis. In our view, the requirement to distribute the net accounting profit annually is an additional obligation to deliver cash and, hence, these instruments do not qualify for equity classification.

3.11.59 Total expected cash flows attributable to the instrument over the life of the instrument

IAS 32.16A(e)   3.11.59.10 In respect of puttable instruments, one of the conditions for equity classification is that the total expected cash flows attributable to the instrument over its life is based substantially on the profit or loss, the change in the recognised net assets or the change in the fair value of the recognised and unrecognised net assets of the entity. In this context, profit or loss and the change in recognised net assets are measured in accordance with relevant IFRSs.

3.11.59.20 In some cases, an instrument may be puttable at a *pro rata* share of the entity's recognised net assets as calculated in its *separate* financial statements. IFRSs do not discuss whether such instruments could qualify for equity classification if the issuer is a parent entity required to present consolidated financial statements in which it consolidates its investments in subsidiaries. IFRSs include no statement that, absent any additional arrangements between the holder of an instrument and subsidiaries of the issuer, puttable instruments issued by a parent should be classified differently in the parent's separate financial statements and consolidated financial statements. Therefore, in our view when the "entity" is a parent, its profit or loss, change in recognised net assets or change in the fair value of the recognised and unrecognised net assets may be measured either on a separate or consolidated basis. Hence, an instrument that is puttable at a *pro rata* share of a parent's recognised net assets as presented in its separate

IFRS financial statements may qualify for classification as equity in both the separate and consolidated IFRS financial statements, provided that all other conditions in the exceptions also are met.

3.11.59.30 Instruments that are puttable at a *pro rata* share of recognised net assets determined in accordance with a different basis of accounting, e.g. local GAAP, still may satisfy the condition in 3.11.59.10 depending on the circumstances. For example, it may be possible to argue that the effect of differences between local GAAP and IFRS is immaterial with regard to their application to the entity, or is temporary and expected to converge over the life of the instrument, such that the total "expected" cash flows are "based substantially" on IFRS profit or loss or change in recognised net assets. In our view, the use of the terms "expected" and "based substantially" indicate that judgement should be exercised in determining whether the requirement is met in the individual circumstances of each specific situation, including consideration of how local GAAP and IFRS apply to the reporting entity's business and the terms of the instrument.

3.11.59.40 When the redemption amount of a puttable instrument is based on the change in fair value of the recognised and unrecognised net assets of the entity, judgement still should be applied to determine whether the total expected cash flows test is met, but, in our experience, it often will be straightforward to determine.

3.11.60 *Reclassification*

IAS 32.16E   3.11.60.10 A puttable instrument or an instrument that imposes on the entity an obligation only on liquidation is reclassified as equity from the date when the instrument has all the features and meets the conditions set out in 3.11.50.20 and 30, and 3.11.51.10 and 20. An instrument is reclassified from equity to financial liabilities from the date when the instrument ceases to have all of the features or meet all of the conditions for equity classification.

3.11.60.20 This indicates a continuous assessment model under which an entity reassesses its classification of instruments whenever there are changes to the capital structure of the entity, e.g. when new classes of shares are issued or when existing shares are redeemed, or when the expectations as to "total expected cash flows" and the evaluation as to whether they are based substantially on IFRS profit or loss or change in recognised net assets changes.

IAS 32.16F(a)   3.11.60.30 When a puttable instrument, or an instrument that imposes on the entity an obligation only on liquidation is reclassified from equity to financial liabilities, the liability is measured initially at the instrument's fair value at the date of reclassification. Any difference between the carrying amount of the equity instrument and the fair value of the financial liability at the date of reclassification is recognised in equity.

IAS 32.16F(b)   3.11.60.40 When a puttable instrument, or an instrument that imposes on the entity an obligation only on liquidation is reclassified from financial liability to equity, the equity instrument is measured at the carrying amount of the financial liability at the date of reclassification.

3.11.60.50 In either case, there is no pre-tax profit or loss impact arising from the reclassification. Any potential income tax accounting implications under IAS 12 *Income Taxes* (see 3.13) resulting from the reclassification should be considered.

3.11.65 *Instruments to be settled in own equity*

IAS 32.21   3.11.65.10 A contract that will be settled by the entity issuing its own equity instruments generally does not create an obligation on the part of the entity to deliver cash or another financial asset. However, IAS 32 imposes additional requirements that have to be met in order to classify such instruments as equity.

IAS 32.11,   3.11.65.20 If a non-derivative contract will or may be settled in the issuer's own equity
16(b)(i), 21,   instruments, then it is a financial liability if it includes a contractual obligation for the
AG27(d)   issuer to deliver a *variable number* of its own equity instruments. Liability classification follows from the fact that, from the holder's perspective, the return is fixed in the same way as if settlement were to be made in cash. As a result, the holder does not have an equity exposure as would be the case if the issuer were obliged to deliver a fixed number of shares.

3.11.65.30 Also, if a contract may be settled either in the issuer's own equity instruments (whether fixed or variable in number) or in cash or other financial assets, at the option of the *holder*, then the instrument is a financial liability or contains a liability component (e.g. a bond convertible into shares at the holder's option).

IAS 32.11,   3.11.65.40 If a derivative contract will be settled by the entity receiving or delivering a
16(b)(ii)   fixed number of own shares for a fixed amount of cash or another financial asset, then the contract is an equity instrument of the entity. A contract that is settled by an entity issuing a variable number of own shares for a fixed amount of cash, or a fixed number of own shares for a variable amount of cash, is a financial asset or liability of the entity.

IAS 32.21   3.11.65.60 A contract is a financial liability if an entity has an obligation to deliver a number of its own equity instruments that varies so that the total fair value of the equity instruments delivered is equal to the amount of the contractual obligation. The amount of that contractual obligation could be fixed, or it could vary in response to changes in another market variable that is unrelated to the market value of the entity's equity instruments, e.g. the gold price. In these circumstances the holder is not exposed to any gain or loss arising from movements in the fair value of the equity instruments. Consequently, in all such instances the entity is using its equity instruments as currency and such contracts are either financial assets or financial liabilities of the entity.

IAS 32.22   3.11.65.70 On the other hand, a contract is an equity instrument if it can be settled only by the entity receiving or delivering a fixed number of its own equity instruments for a fixed amount of cash or another financial asset (the so-called fixed-for-fixed requirement). For example, an issued share option that gives the holder the right to buy a fixed number of the entity's shares for a fixed amount of cash is an equity instrument. IAS 32 also goes on to state that changes in fair value of an instrument that will be settled by the entity delivering a fixed number of its own shares as a result of changes in market interest rates does not impact classification as equity instruments. However, such changes should not affect the amount of cash or other financial assets to be received or paid or the number of equity instruments to be received or delivered.

3.11.65.80 In our view, the requirement that a contract be settled by delivering a fixed number of its own shares for a fixed amount of cash, in order to be classified as equity, also can be met if the number of shares to be delivered and the amount of cash to be received changes over the life of the contract but the change is predetermined at the inception of the contract. For example, consider an option where the parties can exercise the option at predetermined dates (a Bermudan option). At each date the option can be settled by the entity delivering a fixed number of its own shares for a fixed amount of cash, but the number of shares and the amount of cash depends on the date of exercise of the option; the exact terms of the exchange at each exercise date were determined when the entity entered into the contract, i.e. the number of shares to be delivered are fixed for each date at inception. Such a contract is in fact a series of European style option contracts that each will be settled by the entity delivering a fixed amount of its own shares for a fixed amount of cash. Consequently, we believe that such a contract, assuming that it meets the other requirements, should be classified as an equity instrument.

3.11.65.81 Similarly, in our view adjustment clauses that alter the conversion ratio only to prevent dilution (anti-dilution) do not violate the fixed-for-fixed requirements and therefore do not result in the instrument being classified as a financial liability. In this context, anti-dilution refers to the adjustment of the conversion ratio to compensate holders of the instrument for changes in the number of equity instruments outstanding that relate to share issuances or redemptions not made at fair value, e.g. arising from rights issues or bonus issues. Anti-dilution does not comprise any other form of compensation to the instrument holder for fair value losses, e.g. when compensation is given if the share price falls below a certain level.

3.11.65.82 Many convertible bonds include a takeover clause that allows the holder to exercise its conversion option at an enhanced conversion ratio in the event of a change of control of the issuer. A takeover may negatively affect bondholders relative to shareholders, for example, if current shareholders are bought out by an acquirer and the issuer's business is transferred to a new entity or the underlying shares are delisted. In our view, if such a clause is designed to compensate bondholders for the loss of optionality that arises on a takeover and is intended to preserve the relative economic interests of bondholders and shareholders, then, as in the case of an "anti-dilution" clause, it does not violate the fixed-for-fixed criterion.

3.11.65.85 Except as described in 3.11.65.81 – 82, in our view the requirement that a contract be settled by delivering a fixed number of its own shares for a fixed amount of cash cannot be met when the right to the number of shares to be delivered is contingent on *both* the exercise date of the instrument and equity prices or any other index. For example, an entity issues a convertible bond containing a right for the holder to convert the bond into shares of the issuer. The number of shares received at each exercise date is dependent upon the average share prices prevailing three months prior to the exercise date (i.e. a path-dependent option). In our view, an instrument such as a path-dependent option does not meet the fixed-for-fixed requirement as there is variability not only in the date of exercise (as in the example in 3.11.65.80 on European style option contracts) but also variability in the actual number of shares that will be issued at each exercise date.

IAS 32.22   3.11.65.90 Any consideration received or paid for an instrument that is classified as an equity instrument, for example the option premium, is added to or deducted from equity.

IAS 32.23   3.11.65.100 An instrument that creates an obligation or potential obligation for an entity to purchase its own equity instruments for cash or another financial asset gives rise to a financial liability, and the amount of the liability is measured at the present value of the redemption amount (see 3.11.45). This is the case even if the contract itself is an equity instrument. Consequently, even if a contract entered into to purchase an entity's own equity instruments is classified as equity (i.e. a fixed amount of cash for a fixed number of equity instruments), an accounting entry is required to recognise a liability for the present value of the redemption amount with a corresponding debit to equity. In effect, a reclassification is made from equity to reflect the obligation to repurchase the equity instruments in the future. If the contract expires without the obligation being settled, for example, if a written put option expires unexercised, then the carrying amount of the liability at that time is reclassified to equity.

IAS 32.AG29   3.11.65.110 In our view, this applies equally from a consolidated financial statements perspective to an (potential) obligation to purchase *a subsidiary's* equity instruments. This derives from the requirement that when an entity presents NCI or when it classifies a financial instrument (or a component thereof) in consolidated financial statements, the entity considers all terms and conditions agreed between members of the group and the holders of the instrument.

IU 11-06   3.11.65.120 When an entity has a potential obligation to purchase shares from non-controlling interests in a subsidiary through a written put option, in our view the entity recognises a liability for the present value of the strike price of the option. See 2.5.460 for further discussion of written puts/(synthetic) forwards on NCI.

3.11.65.130 However, in our view an obligation or potential obligation (either in the form of forward or option contracts) to purchase an associate's or a jointly controlled entity's equity instruments should be classified as derivative instruments in the separate, individual and/or consolidated financial statements of the investor. This is because associates and jointly controlled entities are not part of the group (see 2.1.50.10).

3.11.67 *Contingent consideration in a business combination*

IFRS 3.40   3.11.67.10 Contingent consideration may be included in the consideration transferred in a business combination (see 2.6.920). IFRS 3 *Business Combinations* requires an obligation to pay contingent consideration to be classified as a liability or equity on the basis of the definitions of an equity instrument and a financial liability in paragraph 11 of IAS 32, or other applicable IFRSs. That means that the "fixed-for-fixed criterion" as described in 3.11.65 has to be met in order for consideration that is settled in own equity instruments to be classified as equity. The subsequent accounting for the contingent consideration is dependent on this classification.

3.11.67.20 In our view, the existence of any contingency regarding whether or not any own shares will be delivered does not necessarily disqualify the contingent consideration from equity classification. We believe that if one of the possible outcomes in respect of the contingency is the delivery of neither shares nor other considerations, then this does not of itself preclude equity classification as the delivery of no consideration does not constitute a "settlement". For example, if the arrangement involved issuing either zero or a single fixed amount of equity shares then the fixed for fixed criterion will be met as the only way that settlement could take place is by delivering a single fixed amount of shares.

IFRS 3.40 3.11.67.30 Also, in our view the classification analysis is performed for an obligation to pay contingent consideration as referred to in IFRS 3 rather than to the entire contract. An entire contract approach generally is not feasible given that a contingent consideration arrangement usually is just one element of an overall sale and purchase agreement that governs all aspects of the business combination. We believe that a single business combination may involve more than one obligation to pay contingent consideration and that each obligation should be analysed separately as to whether it is equity or liability.

3.11.67.40 In our view, two policies are acceptable to analyse the relationships between obligations. An entity should choose an accounting policy, to be applied consistently, to analyse such relationships. We believe that one obligation may be seen as separate from another obligation if there is no necessary relationship between the outcome or settlement of the obligations. For example, non-cumulative obligations to deliver shares based on different profit targets for different years may be seen as independent and therefore separate because there is no necessary link between meeting the target for one year and meeting the target for another year. However, if there were an overlap between the periods, the targets would not be independent. Alternatively, we believe that a policy that views an obligation as separate from another obligation only if there is no underlying causal relationship or significant correlation between the outcome or settlement of the obligations also would be acceptable. Therefore, if the latter policy is chosen, non-cumulative requirements to deliver shares based on different profit targets for different years are seen as a single obligation because the underlying operational and economic factors that influence performance in one year will tend to influence performance in another year. For example, an entity's performance across a number of years may be influenced by the successful development of, or failure to develop, a new product line.

3.11.67.50 To illustrate the principles set out in 3.11.67.40, the following table contains several scenarios and the respective classification assessments:

Scenario	Classification
The vendor receives shares in the acquirer to the value of 50 if the acquiree's cumulative profits over a three-year period are at least 20.	Liability, since there is a single obligation to deliver a variable number of shares.
The vendor receives 50 shares in the acquirer if the acquiree's cumulative profits over a three-year period are at least 20.	Equity, since there is a single obligation to deliver a fixed number of shares.
The vendor receives 50 shares in the acquirer if the acquiree's cumulative profits over a three-year period are at least 20, and 100 shares if profits are at least 40.	Liability, since the arrangement involves settling with either 50 or 100 shares, i.e. a variable rather than a fixed number. The profit targets relate to the same period and therefore they are not independent.
The vendor will receive one share in the acquirer for every 1 of profit in excess of 10.	Liability, the analysis is similar to the previous example except that the number of shares is more obviously variable.
Share-settled contingent consideration is payable in three tranches: 1,000 shares if an earnings target is achieved for 2011; 1,000 shares if an earnings target is achieved for 2012; and 1,000 shares if an earnings target is achieved for 2013. Each target relates to annual earnings of the acquiree and is non-cumulative.	The classification depends on the policy adopted as described in 3.11.67.40. This may be considered three separate obligations to deliver a fixed 1,000 of shares each (equity) or a single obligation to deliver 1,000, 2,000 or 3,000 shares (liability).

3.11.70 **Settlement options in derivative instruments**

IAS 32.26, 27 3.11.70.10 A choice of the manner in which derivative financial instruments are settled (e.g. when the issuer or the holder could opt to settle net or gross) could determine their classification. IAS 32 states that a derivative financial instrument with settlement options is a financial asset or liability unless *all* of the settlement alternatives result in equity classification. Consequently, settlement options, even those that are at the discretion of the entity, could result in instruments being classified as financial assets or liabilities. For example, an entity may issue a warrant that gives the holder the right to acquire a fixed number of the issuer's own equity instruments for a fixed amount of cash. If the warrant expires unexercised, then the issuer will pay to the holder a fixed cancellation fee. Given that the holder may choose to receive cash or shares, the warrant is a financial liability and not an equity instrument of the entity.

3.11.70.20 In another example, Company H issues preference shares at par that are redeemable in five years and do not carry the right to receive dividends. At the end of five years H has the option to redeem the shares, either in a fixed number of own shares or in cash at an amount that is equal to the fair value of the shares. Consequently, H does not have an obligation to transfer cash or another financial asset; nor does the entire instrument meet the definition of a derivative as it fails the initial net investment criterion (see 3.6.190). Therefore the provisions regarding settlement options do not apply and the entire instrument is classified as equity.

3.11.80 *Discretionary payments: dividends and other payments*

IAS 32.19(a), 25, AG26   3.11.80.10 A contractual requirement to pay dividends is an obligation to deliver cash; therefore it gives rise to a financial liability. This does not change even if the agreement to pay is conditional on the entity earning sufficient distributable profits; a restriction on the ability of an entity to satisfy a contractual obligation does not negate this obligation (see 3.11.30).

IAS 32.19   3.11.80.20 Dividends or other payments may be discretionary (i.e. there is no obligation to pay). For example, normally dividends on ordinary shares vary depending on the level of profitability and the entity has discretion in deciding whether or not to pay dividends and how much to pay. Although there may be an expectation that dividends will be paid if a certain level of profitability is achieved, this expectation is not a contractual obligation. Therefore, the entity is able to avoid the transfer of cash or another financial asset.

IAS 32.AG26   3.11.80.30 Generally, when preference shares are non-redeemable, the appropriate classification is determined by the other rights that attach to them, in particular distributions to holders. If the dividends are cumulative, then this suggests that the issuer may delay but cannot avoid the payment of dividends. However, if the issuer has the discretion to avoid the payment of dividends under all circumstances until the liquidation of the entity, then the dividends are discretionary and do not give rise to an obligation. For example, if a non-redeemable preference share has a cumulative dividend, but payment is discretionary, then classification as equity is not precluded.

3.11.90 *Compound instruments*

IAS 32.29, AG31   3.11.90.10 An instrument may contain both a financial liability (e.g. obligation to make interest and/or scheduled principal payments) and an equity component (e.g. a conversion feature in a convertible bond). Such an instrument is a compound instrument.

IAS 32.28   3.11.90.20 The issuer of compound instruments classifies the liability and equity components of the instrument separately as financial liability and equity ("split accounting").

IAS 32.31   3.11.90.30 A typical form of a compound instrument is a convertible bond, in which the holder is entitled to convert the instrument into equity instruments of the entity. A less common form of compound instrument is one in which the equity characteristics lie in the dividend or interest stream rather than in the convertibility of the principal amount. For example, consider a non-cumulative mandatorily redeemable preference share, on which dividends are payable at the discretion of the issuer. In this case the present value of the redemption amount represents the financial liability, with any remaining proceeds being attributed to equity.

IAS 32.31 3.11.90.40 The same split accounting applies to share purchase warrants attached to debt instruments, irrespective of whether they formally are detachable from the debt instruments. The share purchase warrants should be split and accounted for as an equity component by the issuer if the warrants meet the definition of an equity instrument. In this case the amount allocable to the debt instrument is determined first, with any remaining proceeds being attributed to the warrants.

IAS 32.30 3.11.90.50 Subject to 3.11.20.70 and 3.11.150, the initial classification of a convertible instrument into its liability and equity components is not revised subsequent to initial recognition, even if the likelihood of the conversion option being exercised changes over time.

3.11.90.60 See 3.11.190 for a discussion of the measurement of the financial liability and equity components of a compound financial instrument.

3.11.100 *Accounting for early redemption*

IAS 32.AG33 3.11.100.10 On early redemption of a convertible instrument, the redemption payment is allocated to the liability and equity components using a method consistent with the method used initially to allocate the instrument between its debt and equity components (see 3.11.190). The fair value of the liability component at redemption date is compared to its carrying amount, giving rise to a gain or loss on redemption that is recognised in profit or loss. The remainder of the redemption payment is recognised in equity.

3.11.110 *Accounting for conversion*

IAS 32.AG32 3.11.110.10 On conversion of a convertible instrument, which is a compound instrument, the entity derecognises the liability component that is extinguished when the conversion feature is exercised, and recognises the same amount as equity. The original equity component remains as equity, although it may be transferred within equity (see 3.11.410). No gain or loss is recognised in profit or loss.

3.11.110.20 However, issues regarding the recognition of the gain or loss may arise when convertible instruments contain embedded derivatives (see also 3.11.140.50).

3.11.110.30 For example, an entity issues a 10-year convertible bond that is convertible at any time at the option of the holder after five years (American style option). The conversion feature is classified at inception as equity, as it meets the fixed-for-fixed requirements (see 3.11.65.70), and the host debt instrument is carried at amortised cost.

3.11.110.40 A question arises as to whether to treat the liability component as having a 10-year maturity or whether to treat earlier conversion as a prepayment of the liability component. Under the first approach the carrying amount of the liability on conversion would be reclassified to equity (see 3.11.110.10). Under the second approach the liability would be remeasured to par at conversion, with additional interest expense being recognised in profit or loss under paragraph AG8 of IAS 39 (see 4.6.60).

788

3.11.110.50 In our view, such conversion represents in effect a conversion at maturity as the bond does not have a fixed maturity of 10 years due to the operation of the American style option. The convertible bond should be accounted for as a non-prepayable host contract and an American style equity option recognised in equity. Consequently, in our view no prepayment or other adjustment features in the host contract should lead to the recognition of a gain or loss arising from the revision of cash flow estimates (see 4.6.60).

3.11.110.60 As the conversion is arising from the exercise of the equity conversion option, which is an American style option recognised in equity and not remeasured through profit or loss under IAS 32, we believe that no gain or loss should be recognised in profit or loss on conversion of the bond.

3.11.110.70 In another example, the convertible bond in the example in 3.11.110.30 contains a prepayment feature that enables the issuer to call the bond at any time after five years at par. The prepayment option is not accounted for separately if it is closely related to the host contract (see 3.6.260), and if the issuer calls the bond and the holder has not exercised the conversion option, then the conversion option is extinguished. In our view, when the issuer repurchases the bond under the call option it should recognise a catch up to the amortised cost accounting under paragraph AG8 of IAS 39 (see 4.6.60). This is because, in contrast to the example in 3.11.110.30, the issuer's call option is separate from the holder's conversion option.

3.11.110.80 In both examples, the carrying amount of the liability component at conversion is reclassified to equity. However, in the first scenario (see 3.11.110.50) the carrying amount of the liability component would be less than the par amount at the conversion date and in the second scenario (see 3.11.110.70) the carrying amount of the liability component would be adjusted to par under paragraph AG8 of IAS 39 prior to conversion with an impact on profit or loss.

3.11.120 *Amendment to induce early conversion*

3.11.120.10 An entity may amend the terms of a convertible instrument to induce early conversion, for example, by offering a more favourable conversion ratio in the event of conversion before a specified date.

IAS 32.AG35 3.11.120.20 The difference between the fair value of the consideration that the holder receives on conversion of the instrument under the revised terms, and the fair value of the consideration that the holder would have received under the original terms, is recognised in profit or loss when the terms are amended.

3.11.130 *Foreign currency convertible bond#*

3.11.130.10 If a convertible bond is denominated in a currency other than the functional currency of the entity, then an issue arises regarding the classification of the conversion option. For example, an entity with a euro functional currency issues a convertible bond denominated in US dollars. The bond carries a fixed rate of interest and is convertible at the end of 10 years, at the holder's option, into a fixed number of euro-denominated shares of the entity. No settlement alternative is provided to the issuer under the terms of the bond. The conversion option is an obligation for the issuer to issue a fixed number of shares in exchange for a financial asset (the principal amount of the bond) that represents a right to receive an amount of cash that is fixed in US dollar terms but variable in functional currency terms.

3.11.130.20 In our view, an obligation denominated in a foreign currency represents a variable amount of cash. Consequently, contracts, both free-standing and embedded, that will be settled by an entity delivering a fixed number of its own equity instruments in exchange for a fixed amount of foreign currency should be classified as liabilities. In other words, the conversion feature in the convertible bond in 3.11.130.10 should be classified as a liability.

IU 11-06 3.11.130.30 A related issue arises if a convertible bond denominated in a foreign currency is issued by a subsidiary that has a functional currency different from that of its parent, which is convertible into the shares of the parent. In the subsidiary's separate or individual financial statements the conversion feature is a liability since the bond is denominated in a currency other than the subsidiary's functional currency. However, since a group as a whole has no functional currency (see 2.7.30), in our view, two approaches are possible in the consolidated financial statements. We believe that an entity should choose an accounting policy, to be applied consistently, to base the classification in the consolidated financial statements on the functional currency of either the parent or the subsidiary.

3.11.130.40 In addition, in our view:

- if the bond is denominated in a currency other than the functional currency of either the parent or the subsidiary, then the conversion feature is a (derivative) liability;
- the currency in which the shares are denominated is not relevant to the analysis; the only requirement is that the number of shares is fixed; and
- the presentation currency or currencies of the group's consolidated financial statements (see 2.7.60) has no impact on the analysis.

3.11.130.45 Another issue arises in cases of inflation indexation. For example, Company S issued a convertible bond denominated in its functional currency. Both principal and interest payments of the instrument are indexed to changes in the CPI inflation of the economic environment of S. In our view, such indexation creates variability in the amount of cash being exchanged for a fixed number of shares and therefore such conversion feature should be classified as a financial liability. This principle applies even if the functional currency of the entity is the currency of a hyperinflationary economy.

3.11.131 *Forthcoming requirements*

3.11.131.10 In October 2009 the IASB issued Amendment to IAS 32 *Classification of Rights Issues*. The limited amendment to IAS 32 requires that rights, options or warrants to acquire a fixed number of the entity's own equity instruments for a fixed amount of any currency are equity instruments under certain circumstances. See 3.11.455 for further detail.

3.11.140 *Cash settlement option in a convertible bond*

3.11.140.10 Many convertible bonds include a cash settlement option for the issuer in the event of the holder exercising its right to convert the bonds into ordinary shares. For example, an entity with a euro functional currency issues euro-denominated fixed rate bonds with a 20-year maturity, convertible at the option of the holder into a fixed number of the issuer's ordinary shares at any time during the life of the bond. In the event of the holder exercising its conversion option, the issuer has the right to settle either by delivering a fixed number of shares or in cash at an amount equal to the market value of the shares to be issued.

3.11.140.20 Generally a convertible bond is a compound instrument, i.e. having characteristics of both equity and a liability. However, in the example in 3.11.140.10, the convertible bond comprises an obligation to make fixed interest payments, and an obligation to deliver cash to the holder upon redemption of the bond in the event of the holder not exercising its conversion option. These features clearly are characteristics associated with a financial liability.

IAS 32.26 3.11.140.30 In addition, the instrument contains a conversion feature whereby there may be an exchange of a fixed number of shares for a fixed amount of cash. The issuer can settle the conversion option either by paying the holder the market value of the shares in cash or through physical delivery of the shares. Consequently, the conversion option can be settled other than by the issuer exchanging a fixed number of shares for a fixed amount of cash.

3.11.140.40 Since the conversion option is a derivative financial instrument, the settlement option causes it to be classified as a financial liability instead of being an equity instrument. Therefore, in this case the convertible bond is not a compound instrument under IAS 32. Rather, it comprises a liability for the interest and principal amount plus a derivative instrument for the conversion option. The liability should be measured at amortised cost and the derivative, not being closely related to the host, should be measured at fair value through profit or loss; alternatively, the entire instrument is measured at fair value through profit or loss. See 3.6.260 for a discussion of measurement of the accounting for embedded derivatives.

3.11.140.50 In our view, in contrast to the accounting for conversion of a compound instrument (see 3.11.110.10), the conversion of a hybrid instrument that is classified entirely as a financial liability should be accounted for as an extinguishment of a financial liability, and hence the conversion could give rise to a gain or loss in profit or loss. See 3.11.240 for guidance on the reclassification of instruments between liability and equity.

3.11.150 *Restructuring a convertible bond#*

3.11.150.10 Continuing the example in 3.11.140.10 – 40, the issuer might restructure the convertible bond by removing the cash settlement alternative in the conversion option. As a result the issuer would have a contract that requires it to physically deliver a fixed number of shares in exchange for a fixed amount of the bond upon exercise by the holder. Such a contract meets the definition of an equity instrument and consequently the conversion option is classified as such.

3.11.150.20 However, concluding that the restructured conversion option should be presented as equity is only the first step in accounting for the restructuring.

3.11.150.30 Further consideration should be given as to whether or not the restructuring would be considered a significant modification of the terms of the bond, resulting in it being accounted for as a debt extinguishment (see 3.6.1340).

IAS 39.AG62 3.11.150.40 IAS 39 provides specific guidance when there is a modification in the cash flows of a debt instrument (see 3.6.1340). However, when the terms of the conversion option are revised, there is no such cash flow effect. In such circumstances, in our view the impact of the modification from the holder's perspective should be considered. Continuing the example in 3.11.150.10 with a cash settlement option, the holder might receive cash directly from the issuer at an amount equal to the market value of the shares instead of receiving the shares and converting them into cash. The amount of cash accruing to the holder with or without the cash settlement option is almost the same. Consequently, removal of the cash settlement option does not, in our view, represent a substantial modification of the bond. As a result the restructuring does not lead to a derecognition or extinguishment of the "original" convertible bond and the recognition of a "new" convertible bond.

3.11.150.50 However, the restructuring does result in the extinguishment of the derivative component as this is exchanged for an equity component. From the perspective of the holder this comprises an exchange of financial assets. However, as there is no cash transfer in the transaction, the consideration paid usually will be the fair value of the instrument received, i.e. the new conversion option without a cash settlement feature. As the fair value of the "old" conversion option is almost identical at the date of the restructuring to the fair value of the "new" conversion option (see 3.11.150.60), no significant gain or loss will arise.

3.11.150.60 The "old" conversion option would have been measured at fair value through profit or loss until the restructuring of the convertible bond. At the date of restructuring the derivative component is derecognised and a new instrument is recognised in equity at fair value (assuming that the fair value of both options is the same).

3.11.151 *Forthcoming requirements*

3.11.151.10 The IASB published IFRIC 19 *Extinguishing Financial Liabilities with Equity Instruments*. The interpretation addresses the accounting by the debtor in a debt for equity swap transaction. See 3.11.455 for further detail.

3.11.160 *Perpetual instruments*

IAS 32.AG6   3.11.160.10 Perpetual debt instruments normally provide the holder with a contractual right to receive an indefinite stream of interest payments at a market rate of interest with no redemption of principal. Even though the holder will not receive repayment of the principal, such instruments are a liability of the issuer as there is a contractual obligation to make a stream of future interest payments to the holder. On the assumption the terms of the instrument are at market rate the face value or the carrying amount of the instrument reflects the present value of the holder's right to receive these interest payments in perpetuity.

3.11.170 *Preference shares*

IAS 32.AG25,   3.11.170.10 Preference shares that provide for redemption at the option of the holder
   AG26   give rise to a contractual obligation and should be classified as financial liabilities. If preference shares are not redeemable at the option of the holder, then the appropriate classification depends on the other terms and conditions associated with such shares, in particular the attached dividend rights. If dividends are discretionary, this fact supports the classification of the preference shares as equity instruments. If dividends are not discretionary, then they represent a contractual obligation and are a financial liability of the issuer.

3.11.170.20 A typical example of a cumulative perpetual preference share is one with the following characteristics:

- the issuer has an obligation to pay dividends on preference shares only if it pays a dividend on its ordinary shares; and
- the preference dividend is cumulative.

IAS 32.25   3.11.170.30 The fact that dividends are payable only if ordinary dividends, which are discretionary, are paid ("dividend stopper feature") does not create an obligation. However, due to the cumulative feature, the instrument is classified as equity only if: the accumulated dividends can be deferred indefinitely, i.e. until liquidation of the entity; and there is no other feature of the instrument that would lead to liability classification.

3.11.170.40 The terms of certain preference shares provide for the accrual of interest on cumulative discretionary dividends even before such dividends are declared. In other words, interest accrues from that point in time at which the dividend *might* have been declared such that if the dividend is declared, then an amount of interest becomes payable automatically. In our view, the accrual of interest alone does not cause such preference shares to be classified as a liability as long as the dividends remain discretionary, i.e. the entity can avoid the payment of both dividend and interest on unpaid dividends until liquidation of the entity.

3.11.170.50 A preference dividend, in which payment is contingent upon the availability of future distributable profits, differs from a discretionary dividend. With a discretionary dividend the issuer is able to avoid the payment of dividends indefinitely. However, the payment of a contingent dividend cannot be avoided indefinitely. The fact that the issuer, at the present time, might be unable pay the dividend has no bearing on the classification of the preference shares. Consequently, a preference share that bears contingent dividends should be classified as a liability.

IAS 32.25   3.11.170.60 For example, Company K issues preference shares redeemable at the option of the issuer at a fixed redemption price of 100 per share plus any accrued unpaid dividends. There is no fixed redemption date, i.e. the holder has no right to demand repayment at a certain date. The payment of dividends is at the discretion of the issuer. However, the payment of dividends is required if K's parent pays dividends on its ordinary shares. Therefore, the payment of dividends is contingent upon the occurrence of an uncertain future event that is beyond the control of both the issuer and the holder of the instrument. Consequently, a liability should be recognised. In substance, this instrument is a perpetual instrument with variable dividend payments. Therefore, the amount of the initial investment represents the expected value of the variable contingent dividend payments, which are classified as a liability.

3.11.170.70 The classification of the instrument in 3.11.170.60 would be different in the consolidated financial statements of the parent because the payment of dividends at the consolidated level is at the discretion of the parent.

3.11.180 Recognition and measurement

IAS 39.2(d)   3.11.180.10 IFRSs do not have any specific measurement rules related to equity, other than in respect of splitting compound instruments, the cost of equity transactions and own equity instruments acquired and reissued or cancelled (see below). In part this is because the IFRSs on financial instruments generally do not apply to own equity.

3.11.180.20 As a general principle, the definitions of income and expenses exclude transactions with holders of equity instruments. Therefore, no gains or losses should be reported in profit or loss on transactions in equity instruments. All the effects of transactions with owners should be recognised directly in equity. However, certain derivatives on own equity, when they do not meet the definition of equity, will be treated as derivative assets or liabilities and will result in gains and losses recognised in profit or loss (see 3.6.790).

3.11.180.30 Recognition and measurement requirements for equity instruments that are issued in share-based payment transactions are specified in IFRS 2 *Share-based Payment* (see 4.5).

3.11.190 *Compound instruments*

IAS 32.31, 32   3.11.190.10 When allocating the initial carrying amount of a compound instrument to the underlying financial liability and the equity components, an entity first determines the fair value of the liability component, including any embedded derivatives, whether or not they have to be accounted for separately. The fair value of the liability component is determined by reference to the fair value of a similar stand-alone debt instrument (including any embedded non-equity derivatives). The amount allocated to the equity component is the residual after deducting the fair value of the financial liability component from the fair value of the entire compound instrument.

3.11.190.20 For example, Company Y issues 2,000 convertible bonds at the start of year one. The bonds have a three-year term, and are issued at par with a face value of 1,000 per bond, giving total proceeds of 2,000,000. Interest is payable annually in arrears at a nominal annual interest rate of 6 percent. Each bond is convertible at any time until maturity into 250 ordinary shares. When the bonds are issued, the prevailing market interest rate for a similar liability without a conversion option is 9 percent.

3.11.190.30 The present value of the financial liability component is calculated using a discount rate of 9 percent (the market interest rate for similar bonds having no conversion rights):

Present value of the principal – 2,000,000 payable at the end of three years	1,544,367
Present value of the interest – 120,000 payable annually in arrears for three years	303,755
Total liability component	1,848,122
Equity component (balancing figure)	151,878
Proceeds of the bond issue	2,000,000

3.11.190.40 The unwinding of the discount is accounted for as an interest expense. However, when dividends are declared post-conversion of the bonds, these relate to the equity component and are recognised as a distribution of profits.

3.11.190.50 See 3.13.160 for guidance on the recognition of deferred tax liabilities on compound financial instruments.

3.11.200 *Share splits and bonus issues*

3.11.200.10 IFRSs do not require any adjustment to total equity or to individual components of equity presented in the financial statements in the case of a simple split of shares or a bonus issue, although they may have an impact on basic and diluted earnings per share (see 5.3.360). However, the laws of the country of incorporation may require a reallocation of capital within equity.

3.11.200.20 There is no guidance in IFRSs on whether a share dividend should be treated as a share split or bonus issue. See 3.11.450.80 and 4.6.280 for guidance on the treatment of share dividends.

3.11.210 *Prepaid capital contributions*

3.11.210.10 Shareholders may pay for shares before they are issued. An issue then arises as to whether the prepayment should be recognised directly in equity or shown as a liability.

3.11.210.20 If there is any possibility that the entity may be required to repay the amount received, for example if the share issue is conditional on uncertain future events, then in our view the amount received should be shown as a liability. However, if there is no possibility of the prepayment being refunded, so that the entity's obligation is to deliver only a fixed number of shares, then we believe that the amount should be credited to a separate category of equity, for example a prepaid share reserve. The notes to the financial statements should contain disclosure of the prepayment and the terms of the shares to be issued.

3.11.220 *Receivables in respect of equity contributions*

3.11.220.10 An entity may be owed an amount in respect of a contribution for new equity shares which have already been issued or as an equity contribution for which no new shares will be issued (see 3.11.230). In this case an issue arises as to when the equity should be recognised.

3.11.220.20 In our view, the equity and a corresponding receivable is recognised if the receivable meets the definition of a financial asset. This requires the entity to have a contractual right to receive the amount at the reporting date. A contractual right is more than an informal agreement or a non-contractual commitment.

3.11.220.30 If the shareholder is not committed contractually to make the contribution at the reporting date, then no receivable should be recorded in respect of the transaction.

3.11.220.40 If a receivable is recognised but payment is not expected in the short term, then the amount should be discounted and recorded, in both equity and receivables, at the present value of the amount to be received; unwinding of the discount on the receivable should be accounted for as interest income (see 4.6.20).

3.11.220.50 An entity might decide to increase its share capital through a shareholders' resolution to issue new shares. However, in certain jurisdictions this does not establish a contractual right for the entity to receive cash or another financial asset; nor does it contractually bind the shareholders. In our view, unless and until there is a contractual right and the new shares are issued or outstanding, no receivable or outstanding shares should be recognised with respect to the transaction.

3.11.230 *Non-reciprocal capital contributions*

3.11.230.10 Sometimes an entity receives amounts from shareholders in the form of capital contributions, being either cash or other non-monetary assets, which are non-reciprocal (i.e. no financial or non-financial obligation exists). This may happen, for example, when an entity requires additional financing or is in financial difficulty. Amounts might be received from all shareholders or only certain shareholders.

3.11.230.20 IFRSs do not contain any specific guidance on transactions with shareholders. However, in applying the definitions of financial liabilities and equity, in our view the amount received should be accounted for in accordance with its substance as follows:

- If there is any possibility of having to repay the amount received, then a liability should be recognised for the advance.
- If there is no requirement to repay the amount under any circumstances and any repayment is entirely at the discretion of the entity that receives the contribution, then normally the economic substance will be an equity contribution and not income, as generally the shareholder is acting in its capacity as a shareholder in such cases. In our experience it is highly unlikely that an entity would receive a non-reciprocal capital contribution from an unrelated third party.

3.11.230.30 If the amount is treated as equity, then it may be classified as additional paid-in capital or perhaps as share premium or as a separate reserve "contributed assets". However, the classification within equity will often be determined by the legal framework.

3.11.230.40 The recognition criteria for receivables in respect of equity transactions (see 3.11.220) should be applied in determining when a non-reciprocal capital contribution is recognised.

3.11.230.50 If a shareholder forgives debt, then it is likely that the shareholder is acting in its capacity as a shareholder and that the forgiveness of debt should be treated as a capital transaction (see 3.6.1360.20).

3.11.240 *Reclassification of instruments between liability and equity#*

IU 11-06 3.11.240.10 An entity may amend the terms of an instrument such that the classification of the instrument changes from equity to a financial liability or vice versa. For example, Company J has perpetual preference shares, which were issued for 1,000 and which carry the right to receive a discretionary dividend of 10 percent. J amends the terms of the instrument such that redemption will be required in the event of a change in control of the entity. Since the entity no longer has the unconditional ability to avoid payment, as a change in control is not within the control of the entity, the instrument is reclassified as a financial liability. In our view, the financial liability should be measured on initial recognition at fair value at the date of reclassification. If, for example, market interest rates have fallen and the fair value of the instrument on initial recognition as a financial liability is 1,200 then an adjustment of 200 would be recognised in equity on extinguishment of the equity instrument.

3.11.240.20 On the other hand, when the classification of an instrument changes from a financial liability to equity, in our view this represents the extinguishment of a financial liability and the issue of equity instruments and the resulting gain or loss on the extinguishment of the liability should be recognised in profit or loss (see 3.6.1340), or, when appropriate, as an equity contribution (see 3.11.230.50).

> **3.11.245 *Forthcoming requirements***
>
> **3.11.245.10** The IASB published IFRIC 19 *Extinguishing Financial Liabilities with Equity Instruments*. The interpretation addresses the accounting by the debtor in a debt for equity swap transaction. See 3.11.455 for further detail.

3.11.250 Treasury shares

3.11.260 *Recognition and measurement*

IAS 32.33   **3.11.260.10** Generally any amounts paid by an entity to acquire its own equity instruments are debited directly to equity. This applies whether the equity instruments are cancelled immediately or held for resale (i.e. treasury shares). Amounts received on the sale of treasury shares are credited directly to equity. No gains or losses are recognised in profit or loss on any purchase, sale, issue or cancellation of own equity instruments, or in respect of any changes in the value of treasury shares.

IAS 32.4(f),   **3.11.260.20** Own equity instruments held in connection with an equity compensation plan
33, 34   are required to be presented as treasury shares (see 4.5.530 and 1060).

3.11.260.30 Assets held in respect of employee benefit plans other than equity compensation plans may include the employer's own shares. See 4.4.410 for a discussion of the treatment of these shares.

3.11.270 *Treasury shares held for trading purposes*

3.11.270.10 Some entities hold their own equity instruments for trading purposes; for example, they may be part of a portfolio of investments held for trading purposes.

IAS 32.33,   **3.11.270.20** There are no exemptions for treasury shares held for trading purposes. Such
AG36   instruments may not be recognised as assets or measured at fair value with gains and losses recognised in profit or loss, which is the treatment for other trading investments (see 3.6.790).

3.11.280 *Treasury shares held for hedging purposes*

3.11.280.10 Treasury shares may be held for economic hedging purposes, for example to hedge an exposure to an index-linked structured note when the index includes the entity's own share price or to hedge against the cost of a share-based payment arrangement. Holding treasury shares as an economic hedge is not sufficient to override the treasury share accounting requirements even though this may give rise to a profit or loss mismatch. In this example, the index derivative feature in the structured notes will be measured at fair value with all changes therein recognised in profit or loss (see 3.6.790). Any own equity instruments held to hedge the index will be accounted for as treasury shares and changes in the value thereof will not be recognised.

IAS 39.72, 3.11.280.20 In our view, the hedge accounting principles explained in 3.7 are not applicable
AG97 to treasury shares. Treasury shares cannot be designated as a hedging instrument; the only non-derivatives that qualify as hedging instruments are financial assets or liabilities (for foreign exchange risk only), and own equity is not considered to be a financial asset or liability. Also, treasury shares cannot be designated as the hedged item; the hedged risk should be one that could affect reported income, and gains and losses on treasury shares are not recognised in profit or loss.

3.11.290 **Treasury shares held by subsidiaries**

IAS 32.33 3.11.290.10 In consolidated financial statements, treasury share accounting applies to own equity instruments that are held by a consolidated subsidiary.

3.11.290.20 For example, Company S is a subsidiary of Parent P. S has a 2 percent investment in P and S classifies its investment as available for sale. The investment was acquired at a cost of 72. The current fair value of the investment is 87. P would record the following entry in respect of the treasury shares on consolidation of S:

	Debit	Credit
Available-for-sale revaluation reserve	15	
Treasury shares (equity)	72	
Available-for-sale investments		87
To eliminate available-for-sale investment on consolidation and to recognise shares as treasury shares		

3.11.290.30 Continuing the example in 3.11.290.20, assume that in the next period S sells its investment in P for 90 S would recognise a profit of 18 in profit or loss on the sale of the investment. On consolidation, P would record the following entry to eliminate the profit recognised by S:

	Debit	Credit
Profit on disposal of investments	18	
Treasury shares (equity)		18
To eliminate profit recognised by S on consolidation		

3.11.290.40 See 3.11.310 for a discussion of the presentation of any surplus or deficit on the sale of treasury shares. Any current or deferred tax on the transactions also should be recognised in equity (see 3.13.400).

3.11.300 *Treasury shares held by associates*

IAS 1.79,
32.33

3.11.300.10 An associate may have an investment in its investor. The carrying amount of the associate under the equity method will include the investor's share of the associate's investment in the investor's own shares.

IAS 27.4,
32.33

3.11.300.20 In our view, the investor is not required to make any adjustment in respect of treasury shares held by an associate. We do not believe that the investor should reclassify this portion of the carrying amount of the investment in the associate as a deduction from equity. Similarly, if dividends are declared on these equity instruments, then no adjustment should be made to the entity's share of the associate's profit during the year. We believe that the lack of control over an associate, and also the definition of a group (i.e. a parent and all its subsidiaries (see 2.1.50.10)), distinguishes these from cases in which treasury shares are held by a subsidiary. Information about own equity instruments held by associates should be disclosed in the notes to the financial statements.

3.11.310 *Presentation*

3.11.310.10 IFRSs do not mandate a specific method of presenting treasury shares within equity. Laws may prescribe the allocation method. Therefore, an entity should take into account its legal environment when choosing how to present its own shares within equity. Possible presentation alternatives are explained below, although other methods also may be used. An entity should choose a presentation format, to be applied consistently to all treasury shares.

3.11.320 *Total cost of treasury shares as a separate category of equity*

3.11.320.10 In this case:

- the cost of treasury shares purchased is debited to a separate category of equity;
- when treasury shares are sold or reissued, the amount received for the instruments is credited to this category; and
- any surpluses or deficits on sales of treasury shares are shown as an adjustment to share premium or reserves, including retained earnings, or a combination thereof.

3.11.320.20 This method is illustrated in KPMG's series of illustrative financial statements.

3.11.330 *Par value of treasury shares as a separate category of equity*

3.11.330.10 In this case:

- the par value of treasury shares purchased is debited to a separate category of equity;
- when treasury shares are sold or reissued, the par value of the instruments is credited to this category; and
- any premium or discount to par value is shown as an adjustment to share premium or reserves including retained earnings, or a combination thereof.

3.11.340 *Par value of treasury shares as a deduction from share capital*

3.11.340.10 In this case:

- the par value of treasury shares purchased is debited to share capital;
- when treasury shares are sold or reissued, the par value of the instruments is credited to the share capital; and
- any premium or discount to par value is shown as an adjustment to share premium or reserves including retained earnings, or a combination thereof.

3.11.350 Costs of an equity transaction

IAS 32.35 3.11.350.10 Qualifying costs attributable to an equity transaction (e.g. issuing or buying back own shares) are debited directly to equity, net of any tax effects (see 3.13.400).

IU 09-08 3.11.350.20 Listing transactions often involve both listing existing shares and issuing new shares. In our view, the costs directly attributable to issuing new shares should be recognised directly in equity and any costs attributable to listing existing shares should be expensed as incurred.

3.11.350.30 Issuing shares in a private placement is a transaction that results in additional capital being raised and therefore, in our view costs directly related to issuing equity instruments in a private placement should be recognised directly in equity.

IFRS 3.53,
IAS 32.35, 36 3.11.350.40 The requirement to record in equity all costs attributable to an equity transaction applies also to costs incurred on the issue of equity instruments in relation to a business combination (see 2.6.290). In our view similar to a listing of existing shares, secondary offerings and share splits do not result in new equity instruments being issued, so any costs associated with these transactions should be expensed as incurred.

IAS 32.38 3.11.350.50 Qualifying costs that relate to both existing shares and new shares should be allocated on a rational and consistent basis, e.g. based on the number of shares. For example, Company G issues 160 new shares and lists 80 existing shares in an IPO. Total costs related to both existing and new shares are 300. G allocates the cost between the listing of existing shares and the issue of new shares based on the number of shares. Therefore the cost allocated to the new shares is 200 (300 x 160 / 240), which will be recognised directly in equity. The cost allocated to listing the existing shares is 100 (300 x 80 / 240), which will be recognised in profit or loss.

3.11.350.60 Only costs that relate to both listing existing shares and issuing new shares should be allocated as explained in 3.11.350.50. Costs that are directly attributable only to the listing itself, should be recorded in profit or loss as incurred.

3.11.360 *Qualifying costs*

IAS 32.37 3.11.360.10 Only incremental costs that are attributable directly to issuing or buying back own equity instruments are recognised in equity. These costs may be internal or external, but should be incremental. Other costs are recognised in profit or loss even if those costs relate to newly issued shares.

3.11.360.20 For example, assume an entity is issuing new shares and simultaneously listing those shares. The following are examples of costs related to the transaction that we believe should be recognised in equity, if they are incremental costs:

- fees for legal and tax advice related to the share issue;
- cost of preparing and printing the prospectus;
- fees incurred in respect of the valuation of the shares;
- fees incurred in respect of the valuation of other assets (e.g. property) if the valuation is required to be disclosed in the prospectus;
- underwriting fees;
- fees and commissions paid to employees acting as selling agents that relate to the share issue;
- costs incurred in holding press conferences related to the share issue; and
- cost of handling share applications.

3.11.360.25 In our view, few internal costs will meet the incremental test in practice as we believe that this will be difficult to demonstrate.

3.11.360.30 In our view, costs that relate to the listing itself and that are not directly attributable to the new share issue should be expensed. For example, stock exchange registration costs do not relate to the issue of shares but rather to the listing of the issued shares; accordingly, they should be expensed as incurred.

3.11.360.40 In our view, the costs of advertising a share issue should be recognised directly in equity if the advertising relates directly to the share issue, and is not general advertising aimed at enhancing the entity's brand. An example may include incremental costs related to a road-show in which the entity specifically is targeting potential investors. If only a part of the advertising relates to the share issue, then an apportionment of the costs may be appropriate.

3.11.360.50 See 3.6.720 for further guidance on incremental internal transaction costs.

3.11.370 *Costs of anticipated equity transactions*

3.11.370.10 Equity transaction costs may be incurred before the equity instrument is issued or bought back. IFRSs are silent on how to treat costs incurred before the equity transaction has been recorded.

3.11.370.20 In our view, costs that are related directly to a probable future equity transaction should be recognised as a prepayment (asset) in the statement of financial position. The costs should be transferred to equity when the equity transaction is recognised, or recognised in profit or loss if the issue or buyback no longer is expected to be completed.

3.11.380 *Cost of issuing compound instruments*

IAS 32.36, 38   3.11.380.10 In the case of compound instruments, transaction costs are allocated to the individual components in a manner consistent with the allocation of the proceeds. The costs related to the liability component should be dealt with in accordance with the requirements for transaction costs associated with financial liabilities (see 3.6.720), whereas the costs related to the equity component should be reported as a deduction from equity.

3.11.390 *Related tax benefits*

IAS 12.61,   3.11.390.10 The tax effects of any transaction costs that are recognised in equity also
32.39   should be recognised directly in equity.

3.11.390.20 If the tax benefits associated with the transaction costs are not probable, then the deferred tax asset is not recognised (see 3.13.170). In these cases the gross transaction costs should be deducted from equity. If in a subsequent period the tax benefits related to the transaction costs qualify for recognition, then the corresponding credit will be recognised directly in equity.

3.11.400 *Presentation in equity*

3.11.400.10 IFRSs do not specify which component of equity the transaction costs recognised in equity should be charged against. An entity should choose an accounting policy, to be applied consistently, as to the component of equity the transaction costs are recognised.

3.11.400.20 [Not used]

3.11.400.30 See 3.13.370.50 for a discussion of the presentation of income tax effects within equity.

3.11.400.40 If shares are issued at par, then regulatory issues may prevent the amount from being deducted from share capital. In this case the transaction costs may be presented as a deduction from other share premium, other paid-in capital, retained earnings or shown as a separate reserve. If the transaction costs are presented as a deduction from share capital, then we recommend that disclosure of the impact be made. For example, assume shares are issued at their par value of 100. Transaction costs are 10. The suggested note disclosure would be as follows:

Share capital (par value)	100
Transaction costs	(10)
Share capital in the statement of financial position	90

3.11.400.50 The following example illustrates the combined application effect of the approaches explained in 3.11.390 and 3.11.400.40. Company Q issues additional shares for proceeds of 6,000. The total par value of those shares is 600. The costs of the transaction are 1,200. It is probable that Q will receive a tax deduction in future periods in respect of the transaction costs; the tax rate is 30 percent.

3.11.400.60 The entries to record the transactions are as follows:

	Debit	Credit
Cash	6,000	
Share capital		600
Share premium		5,400
To recognise share issuance		
Deferred tax asset (1,200 x 30%)	360	
Share premium	840	
Cash		1,200
To recognise cost and tax impact of share issuance		

3.11.410 Equity presentation

3.11.410.10 There are no specific requirements in IFRSs on how to present the individual components of equity. Therefore, in our view net accumulated losses may be deducted, upon a decision by the shareholders or application of the articles of association, from another component of equity, for example additional paid-in capital, if permitted by applicable laws.

3.11.410.20 Laws in some countries require reserves to be established for specific purposes. For example, banks may be required to set aside amounts for general banking risks or losses on loans. Some entities also establish reserves if national tax laws grant exemptions from, or reductions in, tax liabilities when transfers to such reserves are made. IFRSs neither require nor prohibit the creation of such reserves, which merely are allocations and designations of components of equity. If such reserves are created, then in our view they should be classified as a separate component of equity and created by an appropriation from another category of equity, preferably retained earnings. Transfers to these reserves and their related tax effects should be recognised directly within equity, and should not be recognised in profit or loss. These reserves also may not be recognised as liabilities in the statement of financial position.

3.11.420 *Income tax*

IAS 12.61, 81(a) 3.11.420.10 All changes in equity are recorded net of any related current and deferred tax. The amount of current and deferred tax recognised directly in equity should be disclosed separately. There is no requirement to present the tax impact separately in the statement of changes in equity. In practice the tax effects often are disclosed in the notes to the financial statements (see 2.2.40).

3.11.420.20 Some entities present a separate category of equity for current and deferred taxes charged directly to equity. We prefer to present the tax effects of equity transactions in the same category of equity as the underlying transaction as opposed to the creation of a separate category of equity for taxes (see 3.13.370.50).

3.11.430 *Non-controlling interests*

IAS 1.54, 106, 27.33 3.11.430.10 NCI are required to be presented in the consolidated statement of financial position within equity, separately from the parent's shareholders' equity (see 2.5.300). Therefore, a statement of changes in equity should include an analysis of the amounts attributable to NCI.

3.11.435 **Capital disclosures**

IAS 1.134, 135 3.11.435.10 An entity discloses information that enables users of its financial statements to evaluate the entity's objectives, policies and processes for managing capital. The entity discloses the following:

- Qualitative information about its objectives, policies and processes for managing capital, including a description of what it manages as capital, when an entity is subject to externally imposed capital requirements, the nature of those requirements and how those requirements are incorporated into the management of capital, and how it is meeting its objectives for managing capital.
- Summary quantitative data about what it manages as capital. Some entities regard some financial liabilities (e.g. some forms of subordinated debt) as part of capital. Other entities regard capital as excluding some components of equity (e.g. components arising from cash flow hedges).
- Any changes in qualitative information and quantitative data from the previous period.
- Whether during the period it complied with any externally imposed capital requirements to which it is subject.
- When the entity has not complied with such externally imposed capital requirements, the consequences of such non-compliance.

3.11.440 **Capital maintenance**

3.11.440.10 IFRSs do not establish requirements about what assets or net assets should be retained and what may be distributed. This is a legal issue that will depend on the regulatory environment in which an entity operates.

IAS 1.79(b) 3.11.440.20 If there is a legal prohibition on the distribution of certain reserves, and an entity wishes to indicate these restrictions in the statement of changes in equity, then we recommend transferring the restricted amounts to a separate component of equity, for example, a non-distributable reserve or a capital reserve if the applicable law permits. Any such transfer would be made through the statement of changes in equity (see 2.2 and 3.11.410.20). In any case, the restrictions on distribution should be disclosed in the notes to the financial statements.

3.11.450 **Dividends**

3.11.450.10 Dividends and other distributions to holders of equity instruments are recognised directly in equity.

IAS 10.12   3.11.450.20 A liability for a dividend payable is not recognised until an entity has an obligation to pay dividends. In the case of discretionary dividends, a liability for a dividend payable is not recognised until the dividend is appropriately authorised *and* no longer at the discretion of the entity, i.e. when the entity has an obligation to pay. In our view, it is inappropriate to recognise a liability based only on a constructive obligation. This is consistent with paragraph BC4 of IAS 10 *Events After the Reporting Period* and the definition of a financial liability in IAS 32 (see 3.11.20). Therefore a constructive obligation cannot arise in connection with a dividend.

3.11.450.25 In the case of discretionary dividends the legal requirements of the particular jurisdiction are important in determining of the point at which a liability is recognised. For example, if the relevant law provided that a board decision or announcement required no further approval and was binding on the entity (e.g. the board has no discretion to withdraw its decision or announcement and no legal discretion to avoid making payment), then the dividend liability is recognised on announcement. However, if the entity has discretion to avoid payment until either approved by the shareholders or until actual payment of the dividend then it would be inappropriate to recognise a liability at the time of the board decision or announcement.

3.11.450.30 In our view, an obligation to pay an interim dividend has to be recognised when the entity has an obligation to make the payment and the amount to be paid can be determined reliably, i.e. the shareholders do not have an obligation to pay back the interim dividend.

3.11.450.40 When, in addition to the declaration or the approval process required as a condition for the payment of the dividends, additional conditions (e.g. the holder of the equity instruments continues to hold the securities until a specific date) determine the amount to be paid to the holder, then the liability is recognised when the obligation exists and for the amount that the entity has an obligation to pay. For example, Company U issues subordinated debt that is classified as equity as it is non-redeemable. The interest (dividend) is payable only when a dividend is paid on the ordinary shares and the due date for payment has been reached by the holder. If the debt is redeemed before the due date for payment, then the holder of the debt is entitled to be paid a time-based proportion of the interest since the last payment. In our view, U has a liability for the interest when an ordinary dividend is declared. U will measure the liability for the "interest" (dividend) based on the amount payable on a time basis from the date on which the ordinary dividend is declared.

3.11.450.50 Dividends on shares, or components of shares, that are classified as liabilities are presented in the statement of comprehensive income as a finance cost. Even if the legal form of the payment is a dividend, it is not recognised directly in equity. Financing costs on shares or components of shares classified as liabilities are determined using the effective interest method.

3.11.450.60 IFRSs do not provide any guidance on accounting for share dividends (i.e. the issue of additional shares to shareholders characterised as a dividend).

3.11.450.70 Sometimes shares with a value equal to the cash dividend amount are offered as an alternative to the cash dividend. When the shares are issued, the liability is settled and a credit to equity is recognised as the proceeds of the issue. In our view, this practice is acceptable. Any reallocation of capital within equity will be in accordance with the applicable law.

3.11.450.80 In our view, a share dividend that is not an alternative to a cash dividend should be treated in the same way as a bonus issue, i.e. no entries are required (see 3.11.200).

3.11.452 *Distributions of non-cash assets to owners*

3.11.452.10 IFRIC 17 *Distributions of Non-cash Assets to Owners* addresses specific forms of distributions. The interpretation deals with measurement and presentation issues in this respect.

IFRIC 17.2, 3, BC4, 5 3.11.452.20 A *distribution* is a non-reciprocal transfer of assets from an entity to its owners, commonly referred to as a dividend. There is no restriction placed on the term "distribution" other than that it is non-reciprocal. Neither the reason for the transfer of assets nor its legal characterisation is a factor in determining whether it falls within the scope of the interpretation. Therefore, for example, a distribution that is in effect a return of capital is within the scope of the interpretation.

IFRIC 17.3 3.11.452.30 IFRIC 17 addresses the accounting for distributions of non-cash assets to owners acting in their capacity as owners in the financial statements (separate, individual and/or consolidated) of the entity making the distribution. It also applies to distributions in which each owner may elect to receive either their share of the non-cash asset or a cash alternative. Perhaps the most significant transactions included within the scope of the interpretation are demergers or spin-offs, in which an entity distributes its ownership interests in one or more subsidiaries to existing shareholders.

IFRIC 17.4-7 3.11.452.40 It does not apply to:

- common control transactions (see 5.13);
- distributions of part of the ownership interests in a subsidiary when control is retained; and
- distributions in which owners of the same class of equity instruments are not treated equally.

IAS 18.5, 9, 29, 30, 27.38A, IFRIC 17.8 3.11.452.45 It also does not apply to the financial statements of the recipient of the distribution; recipients apply the requirements of IAS 18 *Revenue* and IAS 27 *Consolidated and Separate Financial Statements* in respect of the receipt of dividends.

IFRIC 17.10   3.11.452.50 A liability for the distribution is recognised in equity when the distribution is authorised and is no longer at the discretion of the entity. This timing will vary depending on the legal requirements of individual jurisdictions (see 3.11.450.20).

IFRIC 17.11, 12, 13   3.11.452.60 The liability for the distribution is measured, initially and until settlement date, at the fair value of the assets to be distributed. Any changes in the measurement of the liability are recognised in equity; this is consistent with the accounting for the liability at the time of initial recognition. For distributions in which the owners may elect to receive either non-cash assets or a cash alternative, the entity considers the fair value of each alternative and their associated probabilities when measuring the liability.

3.11.452.70 Unless required by other IFRSs, the assets to be distributed are not remeasured to fair value when the liability is recognised. Instead, assets to be distributed that are within the measurement scope of IFRS 5 are measured in accordance with that standard (see 5.4.40). Assets to be distributed that are not within the measurement scope of IFRS 5 (e.g. deferred tax assets) continue to be measured in accordance with other IFRSs (e.g. IAS 12).

IFRIC 17. 13-15, BC38   3.11.452.80 At the date on which the distribution occurs (i.e. settlement date), the following takes place:

- The liability is remeasured based on the fair value of the assets to be distributed, with any change therein recognised in equity.
- The liability and the assets distributed are derecognised.
- Any difference between the fair value of the assets distributed and their carrying amount in the financial statements is recognised as a separate line item in profit or loss, with a consequential effect on earnings per share.
- Any amounts recognised in other comprehensive income in relation to the assets distributed (e.g. revaluation reserves) are reclassified to profit or loss or transferred within equity if required in accordance with other IFRSs, on the same basis that would be required if the non-cash assets had been disposed of.

IFRIC 17.BC 39   3.11.452.90 It is expected that the amount recognised in profit or loss at the settlement date will generally not be a loss because if the fair value of the assets had been lower than their carrying amount, then an impairment loss would have been recognised prior to settlement.

3.11.455 *Forthcoming requirements*

3.11.455.10 In November 2009 the IASB issued IFRIC 19 *Extinguishing Financial Liabilities with Equity Instruments*. The interpretation addresses the following issues in respect of the accounting by the debtor in a debt for equity swap transaction that arises as a result of a renegotiation of the terms of a financial liability:

- The interpretation clarifies that equity instruments issued to a creditor to extinguish all or part of a financial liability in a debt for equity swap are "consideration paid" in accordance paragraph 41 of IAS 39.

- An entity should measure equity instruments issued to a creditor to extinguish all or part of a financial liability at the fair value of those equity instruments, unless that fair value cannot be reliably measured, in which case the equity instruments are measured to reflect the fair value of the financial liability extinguished. The equity instruments are initially measured when the financial liability (or part of that liability) is extinguished.
- The difference between the carrying amount of the financial liability (or part of the financial liability) extinguished and the initial measurement amount of the equity instruments issued is recognised in profit or loss (see 3.6.1330). If only part of the financial liability is extinguished by the issue of equity instruments, the entity assesses whether some of the consideration paid relates to a modification of the part of the liability that remains outstanding and allocates the consideration paid between the part of the liability extinguished and the part of the liability that remains outstanding if appropriate. The consideration allocated to the part of the liability that remains outstanding forms part of the assessment of whether there has been a substantial modification of the terms of the remaining liability. Any gain or loss arising from the extinguishment of a financial liability (or a part of a financial liability) in accordance with the interpretation is disclosed as a separate line item in profit or loss or in the notes.

3.11.455.20 The interpretation is applicable for annual periods beginning on or after 1 July 2010; earlier application is permitted. An entity shall apply a change in accounting policy in accordance with IAS 8 *Accounting Policies, Changes in Accounting Estimates and Errors* from the beginning of the earliest comparative period presented.

3.11.455.30 In October 2009 the IASB issued Amendment to IAS 32 *Classification of Rights Issues*. IAS 32 states that a derivative instrument related to an entity's own equity instruments is classified as equity only if it results in the exchange of a fixed number of equity instruments for a fixed amount of cash or another financial asset. As set out in 3.11.130 if the amount of cash is denominated in a foreign currency that amount is variable in the functional currency. Consequently, the instrument does not qualify as an equity instrument.

3.11.455.40 The limited amendment to IAS 32 requires that rights, options or warrants to acquire a fixed number of the entity's own equity instruments for a fixed amount of any currency are equity instruments if the entity offers the rights, options or warrants *pro rata* to all of its existing owners of the same class of its own non-derivative equity instruments.

3.11.455.50 The amendment is applicable for annual periods beginning on or after 1 February 2010; earlier application is permitted.

3.11.460 Future developments

3.11.460.10 The objective of the IASB and FASB's joint project on the distinction between liabilities and equity is to have more relevant, understandable and comparable requirements for determining the classification of financial instruments that have the characteristics of liabilities, equity, or both.

3.11.460.20 In February 2008 the IASB published a DP on *Financial Instruments with Characteristics of Equity*, seeking constituent's views on all the issues addressed in the DP. An ED of proposed new requirements for classifying financial instruments as equity or as an asset/liability is scheduled for the first quarter of 2011.

3.12 Provisions
(IAS 37, IFRIC 1, IFRIC 5, IFRIC 6)

3.12 Provisions
(IAS 37, IFRIC 1, IFRIC 5, IFRIC 6)

Overview of currently effective requirements

- A provision is recognised for a legal or constructive obligation arising from a past event, if there is a probable outflow of resources and the amount can be estimated reliably. *Probable* in this context means more likely than not.

- A constructive obligation arises when an entity's actions create valid expectations of third parties that it will accept and discharge certain responsibilities.

- A provision is measured at the "best estimate" of the expenditure to be incurred.

- If there is a large population, then the obligation generally is measured at its expected value.

- Provisions are discounted if the effect of discounting is material.

- A reimbursement right is recognised as a separate asset when recovery is virtually certain, capped at the amount of the related provision.

- A provision is not recognised for future operating losses.

- A provision for restructuring costs is not recognised until there is a formal plan and details of the restructuring have been communicated to those affected by the plan.

- Provisions are not recognised for repairs or maintenance of own assets or for self-insurance prior to an obligation being incurred.

- A provision is recognised for a contract that is onerous, i.e. one in which the unavoidable costs of meeting the obligations under the contract exceed the benefits to be derived.

Currently effective requirements

This publication reflects IFRSs in issue at 1 August 2010. The currently effective requirements cover annual periods beginning on 1 January 2010. The requirements related to this topic are derived mainly from IAS 37 *Provisions, Contingent Liabilities and Contingent Assets*.

Forthcoming requirements and future developments

When a currently effective requirement will be changed by a new requirement that is issued but is not yet effective, it is marked with a # as a **forthcoming requirement** and the impact of the change is explained in the accompanying boxed text. In respect of this topic no forthcoming requirements are noted.

When a significant change to the currently effective or forthcoming requirements is expected, it is marked with a * as an area that may be subject to **future developments** and a brief outline of the relevant projects is given in 3.12.880.

3.12.10 **Definitions***

IAS 37.10 3.12.10.10 A *provision* is a liability of uncertain timing or amount.

IAS 37.10 3.12.10.20 A *liability* is a present obligation that arises from past events, which is expected to result in the outflow of the entity's resources upon settlement.

IAS 37.11 3.12.10.30 *Accruals* are liabilities to pay for goods or services that have been received or supplied but not yet paid for or invoiced. The uncertainty of timing and amount generally is less for an accrual than for a provision. Examples of accruals are fees for services rendered such as audit or consulting fees and certain employee benefits such as vacation pay.

3.12.20 **Scope***

IAS 37.1, 2, 5 3.12.20.10 This chapter deals with all provisions other than income taxes including income tax exposures (see 3.13), contract losses (see 4.2.300), obligations for employee benefits (see 4.4), liabilities for share-based payments (see 4.5), liabilities for insurance contract obligations (see 5.10), non-onerous leases (see 5.1) and non-onerous executory contracts (see 1.2.60). Financial instruments, including guarantees that are in the scope of IAS 39 *Financial Instruments: Recognition and Measurement*, also are not dealt with in this chapter (see 3.6).

3.12.20.20 While the term "provision" may be used to refer to loan loss allowances or similar impairment estimates, these are not provisions for liabilities but rather adjustments to the measurement of the relevant asset. See 3.6.1370 for guidance on the impairment of loans and other financial assets and 3.10 for guidance on the impairment of tangible and intangible assets.

IFRS 4. IG32(e), IAS 37.1(c) 3.12.20.30 The standard on provisions applies only if another standard does not deal with a specific type of provision. IFRS 4 *Insurance Contracts* applies to contractual rights and obligations under insurance contracts. If an insurer is sued over an insurance policy or a claim, then it may be unclear whether the claim arising in respect of the lawsuit should be accounted for under IFRS 4 or under IAS 37. In our view, for an insurer, the determination of the applicable standard for a lawsuit related to an insurance policy will depend on the basis for the respective claim. Assumptions and estimates that are part of the measurement of the insurance policy liabilities include litigation awards. Therefore, if the lawsuit relates to, for example a dispute as to whether an event is covered by the insurance or the adequacy of a settlement, then we believe the lawsuit should be part of the measurement of the insurance policy liability under IFRS 4 (see 5.10.70). If, however, the lawsuit relates to sales practice (e.g. refusal to provide a certain type of coverage), then this claim would not arise from an insurer's contractual rights and obligations, and we believe that it should be within the scope of IAS 37.

3.12.30 **Recognition***

IAS 37.14, 23 3.12.30.10 A provision is recognised when:

- there is a legal or constructive obligation arising from past events, or in cases of doubt as to the existence of an obligation (e.g. a court case), when it is more likely than not that a legal or constructive obligation has arisen from a past event;
- it is more likely than not that there will be an outflow of benefits; and
- the amount can be estimated reliably.

3.12.40 *Obligating event*

IAS 37.17 3.12.40.10 An integral part of an obligation is that it arises from a past event.

IAS 37.18, 63, 66 3.12.40.20 Expected future operating losses, even if probable, are not provided for unless they relate to an onerous contract (see 3.12.630).

3.12.40.30 Similarly a provision is not recognised for sub-optimal profits. For example, in a regulated industry, good results in one period may result in lower prices being charged in the following period. However, a provision is not recognised in respect of the expected lower revenues because, assuming that the future obligation is not an onerous contract, there is no obligating event.

3.12.40.40 A provision also is not recognised for general business risks. Although losses may be probable, and the amount of the expected losses can be estimated, until there is an event of loss there is no obligating event. For example, Company P has announced to the public a business plan. As part of the plan P is entering new overseas markets. The new markets expose P to significant increases in risk, including currency risk and legal and political uncertainties. Although the plan has been made public, and may be virtually certain of being implemented, even if exit strategies are costly, P does not recognise a provision because there is no obligating event.

3.12.50 *Legal obligation*

IAS 37.10 3.12.50.10 Legal obligations normally arise from contracts or legislation.

IAS 37.22 3.12.50.20 Possible new legislation is reflected only when it is virtually certain to be enacted as drafted. In practice new legislation normally does not give rise to an obligation until it is enacted because of uncertainties with respect to both whether it will be enacted and its final terms.

3.12.60 *Constructive obligation*

IAS 37.10   3.12.60.10 A constructive obligation arises when an entity, by past practice or sufficiently specific communication to affected parties, has created a valid expectation in other parties that it will carry out an action.

3.12.60.20 For example, Company Y operates in the oil industry in a country that has no environmental clean-up requirements. However, Y has published an environmental policy indicating that it will clean up all contaminated sites and, in the past, has cleaned up such sites regardless of whether it legally is required to do so. Therefore, Y has a constructive obligation for clean-up costs because its policy and past practice creates a valid expectation that it will clean up the contamination.

IAS 37.76   3.12.60.30 A management decision alone does not give rise to a constructive obligation, as it does not create a valid expectation in other parties until that decision is communicated to them. Therefore a board decision about a possible restructuring that has not been communicated does not trigger recognition of a provision.

IAS 37.19, C6   3.12.60.40 Business reasons or legal requirements may mean that an entity intends or is required to incur expenditures in the future. However, an intention or future requirement does not result in an unavoidable obligation. For example, an entity may need to fit a purifier in an oil plant or retrain staff to comply with new laws. The expenditure could be avoided by future actions such as relocating its operations or hiring new staff, even if the entity does not plan to do so. Therefore there is no obligating event.

3.12.60.50 In our view, in some cases an unconditional but not legally binding pledge may create a constructive obligation if the donor takes actions that mean that it has little or no alternative to fulfilling its pledge. We believe that this would involve considering not only past practice regarding fulfilling pledges, but also whether the donor's pledge has been communicated sufficiently widely and with sufficient detail so as to create valid expectations of performance. See 5.7.60 for a discussion of the accounting by a recipient for donations.

3.12.70 *Uncertainty about whether an obligation exists*

IAS 37.15, 16   3.12.70.10 In some cases it may not be clear whether an obligation exists or, particularly in the case of a legal claim, an entity may dispute whether there is an obligation even if it is clear that there is a past event.

3.12.70.20 A past event gives rise to a present obligation if it is more likely than not that a present obligation exists at the reporting date. For example, Company F is a fish-canning company. A group is claiming that certain people suffered food poisoning from tuna canned by F. F disputes the claim. If it is more likely than not that F's tuna caused the food poisoning, then F is considered to have a present obligation, even if F is planning to defend its position (see 3.12.740).

3.12.75 *Detection risk*

3.12.75.10 An entity may be subject to penalties only if obligating events are detected. In our view, if an entity is obliged to self report obligating events (e.g. in some countries environmental contamination should be self reported), then the detection risk (i.e. the possibility that the event will not be detected) should not be considered when measuring the obligation. When self reporting is not required and there is uncertainty about the amount of an obligation in respect of a past event, then we believe it may be appropriate to consider detection risk in measuring the provision.

3.12.80 *Subsequent events that give rise to an obligation*

IAS 37.21 3.12.80.10 An event that does not give rise to an obligation initially may give rise to one at a future date due to changes in the law or because an entity's actions create a constructive obligation.

3.12.80.20 For example, assume a new regulation is passed that imposes a requirement on Company V, a motor vehicle manufacturer, to accept back and scrap all vehicles it sells after 1 January 2011. A legal obligation to scrap the vehicles arises when enactment of the new legislation is virtually certain. The obligating events are sales of vehicles. V therefore recognises a provision for the present value of the expected costs of scrapping each vehicle sold after 1 January 2011. This provision is recognised as the vehicles are sold. No provision is recognised for vehicles in inventory at 1 January 2011, although the cost of scrapping would be considered in any net realisable value tests.

3.12.80.30 Extending the example in 3.12.80.20, assume that the legislation requires V to accept back and scrap from 1 January 2011 all vehicles sold by it, *including* those sold before 1 January 2011. An issue arises as to when V has an obligation in respect of vehicles sold before 1 January 2011 and not scrapped by 31 December 2010. In our view, V should recognise a provision once it is virtually certain that the legislation will be enacted; the specific terms of the legislation are known; and it is possible to estimate the number of vehicles that will be in use and the scrapping costs. The obligation arises when the legislation is enacted or becomes virtually certain of being enacted and the obligating events are the past sales.

3.12.90 *Obligation dependent on future events*

IAS 37.19 3.12.90.10 If the existence of an obligation depends on the future actions of the entity, then a provision is not recognised until the obligation is unavoidable.

3.12.90.20 For example, as in the example in 3.12.80.20, a new regulation is passed that imposes an obligation on motor vehicle manufacturers in respect of scrapping costs. However, instead of being responsible for scrapping the vehicles, V will be required to pay a scrapping levy to the government. The scrapping levy in respect of vehicles sold before 2011 will be based on vehicle manufacturers' market share in 2011 regardless of their actual sales in previous periods. V could avoid the obligation, for example by selling vehicles in a different market. Therefore, in our view the obligating event in this case occurs only in 2011 as V makes sales that establish its market share, and therefore its share of the costs of scrapping historical production by all manufacturers.

IFRIC 6   3.12.90.30 In another example, consider a manufacturer that will become liable for waste management costs on historical household equipment based on its share of the market in a measurement period, defined as calendar year 2010. No provision is required to be recognised by manufacturers until 2010 and then only if they participate in the market during this time; it is the entity's participation in the market during the measurement period that is the obligating event. See 3.12.520 for further detail.

3.12.100 *Counterparty*

IAS 37.20   3.12.100.10 An obligation involves another party. However, an entity is not required to be able to identify the counterparty to the obligation before a provision is recognised.

3.12.110 **Measurement***

IAS 37.36   3.12.110.10 The amount recognised for a provision is the best estimate of the expenditure to be incurred. There is no option to have an accounting policy of measuring the provision based on the lowest or the highest anticipated outcome.

IAS 37.39   3.12.110.20 If there is a large population, such as for product warranties, then the provision is measured at its expected value. Expected value considers all possible outcomes weighted based on their probabilities. If there is a continuous range of possible outcomes, and each point in the range is equally likely, then a provision is recognised for the mid-point in the range. The items considered together using an expected value approach should be similar in nature in order for the distribution (probability) calculation to be meaningful.

IAS 37.40   3.12.110.30 If there is a single item, then the most likely outcome usually is the best estimate. For example, if there is a 60 percent probability that Company D will have to pay damages of 600 in a legal case and a 40 percent probability that the claim against D will be dismissed, then the provision is measured at 600 because D will either win (and pay nothing) or lose and pay 600. The provision is not measured at 360 (600 x 60% + 0 x 40%).

IAS 1.125, 37.85(b)   3.12.110.40 In our view, when a provision is measured at its best estimate, which is less than the amount that could be payable, the difference between the two amounts is *not* a contingent liability. For example, Company G has an obligation to rectify a fault in a plant constructed for a customer. The provision should be measured based on the expected repair cost, which may be anywhere between 70 and 130. If the provision is measured at 90, then we believe that the remaining possible amount of 40 is not a contingent liability (see 3.14.30). This is because the unit of accounting is the obligation. The uncertainty regarding the amount of the costs to be incurred is reflected in the measurement although disclosure of the uncertainty regarding measurement should be considered. We believe that there is no separate obligation or past event for the unrecognised portion of the range of possible costs.

3.12.120 *Risk and discounting**

IAS 37.45, 47   3.12.120.10 If the effect is material, then the estimate is discounted at a pre-tax rate that reflects the time value of money and the risks specific to the liability, unless the future cash flows are adjusted for these risks (see 3.12.120.20).

IAS 37.47   3.12.120.20 Risk is reflected by adjusting either the cash flows or the discount rate. In our experience, generally it is easier to adjust the cash flows for risk and to discount the expected cash flows at a risk-free interest rate. Adjusting the discount rate for risk often is complex and involves a high degree of judgement. In our view, the discount rate used should not include an adjustment for an entity's own credit risk. This is because IAS 37 notes that the discount rate reflects the risks specific to the liability. Therefore, we believe that use of the entity's average or incremental borrowing rate, which generally reflects the entity's own credit risk, would not be an automatic proxy for the risk of a specific liability.

3.12.120.30 The risk-free rate may be determined by considering the interest rate on a government bond in the same currency and with a similar maturity to the obligation. In our view, a government bond rate for a country that has a poor credit rating reflecting a risk of default should not be used. This is because, in this circumstance, a government bond rate is not a risk-free rate. In such circumstance, if there are other countries that use the same currency, for example, the country is part of the Eurozone, then we believe that the rate of the country with the lowest yield in that zone should be used as evidence of the risk-free rate. Alternatively, if there are no other countries that use the same currency, then the development of the price for respective credit default swaps may be an indicator for increasing risk in the bond yield, which should be eliminated for purposes of calculating the risk-free rate.

3.12.120.40 If an entity has set aside assets to fund an obligation, and the assets are intended to generate a sufficient return to meet the ultimate obligation, then an issue arises about whether the rate of return on the assets in the fund may be used as a risk-adjusted discount rate for the obligation. The variability of the cash flows on the liability normally is not correlated to the variability of the cash flows on the assets. Therefore, the return on the assets does not reflect the risks specific to the liability and, in our view should not be used to discount the provision.

3.12.130 *Inflation adjustments*

IAS 36.40   3.12.130.10 The standard provides no guidance on whether the discount rate should include the effects of inflation. In our view, if the cash flows are expressed in current prices, then the effects of inflation should not be included in the discount rate (i.e. a real discount rate should be used). If the cash flows include inflation, then the discount rate should include the effects of inflation (i.e. a nominal discount rate should be used).

IAS 37.59 3.12.130.20 For example, Company M entered into a 10-year operating lease agreement in 2007 that requires it to make good any damage done during the lease. The make-good requirements include the requirement to remove leasehold improvements. M has recognised the costs of the leasehold improvement as property, plant and equipment, including the estimated costs of removing the leasehold improvements (see 3.12.450.10). At each reporting date M estimates expected costs to make good the damage done, including costs to remove the leasehold improvements (see 3.12.150). This estimate should reflect the damage done at the reporting date, and be based on the expected costs at the end of the lease term.

3.12.130.30 If M obtains a quote for making good damage incurred as of the reporting date, then, in our view this quote should be adjusted to reflect the expected timing of the expenditure, i.e. at the end of the lease. We believe that this adjustment can be made by applying an inflation rate to the quote obtained and discounting that amount back to the reporting date using a nominal (i.e. including inflation) risk-free rate. In this example, M prepares its financial statements as at and for the year ended 31 December 2010 and obtains a quote for the costs to make good damage done as of that date. The estimated costs as of the reporting date are 100, the nominal risk-free rate is 6 percent and the projected inflation rate is around 4 percent. To estimate the expected costs at the end of the lease term, M should apply the inflation rate to the amount of 100 and discount it back at the nominal risk-free rate for the period of seven years. In this example, the estimated costs at the end of the lease term equal 87 ($(100 \times 1.04^7) / 1.06^7$) after discounting.

3.12.140 *Tax impact*

3.12.140.10 A pre-tax discount rate is used because provisions are measured on a pre-tax basis. Any tax impact is accounted for separately (see 3.13).

3.12.150 **Remeasurement**

IAS 37.36, 59, 3.12.150.10 Provisions are remeasured at each reporting date based on the best estimate
IFRIC 1.4 of the settlement amount. Changes to the best estimate of the settlement amount may result from changes in the amount or timing of the outflows or changes in discount rates.

IFRIC 1.5 3.12.150.20 For those provisions included in the cost of a related asset, the effect of any changes to an existing obligation, including those resulting from changes in the discount rate used, generally are added to or deducted from the cost of the related asset and depreciated prospectively over the asset's useful life (see 3.2.140).

3.12.150.30 For example, Company W enters into an arrangement and obtains the right to operate an airport. In exchange for the right to operate W is required by law to make one-off payments to local residents and businesses as compensation for the loss in the value of their property due to the noise. In our view, the costs to be incurred for this compensation are a cost of obtaining the airport operating licence. We believe that these costs should be capitalised as an intangible asset (a licence) and amortised over the licence period (see 3.3.90 and 210).

IAS 38.21 3.12.150.40 We believe that the intangible asset generally should be recognised from the commencement of the arrangement if the right granted is usable from that date. However, in the unusual case that the estimated costs are not reliably measurable at the commencement of the licence and therefore the provision for payments is not recognised, then we believe that the entity should disclose a contingent liability (see 3.14.60). When the costs can be estimated, then a provision will be recognised. In our view, these costs should be capitalised when they become reliably measurable as part of the cost of the licence.

3.12.150.50 At the date that the obligation can be measured reliably, both the intangible asset and the corresponding liability should be recognised at the same amount, being the present value of the expected future payments to the local residents and businesses as compensation for the loss in the value of their property.

3.12.150.60 The estimate of the costs of compensation may change over time. In our view, changes in the carrying amount of the liability, except for the unwinding of the discount recognised in profit or loss, should be accounted for as an adjustment to the carrying amount of the intangible asset.

3.12.160 *Future events*

IAS 37.48 3.12.160.10 Future events are reflected when measuring a provision if there is sufficient objective evidence that they will occur. For example, a technological development that would make decommissioning less expensive would be considered if there is evidence that the new technology will be available. In our view, an intention to reduce an obligation via negotiation or avoid it by declaring bankruptcy is a future event that should not be anticipated.

3.12.160.20 For example, Parent M owns 100 percent of Subsidiary G. At 31 December 2010 G has net assets of 10. At the 2010 reporting date M determines that its present estimate of G's environmental remediation obligation needs to be increased by 50. M is not required by the legislation to fund G's exposures. M determines that it will not fund G's deficit in the future such that the net assets of G will not be sufficient to fund the full obligation. G intends to enter into negotiations with the relevant authorities to reduce, or be exempted from, the remediation obligation. We believe that the measurement of G's obligation both in its individual financial statements and in M's consolidated financial statements should not be limited to G's net assets. Instead, we believe that G should recognise the full amount of the revised estimate of its environmental obligation. M should continue to consolidate G including its full obligation until it no longer controls G; for example, after any bankruptcy proceedings have removed M's control (see 2.5.490.10).

3.12.170 *Gains*

IAS 37.51   3.12.170.10 Gains from the expected disposal of assets are not considered when measuring a provision.

3.12.170.20 Therefore, if a provision is recognised for a restructuring (see 3.12.230), then gains on the related sale of any assets are not considered in measuring the provision. As a result restructuring costs are likely to be recognised earlier than the gain on the related sale of assets.

3.12.170.30 For example, an entity commits to a restructuring to outsource its distribution activities. This will involve closing one of its warehouses and cancelling leases of equipment used in the warehouse. The entity expects to sell the closed warehouse for a gain that exceeds the cancellation penalties on the equipment leases. The provision for the lease cancellation costs is not reduced by the expected gain from the sale of the warehouse.

3.12.180 *Associated costs*

IAS 37.18, 36   3.12.180.10 Provisions are measured based on what an entity rationally would pay to settle or transfer the obligation. IFRSs do not provide much guidance regarding the types of costs to be included in the measurement of a provision. However, the accrual of costs that need to be incurred to operate in the future is prohibited.

3.12.180.20 In our view, anticipated *incremental* costs that are related directly to the settlement of a provision should be included in the measurement of the provision to the extent that a third party who assumes the liability would require compensation. This is likely to be the case when the incremental costs are probable and can be estimated reliably.

3.12.180.30 Incremental costs are those in addition to normal operating expenses. Therefore, we believe costs that are not incremental should not be included in the measurement of a provision, even if there is a reasonable basis for allocating a portion of these costs to the settlement of the provision. For example, costs to be incurred irrespective of a specific claim, such as salaries of employees in the claims department, are future operating costs, and therefore we believe that they should be excluded from the measurement of a provision.

3.12.180.40 In our view, the above principle applies to both external and internal costs. However, internal costs are less likely to be incremental and therefore normally would not be included in the measurement of a provision.

3.12.180.50 For example, Company G maintains a risk management department that handles damage claims. The costs of the department are unlikely to be incremental for any one claim and therefore should not be included in the measurement of the provision for expected claims. However, if G engages an external adviser to negotiate a settlement of a specific matter, then this cost is incremental and normally would be included in the measurement of the related provision.

3.12.190 **Reimbursements***

IAS 37.53   3.12.190.10 Reimbursements (such as insurance recoveries, indemnities or warranties) are recognised as a separate asset when recovery is virtually certain. The amount recognised is limited to the amount of the related provision.

IAS 1.34   3.12.190.20 For example, one of Company M's customers has established a claim against M for 300 in respect of a defective product that the customer purchased from M. M can recover the cost of the defect and a penalty of 12 percent from the supplier. The supplier has confirmed that it will pay 336 (300 + (300 x 12%)) to M as soon as M has paid the customer. M should recognise a provision for the claim of 300. Since the reimbursement is virtually certain it should be recognised as a separate asset. However, the amount recognised should not exceed the amount of the provision recognised for the claim (i.e. 300). The expense and the reimbursement may be netted in the statement of comprehensive income; however, the asset and the provision are not netted in the statement of financial position and are presented gross. M discloses the unrecognised reimbursement of 36 in the notes to the financial statements.

3.12.190.30 If the amount of a reimbursement cannot be determined, or the party that will make the reimbursement cannot be identified, then the reimbursement generally is not virtually certain. In practice an obligation and the related recovery often are recognised at the same time.

3.12.190.40 If the only uncertainty regarding the recovery of an insured loss is the amount of the recovery, then in our view the reimbursement often will qualify to be recognised as an asset. For example, Company Y has recognised a provision for environmental contamination that it must clean up. Y's insurance company has confirmed that the accident that caused the contamination is an insured event, but has not yet finalised the settlement amount. We believe that Y should recognise its best estimate of the reimbursement, not exceeding the amount of the provision, as a separate asset.

3.12.190.50 [Not used]

3.12.190.55 In some cases compensation for lost revenue may be received in non-cash form, for example, as a non-financial asset. In our view, the difference in nature of the compensation does not result in different accounting outcomes and non-cash compensation should be treated in the same manner as cash compensation, i.e. it should be recognised when the event occurs that gives rise to the claim for compensation and the compensation becomes receivable. For example, Company B is a railway operator and it has a delivery contract with Company G, which builds trains. The contract includes a clause for compensation for delivery delays of any committed purchases of railway cars on a fixed date. B agrees to accept spare parts free of charge in lieu of cash compensation if delays in delivery occur. In this scenario we believe that B should recognise compensation for delays as delays occur and the compensation becomes receivable. The amount of compensation recognised then would become B's cost basis for the spare parts.

3.12.190.60 In certain cases obligations can be settled by a parent company on behalf of its investee. For example, Company G manufactures and sells complex customised equipment and guarantees to reimburse its customers in case of product malfunction. At the end of 2010 G receives a claim for 100 from one of its customers, but it does not have sufficient funds to settle this claim. G's parent M agrees to settle this claim on behalf of G without requiring further reimbursement by G. In our view, the fact that M assumes the obligation without requiring further reimbursement does not exempt G from the requirement to recognise a liability arising from a contractual obligation; therefore G should recognise a provision in respect of the customer's claim of 100. When M agrees to settle the claim on behalf of G without requiring further reimbursement and acts in its capacity as shareholder, G should treat this reimbursement as an increase in equity for the shareholder contribution (see 1.2.110).

3.12.195 *Compensation for impairment of an asset or for lost revenue*

IFRS 4.2-4, A, IAS 39.2(e) 3.12.195.10 Under insurance contracts the policyholder is compensated if a specified uncertain future event (an insured event) adversely affects the policyholder (see 5.10.30). An entity may hold an insurance contract under which it is compensated in some circumstances for impairment of an asset or for lost revenue. The question arises as to how to account for that compensation right. The first step is to determine which standard to apply or analogise to. IAS 39 specifically excludes insurance contracts held from its scope and IFRS 4 does not address the accounting for insurance contracts by policyholders, other than the holders of reinsurance contracts (see 3.6.30 – 35 and 5.10.20). In our view, determining which standard to apply or analogise to depends on whether the compensation right is:

- a right under a financial guarantee contract, and if so whether that financial guarantee contract is an integral part of another financial instrument (see 3.6.35); or
- rights under other types of insurance contracts, e.g. compensation for impairment of property, plant and equipment or compensation for lost profits.

3.12.195.15 We believe that compensation that is not related to a provision (e.g. for impairment of an asset or for lost revenue) is not a reimbursement right within the scope of IAS 37.

3.12.195.20 A contract that requires payment in circumstances other than reimbursing the holder for a loss it incurs because a specified debtor fails to make payment when due in accordance with the original or modified terms of a debt instrument is not an insurance contract. It is a credit derivative that is accounted for in accordance with IAS 39 (see 3.6.30.30 and 3.6.35.10 – 190).

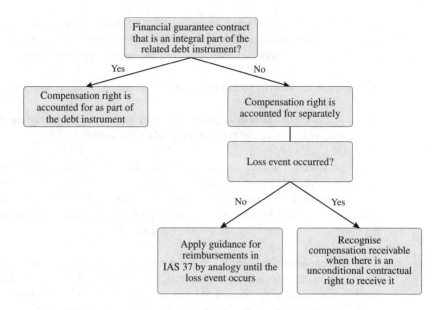

3.12.196 Compensation right under a financial guarantee contract that is an integral element of the related debt instrument

3.12.196.10 If the compensation right under an insurance contract is a financial guarantee contract that the holder determines is an integral element of the related debt instrument, then in our view the compensation right would not be accounted for separately from the related debt instrument. The holder should consider the effect of the protection when determining the fair value of the instrument, in estimating the expected cash receipts and when assessing any impairment losses in respect of the debt instrument (see 3.6.35.200).

3.12.197 Other compensation rights

3.12.197.10 If the compensation right under an insurance contract is either a financial guarantee contract that the holder determines is not an integral element of the related debt instrument or is a right under another type of insurance contract, then in our view the accounting for this compensation right would depend on whether the loss event that creates a right for the entity to assert that a claim has occurred at the reporting date.

3.12.198 Other compensation rights when the loss event has occurred

IAS 16.65, 66 3.12.198.10 IAS 16 *Property, Plant and Equipment* provides specific guidance on compensation for the impairment of property, plant and equipment (see 3.2.430). In our view, a consistent approach should be applied to other insurance contracts that compensate the holder for a loss event related to asset impairment or lost revenue/profit. Therefore, if the loss event that creates a right for the entity to assert a claim has occurred, then we believe that the entity recognises a receivable for the compensation when it has an unconditional contractual right to receive the compensation. The compensation receivable should be measured based on the amount and timing of the expected cash flows discounted at the rate that reflects the credit risk of the insurer. We believe that an entity would have an unconditional contractual right to receive compensation if:

- the entity has an insurance contract under which it can make a claim for compensation; and
- the loss event that creates a right for the entity to assert a claim at the reporting date has occurred and the claim is not disputed by the insurer.

3.12.198.20 If an entity holds an insurance policy that provides for compensation of lost profits or for impairment of an asset when an insured event occurs, then the entity has a contractual right to receive the compensation when such an insured event occurs. Therefore, we believe that the entity should recognise the compensation receivable from the insurance company when the insured event occurs.

3.12.198.30 For example, Company P has an insurance policy that allows it to claim for lost profits in the event of one of its key machines breaking down. Under the terms of the insurance contract the amount of compensation will be 10 for each full day that the machine is out of order. The machine breaks down on 1 October 2010 and P estimates that the machine will be out of order for the next six months. The amount of 10, being compensation receivable, is accrued for each working day that the machine has been out of order, as the loss event that creates a right for P to assert a claim occurs at the end of each working day.

3.12.198.40 In another example, Company Q's building burns down and it claims compensation for the impaired building under its fire insurance policy that covers this loss. The impairment of the building is recognised when the fire occurs. A receivable for the compensation is recognised when Q has an unconditional contractual right to receive compensation, i.e. when the damage has occurred assuming that the loss event is not disputed by the insurer, e.g. asserting arson, which is not covered by the insurance (see 3.2.430).

3.12.199 Other compensation rights when the loss event has not occurred

IAS 8.11, 3.12.199.10 If the loss event that creates a right for the entity to assert a claim at
37.53 the reporting date has not occurred, but an impairment of an asset has been recognised for accounting purposes, then in our view the compensation right is accounted for by analogy to the guidance for reimbursements in IAS 37 since that is the guidance in IFRSs dealing with the most similar issue (see 2.8.6).

IAS 37.53 3.12.199.20 In applying this guidance by analogy the compensation right is recognised when it is virtually certain of being received if the insured event occurs. Also, the amount of the asset recognised for compensation is limited to the amount of the recognised impairment loss, i.e. no net gain is accrued. This is consistent with the requirement in IAS 37 to limit the amount recognised for the reimbursement to the amount of the related provision. In our view, a recognised impairment loss for which there is not yet a contractual right to assert a claim is similar in nature to a provision. A provision is a liability that is a present obligation arising from a past event, of uncertain timing or amount; an impairment recognised in advance of the event that allows an entity to assert a claim is an insured loss related to a past event, but there may be uncertainty about timing or amount of the actual final loss. Therefore, we believe no net gain should be accrued when there is no current right to assert a claim under the insurance contract. During the period between initial recognition of the compensation right and the occurrence of the loss event that creates a right for the entity to assert a claim, the amount of the compensation right recognised should be limited to the difference between the impaired carrying amount of the asset and the amount that the carrying amount of the asset would have been had the impairment not been recognised. In some cases, for example a fire, there will be no gap between recognition of the impairment and the related loss event. In other cases, for example, financial guarantee contracts, there may be a gap between recognition of the impairment and the related loss event.

3.12.199.30 In our view, if the impairment loss recognised includes items not covered by the insurance contract, then the asset recognised for the compensation should be limited to the impairment loss covered by the insurance contract. For example, an impairment loss recognised on an available-for-sale financial asset (see 3.6.1370) may include not only a credit loss covered by a financial guarantee contract, but also other fair value changes that have occurred. We believe that only the credit portion of the impairment loss covered by the financial guarantee contract should be considered when recognising and measuring the asset for the compensation right.

3.12.199.40 When the loss event that creates a right for the entity to assert a claim occurs, the entity applies the treatment discussed at 3.12.198. This involves recognising the amount of compensation that the entity is entitled to receive as a receivable to the extent that it has an unconditional contractual right to receive compensation. Any difference between the carrying amount of the previously recognised compensation right and the compensation receivable is recognised in profit or loss.

3.12.199.50 For example, on 1 January 2008 Bank N purchased a five-year 100 zero-coupon bond issued by Company B.

- The bond matures on 31 December 2012 and on this date B is due to pay N 100. The bond is classified as a loan and receivable in N's financial statements and its amortised cost carrying amount before impairment is 83 at 31 December 2010.
- In December 2010 B's credit rating declines, reflecting recently disclosed operating losses and liquidity shortfalls.
- On 15 December 2010 N enters into a financial guarantee contract with Insurer C, a third party. Under the terms of the financial guarantee contract C will pay to N up to 100 if B has not paid the full 100 to N by 31 January 2013. If B pays N less than the 100 owed, then C will pay N the difference between 100 and the amount received from B. If, after any payment from C to N, B subsequently repays any amount to N, then N is required under the terms of the contract to pay this amount

to C. Therefore, under the terms of the contract, C will not compensate N for an amount greater than the loss incurred by N related to contractual payments due under the terms of the debt instrument.

- At 31 December 2010 the original effective interest rate on the bond is 10 percent and the appropriate discount rate for C is 5 percent, as C has a lower credit risk. At 31 December 2010 N estimates that, as a result of past events, B will repay only 70 out of the 100.

3.12.199.60 N accounts for the impairment and the related compensation right as follows:

- In its 2010 financial statements N recognises an impairment loss of 25 on the bond (83 - (70 x 0.909 x 0.909)). This is based on the revised expected cash flows discounted at the original discount rate of 10 percent for N. The new amortised cost of the bond is 58.
- In its 2010 financial statements N recognises a compensation right of 25. The compensation right is measured based on the expected cash flows of 30 on 1 February 2013, discounted at the appropriate discount rate of 5 percent for C. The asset, which otherwise would be 27 (30 x 0.952 x 0.952), is limited to the amount of the recognised impairment loss of 25, i.e. no net gain is accrued.
- In 2011 N accretes interest at 10 percent (i.e. the original effective interest rate) on the carrying amount of the bond (58) and recognises 5.50 of interest assuming that N's expected cash flows from collection of the bond remain unchanged. N also accretes interest at 5 percent on the compensation right and remeasures the compensation right to reflect additional recovery rights related to interest on the impaired portion of the bond. This calculation is illustrated below for the year to 31 December 2011.
  - The amortised cost of the bond at 31 December 2011 is 63.50, reflecting accretion of interest by N at 10 percent on the carrying value of the bond after impairment (58). N reflects 5.5 of interest income in 2011.
  - N calculates what the amortised cost of the bond would have been if it had not been impaired. This amount is 91 (100 x 0.909). Therefore, at 31 December 2011, the amount of the compensation right recognised is limited to 27.50 (91 - 63.50, or 25 x 1.1). In the absence of the imposed limit the compensation right would have been 28.35 (27 x 1.05).
  - Therefore, N recognises income of 2.50 (27.50 - 25) related to remeasuring of the compensation right. The increase in compensation right of 2.50 recognised is greater than the accretion of the compensation right of 25 at the 5 percent rate appropriate for the insurer (26.25, or 25 x 1.05). This is because N also is recognising an increase in the amount recoverable for interest that N would have accreted on the impaired portion of the loan.

3.12.200 *Environmental and similar funds*

IFRIC 5.9 3.12.200.10 Funds may be set up to assist contributors to the fund to meet their decommissioning or rehabilitation obligations. If a contributor does not have control, joint control or significant influence over the fund, then the contributor should recognise the right to receive compensation from the fund as a reimbursement right (see 3.12.190).

3.12.210 **Use of provisions**

3.12.210.10 [Not used]

IAS 37.61   3.12.210.20 Only expenditures related to the original nature of the provision are offset against the provision.

3.12.220 **Specific application guidance***

3.12.230 *Restructuring***

3.12.230.10 Specific guidance is provided regarding the recognition and measurement of restructuring provisions.

3.12.240 *Definition*

IAS 37.10   3.12.240.10 A *restructuring* is a programme planned and controlled by management that materially changes the scope of the business or the manner in which it is conducted.

3.12.250 *Obligating event*

IAS 37.72   3.12.250.10 A constructive obligation for a restructuring arises only when:

- there is a formal plan for the restructuring specifying:
    - the business or part of a business concerned;
    - the principal locations affected;
    - the location, function and approximate number of employees whose services will be terminated;
    - the expenditure to be incurred; and
    - when the plan will be implemented (see 3.12.290 for additional comments on timing); and
- the entity has raised a valid expectation in those affected that it will carry out the plan by either:
    - starting to implement the plan; or
    - announcing its main features to those affected by it.

IAS 37.1(c),   3.12.250.20 These requirements apply to all restructuring costs other than pension plan
5(d)   changes and redundancy payments (see 4.4.880 and 1040), and the impairment of assets as a result of a restructuring (see 3.10).

IFRS 3.41   3.12.250.30 See 2.6.570.30 for a discussion of restructuring costs of an acquiree in a business combination.

3.12.260 Sale transactions

IAS 37.78   3.12.260.10 An obligation related to the sale of an operation arises only when there is a binding sale agreement. Therefore, even though the decision to sell an operation has been announced, no provision is recognised for obligations arising as a result of the sale until there is a binding sale agreement.

3.12.260.20 Certain sale transactions may be subject to regulatory or shareholder approval. In these cases the sale agreement normally is binding unless the approval is substantive and is considered to be a significant hurdle (see 5.4.30.85 and 87). In our view, a provision triggered by a sale agreement should be recognised once the agreement is finalised if it is more likely than not that the necessary approval will be obtained.

3.12.260.30 To the extent that the planned sale of an operation includes non-current assets (or disposal groups), the requirements for assets held for sale are relevant (see 5.4.20). Non-current assets (or disposal groups) that are classified as held for sale are subject to specific measurement requirements.

3.12.270 Announcement

IAS 37.17(b),
72(b) 3.12.270.10 There are no specific requirements for the contents of the announcement. However, the announcement should be sufficiently explicit to create a valid expectation in those affected that the plan will be implemented.

3.12.270.20 In our view, the announcement should include information about:

- the business or part of the business that is affected;
- the estimated timing; and
- the functions and approximate number of employees affected.

3.12.270.30 In cases when the business is carried out in several locations, the affected locations also should be specified. However, we do not believe that it is necessary for the estimated cost of the restructuring to be included in the announcement, since this is unlikely to be a key factor in raising an expectation that the restructuring will go ahead.

3.12.280 Counterparty

IAS 37.20, 73 3.12.280.10 As noted previously, IFRSs do not require an entity to know the identity of the counterparty to the obligation before a provision is recognised. Therefore, it is not necessary to notify individual counterparties (e.g. each employee or vendor) before a provision is recognised. However, both the plan and the announcement of the plan should have sufficient detail for those affected to identify the potential impact and to understand what their claim may be.

3.12.290 Timing

IAS 37.74 3.12.290.10 For a plan to create a constructive obligation, implementation should begin as soon as possible and it should be completed in a timeframe that would not allow for significant changes to the plan.

3.12.290.20 There is no specified limit on the timing. The time frame should be short enough that the plan is fixed and the possibility of it being changed is small. The longer the time frame, the more difficult it will be to demonstrate that it is highly unlikely that the plan will be changed.

3.12.300 Contractual requirement to restructure

3.12.300.10 An entity may enter into a contractual agreement to undertake a restructuring, for example as a result of an outsourcing arrangement.

3.12.300.20 For example, Company K outsources its IT processing function to Company L, a third party that will take over and restructure K's existing IT department. Under the terms of the outsourcing contract, K agrees to reimburse L for all costs associated with the restructuring. In our view, entering into the outsourcing contract creates a valid expectation in a third party (L) that the restructuring will be undertaken. However, we view the outsourcing agreement as an executory contract. Therefore, we believe that the restructuring costs should be recognised as L performs under the contract, and not upon signing the contract. K would recognise a liability for its obligation to reimburse L once L recognises its restructuring obligation, e.g. upon communication to affected employees.

3.12.310 Group-wide restructuring

3.12.310.10 An entity that has a group-wide restructuring might not meet the criteria for recognising a provision for all of the locations at the same time.

3.12.310.20 In our view, the criteria should be applied to each part of the restructuring programme (e.g. each location) separately. Provisions should be recognised only for those locations that meet the criteria.

3.12.320 Board decision

IAS 37.77 3.12.320.10 Generally a board decision in itself does not establish a constructive obligation, for example with respect to the termination of employees.

3.12.320.20 However, a board decision may require communication with a decision-making body that includes employee representatives (e.g. a supervisory board). In such cases approval of the plan by the supervisory board probably results in a constructive obligation even if there is no direct communication to the affected employees at that time.

3.12.330 *Measurement*

IAS 37.80 3.12.330.10 Restructuring provisions include only incremental costs associated directly with the restructuring. Examples of costs that should be considered in measuring the provision include: employee termination benefits that relate directly to the restructuring (see 4.4.1040); contract termination costs, such as lease termination penalties; onerous contract provisions (see 3.12.630); consulting fees that relate directly to the restructuring; and expected costs from when operations cease until final disposal.

IAS 37.80(b), 81   3.12.330.20 IFRSs prohibit recognition of a provision for costs associated with ongoing activities. Therefore provisions are not recognised for:

- expected future operating costs or expected operating losses unless they relate to an onerous contract (see 3.12.630);
- gains or losses on expected disposals or impairments of assets (see 3.12.350);
- investment in new systems;
- lower utilisation of a facility;
- costs of training or relocating staff;
- staff costs for staff that continue to be employed in ongoing operations;
- loyalty bonuses or amounts paid to staff as an incentive to stay;
- costs of moving assets or operations;
- administration or marketing costs;
- allocations of corporate overheads; or
- costs of changing the name of an entity.

3.12.330.30 For example, Company C is a dairy but also produces cheese. The cheese-making operations are being restructured. The equipment that is used in the cheese-making operations will be redesigned and staff will be trained to use the new equipment. To the extent that the restructuring relates to C's ongoing operations, a provision is not recognised for these costs. Therefore, the costs of redesigning the operation and retraining staff are not included in the restructuring provision. Costs of new equipment and costs of improvements to existing equipment are capitalised when incurred (see 3.2).

3.12.340 Employee termination payments

3.12.340.10 See 4.4.1040 for guidance on accounting for employee termination payments.

3.12.350 Asset disposals or impairment

3.12.350.10 A restructuring also may entail asset disposals or trigger impairment of assets. See 3.10 for a discussion of issues related to the impairment of assets and 5.4 for a discussion of the classification of non-current assets (or disposal groups) as held for sale and their measurement.

3.12.360 Warranties*

IAS 37.C1   3.12.360.10 An entity that has an established practice of repairing or replacing faulty or defective goods that are returned, even if legally it is not obliged to do so, generally has a constructive obligation to repair or replace products. The obligating event is the sale of goods that turn out to be defective or faulty (see also 4.2.140).

IAS 37.C1   3.12.360.20 A warranty provision is measured based on the probability of the goods requiring repair or replacement and the best estimate of the costs to be incurred in respect of defective products sold on or before the reporting date.

3.12.360.30 For example, Company M manufactures and sells luxury vehicles. All vehicles are guaranteed for 12 months. M introduced a new model, the R100, two months before the reporting date. When the financial statements are prepared, no warranty claims have been made in respect of the R100. However, based on previous experience with similar models, it is probable that there will be claims for manufacturing defects. M should recognise a provision in respect of expected claims on the new model. The lack of claim history in respect of the R100 does not change this, as the sale of the defective vehicles is the obligating event. M should consider claim patterns in respect of comparable models to determine the expected number of claims and the anticipated cost.

3.12.360.40 In our view, *incremental* staff costs that are directly attributable to handling individual warranty claims (e.g. amounts paid to contractors for call-outs or overtime pay) should be included in the measurement of provisions. However, costs that are not related to a specific warranty claim (e.g. the cost of maintaining a claims department) are not incremental and therefore should not be included in the measurement of the provision.

3.12.370 *Customer refunds**

IAS 18.16(d), 17, A2(b) 3.12.370.10 An obligation to give refunds is considered in determining whether to recognise revenue. If the right of return does not result in the seller retaining significant risks of ownership and a return is not probable, then revenue may be recognised (see 4.2.150).

IAS 37.C4 3.12.370.20 The obligation to give refunds may be a legal requirement, or a constructive obligation created by a past practice or published policy of giving refunds to dissatisfied customers. If there is an obligation and it is determined that it is an insignificant risk of ownership, then the obligating event is the sale of the product. If it is probable that a certain portion of the goods sold will be returned, then a provision is recognised at the same time as the revenue is recognised, for the best estimate of the cost of refunds, applying the same principles to those for warranty provisions (see 3.12.360).

IU 05-08 3.12.370.30 In some industries, customer refunds may relate to deposits collected for returnable containers. For example, Company K sells gas in returnable cylinders. K accounts for the returnable cylinders as its property, plant and equipment and does not derecognise them as part of a sales transaction (see 3.2). On delivery of gas to customers, K collects a deposit for each cylinder delivered and it has an obligation to refund this deposit when the customers return the cylinders. In our view, a deposit collected from a customer for a returnable container, which is not derecognised as part of a sales transaction, meets the definition of a financial liability as it is a contractual obligation to pay cash to the customer (see 3.6.150.60). Therefore, customer refunds related to deposits collected for returnable containers, which are not derecognised as part of a sales transaction, are outside the scope of IAS 37.

IAS 18.19, IU 05-08 3.12.370.40 In a contrasting example, K derecognised cylinders as part of a sale transaction because it expects many of the cylinders to be retained by customers. However,

K still collected a deposit from customers, and has an obligation to return the deposit to a customer if the customer returns cylinders. The customer has a right but not an obligation to return the cylinders. In our view, a deposit received for containers, which are derecognised as part of a sales transaction, would not meet the definition of a financial instrument, but rather would represent a consideration received for cylinders sold. As the customer has a right to return the cylinders purchased and K is uncertain about the probability of return, we believe that revenue related to cylinders would not be recognised until the criteria for revenue recognition are met (see 4.2.70). Therefore, we believe that customer refunds related to deposits collected for returnable containers, which are derecognised as part of a sales transaction, are outside the scope of IAS 37 as well.

3.12.380 *Gift certificates or vouchers**

3.12.380.10 Retailers may sell gift vouchers that can be exchanged for goods or services. An entity selling such vouchers determines if the voucher is the unfulfilled portion of a contract. Whether an unfulfilled contract exists usually is determined based on the revenue recognition requirements and will arise if there are multiple deliverables with separate revenue streams. See 4.2.430 for further guidance on gift vouchers, including vouchers issued as part of a sales transaction and redeemable against future transactions.

3.12.390 *Self-insurance*

3.12.390.10 Entities may elect not to insure against some risks or to obtain insurance that covers only a certain portion of incurred losses (e.g. due to high deductibles); sometimes this is referred to as self-insurance.

3.12.390.20 A provision is not recognised for future losses or costs associated with self-insurance. However, a provision should be recognised for qualifying costs related to events (insured or not) that occur before the end of the reporting period.

3.12.390.30 For example, Company D operates a chain of fast food outlets and decides not to insure against the risk of third-party liability claims. Instead, D will self-insure this risk. Based on past experience, D expects losses of 100 each year in respect of third-party liability claims for events that occurred within the year. In the first year of self-insurance, actual claims are 80. Assuming that all incurred losses have been reported, a provision cannot be recognised for the additional average claims of 20. Although it may be possible to estimate average annual expected claims reliably, there is no *obligating* event in the current year in respect of average claims in excess of actual claims.

3.12.390.40 However, a provision should be recognised for losses that have been incurred, but not yet reported, at the reporting date (commonly referred to as IBNRs), if there is a probable outflow of economic benefits and a reliable estimate of the losses can be made. For example, if the entity believed that injuries had occurred for which 25 of valid additional claims would be made, then it should accrue that 25. This is because, although the entity has not yet received these claims, an obligating event has occurred. In our view, the calculation should take into account statistical experience of such events and the related amounts. Principles similar to those applied in the insurance industry may be helpful in measuring IBNR provisions.

3.12.400 *Risks assumed on behalf of third parties*

IFRS 4.2(a)   3.12.400.10 Specific requirements apply to obligations arising under an insurance contract (see 5.10). Those requirements are not limited to entities regulated as insurance companies.

3.12.400.20 For example, Company L owns and rents out properties. Under the rental agreement L is responsible for repairing the properties in the case of fire. The rental payment includes a risk premium in respect of the possible loss due to fire. In our view, the properties are L's assets and therefore L should not recognise a provision for expected future damage (e.g. future fires). However, any further obligations (e.g. for damage to tenants' belongings) are an insurance contract and should be accounted for separately (see 5.10).

IFRS 4.A,   3.12.400.30 Insurance contract liabilities arise only when risks are assumed on behalf
B19(c)   of third parties. Risks assumed on behalf of group entities are self-insurance (as described in 3.12.390) in the consolidated group financial statements.

3.12.410 *Captive insurance entities*

3.12.410.10 In some cases separate entities are established for self-insurance arrangements. These may be subsidiaries or SPEs. The administration of the entity often is handled by a third-party insurance entity.

3.12.410.20 The guidance on consolidation (see 2.5) is applicable in determining whether such entities should be consolidated.

3.12.410.30 If the insured entity continues (directly or indirectly) to bear the risk of the insured losses, then generally it should consolidate the captive insurance entity. Therefore, the principles described above for self-insurance would apply, and the insured entity would recognise a provision only when an event of loss occurs, and only for obligations incurred. For example, a self-insured entity would recognise impairment losses for property damaged in a fire rather than a provision to repair the property.

3.12.410.40 If an arrangement transfers the risk of losses to an unrelated third party, then the arrangement has the same economic substance as an insurance contract. Therefore, the arrangement should be accounted for in the same way as an insurance policy. An insurance policyholder recognises premiums as an expense over the period of the insurance. Losses are recognised only once the loss occurs, and reimbursement rights are recognised as separate assets (see 3.12.190).

3.12.410.50 See 5.10.130 for a discussion of the presentation and disclosure of self-insurance arrangements.

3.12.420 *Environmental provisions*

IAS 37.14   3.12.420.10 The recognition and measurement of a provision for environmental obligations follows the general requirements described in 3.12.30 and 110. Therefore, a provision is recognised when there is either a legal or constructive obligation to restore a site, the damage already has occurred, it is probable a restoration expense will be incurred, and the costs can be estimated reliably.

3.12.430 *Obligating event*

IAS 37.10   3.12.430.10 A constructive obligation may arise from published policies, past practices of environmental clean ups or statements about clean-up policies made in the press or to the public.

3.12.430.20 In-house standards and practices result in a constructive obligation only if they are communicated to third parties.

3.12.430.30 For example, although no legal obligation exists, the board of Company G has instructed local management to clean up a site where land and ground water have been contaminated. The estimated cost of the clean up is 250. If G does not have an established practice or published policies that would demonstrably commit it to clean up the site, then no provision should be recognised based on the board decision alone. The board decision and instruction to clean up the site do not result in a constructive obligation if that decision is not communicated externally. The decision still could be reversed and the costs avoided.

IAS 37.22   3.12.430.40 Future changes in environmental legislation are not taken into account unless they are virtually certain of being enacted.

3.12.440 *Measurement*

IAS 37.36   3.12.440.10 A provision is measured at the best estimate of the future clean-up costs. It reflects the amount that the entity would be required to pay to settle the obligation at the reporting date (see 3.12.440.50).

3.12.440.20 In our experience, making the estimate may require specialised knowledge of environmental issues, for example, the quantity and type of contaminants involved, the local geography and remediation costs. The estimates typically need to be made with input from environmental experts.

IAS 37.49   3.12.440.30 Anticipated cost savings arising from future improvements in technology are considered in measuring the provision only if the existence of that technology is reasonably certain.

3.12.440.40 The provision should include estimated incremental direct costs such as amounts paid to consultants, costs of equipment dedicated to the clean up, and costs of employees performing the clean-up effort. In our view, the costs of the following activities should be included when measuring the provision:

- remedial investigation
- risk assessment
- feasibility studies
- remedial action planning
- remediation work
- government oversight
- post-remediation monitoring.

IAS 37.45, 3.12.440.50 Outflows in respect of environmental provisions may occur far in the future.
IFRIC 1.4 Therefore, the effects of discounting are likely to be significant and, if so, the provisions are measured at the present value of expected cash flows and remeasured when changes in interest rates impact the current estimate of the discount rate.

3.12.450 *Decommissioning*

IAS 37.14 3.12.450.10 The obligation to make good environmental or other damage incurred in installing an asset is provided for in full immediately since the damage arises from a past event; the installation of the asset. For example, a provision is recognised for the expected cost of dismantling an oil rig when the rig is installed.

IAS 16.16(c) 3.12.450.20 When an obligation to restore the environment or dismantle an asset arises upon the initial recognition of the asset, the corresponding debit is treated as part of the cost of the related asset and is not recognised immediately in profit or loss (see 3.2.70). The cost of an item of property, plant and equipment includes not only the initial estimate of the costs related to dismantlement, removal or restoration of property, plant or equipment at the time of installing the item, but also amounts recognised during the period of *use* for purposes other than producing inventory (see 3.2.110), for example certain additional obligations for restoration costs.

3.12.450.30 IFRSs do not address how to account for new obligations, for example those triggered by a law enacted after the asset was acquired.

IAS 37.14 3.12.450.40 If an obligation to dismantle or decommission an asset or restore the environment arises, e.g. due to changes in law or intent, after the initial recognition of the asset, then a provision is recognised at the time that the obligation arises. In our view, the estimated cost should be recognised as an adjustment to the cost of the asset and depreciated prospectively over the remaining useful life of the asset assuming that the liability was not created through use of the item, e.g. to produce inventory (see 3.12.150.20). We believe that a new cost is analogous to revision of the estimate of a pre-existing obligation (see 3.2.80). However, the increase in cost may require recognition of an impairment loss if that additional cost is not recoverable (see 3.10).

3.12.450.50 In our view, the same approach should be taken even if the obligation arises only at the end of the useful life of the asset. For example, Company Q operates a brewery close to the city centre. In 2010 due to new town planning restrictions, Q is required to cease operations immediately, move the brewery out of the town centre and clean up the site. Previously Q had not recognised a provision for the clean up, as there was no obligation. Q should recognise a provision for the site clean up when the government informs Q of the need to move and clean up the site. If the brewery will stop operations immediately, then an argument can be made that the clean-up costs should be expensed immediately as it will not benefit future periods. However, because of the requirement to treat decommissioning as an element of the asset's cost, we believe that the provision should not be expensed immediately. The adjusted cost of the brewery will have to be tested for impairment. Further, if the brewery qualifies as an asset held for sale (see 5.4.20) then the requirement to measure the asset at the lower of its carrying amount and fair value less costs to sell may result in an impairment loss being recognised.

3.12.460 Discounting

IAS 37.45   3.12.460.10 Decommissioning, like the remediation of environmental damage, often will take place only far in the future. Therefore, the effects of discounting normally are material for decommissioning liabilities. In some industries, e.g. in oil refining, the useful lives of assets requiring decommissioning might be very long. In our view, if there is an uncertainty about the useful life of the asset, and therefore about the period over which the expected cash outflows related to the end-of-service decommissioning have to be discounted, then this uncertainty should be reflected in measurement of the provision rather than used as a reason for not recognising the decommissioning liability. This is because we believe that uncertainty about the useful life of the assets should not lead to an inability to measure the provision reliably. However, if the useful life of the assets is very long, then the present value of the related decommissioning provision might not be material in early years.

3.12.470 Timing of outflow

3.12.470.10 In determining the expected timing of the outflow, the expected useful life of the related asset should be considered. In our view, assumptions about future events should be supported by objective evidence because of the uncertainty of predicting events far into the future. For example, Company Y has a chemical production plant with an anticipated useful life of 25 years. Clean up is required only when the site is decommissioned. At the end of the useful life it is possible that Y will construct a new production plant with a 25 year useful life on the site, in which case decommissioning will take place only in 50 years. Unless there is persuasive evidence that a new plant will be constructed, we believe that Y should assume that the decommissioning will take place in 25 years.

3.12.470.20 The assumptions also should be consistent with the other assumptions regarding the use of the asset. For example, Company T is required to remove an oil rig as soon as it ceases pumping oil. If the estimated remaining useful life of the oil rig is 10 years, then T should assume that the decommissioning will take place in 10 years, even if there is a possibility that the oil rig may be used for longer.

3.12.470.30 An entity may not be required to, and may not be able to, decommission an asset immediately after it ceases using the asset. In this case, the best estimate of the timing of the cash flows should be used to measure the present value of the obligation.

3.12.475 Decommissioning liability in a foreign currency

3.12.475.10 IFRSs do not provide clear guidance regarding the accounting treatment of exchange differences related to an obligation denominated in a foreign currency to settle a decommissioning obligation. For example, Company B constructs a plant. As the plant is constructed, B incurs a legal obligation to decommission the plant and the costs are denominated in a currency other than B's functional currency.

IAS 21.23, 36, 54 3.12.475.20 Foreign currency denominated obligations are translated at the exchange rates at the reporting date when the obligation is a monetary liability, with translation gains and losses recognised in profit or loss. Non-monetary liabilities denominated in a foreign currency are translated at their historical exchange rate (see 2.7.110.10). In our view, a decommissioning liability is monetary if it is expected to be settled by payment of a fixed or determinable number of units of currency, or non-monetary if it will be settled by providing services (i.e. by the entity carrying out the remedial works itself or by paying another party to do so) or a non-monetary asset.

IAS 36.54 3.12.475.25 If a foreign currency denominated obligation is a monetary liability, then in our view foreign currency denominated cash flows first should be discounted to their present value in the foreign currency using a discount rate appropriate for the currency in which the cash flows are generated; thereafter the present value amount should be translated into the functional currency at the exchange rate at the reporting date. This approach is consistent with that required for impairment calculations (see 3.10.290).

IAS 23.6(e), IFRIC 1.4-7 3.12.475.30 The analysis is complicated further because decommissioning costs are capitalised as part of the costs of the plant (see 3.12.450.20). Generally, changes in estimates for decommissioning are adjustments to the cost basis of the asset other than changes resulting from finance costs (unwinding of the discount). In some cases foreign exchange gains or losses are regarded as borrowing costs (see 4.6.420), but generally under IFRSs they are regarded as revisions of estimates of cash flows.

3.12.475.40 In our view, the entity should choose an accounting policy, to be applied consistently, between:

- capitalising exchange differences related to a decommissioning obligation in a foreign currency as part of property, plant and equipment and depreciating the amount prospectively over the remaining useful life of the asset; or
- recognising exchange differences related to a decommissioning obligation in a foreign currency immediately in profit or loss.

3.12.475.50 We believe that either treatment can be justified since the gains or losses on remeasurement can be viewed as either finance costs that are not eligible for capitalisation, or as revisions of estimated cash flows.

3.12.480 *Past vs future events*

3.12.480.10 A provision is recognised only if there are past events. Therefore a provision reflects only damage incurred at the reporting date; a provision is not recognised for expected future damage.

3.12.480.20 For example, Company U operates a nuclear power plant. Construction of the nuclear power plant was completed at the end of 2009 at a cost of 10,000. The estimated present value of the costs of dismantling the power plant and restoring the site for the damage caused by its construction at the end of its 25-year useful life is 980. In addition, there will be ongoing damage to the environment by the emissions of various pollutants throughout the operating life of the power plant, which is expected to require remediation in 25 years costing approximately 175 for each year of operation. The remediation resulting from ongoing damage will be carried out at the end of the plant's useful life. The obligation to dismantle the power plant and restore the site (980) is created as the power plant is constructed. The obligation in respect of the ongoing emissions arises as the emissions occur, i.e. over the useful life of the power plant. The following are the entries that U should record in respect of the environmental damage:

As the nuclear power plant is constructed:		
	Debit	*Credit*
Nuclear power plant	980	
Obligation for remediation		980
To recognise liability for anticipated cost of site restoration		
and dismantling as part of cost of asset		
At 31 December 2010, assuming a 10 percent discount rate:		
Interest cost (profit or loss)	98	
Obligation for remediation		98
To recognise unwinding of discount for year 1 on liability		
for site restoration and dismantling (980 x 10%)		
Depreciation of power plant (profit or loss)	439	
Accumulated depreciation power plant		439
To recognise depreciation of power plant (10,980 / 25)		

	Debit	Credit
Operating costs (profit or loss)	18	
Obligation for remediation		18
To recognise liability in respect of emissions during		
the period (present value of 175 in 24 years)		

3.12.480.30 In each of the following years during the useful life of the power plant, U will recognise:

- depreciation on the power plant of 439 (10,980 / 25);
- a provision for the present value of the additional obligation for remediation caused by emissions damage during the year; and
- assuming that there is no change in interest rates, the unwinding of the discount based on 10 percent of the accumulated obligation (for decommissioning and emissions damage) at the beginning of the year. Therefore, in 2011 U will recognise an interest cost of 110 ((980 + 98 + 18) x 10%). The unwinding of the discount is presented as a component of interest expense (see 3.12.840).

3.12.490 Changes in estimate

IFRIC 1.5   3.12.490.10 The effect of any changes to an existing obligation for dismantling costs generally is added to or deducted from the cost of the related asset and depreciated prospectively over the remaining useful life (see 3.2.140) of the asset (i.e. treated as a change in estimate (see 2.8.60)).

3.12.500 Environmental and similar funds

3.12.500.10 Sometimes funds are established to finance environmental or other remediation costs. Typically, funds reimburse entities for qualifying costs incurred but do not assume the primary responsibility for the decommissioning obligation. For example, in order to ensure that nuclear power plant operators have funding available to finance decommissioning costs, the government may require operators to make contributions to a fund. A fund may be set up to meet the decommissioning costs of a single contributor, or several contributors. The operator may have no control over the investment decisions of the fund and if the amount in the fund is insufficient to cover the decommissioning costs, then the operator will not be reimbursed for the additional costs.

3.12.500.20 The operator normally continues to bear the primary obligation for the decommissioning and therefore continues to recognise a provision for its obligation.

IFRIC 5.8, 9   3.12.500.30 The operator's investment in the fund is accounted for as an asset. If the fund is a subsidiary, joint venture or associate of the operator, then it is consolidated (see 2.5), proportionately consolidated or accounted for using the equity method as appropriate (see 3.5). Otherwise if the operator does not have control, joint control or significant influence, then it recognises the right to receive compensation from the fund as a reimbursement right. The reimbursement right is measured at the lower of:

- the amount of the decommissioning obligation recognised; and
- the operator's share of the fair value of the net assets of the fund attributable to the operators.

3.12.500.40 The change in the carrying amount of the reimbursement right other than from contributions to and payments from the fund is recognised in profit or loss in the period in which these changes occur.

IFRIC 5.10 3.12.500.50 An obligation to make potential additional contributions, for example in the event of bankruptcy of another contributor, is treated as a contingent liability that is not recognised but disclosed. A liability is recognised only if it is probable that additional contributions will be made.

3.12.500.60 A residual interest in a fund that extends beyond a right to reimbursement, such as a contractual right to distributions once all the decommissioning has been completed, may be an equity instrument (see 3.6.150.70).

3.12.510 *Emissions allowances**

3.12.510.10 Certain jurisdictions operate a "cap and trade" scheme, whereby an entity must deliver emissions certificates to a third party (e.g. a regulator) to be able to emit pollutants legally. The government grants a certain number of emissions certificates to an entity for use during a compliance period. The entity then can trade certificates with other parties to ensure that they have sufficient emissions certificates to match their emissions. IFRSs do not contain specific guidance on accounting for cap and trade schemes involving emissions allowances.

3.12.510.20 In our view, emissions certificates received by a participant in a cap and trade scheme are intangible assets. As these intangible assets are received from the government or government-related entity, the intangible may be measured initially at fair value or at a nominal amount, although we prefer fair value measurement (see 4.3.110.10). Subsequently the allowances should be accounted for using the revaluation or cost model within IAS 38 *Intangible Assets*, and tested for impairment. See 3.3.170 for a more detailed discussion of the accounting for emissions certificates held by entities under such cap and trade schemes.

3.12.510.30 Provisions are measured at the best estimate of the expenditure required to settle the present obligation at the reporting date (see 3.12.110). Under cap and trade schemes, generally entities can settle their obligation created by the emissions of pollutants only by surrendering emissions certificates to the local regulator. Generally, an entity cannot settle its obligation by making a cash payment or by transferring other assets. In our view, in cases when other means of settlement are not possible, the provision could be measured based upon the current carrying amount of the certificates on hand if sufficient certificates are owned to settle the current obligation, as that could be viewed as being the best estimate of the expenditures required to settle the obligation. Otherwise the provision should be based on the current market value of the emissions certificates at the reporting date.

3.12.510.40 If at the reporting date the number of emissions certificates required to settle its obligation exceeds the actual number of certificates on hand, then we prefer to measure the actual shortfall at the current market value of the emissions certificates. Consequently, if an entity chooses to sell emissions certificates during the year and in so doing creates a shortfall in the actual number of certificates held as compared to the total pollutants emitted at that date, then we prefer to remeasure the portion of the obligation related to the actual shortfall at the reporting date at the current market value of the certificates. However, there may be other appropriate methods of measuring the amount of the shortfall.

3.12.520 *Waste Electrical and Electronic Equipment*

3.12.520.10 The European Union's (EU) Directive on Waste Electrical and Electronic Equipment (WE&EE) requires costs of disposing of such equipment in an environmentally acceptable manner to be borne by the producers, or by commercial users in some cases. Each member state is required to transform the EU Directive on WE&EE into national law.

IFRIC 6   3.12.520.20 An entity has an obligation to contribute to waste management costs for historical household equipment (equipment sold to private households before 13 August 2005) based on its share of the market in a measurement period; the measurement period is specified in national law, which may vary from country to country. It is an entity's participation in the market during the measurement period that is the past event that triggers the recognition of an obligation to meet waste management costs.

3.12.520.30 The disposal costs of new WE&EE (sold after 13 August 2005) and historical WE&EE from sources other than private households are allocated in different ways and are considered by the Interpretations Committee to be addressed adequately by the recognition criteria in IFRSs. In our view, the facts and circumstances of each country's national law on the disposal of WE&EE should be analysed to determine the appropriate accounting under IFRSs.

3.12.520.40 In relation to historical WE&EE from sources other than private households, consider an example of a commercial user that owns historical WE&EE and is responsible for its disposal. Under the user's national legislation, assume that responsibility for the disposal of WE&EE is with commercial users unless and until the commercial user replaces the equipment. Upon replacement of the equipment the producer of the new equipment assumes responsibility for disposing of the old equipment, i.e. the responsibility for the disposal of the equipment is transferred from the commercial user to the producer of the replacement equipment. In our view, the following accounting is appropriate assuming that a replacement is acquired:

- The commercial user should recognise a provision and capitalise the cost of disposal as part of the cost of the old equipment when the law is enacted.
- When the WE&EE is replaced, the waste disposal obligation for the equipment that is replaced is transferred to the producer of the replacement equipment. Therefore the producer would recognise a provision for the disposal costs.
- The commercial user would derecognise the obligation and recognise any resulting gain or loss, depending on the amount paid to the producer for taking on the costs of disposal. This payment might be embedded in, and therefore should be separated from, the purchase price of the new (replacement) equipment.

3.12.530 *Obligation to acquire or replace assets*

IAS 37.C6   3.12.530.10 Generally, a legal or constructive obligation is recognised as a liability (provision) if the recognition criteria are met. However, a legal or contractual obligation to acquire or replace assets is recognised as a liability only to the extent of the performance of the obligation, i.e. the extent to which costs of acquiring and replacing the asset have been incurred. For example, an entity is required to build infrastructure to satisfy the conditions of a licence. In our view, this should be treated the same way as an executory contract so that the obligation to incur costs for an item that will qualify for recognition as an asset in the future is not an obligation that requires recognition when the contract is agreed. Rather, an asset and liability will be recognised incrementally in accordance with the performance of the obligation, unless the contract is onerous (see 3.12.630).

3.12.540 *Repairs and maintenance*

IAS 37.C11   3.12.540.10 Repairs and maintenance of own assets cannot be provided for since these are costs associated with the future use of the assets. These costs generally are expensed as incurred.

3.12.550 *Shut downs*

3.12.550.10 Some entities periodically shut down facilities for repairs and maintenance. For example, Company Z operates a chain of hotels. Every three years Z closes the hotel for three months to perform repairs and maintenance. A provision cannot be recognised in respect of future repairs and maintenance, even though the costs can be estimated reliably and the repairs and maintenance are probable because they are necessary for Z to continue in operation. Until the expenditure is incurred, there is no obligating event since the expenditure is avoidable. The cost of repairs and maintenance are expensed when incurred unless the activity creates a separately recognisable component of the hotel (see 3.2.230).

3.12.560 *Legal requirement*

3.12.560.10 The prohibition on recognising a provision for future repairs and maintenance also applies when there is a legal requirement to undertake the specified repairs and maintenance activities.

IAS 37.C11B 3.12.560.20 For example, aviation laws require aircraft overhauls after a fixed number of flight hours. However, the overhaul can be avoided if the aircraft is withdrawn from use when or before it has flown the specified number of hours. Therefore, the expenditure of the overhaul is recognised only when the work is done.

3.12.560.30 As another example, in the United Kingdom entities operating in the water industry agree a programme of maintenance with the regulator. If an entity does not spend the agreed amount within the specified period, then the regulator can require the water company to reduce the amount it charges to customers in future periods. In our view, both the future maintenance cost and any enforced reduction in revenues are amounts that relate to the future costs and therefore a provision should not be recognised for them. Instead the costs and revenue reduction are recognised as they are incurred, unless the revenue reduction results in an onerous contract.

3.12.570 *Major inspection or overhaul costs*

IAS 16.14 3.12.570.10 When assets are subject to a major inspection or overhaul, a component approach to depreciation is applied. The component approach results in the capitalisation of major inspection and overhaul costs and their depreciation over the period until the next major overhaul. See 3.2.230 for an explanation and an example of when the component approach is applied.

3.12.580 *Replacement costs*

IAS 2, 16 3.12.580.10 A provision is not recognised for the cost of replacing items of equipment that will be consumed in operations (e.g. the cost of replacement linen or crockery in the hospitality business).

3.12.580.20 Instead, the cost of the replacement items is recognised as equipment and depreciated if the items will be used for more than one period (see 3.2), or as inventory when they are purchased or produced. See also 3.8.310 for a discussion of using the base stock method to account for such items.

3.12.590 *Third-party maintenance contracts*

3.12.590.10 Sometimes an entity will enter into a contract with an unrelated party to provide maintenance services (e.g. a lessor may agree to maintain a leased asset). In our view, the contract is executory and the service provider should not accrue for the expected cost of meeting its obligations under the contract unless the contract is onerous (see 3.12.630). The relevant costs should be recognised only when the services are performed. See 5.1.30.20 for additional guidance on accounting for the service element of lease payments.

3.12.590.20 Similarly, we believe that the customer is the lessee and should not recognise a provision in advance for the maintenance costs that will be payable under the contract. The maintenance contract is a service contract (an executory contract), and normally obligations under such contracts are not recognised until the service is provided unless the contract is onerous. Rather the customer should accrue the costs only when they are due.

IAS 18.13, 37.18
3.12.590.30 For example, Company D is a manufacturer and retailer of motor vehicles. D offers customers the option of a service contract. Customers who elect to have a service contract pay a higher price for the vehicle. Under the terms of the service contract D maintains and services the vehicle for three years from the purchase date. We believe that D should not recognise a provision for the future service costs, unless the contract is onerous. Instead the portion of the selling price that relates to the service contract should be deferred (see 4.2.40).

3.12.600 Maintenance of leased assets

IAS 17.4
3.12.600.10 Lease contracts sometimes require the lessee to maintain the leased asset. In our view, the appropriate accounting treatment of the maintenance costs depends on the nature of the costs, whether the lease is classified as a finance or an operating lease (see 5.1), and the terms of the lease agreement.

3.12.600.20 In our view, when the lessee is required to restore a leased asset to its original condition at the end of the lease term, the obligation to incur the hand-back cost arises when the damage occurs, which may be as the lessee uses the asset. The accounting for the obligation to restore and maintain the leased asset may vary depending on the nature of the lease agreement as discussed below.

3.12.610 Assets leased under a finance lease

3.12.610.10 The substance of a finance lease is the purchase of an asset and a financing transaction (see 5.1.100). The accounting for a finance lease reflects this substance. Therefore, in our view the lessee should account for any overhauls or repairs and maintenance costs associated with an asset leased under a finance lease in the same way as it would for such costs related to its own assets.

3.12.610.20 As such, the lessee should apply the component approach to accounting for a leased asset that is subject to major repair or overhaul costs (i.e. the costs should be capitalised and depreciated over the useful life of the component (see 3.2.230)). Other repair and maintenance costs should be expensed as incurred.

3.12.620 Assets leased under an operating lease

3.12.620.10 The issues are more complex for an asset leased under an operating lease because the asset and the future obligations under the lease are not reflected in the lessee's statement of financial position. There is no guidance in IFRSs on whether component accounting is appropriate when the principal asset is not recognised in the financial statements.

IAS 37.36   3.12.620.20 In the case of an asset leased under an operating lease with an obligation to return the asset (or parts of the asset) in its original condition, the operating lease payments will not reflect fully the consumption of the asset during the lease term. In other circumstances operating lease payments will include payments that reflect the original condition of the asset and its anticipated condition at the end of the lease term. In our view, the nature of the transaction determines the accounting treatment:

- Apply the component approach and recognise major repair or overhaul costs as a leasehold improvement. This approach may be applied on initial recognition to the extent repair or overhaul costs are included in the lease payments, effectively treating a part of the lease contract as a finance lease (or owned asset) and the other part as an operating lease contract. Other maintenance costs are recognised as an expense when incurred.

- Apply the liability approach and recognise a provision for the maintenance cost over the period of the lease as the original component is consumed, for the contractual obligation to hand back the asset in its original condition. This approach should be applied when the operating lease payments do not include payments for repair or overhaul costs. However, the approach also may be applied when repair or overhaul costs are included in the lease payments. In our view, for this approach to be applied when the operating lease payments do not include repair or overhaul costs, the lease agreement should establish a clear obligation for the lessee to incur expenditure when "damage" occurs; this may be proportionate to the use of the asset. The provision would be based on the extent of the damage at the reporting date.

3.12.620.30 To illustrate the two approaches in 3.12.620.20, assume that Company T leases a property under an operating lease. The property was refurbished two years before the lease commenced. T is required to refurbish fully the building every five years.

3.12.620.40 If the building may be handed back with a five-year old refurbishment then consumption of three years of refurbishment is included in the lease payments and the component approach in 3.12.620.20 may be applied. Under this approach, an asset (and a liability) would be recognised on initial recognition of the lease. Subsequently, when the refurbishment costs are incurred, T would capitalise those costs as leasehold improvements and depreciate the component over the period to the next refurbishment or to the end of the lease, if shorter. The component should not include costs of day-to-day servicing of the building (e.g. cleaning).

3.12.620.50 In our view, if the building is required to be handed back newly refurbished, then the liability approach in 3.12.620.20 should be applied. Under this approach, T would recognise a provision for the refurbishment costs. The provision would be measured at the expected cost of the refurbishment based on the condition of the building at each reporting date. This results in a provision being recognised for the full cost of the refurbishment every five years.

3.12.630 *Onerous contracts*

3.12.640 *Definition*

IAS 37.10   3.12.640.10 An onerous contract is one in which the unavoidable costs of meeting the obligations under the contract exceed the economic benefits expected to be received under the contract.

3.12.640.20 A contract on unfavourable terms is not necessarily onerous. For example, Company B is the lessee of properties under operating leases. The lease payments on a number of the properties exceed normal market rentals for properties in the area. B does not have an onerous contract as long as the lease payments do not exceed the benefits it will derive from the properties (see 3.12.670).

3.12.640.30 Similarly, a contract that is not performing as well as anticipated, or as well as possible, is not onerous unless the costs of fulfilling the obligations under the contract exceed the benefits to be derived.

IFRS 4.B6,   3.12.640.40 A potentially onerous contract may be a contract to provide services
B7,   that is accounted for using the percentage of completion method (see 4.2.310.30).
IAS 11.36, 37,   In these circumstances it is not clear whether the onerous contract guidance
37.66   in IAS 37 applies or whether the guidance on the recognition of expected losses in IAS 11 *Construction Contracts* should be applied. In our view, if a potentially onerous contract is a contract accounted for as the rendering of services under IAS 18 *Revenue* using the percentage of completion method, then an entity should choose an accounting policy, to be applied consistently, between the requirements of IAS 11 (see 4.2.300) and IAS 37 unless the service contract is a fixed fee insurance service contract. A fixed fee insurance service contract (see 5.10) that potentially is onerous is accounted for by applying IAS 37. If an entity elects to apply IAS 11 requirements to other service contracts accounted for using the percentage of completion method, then it should consider full costs (i.e. directly attributable variable costs and fixed allocated costs) in assessing whether a contract is onerous. If it elects to apply IAS 37, then only unavoidable costs of meeting the obligation under the contract (i.e. directly variable and incremental to the performance of the contract) should be considered (see 3.12.660 for further guidance).

3.12.640.50 If an entity is assessing whether a contract for the sale of goods is an onerous contract, then in our view this assessment should be made based on the contract as a whole rather than on an item-by-item basis. This may be relevant when there are "learning curve" costs that mean that inefficiencies are expected in the production of early units (see 3.8.215). However, entities also should consider the requirement for inventory to be tested for impairment on an item-by-item basis. If the contractual sales price is less than the unit cost, then a write down to net realisable value may be required (see 3.8.110.10 and 330). Because this net realisable value test is applied to items of inventory, we believe that a write down to the net realisable value may be required for items produced under a contract that, taken as a whole, is not onerous.

3.12.640.60 For example, Company G builds three trains for a rail system. The contract with the rail system is for the sale of goods and is expected to be profitable overall. However, due to the customisation that requires use of a new technology, learning curve costs on the first of three trains are expected to create a loss as detailed below, when considering only incremental costs (see 3.12.660):

	First	Second	Third
Revenue per train	100	100	100
Projected incremental costs	(110)	(95)	(70)
Projected margin over incremental costs	(10)	5	30

3.12.640.70 Since the contract as a whole is profitable (i.e. the expected margin in excess of incremental costs is 25), in our view it is not onerous. However, as costs are being incurred to build the first unit, the entity should consider its net realisable value and write it down, as necessary. The entity also should consider whether assets used to fulfil the contract are impaired (see 3.10).

3.12.650 *Determining whether a contract is onerous*

IAS 37.10   3.12.650.10 In assessing whether a contract is onerous it is necessary to consider:

- the unavoidable costs of meeting the contractual obligations, which is the lower of the net costs of fulfilling the contract and the cost of terminating it; and
- the economic benefits expected to be received.

IAS 37.67   3.12.650.20 If a contract can be terminated without incurring a penalty, then it is not onerous.

3.12.660 Costs

IAS 37.68   3.12.660.10 In determining the costs of fulfilling a contract, the payments due in the period in which the contract cannot be cancelled should be considered. If there is an option to cancel the contract and pay a penalty, then the present value of the amount to be paid on cancellation of the contract also should be considered, and the contract is measured at the lowest net cost to exit.

IAS 37.68   3.12.660.20 For example, Company F leases office space for an annual rental of 20. The remaining lease term is five years, although after two years F has an option to cancel the lease and pay a penalty of 25. The cost of fulfilling the contract is 75 (the present value of 20 x 5). The cost of terminating the contract is 60 (the present value of (20 x 2 + 25)). The alternative that results in the lowest cost should be used in determining whether the contract is onerous, i.e. 60.

3.12.660.30 In our view, if a contract is for goods, or if an entity recognises and measures onerous service contracts under IAS 37 (see 3.12.640.40), then only unavoidable costs directly associated with meeting the entity's obligations under the contract should be considered in determining whether the contract is onerous and in measuring any resulting provision. We believe that the unavoidable costs of meeting the obligations under the contract are only costs that:

- are directly variable with the contract and therefore incremental to the performance of the contract;
- do not include allocated or shared costs that will be incurred regardless of whether the entity fulfils the contract or not; and
- cannot be avoided by the entity's future actions.

3.12.660.33 For example, Company G services computers and charges clients a fixed monthly fee. On one of the contracts the servicing requirements are significantly higher than anticipated. In determining whether the contract is onerous, we believe that G should consider the direct variable costs that it would need to incur to meet its obligations under the contract, but not costs that relate to the servicing business as a whole.

IAS 37.18 3.12.660.37 In our view, costs that would be incurred regardless of whether the contract is fulfilled or not are not incremental. Costs that are not incremental include fixed and non-cancellable costs, such as depreciation of property, plant and equipment, non-cancellable operating lease costs, and personnel costs for employees who would be retained. We believe that costs that are not incremental should not be considered in the onerous contract analysis as they are costs to operate the business. For example, Company Y provides data transmission services using a network infrastructure, which is purchased partly from external carriers. The network infrastructure lease contracts are non-cancellable and are on fixed payment terms regardless of the volume or number of customers serviced by Y using the network. For management purposes, Y uses a cost allocation methodology whereby the full cost of operating the network, including depreciation of owned equipment, rental of network infrastructure and personnel costs, is allocated to individual customer contracts. Y elected to recognise and measure onerous service contracts under IAS 37. We believe that depreciation of entity-owned equipment, rental of network infrastructure and personnel costs are fixed costs associated with operating the infrastructure and should not be included in the onerous contract analysis.

3.12.660.40 In some cases fulfilling an onerous contract may involve use of an item that is leased under a non-cancellable operating lease. Because the lease is not cancellable, the lease cost should not be considered an unavoidable cost of meeting the obligation under the onerous contract. In the example in 3.12.660.37, Y needs to use the network equipment that is leased under a non-cancellable operating lease. While we believe that the lease cost should not be considered an unavoidable cost of meeting the obligation because this cost will be incurred whether or not the onerous contract exists, we believe that Y should consider whether its lease of the network equipment is itself an onerous contract.

3.12.670 Benefits

3.12.670.10 The expected benefit under a contract is the net present value of the future inflows related to the contract. Estimating the future benefits to be derived may require judgement, possibly based on past experience or expert advice.

3.12.670.20 In considering the expected benefits under a contract it may be necessary to evaluate the entity's expected use of a product. For example, Company C manufactures chocolate and has a contract to buy cocoa beans at a cost of 7,800 per ton. The market price of cocoa beans has fallen to 7,000 per ton. The contract is not onerous unless the expected selling price of the final product (the chocolate) is less than the unavoidable cost of producing the chocolate.

IAS 39.5 3.12.670.30 As another example, assume that Company B, a commercial bakery, has a forward contract to purchase 100 tons of wheat at a price of 13,000 per ton. The forward contract will be settled by physical delivery of the wheat and therefore the contract is not treated as a derivative (see 3.6.90). At the reporting date the market price of wheat has dropped to 10,000 per ton. However, B still expects to make a profit on the sale of the bread that will be made from the wheat. Therefore the contract is not onerous and B should not recognise a provision for the above-market price. Instead B will measure the cost of the wheat at 13,000 per ton when the risks and rewards of ownership transfer.

3.12.680 Leases

3.12.680.10 In our view, when assessing whether a lease is onerous, consideration should be given to any sublease income that could be earned. We believe that this applies even if the entity chooses not to sublease the asset (e.g. to avoid competitors gaining access to the area); or a sublease requires the lessor's approval, provided that the approval cannot be withheld unreasonably. However, if a lease prohibits subleases, then potential sublease income should not be considered.

3.12.690 *Timing of recognition*

3.12.690.10 Usually, a decision to terminate a contract does not result in a legal or constructive obligation. Therefore, in our view costs of cancelling or terminating a contract should not be recognised until the contract actually is terminated, unless the contract becomes onerous.

3.12.700 *Overall loss-making operations*

3.12.700.10 Some contracts may be part of an overall loss-making operation. In our view, a provision should not be recognised for these contracts unless the cash flows related to the contract clearly are distinguishable from the operations as a whole. Otherwise, a provision effectively would be recognised for future operating losses, which is prohibited by IFRSs.

3.12.700.20 For example, Company T is a tour operator. Among other services, T offers cruises on a lake. For this purpose T leases a cruise ship under an operating lease. Due to increased competition for cruises, the costs of leasing the cruise ship exceed the income that T generates from its cruise operations. Given that the operating lease contract relates only to T's cruise operations, and the cash flows related to these operations are separately identifiable, in our view T should assess whether the lease contract is onerous. In performing this analysis T should consider the costs of terminating the lease contract and alternative uses for the ship.

3.12.700.30 However, if T sold package tours, which included a cruise on the lake, and T's overall operations were loss-making, then the losses would relate to the business as a whole rather than specifically to the lease contract. In addition, it is likely that the cash inflows related to the cruise operations would not be clearly distinguishable from those related to the other operations. Therefore, in this case we do not believe that a provision for an onerous contract should be recognised. However, T should consider whether the related recognised assets are impaired.

3.12.710 *Measuring the provision*

IAS 37.66   3.12.710.10 The present value of the obligation under an onerous contract should be recognised as a provision. The amount of the provision is the lower of the cost of terminating the contract and the net cost of continuing with the contract (i.e. the lowest net cost to exit).

IAS 37.68   3.12.710.15 In our view, an onerous contract should be measured using the same approach used for determining whether a contract is onerous (see 3.12.650). For example, an entity may have a choice either to produce goods itself or to purchase them on the market in order to fulfil a contract. In our view, if the entity-specific marginal costs of producing the goods are lower than the cost of purchasing them on the market, then the marginal costs should be used rather than the fair value of the goods on the market. This is consistent with the requirement to measure an onerous contract at the lowest net cost to exit.

3.12.710.16 For example, Company T produces electricity and has a non-cancellable fixed-price contract with a customer. T has a variety of electricity generating facilities, including nuclear, thermal hydro and wind power plants. If there is insufficient capacity, then T can purchase electricity on the market. The revenue under the contract is less than both the incremental cost of producing (i.e. fuel and labour) and the market price for purchasing electricity. The market price for purchasing electricity is higher than the entity-specific incremental costs. We believe that T should measure the onerous contract provision based on the incremental costs of producing electricity.

IAS 37.69   3.12.710.20 In our view, revenues directly related to a contract also should be considered in measuring an onerous contract provision. For example, airline S owns a number of aircraft and has entered into a non-cancellable agreement under which it charters out one of its aircraft for 20 days for a fee of 10 per day. S incurs unavoidable costs of 15 a day to service the aircraft. The unavoidable costs of servicing the aircraft exceed the revenues. The anticipated loss on the contract is 5 per day for the 20 days, i.e. 100 (5 x 20). Before the onerous contract provision is calculated S should test the aircraft for impairment (see 3.12.710.60).

3.12.710.30 In our view, the lower of the cost of fulfilling the contract and of terminating the contract should be considered in measuring the provision, regardless of the entity's intention. Extending the example of S in 3.12.710.20, if S is able to cancel the charter arrangement by paying a penalty of 40, then a provision of 40 rather than 100 should be recognised, regardless of whether S intends to cancel the contract.

3.12.710.35 If a contract for the sale of goods is onerous, then the provision for the contract will be reversed as the contract is fulfilled. Modifying the example in 3.12.640.60 – 70, assume that the revenue per train is 80, not 100. G enters into the agreement in the first quarter of 2011 and will produce and deliver one train in each of the next three quarters. G has the following projected revenues and costs measured on a net present value basis for the purpose of calculating the onerous contract provision:

	Q2	Q3	Q4	Total
Revenue per train	80	80	80	240
Projected incremental costs	(110)	(95)	(70)	(275)
Projected margin over incremental costs	(30)	(15)	10	(35)

3.12.710.36 An onerous contract provision of 35 would be recognised in the first quarter of 2011 when G enters into the contract. In our view, this provision should be reversed as the trains are delivered as follows:

	Q2	Q3	Q4
Revenue per train	80	80	80
Projected incremental costs	(110)	(95)	(70)
Projected margin over incremental costs	(30)	(15)	10
NRV adjustment	(30)	(15)	-
Release of onerous contract provision	30	5	-

3.12.710.37 Therefore, in respect of this contract G would recognise a loss of 35 in the first quarter of 2011, no gain or loss in the second quarter, a loss of 10 in the third quarter and a profit of 10 in the fourth quarter.

3.12.710.40 In our view, direct variable operating costs necessary to fulfil an entity's obligations under a contract that cannot be avoided should be included when measuring the provision for an onerous contract. Costs that could be avoided by the entity's future actions or that are not related directly to the contract should not be included.

3.12.710.50 If a finance lease contract is onerous, then the leased asset is evaluated for impairment (see 3.10.110). An onerous contract provision is not recognised. Although the future lease payments under the contract may exceed the carrying amount of the asset due to future finance costs, an onerous contract provision cannot be recognised for future finance costs. Any component of the future lease payments that relates to services provided under the lease should be evaluated separately to assess whether they give rise to an onerous contract.

IAS 37.69 3.12.710.60 Similarly, in our view if a contract, including an operating lease contract, is onerous, then assets dedicated to the contract, including any capitalised leasehold improvements, should be tested for impairment (see 3.10) before the onerous contract provision is calculated. Therefore, in the case of the airline charter contract discussed in 3.12.710.20 and 30, the fact that the operating costs exceed the revenues to be derived from the aircraft is an impairment indicator. As the aircraft is S's recognised asset, it should test the aircraft for impairment before recognising a provision for an onerous contract.

3.12.720 Regulatory liabilities

3.12.720.10 In many countries utility companies, and other entities operating in regulated industries, have contractual arrangements with the local regulator to charge a price based on a cost-plus model. When costs incurred are lower than budget, some arrangements may require the regulated entity to return any "excess margin" to customers through future price decreases.

3.12.720.20 Under such arrangements the regulator specifies the reduction in future prices, generally based on conditions set out in the agreement. For example, in 2010 an electricity generator U was subject to rate regulation that limits the return on capital to 6 percent. Actual sales and costs resulted in U earning 8 percent and U knows that under the terms of its licence it must reduce 2011 prices to achieve a target return of 4 percent. This expected future rate reduction is equal to 750 of "excess" 2010 revenue.

3.12.720.30 The question is whether a liability for the expected future rate reduction of 750 should be recognised in the 2010 financial statements and if yes, then what type of obligation is being recognised and measured. In our view, when the claw-back of the excess margin is contingent on future activity and sales, U has no contractual obligation to deliver cash to a third party; therefore, it does not have a financial liability within the scope of IAS 32 and IAS 39. However, if U was required to pay the 750 to the local regulator if it stops operating, or to another entity if that entity took over U's licence, then the 750 would be considered a financial liability. Further, since the mechanism for "returning" current year excess revenue is a reduction in prices on future sales, U does not have a present obligation within the scope of IAS 37 and a provision would be recognised only if U had an onerous contract, i.e. if it was obligated to provide future services at a loss.

3.12.720.40 In our view, in the circumstances described in 3.12.720.20 and 30 U also would have to consider, in preparing its 2010 financial statements, if it has satisfied the revenue recognition requirements of IAS 18 in respect of the 750 of excess revenue.

Revenue recognition requires that the risks and rewards of ownership of goods have been transferred and that services have been rendered, and measured by the reference to the stage of completion. If an entity is required to deliver additional goods or services for monies already collected via an adjustment of the sales price, then in our view recognition of revenue related to these additional goods or services would not be appropriate. Instead the excess of 750 would be recognised as deferred revenue. Deferred revenue is recognised in profit or loss as the future discounted goods or services are provided. This approach is similar to the approach for multiple deliverables such as customer loyalty programmes (see 4.2.50 and 360).

3.12.720.50 See 3.3.180 for a discussion of regulatory assets.

3.12.730 *Software modification costs*

IAS 37.19,
C11

3.12.730.10 When an external event, such as the introduction of a new currency, requires an entity to make a modification of its software in order to continue to operate once the new currency is introduced, the entity does not have a present obligation to modify software. In our view, a provision is not recognised, as the entity would be able to avoid this expenditure by its future actions. However, an entity should consider whether costs incurred qualify for capitalisation as either an intangible or fixed asset.

IAS 16.12,
13

3.12.730.20 Costs of modifying existing software are recognised as an expense when incurred unless they increase the expected utility of the asset and therefore qualify for capitalisation.

3.12.740 *Legal claims*

3.12.740.10 In our view, the potential obligating event for a legal claim is the event that gives rise to the claim, rather than receipt of the claim itself.

3.12.740.15 In our view, a present obligation may exist even without an asserted claim against an entity. However, if the entity concludes that the claim is unlikely to be asserted and therefore that the outflow of the resources related to this obligation is not probable, then we believe that this present obligation should be treated as a contingent liability. For example, a person slips on a wet floor in a shop and injures their left ankle. The shop provided details if the person wished to assert a claim; however, the person has not contacted the shop and did not indicate that this would be done. Based on its past experience, the shop considers it unlikely that the claim will be asserted. Even though the person does not raise a claim against the shop, the shop has a present obligation if the accident occurred due to management's failure to mark the wet area. However, the outflow of resources in respect of this present obligation is not probable in this example; therefore, we believe that the shop has a contingent liability even though it has a present obligation to compensate the injured customer as a result of a past event.

3.12.740.17 Conversely, the assertion of a claim is not, in our view determinative evidence that a present obligation exists. While receipt of the claim will require assessment of whether there is a present obligation, we believe that the claim itself is not sufficient to create an obligation.

3.12.740.20 For many legal claims it is clear whether there is a past event. What may not be clear is whether an entity has an obligation as a result of the past event (e.g. the entity may not accept responsibility for the event), or whether there is a probable outflow (e.g. the entity may expect to defend the claim successfully).

3.12.740.30 If an entity disputes a legal claim and legal opinion supports the view that the defence will more likely than not be successful, then the legal claim gives rise to a contingent liability (see 3.14.10). In these cases no provision is recognised. When it is probable that the entity is liable and that there will be an outflow of resources to settle the claim, a provision is recognised, unless the amount cannot be measured reliably. In such cases, a contingent liability would be disclosed instead.

3.12.740.35 In our view, if the entity believes that there is no past obligating event, then expected legal costs to be incurred in defending the claim should not be accrued as a provision, even if these expected legal costs are incremental. We believe that the claim is not an obligating event with respect to the future legal costs if there is no past obligating event for the underlying claim. Instead, we believe that in such cases the probable future legal costs are future operating expenses and should be expensed when incurred. In contrast, if the entity concludes that there is a past obligating event with respect to the underlying claim, then we believe that any incremental legal costs expected to be incurred in settling the claim should be included in measuring the provision.

3.12.740.40 In our view, if an entity has been unsuccessful in defending a claim, but intends to appeal against the decision in a higher court, then a provision should be recognised for the expected amount of the claim because, since the entity was unsuccessful in defending the claim, it cannot be argued that there is no obligation or that an outflow is not probable. In this case any incremental legal costs expected to be incurred in settling the claim should be included in measuring the provision as the related obligation meets the definition of a present rather than possible obligation.

3.12.750 *Liabilities arising from financial guarantees*

IAS 39.2(e), 3.12.750.10 Financial guarantee arrangements such as certain letters of credit are within
47(c) the scope of IAS 39 unless the issuer of the contract previously has asserted explicitly that it regards such contracts as insurance contracts, and has used accounting applicable to insurance contracts, in which case the issuer may choose to apply either IAS 39 or IFRS 4 to such contracts (see 3.6.30). Generally, when a financial guarantee recognised under IAS 39 or IFRS 4 becomes probable of being exercised, then the provision is measured in accordance with IAS 37. However, the remaining elements of this standard, e.g. the disclosure requirements, do not apply. See 3.12.360 for a discussion of non-financial guarantees for products or services.

3.12.755 *Tax exposures*

3.12.760 *Income tax*

3.12.760.10 In our view, obligations for possible income tax exposures are treated as current tax liabilities, and not provisions (see 3.13.580).

IAS 12.88   3.12.760.20 In our view, an entity should choose an accounting policy, to be applied consistently, as to whether it accounts for interest and penalties on tax exposures under IAS 12 *Income Taxes* or under IAS 37. If IAS 37 is elected, then an entity should recognise a provision for the best estimate of interest and penalties payable related to previous tax years, if there is a probable outflow of resources and the amount can be estimated reliably. The provision is discounted if the effect of discounting is material. The interest and penalties will then be presented as other provisions (liabilities) in the statement of financial position and as interest and operating expenses respectively in the statement of comprehensive income. See 3.13.580 for further discussion of income tax exposures.

3.12.760.30 In some countries entities are subject to taxes that are calculated as a percentage of net revenues less certain specified costs. The list of deductible costs varies depending on the jurisdiction. Whilst IAS 12 defines the taxable profit as a profit or loss for a period, determined in accordance with the rules established by taxation authorities, upon which income taxes are payable, in some cases it may be difficult to determine whether a taxable amount should be considered to be a "taxable profit", and therefore whether a tax is an income tax in the scope of IAS 12. In our view, this determination will be based on the facts and circumstances of the particular case, including among other factors the relative significance of the deductions (see 3.13.10).

3.12.765 *Taxes related to share-based payment transactions*

3.12.765.10 See 4.5.140 for a discussion of the taxes related to share-based payment transactions.

3.12.770 **Presentation and disclosure**

IAS 1.54,   3.12.770.10 Provisions are disclosed as a separate line item in the statement of
70   financial position. Provisions that will be utilised within one year are classified as current liabilities.

3.12.780 *Classes of provisions*

IAS 37.84   3.12.780.10 Each class of provision is disclosed separately. The extent of disaggregation that is required will depend on the significance and nature of the individual provisions. Categories of provisions that generally should be disclosed separately include provisions for: litigation, warranties, environmental obligations, onerous contracts and restructuring costs.

3.12.790 *Movements schedule*

IAS 37.84 3.12.790.10 Movements in each class of provisions during the reporting period are disclosed. Comparative period information is not required.

3.12.790.20 All movements are disclosed separately on a gross basis. Amounts that are reversed or used during the period may not be netted off against additional provisions recognised during the period. For example, if the provision for litigation for some matters has increased, but for others has decreased, the gross amount of the increases and decreases are shown.

3.12.800 *Description of provisions*

IAS 37.85 3.12.800.10 Narrative information is required about the nature of provisions, the expected timing of the outflows, and uncertainties and assumptions made in measuring the provisions. The disclosure of uncertainties may be general in nature. In our view, for a legal claim normally it would be sufficient to say that the outcome depends on court proceedings.

IAS 1.125 3.12.800.20 However, an entity also should consider the requirement to disclose key assumptions about the future, and other sources of estimation uncertainty that have a significant risk of causing a material adjustment to the carrying amounts of assets and liabilities within the next financial year (see 2.4.180).

IAS 1.38 3.12.800.30 Comparative information should be included in the narrative information when it is relevant to an understanding of the current period's financial statements. For example, when a provision for a matter was made in a previous reporting period, it may be useful to the readers to be given comparative narrative information to put the provision in its proper context.

3.12.810 *Disclosure exemption*

IAS 37.92 3.12.810.10 There is an exemption from the disclosure requirements for provisions in extremely rare cases if providing the disclosure would seriously prejudice a dispute. For example, this exemption may apply to pending litigation, disputes with tax authorities and claims subject to arbitration.

3.12.810.20 The exemption applies only to the disclosures required by IAS 37, and not to disclosures that may be required by other IFRSs, for example disclosures regarding income tax liabilities or related party transactions.

3.12.810.30 The exemption often would not apply in consolidated financial statements because, for example, disclosure of litigation provisions generally is made in aggregate and as such it is unlikely that the disclosure would harm the entity's position in any one case.

3.12.820 *Presentation of onerous contract provisions*

IAS 1.32   3.12.820.10 In our view, when an entity has an onerous contract, any provision recognised should be presented as a liability. It should not be netted against the carrying amount of any related assets.

3.12.830 *Environmental and similar funds*

IFRIC 5.7   3.12.830.10 A fund that is established to finance the costs associated with a provision is not offset against the related provision. Therefore, the operator recognises an obligation for decommissioning as a provision and recognises its interest in the fund as a separate asset, unless the fund relieves the contributor of its obligation to pay decommissioning costs (see 3.12.500).

3.12.840 *Effects of discounting*

IAS 37.60,   3.12.840.10 The unwinding of the discount is presented as a component of interest
IFRIC 1.8   expense. This cost is not a qualifying borrowing cost that is eligible for capitalisation.

3.12.850 *Reversals and other changes in estimate*

3.12.850.10 A reversal of a provision is a change in estimate (see 2.8.60). Therefore, in our view the reversal should be presented in the same line item of the statement of comprehensive income as the original estimate. For example, changes in provisions, whether they are additional amounts (debits) or reductions in amounts charged previously (credits), should be presented in distribution expenses if the original estimate was recorded in that classification. However, in some instances (e.g. on the basis of the size and incidence of the change in estimate) we believe that the effect of a reversal may be presented in other income (see 4.1.150).

IAS 1.98(g)   3.12.850.20 Reversals of provisions are disclosed separately. Significant reversals of provisions may raise questions regarding the reliability of management estimates and should be explained in the notes; this disclosure also may be required due to the size or incidence of the reversal (see 4.1.80).

3.12.860 *Reserves for general business risks*

3.12.860.10 A provision cannot be recognised for costs associated with the risk of future losses. If an entity wishes to reflect risks not covered by provisions in the financial statements, then in our view it may establish a separate component of shareholders' equity, e.g. a non-distributable reserve, depending on the shareholders' approval, as may be required by the articles of incorporation or law. Amounts may be transferred to this reserve directly from retained earnings or from another category of equity. Any such transfers would be disclosed as part of the movements in equity (see 3.11.410).

3.12.870 *Restructuring provisions*

3.12.870.10 An issue often arises as to whether restructuring costs may be presented as a separate line item in the statement of comprehensive income, particularly in cases when expenditures are classified according to their function. See 4.1.70, 82 and 84 for a detailed discussion of this issue.

3.12.880 **Future developments**

3.12.880.10 In June 2005 the IASB published an ED *Proposed Amendments to IAS 37 Provisions, Contingent Liabilities and Contingent Assets and IAS 19 Employee Benefits* (the 2005 ED). The proposed amendments would result in significant changes from current practice in accounting for provisions, contingent liabilities and contingent assets. As part of its redeliberations of the proposals in the 2005 ED, some of the main decisions that the IASB has reaffirmed are that:

- the existence of a present obligation distinguishes a liability from a business risk; and
- the term "stand ready obligation" would be used to describe situations when there is an uncertainty about the outflow of economic benefits required to settle a present obligation, but not when there is an uncertainty about its existence.

3.12.880.20 The IASB also determined that its final conclusions about the probability recognition criterion (i.e. "more likely than not") would depend on further redeliberations of the measurement requirements. However, the IASB indicated its intention to remove the recognition threshold by adopting a model in which probability would be factored into the measurement of a provision, not into whether or not it is recognised.

3.12.880.30 In January 2010 the IASB published ED/2010/1 *Measurement of Liabilities in IAS 37* (the 2010 ED) which is a limited re-exposure of the 2005 ED focused on:

- a high-level measurement objective for liabilities and certain aspects of application of that measurement objective; and
- the measurement of obligations involving services, e.g. decommissioning. The 2010 ED proposes that service-related obligations would be measured by reference to the price that a contractor would charge to undertake the service, i.e. including a profit margin. This would be irrespective of the entity's intentions with regard to settling the obligation, i.e. irrespective of whether the entity intends that the work will be carried out by an in-house team or by external contractors.

3.12.880.40 A final standard is scheduled for the first half of 2010.

3.12.880.50 In June 2010 the IASB published ED/2010/6 *Revenue from Contracts with Customers*, which provides guidance on the accounting for onerous performance obligations that arise in contracts with customers. If finalised as proposed, then this guidance would supersede the existing guidance in IAS 37 for these business arrangements. A final standard is scheduled for the second quarter of 2011.

3.12.880.60 In July 2010 the IASB issued ED/2010/8 *Insurance Contracts*. The ED addresses accounting for insurance contracts issued by insurers and reinsurance contracts held by insurers; it does not address policyholder accounting. A final standard is scheduled for the second quarter of 2011.

3.12.880.70 In December 2007 the IASB activated a joint project with the FASB to address the underlying accounting for emissions trading schemes. An ED is expected no earlier than the second half of 2011.

3.13 Income taxes
(IAS 12, SIC-21, SIC-25)

3.13 Income taxes
(IAS 12, SIC-21, SIC-25)

Overview of currently effective requirements

- Income taxes are taxes based on taxable profits and taxes that are payable by a subsidiary, associate or joint venture upon distribution to investors.

- The total income tax expense recognised in a period is the sum of current tax plus the change in deferred tax assets and liabilities during the period, excluding tax recognised outside profit or loss (i.e. either in other comprehensive income or directly in equity) or arising from a business combination.

- Current tax represents the amount of income taxes payable (recoverable) in respect of the taxable profit (loss) for a period.

- Deferred tax is recognised for the estimated future tax effects of temporary differences, unused tax losses carried forward and unused tax credits carried forward.

- A temporary difference is the difference between the tax base of an asset or liability and its carrying amount in the financial statements.

- A deferred tax liability is not recognised if it arises from the initial recognition of goodwill.

- A deferred tax liability (asset) is not recognised if it arises from the initial recognition of an asset or liability in a transaction that is not a business combination, and at the time of the transaction affects neither accounting profit nor taxable profit.

- Deferred tax is not recognised in respect of investments in subsidiaries, associates and joint ventures if certain conditions are met.

- A deferred tax asset is recognised if it is probable that it will be realised.

- Income tax is measured based on rates that are enacted or substantively enacted at the reporting date and, in the case of deferred tax, the expected manner of settlement (liability) or recovery (asset).

- Deferred tax is measured on an undiscounted basis.

- Deferred tax is classified as non-current in a classified statement of financial position.

> - **Income tax related to items recognised outside profit or loss is itself recognised outside profit or loss.**

Currently effective requirements

This publication reflects IFRSs in issue at 1 August 2010. The currently effective requirements cover annual periods beginning on 1 January 2010. The requirements related to this topic are derived mainly from IAS 12 *Income Taxes*, SIC-21 *Income Taxes – Recovery of Revalued Non-Depreciable Assets* and SIC-25 *Income Taxes – Changes in the Tax Status of an Entity or its Shareholders*.

Forthcoming requirements and future developments

When a currently effective requirement will be changed by a new requirement that is issued but is not yet effective, it is marked with a # as a **forthcoming requirement** and the impact of the change is explained in the accompanying boxed text. In respect of this topic no forthcoming requirements are noted.

When a significant change to the currently effective or forthcoming requirements is expected, it is marked with a * as an area that may be subject to **future developments** and a brief outline of the relevant projects is given in 3.13.1010.

3.13.10 Scope

IAS 12.1, 2 3.13.10.10 The scope of IAS 12 is limited to income taxes, which are taxes based on taxable profits, as well as taxes, for example withholding taxes, that are payable by a subsidiary, associate or joint venture upon distribution to the investor. Taxes that are not based on taxable profits are not within the scope of IAS 12; examples include social taxes payable by an employer based on a percentage of employees' wages, which may be employee benefits (see 4.4), and taxes payable on capital and reserves. In our view, taxes that are not income taxes generally should be accounted for as provisions (see 3.12) or as financial liabilities (see 3.6) as appropriate.

IAS 12.4 3.13.10.20 Also excluded from the scope of IAS 12 are government grants, including the forgiveness of income tax liabilities (see 4.3.30) and investment tax credits (ITCs) (see 3.13.590).

IAS 12.5 3.13.10.30 In some cases it is not clear whether a tax is based on *taxable profit*, which is the profit (loss) for a period, determined in accordance with the rules established by the taxation authorities, upon which income taxes are payable (recoverable).

3.13.10.40 For example, companies in South Africa currently pay a secondary tax (STC) on dividends paid to shareholders; the tax is levied on the entity paying dividends and is not a shareholder withholding tax. The introduction of the STC was accompanied by a reduction in the corporate income tax rate. In our view, the STC is in substance an income tax since it taxes profits, even though the timing of the payment is linked to the payment of dividends (see 3.13.410).

3.13.10.50 In another example, companies in Estonia pay a tax levied on dividends paid to natural persons and non-residents and on certain other payments including employee fringe benefits that generally are non-deductible expenses for tax purposes. However, companies pay no income tax. The Estonian tax system is an extreme example of a dual income tax rate system, with a zero tax rate on undistributed taxable income and a higher rate on distributed income. In our view, the income tax effect of dividends should be recognised in an entity's profit or loss when a liability to pay the dividend is recognised (see 3.13.15.30 and 330). See 3.13.410 – 427 for a discussion of the presentation of tax effects of distributions.

IU 03-06; 3.13.10.55 Taxable profit is not the same as accounting profit, but taxes do not need
IU 05-09 to be based on a figure that is exactly accounting profit to be within the scope of the standard. However, the term "taxable profit" implies that taxes within the scope of IAS 12 are levied on a net rather than a gross amount. Therefore, for example, taxes based on revenue (a gross figure), on a fixed amount per unit of production or on notional income derived from tonnage capacity would not, in our view be within the scope of IAS 12.

3.13.10.60 A variety of complex tax regulations are created by different tax authorities under which regulations levies are not calculated based on taxable profit; such levies may take the form of royalties, extraction taxes and corporate taxes, or a combination thereof. These types of levies are particularly prevalent in the extractive industries, but are not limited to that particular industry and might be found in many jurisdictions.

3.13.10.70 For example, levies may be based on a percentage of "operating profit" as determined on a mine-by-mine, field-by-field, ship-by-ship or other basis, after allowing for the deduction of certain expenses. In other cases these taxes are imposed in a way that may be viewed as creating a joint venture between the producing entity and the government. An assessment of whether a levy is within the scope of IAS 12 is performed based on its terms and conditions.

3.13.10.80 Whether or not a levy is within the scope of IAS 12 results in recognition, measurement, presentation and disclosure consequences; for example, the definition of an obligating event may give rise to later recognition of the corresponding liability under IAS 37 *Provisions, Contingent Liabilities and Contingent Assets* than under IAS 12. In any event, the classification of items such as levy schemes is not an accounting policy choice. Therefore an entity operating in multiple jurisdictions, or even in a single jurisdiction under multiple regulations with different terms, may have to recognise, measure and classify each tax differently.

3.13.15 Current tax: recognition and measurement

3.13.15.10 Current tax represents the amount of income taxes payable (recoverable) in respect of the taxable profit (loss) for a period. A current tax liability (or asset) is recognised for income tax payable (or paid but recoverable) in respect of all periods to date.

IAS 12.46   3.13.15.20 As in the case of deferred tax, the measurement of current tax liabilities and assets is based on tax law that is enacted or substantively enacted by the reporting date, which in certain circumstances may include announcements of future changes; otherwise the effects of future changes in tax laws or rates are not anticipated (see 3.13.310).

IAS 12.46,   3.13.15.30 Generally current tax liabilities (assets) are measured at the amount expected
52A, 52B   to be paid (recovered). However, any income tax consequences of dividends on the tax rates are recognised when a liability to pay the dividend is recognised. For example, in jurisdiction X the tax rate applicable to undistributed investment income is 50 percent and the tax rate applicable to distributed investment income is 30 percent. Company F earns investment income of 100 in year 1 and pays a dividend of 80 in year 2. F has a history of annual dividend payments and it intends to continue this policy in the future. F did not recognise the dividend as a liability at the end of year 1 because the dividend was approved after the reporting date. In this case the specific requirement in relation to the tax consequences of dividend payments takes precedence over the general requirement regarding the amount expected to be paid (recovered). Therefore, in year 1 F recognises current tax expense of 50 (100 x 50%); in year 2 F recognises current tax income of 16 (80 x (30% - 50%)) as a result of the dividend.

IAS 12.46   3.13.15.40 In some tax jurisdictions, entities are able to negotiate the payment of large tax balances, so that the payment of amounts that ordinarily would be settled within 12 months under the tax legislation is deferred. Typically a series of payments is negotiated with the tax authorities. When the restructured tax liability does not bear interest at a market rate, an issue arises as to whether the liability is discounted to net present value at the date that the terms of payment are agreed. In our view, an entity should discount restructured tax liabilities. The same rationale applies to current tax receivables of an entity with deferred payment terms. Conversely, deferred tax amounts should not be discounted (see 3.13.350.10).

IAS 12.80(b)   3.13.15.45 Actual taxes payable (receivable) might differ from amounts recognised as current tax liabilities (assets). Such adjustments reflect changes in the estimated amounts to be paid to (recovered from) the tax authorities which arise in the course of an entity finalising its tax position for prior years. Unless there is an indication that the adjustment is the result of an error, such changes to current tax are treated as a change in estimate and recognised in the tax expense of the period the adjustment occurs (see 2.8), resulting in a separately disclosed component of tax expense (income) in the notes.

IAS 32.11, 13,   3.13.15.50 Current (and deferred) tax assets and liabilities are not financial instruments
AG11, AG12,   as they arise from tax legislation and not from a contract between the taxable entity and
39.14   the tax authorities. Therefore, income tax assets and liabilities are not subject to the measurement requirements of IAS 39 *Financial Instruments: Recognition and Measurement* (see 3.6.150.90).

3.13.15.60 However, IAS 12 is silent on the derecognition of tax assets in situations when, for example, an entity transfers its right to receive cash from the tax authorities to another party. In our view, an entity may apply the derecognition requirements of IAS 39 by analogy in such situations to assess whether it is appropriate to derecognise tax assets (see 3.6.1070 and 1330).

3.13.20 Deferred tax: recognition and measurement

3.13.20.10 Deferred tax is recognised for the estimated future tax effects of temporary differences, unused tax losses carried forward and unused tax credits carried forward. See 3.13.15.45 for a discussion of adjustments to current taxes, which also applies to deferred taxes.

3.13.30 *Temporary differences*

IAS 12.5   3.13.30.10 A temporary difference is the difference between the tax carrying amount (or tax base) of an asset or liability and its carrying amount in the financial statements that will result in taxable or deductible amounts in future periods when the carrying amount is recovered or settled. Therefore, in determining the amount of deferred tax to recognise, the analysis focuses on the carrying amounts in the statement of financial position (i.e. a "balance sheet approach") rather than on the differences between profit or loss and taxable profits (i.e. "an income statement approach"). Temporary differences may be either taxable (will result in taxable amounts in future periods) or deductible (will result in deductions in future periods).

IAS 12.IE.A.1   3.13.30.20 For example, Company R accrues interest of 100, which will be taxed only when R receives the cash payment. The statement of financial position under IFRSs includes an asset (receivable) of 100. However, the tax statement of financial position does not include an asset because the interest is not yet taxable (tax base equals zero). This difference results in a deferred tax liability (taxable temporary difference) because the amount will be taxed in a future period, i.e. when the cash is received.

IAS 12.20, 62   3.13.30.30 In another example, Company B revalues its main production plant above its original cost because its accounting policy is to measure property, plant and equipment at fair value (see 3.2.300). The tax statement of financial position shows no such revaluation and the revaluation itself will not be taxed (tax base of the revaluation equals zero). This difference results in a deferred tax liability because B will use the plant to generate future economic benefits that are expected to result in taxable profits, but the corresponding tax deduction (i.e. depreciation charge) will be limited to the original cost of the plant. Therefore, the revaluation will be taxed indirectly and a deferred tax liability (taxable temporary difference) results, for which the income tax expense is recognised in other comprehensive income because the revaluation also is recognised in other comprehensive income. See 3.13.110.80, 390 and 440 for a discussion of other tax accounting issues associated with revaluations.

3.13.30.40 In another example, Company C's property, plant and equipment is revalued for tax purposes, with the revaluation surplus being deductible in future years. No revaluation is recognised under IFRSs in accordance with C's accounting policy for property, plant and equipment. This difference results in an increase in a deferred tax asset, a reduction in a deferred tax liability, or both, because C will receive future tax deductions for the additional value recognised for tax purposes. In our view, to the extent that the tax base is increased to the same level as the carrying amount under IFRSs, this increase represents the reversal of the previously recognised taxable temporary difference rather than the origination of a deductible temporary difference, i.e. there are not separate temporary differences for the property, plant and equipment and its subsequent revaluation (see 3.13.390.30 and 40).

IAS 12.7, 8, **3.13.30.50** In another example, Company D enters into a pay-fixed receive-floating inter-
15, 24 est rate swap with an initial fair value of zero, which it does not designate as a hedging instrument. The swap is taxed on a cash basis. That is, if D makes a net payment under the swap, then D receives a tax deduction; conversely if D obtains a net receipt under the swap, then the receipt is taxable. Remeasurement of the interest rate swap results in temporary differences as follows:

- If the swap has a positive fair value of 100 at the reporting date, i.e. the swap is an asset, then this indicates that D expects to obtain net cash receipts in the future. The tax base of the asset is zero. A taxable temporary difference of 100 arises, resulting in a deferred tax liability.
- If the swap has a negative fair value of 100 at the reporting date, i.e. the swap is a liability, then this indicates that D expects to make net cash payments in the future. The tax base of the liability is zero. A deductible temporary difference of 100 arises, resulting in a potential deferred tax asset.

3.13.30.60 In other cases cash flow hedging of a forecast transaction (see 3.7.60) that results in the recognition of a non-financial asset (liability) can give rise to temporary differences to the extent that a basis adjustment affects the carrying amount of the asset (liability) but not its tax base; see 3.7.80.40 for further guidance on basis adjustments.

3.13.30.70 For example, Company S enters into a foreign currency forward contract (forward) to hedge the currency exposure on a future purchase of inventory. When the inventory is purchased, the cost of the inventory translated at the spot rate is 100, which also is the tax base of the inventory. S receives a net amount of 10 on settlement of the forward (i.e. immediately prior to settlement the forward was an asset with a fair value of 10), which is taxed on receipt. Assume for simplicity that the hedge is fully effective.

3.13.30.80 In this case, remeasurement of the forward prior to settlement results in the recognition of a gain of 10, which is recognised in other comprehensive income, and a taxable temporary difference of 10 arises. On settlement of the forward, the net receipt of 10 is taxed. If S's policy is to transfer the deferred gain on the forward of 10 from other comprehensive income to the carrying amount of inventory i.e. make a basis adjustment (see 3.7.80), then the initial carrying amount of the inventory is 90 and a temporary difference of 10 arises. Conversely, if S's policy is to transfer the deferred gain of 10 to profit or loss as the inventory affects profit or loss, then the initial carrying amount of the inventory is 100 and no temporary difference arises.

3.13.40 *Determining the tax base*

IAS 12.5, 7-9   3.13.40.10 The tax base of an asset or a liability is the amount attributed to that asset or liability for tax purposes. The tax base of an asset is the amount that will be deductible for tax purposes against any taxable economic benefits that will flow to an entity when it recovers the carrying amount of the asset. The tax base of a liability is its carrying amount, less any amount that will be deductible for tax purposes in future periods. Some items have a tax base even though they are not recognised as assets or liabilities (see 3.13.70).

IAS 12.5, 7, 8, 24   3.13.40.20 In our view, in determining the tax base of an asset or a liability, no assessment is carried out as to how probable it is that the respective amounts will ultimately be deducted or taxed (see 3.13.100). Instead, the probability assessment is part of the analysis required for the recognition of deferred tax assets (see 3.13.170.10).

3.13.40.30 For example, tax law provides for the acquisition cost of an asset of 150 to be deducted from taxable profit by way of depreciation over the asset's useful life. Company T expects that it will suffer ongoing losses over the entire foreseeable future. In our view, the tax base of the asset is 150 despite the fact that T may not be able in the future to obtain a tax benefit from the depreciation of the asset (i.e. from the tax base). However, the expectation of ongoing losses makes it unlikely that T will be able to obtain a benefit and therefore no deferred tax asset will be recognised in respect of any deductible temporary difference arising from the tax base of 150.

3.13.40.40 In another example, tax law provides that a tax deduction will be available on the sale of an asset subject to prior utilisation of tax losses carried forward. For example, Company M acquires an asset for 150 and revalues it to 200 subsequently. Upon disposal of the asset, M receives a tax deduction of 150 in all cases. In addition, if M has utilised its tax losses carried forward, then M receives a further tax deduction of 50 on disposal of the asset (the conditional deduction). We prefer that an entity consider that the tax base of the asset is 200. The uncertainty regarding whether the entity will benefit from the conditional deduction or utilise tax losses carried forward is factored into the entity's assessment of whether any deferred tax asset related to the tax losses is recoverable (see 3.13.170.10). An alternative view would be to treat the conditional deduction as a separate tax credit. Under this approach, two separate temporary differences would exist: a taxable temporary difference of 50 associated with the asset (200 - 150) and a deductible temporary difference of the same amount, associated with the tax credit.

3.13.50 *Management's intention*

IAS 12.51   3.13.50.10 In some jurisdictions different tax deductions are available for an asset depending on the way in which its carrying amount is recovered. In such cases the tax base of an asset is determined based on management's intent.

3.13.50.20 In some jurisdictions no deduction is allowed when an asset is depreciated, but is allowed when the asset is disposed of, abandoned or scrapped. When the asset is recovered through use and then scrapped at the end of its useful life, in our view the tax base should be determined assuming that the carrying amount is recovered through use and scrapping together. Therefore, we believe that the tax base would include the tax deduction that will be received when the asset is scrapped.

3.13.50.30 For example, an item of plant and equipment is purchased for 100. The asset will be depreciated for accounting purposes over its 10-year useful life to a residual value of zero. No tax deductions will be received while the asset is being used. However, when the asset is sold or scrapped, a tax deduction is received for the initial cost of the asset of 100. In our view, the tax base of the asset is 100.

3.13.50.40 In another example, an intangible asset arising from the right to mine a specific area for 40 years is acquired for 100. The asset is not depreciable for tax purposes, but is depreciated for accounting purposes. If the right is used until expiry, then at the expiry date a tax deduction will be received for the initial cost of 100. However, no deduction is available if the asset is disposed of or abandoned in the future. In our view, if management's intention is to use the intangible asset until it expires, then the tax base is 100. However, if management's intention is to sell the asset after 10 years, then the tax base of the intangible asset is zero.

3.13.50.50 Management's intent normally needs to be demonstrated clearly in order for it to be reflected in the determination of the tax base. However, in our view it is not always required that the reporting entity perform a formal act demonstrating this intention. Rather, depending on the facts and circumstances, we believe that it may be sufficient to assume that management will act in the most economically advantageous way.

3.13.50.60 For example, if the only way to obtain a tax deduction was upon disposal, then we believe that it should be assumed that management would sell the asset for an immaterial amount rather than merely scrap the asset and thus forfeit a tax benefit.

3.13.50.70 In another example, the estimation of a positive residual value to property, plant and equipment under IAS 16 *Property, Plant and Equipment* is, we believe, a demonstration of management's intention to sell the asset at the end of its useful life.

3.13.50.80 Management's intentions also may be relevant in determining the tax rates to be applied in calculating deferred tax assets and liabilities (see 3.13.230).

3.13.60 *Financial liabilities*

IAS 12.23   3.13.60.10 Due to the requirement in IAS 39 to recognise a financial instrument at fair value initially or the requirement in IAS 32 *Financial Instruments: Presentation* to split compound financial instruments into a financial liability and an equity component, the carrying amount of the financial liability component may not equal its par or nominal value. In most tax jurisdictions, this will result in a temporary difference, as in many jurisdictions the tax base will be the sum of the liability and equity components for a compound instrument. A taxable temporary difference will arise that needs to be assessed for deferred tax liability recognition (see 3.13.90 and 160).

3.13.60.20 As required by IAS 32, a financial liability for the present value of the redemption amount typically is recognised by an entity that has committed to acquire its own shares or the shares held by a non-controlling interest holder in a subsidiary. This also applies to contracts under which a non-controlling interest holder can put an entity's shares or shares of a subsidiary back to the entity (see 2.5.460). For example:

- Company Z enters into a transaction on 1 May 2010 to obtain control of Company S whereby Z acquires 60 percent of S's shares from Company M (M wholly owns S before this transaction).
- At the same date, Z writes a put ("written put") to M whereby on 1 May 2011 M is entitled to put all of its shares in S (40 percent) at a formulaic price based on earnings before interest, tax, depreciation and amortisation (EBITDA).

3.13.60.30 Assume that based on the best estimate of the redemption amount (variable based on EBITDA), the fair value of the liability on 1 May 2010 is 500; a financial liability for 500 will be recognised in the financial statements. In Z's tax jurisdiction, as in many others, no tax deduction in relation to the written put liability is available.

3.13.60.40 In our view, consistent with the definition of the tax base of a liability, the tax base of the written put liability is equal to its carrying amount of 500 less the deductible amount of zero; therefore no temporary difference exists and no deferred tax should be recognised.

3.13.70 *Absence of a recognised asset or liability*

IAS 12.9   3.13.70.10 *Temporary differences* are differences between the carrying amount of an asset or liability in the statement of financial position and its tax base. However, in our experience it is quite common for entities to be entitled to future tax deductions that relate to transactions that do not give rise to the recognition of any asset or liability in the statement of financial position (e.g. the transaction might give rise to the recognition of equity or a gain or loss in the statement of comprehensive income). In our view, generally the future tax allowance available should be compared to the related carrying amount of zero in the statement of financial position, therefore concluding that a temporary difference exists; however, see the treasury shares example in 3.13.70.50.

3.13.70.20 For example, Group X has undertaken a "structured" transaction whereby the group's investment in a Thai Subsidiary (B) was sold from one group company (M1) to another (M2). Both M1 and M2 are registered in Thailand and are wholly-owned subsidiaries. The sale was executed at fair value, which resulted in a profit for M1 (i.e. fair value exceeded the carrying amount in M1). One of the key tax outcomes of this transaction was the creation of a tax deductible "premium" (effectively the profit on the sale) in M2. For tax purposes, this amount is amortised systematically over 10 years.

3.13.70.30 On consolidation the impact of the intra-group transaction is eliminated. While this transaction eliminates and the premium does not exist in the consolidated financial statements, annual tax deductions will be available to the group arising from the tax deductibility of the premium amortisation. Additionally M1 will have a current tax liability for the tax on the capital profit from the sale. In Thailand the tax rate for capital profits is the same as that on taxable income.

3.13.70.40 In our view, even though the intra-group transaction (and consequently the capital profit and premium) is eliminated on consolidation, IAS 12 applies in this situation as it is applicable to accounting for income taxes overall. In our view, a deductible temporary difference exists despite there being no recognised asset or liability for accounting purposes; this is in accordance with paragraph 9 of IAS 12, which states that some items have a tax base even though they are not recognised as assets or liabilities, for example research costs that are expensed immediately for accounting purposes but are tax deductible over a future period of time. Therefore, subject to recoverability, a deferred tax asset for the deductible temporary difference related to the tax deductible premium should be recognised by Group X as it is not subject to the initial recognition exemption (see 3.13.110) because taxable profit is impacted by the transaction that gives rise to the temporary difference.

3.13.70.50 Another scenario that raises difficulty in determining whether a temporary difference exists when no asset or liability is recognised in the statement of financial position is treasury shares in tax jurisdictions where a tax deduction is available in relation to treasury shares (e.g. in case of disposal of the treasury shares).

IAS 32.33   3.13.70.60 For example, Company Y purchases treasury shares on the market for 1,000. Y intends to "hold" the shares (from a legal perspective), i.e. not to cancel them, for a number of reasons, e.g. selling on the market, exchanging the shares as consideration for the acquisition of a business etc. Regardless of the purpose, the acquisition of treasury shares is deducted from equity. In Y's tax jurisdiction, proceeds from the sale of treasury shares (if ever disposed of) are taxed and the original cost is deducted from this taxable income.

3.13.70.70 In the absence of any clear guidance in IFRSs, in our view there are two approaches to this issue. An entity should choose an accounting policy based on one of these approaches, to be applied consistently, to determine whether a temporary difference exists.

3.13.70.75 Under one approach, the tax base of the treasury shares is compared to the amount deducted from equity for determining whether a temporary difference exists. Therefore in Y's case, the tax base of 1,000 will be compared to the acquisition cost of 1,000 deducted from equity; therefore, there is no temporary difference at inception between the tax base and the carrying amount of the equity component recognised in the statement of financial position. See 3.13.400 for a discussion of the presentation of tax effects of transactions involving an entity's own shares and 3.13.360 for a discussion of other presentation items.

IAS 12.9, 24 3.13.70.80 Under another approach, it is argued that whereas there is a tax base of 1,000, there is no corresponding asset or liability recognised in the statement of financial position. Hence, a deductible temporary difference of 1,000 arises. However, because of the initial recognition exemption (see 3.13.110), no deferred tax asset is recognised in respect of this temporary difference.

3.13.70.90 However, if Y is holding the treasury shares to settle a share-based payment transaction and expects to receive a tax deduction based on the cost of the treasury shares, then the cost of the treasury shares will be factored into measurement of the tax base of the share-based payment transaction (see 3.13.630.15).

3.13.80 *Other differences*

3.13.80.10 In some cases a difference arises between IFRSs and the corresponding tax treatment that is not a temporary difference because an item that impacts the financial accounting will not be taxable or deductible in the future. While there is no definition of such items in IFRSs, often in practice they are referred to as "permanent" differences.

IAS 12.7 3.13.80.20 For example, one of Company D's investees has declared a dividend of 100 and D has recognised a receivable in its financial statements. In D's jurisdiction dividends are tax-exempt. In this case, no deferred tax liability is recognised, following either of these analyses:

- The tax base of the receivable is zero and therefore there is a temporary difference of 100; however, the tax rate that will apply is zero when the cash is received. Therefore, no deferred tax liability is recognised.
- The tax base of the receivable is 100 since, in substance, the full amount will be tax deductible (i.e. the economic benefits are not taxable). Therefore, no deferred tax liability is recognised as the tax base is equal to the carrying amount of the asset.

3.13.90 **Liability recognition**

IAS 12.15 3.13.90.10 A deferred tax liability is recognised for all taxable temporary differences, unless the deferred tax liability arises from:

- the initial recognition of goodwill; or
- the initial recognition of an asset or liability in a transaction that:
  - is not a business combination; and
  - at the time of the transaction, affects neither accounting profit nor taxable profit (see 3.13.110).

IAS 12.39 3.13.90.20 An additional exemption applies to taxable temporary differences related to investments in subsidiaries, associates and joint ventures, if certain criteria are met (see 3.13.510).

3.13.100 *Full liability recognition*

IAS 12.15   3.13.100.10 The standard requires all taxable temporary differences to be recognised as a deferred tax liability and does not allow the partial recognition method. Therefore, it is not relevant under IFRSs that some, or all, of the differences may not be expected to crystallise in the future.

IAS 12.20   3.13.100.20 For example, Company E owns machinery with a revalued carrying amount of 150 and a tax base of 80 (original cost was 100). When the machinery is sold, any capital gain is deductible against the cost of similar replacement assets. E expects its business to grow and the machinery will be replaced. Therefore E does not expect the difference of 50 between the carrying amount and the original cost to crystallise and generate a tax liability. Nevertheless, IFRSs require the deferred tax liability to be recognised.

3.13.110 Initial recognition exemption

IAS 12.15,   3.13.110.10 Deferred tax is not recognised for certain temporary differences that arise
22(c), 24,   upon the initial recognition of assets and liabilities. The exemption is not conceptual in
32A, 33   nature and is one of the more difficult aspects of the standard to apply. The exemption applies to:

- a deferred tax liability (but not a deferred tax asset) that arises from the initial recognition of goodwill (see 3.13.690); and
- a deferred tax asset or liability that arises from the initial recognition of an asset or liability in a transaction that is not a business combination, and at the time of the transaction affects neither accounting profit nor taxable profit (see 3.13.110.60 and 170.20).

3.13.110.20 – 55 [Not used]

IAS 12.15(b),   3.13.110.60 The initial recognition exemption applies also to an asset or liability in a
22   transaction that is not a business combination and, at the time of the transaction, affects neither accounting profit nor taxable profit. For example, Company F acquires a building for 100. The cost of the building never will be deductible for tax purposes, even upon its eventual disposal. Therefore the tax base is zero and a taxable temporary difference of 100 arises. In the absence of the exemption, the carrying amount of the building would be grossed up for the effect of the taxable temporary difference. However, no deferred tax liability is recognised since IFRSs regard grossing up as resulting in less transparent financial statements.

IAS 12.22   3.13.110.70 If the exemption applies and no deferred tax is recognised initially, then no deferred tax will be recognised subsequently as the carrying amount of the asset changes. Continuing the example in 3.13.110.60, at the end of year one the carrying amount of the building is 95 after recognising depreciation. No deferred tax is recognised for the difference of 5 created in year one.

3.13.110.80 In our view, the situation would be different if the asset was revalued subsequent to initial recognition. Continuing the example in 3.13.110.60, F revalues the building at the end of year three, when the original cost less accumulated depreciation is 85 and the new carrying amount after revaluation is 120. We believe that the revaluation is a subsequent event in the life of the recognised asset for the purpose of applying deferred tax accounting. Therefore a new temporary difference is created, the initial recognition exemption is irrelevant for the consequences of the revaluation, and a deferred tax liability should be recognised as a result of the revaluation. In our view, an entity should choose an accounting policy, to be applied consistently, to either measure that deferred tax liability:

- based on the excess of the revaluation over the original cost (120 - 100 = 20 in this example); or
- based on the impact of the revaluation, i.e. the difference between the revalued amount and the original cost less accumulated depreciation (120 - 85 = 35 in this example).

3.13.110.90 See also 3.13.30.30 for an example of the recognition of deferred tax in respect of asset revaluations in general.

3.13.110.100 In our view, if assets or liabilities with temporary differences that did not give rise to the recognition of any deferred taxes because of the initial recognition exemption subsequently are acquired in a business combination, then a deferred tax liability or asset is recognised.

3.13.110.110 At the end of year one in the example in 3.13.110.60 (i.e. before the revaluation), F is acquired by Company M in a business combination. The fair value of the building upon acquisition is 95, which is equal to the carrying amount in F's financial statements. The tax status of the building has not changed and its tax base is zero. The building is recognised by M in its consolidated statement of financial position for the first time at the time of the business combination. As the building is acquired in a business combination, we believe that there is no exemption and a deferred tax liability is recognised by M in its consolidated statement of financial position.

3.13.120 *Partial deductions*

3.13.120.10 In some cases the cost of an asset is partially deductible for tax purposes. For example, Company G acquires machinery for 200. For tax purposes, 80 percent of the cost can be deducted; the remaining 20 percent can never be deducted, even upon disposal.

3.13.120.20 In our view, the asset should be split into two parts for the purpose of calculating deferred tax:

- The initial recognition exemption applies to a cost of 40 (200 x 20%). Therefore no deferred tax will be recorded on initial recognition or as this portion of the asset is depreciated subsequently.

- The general requirements should apply to a cost of 160 (200 x 80%). This means that no deferred tax will be recognised initially because the carrying amount and tax base of the asset are both 160. However, if a temporary difference arises as the asset is depreciated, then deferred tax should be recognised.

3.13.120.30 If the original cost of an asset is partially deductible for tax purposes and that asset is revalued subsequent to initial recognition, then in our view the entity may calculate deferred tax by splitting the revalued amount in proportion to the deductible and non-deductible portions of the asset, and considering the two parts of the revaluation separately, consistent with the views expressed in 3.13.110.80 and 120.20.

3.13.120.40 Continuing the example in 3.13.120.10, suppose that G revalues for accounting purposes the machinery that it purchased for 200. The revaluation for accounting purposes has no effect on the tax base of the machinery, which remains at 160. For simplicity, assume that both tax and accounting depreciation are zero at the date of revaluation.

3.13.120.50 Firstly, suppose that G recognised an impairment loss that reduced the carrying amount of the machinery down to 180. In this case, subject to recoverability, a deferred tax asset is calculated on a deductible temporary difference of 16, as follows:

- The initial recognition exemption applies to the revalued amount of 36 (180 x 20%) since this part of the revaluation is a subsequent change in the initially unrecognised deferred tax liability.
- The revalued amount of 144 (180 x 80%) is compared to the tax base of 160 (200 x 80%), giving a deductible temporary difference of 16.

3.13.120.60 Secondly, suppose that G revalues the machinery upwards to 220. In this case, a deferred tax liability is calculated on a taxable temporary difference of 20, as follows:

- The revalued amount of 44 (220 x 20%) is compared to the original cost of 40 (200 x 20%), giving a taxable temporary difference of 4. This is a new temporary difference and the initial recognition exemption is not relevant (see 3.13.110.80).
- The revalued amount of 176 (220 x 80%) is compared to the tax base of 160 (200 x 80%), giving a taxable temporary difference of 16.

3.13.130 *Finance leases*

3.13.130.10 The treatment of finance leases in relation to the initial recognition exemption is particularly difficult, depending on the treatment allowed by the tax authorities. The following examples illustrate this issue.

3.13.140 *Lessee receives tax deduction for lease payments*

IAS 12.7-9 3.13.140.10 For example, Company H enters into a finance lease and records an asset and a corresponding liability in its statement of financial position. For tax purposes the lease payments, which are not spread evenly over the lease term, are deductible on a cash basis. Although there is an asset under IFRSs, there is no corresponding asset for tax purposes, and therefore a temporary difference arises on the initial recognition of the asset. Similarly, there is a liability recognised under IFRSs that has a tax base of zero, and therefore a temporary difference arises on the initial recognition of the liability. Also, the transaction does not affect either accounting or taxable profit upon initial recognition. Therefore, under one interpretation of the initial recognition exemption, deferred tax would not be recognised in respect of the asset and the liability, either initially or as the asset is depreciated and the liability is repaid. This would give rise to the following entries:

	Debit	*Credit*
Property, plant and equipment	100	
Lease liability		100
To recognise finance lease liability and related asset		
Depreciation (profit or loss)	10	
Property, plant and equipment		10
To recognise depreciation in respect of year one		
Interest expense (profit or loss)	8	
Lease liability	12	
Cash		20
To recognise lease repayment in respect of year one		

3.13.140.20 Under the "no recognition" interpretation, at the end of year one no deferred tax liability would be recognised under the initial recognition exemption even though H will generate future economic benefits of 90 (100 - 10) through use of the asset, but will be entitled to deductions of only 88 (100 - 12), thus creating a taxable temporary difference of 2. In our view, the non-recognition of this taxable temporary difference is not an appropriate application of the exemption. We believe that the asset and liability that arise for accounting purposes under a finance lease are integrally linked, and should be regarded as a net package (the finance lease) for the purpose of recognising deferred tax. This is consistent with how a lease transaction is viewed for tax purposes. In our view, the example should be analysed as follows:

- Upon initial recognition of the transaction, a taxable temporary difference of 100 arises on the asset, and a deductible temporary difference of 100 arises on the liability, giving a net temporary difference of zero. Therefore no deferred tax is recognised. The initial recognition exemption does not apply because there is no temporary difference.
- At the end of year one, a taxable temporary difference of 90 exists on the asset, and a deductible temporary difference of 88 exists on the liability, giving a net tax-

able temporary difference of 2 in respect of which a deferred tax liability should be recognised.

3.13.140.30 This would give rise to the following additional entry at the end of year one, based on a tax rate of 50 percent:

	Debit	Credit
Income tax expense	1	
Deferred tax liability		1
To recognise deferred tax at end of year one		

3.13.140.40 The deferred income tax expense is the difference between the total tax amount in the IFRS profit or loss and the amount resulting from application of the statutory tax rate to the accounting profit as illustrated by the following:

	Book value
Profit (assumed)	100
Depreciation	(10)
Interest expense	(8)
Profit before tax	82
Current tax expense	(40)[1]
Deferred tax expense	(1)
Total tax expense	(41)

Notes

(1) The current tax of 40 is derived from taxable profit of 80 (profit of 100 minus lease payments of 20) taxed at the rate of 50 percent.

3.13.145 *Lessor deducts tax depreciation on leased asset*

3.13.145.10 Company J leases an asset it owns and previously recognised in its statement of financial position to a third party under a finance lease. J therefore derecognises the asset and recognises a receivable at an amount equal to the net investment in the lease. For tax purposes, the lease receipts are taxed on a cash basis. In addition, J retains title to the leased asset during the lease term and, for tax purposes, deducts the cost of the asset on a straight-line basis over ten years.

3.13.145.20 Similar to the position of the lessee discussed in 3.13.140, in our view the finance lease asset and the tax deductions that arise on the leased asset are integrally linked and should be considered together for the purpose of recognising deferred tax. For example, assume that J measured the leased asset at 100 immediately prior to commencement of the lease, and recognises a receivable with a carrying amount of 100 on commencement of the lease. In that case, no temporary difference arises on commencement of the lease, as follows:

	Carrying amount	Tax base	Net
Finance lease receivable	100	-	100
Leased asset (PPE)	-	(100)	(100)
	100	(100)	-

3.13.145.30 In later years, a temporary difference will arise to the extent that the carrying amount of the finance lease receivable differs to the tax base of the leased asset. In effect, the tax base of the leased asset is attributed to the finance lease receivable.

3.13.150 *Decommissioning provisions*

3.13.150.10 Another area of difficulty in relation to the initial recognition exemption is the treatment of decommissioning provisions that are capitalised as part of the cost of property, plant and equipment (see 3.2.20). For example, Company K recognises a provision for site restoration, which is capitalised; for tax purposes the expenditure will be deducted only when incurred and therefore the tax base of the liability is zero (as is the related portion of the asset). This deductible temporary difference arises on initial recognition of the provision, but does not affect either accounting or taxable profit. Therefore, under one interpretation of the initial recognition exemption, deferred tax would not be recognised in respect of the provision, either initially or as the asset is depreciated. This would give rise to the following entries:

	Debit	Credit
Property, plant and equipment	100	
Provision		100
To recognise provision and related asset		
Depreciation (profit or loss)	10	
Property, plant and equipment		10
To recognise depreciation in respect of year one		

3.13.150.20 Under the "no recognition" interpretation, at the end of year one no deferred tax asset would be recognised under the initial recognition exemption even though K will generate future economic benefits of 90 (100 - 10) through the use of the asset, but will be entitled to deductions of 100, thus creating a deductible temporary difference of 10. In our view, the non-recognition of this deductible temporary difference is not an appropriate application of the exemption. Consistent with our analysis for finance leases (see 3.13.140.20), in our view the asset and liability that arise in accounting for a decommissioning provision are integrally linked, and should be regarded as a net package for the purpose of recognising deferred tax.

3.13.150.30 This would give rise to the following additional entry at the end of year one, based on a tax rate of 50 percent:

	Debit	Credit
Deferred tax asset	5	
Income tax expense		5
To recognise deferred tax at end of year one		

3.13.160 *Compound financial instruments*

IAS 12.23   3.13.160.10 A difference in debt or equity classification between the financial statements and the tax statement of financial position that creates a temporary difference does not trigger the initial recognition exemption.

IAS 12.23,   3.13.160.20 The standard refers to compound financial instruments in general, which have
62(d), IE.A.9,   both a financial liability and an equity component, but illustrates only the example of
IE.Ex4   a convertible bond. For example, Company L issues convertible debt for proceeds of 100; a liability of 80 is recognised and the remaining 20 is recognised as equity (see 3.11.190). For tax purposes the carrying amount of the liability is 100. The temporary difference arises from a difference in the classification of the instrument rather than from a difference in the initial recognition – the total carrying amount in both cases is 100. Therefore the initial recognition exemption does not apply and deferred tax in respect of the taxable temporary difference of 20 is recognised in equity.

3.13.160.30 Compound financial instruments include many types of financial instruments, the common characteristic being that there is a liability and an equity component. In our view, the specific requirements mentioned in 3.13.160.20, that apply to taxable temporary differences for which the initial recognition exemption is overridden, should not be restricted to taxable temporary differences arising from a convertible bond, as illustrated in the standard, but should extend to all temporary differences arising from the initial recognition of any compound financial instrument. This includes, for example, any deductible temporary difference arising from a mandatorily convertible bond in a jurisdiction where the tax deduction is based on the interest calculated on the par value of the bond.

3.13.160.40 For example, Company Z issues a mandatorily convertible bond paying non-discretionary interest. This compound financial instrument will be separated at inception between a financial liability (the interest strip) and an equity component (as a residual). Assume the following characteristics/values of the mandatorily convertible bond at inception:

Liability component	18
Equity component	82
Interest cash outflows over the life of the convertible bond, which will be tax deductible when paid	20

3.13.160.50 No amount will be repaid upon maturity as the bond is mandatorily convertible. The only cash flows exchanged is the interest of 20 paid to the bond holders, which accounts both for the repayment of the principal and for the interest on the liability recognised by Z. All these cash flows are deductible for tax purposes in Z's tax jurisdiction, where the tax rate is 30 percent.

IAS 12.8 3.13.160.60 We believe that the tax base of the liability component of the bond is zero, which is the difference between the carrying amount of the liability component less all repayments deductible for tax purposes (20 which actually exceeds the carrying amount of 18). Therefore a deductible temporary difference of 18 arises from the initial recognition of the mandatorily convertible bond, which, in accordance with the specific requirements on compound financial instruments that override the initial recognition exemption, should give rise to recognition of a deferred tax asset of 5.4 (18 x 30%), subject to recoverability.

3.13.160.70 In our view, the same principle would apply when an entity has received a low-interest loan from a shareholder. For example, Company M receives a loan of 100 from its parent that is repayable after six years; no interest is payable on the loan. In order to recognise the capital contribution arising from the loan not charging interest (see 3.6.730), M recognises a liability of 70 and a capital contribution of 30. For tax purposes the carrying amount of the loan is 100. Once again the temporary difference arises from a difference in initial classification rather than from a difference in recognition and therefore we believe that a taxable temporary difference of 30 arises.

3.13.170 Asset recognition

IAS 12.24 3.13.170.10 Unlike deferred tax liabilities, a deferred tax asset is recognised in respect of deductible temporary differences only to the extent that it is *probable* that taxable profit will be available against which the deductible temporary differences can be utilised. Additionally, similar to deferred tax liabilities, no deferred tax asset is recognised if it arises from the initial recognition of an asset or liability in a transaction that:

- is not a business combination; and
- at the time of the transaction, affects neither accounting profit nor taxable profit.

IAS 12.IE.B.7 3.13.170.20 The issues that arise in respect of the initial recognition exemption for deferred tax assets are similar to those in respect of deferred tax liabilities (see 3.13.90). For example, no deferred tax asset is recognised in respect of non-taxable government grants, whether deducted from the cost of the asset or presented as deferred income (see 4.3.120), since the temporary difference arises at the time of the transaction and affects neither accounting nor taxable profit.

IAS 12.44 3.13.170.30 Also, similar to taxable temporary differences, an additional exemption exists in respect of deductible temporary differences related to investments in subsidiaries, associates and joint ventures (see 3.13.510).

IAS 12.24 3.13.170.40 Although an entity is required to consider the probability of realising the benefit of deductible temporary differences, "probable" is not defined in IAS 12. In our experience, entities often use a working definition of "more likely than not", which is consistent with the definition of probable in respect of provisions (see 3.12.30). However, IAS 12 does not preclude a higher threshold from being used. In our view, a single definition of "probable" should be developed and applied throughout a group for the purpose of recognising deferred tax assets (e.g. more likely than not, or more than 60 percent likely). However, in our view a virtually certain threshold, as used in the test for contingent assets, should not be used. (see 3.14.40).

IAS 12.28, 29 3.13.170.50 In considering whether taxable profit will be available in the future, an entity considers:

- taxable temporary differences that will reverse (i.e. will become taxable) in the same period that deductible temporary differences reverse (i.e. will become deductible);
- the periods into which a tax loss arising from a deductible temporary difference can be carried back or forward;
- the probability of generating taxable profits in the periods that the deductible temporary differences reverse; and
- tax planning opportunities.

3.13.180 *Taxable temporary differences*

IAS 12.28 3.13.180.10 In considering the availability of taxable temporary differences in order to recognise a deferred tax asset, it is necessary to estimate the periods in which the reversals are expected to occur. For example, Company N has a possible deferred tax asset of 100 in respect of a liability for employee benefits. For tax purposes the expenditure is deducted as incurred, which is expected to be in two years' time. N also has a deferred tax liability of 300 in respect of property, plant and equipment, of which 150 is expected to reverse in two years' time and the remaining 150 in four years' time. Therefore N can recognise the deferred tax asset on the basis that the reversing deferred tax liability will generate sufficient taxable profit to enable the deferred tax asset to be utilised.

IAS 12.28, 29 3.13.180.20 Changing the facts in the example in 3.13.180.10, the employee benefit expenditure is expected to be incurred in 10 years' time and there are no existing taxable temporary differences that are expected to reverse in the same period. However, N expects to continue investing in property, plant and equipment and fully expects that future taxable temporary differences, sufficient to absorb the deductible temporary difference, will be available 10 years from now. In this case the standard is specific that taxable temporary differences expected to arise in the future cannot be taken into account because the deductions associated with such differences (deduction of tax depreciation) also require taxable profit in order to be utilised. Therefore, subject to an analysis of other sources of taxable profit, N is not able to recognise a deferred tax asset.

3.13.180.30 In some cases it is not clear when a deductible temporary difference reverses. For example, Company O is a retailer that recognises an allowance for doubtful debts. For tax purposes the allowance cannot be deducted; instead, actual bad debts are deducted in accordance with criteria established by the tax authorities. Since the allowance for doubtful debts remains constant or grows slightly year on year, O believes that the deductible temporary difference will never reverse as long as it remains in business. In our view, the allowance reverses each year and is replaced by a new allowance against new trade receivables. Therefore, in assessing whether a deferred tax asset should be recognised, O considers the recoverability in the following year.

3.13.190 *Future taxable profits*

3.13.190.10 In our view, the assessment of whether a deferred tax asset should be recognised on the basis of the availability of future taxable profits should take into account all factors concerning the entity's expected future profitability, both favourable and unfavourable. If an entity has a stable earnings history, there is no evidence to suggest that current earnings levels will not continue into the future, and there is no evidence to suggest that the tax benefits will not be realised for some other reason, then in our view a deferred tax asset should be recognised.

3.13.190.20 For example, Company P has a deductible temporary difference in respect of a liability for employee benefits, the majority of which is expected to reverse in 20 years' time. P prepares budgets and forecasts for a period of only two years into the future. However, P has a history of being profitable and based on an assessment of P's business prospects, there is no reason to believe that it will not be profitable in the future. We believe that a deferred tax asset should be recognised notwithstanding the limited period for which budgets and forecasts are available.

IAS 12.24, 3.13.190.30 In another example, Company Q is a wine maker and the land from which it
36(a), operates is vital to its operations. The land is revalued for tax purposes (but not under
SIC-21.5 IFRSs) and the revaluation surplus is deductible from the sales proceeds when the land is sold. Therefore, the tax revaluation creates a deductible temporary difference that will reverse when the land is sold (see 3.13.30.40). However, Q needs to maintain possession of the land on which the grapes are grown in order to continue its business of producing wine; therefore, it is not possible to forecast when or if the land will be disposed of. We believe that the difficulty of estimating the timing of the reversal of the temporary difference is not in itself a reason for not recognising a deferred tax asset, but it is a factor

that is relevant in assessing the probability of the availability of future tax benefits. If the fair value of the land is higher than its revalued tax base, then in our view it is probable that a taxable profit will be available to offset the deductible temporary difference. For example, if the carrying amount of the land is 60, but its estimated fair value is 100 and the revalued tax base is 70, taxable profit of 30 would be generated upon sale; in that case, a deferred tax asset should be recognised for the deductible temporary difference of 10 (70 - 60).

IAS 12.29(a)   3.13.190.40 When assessing the availability of future taxable profits, an entity does not include in that assessment new deductible temporary differences that originate in future periods.

3.13.190.50 For example, Company S, which has a calendar year end, has a deductible temporary difference of 400, which is expected to reverse over the next three years. S assesses its expected future profits in order to determine whether or not to recognise the deferred tax asset; S's tax rate is 40 percent.

	Year 1	Year 2	Year 3
Future taxable profits	250	150	150
Of which new deductible differences	(200)	(120)	(100)
Future taxable profits available for recovery of deferred tax assets	50	30	50

3.13.190.60 Although S expects to generate sufficient future taxable profits in the next three years, a large part of those profits are due to the origination of new deductible temporary differences. For the purpose of assessing recoverability of the deferred tax asset, S determines future taxable profits arising in the relevant period exclusive of the effects of originating temporary differences. These future profits of 130 (50 + 30 + 50) support the recognition of a deferred tax asset of 52 (130 x 40%). The recognition of the remaining 108 (160 - 52) would depend on the availability of other sources of taxable profits, such as tax planning opportunities (see 3.13.200).

3.13.200 Tax planning opportunities

IAS 12.30   3.13.200.10 *Tax planning opportunities* are described as actions that an entity would take in order to create or increase taxable income for a specific period in order to utilise an expiring tax loss or tax credit carried forward. An example includes deferring the claim for certain deductions from taxable profits to a later period. However, these opportunities do not include creating taxable profit in the future from future originating temporary differences (see 3.13.190.40).

3.13.200.20 In our view, it should be management's intention to take advantage of tax planning opportunities, or at least it should be more likely than not that they will take advantage of these opportunities, before they can be used to justify the recognition of deferred tax assets. In most cases it can be presumed that the entity will take advantage of any opportunity to reduce its overall tax burden. However, when taking advantage of the opportunities involves, for example, making an irrevocable election that may have other, disadvantageous, implications for the future, thought should be given as to whether management actually believes it probable that they will make the election (see also 3.13.50 and 710.10).

3.13.200.30 Including or excluding entities from a tax group, i.e. a group of entities that are treated as a single entity for tax purposes, may qualify as a tax planning opportunity. In some situations entities, for example a parent and its subsidiaries, automatically are included in the same tax group. If this is the case, then in our view income taxes are determined on a combined basis. If, however, participation within a tax group is discretionary, then we believe management's intention is taken into account as described in 3.13.200.20 when evaluating whether discretionary elections related to tax groups would qualify as a tax planning opportunity.

3.13.210 *Unused tax losses and tax credits*

3.13.210.10 The requirement to consider the sources of taxable profit in respect of deductible temporary differences applies equally in assessing whether a deferred tax asset arising from unused tax losses and unused tax credits may be recognised. See 3.13.590 for a discussion of tax credits in respect of specific investments.

IAS 12.34 3.13.210.20 A deferred tax asset is recognised for the unused tax losses and unused tax credits carried forward to the extent that it is probable that future taxable profits will be available.

3.13.210.30 In our view, in determining whether probable future taxable profits are available, the probability threshold is applied to portions of the total amount of unused tax losses or tax credits, rather than to the entire amount.

3.13.210.40 For example, Company R has cumulative tax losses of 1,000 carried forward at 31 December 2010. The applicable tax rate in R's tax jurisdiction is 30 percent. R expects recovery of a portion of that amount in 2011 because it has just signed a major contract that will be performed during 2011. However, it is uncertain whether that contract will be extended for subsequent years. At 31 December 2010, R assesses that it is highly probable that a taxable profit of 400 will be available in 2011, but it is not yet probable that any further taxable profit will be available from 2012 onwards. Therefore R believes that it is not more likely than not that the total 1,000 tax losses will ever be fully recovered.

3.13.210.50 In determining whether it should recognise a deferred tax asset, R should assess whether any portion of the tax losses carried forward is recoverable through probable future taxable profits. Therefore, as at 31 December 2010 R should recognise a deferred tax asset of 120 (400 x 30%).

IAS 12.34-36 3.13.210.60 The standard provides the following additional guidance:

- When an entity has a history of recent losses, a deferred tax asset is recognised only to the extent that the entity has sufficient taxable temporary differences or there is convincing evidence that sufficient taxable profit will be available against which the tax losses or tax credits can be utilised.
- An entity considers whether any unused tax losses arise from identifiable causes that are unlikely to recur; if so, this makes it easier to justify recognition of the resulting deferred tax asset.

3.13.210.70 For example, Company T was established one year ago and is in its "start-up" phase. In its first year of operations T has a loss of 500 for tax purposes. T expects to be profitable by its third year of operations, and expects all tax losses to be utilised by the end of its fifth year of operations.

3.13.210.80 In our view, T should not recognise a deferred tax asset in respect of the tax losses because we believe that it is not appropriate to forecast profits when a business is in a start-up phase, unless there is convincing evidence that future taxable profits will be available (e.g. signed contracts are in place and it is clear that the business can operate at a cost level that will result in taxable profits).

IAS 12.82 3.13.210.90 When the recoverability of a deferred tax asset depends on future taxable profits in excess of the profits arising from the reversal of existing taxable differences and if an entity has suffered a tax loss in the current or preceding period in a tax jurisdiction in respect of which a deferred tax asset has been recognised in the financial statements, both the amount of the deferred tax asset and the nature of the evidence supporting its recognition is disclosed.

3.13.220 Measurement

IAS 12.47, 51 3.13.220.10 Deferred tax assets and liabilities are measured based on:

- the expected manner of recovery (asset) or settlement (liability); and
- the tax rate expected to apply when the underlying asset (liability) is recovered (settled), based on rates that are enacted or substantively enacted at the reporting date.

3.13.220.20 In our view, the tax rate expected to apply is based on the statutory tax rate and not an entity's effective tax rate. For example, Company U is subject to a statutory tax rate of 30 percent. However, after tax deductions it usually pays tax of around 20 percent. We believe that deferred tax should be recognised using the tax rate of 30 percent and U should not anticipate future deductions.

3.13.230 *The expected manner of recovery or settlement*

IAS 12.52 3.13.230.10 In some tax jurisdictions the applicable tax rate depends on how the carrying amount of an asset or liability is recovered or settled. In such cases management's intentions are key in determining the amount of deferred tax to recognise. For example, Company V owns an operating plant that it intends to continue to use in its operations. If the plant was sold, then any gain would attract capital gains tax of 20 percent; the income tax rate is 30 percent. In this case deferred tax is measured using a rate of 30 percent because the carrying amount will be recovered through use. Even if the plant is revalued, deferred tax would be measured at a rate of 30 percent because as the plant is recovered through operations and taxable operating income is generated, it will be taxed at a rate of 30 percent.

3.13.240 *Dual intention*

3.13.240.10 In many cases an entity will have a dual intention with respect to assets (i.e. to operate the asset and then to sell it). In that case the carrying amount will be recovered in two ways and the calculation of deferred tax should reflect that dual intention. If different tax rates apply to usage and sale of the asset, then in our view deferred tax should be calculated using what is sometimes called a "blended rate" approach.

3.13.240.20 For example, assume that Company P acquires an asset as part of a business combination. P determines that the fair value of the asset on the acquisition date is 150. For accounting purposes, P depreciates the asset over five years to its expected residual value of 50. The asset is not depreciated for tax purposes, rather, a tax deduction is given on sale. P expects to sell the asset for its residual value, at which time it will receive a tax deduction of 100. The statutory tax rate for income is 30 percent and the statutory tax rate on capital gains is 10 percent.

3.13.240.30 We prefer in these circumstances to treat the asset as having a single tax base of 100. This results in a single temporary difference of 50 (carrying amount of 150 less tax base of 100). Considering the expected manner of recovery of the carrying amount of 150, a deferred tax liability of 25 is recognised in the acquisition accounting as follows:

	Carrying amount	Tax base	Temporary difference	Deferred tax
Use (tax rate = 30%)	100	0	100	30
Sale (tax rate = 10%)	50	100	(50)	(5)
Total	150	100	50	25

3.13.240.40 Alternatively, it could be argued that the use and sale consequences should be considered separately, having regard to the manner in which P expects to recover the carrying amount of the asset. Separate consideration of the two components of the calculation shown in 3.13.240.30 would result in recognition of a deferred tax asset of 5, subject to recoverability (see 3.13.170.10) and a deferred tax liability of 30.

	Carrying amount	Tax base	Temporary difference	Deferred tax
Use (tax rate = 30%)	100	0	100	30
Sale (tax rate = 10%)	50	100	(50)	(5)

P recognises a deferred tax asset of 5 (subject to recoverability) and a deferred tax liability of 30.

3.13.240.50 A third, less common, approach is to treat the asset as having a single tax base of 100, but first to apply the usage tax rate to the "top slice" of the temporary difference and then to apply the sale tax rate to any "bottom slice" of the temporary difference. The top slice is the lower of the portion of the carrying amount that will be recovered through usage and the temporary difference; the bottom slice is the temporary difference less the top slice. In this example the carrying amount that will be recovered through usage is 100 and the temporary difference is only 50 resulting in a top slice of 50. Applying the usage rate of 30 percent results in a deferred tax liability of 15 on initial recognition. Subsequently, as the carrying amount of the asset reduces, the temporary difference falls to zero and the deferred tax liability is released. When the carrying amount falls below the tax base, a deductible temporary difference arises for the first time and this is recognised at the sale rate of 10 percent.

3.13.240.60 In the case of the third approach, this can be seen more clearly if the figures in the example in 3.13.240.50 are varied. For example, if the deduction available on sale had been only 40 such that the taxable temporary difference was 110, then the usage rate would have been applied to the first 100 of the temporary difference and the sale rate would have been applied to the remaining 10 of the temporary difference.

3.13.240.70 The three approaches in 3.13.240.20 – 50 all result in the use of a blended rate.

3.13.250 Non-depreciable property, plant and equipment

3.13.250.10 In another example, Company X owns a piece of land that is not depreciated. For tax purposes, the cost of the land is 300 and it is depreciated over 15 years. At the end of the reporting period the carrying amount of the land under IFRSs is 300, and the carrying amount for tax purposes is 150. X revalues the land to 400 in accordance with the revaluation model for property, plant and equipment (see 3.2.300); the revaluation is not recognised for tax purposes. If the land is ever sold, then any recovery of the original cost will be taxed at the income tax rate of 30 percent; the proceeds in excess of the original cost will not be taxed.

SIC-21.5 3.13.250.20 When a non-depreciable item of property, plant and equipment is revalued, the deferred tax on the revaluation is measured using the tax rate that applies upon disposal. Therefore the deferred tax calculations are as follows:

- Prior to the revaluation X has recognised a deferred tax liability of 45 (150 x 30%).
- As a result of the revaluation X will not recognise any further deferred tax liability because there will never be any taxation consequences arising from the revaluation above original cost.

3.13.260 *Non-amortisable intangibles*

3.13.260.10 The question of which tax rate to use also arises in the context of non-amortisable intangible assets.

3.13.260.20 For example, if a company acquires, in a business combination, a licence that is renewable without limitation, and therefore has an indefinite useful life, then the carrying amount of the licence will be the fair value allocated to the licence in the purchase price allocation until an impairment is triggered, or the licence is sold. If the fair value of the licence determined in the purchase price allocation is higher than its tax base, then a temporary difference arises and a deferred tax liability is recognised.

3.13.260.30 The tax rate for use of the asset may differ from the tax rate applicable to the sale of the asset. In our view, although SIC-21 is not directly applicable because its scope is limited to non-depreciable assets, the consensus in SIC-21 may be applied by analogy to non-amortisable assets through the hierarchy for the selection of accounting policies (see 2.8.6). This would result in measuring the deferred tax liability at the sale rate.

3.13.270 *Investment property**

SIC-21.4   3.13.270.10 The requirements in respect of the revaluation of non-depreciable assets apply also to investment property that is accounted for at fair value and that would be considered non-depreciable *if* it fell within the scope of IAS 16 (see 3.2.10). The implications of this are as follows:

- If an investment property comprises a building only, then deferred tax should be recognised on changes in fair value that are recognised because a building would be depreciated if it were accounted for as property, plant and equipment. The amount of deferred tax recognised should be based on the manner in which the carrying amount of the building is expected to be recovered (see 3.13.230).
- If an investment property comprises land only, and assuming that the land would not be depreciated, then deferred tax should be recognised based on the consequences of the disposal of that land.
- If a single investment property comprises land and buildings, then the valuation should be split into its component parts in order to determine the amount of deferred tax. In some cases this may result in additional valuation work being required in order to determine that split.

3.13.270.20 For example, Company Y acquired an investment property that comprises a beach-front plot of land with a two-star hotel. The cost of the investment property was

600, which Y split 540 for the land and 60 for the building. For tax purposes the property, including land, is depreciated over 20 years. A year later Y employs an independent valuation specialist in order to establish the fair value of the property; the valuation specialist concludes that the fair value is 700. The income tax rate in Y's jurisdiction is 35 percent; there is no capital gains tax. In order to calculate deferred tax, Y asks the valuation specialist to provide information about the respective fair values of the land and building components. The valuation specialist reports that the land component is 650 and the hotel component is 50. Therefore upon revaluing the property Y recognises deferred tax as follows:

- The building has a carrying amount of 50 under IFRSs and a tax carrying amount of 57 (60 - 3 for depreciation in year one). Therefore, a deferred tax asset of 2 (7 x 35%) arises at the end of year one.
- The land has a carrying amount of 650 under IFRSs and a tax carrying amount of 513 (540 - 27 for depreciation in year one). Since there is no capital gains tax, at the end of year one the taxable temporary difference is limited to the difference between the original cost and the tax carrying amount (i.e. 27 (540 - 513)), and a deferred tax liability of 9 (27 x 35%) arises.
- Therefore, the net deferred tax liability is 7 (2 - 9).

3.13.275 *Special tax regimes for investment property companies*

3.13.275.10 In some jurisdictions entities may elect to take advantage of special tax regimes for investment property companies. Typically, the entity will pay a one-off amount to the tax authorities in order to enter the special tax regime, i.e. an "entry tax". The entry tax may be based on a percentage of the value of the entity's investment property portfolio, or may be equivalent to the current tax that would be payable if the entity were to dispose of its portfolio on the date that it enters the special tax regime. Once it has entered the special tax regime, an entity within such a regime may pay income taxes at a rate that is lower than the prevailing rate, or may be exempt from income taxes. See 3.13.430 for a discussion of changes in tax status.

3.13.275.20 There may be a delay between the date of the management decision to enter the special tax regime and the date that the entity actually enters the special tax regime. In our view, the entity should measure deferred taxes at the entry tax rate from the date of the management decision provided that there are no substantive conditions for entry to the regime that are outside the control of the entity. Conversely, if entry to the special tax regime is subject to conditions that are not within the control of management, e.g. shareholder approval, regulatory approvals etc., then in our view the entity should consider whether those conditions are substantive. Depending on the outcome of that assessment, it may be necessary to continue to calculate deferred tax at the prevailing tax rate until such time the substantive conditions are met.

3.13.275.30 For example, Company Z is an unlisted investment property company in a jurisdiction in which the normal corporate tax rate on income and asset disposals is 30 percent. However, a special tax regime for listed investment property companies exists under which investment property companies pay no income taxes. In order to enter the special tax regime, Z must pay a one-off entry tax calculated as the tax that would arise on disposal of its entire property portfolio, at the special entry tax rate of 20 percent. The management of Z decides in July 2010 that Z will enter the special tax regime with effect from 1 April 2011. Management considers that the only substantive condition for entry to the special tax regime that Z does not meet at the date of its decision is the listing condition. As at 31 December 2010, we believe that Z should measure deferred tax at the normal tax rate of 30 percent if it remains unlisted, or recognise the entry tax measured at 20 percent as a liability if it has completed its listing at that date.

3.13.280 *Corporate structure*

IAS 12.51, 52   3.13.280.10 The tax treatment of an asset may be different depending on whether the asset is treated as an individual asset or as part of a corporate structure. For example, in some jurisdictions it is more tax-efficient to dispose of the shares of the entity that holds the asset, rather than to dispose of the underlying asset itself. In our view, the tax base in consolidated financial statements should be determined based on the tax treatment of individual assets and liabilities on an item-by-item basis.

IAS 12.39, 44   3.13.280.20 In our view, this principle applies even upon classification of the corporate structure as a disposal group held for sale or distribution (see 5.4.20 and 35). We believe that any deferred taxes on the individual assets/liabilities should not be impacted by the corporate structure of the corresponding disposal group. However, classification as a disposal group should be considered when analysing whether a deferred tax on the corporate structure itself should be recognised.

IAS 12.15, 39, 44   3.13.280.30 For example, Subsidiary E has two individual assets, B and C, and no liabilities. E meets the criteria in IFRS 5 *Non-current Assets Held for Sale and Discontinued Operations* to be classified as a disposal group. The carrying amounts of the asset B and asset C in Parent P's consolidated financial statements after applying the measurement requirements in IFRS 5 are 300 and 400 respectively. The tax bases of the assets in accordance with the tax accounts of E are 200 for each asset. When P disposes of the shares in E, an amount of 800 will be deductible for tax purposes. We believe that P should not consider the tax base of 800 in its consolidated financial statements for the asset B and asset C, but rather the tax base of 200 for each asset. Consequently, despite the planned disposal of E, P continues to recognise a deferred tax liability based on the taxable temporary difference of 300. However, the difference between the consolidated net assets of E of 700 and the tax base of P's investment in E of 800 represents a temporary difference of 100 that leads to the recognition of a deferred tax asset (see 3.13.510), subject to recoverability (see 3.13.170).

3.13.280.40 In an extreme case, an asset (e.g. a building) might be held by a group as the sole asset within a corporate shell for tax planning reasons. This asset, when sold individually, would not be tax deductible and therefore has a tax base of zero. However, the original cost of the investment in the shares of the corporate shell is tax deductible when disposed of by the holding company. In our view, in determining deferred tax from the perspective of the group financial statements the carrying amount of the underlying asset needs to be compared to its tax base of zero and not to the tax base of the investment in the corporate structure.

3.13.290 *Financial assets*

3.13.290.10 In our view, the tax treatment of financial assets should be consistent with management's intention for the financial asset. Therefore, for financial assets classified as held for trading, we believe that the entity should assume that the carrying amount of the asset will be recovered through sale. For financial assets classified as available for sale, in our view management should determine whether its intention is to recover the carrying amount of the asset through sale or through the receipt of dividends and the repayment of capital (see 3.13.520.15). When there is a dual intention with respect to the recovery of the carrying amount of an available-for-sale financial asset, a more detailed analysis will be required following the same methodology as illustrated above (see 3.13.240).

3.13.290.20 When the financial asset is an investment in a subsidiary, associate or jointly controlled entity, special recognition criteria apply to determine whether any deferred tax should be recognised (see 3.13.510).

3.13.300 **Split tax rates**

IAS 12.49 3.13.300.10 When different statutory tax rates apply to different levels of taxable income, it is necessary to determine the average statutory rates that are expected to apply when the temporary difference reverses. For example, Company F pays tax at 20 percent on the first two million of taxable profit in any year, and 30 percent on taxable profit in excess of two million. In our view, it is necessary to prepare forecasts in order to estimate the tax rate that will apply when temporary differences reverse; in each period the forecast should be updated and the balance of deferred tax should be revised as a change in estimate (see 2.8.60), if necessary.

3.13.300.20 We believe that the example in 3.13.300.10 is different from using an effective tax rate to recognise deferred tax (see 3.13.220) because in this case the statutory rate varies depending on the level of taxable income, not depending on what tax deductions are available.

3.13.300.30 In another example, Country B taxes profits realised in the local market at 20 percent, whereas profits from exports are taxed at 10 percent; deductions in respect of capital assets used to support the business in both markets (e.g. property, plant and equipment) are taxed at a weighted average rate based on the proportion of profits earned in each market. In our view, similar to the previous example, it is necessary to prepare forecasts, which should be updated at each reporting date, in order to estimate the tax rate that will apply when temporary differences associated with both markets reverse.

IAS 12.49 3.13.300.40 Similar considerations apply when the statutory tax rate is subject to a minimum alternative rate. For example, Company R may be required to pay tax calculated as the higher of 20 percent of taxable profit and 2 percent of gross income, when the range of deductions allowable in determining taxable profit is larger than the range of deductions allowable in determining gross income. Generally, IAS 12 requires tax balances to be calculated using the rate expected to apply, which is the guiding principle in this circumstance. In our view, it may be appropriate to apply by analogy the IAS 12 guidance on split tax rates to such arrangements.

3.13.310 *Enacted or substantively enacted*

IAS 12.47, 48 3.13.310.10 In most cases the calculation of deferred tax will be based on tax rates that have been enacted. However, in some jurisdictions it may be clear that a change in tax rate is going to be enacted even though the legal process necessary in order to effect the change has not yet been completed.

3.13.310.20 For example, the president of Country Z indicated to the public in July 2010 that they would like to reduce the corporate tax rate from 40 to 30 percent. The issue was debated by the government in August and September, and on 30 November the government announced formally that the reduction in tax rate would take effect in January 2011. However, the change in tax rate was not written into law until a presidential decree confirming the change in law was signed in February 2011. In Country Z the signing of a presidential decree is a mere formality and the president cannot override decisions announced formally by the government. Therefore, in our view the tax rate of 30 percent is substantively enacted on 30 November 2010 and should be used in the calculation of deferred tax from that date.

IAS 10.22 3.13.310.30 If the example had been different and the president of Country Z had the power to override or veto decisions made by the government, then in our view the new tax rate of 30 percent should not be used until enacted in February 2011. However, if the new tax rate is enacted prior to authorisation of the financial statements, then the notes should include disclosure of this non-adjusting event (see 2.9.30).

3.13.310.40 In some countries, entities are able to negotiate a rate of tax with the government that is different from the general statutory rate. In our view, the negotiated rate should not be used in the determination of deferred tax until a formal agreement is in place confirming that rate. This is because the negotiated rate is not "enacted" or "substantively enacted" for that particular entity until agreement has been reached with the government.

3.13.320 *Tax holidays*

IAS 12.47 3.13.320.10 Some countries provide tax holidays (i.e. periods in which no tax is payable) for entities in a start-up phase or which meet certain investment criteria. In our view, it is not appropriate to base the recognition of deferred tax on the tax rate that applies when a temporary difference originates; instead, we believe that the entity should consider the rate of tax expected to apply when the underlying asset (liability) is recovered (settled).

3.13.320.20 For example, Company C has a two-year tax holiday; from the third year a tax rate of 33 percent applies. At the start of the tax holiday C purchased a machine for 100 that will be operated, and therefore depreciated, over its estimated useful life of five years; for tax purposes the machine is depreciated over four years. In this example the temporary difference originates partly during the tax holiday in years one and two, and reverses only in year five.

3.13.320.30 Therefore, we believe that deferred tax should be provided during the tax holiday, i.e. in years one and two, applying a 33 percent tax rate, as shown in the following table.

End of year	Asset balance		Temporary difference	Deferred tax balance	Deferred tax movement
	Book	Tax			
1	80	75	(5)	(2)	(2)
2	60	50	(10)	(3)	(1)
3	40	25	(15)	(5)	(2)
4	20	-	(20)	(7)	(2)
5	-	-	-	-	7

3.13.320.40 If a tax holiday is available for a limited period of time but commences only when cumulative taxable profit exceeds zero and an entity is currently in a tax loss position, then in our view deferred tax assets and liabilities should be measured at the statutory tax rate prior to the commencement of the tax holiday; that is until the date that all tax losses carried forward are utilised.

3.13.330 *Tax rate dependent upon profit distribution*

IAS 12.47, 52A, 52B 3.13.330.10 When income taxes are payable at a higher or lower rate if part or all of the net profit or retained earnings is distributed, deferred tax is based on the tax rate applicable to undistributed profits. When a liability for the payment of dividends is recognised in the financial statements, the tax consequences of the distribution also are recognised. In this case the specific requirement in relation to the tax consequences of dividend payments takes precedence over the principle that deferred taxes are measured at the amount expected to be paid (recovered). See 3.13.410 – 427 for a discussion of presentation of the tax effects of profit distribution.

3.13.340 *Tax exempt reserves*

3.13.340.10 In some countries, the tax authorities allow gains on the disposal of property, plant and equipment to be added to a tax-exempt reserve that is taxed only when the reserve is distributed in the form of dividends or upon liquidation.

3.13.340.20 For example, in Country E any capital gain on the disposal of certain machines is not taxable, provided that the capital gain is not distributed and is recorded in a "reserve not available for distribution". If the capital gain is distributed, then it is taxed at the income tax rate of 40 percent. An entity in Country E sells a machine with a carrying amount of 250 for 350, earning a gain on disposal of 100. For tax purposes, the 100 gain on disposal will be taxed in future periods only if distributed. The income tax consequences of the disposal gain should be calculated at the income tax rate for undistributed earnings, which is zero in this case; therefore no deferred tax liability is recognised (100 x 0%). Income tax payable of 40 (100 x 40%) is recognised only when a liability to distribute the reserve is recognised.

3.13.340.30 In some countries the tax authorities allow revaluations for tax purposes, whereby part of the tax revaluation is recorded in a tax-exempt reserve, which will be taxed only upon distribution of dividends out of this tax-exempt reserve. The issue is whether a deferred tax asset should be recorded in the period in which the tax revaluation takes place.

3.13.340.40 For example, in Country F entities may revalue property, plant and equipment for tax purposes, and subsequent depreciation based on the revalued amount is tax deductible at the income tax rate of 40 percent. The revaluation is taxed immediately at 25 percent and credited to a revaluation reserve in equity (for tax purposes). Upon distribution of the revaluation reserve further income tax is payable at a rate of 15 percent (the normal income tax rate of 40 percent less the 25 percent tax paid already). In accordance with C's accounting policy for property, plant and equipment, no revaluation is recognised under IFRSs (see 3.2.300).

3.13.340.50 Assuming that the carrying amount under IFRSs equalled the tax base prior to a revaluation of 100, the entries are:

	Debit	Credit
Income tax (profit or loss)	25	
Income tax payable		25
To recognise current tax (100 x 25%)		
Deferred tax asset	40	
Income tax (profit or loss)		40
To recognise deferred tax asset (100 x 40%)		

3.13.340.60 No deferred tax liability is recognised for the additional tax to be paid on distribution until the related dividend is recognised (see 3.13.330.10). The recognition of the deferred tax consequences of the tax revaluation, in this example in profit or loss, is discussed in 3.13.390.30.

3.13.350 *Discounting*

IAS 12.53 3.13.350.10 Deferred tax amounts are not discounted. Instead, the nominal amount is presented in the statement of financial position even if the effect of discounting would be material. Conversely current tax liabilities (assets) are in some cases discounted (see 3.13.15.40).

3.13.360 **Classification and presentation of current and deferred taxes***

3.13.370 *General*

IAS 1.54 3.13.370.02 Tax assets and tax liabilities are presented separately from other assets and liabilities in the statement of financial position. In addition, current tax assets and current tax liabilities should be distinguished from deferred tax assets and deferred tax liabilities in the statement of financial position whether or not an entity presents a classified statement of financial position. See 3.1.10 for a discussion of the presentation of a classified statement of financial position.

IAS 1.54, 56 3.13.370.04 Deferred tax liabilities and assets always should be classified as non-current when a classified statement of financial position is presented (see 3.1.10), even though it may be expected that some part of the deferred tax balance will reverse within 12 months of the reporting date. In addition, deferred tax liabilities and assets are presented separately from current tax liabilities and assets.

IAS 1.82(d), 12.77, 77A 3.13.370.06 The total tax expense (income) related to profit or loss from ordinary activities is presented in profit or loss as a separate line item in the statement of comprehensive income or in the separate income statement, if presented.

IAS 12.78 3.13.370.08 There is no guidance in the standard on where exchange differences arising from deferred or current foreign currency tax liabilities/assets should be presented in profit or loss. For deferred taxes, such differences may be classified as deferred tax expense (income) if that presentation is considered to be the most useful to financial statement users. In our view, this treatment should apply equally to current taxes.

IAS 12.57, 58, 61A 3.13.370.10 Accounting for the current and deferred tax effects of a transaction or other event is consistent with the accounting for the transaction or event itself. Therefore, generally current and deferred tax is recognised in profit or loss, except to the extent that it arises from:

- a business combination; or
- items recognised in the current or previous period, outside profit or loss, i.e. either in other comprehensive income or directly in equity.

IAS 12.58, 67 3.13.370.20 Deferred tax recognised as part of acquisition accounting for an entity acquired in a business combination is adjusted against goodwill upon initial recognition, unless the deferred tax asset is a previously unrecognised asset of the acquirer, in which case the acquirer recognises the deferred tax asset as a gain in profit or loss (see 3.13.670).

IAS 12.68A-C, 3.13.370.30 When an entity pays remuneration for goods or services in shares, share
IE.Ex5 options or other equity instruments that are considered to be share-based payments (see 4.5), any deferred tax on temporary differences arising from such transactions is recognised in profit or loss except when the underlying transaction is a business combination or is recognised outside profit or loss. A temporary difference may arise, for example, when the entity receives a tax deduction for share-based payments at the exercise date, whereas the expense is recognised in profit or loss over the vesting period. However, to the extent that the tax deduction (or estimated future tax deduction) for that share-based payment transaction exceeds the amount of the related cumulative remuneration expense, the excess of the associated deferred tax is recognised directly in equity (see 3.13.630).

IAS 12.63 3.13.370.40 When an enacted or substantively enacted tax rate changes, an entity should undertake a detailed review of the components of the net deferred tax position to determine whether any items comprising the balance previously were charged or credited to other comprehensive income (e.g. for available-for-sale securities or the revaluation of property, plant and equipment) or equity. The change in the net deferred tax position arising as a result of a change in tax rates related to these items, if any, would be recorded outside profit or loss (i.e. in other comprehensive income or directly in equity). Only in exceptional circumstances might an entity recognise outside profit or loss part of the change in the net deferred tax position using a reasonable *pro rata* allocation (see 3.13.400).

IAS 1.90, 91, 3.13.370.50 As discussed in more detail in 4.1.210, an entity may present each component
IG6 of other comprehensive income either net of the related tax effects, or gross of tax with the tax effects shown separately. There is no explicit guidance under IFRSs as to the reserve in equity in which deferred tax should be recognised. In practice deferred tax generally is recognised in the same reserve as the underlying item to which it relates. For example, deferred tax related to a revaluation of property, plant and equipment usually is recognised in the revaluation reserve.

3.13.380 *Change in accounting policy*

IAS 12.61A, 3.13.380.10 Generally, changes in the carrying amount of deferred tax balances that relate
62A to changes in the underlying temporary differences are recognised in profit or loss. Other changes, for example those resulting from changes in tax rates, are recognised in profit or loss unless they relate to items previously recognised outside profit or loss.

3.13.380.20 When an entity applies a new accounting policy retrospectively (see 2.8.10) the impact on assets and liabilities, including related changes to deferred tax assets and liabilities, is credited or charged directly to equity. However, it is unclear where subsequent adjustments to the deferred tax recognised as part of a change in accounting policy should be recognised.

3.13.380.30 We prefer for any subsequent changes in deferred taxes recognised originally directly in equity as a result of a change in accounting policy to be recognised as if the new accounting policy always had been applied. Depending on the policy in question, and therefore on how the underlying transaction is accounted for, the change in deferred tax will be recognised either in profit or loss, in other comprehensive income or directly in equity.

3.13.380.40 Alternatively the entity should choose an accounting policy, to be applied consistently, to recognise any subsequent changes in deferred taxes, recognised originally directly in equity as a result of a change in accounting policy, directly through equity.

IAS 23.27-29A 3.13.380.50 For example, on 1 January 2009 Company B adopted the revision of IAS 23 *Borrowing Costs* and changed its accounting policy from expensing all borrowing costs as incurred to capitalising qualifying borrowing costs. B elected to apply the new policy to borrowing costs related to all qualifying assets for which the commencement date for capitalisation is on or after 1 January 2007 (see 4.6.350). In 2007, B recognised 200 in interest expense on qualifying assets; it had no qualifying interest expense in earlier years. Construction was suspended during 2008 so no qualifying interest expense was incurred in 2008. Activities were resumed in 2009 and qualifying interest costs of 150 were incurred during 2009 and capitalised as part of the cost of the property, plant and equipment. The item was put into use in early 2010. For tax purposes, interest is deductible on a cash basis. The applicable tax rate is 40 percent.

3.13.380.60 B presents one year of comparative information in its financial statements; therefore, for 2009, it presents 2008 comparative information. In its 2009 financial statements, B restates the opening statement of financial position at 1 January 2008 by increasing property, plant and equipment by 200, increasing opening retained earnings by 120 and recognising deferred tax liabilities of 80 (temporary difference of 200 x 40%). For 2009 B capitalises 150 as part of the cost of the property, plant and equipment under construction and recognises an additional deferred tax liability of 60 (150 x 40%).

3.13.380.70 At the beginning of 2010 the applicable tax rate is decreased unexpectedly to 30 percent. Therefore Company B recalculates its deferred tax liability as follows:

In respect of:	
200 capitalised as an adjustment of opening retained earnings in 2008	20
150 capitalised in 2009	15
Total change in deferred tax liability	35

3.13.380.80 The change in deferred tax liability of 15 that relates to 2009 is recognised in profit or loss in 2010, since it relates to items recognised in profit or loss (interest and depreciable property, plant and equipment).

3.13.380.90 The change in deferred tax liability of 20 relates to the cumulative effect on opening retained earnings of a change in accounting policy that was recognised directly in equity (retained earnings). We prefer that the decrease of 20 be recognised in profit or loss as deferred tax income, on the basis that it is a current period remeasurement of a tax liability related to items that would have been recognised in profit or loss had the policy of capitalising qualifying borrowing costs always been applied. Alternatively, the entity could recognise the decrease of 20 in retained earnings. In our view, an entity should choose an accounting policy, to be applied consistently, in these circumstances.

IAS 12.57, 58, 61A   3.13.380.100 Whereas we believe that the situation is not clear for subsequent changes in deferred tax balances resulting from changes in accounting policies or other retrospective adjustments to retained earnings, in other circumstances involving items recognised outside profit or loss (e.g. the revaluation of property, plant and equipment), the standard is quite explicit that any subsequent changes is recorded outside profit or loss (see 3.13.370.10).

3.13.385 *Reassessment of recoverability of deferred tax assets*

IAS 12.37   3.13.385.05 At the end of every reporting period, an entity assesses whether it has any previously unrecognised deferred tax assets that now fulfil the recognition criteria of probable future taxable profits (see 3.13.170). The entity recognises any previously unrecognised deferred tax assets to the extent that it has become probable that future taxable profit will allow the deferred tax assets to be recovered.

3.13.385.10 In our view, if a deferred tax asset previously considered not recoverable is recognised, then the presentation of the deferred tax income should follow the presentation of the item that gave rise to the potential deferred tax asset originally.

3.13.385.20 For example, management reassesses the recoverability of a deferred tax asset associated with tax losses carried forward and previously not recognised. Management concludes that the deferred tax asset is recoverable following the revaluation of an available-for-sale financial asset. The revaluation of the available-for-sale financial asset is recognised in other comprehensive income in accordance with IAS 39. In our view, the deferred tax income associated with the tax losses carried forward should be recognised in profit or loss, notwithstanding that the revaluation of the available-for-sale financial asset and its related deferred tax are recognised in other comprehensive income, because the item that gave rise to the deferred tax asset was the tax loss of a prior period.

3.13.385.30 See 3.13.455 for a discussion of the allocation of income taxes between continuing and discontinued operations.

3.13.390 *Revaluations*

IAS 12.62, 64   3.13.390.10 Whether or not the deferred tax related to a revaluation is recognised in or outside profit or loss depends on the treatment of the revaluation under IFRSs. For example, Company H revalues property, plant and equipment and recognises the revaluation in other comprehensive income in accordance with the revaluation model (see 3.2.300); in this case the related deferred tax also is recognised in other comprehensive income (see 3.13.30.30).

3.13.390.20 In the example in 3.13.390.10, subsequent changes in the temporary difference that arise as the asset is depreciated are recognised in profit or loss and the balance in the revaluation reserve is not adjusted. However, in the case of property, plant and equipment, an entity is permitted but not required to make transfers from the revaluation reserve to retained earnings as the revaluation is realised (e.g. through depreciation); in such cases any transfer would be made net of the related deferred tax (see 3.2.410).

3.13.390.25 Additional considerations apply when IFRSs require valuation gains recognised initially in other comprehensive income to be reclassified to profit or loss. For example, Company J acquires an available-for-sale financial asset for 100 in 2010, which it revalues to 120 at 31 December 2010. J sells the asset for 120 on 1 January 2011, reclassifying the gain of 20 to profit or loss. J pays tax on the gain of 20 at the applicable tax rate of 25 percent. As at 31 December 2010 J will recognise a deferred tax liability of 5 in other comprehensive income. In our view, J should, in effect, reclassify this tax amount on disposal of the asset in 2011, by crediting the deferred tax liability of 5 to other comprehensive income and charging current tax of 5 to profit or loss. In our view, J should not net off the reclassified gain of 20 against the tax charge of 5 in profit or loss, but should present a pre-tax gain of 20 and a current tax expense of 5.

IAS 12.65   3.13.390.30 The situation is different when the revaluation is carried out for tax rather than for accounting purposes, e.g. when the tax authorities permit or require adjusting the tax base of property, plant and equipment. In such cases the change in deferred tax is recognised in profit or loss (see 3.13.340.40) unless the tax revaluation is linked to an accounting revaluation, either in the past or in a future period, that was (or will be) recognised in other comprehensive income.

3.13.390.40 In our view, it may be appropriate to apply the IAS 12 guidance on tax revaluations by analogy to other situations in which the tax base of an asset changes but its carrying amount remains the same. For example, in some jurisdictions the tax base of an asset may be changed if the asset is transferred from a wholly-owned group entity to another group entity that is not wholly owned, to the extent of the non-controlling interest in the receiving entity. Suppose that Company M transfers an item of property that has a carrying amount and tax base of 1,000 to its 75 percent subsidiary, Company N. The carrying amount of the property in M's consolidated financial statements will be unchanged at 1,000. However, in accordance with applicable local tax legislation, the tax base of the asset is reduced to 750, i.e. by the extent of the non-controlling interest in N. In our view, M should recognise a deferred tax liability and deferred tax expense in consolidated profit or loss at the time of the transfer to reflect the decrease in the tax base of the property.

902

3.13.395 *Defined benefit post-employment plans*

3.13.395.10 IFRSs do not specify how income taxes in relation to defined benefit post-employment plans should be allocated between other comprehensive income and profit or loss, e.g. if an entity receives a tax deduction for contributions that it makes to the plan rather than for the related net pension expense that it recognises in profit or loss. In our view, if an entity opts to recognise actuarial gains and losses in other comprehensive income, then one acceptable approach is to allocate income taxes first to profit or loss, to the extent of the related pension expense recognised in profit or loss multiplied by the relevant statutory tax rate, and to recognise the residual balance in other comprehensive income. This approach follows the IFRS 2 *Share-based Payment* guidance on the allocation of deferred taxes arising on equity-settled share-based payment expense by analogy (see 3.13.630).

3.13.400 *Transactions involving an entity's own shares*

3.13.400.10 Since transactions involving an entity's own shares (e.g. the issue, purchase and reissue of treasury shares) are recognised in equity, the resulting deferred tax (if any) also is recognised in equity. For example, Company J issues shares and incurs transaction costs of 100 (recognised in equity), which are deductible for tax purposes (the tax rate is 30 percent). However, J has tax losses and the deduction cannot be utilised in the current year. J has determined that it is probable that the tax losses will be utilised before they expire (see 3.13.210), and accordingly the deferred tax asset is recognised in full. Therefore, the credit for the amount of the deferred tax asset related to the transaction costs of 30 should be recognised directly in equity.

IAS 12.63 3.13.400.20 Changing the facts of the example in 3.13.400.10, J has total tax losses of 150, which includes the 100 in respect of the transaction costs. After considering the probability of utilising the tax losses before they expire, J concludes that an asset for only 50 percent of the losses should be recognised. In this case it is very difficult to attribute the part of the tax loss recognised to specific items, and an entity is allowed to make a reasonable allocation between profit or loss and equity. In our view, for this example, it would be reasonable to conclude that 50 percent of tax attributable to the transaction costs are recoverable and therefore that 15 (100 x 50% x 30%) should be recognised in equity.

IAS 12.61A 3.13.400.30 The requirement to recognise outside profit or loss the tax effect of items recognised outside profit or loss extends beyond the initial recognition of a deferred tax liability (or asset) to any subsequent revisions to the tax balance. If, in the following year, J revises its estimate and concludes that the full deferred tax asset should be recognised, then the additional 15 of deferred tax related to the transaction costs also would be recognised in equity.

3.13.400.40 Continuing the example in 3.13.400.10, when the transaction costs are actually deducted for tax purposes, a current tax asset will arise, which will be offset by the reversal of the deferred tax asset. In our view, both the current tax and the related deferred tax reversal should be recognised in equity, resulting in a net effect of zero on equity.

IAS 12.5, 9, 61A 3.13.400.50 In another example, Company K acquires its own shares for 100 for the purpose of using them as consideration in acquiring a subsidiary at a later date; at the reporting date the fair value of the shares has increased to 120. When K disposes of the shares by using them as consideration in acquiring a subsidiary at a later date, taxable income of 120 arises and the original cost of 100 is offset against this taxable income. K will be taxed on the difference of 20. In our view, any tax effect on this difference should be recognised in equity since the underlying item (i.e. the share transaction) was recognised in equity.

3.13.410 *Income taxes triggered by the payment of dividends*

IAS 12.52B 3.13.410.10 Income taxes that are linked to the payment of dividends generally are linked more directly with past transactions and events than with the actual distribution to shareholders. Therefore the classification between profit or loss, other comprehensive income and equity follows the same general principles as outlined above.

3.13.420 *Dividend withholding tax*

IAS 12.65A 3.13.420.10 In some countries a dividend withholding tax is payable on distributions to shareholders. Such taxes are not attributable to the entity paying the dividend; rather, they are collected by the entity and paid to the tax authorities on behalf of the shareholder. Therefore, such taxes are recognised directly in equity as part of the distribution to shareholders. For example, Company M declares a dividend of 200, 20 percent of which is payable to the tax authorities.

3.13.420.20 M will record the following entry:

	Debit	Credit
Distribution (equity)	200	
Liability (to shareholders)		160
Liability (to the tax authorities)		40
To recognise distribution of dividend and resulting		
withholding tax		

3.13.420.25 See 3.13.510 for a discussion of accounting for potential income tax effects of such distributions in financial statements of M's parent.

IAS 12.2 3.13.420.30 In our view, withholding taxes attributable to investment income (e.g. dividends received) should be recognised as part of income tax expense, with the investment income recognised on a gross basis. This is on the basis that neither IAS 18 *Revenue* nor IAS 12 provides any mechanism for income tax paid to be offset against the underlying income.

3.13.423 *Dividend credits*

3.13.423.10 In some tax jurisdictions an entity may "attach" credits to a dividend payment that are used by the shareholder to offset tax payable on the dividend. The purpose of such credits is to provide relief from double taxation since the profits from which the dividend is paid have been taxed already at the entity level.

3.13.423.20 For example, in Country T shareholders are taxed on the gross amount of the dividend plus any credit attached, but then receive a deduction against tax payable for the amount of the credit; the statutory tax rate is 30 percent. Company B receives a dividend of 100 from Company C, with an "attached" dividend credit of 43 (calculated as 30 / (100 - 30)%).

3.13.423.30 B's tax is calculated as follows:

Dividend received	100
Dividend credit received	43
Taxable income	143
Income tax at 30 percent	43
Less deduction	(43)
Tax payable	-

3.13.423.40 The issue for accounting purposes is how B should present the dividend received in profit or loss, net or gross of the dividend credit:

	Net	*Gross*
Profit before tax	100	143
Income tax	-	(43)
Net profit	100	100

3.13.423.50 In our view, the net presentation is more appropriate because the dividend credit is simply a mechanism to ensure that certain dividends (or parts thereof) are tax-exempt. We believe that the net presentation reflects that substance.

3.13.427 *Foreign investment*

3.13.427.10 Many jurisdictions provide tax relief for entities with an element of foreign ownership. This relief may be structured in a variety of ways. In general, as in the case of dividend credits (see 3.13.423), when the result of a tax scheme is to reduce the effective tax rate attributable to certain income, in our view any benefit should be recognised as part of income taxes.

3.13.427.20 For example, in Country F the statutory tax rate is 35 percent. However, when a dividend is received by an overseas shareholder, that shareholder receives a cash rebate directly from F's tax authorities of 20 percent of the underlying taxes paid. This has the effect of reducing the effective tax rate on that dividend income to 28 percent (35% x 80%). Overseas shareholder G (who resides in Country F for tax purposes) receives a dividend of 100 from Company H, and thereby becomes entitled to receive a cash rebate of 7 (100 x 35% x 20%). We believe that G's statement of comprehensive income should be presented as follows:

Profit before tax	100
Income tax	(28)
Net profit	72

3.13.427.30 If G was the parent of H, then on consolidation we believe that the effect of the rebate should continue to be disclosed as part of income taxes since the overall effect is still to reduce the group's effective tax rate.

3.13.430 *Change in tax status*

SIC-25.4   3.13.430.10 The recognition of changes in current and deferred tax caused by a change in the tax status of an entity or its shareholders follows the general principles outlined above. The change in current and deferred tax is recognised in profit or loss except to the extent that it relates to an item (e.g. a revaluation of property, plant and equipment) recognised outside profit or loss in the current or in a previous period. See 3.13.275 for a discussion of timing of recognition when entering a special tax regime.

3.13.440 *Privatisation*

IAS 12.65,   3.13.440.10 A privatisation sometimes involves the creation of a new entity and may be
SIC-25.4   accounted for as a common control transaction using book values (see 5.13). When, for tax purposes, new values are assigned to the assets and liabilities subject to the privatisation, temporary differences may arise. In our view, such temporary differences are considered to arise from a change in tax base. As this change does not relate to a revaluation for accounting purposes, and in addition the transaction is similar to a change in tax status, the deferred tax resulting from the temporary differences is recognised in profit or loss, except to the extent that it relates to an item recognised outside profit or loss in the current or in a previous period.

IAS 12.65   3.13.440.20 For example, Government N privatises its electricity network by forming Company O into which all assets and liabilities related to its electricity network are transferred. Subsequent to the transfer the shares in O are sold to new owners in the private sector. Under IFRSs the assets and liabilities are transferred at book value; however, new tax bases are set by the tax authorities at the date of the transaction, which gives rise to additional temporary differences. We believe that the additional deferred tax should be recognised in profit or loss of O, assuming that none of the tax basis changes relate to items that are expected to be revalued for accounting purposes in future periods.

3.13.450 [Not used]

3.13.455 *Discontinued operations*

IFRS 5.33   3.13.455.10 There is no explicit guidance in IAS 12 on the allocation of income tax income and expense between continuing and discontinued operations when an entity presents discontinued operations in accordance with IFRS 5 (see 5.4). Complexities can arise in practice.

3.13.455.20 For example, Company G has two principal lines of business, A and B. For several years A has been profitable and B has been loss-making. Tax losses in B have exceeded the taxable income in A and overall, G has accumulated tax losses carried forward. However, G previously has not recognised a deferred tax asset, as management considered that there would be insufficient taxable profit to utilise the losses. G then abandons B's line of business and presents B as a discontinued operation. Management concludes that the tax losses carried forward generated in the past by B will be utilised against future profits in A; therefore G recognises a deferred tax asset. A question arises as to whether the deferred tax income arising on recognition of this deferred tax asset should be presented as part of discontinued operations, as the tax losses arose originally in B, or as part of continuing operations, as the tax losses will be utilised against future profits in A. In our view, either presentation is acceptable.

3.13.460 *Offsetting*

IAS 12.71   3.13.460.03 Current tax assets and current tax liabilities are offset only when:

- the entity has a legally enforceable right to set off current tax assets against current tax liabilities; this normally will be the case only when the tax payable or receivable relates to income taxes levied by the same taxation authority and the taxation authority permits the entity to make or receive a single net payment; and
- the entity intends either to settle on a net basis, or to realise the asset and settle the liability simultaneously.

IAS 12.73   3.13.460.05 Thus, within a group, current tax assets and current tax liabilities of different group entities are offset only if the entities concerned have a legally enforceable right to make or receive a single net payment, and the entities intend to make or receive such a net payment or to recover the asset and settle the liability simultaneously.

IAS 12.74   3.13.460.10 Deferred tax liabilities and assets are offset if the entity has a legally enforceable right to offset current tax liabilities and assets, and the deferred tax liabilities and assets relate to income taxes levied by the same tax authority on either:

- the same taxable entity; or
- different taxable entities, but these entities intend to settle current tax liabilities and assets on a net basis, or their tax assets and liabilities will be realised simultaneously for each future period in which these differences reverse.

IAS 12.75   3.13.460.20 The standard further explains that the offset requirements allow an entity to avoid having to schedule the timing of reversal of temporary differences. In our view, this relates only to the presentation of deferred tax liabilities and assets, and not to the underlying recognition criteria (see 3.13.90 and 170).

3.13.460.30 For example, Company P has a deferred tax asset of 100 in respect of a provision for environmental remediation. For tax purposes the expenditure is deductible as incurred, which is expected to be in two years' time. P also has a deferred tax liability of 300 in respect of property, plant and equipment, of which 150 is expected to reverse in two years' time and the remaining 150 in four years' time. Following the recognition criteria, P can recognise the deferred tax asset on the basis that the reversing deferred tax liability will generate sufficient taxable profit to enable the deferred tax asset to be utilised. Following the offset criteria, in the statement of financial position P will present a net deferred tax liability of 200.

3.13.470 Specific application issues

3.13.470.10 The commentary that follows considers some specific application issues in accounting for deferred tax that cause difficulties in practice.

3.13.480 – 490 [Not used]

3.13.500 *Intra-group transactions*

IAS 12.IE.   3.13.500.10 Intra-group transactions are eliminated upon consolidation (see 2.5.370). It
A.14, B.11   may be intuitive to reverse not only the transaction itself, but also the tax effects thereof in order to eliminate the transaction fully in the consolidated financial statements. However, the tax effects are not eliminated unless the transacting entities are subject to the same tax rate. This is because the transaction creates a real asset or liability from the point of view of the group.

3.13.500.20 For example, Company V sells inventory to fellow subsidiary Company W for 300, giving rise to a profit of 50 in V's separate financial statements. V pays current tax of 15 on the profit. Upon consolidation the profit of 50 is reversed against the carrying amount of the inventory of 300. Therefore, the carrying amount of the inventory on consolidation is 250. However, the carrying amount of the inventory for tax purposes will depend on the legislation in W's jurisdiction. Assuming that the carrying amount of the inventory for tax purposes is 300, a deductible temporary difference of 50 arises, which should be recognised on consolidation at W's tax rate, subject to the general asset recognition requirements (see 3.13.170).

3.13.500.25 In another example, Parent P bills royalties for 300 to its Foreign Subsidiary S. S expenses the cost and receives tax relief immediately while P recognises the income over a period of three years for tax purposes, i.e. 100 per year. On consolidation, expenses, income and deferred income are eliminated. However a taxable temporary difference of 200 arises at the end of the first year of the arrangement, which should be recognised on consolidation at P's tax rate, being the rate that will apply when the temporary difference reverses.

3.13.500.30 In some jurisdictions, an intra-group transfer of an asset to an entity that is not wholly owned by the group may result in a change in tax base (see 3.13.390.30 and 40).

3.13.510 *Investments in subsidiaries, branches, associates and joint ventures*

IAS 12.38 3.13.510.05 The difference between the tax base of a parent or investor's investment in a subsidiary, branch, associate or joint venture and the carrying amount of the related net assets or investment in the parent or investor's consolidated financial statements is a temporary difference, even though that investment may be eliminated in the consolidated financial statements. Such temporary differences can arise, for example, as a result of the existence of undistributed profits of a subsidiary, branch, associate or joint venture that affect the carrying amount of the investment but not its tax base.

IAS 12.39 3.13.510.10 *Taxable* temporary differences in respect of investments in subsidiaries, branches, associates and joint ventures are not recognised if:

- the investor is able to control the timing of the reversal of the temporary difference; and
- it is probable that the temporary difference will not reverse in the *foreseeable future*.

IAS 12.44 3.13.510.20 *Deductible* temporary differences in respect of investments in subsidiaries, branches, associates and joint ventures are recognised only to the extent that it is probable that:

- the temporary difference will reverse in the foreseeable future; and
- taxable profit will be available against which the temporary difference can be utilised.

3.13.520 *The timing and nature of reversal*

IAS 12.51 3.13.520.10 The temporary differences associated with investments in subsidiaries, branches, associates and joint ventures will fluctuate from period to period, for example due to movements in exchange rates and the profitability of the investee. In our view, the reversal of a temporary difference means its crystallisation rather than its fluctuation. For example, we believe that changes in exchange rates do not cause the reversal of a temporary difference but change the amount of the temporary difference. Conversely, the disposal of an investee or the payment of dividends by the investee reverses the temporary difference, either in full or partially.

3.13.520.15 The reversal of temporary differences associated with investments in subsidiaries, branches, associates and joint ventures can occur through sale, dividend, by other means such as liquidation, or a combination of those means of reversal. In our view, an entity should measure deferred taxes based on the most likely manner of reversal taking into account management's intent and all relevant facts and circumstances.

3.13.520.16 For example, Company C purchases a 30 percent equity interest in Associate K for 500. The tax base of the investment is different from its carrying amount due to undistributed profits and dilution gains, resulting in a temporary difference (see 3.5.730). Management believes that the portion of the temporary difference that relates to undistributed profits will be reversed through dividends; however, management believes that the portion of the temporary difference related to the dilution gains will only reverse if the investment is disposed of or liquidated, or the investee makes a distribution of capital. Management has no plans to dispose of its investment in K; accordingly, management does not consider the tax rate for sale to be applicable. In C's tax jurisdiction, distributions of capital are treated differently for tax purposes from dividend distributions of undistributed profits. We believe that the measurement of the deferred tax liability should take into account those different rates. For example, to the extent that the temporary difference relates to undistributed profits and is expected to reverse via dividends, the rate applicable to dividends from undistributed profits should be applied. To the extent that the temporary difference will only reverse via sale, liquidation or a distribution of capital, the relevant rate(s) should be used.

3.13.520.20 Sometimes when a taxable temporary difference associated with an investment in a subsidiary, branch, associate or joint venture crystallises, a related tax deduction will be recognised. For example, payment of a dividend may reverse a temporary difference associated with an investment in a subsidiary and also generate a dividend credit or other tax benefit for the parent. In our view, the tax effect of the reversal of the temporary difference should be considered net of the tax benefit related to the dividend (see 3.13.427).

3.13.530 *The foreseeable future*

IAS 12.39, 44   3.13.530.10 In order to avoid recognising a tax liability for temporary differences, the reversal of the temporary difference in the foreseeable future should not be probable; however, the term "foreseeable future" is not defined. In our view, it is necessary to consider in detail a period of 12 months from the reporting date, and also to take into account any transactions that are planned for a reasonable period after that date.

3.13.530.20 In practice the assessment of "foreseeable future" should be made on a case-by-case basis, taking into account the entity's history and the certainty of its plans. For example, Company X plans to draw dividends of 200 from Company Y in 18 months' time; X estimates that 150 of that amount will relate to post-acquisition earnings already recognised in the financial statements. We believe that 18 months is within the foreseeable future and, the deferred tax related to the planned 150 distribution should be recognised.

IAS 21.15   3.13.530.30 When a loan to an investee is accounted for as an integral part of the investor's investment, in our view it should be assumed that any temporary difference associated with the loan will not reverse in the foreseeable future through repayment. This is because the requirement for net investment accounting requires that repayment should not be planned or likely to occur in the "foreseeable future" in order to allow classification as part of the investment (see 2.7.150).

3.13.540 *Investments in subsidiaries or branches*

IAS 12.39, 44   3.13.540.10 Since an entity controls an investment in a subsidiary or branch, generally there is no need to consider whether the entity can control the timing of the reversal of a taxable temporary difference. The key issue is whether the temporary difference will reverse in the foreseeable future, and if so, how it will reverse; and in relation to a deductible temporary difference, whether the asset recognition criteria are met.

IAS 12.51   3.13.540.20 For example, if Subsidiary N pays dividends to Parent B, then a dividend tax of 10 percent will be incurred. However, if B disposes of its investment, then tax of 30 percent will be incurred on the reversal of the temporary difference. The measurement of deferred tax should reflect the manner in which the entity expects to recover the carrying amount of the investment. If B plans to dispose of its investment in N within the next year, then the deferred tax liability is calculated using a tax rate of 30 percent.

3.13.550 *Investments in associates*

IAS 12.42   3.13.550.10 An investor does not control an associate (see 3.5) and therefore generally is not in a position to control the timing of the reversal of a temporary difference related to the investment in the associate. Therefore, a deferred tax liability is recognised unless the investor can otherwise control the timing of the reversal of the temporary differences, for example if the associate has agreed that profits will not be distributed in the foreseeable future.

3.13.550.20 In our view, if the investor does not control the reversal of a temporary difference, and recognises a deferred tax liability, then the measurement of the deferred tax liability should be analysed as follows:

- If the entity has a plan to dispose of its investment in the associate in the foreseeable future, then the deferred tax should be based on the tax consequences of disposal, taking into account any recovery of the carrying amount through dividends until the date of disposal.
- In other cases, the entity should determine the most likely manner of recovery of the temporary difference, for example, dividend, payment out of capital or liquidation. If different tax rates apply to different manners of reversal of different elements of the temporary difference, then such differences should be taken into account in measuring the deferred tax liability (see 3.13.520.15).

3.13.550.30 For example, Company C acquired a 25 percent equity interest in Associate D for 1,000. Since the acquisition D has followed a dividend policy of distributing a third of its profit for the year, but there is no shareholders' agreement in this respect. At the end of 2010 the carrying amount of D in C's consolidated financial statements is 1,500. For tax purposes the investment has a cost of 1,000. The tax laws under which C operates stipulate that dividends received from associates are tax exempt. On disposal of the investment, any realised capital gains are subject to tax at a rate of 40 percent. C has no intention of selling its investment in D. We believe that no deferred tax will be recognised since there is no intention to dispose of the investment in the foreseeable future.

3.13.550.40 Changing the facts of the example in 3.13.550.30, C expects the temporary difference to reverse via dividends. Dividends received by C are taxed at a rate of 20 percent. We believe that a taxable temporary difference of 100 ((1,500 - 1,000) x 20%) should be recognised.

3.13.560 *Investments in joint ventures*

3.13.560.10 Whether or not a joint venturer is in a position to control a joint venture's dividend policy will depend on the terms of the joint venture agreement. In our view, a venturer's ability to veto the payment of dividends is sufficient to demonstrate control for the purpose of recognising deferred tax.

3.13.570 **Foreign currencies and hyperinflation**

IAS 12.41 3.13.570.10 Sometimes temporary differences are created when changes in exchange rates lead to changes in the tax basis rather than the book basis (see 2.7.140). For example, Company Q based in the United Kingdom may have some operations in Germany for which sterling is the functional currency (see 2.7.30). As a result, non-monetary property, plant and equipment in Germany is translated into sterling once, using the historical rate at the transaction date.

3.13.570.20 If the asset is part of a unit paying tax in Germany, then the tax basis in euro is retranslated from euro to sterling at each reporting date using a current rate. This translation difference may create temporary differences. Deferred tax is recognised for this temporary difference in accordance with the general principles for recognising income tax assets and liabilities (see 3.13.90 and 170).

IAS 12.41, 3.13.570.30 This applies even when the non-monetary assets are part of a foreign branch
IE.A.17, B.13 that has the same functional currency as its parent. In that case the special recognition criteria regarding subsidiaries, associates and joint ventures (see 3.13.510) do not apply because the non-monetary assets are those of the entity itself, not the overall investment.

3.13.570.40 [Not used]

3.13.570.50 The foreign currency translation reserve arising from the translation of foreign operations in the consolidated financial statements does not in itself give rise to the recognition of deferred tax assets or liabilities. The foreign currency translation reserve is neither an asset nor a liability and does not give rise to temporary differences. However, exchange differences arising on the translation of the financial statements of foreign operations might have associated tax effects that affect the financial statements. For example, when an entity intends to sell an investment in a subsidiary in the foreseeable future, it recognises deferred taxes on temporary differences arising from that investment (see 3.13.280.30). If part of these differences arises from the translation of the financial statements of foreign operations, then the deferred tax effect in respect of these differences will be recognised in other comprehensive income (see 3.13.370.10).

IAS 12.5 3.13.570.60 In some jurisdictions foreign currency gains and losses are netted for tax purposes, and the net gain (or loss) is taxable (or deductible) in instalments over several years. In our view, if a single tax base exists under applicable tax law, then it is appropriate to present a net deferred tax asset (liability).

IAS 12.IE. 3.13.570.70 Temporary differences arise when current purchasing power adjustments
A.18 are made to assets of entities operating in hyperinflationary economies (see 2.4.20) if the value in the financial statements is increased but the tax base remains stated in the historical measuring unit. Such temporary differences are recognised in full.

3.13.580 *Income tax exposures*

3.13.580.10 The term "income tax exposures" generally refers to positions taken by an entity that may be challenged by the tax authorities, and which may result in additional taxes, penalties or interest, changes in the tax basis of assets or liabilities, or changes in the amount of available tax losses carried forward that would reduce a deferred tax asset or increase a deferred tax liability. Whether or not an income tax exposure is present depends on both the specific position taken by an entity as well as on the applicable tax law. Therefore, income tax exposures often occur when the applicable tax law is not very clear or is not consistently understood, or in tax regimes where the amounts finally payable to the tax authorities are the outcome of lengthy negotiations involving a high degree of subjectivity and discretion, or are even random. Examples of tax exposures include:

- deductions taken on tax returns that may be disallowed by the tax authorities;
- transactions structured to utilise existing tax losses carried forward that may otherwise expire unused; and
- transactions that could affect an entity's non-taxable or tax-exempt status.

IAS 12.5 3.13.580.20 Income tax exposures are not discussed directly in IFRSs. However, the following definitions are relevant:

- Current tax is the amount of income tax payable (recoverable) in respect of the taxable profit (tax loss) for a period.
- Deferred tax liabilities are the amounts of income taxes payable in future periods in respect of taxable temporary differences.

IAS 12.88 3.13.580.30 To the extent that a tax exposure affects the calculation of income tax in respect of the current or prior periods, it falls within the definition of current tax (see 3.13.15.45). To the extent that a tax exposure affects the carrying amount of an asset or liability for accounting or tax purposes, it falls within the definition of deferred tax.

IAS 12.46 3.13.580.40 Potential tax exposures are analysed individually and separately from the calculation of income tax, and in our view the amount of tax provided for should be determined in accordance with IAS 12 since we believe that tax exposures are income taxes within the scope of that standard. In our view, consistent with the definition of a current tax liability (or asset), the amount to be provided for is the best estimate of the tax amount expected to be paid.

IAS 12.88 3.13.580.50 Interest and penalties arising from income tax exposures, although not covered by the definition of income taxes, are amounts due to the tax authorities that are closely related to income taxes. In our view, in the absence of clear guidance, if and only if an income tax exposure is present (see 3.13.580.40), an entity should choose an accounting policy, to be applied consistently, as to whether it accounts for such interest and penalties under IAS 12 or under IAS 37 (see 3.12.760 and 3.13.10.80). As a result, these amounts, when recognised, will be presented in the statement of financial position and in the statement of comprehensive income consistent with their nature and the standard applied:

- as other provisions (liabilities) in the statement of financial position and as operating and interest expenses respectively in profit or loss when IAS 37 is applied; or
- as current/deferred tax payables in the statement of financial position and as income tax expense in the statement of comprehensive income when IAS 12 is applied.

3.13.580.60 In our view, this accounting policy choice is not available for interest and penalties on items other than income tax exposures, i.e. when the uncertainties referred to above are not present or are insignificant. In these circumstances, interest and penalties that relate to income tax obligations should be determined separately and presented according to their nature in the statement of financial position and statement of comprehensive income, in the same way as other operating expenses or interest payable, rather than as current tax payable. If payment is delayed, then the effect of discounting should be considered in accordance with IAS 37 (see 3.13.15.40).

3.13.580.70 Exposures related to taxes that are not income taxes, for example taxes on sales such as value added tax, should be recognised and measured in accordance with IAS 37 unless dealt with specifically in another standard, for example IAS 19 *Employee Benefits* for social security taxes.

3.13.590 *Investment tax credits*

3.13.600 *Scope exclusion*

IAS 12.4 3.13.600.10 Accounting for ITCs is not addressed directly in IFRSs. However, IAS 12 applies to all temporary differences arising from ITCs (see 3.13.10).

3.13.610 *Definition*

3.13.610.10 There is no formal definition of ITCs under IFRSs. In our view, it is necessary to consider the substance of a tax incentive to determine if it is more akin to a credit received for investment in a certain area or simply a reduction in the applicable tax rate. For example, Company E receives a tax incentive for a period of five years, which does not relate to specific expenditure being made or any spending on a particular asset. However, in order to continue being eligible for the tax incentive E must achieve a certain profit and employ a certain number of staff. In our view, this tax incentive is not an ITC in substance because it does not relate to specific expenditure or required spending on a particular asset. In this example, we believe that the tax incentive is a reduction in the applicable tax rate during the period that it is received.

3.13.610.20 In another example, Company F acquires a certain machine and thereby qualifies to receive a credit against its tax of 100 per year for the next five years as long as no dividends are declared during that period. We believe that this credit is an ITC.

3.13.610.30 In another example, Company G acquires a certain machine and receives a tax deduction equal to 150 percent of its cost (referred to as "bonus depreciation") as an incentive to invest in that kind of machinery; there are no additional requirements to be fulfilled. We believe that the additional tax deduction received is an ITC.

3.13.620 *Accounting*

3.13.620.10 ITCs are excluded from the scope of both IAS 12 (see 3.13.10) and IAS 20 *Accounting for Government Grants and Disclosure of Government Assistance*. However, in practice entities generally account for ITCs using one of these two standards by analogy. In our view, management needs to choose an approach that best reflects the economic substance of the specific ITC. When conditions are attached to the grant of an ITC, application of IAS 20 by analogy might be more appropriate. Details of following these two standards by analogy are as follows:

- Following IAS 12 by analogy, ITCs are presented in profit or loss as a deduction from a current tax expense to the extent that an entity is entitled to claim the credit in the current reporting period. Any unused ITC is recognised as a deferred tax asset and income if it meets the recognition criteria (see 3.13.170).
- Following IAS 20 by analogy, ITCs are recognised as income over the periods necessary to match them with the related costs that they are intended to compensate. The ITC initially is shown in the statement of financial position as a receivable from the government and deferred income and subsequently presented in profit or loss either as "other income" or deduction from the related expense as appropriate.

3.13.630 **Share-based payments**

IAS 12.68A, 3.13.630.10 In some tax jurisdictions, an entity may receive a tax deduction that differs
68B, IE.Ex5 in amount or timing from the cumulative share-based payment expense recognised

in profit or loss. Generally this will give rise to the recognition of deferred tax on the temporary differences. In our view, the deferred tax should be recognised for each share-based payment arrangement as the services are received over the vesting period.

3.13.630.15 For measurement purposes the entity has to determine the amount of tax deduction to which it will be entitled based on the manner in which it expects to settle the award and in accordance with applicable tax legislation.

- In some cases the tax deduction may be based on the intrinsic value of the equity instrument at a future date. If this is the case, then the expected future tax deduction should be estimated based on the information available at the reporting date, including share price, exercise price and number of options expected to be exercised. The information used to estimate the deductions available in future periods needs to be consistent with that applied in measuring the share-based payment expense, although some information may result in an adjustment to deferred tax but not to the share-based payment expense, e.g. failure to meet a market condition in the case of an equity-settled share-based payment arrangement.
- In other cases the entity may settle the share-based payment transaction through the transfer of treasury shares and receive a tax deduction based on the cost of the treasury shares. If this is the case, then the expected future tax deduction should be estimated based on the cost of the treasury shares. It should be noted however, that in this case the temporary difference arises in relation to the share-based payment expense, not the treasury shares as such. See 3.13.70.50 – 90 for a discussion of the tax base of treasury shares.

IAS 12.68C 3.13.630.20 A particular issue arises if the amount of the tax deduction (or estimated future tax deduction) exceeds the amount of the related cumulative share-based payment expense. Such a situation indicates that the tax deduction relates not only to remuneration expense, but also to an equity item. In this situation the excess of the associated income tax is recognised directly in equity. Any subsequent reduction in the excess also is recorded in equity.

3.13.630.23 IFRSs provide specific guidance on calculating income tax in relation to equity-settled share-based payment expense when the tax deduction is received after recognition of the expense. However, in some jurisdictions current tax deductions are available based on the intrinsic value of a share-based payment award at the grant date. In these circumstances we prefer to recognise deferred tax between points in time at which the share-based payment expense is recognised and the associated tax deduction is given, thereby applying a similar approach of recognising deferred tax irrespective of whether the tax deduction is received before or after the related expense is recognised. A second approach is to recognise the current tax deduction entirely in equity at grant date and then to release it to profit or loss over the vesting period, such that no deferred tax is recognised. A third approach is to recognise a deferred tax liability at the time that the tax deduction is received and build up a deferred tax asset as the share-based payment expense is recognised. The resulting asset and liability then would be offset at the end of the vesting period. In our view, an entity should choose an accounting policy, to be applied consistently, as to which approach to apply. The initial recognition exemption in IAS 12 does not apply in such circumstances as the related temporary difference only develops over time.

3.13.630.27 In the case of a cash-settled share-based payment arrangement for which tax relief is received on the amount of the ultimate payment when it is made, a question arises as to whether the temporary difference should reflect the carrying amount of the share-based payment liability, which is measured at fair value under IFRS 2, or the intrinsic value based on the price of the underlying share at the reporting date. Determining the temporary difference by reference to fair value would be consistent with general practice for calculating deferred tax on revalued items (see 3.13.40). Conversely, the guidance on deferred tax in IFRS 2 refers explicitly to intrinsic value in the case of equity-settled share-based payments. In our view, an entity should choose an accounting policy, to be applied consistently, in these circumstances.

3.13.630.30 A further issue arises in relation to first-time adopters of IFRSs that elect not to apply IFRS 2 retrospectively to share options granted to employees before 7 November 2002. For example, Company X makes that election and, as a result, no adjustment to retained earnings in the opening IFRS statement of financial position of X is made and no expense will be recognised in profit or loss subsequently in respect of the options issued before 7 November 2002. If the options are exercised, then the share issue will be recognised directly in equity. In its tax jurisdiction, X will receive a tax deduction, based on the intrinsic value of the options at exercise date, when the employees exercise their options and receive the shares. However, similar to a situation in which an entity receives a tax deduction at grant date (see 3.13.630.23), as there is no asset, liability or expense in the financial statements to which the tax deduction relates, the question arises as to whether a temporary difference arises and a deferred tax asset may be recognised.

3.13.630.40 An entity should choose an accounting policy, to be applied consistently, to make such a determination using one of the following approaches:

- Identify the difference between the tax base of the share options and their carrying amount of zero as a temporary difference on which a deferred tax asset should be recognised, subject to recoverability (see 3.13.170). In accordance with the principle in IAS 12 the tax consequences of a transaction should be recognised in a manner consistent with the accounting for the transaction itself; the deferred tax asset will be recognised in equity, as the underlying transaction will affect equity upon exercise of the options and issue of the shares. The initial recognition exemption in IAS 12 is not available as the difference only develops over time.
- Alternatively, the entity may elect not to identify a temporary difference and consequently not to recognise any deferred tax on the basis that the share-based payments granted prior to 7 November 2002 have not been recognised in the IFRS financial statements and hence there is no carrying amount, rather than a carrying amount of zero, recognised for accounting purposes.

3.13.635 *Tax groups*

3.13.640 *Tax consolidated groups*

3.13.640.10 In many countries, tax consolidation systems permit groups comprising a parent entity and its wholly-owned subsidiaries (subsidiaries that are not wholly owned, or not directly owned also might be eligible if certain criteria are met) to elect to be treated as a single entity for income tax purposes. The tax consolidation systems generally are elective rather than compulsory. Generally, under these systems, a tax-consolidated group prepares a single consolidated annual tax return. In most cases the parent entity will become liable for the income tax liabilities of the entire group.

3.13.640.20 The entities in a tax-consolidated group may or may not enter into a tax-sharing agreement (including a tax funding or contribution agreement) in order to allocate tax expenses to subsidiaries on a predetermined, ongoing basis.

3.13.640.30 In our view, in the absence of specific guidance in IFRSs, an entity should choose an accounting policy, to be applied consistently, to accounting for income taxes in the separate or individual IFRS financial statements of entities within a tax group. Various approaches are acceptable under IFRSs.

3.13.640.40 Below are examples of such approaches that might be applied.

3.13.650 Approach 1

3.13.650.10 Current and deferred income taxes are recognised by each entity within the group, regardless of who has the legal liability for settlement or recovery of the tax.

3.13.650.20 Under this approach, the view is taken that in substance each entity in the tax-consolidated group remains taxable, since income taxes are payable and recoverable on the subsidiary's profits or losses as determined in accordance with the applicable tax rules, even if they are payable or recoverable by the parent entity and not the subsidiary itself.

3.13.650.30 Current and deferred tax amounts for each entity within the tax group are determined and recognised under a systematic, rational and consistent method. Any difference resulting from current and deferred taxes recognised and the amounts paid to or received from the parent entity is disclosed in the tax reconciliation or recognised as a contribution from or a distribution to the parent entity.

3.13.650.40 An entity should choose an accounting policy, to be applied consistently, for measuring the current and deferred taxes to be recognised by each entity within a tax-consolidated group. In our view, there are several acceptable ways to measure the current and deferred taxes to be recognised by each entity within a tax-consolidated group, including:

- a "stand-alone taxpayer" approach, whereby current and deferred taxes are recognised as if the entity was taxable in its own right;
- a "separate taxpayer within the group" approach, whereby current and deferred taxes are measured on the basis that the entity is part of a tax group; this results in adjustments related to the entity's transactions that have tax consequences for the entity but do not have tax consequences (or have different tax consequences) at the group level (e.g. intra-group transfers of inventories or property, plant and equipment, management fees); and
- a "group allocation" approach, whereby current and deferred taxes of the tax group are allocated in a systematic manner.

3.13.650.50 Various allocation methods might be applied. However, in our view any method that results in: only current taxes being allocated to an entity in the group that has taxable temporary differences; no deferred taxes being allocated to an entity with temporary differences because the tax group has none; current taxes being allocated only to entities with accounting profit; or current taxes and deferred taxes being allocated on a basis inconsistent with IAS 12 (e.g. sales revenue, total assets, net assets, operating profit), is not appropriate.

3.13.660 Approach 2

3.13.660.10 Under this approach, current income taxes are recognised in each entity (subsidiaries and parent entity) based on the amounts actually paid by the individual legal entities, generally based on a contractual agreement between the entities within the group. Deferred income taxes also are recognised in each entity's (subsidiaries and parent entity) financial statements based on the amounts expected to be settled by the entity in the future.

3.13.660.20 In our view when electing one of these approaches, entities should be consistent with how they account for other aspects of common control transactions and, more generally, with their accounting policies for separate or individual financial statements. In our view, an entity should elect, apply and disclose its policy in its separate or individual financial statements if it is part of a tax consolidation group.

3.13.665 *Group relief*

3.13.665.10 In other jurisdictions, each entity within a group prepares its own tax return and is liable for any tax payable. However, an entity that makes tax losses may transfer those losses to another entity within the same group. Practice varies as to whether the receiving entity pays the surrendering entity. In our view, if entities within a group transfer tax losses between themselves for no payment, then in their separate financial statements the entities should choose an accounting policy, to be applied consistently, as to whether to disclose such transfers in their tax reconciliations or recognise them as contributions/distributions as appropriate.

3.13.665.20 For example, suppose that Subsidiary S is subject to a tax rate of 25 percent and has taxable losses of 100. Initially S recognises a deferred tax asset of 25. S agrees to transfer its taxable loss of 100 to Company P, its parent, at the end of the year. If P pays 25 to S in consideration for the transfer, then S will record the cash receipt against its deferred tax balance (case one below). Conversely, if P pays nothing in consideration for the transfer, then either S will record the transfer of its tax asset as a distribution (case two below); or S will write off its deferred tax asset and disclose the transfer in its tax reconciliation (case three below). In the latter case S will make no net entry in relation to its taxable losses. The entries for S for the initial recognition of the deferred tax in cases one, two and three are:

	Debit	Credit
Deferred tax asset	25	
Tax income		25
To recognise initially deferred tax on tax losses		
(100 x 25%)		
Case 1		
Cash	25	
Deferred tax asset		25
To recognise entry for S if P pays 25 to S in consideration		
for tax loss transfer		
Case 2		
Equity	25	
Deferred tax asset		25
To recognise entry for S if P pays nothing to S in		
consideration for tax loss transfer		
Case 3		
Profit or loss	25	
Deferred tax asset		25
To recognise entry for S if P pays nothing to S in		
consideration for tax loss transfer		

3.13.670 *Business combinations*

3.13.680 *General principles*

IAS 12.19, 15, 24   3.13.680.10 Generally an entity recognises deferred tax assets and liabilities for temporary differences that arise in respect of recognised identifiable assets and liabilities in a business combination. However, deferred tax liabilities are not recognised for differences related to the initial recognition of goodwill (see 3.13.110) and, when the relevant criteria are met, for temporary differences related to acquired investments in subsidiaries, branches and associates, and interests in joint ventures (see 3.13.510). Additionally, deferred tax assets arising in a business combination are recognised at the acquisition date only to the extent that it is probable, at that date, that future taxable profits will be available against which the related deductible temporary differences can be utilised (see 3.13.170). See 2.6 for general guidance on the accounting for business combinations.

IAS 12.19, 3.13.680.20 Deferred taxes are recognised in accordance with the principles in IAS 12 in
26(c) the acquisition accounting for unused tax losses and unused tax credits of the acquiree, and on temporary differences between the tax bases of identifiable assets acquired and liabilities assumed in a business combination and the related amounts recognised in the acquisition accounting. Assets acquired and liabilities assumed in a business combination are measured in the acquisition accounting in accordance with IFRS 3 *Business Combinations*, but in some jurisdictions, depending on how the transaction is structured, the tax bases of those assets and liabilities may not be affected by the business combination or the tax bases may be measured in a different way, which can give rise to temporary differences. Such temporary differences arise for different reasons. For example,

IAS 12.15(b), • *Recognition.* Temporary differences to which the acquiree applied the initial recogni-
24 tion exemption do not meet the criteria for that exemption from the perspective of an acquirer in a business combination. Additionally, temporary differences may arise related to assets and liabilities that were not recognised in the acquiree's financial statements.

IAS 12.19 • *Measurement.* Amounts recognised in respect of acquisition accounting for assets acquired and liabilities assumed differ from those recognised in the acquiree's financial statements.

• *Assessment of recoverability.* The acquirer's assessment of whether deferred tax assets are recoverable may differ from that of the acquiree due to changed circumstances of the combined entity compared to those of the acquiree on a stand-alone basis.

3.13.680.30 The interaction of the acquirer's and acquiree's tax attributes, including, for example, current and deferred tax balances, tax rates, taxable income and tax jurisdiction, may impact the deferred tax recognised in the acquisition accounting as well as the acquirer's existing temporary differences.

IAS 12.66, 67 3.13.680.40 Generally, the effects of the acquisition on the acquiree's deferred taxes are recognised as part of the acquisition accounting, while the effects of the acquisition on the acquirer's deferred taxes are recognised separately from the acquisition accounting.

3.13.690 *Accounting for the tax effects of goodwill*

IAS 12.15(a) 3.13.690.10 Deferred tax liabilities are not recognised at the acquisition date for taxable temporary differences that arise between the tax base of goodwill and its financial statement carrying amount, i.e. in cases in which the carrying amount of goodwill is greater than its tax base (see 3.13.850).

IAS 12.15(a), 3.13.690.20 A temporary difference also may arise on the initial recognition of goodwill if
21, 21A the goodwill is not tax deductible. No deferred tax liability is recognised on this temporary difference, because goodwill is measured as a residual and the recognition

of a deferred tax liability would gross up the amount of goodwill. If in subsequent periods the temporary difference decreases, for example due to the impairment of goodwill, then the exemption still applies and no deferred tax is recognised. In our view, this guidance also applies to a portion of goodwill that is only partially deductible (see 3.13.690.40).

IAS 12.15(a), 21B   3.13.690.30 It is necessary to distinguish this situation from scenarios in which goodwill is tax deductible, but no temporary difference arises because the carrying amount of goodwill in the IFRS financial statements equals its tax base. If in subsequent periods the carrying amount and the tax base of such goodwill differ (e.g. due to impairment for accounting purposes that is not deductible for tax purposes until later periods), then deferred tax is recognised (see 3.13.850.20).

3.13.690.40 IFRSs do not provide explicit guidance in respect of goodwill that is only partially tax deductible when recognised initially. In our view, goodwill with a carrying amount higher than its tax base should be split into two parts:

- To the extent that the carrying amount equals the tax base, no temporary difference arises. If in subsequent periods temporary differences arise, then deferred tax is recognised in relation to this portion of the goodwill, subject to realisability (see 3.13.850).
- The excess of the carrying amount of goodwill over the tax base is not tax deductible and the exemption for not recognising deferred tax for goodwill applies both initially and subsequently to any temporary differences that arise in respect of the non-tax deductible portion of the goodwill.

IAS 12.32A   3.13.690.50 Subject to the existence of appropriate future taxable income, an entity recognises deferred tax assets in respect of the initial recognition of goodwill for which the tax base of that goodwill is in excess of its carrying amount. In our view, an appropriate method of determining the amount of deferred tax asset to recognise in such a situation is by determining an adjustment to both deferred taxes recognised in acquisition accounting and to goodwill such that the deferred tax asset recognised for goodwill equates to the related temporary difference multiplied by the relevant tax rate. This may be done by resolving the following equation:

> Deferred tax asset recognised for tax-deductible goodwill in excess of accounting goodwill = net temporary difference initially calculated x (tax rate / (1 - tax rate)

3.13.690.60 For example, Company B acquires Company X. Goodwill for financial reporting purposes before any adjustment for deferred tax assets arising on goodwill is 600. Tax deductible goodwill of 900 arises in the business combination. The relevant tax rate is 40 percent. Using the formula above, the deferred tax asset to be recognised and associated adjustment to accounting goodwill is 200 ((900 - 600) x (40% / (1 - 40%)). Accordingly, goodwill recognised in the acquisition accounting is 400 (initially-determined goodwill of 600 less the adjustment to goodwill of 200). The deferred tax asset of 200 equates to the temporary difference of 500 (900 - 400) related to the goodwill multiplied by the relevant tax rate of 40 percent.

IAS 12.11 3.13.690.70 Deferred taxes are determined separately for each tax-paying component in each tax jurisdiction. Accordingly, an entity determines the carrying amount and tax base of goodwill separately for each tax-paying component rather than at the reporting entity level.

3.13.700 *Accounting for the tax effects of a gain on a bargain purchase*

IFRS 3.34, 3.13.700.10 A gain on a bargain purchase is determined after deferred taxes have been
IAS 12.38-45 recognised in the acquisition accounting. The gain may create or change a temporary difference. For example, in a bargain purchase the tax base of the acquirer's investment in the acquiree may be less than the related carrying amount of the identifiable net assets recognised in the consolidated financial statements, in which case the acquirer assesses whether a deferred tax liability is recognised for such a temporary difference (see 3.13.540). In our view, since the gain is recognised immediately in profit or loss, the related tax effects of the resulting temporary difference, if any, also should be recognised in profit or loss. See 2.6.900 for a discussion of the gain on a bargain purchase.

3.13.710 *Recognition of acquiree's deferred tax assets*

IAS 12.29(b), 3.13.710.10 In assessing whether to recognise deferred tax assets of the combined entity,
30 the acquirer considers tax planning opportunities that the combined entity would take if necessary to realise a tax benefit that otherwise may not be realised, e.g. due to the expiration of an unused tax loss. If an acquirer is permitted under tax law to include the acquiree in its tax group, then the possibility of so doing may need to be considered in the acquirer's evaluation of qualifying tax planning opportunities (see 3.13.200.20).

3.13.710.20 In some situations tax law restricts acquired tax benefits from being recovered through future taxable income of the combined entity subsequent to the acquisition. In such cases only the acquiree's separate past and expected future results of operations are used in determining whether recognition of the acquiree's existing deferred tax assets is appropriate. A similar situation arises when the combined entity is not permitted to include the acquirer and acquiree in the same tax group; in those circumstances taxes payable resulting from the reversal of existing taxable temporary differences of the acquirer would not be reduced by reversing deductible temporary differences of the acquiree.

3.13.710.30 Care should be taken to distinguish tax planning opportunities from post-acquisition events or the acquirer's post-acquisition actions (see 3.13.820). Tax planning opportunities affect the realisation of deferred tax assets; post-acquisition events or the acquirer's post-acquisition actions affect temporary differences and are not anticipated in determining the recognition or measurement of deferred taxes in the acquisition accounting. See 3.13.840 for a discussion of subsequent changes to deferred tax benefits of the acquiree.

3.13.720 *Changes in the recognition of acquirer's deferred tax assets at the acquisition date*

IAS 12.67   **3.13.720.10** A frequent consequence of the interaction of the tax positions of the acquirer and acquiree is a change in the assessment of the realisability of the acquirer's deferred tax assets. For example, the acquirer might determine that, as a result of the business combination, it is able to utilise the benefit of its tax losses, for which it previously did not recognise a deferred tax asset, against the future taxable profit of the combined entity. Such changes are recognised separately from the acquisition accounting. Also changes to the acquirer's deferred taxes occurring subsequent to the acquisition date are recognised outside of the acquisition accounting. In our view, the deferred tax consequence of an acquisition for the acquirer is determined as the difference between the acquirer's net deferred tax asset or liability measured just prior to the acquisition and its net deferred tax asset or liability measured on those same temporary differences just after the acquisition.

3.13.720.20 See 3.13.200.20 and 635 for a discussion of the general principles of asset recognition and tax groups.

3.13.720.30 For example, Company P acquires 100 percent of Company S in a business combination. P has cumulative tax losses of 200 at the acquisition date. Prior to the acquisition, P's management had determined that it was less than probable that P would realise its deferred tax assets. In making that determination, P's management considered future taxable profits, the existence of taxable temporary differences and tax planning opportunities. P's losses have an indefinite carryforward period. The tax rate applicable to both Companies P and S is 40 percent. Goodwill arising in the business combination is not tax deductible.

3.13.720.40 Amounts recognised in the acquisition accounting and related tax bases in respect of the acquisition of S are as follows:

	Financial statements	Tax base
Identifiable net assets acquired (excluding deferred tax)	500	400
Deferred tax liability ((500-400) x 40%)	(40)	-
Goodwill	240	-
Consideration transferred	700	

3.13.720.50 S has no unused tax losses or tax credits. All of the taxable temporary differences of S relate to finite-lived assets. In its consolidated financial statements to record the acquisition of S, P recognises identifiable net assets acquired of 460 and goodwill of 240.

3.13.720.60 Under local tax law P and S will be included in the same tax group. There is no restriction on utilising the tax losses of P against the taxable profits of other entities in that tax group. The reversal of the taxable temporary differences of S plus the anticipated profits projected to be generated by S subsequent to the acquisition provide evidence of the recoverability of P's unused tax losses. P recognises the deferred tax asset of 80 (200 of tax losses at the applicable tax rate of 40 percent) as tax income in profit or loss separately from the business combination.

3.13.720.70 If P is not able to include S in the same tax group and is unable otherwise to support a conclusion that it is probable that it will be able to recover its unused tax losses against the taxable profit of S, then the deferred tax asset in respect of P's losses remains unrecognised as of the acquisition date.

3.13.730 *Acquiree's investments in subsidiaries, branches and associates, and interests in joint ventures*

IAS 12.39 3.13.730.10 The difference between the tax base of the acquirer's investment in the acquiree and the carrying amount of the acquiree in the acquirer's consolidated financial statements is a temporary difference, even though that investment is eliminated in the consolidated financial statements (see 3.13.510.05).

3.13.730.20 The determination of whether a deferred tax liability (asset) is recognised for a taxable (deductible) temporary difference at the acquisition date is made by the acquirer without regard to the previous assertions of the acquiree about meeting the criteria in paragraph 39 and 44 of IAS 12 (see 3.13.510). If the relevant criteria are met, then no deferred tax liability is recorded at acquisition. If the criteria are not met, then a deferred tax liability is recognised in the acquisition accounting. In our experience, the tax base of the investment and the carrying amount of the related net assets in the consolidated financial statements frequently both are the fair value at the acquisition date, i.e. no temporary difference related to the investment exists at acquisition. Accordingly, a temporary difference associated with an investment in a subsidiary occurs often when the acquiree has existing subsidiaries.

3.13.730.30 Subsequent changes in an entity's assessment of whether a deferred tax asset or liability is recognised for temporary differences are accounted separately from the acquisition accounting. For example, if a deferred tax liability is not recognised at the acquisition date because the acquirer determines that it is probable that the temporary difference will not reverse in the foreseeable future, then subsequent recognition of a deferred tax liability due to a change in circumstances is recognised outside the business combination.

IAS 12.44 3.13.730.40 A deferred tax asset is recognised for a deductible temporary difference related to investments in subsidiaries, branches, associates and joint ventures only if it is probable that the temporary difference will reverse in the foreseeable future (see 3.13.510.20), subject to realisability. Situations also may arise in which the acquirer does not initially recognise a deferred tax asset at the acquisition date as it does not meet the *foreseeable future* requirement (see 3.13.530), but subsequently recognises that deferred tax asset. In such circumstances, the related benefit is recorded as a reduction to income tax expense separately from the acquisition accounting, unless it is considered a measurement period adjustment (see 3.13.840).

3.13.740 *Anticipated changes in tax rates*

IAS 12.46   3.13.740.10 The future enactment or substantive enactment of a change in tax rates is not anticipated for purposes of measuring deferred taxes in a business combination. Deferred tax assets and liabilities are measured based on rates that are enacted or substantively enacted at the acquisition date (see 3.13.310). This applies even if expected tax rate changes were considered in negotiating the consideration transferred or a change in tax rates was substantively enacted after the acquisition date but during the measurement period. The effect of changes in tax rates is recognised separately from the acquisition accounting in the period in which the change is enacted or substantively enacted.

3.13.750 *Income tax issues related to consideration transferred and identifiable assets acquired and liabilities assumed*

3.13.760 Contingent consideration

3.13.760.10 When determining the income tax effects of contingent consideration, an entity considers all relevant factors, which may include the nature, measurement and timing of any tax deduction in respect of the contingent consideration and the classification of the related contingent consideration. See 2.6.10.10 for a discussion of contingent consideration.

3.13.760.20 The tax treatment of contingent consideration may vary depending on the jurisdiction in which a business combination takes place and may depend on the legal form of the transaction. For example, contingent consideration may affect the tax base of the identifiable assets and liabilities acquired or of goodwill deductible for tax purposes, or may affect only the tax base of an acquired investment in a subsidiary.

IAS 12.66   3.13.760.30 If a liability (asset) in relation to contingent consideration recognised in the acquisition accounting will result in amounts that are deductible (taxable) in future periods, then generally deferred taxes are recognised for the resulting temporary differences. In our view, the tax effects of such contingent consideration are recognised in the acquisition accounting consistent with the recognition of the contingent consideration.

IAS 12.38-45   3.13.760.40 When contingent consideration affects the tax base of an acquired investment in a subsidiary, the acquirer considers whether it is appropriate to recognise deferred taxes in relation to a temporary difference related to that investment or whether the exception to the recognition of deferred tax in relation to such investments applies (see 3.13.730).

IAS 12.61A   3.13.760.50 Changes in the fair value subsequent to the acquisition date of contingent consideration that is classified as an asset or liability generally are recognised in profit or loss. The deferred tax effects of changes in temporary differences are recognised in the same manner as the related changes in the fair value of the contingent consideration, i.e. in profit or loss.

3.13.760.60 For example, Company P acquires Company S in a business combination for which the acquisition date is 30 June 2010. In addition to consideration transferred at the acquisition date, an amount of 300 potentially is payable in cash dependent on the future earnings of S. As the contingent consideration is payable in cash upon settlement, it is classified as a liability and changes in fair value are recognised in profit or loss. The fair value of the contingent consideration is 140 at the acquisition date. Before accounting for the tax effects of the contingent consideration, goodwill is calculated as 600 for financial reporting purposes, of which 400 is tax deductible. P anticipates adequate future taxable income to support recognition in full of all deferred tax assets arising from its deductible temporary differences.

3.13.760.70 If the payment of contingent consideration affects the tax base of the goodwill, then the recognition of deferred taxes in the acquisition accounting depends on whether the related temporary difference is a taxable or deductible temporary difference, i.e. on whether goodwill for accounting purposes exceeds that for tax purposes or vice versa (see 3.13.690). In the fact pattern described in 3.13.760.60 the resulting tax goodwill at the acquisition date, assuming settlement of the related liability at its carrying amount at that date, is 540 (400 + 140). Accordingly, no deferred tax is recognised for the resulting taxable temporary difference due to the exemption for initial recognition of goodwill (see 3.13.690.40).

3.13.760.80 In a contrasting example, assume that the payment of contingent consideration attracts a tax deduction when the related liability is settled. The applicable tax rate is 40 percent. In this example, a deferred tax asset of 56 (140 x 40%) related to the contingent consideration is recognised as part of the acquisition accounting, thereby reducing the goodwill recognised in the business combination.

3.13.760.90 Subsequent to the acquisition date, the fair value of the contingent consideration is remeasured to 250. P recognises the change in the fair value of the contingent consideration and related tax effects in profit or loss.

3.13.770 Equity-settled replacement awards issued in a business combination

3.13.770.10 If an acquirer issues an equity-settled replacement award (see 4.5) that will result in a tax deduction at a later date, then a deferred tax asset is recognised as part of acquisition accounting for the deductible temporary difference that relates to the portion of the award attributed to pre-combination employee service. For portions of the award attributable to post-combination employee service, a deferred tax asset is recognised in the period that the cost is recognised for financial reporting purposes following the same principles discussed in 3.13.370.30.

3.13.770.20 The deferred tax asset recognised as part of the acquisition accounting subsequently may be remeasured for changes in the amount expected to be received as a tax deduction, for example due to fluctuations in the market price of the related shares. IAS 12 does not stipulate how such changes in the deferred tax asset arising from the expected tax deduction should be recognised. In our view, an entity should choose an accounting policy, to be applied consistently, to:

- recognise all such changes in profit or loss;
- recognise all such changes directly in equity; or
- recognise the effect of estimated future tax deductions in excess of a certain amount directly in equity and other such changes in profit or loss.

3.13.770.30 See 3.13.370.30 for a discussion of classification and presentation of current and deferred taxes.

3.13.770.40 An entity that adopts the "asymmetric" accounting policy in 3.13.770.20 recognises changes in the expected tax deduction differently depending on whether the total estimated tax deduction attributed to the pre-combination service element of an award exceeds the amount of the acquisition-date market-based measure of that element of the award. To the extent that the expected tax deduction exceeds the market-based measure, the related tax effects are recognised in equity; all other such changes are recognised in profit or loss.

3.13.780 The settlement of a pre-existing relationship

IFRS 3.51,   3.13.780.10 Pre-existing relationships between the acquirer and the acquiree effectively
B51-B53   are settled as a result of the business combination transaction and are accounted for separately from the business combination as a gain or loss at the acquisition date (see 2.6.780). An entity also recognises the tax effects of the settlement outside the business combination.

3.13.780.20 The tax treatment of the settlement of a pre-existing relationship will vary depending on the tax laws of the relevant jurisdiction. If the tax treatment is the same as that for accounting, then the current tax income or expense is recognised in the same manner as the related settlement loss or gain. If, however, the tax treatment of the set-tlement gain or loss differs from the accounting treatment, then a temporary difference may arise. The accounting for that temporary difference will depend on the tax treat-ment of the gain or loss, which might, for example result in an adjustment to goodwill deductible for tax purposes or other intangible asset, or an adjustment to the tax base of the acquirer's investment in its subsidiary.

3.13.790 Acquisition-related costs

IFRS 3.53   3.13.790.10 Acquisition-related costs are expensed as incurred or as services are received unless the costs are related to the issue of debt or equity securities. Acquisition-related costs may include finder's fees, advisory, legal, accounting, valuation and other profes-sional or consulting fees (see 2.6.520).

3.13.790.20 For tax purposes, these costs may be immediately deductible, capitalised, included as part of goodwill deductible for tax purposes or included in the tax base of the investment acquired. The ultimate tax treatment might depend on the treatment of the business combination for tax purposes and whether the business combination ultimately is consummated.

3.13.790.30 When determining the accounting prior to the acquisition date for the tax effects of acquisition-related costs incurred, an entity considers the expected ultimate tax treatment of those costs. Accordingly, if an entity expects that the transaction costs will result in a tax deduction subsequent to incurring such costs, then the entity recognises a deferred tax asset with respect to those costs, subject to realisability. Conversely, if an entity expects that the transaction costs will be treated as part of the cost of investment for tax purposes and the entity does not expect that it will recognise deferred taxes on temporary differences related to that investment, then no deferred tax asset will be recognised.

3.13.790.40 The deferred tax effects related to acquisition-related costs are recognised outside of the business combination because those costs themselves are accounted for separately from the acquisition accounting.

3.13.800 Tax indemnifications

IFRS 3.27, 28, 57   3.13.800.10 Entities may enter into indemnification arrangements whereby the seller of a business will agree contractually to reimburse the acquirer in respect of certain tax liabilities of the acquiree. In our view, the acquirer accounts for such income tax exposures under IAS 12 (see 3.13.580.40). See 2.6.670 for a discussion of indemnification assets in a business combination.

3.13.810 Identifiable intangible assets

3.13.810.10 Identifiable assets for tax purposes might not match exactly the identifiable assets or goodwill recognised for accounting purposes. For example, an entity may receive tax deductions for a single "tax intangible", which for accounting purposes is recognised as several different identifiable intangible assets and goodwill as a residual.

3.13.810.20 For example, Company P acquires Company S's business, as opposed to the acquisition of the legal entity. In the acquisition accounting, P recognises various identifiable intangible assets (A, B and C), each with a carrying amount of 100 with goodwill of 200 as a residual. P is entitled to a total tax deduction of 500 in respect of the identifiable intangible assets and goodwill ("tax intangible"). Economically the tax intangible is a combination of some of the identifiable intangible assets recognised for accounting purposes and a component of goodwill. In our view, the deduction attached to the tax intangible should be treated as the combined tax base of the relevant intangible assets (A, B and C) and of a component of goodwill for the purpose of determining any temporary difference arising from the business combination.

3.13.820 Income tax issues related to subsequent measurement and accounting

3.13.820.10 An entity recognises deferred taxes that result from a business combination as part of the acquisition accounting. However, in our view the tax effect of post-acquisition events, or the acquirer's post-acquisition actions, should not be anticipated.

IAS 12.66 3.13.820.20 For example, an acquirer might complete a business combination and plan to restructure the acquired business shortly after the acquisition in order to transfer non-tax deductible goodwill or another intangible asset to a jurisdiction with more favourable tax treatment. We believe that the tax consequences of this post-acquisition restructuring should not be recognised as part of the acquisition accounting.

3.13.830 Measurement period

IFRS 3.45-50 3.13.830.10 In certain circumstances the acquirer may adjust provisional amounts recognised in the acquisition accounting if new information is obtained about facts and circumstances that existed at the acquisition date that if known would have affected the measurement of the amounts recognised (see 2.6.960).

IFRS 3.45 3.13.830.20 Amounts included in the acquisition accounting may be subject to changes in estimates related to the tax attributes of the acquiree as well as changes in estimates related to amounts included in respect of the carrying amounts of assets acquired and liabilities assumed. These changes may affect temporary differences on which deferred taxes were recognised as part of the acquisition accounting. Tax-related amounts included in the determination of deferred taxes in the acquisition accounting may be based on estimates as well. For example, an entity may need to estimate the tax base at the acquisition date of significant capital assets or the amount and availability of unutilised tax losses. These estimated amounts may be revised as more information is available. Changes in estimates of tax-related amounts are accounted for in the same manner as changes in estimates of other amounts recognised in the acquisition accounting (see 2.6.960).

3.13.840 Changes in the acquiree's deductible temporary differences, unused tax losses or unused tax credits acquired in a business combination

3.13.840.10 The accounting for subsequent changes in the recognition of acquired deferred tax assets depends on:

- whether such changes occur during or after the end of the measurement period; and
- whether such changes result from new information about facts and circumstances that existed at the acquisition date or result from events that occur subsequent to the business combination.

IAS 12.68A 3.13.840.20 Measurement period changes in the recognition of acquired deferred tax assets that result from new information about facts and circumstances that existed at the acquisition date generally are recognised by adjusting the acquisition accounting retrospectively (see 2.6.960). However, if recognition of such deferred tax assets during the measurement period results in the carrying amount of goodwill recognised in the business combination being reduced to zero, then any remaining deferred tax benefit is recognised in profit or loss (see 3.13.700).

IAS 12.68B 3.13.840.30 If taxes recognised in the acquisition accounting are adjusted due to events that occur after the acquisition date, then subsequent recognition or derecognition of the acquiree's tax benefits is recognised separately from the acquisition accounting, even if the event occurs during the measurement period. Such events might include changes in enacted or substantively enacted tax laws and changes in expected levels of future taxable income caused by events occurring subsequent to the acquisition date.

IAS 12.68(b) 3.13.840.40 For example, at the acquisition date, management concludes that full recognition is appropriate for an acquired deferred tax asset. During the measurement period the acquiree loses a significant customer, an event that will result in significantly less future taxable income than was estimated at the acquisition date. As a result, management concludes that realisation of the acquired deferred tax asset is not probable and derecognises the deferred tax asset. Since this change is the result of an event that occurred subsequent to the acquisition date, the entity accounts for the derecognition as an adjustment to income tax expense, instead of an adjustment to acquisition accounting.

3.13.850 Recognition of deferred taxes related to goodwill subsequent to a business combination

IAS 12.21B 3.13.850.10 Even when deferred taxes are not recognised in respect of goodwill at the acquisition date (see 3.13.690), they may need to be recognised subsequently. Such recognition may be required as a result of changes in the difference between the tax base of goodwill and the related financial statement carrying amount that arise subsequent to the acquisition. Whether and how those subsequent changes are recognised depends on:

- whether goodwill has a tax base (i.e. whether goodwill is deductible for tax purposes); and
- and whether the financial statement carrying amount of the goodwill at the acquisition date is less than, equal to, or greater than the tax base of goodwill at the acquisition date.

IAS 12.21B 3.13.850.20 When goodwill deductible for tax purposes has a tax base equal to or less than its carrying amount on initial recognition in a business combination, no deferred taxes are recognised in the acquisition accounting (see 3.13.690.20). However, if in subsequent periods a temporary difference arises or changes, for example due to amortisation of the goodwill for tax purposes or impairment of the carrying amount of goodwill for financial reporting purposes in later periods, then deferred tax is recognised, subject to a realisability assessment for deferred tax assets.

3.13.850.30 For example, Company R recognises goodwill of 400 as part of its accounting for a business combination. The goodwill is deductible for tax purposes; the carrying amount of the goodwill for tax purposes also is 400. In this case, no deferred tax is recognised at the date of initial recognition. If the goodwill is deductible for tax purposes over 10 years on a straight-line basis and no amortisation is recognised in the IFRS financial statements, then temporary differences will arise after the date of initial recognition of the goodwill. At the end of year one the carrying amount of the goodwill under IFRS is still 400 and the carrying amount for tax purposes would be 360 (400 - 40). If the tax rate is 25 percent then this would result in the recognition of a deferred tax liability of 10 ((400 - 360) x 25%).

IAS 12.21A   3.13.850.40 There is no tax effect from the impairment of non-deductible goodwill.

3.13.860 *Accounting for the tax effects of a reverse acquisition*

3.13.860.10 In the case of a reverse acquisition (see 2.6.170), in the consolidated financial statements, deferred tax is recognised as part of the acquisition accounting on the difference between the tax bases and the fair values of the identifiable assets and liabilities of the accounting acquiree, notwithstanding that the accounting acquiree is the legal acquirer.

IAS 12.66, 67   3.13.860.20 Similarly, changes to the accounting acquirer's deferred tax assets/liabilities generated by a reverse acquisition should in our view be recognised in profit or loss and not as part of the acquisition accounting, notwithstanding that the accounting acquirer is the legal acquiree.

IFRS 3.17   3.13.860.30 For example, Company Y and Company Z complete a business combination in which Z acquires 100 percent of the share capital of Y. However, Y is considered to be the acquirer for accounting purposes in accordance with IFRS 3. In Y and Z's jurisdiction, the tax bases of the legal acquiree's assets and liabilities are adjusted to reflect the cost of the legal acquirer's investment. The cost of Z's investment in Y is "pushed down" to adjust the tax bases of Y's assets and liabilities, notwithstanding that Y is the acquirer for accounting purposes. In our view, in the consolidated financial statements, the resulting adjustments to Y's deferred tax assets and liabilities should be recognised in profit or loss and not against goodwill.

3.13.870 *Business combination achieved in stages*

3.13.880 Changes in deferred tax recognised on a previously held investment in an associate or interest in a joint venture

IAS 12.58   3.13.880.10 An entity that obtains control over a previously held investment in an associate or interest in a joint venture in a business combination achieved in stages may change its assessment about the recognition of deferred taxes in relation to that investment (see 3.13.510). For example, an entity may have been unable to control the timing of reversal of a temporary difference related to its investment in an associate and hence recognised deferred taxes on a temporary difference related to that investment. If the entity acquires an additional interest in that associate such that it obtains control, then it may be able to assert that it can control the timing of reversal of the temporary difference and that it is not probable that such reversal will occur in the foreseeable future. In our view, as such changes in deferred taxes are an indirect consequence of the business combination, they should be recognised separately from the acquisition accounting.

3.13.890 Tax consequences of remeasuring a previously held associate or joint venture

IFRS 3.41, 42,
IAS 12.58

3.13.890.10 A business combination that is achieved in stages requires the acquirer to remeasure to fair value its previously held equity interest at the acquisition date (see 2.6.1020).

IAS 12.58

3.13.890.20 The remeasurement of an equity-accounted investee or proportionately consolidated joint venture upon obtaining control of the investee increases or decreases the financial statement carrying amount of the previously held investment. In some jurisdictions, such a transaction may not cause a change in the tax base of the investment, and therefore in such cases the temporary difference related to the investment changes. In our view, any deferred tax income or expense in respect of the change in temporary difference related to the entity's investment should be recognised separately from the acquisition accounting. This treatment is consistent with the gain or loss upon remeasurement of the previously held investment, which is recognised separately from the acquisition accounting.

3.13.900 Changes in ownership interests while retaining control

IAS 27.30

3.13.900.10 Changes in the parent's ownership interest in a subsidiary while retaining control are accounted for as equity transactions (see 2.6.530).

3.13.900.20 Examples of the tax effects of transactions with the non-controlling interests include current tax payable by the parent on the sale of shares to these parties and the effects of changes in the composition of the *tax group*. Membership of such tax groups frequently is restricted to subsidiaries in which the parent has a minimum ownership interest. Accordingly, transactions with the non-controlling interests may affect the tax attributes of a tax group or its members due to a change in the parent's ownership interest, including:

- a change in the ability to recognise deferred tax assets, for example the anticipated future profits a subsidiary that becomes a member of a tax group may provide evidence that supports the recognition of previously unrecognised deferred tax assets;
- a change in tax rates, for example adding an entity to a tax group may increase overall taxable profits to a level that results in different tax rate applying the profits of the entire tax group; and
- a change in tax bases of assets and liabilities, for example in some jurisdictions, an entity becoming part of a tax group may have its assets and liabilities rebased for tax purposes.

3.13.900.30 Because a change in a parent's ownership interest in a subsidiary while retaining control is accounted for as an equity transaction, in our view the direct tax effects of the transaction are recognised directly in equity. For example, if a parent is taxed on the gain on sale of part of its interest in a subsidiary in a transaction in which the entity does not lose control of that subsidiary, then the tax effect of the gain on the sale is recognised in equity.

3.13.900.40 In addition, there may be additional tax effects that are indirectly related to the transaction. In our view, those tax effects should be recognised separately from the accounting for the equity transaction. In order to determine whether a tax effect is a direct or an indirect effect of an equity transaction, an entity considers all relevant indicators. Factors that may indicate that a tax effect of a transaction is indirect include:

- the tax effect depends on a specific election or action of the entity, rather than being an automatic consequence of the transaction with the non-controlling interest; and
- the tax effect depends on the entity-specific attributes of the parent or its subsidiaries, rather than being an effect of the transaction with the non-controlling interest that would apply to a market participant. For example, a change in an entity's assessment of recoverability of deferred tax assets is dependent on the financial condition of the members of that tax group.

3.13.900.50 The type of transaction will determine whether the direct tax effects of these transactions are current or deferred. For example, if an entity's subsidiary sells its own shares to a third party, then the transaction might not result in a current tax effect for the parent but rather increases the temporary difference related to the investment in the subsidiary. As such, this transaction would result in the recognition of deferred tax, which would be recognised in equity. However, if an entity sells a portion of its interest in a subsidiary to a third party at a taxable gain, then that would result in a current tax effect that is recognised in equity.

3.13.900.60 In our view, similar to the accounting for the tax effects of business combinations discussion in 3.13.820.10, the tax effect of events that occur, or actions that are undertaken, subsequent to a transaction with a non-controlling interest should not be anticipated.

3.13.1000 **Disclosure**

IAS 12.79-88 3.13.1000.10 Extensive disclosures regarding deferred tax are required, which are illustrated in KPMG's series of illustrative financial statements. This commentary focuses on areas of uncertainty in practice.

IAS 12.81(c),
85 3.13.1000.20 A reconciliation between the applicable statutory tax rate and the entity's effective tax rate (expressed in percentages or in absolute numbers) is required. The applicable tax rate can be determined in one of two ways for a group that operates in multiple tax jurisdictions:

- based on the statutory tax rate applicable to the parent entity; in this case the reconciliation will include a separate line item representing the effect of tax rates in different jurisdictions; or

- using the average statutory tax rate applicable to the group, calculated on a weighted average basis.

IAS 12.81(f),   3.13.1000.30 Unrecognised temporary differences in respect of investments in subsidiaries,
87, IE.Ex3   associates and joint ventures (see 3.13.510) are disclosed. The disclosure is not the amount of unrecognised deferred tax; rather, it is the gross temporary difference. For example, Company P has acquired Company Q and has recognised Q's post-acquisition earnings of 500 in its consolidated financial statements. If these earnings were distributed, then tax of 50 would be payable by P. P did not recognise this deferred tax since it met the criteria for non-recognition. In the notes to the financial statements of P the temporary difference of 500 should be disclosed. In addition, entities are encouraged to disclose the tax consequences of a distribution, being 50 in this example.

IAS 12.81(g)   3.13.1000.40 An entity is required to disclose, in respect of each *type* of temporary difference, the amount of deferred tax assets and liabilities recognised in the statement of financial position. In our view, this could be interpreted in one of two ways:

- Disclosure based on the statement of financial position captions (e.g. disclosure of deferred tax assets and deferred tax liabilities (separately) in respect of property, plant and equipment). This method of presentation is shown in KPMG's series of illustrative financial statements.
- Disclosure based on the reason for the temporary difference (e.g. excess of wear and tear tax deductions over depreciation and amortisation).

IAS 12.81   3.13.1000.50 In our view, it is not appropriate to disclose gross deductible temporary differences because, under IFRSs, it is *recognised* temporary differences that are required to be disclosed. The following example illustrates the two methods of disclosure:

Deductible temporary differences	Inappropriate	Appropriate
Property, plant and equipment	1,000	800
Intangible assets	400	300
Valuation allowance	(300)	-
Total deductible temporary differences	1,100	1,100

3.13.1010 **Future developments**

3.13.1010.10 In March 2009 the IASB published ED/2009/2 *Income Tax*, in which it proposed to replace IAS 12 with a new IFRS. In light of responses to the ED, the IASB narrowed the scope of the project to focus on resolving problems in practice under IAS 12, without changing the fundamental approach under IAS 12 and preferably without increasing divergence with US GAAP. An ED is scheduled for the second half of 2010.

3.13.1010.10 The overall objective of the comprehensive financial statement presentation project is to establish a global standard that prescribes the basis for presentation of financial statements of an entity that are consistent over time, and that promote comparability between entities. In July 2010 the IASB posted a staff draft of a proposed ED reflecting tentative decisions made to date to obtain further stakeholder feedback. The staff draft proposes that deferred tax assets and liabilities be presented as current or non-current according to the classification of the related asset or liability. An ED is scheduled for the first quarter of 2011.

3.14 Contingent assets and liabilities
(IAS 37)

3.14 Contingent assets and liabilities

(IAS 37)

Overview of currently effective requirements

- Contingent liabilities are present obligations with uncertainties about either the probability of outflows of resources or the amount of the outflows, and possible obligations whose existence is uncertain.

- Contingent liabilities are not recognised other than in connection with a business combination.

- Details of contingent liabilities are disclosed in the notes to the financial statements unless the probability of an outflow is remote.

- Contingent assets are possible assets whose existence is uncertain.

- Contingent assets are not recognised in the statement of financial position. If an inflow of economic benefits is probable, then details are disclosed in the notes.

Currently effective requirements

This publication reflects IFRSs in issue at 1 August 2010. The currently effective requirements cover annual periods beginning on 1 January 2010. The requirements related to this topic are derived mainly from IAS 37 *Provisions, Contingent Liabilities and Contingent Assets*.

Forthcoming requirements and future developments

When a currently effective requirement will be changed by a new requirement that is issued but is not yet effective, it is marked with a # as a **forthcoming requirement** and the impact of the change is explained in the accompanying boxed text. In respect of this topic no forthcoming requirements are noted.

The currently effective or forthcoming requirements may be subject to **future developments** and a brief outline of the relevant project is given in 3.14.80.

3.14.10 Definitions

IAS 37.10, 29 3.14.10.10 A *contingent liability* is a liability of sufficient uncertainty that it does not qualify for recognition as a provision (see 3.12), unless acquired in a business combination (see 3.14.30.20). The uncertainty may arise due to any of the following reasons:

- It is a *possible* obligation, i.e. one whose existence will be confirmed by the occurrence or non-occurrence of uncertain future events not wholly within the control of the entity. For example, when an entity is jointly and severally liable for an obligation, the portion of the obligation that is expected to be met by other parties is an example of a possible obligation.
- It is a *present* obligation, but it is *not* more likely than not that there will be an outflow of resources embodying economic benefits, so that the probability of an outflow is 50 percent or less. An example is a claim against an entity, when the entity concludes that it is liable, but that it is likely to defend the case successfully.
- It is a *present* obligation, but its amount cannot be estimated reliably. These cases are expected to be extremely rare.

3.14.10.15 In our view, when a provision is measured at its best estimate, which is less than the amount that could be payable, the difference between the two amounts is *not* a contingent liability (see 3.12.110.40).

IAS 37.10   3.14.10.20 A *contingent asset* is a possible asset that arises from past events and whose existence will be confirmed by the occurrence or non-occurrence of uncertain future events not wholly within the control of the entity.

3.14.20 Recognition

3.14.30 *Contingent liabilities*

IFRS 3.37(c),   3.14.30.10 Contingent liabilities are not recognised in the statement of financial position
IAS 37.27   unless they were assumed in a business combination.

IAS 37.30   3.14.30.15 Contingent liabilities are reviewed continuously to assess whether an outflow of resources has become probable. If the recognition criteria are met, then a liability is recognised in the financial statements in the period in which the change in probability occurs.

IFRS 3.23,   3.14.30.20 Contingent liabilities assumed in a business combination are recognised in
56   accordance with the requirements of IFRS 3 *Business Combinations*. An acquirer recognises a contingent liability assumed in a business combination if it is a present obligation and its fair value can be measured reliably. Subsequently they are measured at the higher of the amount that would be recognised as a provision (see 3.12.110) and the amount recognised on acquisition, less any subsequent amortisation when appropriate. An example of accounting for a contingent liability assumed in a business combination related to a legal case is included in 2.6.900. A contingent liability that is a *possible* obligation is not recognised even if its fair value can be measured reliably.

3.14.30.30 [Not used]

IAS 37.14   3.14.30.40 If a present obligation relates to a past event (i.e. more likely than not), the possibility of an outflow is probable and a reliable estimate can be made, then the obligation is not a contingent liability, but instead is a liability for which a provision is required (see 3.12.30).

IAS 37.53 3.14.30.50 The expectation that an outflow related to an obligation will be reimbursed, for example, that an environmental obligation will be covered by an insurance policy, does not affect the assessment of the probability of an outflow for the obligation.

IFRS 3.27 3.14.30.55 If a seller is obliged contractually to indemnify the acquirer for a specific liability assumed in a business combination, then IFRS 3 requires the acquirer to recognise an asset at the same time, measured using the same measurement basis as the related liability. See 2.6.910 for detailed guidance on indemnification assets under IFRS 3.

3.14.30.60 An acquisition agreement in a business combination may require the seller to provide an indemnity of a specific contingent liability assumed by the acquirer in the acquisition. For example, in the event that a legal claim recognised by the acquirer as a contingent liability on acquisition is not settled subsequently in favour of the acquirer, the seller is required to reimburse the acquirer for any costs incurred in respect of the contingent liability. The existence of such an indemnity should not affect the amount recognised by the acquirer as a contingent liability in the accounting for the acquisition; however, it may give rise to an indemnification asset (see 2.6.910).

3.14.30.70 [Not used]

IAS 10.8, 14 3.14.30.80 If events after the reporting date confirm the existence of a liability, including the case in which the liability affects the entity's ability to continue as a going concern, then adjustments may be required (see 2.9.20).

IAS 39.2(e), 47(c) 3.14.30.90 Financial guarantee contracts such as certain letters of credit are within the scope of IAS 39 *Financial Instruments: Recognition and Measurement* (see 3.6.35) unless the issuer of the contract has previously asserted explicitly that it regards such contracts as insurance contracts, and has used accounting applicable to insurance contracts, in which case the issuer may choose to apply either IAS 39 or IFRS 4 *Insurance Contracts* (see 5.10.20) to such contracts. Generally, when a financial guarantee recognised under IAS 39 or IFRS 4 becomes probable of being exercised, the provision is measured in accordance with IAS 37. However, the remaining requirements of IAS 37, e.g. disclosures, do not apply. Non-financial guarantees related to products or services are addressed in 3.12.360 that deals with warranties.

3.14.40 *Contingent assets*

IAS 37.31, 33 3.14.40.10 Contingent assets are not recognised in the statement of financial position because this may result in the recognition of income that may never be realised.

IAS 37.33, 35 3.14.40.20 When realisation of a contingent asset is virtually certain, it is no longer considered contingent and is recognised as an asset. In our view, virtually certain generally should be interpreted as a probability of greater than 90 percent. An item previously regarded as a contingent asset may become virtually certain of being realised, and therefore qualify for recognition as an asset. In this case an asset is recognised in the period in which the change from less than virtually certain to virtually certain occurs (see also 2.9.30.15).

3.14.40.30 For example, Company L leases a property to Company B under an operating lease. The contract is non-cancellable for 10 years. On 30 November 2009, before the end of the contract, B withdraws from the contract and is required to pay a cancellation penalty of 450. In our view, generally L should recognise a receivable of 450 and corresponding income once B cancels the contract.

3.14.40.40 However, an asset should not be recognised until the contract is cancelled. For example, if in the above example in 3.14.40.30, B had cancelled the contract on 28 February 2010, then L would not recognise a receivable for the cancellation penalty as at 31 December 2009. The event that gives rise to the asset is the cancellation of the contract. Therefore, if the cancellation happens only after the reporting date, then an asset is not recognised at the reporting date (see 2.9.30).

3.14.50 Disclosure

3.14.60 *Contingent liabilities*

IAS 37.86, 91   3.14.60.10 Contingent liabilities are disclosed unless the likelihood of an outflow of resources embodying economic benefits is remote. Disclosures include the nature of the contingency, when practicable, the estimated financial effect, an indication of the uncertainties and the possibility of any reimbursement. When disclosure is impractical, that fact is stated.

3.14.60.20 The type of information that should be disclosed in respect of a contingent liability related to a legal claim includes:

- an explanation of the claim;
- the fact that no liability has been recognised;
- an explanation of why the entity does not accept liability under the claim;
- information about the estimated amount of the liability or an explanation of why this cannot be estimated reasonably; and
- information about any reimbursements that may be claimed if the defence is not successful, e.g. amounts that are reimbursable under an insurance policy.

IAS 37.92   3.14.60.30 In the extremely rare case that disclosure could prejudice seriously the entity's position in a dispute with another party, the entity need only disclose the general nature of the dispute and the reasons for not disclosing the information (see 3.12.810).

IAS 1.25   3.14.60.40 If crystallisation of a contingent liability would affect an entity's ability to continue as a going concern, then additional disclosures are required.

3.14.70 *Contingent assets*

IAS 37.89-91   3.14.70.10 Contingent assets are disclosed when an inflow of economic benefits is considered more likely than not to occur. The disclosure includes the nature and, when practicable, the estimated financial effects of the contingent asset. When disclosure is not practical, that fact is stated. The disclosures about contingent assets should avoid giving misleading indications of the likelihood of income arising.

IAS 37.92   3.14.70.20 Consistent with contingent liabilities, in the extremely rare case that disclosure of a contingent asset could prejudice seriously the entity's position in a dispute with another party, the entity need only disclose the general nature of the dispute and the reasons for not disclosing the information.

3.14.80 **Future developments**

3.14.80.10 In June 2005 the IASB published ED *Proposed Amendments to IAS 37 Provisions, Contingent Liabilities and Contingent Assets and IAS 19 Employee Benefits.* The proposed standard would result in significant changes from current practice in accounting for provisions, contingent liabilities and contingent assets.

3.14.80.20 Under the proposals, contingent liabilities and contingent assets would no longer exist. Instead the term "contingency" would be used to describe uncertainty about the level of benefits (obligations) inherent in an asset (liability), rather than uncertainty about whether the asset (liability) exists. Probability would not be a criterion for the recognition of an asset or liability (see 3.12.880.10). A final standard is scheduled for the first half of 2011.

4.1   General

(IAS 1)

Chapter 4

4. Specific statement of comprehensive income items

4.1 General
(IAS 1)

Overview of currently effective requirements

- A statement of comprehensive income is presented as either a single statement or an income statement (displaying components of profit or loss) with a separate statement of comprehensive income (beginning with profit or loss and displaying components of other comprehensive income).

- An analysis of expenses is required, either by nature or by function, in the statement of comprehensive income or in the notes.

- While IFRSs require certain items to be presented in the statement of comprehensive income, there is no prescribed format.

- Material items of income or expense are presented separately either in the notes or, when necessary, in the statement of comprehensive income.

- The presentation or disclosure of items of income and expense characterised as "extraordinary items" is prohibited.

- Items of income and expense are not offset unless required or permitted by another IFRS, or when the amounts relate to similar transactions or events that are not material.

- In our view, components of profit or loss should not be presented net of tax unless required specifically.

- Reclassification adjustments from other comprehensive income to profit or loss are disclosed in the statement of comprehensive income or in the notes to the financial statements.

- Amounts of income tax related to each component of other comprehensive income are disclosed in the statement of comprehensive income or in the notes.

Currently effective requirements

This publication reflects IFRSs in issue at 1 August 2010. The currently effective requirements cover annual periods beginning on 1 January 2010. The requirements related to this topic are derived mainly from IAS 1 *Presentation of Financial Statements*.

Forthcoming requirements and future developments

When a currently effective requirement will be changed by a new requirement that is issued but is not yet effective, it is marked with a # as a **forthcoming requirement** and the impact of the change is explained in the accompanying boxed text. In respect of this topic no forthcoming requirements are noted.

When a significant change to the currently effective or forthcoming requirements is expected, it is marked with a * as an area that may be subject to **future developments** and a brief outline of the relevant project is given in 4.1.220.

4.1.10 **Format of the statement of comprehensive income***

IAS 1.81   4.1.10.05 Comprehensive income is presented in either (see 2.1.10.10):

- a single statement of comprehensive income (which includes all components of profit or loss and other comprehensive income); or
- the form of two statements, being an "income statement" (which displays components of profit or loss) followed immediately by a separate "statement of comprehensive income" (which begins with profit or loss as reported in the income statement and displays components of other comprehensive income to sum to total comprehensive income for the period).

IAS 1.82-84   4.1.10.10 While the formats of the statement of comprehensive income are not prescribed, certain items are required to be presented in the statement of comprehensive income. In practice there is limited flexibility as to the order of these items, which tends to follow the order of the items set out in IAS 1.

IAS 1.45   4.1.10.20 The chosen format of the statement of comprehensive income is applied consistently. In our view, if an entity has no items of other comprehensive income, then it may present a single performance statement ending at a line "profit or loss for the year and total comprehensive income" (or similar) that is titled "statement of comprehensive income"; such a statement should not be titled "income statement".

IAS 1.85   4.1.10.30 Additional line items, headings and subtotals are presented when this is necessary for an understanding of the entity's financial performance (see 4.1.80).

4.1.10.40 Both formats for presenting the statement of comprehensive income are illustrated in KPMG's series of illustrative financial statements.

4.1.20 **Classification of expenses***

IAS 1.99, 100 4.1.20.10 Expenses are classified according to their nature (e.g. staff costs, depreciation and amortisation) or function (e.g. cost of sales, distribution and administration). This analysis may be presented in the statement of comprehensive income or in the notes. We prefer the analysis to be presented in the statement of comprehensive income. If an entity chooses to present the analysis of expenses in the notes to the financial statements, then it ensures that its presentation in the statement of comprehensive income is not misleading and is relevant to an understanding of the financial statements (see 4.1.82).

IAS 1.99, 105 4.1.20.20 IAS 1 requires management to select the most relevant and reliable presentation of expenses; an entity's choice often depends on the nature of the entity and the industry in which it operates.

IAS 1.45 4.1.20.30 The chosen classification generally is applied consistently from one period to the next. A change of classification is made only if a new or revised IFRS requires a change in presentation or if the change will result in more relevant information, for example following a significant change in the nature of operations (see also 2.8.70).

4.1.20.40 In our view, presentation of the effect of a particular event or circumstances as a single amount in the statement of comprehensive income that overrides the requirement to classify expenses either by nature or function can be justified only in very rare cases.

4.1.30 *Classification by function*

IAS 1.103 4.1.30.10 When expenses are classified according to function, expenses are allocated to, for example, cost of sales, distribution or administrative activities. Only in the rare cases that expenses cannot be allocated to a specific function are they classified as "other expenses".

4.1.30.20 There is no guidance in IFRSs on how specific expenses are allocated to functions. An entity establishes its own definitions of functions such as cost of sales, distribution and administrative activities, and apply these definitions consistently. It may be appropriate to disclose the definitions used.

4.1.30.30 All expenses, including staff costs, depreciation and amortisation, are allocated to the appropriate functions. In our view, staff costs, depreciation and amortisation can be allocated to specific functions in almost every case.

4.1.30.40 In our view, cost of sales includes only expenses directly or indirectly attributable to the production process, such as direct materials, labour costs, the depreciation of assets used in manufacturing, and repair and maintenance costs related to production. Other costs not attributable to the production process, such as marketing and advertising expenses, are classified as selling and distribution costs.

IAS 1.104 4.1.30.50 Additional information based on the nature of expenses (e.g. depreciation, amortisation and staff costs) is disclosed in the notes to the financial statements.

4.1.40 *Classification by nature*

IAS 1.102   4.1.40.10 When classification by nature is used, expenses are aggregated according to their nature (e.g. purchases of materials, transport costs, depreciation and amortisation, staff costs and advertising costs).

4.1.50 Employee benefits and restructuring expenses

4.1.60 *Employee benefits (staff costs)*

IAS 1.102,   4.1.60.10 Staff costs are presented separately if expenses are classified by nature. In
104   addition, staff costs are required to be disclosed in the notes if expenses are classified by function.

4.1.60.20 IAS 1 does not contain specific guidance on what to include in staff costs. In our view, staff costs comprise all costs directly attributable to personnel, including salaries, social security expenses, pension costs, health benefits and share-based compensation received in the capacity as an employee.

4.1.60.30 In some countries, housing and other infrastructure assets (e.g. schools) are provided to staff and their families. In this case, in our view any rent paid by the entity should be included in staff costs. If the property is owned by the employer, then in our view depreciation and maintenance of the property also should be included in staff costs.

4.1.70 *Restructuring expenses*

IAS 1.BC56   4.1.70.10 In our view, if an entity chooses to disclose "results of operating activities" (see 4.1.90), then restructuring costs normally should be presented as part of operating results as they represent costs of restructuring ongoing operations. If the restructuring charge is significant, then it may be appropriate to disclose the effect(s) of the restructuring charge either in the statement of comprehensive income or in the notes to the financial statements.

4.1.80 Additional line items*

IAS 1.85, 86   4.1.80.10 An entity presents additional items of income or expense, headings or subtotals when relevant to an understanding of the entity's financial performance. Additional line items are described appropriately in accordance with their nature or function, consistent with the way that the entity presents its analysis of expenses. Factors to consider when determining whether to present additional items include materiality and the nature and function of the components of income and expenses.

IAS 1.29-31,   4.1.80.20 Materiality is a factor when making judgements about disclosure, for example
86   when items may be aggregated, and about the use of additional line items, headings and subtotals. It also is relevant to the positioning of these disclosures – an item may be sufficiently material to warrant disclosure in the statement of comprehensive income or it may warrant disclosure only in the notes to the financial statements. In some cases

950

this may mean that a specific disclosure requirement in an IFRS need not be satisfied if the information is not material.

IAS 1.7, 8.5   4.1.80.30 Omissions or misstatements of items are material if they could, individually or collectively, influence the economic decisions of users taken on the basis of the financial statements. Materiality depends on the size and nature of the omission or misstatement judged in the surrounding circumstances. The size or nature of the item, or a combination of both, could be the determining factor.

IAS 1.17(c),   4.1.80.40 In our view, when assessing materiality the effect of a transaction or an event
86, 97, 98   as a whole should be considered even if, for presentation purposes, the effect will be allocated to different line items for the purpose of classification by nature or function. For example, Company P has incurred restructuring costs related to various parts of its business. If P analyses its expenses by function, then it will allocate the total restructuring costs to the identified functions to ensure that the analysis of expenses is presented using a consistent classification method. However, in assessing materiality, the total restructuring costs are assessed, instead of the allocated amounts being assessed in isolation from each other.

4.1.82 *Presentation and disclosure*

IAS 1.29, 30,   4.1.82.10 Disclosure in the notes to the financial statements is sufficient for many items
97   that are material individually. We prefer separate presentation to be made in the statement of comprehensive income only when necessary for an understanding of the entity's financial performance. In such cases the notes to the financial statements should disclose an additional explanation of the nature of the amount presented.

IAS 1.29, 45,   4.1.82.20 Individually material items are classified in accordance with their nature or
99   function, consistent with the classification of items that are not individually material. In our view, the nature of an item does not change merely because it is individually material. We believe that consistent presentation by classification requires individually material items to be presented within, or adjacent to, the remaining aggregated amounts of the same nature or function (see 4.1.20). For example, a separately presented material impairment loss on an investment is classified as finance costs if other impairment losses on similar investments are included in that line item.

4.1.82.30 We prefer the inclusion of a subtotal of all items classified as having the same nature or function. For example, when an individually material cost of sale (e.g. a write-down of inventory damaged in a fire) is presented separately from "other cost of sales", we prefer that a subtotal for the line item "cost of sales" also be presented.

4.1.82.40 When the effect of a particular transaction, event or circumstance is pervasive, affecting a number of line items, it may be appropriate to disclose in the notes to the financial statements the total impact of the event. In this case, in our view an analysis of related amounts and the line items affected is disclosed in the notes, together with a description of the circumstances. An entity also may wish to disclose in the statement of comprehensive income the related element of each line item affected. This may be achieved in a number of ways, for example by sub-analysing (and subtotalling) the appropriate line items or by presenting the individually material items in a separate column, together with a column in which the total for each line item is presented.

4.1.82.50 Set out below are extracts from statements of comprehensive income illustrating possible presentations of individually material items.

Example 1 – Parenthesis

Cost of sales (including loss of inventory destroyed in fire of 175)	1,000

Example 2 – Subtotal

Revenue		1,600
Cost of sales		
Loss of inventory destroyed in fire	175	
Other cost of sales	825	
		(1,000)
Gross profit		600

Example 3 – Columns

	Excluding restructuring	Restructuring costs	Total
Raw materials and consumables	2,500	50	2,550
Employee benefit expense	1,000	200	1,200
Depreciation and amortisation	750	100	850
Other expenses	400	50	450

4.1.82.60 [Not used]

<table><tr><td>IAS 1.38,
40-44</td><td>4.1.82.70 When an item of income or expense is presented or disclosed separately in the current period, comparable amounts recognised in the comparative period are presented or disclosed as comparative information. This may arise, for example, when expenses in respect of a single event or transaction are recognised in both the current and comparative periods. The presentation of comparative amounts for an individually material item of income or expense may be appropriate even if the item was not presented or disclosed separately in the annual financial statements of the prior period.</td></tr></table>

4.1.84 Use of the description "unusual" or "exceptional"*

<table><tr><td>IAS 1.17(c),
97</td><td>4.1.84.10 IFRSs do not describe events or items of income or expense as "unusual" or "exceptional".</td></tr></table>

4.1.84.20 In our view, an item is not exceptional or unusual merely because there is a requirement to present or disclose that item separately, either in the statement of comprehensive income or in the notes to the financial statements.

4.1.84.30 In our view, if the description exceptional is used, then its use should be infrequent and reserved for items that justify a prominence greater than that achieved by separate presentation or disclosure. For example, it may be appropriate to characterise items such as costs associated with a natural disaster as unusual or exceptional.

4.1.84.40 When an item is characterised as exceptional, in our view the description used should include the nature of the item (e.g. exceptional impairment loss on property affected by earthquake), and the notes to the financial statements should include an additional explanation of the nature of the amount and its characterisation as exceptional. We believe that the description of an item simply as an exceptional item does not meet the requirement for amounts to be classified by their nature or function.

4.1.84.50 In our view, when classifying expenses by nature or function, any amount described as unusual or exceptional should be classified in the same way as non-exceptional amounts of the same function or nature (see 4.1.20).

4.1.84.60 If an entity chooses to use a descriptor that is not defined in IFRSs (e.g. exceptional), then we prefer that the term be used consistently and that its use is described in the notes to the financial statements.

4.1.84.70 Describing items of a similar nature or function as exceptional in consecutive periods is inconsistent with a characterisation of these items as unusual or non-recurring, unless the amounts relate to a single transaction or event that is recognised over several financial periods.

4.1.84.80 A restructuring is one example of an event that may give rise to amounts that are individually material. In our view, such events are not unusual and generally should not be described as exceptional. However, it may be appropriate nonetheless to disclose or present the effect(s) of a significant restructuring separately, either in the statement of comprehensive income (following an appropriate presentation (see 4.1.82)) or in the notes to the financial statements.

4.1.86 Extraordinary items

IAS 1.87 4.1.86.10 IFRSs make no distinction between ordinary and extraordinary activities. The presentation, disclosure or characterisation of items of income and expense as "extraordinary items" in the statement of comprehensive income or in the notes is prohibited.

4.1.90 Operating result

IAS 1.82, 4.1.90.10 The disclosure of the results of *operating* activities is not required as a separate
BC55, BC56 line item in the statement of comprehensive income. However, entities may provide a subtotal before profit or loss for the year voluntarily. In our view, "results from operating activities" may be an appropriate subtotal.

IAS 7.6   4.1.90.20 The terms "operating" and "non-operating" are not defined in the context of the statement of comprehensive income. However, the standard on the statement of cash flows defines operating activities as "the principal revenue-producing activities of an entity...". If an entity wishes to present a subtotal for operating result, then this definition may be an appropriate starting point in determining the components of operating income.

IAS 1.BC56   4.1.90.30 Only items that clearly are not related to operating activities are presented outside of operating result.

4.1.90.40 In our view, gains and losses on the disposal of property, plant and equipment generally are part of the operating activities of an entity and should be shown below gross profit but within operating results, perhaps as part of other operating income or expense. This is an example of when the effect of a single transaction is classified differently in each of the statement of cash flows and the statement of comprehensive income. The cash proceeds from the sale would be presented within investing activities in the statement of cash flows and not as an operating cash flow (see 2.3.20).

4.1.100 Sales of financial investments

4.1.100.10 Gains (losses) on the disposal of financial investments generally are included in finance income (finance costs).

4.1.100.20 In our view, entities that trade routinely in financial instruments, or for which investing activities are part of the ordinary operations, should present the net results of these activities within operating result. The gross proceeds on disposal of investments generally are not presented as revenue in the statement of comprehensive income.

4.1.110 Share of profit of equity accounted investees

IAS 1.82,   4.1.110.10 The share of profit or loss of equity accounted investees (associates and
IG6, 28.38   equity accounted joint ventures) attributable to an investor (i.e. after tax and non-controlling interests) is presented as a separate line item before tax in the statement of comprehensive income. This presentation generally results in a reconciling item in the tax rate reconciliation (see 3.13.1000.20).

4.1.120 Alternative earnings measures

4.1.120.10 An entity may wish to present alternative earnings measures such as EBITDA (earnings before interest, tax, depreciation and amortisation), EBIT (earnings before interest and tax) or headline earnings in the statement of comprehensive income. IFRSs do not prohibit alternative earnings measures being presented, but when expenses are classified by either their nature or function in the statement of comprehensive income, sometimes this precludes the presentation of alternative earnings measures in the statement of comprehensive income, e.g. the use of EBITDA where depreciation is not disclosed separately in a presentation by function.

4.1.120.20 National regulators in the European Union (EU) and elsewhere may have more restrictive requirements. In some jurisdictions regulations may prohibit various presentation formats, and therefore these requirements also are considered. For example, according to the United States Securities and Exchange Commission *Final Rule: Conditions for Use of Non-GAAP Financial Measures* (e.g. EBITDA, "special" earnings per share), such measures are shown outside of the financial statements.

4.1.120.30 In the EU the Committee of European Securities Regulators has issued a *Recommendation on Alternative Performance Measures* (APMs). While the recommendation does not prohibit the presentation of APMs, it provides guidance to ensure that their use is not misleading.

4.1.120.40 In our view, if an alternative measure of performance such as EBITDA or EBIT is presented in the financial statements, then a definition, and possibly a reconciliation of the earnings measure to subtotals in the statement of comprehensive income, should be given so that users are clear regarding the elements of revenue and expense that are included in and excluded from the measure.

4.1.130 *EBITDA*

4.1.130.10 The presentation of EBITDA as the primary disclosure in the statement of comprehensive income depends on the classification of expenses adopted, and whether that classification is given in the statement of comprehensive income or in the notes.

4.1.130.20 In our view, the presentation of EBITDA usually is possible by presenting a sub-analysis of earnings while classifying items of income and expense to the appropriate line items.

4.1.130.30 For example, the statement of comprehensive income could be presented as follows:

Extract from the statement of comprehensive income		
Revenue		500
Expenses (classified by nature or function either in the statement of comprehensive income or in the notes)		(400)
Analysis of profit from operations:		
Profit before interest, tax, depreciation and amortisation (EBITDA)	120	
Depreciation and amortisation	(20)	
Results from operating activities		100

4.1.130.40 As an alternative an entity could disclose EBITDA as a footnote to the statement of comprehensive income beneath earnings per share, in a note to the financial statements, or as supplemental information (see 5.8).

4.1.130.50 If an entity elects to classify its expenses by nature, then it also is possible to present EBITDA as a subtotal in the statement of comprehensive income. For example:

Extract from the statement of comprehensive income	
Revenue	500
Other income	10
Raw material and consumables used	(210)
Staff costs	(100)
Other expenses, other than depreciation and amortisation	(80)
Profit before interest, tax, depreciation and amortisation (EBITDA)	**120**
Depreciation and amortisation	(20)
Results from operating activities	100

4.1.140 *EBIT*

4.1.140.10 It is possible to show EBIT in the statement of comprehensive income, regardless of the classification of expenses or the entity's definition of interest for the purposes of EBIT. For example, an entity that excludes foreign exchange gains and losses from its definition of interest, and includes these gains and losses in finance income and finance costs, might present EBIT as follows:

Extract from the statement of comprehensive income		
Results from operating activities		100
Net foreign exchange losses	(30)	
Profit before interest and tax (EBIT)	**70**	
Interest income	20	
Interest expense	(30)	
Net finance results		(40)
Profit before tax		60

IAS 1.82 4.1.140.20 Although finance costs are presented separately in the statement of comprehensive income, in our view the above split between interest and other finance costs is acceptable. Some entities that present EBIT include all finance costs in the interest line. In our view, this also is acceptable as long as the definition of EBIT is clear.

4.1.150 Changes in estimates

IAS 1.35 4.1.150.10 In our view, changes in estimates, for example reversals of provisions or impairment losses, generally should be presented in the same line item (classification) within the statement of comprehensive income as the original estimate.

IAS 8.39 4.1.150.20 Therefore, if the original estimate was classified as cost of sales, then changes in the estimate, whether they are additional charges (debits) or reductions in amounts previously charged (credits), also should be presented in cost of sales. The nature and amount of a change in accounting estimate that affects the current period or is expected to have an impact on future periods should be disclosed.

4.1.150.30 Sometimes, however, it may be acceptable to present the effect of a reduction in an estimate of an expense within other income even if the original estimate was classified as other expenses. This might be appropriate when, for example, the reversal is significant and otherwise would result in the line item "other expenses" being a net credit. In this situation we prefer "other income" and "other expenses" to be presented in consecutive line items.

4.1.160 Income tax

IFRS 5.33,   4.1.160.10 In our view, all items of profit or loss are required to be presented in the
IAS 12.77,   statement of comprehensive income before the effect of income tax (i.e. gross) un-
28.11   less specifically required to be presented after the effect of income tax, e.g. share of profit of equity accounted investees (see 4.1.110) and amounts related to discontinued operations (see 5.4.220).

4.1.170 Offsetting

IAS 1.32-35   4.1.170.10 Items of income and expense are offset when required or permitted by an IFRS; or when gains, losses and related expenses arise from the same transaction or event or from similar individually immaterial transactions and events. For example, in our view if an entity buys and then within a short timeframe sells foreign currency, then the transactions should be presented on a net basis in the statement of comprehensive income.

4.1.170.20 In our view, when a financial asset and financial liability qualify to be offset (see 5.6.490), then the related income and expense items also should be offset.

4.1.175 *Finance costs*

IFRS 7.IG13,   4.1.175.10 Finance costs are required to be presented as a separate line item in the
IAS 1.82(b)   statement of comprehensive income. In our view, the presentation should not be of "net finance results" unless finance costs and finance income also are presented as separate line items in the statement of comprehensive income, with the net amount being a subtotal of finance costs and finance income. See 4.6.540 for further guidance.

4.1.180 *Pro forma*

4.1.180.10 When there have been significant changes in the structure of an entity (e.g. following a major business combination), the entity may wish to present a *pro forma* income statement. IFRSs do not prohibit such presentation, but in our view any *pro forma* information should be identified clearly as such and presented in a manner that is not misleading. Also, the basis of preparation of the *pro forma* information should be explained clearly.

4.1.180.20 Although a *pro forma* income statement may be appropriate as supplemental information, it is not a substitute for an income statement that complies with IFRSs.

4.1.180.30 See 2.1.80 for further guidance on the presentation of *pro forma* information.

4.1.190 Other comprehensive income*

IAS 1.7, 82 4.1.190.10 Other comprehensive income comprises items of income and expense, including reclassification adjustments, that are not recognised in profit or loss as required or permitted by IFRSs. Examples include the revaluation of property, plant and equipment (see 3.2.300) and intangible assets (see 3.3.280), foreign exchange differences on the translation of foreign operations (see 2.7.230 and 300), the effects of cash flow hedging (see 3.7.80), the remeasurement of available-for-sale financial assets (see 3.6.830), the immediate recognition of actuarial gains and losses on defined benefit plans (see 4.4.560) and the share of other comprehensive income of associates and joint ventures accounted for using the equity method (see 3.5.500).

4.1.200 *Reclassification adjustments*

IAS 1.93, 96 4.1.200.10 Certain items initially recognised in other comprehensive income subsequently are reclassified (formerly referred to as "recycled") to profit or loss. Generally IFRSs specify when amounts recognised previously in other comprehensive income are reclassified to profit or loss. For example, unrealised gains on available-for-sale financial assets initially recognised in other comprehensive income are reclassified to profit or loss when these financial assets are disposed of (see 3.6.830.20). However, there are instances in which components of other comprehensive income are not reclassified to profit or loss in subsequent periods. Examples include revaluations of property, plant and equipment (see 3.2.300) and intangible assets (see 3.3.280), and actuarial gains and losses in respect of defined benefit plans recognised directly in other comprehensive income (see 4.4.560). Changes in the valuation of property, plant and equipment and intangible assets may be transferred to retained earnings in subsequent periods as the asset is used or when it is derecognised (see 3.2.410 and 3.3.310 respectively).

IAS 1.92, 4.1.200.20 Reclassification adjustments to profit or loss of amounts recognised previously
94, IG6 in other comprehensive income are disclosed separately for each component of other comprehensive income. An entity may present these reclassification adjustments either in the statement of comprehensive income or in the notes to the financial statements. If the entity chooses the latter approach, then it presents the components of other comprehensive income after any related reclassification adjustments.

4.1.210 *Effect of income tax*

IAS 1.90 4.1.210.10 The amount of income tax related to each component of other comprehensive income, including reclassification adjustments, is disclosed either in the statement of comprehensive income or in the notes to the financial statements.

IAS 1.91 4.1.210.20 An entity may present components of other comprehensive income either net of the related tax effects, or gross of tax with a separate line item for the tax effects related to those components. The latter presentation is illustrated in KPMG's series of illustrative financial statements.

4.1.220 Future developments

4.1.220.10 In May 2010 the IASB published ED/2010/5 *Presentation of Items of Other Comprehensive Income – Proposed Amendments to IAS 1*, which proposes to:

- change the title of the statement of comprehensive income to statement of profit or loss and other comprehensive income; however, an entity is still allowed to use other titles;
- present comprehensive income and its components in a single statement of profit or loss and other comprehensive income, with items of other comprehensive income presented in a separate section from profit or loss within that statement, thereby eliminating the alternative permitted by current IAS 1 to present a separate income statement; and
- present separately the items of other comprehensive income that would be reclassified to profit or loss in the future from those that would never be reclassified to profit or loss.

4.1.220.20 The final amendments are scheduled for the fourth quarter of 2010.

4.1.220.30 The overall objective of the comprehensive financial statement presentation project is to establish a global standard that prescribes the basis for presentation of financial statements of an entity that are consistent over time, and that promote comparability between entities. The financial statement presentation project is conducted in three phases:

- Phase A was completed in September 2007 with the release of a revised IAS 1;
- Phase B is in progress and addresses the more fundamental issues related to financial statement presentation; and
- Phase C has not been initiated, but is expected to address issues related to interim financial statements.

4.1.220.40 In July 2010 the IASB posted a staff draft of a proposed ED reflecting tentative decisions made to date in respect of phase B to obtain further stakeholder feedback. An ED is scheduled for the first quarter of 2011.

4.2 Revenue

(Framework, IAS 11, IAS 18, IFRIC 13, IFRIC 15, IFRIC 18, SIC-27, SIC-31)

4.2 Revenue

(Framework, IAS 11, IAS 18, IFRIC 13, IFRIC 15, IFRIC 18, SIC-27, SIC-31)

Overview of currently effective requirements

- Revenue is recognised only if it is probable that future economic benefits will flow to the entity and these benefits can be measured reliably.

- Revenue includes the gross inflows of economic benefits received by an entity for its own account. In an agency relationship, amounts collected on behalf of the principal are not recognised as revenue by the agent.

- When an arrangement includes more than one component, it may be necessary to account for the revenue attributable to each component separately.

- Revenue from the sale of goods is recognised when the entity has transferred the significant risks and rewards of ownership to the buyer and it no longer retains control or has managerial involvement in the goods.

- Revenue from service contracts is recognised in the period that the service is rendered, generally using the percentage of completion method.

- Construction contracts are accounted for using the percentage of completion method. The completed contract method is not permitted.

- Revenue recognition does not require cash consideration. However, when goods or services exchanged are similar in nature and value, the transaction does not generate revenue.

Currently effective requirements

This publication reflects IFRSs in issue at 1 August 2010. The requirements related to this topic are derived mainly from IAS 18 *Revenue*, IAS 11 *Construction Contracts*, IFRIC 13 *Customer Loyalty Programmes*, IFRIC 15 *Agreements for the Construction of Real Estate* and IFRIC 18 *Transfers of Assets from Customers*.

Forthcoming requirements and future developments

When a currently effective requirement will be changed by a new requirement that is issued but is not yet effective, it is marked with a # as a **forthcoming requirement** and the impact of the change is explained in the accompanying boxed text. The forthcoming requirements related to this topic are derived from the *Improvements to IFRSs 2010*. A brief outline of the impact of the *Improvements to IFRSs 2010* is given in 4.2.385, and a brief outline of the relevant project is given in 1.1.85.

The currently effective requirements may be subject to **future developments** and a brief outline of the relevant projects, which may affect several aspects of revenue recognition, is given in 4.2.730.

4.2.10 **Scope and definition**

4.2.10.10 IFRSs contain general principles for revenue recognition that apply to all entities, with additional guidance in respect of certain types of transactions, e.g. IFRIC 13 in respect of customer loyalty programmes. While IFRIC 12 *Service Concession Arrangements* (see 5.12) and IFRIC 15 include revenue recognition guidance that is specific to an industry, in general IFRSs contain limited industry-specific guidance on revenue recognition. For example, there is no specific guidance for the recognition of revenue and costs by entities in the software industry.

4.2.10.20 The appendix to IAS 18 contains examples illustrating how to apply the general guidance in the standard to specific types of transactions. The appendix accompanies, but is not part of, the standard.

IAS 1.34, 18.7 4.2.10.30 The definition of revenue is similar to the *Framework for the Preparation and Presentation of Financial Statements* (the Framework) definition of income (see 1.2.30). Revenue is income that arises in the course of the ordinary activities of the entity (e.g. the sale of inventory). Other income (i.e. income that does not arise in the course of the ordinary activities of the entity) is not revenue but is a gain, and falls outside the scope of IAS 18 (see 3.2.440.30).

IAS 16.68A 4.2.10.40 Generally the sale of an item of property, plant and equipment by an entity results in the recognition of a gain or loss. However, if on a routine basis an entity rents out property, plant and equipment and then sells it, then the proceeds from such sale are recognised as revenue (see 3.2.440.37).

4.2.10.50 In our view, the general revenue recognition criteria (e.g. evaluating the extent to which risks and rewards are transferred) are considered to determine the timing of recognition of any gain or loss.

4.2.10.60 Contributions by shareholders in their capacity as shareholders do not generate revenue or income. For example, in our view the forgiveness of a loan granted by a shareholder generally should not be treated as income, but rather as a capital contribution, unless the shareholder was not acting in the capacity of a shareholder (see 3.11.230). A similar assessment may need to be carried out for loans forgiven by fellow subsidiaries, as the waiver might have been instigated by the common parent.

4.2.20 **Measurement**

IAS 18.9-11   4.2.20.10 Revenue is measured at the fair value of the consideration received, taking into account any trade discounts and volume rebates. The amount of revenue recognised is discounted to the present value of consideration due if payment extends beyond normal credit terms.

IAS 18.11,   4.2.20.20 In our view, when payment for goods sold or services provided is deferred
39.38, AG35,   beyond normal credit terms, and the entity does not charge a market interest rate, the
AG53   arrangement effectively constitutes a financing arrangement and interest should be imputed if the impact is material. In these cases the amount of revenue recognised on the goods sold or services provided will be less than the amount that ultimately will be received.

IAS 39.AG64   4.2.20.30 When a current cash price is available, the imputed rate of interest is the rate that exactly discounts the amount to be received in the future to the current cash sales price. In practice the price for normal credit terms often is treated as the cash price equivalent.

4.2.20.40 When a current cash sales price is not available, the imputed rate of interest is a market rate for a similar instrument, giving consideration to the counterparty's credit risk. For example, Company M sells a car to Company B for 1,100 and payment is due in 12 months. M will not charge B any interest. Current market interest rates for a similar level of risk are 10 percent. The fair value of the consideration, and therefore the revenue recognised on the sale of the car, is 1,000, calculated as the present value of the future payment of 1,100. The difference of 100 should be recognised as interest income over the period of financing, using the effective interest method (see 4.6.30). Because M will receive the revenue only in a year, which is outside normal credit terms, the revenue recognised for the sale transaction is less than the amount that will be received.

4.2.20.50 The length of normal credit terms will depend on the industry and the economic environment.

4.2.20.60 In contrast, when payment is received in advance of the related goods being sold or the services rendered, in our view generally revenue should not be adjusted for the time value of money. One of the reasons for this approach is that the entity already has received the consideration due, so there are no future cash flows.

IAS 18.12   4.2.20.70 Revenue is recognised by an entity when goods or services are rendered in exchange for dissimilar goods and services. Revenue is measured at the fair value of the goods or services received, adjusted by the amount of any cash or cash equivalents received or paid. If the fair value of goods or services received cannot be measured reliably, then revenue is measured at the fair value of goods or services given up, adjusted by the amount of any cash or cash equivalents received or paid. When goods and services are exchanged for goods or services that are similar in nature and value, the exchange is considered to lack commercial substance and is not treated as a transaction that generates revenue. See 5.7 for further guidance on non-monetary transactions.

4.2.30 **Linked transactions**

4.2.30.10 In general, this section refers to revenue recognition in the context of a single transaction. However, in some cases two or more transactions may be linked so that the individual transactions have no commercial effect on their own. In these cases the combined effect of all such transactions together is analysed as one arrangement.

4.2.30.20 In the context of revenue recognition, the following could indicate that transactions might be linked:

- The transactions are entered into at the same time or as part of a continuous sequence and in contemplation of one another.
- The transactions, in substance, form a single arrangement that achieves or is designed to achieve an overall commercial effect.
- One or more of the transactions, considered on its own, does not make commercial sense, but they do when considered together.
- The contracts include one or more options or conditional provisions for which there is no genuine commercial possibility that the option(s) or conditional provision(s) will, or alternatively will not, be exercised or fulfilled.
- The occurrence (or non-reversal) of one transaction is dependent on the other transaction(s) occurring.

4.2.30.30 For example, Company D sells a subsidiary to Company E. The purchase and sale agreement includes a manufacture and supply agreement. According to the manufacture and supply agreement, D agrees to supply specific products to E. The selling price of the products covers all of D's manufacturing costs (direct and indirect), transportation costs, duties and other taxes, and insurance costs, but includes no profit margin to D. The manufacturing and supply agreement commences upon completion of the purchase and sale agreement and ends five years later. Other relevant facts include:

- D has no similar manufacturing and supply agreement with other customers.
- It is believed that D would not have received the same price for the sale of the subsidiary if the purchase and sale agreement had not been entered into simultaneously with the manufacturing and supply agreement.
- Each year E provides D with a two-year non-binding forecast of the expected order quantities and a 12-month rolling forecast is provided on a monthly basis.

4.2.30.40 The agreement includes two transactions: (1) the disposal of a subsidiary; and (2) a manufacture and supply agreement of goods. In our view, the transactions are linked and should be analysed together as one arrangement, which contains separately identifiable components. Therefore, a portion of the proceeds on the sale of the subsidiary should be deferred and recognised as the goods are delivered. Any subsequent changes in the estimate of goods to be delivered are changes in estimates and should be accounted for as such (see 2.8.60).

4.2.40 **Overall approach**

4.2.40.10 Revenue may be generated by:

- the sale of goods, including goods produced or purchased by the entity for resale (see 4.2.100);
- construction contracts, which are specifically negotiated contracts for the construction of an asset or a combination of assets if those assets are closely interrelated or interdependent in terms of their design, technology and function or ultimate purpose or use (see 4.2.230);
- the rendering of services, typically involving the performance of a contractually agreed task (see 4.2.310); and
- the use of an entity's assets that generates fees such as royalties, dividends and interest; see 4.6 for guidance on dividends and interest.

IAS 18.14, 20   4.2.40.20 In order to recognise revenue, the entity (seller) should have supplied the goods, or performed the services, as agreed. The required actions may be specified in a formal contract such as a purchase order or service agreement. However, revenue recognition does not require written or formal evidence of an arrangement; for example, revenue may be recognised even if a formal purchase order is not prepared. Furthermore, the form and contents of the contract may not correspond with performance and revenue recognition.

4.2.40.30 The general steps involved in the recognition of revenue are illustrated in the diagram below; the detailed revenue recognition criteria are discussed in the sections that follow. While the diagram assumes that the contract has a number of components, in many cases the contract will have only a single component; in that case the entity will go straight to Step 3: recognise revenue (see 4.2.70):

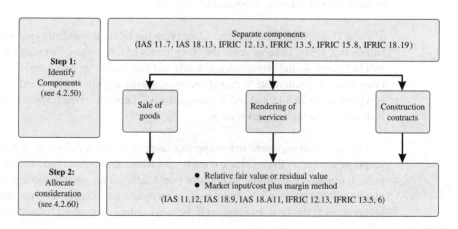

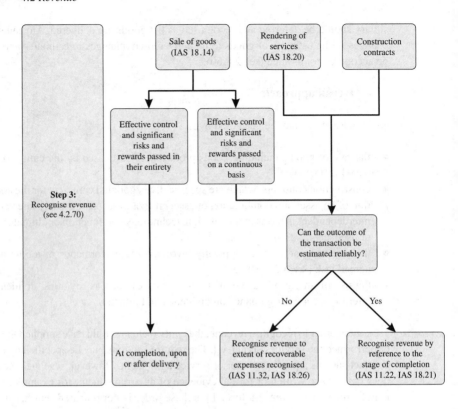

4.2.50 *Step 1: Identify components*

IAS 18.35(b) 4.2.50.10 The first step in recognising revenue is to determine whether a single arrangement comprises separately identifiable components. However, when revenue recognition for the components occurs at the same time and the components belong to the same category of revenue for disclosure purposes, generally there is no need to identify the separate components of the transaction because doing so has no impact on the timing or disclosure of revenue recognition.

4.2.50.20 This process also involves identifying the relevant standards and/or interpretations that apply. In some cases the components of a revenue-generating transaction will fall under a single standard, e.g. a sale and subsequent servicing under IAS 18; in other cases they will relate to more than one standard, e.g. construction and subsequent servicing under IAS 11 and IAS 18, respectively. The scope of the respective standards is discussed throughout this section.

4.2.50.30 In an arrangement that comprises more than one activity, e.g. it may be appropriate to identify the separable components within the contract and allocate revenue to each separately identified component (see 4.2.60). If no separable components are identified, then it may not be appropriate to recognise any revenue until completion (or acceptance) of the final deliverables if the transaction is accounted for under IAS 18.

IAS 18.13 4.2.50.40 The identification of components within a single arrangement is consistent with the general principles in IAS 18, i.e. the requirement that it may be necessary to apply the revenue recognition criteria to the separately identifiable components of a single transaction in order to reflect the substance of the transaction.

4.2.50.50 This general principle is expressed explicitly in a number of recent interpretations:

- IFRIC 13 in respect of customer loyalty programmes (see 4.2.360);
- IFRIC 15 in respect of real estate sales (see 4.2.440); and
- IFRIC 18 in respect of transfers of property, plant and equipment from customers (see 4.2.640).

IFRIC 18.15 4.2.50.60 IAS 18 does not provide detailed guidance on how separate components within a contract or agreement should be identified. However, in our view an entity should consider the requirements of IAS 11 in respect of combining and segmenting construction contracts (see 4.2.240), and the following test contained in IFRIC 18, by analogy to other types of contracts:

- the component has stand-alone value to the customer; and
- the fair value of the component can be measured reliably.

4.2.50.61 IFRIC 18 does not define, nor does it provide guidance about application of the term "stand-alone value". One view is that a delivered element has stand-alone value if a vendor sells the item on a stand-alone basis or the customer could resell it. Another view is that an item has stand-alone value if the customer derives value from that item that is not dependent on receiving other deliverables under the same arrangement.

4.2.50.62 In our view, both of these interpretations of stand-alone value are acceptable. We believe that an entity should choose an accounting policy, to be applied consistently, in determining the definition of stand-alone value. Regardless, of the policy applied, the determination of whether a component within an arrangement has stand-alone value to the customer depends upon facts and circumstances and requires judgement.

4.2.50.70 In some cases a contract may identify separate components, but it may be appropriate to account for them as a single transaction. For example, supply or service transactions may involve charging a non-refundable initial fee with subsequent periodic payments for future products or services. The initial fees may, in substance, be wholly or partly an advance payment for future products or services or the ongoing rights or services being provided are essential to the customers receiving the expected benefit of the upfront payment. In these cases the upfront fee and the continuing performance obligation related to the services to be provided should be assessed as an integrated package. In our view, in these circumstances upfront fees, even if non-refundable, are earned as the services are performed over the term of the arrangement or the expected period of performance and generally should be deferred and recognised systematically over the periods that the fees are earned. Determining when to recognise initial fees as revenue depends upon facts and circumstances and requires judgement (see 4.2.320).

4.2.50.80 The terms, conditions, and amounts of these upfront fees typically are negotiated in conjunction with the pricing of all elements of the arrangement, and the customer would ascribe a significantly lower, and perhaps no, value to elements apparently associated with the upfront fee in the absence of the entity's performance of other contract elements.

4.2.50.90 For example, Biotechnology Company U agrees to provide research and development services to a customer for a specified period of time. The customer needs to use certain technology owned by U. The technology is not sold or licensed separately without the related research and development activities. Under the terms of the arrangement, the customer is required to pay a non-refundable "technology access fee" in addition to periodic payments for research and development activities over the term of the contract.

4.2.50.100 We believe that the activity completed by U (i.e. providing a license to access the technology to the customer) is not a significant revenue-earning event and has no stand-alone value to the customer. The customer is purchasing the ongoing rights, products, or services being provided through U's continuing involvement and the revenue earning process is completed by performing under the terms of the arrangement, not simply by originating a revenue-generating arrangement. This is supported by the fact that U does not sell the initial rights, products or services separately (i.e. without the company's continuing involvement). The upfront fee should be recognised systematically over the period that the research services are provided since that is the period over which the fees are earned.

4.2.50.110 See also 4.2.200 and 4.2.320 for further examples.

4.2.60 *Step 2: Allocate consideration*

4.2.60.10 When a contract or agreement includes more than one component, the second step in recognising revenue is to allocate the overall consideration to the different components. However, to the extent that revenue recognition for components occurs at the same time and the components belong to the same category of revenue for disclosure purposes, generally no allocation of revenue is necessary because those components are accounted for collectively.

IFRIC 13.5-7, 4.2.60.20 While IAS 18 largely is silent on the allocation of revenue to components, there
BC14, 15.8 is specific allocation guidance included in recent interpretations such as IFRIC 13 in respect of customer loyalty programmes, and IFRIC 15 in respect of real estate sales. Under these interpretations, revenue could be allocated to components using either of the following methods:

- relative fair values; or

- fair value of the undelivered components (residual or fair value method).

IFRIC 13.5-7, 4.2.60.30 Using relative fair values, the total consideration is allocated to the different
AG3, 15.8 components based on the ratio of the fair values of the components relative to each other. For example, assume a transaction comprises two components, X and Y. If the fair value of component X is 100 and of component Y is 50, then two thirds of the total consideration would be allocated to component X. If the total consideration is 120, then revenue of 80 would be allocated to component X and 40 to Y.

4.2.60.40 Using the residual method, the undelivered components are measured at fair value, and the remainder of the consideration is allocated to the delivered component. For example, assume a transaction consists of two components, X and Y; at the reporting date only component X has been delivered. If the fair value of component Y is 90 and the total consideration is 120, then revenue of 30 would be allocated to component X and 90 to Y.

4.2.60.50 [Not used]

4.2.60.60 In our view, the reverse residual method, in which the delivered components are measured at fair value, and the remainder of the consideration is allocated to the undelivered component(s), is not an appropriate basis for allocating revenue. Application of the reverse residual method may result in excessive revenue being allocated to the delivered components of a transaction.

IFRIC 12. 4.2.60.70 In our view, if a single contract comprises one or more components within
BC31, the scope of IAS 18 and one or more components within the scope of IAS 11, then
15.BC13 the allocation of revenue, based on the methodologies described in 4.2.60.20, to the various components might result in different profit margins on different components of a single contract. To the extent that components of a single contract fall within the scope of IAS 11, that standard includes specific guidance on the extent to which further separation of the construction component of the contract is required (see 4.2.240).

4.2.60.80 In some cases the allocation of revenue to the different components of an arrangement might result in revenue being recognised even though the related consideration will not be paid by the customer until future services are performed by the entity (seller). For example, Company L sells equipment and installation services in a bundled arrangement for 950. The fair value of the installation services is 100 based on the price charged by other vendors. L also sells the equipment without installation services for 900. The payment terms are 650 payable upon delivery of the equipment, and the remaining 300 once installation is complete. Applying the relative fair value method (see 4.2.60.20), revenue would be allocated as follows:

- Equipment 855: (900 / 1,000) x 950
- Installation 95: (100 / 1,000) x 950.

IAS 18.14(d)   4.2.60.90 We prefer that the entity recognises 855 as revenue when the equipment is delivered, as long as the other criteria in IAS 18 for the sale of goods are met (see 4.2.70 and 100).

IAS 18.IE11,   4.2.60.100 When applying either the relative fair value method or the residual method,
IFRIC   IAS 18 refers to estimating the value of a component of revenue based on the expected
13.AG3   cost of delivery plus a reasonable margin (cost-plus-margin method). In our view, the cost-plus-margin method generally should be applied only when it is difficult to estimate the value of a component based on market inputs because of a lack of such inputs; such inputs may be either direct (sales prices for homogenous products) or indirect (e.g. sales prices for similar products).

4.2.70 Step 3: Recognise revenue

IAS 11.22,   4.2.70.10 Apart from the recognition of interest, dividends (see 4.6) and royalties, revenue
18.14, 20   recognition can be categorised under three headings: sale of goods, construction contracts and the provision of services. There are three common recognition requirements:

- it is probable that the economic benefits of the transaction will flow to the entity;
- the revenue can be measured reliably; and
- the costs (both incurred to date and expected future costs) are identifiable and can be measured reliably.

4.2.80 Probability of future economic benefits

IAS 18.18   4.2.80.10 The probability of future economic benefits relates to the collectibility of the revenue. In some cases revenue recognition may not be appropriate until the consideration is received or the cause of uncertainty is removed.

IAS 18.18,   4.2.80.20 When recoverability of an amount included in revenue in a prior reporting
39.58-70   period becomes uncertain, the uncollectible amount is recognised separately as an expense, rather than as a reduction of revenue. See 3.6.1440 for a discussion of the impairment of receivables.

4.2.90 Timing of revenue recognition

4.2.90.10 In our view, in assessing the timing of revenue recognition, the criteria in IAS 18 should be assessed from the point of view of the seller of the goods or services. For example, Company X sells widgets to Wholesaler W, who then sells them to the end customers. There is no agreement for W to return any unsold widgets to X and neither does X offer any vendor's guarantee to W. X's marketing campaigns are directed at the end customers of the widgets, although its sales are through W. We believe that it would not be appropriate for X to recognise a sale only when a customer buys a widget from W unless the sales arrangement between X and W is a sell-through arrangement (see 4.2.160). On the basis that W is acting as a principal, X should recognise revenue when the criteria in IAS 18 are met from its point of view.

4.2.90.20 The timing of the receipt of payment and the pattern of costs incurred by the entity (seller) often are not the determining factors when considering the timing of revenue recognition, although they may affect the measurement of revenue. For example, a customer purchases a particular item from a retailer, which is not in inventory, and pays in advance. The retailer agrees to order the item. In this case no revenue should be recognised by the retailer until the item has been received and shipped or delivered to the customer.

IAS 18.14, 20   4.2.90.30 Revenue is recognised only once the risks and rewards of ownership have been transferred or, for sales of services, revenue is recognised by reference to the stage of completion of the transaction (see 4.2.310), if all of the other conditions for revenue recognition have been met. For example, Company W sells prepaid phone cards that are used on the landlines provided by Telecommunications Company P. W owes payments to P based on the actual time that W's customers use P's network. In our view, revenue from the sale of the cards should be recognised by W over the period that the cards are used (based on the costs incurred by W, or other evidence that shows actual use) and not on receipt of the proceeds of the sale of the cards.

IAS 18.19   4.2.90.40 In the case of sale of goods, the costs related to completing performance should be reliably measurable prior to recognising revenue. If they are not, then revenue recognition is deferred, not only for the portion of the sale to be completed, but also for the goods that already have been delivered. In very limited circumstances it may be appropriate to recognise all the revenue while accruing costs related to fulfilling the agreement. In our view, this would be appropriate only when the costs to complete, as well as the significance of the remaining component to the product, are insignificant. For example, this approach may be appropriate for the costs of fulfilling product warranties (see 4.2.140).

IAS 18.26   4.2.90.45 In the case of rendering of services, if the costs related to completing performance are not reliably measurable, then revenue is recognised only to the extent of the expenses recognised that are recoverable.

4.2.90.50 Revenue should be reliably measurable in order to be recognised. When revenue depends on the results of uncertain future events, the specific facts and circumstances need to be considered in order to verify whether revenue can be measured reliably. For example, Company B, a private equity investment company, earns management fees for the management services that it performs for a number of investments. These fees are subject to a claw-back provision on an individual investment basis, determined upon sale of the investment. Because calculation of the final performance fees is not possible before the results of each of B's investments are known, B applies a valuation technique to determine each year the fee to be charged. In our view, even though a valuation model has been used, normally it is not possible to estimate the result of an investment reliably before its maturity. Therefore, in this situation, the management fees that are subject to a claw-back provision should not be recognised as revenue. In a situation in which the performance period is completed shortly after the reporting date such that no further claw-back is possible, we believe that it would be much more likely that a reliable determination of the investment result could be made. Therefore, judgement is required to assess the reliable determination of the investment results, and the requirements of IAS 10 *Events after the Reporting Period* (see 2.9) should be considered.

4.2.100 Sale of goods

IAS 18.14   4.2.100.10 In addition to the general recognition tests (see 4.2.70), the following criteria also should be met for the sale of goods before revenue can be recognised:

- there is no continuing managerial involvement over the goods to the degree usually associated with ownership; and
- the significant risks and rewards of ownership of the goods have been transferred to the buyer and there is no effective control over the goods.

4.2.110 *Managerial involvement and effective control*

IAS 18.14   4.2.110.10 In order to recognise revenue the entity (seller) should not maintain effective control over, or managerial involvement to the extent normally associated with ownership of, the goods. These criteria are especially important in analysing non-standard transactions, e.g. bill and hold sales, when delivery is delayed at the buyer's request but the buyer takes title and accepts billing.

IAS 18.IE1   4.2.110.20 Revenue is not recognised when there is simply an intention to acquire or manufacture the goods in time for delivery. For bill and hold transactions revenue is recognised when the customer takes title, provided that:

- it is probable that delivery will be made;
- the item is on hand, identified and ready for delivery to the buyer at the time that the sale is recognised;
- the buyer specifically acknowledges the deferred delivery instructions; and
- the usual payment terms apply.

4.2.110.30 For example, Company X offers customers financial incentives to place purchase orders before they actually need the goods. X offers to hold the goods for the customers until they request delivery, as customers cannot store the out-of-season merchandise. In most cases X pays the cost of storage, shipment and insurance on the goods.

4.2.110.40 In our view, X should not recognise the revenue prior to delivery, since the customer simply takes advantage of the inducements offered and delivery is not delayed at the customer's request. The entire transaction was initiated by X. X pays for the cost of storage, shipment and insurance on the goods, and we believe the significant risks and rewards have not passed to the customer.

4.2.110.50 Consideration of the "usual payment terms" often will depend on historical evidence of how such sales are transacted normally. If there is no precedent for such

974

a sale and the terms of payment appear abnormal, then this may indicate that revenue should not be recognised.

4.2.120 *Significant risks and rewards of ownership*

IAS 18.14-17, 4.2.120.10 In most cases transfer of the significant risks and rewards of ownership will
IFRIC 15.17 correspond to the transfer of legal title or physical delivery. However, in some cases the transfer of risks and rewards of ownership could occur at a point different from the transfer of legal title or the passing of possession, or might be on a continuous basis rather than at a point in time.

4.2.120.20 In our experience, there generally is no time lag between the seller transferring and the buyer accepting the significant risks and rewards of ownership. The transfer of risks and rewards of ownership from the seller to the customer occurs at the same point in time; however, at times judgement is required to determine the exact timing of transfer from the seller's perspective (see 4.2.90.10).

4.2.120.30 In evaluating the point at which the risks and rewards of ownership transfer from the seller to the buyer, one of the considerations is the shipment terms. Standard trade definitions (Incoterms of the International Chamber of Commerce) that are used frequently in international purchase and sales contracts are Free on Board (FOB), Cost, Insurance and Freight (CIF) and Delivered Duty Unpaid (DDU) (see 3.8.90).

4.2.120.40 In the case of FOB and CIF, generally the significant risks and rewards of ownership are transferred to the buyer when the goods are loaded onto the ship, or other delivery vehicle, at the port of the seller. In the case of DDU, the significant risks and rewards of ownership are transferred to the buyer when the goods are delivered to the port of the buyer. The sale is recognised when these events occur, provided that the other conditions for revenue recognition have been met.

4.2.120.50 See 4.1.130 – 220 for further guidance on the significance of risks and rewards transferred.

4.2.130 *Significant performance obligations*

IAS 18.16, 4.2.130.10 Revenue is recognised once all significant performance obligations have been
A2(a) met. For example, when goods are subject to installation or inspection (and that is a significant part of the contract), revenue is recognised once the installation or inspection is complete.

4.2.130.20 For example, an entity manufactures, sells and installs complex machinery for customers and the complete package costs 20,000. Installation can be performed only by the manufacturer. In our view, when the entity agrees to carry out the installation as well as supply the goods, revenue should not be recognised until installation is complete. The customer cannot use the machinery until it is installed, and therefore the significant risks and rewards of ownership have not passed.

4.2.130.30 In a contrasting example, a manufacturer may enter into two separate and distinct performance obligations with a customer integrated in one contract: one for the machinery and another for installation (see 4.2.50). In this example, the installation is routine and could be performed by the customer or another third party. In this case the risks and rewards of ownership of the machinery have passed upon delivery and the revenue related to the delivery of the machinery should be recognised upon delivery.

4.2.140 *Warranty obligations*

IAS 18.16(a) 4.2.140.10 When the selling price of goods includes a standard warranty, e.g. a 12-month warranty on whiteware such as fridges and washing machines, normally this does not result in the retention of significant risks of ownership by the seller, and consequently would not preclude the recognition of revenue. Even if the warranty period extends beyond a standard period, this does not normally prevent revenue recognition for the item sold. Instead, this is treated as a multiple component arrangement, with the consideration received or receivable allocated between the delivered item and the extended warranty. However, an abnormal warranty obligation, e.g. a warranty related to the amount of revenue that use of the asset will generate for the buyer, may indicate that the significant risks and rewards of ownership have not passed to the buyer, or that the seller has not performed all of its obligations in delivering a product that the buyer can use. See 3.12.360 for a discussion of warranty provisions.

4.2.140.20 See also 4.2.460.10 in respect of real estate rental guarantees.

4.2.150 *Right of return by the buyer*

IAS 18.16, 4.2.150.10 When the buyer has a right of return and there is uncertainty about the
A2(b) possibility of return, revenue is not recognised until the shipment has been accepted by the customer, or the goods have been delivered and the time period for rejection has elapsed.

4.2.150.20 In our view, an entity considers historical experience in assessing the possibility of return. If, based on past experience, the entity can make a reliable estimate of the amount of goods that will be returned, then it would be appropriate to recognise revenue for the amount that is expected to be received for items that are not returned (assuming that the other conditions for revenue recognition are met).

4.2.160 *Receipt of revenue is contingent on a sale by the customer (sell-through arrangements)*

IAS 18.16, 4.2.160.10 In some cases the receipt of revenue by an entity is contingent upon the
A2(c) customer making a sale of the goods. Examples include situations in which inventory has been transferred to another entity (a consignee) who holds it on consignment at its premises, or when sales are made to distributors or other parties acting as agents. Revenue is recognised only when the inventory has been sold by the consignee to third-party customers.

4.2.170 *Repurchase options*

IAS 18.IE5 4.2.170.10 At the time of the sale, an entity (seller) may enter into an agreement to re-purchase the same goods at a later date or the seller may have an option to repurchase the goods at a later date. An entity also may provide a guarantee to pay the customer any shortfall between the residual value of an item, for example a car, at a certain point in the future and a guaranteed amount. Such transactions are considered to be linked (see 4.2.30). When the seller enters into a sale and repurchase agreement, the terms of the agreement need to be analysed to determine whether, in substance, the seller has transferred the risks and rewards of ownership to the customer.

4.2.170.20 In our view, if the seller has a repurchase option or obligation, then it is ap-propriate to consider the guidance for lease accounting to determine whether risks and rewards have been transferred and a sale should be recognised (see 5.1). Finance leases are distinguished from operating leases based on the extent to which risks and rewards of ownership are transferred to a lessee.

4.2.170.30 In our experience, the following are factors that may indicate that the entity (seller) has transferred substantially all of the risks and rewards of ownership to the customer even if a repurchase right or obligation is retained:

- the period from sale to repurchase is for the major part of the economic life of the asset;
- the difference between the proceeds received on the initial transfer and the amount of any residual value guarantee or repurchase price, measured on a present value basis, amounts to substantially all of the fair value of the asset at the sale date;
- insurance risk is borne by the customer; however, if the customer bears the insurance risk but the seller bears the remaining risks, then in our view the risks and rewards probably have not transferred to the buyer; and
- the repurchase price is equal to the market value at the time of the buy-back.

4.2.170.40 In our view, if an initial sale of a good is concluded with a customer and a buy-back agreement or a repurchase option follows at a later date, then the substance of both transactions should be considered. If the transactions are linked (see 4.2.30), then the transactions should be assessed together. If a seller of goods has no obliga-tion to enter into a buy-back agreement with a buyer at the date of the sale of the goods, then this might indicate that the two transactions (sale and later buy-back) are not linked. In our view, the obligation to enter into a buy-back agreement might either be a contractual (written or oral) obligation or a constructive obligation. For example, the entity (seller) has established a constructive obligation if it frequently agrees to enter into a buy-back agreement if a customer asks for it and therefore the retailer (customer) realistically can expect the buy-back agreement when the goods are sold (bought).

4.2.170.50 In another example, Company R purchases copper for its own use from supplier X and borrows from Bank B to pay X. R also enters into a separate sale and repurchase arrangement to sell the copper to a financial institution, using the proceeds to repay the bank loan, and immediately repurchase an equivalent amount of copper from the financial institution on deferred payment terms. R has no legal obligation to repurchase the copper that it sells to the financial institution. The overall commercial effect of the sale and repurchase transactions is to reduce R's financing costs. Although there is no contractual linkage between the sale and purchase transactions, in our view the combined outcome of the sale and repurchase transaction with the financial institution should be considered together as the transactions are linked (see 4.2.30). Although R has no legal obligation to repurchase the copper sold to the financial institution, R has established a constructive obligation through the pattern of sales and purchases completed to date. We believe that the sale and repurchase transactions result in no net change in the distribution of the risks and rewards of ownership of the copper and, accordingly, give rise to no gross inflow of economic benefits to R and no increase in R's equity. Therefore, the sale and repurchase transactions should be accounted for as a financing arrangement and the transactions should be classified as cash flows from financing activities in the statement of cash flows (see 2.3.20).

4.2.170.60 If the overall effect of the agreements is that the entity (seller) has not transferred the risks and rewards of ownership of the asset, then the transaction is considered to be a financing arrangement and no revenue is recognised with respect to the initial "sale".

4.2.170.70 If the customer is required to sell a similar asset back to the entity (seller) at the end of the buy-back period, then the assessment of the transfer of risks and rewards would be evaluated in the same manner as discussed in 4.2.180.

4.2.180 Residual value guarantees

IAS 17.10(d), 18.14(d) 4.2.180.10 A seller may offer a guaranteed residual or reimbursement to the customer. Such guaranteed residual amounts may preclude revenue recognition if significant risks are retained. In our view, not retaining significant risks requires that a guaranteed residual amount at or near the end of the useful life of the asset, measured on a present value basis, should transfer substantially all (as that term is used in the context of evaluating the classification of a lease agreement) of the initial sales price risk to the customer. For example, if a sales arrangement for an asset with a useful life of eight years contains a guaranteed residual value after six years amounting to a present value of 20 percent of the initial sales price, then only 80 percent of the initial sales price risk would have been transferred. We believe that this would not qualify as the transfer of significant ownership risks.

4.2.180.20 Similar principles as for leasing transactions should be applied to a reimbursement or a residual value guarantee to judge whether the amount is insignificant (see 5.1.30). When the guaranteed repurchase price or residual value guarantee will be determined using a formula or model, in our view the entity should estimate the residual value guarantee at the date of the transaction based on the expected amount of the residual value.

4.2.180.30 In our view, a residual value guarantee also would be considered insignificant if the guarantee is significantly out of the money at the date of the sales transaction. A guaranteed residual amount before the end of the useful life of the asset should be evaluated by reference to the residual value at the same date. For example, a guarantee of 50 percent of the value of the asset after two years could represent an insignificant risk if the probability of exercise is very low because it is highly probable that market value will be in the range of 70 to 80 percent.

4.2.180.40 In our view, valuating the significance of a residual value guarantee also should take into account the seniority of the guarantee. For example, if the guarantee is for a small percentage of the expected residual value and it is a "last loss guarantee", then the expected value will be very low, because substantially all of the estimated residual value would have to be lost before the guarantee takes effect.

4.2.180.50 If the entity (seller) does not retain more than an insignificant residual value guarantees, and transfers the significant risks and rewards of ownership to the customer, then the transaction is a sale and the related revenue is recognised, provided that the other conditions for revenue recognition also are met. Liabilities are not recognised in respect of commitments to purchase assets as these are executory contracts. Any call and put option will be outside of the scope of the financial instruments standards if physical settlement is required (see 3.6.90). However, a provision for an onerous contract may be required (see 3.12.630).

IAS 18.IE5, 4.2.180.60 If the significant risks and rewards of ownership remain with the entity (seller),
IFRIC 4.6 then the transaction is not a sale and no revenue is recognised. The transaction is, in substance, a financing arrangement. An arrangement may contain a lease even though the agreement is not in the legal form of a lease, in particular when the arrangement conveys the right to use the asset and the buyer obtains the ability or right to control the use of a specific asset (see 5.1.510). Therefore, IAS 17 *Leases* is likely to apply because it covers asset-specific financing when the use of the asset is granted to another party (see 5.1). In these cases the characteristics of the transaction suggest that the seller acts as a lessor in an operating lease for the period between the legal sale and the repurchase date. The fact that the customer pays for the goods or that title transfers is not conclusive if the substance of the transaction is a financing agreement.

4.2.180.70 For example, Company K sells equipment to its customers and at the same time agrees that it will repurchase the equipment after three years at its market value, which will reflect market conditions at that time and the extent of use and condition of the equipment. Customers pay the full purchase price at the sale date and there are no restrictions on the extent to which they can use the asset, and no requirements in relation to its general upkeep and maintenance. Comparable second-hand equipment is freely available in an active market (i.e. it is not specialised).

4.2.180.80 In our view, K recognises revenue on the sale because the risks and rewards of ownership, including residual value risk, have been transferred to the customer. The only obligation of K is to buy back the equipment at its market value, which in our view is an executory contract.

4.2.180.90 In an alternative arrangement, the customer settles the purchase price by 24 equal monthly instalments and K agrees to repurchase the equipment after three years at a specified price, which results in K obtaining a market rental rate for the use of the equipment over three years, less a lender's return payable by K on the net temporary cash flow benefit it enjoys from the overall arrangement. The customer is required to maintain the equipment to a specified level, and restrictions are placed on use of the asset. If the customer defaults on its payments, then K has the right to repossess the equipment.

4.2.180.100 In this example, we believe that the sale and repurchase agreement are considered to be linked (see 4.2.30). While the benefits and risks arising from the use of the asset over the three-year period are transferred to the customer, K retains some effective control over the equipment via the restriction of use placed on the customer as well as the residual value risk. For example, if the market value of the equipment at the date of repurchase is less than the residual capital amount outstanding, then K has no recourse to the customer; equally, if the residual value is greater than the residual amount, then K retains that benefit.

4.2.180.110 K should consider whether the arrangement falls within the scope of IAS 17 (see 5.1.15), as it may be appropriate to account for the equipment as being subject to a lease. If the transaction is a lease, then K would recognise the payments received over the lease term.

4.2.190 Layaway sales

IAS 18.IE3 4.2.190.10 Layaway sales are sales of goods under which the goods are delivered only when the customer makes the final payment in a series of instalments. Revenue from layaway sales generally is recognised when the goods are delivered to the customer.

4.2.190.20 For example, Company R is a retailer that offers layaway sales to its customers. R retains the merchandise, segregating it from items for sale, and collects a cash deposit from the customer. R does not require the customer to enter into an instalment agreement or other fixed payment commitments when the initial deposit is received; however, R sets a time period within which the customer should finalise the purchase. The merchandise is not delivered to the customer until the customer pays the full purchase price. In the event that the customer fails to pay the remaining purchase price, the customer forfeits the amount paid and R, under the laws of its jurisdiction, is allowed to keep the forfeited funds. In the event that the merchandise is lost, damaged or destroyed, R either should refund the amounts paid by the customer or provide replacement merchandise.

4.2.190.30 R generally will recognise revenue from such sales only when the merchandise is released to the customer. However, when experience indicates that most of these sales are consummated, revenue may be recognised when a significant deposit is received, provided that the goods are on hand, identified and ready for delivery to the buyer. "Significant" is not defined in IFRSs, but in our view the deposit should be large enough to conclude that the particular sale is virtually certain to be finalised, similar to the requirements for recognising a contingent asset (see 3.14.40), having regard to the entity's past history.

4.2.190.40 This requirement should be applied to individual sales when the deposit received is significant, not as a general threshold for recognising layaway sales. For example, a fashion retailer requires a 5 percent deposit on all layaway sales and experience shows that 95 percent of the sales are consummated. In this case revenue should not be recognised as the size of the deposit is not significant. However, if on one such sale a significant deposit has been received, then the criteria to recognise revenue may be met.

4.2.200 *Non-refundable payment before delivery*

4.2.200.10 See 4.2.50.70 – 80 for general information about the analysis of upfront payments.

4.2.200.20 For example, Company H grants a licence to Company B for a non-refundable fee of 2,000 that is paid to H at inception of the arrangement. This licence allows B to sell H's software to third parties and B's initial 2,000 of purchases will be offset against the licence fee. B may make further purchases without renewing the licence once software with a cumulative sales value of 2,000 has been sold by H to B. The price of the individual software items is not fixed at the inception of the arrangement.

4.2.200.30 H is required to make upgrades to existing products and new products available to B as and when they become available. All copies of the software are supplied to B as required.

4.2.200.40 B has an unlimited right of return for products that it has acquired from H until B makes a sale to one of its own customers. The software is for a new market, and the level of potential returns cannot be estimated reliably.

4.2.200.50 In considering whether the 2,000 can be recognised as revenue by H on receipt, H concludes that the amount of the revenue can be measured reliably and it is probable that economic benefits associated with the revenue will flow to H, as the payment is non-refundable and paid in advance.

4.2.200.60 However, in our view although the transaction has been described as granting a licence, the substance of the arrangement is that the arrangement is a prepayment for the supply of software by H to B. The purchase price of future software supplies will be offset against the 2,000 payment until the value of B's purchases exceeds this amount. It is only at that point that B will need to pay for any further supplies.

4.2.200.70 In our view, H should recognise revenue only when copies of the software are sold by B to end users. H retains the risks and rewards of ownership of the software until it is sold to the end users, indicated by the following:

- At inception H has not performed any of the activities that it is required to carry out under the terms of the agreement (i.e. supply the software). As the goods will be subject to upgrades and new products may be developed, it is not clear what the goods will be.
- B has an unlimited right of return until the point at which it makes a sale to one of its own customers. As the software is designed for a new market, the level of returns cannot be estimated reliably.
- The software prices are not fixed at inception of the contract.
- Copies of the software are delivered individually as B requires them.

4.2.210 *Pre-production costs related to supply agreements*

4.2.210.10 In some cases an entity may manufacture a product that is to be used only for manufacturing a certain component for a customer, for example, e.g. a mould. Even if the mould is not sold directly to the customer, the cost of production of the mould often will be recovered from the customer. In these cases the entity considers whether it in fact retains the risks and rewards of ownership of the mould.

4.2.210.20 For example, Company M manufactures a plastic component for motor vehicle manufacturer P. M is not able to use the mould used in the manufacture of that component to manufacture components for other customers or for any other purpose; nor may it sell the mould. The costs for the production of the mould form a substantial part of the production cost of the component. P agrees to compensate M for the cost of the mould, either through the price of individual components of the units, or via an upfront payment. The mould costs are to be recovered through unit sales. If P fails to purchase the agreed number of components, then P is required to reimburse M for the remaining mould production costs. If M fails to deliver ordered items under the supply contract, then it still will be entitled to claim the cost of the mould from P, but may be liable for further damages and claims.

4.2.210.30 In our view, the agreement between M and P consists of two components that are integrated in a single agreement: construction of the mould and the subsequent delivery of the components that are produced using the mould. The two components should be accounted for separately.

4.2.210.40 In our view, while M retains physical control over the mould, the following indicate that the risks and rewards of ownership of the mould are transferred to P when P approves the mould:

- M does not bear the risk of future changes in the value of the mould as it is entitled to recover the full cost of production of the mould from P, regardless of the number of parts actually ordered by P.
- M is not exposed to the risk of the mould being idle as a result of reduced needs of P, as it will be entitled to claim any unrecovered mould costs from P. The reimbursement of the costs to manufacture the mould does not depend on M's performance in the delivery phase of the contract.

- The fact that M may be required to insure the mould does not necessarily indicate that it actually bears the risk of loss of the mould, which would be indicative of its economic ownership. This may be a practical issue as it has physical custody of the mould.
- While M continues to use the mould to manufacture the components, M retains no continuing managerial ownership or control usually associated with ownership. M is not able to use the mould to manufacture components for other customers or for any other purpose; nor may it sell the mould. Further, M may not increase or reduce the capacity of the mould. M is able only to use the mould to fulfil its obligations under the delivery contract.

4.2.210.50 In our view, to the extent that the other recognition criteria are met, M should recognise revenue on acceptance of the mould by P.

4.2.210.60 In our view, if reimbursement for the cost of the mould depends on the performance of M, and M is not unconditionally entitled to recover the production costs of the mould, then the two components of the transaction would be integrated economically and could not be accounted for separately. This would be the case if M was to recover the cost of production of the mould through subsequent orders, but M did not deliver the components or P did not order the anticipated quantity. In this case M retains the significant risks of ownership, as it is not contractually able to recover its costs if it does not perform or if P no longer requires the components.

4.2.210.70 The contracts also would be considered to be integrated, and accounted for as a single contract, if the revenue attributed to the sale of the mould was far below or in excess of a reasonable price, e.g. below or in excess of fair value or cost plus reasonable profit, with a resulting adjustment to the selling price of the components produced. If the contracts are considered to be integrated, and the mould is considered to be an asset of M, then it may be necessary to recognise a portion of the consideration as a lease payment for the mould.

4.2.210.80 In the fact pattern discussed in 4.2.210.20 – 70, the mould is the asset of the customer (P in this example). However, in other transactions it might be appropriate to conclude that the mould is the asset of the manufacturer (M in this example), who is obliged to use the mould to provide ongoing access to the customer to a supply of goods (components). This might be the case if the manufacturer has continuing managerial ownership or control usually associated with ownership, for example, if the manufacturer also is able to use the mould to manufacture components for other customers or for any other purpose or is able to sell the mould. In that case the manufacturer would recognise the asset and would recognise a corresponding amount of revenue on an appropriate basis (see 3.2.20.30 and 4.2.640).

4.2.220 *Sale and leaseback transactions*

4.2.220.10 In our view, when an entity enters into a sale and leaseback transaction, the entity (seller) considers both the sale and the leaseback transactions to determine whether it has transferred substantially all of the risks and rewards of ownership of the asset. When the leaseback does not transfer substantially all of the risks and rewards of ownership back to the seller-lessee, the seller-lessee recognises a sale and the leaseback is considered to be an operating leaseback; otherwise the leaseback is treated as a finance leaseback and no sale is recognised by the seller-lessee (see 5.1.470). In our view, the net transaction does not have to satisfy all of the revenue recognition requirements in IAS 18 because the leaseback results in the transaction falling within the scope of IAS 17.

IAS 40.67   4.2.220.20 IAS 18 also is applied to disposals of investment property to determine the date of disposal (see 3.4.260). However, IAS 17 applies to a disposal effected by entering into a finance lease, as well as to a sale and leaseback.

4.2.230 **Construction contracts**

IAS 11.3   4.2.230.10 A *construction contract* is a contract specifically negotiated for the construction of an asset or a combination of assets that are closely interrelated or interdependent in terms of their design, technology and function or their ultimate purpose or use. Construction contracts are classified either as fixed price contracts or as cost-plus contracts:

- A fixed price contract is a construction contract in which the contractor agrees to a fixed contract price, or a fixed rate per unit of output, which in some cases is subject to cost escalation clauses.
- A cost plus contract is a construction contract in which the contractor is reimbursed for allowable or otherwise defined costs, plus a percentage of these costs or a fixed fee.

4.2.230.20 IAS 11 is intended for more than construction work in the narrow sense of constructing a building. In our view, construction of both complete assets and components that are for use in a larger asset may be accounted for as construction contracts if they are complex custom-designed items. For example, the construction of components of aircraft specifically designed for customers is likely to comprise construction contracts provided that the general considerations below are met, if the components are complex custom-designed pieces of equipment.

4.2.230.30 The construction or development of certain intangible assets also may fall within the scope of IAS 11, for example the development of custom software and technology products.

4.2.230.40 The general application of IAS 11 is discussed below; see 4.2.500 for a discussion of more detailed application issues.

4.2.240 *Combining and segmenting construction contracts*

IAS 11.7, 8   4.2.240.10 Usually construction contract accounting is applied separately to each construction contract. The components of a contract are accounted for as separate contracts when each segment functions on a stand-alone basis and all of the following criteria are met:

- separate proposals were submitted for each component;
- each component was subject to separate negotiation and could have been accepted or rejected; and
- the costs and revenue for each component can be identified.

IAS 11.9 4.2.240.20 A group of contracts (whether with a single customer or not) is treated as a single construction contract when they do not function on a stand-alone basis and:

- they were negotiated as part of a single package;
- the contracts effectively are part of a single project with an overall profit margin; and
- the contracts are performed concurrently or in continuous sequence.

4.2.240.30 Sometimes a contract for a single complex custom-designed item may specify certain milestones (e.g. a development and a production phase). Generally the contract price is negotiated for the whole contract and customers are not able to reject the development phase and accept the production phase (or *vice versa*). In our view, because separate negotiations are not conducted in respect of the various phases and separate proposals are not submitted for the development and production phases, the contract in this case is not split into the development and the production phase.

4.2.250 *Multiple items or units*

4.2.250.10 A construction contract may deal with the construction of a number of assets that are closely interrelated or interdependent in terms of their design, technology and function or ultimate purpose. A contract also may be for the construction of a system with component parts. A system is a single integrated unit and not just multiple units of a standard product. For example, the sale and installation of a radar system that requires the installation of 100 units, all of which are required in order for the system to work, would in our view fall within the definition of a construction contract. However, the sale of 100 radar towers that each operates independently of one another is not a system that would be a single construction contract. However, each radar tower may itself be a construction contract if it is considered to be a complex, custom-designed piece of equipment. See 4.2.510 for further discussion of this topic.

IAS 11.22 4.2.250.20 Once the revenue recognition criteria are satisfied, both contract revenue and contract costs of both fixed price and cost-plus construction contracts are recognised by reference to the stage of completion of the contract. The completed contract method is not permitted. Any costs incurred or consideration received in excess of the stage of completion generally is deferred.

IAS 11.32 4.2.250.30 When the outcome of a construction contract cannot be estimated reliably, no profit is recognised, but revenue is recognised to the extent of costs incurred that are probable of recovery. Costs are recognised as an expense as incurred.

4.2.260 *Recognition of contract revenue and expenses*

4.2.260.10 Revenue for cost-plus contracts is recognised when the general revenue recognition criteria are met (see 4.2.70).

IAS 11.23 4.2.260.20 In addition to the general revenue recognition criteria, the following criteria also should be met for fixed price construction contracts:

- the outcome of the contract can be estimated reliably; and
- the stage of completion of the contract can be measured reliably.

IAS 11.25-27 4.2.260.30 Contract revenue and expenses are recognised in accordance with the stage of completion of the contract. Under the stage of completion method, contract costs, revenue and the resulting profit are recognised in the period that the work is performed. Contract costs incurred that relate to future activities are deferred and recognised as inventory.

IAS 11.42-44 4.2.260.40 The gross amount due from customers for all contracts in progress for which costs incurred plus recognised profits or net of recognised losses exceed progress billings is presented as an asset separately in the statement of financial position. A liability is presented for the gross amount due to customers for all contracts in progress for which progress billings exceed costs incurred plus recognised profits or net of recognised losses. There is no guidance on the characterisation of the asset or liability related to construction contracts in progress. We prefer to present the asset as an accounts receivable, or in the case of a liability, as deferred revenue.

4.2.270 *Contract revenue*

IAS 11.11, 12 4.2.270.10 Contract revenue comprises:

- the initial amount of revenue agreed in the contract; and
- variations in contract work, claims and incentive payments, to the extent that it is probable that they will result in revenue and the additional revenue is reliably measurable.

4.2.270.20 Revenue measurements are based on estimates that are revised as events and uncertainties are resolved. Amounts may increase or decrease based on variations to the original contract, penalties on delays, cost escalation clauses and other similar items.

IAS 11.12(c) 4.2.270.30 Any penalty for late delivery is a reduction to contract revenue and is accounted for under IAS 11, rather than as a provision or contingent liability (see 3.12 and 3.14, respectively).

IAS 11.12 4.2.270.40 Revenue is recognised at the fair value of the amount receivable.

IAS 11.41 4.2.270.50 "Retentions" are common in the construction industry. Retentions usually are determined as a fixed percentage of the total contract price that is paid only once a specified time period has elapsed from the date of completion of the contract and all defects have been corrected. When revenue on a contract is recognised, but will be received only after the expiry of a specified period of time, for example in the case of a retention, in our view interest should be imputed and the expected cash receipts discounted to determine the fair value of the amount receivable (see 4.2.20).

4.2.280 *Contract costs*

IAS 11.16-19, 21   4.2.280.10 Contract costs include the costs attributable to a contract from the date of securing the contract to the final completion of the contract. Contract costs comprise:

- costs that relate directly to the contract, for example labour, materials, direct design and assistance, cost of rectification and guarantee work, royalties paid for the use of intellectual property and depreciation of property, plant, and equipment used directly on the contract;
- costs that are attributable to contract activity in general, for example insurance and overheads, and that can be allocated to the contract on a systematic and rational basis based on normal contract activity; and
- other costs that are chargeable specifically to the customer, for example general administrative and development costs that are reimbursed under the terms of the contract.

4.2.280.20 General and administration costs should be treated as contract costs if the costs relate directly to either performance under a specific contract in progress or the seller's contracting activities.

IAS 11.18   4.2.280.30 Construction contract projects often are financed by advances from customers. Otherwise long-term funding may be required. Borrowing costs directly attributable to the construction of a "qualifying asset" are capitalised and included as contract costs in accordance with IAS 23 *Borrowing Costs* (see 4.6.350).

IAS 11.21   4.2.280.40 A contractor may incur costs prior to securing the contract, including costs for assigned tenders and tenders that are not yet awarded. Examples of these costs include sales costs attributable to a particular tender presentation, and legal and consultancy fees that can be attributed to a specific contract.

4.2.280.50 Costs that are related directly to securing a contract and other pre-contract costs are included as part of contract costs only when it is probable that the contract will be obtained and the costs can be identified separately and measured reliably. These direct costs are not presented separately as intangible assets, but rather as amounts due to or from contract customers.

4.2.280.60 If pre-contract costs are expensed in the period in which they were incurred, then they are not reinstated subsequently as contract costs when the contract is obtained.

IAS 11.20   4.2.280.70 Costs that cannot be allocated directly to contracts or attributed to contract activity include selling costs, general administrative costs and other costs that are not reimbursable under the terms of specific contracts. For example, in negotiating a contract to construct a plant for the government of Country X, Company Z agrees to move a portion of its production facilities of an unrelated product to Country X. In our view, even though the costs to move the plant are incurred in order to secure a particular contract, they do not relate directly to that contract and should be recognised separately and not as a contract cost.

4.2.290 Stage of completion

IAS 11.30   4.2.290.10 No specific method is mandated for assessing the stage of completion. An entity may use the more appropriate of input measures (consideration of the efforts devoted to a contract), or output measures (consideration of the results achieved). The following are methods that can be used to determine the stage of completion, depending on the nature of the contract:

- surveys of work performed (output measure);
- completion of a physical proportion of the contract work (output measure); or
- percentage of contract costs incurred in relation to total estimated contract costs (input measure).

4.2.290.20 An example of an output measure is when 60 miles of a 300-mile railway track have been completed: the contract is 20 percent complete, assuming that each mile is equivalent. As an example of an input measure, if estimated contract costs total 2,000 and 800 of costs have been incurred to date, then the contract is 40 percent complete.

4.2.290.30 In our view, output measures are the more appropriate measure of the stage of completion as long as a reliable measure of output can be established. For example, a contract may require technical inspections at various stages, which are considered to be identifiable milestones, and the revenues related to these milestones can be established.

4.2.290.40 In our view, an input method should be used only if a reliable output measure cannot be established. If an input method is used, then only those contract costs that reflect the work performed to date should be included in determining the stage of completion, and advance payments made to suppliers should be excluded.

IAS 11.30   4.2.290.50 Progress billings often are not an appropriate measure of revenue recognition, as revenue recognition should reflect the actual stage of completion, while billing schedules do not necessarily reflect the actual status of the work.

4.2.300 Expected contract losses

IAS 11.36   4.2.300.10 When it is probable that the total contract costs will exceed contract revenue, the expected loss is recognised as an expense immediately. Expected losses are determined by reference to the latest estimates of contract revenue, contract costs and contract outcome.

4.2.310 **Service contracts**

IAS 18.21 4.2.310.10 Service contracts generally are accounted for in the same way as construction contracts (see 4.2.230) and the requirements of IAS 11 are applied to determine the stage of completion for recognising revenue. The appendix to IAS 18 includes examples of when service contract revenue is deferred or recognised unevenly (e.g. non-refundable initiation fees). Therefore, both IAS 11 and the guidance in the appendix to IAS 18 should be considered in determining revenue recognition for sales of services.

IFRIC 15.6 4.2.310.20 If a construction contract includes a service element and a construction element, then the contract will need to be split into the servicing component that falls under IAS 18 and the construction component that falls under IAS 11 (see 4.2.60.70). See 4.2.440.110 for guidance on the identification of separable components in a contract.

IAS 11.36, 4.2.310.30 A contract to provide services that is accounted for using the percentage of
37, 37.66 completion method may potentially be an onerous contract. In these circumstances it is not clear whether the onerous contract guidance in IAS 37 *Provisions, Contingent Liabilities and Contingent Assets* applies or whether the guidance on the recognition of expected losses in IAS 11 should be applied. In our view, an entity should choose an accounting policy, to be applied consistently, between the requirements of IAS 11 (see 4.2.300) and IAS 37 (see 3.12.630) unless the service contract is a fixed fee insurance service contract (see 5.10).

4.2.320 *Timing*

IAS 18.IE17, 4.2.320.10 Fees for providing continuing services, whether they are part of an initial fee
IE18 or are charged as a separate fee, are recognised as revenue as the services are rendered. Any initial or entrance fee is recognised as revenue when there is no significant uncertainty as to its collection and the entity has no further obligation to perform any continuing services.

IAS 18.25 4.2.320.20 When services are performed through an indefinite number of repetitive acts over a specified period of time, revenue is recognised on a straight-line basis over the specified period unless some other method better represents the stage of completion. When a specific act is much more significant than any other acts, revenue is recognised only after the significant act is performed.

4.2.320.30 For example, Company W operates an electronic payment processing service on behalf of retailers who accept payment by credit card. One-off costs are incurred by W at inception of the arrangement for adding the retailer to its processing system. Charges to retailers for the service comprise a set-up fee at inception of the arrangement of 360, followed by annual charges of 240 per year beginning on the first anniversary of the arrangement. W makes a reasonable profit from the ongoing services based on the annual charge of 240.

4.2.320.40 Although the initial charge of 360 is described as an initial set-up fee, no separate charge is made for providing the first year's services. In our view, W should recognise 120 as revenue (360 total less 240 deferred based on normal annual charges) when a retailer is added to its processing system and the balance of 240 over the first year, being the period during which services are provided or made available. In subsequent years, the annual fee should be recognised as revenue over the service period.

IAS 18.IE11, IE18   4.2.320.50 In some cases an initial fee is levied followed by, or including, separate fees for services, but the separate fees do not cover the cost of the continuing services together with a reasonable profit. In these cases part of the initial fee, sufficient to cover the costs of continuing services and to provide a reasonable profit on those services, is deferred and recognised as revenue as the services are rendered.

4.2.320.60 If in the previous example the initial fee was 1,200 and subsequent fees were 50 per year, which resulted in the ongoing service being loss-making, then in our view it would be necessary to defer at least part of the initial fee of 1,200 and recognise it as revenue in future periods.

4.2.320.70 In our view, the entity may consider market transactions to determine the amount to be deferred (see 4.2.60). If there are no market transactions, but there is a period during which W expects to provide services to these customers or a period which reasonably can be estimated, then we believe that it may be appropriate to spread the deferred fee over that expected or estimated period. Alternatively, a realistic maximum potential period taking into account the possibility of a contract termination by W may be estimated and revenue recognised over that period.

4.2.320.80 For example, Company C agrees to distribute films for a film producer. C earns a non-refundable upfront fee of 250 in exchange for a commitment to distribute the films. The fee is received before filming commences. C earns a 10 percent sales commission, but no commission is earned on the first 2,500 of sales.

4.2.320.90 In our view, the two elements of the transaction are linked. The upfront fee is an integral part of the distribution deal because, even if the 10 percent commission is a market rate, the first 250 worth of commission will not be earned by C as it has, in substance, been prepaid for these commissions by the upfront fee. Even though the fee is non-refundable, the 250 non-refundable fee should be deferred and recognised on the same basis as the commission from distribution.

IAS 17.3   4.2.320.100 A common form of a service agreement is a maintenance agreement, in particular for vehicles. Vehicle maintenance agreements may be provided either on a stand-alone basis, or as part of a vehicle lease or sales contract. When a service contract is included as part of an equipment sale or lease, the maintenance agreement is separated from the sales or lease agreement.

IAS 18.IE11   4.2.320.110 Revenue for the service contract is recognised during the period over which the maintenance services are performed using the stage of completion method. The amount of the total consideration to be deferred is based on the expected cost of performing the service plus a reasonable profit on those services, which often is based on previous experience.

4.2.330 Specific application issues

4.2.340 *Sales incentives*

4.2.340.10 An entity (seller) may provide incentives to a customer as part of an arrangement. Examples of sales incentives offered by a seller include cash incentives, discounts and volume rebates, free/discounted goods or services, customer loyalty programmes, loyalty cards and vouchers.

4.2.340.20 The following simplified illustration depicts in general terms the treatment of sales incentives:

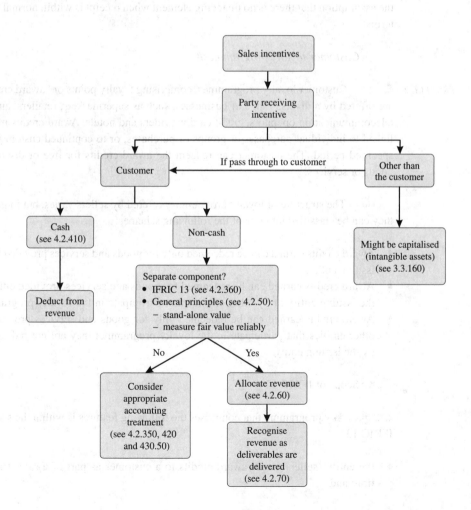

4.2.350 *Early settlement discounts*

4.2.350.10 In our view, if it is probable that an early settlement discount will be taken, and the amount can be measured reliably, then the discount is recognised as a reduction of revenue as the sales are recognised. For example, Company J sells goods on credit to customers and normal credit terms are 60 days. J grants a 2 percent discount if customers pay within 10 days of the invoice date. In our view, the settlement discount and the expected cash flows should be estimated at the time of sale, and the expected discount recognised as a reduction of revenue.

4.2.350.20 In theory the difference between the discounted amount and the full invoice amount represents finance income in respect of all discounts not taken. However, in practice, when such discounts are not taken, the amount of revenue recognised generally is the higher amount receivable before discount, provided that receipt is not deferred beyond normal credit terms (see 4.2.20). This approach is consistent with the assumption that there is no financing element when receipt is within normal credit terms.

4.2.360 *Customer loyalty programmes#*

IFRIC 13.1, 2 4.2.360.10 Customer loyalty programmes, comprising loyalty points or "award credits", are offered by a diverse range of businesses, such as supermarkets, retailers, airlines, telecommunication operators, credit card providers and hotels. Award credits may be linked to individual purchases or groups of purchases, or to continued custom over a specified period. The customer can redeem the award credits for free or discounted goods or services.

4.2.360.20 The structure of loyalty programmes offered by sellers varies, but in general they can be classified into one of the following schemes:

- Award credits earned can be redeemed only for goods and services provided by the issuing entity.
- Award credits earned can be redeemed for goods and services provided either by the issuing entity or by other entities that participate in the loyalty programme.
- Award credits earned can be redeemed only for goods and services provided by other entities that participate in the loyalty programme; they are not redeemable by the issuing entity.

4.2.370 Scope of IFRIC 13

4.2.370.10 Any programme that comprises the following features is within the scope of IFRIC 13:

- the entity (seller) grants award credits to a customer as part of a sales transaction; and

- subject to meeting any other conditions, the customer can redeem the award credits for free or discounted goods or services in the future.

4.2.370.20 Therefore, the scope of IFRIC 13 is not limited to loyalty points programmes but captures a wide range of sales incentives that might include, for example, vouchers, coupons, discounts on renewals, and volume rebates. For example, a customer receives a complimentary product with every tenth product bought from the entity (seller). As the customer purchases each of the first ten products, they are earning the right to receive a free good in the future, i.e. each sales transactions earns the customer credits that go towards free goods in the future.

4.2.370.30 In another example, Company B launches a customer volume discount pro-gramme. The discount programme assigns points to the products and services offered by B. After reaching a certain number of points, customers receive a defined discount level for future purchases. Points earned are accumulated over a rolling eight-quarter period. After nine quarters, points earned in the first quarter are dropped, and points are rolled forward into the ninth quarter. In our view, this volume discount programme falls within the scope of IFRIC 13 because current sales transactions go towards earning a discount on future sales transactions.

4.2.370.40 Not all forms of loyalty card schemes will be within the scope of IFRIC 13. For example, Company R offers its customers a VIP card, a form of loyalty card. For an annual fee of 150, VIP card members are entitled to various levels of discount on the goods sold by R. Although the VIP card gives customers the right to receive dis-counted goods and services in the future, the purchase of the annual membership is not a *separate* sales transaction; rather, the current sales transaction is the purchase of the future discounts. Therefore, this arrangement is not within the scope of IFRIC 13, and the revenue from the sale of the VIP card should be recognised on an appropriate basis over the period of its validity.

4.2.380 Allocation of revenue to award credits

IFRIC 13.5, 6   4.2.380.10 An entity recognises the award credits as a separately identifiable component of revenue (see 4.2.50) and defers the recognition of revenue related to the award cred-its. The revenue attributed to the award credits takes into account the expected level of redemption.

IFRIC 13.   4.2.380.20 The consideration received or receivable from the customer is allocated between
BC14   the current sales transaction and the award credits by reference to fair values. IFRIC 13 itself does not prescribe a particular allocation method, but the basis for conclusions to the interpretation refers to the following methods, noting that the selection of one of the methods is a matter of judgement:

- relative fair values; or
- fair value of the award credits (residual or fair value method).

4.2.380.30 In our view, the reverse residual method, in which the current sales transaction is measured at fair value, and the remainder of the consideration is allocated to the award credits, is not an appropriate basis for allocating revenue (see also 4.2.60.60) as IFRIC 13 requires the consideration allocated to the award credits to be measured by reference to the fair value of the award credits.

IFRIC 13.
AG2

4.2.380.40 In estimating fair value, the entity (seller) takes into account:

- the fair value of awards offered to customers who have not earned award credits; and
- the proportion of award credits expected not to be redeemed, i.e. expected forfeitures.

IFRIC 13.
AG3

4.2.380.50 Other estimation techniques may be available. For example, if an entity (seller) pays a third party to supply the awards, then the fair value of the award credit could be estimated by reference to the amount that the entity pays plus a reasonable profit margin. However, judgement is required to select and apply the estimation technique that is most appropriate in the circumstances.

4.2.385 *Forthcoming requirements*

IFRIC 13.
AG2

4.2.385.10 The *Improvements to IFRSs 2010* clarified the terminology used in respect of the values of awards and award credits in a customer loyalty programme. Prior to the amendment, IFRIC 13 used the term "fair value" in relation to both the value of award credits and the value the awards for which such award credits could be redeemed. IFRIC 13 as amended states that the fair value of award credits takes into account the amount of discounts or incentives that otherwise would be offered to customers that have not earned the award credits. This amendment is effective for annual periods beginning on or after 1 January 2011. Early application is permitted. A brief outline of the annual improvements process is given in 1.1.85.10.

4.2.390 Recognition of revenue

4.2.390.10 The revenue from award credits is recognised as the entity (seller) fulfils its obligation to provide the free or discounted goods or services:

- Continuing the example in 4.2.370.20 (free product received after ten products purchased), revenue related to the complimentary product would be recognised when the customer receives that product.
- Continuing the example in 4.2.370.30 (customer volume discount programme), revenue related to the discount would be recognised on an appropriate basis over the period that the discount is received.

IFRIC 13.
AG2, BC16

4.2.390.20 Any subsequent change in the estimates of awards expected to be redeemed are trued-up for differences between the number of awards expected to be redeemed and the actual number of awards redeemed; the amount of revenue deferred at the time of the original sale is not recalculated.

4.2.390.30 For example, Company X runs a loyalty scheme, rewarding a customer's spend at its stores. Under this scheme, customers are granted 10 loyalty points (or award credits) for every 100 spent in X's store. Customers can redeem their points for a discount off the price of a new product in X's stores. The loyalty points are valid for five years and 50 points entitle a customer to a discount of 50 on the retail price of the product in X's store.

4.2.390.40 During 2010 X has sales of 1,000,000 and grants 100,000 loyalty points to its customers. Based on the expectation that only 80,000 loyalty points will be redeemed, management estimates the fair value of each loyalty point granted to be 0.80. During 2010 30,000 points were redeemed in exchange for new products, and at the end of the reporting period management still expected a total of 80,000 points to be redeemed, i.e. a further 50,000 points will be redeemed.

4.2.390.50 X records the following entries in 2010 in relation to the loyalty points granted in 2010:

	Debit	Credit
Cash	1,000,000	
Revenue		920,000
Deferred revenue (100,000 x 0.80)		80,000
To recognise revenue in relation to goods sold and		
deferred revenue for loyalty points awarded		

4.2.390.55 At the end of the reporting period, the balance of the deferred revenue is 50,000 ((50,000 / 80,000) x 80,000). Therefore, the difference in the deferred revenue balance is recognised as revenue for the year:

	Debit	Credit
Deferred revenue (80,000 - 50,000)	30,000	
Revenue		30,000
To recognise revenue in relation to 30,000 points		
redeemed in 2010		

4.2.390.60 During 2011 35,000 points are redeemed, and at the end of the year management expects a total of 85,000 points to be redeemed, i.e. an increase of 5,000 over the original estimate. The fair value of each award credit does not change, but the redemption rate is revised based on the new total expected redemptions. At the end of the year, the balance of deferred revenue for 20,000 loyalty points (85,000 - 30,000 - 35,000) is 18,824 ((20,000 / 85,000) x 80,000). X records the following entry in 2011 in relation to the loyalty points granted in 2010:

	Debit	Credit
Deferred revenue (50,000 - 18,824)	31,176	
Revenue		31,176
To recognise revenue in relation to points redeemed		
in 2011		

4.2.390.70 The reversal of deferred revenue in 2011 comprises two elements:

- A downwards adjustment of 1,765 to the 2010 reversal based on the revised expectation of redemptions: ((30,000 / 85,000) x 80,000) - 30,000.
- A reversal of 32,941 in relation to redemptions in 2011, based on the revised expectation of redemptions: (35,000 / 85,000) x 80,000.

4.2.390.75 Alternatively, on a cumulative basis 61,176 has been released, which can be calculated as (65,000 / 85,000) x 80,000.

IFRIC 13. 4.2.390.80 If a third party supplies the awards, then an assessment is required of whether *BC19, BC20* the entity acts as an agent or as a principal in the arrangement (see 4.2.660). If the entity acts as an agent, then the net amount retained is recognised as revenue, i.e. the difference between the revenue allocated to the award credits and the amount that the entity pays to the third party to supply the awards.

IFRIC 13. 4.2.390.90 For example, Company L participates in a customer loyalty programme oper-
IE10 ated by a third party. Under the programme, members earn points for purchases made in L's stores. Programme members redeem the accumulated award points for goods supplied by the third party. L has fulfilled its obligation to programme members once the members have been granted points when making purchases in its stores. The obligation to supply the redeemed goods lies with the third party. At the end of 2010 L has granted award points with an estimated fair value of 1,000, and owes the third party an amount of 700. Revenue is recognised as follows:

- If L is acting as an agent, then it recognises revenue of 300 in relation to the award points when its products are sold to customers.
- If L is acting as a principal, then it recognises revenue of 1,000 and an expense of 700 when its products are sold to customers.

996

4.2.390.100 If in the example programme members had the option of claiming their award from either L or the third party, then L would fulfil its obligation and recognise revenue only when the member claims their award, either from L or from the third party.

IFRIC 13.9 4.2.390.110 When the unavoidable costs of meeting the obligations to supply the award credits exceed the consideration received the entity has an onerous contract and a provision should be recognised in accordance with IAS 37 (see 3.12.630).

4.2.400 *Free/discounted goods or services*

4.2.400.10 In our view, the provision of free or discounted goods or services also is a form of identifiable benefit that is required to be identified as a separate component of the sales transaction (see 4.2.50). In such cases revenue is recognised and is allocated to all goods or services, including those provided free of charge.

4.2.400.20 For example, Company Y is offering a buy-one-get-one-free promotion on a specific product line. The selling price of the item is 25. In this example the free product has stand-alone value to the customer and is a separately identifiable component of the sales transaction (see 4.2.50). Therefore, the consideration received of 25 is allocated between the two separate components: the product purchased by the customer and the product provided free of charge.

4.2.400.30 The terms of any agreement to provide free or discounted goods or services should be analysed to determine if, in substance, they constitute customer loyalty programmes (see 4.2.360).

IAS 18.13, 4.2.400.40 For example, Company X hosts a promotion that allows a customer to pre-
IFRIC 13.5, pay for nine products and get the tenth product for free, i.e. the customer buys
18.15, 16 ten products and pays for only nine. One view is that the purchase of ten products is considered to be a single sales transaction; the free product is granted to the customer together with the current sales transaction, and therefore it is not within the scope of IFRIC 13 (see 4.2.370). Another view is that as part of a sales transaction (purchasing nine products) the customer has been granted a free product to be redeemed in the future; therefore the transaction is within the scope of IFRIC 13 (see 4.2.370). Whichever approach is taken, we would expect the accounting outcome for the purchase of the ten products to be similar. The free product granted is considered to be a separate identifiable component as it has a stand-alone value to the customer and we assume that its fair value can be measured reliably (see 4.2.50.60). Therefore, revenue is allocated to each separately identifiable component (ten purchases) and revenue is recognised as the products are redeemed by the customer.

4.2.400.50 Similarly, if an entity (seller) grants goods or services from third parties to a customer prior to or concurrent with the sale of other goods or providing services, then the arrangement should be analysed to determine if it includes separately identifiable components (see 4.2.50). If separate components are identified, then revenue is allocated to the separately identifiable components and revenue is recognised on each component when the recognition criteria are fulfilled.

4.2.410 *Cash incentives*

4.2.410.10 A cash sales incentive should be distinguished from arrangements in which a payment is made by an entity to a customer for an identifiable benefit that is separable from the supply contract. If that transaction could have been entered into with a third party independent of the supply contract, then generally the payment would be identified as a separate component of the transaction (see 4.2.50). In contrast, a cash sales incentive is not a separately identifiable component of the transaction.

4.2.410.20 For example, Company X is running a promotion in which customers receive a cash payment of 30 for entering into a contract. The cash payment in this example effectively is a discount on the usual price of the goods or service, i.e. the discount is linked to the sales contract (see 4.2.30); it is not a transaction that could have been entered into with a third party independent of the transaction with the customer.

4.2.410.30 If the benefit that the entity (seller) receives from the customer in return for the cash payment is the "right" to perform under a contract, then in our view it is not sufficiently separable for revenue to be recognised for that component even if it is an exclusive contract, i.e. the right would not be identified as a separate component of the transaction (see 4.2.50).

4.2.410.40 Continuing the example in 4.2.410.20, even if, for example, the contract with the customer is for a fixed term and the entity (seller) will receive a minimum amount of revenue under the contract, we believe that the cash payment of 30 should be accounted for as part of the sales transaction.

4.2.410.50 If the example in 4.2.410.20 were different such that the entity (seller) made the cash payment of 30 to a third party, e.g. to a selling agent, then the payment should be assessed to determine whether an intangible asset in respect of subscriber acquisition costs should be recognised (see 3.3.160), or whether the amount should be recognised as an expense when incurred.

4.2.410.60 In our view, cash incentives paid to the customer are rebates under IFRSs and should be recognised as a reduction from revenue. The fact that cash incentives are payments made to the customer at inception or renewal of an arrangement does not change the character of the payment and it is considered to be part of the overall consideration. In these circumstances the entity (seller) recognises an asset, if the recognition criteria are fulfilled (see 4.2.70). The asset reflects the fact that the seller has paid the cash incentive and will receive payment later, when the customer pays in accordance with the contract. Revenue will be recognised at a reduced amount taking into account the rebate provided by the cash incentive. In the example in 4.2.410.20, revenue would be reduced by 30.

4.2.420 *Volume rebates*

IAS 18.10   4.2.420.10 Sales agreements may include rebates payable to the customer if sales reach a certain volume. For example, if a customer purchases a certain value of goods, then a refund of a specified percentage will be granted. In our view, if it is probable that the rebate will be granted and the amount can be measured reliably, then the rebate is recognised as a reduction of revenue as the sales are recognised, i.e. before the threshold is met.

4.2.420.20 For example, Company V sells goods and grants a 15 percent rebate to each customer that spends at least 100,000 during a calendar year, which also is V's financial year. Usually the majority of sales take place in the fourth quarter. V concludes that it is probable that a particular customer will purchase 110,000 worth of goods over the full year, reflecting its past experience and the current year's forecasts.

4.2.420.30 In our view, the amount of revenue recognised during the year should reflect the expected sales to the customer for the full year. The same principle is applied when V prepares interim financial statements (see 5.9.100). Therefore, V applies a 15 percent rebate to measure revenue during the first quarter, based on the expected sales of 110,000 for the full period.

4.2.420.40 If it is probable that the criteria for the rebate will not be met, then we believe that the rebate should not be recognised until payment is probable. In our view, the rebate should be recognised as a reduction in revenue at the time that the rebate can be estimated.

4.2.430 *Gift certificates and vouchers*

4.2.430.10 Retailers may sell gift vouchers that can be exchanged for goods or services, or sometimes even cash. For example, a gift voucher is sold and can be exchanged for (specific) goods or services available in the store, but not for cash.

4.2.430.20 In our view, the voucher represents an advance payment by the customer and the entity (seller) has an unfulfilled obligation to deliver the (specific) goods or services. Revenue should be recognised when the (specific) goods are collected by the customer or the services have been rendered (and the other revenue recognition criteria have been met). The unredeemed gift vouchers would also be recognised as revenue if the amount is non-refundable and the entity concludes, based on evidence, that the likelihood of the customer requiring the entity to fulfil its performance obligation is remote. In our view, a portfolio approach covering all gift vouchers is not appropriate. Instead, the entity should assess all vouchers on a category-by-category basis.

4.2.430.30 If the customer has the right to receive cash, then the obligation resulting from an unredeemed gift voucher is a financial liability rather than deferred revenue and is subject to the derecognition requirements of IAS 39 *Financial Instruments: Recognition and Measurement* (see 3.6.1330).

IFRIC 13.
AG2 4.2.430.40 When vouchers are issued as part of a sales transaction and are redeemable against future transactions, IFRIC 13 is likely to apply and the amount of revenue recognised from the initial sale would be net of the fair value of the voucher issued (see 4.2.380.20). For example, customers spending over 50 in a single transaction

are given a voucher that entitles them to receive 5 off their next purchase over 20. Assuming that the fair value of the voucher is 3, the retailer would recognise revenue of 47 associated with the initial sale transaction and defer 3 until the voucher is redeemed by the customer. However, if the entity has a past practice of routinely granting customers 5 off purchases over 20 without needing a discount voucher, then this is taken into account in determining the fair value of the discount award (see 4.2.380.50), which in some cases may result in the full 50 being recognised at the date of the initial sale.

4.2.430.50 In some cases discount vouchers may be distributed to customers on a discretionary basis rather than as part of a sales transaction. As the discretionary vouchers were not granted as part of a sales transaction, no liability is recognised for the vouchers distributed as there is no performance obligation; the voucher requires customers to make a purchase in order to obtain the discount. Therefore, the vouchers are treated as discounts against revenue when the vouchers are redeemed by customers. However, the entity should assess whether the level of discounts awarded could have resulted in one or more onerous contracts in accordance with IAS 37 (see 3.12.630).

4.2.440 *Real estate*

IFRIC 15.4, 6   4.2.440.10 IFRIC 15 focuses on the accounting for revenue and associated expenses by entities that undertake the construction of real estate directly or through subcontractors. IFRIC 15 provides guidance on determining whether revenue from the construction of real estate should be accounted for in accordance with IAS 11 or IAS 18, and the timing of revenue recognition.

IFRIC 15.10-   4.2.440.20 IFRIC 15 clarifies that IAS 11 is applied to agreements for the construction of
12   real estate that meet the definition of a construction contract in accordance with IAS 11 (see 4.2.230), i.e. agreements in terms of which the buyer is able to specify the major structural elements of the design of the real estate before construction begins and/or specify major structural changes once construction is in progress, regardless of whether or not this ability is exercised. If the agreement does not meet the definition of a construction contract, then it is in the scope of IAS 18 (see also 4.2.2.90 and 500). In making this assessment, an entity also should consider the surrounding facts and circumstances, and the legal requirements of the relevant jurisdiction.

4.2.440.30 Some pre-completion contracts for the sale of residential properties may allow customers to specify a degree of customisation of the apartments (e.g. paint, appliances, fittings), but if this is small in relation to the project as a whole, then in our view the contract is not a construction contract because such minor variations do not constitute "major structural elements of the design". For example, we believe that an off-the-shelf house design under which cosmetic details and optional extras may be specified by the customer is not sufficient customisation to fall within construction contract accounting.

4.2.440.40 When the conditions in 4.2.440.20 are not met, the construction of an apartment building and the sale of individual apartments within that building are considered to be separate events. Accordingly, the sale of the units would be accounted for under IAS 18, which has a number of criteria for revenue recognition on the sale of real estate (see 4.2.450).

4.2.440.50 A real estate developer may form a mutual entity or fund to develop the property and facilitate the subsequent administration thereof. During development, or once it is complete, the developer sells shares in the entity rather than title to the underlying property. Often the shares in the entity are sold only once development has commenced; the shares issued can be sold freely on the secondary market.

4.2.440.60 In our view, these arrangements often are similar to the development and subsequent sale of a property, even though in these cases the developer is selling units in the entity that owns the property, rather than the property itself. We believe that even if the developer has a construction contract with the legal entity created to own the property, the developer should not account for the project as a construction contract. The developer should recognise revenue for the sold apartments (demonstrated by the sale of the shares to the investors) either in its entirety, e.g. upon completion of construction or upon delivery, or by reference to the stage of completion, depending on when the developer transfers to the buyer effective control and the significant risks and rewards of the work in progress (see 4.2.450).

4.2.440.70 Similarly, an entity may enter into contracts to construct buildings, semi-industrial warehouses and/or offices and sell its interest in the property to a third party, for example a real estate fund, once a reasonable occupancy rate of the premises has been achieved. In some cases the occupancy rate is achieved (and thus the project sold) before actual construction commences through pre-construction leasing.

4.2.440.80 In our view, the revenue-generating activity of the entity in this example is selling properties, both in progress and completed. In most cases the contracts are not specifically negotiated with the ultimate buyer, and construction often commences before a sales agreement or contract is negotiated. Work in progress and production costs should be recognised as inventory (see 3.8). Recognition of the revenue for the sale of the project will be in accordance with IAS 18. Accordingly, the entity should recognise revenue either in its entirety, e.g. upon completion of construction or upon delivery, or by reference to the stage of completion, depending on when the developer transfers to the buyer effective control and the significant risks and rewards of the work in progress (see 4.2.450).

4.2.440.90 The same analysis should be applied if the developer in the example in 4.2.440.50 sells shares in the entity before construction has been completed.

IFRIC 15.15, 4.2.440.100 When an entity is contracted to assemble materials supplied by others and
BC22 is not required to acquire and supply construction materials, i.e. it does not have inventory risk for the construction materials, the agreement is a service contract. Revenue is recognised by reference to the stage of completion of the contract activity when all of the revenue recognition criteria of IAS 18 are satisfied (see 4.2.310).

4.2.440.110 In general, the accounting for revenue arising from the construction of real estate can be summarised as follows:

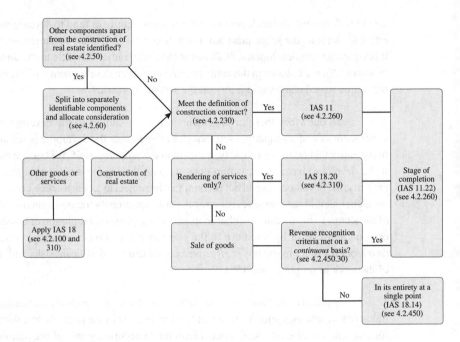

IAS 18.13,
IFRIC 15.8,
BC11

4.2.440.120 In addition to the construction of real estate, an entity may be contracted to deliver goods or services, e.g. property management services or the sale of land. The arrangement should be analysed to determine if it includes separately identifiable components (see 4.2.50). Each separately identifiable component is assessed on an individual basis to determine if it is within the scope of IAS 11 or IAS 18. The consideration received is allocated to the separately identifiable components on an appropriate basis (see 4.2.60).

IFRIC 15.IE1-
IE3

4.2.440.130 For example, Company Y submits design plans for an office block for building permission. Y enters into a sale agreement with a buyer for the sale of land and the construction of the office block. Under the terms of the sale agreement the buyer cannot influence the design of the offices except for minor design variations; and the buyer is not able to put the land or the incomplete office block back to Y. The construction of the office block commences once the building permission is received. Y is given access to the land to undertake the construction of the office block. The sale agreement is analysed as follows:

- The sale of the land is a sale of goods within the scope of IAS 18 (see 4.2.450).
- The construction of the office block is not a construction contract in accordance with IAS 11 because all of the major structural decisions were made by Y and were submitted to the planning authority before the buyer signed the sale agreement, and the buyer can make only minor variations to the design. Therefore, the construction of the office block is a sale of goods within the scope of IAS 18. Revenue for

the construction of the office block would be recognised either in its entirety, e.g. upon completion of construction or upon delivery, or by reference to the stage of completion depending on when Y transfers to the buyer effective control and the significant risks and rewards of the work in progress (see 4.2.450).

IFRIC 15.IE4 4.2.440.140 Continuing the example in 4.2.440.130, assume that construction of the office block commenced prior to Y signing the sales agreement with the buyer. In this case, there are three components identified in the sale agreement: the sale of land, the sale of the partially constructed office block, and finalising construction of the office block. Y would apply the revenue recognition criteria separately to each component (see 4.2.440.110).

4.2.450 *Sales of real estate within the scope of IAS 18*

IAS 18.14, 4.2.450.10 When effective control and the significant risks and rewards of ownership of
IFRIC 15.17, real estate are transferred to the buyer, revenue from sales of real estate is recognised
18 either:

- in its entirety at a single point of time when all of the revenue recognition criteria of IAS 18 (see 4.2.100) are satisfied, e.g. upon completion of construction or upon delivery (sales of goods approach); or
- by reference to the stage of completion (see 4.2.260) of the contract activity when all of the revenue recognition criteria of IAS 18 (see 4.2.100) are satisfied *continuously* as construction progresses (continuous transfer approach).

4.2.450.20 In our view, consideration of the significant risks and rewards of ownership generally will include price (market) risk related to the property and, in transactions in which the property is being developed, construction risk. In an arrangement in which an entity transfers a completed property to the buyer upon completion, typically revenue is recognised when legal title is transferred to the buyer as this demonstrates the transfer of the risks and rewards of ownership of the property.

IFRIC 15.IE8 4.2.450.30 In some jurisdictions ownership of the work in progress is transferred to the buyer as construction progresses, regardless of the stage of completion. The buyer would retain the work in progress and the entity has the right to be paid for the work performed should the agreement be terminated. This is an indication that control is transferred along with ownership of the work in progress. The entity would recognise revenue under the continuous transfer approach by reference to the stage of completion of the contract activity (see 4.2.260).

IFRIC 15.20 4.2.450.40 An entity considers all relevant facts and circumstances when determining whether the revenue recognition criteria are met continuously as construction progress. In our view, when considering the facts and circumstances of each agreement, an indicator approach is taken. The entity will need to exercise judgement to determine whether the facts and circumstances, taken individually or collectively, indicate that it is appropriate to recognise revenue as the construction activity progresses or to wait until the property is completed and physically transferred to the buyer.

4.2.450.50 The following factors are pertinent to the question of whether continuous transfer is, or is not, occurring while the construction activity progresses.

IFRIC 15.IE3,
IE8, IE11 4.2.450.60 Factors that collectively or individually may indicate that continuous transfer is occurring while construction progresses include:

- the construction activity takes place on land owned by the buyer;
- the buyer cannot put the incomplete property back to the developer;
- if the agreement is terminated before construction is complete, then the buyer retains the work in progress and the developer has the right to be paid for the work performed; and/or
- the agreement gives the buyer the right to take over the work in progress, perhaps with a penalty, during construction, e.g. to engage a different entity to complete the construction.

IFRIC 15.IE6 4.2.450.70 Factors that collectively or individually may indicate that continuous transfer is not occurring while construction progresses include:

- the sales agreement gives the buyer the right to acquire a specified unit in an apartment building when it is ready for occupation; and/or
- the deposit paid by the buyer is refundable if the developer fails to deliver the completed unit in accordance with the contractual terms.

IFRIC 15.IE6,
IE7, IE11 4.2.450.80 Factors that may be present in both a sales of goods approach and a continuous transfer approach and therefore do not appear to be indicative of either include:

- the buyer is required to make progress payments between the time of initial agreement and contractual completion;
- the balance of the purchase price is paid only on contractual completion, when the buyer obtains possession of its unit;
- the buyer's interest in the completed property can be transferred to others prior to completion; and/or
- The developer has physical control over access to the construction site during the period of construction activity (see 4.2.460.30)

IFRIC 15.
IE11 4.2.450.90 A factor that we expect often would be present in a continuous transfer agreement under paragraph 14 of IAS 18 is that the land on which the construction activity takes place is beneficially owned by the buyer at the time of that activity. Usually the owner of the land would have rights in respect of any structures located on that land, even if temporarily their access to the site is restricted while construction activity is in progress. Consequently, activity that falls under the continuous transfer approach may be economically similar to a real estate construction contract that falls within IAS 11, absent only the buyer's ability to specify the major structural elements of the design of the property.

IFRIC 15.IE2,
IE4 4.2.450.100 Such beneficial land ownership need not necessarily be in the form of a freehold interest, as in some jurisdictions title to the land may be in the form of a long-

term leasehold interest that gives the lessee the right to develop the land. The interest in the land typically would have arisen in one of the following ways:

- the interest in the land already was owned by the buyer before the entity was engaged to construct the property; or
- the interest in the land was sold to the buyer by the developer as part of the agreement to construct the building, and was identified as a separate component from the construction activity, in respect of which the sale of goods criteria under paragraph 14 of IAS 18 were met before the property was completed.

4.2.450.110 However, as indicated above, even if the construction activity takes place on the customer's land, a careful consideration of all facts and circumstances of the arrangement is required in order to determine whether revenue recognition criteria are met continuously as construction progresses.

IFRIC 15.IE5, 4.2.450.120 When the property is a unit (apartment) in a multi-unit building, the question
IE6, IE7 of land ownership by the buyer of an individual unit during the construction period generally is less straightforward and may vary from one legal jurisdiction to another. It may be common for agreements to buy individual units in multi-unit buildings to fall into the category of sales of goods approach, i.e. that in many such cases, revenue will be recognised by the developer on the later of the completion of the building and the sales agreement.

IFRIC 15.IE8 4.2.450.130 Conversely, certain jurisdictions require the developer to transfer to the buyer ownership of the real estate in its current state of completion and any additional construction becomes the property of the buyer as construction progresses. In such jurisdictions, IFRIC 15 also allows for the possibility that revenue may be recognised on the sale of units in a multi-unit building continuously as the construction activity progresses. Even in such jurisdictions all of the terms of the agreement should be considered and judgement should be applied to determine whether it is appropriate to apply the continuous transfer approach to such agreements.

4.2.460 Continuing involvement

IFRIC 15. 4.2.460.10 In some cases, although the construction of the property is completed and
IE10 the buyer has taken possession, the agreement for the construction of the property may include a degree of continuing involvement by the seller such that control and the significant risks and rewards of ownership have not been transferred to the buyer, e.g. a guarantee by the seller of a minimum return or occupancy level. In our view, for those arrangements in which revenue is recognised by reference to the stage of completion under the continuous transfer approach, the issue of any rental guarantee will result in the deferral of revenue, up to the amount of the outstanding rental guarantee. Conversely, for those arrangements in which revenue is recognised in its entirety, revenue recognition would be precluded by the issue of a significant rental guarantee (see also 4.2.120).

4.2.460.20 In our view, the guidance in IAS 17 should be applied in evaluating whether the seller has transferred the risks and rewards of ownership to the buyer (see 5.1) when the seller retains continuing involvement in the property, or provides guarantees of returns and occupancy levels.

IFRIC 15.
IE11

4.2.460.30 Having access to the land and work in progress in order to fulfil an entity's contractual obligation to deliver the buyer a completed property if the control of the work is transferred continuously to the buyer does not imply that the entity has retained continuing managerial involvement with the property to the degree associated with ownership. The entity may have control over the activities related to the performance of its contractual obligation but not over the property itself.

4.2.470 Contingent consideration

4.2.470.10 In some cases contingent consideration may be included in the selling price of a property. The entity (seller) should consider the nature of the contingent consideration in determining whether it has transferred substantially all of the risks and rewards of ownership of the asset and the degree of potential continuing involvement by the seller, if any.

4.2.480 [Not used]

4.2.490 *Selling and marketing costs*

4.2.490.10 During construction a real estate developer may incur selling and marketing costs that relate to a specific real estate construction project. Examples of such costs include advertising, sales commissions, and bank fees in order to list the property so that buyers can obtain mortgages. Generally selling costs are neither capitalised as inventory in accordance with IAS 2 *Inventories* (see 3.8.220.20) nor included in the costs of a construction contract in accordance with IAS 11 (see 4.2.280). Additionally, advertising and other costs incurred in obtaining customer contracts should be expensed as incurred (see 3.3.150). In our view, only in limited circumstances will direct and incremental costs recoverable as a result of securing a specifically identifiable contract with a customer qualify for capitalisation as an intangible asset in accordance with IAS 38 *Intangible Assets*; judgement will be required in making this assessment, which will depend on the specific facts and circumstances.

4.2.500 *Specific application issues for construction contracts*

4.2.510 *Bulk orders*

4.2.510.10 Sometimes entities receive orders to manufacture numerous items of a particular custom design. In these cases the entity considers:

- whether the construction of the assets produced under the contract would qualify as a construction contract; and
- if the assets qualify, then whether each unit is considered to be a construction contract or the entire order is considered to be one construction contract to manufacture a number of items.

4.2.510.20 For example, in our view an order for 100 aircraft should be treated as one overall contract, to which construction contract accounting is applied, if:

- there is a binding contract for the total order (i.e. 100 aircraft);
- the items ordered are custom-designed, for example when the 100 aircraft (although based on a standard platform) are modified and tailored to a high degree to the customer's specific needs;
- the penalties, in the event that the total order is cancelled, cover at least the costs incurred until the contract is cancelled; and
- all 100 aircraft are negotiated and total consideration is determined as part of a complete package (see 4.2.240).

4.2.520 *Learning curve costs*

4.2.520.10 "Learning curve costs" are common in contracts for multiple units of a custom-designed item. Learning curve costs is an industry accepted phrase. Losses may be incurred on the manufacture of the earlier units, while later production is more profitable as a result of construction efficiencies.

4.2.520.20 In our view, when the contract is within the scope of IAS 11 and is considered to be a single contract to manufacture numerous units, the learning curve costs are costs that relate to future contract activity and therefore are recognised evenly over the period of the contract under which these costs are expected to be recovered. As a result the learning curve costs are allocated evenly to each unit in the contract. When the contract is considered to be a construction contract, but firm orders have been received only for a portion of the units, the learning curve costs are spread only over those units for which a firm order has been received.

4.2.520.30 In our view, if the contract for 100 aircraft in 4.2.510.20 is treated as a single construction contract under IAS 11, then the learning curve costs incurred in producing the earlier aircraft are spread evenly over the entire contract. If IAS 18 was applied, then losses might be recognised on the earlier units, while later production would be more profitable once efficiencies in the construction process were achieved. In line with the requirements of IAS 2 (see 3.8.110 – 330), losses might need to be recognised prior to the sale, i.e. during production, if it would mean that costs are being capitalised that are not recoverable when accounting for revenue under IAS 18. See 3.8.215 for further discussion of learning curve costs.

4.2.530 *Recurring and non-recurring costs*

4.2.530.10 In some cases entities may enter into long-term programmes for the development and manufacture of components or assets. These long-term programmes do not meet the definition of construction contracts if the criteria discussed in 4.2.440.20 are not met. These programmes often are divided into multiple phases including:

- *Non-recurring phase.* Period during which the design, development and production preparation activities are performed. During this phase production orders may not have been received.
- *Recurring phase.* Period during which the components and assets are manufactured, either per shipsets (working packages that are technically defined) or in small series of several shipsets, depending on the specification of the agreed purchase orders.

4.2.530.20 The entity considers whether any part of the agreement is a construction contract and therefore is accounted for under IAS 11. In some cases a general agreement (framework) is negotiated with the customer that covers both the non-recurring phase and the recurring phase and, under this framework, the contractor usually is compensated for non-recurring activities only during the recurring phase, because the price per item includes compensation for the non-recurring costs. However, the customer may not be obliged to purchase a specified quantity and therefore no construction contract exists in respect of the full programme.

4.2.530.30 The agreement for the non-recurring phase may or may not be a construction contract under IAS 11. If it is a construction contract, then the costs of the non-recurring phase are treated as contract costs and the costs and related revenue are recognised in accordance with IAS 11. If there is no binding agreement for the recovery of the costs of the non-recurring phase or other indicators for a construction contract are not present, then the costs incurred during the non-recurring phase are capitalised and deferred only if they qualify for capitalisation as an intangible asset (see 3.3).

4.2.530.40 During the recurring phase, there still may be uncertainty regarding the quantity of items to be sold. A binding sales agreement (and therefore potentially a construction contract) is created only once a firm purchase order exists. Therefore, revenue recognition is based on the agreed number of firm purchase orders. If the non-recurring costs were recognised as an intangible asset, then the intangible asset would be amortised and included in construction work in progress inventory. However, treatment as a construction contract is subject to meeting the additional requirements discussed above.

4.2.530.50 Even if the order is accounted for as a construction contract, the results of the first purchase orders (contract) still may be a loss. This is because start-up costs or high (inefficient) production costs, not eligible for deferral, may be incurred that should be written off as incurred.

4.2.540 Software revenue

4.2.540.10 IFRSs do not provide specific guidance on revenue recognition for software-related transactions.

4.2.540.20 Often, software sales arrangements provide for sale of the software, together with subsequent servicing or licence arrangements. The substance of the transaction should be considered to determine whether the various components are linked and therefore accounted for as a single contract (see 4.2.30).

4.2.540.30 The general revenue recognition rules are applied to each component, for example:

- If the software entity is selling software products, then the principles for the sale of goods apply (see 4.2.100).
- If the software entity provides services related to software sold (e.g. upgrades or support), then revenue from these services should be deferred and recognised when the services are provided (see 4.2.310).
- If the software entity is developing customised software, then revenue is recognised by reference to the stage of completion of the development, in a similar manner to services and construction contracts (see 4.2.230).
- When the software entity enters into a licensing arrangement, the revenue is accounted for in accordance with the substance of the arrangement (see 4.2.570).

4.2.540.40 For example, Company K develops anti-virus software and sells non-renewable licences for the use of the software. The licensee receives the following during the licence period, which generally is two years:

- use of the software over the period of the licence;
- technical support in case of problems in installing and running the software; and
- an unlimited quantity of updates of the virus database, but not of the software itself.

4.2.540.50 The various elements of the product (as above) are not sold separately.

4.2.540.60 Once the licence period ends, users who want to continue using the software are required to pay the full fee again.

4.2.540.70 In our view, the components of the licence fee are linked (see 4.2.30) and are not separately identifiable; each component on its own has no stand-alone value to the customer (see 4.2.50.60) because the software on its own would be useless without the regular virus upgrades. We believe that the whole fee should be recognised as revenue over the licence period on a straight-line basis, unless there is another more appropriate method.

4.2.540.80 In our view, the stage of completion method is not always appropriate for the recognition of revenue for software licences and sales if the sale cannot be separated from any installation or services sold. In many cases the costs to complete the transaction and the direct costs incurred can be measured reliably. However, one of the costs incurred by the entity is that related to the cost of initial development of the software package. This cost would be related to all software and licences sold by the entity and not only to a single package sold to a single customer.

4.2.550 *Right of use of assets*

4.2.550.10 Sometimes the right to use an asset may be transferred in an agreement for the supply of goods or services (or both) that is not characterised as a lease. Additionally, IFRSs do not provide specific guidance on the circumstances in which revenue is not recognised on a sale transaction (i.e. a failed sale). In our view, the supply arrangement should be analysed to determine whether a right to use the asset is conveyed. This right also may be present in a failed sale. In our view, when the substance of such an arrangement is, or includes, a lease, lease accounting should be applied.

IFRIC 4.13 4.2.550.20 Under IFRIC 4 *Determining whether an Arrangement contains a Lease*, a supply arrangement is, or contains, a lease when specified criteria are satisfied. If an arrangement contains a lease, then the lease element is accounted for as either an operating lease or a finance lease in accordance with IAS 17. At the inception of such an arrangement, payments are split into lease payments and payments related to the other elements of the arrangement based on their relative fair values.

4.2.550.30 See 5.1 for further guidance on determining whether an arrangement contains a lease and accounting for a lease as either an operating lease or a finance lease.

4.2.560 *Outsourcing contracts*

4.2.560.10 Outsourcing contracts in practice offer a variety of different features. For example, Service Provider M enters into a 10-year contract with Manufacturing Company P to design and build a new IT platform to replace the various IT systems existing in P, and furthermore to outsource and run P's new IT platform after implementation (recurring service). As part of the outsourcing contract, all of P's existing IT hardware (computers, servers, laptops) as well as the personnel in P's IT department will be transferred to M.

4.2.560.20 In order to determine the proper accounting treatment for outsourcing contracts, a service provider should consider the substance of the contract:

- Certain outsourcing contracts contain an integrated set of activities and assets that are transferred. In the above example, the transfer of P's IT personnel and IT hardware might indicate that an integrated set of activities and assets is transferred to M. As a consequence, it should be determined whether the outsourcing contract falls within the scope of IFRS 3 *Business Combinations*. When the contract is indeed a business combination, the contract should be accounted for in accordance with IFRS 3 (see 2.6.50).
- As in this example, often outsourcing contracts include assets (e.g. an IT platform or other IT hardware) and therefore IFRIC 4 should be considered. If it is determined that the outsourcing contract contains leased assets, then the asset should be accounted for in accordance with IAS 17 (see 4.2.550 and 5.1). Equally relevant is considering whether the asset is property, plant or equipment of the service provider (see 3.2).
- When an outsourcing contract includes a public-to-private infrastructure service concession involving a public service obligation, the contract might be classified as a service concession agreement (see 4.2.580).
- A contract may include multiple elements, and the identification and recognition of those separate elements may be required (see 4.2.40).

IAS 18.20, 25 4.2.560.30 Outsourcing contracts that are service arrangements are accounted for under IAS 18. In the example in 4.2.560.10, this means that M's running of P's new IT platform after implementation should be accounted for as revenue as the services are rendered. In our view, in order to determine the amount of revenue earned it will be necessary to assess the most appropriate measure of performance, although in some cases this could be complex because of the mix of services provided. In some cases an output-based measure of performance will be appropriate, for example the number of transactions processed. In other cases when services are performed through an indefinite number of acts over a specific period, it may be appropriate to recognise revenue on a straight-line basis over that period. In the above example, revenue from the continuous maintenance of the IT platform might be recognised on a straight-line basis (see also 4.2.320).

IAS 18.13 4.2.560.40 Many contracts will require the outsource company to construct a specific asset as part of the service (as in the above example). It should be assessed whether the construction of the asset represents a separate component that should be accounted for separately. The construction of the specific asset, when separable, generally is accounted for in accordance with IAS 11 (see 4.2.230).

4.2.570 *Licence fees and royalties*

IAS 18.30, 4.2.570.10 Licence fees and royalties are paid for the use of an entity's assets, e.g. trade-
A20 marks, patents, software, music and motion picture films. Fees often are recognised on a straight-line basis.

IAS 17.2 4.2.570.20 Licence fees and royalties have to be distinguished from leases (e.g. for a building) although both may have similar characteristics.

4.2.570.30 An entity determines whether the transaction is, in substance, a sale of the asset or rights or is a licensing arrangement. The arrangement would in substance be a sale, with revenue recognised on transfer of the rights to the licensee, in the following circumstances:

- the rights to the asset are assigned to the licensee in return for a fixed fee or non-refundable guarantee;
- the contract is non-cancellable;
- the licensee is able to exploit its rights to the asset freely (i.e. the licensor no longer retains managerial control); and
- the licensor has no remaining obligations to perform.

4.2.570.40 For example, an entity sells film rights through a distributor who enters into licence agreements with customers. The licence period commences once the master tape is made available to the distributor. The entity has no further obligations and has no control over how the distributor distributes the film. In our view, all of the revenue from the sale of the film should be recognised when the licence period begins. Until that time ownership of the rights has not passed.

4.2.570.50 In other cases the proceeds are considered to relate to the right to use the asset over the licence period and the revenue is recognised over that period.

4.2.570.60 In some cases an entity may be entitled to a percentage of the revenues generated by the asset, but will be guaranteed a certain minimum. The guaranteed minimum fee may be recognised in a manner similar to a sale.

4.2.570.70 However, in our view in most cases it is unlikely that the entity will be able to recognise revenue equal to the guaranteed amount on transfer of the rights. Often the entity still retains significant risks and rewards of ownership because it continues to earn additional revenues based on the performance of the asset.

4.2.570.80 For example, Company B grants licences to Company G to broadcast a number of films on television. B cannot grant the licences to any other party. The licence fee is payable in instalments over a three-year period, based on a percentage of the advertising revenue generated from the films, with a minimum guaranteed fee payable over three years.

4.2.570.90 In our view, while B receives a minimum guaranteed amount, it still earns a percentage of the advertising revenues earned by G and therefore B still retains risks and rewards of ownership. In this case revenue does not arise from the initial transfer of the rights to the films, but rather from the use of the films. This is different from the case in which the rights to the asset are assigned to the licensee in return for a fixed fee or non-refundable guarantee referred to in 4.2.570.40. B will recognise the revenue when the film is shown and the amount of advertising revenue is reliably measurable. If the amount of the recognised revenue from this contract at the end of the term of the agreement is lower than the guaranteed minimum payment, then the difference would be recognised as revenue in that period.

4.2.580 Concession arrangements

4.2.580.10 IFRSs currently do not provide specific guidance on the recognition and measurement of concession arrangements by a grantor, including any fees received from the concession operator. In our view, the concession grantor should recognise any guaranteed minimum fee as revenue on a straight-line basis over the concession period, unless another method can be shown to be more appropriate. Any fees contingent on the concessionaire's sales or other income should be recognised when earned, i.e. when sales exceed the minimum amount agreed in the concession agreement.

4.2.580.20 See 5.12 for a discussion of the accounting for service concession arrangements by *operators*.

4.2.590 Financial services and related fees

IAS 18.IE14   4.2.590.10 Financial service fees may be considered an integral part of the effective yield of the instrument (see 4.6.300); otherwise, they are recognised in accordance with the general requirements above.

4.2.600 *Product financing arrangements*

SIC-27 4.2.600.10 IFRSs do not deal specifically with product financing arrangements, other than those involving the legal form of a lease.

4.2.600.20 SIC-27 *Evaluating the Substance of Transactions Involving the Legal Form of a Lease* identifies circumstances in which a transaction in the form of a lease is not accounted for as a lease. Often these arrangements do not convey the right to use an asset, but may be designed to achieve a tax advantage that is shared with another entity in the form of a fee.

4.2.600.30 SIC-27 highlights that it is necessary to distinguish between fees earned on the execution of a significant act and fees related to future performance and risks retained. Whether the fee is recognised immediately upon entering into the transaction or over the period of the transaction depends on whether or not the fee is contingent on future actions of the entity, including refraining from certain actions.

4.2.600.40 In our view, there is an initial presumption that any tax benefit received by an entity passed on as a fee is to be recognised over the period covered by the transaction rather than recognised immediately as revenue. In order to recognise any fee immediately, the risk of forfeiture would need to be remote.

4.2.600.50 In our view, when the entity is exposed to the risk of changes in tax legislation, i.e. when part or all of the tax benefit would not be received in the event of a change in tax legislation, it would not be appropriate to recognise the fee immediately.

4.2.600.60 In some cases financing also is obtained in addition to the tax benefit or fee. In our view, when this benefit is received in the form of a lower interest rate, it may be appropriate to present the benefit as a reduction in finance charges instead of revenue, provided that the benefit was received in the form of a lower interest rate.

4.2.610 *Upfront fees in the investment funds industry*

4.2.610.10 In the funds industry usually there are two separate contracts: the first between the investor and the fund's manager (brokerage or sales contract, whereby the fund manager is acting as an agent for the fund); and the second between the fund's manager and the fund itself (investment management contract). It could be questioned whether the upfront fee receivable by a fund manager for the sale of units of a (retail) fund relates to the provision of ongoing investment management service of the fund manager or to two services, i.e. a brokerage service and an investment management service.

4.2.610.20 Upfront fees receivable by a fund manager for the sale of units of a (retail) fund, in our view may relate to a separately identifiable brokerage service, as evidenced by the fact that third parties also undertake this service, as well as to investment management services. When a brokerage service can be identified and measured reliably, revenue may be recognised when the brokerage service is rendered. In this case revenue for the fund manager's services (i.e. brokerage service and investment management service) should be accounted for separately.

4.2.610.30 In our view, in the insurance industry generally there is no separately identifiable brokerage service as insurers enter into a single contract with policyholders (investors) and the contract is sold as a net package. However, when the brokerage service is separately identifiable, revenue should be measured at the fair value of the consideration received (or receivable), i.e. based on the amount that the market would charge for similar brokerage services that are not associated with an investment management contract.

4.2.620 *Credit guarantees*

IFRS 4.4(d) 4.2.620.10 Financial guarantees issued by an entity may be accounted for under IAS 39 (see 3.6.35) or, in certain circumstances, under IFRS 4 *Insurance Contracts* (see 5.10.30). IFRS 4 provides limited guidance related to revenue recognition. An exception exists for an insurance contract that is entered into or retained on transferring to another party financial assets or financial liabilities within the scope of IAS 39. Such guarantees are accounted for under IAS 39.

IAS 39.9 4.2.620.20 For credit guarantees that are accounted for as derivatives, the credit derivative is measured as a financial instrument (see 3.6.30). On initial recognition an issuer of credit derivatives measures these derivatives at fair value, which usually is equal to the value of the commission received. Subsequently, these instruments are measured at fair value through profit or loss. In the case of a credit derivative that remains out of the money for its term (i.e. the issuer is not required to make payments to the holder), the treatment will have the effect of recognising the commission received as revenue over the term of the credit derivative, though not on a straight-line basis.

4.2.630 *Advertising*

IAS 18.IE12 4.2.630.10 Revenue for advertising services generally should be recognised only when the related advertisement appears before the public. However, any production commissions are recognised by reference to the stage of completion.

4.2.630.20 For example, an entity produces, publishes and distributes telephone directories annually, which display advertisements placed by third parties. In our view, the revenue received by the entity from the sale of advertisements should be recognised only when the telephone directories are distributed to the public, despite the fact that the advertisements are arranged and consideration is received during prior periods. The related costs are recognised in profit or loss at the same time as the revenue is recognised to the extent that the costs were recognised as inventory (see 3.8). If the directories are delivered over an extended period, for example over several reporting periods, then in our view it would be appropriate to measure the stage of completion based on the proportion of directories delivered in a period. See also 3.8.60.

4.2.640 *Transfers of assets from customers*

IAS 18.13, 4.2.640.10 IFRIC 18 provides guidance on transfers of property, plant and equipment
IFRIC 18.13, (or cash to acquire it) for entities that receive such assets from their customers in return
14 for a network connection and/or an ongoing supply of goods or services. When an asset
is recognised, at fair value, by an entity that receives a contribution within the scope of
IFRIC 18 (see 3.2.20.30), a corresponding amount is recognised as revenue.

4.2.641 *Scope of IFRIC 18*

IFRIC 18. 4.2.641.10 IFRIC 18 provides guidance on accounting for transfers of items of property,
BC5, plant and equipment or cash to acquire or construct such property, plant and equipment.
IAS 8.11, 12 For transactions involving the transfer of assets other than property, plant and equipment or cash to acquire or construct such property, plant and equipment, for example,
transfers of intangible assets such as software, patents, licences or intellectual property
rights, entities consider the criteria in IAS 8 *Accounting Policies, Changes in Accounting Estimates and Errors* in order to determine whether IFRIC 18 or other appropriate
guidance should be applied by analogy.

IFRIC 18.7 4.2.641.20 Arrangements within the scope of IFRIC 12 *Service Concession Arrangements*
and IAS 20 *Accounting for Government Grants and Disclosure of Government Assistance* are excluded from the scope of IFRIC 18.

IFRIC 18.3 4.2.641.30 In some transactions in the scope of the interpretation, the party that transfers the
assets (the transferor) may be different from the party that will receive access to a supply
of goods or services (the ultimate customer). For example, a property developer builds a
residential complex in an area that is not connected to the water mains. To connect to the
water mains, the property developer is required to install a network of pipes and to transfer
them to the water supply company, which will supply future services to the residents of
the complex. This fact does not affect the accounting outcome under IFRIC 18.

4.2.642 *Timing of revenue recognition*

IFRIC 18.14- 4.2.642.10 In determining the timing of revenue recognition, the entity (recipient)
21 considers:

- what performance obligations it has as a result of receiving the customer contribution;
- whether these performance obligations should be separated for revenue recognition
  purposes (see 4.2.50); and
- when revenue related to each separately identifiable performance obligation should
  be recognised (see 4.2.40.30).

IFRIC 18. 4.2.642.20 Comprehensive guidance on how to determine the entity's performance obliga-
BC18 tions is not provided by the interpretation. In practice it may be difficult to determine
whether the entity only has to connect the customer to a network, or it has to provide
ongoing access to a supply of goods and services, or both.

4.2.642.30 IFRIC 18 does not specify whether the analysis of performance obligations starts with evaluating whether the connection is a separately identifiable service or with determining whether any additional performance obligations arise from the transaction. In our view, both of those approaches are acceptable and an entity should choose an accounting policy, to be applied consistently, for determining separately identifiable components of such arrangements.

IFRIC 18.17, 4.2.642.40 All relevant facts and circumstances should be evaluated when determining
IE3 whether additional performance obligations arise from the transfer including:

- whether or not the customer providing the contribution is charged the same fee for the supply of goods or services as is charged to other customers that are not required to make such customer contributions;
- whether customers have the ability to change the supplier of goods or services at their discretion; and
- whether a successor customer needs to pay a connection fee when the customer that made the customer contribution discontinues the service, and if so, the amount of such connection fee relative to the fair value of asset contributed.

IFRIC 18.17 4.2.642.50 In our view, in determining whether a rate charged to a customer includes a discount, the entity should compare rates for ongoing services charged to customers that make a contribution with the rates charged to customers that do not.

IFRIC 18.20 4.2.642.60 If it is determined that some or all of the revenue arising from the customer contribution relates to the ongoing supply of goods or services, then revenue is recognised as those services are delivered. Typically such revenue is recognised over the term specified in the agreement with the customer. If, however, no such term is specified, then the period of revenue recognition is limited to the useful life of the transferred asset (see 4.2.90).

4.2.646 *Cash contributions*

4.2.646.10 Instead of property, plant and equipment, an entity may receive cash that must be used to construct or acquire an item of property, plant and equipment in order to connect the customer to a network and/or provide the customer with ongoing access to a supply of goods or services.

IFRIC 18.21 4.2.646.20 The accounting for such cash contributions depends on whether the item of property, plant and equipment to be acquired or constructed is recognised as an asset of the entity upon acquisition/completion:

- If the asset is not recognised by the entity, then the cash contribution is accounted for as proceeds for providing the asset to the customer under IAS 11 or IAS 18, as applicable.
- If the asset is recognised by the entity, then the asset is recognised and measured as it is constructed or acquired in accordance with IAS 16 *Property, Plant & Equipment*; the cash contribution is recognised as revenue following the guidance in 4.2.642.

4.2.650 Gross or net presentation

IAS 18.7, 8 4.2.650.10 Revenue represents the amounts receivable by the entity for its own account. Therefore, revenue is stated at its *gross* amount and is measured before deducting related costs such as costs for materials and salaries.

4.2.660 *Agency relationships*

IAS 18.8 4.2.660.10 In an agency relationship, amounts collected on behalf of and passed on to the principal are not revenue of the agent. The revenue of the agent is the amount of commission, plus any other amounts charged by the agent to the principal or other parties.

4.2.660.20 The principal in an agency relationship recognises the gross amount charged to the ultimate customer as revenue. Commission paid to the agent is accounted for as an expense by the principal.

IAS 18.IE21 4.2.660.30 Determining whether an entity is acting as an agent or principal is based on an evaluation of the risks and responsibilities taken by the entity, including inventory risk and responsibility for the delivery of goods or services. Judgement is required and all relevant facts and circumstances must be considered.

4.2.660.40 A common example of an agency relationship is a travel agent. Travel agents sell airline tickets to the public generally at a price determined by reference to the market rate, but often pay the airline a discounted amount. The travel agent does not bear any general inventory risk because it does not carry tickets in inventory and only purchases tickets when it receives orders or bookings from customers.

4.2.660.50 In this case the travel agent does not bear any inventory risk nor is it responsible for carrying out the services related to the ticket itself, as this is the responsibility of the airlines. In our view, the travel agent provides a service on behalf of various airlines and other suppliers and earns a fee. The travel agent's revenue should reflect only the fee and not the gross amount billed to the customer. In some cases travel agents may bear some credit risk, for example when corporate customers have an account with the travel agent and settle the account only after the travel agent has paid the airline for the ticket. In our view, the fact that the agency sometimes bears credit risk is not a determining factor and does not compel the agency to reflect the gross billing as revenue.

IAS 18.IE21 4.2.660.60 Usually an entity working as an agent or broker does not have exposure to the significant risks and rewards of ownership of goods or rendering of services. An entity having exposure to the significant risks and rewards associated with the sale of goods or rendering of services is acting as a principal. The following features should be considered to determine if an entity is acting as a principal or an agent. None of the indicators noted below should be considered presumptive or determinative, but an overall assessment would need to take into account the direction of the majority of indicators:

- Indicators that an entity is acting as a *principal* include that it:
  - has primary responsibility for providing the goods and services to the customer or for fulfilling the order;
  - has inventory risk before or after the customer order, during shipping or on return;
  - has discretion in establishing prices (directly or indirectly); and
  - bears the customer's credit risk for the amount receivable from the customer.
- An indicator that an entity is acting as an *agent* is that it performs services for compensation on a commission or fee basis, which is fixed either in terms of an amount of currency or a percentage of the value of the underlying goods or services provided by the principal.

4.2.660.65 The additional indicators listed below also may be useful in determining whether an entity is acting as a principal, i.e. the entity:

- modifies the product or performs part of the services;
- has discretion in selecting the supplier used to fulfil an order;
- is involved in determining product or service specifications.

4.2.660.70 For example, Company V operates an internet site from which it will sell Company T's products. Customers place orders directly on the internet site and provide credit card details for payment. V receives the order and authorisation from the credit card company, and passes the order on to T, who ships the product directly to the customer. V does not take title to the product and has no risk of loss or other responsibility for the function or delivery of the product. T is responsible for all product returns, defects and disputed credit card charges. The product typically is sold for 175 from which V receives a commission of 25. In the event that a credit card transaction is rejected, V loses its margin on the sale (i.e. the 25).

4.2.660.80 We believe that V should recognise its fee of 25 as revenue, as it does not take title to the product or take on any of the risks and rewards of ownership of the product. In addition, its credit risk is limited to its fee of 25.

4.2.660.90 In another example, a film distributor agrees to distribute films on behalf of a producer and the only risk borne by the distributor is the responsibility for replacing the film if it is lost in transit. We believe that when the cost of a replacement copy is small, this risk is not material. In this case the distributor does not take ownership of the films, is not at risk if the films are faulty, does not determine prices, and does not take any credit risk other than in relation to its commission. Therefore, we believe that the distributor should report, as revenue, only its distribution fee and should not include amounts collected from theatres on behalf of the producer as revenue.

4.2.670 *Amounts incurred or collected on behalf of customers*

4.2.670.10 It is necessary to distinguish between amounts received from customers in exchange for goods or services provided to them, and amounts received on behalf of third parties from customers. Amounts received on behalf of third parties should be accounted for as a payable in the statement of financial position until settled and should not gross up revenue and expenses (e.g. sales taxes). Similarly, amounts prepaid to third parties on behalf of customers should be recognised as a receivable until recovered and also should not gross up revenues and expenses.

4.2.670.20 Conversely, amounts received from customers in exchange for services rendered should be recognised as revenue (see 4.2.660). For example, the principal activity of Company S is structuring finance transactions, for which it earns a fee. When developing and executing the transactions, S hires tax lawyers to advise on the transactions and to draft documentation.

4.2.670.30 In our view, S should report revenue gross (i.e. not deducting legal fees). The legal fees are S's operating costs that are incurred to generate fee revenue, regardless of whether transactions are successful or not. S does not incur the legal fees on behalf of its clients nor is it collecting fees on behalf of the lawyer.

4.2.670.40 To determine whether revenue should be presented gross or net of costs incurred, the entity considers whether it is acting in the capacity of an agent or a principal. In our view, in these cases the entity should consider:

- when the seller has the freedom to determine the amount to charge to the customer, this indicates that the seller acts as the principal, while a requirement to pass on the actual costs incurred indicates that the seller acts as an agent; and
- when the seller is exposed to changes to the actual costs and cannot pass on price changes to the customer, this indicates that the seller is acting as a principal.

4.2.680 *Transport costs*

4.2.680.10 Sellers often incur transport costs on the delivery of goods sold to customers. For example, Company E sells steel (both domestically and to foreign markets) and arranges the transport of that steel to its customers. E enters into contracts for the transport directly with the transporter. For domestic sales, customers of E can choose to arrange for their own transportation or they can arrange transportation through E; E recharges its customer the actual cost plus a fee. With respect to export sales, transportation services are included in the price in the sales contract. E does not charge the export customer separately for delivery expenses, but merely includes an export charge to the customer, which is calculated by E to include recovery of the expected transport charges.

4.2.680.20 We believe that E acts as an agent with respect to the transport costs for its domestic customers, as the customer bears the risk for any changing transport prices and E will not absorb changes in transport prices. In our view, while E bears the credit risk of the customers, it is not a significant risk in this case. Therefore, we believe that E should report revenue from domestic sales (including the commission charged for transport costs) net of transport costs incurred.

4.2.680.30 The selling price of the export goods is set to recover the expected transport costs. E bears the price risks related to the transport, as it will not pass any unexpected transport price fluctuations onto the customer when billing for the transaction. Further, E has the freedom to set and change the prices it charges to the customer in respect of the transport costs (as these are costs that are included in the determination of the overall selling price). We believe, E is acting as the principal in respect of the transport for export goods and therefore revenue should be presented on a gross basis. The transport costs should be presented as part of cost of sales.

4.2.690 *Lease arrangements*

4.2.690.10 In another common example, an entity leases out property and the fixed monthly rent payment includes both the right to use the premises and the water and electricity usage. In our view, it would not be appropriate to net the utility costs against revenue or otherwise allocate a portion of revenue as reimbursement of the utility costs. This is because, in this case, the landlord bears the risks of price and volume fluctuation associated with the actual consumption of water and electricity by the tenant.

4.2.690.20 If, however, the rent includes only the right to use the premises and the tenant also agrees to refund the landlord for all electricity and water costs, then revenue would include only the fixed rental charged. In this case the property owner has no risks beyond credit risk related to the actual consumption of water and electricity and the related costs, and we believe is acting as an agent on behalf of the utility companies.

4.2.700 *Sales taxes*

IAS 18.IE21 4.2.700.10 Revenue does not include sales taxes, value added taxes (VAT) or goods and service taxes when the entity is acting as a collection agent on behalf of the tax authorities.

4.2.700.20 In some jurisdictions, excise duties or taxes are levied on particular goods and services, for example, oil and gas products, tobacco products or alcoholic drinks. Excise duties may be computed as a percentage of either the selling price or the production cost.

4.2.700.30 IFRSs do not address specifically the accounting for excise duties. In our view, an analogy with sales tax often is relevant, but the appropriate accounting treatment will depend on the local regulatory requirements. An entity should consider whether it is acting in a manner similar to that of an agent or a principal.

4.2.700.40 For example, excise duties may be determined based on production levels and are payable to the authorities regardless of whether goods are sold (i.e. the tax payments are not refunded by the authorities if the goods are not sold). In our view, in these cases the tax is another production cost to be recovered in the pricing of the goods. Accordingly, the sales price effectively would be gross of the excise duties recouped from customers. As a result, the excise duties are included in the revenue line item, with an equal amount included in the cost of goods sold line item.

4.2.700.50 In another example, duties calculated as a percentage of the selling price may be recouped from the authorities if the buyer defaults. In our view, the seller is likely to be acting as an agent because it does not bear any risk, including credit risk. Under this approach the amount of excise tax is excluded from revenue and amounts collected are reported as a liability.

4.2.700.60 In another example, the tax authorities in Country X impose an export tax on certain commodities sold to overseas customers; an entity cannot reclaim the tax if the customer defaults. In our view, in this example an entity acts as a principal rather than as an agent for the tax authorities. Therefore, similar to the example in 4.2.700.40, the sales price effectively is gross of the export tax recouped from customers. As a result, the export tax is included in the revenue line item, with an equal amount included in expenses.

4.2.700.70 In practice, this might lead to different accounting by entities within a multi-national group as the approach taken should vary depending on the different tax regimes in various jurisdictions. Depending on how the legal or regulatory requirements are applied, the determination of whether an entity is acting as an agent or principal may require significant judgement. In our view, if excise taxes are significant, then the entity should disclose the line item(s) in which they are included.

4.2.710 *Allowances received from suppliers*

IAS 1.34 4.2.710.10 Some transactions do not generate revenue, but are incidental to the main revenue-generating activities of an entity. The results of these transactions are presented by netting any income with related expenses arising from the same transaction when this reflects the substance of the transaction or event.

4.2.710.20 For example, an entity (retailer) may receive consideration from suppliers as a reimbursement of costs incurred. This consideration may be in the form of cash payments or rebates. In our view, allowances should be treated as follows:

- Consideration received for assets or services delivered to the supplier by the retailer should be recognised in profit or loss. It may be presented as revenue by the retailer, if it relates to goods or services sold or delivered in the course of the ordinary activities of the entity, or presented as other income if the activities are incidental to the retailer's main operations (see 4.2.10.30).

  For example, Retailer G receives a payment from a supplier in respect of the rental of space in its store, including freezer space and prime aisle space. The inventory located in these areas is owned by G; however, the rent is not dependent upon the sale of the supplier's products. We believe, G is rendering services (the provision of space) to the supplier and the rental income should be presented either as revenue (if the activity is not incidental in nature), or as other income.

- Consideration that is a reimbursement of costs incurred by the retailer to sell the manufacturer's products should be presented as a reduction of that cost incurred by the entity.

  As an example, Retailer C distributes product X. The supplier of product X agrees to reimburse C for certain marketing costs incurred by C, with payment made on a quarterly basis. We believe, the reimbursement of any costs by the supplier would not qualify as revenue of C and should be offset in profit or loss against the marketing costs that have been incurred by C.

  In our view, when the consideration received exceeds the expense incurred by the entity, this excess amount should be recognised as a reduction of the retailer's cost of sales.

- Consideration that represents a reduction of the prices of the manufacturer's products or services, e.g. trade discounts, rebates and other similar items, should be presented as a reduction of the retailer's inventory and therefore of cost of sales (see 3.8.160).

4.2.720 **Presentation and disclosure**

IAS 1.81   4.2.720.10 Revenue is presented as a separate item in the statement of comprehensive income.

IAS 18.1, 29   4.2.720.20 In IAS 18, interest and dividends also are referred to as revenue. In practice, entities other than financial institutions generally present interest and dividends received within finance income (see 4.6.540). Revenue also may include rental income earned by a lessor (see 5.1.320).

IAS 11.39(a), 18.35(b)   4.2.720.30 In addition to the above, revenue arising from the following categories is disclosed separately:

- sale of goods;
- services rendered;
- royalties; and
- construction contracts.

IAS 18.35(c)   4.2.720.40 Revenue from barter transactions is disclosed separately.

IAS 11.39, 18.35(a)   4.2.720.50 Accounting policies adopted for revenue recognition are required to be disclosed, including disclosure of the methods used to determine contract revenue (which will depend on whether contracts are fixed price or cost-plus contracts), and the methods used to determine the stage of completion for construction contracts and the rendering of services.

SIC-27.10(b)   4.2.720.60 The accounting treatment of fees received on a product financing arrangement is disclosed, as is the amount recognised as income during the period. It is likely that these fees will be presented as part of "other income" when financing transactions are not considered to be part of the entity's ordinary activities.

4.2.730 **Future developments**

4.2.730.10 The IASB and the FASB are working on a joint project to develop a comprehensive set of principles for revenue recognition. In June 2010 the IASB published ED/2010/6 *Revenue from Contracts with Customers*, which would replace IAS 11, IAS 18 and a number of interpretations, including IFRIC 18 and SIC-31. The ED proposes a single revenue recognition model in which an entity recognises revenue as it satisfies a performance obligation by transferring control of promised goods or services to a customer. The ED does not propose to retain current requirements that revenue is not recognised if the goods or services exchanged are of a similar nature and value. The model would be applied to all contracts with customers except leases, financial instruments, insurance contracts and non-monetary exchanges between entities in the same line of business to facilitate sales to customers other than the parties to the exchange. A final standard is scheduled for the second quarter of 2011.

4.2.730.20 In May 2009 the IASB published ED/2009/5 *Fair Value Measurement* (the 2009 ED). The proposals in the 2009 ED are intended to replace the fair value measurement guidance contained in individual IFRSs with a single, unified definition of fair value, as well as provide further authoritative guidance on the application of fair value measurement in inactive markets. The 2009 ED proposes a framework for measuring fair value and disclosures about fair value measurements. The proposals in the 2009 ED explain how to measure fair value when it already is required or permitted by existing IFRSs; they do not introduce new fair value measurements, nor do they eliminate the practicability exceptions to fair value measurements that exist currently in certain standards.

4.2.730.30 In June 2010 the IASB published ED/2010/7 *Measurement Uncertainty Analysis Disclosure for Fair Value Measurements* (the 2010 ED). The 2010 ED expands on the proposal in the 2009 ED for an entity to disclose a measurement uncertainty analysis (or sensitivity analysis) for assets and liabilities measured at fair value categorised within Level 3 of the fair value hierarchy. The 2010 ED proposes that an entity consider the effect of correlation between unobservable inputs, if relevant.

4.2.730.40 A final standard on fair value measurement and disclosure, which is expected to be converged with a forthcoming amended standard under US GAAP, is scheduled for the first quarter of 2011.

4.3 Government grants
(IAS 20, IAS 41, SIC-10)

4.3 Government grants
(IAS 20, IAS 41, SIC-10)

Overview of currently effective requirements

- Government grants that relate to the acquisition of an asset, other than a biological asset measured at fair value less costs to sell, may be recognised either as a reduction in the cost of the asset or as deferred income, and are amortised as the related asset is depreciated or amortised.

- Unconditional government grants related to biological assets measured at fair value less costs to sell are recognised in profit or loss when they become receivable; conditional grants for such assets are recognised in profit or loss when the required conditions are met.

- Other government grants are recognised in profit or loss when the entity recognises as expenses the related costs that the grants are intended to compensate.

Currently effective requirements

This publication reflects IFRSs in issue at 1 August 2010. The currently effective requirements cover annual periods beginning on 1 January 2010. The requirements related to this topic are derived mainly from IAS 20 *Accounting for Government Grants and Disclosure of Government Assistance* and IAS 41 *Agriculture*.

Forthcoming requirements and future developments

When a currently effective requirement will be changed by a new requirement that is issued but is not yet effective, it is marked with a # as a **forthcoming requirement** and the impact of the change is explained in the accompanying boxed text. In respect of this topic no forthcoming requirements are noted.

When a significant change to the currently effective or forthcoming requirements is expected, it is marked with a * as an area that may be subject to **future developments** and a brief outline of the relevant projects is given in 4.3.170.20 – 50. In addition, a brief outline of a further project is given in 4.3.170.10 that may affect all aspects of the accounting for government grants.

4.3.10 Definitions

IAS 20.3 4.3.10.10 Government grants are transfers of resources to an entity by a government entity in return for compliance with certain past or future conditions related to the operating activities of the entity, e.g. a government subsidy.

SIC-10   4.3.10.20 Government assistance meets the definition of a government grant even if the conditions are only a requirement to operate in certain regions or industry sectors.

IAS 20.3,   4.3.10.30 IAS 20 establishes accounting requirements only for government assistance
34-38   in the form of grants. Therefore, the distinction between government grants and other forms of government assistance is important. Government assistance is not considered a government grant if the assistance cannot reasonably have a value placed upon it, or is a transaction with a government body that cannot be distinguished from the normal operating transactions of the entity. Therefore, when a government provides free technical or marketing advice or other services or guarantees, the assistance normally is not recognised in the financial statements. Similarly, a government procurement contract, or similar arrangement, whereby a government body agrees to buy certain output produced by an entity, normally is not distinguished from the normal operations of the entity and is not treated as a government grant. The extent of government assistance that does not take the form of a grant is, however, disclosed if it is significant and benefits the entity directly.

IAS 20.3   4.3.10.40 In addition, if the government provides support to an entity and also is a shareholder in that entity, then an assessment needs to be carried out as to whether the government is acting in its capacity as shareholder or as government (see also 3.6.1360.20). If there is no requirement attached to a contribution from the government to comply with certain conditions related to the operating activities of the entity, then that contribution is most likely not a government grant. For example, a local bus company receives buses from the government; the government also is the sole shareholder of the bus company and a similar contribution is not available to other bus companies. There are no further conditions attached to the contribution of the buses, but there is a general expectation that the company will provide bus services to the local community. In order to determine the proper accounting for the contributed assets, the economic substance of the transaction needs to be analysed. In our view, providing public transportation in the local area is an objective of the company itself, and not a condition of the contributed assets. In addition, the contribution is not available to other companies. Therefore, we believe that in this example the contributed assets do not meet the definition of a government grant; the government is acting in its capacity as a shareholder and the asset contribution should be recognised as a capital contribution. See 1.2.110 for a discussion of the evaluation of shareholder transactions.

4.3.20 *Forgivable loans*

IAS 20.10   4.3.20.10 A government may extend a loan that will be forgiven if certain conditions are met (a forgivable loan). A forgivable loan is treated as a government grant only when there is reasonable assurance that the entity will meet the terms for forgiveness of the loan. Otherwise the loan is recognised as a liability (see also 4.3.100).

4.3.20.20 For example, Company C is launching an airline. Government Z provides C with financing to fund the launch. The financing is in the form of a loan that will be repayable by C if the business is successful, but the amount advanced will not be repaid if the airline is launched but the business is unsuccessful. In our view, C should recognise the amount received as a liability. The liability would become a government grant (forgivable loan) if, and only if, the venture does not succeed, i.e. when it is reasonably assured that the business is not successful.

4.3.30 *Waiver of expenses*

4.3.30.10 In some cases, instead of providing a cash grant, a government may waive amounts payable by the entity (e.g. a liability for taxes). In our view, these qualify as government grants because in substance there is a transfer of resources, although it is in the form of a waiver of expenses.

4.3.40 **Recognition and measurement**

IAS 20.7   4.3.40.10 Government grants are recognised when there is reasonable assurance that the entity will comply with the relevant conditions and the grant will be received.

IAS 20.12   4.3.40.20 Grants are recognised in profit or loss on a systematic basis when the entity recognises, as expenses, the related costs that the grants are intended to compensate.

IAS 20.17   4.3.40.30 Grants that relate to the acquisition of an asset are recognised in profit or loss as the asset is depreciated or amortised. See 4.3.130 for a discussion of the presentation of such grants in the statement of financial position and in the statement of comprehensive income.

IAS 20.18   4.3.40.40 If a grant relates to a non-depreciable asset, then an entity considers the conditions related to the grant. For example, an entity is granted land on the condition that it operates a building on that land. The entity recognises the land at its fair value. In this case the grant is recognised in profit or loss as the cost of operating the building to meet the conditions of the grant is incurred (e.g. as the building is depreciated).

4.3.40.50 In some cases a grant may relate to an asset that will be used to fulfil the conditions of the grant and for other activities of the entity. In our view, the grant is recognised in profit or loss systematically based on the cost incurred in meeting the conditions of the grant, i.e. excluding the cost of activities that are not related to the conditions of the grant.

4.3.40.60 For example, Company D receives a grant of land. D recognises the land at its fair value. The conditions of the grant require the entity to construct on the land and to operate, for a given period, a sports stadium. D assesses whether the arrangement is in the scope of IFRIC 12 *Service Concession Arrangements* (see 5.12.01 – 45) and concludes that it is not. The piece of land is larger than required to construct the stadium and D disposes of the excess land to a third party. In our view, the whole of the grant, i.e. the value of all the land granted, should be recognised systematically based on the costs incurred in fulfilling the conditions of the grant, i.e. the costs of operating the stadium.

IAS 20.20 4.3.40.70 A grant that is compensation for expenses or losses already incurred, or for which there are no future related costs, is recognised in profit or loss in the period in which it becomes receivable. Therefore, if a government provides an entity with annual grants that do not relate to future costs, then the grant in respect of each period is recognised as it becomes receivable.

4.3.50 *Non-monetary grants*

IAS 20.23 4.3.50.10 If a government grant is in the form of a non-monetary asset, then an entity chooses an accounting policy, to be applied consistently, to recognise the asset and grant at either the fair value of the non-monetary asset or at the nominal amount paid. For example, Government X gives Company Y an item of property, plant and equipment with a fair value of 50 for no consideration. Y measures both the item of property, plant and equipment and the grant either at 50, or at nominal value, which in this case is zero. We prefer that both the asset and the grant are measured at fair value.

4.3.60 *Grants related to biological assets*

IAS 41.34, 4.3.60.10 As an exception to the general recognition principle, an unconditional govern-
35, 37 ment grant related to biological assets that are measured at fair value less costs to sell (see 3.9.95) is recognised in profit or loss when it becomes receivable. If the government grant is conditional, then it is recognised in profit or loss when the condition is met. IAS 20 applies to government grants related to biological assets to which the cost exemption applies (see 3.9.10).

4.3.70 *Grants related to other assets measured at fair value with changes therein recognised in profit or loss*

4.3.70.10 Although there is specific guidance on accounting for government grants related to biological assets that are measured at fair value less costs to sell (see 4.3.60), there is no similar guidance for government grants related to other assets that are measured at fair value with changes therein recognised in profit or loss (e.g. investment property for which the entity applies the fair value model (see 3.4.150)). In our view, in such cases, the treatment required for government grants related to biological assets should be applied by analogy. Therefore, we believe that a grant related to an asset measured at fair value with changes therein recognised in profit or loss should be recognised in profit or loss when it becomes receivable, provided that any attached conditions are fulfilled.

4.3.70.20 For example, on 25 January 2010 Local Government F grants Company G a property with a fair value of 450; ownership of the property is transferred to G at the same time. G classifies the property as investment property, which it measures at fair value. The fair value of the property at 31 December 2010 is 480. There are no conditions attached to the grant. We believe that the government grant of 450 should be recognised in profit or loss on 25 January 2010. A gain on revaluation of the property of 30 is recognised on 31 December 2010 when the investment property is revalued in accordance with the requirements of IAS 40 (see 3.4).

4.3.70.25 In another example, on 30 September 2010 Company H purchases a residential building, which is partially funded by a grant from local government. H classifies the building as investment property and measures it at fair value. The grant is repayable if specified works intended to improve the energy efficiency of the building are not completed by 30 June 2011. The specified works are finalised in May 2011. At the end of the 2010 annual reporting period H revalues its investment property and recognises any changes therein in profit or loss. Notwithstanding the fact that H received the grant attached to the building before the end of the annual reporting period, H defers the recognition of the grant in profit or loss until the date the conditions are met. Accordingly H recognises income from the grant upon completion of the specified works in May 2011 (see 4.3.90 for a discussion of repayable grants).

4.3.80 *Grants in the form of a waiver of expenses*

4.3.80.10 In our view, the normal recognition principles apply to grants in the form of a waiver of expenses. Therefore, we believe that such grants should be recognised in profit or loss on a systematic basis when the entity recognises as expenses the related costs that the grant is intended to compensate.

4.3.80.20 For example, if a grant is in the form of a waiver of current taxes payable, and the expenditure to which the grant relates is incurred in the period in which the tax is waived, then the benefit of the tax relief should be reflected in that period. If the expenditure will be incurred in a future period, then the benefit of the tax relief should be deferred in the statement of financial position until the expenditure is incurred. Similarly, if the grant relates to the acquisition of an asset, then the benefit of the tax relief should be deferred in the statement of financial position and recognised in profit or loss as the related asset is depreciated.

4.3.80.30 See 4.3.150 for guidance on the presentation of grants in the form of a waiver of expenses.

4.3.90 *Repayment*

4.3.90.10 A government grant may be required to be repaid under certain conditions, e.g. if the actual costs to which the grant relates are lower than expected.

4.3.90.20 [Not used]

IAS 20.32 4.3.90.30 If the amount is recognised as a government grant and subsequently some or all of the amount becomes repayable unexpectedly, then the repayment is accounted for as a change in estimate (see 2.8.60). In our view, the effect of the change in estimate should be recognised in the period in which management concludes that it no longer is reasonably assured that the terms for forgiveness will be met. In our view, a financial liability should be recognised at the same time for the amount of the repayment, based on the general requirements of IAS 39 *Financial Instruments: Recognition and Measurement*, i.e. at fair value (see 3.6.710). The amount would differ from the face value of the grant if the interest rate is not a market rate of interest (see also 4.3.100). In our view, the repayable portion of the credit recognised previously should be reversed as follows:

- the credit may have been shown as deferred income or a credit to an asset, in which case the reversal should be against the appropriate line item in the statement of financial position; and/or
- the credit may have been recognised as a reduction in depreciation or amortisation of an asset or as income, in which case the reversal should be against the appropriate line item within profit or loss.

IAS 20.33   4.3.90.40 The entity also considers whether the change in circumstances that gave rise to the repayment of the loan is an indication of impairment (see 3.10.110).

4.3.90.50 In some circumstances, a financial liability in respect of a grant that becomes repayable may be forgiven (see 4.3.20 for a discussion of forgivable loans). In our view, if there is reasonable assurance that the entity will meet the terms for forgiveness of such a loan, then it should be accounted for as a government grant and the amount received recognised over the compliance period. Otherwise we believe that the loan should be treated as a financial liability.

4.3.100 *Low-interest loans*

IAS 20.10A,   4.3.100.10 Low-interest or interest-free loans from a government are recognised and
39.43, AG64   measured in accordance with IAS 39. IAS 39 requires loans at below-market rates to be measured initially at their fair value (i.e. the present value of the future cash flows discounted at a market interest rate) and interest to be imputed on the loan in subsequent periods (see 3.6.730). The benefit that is the government grant is measured as the difference between the fair value of the loan on initial recognition and the amount received, which is accounted for according to the nature of the grant.

4.3.100.20 – 30 [Not used]

4.3.100.40 In some situations a government may provide a loan at market rate that will be modified to a lower rate when the entity spends the funds provided on qualifying research and development activities. In our view, the difference between the fair value of the loan at a market interest rate and the fair value of the low-interest rate loan should be accounted for as a government grant. Payments on research activities are expensed as incurred, while payments on development activities are capitalised when the criteria set out in IAS 38 *Intangible Assets* are met (see 3.3.120). Therefore, in this situation, we believe that the part of the government grant related to research activities and development costs that are not capitalised should be recognised in profit or loss when the related costs are incurred; we also believe that an entity should choose an accounting policy, to be applied consistently, either to deduct the grant related to capitalised development costs from the related intangible asset, or to recognise such grants as deferred income and release them to profit or loss as the capitalised development costs are amortised (see 4.3.130 in respect of the presentation of grants related to assets). In this way the benefit of the grant is recognised on a systematic basis as the entity recognises, as expenses, the related costs that the grant is intended to compensate.

4.3.110 *Emissions allowances**

4.3.110.10 IFRSs do not have any specific guidance on accounting for emissions allowances received in a cap and trade scheme. In our view, if an allowance is received from a government for less than its fair value, then the entity should choose an accounting policy, to be recognised consistently, either to recognise the resulting government grant at fair value (as the difference between the fair value of the allowance and the consideration (if any) paid) or at the nominal amount paid for the certificate. We prefer the allowance and the grant to be measured at fair value (see 3.3.170). The grant then is recognised as deferred income and recognised in profit or loss on a systematic basis over the compliance period regardless of whether the allowance received continues to be held by the entity. Disposals of certificates or changes in their carrying amount (e.g. due to impairment (see 3.10)) do not affect the manner in which grant income is recognised. As an alternative to the deferred income approach, we believe that an entity may present an allowance net of the deferred government grant. See 3.12.510 for further discussion of the accounting for emissions allowance schemes.

4.3.120 **Presentation and disclosure**

4.3.130 *Presentation of grants related to assets*

IAS 8.13, 20.24   4.3.130.10 Government grants related to assets other than biological assets measured at fair value less costs to sell (see 4.3.60) and other assets measured at fair value with changes therein recognised in profit or loss (see 4.3.70), may be either deducted from the cost of the asset (net presentation), or presented separately as deferred income that is amortised over the useful life of the asset (gross presentation). In our view, this approach also applies to grants related to assets held by a lessee under a finance lease. An entity chooses a presentation format in the statement of financial position, to be applied consistently to all government grants related to assets.

IAS 20.27   4.3.130.15 If net presentation in the statement of financial position is used, then the grant reduces the cost and therefore reduces the depreciation expense recognised. However, if an entity presents government grants related to assets (other than biological assets measured at fair value less costs to sell and other assets measured at fair value with changes therein recognised in profit or loss) gross in the statement of financial position, then IAS 20 does not require a specific presentation in the statement of comprehensive income. In our view, an entity should choose an accounting policy, to be applied consistently, to present such grants either as income or as a reduction in the related expense.

4.3.130.20 For example, Company F received a government grant of 200 to acquire machinery. The machinery costs 700 and has an estimated useful life of five years. If F presents the grant as a deduction from the cost of the machinery, then the asset is shown in the statement of financial position at its net cost of 500 (700 - 200). The grant is recognised in profit or loss over the useful life of the depreciable asset and presented as a reduction to the annual depreciation expense, which expense amounts to 100 (500 / 5).

4.3.130.30 If the grant is presented as deferred income, then the machinery is shown at its gross cost of 700 and annual depreciation on the machinery is 140 (700 / 5). In addition, F presents deferred income of 200. Each year, 40 (200 / 5) is recognised in profit or loss.

4.3.130.35 In our view, the choice of net or gross presentation (see 4.3.130.10) has no impact on the timing of recognition in the statement of comprehensive income.

4.3.130.40 Continuing the example in 4.3.130.20 – 30, assume that the machinery is used in F's production plant for producing inventories for sale in the ordinary course of business. The depreciation of the machinery is reflected in the cost of inventories. In accordance with F's accounting policies, the machinery is shown at its gross cost, i.e. the grant is presented as deferred income. In our view, the amortisation of the deferred income should be included in the cost of inventory. This means that the amortisation of the deferred income will be recognised in profit or loss at the same time as the depreciation on the machinery, i.e. as inventory is sold. This approach is consistent with the principle in IAS 20 that the benefit of a government grant is recognised at the same time as the expenses to which it relates.

4.3.130.50 In our view, if an entity presents government grants as a deduction from the related asset, but the grant is received before the asset is recognised, then the grant should be shown as deferred income until the asset is constructed or acquired.

4.3.130.60 The deferred income generally is classified as a non-current liability. The portion that will be recognised in profit or loss in the next year (i.e. 40 in the example of F in 4.3.130.30) is shown as a current liability.

4.3.140 *Presentation of grants related to income*

IAS 8.13, 4.3.140.10 An entity chooses a presentation format, to be applied consistently, either
20.29 to offset a grant related to income against the related expenditure, or to include it in other income. For example, Company P receives a government grant of 100 to fund research costs of 500. P has a choice of presenting net research costs of 400, or gross research costs of 500 and other income of 100. Regardless of P's choice, it is applied consistently.

4.3.150 *Presentation of grants in the form of a waiver of expenses*

4.3.150.10 In our view, either a net or gross approach may be used to present a grant in the form of a waiver of expenses.

4.3.150.20 For example, when the grant is in the form of a waiver of taxes, then we believe that the entity should choose a presentation format, to be applied consistently, either to recognise the benefit of the government grant in the tax line or "gross up" the tax line and present the benefit in profit or loss in the same way as other government grants (i.e. as other income, a reduction of the related expense, or a reduction in the carrying amount of the related asset and depreciation on the asset, as appropriate).

4.3.160 *Related party disclosures*

4.3.160.10 If the government also is a shareholder, then additional related party disclosures are required (see 5.5).

4.3.170 **Future developments**

4.3.170.10 The IASB is considering amending IAS 20 in order to resolve inconsistencies between the standard's recognition requirements and the Framework. Work on this project has been deferred pending the completion of work on other related projects such as related parties, revenue recognition and emissions trading schemes.

4.3.170.20 In December 2007 the IASB activated a joint project with the FASB to address the accounting for emissions trading schemes. This project interacts with the project to revise IAS 20 (see 4.3.170.20) with regard to emissions trading schemes granted by the government. An ED is expected no earlier than the second half of 2011.

4.3.170.30 In May 2009 the IASB published ED/2009/5 *Fair Value Measurement* (the 2009 ED). The proposals in the 2009 ED are intended to replace the fair value measurement guidance contained in individual IFRSs with a single, unified definition of fair value, as well as provide further authoritative guidance on the application of fair value measurement in inactive markets. The 2009 ED proposes a framework for measuring fair value and disclosures about fair value measurements. The proposals in the 2009 ED explain how to measure fair value when it already is required or permitted by existing IFRSs; they do not introduce new fair value measurements, nor do they eliminate the practicability exceptions to fair value measurements that exist currently in certain standards.

4.3.170.40 In June 2010 the IASB published ED/2010/7 *Measurement Uncertainty Analysis Disclosure for Fair Value Measurements* (the 2010 ED). The 2010 ED expands on the proposal in the 2009 ED for an entity to disclose a measurement uncertainty analysis (or sensitivity analysis) for assets and liabilities measured at fair value categorised within Level 3 of the fair value hierarchy. The 2010 ED proposes that an entity consider the effect of correlation between unobservable inputs, if relevant.

4.3.170.50 A final standard on fair value measurement and disclosure, which is expected to be converged with a forthcoming amended standard under US GAAP, is scheduled for the first quarter of 2011.

4.4 Employee benefits
(IAS 19, IFRIC 14)

4.4 Employee benefits
(IAS 19, IFRIC 14)

Overview of currently effective requirements

- IFRSs specify accounting requirements for all types of employee benefits, and not just pensions. IAS 19 deals with all employee benefits, except those to which IFRS 2 applies.

- Post-employment benefits are employee benefits, which are payable after the completion of employment (before or during retirement).

- Short-term employee benefits are employee benefits that are due to be settled within one year after the end of the period in which the services have been rendered.

- Other long-term employee benefits are employee benefits that are not due to be settled within one year after the end of the period in which the services have been rendered.

- Liabilities for employee benefits are recognised on the basis of a legal or constructive obligation.

- Liabilities and expenses for employee benefits generally are recognised in the period in which the services are rendered.

- Costs of providing employee benefits generally are expensed unless other IFRSs permit or require capitalisation, for example, IAS 2 or IAS 16.

- A defined contribution plan is a post-employment benefit plan under which the employer pays fixed contributions into a separate entity and has no further obligations. All other post-employment plans are defined benefit plans.

- Contributions to a defined contribution plan are expensed as the obligation to make the payments is incurred.

- A liability is recognised for an employer's obligation under a defined benefit plan. The liability and expense are measured actuarially using the projected unit credit method.

- Assets that meet the definition of plan assets, including qualifying insurance policies, and the related liabilities are presented on a net basis in the statement of financial position.

- Actuarial gains and losses of defined benefit plans may be recognised in profit or loss, or immediately in other comprehensive income.

- If actuarial gains and losses of a defined benefit plan are recognised in profit or loss, then as a minimum gains and losses that exceed a "corridor" are required to be recognised over the average remaining working lives of employees in the plan. Faster recognition (including immediate recognition) in profit or loss is permitted.

- Liabilities and expenses for vested past service costs under a defined benefit plan are recognised immediately.

- Liabilities and expenses for unvested past service costs under a defined benefit plan are recognised over the vesting period.

- If a defined benefit plan has assets in excess of the obligation, then the amount of any net asset recognised is limited to available economic benefits from the plan in the form of refunds from the plan or reductions in future contributions to the plan, and unrecognised actuarial losses and past service costs.

- Minimum funding requirements give rise to a liability if a surplus arising from the additional contributions paid to fund an existing shortfall with respect to services already received, is not fully available as a refund or reduction in future contributions.

- If insufficient information is available for a multi-employer defined benefit plan to be accounted for as a defined benefit plan, then it is treated as a defined contribution plan and additional disclosures are required.

- If an entity applies defined contribution plan accounting to a multi-employer defined benefit plan and there is an agreement that determines how a surplus in the plan would be distributed or a deficit in the plan funded, then an asset or liability that arises from the contractual agreement is recognised.

- If there is a contractual agreement or stated policy for allocating a group's net defined benefit cost, then participating group entities recognise the cost allocated to them. If there is no agreement or policy in place, then the net defined benefit cost is recognised by the entity that is the legal sponsor.

- The expense for long-term employee benefits is accrued over the service period.

- Redundancy costs are not recognised until the redundancy has been communicated to the group of affected employees.

Currently effective requirements

This publication reflects IFRSs in issue at 1 August 2010. The currently effective requirements cover annual periods beginning on 1 January 2010. The requirements related to this topic are derived mainly from IAS 19 *Employee Benefits* and IFRIC 14 *IAS 19 – The Limit on a Defined Benefit Asset, Minimum Funding Requirements and their Interaction.*

Forthcoming requirements and future developments

When a currently effective requirement will be changed by a new requirement that is issued but is not yet effective, it is marked with a # as a **forthcoming requirement** and the impact of the change is explained in the accompanying boxed text. The forthcoming requirements related to this topic are derived from *Prepayments of a Minimum Funding Requirement (Amendments to IFRIC 14: IAS 19 – The Limit on a Defined Benefit Asset, Minimum Funding Requirements and their Interaction).* The amendments to IFRIC 14 are effective for annual periods beginning on or after 1 January 2011; earlier application is permitted. A brief outline of the impact of the amendments to IFRIC 14 on this topic is given in 4.4.743.

When a significant change to the currently effective or forthcoming requirements is expected, it is marked with a * as an area that may be subject to **future developments** and a brief outline of the relevant projects is given in 4.4.1160.

4.4.10 Scope

IAS 19.7,
IFRIC 14.5, 6

4.4.10.10 Employee benefits are all forms of consideration given by an entity in exchange for services provided by employees and include benefits provided directly to employees, to their dependants or to others. IAS 19 deals with all employee benefits except those to which IFRS 2 applies. IFRIC 14 applies to all post-employment and other long-term employee defined benefit plans. The interpretation also may be applicable for entities that have plan deficits.

4.4.20 *Share-based payment or employee benefit*

4.4.21 *Equity instruments of other entities*

4.4.21.10 Equity-settled and cash-settled entity and group share-based payment transactions are within the scope of IFRS 2 (see 4.5.20). However, if employees of an entity are granted rights to equity instruments in an entity that is not a group entity (e.g. joint venture, associate or other entity), then in our view the transaction is not a share-based payment transaction (see 4.5.873). Since a benefit is provided to employees, we believe that such a transaction is an employee benefit within the scope of IAS 19.

4.4.23 *Tax payments*

4.4.23.10 In some countries a share-based payment arrangement may be subject to a tax payment and the employer may pay employees an amount of cash to cover social taxes and/or income taxes related to share-based payment transactions in addition to the share-based payment arrangement. In our view, if the cash payment is not based on the price or value of the entity's shares, then this portion of the plan should be treated as an employee benefit under IAS 19. In our view, if the cash payment is based on the value of the entity's shares, then it may be appropriate to treat this portion of the plan as a cash-settled share-based payment transaction within the scope of IFRS 2 *Share-based Payments* (see 4.5.140.20).

4.4.25 *Cash payments based on estimates of fair value*

4.4.25.10 Arrangements involving payments tied to the performance of an entity require careful evaluation of the substance of the transaction. For example, an arrangement in which employees of an entity receive a cash payment based on the increase in the entity's net assets may be a profit-sharing arrangement or a share-based payment arrangement depending on the facts and circumstances (see 4.5.150.10). In our view, if the net asset value of the entity does not reflect the fair value of its equity instruments (e.g. the change in net assets represents primarily the profit or loss from operations and does not include fair value changes of assets and liabilities), then the transaction is, in substance, a profit-sharing arrangement that should be accounted for as an employee benefit (see 4.4.60).

4.4.27 *Components with different features*

4.4.27.10 In our view, the components of a payment to an employee should be accounted for separately if the award contains both an employee benefit and a share-based payment. For example, a payment to an employee may have both a cash and a share component. The terms of a bonus plan may require settlement of 75 percent of the award in a fixed amount of cash and 25 percent in shares. We believe that the 75 percent cash bonus is an employee benefit within the scope of IAS 19, while the 25 percent bonus that is paid in shares represents a share-based payment within the scope of IFRS 2 (see 4.5.210.10).

4.4.27.20 Certain arrangements, such as profit-sharing plans may provide, at the discretion of the employee, a choice of two settlement alternatives that are mutually exclusive, e.g. one equity-settled share-based payment component that would be a share-based payment transaction within the scope of IFRS 2 and one profit-sharing component, that, if granted separately, would be an employee benefit within the scope of IAS 19. In our view, the entire arrangement should be accounted for as a share-based payment applying IFRS 2 requirements for compound instruments by analogy (see 4.5.210.20 and 660.60).

4.4.28 *Cash payments depending on the share price vs being based on the share price*

4.4.28.10 A cash payment may depend, but not be based on the share price. Judgement is required to define the border between "depending on" and "being based on". For example, an employee is entitled to a cash payment of 100 if the share price remains at least at the current share price of 8 over the next year. If the share price falls, then the employee is not entitled to the payment. In our view, while this cash payment depends on the share price, it is not based on the share price. Therefore, we believe that the cash payment is not a share-based payment but an employee benefit within the scope of IAS 19 (see 4.5.170.10).

4.4.28.20 A cash payment may be based on but not equal to the share price. If an employee is entitled to a payment equal to the share price at vesting date, then the employee participates one-to-one in the share price increases. In our view, a payment determined as a linear function of the share price or its movements is based on the share price and therefore is a share-based payment. For example, if the employee is entitled to 60 percent of the share price or to 200 percent of the share price, then we believe that the payment meets the definition of being based on the value of the equity instruments and therefore is a share-based payment (see 4.5.170.20).

4.4.29 *Tax levied on employers*

4.4.29.10 In some countries a tax may be levied on employers with respect to employee benefits within the scope of IAS 19 (e.g. cash bonuses). The question arises as to whether the tax liability levied on the employer is within the scope of IAS 19 or IAS 37 *Provisions, Contingent Liabilities and Contingent Assets*. IFRSs are not clear in this regard. In our view, an entity should choose an accounting policy, to be applied consistently, as to the standard to be applied for tax liabilities levied on the employer. It can be argued that the tax liability would be considered an employee benefit to be accounted for in accordance with IAS 19, with the rationale being that the tax liability levied on the employer is part of the benefit to which it relates, e.g. a tax levied on an employer in respect of a cash bonus is part of the bonus. However, such arrangements also may be considered to be within the scope of IAS 37 based on the tax liability being treated separately from the bonus. When this is the case, the timing of the recognition of the cash bonus (see 4.4.60 and 1020) and the tax levy (see 3.12.30.10) might be different.

4.4.30 Short-term employee benefits

IAS 19.7 4.4.30.10 Short-term employee benefits are those benefits (other than termination benefits) due to be settled within one year after the end of the period in which the services have been rendered, and are accounted for using normal accrual accounting. Benefits due to be settled after such time are long-term employee benefits (see 4.4.970). In our view, due to be settled within one year should be interpreted to include situations in which an employee could require settlement within one year after the end of the period in which the services have been rendered (see also 4.4.980.29). In our view, the end of the period should be considered the end of the current reporting period when the service period spans more than one reporting period (see 4.4.980.10).

4.4.40 *Compensated absences*

IAS 19.11 4.4.40.10 An employer accrues the obligation for paid absences if the obligation both relates to employees' past services and accumulates (i.e. can be carried forward to a future period).

IAS 19.13   4.4.40.20 A liability is recognised whether or not the benefits are vesting (i.e. whether or not employees are entitled to payment of their unused benefits if they leave). For example, if entitlement to vacation pay accumulates, then it is accrued even if it does not vest (i.e. even if employees do not get paid for unused vacation when they leave).

4.4.40.30 In most cases an entitlement to maternity or paternity leave is contingent upon a future event and does not accumulate. Therefore, these costs are recognised only when the absence commences. In our view, this applies even if employees are required to complete a minimum service period before being entitled to the benefit, or if the length of the leave entitlement depends on the period of service.

4.4.40.40 Similarly, no accrual is recognised for amounts to be paid to employees in future periods in respect of public holidays because the entitlement to pay does not accumulate.

4.4.50 *Measurement*

IAS 19.14   4.4.50.10 The amount of the liability is that which the entity expects to pay in respect of the unused entitlement.

4.4.50.20 Therefore, the accrual for vacation pay should be based on the expected amount of unused vacation pay, i.e. the number of days' leave at each reporting date that employees are entitled to, but have not used, and that can be used (or paid) in future periods.

4.4.50.30 If the benefits are vesting (i.e. employees will receive payments for unused benefits when they leave), then a liability is recognised for the total amount.

4.4.50.40 In measuring an obligation for non-vesting benefits, the possibility that employees may leave before they use their entitlement should be taken into account. For example, an entity would recognise a liability for an entitlement to sick leave that can be carried forward to future periods, but that will not be paid for if the employee leaves, only to the extent that it expects employees to take sick leave in the future.

4.4.60 *Profit-sharing and bonus plans*

IAS 19.17   4.4.60.10 A provision is recognised for the expected cost of bonus or profit-sharing plans when an entity has a present legal or constructive obligation and a reliable estimate of the obligation can be made. See 2.9 for guidance on determining whether a liability should be recognised at the reporting date.

4.4.60.20 Some bonus plans may have aspects that are similar to long-term benefits (see 4.4.970). For example, under a bonus plan employees are entitled to higher bonuses the longer they remain with the entity. However, the bonuses are calculated and paid quarterly. Such a bonus plan raises the following questions:

- does one year of service earn the employee the right to one year of benefit; or
- does continuous employment earn the right to an accumulated benefit?

4.4.60.30 In our view, such an arrangement is more like a salary benefit and the incremental bonus should be treated in the same way as expected future salary increases. Therefore, the benefit is a salary benefit based on the current year's service, which is settled in full within one year after the period in which the services are provided.

4.4.70 *Measurement*

4.4.70.10 The amount provided is the best estimate of the amount that the entity expects to pay in cash.

IAS 19.18, 4.4.70.20 If payment is conditional (e.g. on the employee remaining in service), then
BC14 the conditions (and the possibility of forfeiture) are taken into account in measuring the obligation.

4.4.70.30 For example, Company P with a reporting date of 31 December 2010 offers its employees a profit-sharing plan. P will pay, on 31 March 2011, an amount to participants in respect of services provided during 2010 provided that they remain in employment on that date. The total amount payable to employees is calculated as 5 percent of the profit for 2010. Each employee's entitlement is determined at 31 December 2010; there is no reallocation of the bonus entitlement for participants who are no longer employed at 31 March 2011. P estimates that 3 percent of the participants will cease employment between 31 December 2010 and 31 March 2011. P will offer its employees a similar plan in future periods.

IAS 19.10 4.4.70.40 As the amount payable is calculated in respect of achieving a performance condition at 31 December 2010 and there will be a similar plan each year, in our view the amount payable by P in respect of services received in 2010 is accrued over the 12-month service period in 2010, i.e. excluding the three-month "loyalty" period between 31 December 2010 and 31 March 2011. The measurement of the obligation at 31 December 2010 includes an estimate of expected forfeitures, i.e. the 3 percent of participants who are expected to cease employment between 31 December 2010 and 31 March 2011.

4.4.70.50 If the conditions on which payment is conditional result in payment being due to be settled more than 12 months after the period in which the services are rendered, then the profit-sharing or bonus plan is an other long-term employee benefit (see 4.4.1020).

4.4.80 *Low-interest loans*

IAS 19.8 4.4.80.10 Loans given to employees at lower than market interest rates generally are short-term employee benefits. IFRSs do not address directly how to account for such low-interest employee loans.

IAS 39.43 4.4.80.20 Loans granted to employees are financial instruments within the scope of IAS 39 *Financial Instruments: Recognition and Measurement*. Therefore low-interest loans to employees are measured at the present value of the anticipated future cash flows discounted using a market interest rate (see 3.6.740.10). In our view, any difference between the fair value of the loan and the amount advanced is an employee benefit.

4.4.80.30 In our view, loans to employees at below-market interest rates by an entity that is in the business of making loans, such as a bank, also should be measured initially at fair value.

4.4.80.40 Determining the fair value of loans to employees will require assumptions to be made regarding employee turnover and, if the loans do not have a fixed maturity, then of estimated repayment dates also. In our view, if expectations about repayment dates or employee turnover change, then the calculation should be revised and any adjustment should be treated as a change in estimate (see 2.8.60).

4.4.80.50 If the favourable loan terms are not dependent on continued employment, then in our view there should be a rebuttable presumption that the interest benefit relates to past services, and the cost should be recognised in profit or loss immediately. If the benefit relates to services to be rendered in future periods (e.g. if the interest benefit will be forfeited if the employee leaves or is a bonus for future services), then in our view the amount of the discount may be treated as a prepayment and expensed in the period in which the services are rendered. If the services will be rendered more than 12 months into the future, then the entire benefit is a long-term benefit (see 4.4.970).

IAS 24.9, 17, 18 4.4.80.60 Loans to key management personnel, whether or not they are at below-market interest rates, are related party transactions that require additional disclosure (see 5.5).

4.4.80.70 The issue of shares to employees using the proceeds of a loan made by the issuer, when the loan has recourse only to the shares, is an option grant and not an employee benefit (see 4.5.540.20).

4.4.90 *Non-monetary benefits*

IAS 19.10 4.4.90.10 The recognition and measurement of short-term employee benefits generally is based on the amount paid by an entity to provide benefits to the employee. However, if the benefit is in the form of a benefit in kind, e.g. free or discounted goods or services, then in our view the measurement could be based on the employer's net marginal cost of providing such benefit, unless other standards specifically require fair value measurement of the asset or obligation (e.g. the benefit represents a share-based payment within the scope of IFRS 2 or the benefit is in the form of low-interest loans to employees (see 4.4.80)).

4.4.90.20 For example, Company C owns apartments that it leases to its employees at below-market rental rates. An issue arises as to whether the below-market element of the rental should be recognised as an employee benefit. While the accounting requirements for low-interest loans require financial assets to be measured at fair value, there are no similar requirements in IFRSs for non-monetary benefits. Therefore, in our view C is not required to impute a notional income (the difference between a market rental and the rental actually charged) in order to impute a corresponding expense, which would represent the employee benefit. Even if the core business of C is investment property, the benefit provided to the employees in the form of free or discounted rental property would not give rise to revenue.

4.4.100 Scope of post-employment benefits

IAS 19.7 4.4.100.10 Post-employment benefits include all benefits payable after employment (before or during retirement), for example, pensions, medical benefits after employment and severance payments.

4.4.100.20 Some plans are established specifically to provide benefits both during and after employment. For example, Company K has a fund for vacation pay. Any surplus in the fund is used to make pension payments. In our view, a plan that is established specifically to pay benefits both during and after employment should be treated as a long-term employee benefit plan (see 4.4.970) rather than as a post-employment benefit plan.

4.4.100.25 If a plan offers different benefits (i.e. under different benefit formulae) to different groups of beneficiaries, active employees and retirees, and is funded by separate pools of assets or a single pool of assets but with appropriate controls in place, then the benefits offered during employment and post-employment should be accounted for separately as the separate promises are made to employees and retirees, and under different benefit formulae. As such, benefits offered to retirees are accounted for as a post-employment benefit (see 4.4.160.10 and 870.10).

IAS 19.126, 130 4.4.100.30 Long-term disability benefits are an example of other long-term employee benefits (see 4.4.970 and 1000). However, if a long-term disability benefit is payable only after termination of employment, then in our view the benefit is a post-employment benefit. In addition, in our view a long-term disability benefit that is payable only if an employee remains employed but is no longer providing services also should be accounted for as a post-employment benefit. We believe that this is in substance the same as if there is cessation of employment for the employee.

4.4.110 *Constructive obligations*

IAS 19.52 4.4.110.10 Post-employment benefit plans include not only formal arrangements but also informal arrangements that give rise to *constructive obligations*. Therefore, the accounting treatment should be the same, regardless of whether an obligation is legal or constructive.

IAS 19.52 4.4.110.20 Constructive obligations arise when an entity has no realistic alternative but to pay the employee benefits. A constructive obligation may arise from informal past practices or communication with employees. See 4.4.120 on classification, 4.4.280 on actuarial assumptions, 4.4.290 on benefits and 3.12.60 for general guidance on constructive obligations.

4.4.120 **Classification as a defined benefit or a defined contribution plan***

IAS 19.25　4.4.120.10 Post-employment plans are classified as either a defined contribution or a defined benefit plan. The classification determines the accounting treatment.

IAS 19.7　4.4.120.20 A plan is classified as a defined contribution plan if the entity pays fixed contributions into a separate entity and will have no further obligation (legal or constructive) to pay further amounts. All other plans are defined benefit plans.

IAS 19.7,　4.4.120.30 The classification of employee benefit plans is based on the employer's
BC5　obligation to make further contributions, rather than on the basis of the benefit to which the employees are entitled.

4.4.120.40 Employee benefit plans may promise employees a defined benefit, for example, payment of a specified amount or an amount to be determined using a specified formula such as a percentage of average or final salary. In many cases the employer's current funding obligation (e.g. under local social legislation) is limited to a fixed amount or satisfaction of a funding level that is lower than the estimate calculated in accordance with IFRSs of the present value of the future obligation. In our view, a requirement to satisfy only current funding requirements does not provide a sufficient basis for classification of the plan as a defined contribution plan.

4.4.120.50 In some cases it may be difficult to determine whether a plan that has promised specified benefits to employees is a defined benefit or a defined contribution plan for the employer. If the plan bears all the risk of funding shortfalls and members would have to accept reduced benefit levels in the event of a shortfall, then the plan is likely to be a defined contribution plan.

4.4.120.60 However, when a defined benefit promise has been made to employees (either by the employer or by the pension plan), then in our view it generally is very difficult for the employer to demonstrate that it does not have a constructive obligation to fund any shortfalls.

4.4.120.70 An employer may settle a defined benefit promise by arranging for an independent insurance company to assume the actuarial risk and the primary obligation to the employees (see 4.4.770). The employer retains only a contingent obligation to make additional payments if the third party defaults. If the risk of the employer having to make additional payments is remote, then in our view such a plan normally is a defined contribution plan and the employer's potential obligation is a contingent liability that would not be recognised (see 3.14).

4.4.120.80 See 4.4.160.10 for a discussion of group plans with pooled assets and with both a defined contribution and a defined benefit component.

4.4.130 *Impact of vesting conditions*

4.4.130.10 When a plan that has characteristics of a defined contribution plan contains vesting conditions (e.g. a service condition), there is a potential for the employer to benefit (from refunds or reduced future contributions) if the vesting conditions are not met. In our view, such a plan nevertheless may be classified as a defined contribution plan, as long as the employer bears no downside risk and would not be required to make additional contributions to cover shortfalls.

4.4.140 *Severance payments*

4.4.140.10 Severance payments and other amounts that always are payable on cessation of employment, regardless of the reason for the employee's leaving, are post-employment benefits. For example, Company B makes payments to its employees upon cessation of employment regardless of the reason the employee leaves B's employment. The employee is entitled to one week's salary for each year of service provided, based on the employee's final salary. As the amount is payable upon cessation of employment regardless of the reason for leaving, the plan is a post-employment benefit plan.

4.4.140.20 The normal principles apply in determining whether such post-employment plans give rise to defined benefit or defined contribution plans. Often the amount of the payments is based on factors such as the number of years of service or final salary. Therefore, these plans often give rise to a defined benefit plan. The principles set out in 4.4.260 – 950.50, including the requirements to discount the obligation and to use the projected unit credit method, apply to any defined benefit arrangements and therefore also to these plans.

4.4.150 *Multi-employer plans*

IAS 19.7   4.4.150.10 Multi-employer plans are plans that pool the assets contributed by various entities to provide benefits to employees of more than one entity. In multi-employer plans, benefit levels are not determined based on the identity of the employer.

IAS 19.29   4.4.150.20 Multi-employer plans are classified and accounted for in the same way as single-employer plans, considering the characteristics of the scheme and the obligation of the employer.

IAS 19.30, 32   4.4.150.30 When sufficient information is available for a multi-employer defined benefit plan, an entity accounts for its proportionate share of the defined benefit obligation, plan assets and post-employment benefit cost associated with the plan in the same manner as for any other defined benefit plan. If insufficient information is available for a multi-employer defined benefit plan to be accounted for in accordance with the requirements for defined benefit plans, then it is treated as a defined contribution plan and additional disclosures are required.

4.4.150.40 In our view, sufficient information is available for defined benefit accounting to be applied for participation in a multi-employer defined benefit plan when the participant in the multi-employer plan:

- has access to information regarding all components of the plan, e.g. plan assets, plan obligations, actuarial gains or losses, service costs and interest costs, and not only knowledge of the net deficit or surplus (i.e. an actuarial valuation on an IAS 19 compliant basis for the plan as a whole is available to participating entities); and

- the stated basis for allocating the deficit or surplus is reasonably stable. In order for the stated basis for allocating the deficit or surplus to be reasonably stable, the methodology for allocating the deficit or surplus should remain consistent and the allocation should not result in significant variability of the entity's proportion of the deficit or surplus.

4.4.150.50 In our view, the assessment of whether the stated basis for allocating the deficit or surplus is reasonably stable should be made in relation to the entity participating in the plan. As such, the magnitude of the entity's share of the plan may impact this assessment.

4.4.150.60 For example, a plan may allocate the deficit or surplus based on a plan-wide contribution rate that is calculated based on each entity's relative percentage of pensionable earnings. A plan participant estimates that its relative percentage of pensionable earnings may increase or decrease by five percentage points from year to year. If the participant's share of the plan is significant, then it may determine that a five percentage point change in its relative percentage of pensionable earnings would not result in significant variability in the proportion of the deficit or surplus that would be allocated. However, a participant that does not have a significant share of the plan may determine that a five percentage point change in its relative percentage of pensionable earnings would result in significant variability, and therefore this may not be considered a reasonably stable basis for allocating the deficit or surplus.

IAS 19.32, 32A, 32B   4.4.150.70 If an entity applies defined contribution plan accounting to a multi-employer plan for which there is a contractual agreement between the multi-employer plan and its participants that determines how a surplus in the plan would be distributed or a deficit in the plan funded, then the asset or liability that arises from the contractual agreement is recognised. Any changes in the amount of the obligation (or asset) are recognised in profit or loss. In our view, if a participant applies defined contribution accounting to a multi-employer plan and recognises a surplus or deficit based on a contractual agreement for allocation of the surplus or deficit, then it cannot apply the corridor method to the allocated amount, or recognise the allocated amount outside profit or loss in the period that it is allocated.

IAS 19.32B   4.4.150.80 An entity participating in a multi-employer plan discloses information about the contingent liability arising in the following circumstances in accordance with IAS 37:

- actuarial losses related to other participating entities because each entity that participates in a multi-employer plan shares in the actuarial risks of every other participating entity; or
- any responsibility under the terms of a plan to finance any shortfall in the plan if other entities cease to participate.

4.4.160 *Group plans*

IAS 19.34 4.4.160.05 Defined benefit plans in which entities under common control share risks are group plans rather than multi-employer plans.

4.4.160.10 Group plans are classified as either a defined contribution plan or a defined benefit plan in accordance with the terms of the plan (see 4.4.120). However, IAS 19 does not address specifically group plans that have both defined contribution and defined benefit components, e.g. defined benefit for all employees of some group entities and defined contribution for all employees of other group entities. For example, Companies C and B are under the common control of Parent P. C and B participate in a single plan for the benefit of their employees; C's employees are entitled to a defined contribution award upon retirement and B's employees are entitled to a defined benefit award upon retirement. The contributions made by C and B and their employees are held in a single asset pool in a trust. In our view, in order to account for the defined contribution and defined benefit components of the plan separately (i.e. C to account for the scheme as a defined contribution plan, while B accounts for it as a defined benefit plan, if a contractual agreement or stated policy exists for charging the IAS 19 cost for the plan as a whole (see 4.4.160.20)), as a minimum there should be controls in place within the trust that prevent any use of assets related to defined contribution members to settle obligations related to defined benefit members, or vice versa. If such restrictions on availability are not in place, then we believe that the scheme as a whole should be accounted for as a single plan and defined benefit accounting should be applied at a group level (see 4.4.160.20).

IAS 19.34A 4.4.160.20 If a contractual agreement or stated policy exists for charging the IAS 19 cost for the plan as a whole, then an entity recognises the defined benefit cost allocated to it under the agreement or policy. If there is no contractual agreement or stated policy in place, then the net defined benefit cost is recognised by the group entity that is legally the sponsoring employer for the plan.

4.4.170 *Contractual agreement or stated policy exists*

4.4.170.10 In our view, the net defined benefit cost to be allocated to and recognised by group entities under a contractual agreement or a stated policy is, in aggregate, equal to the amount recognised at the group level in profit or loss, and, if relevant, the amount of actuarial gains and losses recognised in other comprehensive income (see 4.4.510).

4.4.170.20 IFRSs are silent as to how the net defined benefit cost allocated should be recognised in the financial statements of group entities (see 2.1.60 and 70). In our view, participants in a group plan generally should not recognise any of the allocated amount outside profit or loss; instead they should recognise it as a single expense within personnel expenses (see 4.4.1140). However, there may be circumstances in which recognition of a portion of the allocated amount outside profit or loss is appropriate; for example, if there is a reasonable basis of allocating actuarial gains and losses to group entities and the policy at group level is for the recognition of actuarial gains and losses outside profit or loss.

4.4.170.30 For example, Company G participates in a group defined benefit plan for which the net defined benefit cost is allocated to group entities in accordance with a stated policy. The stated policy is that the cost allocated to participating entities is based on the obligation attributable to the plan participants. This assessment includes identifying which specific participating entities have incurred an obligation for particular plan members. The stated policy is intended to reflect as closely as possible each group entity's share of the underlying financial position and performance of the plan, including any actuarial gains and losses attributable to those entities. In our view, it may be appropriate for G to apply full defined benefit accounting to its share of each component of the net defined benefit cost, and therefore to have the option to recognise allocated actuarial gains and losses in other comprehensive income in its financial statements. For complex group plans it may be necessary to involve an actuary to determine the group entities to which the defined benefit obligation relates.

4.4.170.40 In another example, Company B participates in a group defined benefit plan for which 90 percent of the defined benefit obligation is attributable to its active employees and retirees. B is not the legal sponsor of the plan and the net defined benefit cost is allocated to group entities in accordance with a stated policy. In accordance with the stated policy, the net defined benefit cost is allocated based on an assessment of either the defined benefit obligation or the current service cost attributable to other participants, with the balance allocated to B. In our view, it may be appropriate for B to apply full defined benefit accounting to its share of each component of the net defined benefit cost, and therefore to have the option to recognise allocated actuarial gains and losses in other comprehensive income. We believe that this would be appropriate on the basis that 90 percent of the defined benefit obligation is attributable to B's active employees and retirees, and not simply as a result of the stated policy to allocate this amount.

IAS 19.34B 4.4.170.50 In our view, an entity that applies full defined benefit accounting to its allocated cost in its financial statements is not required to provide disclosures in respect of that allocated amount, i.e. the entity is required to provide disclosures only in respect of the group plan as a whole.

4.4.180 *No contractual agreement or stated policy in place*

4.4.180.10 If there is no contractual agreement or stated policy in place, then the net defined benefit cost is recognised by the group entity that legally is the sponsoring employer for the plan. The other participants in the plan recognise in profit or loss an amount equal to their contributions payable for the period. In our view, the net defined benefit cost recognised by the legal sponsor should be equal to the net defined benefit cost for the plan as a whole less the contributions of other plan participants (referred to subsequently as "net cost").

4.4.180.20 IFRSs do not address how the net cost should be recognised by the legal sponsor. In our view, when the policy at group level is to recognise actuarial gains and losses in profit or loss, the legal sponsor should recognise its net cost in profit or loss. When the policy at group level is to recognise actuarial gains and losses immediately in other comprehensive income, in our view the appropriate accounting treatment by the legal sponsor will depend on the facts and circumstances of the plan, and in particular the basis of the contributions made by other entities.

4.4.180.30 For example, Company C is the legal sponsor of a group plan for which the contributions of participants relate only to their current service cost for the period. At the group level, actuarial gains and losses are recognised immediately in other comprehensive income. As the actuarial gains and losses for the plan as a whole largely are attributable to C, in our view it may be appropriate for C to elect to apply the group policy for recognition of actuarial gains and losses and recognise actuarial gains and losses in other comprehensive income in its financial statements. The remaining defined benefit cost, net of the contributions of other entities, is recognised in profit or loss.

4.4.180.40 A situation may arise in which the contributions of participants other than the legal sponsor may exceed the defined benefit cost of the plan as a whole recognised in profit or loss, and at group level actuarial gains and losses are recognised in other comprehensive income. IFRSs do not provide guidance on the treatment by the legal sponsor of the excess of contributions received. The appropriate accounting treatment by the legal sponsor will depend on the facts and circumstances of the plan.

4.4.180.50 If the legal sponsor also recognises actuarial gains and losses outside profit or loss, then one approach would be to apply contributions of other entities first against the amount recognised in profit or loss in the current period, with the excess contributions offset against actuarial gains and losses recognised outside profit or loss, because the contributions may include an element of funding a deficit related to actuarial losses recognised in prior periods. For example, Company D is the legal sponsor of a group plan for which the net defined benefit cost is 100, including actuarial losses of 20. Contributions by other participants are 90. D recognises actuarial gains and losses outside profit or loss in its individual financial statements. Under this approach, in D's individual financial statements the contributions first would be offset against the amount recognised in profit or loss of 80, with the remaining contribution of 10 being recognised in other comprehensive income, as an adjustment of recognised actuarial gains and losses.

4.4.185 *Introduction or removal of stated policy*

4.4.185.10 If a legal sponsor introduces a stated policy or removes a stated policy, then the general principles of changes in the classification of a pension plan should be applied to the respective recognition and derecognition of a share of an existing deficit or surplus (see 4.4.950). Accordingly, if the plan has a deficit and a stated policy is removed by a legal sponsor, then other participants will derecognise their portion of the deficit and recognise a settlement gain (4.4.950.20) whereas the sponsor will recognise an additional deficit in profit or loss as past service cost (4.4.950.50). If the opposite occurs, then an introduction of a stated policy would result in a settlement gain by the legal sponsor and past service costs for other participants.

4.4.190 *State plans*

IAS 19.37 4.4.190.10 State plans are established by legislation to cover all, or specific groups of, entities and are not operated by the employer.

IAS 19.36, 38 4.4.190.20 State plans are accounted for in the same way as multi-employer plans. If the employer has an obligation only to pay contributions and has no legal or constructive obligation to pay future benefits, then state plans are defined contribution plans. Otherwise they are defined benefit plans.

4.4.190.30 Generally, there is insufficient information available about state plans to apply defined benefit accounting. Therefore defined contribution accounting normally is applied to state plans.

4.4.200 *Minimum benefit guarantees**

4.4.200.10 In certain cases a plan that otherwise would be a defined contribution plan contains certain minimum benefit guarantees. For example, the employer may guarantee a minimum return on the investment of contributions. In our view, a minimum benefit guarantee causes a plan to be a defined benefit plan.

4.4.210 **Accounting for defined contribution plans***

IAS 19.44 4.4.210.10 The entity accounts for its contributions to defined contribution plans on an accrual basis.

4.4.220 *Prepayments and accruals*

4.4.220.10 An asset or liability may result from advance payments or payments due, respectively, to a defined contribution fund.

4.4.230 *Refund of contributions or contribution holiday*

4.4.230.10 In unusual cases an entity may be entitled to a refund of contributions or to a contribution holiday in respect of a defined contribution plan; for example, if an employee forfeits benefits as a result of failing to meet the required service conditions.

4.4.230.20 An entity may be entitled to a refund of contributions or a contribution holiday in respect of past services; for example, when past contributions made to a plan exceed the contribution due for services provided and the excess of contributions are available as a refund of contributions or a contribution holiday. In our view, a refund of contributions or a contribution holiday for past services, which already have been recognised as personnel expenses, should be recognised in profit or loss when it is receivable. In our view, a refund that will accrue in future periods for services to be provided after the reporting date (e.g. in the form of a contribution holiday or a reduction in future contributions) should not be anticipated. Rather, the benefit should be recognised by way of a lower (or no) contribution expense in those future periods.

4.4.240 *Refund or contribution holiday related to a multi-employer plan*

4.4.240.10 In our view, an asset should not be recognised in respect of an anticipated refund of contributions or a contribution holiday for a defined benefit multi-employer plan that is accounted for as a defined contribution plan because insufficient information is available to apply defined benefit accounting. This is because the factors that give rise to the exemption from defined benefit accounting (i.e. the inability to obtain sufficient information to calculate the entity's proportionate share), and therefore the exemption from recognising an asset or liability, applies until the refund is received or receivable. However, the surplus and the implications (i.e. the expected reduction in contributions) should be disclosed.

4.4.250 **Vesting conditions and advance contributions**

4.4.250.10 When contributions are made to a defined contribution plan in advance of services being rendered, or when a defined contribution plan has vesting conditions, in our view the contributions should be recorded as a prepayment. The prepayment should be expensed as the employees provide services that entitle them to the benefits. In our view, the allocation over the service period should be based on the plan's benefit formula in the same way as for a defined benefit plan (see 4.4.270.40).

4.4.250.20 For example, Company Y makes contributions to a defined contribution plan on behalf of its employees. Each employee's vested interest is 100 percent if employment terminates after age 60; 75 percent if employment terminates after age 55; and 50 percent if employment terminates before age 55. Therefore, half the benefits vest immediately, an additional 25 percent vests at age 55 and the remainder vests at age 60. For employees younger than 55, an employment cost should be recognised immediately for 50 percent of the contribution. In our view, the remainder should be recognised initially as a prepayment, and a personnel expense should be recognised over the vesting period (i.e. 25 percent over the period until the employee reaches the age of 55, and the remaining 25 percent over the period until the employee reaches the age of 60). For employees between the ages of 55 and 60, 75 percent should be recognised immediately and the remainder over the period to age 60. For employees over the age of 60 the entire contribution should be recognised immediately.

4.4.260 **Accounting for defined benefit plans***

4.4.265 *Valuation of defined benefit plan liabilities and assets*

4.4.265.10 IFRSs establish requirements regarding the basis of the valuation as well as principles about the actuarial assumptions that should be used in valuing defined benefit plans.

IAS 19.51 4.4.265.20 Estimates, averages and computational short-cuts may be used only if they provide a reliable approximation of the detailed computations that are required. In our view, computational short-cuts may be appropriate in practice when performing a roll forward of a previous valuation, e.g. from valuation date to a subsequent reporting dates (see 4.4.330).

4.4.270 *Measurement of the obligation**

IAS 19.64 4.4.270.10 The projected unit credit method is used to determine the present value of the defined benefit obligation. This method involves projecting future salaries and benefits that an employee will be entitled to at the expected date of leaving.

4.4.270.20 For example, Company F operates a defined benefit plan that provides an annual pension of 1/60 of final salary for each year of service. The total expected annual salary on retirement of employees covered by the plan is 600,000. All the employees are expected to retire in 10 years and have worked for 5 years to date. After retirement the employees are expected to live for 15 years.

4.4.270.30 The defined benefit obligation is the present value of the expected payment of 750,000 (5/60 x 600,000 x 15). The employee cost for the period (current service cost) is equal to (1/60 x 600,000 x 15) discounted to its present value, adjusted for the actuarially determined probability of the outcome.

IAS 19.67 4.4.270.40 Benefits are attributed to periods of service in accordance with the plan's benefit formula, unless that formula is back-end loaded (i.e. service in later periods will lead to a materially higher level of benefit than service in earlier periods), in which case a straight-line attribution is used.

IAS 19.70 4.4.270.50 In determining whether straight-line attribution is required, an entity considers whether an employee's service throughout the period ultimately will lead to benefits at that higher level.

4.4.270.60 For example, Company G sponsors a pension plan in which employees earn defined benefits for service provided between the ages of 25 and 65. As part of the pension plan, G offers an early retirement scheme under which employees earn early retirement benefits for service provided between the ages of 47 and 62. The early retirement benefits are earned regardless of the period of service prior to the age 47 (i.e. an employee joining G at age 46 is entitled to the same early retirement benefit as an employee who has been employed since the age of 26). As services provided from the age of 47 to 62 lead to the early retirement benefit, the obligation for the early retirement scheme should be attributed to services provided from the age of 47 through age 62.

IAS 19.67, 70 4.4.270.70 If a straight-line attribution is used, then benefits are attributed from the date that service first leads to benefits under the plan until the date that further service by the employee will lead to no material amount of further benefits under the plan, other than

1056

from salary increases. This method of attribution is required because the employee's service throughout the period ultimately will lead to benefits at a higher level.

4.4.270.71 Careful evaluation should be given to the terms of the plan to determine the date that service first leads to benefits under the plan, as it may not be necessarily the date of hire. For example, Company H offers post-employment medical benefits to its retirees under two conditions, that they:

- provided 20 years of service; and
- were employed at the age of 60.

4.4.270.73 The start of the attribution period may differ depending on whether the benefit is earned after 20 years of cumulative service or 20 years of consecutive service. In the cumulative service (first) scenario, the employee may leave at the age of 35 after seven years of service and return at the age of 38 and still earn the benefit. If 20 years of cumulative service is required, then the benefit would be attributed from the date of original hire, i.e. 28, as the services provided from that date contribute to the benefits earned. However, if 20 years of consecutive service is required, then the attribution would start from the age of 40 as the first seven years of employment did not give rise to benefit entitlement. However all facts and circumstances need to be considered, e.g. an entity does not re-hire former employees in practice, to ensure the appropriate attribution period is used.

4.4.270.75 IFRSs are silent as to whether the benefits attributed previously to earlier years of service should be revised when the structure of benefits offered by a plan is amended but benefits earned from the past service are unchanged. In our view, if an amendment offers improved benefits for future services and benefits accrued in respect of past service remain unaffected, then the benefits should not be attributed over the entire service period but rather split into two distinct periods. For example, a defined benefit plan offers different benefit accrual rates for different groups of participants, e.g. one category accrues a benefit of 1/60 of the final salary per year whereas the other accrues a benefit of 1/50. On 1 January 2010, the plan is amended to offer all members benefits at the more advantageous accrual rate (i.e. 1/50) and this change applies prospectively, i.e. only to benefits earned after 1 January 2010. In our view, since the benefits earned in respect of service provided until 31 December 2009 are not affected by the amendment, the benefits should not be attributed over the entire working lives of members but rather should be attributed over two distinct periods, i.e. before and after the amendment.

IAS 19.67, 83(a) 4.4.270.80 The measurement of plan liabilities reflects expected future salaries. Therefore, for average salary plans, the *projected* average salary rather than the current average salary is used in measuring the liability. Similarly, even if the plan benefits are expressed in terms of current salaries, expected future salaries should be taken into account.

4.4.280 *Actuarial assumptions*

IAS 19.72 4.4.280.10 The actuarial assumptions represent the entity's best estimates of the future variables and should be unbiased (neither imprudent nor excessively conservative) and mutually compatible (e.g. the economic relationship between increases in salaries and future inflation-linked pension increases should reflect the same expectations).

IAS 19.76, 77 4.4.280.20 The financial assumptions are based on the current market expectations of future events (e.g. medical cost inflation), and are determined in nominal (stated) terms unless real (inflation-adjusted) terms would be more appropriate.

IU 01-08 4.4.280.30 Certain pension promises may be based on achieving specific performance hurdles, e.g. additional pensionable earnings from performance bonuses. Such performance targets are considered variables (actuarial assumption) that will affect the ultimate cost of providing the post-employment benefit. As such they should be included in the determination of the pension benefit.

IU 05-08 4.4.280.40 A plan may give its members the option to choose to receive a lump sum payment at retirement instead of ongoing payments. In our experience, the expectation of such election generally is covered by the actuarial assumptions underlying the measurement of the defined benefit obligation. However, we recognise that there may be circumstances in which settlement accounting may be more appropriate, e.g. in a situation in which a large number of individuals choose the lump sum payment option at the same time in response to the employer's action. Therefore consideration should be given to the facts and circumstances of the arrangement.

4.4.290 *Benefits*

IAS 19.83 4.4.290.10 The calculation takes into account not only the stated plan benefits, but also any constructive obligations. Constructive obligations include those established by informal practices, which the entity has no realistic alternative but to continue, such as "discretionary" inflationary increases in pensions that would be very difficult for an employer to stop granting.

IAS 19.83 4.4.290.20 Also, the assumptions take into account estimated future salary increases and include any future changes in state benefits that affect benefits payable under the plan and for which there is reliable evidence that the change will occur.

4.4.290.30 Although estimates of early retirements are made, future redundancies are not taken into account until the employer is committed to make the redundancies (see 3.12.230). When the employer becomes committed to the redundancies, the impact on the defined benefit plan may need to be treated as a curtailment (see 4.4.880).

4.4.300 *Discount rate*

IAS 19.78 4.4.300.10 The obligation for estimated future payments is measured on a discounted basis. The obligation is discounted using a high quality corporate bond rate or a government bond rate when there is an insufficiently deep high quality corporate bond market. The currency and maturity of the bond should match the currency and maturity of the pension obligation.

4.4.300.20 In our view, "high quality" should be interpreted as at least an AA (Standard & Poor's rating) or Aa2 (Moody's rating) bond.

IU 06-05   4.4.300.30 In our view, an entity in a country without a sufficiently deep high quality corporate bond market cannot construct a synthetic equivalent using a bond market in another country's currency and notional or actual currency swaps. We believe that the hierarchy specified in the standard, which requires a default to the government bond rate, means that the government bond rate should be used. IAS 19, however, is not specific as to what level of government should be used to determine the appropriate government bond rate.

IU 06-05   4.4.300.40 In our view, when an entity operates in a country in which a sufficiently deep high quality corporate bond market does not exist locally, the entity may be able to determine a discount rate by reference to high quality corporate bond yields in other countries sharing the same currency.

IAS 19.81   4.4.300.50 If bonds with a maturity that matches the maturity of the pension obligation are not available, then an appropriate discount rate is estimated by extrapolating interest rates on shorter-term bonds using the yield curve and considering any available evidence about likely longer-term interest rates.

IAS 19.BC31   4.4.300.60 In our view, the incremental borrowing rate of an entity is not an appropriate rate to use because it reflects the credit quality of the entity.

4.4.305 *Determination of a discount rate in changing market conditions*

4.4.305.10 Approaches to determining an IAS 19 discount rate may vary from entity to entity. In our experience, the prevalent methods are a yield curve approach, a bond matching model, or a market index approach under which an entity selects a representative discount rate from a published index representing high quality corporate bonds (see 4.4.300.20).

IAS 8.39   4.4.305.20 In our experience, entities generally determine discount rates for employee defined benefit plans using methodologies and data sources that are consistent from period to period. It may be appropriate, in certain circumstances, to consider the appropriateness of previously used methodologies, in particular in response to any significant changes in market conditions. In our view, a change in the method used to select a discount rate may be appropriate when that change results in a more reliable estimate. We believe that this would be a change in estimate as opposed to a change in accounting policy in accordance with IAS 8 *Accounting Policies, Changes in Accounting Estimates and Errors*. If an entity changes its approach to determining a discount rate, then it provides disclosures in accordance with IAS 8. The nature and amount of a change in an accounting estimate that affects the current period or is expected to have an impact on future periods is disclosed (see 4.4.920).

4.4.305.30 In our view, any adjustments and changes to the previously used methodologies require careful assessment. We believe that it may be appropriate for an entity to exclude certain bonds from those to be included in a yield curve, a bond matching model or a market index to more reliably reflect changing market conditions, for example, by excluding "outlier" bonds from an index. Such adjustments should be made on an objective and rational basis. For example, some entities express this in terms of the number of standard deviations of a bond's yield compared to the median or mean.

4.4.305.40 We believe, however, that certain approaches would not be appropriate, for example, weighting the yields on outlier bonds differently than bonds deemed to be more representative of the overall market, as such weighting would be arbitrary and, accordingly, would not be consistent with the measurement requirements of IAS 19. Similarly, eliminating bonds issued by financial institutions solely on the basis that they are issued by financial institutions may be difficult to support as these bonds are an integral part of the market; however, if elimination of bonds issued by such entities is a consequence of the use of a systematic and rational method of eliminating outliers, then this might be acceptable. Additionally, we believe that averaging observed bond yields for some period of time, for example, a period of time before and after the end of the reporting period, would be inconsistent with the requirement in paragraph 78 of IAS 19 to determine an appropriate discount rate by reference to market yields at the end of the reporting period.

4.4.305.50 We also believe that consideration should be given to adjustments for downgrades subsequent to the end of the reporting period. In some cases, bonds that are included in data underlying a yield curve or bond matching model may be downgraded by a credit rating agency subsequent to the end of the reporting period so that the bonds no longer meet the criteria to be considered high quality (see 4.4.300.20). In other circumstances, the market index may include corporate bonds that no longer are high quality. When either of these circumstances occur, the facts and circumstances should be evaluated to determine if there is an adjusting event or non-adjusting event after the end of the reporting period as defined in IAS 10 *Events after the Reporting Period* (see 2.9).

4.4.310 *Expected return on plan assets*

IAS 19.106 4.4.310.10 The expected return on plan assets reflects the best estimate at the beginning of the period of future market returns on plan assets over the life of the obligation. The expected return on plan assets reflects changes in the fair value of plan assets held during the period as a result of actual contributions made and actual benefits paid during the period.

4.4.310.20 In our view, expected rates of return need to be reviewed and revised, if necessary, at each valuation date to reflect changes in anticipated market returns. We believe that estimates should reflect management's expectations of changes in asset allocation in the next period. However, we do not believe that it would be appropriate to change the expected rate of return if the asset allocation changes unexpectedly during the period. Nevertheless, any resultant difference between the expected and actual rates of return would be reported as part of actuarial gains and losses.

1060

4.4.310.30 The expected return on assets denominated in a foreign currency other than the functional currency of the plan takes into account the economic environment of the underlying investment. In our view, the expected return in the foreign currency should be translated into the functional currency based on applicable forward, rather than spot, exchange rates.

4.4.320 *Interaction between measurement of plan assets and obligations*

IAS 19.78   4.4.320.10 The discount rate used to determine the obligation is the rate on high quality corporate bonds; the expected return on plan assets cannot be used instead.

4.4.325 *Sharing of a surplus*

IAS 19.85,   4.4.325.10 The terms of a plan may include specific surplus-sharing provisions or the
IU 11-07   terms of allocation may be defined in a separate agreement between the employer and the employees; for example, when a plan has a surplus, the terms of the plan indicate that 30 percent of the future surplus should be allocated to employees and the remainder to the employer (see 4.4.700). In our view, the portion of the surplus allocated to the participants in a defined benefit plan should be considered in measuring the defined benefit obligation. Any change in the amount of surplus allocated to employees may be considered either a past service cost or an actuarial gain/loss depending on the circumstances that gave rise to the change in the surplus (see 4.4.700.10).

4.4.330 **Timing and frequency of valuations**

IAS 19.56, 57   4.4.330.10 The timing or frequency of actuarial valuations is not mandated by IFRSs. Actuarial valuations are required to be regular enough for the amounts recognised in the financial statements not to differ from the amounts that would be determined at the reporting date. Thus a valuation a few months before the reporting date is acceptable if it is adjusted for material subsequent events (e.g. discount rate changes) up to the reporting date.

IAS 34.B9   4.4.330.15 The preparation of interim financial information generally does not involve obtaining an updated actuarial valuation, although an entity may obtain one at each interim reporting date (see 5.9.150.10). However, material changes to the plan, including a curtailment or settlement as well as unexpected significant changes in market conditions, should be adjusted for in the interim calculation (see 5.9.150.20). In our view, the impact of market conditions should be taken into consideration when deciding whether it is appropriate to obtain an updated actuarial valuation at the interim reporting date. In our experience, materiality of market changes is assessed in practice either on a gross basis (i.e. change is material to asset or defined benefit obligation) or on a net basis (i.e. change is material to deficit/surplus).

4.4.330.20 IFRSs are silent on the treatment of a change in the timing of actuarial valuations. In our view, as the change in the timing of an actuarial valuation does not change the measurement objective, it is not a change in accounting policy (see 2.8).

In our view, such a change can be made if the measurement of the obligation still would not be materially different from measurement based on an actuarial valuation obtained at the reporting date. For example, Company D previously measured its defined benefit obligation based on an actuarial valuation obtained at the reporting date; the most recent actuarial valuation was obtained at 31 December 2009. We believe that D may measure the obligation based on an actuarial valuation obtained at 30 September 2010 if it adjusts the obligation for material subsequent events up to 31 December 2010.

4.4.330.30 In our view, asset values should be determined at the annual reporting date, even if the valuation of the obligation is done in advance and is adjusted forward, since these values normally are readily determinable. Similarly, the expected return on plan assets should be determined based on the value of the assets at the beginning of the period (see 4.4.310.10 and 4.4.480.10).

IAS 34.B9   4.4.330.40 For interim financial statements a greater degree of estimation may be appropriate (see 5.9.150).

4.4.340 *Qualifications of valuer*

IAS 19.56   4.4.340.10 IAS 19 encourages but does not require the involvement of a qualified actuary in the measurement of all material defined benefit obligations.

IAS 19.57   4.4.340.20 There are no prohibitions on related parties performing the valuation. Therefore, for example, a suitably qualified employee of the parent may perform an actuarial valuation for an associate or subsidiary.

4.4.350 **Plan assets of a defined benefit plan**

4.4.360 *Definition*

IAS 19.7   4.4.360.10 Plan assets comprise:

- assets held by a legally separate fund, which:
  - can be used solely to pay or fund employee benefits;
  - are not available to the employer's creditors (even in case of a bankruptcy); and
  - cannot be returned to the entity except as reimbursement for employee benefits paid or when the fund is in surplus; and
- qualifying insurance policies (see 4.4.770).

4.4.370 *Nature of plan assets*

4.4.370.10 [Not used]

4.4.370.20 If assets meet the criteria for classification as plan assets, then any special characteristic (e.g. due to their location or age) may impact their values. Differences between the carrying amount of the asset and the value recognised upon contribution may result in the recognition of gains or losses on contribution (see 4.4.410.30).

4.4.370.30 While there is no explicit requirement in IFRSs regarding the nature of plan assets, there may be such requirements in local pension regulations, which may have to be considered.

4.4.380 *Restriction on availability*

4.4.380.10 In our view, the restriction on the availability of the assets to creditors of the sponsor applies both to claims arising from liquidation or similar court proceedings and from normal operations.

4.4.380.20 In our view, the protection from claims of other parties to the assets should not be capable of being overridden by other contracts (e.g. mortgages) or legislation. There should be legal restrictions that prevent the assets from being made available to the entity or its creditors under any circumstances, other than for permitted purposes (as discussed in 4.4.360).

4.4.390 *Reimbursement for benefits paid*

IAS 19.104A-   4.4.390.10 Reimbursement of plan assets to a sponsor should relate to benefits that have
104D   been paid. Therefore, in our view the definition of plan assets is not met if an entity has the ability to receive reimbursement in advance, *before* the reimbursable benefit payments are made.

4.4.395 *Operating assets of the reporting entity*

IAS 19.7,   4.4.395.10 It is possible for operating assets of the reporting entity to be plan assets.
103, BC68   IAS 19 does not impose any additional conditions in order for such assets to be classified as plan assets. However, when determining whether operating assets of the reporting entity qualify as plan assets, in addition to meeting the general criteria for treatment as plan assets (see 4.4.360 and 400.10), in our view it is necessary for the plan to have the ability to use those assets to fund employee benefit payments both legally and in substance. A careful analysis of the facts and circumstances may be required in performing this assessment. For example, if the operating assets in question are critical to the continued existence of the reporting entity or highly specialised and/or transferability restrictions are imposed on the plan in connection with those assets, then the plan may not have the ability to use those assets to fund employee benefits both legally and in substance. See 4.4.410.40 for consideration of sale and leaseback arrangements and 4.4.400 for a discussion of classifying financial instruments issued by the reporting entity as plan assets.

4.4.400 *Financial instruments issued by the reporting entity*

IAS 19.7, 103,   4.4.400.10 Plan assets include *transferable* financial instruments issued by the reporting
BC67A, BC68   entity when the criteria for treatment as plan assets are met (see 4.4.360 – 370). Examples

of such transferable financial instruments may include shares issued by the reporting entity (including by its subsidiaries) or loans granted by post-employment benefit plans to the reporting entity (or its subsidiaries) (see 4.4.1095). In our view, transfer would need to be possible both legally and in substance. IAS 19 precludes non-transferable financial instruments issued by the reporting entity from being plan assets in all cases.

4.4.400.20 In our view, if a reporting entity controls the voting rights of shares contributed to and held by the fund, then this does not preclude the shares from being plan assets; however, the lack of voting rights would be taken into account when determining the fair value of the shares (see 4.4.370.20).

4.4.400.30 In our view, insurance policies issued to the plan by the sponsor or a related party of the sponsor also qualify for treatment as plan assets if they are transferable and the other criteria for treatment as plan assets are met (see 4.4.790).

IAS 19.103 4.4.400.40 Plan assets exclude contributions receivable from the employer and other financial instruments issued by the employer and held by the fund that cannot be transferred to third parties (e.g. non-transferable loans by the fund to the employer (see 4.4.1095)).

4.4.400.50 In our view, the requirement for financial instruments to be transferable to qualify as plan assets applies to instruments issued by all entities that are part of the group (parent, intermediate and ultimate parent, and subsidiaries), in both separate and consolidated financial statements. We also believe that non-transferable financial instruments of associates and joint ventures in which group entities have invested are not qualifying plan assets.

4.4.405 *Replacement assets*

4.4.405.10 In some cases assets of the fund can be returned to the sponsor in situations other than when it is for reimbursement of employee benefits paid or when the fund is in surplus. In these cases, the sponsor typically is required to provide replacement assets to the fund. In our view, a sponsor's ability to replace existing plan assets does not preclude classification of the assets as plan assets, if the current fair value of the replacement assets must be equal to or higher than the fair value of the assets replaced and the trustees of the fund must agree to the substitution. We believe that this is similar to the sale of the assets by the fund. However, it is critical in this fact pattern that the sponsor delivers equivalent or greater current fair value in order to be considered similar to a sale. This is because any below-market exchange represents a transfer of value to the sponsor, which would preclude the assets from qualifying as plan assets.

4.4.410 **Measurement***

IAS 19.54(d) 4.4.410.10 Plan assets are measured at fair value. In our view, when plan assets have a quoted market price, they should be measured at the bid price, based on the requirements for measuring the fair value of financial instrument assets (see 3.6.940.40).

4.4.410.20 The requirement to measure plan assets at fair value overrides the requirements of other standards. Therefore, in our view if the plan has a controlling interest in another entity, then the investment is measured at fair value and the underlying entity is not consolidated. Similarly, shares of the plan sponsor (employer) that qualify as plan assets are measured at fair value and not presented as a deduction from equity, which normally is the treatment of treasury shares (see 3.11.250).

4.4.410.30 Plan assets may include non-financial assets such as property; in our view they also are measured at fair value, even if they were transferred to the fund by the plan sponsor in settlement of contributions due to the fund and previously were measured at cost by the sponsor. For example, a sponsor may contribute property to a plan with a cost basis of 100 and a fair value of 160 in settlement of contributions due to the fund of 160. The gain of 60 arising on the contribution of the asset could be viewed either as an actuarial gain, or as a gain recognised in profit or loss by the sponsor in the period that the asset is contributed. As the sponsor has transferred risks and rewards of ownership to the fund and the plan assets are not consolidated by the sponsor, in our view the gain of 60 should be recognised in profit or loss of the sponsor in the period that the asset is contributed.

4.4.410.40 In some cases the sponsor may continue to use the asset after the asset has been contributed into the plan (e.g. lease back of a contributed office building). In such cases the sponsor considers the requirements for the transfer of risk and rewards of ownership, which may impact whether a gain should be recognised (see 4.2.120).

4.4.420 *Presentation of the interest in a fund*

IAS 19.BC 68D-1 4.4.420.10 The employer offsets qualifying plan assets against the related obligation to employees; it does not consolidate the fund that holds the plan assets.

4.4.430 *Assets that do not meet the definition of plan assets*

4.4.430.10 In our view, investments held by employee benefit plans that do not meet the definition of plan assets should be accounted for by the sponsor in the same way as other financial assets of the sponsor (see 3.6) but also might give rise to a reimbursement right (see 4.4.840.10). If the investments include shares of the sponsoring entity itself, then the normal principles in respect of treasury shares would apply (see 3.11.250).

4.4.440 Accounting for defined benefit plans

4.4.450 *Profit or loss**

IAS 19.61 4.4.450.10 The total cost of a defined benefit plan is the entire periodic change in the plan liabilities less plan assets, aside from certain changes not recognised fully. The total cost comprises the following:

- current service cost, including the current period impact of the asset ceiling, when actuarial gains and losses are recognised through profit or loss;

- interest cost;
- expected return on plan assets, including on any reimbursement right recognised as an asset;
- certain actuarial gains and losses;
- certain past service costs; and
- the effect of any curtailments or settlements.

4.4.460 *Current service cost*

IAS 19.7   4.4.460.10 The current service cost is the increase in the present value of the defined benefit obligation attributable to the current period's service.

4.4.470 *Interest cost*

IAS 19.82   4.4.470.10 The interest cost is the unwinding of the discount on the present value of the defined benefit obligation. It is determined by multiplying the discount rate at the beginning of the period by the present value of the defined benefit obligation during the period, taking account of any material changes in the obligation. In our view, the obligation at the beginning of the period needs to be adjusted only for significant changes (e.g. significant past service costs, settlements and curtailments).

4.4.480 *Expected return on plan assets**

IAS 19.7, 106,   4.4.480.10 The expected return on plan assets includes interest, dividends and other
107, IU 03-07   income expected to be derived from the plan assets, and expected realised and unrealised gains and losses from changes in their value. Anticipated administration costs and taxes payable by the fund generally are deducted to calculate the expected return. However, in our view consideration should be given to the nature of any taxes payable by the plan to determine whether it is more appropriate for taxes to be included in the measurement of a defined benefit obligation rather than as part of the expected return on plan assets. The expected return on plan assets is determined based on market expectations at the beginning of the period, by multiplying the expected return by the plan assets at the beginning of the period, taking account of any contributions made into and benefits paid out of the plan during the period (see 4.4.310.10).

4.4.480.20 While IFRSs provide specific guidance on the treatment of taxes payable by the plan, the accounting for taxes paid by the sponsor in respect of the plan is not addressed specifically. In our view, such taxes generally are not income taxes (see 3.13.10) as they usually are not based on the income of a plan. We believe that taxes payable by the sponsor are similar to the administrative costs of running a defined benefit plan, and similar to the treatment of taxes payable by the plan, a consideration of the nature of taxes payable by the sponsor also is relevant (see 4.4.480.10). In our view, an entity has a choice of either:

IU 03-07
- recognising the expense in the rate of return on plan assets; in this case taxes are expensed as incurred; or

- estimating the net present value of expected future taxes related to services provided in the current year and including the cost in the service cost and therefore as part of the defined benefit obligation.

4.4.480.30 We believe that the entity should choose an accounting policy, to be applied consistently, to income taxes payable by the sponsor. If an entity elects an accounting policy of including in service cost an estimation of the net present value of expected future taxes related to services provided in the current year, then in our view any difference between the estimate of taxes payable and actual taxes paid is an experience adjustment and may be treated as actuarial gains and losses (see 4.4.490).

4.4.490 *Actuarial gains and losses*

4.4.500 *Determination of actuarial gains and losses*

IAS 19.7 4.4.500.10 Actuarial gains and losses arise from differences between the actual and expected outcome in the valuation of the obligation and the assets. Actuarial gains and losses may result from experience adjustments (due to differences between assumptions and what actually occurred) or from changes in assumptions. For example, experience adjustments include differences between assumptions as to future salary levels of plan participants and actual final salary levels, as compared to a change in assumptions as to future salary levels based on trends in employee compensation.

4.4.500.20 To determine actuarial gains and losses, a schedule is prepared of movements in the obligation and the plan assets. The difference between the opening balance, adjusted for expected movements during the period, and the closing balance, represents the actuarial gains or losses for the period.

4.4.500.30 The following example, which assumes there are no actuarial gains or losses at 31 December 2009, illustrates the calculation of the cumulative actuarial gains and losses at 31 December 2010 for Company W's defined benefit plan:

Plan assets	
Fair value at 31 December 2009 (actual market values at 31 December 2009)	14,000
Expected return (based on actuarial calculation at 1 January 2010; 14,000 x 7%)	980
Contributions for the period (actual amounts received by the fund)	1,050
Employee benefits paid during the period (actual benefits paid by the fund)	(1,500)
Expected fair value of assets at 31 December 2010	14,530
Actual fair value at 31 December 2010 (based on market values at 31 December 2010)	14,920
Cumulative (unrecognised) actuarial gain on plan assets at 31 December 2010	390

Defined benefit obligation

Obligation at 31 December 2009 (actual obligation based on actuarial calculation at 31 December 2009)	15,000
Interest cost (based on interest rates and obligation at 1 January 2010; 15,000 x 6%)	900
Current service cost (based on actuarial calculation at 1 January 2010)	800
Employee benefits paid during the period (actual benefits paid by the fund)	(1,500)
Expected obligation at 31 December 2010	15,200
Obligation at 31 December 2010 (actual obligation based on actuarial calculation at 31 December 2010)	17,410
Cumulative (unrecognised) actuarial loss on plan obligations at 31 December 2010	2,210

The interest cost is based on the obligation at the beginning of the year assuming that there are no material changes during the year. For purposes of this example the expected return on plan assets is based only on plan assets at the beginning of the period and does not take into account contributions made into and benefits paid out of the plan during the period.

4.4.510 Recognition of actuarial gains and losses*

4.4.510.10 An entity chooses an accounting policy of recognising actuarial gains and losses in profit or loss, or alternatively immediately in other comprehensive income. If actuarial gains and losses are recognised in profit or loss, then an entity may choose to recognise cumulative gains and losses using the "corridor method" or choose a method that results in faster recognition.

IAS 19.93   4.4.510.20 The policy chosen is applied consistently to *all* defined benefit plans and from period to period.

4.4.520 Recognition of actuarial gains and losses in profit or loss

4.4.530 Corridor method*

IAS 19.92   4.4.530.10 Under the corridor method, actuarial gains and losses are recognised when the cumulative (unrecognised) amount thereof at the *beginning of the period* exceeds a "corridor". The corridor is 10 percent of the greater of the present value of the obligation and the fair value of the assets. The corridor is calculated separately for each plan.

4.4.530.20 In the example in 4.4.500.30, the corridor at 31 December 2010, used to determine the minimum amortisation of net cumulative (unrecognised) actuarial gains and losses in 2011, is 1,741 (the greater of 1,492 (10 percent of the fair value of the actual plan assets at the beginning of 2011 of 14,920) and 1,741 (10 percent of the actual obligation at the beginning of 2011 of 17,410)). Based on the above calculation, there is a net actuarial loss at 1 January 2011 of 1,820 (2,210 - 390). So the net cumulative (unrecognised) actuarial loss exceeds the corridor and a portion is required to be recognised during 2011.

IAS 19.93 4.4.530.30 The net cumulative (unrecognised) actuarial gain or loss at the beginning of the period in excess of the corridor is amortised on a straight-line basis over the expected average remaining working lives of the employees participating in the plan. This represents the minimum amount of cumulative actuarial gains and losses that should be recognised (see 4.4.590.10).

4.4.540 Faster recognition in profit or loss

4.4.540.10 An entity is permitted to recognise actuarial gains and losses in profit or loss in any systematic method that results in faster recognition than using the corridor method as described in 4.4.530. Therefore, an entity should choose an accounting policy, to be applied consistently, for example to:

- recognise all or a stated percentage of the actuarial gains and losses immediately in profit or loss regardless of the corridor (subject to the minimum recognition requirement);
- amortise all actuarial gains and losses into profit or loss over the expected remaining working lives of the employees in the plan, or a shorter period; or
- not recognise any actuarial gains and losses that are within the corridor but recognise all other actuarial gains or losses immediately.

4.4.540.20 In practice most entities that use the corridor method recognise the minimum amount of actuarial gains or losses (i.e. spread actuarial gains and losses outside the corridor over the anticipated remaining working lives of the related employees).

4.4.540.30 Continuing the example in 4.4.500.30, the net cumulative (unrecognised) actuarial loss in excess of the corridor at 1 January 2011 is 79 (1,820 - 1,741). If W wishes to recognise only the minimum amount, then this excess would be spread over the average remaining working lives of employees. If this is 10 years, then the actuarial loss to recognise in 2011 is 7.9 (79 / 10). The amount of the excess and the amortisation are recalculated each reporting period.

4.4.550 *Recognition at the reporting date*

4.4.550.10 IFRSs are silent regarding whether it would be acceptable to recognise immediately in profit or loss actuarial gains and losses *at the reporting date*, rather than those at the beginning of the period. In our view, an entity's accounting policy choice, to be applied consistently, could include recognition of the actuarial gains or losses at the reporting date, as that policy results in faster recognition than using the corridor method as described in 4.4.530. To ensure that the policy is applied consistently, we believe that it would be necessary to update the actuarial computations at each annual reporting date.

4.4.560 *Immediate recognition of actuarial gains and losses in other comprehensive income*

IAS 19.93A, 4.4.560.10 An entity may choose an accounting policy of recognising actuarial gains and *93B* losses in the periods in which they occur *outside* profit or loss (i.e. in other comprehensive income). If this accounting policy is selected, then actuarial gains and losses are presented in the statement of comprehensive income (see 4.1).

4.4.560.20 The actuarial gains and losses recognised in other comprehensive income may not be reclassified to profit or loss.

IAS 8.14, 4.4.560.30 In our view, an entity that has an existing accounting policy of immediate
19.93 recognition of actuarial gains and losses in profit or loss or other comprehensive income cannot in the future adopt an accounting policy of recognising actuarial gains and losses under the "corridor" approach as this does not provide reliable and more relevant information about the effects of transactions. However, in our view an entity that previously chose to recognise actuarial gains and losses immediately in profit or loss may change to immediate recognition of actuarial gains and losses in other comprehensive income.

4.4.570 *Expected average remaining working lives*

IAS 19.93 4.4.570.10 In order to calculate the minimum amount of cumulative actuarial gains and losses that should be recognised (see 4.4.530.30) the entity must calculate the expected average remaining working life of employees participating in the plan; the term *participating* is not defined in IAS 19.

IAS 19.93 4.4.570.20 We prefer that the average remaining working life of participating employees be determined considering only active employees in the plan. We also prefer that when a plan includes retirees whose benefit entitlement still is increasing, these retirees also should be considered.

4.4.572 Retired employees

4.4.572.10 We understand that the average remaining working life sometimes is calculated considering the remaining working life of all participants in the plan, i.e. including both active and retired employees, with the latter having a remaining working life of zero if their benefits are no longer increasing. However, in our experience, this is less common in practice.

4.4.572.20 For example, in a situation in which substantially all of the participants in a plan are retired, we believe that both active and retired employees should be considered and an average remaining working life of zero should be attributed to retired employees. In a plan with only retired participants, all the actuarial gains or losses outside the corridor would be recognised in the following year (if the corridor method is applied) or in the current year (if an approach of immediate recognition is applied) as the average remaining working life is zero.

4.4.575 Deferred members of a defined benefit plan

4.4.575.10 Sometimes members of a defined benefit plan may no longer be accruing benefits in the plan in respect of their current service; these commonly are referred to as deferred members. Deferred members may be current employees of the entity (i.e. they are active employees of the entity but are not accruing benefits in the plan for their current service) or former employees. The benefit entitlement of deferred members under the defined benefit plan in respect of past service still may be increasing or may be frozen. IFRSs do not provide guidance on whether/how deferred members should be taken into account in determining the average remaining working lives of employees participating in the plan.

4.4.575.20 In our view, deferred members who are former employees of the entity are analogous to retired employees and accordingly should be treated in the same way as retired employees when determining the average remaining working lives of employees (see 4.4.570).

4.4.575.30 In our view, there are a number of alternatives for how deferred members who are current employees of the entity may be taken into consideration when determining the average remaining working lives of employees, including:

- do not consider them when determining the average remaining working lives of employees;
- consider them when determining the average remaining working lives of employees and attribute to them their expected remaining working life with the entity; or
- consider them when determining the average remaining working lives of employees but attribute to them a remaining working life of zero.

4.4.580 *Anticipated future events*

IAS 19.83   4.4.580.10 The benefits under a plan may depend on the outcome of future events (e.g. future salary levels or fulfilment of service conditions). These anticipated future events are considered in measuring the employee benefit obligation if the entity has a legal or constructive obligation to pay the benefits. A change in expectations gives rise to actuarial gains or losses.

IAS 19.86   4.4.580.20 Other future changes that the employer currently has a constructive obligation to make (e.g. inflation increases) also are reflected in the measurement of the obligation. However, future changes to the terms of a plan, as long as the employer does not have a constructive obligation to make these changes, are not anticipated in the measurement of the obligation. Therefore, if the terms of a plan are changed from covering a select group of employees to covering all employees, then the change is treated as a plan amendment that may give rise to a past service cost (see 4.4.600), or as a new plan, rather than as an actuarial loss.

4.4.590 *Review of actuarial gains and losses*

IAS 19.92   4.4.590.10 The calculations of the amount of actuarial gains and losses to recognise are reviewed at least on an annual basis. Therefore the amount of amortisation of actuarial gains and losses year-on-year is unlikely to be consistent. Depending on the policy selected, if the cumulative unrecognised gains and losses fall within the corridor, then amortisation may stop and restart again if they fall outside the corridor in a subsequent period.

4.4.600 *Past service cost*

IAS 19.7   4.4.600.10 Past service cost is the change in the present value of the obligation, in respect of prior periods' service, due to changes in benefit entitlement. Examples of plan amendments that may give rise to past service cost include:

- changing the retirement age from 65 to 60;
- increasing the benefits that are payable on early retirement;
- changing the final salary on which the pension is based to include bonuses; and
- expanding the employee groups covered by the plans, with retrospective effect.

4.4.600.20 In our view, in order for a change to be a plan amendment, there has to be a change in the agreement between the employer and the employee. This is because the focus of the definition for past service cost is on benefits received and not on the net employer cost.

4.4.600.30 For example, in December 2003 Medicare legislation was passed in the United States that made reimbursements available to sponsors of qualifying benefit plans. In our view, that legislation introduced in December 2003 is not a plan amendment as it had no direct impact on the benefit received by the employees and did not lead to a change in the agreement between the employer and the employees. Therefore, we believe that the effect of the US Medicare legislation should be treated as an actuarial gain. Since the benefit is provided as a government subsidy for costs incurred, we believe that the Medicare benefit should be accounted for as a reimbursement right (see 4.4.840).

IAS 19.BC55,   4.4.600.35 In general, the source of the change does not affect the accounting. Therefore,
IU 11-07   accounting for changes caused by government is the same as for changes made by an employer (see 4.4.900.50).

4.4.600.37 Sometimes it is difficult to determine whether a change in the defined benefit obligation is the result of a benefit change or is an actuarial gain/loss. For example, Company P is the sponsoring entity of a defined benefit plan in which benefits are based on final salary. During 2010 the salaries of P's employees are reduced by 10 percent. As a result, the present value of the defined benefit obligation reduces. The question arises as to whether the reduction in the defined benefit obligation is a negative past service cost (see 4.4.620) or an actuarial gain (see 4.4.500). In our view, the reduction in the defined benefit obligation as a result of the salary reduction is an actuarial gain; there has been no change to the benefit entitlement as the employees still receive the same percentage of final salary. Instead the defined benefit obligation reduction is the result of a difference between previous and revised actuarial assumptions about final salary.

IAS 19.96   4.4.600.40 If entitlements to enhanced benefits are not conditional on future service and therefore vest immediately, then the expense and an increase in the obligation are recognised in full immediately. To the extent that the benefits are not vested, the expense is amortised on a straight-line basis over the period until they vest.

4.4.600.50 For example, Company E increases the pension for all of its employees from 2 percent of final salary for each year of service to 2.5 percent for those employees who provide at least five years of service. The present value of the additional benefits for services rendered in the past is 150 for employees with more than five years of service and 120 for employees with less than five (on average two years of service). E recognises the vested benefits of 150 immediately. The 120 that is not vested is recognised on a straight-line basis over the average vesting period of three years (5 - 2).

4.4.600.60 In our view, past service cost also includes granting entitlements to employees joining a plan, for example, in connection with a group reorganisation, when members of one defined benefit plan may transfer to another defined benefit plan and their past service entitlements also are transferred. In our view, the gain or loss arising on the introduction of new members to a plan, together with past service entitlement, meets the definition of a past service cost and not actuarial gains or losses. We believe that this past service cost should be calculated net of any related assets transferred, i.e. the past service cost is equal to the increase in the obligation in respect of the transferred employees less the fair value of the related assets transferred.

4.4.610 *Timing of recognition*

IAS 19.52   4.4.610.10 In our view, a change in the obligation in respect of a past service cost should be recognised when an entity has a legal or constructive obligation to make the plan amendment. For example, on 1 November 2010 Company X decides to increase pensions of all employees by 7 percent with effect from 1 July 2011. X communicates the decision to the employees at 31 December 2010 and therefore should recognise the past service cost at that date, since it has no realistic alternative but to pay the increased benefits as a result of its communication.

IAS 19.99   4.4.610.20 An entity establishes its amortisation schedule for past service cost when the benefits are introduced or changed.

4.4.620 *Negative past service cost*

4.4.620.10 Past service cost normally results in an increase in the liability (i.e. benefits are improved), but if benefits are reduced (e.g. if an entity retroactively reduces its accrual rate of pensionable earnings), then those changes result in a reduction of the liability (negative past service cost).

IAS 19.BC 62B   4.4.620.20 When a benefit reduction occurs, this can have an impact in respect of future service, past service or both. As such, it is important to determine whether a reduction of benefits gives rise to a negative past service cost or a curtailment. A plan amendment that reduces benefits in respect of past service is a negative past service cost and is recognised over the vesting period. Changes that result in a significant reduction in the *number of employees* covered by a plan, or that mean a significant element of *future service* by the current employees no longer earns benefits or earns only reduced benefits, are treated as curtailments (see 4.4.880). As explained in 4.4.890.50, if an amendment to a benefit plan affects the extent to which future salary increases after the reporting date are linked to benefits payable for past service, then that part of the amendment is a curtailment. In other words, the removal of the link to future pensionable earnings growth, or a reduction in the definition of pensionable earnings, is exclusively a future service change, and so the reduction in the defined benefit obligation of such a future service change is accounted for as a curtailment gain. As such, if a plan amendment affects the benefit for future service only, e.g. if an entity changes its pension plan from a final salary plan to an average salary plan (fixing average salary to the date of change at the current salary level at that date) or an entity introduces a cap on the pensionable earnings, then that resulting reduction in the liability is wholly a curtailment gain.

IAS 19.111A 4.4.620.30 If a reduction in benefits affects the benefits from both past and future service, and as a consequence results in both a curtailment and negative past service cost, then the effects are accounted for separately (see 4.4.890.50).

4.4.620.32 For example, Company K operates a defined benefit pension plan in which employees accrue 1 percent of their final salary for each year of service. On 1 January 2010 the plan is amended, with retrospective effect, to offer employees benefits at the less advantageous accrual rate of 0.75 percent of their *current* salary for each year of service, with current salary for service to date deemed to be the same as salary on the date of the change. This change was agreed by negotiation and no further approvals are pending. As a result of the changes introduced with the plan amendment the defined benefit obligation decreases, in part as a result of change in the accrual rate with retrospective effect (negative past service cost) and in part as a result of change in pensionable salary (curtailment gain). Therefore the plan amendment gives rise to both curtailment and negative past service cost; the effect of each needs to be quantified separately, considering that the curtailment gain would be recognised immediately whereas negative past service cost would be recognised over the vesting period. In our experience, such calculations may be complex and different outcomes may be reached depending on the order in which the curtailment and negative past service cost are factored into the calculations.

4.4.620.34 Continuing the example in 4.4.620.32, assuming that a projected final pensionable salary prior to an amendment is 1,000 but as a result of an amendment the projected pensionable salary is reduced to 900; the benefit for an employee with 10 years of service would reduce from 100 (calculated as 1,000 x 10 x 1%) to 67.5 (calculated as 900 x 10 x 0.75%). If the curtailment is considered first, before negative past service cost, then the curtailment portion resulting from a change in the salary plan from final to current would be 10 (calculated as 100 (1,000 x 10 x 1%) less 90 (900 x 10 x 1%)) and the remaining reduction of 22.5 (calculated as 90 less 67.5) would be negative past service cost. In contrast, if the negative past service cost is considered first, before curtailment, then the negative past service cost portion resulting from the reduction in the accrual rate would be 25 (calculated as 100 (1,000 x 10 x 1%) less 75 (1,000 x 10 x 0.75%)) and the remaining reduction of 7.5 (calculated as 75 - 67.5) would be a curtailment gain.

IAS 19.101 4.4.620.35 When there are multiple amendments to the same plan, careful consideration of the specific facts and circumstances of those plan amendments is required. In our view, there is an initial presumption that the amendments should be considered and accounted for in aggregate rather than each in isolation. However, this presumption may be rebutted if it can be demonstrated that the amendments were negotiated separately with separate member groups (e.g. employees vs retirees) as opposed to being negotiated as a package.

IAS 19.96 4.4.620.40 Past service costs that reduce the obligation are accounted for in the same way as a past service cost that increases it. Therefore, if the benefits are vested, then a reduction in the liability and income is recognised immediately; if the benefits are not yet vested, then the gain resulting from the reduction in benefits is spread over the vesting period.

4.4.630 Statement of financial position

IAS 19.54 4.4.630.10 The effect of defined benefit accounting on the statement of financial position is that a liability is recorded as the present value of the obligation less the fair value of the plan assets less (plus) unrecognised past service cost and unrecognised actuarial losses (gains).

4.4.640 Example

4.4.640.10 The example in 4.4.640.20 – 70 illustrates the accounting for a defined benefit plan.

4.4.640.20 The following information pertains to Company K's pension plan:

Plan assets at 1 January 2010	100,000
Defined benefit obligation at 1 January 2010	100,000
Unrecognised net actuarial loss at 1 January 2010	20,000
Average remaining working life of employees at 1 January 2010	10 years
Service cost for 2010	9,000
Discount rate at 1 January 2010	10%
Expected return on plan assets at 1 January 2009	10,000
Contributions by K to the plan in 2010	8,000
Benefits paid by the plan in 2010 to retirees	7,000
Net actuarial loss arising in 2010	2,000

4.4.640.30 K chooses to recognise the minimum amount of actuarial gains and losses under the corridor method (see 4.4.530).

4.4.640.40 The following entries are made in respect of the pension plan for the year ending 31 December 2010:

	Debit	Credit
Pension expense	9,000	
Pension liability		9,000
To recognise current service cost		
Pension expense	10,000	
Pension liability		10,000
To recognise interest cost (100,000 x 10%)		
Pension liability	10,000	
Pension expense		10,000
To recognise expected return on plan assets		
Pension expense	1,000	
Pension liability		1,000
To recognise portion of actuarial loss that exceeds corridor ((20,000 - 10,000) / 10)		
Pension liability	8,000	
Cash		8,000
To recognise contributions for the year		

4.4.640.50 The pension cost recognised for the year is 10,000, made up as follows:

Current service cost	9,000
Interest cost	10,000
Expected return on plan assets	(10,000)
Actuarial loss recognised	1,000
Net cost for the year	10,000

4.4.640.60 The amount recognised in the statement of financial position at 31 December 2010 is a net asset of 18,000. This represents the opening statement of financial position balance (net asset at 1 January 2010), plus the expense for the year, less contributions, as follows:

Obligation at 1 January 2010	100,000
Plan assets at 1 January 2010	(100,000)
Unrecognised actuarial loss	(20,000)
Statement of financial position net asset at 1 January 2010	(20,000)
Net cost for the year	10,000
Contributions paid	(8,000)
Statement of financial position net asset at 31 December 2010	(18,000)

4.4.640.70 Neither the benefits paid to employees directly by the plan nor the actuarial gains and losses arising in the current year affect the net cost for the year, or the roll forward of the opening to closing statement of financial position balances. The net unrecognised actuarial loss at 31 December 2010 is 21,000 (20,000 + 2,000 - 1,000). Since there is a net asset the sponsor applies the asset ceiling test to determine whether a net plan asset is recognised (see 4.4.660).

IAS 19.120A   4.4.640.75 Although IFRSs generally do not distinguish between funded and unfunded
(d), (q),   plans, IAS 19 requires disclosure of defined benefit obligations arising from plans
BC85A   that are unfunded separately from plans that are wholly or partly funded. In addition, an entity discloses its best estimate of contributions expected to be paid to the plan during the annual period beginning after the reporting date. With reference to the term "contributions" some believe that this requirement relates only to funded plans. However, in our view information about the entity's cash flows in the immediate future is useful, and therefore we encourage providing this information for both funded and unfunded plans; in the latter case we also encourage disclosure of expected benefits to be paid. The amounts may be aggregated, with disclosure that both elements are included. Even if expected benefits payments from the unfunded plans are not disclosed, the best estimate of contributions expected to be paid to the funded plans should as a minimum always be disclosed.

4.4.650 *Foreign currency denominated obligation*

4.4.650.10 A net obligation under a pension plan may be denominated in a foreign currency; for example, a reporting entity may have an obligation to employees working abroad, and that obligation is denominated in the local currency of the country in which they work. An issue arises as to whether the obligation should be translated to the reporting entity's functional currency before or after applying the corridor and measuring the obligation. In our view, the net obligation first should be calculated in the currency in which it is denominated and the resulting obligation should be translated into the reporting entity's functional currency. As a result, foreign exchange gains and losses are recognised immediately rather than entering into the determination of actuarial gains or losses. In our view, the same treatment would apply to all plans that have functional currency different than that of the reporting entity, regardless of whether or not the corridor method is applied.

4.4.660 Asset ceiling

IAS 19.58   4.4.660.10 If the statement of financial position amount turns out to be an asset, then the amount recognised is limited to the present value of available contribution reductions or refunds plus unrecognised actuarial losses and unrecognised past service costs. Further requirements ensure that a gain (loss) is not recognised solely as a result of an actuarial loss (gain) or a past service cost in the current period.

4.4.660.20 For example, Company E's defined benefit plan has the following characteristics:

Present value of obligation	11,000
Fair value of plan assets	(12,400)
Unrecognised actuarial losses	(1,100)
Unrecognised past service cost	(700)
Computed net asset	(3,200)

4.4.660.30 The present value of available reductions in future contributions as a result of the plan surplus is 1,000. E does not have an unconditional right to a refund. The ceiling on the asset that may be recognised is calculated as follows:

Unrecognised actuarial losses	1,100
Unrecognised past service cost	700
Present value of available reductions in future contributions	1,000
Ceiling on asset to be recognised	2,800

4.4.660.40 Therefore E will recognise an asset of 2,800 in the statement of financial position and have an unrecognised surplus of 400 (3,200 - 2,800).

4.4.660.45 If in the example at 4.4.660.20 – 40 Company E had unrecognised actuarial gains of 1,100 instead of unrecognised actuarial losses of 1,100, then the asset recognised would be 1,000. This is the amount of the computed net asset ((11,000 + 1,100) - (12,400 + 700)). In this case the ceiling on the asset that may be recognised would be 1,700 (1,000 + 700), which is higher than the computed net asset. Therefore, in this case the asset ceiling has no effect on the asset recognised.

IAS 19.61   4.4.660.50 When an entity elects to recognise actuarial gains and losses in other comprehensive income in the periods in which they occur (see 4.4.510), the impact of the asset ceiling also is recognised outside profit or loss in other comprehensive income. When this policy choice is elected, adjustments arising from the asset ceiling recognised in other comprehensive income may not be reclassified to profit or loss.

4.4.670 Benefits available

IFRIC 14.7, 8   4.4.670.10 Issues often arise in practice about whether a surplus is available to the entity. An economic benefit is available to an entity if, in accordance with the terms of the plan and applicable statutory requirements, it is realisable during the life of the plan or on the settlement of the plan liabilities (see 4.4.740.30).

4.4.670.20 Determining whether the economic benefit is available to an entity will require a detailed analysis of the facts in each case, including the rules of the plan and applicable legislation (see 4.4.695).

4.4.680 [Not used]

4.4.690 *Intended use of surplus*

IFRIC 14.9   4.4.690.10 The economic benefit available does not depend on how the entity intends to use the surplus. An entity determines the maximum economic benefit that is available from refunds, reductions in future contributions or a combination of both, but not based on mutually exclusive assumptions.

4.4.690.15 In our view, unless agreement is required an entity does not have to have made a request, or intend to make a request, for a refund or reduction in future contributions in order to factor in these methods of realising benefits when applying the asset ceiling. This is because the asset ceiling test is not based on management intentions.

4.4.690.20 Sometimes an employer may decide to use an available surplus to improve the plan benefits. In our view, unless there is a legal or constructive obligation to improve the benefits, the surplus should be considered as being available to the employer in determining the amount of the asset to recognise.

4.4.690.30 When there is a legal or constructive obligation to enhance the benefits, any resulting increase in the obligation should be treated as a past service cost (see 4.4.600).

4.4.695 *The economic benefit available as a refund*

IFRIC 14.11   4.4.695.10 A refund is available to an entity only if the entity has an unconditional right to a refund:

- during the life of the plan, without assuming that the plan liabilities are settled;
- over time until all members have left the plan, assuming the gradual settlement of the plan liabilities; or
- upon plan wind-up, assuming the full settlement of the plan liabilities in a wind-up.

The economic benefit available as a refund under each of these scenarios might vary (see 4.4.745).

IFRIC 14.11
(b)   4.4.695.15 In our view, if the trustees, or any other third party responsible for governing the plan, have an unconditional right to wind up the plan at any time, then the entity may not have an unconditional right to a refund assuming the gradual settlement of the plan liabilities over time, which would support recognition of an asset. (The entity may have an unconditional right to a refund assuming wind-up but, as explained in 4.4.745.25, this may not support recognition of an asset.) In our view, an unconditional right of the entity to a refund should not be assessed based on probability or past practice. In our experience, in analysing whether an entity has an unconditional right to a refund, care should be taken to understand the rules of the plan, terms of the trust deed and applicable legislation that may influence the existence of such right. In analysing trustees' rights to put the plan into wind-up, consideration should be given to whether such right can be exercised "with cause" or "without any cause". In the latter case, the unconditional right of the entity to a refund after gradual settlement over time is presumed

not to exist unless there is evidence to the contrary. However, if the trustees can exercise their right only "with cause" and such cause is within the entity's control, then in our view the entity may have an unconditional right to a refund under this scenario as the entity can avoid by its own actions the trustees' wind-up of the plan. In our experience, determining whether an economic benefit is available as a refund can be complex and often depends on entity and country specific facts and circumstances.

4.4.695.17 For example, if the trustees have an unconditional right to wind up the plan in the event of a change in control of Company P, the sponsoring entity, then in our view P does not have an unconditional right to a refund assuming the gradual settlement of the plan liabilities over time, since we believe that a change in control event is an uncertain future event that is not within the control of the entity (see 3.11.40.36). If on the other hand the trustees had an unconditional right to wind up the plan in the event of a change in control of P only in the event that P reduces its contributions to the scheme, then in our view this does not preclude P from having an unconditional right to a refund under this scenario; P can avoid the trustees' wind up of the scheme by not reducing contributions to the scheme, since P reducing its contributions to the scheme is within P's control.

IFRIC 14.12   4.4.695.20 If the entity's right to a refund of a surplus depends on the occurrence or non-occurrence of one or more uncertain future events not wholly within its control, the entity does not have an unconditional right and does not recognise an asset.

4.4.700 *Sharing of benefits*

4.4.700.10 If any surplus is required to be shared between the employer and employees, or when past practice has established a valid expectation that the benefit will be shared, then in our view the portion that will be made available to the employees increases the defined benefit obligation, and as a consequence decreases the amount that could be recognised as a net asset by the employer (see 4.4.325.10).

4.4.710 [Not used]

4.4.720 *Taxes on the surplus*

4.4.720.10 If an entity will be required to pay income tax on the realisation of a surplus, then it may be required to recognise a related deferred tax liability (see 3.13).

IFRIC 14.13   4.4.720.20 If a refund will be subject to a tax other than income tax, then the available surplus is determined net of tax.

4.4.730 [Not used]

4.4.740 *Minimum funding requirements#*

4.4.740.10 Some entities are subject to requirements that specify a minimum level of contributions to be made to a post-employment benefit plan over a period of time (a minimum funding requirement). Under a minimum funding requirement an entity may have a present obligation to make additional contributions to a plan. If the fair value of plan assets is in excess of the defined benefit obligation, or would be once the committed contributions were made (see 4.4.747), then the entity considers whether the asset ceiling may limit the amount that the entity may recognise as an asset. If this additional contribution could be recovered as a refund, either from the ongoing plan or on settlement or termination of the plan, then normally the net plan asset would qualify for recognition (see 4.4.350). However, if this amount could not be recovered as a refund but only through a reduction in future contributions, then the minimum funding requirement may limit the amount of the asset that can be recognised. As a result, some or all of the additional contribution may have to be recognised in profit or loss in the current period if it is not recoverable.

4.4.740.20 For example, under a minimum funding requirement Company Q has a present obligation to make additional contributions in respect of services it has received to date. The minimum funding requirement also limits the reduction in future contributions based on a ratio calculated as a percentage of plan assets divided by the obligations to employees as determined under statutory requirements. If the plan is over-funded by a specified percentage, for example, 110 percent, then Q is entitled to a reduction in future contributions. Currently Q has a funding ratio that is less than 110 percent, and therefore it is required to make additional (above the normal) contributions to raise the asset-to-liability ratio to the minimum funding level. Q is allowed to make contributions over the next several years and is not entitled to a reduction in future contributions. However, Q has projected that, in respect of services it has received to date, a reduction in future contributions will be available to it in the future based on its expected return on plan assets, future expected service costs and current minimum funding scheduled payment requirements. The question arises as to whether the economic benefit is available to Q such that it can recognise an asset.

IFRIC 14.8 4.4.740.30 The economic benefit, in the form of a refund from the plan or a reduction in future contributions, may be considered as being available even if it is not immediately realisable at the reporting date. Therefore, because a reduction in future contributions will be available to the entity in the future, an asset can be recognised.

4.4.743 *Forthcoming requirements*

4.4.743.10 The amendments to IFRIC 14, published in November 2009, address the treatment of prepayments when there is a minimum funding requirement.

4.4.743.20 Current IFRIC 14 states that a surplus in a plan, whether created by a prepayment or otherwise, is not regarded as an economic benefit available as a reduction in future contributions if the future minimum funding contribution required in respect of future accrual of benefits exceeds the future IAS 19 service cost. Therefore, prior to these amendments, under current IFRIC 14 (and if the entity did not have an unconditional right to a refund of surplus) a prepayment is recognised as an expense.

4.4.743.30 Under the amended IFRIC 14 such a prepayment is recognised as an asset, on the basis that the entity has a future economic benefit from the prepayment in the form of reduced cash outflows in future years in which minimum funding requirement payments would otherwise be required. The essence is that the prepayment reduces future contributions that cover not only future service costs but also future excess of minimum funding requirement contributions over service cost.

4.4.743.40 The amendments to IFRIC 14 are effective for annual periods beginning on or after 1 January 2011; earlier application is permitted. The amendments are to be applied from the beginning of the earliest comparative period presented in the first financial statements in which the entity applies IFRIC 14. If the entity had previously applied IFRIC 14 before it applies the amendments, then it recognises the adjustment resulting from the application of the amendments in retained earnings at the beginning of the earliest comparative period presented. For example, an entity with a calendar year end, with one year's comparatives presented, previously applied IFRIC 14 in its 2008 financial statements. It applies the amendments for the first time in its 2011 financial statements. In this case the entity will recognise the resulting adjustment in retained earnings on 1 January 2010, calculated to apply the amendments from 1 January 2007.

4.4.745 *Measurement of economic benefit*

4.4.745.10 [Not used]

IFRIC 14.11, 4.4.745.20 The economic benefit available as a refund of plan surplus is measured as
13, 14 the amount of the surplus at the reporting date (i.e. the fair value of the plan assets less the present value of the defined benefit obligation) that the entity has a right to receive as a refund, less any associated costs. In measuring the amount available when the plan is wound up, the costs of settling the liabilities and making the refund are taken into account. The entity also would need to have an unconditional right to the refund (see 4.4.695).

4.4.745.25 In our experience, even if the entity has an unconditional right to a refund assuming the wind-up, the costs to settle plan liabilities often may be too high to result in the recognition of an asset.

IFRIC 14.16, 4.4.745.30 The economic benefit available as a reduction in future contributions is
20 measured as follows:

- If there is no minimum funding requirement, then as the lower of the surplus in the plan, and the present value of the future service cost to the entity for each year over the shorter of the expected life of the plan and the expected life of the entity.
- If there is a minimum funding requirement, then as equal to the present value of the estimated future service cost to the entity in each year less the estimated minimum funding contribution required in respect of the future accrual of benefits in the given year.

4.4.747 When a minimum funding requirement may give rise to a liability

IFRIC 14.24   4.4.747.10 If a plan has a funding shortfall on the minimum funding basis in respect of services already received, then it may mean that the employer has to pay additional contributions to cover this shortfall. Such minimum funding requirements have to be recognised as a liability if a surplus arising from the payment of the extra contributions is not fully available as a refund or reduction in future contributions.

IFRIC 14.26   4.4.747.20 The liability that results from a minimum funding requirement and any subsequent remeasurement of that liability is recognised immediately in accordance with the entity's accounting policy with respect to the asset ceiling test (see 4.4.510.10).

IFRIC 14.25   4.4.747.30 In addition, an entity also considers whether the deferral of any actuarial gains or losses would be overridden before determining the liability from minimum funding requirements (see 4.4.750).

4.4.750 *Prohibition on recognising a gain or loss as a result of actuarial losses and past service cost*

IAS 19.58A   4.4.750.10 The normal deferral of actuarial gains or losses due to the corridor is overridden in order to ensure that an entity does not recognise a gain (loss) solely as a result of an actuarial loss (gain) when the asset ceiling affects the measurement of a net pension asset. Therefore an entity recognises immediately the following gains and losses, to the extent that these gains or losses arise while the ceiling test affects the measurement of the net pension obligation:

- Net actuarial losses and past service costs to the extent that they exceed any reduction in the present value of economic benefits available in the form of refunds from the plan, or reductions in future contributions to the plan.
- Net actuarial gains less past service costs to the extent that they exceed any increase in the present value of economic benefits available in the form of refunds from the plan, or reductions in future contributions to the plan.

4.4.750.20 For example, Company C's pension fund had a net surplus of 700 at 31 December 2009. There were no unrecognised actuarial gains or losses. Under the terms of the plan, any surplus in the fund will benefit the employees. Therefore, applying the asset ceiling test, C does not recognise a net asset in its statement of financial position at 31 December 2009.

4.4.750.30 During 2010 the return on plan assets is lower than expected and an actuarial loss of 90 occurs. As a result the surplus at 31 December 2010 has decreased to 610. Normally C would not recognise the actuarial loss. Because of the asset ceiling, C now recognises an asset of 90 (the amount of unrecognised actuarial losses). This would result in income of 90 being recognised due to the actuarial losses. Therefore, C also accelerates recognition of 90 of actuarial losses. In effect, it recognises no net gain and no net asset, and it has no unrecognised actuarial gains or losses.

4.4.755 *Multi-employer plans*

4.4.755.10 The principles in 4.4.660 – 750 also apply in determining whether a surplus is available to an employer that participates in a multi-employer plan to which defined benefit accounting is applied.

4.4.760 **Current funding level deficit**

4.4.760.10 There are no special accounting requirements that apply when a plan has a deficit based on the current level of funding.

4.4.770 **Insured benefits**

4.4.780 *General principles*

IAS 19.39 4.4.780.10 When employee benefits are insured, the accounting treatment depends on the nature of the obligation retained by the employer.

IAS 19.39, 42, 113 4.4.780.20 If an employer purchases an insurance policy from an unrelated third party and in so doing settles its legal and constructive obligations under a defined benefit plan (e.g. the insurance policy is in the name of a specified plan participant and the employer does not have any legal or constructive obligation to cover any loss on the policy), then the purchase of the insurance policy is treated as a settlement of some or all of the employer's obligations. The premiums paid under the policy are recognised as an expense (in effect defined contribution accounting). See 4.4.830 for guidance on purchases of insurance policies based on current salary and other policies that do not cover the entire obligation.

4.4.780.30 If the employer retains an indirect obligation (e.g. if actuarial risk will be transferred back to the employer by way of increased premiums, or the employer retains an obligation to pay the benefits through a plan), then the plan continues to be treated as a defined benefit plan. The insurance policy is treated as a plan asset, or as a separate asset, depending on the circumstances as explained in 4.4.790.

4.4.780.40 [Not used]

4.4.780.50 See 4.4.120.70 for additional guidance on determining whether an employer has a legal or constructive obligation.

4.4.790 *Insurance policies that qualify as plan assets*

IAS 19.7 4.4.790.10 Insurance policies may be held by the plan or by the sponsor. If the policy is held by the sponsor (i.e. benefits the sponsor), then the policy is treated as a plan asset if it is a qualifying insurance policy, i.e. if:

- it is not issued by a related party of the entity (see 5.5.30); and

- the proceeds of the policy:
  - can be used only to fund defined benefit obligations;
  - are not available to the employer's creditors (even in the case of bankruptcy); and
  - cannot be returned to the entity except as reimbursement for employee benefits paid or when the proceeds are surplus to requirements.

IAS 19.7, 4.4.790.20 IFRSs require financial instruments issued by the reporting entity to the plan
IU 01-08 to be transferable in order to be treated as plan assets. In our view, this requirement also applies to insurance policies issued to the plan by the sponsor or a related party of the sponsor (see 5.5).

IU 01-08 4.4.790.30 In our view, the requirements that should be met for insurance policies held by the sponsor to qualify as plan assets are not applicable to policies held by the plan. This is because we believe that the definition of qualifying insurance policies applies only to policies issued by related parties *to* the sponsor and not to policies issued *by* the sponsor or a related party of the sponsor to the plan. The table below illustrates the classification of insurance policies as plan assets.

Held by: Issued by:	Sponsor	Pension plan
Related party	Do not qualify as plan assets (definition of qualifying insurance policy in IAS 19.7)	Qualify as plan assets if *transferable*
Unrelated party	Qualify as plan assets (definition of qualifying insurance policy in IAS 19.7)	Qualify as plan assets (definition of assets held by a long-term employee benefit fund in IAS 19.7)

4.4.800 *Measurement*

4.4.810 *Insurance policies that are plan assets*

IAS 19.54(d) 4.4.810.10 An insurance policy that is a plan asset is measured at fair value. A qualifying insurance policy is included with other plan assets held by the fund that are deducted from the related defined benefit obligation.

IAS 19.104 4.4.810.20 When the timing and amount of payments under a qualifying insurance policy exactly match the benefits payable under a plan, the present value of the related obligation is determined and is deemed to be the fair value of the insurance policy. In practice, the fair value of such insurance policies held by the fund will be determined generally on the same basis.

4.4.820 *Insurance policies that are not plan assets*

IAS 19.104C 4.4.820.10 A right to reimbursement that arises from an insurance policy that is not a plan asset is recognised as a separate asset, rather than as a deduction in determining the net defined benefit liability. However, in all other respects, the insurance policy is treated in the same way as plan assets. In particular, net cumulative actuarial gains (losses) on the reimbursement right are considered in measuring the defined benefit obligation (see 4.4.490 and 840 for additional guidance).

4.4.830 *Current salary policies and other limited cover*

4.4.830.10 An employer may buy insurance policies each period to settle all of its defined benefit obligations. In this case recognising as an expense the cost of the policies purchased (in effect, defined contribution accounting) will have the same effect as applying defined benefit accounting and recognising a settlement gain or loss. Although the accounting may be similar to defined contribution accounting, the disclosure requirements for defined benefit plans still may be relevant.

IAS 19.39   4.4.830.15 An assessment of whether an employer settles all of its defined benefit obligations through the purchase of insurance policies is made on a plan-by-plan basis. For example, an entity has a pension plan with an annual benefit based on current salary levels. The entity pays an annual premium under an insurance policy based on the same current salary levels and the insurer guarantees all of the benefits earned to date by employees based on current salary levels. If the entity does not retain an indirect obligation in respect of the plan (see 4.4.780.30), then it may be appropriate for the entity to treat the plan as a defined contribution plan. This is because the entity may have settled all of its obligations with regard to benefits earned to date through the purchase of insurance policies.

4.4.830.20 However, an insurance policy may not cover the employer's entire obligation. For example, Company Q has a pension plan with a payment based on final salary. Q pays premiums under an insurance policy based on current rather than projected salary levels. The insurer, R, guarantees all the benefits earned to date based on current salary levels. Defined benefit obligations are based on projected rather than current salary levels (see 4.4.270). Therefore there is a difference between Q's defined benefit obligation and the obligations assumed by the insurer under the insurance policy.

IAS 19.39   4.4.830.30 An insured benefit cannot be treated as a defined contribution plan if the employer has an obligation to make payments if the insurer does not pay *all* future employee benefits related to employee service in the current and prior periods. Therefore, in our view the resultant plan should be accounted for as a defined benefit plan, even if some of its obligations have been settled and are no longer recognised. In this case while the insurance policy purchased by Q is based on current rather than projected salary levels, resulting in Q having a defined benefit plan, in our view to the extent that the liability (based on current salary levels) is settled by the purchase of an insurance policy this is treated as a partial settlement (see 4.4.880).

4.4.840 **Reimbursement rights**

IAS 19.104A   4.4.840.10 When an entity will be reimbursed for expenditures required to settle a defined benefit obligation, but the reimbursement right does not give rise to a plan asset (see 4.4.390), it is recognised as a separate asset when recovery is virtually certain. For example, an insurance policy that is not a plan asset generally gives rise to a reimbursement right.

IFRS 4.IG2   4.4.840.20 In our view, the reimbursement right must be due from a party outside the group (which may include a joint venture or associate (see 4.5.120.10)). Therefore a right to receive assets from another group entity (e.g. parent or subsidiary) to fund employee benefit obligations is not treated as a reimbursement right in the consolidated financial statements. However, it may be appropriate to recognise a reimbursement right in the separate financial statements of the sponsor providing that the criteria in paragraph 104A of IAS 19 are met.

IAS 19.104A   4.4.840.30 Reimbursement rights are accounted for in the same way as plan assets (i.e. they are measured at fair value and expected return on a reimbursement right is accounted for in the same way as expected rate of return on plan assets). Actuarial gains and losses arising on reimbursement rights are included with the actuarial gains and losses arising on the related obligation, and are taken into account in determining the corridor (see 4.4.530). However, reimbursement rights are presented as a separate asset and are not netted against the related defined benefit obligation.

4.4.840.40 For example, Company O operates a defined benefit pension scheme for all of its employees. O outsources certain of its employees to Company P, a third party. The outsourced employees continue to participate in O's pension plan but O is entitled to recover the costs of the outsourced employees, including costs associated with the defined benefit plan, from P. O accounts for the full obligation under the defined benefit plan as explained in 4.4.840.30. If it is virtually certain that P will reimburse O for the pension costs, then O recognises an asset for the reimbursement, which is accounted for in the same way as a plan asset. However, O shows the reimbursement right as a separate asset, and not deduct it from the carrying amount of the pension obligation.

4.4.840.50 In another example, the US Medicare legislation introduced in December 2003 provided a government subsidy to plan sponsors for costs incurred under plans that are actuarially equivalent to the Medicare Prescription Drug Act. In our view, the initial recognition of the new Medicare benefit should be accounted for as an actuarial gain that gives rise to a reimbursement right and not as a plan amendment (see 4.4.490, 600.35 and 37).

4.4.840.60 For example, Company M provides post-retirement medical benefits to its employees. The defined benefit obligation at 31 December 2003 is 150, excluding any effects of the US Medicare legislation, and the plan assets are 50. There are no unrecognised actuarial gains or losses at 31 December 2003 and, absent the new legislation, a net obligation of 100 (net of plan assets of 50) would be recognised in the 2003 financial statements.

4.4.840.70 M determines that its plan is actuarially equivalent to the Medicare Prescription Drug Act and that, based on its actuarial assumptions about expected costs, it will receive a subsidy of 20. As the definition of a plan asset is not fulfilled the reimbursement right is recognised as a separate asset. Since the creation of the reimbursement right is an unrecognised actuarial gain, if the entity recognises actuarial gains and losses using the corridor method (see 4.4.530), then the following entry is made:

	Debit	Credit
Reimbursement right (separate asset)	20	
Defined benefit liability (unrecognised actuarial gains		
(statement of financial position))		20
To recognise reimbursement right asset		

4.4.840.80 Accordingly, to the extent that the actuarial gain arising from introduction of the Medicare subsidy remains unrecognised, the defined benefit liability would be grossed up, i.e. a separate asset of 20 is recognised and the defined benefit liability is recognised at 120 (150 for the underlying net defined benefit obligation plus an unrecognised actuarial gain of 20, less plan assets of 50).

4.4.840.90 As the unrecognised net actuarial gain of 20 is above the 10 percent corridor, the excess amount would be required to be amortised, in accordance with the entity's usual amortisation policy, in 2004.

4.4.850 *Refunds of contributions*

4.4.850.10 When an entity receives a refund of contributions paid to a defined benefit plan, the refund should be recognised as a reduction in the net pension asset or an increase in the net pension liability. Receipt of the cash does not trigger recognition of income, as the measurement of the net obligation (or asset) would have included a "receivable" for the expected refund.

4.4.850.20 However, if there was a surplus in the fund that previously was not regarded as recoverable, and therefore not recognised, then the refund gives rise to a gain. IFRSs are silent as to how the gain should be recognised, but in our view it should be treated as an actuarial gain and, depending on the policy chosen with respect to the recognition of actuarial gains and losses, recognition of the gain as a reduction of pension expense may have to be deferred.

4.4.860 Death-in-service benefits

4.4.860.10 Employers may offer death-in-service benefits to employees as part of their employment packages. These benefits may be offered:

- through a post-employment plan, within which the benefits may or may not be insured; or
- on a stand-alone basis, which may or may not be insured.

IU 01-08   4.4.860.20 Often, the actuarially determined measurement of the obligation for a post-employment plan reflects expected death in service. In our view, expected death-in-service benefits should be treated consistently in measuring the post-employment benefit obligation and the death-in-service obligation. Therefore, we believe that if death-in-service benefits are provided through a post-employment plan and are not insured, and the measurement of the post-employment benefit plan obligation reflects expected death in service (i.e. is reduced for retirement benefits that will not be paid due to death in service), then the entity should recognise the cost of death-in-service benefits. This is done by including their present value in the post-employment benefit obligation and recognising the service cost as the service that gives rise to the entitlement is provided.

4.4.860.30 When death-in-service benefits are provided through a post-employment plan and are insured, in our view an entity should choose an accounting policy to be applied consistently. In such cases the sponsor may choose either to:

- recognise the cost of the benefits by including their present value in the post-employment benefit obligation and recognise the insurance policy as a plan asset or reimbursement right (see 4.4.840); or
- recognise the cost of the benefit as the insurance premiums are payable.

4.4.860.40 In our view, when death-in-service benefits offered on a stand-alone basis are insured or re-insured with third parties, the cost of the benefit should be recognised as the insurance premiums are payable. We believe that when death-in-service benefits offered on a stand-alone basis are not insured or reinsured with third parties, the benefit should be recognised as an expense to the extent that deaths have occurred at the reporting date.

4.4.870 **Inter-related post-employment benefit plans**

4.4.870.10 An entity may have more than one post-employment benefit plan. In our view:

- If the post-employment benefits are financed through a single scheme, funded by one asset pool and (therefore) sharing the same investment risk, then ordinarily they should be considered and reported as a single plan and the terms of each component of the plan should be disclosed separately.
- The fact that there are the same beneficiaries in two different plans does not automatically result in a single plan even if one plan may have certain rights to the surplus in the other plan. For example, access of an unfunded post-employment medical benefit plan under specific circumstances to part of the surplus of another post-employment plan generally does not result in a plan asset in the medical benefit plan if the amount of the surplus is not transferred but only "reserved", i.e. the surplus "reserved" for the medical benefit plan would decline if the investments decreased or the defined benefit obligation increased in the original post-employment benefit plan. Treating such an arrangement as one plan could result in disguising the true position of the arrangement because the "unreserved" surplus of the post-employment plan could be offsetting the deficit of the medical plan. However, if there is a right of offset,

then the "reserved" surplus may be a plan asset of the medical plan. In such case consideration needs to be given to the entity's legally enforceable right to use a surplus in one plan to settle obligations under another plan and its intention to settle the plans on a net basis (see 4.4.1120.20).

- If the benefits are funded through *different funds* or administered by one fund but have different arrangements, subject to *different investment risk*, then they should be considered as separate plans. They may be combined in preparing disclosures for the financial statements if all are in a net surplus or a net liability position. Otherwise, offsetting is appropriate only if there is a legal right of offset between underfunding in one plan and overfunding of another plan (see 4.4.1120).

4.4.870.20 For example, Company H is required by law to make severance payments to employees when they retire or leave. Severance payments reduce pension entitlement. If the anticipated severance payments are such that no pension payments will be required, then the defined benefit asset or obligation should reflect only the severance payments. If pension payments will be required in addition to the severance payments, then the pension liability should reflect the amounts that will be payable as a top-up to the severance payment. In any case the calculation of the severance liability and the pension liability should reflect consistent actuarial assumptions, such as estimated future salary increases, but may have different inputs (e.g. benefits may be based on the final salary for the pension scheme, but on the average salary for the severance liability).

4.4.880 Settlements and curtailments*

IAS 19.109   4.4.880.10 Settlements and curtailments trigger immediate recognition of the consequential change in the present value of the obligation and in the market value of the assets together with any previously unrecognised actuarial gains and losses or past service costs that relate to obligations impacted by the settlement or curtailment.

4.4.890 *Scope of settlements and curtailments*

IAS 19.112   4.4.890.10 A *settlement* is an early settlement of all or part of the plan obligation.

IAS 19.111   4.4.890.20 A *curtailment* occurs when the entity is demonstrably committed to reduce significantly the number of employees in the plan or amends the terms of the plan so that the benefits for future services are reduced or eliminated. A change in future benefits is treated as a curtailment, rather than an actuarial gain or loss, if the effect of the remeasurement is significant.

4.4.890.30 In some cases a settlement and a curtailment may occur together. For example, as part of a restructuring some benefits may be eliminated, generally via payment (a settlement), and some future benefits may be reduced (a curtailment). A settlement also may occur without a curtailment (e.g. when an employer purchases an insurance contract under which the employee is the beneficiary (see 4.4.770)). Similarly, a curtailment may occur without a settlement.

4.4.890.33 In our view, the absence of a lump-sum payment, or the fact that an actual transfer of plan assets has not yet occurred, does not preclude recognition of a settlement. However, careful evaluation of facts and circumstances is required to determine whether the entity has entered into a transaction that eliminates all further legal or constructive obligations for part or all of the benefits under a plan (see 4.4.900).

IAS 19.114 4.4.890.35 Generally a settlement occurs together with a curtailment if a plan is terminated such that the obligation is settled and the plan ceases to exist. However, the termination of a plan is not a curtailment or settlement if the plan is replaced by a new plan that offers benefits that are, in substance, identical. For example, as part of a restructuring, benefits and assets for a group of participants in a multi-employer plan are transferred to a new plan without any amendments being made to the accrued benefits or future benefits. In substance, this is only restructuring the existing arrangement with no change in benefits for the employees or obligation of the employer. Consequently, the inherited deficit also is carried over to the new plan.

4.4.890.36 In some cases a curtailment may be followed by a settlement, for example, if a plan amendment is executed in stages and the criteria for curtailment are met before the settlement occurs. In our experience this is common when changes to a plan are caused by the government. However, careful evaluation of the facts and circumstances of the arrangement is required to assess when the criteria for curtailment and settlement are met (see 4.4.900).

4.4.890.40 Changes to a plan that are not settlements or curtailments give rise to past service costs (see 4.4.600), even if they occur as a result of a restructuring or a business combination.

IAS 19.111A, 4.4.890.50 The definition of past service costs excludes plan amendments that impact
BC62B future service. Careful analysis will be needed to understand whether past as well as future services are affected. Therefore, if an entity amends the terms of a defined benefit plan such that it affects entitlements from both past as well as future services for the same group of employees so that the benefits are reduced, then in our view only the effect of the reduction related to future service is accounted for as a curtailment; the effect of any reduction for past service is accounted for as a negative past service cost. In accordance with paragraph BC62B of IAS 19, an employee is entitled to future salary increases after the reporting date only as a result of future service. As such, if a change to a benefit plan affects the extent to which future salary increases after the reporting date are linked to benefits payable for past service, then all of the effect of that change to the present value of the defined benefit obligation is treated as a curtailment, and not as a negative past service cost. A plan amendment falls under negative past service accounting (see 4.4.620) to the extent that it affects the entitlements from past service.

4.4.900 *Timing of recognition*

IAS 19.109 4.4.900.10 An entity recognises gains or losses on the curtailment or settlement of a defined benefit plan when the curtailment or settlement occurs.

IAS 19.111   4.4.900.20 A curtailment occurs when an entity either:

- is demonstrably committed (i.e. committed with no realistic possibility of withdrawal) to make a significant reduction in the number of employees covered by a plan; or
- amends the terms of a defined benefit plan so that a significant element of future service by current employees will either no longer qualify for benefits or qualify only for reduced benefits. In our view, an amendment of the terms of a plan may occur prior to the formal signing of the amended terms provided that the employer has a right to enforce the amended terms of the plan and is not in the process of negotiations with an uncertain outcome that is outside the entity's control.

4.4.900.30 In certain circumstances it may be necessary to defer recognition of a curtailment to a later date as a result of matters that are outside of the entity's control, for example, if the employer is in the process of negotiations to amend the terms of a defined benefit plan with an uncertain outcome that is outside the entity's control, or if the approval by another party, substantive in nature, is required.

IAS 19.111   4.4.900.40 The effects of a curtailment that are linked with a restructuring generally are recognised at the same time as the related restructuring (see 3.12.230). This is because the recognition criteria for a restructuring provision require there to be a detailed plan for the restructuring and the main features of the plan to have been announced to those affected by it (i.e. the employees). Once these criteria are met, the entity normally will be committed to the restructuring, and therefore to the related curtailment, with no realistic possibility of withdrawal, and the related curtailment gain or loss also is recognised unless the deferral is appropriate due to ongoing negotiations or pending approval (see 4.4.900.10).

IU 11-07   4.4.900.50 Although generally accounting for changes to a plan caused by a government is the same as accounting for changes made by an employer (see 4.4.600.35), such changes often can be driven by changes in legislation. When a curtailment is triggered by changes in law, the sponsor is not considered to be committed to a change until the law is enacted.

4.4.900.60 In our view, a *commitment* to settlement in itself may not be determinative, as settlement occurs only when the sponsor's legal or constructive obligation for part or all of the benefits provided under a defined benefit plan is eliminated. In other words, if the employer continues to be exposed to certain actuarial risks, e.g. mortality, then that would indicate that the settlement has not yet occurred. However, the possible measurement consequences of the commitment would need to be considered.

4.4.900.70 In our view, the occurrence of a settlement relates to the transfer of an obligation rather than the actual payment. Nevertheless, payment may be considered an indicator of whether a settlement has occurred (see 4.4.890.33).

4.4.910 *Calculation of gain or loss*

IAS 19.110   4.4.910.10 An entity remeasures plan assets and the defined benefit obligation using current actuarial assumptions (e.g. current discount rate, current market prices) before computing the settlement or curtailment gain or loss.

IAS 19.109   4.4.910.15 The settlement or curtailment gain or loss comprises:

- any resulting change in the present value of the defined benefit obligation;
- any resulting change in the fair value of plan assets; and
- any related unrecognised actuarial gains and losses and unrecognised past service costs.

IAS 19.109(c)   4.4.910.20 Unrecognised actuarial gains and losses and unrecognised past service costs related to the curtailed portion of the liability are allocated in determining the gain or loss. In our view, the actuarial gains and losses and past service costs used in the calculation should be those at the date of the curtailment or settlement, rather than at the end of the previous period.

IAS 19.92(c)   4.4.910.30 In our view, all unrecognised actuarial gains and losses related to a curtailment, and not just those outside the corridor, should be included in the calculation of the curtailment gain or loss.

IAS 19.115   4.4.910.40 There are no detailed requirements as to how actuarial gains and losses and past service costs should be allocated in determining the curtailment gain or loss; an example is given in the standard of a curtailment that relates only to some employees in a plan. In this example, a proportionate allocation is made based on the change in the obligation before and after the curtailment, unless another basis is more rational in the circumstances. In our view, this approach also would be appropriate if a curtailment relates to all employees in a plan.

IAS 19.92, 93   4.4.910.50 In our view, if a curtailment occurs as a result of the closure of a plan to future accrual of benefits and is not accompanied by a settlement, then the entity's standard accounting policy for recognition of actuarial gains and losses (see 4.4.510) continues to apply to any actuarial gains or losses that occur subsequently.

4.4.920 Change in estimate

4.4.920.10 In general under IFRSs, a change in estimate is recognised in profit or loss for the current and future periods (see 2.8.60). In our view, changes in the amount of a defined benefit obligation as a result of changes in the method of measuring the obligation (e.g. as a result of using a different measurement method under the projected unit credit method) are actuarial gains or losses.

4.4.920.20 Therefore the adjustment resulting from a change in estimate in respect of a defined benefit plan will become part of the actuarial gains and losses and is subject to the corridor in the same way as other actuarial gains and losses. This means that the speed at which the amount is recognised in the statement of comprehensive income will depend on the entity's accounting policy for recognising actuarial gains and losses and, if applicable, the size of the corridor (see 4.4.510).

4.4.920.30 However, also see 4.4.270.40 for guidance on back-end loaded benefit formulas. In our view, benefits are attributed to periods of service in accordance with the plan's benefit formula; any changes in the overall approach to measurement of the obligation (e.g. changing from using the projected unit credit method to attribute the benefits to periods of service to using a straight-line attribution method) would not be a change in estimate and would need to be considered as a correction of an error, unless the plan's benefit formula changed. We believe there is a distinction between changing the method in measuring the obligation (see 4.4.920.10) and changing the overall approach to measurement of the obligation, which would change the overall attribution method.

4.4.930 **Errors**

4.4.940 *Classification error*

4.4.940.10 An incorrect classification of an employee benefit plan (e.g. as a defined contribution plan instead of a defined benefit plan) is an error.

4.4.940.20 Calculation errors also may arise if the assumptions used in the calculation are incorrect; for example, if certain eligible employees were not included in the calculation of the obligation.

IAS 8.42 4.4.940.30 Material prior period errors are prior period adjustments (see 2.8.40). The effect of the corridor on the retrospective correction of an error should be considered.

4.4.950 **Change in classification**

4.4.950.10 A plan may be reclassified from a defined benefit plan to a defined contribution plan or *vice versa*. There is no specific guidance on how to account for any gain or loss that might arise in this situation.

4.4.950.20 In our view, when the classification of a plan changes from defined benefit to defined contribution, the change in classification should be accounted for as a settlement of the defined benefit plan (see 4.4.880). Therefore any unrecognised actuarial gains and losses or past service costs should be recognised in profit or loss immediately.

4.4.950.30 The facts and circumstances resulting in the reclassification of a defined contribution plan to a defined benefit plan may impact the accounting treatment of that change. For example, if information becomes available to account for a multi-employer plan as a defined benefit plan (see 4.4.150), then in our view this should be treated as a change in estimate following the specific requirements for changes in estimates related to defined benefit plans (i.e. treated as actuarial gains or losses in the period) (see 4.4.920).

4.4.950.40 We believe that any deficit or surplus at the date of reclassification of the plan should be included in the calculation of actuarial gains and losses as if the gain or loss arose in the first year in which defined benefit accounting is applied as a result of new information becoming available. The treatment of the inherited gain or loss will depend on the entity's accounting policy choice for the recognition of actuarial gains and losses. For example, if the entity has elected a policy of immediate recognition of actuarial gains and losses in other comprehensive income, then the gain or loss would be recognised in other comprehensive income in the first year in which defined benefit accounting is applied. See 4.4.490 for a discussion of recognition and measurement of actuarial gains and losses.

4.4.950.50 In other cases the reclassification of a plan from defined contribution to defined benefit may result from a change to the terms of the plan; for example, new laws may change the obligation of the employer even if it does not change the benefit to be received by the employee. In our view, if a change to the terms of a plan results in its reclassification from a defined contribution to a defined benefit plan, then this should be treated as the introduction of a new defined benefit plan. If, under the revised terms of the plan, the present value of the defined benefit obligation differs from the previous defined contribution obligation, then that change should be treated as past service cost (see 4.4.600).

4.4.960 Business combinations

IFRS 3.26, IAS 19.108 4.4.960.10 Generally an acquirer measures assets acquired and liabilities assumed in a business combination at fair value; an acquired entity's pension arrangements are measured at the present value of the obligation less the fair value of plan assets at the acquisition date (see 2.6.680). The present value of the obligation and the fair value of the assets are measured in accordance with IAS 19 taking into account any IFRIC 14 implications. The acquirer does not carry forward unrecognised actuarial gains or losses or unrecognised past service costs of the acquiree at the acquisition date.

4.4.960.20 If this results in a net asset, then the amount of the asset recognised is restricted to the amount recoverable as refunds or as reductions of future contributions.

4.4.970 Other long-term employee benefits

4.4.980 *Scope of long-term employee benefits*

IAS 19.7, 126, 128 4.4.980.10 An employee benefit, other than a post-employment benefit or a termination benefit, that is *due to be settled* more than 12 months after the end of the period in which the employee services were rendered, is an *other long-term employee benefit*. Such benefits may include paid long-service leave, other long-service benefits (e.g. a bonus or extra salary after 20 years of service) and profit-sharing and other bonus schemes due to be settled more than 12 months after the end of the period in which the employee services were received by the entity. In our view, the *end of the period* is considered the end of the current reporting period when the service period spans more than one reporting period (see examples provided in 4.4.980.24 and 28). While the definition of long-term employee benefits relates to benefits due to be settled *during* employment, in our view a long-term disability benefit that is payable only if an employee remains employed but is no longer providing services also should be accounted for as a post-employment benefit (see 4.4.100.30).

IAS 19.7, BC4C 4.4.980.20 Long-term benefits are *accounted* for as such in their entirety; these benefits are not split between the short- and long-term portions for measurement purposes; however, see 4.4.1110 for a discussion of the presentation of long-term employee benefits as current or non-current (see also examples provided in 4.4.980.24 and 28).

4.4.980.24 For example, Company M has a three-year annual bonus plan under which employees receive a bonus based on the financial performance of an entity in the financial year. However, bonuses are paid 30 days after the end of the third year only to employees who are still in employment with the entity at the end of year three. The plan is designed to provide an incentive for employees to remain committed to the entity and is commonly referred to as a profit-sharing benefit (see 4.4.1020). In such an arrangement we believe that each reporting period is considered a distinct service period and the classification is assessed for such a scheme in its entirety at the introduction of the plan. In addition, for years one and two the employee can require settlement, only after more than 12 months from the end of the (reporting) period in which the employee rendered the related service. Considering the above, this arrangement should be classified as a long-term employee benefit for measurement purposes. The liability is presented in the statement of financial position as non-current at the end of years one and two, and as current at the end of year three (see 4.4.1110.40). We believe that the timing of the physical payment of the bonus is not relevant in the determination of whether the benefit is short-term or long-term, e.g. if part of the bonus is paid on account once the financial statements for years one and two are finalised.

IAS 19.7, 126 4.4.980.28 In another example, Company N has a retention plan providing employees with a one off benefit of 15 additional days of annual leave after they have rendered five years of continuing service to the entity. The additional leave vests only at the end of year five, i.e. the employees are not entitled to a portion of the leave before the end of year five. Such an arrangement is commonly referred to as long-service leave. Since the employee can require a settlement only after the end of year five, i.e. in years one to four, more than 12 months from the end of the (reporting) period in which the employees rendered the related service, this arrangement is classified at the outset and throughout its life as a long-term employee benefit for measurement purposes. The liability is presented in the statement of financial position as non-current for those employees within the first four years of providing services, and as current for employees within the fifth year of providing service. A similar treatment would apply to a plan providing employees with a one-off jubilee/milestone anniversary benefit of one month's salary after they have rendered five years of continuing service to the entity.

4.4.980.29 In a contrasting example, often an employee's annual benefit entitlements (e.g. salary, annual leave entitlement) will depend on seniority and/or length of service. In our view, higher salaries and annual leave entitlements based on seniority/length of service are short-term employee benefits. For example, Company P has a policy of promoting employees to manager level after five years and to senior manager after a further five years. Prior to promotion to manager, employees receive an annual salary of 20,000 and an annual leave entitlement of 25 days. Managers receive an annual salary of 25,000 and an annual leave entitlement of 30 days. Senior managers receive an annual salary of 30,000 and an annual leave entitlement of 35 days. In this example, future salary increases/annual leave entitlements are not anticipated in measuring current employee costs, e.g. the annual expense in respect of a manager's salary is 25,000. We believe that the fact that annual salary/leave entitlement increases as employees' length of service/seniority increases does not make the additional benefit a long-term benefit.

4.4.980.30 In our view, benefits that are payable on the earlier of termination of employment or on a specified date more than a year after the end of the year in which services are provided should be treated as other long-term benefits and not as post-employment benefits. For example, Company Y makes lump-sum payments to expatriate employees of one month's salary for each year of service. The amounts are paid every five years, or at the date of termination of employment if the employee leaves within the five-year period. Since the benefits are payable during employment, we believe that they should be treated as long-term benefits and not as post-employment benefits. In our view, even if there is an obligation to pay cash, the benefits payable during employment are an obligation to provide employee benefits under IAS 19 and are not a financial liability (see 3.6.20), as obligations to provide employee benefits are outside the scope of the financial instruments standards.

4.4.990 *Accounting treatment*

IAS 19.128   4.4.990.10 Other long-term employee benefits are accounted for in a manner similar to post-employment benefits, except that all actuarial gains and losses and past service costs are recognised immediately in profit or loss. Neither the corridor method nor immediate recognition of actuarial gains and losses in other comprehensive income may be applied for other long-term benefits. Thus the employer's statement of financial position includes a liability for the present value of the obligation less the fair value of any plan assets.

4.4.990.15 In our view, similar to post-employment defined benefit plans, the adjustments resulting from a change in estimate in respect of other long-term employee benefits becomes part of the actuarial gains and losses (see 4.4.920). However, consistent with the treatment of other long-term employee benefits, those actuarial gains and losses are recognised immediately in profit or loss (see 4.4.990.10).

4.4.990.20 The example in 4.4.990.30 – 60 illustrates the accounting for long-term employee benefits.

4.4.990.30 On 1 January 2010 Company P introduced a benefit of an extra month's salary after a further five years of service for those employees working for P at 1 January 2010. The aggregate current monthly salaries of the employees eligible for the benefits is 480,000 and 60 percent of the employees are expected to work for five years and receive the benefit. The expected annual salary increase over the next five years is 3 percent. The interest rate on high quality corporate bonds is 10 percent.

4.4.990.40 The statement of financial position obligation at 31 December 2010 for the eligible employees is calculated as follows:

Projected salary level after five years (future value of current salary with a 3 percent increase:	
Key i = interest rate; n = numbers of years of service	
PV = 480,000, i = 3 percent, n = 4)	540,244
Present value of projected salary level at 31 December 2010 (present value of 540,244: FV = 540,244, i = 10%, n = 4)	368,994
Adjusted benefit to take into account probability of employee working for the required five additional years (368,994 x 60%)	221,396
Benefit attributable to current year (221,396 / 5 years)	44,279
Fair value of plan assets at 31 December 2010	-
Amount to be recognised as a liability at 31 December 2010	44,279

4.4.990.50 Therefore an employee cost and a corresponding liability of 44,279 are recognised at 31 December 2010.

4.4.990.60 In 2011 the calculation will be the same as in 4.4.990.40. Assuming that the interest rate and the anticipated level of employees expected to work for the five years is constant, this will result in a liability of 97,413 (present value of anticipated payment, i.e. 368,994 x 1.1 x 60% x 2 / 5). The statement of comprehensive income will reflect an interest cost of 4,428 (44,279 x 10%) and a service cost of 48,706 (97,413 - 44,279 - 4,428).

4.4.1000 *Long-term benefits that are not service related*

IAS 19.130   4.4.1000.10 When the amount of a long-term benefit is not dependent on the length of service, the benefit is recognised only when the event that gives rise to an obligation to make the payment occurs. A liability for long-term disability benefits (see 4.4.980.10) is recognised only when an event occurs that causes long-term disability, if the level of benefit is not dependent on years of service, e.g. disability benefit that is a flat percentage of salary at the time of disability. In our view, the lack of an explicit service period does not automatically lead to the conclusion that the benefit is not dependent on a service period, e.g. when a benefit is to be paid to an employee when a specific age is reached.

4.4.1000.20 When the amount of a disability benefit is dependent on the length of service, in our view the accounting treatment is consistent with that for death-in-service benefits (see 4.4.860).

4.4.1010 *Defined contribution long-term benefit plans*

IAS 19.126-131   4.4.1010.10 Although IFRSs imply that all long-term employee benefit plans are defined benefit plans, they do not preclude specifically defined contribution accounting for other long-term benefits. In some situations in practice, other long-term employee benefit plans have the nature of defined contribution plans. In our view, defined contribution accounting should be used for these plans.

4.4.1020 *Long-term profit-sharing and bonus plans*

IAS 19.130   4.4.1020.10 As with post-employment benefits, the cost of long-term employee benefits is attributed to the period in which the services are rendered that give rise to the obligation.

4.4.1020.20 An entity should consider the substance of a long-term profit-sharing or bonus plan in determining the attribution of benefits to periods of service (see 4.4.270).

4.4.1020.30 For example, Company T has a bonus plan in which bonuses are based on the performance of T, as calculated on an annual basis. The bonus plan commences in 2010 and continues through 2014. The bonus is payable in cash to employees in two tranches, and there is a clawback feature whereby payment is conditional on the employee remaining in service for a specified time after the end of the period in which the services have been rendered. Employees receive 50 percent of the bonus if they remain in service six months after the period in which services have been provided, and the remainder of the bonus is paid if the employee remains in service 18 months after this period. For example, in respect of the 2010 bonus, 50 percent of the bonus is payable on each of 30 June 2011 and 30 June 2012 if the employee remains in service on those dates.

IAS 19.7   4.4.1020.35 As the employee becomes entitled to a portion of the annual bonus more than 12 months after the end of the reporting period in which the employee renders the service, the annual bonus plan is classified in its entirety as a long-term employee benefit.

4.4.1020.40 In our view, there are two alternatives available to P with regard to how the benefit is attributed. Which of the two alternatives is most appropriate will depend on how management views the substance of the annual bonus arrangement, i.e. the weight put on it being a recurring annual plan against a "stay period" being required:

IAS 19.67   • *Attribute to 2010 only.* In substance, the plan may be considered to be an annual bonus with deferred payment terms, which is being earned in each period from 2010 through 2014 in exchange for services provided in each of the respective periods. IAS 19 requires benefits to be attributed over the period of service under the plan's benefit formula, which is 12 months in an annual bonus plan. Under this alternative, after the 12-month period the employee's further service leads to no material amounts of further benefits under the plan. Accordingly, the benefit would be attributed to the period in which the services are provided (e.g. during 2010 in respect of the 2010 annual bonus). No amounts would be recognised in 2010 in respect of the 2011 through 2014 annual bonuses (see 4.4.270.40). We believe that the amount that would be recognised in 2010 is the present value of the amounts to be paid on 30 June 2011 and 30 June 2012, as adjusted for estimates of forfeitures occurring during the conditional employment periods. Changes in estimated forfeitures would be treated as a change in estimate (see 2.8.60).

IAS 19.67 • *Attribute over extended service period.* Alternatively, this plan's benefit formula may be considered to be back-end loaded with a service period longer than the annual performance year. Under this alternative, the extended employee "stay period" in this example results in the employee receiving a material amount of further benefits under the plan by staying to receive the full amount; the employee receives either nothing or the entire amount of the award. Under this alternative the substance indicates that the service period is longer than the annual performance year. The fact that 50 percent of the 2010 bonus requires six months of service in 2011 and the other 50 percent requires 18 months of service in 2011 and 2012 may imply that the post 2010 employee service is leading to material amounts of further benefits, since part of the bonus will be forfeited if the employee leaves before the payment date. As such, the two payments of the 2010 bonus would be considered separately and 50 percent of the 2010 bonus benefit would be attributed over 18 months (i.e. from 1 January 2010 to 30 June 2011) and the remaining 50 percent would be attributed over 30 months (i.e. from 1 January 2010 to 30 June 2012). Under such an approach, the benefit would be attributed over the extended service period as opposed to the annual service period only.

4.4.1020.45 In our view, the two alternatives in 4.4.1020.40 are available only when there is an ongoing annual bonus arrangement, as opposed to a one-off bonus, to support a view that the substance is of a twelve-month service period.

4.4.1020.50 In our view, under both alternatives, the present value of the amount to be paid on 30 June 2011 should be presented as a current liability at 31 December 2010 (see 4.4.1110).

4.4.1030 [Not used]

4.4.1040 Termination benefits*

4.4.1040.10 Generally, post-employment benefits are accrued over the service period. However, an obligation for termination benefits is regarded as arising from the termination and not from the employees' service. Due to this difference in attribution the obligation for termination benefits is not recognised until the entity is committed to the termination without realistic possibility of withdrawal. Therefore, it is important to distinguish termination benefits from other post-employment benefits.

4.4.1040.20 In our view, the terms of an early retirement arrangement require careful evaluation to determine whether the arrangement, or part of the arrangement, is a post-employment benefit rather than a termination benefit.

4.4.1040.30 For example, in some jurisdictions there are collective agreements on early retirement. Such schemes usually are designed to create an incentive for employees to transition into early retirement, thereby providing younger people with an opportunity to obtain employment. Such plans are not necessarily linked to a reorganisation or restructuring, but rather are at the option of the employee or employer. In our view, the classification of such a plan depends on whether a constructive obligation (see 4.4.110) exists, considering all the facts and circumstances. In particular, informal past practices or communications with employees may indicate the existence of a constructive obligation (e.g. employees' requests have not been refused in the past despite the fact that the employer may legally be able to refuse the request), which would result in accounting as a post-employment benefit plan rather than a termination benefit.

4.4.1050 *Scope of termination benefits*

IAS 19.7   4.4.1050.10 Termination benefits are those benefits that are payable as a result of an entity terminating employment before the normal retirement date or an employee's decision to accept an offer of voluntary redundancy.

IAS 19.132   4.4.1050.20 For example, Company N has a restructuring and, for a limited period of time, offers an early retirement package to all employees aged 55 to 57. Employees younger than 57 who accept the offer must continue to work until they reach age 57. In our view, the amount of the enhancement in retirement benefits for those employees accepting voluntary early retirement normally should be treated as termination benefits and not as post-employment benefits. Even though there is a continuing service requirement, the event that gives rise to the payment is the offer of early retirement, not the employees' services. Salary and normal retirement benefits related to service between the ages of 55 and 57 are not treated as termination benefits. Instead these costs are recognised as the related services are performed.

4.4.1050.30 In another example, assume that Company J, a restaurant, employs waiters and waitresses on short-term contracts and pays them a lump sum at the end of the contract period. In our view, the lump sum payments should be treated as post-employment benefits, rather than termination benefits, because the employees are entitled to the payments whenever they leave. The obligation does not accrue as a result of the decision to terminate employment. Therefore the expense in respect of the lump-sum payment is recognised over the service period.

4.4.1050.35 In another example, assume that Company P offers a manager a two-year contract with a right to renewal. P has the right to reject the renewal but in that case P will pay the employee a specified amount. In our view, the payment would be a termination benefit, as it is a one-off payment and the triggering event is the termination of the contract, rather than an amount related to the service obligation.

4.4.1050.40 If there is a service obligation as a condition of the payment, then the payment may be a stay bonus rather than compensation for termination.

IAS 19.135 4.4.1050.45 Termination benefits are typically lump-sum payments but also may include enhanced pension. For example, Company M offers its CEO an enhanced pension package that increases the net present value of his pension entitlement to 300,000; his original pension entitlement per employment contract had a net present value of 200,000. This enhanced pension entitlement of 100,000 has been negotiated as part of the termination agreement, as the CEO's employment will be terminated a year before the end of his five-year contract. In our view, since the additional entitlement was negotiated as part of a termination agreement, the termination rather than the employee service is considered the obligating event, and therefore the enhanced pension entitlement of 100,000 is a termination benefit. Although the last year's salary would be forgone by the CEO, M should recognise the full amount of 100,000 as a liability in the year in which M becomes demonstrably committed to the termination and should not net the amount against salary savings. See 4.4.1135.10 for disclosure requirements.

4.4.1060 *Recognition*

IAS 19.133-138 4.4.1060.10 Expenses and liabilities for termination benefits are recognised immediately when the employer has an obligation to make the payment. Termination benefits do not provide an entity with future economic benefits; therefore capitalisation is not permitted. The cost is not spread over any remaining service period.

IAS 19.133-134, 37.72 4.4.1060.20 Two tests need to be met for a termination provision to be recognised: there must be a formal plan in sufficient detail; and the entity must be demonstrably committed to the plan without realistic possibility of withdrawal.

4.4.1060.30 For example, Company H is involved in contract cleaning. One of its major contracts is up for renewal next year and H does not expect the customer to renew the contract. In our view, the estimated costs of terminating the employees dedicated to the contract should not be recognised on the basis of probable non-renewal. There is no obligating event (e.g. the contract may be renewed or H may find replacement business and not need to make redundancies).

4.4.1060.40 In another example, Company O is considering offering to its employees voluntary redundancies (see 4.4.1070) as part of a restructuring plan. O has prepared a formal detailed plan under which employees may request a voluntary redundancy *if* it is offered by the entity, i.e. O retains a right of refusal to provide voluntary redundancies to employees that apply for it. The formal plan has been communicated to employees. In our view, as O has the ability to refuse to provide voluntary redundancies, it is not demonstrably committed to the plan without realistic possibility of withdrawal and therefore would not recognise an obligation for voluntary redundancies.

4.4.1060.50 In our view, the specific employees who will be made redundant do not have to be informed that they are being made redundant (i.e. communicating a restructuring or termination plan to an employee group that includes the affected employees is sufficient to raise a valid expectation).

4.4.1060.60 See 3.12.230 for guidance on the recognition of other costs associated with a restructuring. Sometimes, the timing of recognition of a liability for redundancies may differ from the timing of recognition of the other costs associated with a restructuring. For example, Company Q has met the criteria for recognising a restructuring provision, but has not yet communicated to the affected employees that the restructuring will involve redundancies. Therefore Q has an obligation for the restructuring costs before it has an obligation for the related employee termination costs.

4.4.1070 *Voluntary redundancies*

IAS 19.140   4.4.1070.10 The liability for voluntary redundancies is measured at the best estimate of the anticipated outflow considering expected acceptances of the offer.

4.4.1070.20 The general recognition requirements for termination benefits in 4.4.1060 also apply to voluntary redundancies. However, a liability is recognised only if it is probable that the offer will be accepted and the number of acceptances can be estimated reliably.

4.4.1070.30 For example, Company W's managing director can resign and receive a large payout if certain events, including a buy-out, occur. W has been acquired and the managing director has indicated the intention to resign. This is a termination benefit similar to a voluntary redundancy. The triggering event has occurred and it is probable that the managing director will take the benefit. Therefore, in our view a liability for the severance benefit should be recognised.

4.4.1080 *Measurement*

4.4.1080.10 Costs related to future services from employees who keep working after the redundancy has been announced, e.g. during a notice period, are not be recognised as a termination obligation.

4.4.1080.20 Also, costs that are associated with ongoing activities are not recognised as a termination obligation. For example, Company M operates a chain of restaurants and decides to turn them into franchises. The restaurant managers, currently employees, will receive a redundancy payment if they agree to become franchisees. If they do not accept the offer, then they will remain as employees. Even if the plan has been communicated to the employees, no liability is recognised. The employees are being paid to become franchisees, and therefore the cost is associated with the ongoing activities.

4.4.1090 **Consolidation of employee benefit plans and employee benefit trusts**

4.4.1090.10 Post-employment benefit plans are classified as defined benefit or defined contribution plans (see 4.4.120); defined benefit plans are accounted for as set out in 4.4.440 (i.e. the resulting obligation is presented on a net basis in the statement of financial position). The plans are not subject to normal consolidation principles.

4.4.1090.20 An employer also may set up a separate entity to provide other long-term employee benefits (see 2.5.150.20). Often the entity holds assets that are transferred to it by the employer. The assets then are used by the entity to settle its obligations to employees. For example, an employee benefit trust may hold cash that will be used to pay bonuses. The employer often has control over the entity.

4.4.1090.30 There is no guidance in IFRSs on how to account for such plans. In our view, if the separate entity is determined to be an employee benefit plan, then an employer does not consolidate the plan (regardless of whether it is a post-employment benefit plan or an other long-term employee benefit), even if the plan holds assets that do not qualify as plan assets. The employer should account for its obligation under the employee benefit plan to provide the benefits in the same way as employee benefits that are settled directly by the employer (i.e. the employer should recognise an obligation for the compensation that employees are entitled to receive based on services performed at each reporting date).

4.4.1090.40 In our view, assets held by the fund that meet the definition of plan assets (see 4.4.350) should be measured at fair value and netted against the related liability. In our view, assets other than loans to the sponsor (see 4.4.1095) that do not meet the definition of plan assets (e.g. because of transferability restrictions) should be accounted for in accordance with the relevant IFRS, e.g. in accordance with IAS 39 for financial instruments. See 3.6.460 or 3.11.250 for guidance if those financial instruments are treasury shares. These financial instruments should be shown separately in the employer's statement of financial position.

4.4.1095 *Loans granted to and by post-employment/other long-term benefit plans*

4.4.1095.10 Sometimes a post-employment/other long-term benefit plan may grant loans to, or receive loans from, the sponsoring entity. The following examples illustrate what in our view is the appropriate accounting treatment for such loans.

4.4.1096 *Pension plan grants loan to sponsor that meets the definition of a plan asset*

4.4.1096.10 In this example the pension plan grants a 10-year loan of 100 to Company P, the sponsoring entity, at a market rate of interest. The loan meets the criteria for classification as plan assets (see 4.4.360). We believe that the following entries should be made in the consolidated financial statements of P on initial recognition of the loan:

	Debit	Credit
Cash	100	
Loan payable		100
Plan assets (loan receivable)	100	
Plan assets (cash)		100
To recognise initial loan		

IAS 19.140 4.4.1096.20 The net effect on plan assets is zero, since the cash transferred of 100 and the fair value of the loan receivable of 100 offset each other equally.

4.4.1098 *Pension plan grants loan to sponsor that does not meet the definition of a plan asset*

4.4.1098.10 In this example the pension plan grants a 10-year loan of 100 to Company P, the sponsoring entity, at a market rate of interest; the loan is not transferable. The loan does not meet the criteria for classification as plan assets (see 4.4.360). We believe that the following entries should be made in the consolidated financial statements of P on initial recognition of the loan:

	Debit	Credit
Cash	100	
Plan assets (cash)		100
To recognise impact of loan from pension plan		

IAS 1.17(c), 4.4.1098.20 The net effect on plan assets is a decrease of 100, since the cash trans-
19.140 ferred to P of 100 decreases plan assets and the loan receivable by the plan from P does not meet the criteria for classification as plan assets. We believe that in P's statement of financial position it should recognise neither the loan payable to the plan of 100 nor the loan receivable by the plan of 100. We believe that recognition of the loan receivable by the plan would result in P recognising a receivable from itself. Consequently, the plan assets decrease by the cash receipt of the sponsor and neither loan is recognised in the statement of financial position. However, an entity considers whether such loans should be disclosed.

4.4.1100 Presentation and disclosure

4.4.1110 *Current/non-current presentation*

IAS 19.118 4.4.1110.10 A distinction between current and non-current assets and liabilities arising from post-employment benefits is not required.

4.4.1110.20 In practice assets and liabilities related to defined benefit plans generally are presented as non-current, but if the distinction between the current and non-current portions is clear, then split presentation is permitted. For example, an entity may choose to present as the current portion of its employee benefit obligation an amount equal to its contributions payable to a plan within the next 12 months. However, we prefer the total liability to be presented as non-current unless it is part of a disposal group that is held for sale or distribution (see 5.4.20 and 35).

4.4.1110.30 Assets and liabilities related to defined contribution plans normally are current and are presented as such.

IAS 1.69,   4.4.1110.40 Long-term employee benefits are accounted for as such in their entirety
19.BC4C   (see 4.4.970). However, an entity distinguishes between current and non-current portions
of obligations arising from long-term employee benefits if it does not have the ability to
defer payment beyond 12 months from the reporting date. For example, an employee is
eligible to receive an additional five weeks' leave after providing 10 years of continuous
service to an employer; if the additional leave is not taken during employment, then
it will be paid upon termination of employment. The additional leave is a long-term
employee benefit even after the benefit becomes unconditional (i.e. after the employee
provides 10 years of continuous service). However, after the end of year nine the entity
no longer has the ability to defer settlement of the obligation beyond 12 months from
the reporting date, and therefore we believe that it should be presented as current in the
statement of financial position.

4.4.1120 *Offsetting*

IAS 19.54   4.4.1120.10 Assets that meet the definition of plan assets and the related liabilities are
presented on a net basis in the statement of financial position. All other assets and obligations are presented on a gross basis.

IAS 19.116   4.4.1120.20 Net liabilities and net assets arising on different plans are presented separately,
except in the rare circumstances when there is a legal right of offset and an intention to
settle the plans on a net basis.

4.4.1130 **Statement of comprehensive income presentation***

IAS 19.120(f),   4.4.1130.10 The components of the statement of comprehensive income charge for
BC4(j)   defined benefit obligations do not have to be charged or credited in the same line item.
An entity should choose an accounting policy, to be applied consistently, either to
include interest cost and expected return on plan assets with interest and other financial income respectively, or to show the net total as personnel expenses. However,
regardless of the accounting policy chosen, disclosure is required of the line items
in which the components of the post-employment cost are recognised.

4.4.1130.20 In our view, when the corridor method is used, actuarial gains and losses
of a defined benefit plan should not be split between those related to investments and
those related to the obligation, even if interest and the expected return on plan assets
are presented separately. Instead, actuarial gains and losses recognised in profit or loss
should be classified in the same item as current service costs. However, when the corridor method is not used, e.g. full recognition of actuarial gains and losses in profit or
loss, in our view such presentation would not be required.

4.4.1135 *Disclosure*

4.4.1135.10 IAS 24 *Related Party Disclosures* requires disclosure of key management compensation in total and for each of the following categories: short-term employee benefits,
post-employment benefits, other long-term benefits and termination benefits (see 5.5.110).

4.4.1140 *Group plans*

4.4.1140.10 If there is a contractual agreement or a stated policy for charging the costs of a group plan, then an entity that participates in that plan recognises the defined benefit cost allocated to it under the agreement or policy. In such a case questions may arise regarding how to account for and present the allocated cost. In our view, the amount of the allocated cost recognised in profit or loss (see 4.4.170) generally should be presented as a single expense within personnel expenses.

IAS 19.34A 4.4.1140.20 If there is no such contractual agreement or stated policy, then the net defined benefit cost is recognised by the group entity that is legally the sponsoring employer for the plan. In our view, any amount of the net defined benefit cost recognised in profit or loss by the legal sponsor (see 4.4.180) generally should be presented as a single expense within personnel expenses.

4.4.1150 **Curtailments or settlements**

IAS 19.120(e) 4.4.1150.10 In our view, when a curtailment or settlement arises as a result of the disposal of an operation, including a subsidiary, the resulting gain or loss may be shown as an adjustment to the gain or loss on disposal of the operation or as a component of personnel expenses. In our view, an entity should choose a presentation format, to be applied consistently, in respect of the presentation of curtailment or settlement gains or losses. Whichever presentation is adopted, the amount and nature of the curtailment or settlement gain or loss should be disclosed separately.

4.4.1160 **Future developments**

4.4.1160.10 In July 2006 the IASB announced a project to revisit fundamentally the accounting for employee benefits under IAS 19. The project is divided into two phases, with the first phase focusing on improvements in defined benefit plan accounting.

4.4.1160.20 In April 2010 the IASB published ED/2010/3 *Defined Benefit Plans – Proposed Amendments to IAS 19* as part of the first phase of the project. The ED proposes significant changes to the recognition, presentation and disclosure of defined benefit plans and also changes to their measurement. The proposals in the ED would apply equally to all long-term employee benefits and would require all changes in the value of the defined benefit obligation and in the value of plan assets to be recognised in the financial statements in the period in which they occur. The proposals would remove both the option of using the "corridor method" for recognising actuarial gains and losses and deferred recognition of non-vested past service costs.

4.4.1160.30 The changes in the net defined benefit liability (asset) would be split into the following components:

- service costs – to be recognised in profit or loss;

- net interest income or expense – to be recognised in profit or loss as part of finance costs; and
- remeasurements of the defined benefit liability (asset) – to be recognised in other comprehensive income.

4.4.1160.40 The finance costs component would comprise net interest on the net defined benefit liability (asset), determined by applying the discount rate that is used to discount the defined benefit obligation to the net defined benefit liability (asset) – any return on plan assets in excess or below that discount rate would be recognised as a remeasurement in other comprehensive income.

4.4.1160.50 A final standard on this initial phase of the employee benefits project is scheduled for the first quarter of 2011. The next phase of the project is expected to be carried out in conjunction with the FASB. This next phase is not intended to begin until 2011 at the earliest.

4.4.1160.60 In June 2005 the IASB published an ED *Proposed Amendments to IAS 37 Provisions, Contingent Liabilities and Contingent Assets and IAS 19 Employee Benefits*. The ED proposes amendments to the definition and recognition of termination benefits in IAS 19, which complement the proposed amendments to IAS 37 in relation to restructuring (see 3.12.880.10). The ED proposes to clarify the definition of termination benefits to include benefits payable in exchange for an employee's decision to accept voluntary redundancy only if voluntary redundancy is offered for a short period of time. Final amendments are scheduled for the third quarter of 2010.

4.4.1160.70 In May 2009 the IASB published ED/2009/5 *Fair Value Measurement* (the 2009 ED). The proposals in the 2009 ED are intended to replace the fair value measurement guidance contained in individual IFRSs with a single, unified definition of fair value, as well as provide further authoritative guidance on the application of fair value measurement in inactive markets. The 2009 ED proposes a framework for measuring fair value and disclosures about fair value measurements. The proposals in the 2009 ED explain how to measure fair value when it already is required or permitted by existing IFRSs; they do not introduce new fair value measurements, nor do they eliminate the practicability exceptions to fair value measurements that exist currently in certain standards.

4.4.1160.80 In June 2010 the IASB published ED/2010/7 *Measurement Uncertainty Analysis Disclosure for Fair Value Measurements* (the 2010 ED). The 2010 ED expands on the proposal in the 2009 ED for an entity to disclose a measurement uncertainty analysis (or sensitivity analysis) for assets and liabilities measured at fair value categorised within Level 3 of the fair value hierarchy. The 2010 ED proposes that an entity consider the effect of correlation between unobservable inputs, if relevant.

4.4.1160.90 A final standard on fair value measurement and disclosure, which is expected to be converged with a forthcoming amended standard under US GAAP, is scheduled for the first quarter of 2011.

4.5 Share-based payments

(IFRS 2)

4.5 Share-based payments
(IFRS 2)

Overview of currently effective requirements

- Goods or services received in a share-based payment transaction are measured at fair value.

- Goods are recognised when they are obtained and services are recognised over the period that they are received.

- Equity-settled transactions with employees generally are measured based on the grant-date fair value of the equity instruments granted.

- Equity-settled transactions with non-employees generally are measured based on the fair value of the goods or services received.

- For equity-settled transactions an entity recognises a cost and a corresponding increase in equity. The cost is recognised as an expense unless it qualifies for recognition as an asset.

- Market conditions for equity-settled transactions are reflected in the initial measurement of fair value. There is no "true up" (adjustment) if the expected and actual outcomes differ because of the market conditions.

- Like market conditions, non-vesting conditions are reflected in the initial measurement of fair value and there is no subsequent true up for differences between the expected and the actual outcome.

- Initial estimates of the number of equity-settled instruments that are expected to vest are adjusted to current estimates and ultimately to the actual number of equity-settled instruments that vest unless differences are due to market conditions.

- Choosing not to meet a non-vesting condition within the control of the entity or the counterparty is treated as a cancellation.

- For cash-settled transactions an entity recognises a cost and a corresponding liability. The cost is recognised as an expense unless it qualifies for recognition as an asset.

- The liability is remeasured, until settlement date, for subsequent changes in the fair value of the liability. The remeasurements are recognised in profit or loss.

- Modification of a share-based payment results in the recognition of any incremental fair value but not any reduction in fair value. Replacements are accounted for as modifications.

- Cancellation of a share-based payment results in acceleration of vesting.

- Classification of grants in which the entity has the choice of equity or cash settlement depends on whether or not the entity has the ability and intent to settle in shares.

- Grants in which the counterparty has the choice of equity or cash settlement are accounted for as compound instruments. Therefore the entity accounts for a liability component and an equity component separately.

- A share-based payment transaction in which the receiving entity, the reference entity and the settling entity are in the same group from the perspective of the ultimate parent is a group share-based payment transaction and is accounted for as such by both the receiving and the settling entities.

- A share-based payment that is settled by a shareholder external to the group also is in the scope of IFRS 2 from the perspective of the receiving entity, as long as the reference entity is in the same group as the receiving entity.

- A receiving entity without any obligation to settle the transaction classifies a share-based payment transaction as equity settled.

- A settling entity classifies a share-based payment transaction as equity settled if it is obliged to settle in its own equity instruments and as cash settled otherwise.

Currently effective requirements

This publication reflects IFRSs in issue at 1 August 2010. The currently effective requirements cover annual periods beginning on 1 January 2010. The requirements related to this topic are derived mainly from IFRS 2 *Share-based Payment*.

Forthcoming requirements and future developments

When a currently effective requirement will be changed by a new requirement that is issued but is not yet effective, it is marked with a # as a **forthcoming requirement** and the impact of the change is explained in the accompanying boxed text. The forthcoming requirements related to this topic are derived from:

- *Improvements to IFRSs 2010.* A brief outline of the impact of the *Improvements to IFRSs 2010* on this topic is given in 4.5.1098, and a brief outline of the annual improvements process is given in 1.1.85.
- IFRS 9 *Financial Instruments.* A brief outline of the impact of IFRS 9 on this topic is given in 4.5.1023.

When a significant change to the currently effective or forthcoming requirements is expected, it is marked with a * as an area that may be subject to **future developments** and a brief outline of the relevant projects is given in 4.5.1180.

4.5.10 Basic principles

4.5.10.10 In share-based payment transactions, an entity receives goods or services from a counterparty and grants equity instruments (equity-settled share-based payment transactions) or incurs a liability to deliver cash or other assets (cash-settled share-based payment transactions) as consideration. A counterparty can be an employee or any other third party. The equity instruments granted may be equity instruments of the entity or another group entity. In a cash-settled share-based payment transaction the liability is based on the price or value of an equity instrument of the entity or another group entity.

4.5.10.20 Equity-settled share-based payment transactions with non-employees generally are measured at the fair value of the goods or services received (direct measurement) rather than at the fair value of the equity instruments granted at the time that the goods or services are received. If in rare cases the fair value of the goods or services received cannot be measured reliably, then the goods and services received are measured by reference to the fair value of the equity instruments granted (indirect measurement). See 4.5.370 for further details.

4.5.10.25 Share-based payment transactions, in particular those with employees, often are conditional upon the achievement of conditions. The standard distinguishes between vesting conditions and non-vesting conditions:

- A condition is a vesting condition if it determines whether the entity receives the services that entitle the counterparty to receive the payment. Therefore a vesting condition requires the counterparty to stay in service with an entity for a period of time (service condition).
- A service condition can be combined with the achievement of a performance condition. A performance condition can be based on the price of the entity's equity instruments (market condition), e.g. achieving a certain share price target, or it can be any other performance target (non-market performance condition), e.g. achieving a certain profit target.
- A non-vesting condition is a condition other than a vesting condition that determine whether a counterparty receives an equity instrument granted (see 4.5.10.50).

4.5.10.27 The respective types of conditions are dealt with differently in accounting for share-based payment transactions. See 4.5.380 for further details.

4.5.10.30 Equity-settled share-based payment transactions with employees require indirect measurement and each equity instrument granted is measured on its respective grant date. The impact of any market conditions and non-vesting conditions are factored into the grant-date fair value of each equity instrument. Any service or non-market perform-ance condition is not taken into account in determining the grant-date fair value of the share-based payment. Instead, the number of equity instruments expected to satisfy the service and non-market performance conditions is estimated. The product of this estimate, i.e. grant-date fair value per equity instrument times the number of equity instruments expected to satisfy the service and non-market performance conditions, is the estimate of the total share-based payment cost. This cost generally is recognised as an expense over the vesting period with a corresponding entry in equity. If the payment is not subject to a service condition, then it is recognised immediately. If the cost of the goods or services received meets the criteria for asset recognition, then it is capitalised as an asset or as part of cost of another asset. See 4.5.430 for further details.

4.5.10.40 Subsequent to initial recognition and measurement, the estimate of the number of equity instruments expected to satisfy the service and non-market performance conditions is revised during the vesting period such that the cumulative amount recognised is based on the number of equity instruments that are expected to satisfy the service and non-market performance conditions. No adjustments are made in respect of market conditions, i.e. neither the number of instruments nor the grant-date fair value is adjusted if the outcome of the market condition differs from the initial estimate. See 4.5.430 for further details.

4.5.10.50 Non-vesting conditions are conditions other than vesting conditions that determine whether a counterparty receives a share-based payment granted. Non-vesting conditions are reflected in the measurement of the grant-date fair value of the share-based payment. Non-vesting conditions that the counterparty can choose to meet, e.g. paying contribu-tions towards the purchase (or exercise) price on a monthly basis or complying with transfer restrictions; and non-vesting conditions that the entity can choose to meet, e.g. continuing the plan, result in accelerated recognition of unrecognised cost if such condi-tions are not met. A non-vesting condition that neither the entity nor the counterparty can choose to meet, for example, a target based on a commodity index, has no impact on the accounting if it is not met, i.e. there is neither a reversal of the cost recognised previously nor an acceleration of recognition. See 4.5.470 for further details.

4.5.10.60 Only modifications of an equity-settled share-based payment arrangement that are beneficial to the counterparty are accounted for. If the fair value of the equity instru-ments granted has increased, then the incremental fair value at the date of modification is recognised in addition to the grant-date fair value. Modifications that are not beneficial to the counterparty do not affect the amount of the cost. However, reductions in the number of equity instruments granted are accounted for as cancellations. See 4.5.690 for further details.

4.5.10.70 Cancellations by the entity or by the counterparty are treated as an accelera-tion of vesting. If an entity grants new equity instruments to replace cancelled equity instruments, then this cancellation and replacement is accounted for in the same way as a modification. See 4.5.800 for further details.

4.5.10.80 Cash-settled share-based payment transactions are measured initially at the fair value of the liability and are recognised as an expense or capitalised as an asset if the asset recognition criteria are met. If the payment is subject to a service condition, then the amounts are recognised over the service period. At the end of each reporting period until settlement date the recognised liability is remeasured at fair value with changes recognised in profit or loss. If the payment is not subject to a service condition, then it is recognised immediately. See 4.5.630 for further details.

4.5.10.90 Some share-based payment transactions provide one party with the choice of settlement in cash or in equity instruments. If the entity has the choice of settlement, then the transaction is accounted for as an equity-settled or cash-settled share-based payment transaction, depending on whether the entity has the intent and ability to settle in equity instruments. A present obligation to settle in cash exists, for example, if the entity has past practice or a stated policy of settling in cash. If the counterparty has the choice of settlement, then the entity has granted a compound instrument comprising a debt component and an equity component. See 4.5.650 for further details.

4.5.10.100 A share-based payment transaction in which the receiving entity, the reference entity and the settling entity are in the same group from the perspective of the ultimate parent is a group share-based payment transaction from the perspective of the receiving and the settling entities. In a group share-based payment arrangement in which the parent grants its own equity instruments to the employees of its subsidiary, the share-based payment is recognised in the consolidated financial statements of the parent and the separate financial statements of the parent and the subsidiary. See 4.5.820 for details.

4.5.10.110 More detailed discussions on recognition and measurement are provided for each of the following types of share-based payment transactions:

- equity-settled share-based payment transactions, including shares or share options (see 4.5.370);
- cash-settled share-based payment transactions (see 4.5.630);
- transactions in which there is a choice of cash or equity settlement by either the entity or the counterparty (see 4.5.650); and
- group share-based payment transactions (see 4.5.820).

4.5.20 Scope

IFRS 2.A 4.5.20.03 The standard does not contain a stand-alone definition of a share-based payment but provides a complex two-step definition using the terms "share-based payment arrangement" and "share-based payment transaction." A share-based payment arrangement is an agreement between the entity (or another group entity or any shareholder of any group entity) and another party (including an employee) that, provided the specified vesting conditions are met, entitles the other party to receive:

- cash or other assets of the entity for amounts that are based on the price (or value) of equity instruments (including share or share options) of the entity or another group entity; or

- equity instruments (including shares or share options) of the entity or another group entity.

IFRS 2.A 4.5.20.07 A share-based payment transaction is a transaction in which the entity:

- receives goods or services from the supplier of those goods or services (including an employee) in a share-based payment arrangement; or
- incurs an obligation to settle the transaction with the supplier in a share-based payment arrangement when another group entity receives those goods or services.

4.5.20.10 [Not used]

4.5.20.13 This chapter primarily addresses situations in which the entity that receives the goods or services in a share-based payment transaction (receiving entity) also is the entity that has the obligation to settle the share-based payment transaction (settling entity). Transactions in which the receiving entity and the settling entity are not the same, but are in the same group (group share-based payment arrangements), are addressed in 4.5.820.

IFRS 2.5 4.5.20.15 The most common items received in exchange for a share-based payment are employee services. However, services also can be provided by parties other than employees, such as consultancy services. Goods also can be acquired in a share-based payment transaction.

4.5.20.20 Transactions settled in shares or other equity instruments are referred to as equity-settled share-based payment transactions. Transactions that create an obligation to deliver cash or other assets are referred to as cash-settled share-based payment transactions. See 4.5.820 for a discussion of the terms equity-settled and cash-settled in group share-based payment arrangements.

4.5.20.30 If a transaction is within the scope of IFRS 2, then the requirements of the standard specify both the initial and subsequent accounting for the equity instruments issued or liability incurred.

IFRS 2.2, 13A 4.5.20.40 IFRS 2 also applies to transactions in which an entity cannot identify specifically the goods or services received in return for a share-based payment. In the absence of specifically identifiable goods or services, other circumstances may indicate that goods or services have been received. In particular, if the identifiable consideration received is less than the fair value of the equity instruments granted or liability incurred, then typically this circumstance indicates that other consideration (i.e. unidentifiable goods or services) have been (or will be) received. For example, a grant of shares at a discount may indicate that unidentifiable goods or services have been or will be received that should be accounted for under IFRS 2.

4.5.20.50 If the share-based payment is consideration for services, then in some cases it might be difficult to determine whether it is the entity or the entity's shareholders that receive the service. For example an entity's shareholder grants a share-based payment to members of the entity's management. The non-market performance condition is completion of a pending sale of the entity. In our view, management's services are received by the entity rather than received by the shareholders, because it is one of management's normal duties to act in the best interest of the entity's shareholders. The entity also might benefit from the sale in other ways, such as additional sources of financing, enhanced liquidity, access to new markets etc. Therefore this share-based payment should be reflected in the financial statements of the entity.

4.5.20.60 – 70 [Not used]

IFRS 2.A 4.5.20.72 An equity instrument is a contract that evidences a residual interest in the assets of an entity after deducting all of its liabilities. The most common examples are ordinary shares and written call options, or warrants, issued over ordinary shares (share options).

4.5.20.73 A share-based payment involving preference shares and circumstances in which there is more than one class of ordinary shares will need to be considered to determine if the shares include a right to a residual interest in an entity and therefore are equity (see 4.5.190.10).

IFRS 2.A, 4.5.20.74 The issue of what is an equity instrument of the entity is of particular inter-
B50 est in consolidated financial statements. In the consolidated financial statements equity instruments of the entity comprise the equity instruments of any entity that is included in the group, i.e. the parent and its subsidiaries (see 4.5.190.10 for the relevance of classification of instruments under IAS 32 *Financial Instruments: Presentation*).

IFRS 2.A 4.5.20.76 If the entity does not settle in its own equity instruments but in a payment of cash or other assets, then the amount should be based on the price (or value) of its equity instruments in order to qualify as a share-based payment.

IFRS 2.IG18, 4.5.20.78 A common example of a cash payment based on an equity instrument of the
IG19 entity is when an entity grants share appreciation rights (SARs) to its employees. SARs entitle the holder to receive a payment that equals the increase in value of the shares from a specified level over a specified period of time, for example, from grant date to settlement date. In this case the counterparty directly participates in changes of the value of the underlying equity instrument and accordingly, the cash payment is based on the price or value of the equity instrument. Another common example is a payment based on the value of an equity instrument at a specific date, for example at vesting date or settlement date, rather than on the increase in value.

4.5.20.79 Sometimes it is difficult to assess whether the payment is based on the price or value of the equity instrument. See 4.5.170 for a more detailed discussion of the distinction between a payment that "depends on" vs "is based on" the price or value of the equity instrument.

4.5.20.80 [Not used]

4.5.20.90 Sometimes arrangements involve entities that are outside the reporting entity:

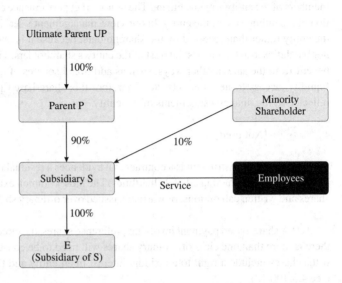

4.5.20.100 For example, in the diagram in 4.5.20.90, if Subsidiary S is the reporting entity and Parent P grants its own equity instruments to the employees of S or if S grants equity instruments of P to its own employees, then from the perspective of S's separate and consolidated financial statements this is a share-based payment arrangement involving an entity outside the reporting entity. This is because P is not part of the reporting entity when S prepares its separate or consolidated financial statements. Share-based payment arrangements that involve entities outside the reporting entity are referred to as "group share-based payment arrangements", if the other entity is, from the perspective of Ultimate Parent UP, in the same group as the reporting entity. See 4.5.820 for guidance on these arrangements.

4.5.30 [Not used]

4.5.40 *Transactions outside the scope of IFRS 2*

4.5.50 *Transactions with shareholders*

IFRS 2.2, 4 4.5.50.10 Transactions with employees or other parties in their capacity as shareholder are outside the scope of IFRS 2.

IFRS 2.4 4.5.50.20 If employees or other parties who are also shareholders participate in a transaction with the entity, then it may be difficult to determine in which capacity they act: as suppliers of goods or services to the entity or as shareholders of the entity. For example, if all shareholders have been offered the right to participate in a transaction, then this is an indication that the employees or other parties do not act as suppliers but as shareholders.

4.5.60 *Transactions covered by other IFRSs*

IFRS 2.5, 6   4.5.60.10 The following share-based payment transactions are covered by other IFRSs and therefore are outside the scope of the share-based payment standard:

- share-based consideration paid in a business combination as defined by IFRS 3 *Business Combinations* (see 2.6.10 and 4.5.70), in a combination of entities under common control (see 5.13) or in connection with the contribution of a business on the formation of a joint venture as defined by IAS 31 *Interests in Joint Ventures* (see 3.5.90);
- share-based consideration for certain commodity contracts that are within the scope of the financial instruments standards (see 3.6.90 and 4.5.90); and
- the issue of equity instruments in return for financial instruments of equal fair value (see 3.6).

4.5.70 Business combinations

IFRS 2.5   4.5.70.10 Share-based consideration paid for net assets acquired in a business combination is outside the scope of IFRS 2. Situations in which employees are also shareholders may require judgement to determine whether a share-based payment transaction represents payment for future services or for control of the acquiree (see 2.6.400).

4.5.70.20 In our view, the exclusion for business combinations extends beyond business combination transactions as defined in IFRS 3, and we believe that the following transactions also are outside the scope of IFRS 2:

- acquisition of non-controlling interests after control is obtained (see 2.5.380); and
- acquisition of significant influence (see 3.5.10).

IFRS 3.B51,   4.5.70.30 IFRS 3 provides additional guidance on determining whether equity instru-
B55   ments issued in a business combination are:

- part of the consideration transferred in exchange for control of the acquiree, and therefore within the scope of IFRS 3;
- in return for service to be recognised in the post-combination period, and therefore within the scope of IFRS 2; or
- a modification of a pre-combination share-based payment (see 2.6.420).

4.5.80 [Not used]

4.5.90 Commodity contracts

IFRS 2.6   4.5.90.10 Share-based consideration for commodity contracts that can be settled net in cash or other financial instruments, that are not for the purpose of the entity's expected purchase, sale or usage requirements, are within the scope of the financial instruments standards (see 3.6.90) and outside the scope of the share-based payment standard.

4.5.100 *Scope issues in practice*

4.5.110 *Share-based payment vs shareholder transaction*

4.5.110.03 Paragraph 4 of IFRS 2 does not limit situations in which the counterparty acts in its capacity as a shareholder to transactions in which all existing shareholders are granted the same rights and restrictions. Distinguishing a share-based payment from a shareholder transaction can be difficult when the counterparty purchases the equity instruments at the same amount as other shareholders; for example, an employee share purchase plan (ESPP) may not appear to fall within the guidance provided in IFRS 2. See 4.5.530 for further discussion of ESPPs.

4.5.110.05 Factors that in our view may be relevant in determining whether a purchase of shares is within the scope of the share-based payment standard include the following:

- the plan specifies that the realisation of a benefit is subject to future services; and
- the plan includes buy-back terms that do not apply to non-employee shareholders.

4.5.110.06 For example, an employee may purchase a share at a price that appears to be fair value, but may be required to sell the share back at the lower of fair value and the amount paid if they leave before a specified date.

4.5.110.07 In another example, senior management of companies owned by private equity funds sometimes purchase equity instruments with vesting being conditional on an exit event (e.g. an IPO or a sale of the company).

4.5.110.08 Considering the indicators in 4.5.110.05 in relation to the transactions described in 4.5.110.06 and 07:

- The arrangement contains a benefit that is subject to future services, because the employee can benefit from future increases in the value of the shares only by providing services for the specified period or by being employed when the exit event occurs.
- There is an apparent inconsistency in these arrangements between the proposition that the purchase of the shares is at fair value and the inclusion of the requirement to sell the shares back at the lower of fair value and purchase price. This requirement is, in effect, a right that allows the entity to re-acquire the shares, which has a positive value to the entity and has a negative value to the employee. If the amount paid was fair value of a share without this condition, then the employee appears to have overpaid in purchasing the share from the entity by the value of the entity's right to re-acquire the shares. If the requirement to sell back was not imposed on non-employee shareholders, then this may call into question the validity of the assertion that the purchase was at fair value in the first place.

4.5.110.09 If applying these indicators results in the conclusion that a share purchased at fair value is a share-based payment, then a second issue is whether there is any cost to recognise. Even if there is no cost to recognise, for example because the purchase price is equal to the grant-date fair value of the equity instruments granted, in our view the disclosure requirements of IFRS 2 still apply.

IFRS 2.4 4.5.110.10 However, sometimes a privately-held entity, such as a wholly employee-owned entity, may require employees (e.g. by virtue of the entity's articles of association (see 4.5.330.25)), to sell shares back to the entity, if they cease to be employees, even if these shares previously were purchased at fair value in a transaction that was a transaction with shareholders and not a share-based payment transaction. In our view, if in such circumstances the obligation to resell the shares requires the entity to pay fair value at the time of repurchase and the acquisition of the shares did not involve a share-based payment, then the repurchase/resale requirement does not result in the transaction being a share-based payment since there is no consideration received/paid beyond the shareholder transaction. However, the requirement to repurchase may affect the classification and measurement of these shares (see 3.11.50).

4.5.120 *Share-based payment vs employee benefit*

IAS 27.4 4.5.120.10 The requirement to treat transactions involving instruments of another entity as a share-based payment applies only to transactions involving equity instruments of a group entity (see 4.5.820). The determination of whether another entity is a group entity is based on the definition of a group as defined in paragraph 4 of IAS 27 *Consolidated and Separate Financial Statements*, i.e. a parent and all its subsidiaries.

4.5.130 [Not used]

4.5.140 Tax payments

4.5.140.10 In some countries a share-based payment arrangement may be subject to a tax payment. The tax often is based on the difference between the share price and the exercise price, measured at the exercise date. Alternatively, the tax may be calculated based on the grant-date fair value of the grant. In many cases the tax obligation is a liability of the employee and not the employer, although the employer may have an obligation to collect it or withhold it (see 4.5.320.30).

IFRS 2.1 4.5.140.20 The employer may pay employees an amount of cash to cover social taxes and/or income taxes related to share-based payment transactions in addition to the share-based payment arrangement. In our view, if the cash payment is not based on the price or value of the entity's shares, then this portion of the plan should be treated as an employee benefit under IAS 19 *Employee Benefits* (see 4.4.23.10). If the cash payment is based on the value of the entity's shares, then it may be appropriate to treat this portion of the plan as a cash-settled share-based payment transaction.

4.5.140.30 In some jurisdictions, the employer rather than the employee (see 4.5.140.10) may have the legal obligation to pay taxes on employee awards. If the employer is only the collection agent, and not the primary obligor for the tax, then the guidance in 4.5.320.30 would apply. However, if the employer is the obligor for the tax, then the employer recognises the cost and liability. In our view, an entity should choose an accounting policy, to be applied consistently, to treat the employer's obligation to pay the taxes either as a provision in accordance with IAS 37 *Provisions, Contingent Liabilities and Contingent Assets* or under IFRS 2. We believe that treatment as a provision would be appropriate if the obligation is of uncertain timing or amount, as this tax is not an income tax and therefore is not in the scope of IAS 12 *Income Taxes*.*

4.5.140.35 One of the alternatives discussed in 4.5.140.30 is to account for the tax obligation under IFRS 2. If the amount of the tax is based on the price or value of the entity's equity instruments, then we believe that it should be accounted for as a cash-settled share-based payment. However, if the amount is not based on the value of an equity instrument, then it may be appropriate to consider the tax as an incidental expense associated with granting the share-based payment; the objective to IFRS 2 notes that the standard addresses share-based payments including associated expenses.

IFRS 2.BC72 4.5.140.40 The employer may be able to require the employee to reimburse the employer for tax paid by the employer. In our view, if the employer elects to collect the tax from the employee, then this agreement with the employee may be accounted for as a reimbursement right in accordance with IAS 37 (see 3.12.190).* Alternatively, we believe that the recovery can be treated as an adjustment to the exercise price because from the entity's perspective it is a cash inflow from the employee that is conditional upon exercise of the share-based payment. If the recovery is treated as an additional exercise price, then the estimation of the actual exercise price would affect the determination of the grant-date fair value. Differences between the estimated and the actual exercise price would not be "trued up". If the reimbursement approach is taken, then the estimated recovery would be trued up to the actual amount recovered. In our view, the accounting policy choice regarding the treatment of the reimbursement right is independent of the accounting policy choice regarding accounting for the employer's obligation (see 4.5.140.30).

4.5.150 Cash payments based on approximations of price or value

4.5.150.10 Sometimes a payment is not based on the price or value of the entity's equity instruments but on an approximation of that measure. For example, employees of an entity receive a cash payment based on the increase in the *net assets* of an unlisted entity (i.e. the change in shareholders' equity). It is necessary to determine whether such an arrangement is a profit-sharing arrangement or a share-based payment arrangement. In our view, if the net asset value of the entity does not reflect the fair value of its equity instruments (e.g. the change in net assets represents primarily the profit or loss from operations and does not include fair value changes of assets and liabilities), then the transaction is, in substance, a profit-sharing arrangement that should be accounted for as an employee benefit (see 4.4.60). We expect that this will be the more typical situation.

4.5.150.15 However, if the changes in net assets include substantially all changes in the fair value of the net assets and the net asset value reflects the fair value of the equity instruments, then this represents, in substance, the fair value of an equity instrument. Accordingly, in our view the transaction should be accounted for as a share-based payment. Judgement is needed on a case-by-case basis and we believe that only in limited circumstances will the change in net assets be substantially the same as the change in the value of an entity's shares.

4.5.150.20 Sometimes newly listed or unlisted entities use an earnings basis for estimating the fair value of the entity's equity instruments. If such a measure uses a pre-determined formula, for example a fixed multiple of EBITDA, to specify how the cash payment at settlement will be determined, then in our view such a payment is unlikely to be based on the price or value of an entity's equity instruments. This is because a market multiple generally will change over time. Accordingly, such payments generally should not be considered to be share-based payments, unless in limited cases the facts and circumstances provide evidence that the payment amount is based on the price or value of the entity's equity instruments. If the payment to an employee is not a share-based payment, then it would be considered an employee benefit in the scope of IAS 19.

4.5.160 Date of determination of cash payments

4.5.160.10 IFRS 2 does not specify the date that is relevant for the assessment of whether or not the payment is based on the price or value of the entity's equity instruments. In principle, a payment could be based on the price or value of the equity instrument at grant date, at vesting date, at settlement date or at another date. If an equity instrument is purchased at fair value on grant date and is redeemable only at the amount paid for it, then there is no net payment to the buyer. However, in our view, if the payment on settlement date changes from being based on the value of an entity's equity instruments on the date the equity instruments are granted to be being based on the value of the entity's equity instruments on settlement date, then the payment meets the definition of a share-based payment.

4.5.160.20 For example, Company C grants a share to its employees in exchange for a cash payment at fair value. The employer is required to redeem the share at the end of employment. If the redemption occurs within the first three years after grant date, then the redemption amount equals the value of the share at grant date. If the redemption occurs after the three-year period, then the redemption amount becomes the current value of the share on redemption, i.e. on settlement date. We believe that the transaction is a share-based payment since the redemption amount is based on the value of the equity instrument and the net payment is in return for services, since the employees can participate in value increases only if they stay employed for a period of three years.

4.5.170 Cash payments *depending on* the share price vs *being based on* the share price

4.5.170.10 A cash payment may depend on, but not be based on, the share price. For example, an employee is entitled to a cash payment of 100 if the share price remains at least at the current share price of 8 over the next year. If the share price falls below 8, then the employee is not entitled to the payment. In our view, while this cash payment depends on the share price, it is not based on the share price. Therefore, we believe that the cash payment is not a share-based payment, but is likely to be an employee benefit in the scope of IAS 19 (see 4.4.29.10).

4.5.170.20 If, in contrast, an employee is entitled to a payment equal to the share price at vesting date, then the employee participates one-to-one in the share price increases. In our view, a payment determined as a linear function of the share price or its movements is based on the share price, and therefore is a share-based payment. If the employee is, for example, entitled to 60 percent of the share price or to 200 percent of the share price, then we believe that the payment also meets the definition of being based on the value of the equity instruments and therefore is a share-based payment.

4.5.170.30 If the mechanism to determine the amount of the cash payment is designed as something in between these extremes, then judgement is required to determine whether the mechanism is sufficiently linked to the price or value of the equity instruments. Therefore, judgement is required to define the border between "depending on" and "being based on".

4.5.170.40 For example, Company B grants a cash bonus to its employees. The amount of the bonus depends on the share price achieved at the end of the year, as follows:

- if the share price is below 10, then the bonus amount is zero (level 1);
- if the share price is between 10 and 12, then the bonus amount is 1,000 (level 2); and
- if the share price is above 12, then the bonus amount is 1,500 (level 3).

4.5.170.50 In the example in 4.5.170.40, changes in the share price within a band (e.g. between 10 and 12) will not result in a change in the bonus amount. We believe that the cash payment is not share-based because the size of the gaps between share price levels means that there is not sufficient linkage between the two. Therefore, we believe that the bonus is not a share-based payment in the scope of IFRS 2.

4.5.180 Capped payments

4.5.180.10 An arrangement may provide for a payment to be made that is based on the share price of an entity, but is subject to a cap. For example, Company E provides a bonus arrangement to its employees. The bonus is calculated as a fixed percentage of the share price of E (see 4.5.170.20). However, if the share price exceeds a certain amount, then the payment is capped at a fixed amount. In our view, the arrangement should be accounted for as a cash-settled share-based payment if the payment is expected to be based largely on the share price of E; otherwise it should be accounted for as an employee benefit.

4.5.180.20 In order to determine whether the payment is expected to be based largely on E's share price, in our view the level of the cap and the expected volatility should be compared to the share price at grant date. If, at grant date, the cap is well in excess of the expected growth in E's share price in light of expected volatility, then we believe that the payment at grant date is based largely on E's share price. In our view, the assessment of whether the payment is expected to be based largely on an entity's share price (i.e. the significance of the cap relative to the expected volatility) should be made at each grant date of a new grant and should be reassessed subsequently only if the grant is modified (see 4.5.690).

4.5.190 Relevance of classification under IAS 32 of instruments granted

IFRS 2.31, A, BC106- BC110, IAS 32.11 4.5.190.10 Cash-settled share-based payment transactions include only amounts based on the price or value of the entity's *shares or other equity instruments*. An equity instrument is a contract that evidences the residual interests in the assets of an entity after deducting all of its liabilities (see 1.2.30.20). Under the financial instruments standards, some instruments issued in the legal form of shares may be classified as liabilities. Some potential share-based payment arrangements require payments based on the change in the price of a share instrument that is a residual interest in an entity, but which would be classified as a liability under the financial instruments standards. The term equity instrument is defined in IFRS 2 without reference to IAS 32, and it appears that classification under IAS 32 is not relevant. For example, IFRS 2 includes as an illustration of a cash-settled share-based payment a grant of puttable or redeemable shares or options over them. Such instruments generally would be classified as a financial liability under IAS 32. Under IFRS 2, payment based on the value of a puttable or redeemable share is a cash-settled share-based payment.

4.5.200 Deemed equity

4.5.200.10 An arrangement may require a cash payment to be made based on the price of a deemed share or a synthetic instrument. For example, a cash award may be based on the price (or value) of an amount that is a measure of equity of a business division that is not a separate legal entity. In our view, if the deemed equity or synthetic instrument meets the definition of equity under IFRSs (see 1.2.30.20), then the arrangement meets the definition of a cash-settled share-based payment. We believe that the reference to equity instruments in IFRS 2 does not require the instruments to be in the legal form of shares or other equity instruments. This view is based, in part, on the view that the definition of a business in IFRS 3 does not require a separate legal entity (see 2.6.70).

4.5.210 Components with different features

4.5.210.10 In our view, an award that contains both an employee benefit and a share-based payment should be separated and each component should be accounted for separately. For example, Company B grants a bonus payment to an employee that has both a cash and a share component. The terms of the bonus plan require settlement of 75 percent of the award in a fixed amount of cash and 25 percent in shares; the total value of the bonus payment is 1,000, to be settled by 750 in cash and the remaining amount of 250 in a variable number of shares at their current share price at settlement date. We believe that the 25 percent bonus that is paid in shares is a share-based payment within the scope of IFRS 2, while the cash bonus is an employee benefit within the scope of IAS 19 (see 4.4.27.10).

4.5.210.20 If one arrangement provides a choice of two settlement alternatives that are mutually exclusive and at the discretion of the employee, in which only one of the alternatives would be accounted for under IFRS 2, then in our view the entire arrangement should be accounted for as a share-based payment applying the requirements for compound instruments by analogy. This is because such an arrangement is neither clearly in the scope of IAS 19 nor clearly in the scope of IFRS 2, but the requirements in IFRS 2 for compound instruments seem similar and therefore applicable by analogy. For example, Company B grants a payment to its employees conditional on a three-year service period. At the end of the service period, the employees will receive a bonus based on a pre-determined percentage of the excess of the profit of B above 5,200. Each employee can choose to be paid in cash or to receive equity instruments of the entity to a value of 150 percent of the cash payment provided that they work for a further three years. We believe that the entire arrangement should be accounted for as a share-based payment and that the profit-sharing component should be separated using the guidance in IFRS 2 for compound instruments (see also 4.5.660.60).

4.5.210.30 See 4.4.20 for other examples of share-related payments that are accounted for under IAS 19.

4.5.220 *Share-based payment vs financial instrument*

4.5.220.10 Some share-based payment arrangements may be in the form of financial instruments that appear to be outside the scope of IFRS 2. While the classification and subsequent measurement requirements of IFRS 2 are similar to those of the financial instruments standards, there are some differences. Therefore it is important to determine which standard applies.

4.5.230 Shares as legal mechanism

4.5.230.10 Sometimes the share transaction in itself is not the share-based payment. In our view, if the issuance of shares represents only a legal mechanism to effect a share-based payment, then it is not itself a share-based payment. For example:

- Company S sells redeemable preference shares to its senior executives for a nominal amount.
- The preference shares are redeemable by the entity at the nominal amount only if the executives leave the company.

- Redeemable preference shareholders are entitled to dividends, which are paid in the form of ordinary shares. The amount of the dividends payable is determined as 1 percent of S's profit for the year.
- The ordinary shares themselves do not contain vesting conditions.

4.5.230.20 We believe that the redeemable preference shares in the example in 4.5.230.10 represent only a legal mechanism to effect a share-based payment, being the issue of equity instruments in the form of ordinary shares, and are not themselves share-based payments. The identified share-based payment, being the issue of dividends in the form of ordinary shares, should be accounted for under IFRS 2 as an equity-settled share-based payment arrangement. See also the example in 4.5.250.10.

4.5.240 Forfeiture payment based on the lower of subscription price and fair value

4.5.240.10 Sometimes a share purchase at fair value is a share-based payment. For example:

- Company T sells ordinary shares to employees for cash consideration (subscription price) equal to the fair value of the shares.
- The shares are subject to a condition that allows the entity to reacquire the share when employment terminates.
- For the purposes of determining the re-acquisition right exercise price, notionally the shares vest after five years of service.
- The re-acquisition right exercise price of *vested* shares (i.e. after five years) is the fair value of the shares on the date of exercise. The exercise price of the reacquisition right for *unvested* shares (i.e. before five years) is the lower of the original subscription price plus 6 percent annual interest (not compounded) for each year from the purchase of the shares to the exercise date of the reacquisition right, and the fair value at the date of exercise.

4.5.240.20 Assume in the example in 4.5.240.10 that the subscription price of the ordinary share was 50, the share price at the end of three years is 67 and the share price at the end of five years is 70. If the employee were to leave T at the end of three years, then T could acquire each of the employee's shares for 59 (50 x 118%) rather than for 67. However, if the employee were to leave T at the end of five years, then T could acquire each of the employee's shares for 70, not 65 (50 x 130%).

4.5.240.30 In the example in 4.5.240.10 the exercise price of the re-acquisition right depends on whether the shares are considered vested or unvested. Shares vest (i.e. the re-acquisition right exercise price varies) with employment. The exercise price for unvested shares limits the amount of fair value appreciation in which the employee can participate, but exposes the employee to all of the downside risk; and the ability to participate in fair value increases is dependent on future service. Therefore, in our view a share-based payment exists because, for the re-acquisition right exercise price to equal fair value and the employee to benefit from increases in the share price, the employee must provide five years of services to the entity. As the employees have written the entity a re-acquisition right, this is an award in which the entity has a choice of settlement (see 4.5.340.10 and 680.10).

4.5.250 Requirement to purchase and hold shares

4.5.250.10 An employee may be required to purchase shares in order to participate in a share-based payment arrangement. If the employee pays fair value for the shares and the shares do not contain vesting conditions, then in our view the acquisition of shares by the employee does not form part of the share-based payment transaction, but rather should be accounted for as an equity transaction in accordance with the financial instruments standards (see 3.11). However, we note that it often is difficult to determine whether shares are issued at fair value and entities should consider all the facts and circumstances in determining whether the purchase of shares by employees is outside the scope of IFRS 2.

4.5.250.20 For example, Company B grants a share-based payment in the form of share options to its employees. In order to receive the share options, an employee is required to purchase a specified number of participation shares at fair value and hold the participation shares throughout the vesting period of the share-based payment. The employees are free to sell the participation shares during the vesting period; however if the employees sell the shares, then the share options are no longer available to them (see 4.5.470.20). We believe that the acquisition of shares by the employees does not form part of the share-based payment transaction, but rather should be accounted for as an equity transaction in accordance with the financial instruments standards. In this example, the employees are required to hold the participation shares for a specified period of time in order to exercise the share-based payment. The requirement to hold the participation shares in order to exercise the share-based payment is treated as a non-vesting condition of the share-based payment arrangement (see 4.5.380.40).

4.5.260 *Share plans with cash alternatives at the discretion of the entity*

IU 05-06 4.5.260.10 Some share-based payment arrangements provide the entity with a choice of settlement, but the amount of the cash settlement does not vary with changes in the share price of the entity. For example, Company B grants its employees a fixed bonus that B may choose to settle in shares or cash. As the cash settlement alternative does not vary with the value of the entity's shares or other equity instruments of the entity, the question arises as to whether such an arrangement is within the scope of the share-based payment standard. In our view, as consideration may be equity instruments of the entity and as plans that give the entity a choice of settlement are addressed specifically by the share-based payment standard, such plans are within the scope of IFRS 2. In contrast to the example in 4.5.210.20, in this case B would not account for two components separately, but for the entire arrangement either as equity settled or as a cash-settled liability, depending on B's past practice or stated policy to settle in cash or equity (see 4.5.685).

4.5.270 **Classification of share-based payment transactions**

4.5.270.05 This section addresses classification of share-based payment transactions in which the entity receiving the services also is the entity settling the transaction. See 4.5.890 for classification issues in group share-based payment arrangements.

IFRS 2.B49 4.5.270.10 Generally, the classification as cash or equity settled is based on the entity's obligation to the counterparty (i.e. whether the entity is or can be required to settle in equity instruments or settle in cash) and the entity's intended settlement method. However, classification is not affected by how an entity obtains shares that it will use to settle its obligations. For example, in order to settle the obligation to transfer shares to the counterparty an entity may expect to buy shares in the market, either because it is prohibited from issuing new shares or because it wishes to avoid dilution.

IFRS 2.31 4.5.270.20 All terms and conditions of the arrangement should be considered when determining whether a share-based payment transaction is equity settled or cash settled. For example, a share-based payment transaction in which the employees are granted the right to shares that are redeemable (e.g. shares that are redeemable upon cessation of employment) is a cash-settled share-based payment arrangement, as the arrangement ultimately may be settled in cash (see 4.5.330 regarding redeemable shares).

4.5.280 *Classification issues in practice*

4.5.290 *Redemption feature applicable only on forfeiture*

4.5.290.10 Equity instruments that are subject to redemption features once the equity instruments are vested (which affect the classification assessment and may result in cash-settled classification) are discussed in 4.5.340. If the redemption feature applies to unvested equity instruments upon forfeiture only, then in our view the assessment of classification may be different if the buy-back is only a mechanism for repaying an initial purchase price.

4.5.290.20 For example, the employees of Company G are eligible to purchase shares from G at a discount from the market price and the employees become unconditionally entitled to the shares if they satisfy a service vesting condition. If the award is forfeited because employment terminates, then the employee is required to sell the shares back to G for an amount equal to the original purchase price. The discount from the grant-date fair value of the shares is a share-based payment with protection from a decline in value that is recognised over the service period. We believe that the requirement for the employee to sell the shares back to G at the original purchase price if the vesting condition is not satisfied does not result in the share-based payment being classified as cash settled.

4.5.290.30 As the employee is not unconditionally entitled to the shares during the vesting period, in our view the entity should recognise the purchase price received as a deposit liability until the share-based payment vests; i.e. the entity initially should recognise a liability to refund the purchase price rather than reflect this in equity as an issuance of shares.

4.5.300 *Cashless exercise in a variable number of shares*

4.5.300.10 An arrangement may require or permit the cashless exercise of options. For example, Company F grants an employee 10 options that entitle the employee to purchase shares after three years at an exercise price of 100. At exercise date the share price is 200. A cashless exercise arrangement permits the employee to:

- pay an exercise price of 1,000 and receive 10 shares worth 2,000 (i.e. net value of 1,000); or
- receive 5 shares worth 1,000 for no cash consideration (i.e. cashless exercise) by tendering all 10 options. The cash exercise price of 500 on these 5 shares is *paid* by tendering unexercised options with an intrinsic value of 500 ((200 - 100) x 5).

IFRS 2.BC 4.5.300.20 In our view, cashless exercise does not change the classification as equity-
106 settled as long as the recipient has no ability to require a cash payment for the equity instruments tendered. This is because an *equity-settled transaction* is a transaction in which the entity receives goods or services as consideration for equity instruments of the entity. Therefore a transaction that is settled in a variable number of shares generally is classified as an equity-settled share-based payment transaction, even though this classification may differ from the debt vs equity classification under the financial instrument standards (see 3.11.10).

4.5.310 *"Shares to the value of"*

4.5.310.10 For the same reason as given in 4.5.300.20, we believe that a payment that is settled in equity instruments is a share-based payment, provided no scope exemption applies, even if the design of the payment is to grant shares with a value equal to a certain cash amount. For example, a share-based payment in which the counterparty receives a specified amount of money settled in shares (shares to the value of) at the end of the vesting period would be classified as equity settled.

4.5.310.20 In our view, classification as equity settled applies even if the amount of money itself is variable. For example, Company C, a listed entity, grants shares to its CEO, conditional on a one-year service period. The value of the grant depends on the share price level achieved at the end of the year and the share price on vesting date. If the share price is above 100 at the end of the year, then the CEO receives 1,000 settled in shares. If the share price is above 120 at the end of the year, then the CEO receives 2,000 settled in shares. We believe that C should classify the arrangement as equity settled because equity instruments are issued in exchange for services.

4.5.320 *Entity facilitates the sale of equity instruments*

4.5.320.10 An entity may facilitate the sale of shares or other equity instruments granted. For example, an entity might offer to act as an agent for employees. In our view, if the employer bears no risk in respect of the sale of the shares (e.g. share price fluctuations, credit risks etc.), then classification of the transaction as an equity-settled share-based payment arrangement is not precluded.

4.5.320.20 Determining whether the entity is settling the arrangement in cash or acting as an agent requires an analysis of all terms and conditions. We believe that the following conditions are indicators of an agency relationship (i.e. that the equity instruments are sold on behalf of the recipient of the shares):

- the shares are sold to the market via an independent, third party brokerage firm;
- the entity has not agreed (explicitly or constructively) to purchase the underlying shares from the brokerage firm;
- the entity does not guarantee, or underwrite in any way, the arrangement between the owner and the brokerage firm; and
- the entity is obliged to remit only the payments received from the broker and cannot be obliged to pay if the shares are not sold (e.g. in the event of unexpected market suspensions).

4.5.320.30 In some countries the employee may be subject to taxes upon the receipt of a share-based payment arrangement. In many cases the tax obligation is a liability of the employee and not the employer, although the employer may have an obligation to collect or withhold it. Some share-based arrangements may allow the employer to sell the number of shares required to settle the tax obligation. In our view, if the entity is acting simply as an agent for the employee and therefore bears no risk associated with the shares, then the settlement of the tax obligation via a sale by the employer of a portion of the shares does not mean that the tax portion is a cash-settled share-based payment (see also 4.5.140.20). If in contrast the entity is not acting simply as an agent, i.e. it bears risk associated with the shares, then in our view the tax portion would be classified as a cash-settled share-based payment while the remainder would be classified as equity settled.

4.5.330 *Redeemable, puttable and callable shares*

IFRS 2.41 4.5.330.10 IFRS 2 provides guidance on classification as equity settled or cash settled for transactions in which the issuer has the choice of settlement. Classification as equity settled is appropriate if the entity has the intent and a substantive ability to settle in shares, and has no past practice of settling in cash (see 4.5.680.10).

IFRS 2.31 4.5.330.20 Classification as equity settled is precluded if the instruments issued have a put right, or are convertible into instruments with put rights or redemption requirements. For example, an employee is granted options that, when exercised, result in the issuance of shares that are redeemable at the then-current market price. In this case the share-based payment transaction is classified as cash settled (see 4.5.630).

4.5.330.25 An entity may make a share-based payment using equity instruments that are redeemable, either mandatorily or at one party's option. The label under which these arrangements are seen in practice varies and includes "buy-back arrange-ment", "sell-back arrangement", "put options" or "call options". While sometimes the redemption features are included in the share-based payment agreement, they also may be part of the entity's articles of association or a separate agreement. In our view, redemption features that are associated with the instrument granted as part of a share-based payment form part of the terms and conditions of the share-based payment arrangement.

4.5.330.30 The fair value of a cash-settled share-based payment is remeasured at each reporting date and ultimately on settlement date (see 4.5.630.20). In our view, for a grant of options to acquire redeemable shares, the settlement of the share-based pay-ment occurs only upon redemption of the shares and not upon exercise of the options. Therefore, we believe that an entity should recognise compensation cost and a cor-responding cash-settled liability equal to the grant-date fair value of the options; this liability should be remeasured at each reporting date (see 4.5.630.20). Upon exercise of the options, the entity should continue to remeasure the cash-settled liability to fair value. The entity should remeasure the cash-settled liability through profit or loss until the shares are redeemed.

4.5.330.40 The requirement to classify transactions involving puttable or redeemable shares as cash-settled share-based payment transactions is not limited to instruments with put or redemption terms that are exercisable immediately. Therefore, in our view instruments that require a minimum holding period before put rights are exercisable should be classified as cash settled, regardless of the length of the minimum holding period.

4.5.340 *Equity instruments redeemable at the entity's option*

4.5.340.10 Even when the equity instruments are not puttable or redeemable, in our view the entity should consider whether the overall effect of the arrangements is that, in sub-stance, the employer has a substantive choice of cash or equity settlement. A question may arise when, for example, the employee is required to offer shares back on ceasing employment and, although not required, the employer has a stated policy or past practice of accepting the offer and buying the shares back.

4.5.340.20 However, a past practice of repurchasing shares issued in an equity-settled share-based payment transaction does not automatically require classifying future similar transactions as cash settled as it can depend on the nature of the repurchase arrangements of each transaction. In our view, when there is no mandatory redemption feature and a repurchase arrangement is available to all shareholders, including non-employees, and is *substantive*, in rare circumstances it may be appropriate to "de-link" the repurchase arrangement from the share-based payment, because it is considered more a shareholder-related term and condition. If the repurchase arrangement is de-linked in this manner, then it is not considered in the classification of the share-based payment, which is classified as equity settled from grant date. For example:

- Company B, an unlisted company, has established a discretionary share buy-back arrangement. Each year a share-dealing window operates around the Annual General Meeting date. A letter is distributed to all shareholders that advises them of the procedures for buying and selling B's shares and the fixed price at which the shares will be bought back as determined by an independent third party.
- These buy-back arrangements are available to all shareholders. Employees can leave B's employment and keep the shares that they have obtained through the share-based payment arrangements. Shareholders include employees, former employees, descendants of former employees and a pool of individual shareholders (i.e. not related to employees).
- Notwithstanding the existence of the buy-back arrangement, B is not obliged to repurchase the shares.

IFRS 2.29   4.5.340.30 We believe that in the example in 4.5.340.20 B would classify the equity instruments issued to its employees under a share-based payment arrangement as equity settled as the buy-back arrangement available to all other shareholders is substantive and B is not obliged to repurchase the shares from the employee (i.e. there is no mandatory redemption feature). B also should consider the terms of the buy-back arrangement to determine whether the offer to buy back shares is a written put within the scope of the financial instruments standards.

4.5.340.40 In a contrasting example:

- Company C, an unlisted company, plans to issue shares to its employees.
- These equity instruments will be subject to discretionary share buy-back arrangements; C plans to make this buy-back available to all shareholders, but has not yet done so.
- Notwithstanding the proposal to establish a broad-based buy-back arrangement, C is not obliged to repurchase the shares. However, unlike in the example in 4.5.340.30, C is owned currently by a single shareholder. Following the share issue, a small percentage of C's shares will be held by other shareholders (i.e. employees). If they leave C's employment, then employees must offer their shares for sale to other employees or C, but C still is not obliged to repurchase the shares. Therefore a body of ex-employee shareholders may in due course develop.

4.5.340.50 In the example in 4.5.340.40 we believe that there is not sufficient evidence to support a conclusion that it is appropriate to de-link the buy-back arrangement from the terms of the share-based payment arrangement. Therefore, considering the proposed buy-back arrangement as a shareholder arrangement rather than a term of the employee share-based payment is not appropriate because there is no body of existing shareholders outside the employee pool to demonstrate that the buy-back arrangement relates other than to employees who receive shares in their role as employees. In our view, the possible future development of a substantial external shareholding body should not be anticipated and the share-based payment should be classified following the requirements for share-based payment transactions in which the entity has the choice of settlement (see 4.5.650).

4.5.350 *Contingently cash-settleable equity instruments*

IAS 37.14   4.5.350.10 While the share-based payment standard provides guidance regarding the classification of share-based payments that are cash-settleable by the entity, it does not provide guidance regarding the classification of a share-based payment in which equity instruments are cash-settleable only upon the occurrence of a contingent event. In our view, if an entity issues a share-based payment that is contingently cash-settleable and the contingency is not within the control of the issuer or the counterparty, then it should determine whether to classify the share-based payment as cash or equity settled based on the liability recognition criteria of IAS 37. This is because IFRS 2 does not base classification solely on the legal right to avoid cash payment; for example, the standard also considers the intended manner of settlement. Therefore, in respect of contingently cash-settleable share-based payment arrangements, we believe that an entity is not required to analogise to the guidance in IAS 32 on the classification of instruments as a liability or equity.

4.5.350.20 Based on the classification guidance in IAS 37, we believe that when determining whether a liability to the employee exists, the contingent feature would affect the classification only if the contingent event is probable, i.e. more likely than not (see 3.12.30.10). If the event's likelihood of occurrence is less than probable and the share-based payment otherwise would be classified as equity settled, then we believe that it should be classified as equity settled. In our view, after initial classification the entity should reassess at each reporting date the probability of cash outflow in order to determine whether the share-based payment is equity or cash settled. The accounting should be adjusted, if necessary, and the principles for modifications that change the classification of an arrangement should be applied (see 4.5.760).

4.5.350.30 A further issue arises when the contingent event is a change in the control of the entity. Often a change in control requires approval of the entity's board and/ or the shareholders. Generally IFRS 2 regards shareholders as part of the entity, such as when it requires attribution to the entity of equity-settled grants made directly by the shareholders (see 4.5.840). Therefore the shareholders of an entity generally are regarded as part of the entity for the purposes of the standard, unless it is clear that they are acting as an investor and not on behalf of the entity. In our view, in respect of a change in control, shareholders should be regarded as separate from the entity since generally they make decisions regarding whether to sell or retain their shares as investors based on the terms offered. Therefore we believe that a change in control would not be regarded as an event within the control of the entity and should be considered a contingent event. This is consistent with our view on the impact of a change in control clause of a financial instrument as debt or equity under the financial instruments standards (see 3.11.240.10).

4.5.350.40 For example, on 1 January 2010 Company K issues share options to employees that vest after three years of service; the options are exercisable until 31 December 2014. If there is a change in control of K prior to 31 December 2014, then K must settle the share options in cash at their fair value at that date. Based on the approach described in 4.5.350.30, this share option is not cash-settleable at the option of the entity but is a contingently cash-settleable option that would be recognised as an equity-settled share-based payment unless it becomes probable that there would be a change in control of K prior to 31 December 2014.

4.5.360 *Arrangements denominated in a currency other than the issuing entity's functional currency*

4.5.360.10 There is no specific guidance on the classification of share-based payment arrangements that are denominated in a currency other than the issuing entity's functional currency. For example, shares of Company C are traded and quoted in euro, which also is C's functional and presentation currency. C issues options on its shares to employees of its US subsidiary with a fixed exercise price that is denominated in US dollars. As the functional currency of C is the euro but the exercise price is denominated in US dollars, C will receive a variable amount of cash upon exercise of the options for a fixed number of shares. Under IAS 32, contracts that will be settled by an entity by delivering a fixed number of its own equity instruments for a variable amount of cash are classified as financial liabilities (see 3.11.65.40). In the absence of specific guidance in IFRS 2, the question arises as to whether the classification of the share-based payment should be consistent with that which would be required under the financial instruments standards. In our view, classification under IFRS 2 should be based on what consideration the entity is providing to its employees (see 4.5.300.20, 310.10 and 310.20). As C is providing equity instruments to employees in exchange for services, we believe that the arrangement should be classified as equity settled. As there are a number of identified differences between the share-based payments standard and the financial instruments standards, we do not believe that an analogy to the financial instruments standards is required in respect of these arrangements.

4.5.360.20 In our view, in determining the grant-date fair value of the foreign currency denominated option, the exercise price should be translated into the entity's functional currency at the exchange rate on that date (euro). We believe that the grant-date fair value should not be remeasured for subsequent changes in exchange rates.

4.5.370 **Equity-settled transactions with employees**

4.5.380 *Classification of conditions*

IFRS 2.IG4A, IG24 4.5.380.10 Conditions that determine whether the counterparty receives the share-based payment are separated into vesting conditions and non-vesting conditions. Vesting conditions are all conditions that determine whether the entity receives the services that entitle the counterparty to the share-based payment, and may be differentiated further between service or performance conditions. Performance conditions are either market conditions or non-market performance conditions. All other conditions are considered non-vesting conditions.

Conditions that determine whether the entity receives the services that entitle the counterparty to the share-based payment:			Conditions that do not determine whether the entity receives the services that entitle the counterparty to the share-based payment:		
Vesting conditions			Non-vesting conditions		
Service conditions	Performance conditions		Conditions that the entity can choose to meet	Conditions that the counterparty can choose to meet	Conditions that neither of the parties can choose to meet
	Market conditions	Non-market performance conditions			

IFRS 2.A   4.5.380.20 Service conditions require the counterparty to complete a specified period of service.

IFRS 2.A   4.5.380.30 Performance conditions require the counterparty to meet specified performance targets in addition to completing a specified period of service, i.e. they must include a service condition. Performance conditions are either market conditions or non-market performance conditions:

- *Market conditions.* Vesting or exercisability of an equity instrument is related to the market price of the entity's equity instruments, the market price of the entity's equity instruments relative to a stock-exchange index or an index of market prices of equity instruments of other entities. Examples of market conditions include a specific share price or total shareholder return, measured based on the share price of an entity as adjusted for the reinvestment of dividends, or based on the share price of an entity relative to a stock-exchange index.
- *Non-market performance conditions.* Vesting or exercisability of an equity instrument is related to specific performance targets unrelated to the market price, e.g. a specified increase in profit or an earnings per share (EPS) target.

IFRS 2.BC   4.5.380.40 There are three types of non-vesting conditions:
171B, IG24

- Non-vesting conditions that the entity can choose to meet, e.g. continuation of the plan by the entity.
- Non-vesting conditions that the counterparty can choose to meet, e.g. participation in a share purchase programme by paying monthly contributions or transfer restrictions after vesting.
- Non-vesting conditions that neither the entity nor the counterparty can choose to meet, e.g. an award can be exercised only when the price of gold does not exceed a specified price.

4.5.380.50 See 4.5.470 for a discussion of the impact of non-vesting conditions on recognition and measurement of share-based payments.

1136

4.5.390 *Classification of conditions in practice*

4.5.400 *Initial public offerings (IPOs)*

IFRS 2.IGEx2   4.5.400.10 The requirement for an IPO affects share-based payment in different ways depending upon how the IPO condition is expressed. If the IPO condition is required to occur during the service period, then it would be a performance condition. For example, a grant of share options has a three-year service condition. However, the options cannot be exercised until an IPO occurs. If employees leaving the entity after the service period but before the IPO retain the options, then in our view the condition of an IPO is not a vesting condition. In another example, if the options do not vest until an IPO occurs and employees leaving before the IPO forfeit the options, then in our view this effectively is an award that contains both a service condition and a non-market performance condition, assuming that there is no minimum IPO price. Such an arrangement should be accounted for as a grant with a variable vesting period (i.e. the length of the vesting period varies depending on when a performance condition is satisfied, see 4.5.460) based on a non-market performance condition. Accordingly, the condition would not be reflected in the grant-date measurement of fair value and the cost would be recognised over the expected vesting period and trued up to the actual vesting period and the actual number of equity instruments granted. However, if the expected IPO condition influences the length of the estimated vesting period, then it might affect inputs in measuring the grant-date fair value, e.g. interest rate. If there is a minimum IPO price, then it is necessary to consider whether the IPO is a market condition (see 4.5.380.30).

4.5.400.20 If the arrangement is accounted for as a grant with a variable vesting period, then the entity estimates at grant date whether the employees will complete the requisite service period and the IPO will occur. In our view, the entity would recognise a share-based payment when it believes the IPO to be more likely than not and the employees are expected to remain in employment until the IPO occurs. For example, if the entity expects at grant date that the IPO is not likely to occur within the next nine years, which is the maximum length of the vesting period, then no cost is recognised until the IPO is expected to be more likely than not.

4.5.410 *Cap in exercisability*

IFRS 2.A   4.5.410.10 The exercisability of a share-based payment may be limited to a cap. For example, an employee is granted 1,000 share options with an exercise price of 10 per option. The employee may exercise the options at the end of the year subject to a service condition and a cap that depends on the employee's salary and the profit realised per option. If, for example, the limit is that the intrinsic value on exercise cannot exceed annual salary and the share price at exercise date is 60 and the employee's salary is 10,000, then the cap limits the number of exercisable options to 200 (10,000 salary divided by a profit of 50 per option): the remaining options lapse. In our view, in a case in which the cap reduces the number of exercisable options when the share price increases, the cap meets the definition of a market condition rather than a non-vesting condition. This is because it is a condition upon which the exercise price, vesting or the exercisability of an equity instrument depends that is related to the market price of the equity instrument, even though usually market conditions are designed to reward, rather than penalise, increases in share price.

4.5.420 *Recognition*

IFRS 2.14   4.5.420.10 If the employee is not required to satisfy a specified vesting condition before becoming unconditionally entitled to the instruments granted, then the equity instruments vest immediately. Therefore there is a presumption that the services rendered as consideration for these instruments have been received and the fair value of these instruments is recognised immediately with a corresponding increase in equity.

IFRS 2.15,   4.5.420.20 If the equity instruments do not vest until the employee completes a period
IGEx1, IGEx2,   of service, then the entity presumes that services are to be provided in the future. The
IGEx5, IGEx6   entity accounts for the services as they are received during the vesting period.

IFRS 2.15,   4.5.420.30 When allocating the cost of share-based payment awards that require the
BC38   achievement of both service and performance conditions (see 4.5.380.30), in our view generally no greater significance should be placed on either the performance or the service condition and the share-based payment cost should be recognised on a straight-line basis over the vesting period. Similar to the observation that generally it is not possible to identify the services received in respect of the individual components of an employee's remuneration package (e.g. services received in respect of healthcare benefits vs a company car vs share-based payment arrangements), it is very difficult to determine whether more services were received in respect of any given performance period as compared to the service period. Therefore, we believe that even if a grant is subject to a four-year service condition and a challenging one-year performance condition, both beginning at the same time, e.g. increase in revenues by 20 percent while revenues have not increased by more than 10 percent over the last five years, this is not sufficiently compelling evidence to apply a method other than the straight-line method over four years.

4.5.420.40 In another example, Company S issues to its employees share options that vest upon the achievement of an EPS target after one year. In addition, the employee must remain employed with S for another two years after the EPS target is achieved. We believe that S should recognise the share-based payment cost on a straight-line basis over the three-year period in the absence of compelling evidence that a different recognition pattern is appropriate.

4.5.430 *Modified grant-date method*

IFRS 2.19-21,   4.5.430.10 The modified grant-date method is used to recognise and measure equity-
IG9   settled share-based payment transactions. Under this method the fair value of the equity instruments is measured at grant date, with some true up (adjustment) for instruments that do not vest (commonly known as "forfeiture").

IFRS 2.2A,   4.5.430.20 The modified grant-date method requires entities to distinguish between the
19-21A, IG9   following types of conditions:

- vesting conditions
  - service conditions
  - performance conditions
    - market conditions
    - non-market performance conditions
- non-vesting conditions.

4.5.430.30 See 4.5.380 for further details regarding the definition and classification of conditions.

4.5.430.40 The following diagram provides a simplified overview of the treatment of different types of conditions in the modified grant-date method:

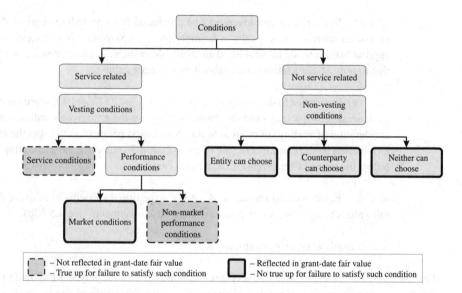

IFRS 2.21 4.5.430.50 Market conditions are reflected as an adjustment (discount) to the initial estimate of fair value at grant date of the instrument to be received and there is no true up for differences between estimated and actual vesting due to market conditions. The same applies to non-vesting conditions, which are discussed in more detail in 4.5.470.

IFRS 2.20 4.5.430.60 The impact of service conditions and non-market performance conditions on vesting is estimated at grant date, but it is not reflected in the grant-date fair value itself. Instead, the accounting for the share-based payment is based on the number of equity instruments for which the service and non-market performance conditions are expected to be met. Subsequently these estimates are trued up for differences between the number of instruments expected to vest and the actual number of instruments vested. There is no true up for options that are forfeited because they vest but are not exercised.

4.5.430.70 Under the modified grant-date approach, estimated share-based payment cost is trued up for forfeiture due to an employee failing to provide service. When an employee resigns before the end of the vesting period, the requested services have not been rendered and the termination is treated as a forfeiture. However, the standard is not explicit regarding whether forfeiture applies when an employer terminates services of the employee and therefore prevents the required service from being provided. In our view, there are two acceptable approaches:

- treat as a forfeiture as the employer has not received the agreed services; or
- treat as a cancellation as it is the employer who is precluding the service from being provided; see 4.5.800 for the accounting consequences of cancellations.

4.5.430.75 We prefer to treat a failure to provide service triggered by termination by the employer as a forfeiture.

4.5.430.80 Similarly, an employee may be precluded from providing services due to a sale of an operation that results in termination of employment. In our view, the same approaches discussed in 4.5.430.70 are available in such circumstances, i.e. we believe that treatment as forfeiture or as cancellation is acceptable.

4.5.430.85 In contrast to the situations addressed in 4.5.430.70 and 80, share-based payment arrangements may contain clauses setting out the employee's entitlement (e.g. acceleration of vesting) in relation to the share-based payment in the specific event of termination by the employer or sale of an operation. In our view, the accounting should reflect the terms of the arrangement in such cases.

4.5.430.90 Equity-settled transactions are not remeasured subsequent to grant date for fair value changes, unlike cash-settled share-based payments (see 4.5.630).

4.5.435 *Implicit service condition*

IFRS 2.A, 4.5.435.10 The definition of a service condition is that the employee is required to deliver
BC171A a specified period of service. However, the service requirement can be implicit rather than explicit.

4.5.435.20 Even if a share-based payment arrangement does not contain an explicit requirement to provide services and also does not contain an explicit leaver clause (i.e. a clause that specifies whether the employee retains their entitlement after they leave the entity), the arrangement still may contain a service condition, i.e. an implicit service condition. All terms and conditions of a share-based payment arrangement are considered for an assessment of whether the arrangement contains an implicit service condition. If the employee can benefit from the fair value increases only by remaining employed, then in our view there is an implicit service condition embedded in the share-based payment.

4.5.440 *Multiple vesting conditions*

4.5.440.10 The standard provides examples in which share-based payments are subject to a single performance condition, i.e. a service requirement and one performance target.

Examples in which a share-based payment is subject to two performance conditions are not included. In practice, it is not unusual for a share-based payment arrangement to contain two performance conditions, often one market condition and one non-market performance condition. In some cases, both conditions need to be satisfied ("and" conditions); in other cases only one condition needs to be satisfied ("or" conditions).

4.5.443 Multiple cumulative performance conditions ("and" conditions)

4.5.443.10 In our view, in a share-based payment subject to both market and non-market performance conditions, the grant-date fair value used to measure the share-based payment should reflect the probability of not achieving the market condition.

4.5.443.20 In our view, if the non-market performance condition is not satisfied, then the entity should true up the cumulative share-based payment cost.

4.5.445 Multiple alternative performance conditions ("or" conditions)

4.5.445.10 Some share-based payment arrangements may require the satisfaction of both a service condition and at least one of two performance conditions, for example, one market condition or one non-market performance condition, in order for the share-based payment arrangement to vest. Such arrangements with multiple vesting conditions sometimes are referred to as containing "multiple interactive vesting conditions". Share-based payment arrangements containing multiple interactive vesting conditions raise complicated accounting issues, as there is limited guidance in relation to grants of share-based payments that combine market and non-market performance conditions.

IFRS 2.15, 21, 4.5.445.20 The implementation guidance in IFRS 2 contains an example of a share-based
IGEx4 payment in which the exercise price varies with a non-market performance condition. This example illustrates that a switching approach should be taken when there are multiple mutually exclusive outcomes in a share-based payment arrangement. In our view, this switching approach should be followed by analogy for a grant with multiple interactive vesting conditions. At grant date the entity should estimate the fair value of the equity instruments for each possible outcome and account for the share-based payment based on the most likely outcome at each reporting date. The following table sets out all the possible outcomes:

Possible outcomes (see 4.5.445.40)	Market condition	Non-market performance condition
Scenario 1	Met	Not met
Scenario 2	Not met	Met
Scenario 3	Not met	Not met
Scenario 4	Met	Met

4.5.445.30 In estimating the fair value for each possible outcome, one fair value ignoring the probability of not achieving the market condition is calculated at grant date for the award assuming that all vesting conditions are met. In the discussion below, this is referred to as the "non-adjusted fair value". That fair value is used, with an adjustment to reflect the probability of not achieving the market condition, to measure the fair value of the award with the market condition; this is referred to below as the "adjusted fair value". The non-adjusted fair value of the award is used to measure the fair value of the award with the non-market performance condition; with regard to the non-market performance condition, the estimate of the number of awards expected to vest is trued up to the actual number of instruments that vest due to the satisfaction of the non-market performance condition (see 4.5.430.60).

4.5.445.40 In our view, the entity should recognise the share-based payment cost based on the fair value of the equity instrument for the most likely outcome over the expected period of the most likely condition. Effectively this means that:

- If vesting is achieved through the market condition only (scenario 1 in 4.5.440.20), then the total cost recognised will be based on the fair value that reflects the grant-date estimate of the probability of achieving (or not achieving) the market condition, i.e. the adjusted fair value.
- If vesting is achieved through the non-market performance condition only (scenario 2 in 4.5.440.20), then the eventual total cost recognised will be based on the fair value related to the non-market performance condition; i.e. the non-adjusted fair value.
- If neither the market nor the non-market performance condition event is achieved (scenario 3 in 4.5.440.20), then we believe that the entity should recognise the share-based payment cost based on the adjusted fair value; i.e. the fair value that was adjusted to reflect the probability of achieving the market condition. This is because there is no "true up" for differences between estimated and actual vesting due to market conditions (see 4.5.430.50).
- If both conditions are met (scenario 4 in 4.5.440.20), then we believe that the share-based payment cost should reflect the grant-date fair value without adjustment to reflect the probability of achieving the market condition. This is because we believe that, when both conditions are met, the share-based payment cost should not ignore the non-market fair value increment.

4.5.448 Separate grants

IFRS 2.IG11   4.5.448.10 A share-based payment arrangement may include several awards that should be accounted for separately. For example, a grant may contain one award that grants shares that vest subject to a one-year service condition and a market condition, and another award that grants shares that vest subject to a one-year service condition and a non-market performance condition. In our view, these two awards should be accounted for as separate share-based payments since their vesting is not interdependent. See also 4.5.600.60 for a discussion of the treatment of dividends when vesting terms differ from the terms of the related share-based payment.

4.5.450 [Not used]

4.5.460 *Market condition with variable vesting period*

IFRS 2.15(b),   4.5.460.10 In some share-based payment arrangements the length of the vesting period
IGEx6   needs to be estimated. For example, a share-based payment is subject to the condition
that the employee remains in service until the share price achieves a certain target
price at any time within the next five years. If the entity estimates that it will be met
at the end of year 3, then the grant-date fair value is recognised over three years. The
standard prohibits a subsequent revision of the expected length of the vesting period if
the performance condition is a market condition. Therefore, in this scenario the entire
grant-date fair value of the equity instruments granted is recognised in years 1 to 3, even
if at the end of year 3 the market condition is not met.

4.5.460.20 Continuing the example in 4.5.460.10, it is unclear how to account for the reverse scenario, i.e. when the market condition is met earlier than expected. If the market
condition is met in year 2, then in theory all the expected services have been provided.
Therefore it could be argued that no cost should be recognised subsequent to that date,
and that instead recognition should accelerate at that date. In our view, the standard's
explicit prohibition of revising the length of the vesting period should prevail, i.e. cost
should continue to be recognised in accordance with the original three-year estimate,
even though we believe that accelerated recognition would better reflect the economics
of the scenario.

4.5.470 *Non-vesting conditions*

IFRS 2.21A,   4.5.470.10 Like market conditions, non-vesting conditions (see 4.5.380.40) are reflected
IG24   in measuring the grant-date fair value of the share-based payment and there is no true up
for differences between expected and actual outcome of non-vesting conditions. Therefore, if all service and non-market performance conditions are met, then the entity will
recognise the share-based payment as a cost even if the counterparty does not receive
the share-based payment due to a failure to meet a non-vesting condition.

4.5.470.20 When either the entity or the counterparty can choose whether to meet a non-
vesting condition and one chooses not to do so during the vesting period, the failure
to meet the condition is treated as a cancellation. Under cancellation accounting, the
amount of the cost that otherwise would have been recognised over the remainder of
the vesting period is recognised immediately in profit or loss (see 4.5.800).

4.5.470.30 For example, when an employee stops contributing to a share purchase plan
by monthly deductions from salary (i.e. the counterparty chooses not to meet a non-
vesting condition), then the unrecognised amount of the grant-date fair value of the
equity instruments granted is recognised immediately (see 4.5.530 for a discussion of
whether a plan is an ESPP or an option plan).

4.5.470.40 When neither the entity nor the counterparty can choose whether to meet a
non-vesting condition, there is no change to the accounting if the non-vesting condition
is not satisfied, and the entity recognises the compensation cost over the vesting period.

4.5 Share-based payments

4.5.480 Determination of grant date

IFRS 2.11 4.5.480.10 The determination of grant date is important since this is the date at which the fair value of equity instruments granted is measured. Usually the grant date also is the date when recognition of the employee services received begins. However, this is not always the case (see 4.5.510.20).

IFRS 2.A 4.5.480.20 Grant date is the date at which the entity and the employee agree to a share-based payment arrangement, and requires that the entity and the employee have a shared understanding of the terms and conditions of the arrangement. If the agreement is subject to an approval process, then grant date cannot be before that approval is obtained. When a grant is made subject to approval, for example by a board of directors, grant date normally is when that approval is obtained.

4.5.490 Meaning of "agreement"

IFRS 2.16, IG2 4.5.490.10 In order for the employer and the employee to *agree* to a share-based payment transaction, there must be both an offer and an acceptance of that offer. The grant date is not reached until there is acceptance of the offer. The acceptance may be explicit (e.g. by signing a contract) or implicit (e.g. by commencing to render services).

4.5.490.20 For example, Company Q establishes a three-year share-based payment arrangement in which an employee must specify a monthly deduction percentage from their salary for buying shares at the then-current fair value (participation shares). For each participation share, the employee will receive an additional free share (matching share). Employees can state their monthly deduction in January 2010 for the entire three-year period, i.e. January 2010 to December 2012. An employee is required to make an explicit annual statement in January of each year in which they confirm the deduction percentage or amount. New joiners to the company can participate in the plan from the beginning of the next calendar year. The employee also has the right to reduce the monthly deductions at any time. If, for example, an employee stops the deductions from May 2010 onwards, then they will not lose entitlement to the matching shares received previously; however, they cannot increase the deduction amount subsequently during 2010. The employee can rejoin in January 2011 or January 2012 by stating a new monthly deduction percentage. In our view, in this example, the statement of the deduction or investment amount is a required explicit acceptance. Therefore, we believe that grant date for the share-based payment of the matching shares could not be earlier than January each year as it is the date on which both parties agree to the arrangement.

4.5.490.25 In our view, 1 January each year is a new grant date in the example in 4.5.490.20 as employees may increase or decrease their contributions and new employees are permitted to join at that date. In our view, in this example, there is only one grant date per year since we believe that an ability to reduce but not increase contributions does not create new acceptance at each monthly purchase date of participation shares. This is because the absence of a reduction is not an implicit acceptance, and an explicit acceptance already has been made. We believe that the ability to reduce or stop deductions entirely is a cancellation right rather than an indication of a separate grant date because it is a one directional change.

4.5.490.30 In a broad-based unilateral grant of a share-based payment, often there is a period of time between board approval and communication of the terms of the award to individual employees. In some entities the terms and conditions of the awards are communicated to each employee by their direct supervisor. Due to the varying schedules of employees and employers, it is possible that different employees may be informed of their awards on different dates. In some circumstances the number and geographic dispersion of employees results in communication spanning several days or weeks. As a result, awards approved at a single board meeting may be subject to several different grant dates. However, using a single grant date for the purposes of valuing share-based payment transactions with the same terms that are granted at approximately the same date may not result in a material difference from the aggregate fair value that otherwise would be determined on the grant date of each individual award.

4.5.490.40 For example, each year on the first day of the year, multinational Company X issues share options to all employees who were employed by X for the three months prior to the end of the previous year. The number of options that each employee receives is based on their employee class and is a set amount each year. The exercise price of the share options always is 10 percent less than the market price on the day that the share plan is approved by the Board, which is on the first day of the year. X's human resources policy requires that remuneration information be communicated to employees by their immediate superiors; once the share plan has been approved by the Board, the immediate superior of each employee is responsible for communicating the grant to the employee. On the day after the share plan was approved, X placed information regarding the share plan on the employee website. In our view, grant date is the board approval date since the award is unilateral, communication to employees is purely administrative and soon after the board meeting X issues an entity-wide communication regarding the grant of the award, including the specific terms and conditions.

IU 05-06 4.5.490.50 A shared understanding may not require finalisation of all terms and conditions. For example, an offer may not specify the actual exercise price, but instead will state the formula that determines how the actual exercise price will be established. In our view, when the outcome is based on *objective* factors and different knowledgeable parties, independently of each other, would be able to make consistent calculations, then there is a shared understanding without having specified the actual grant terms. If, for example, the exercise price is based on the market price at a specified later date but the outcome of all other factors is known already, then there is a shared understanding at the date of the agreement of the way in which the exercise price will be determined.

4.5.490.60 In our view, generally there will not be agreement on terms and conditions if the outcome is based primarily on *subjective* factors, for example if the number of shares to be awarded is a discretionary determination of a compensation committee at the end of the service period. Similarly, if the number of instruments issued to employees is determined based primarily on a subjective evaluation of the individual's performance over a period, then we believe that there is not a shared understanding until the number of instruments has been determined. The assessment of whether or not the evaluation of an individual's performance is primarily subjective may be difficult and requires judgement.

4.5.490.70 The determination of grant date can be illustrated as follows:

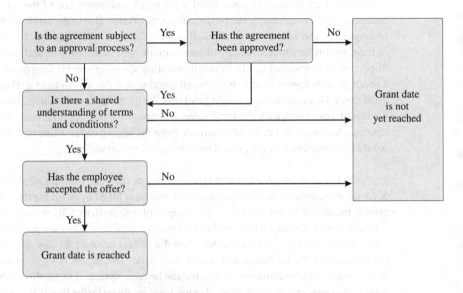

4.5.500 Discretion clauses

4.5.500.10 Some share-based payment arrangements may provide a remuneration committee (or an equivalent) with differing degrees of discretion to amend the terms of awards. If a share-based payment arrangement contains a "discretion clause", then it is necessary to consider the impact of the discretion clause on the determination of the grant date of the share-based payment (see 4.5.480), and whether modification accounting should be applied if discretion is exercised after grant date. In our view, when the terms of a share-based payment arrangement provide the remuneration committee with discretion to amend the terms of an award, a determination as to whether there is a shared understanding with employees should be based on an analysis of the degree of subjectivity (i.e. discretion) afforded the remuneration committee, as well as the factors over which the remuneration committee has discretion.

4.5.500.15 We believe that arrangements with discretion clauses should be categorised into the following three categories (referred to as "buckets") depending on the degree of discretion available to the remuneration committee:

4.5.503 Delayed grant date ("bucket 1")

4.5.503.10 If the discretion clause provides the remuneration committee with significant subjectivity such that there is no shared understanding of the terms and conditions prior to finalisation of the award, then grant date is not achieved until the period for exercising the discretion has passed. In our view, clauses that would be invoked only "with cause" or in exceptional circumstances generally would not delay grant date. For example, a clause that is intended to be invoked with cause may be in relation to a specific employee action or an event that was not anticipated when the original performance condition was set, such as adjusting a revenue performance condition upon the disposal of a significant business unit.

4.5.503.20 If an entity has the discretion to reduce or eliminate an award, then we believe that this will delay grant date. However, this does not result in delaying recognition for the share-based payment (see 4.5.510.20).

4.5.505 No delay to grant date, no modification ("bucket 2")

4.5.505.10 Arrangements may contain clauses that largely are objective such that these may give little, if any, discretion to either the employee or the remuneration committee. In our view, such clauses that largely are objective do not result in a delay in grant date. In our view, subsequent invocation of the clause does not result in modification accounting if the changes are for predetermined adjustments (see 4.5.508.10). Examples of predetermined adjustments are changes in the exercise price of options to reflect changes in capital structures such as share splits or the recalculation of performance requirements.

4.5.505.20 If the discretion clause does not result in a delay in grant date, then it is necessary to consider whether invocation of the clause would result in modification accounting (see 4.5.690).

4.5.508 No delay to grant date, modification ("bucket 3")

4.5.508.10 In our view, modification accounting should be applied if a discretion clause is invoked and results in changes other than predetermined adjustments.

4.5.510 *Determination of vesting period*

IFRS 2.A   4.5.510.10 The vesting period is the period during which all the specified vesting conditions are to be satisfied in order for the employees to be entitled unconditionally to the equity instrument. Normally this is the period between the grant date and the vesting date.

IFRS 2.IG4   4.5.510.20 However, services should be recognised when received and the grant date may occur after the employees have begun rendering services. Grant date is a measurement date only. When the grant date occurs *after* the service commencement date, the entity estimates the grant-date fair value of the equity instruments for the purpose of recognising the services from service commencement date until grant date. A possible method of estimating the fair value of the equity instruments is by assuming that grant date is at the end of the reporting period. Once the grant date has been established, the entity revises the earlier estimates so that the amounts recognised for services received are based on the grant-date fair value of the equity instruments. In our view, this revision is treated as a change in estimate (see 2.8.60).

4.5.520 *Graded vesting*

IFRS 2.IG11   4.5.520.10 In some situations the equity instruments granted vest in instalments over the specified vesting period (e.g. 100 options are granted and 25 options vest each year over the following four years). Assuming that the only vesting condition is service from the grant date to the vesting date of each tranche of 25 options, each instalment is accounted for as a separate share-based payment arrangement (i.e. four separate option grants with one-, two-, three- and four-year vesting periods, respectively). As a result, even though all four grants are measured at the same grant date, there will be four fair values and the total cost recognised each year will be different as both the fair value and the vesting periods are different.

4.5.530 *Determination of the type of equity instruments granted*

IFRS 2.IG17   4.5.530.10 In an ESPP the employees usually are entitled to purchase shares at a discounted price. The terms and conditions can vary significantly and some ESPPs include option features.

4.5.530.20 Determining whether a plan is a true ESPP or an option plan affects the determination of the grant date, the number of instruments to account for and the measurement of the grant-date fair value. For example, on 1 January 2010 Company T grants the right to purchase shares at a 20 percent discount to its share price. This grant is made to 1,000 of its employees; 700 employees purchase shares. If the substance of the offer is an ESPP, then grant date is the date when the employees accept the offer (e.g. February 2010) and recognition is based on the 700 employees accepting the offer. However, if, in an alternative scenario, the substance of the offer is an option grant, then grant date is not dependent on the explicit acceptance by the employees and therefore is already achieved on 1 January 2010. Recognition is based on the "option" instruments granted to the 1,000 employees and not on the 700 employees that exercise their options (e.g. at the end of a two-year vesting period).

4.5.530.30 In our view, the predominant feature of the share-based payment arrangement determines the accounting for the entire fair value of the grant. That is, depending on the predominant features a share purchase plan is either a true ESPP or an option plan. All terms and conditions of the arrangement should be considered when determining the type of equity instruments granted and judgement is required.

IFRS 2.B1-   4.5.530.40 Options are characterised by the *right*, but not the *obligation*, to purchase a
B41   share at a fixed price. An option has a value (i.e. the option premium) since the option holder has the benefit of any future gains and has none of the risks of loss beyond any option premium paid. The value of an option is determined in part by its duration and by the expected volatility of the share price during the term of the option. In our view, the principal characteristic of an ESPP is the right to buy shares at a discount to current

market prices. ESPPs that grant short-term fixed purchase prices do not have significant option characteristics since they do not allow the grant holder to benefit from volatility. We believe that ESPPs that provide a longer-term option to purchase shares at a fixed price are, in substance, option agreements, and should be accounted for as options.

4.5.530.50 For example, employees are entitled to purchase shares at a fixed price from the date of communication of the plan until two years later. Whether the predominant feature in this agreement is the option feature requires judgement based on all of the terms and conditions of the plan. In the absence of other indicators we believe that this effectively is an option and should be accounted for as an option plan and not as an ESPP.

4.5.540 *Share purchases funded through loans*

4.5.540.10 Share purchase arrangements can be structured in many different ways and all terms and conditions should be analysed when determining the type of equity instruments granted. Consider the following example of a share-based payment arrangement that is structured as a share purchase arrangement:

- The employees received a right to and did purchase shares immediately.
- At the same time, the employees received a loan for the amount of the exercise price. The loan accrues interest at a market rate.
- The employees receive a right to settle the loan in full by tendering the shares purchased either directly or via a right to put the shares back at original purchase price plus market interest.

4.5.540.20 In the example in 4.5.540.10, the put option feature on the shares removes any risk for the employee for share price decreases while all rewards above the market rate of interest are retained. In our view, this plan is, in substance, an option and the transaction should be accounted for as such. In general we believe that it is difficult to support recognition of shares and the loan as outstanding when the shares were paid for by a loan from the issuer to the buyer. If the substance of a share purchase arrangement is an option, then neither the shares nor the loan are outstanding until the options are exercised by paying the exercise price for the shares or the put option expires. Accordingly, until exercise of the options, the shares issued to employees are treated as treasury shares and no loan receivable from the employees is recognised until this time.

IU 11-05 4.5.540.30 In our view, in assessing whether shares paid for by a loan from the issuer are in substance a grant of options, an entity should consider whether it has full recourse to the employees in respect of the balance of the loan. For example, if the share price falls below the outstanding balance of the loan, then does the entity have recourse to the personal assets of the employee, and will it pursue collection of the full loan balance? We believe that it is appropriate to account for the transaction as the issue of shares and a loan receivable only when it can be demonstrated clearly that the entity has and will pursue full recourse to the employees in respect of the loan.

4.5.540.40 [Not used]

4.5.540.50 Whether the entity has full recourse to the employees in respect of the loan should be assessed based on all of the terms and conditions of the arrangement. In our view, in order for the loan to be considered full recourse, it should be documented as a full recourse loan and there should be no evidence that would indicate otherwise, for example a past history of the entity waiving all or a portion of similar loans. The following are examples of indicators that may support the conclusion that a loan is full recourse:

- The loan is reported by the entity to a credit agency in the same manner as commercial loans.
- The entity requests financial information from the employee in order to assess their ability to repay the loan.
- The entity has an ongoing process for monitoring the collectibility of the loan.
- If applicable, the entity has a past history of collection in full of other employee loans (e.g. housing loans).

4.5.540.55 For example, Company C issues shares to its employees at the market price on the date of issue and the purchases are funded through a loan provided by the entity to its employees. C has recourse to all of the employees' assets and not just the shares purchased with the loan. If C achieves a two-year cumulative EPS growth target of 15 percent, then 25 percent of the loan balance will be waived, i.e. the share purchase price will be reduced retrospectively by 25 percent. C has the intent and ability to pursue full collection of the outstanding loan balance and a past practice of collecting loans from employees.

IFRS 2.IGEx4 4.5.540.60 In the example in 4.5.540.55 we believe that the arrangement is an issue of shares and a loan (e.g. the loan is full recourse and therefore the arrangement is not in substance an option grant but rather should be treated as a share purchase). The employee may earn a discount to the share price subject to the achievement of a non-market performance condition. This is because the employee receives a waiver of 25 percent of the share price if a cumulative EPS target is met. In our view, the potential retrospective adjustment to the share purchase price is a share-based payment and not an employee benefit under IAS 19. This is consistent with the example in IFRS 2 of a reduction in the exercise price of an option as a result of achieving a non-market performance condition, i.e. the shares ultimately can be purchased by the employees at a discount from the purchase price specified originally.

4.5.540.70 We believe that, as the employee receives equity instruments (i.e. shares that may be purchased at a discount) and does not receive a payment based on the price (or value) of the entity's shares or other equity instruments, the share-based payment in the example in 4.5.540.60 should be classified as equity settled (see 4.5.530.30).

4.5.540.80 In our view, since the structure in 4.5.540.60 is viewed as a share purchase, the loan receivable should be accounted for separately from the share-based payment and should be recognised and measured in accordance with the financial instruments standards. Under those standards, the initial and subsequent measurement of the loan should reflect the likelihood of the employee receiving a discount as a result of the achievement of the non-market performance condition (see 3.6.730 and 4.4.80).

4.5.540.90 If the loan issued to the employee does not bear interest at a market rate, then in our view the low-interest loan is a benefit conveyed to the employees that could be accounted for in accordance with the share-based payment standard. Alternatively, the discount may be accounted for as an employee benefit (see 4.4.80). We prefer for the low-interest loan to be accounted for as a share-based payment when the low or interest-free loan is granted only to finance a share purchase and otherwise would not be available to the employee.

4.5.540.100 In other arrangements a share purchase by employees may be funded only partially through a loan from the entity, e.g. the entity issues a loan to employees for 70 percent of the market price of its shares and the employee is required to pay in cash the remaining 30 percent of the purchase price. The entity has recourse only to the shares and the employees receive a right to settle the loan by tendering the shares purchased either directly or via a right to put the shares back to the entity. If the market price of the shares is less than the amount of the loan when the shares are to be tendered to the entity, then the entity receives the shares as settlement of the loan in full, i.e. the entity accepts the risk that its share price will decrease by greater than 30 percent. If the cash payment by the employee represents substantially all of the reasonably possible loss based on the expected volatility of the shares, then in our view the fact that the loan is recourse only to the shares does not preclude accounting for the transaction as the issuance of shares and a loan. This is because, subsequent to the date of issuance, the employee is not only able to benefit from increases in the entity's share price but also is at risk for substantially all of the reasonably possible decreases in the share price.

4.5.545 Accounting for interest and dividends in a grant of share options

4.5.545.10 As a consequence of treating a share purchase funded through a non-full recourse loan as an option, an issue arises as to how to account for the share purchase, the loan issued, any interest on the loan and any dividends on the shares.

4.5.545.20 In our view, the share purchase, loan issue, interest and dividends should be accounted for in accordance with the substance of the arrangement. If the share purchase funded through a non-full recourse loan is in substance a share option, then we believe that neither the loan nor the shares should be recognised as outstanding and the repayment of the loan by the employee should be treated as the payment of the exercise price.

4.5.545.30 Consequently, we believe that interest is not accrued over the vesting period but recognised only as part of the exercise price when received. Interest therefore decreases the grant-date fair value of the option due to an increased exercise price. The right to receive dividends also should be taken into account in estimating the grant-date fair value of the option (see 4.5.600.40), i.e. the entitlement increases the grant-date fair value compared to an option without dividend entitlement.

4.5.545.40 However, we believe that forfeitable dividends declared but not paid out before exercise of the option should be recognised only when the loan amount, reduced for the dividends declared, becomes a recognised receivable upon exercise. This is because the obligation to pay the dividends only reduces the unrecognised receivable due from the employee rather than being a liability in its own right; this treatment is different to dividends declared on unvested shares (see 4.5.600.80). In our view, the entity should choose an accounting policy upon exercise, to be applied consistently, between recognising the dividends by netting the amount with the proceeds from the exercise price or by recognising a separate distribution in equity.

4.5.550 *Free shares*

4.5.550.10 In some share-based payment arrangements, employees are entitled to shares for no cash consideration; however, the grant is conditional upon the fulfilment of specified vesting conditions. When the holders of such shares have the same rights as holders of shares not subject to a vesting condition, the value of the shares granted is equal to the value of vested shares. However, when the holders of such shares are not entitled to dividends during the vesting period, an adjustment is required for the expected future dividends that will not be received by employees.

4.5.560 **Measurement**

4.5.570 *Determining the fair value of equity instruments granted*

IFRS 2.11   4.5.570.10 Share-based payment transactions with employees are measured by reference to the fair value of the equity instruments granted.

IFRS 2.16, 17   4.5.570.20 The fair value of the equity instruments granted is determined as follows:

- If market prices are available for the equity instruments granted, then the estimate of fair value is based on these market prices.
- If no market prices are available for the equity instruments granted, then the fair value of equity instruments granted is estimated using a *valuation technique*.

4.5.580 No track record of market price

IFRS 2.B4,   4.5.580.10 In many situations a market price for equity instruments (e.g. share options)
B26-B30   will not exist as equity instruments issued to employees often have terms and conditions different from those instruments traded in the market and therefore a valuation technique is used. A valuation technique requires estimation of a number of variables, including the expected future volatility of the entity. In our view, if no equity instruments of the entity are traded, then an implied volatility should be calculated, for example based on

actual experience of similar entities that have traded equity instruments. We believe that an entity, even one without a historical track record (e.g. a newly listed entity), should not estimate its expected volatility at zero. In rare cases an entity may be unable to estimate, at grant date, expected volatility and therefore the fair value of the equity instruments cannot be measured; in such rare cases the use of the intrinsic value may be required (see 4.5.610).

4.5.590 Post-vesting restrictions

IFRS 2.B3,
IU 11-06
4.5.590.10 Post-vesting restrictions are included in the grant-date measurement of fair value to the extent that the restriction affects the price that a knowledgeable, willing market participant would pay for that share. For example, shares are granted to employees conditional on one year of service. After the service period the employees are entitled unconditionally to the shares. However, under the arrangement they are not allowed to sell the shares for a further five-year period. The five-year restriction on the sale of the shares is a post-vesting restriction, which is a non-vesting condition (see 4.5.380.40), and is taken into account in the grant-date fair value measurement.

IFRS 2.B3,
B10, BC168,
IU 11-06
4.5.590.20 In our view, it is not appropriate to determine the fair value of equity instruments, issued only to employees and subject to post-vesting restrictions, based on an approach that looks solely or primarily to an actual or synthetic market consisting only of transactions between an entity and its employees and in which prices, for example, reflect an employee's personal borrowing rate. This is because the objective of IFRS 2 is to estimate the fair value of an equity instrument and not the value from the employee's perspective. We believe that factors that affect only the employee's specific perspective of the value of the equity instruments are not relevant to estimating the price that would be set by a knowledgeable, willing market participant. Therefore hypothetical transactions with actual or potential market participants willing to invest in restricted shares should be considered.

4.5.600 *Dividends*

IFRS 2.B31
4.5.600.10 The treatment of expected dividends in measuring the fair value of the equity instruments depends on whether or not the employee is entitled to dividends.

IFRS 2.B34
4.5.600.20 If the employees are not entitled to dividends declared during the vesting period, then the fair value of these equity instruments is reduced by the present value of dividends expected to be paid compared with the fair value of equity instruments that are entitled to dividends.

IFRS 2.B32
4.5.600.30 If the employees are entitled to dividends declared during the vesting period, then, in our view the accounting treatment depends on whether the dividends are forfeitable, i.e. whether dividends have to be paid back if vesting conditions are not met.

4.5.600.40 We believe that forfeitable dividends should be treated as dividend entitlements during the vesting period. If the vesting conditions are not met, then any true up of the share-based payment would recognise the profit or loss effect of the forfeiture of the dividend automatically because the dividend entitlements are reflected in the grant-date fair value of the award (see 4.5.430 for a discussion of when true up applies).

IFRS 2.B31- B36 4.5.600.45 In our view, two approaches are acceptable in accounting for non-forfeitable dividends.

4.5.600.50 One approach is to treat non-forfeitable dividends as a dividend entitlement during the vesting period when determining the grant-date fair value of the share-based payment. The value of the dividend right is reflected in the grant-date fair value of the share-based payment, and therefore increases the cost of the share-based payment. If the share-based payment does not vest, then in our view the total amount previously recognised as a share-based payment cost should be split into: (a) the value for the non-forfeitable dividends; and (b) the balance of the share-based payment. We believe that only the balance of the share-based payment (the amount excluding the non-forfeitable dividends) would be subject to any true up for failure to satisfy vesting conditions (see 4.5.430.60) in order to reflect the benefit retained by the employee as an expense in the statement of comprehensive income.

4.5.600.60 The other approach is to view non-forfeitable dividends as a payment for services with vesting conditions different from the vesting conditions of the underlying share-based payment. Under this view the dividend rights would be considered to be a benefit (e.g. IAS 19 if employee services) rather than a share-based payment as dividend amounts are unlikely to be based on the price or value of the entity's equity instruments. Accordingly the grant-date fair value of the share-based payment would be lower than under the approach in 4.5.600.50.

4.5.600.65 Since dividends generally are considered to be part of the measurement of grant-date fair value we prefer the approach in 4.5.600.50, i.e. to treat dividend entitlements as part of the share-based payment except if there is evidence that the share component of the transaction is a merely a mechanism to deliver the dividend payments.

4.5.600.70 In our view, regardless of whether the dividends are forfeitable or non-forfeitable, dividends declared during the vesting period should be accounted for in accordance with the requirements of other IFRSs (see 3.11.450), i.e. as a distribution. Therefore neither the declaration nor the payment of the dividends results in additional cost directly because we believe that the recognition of cost for the grant of dividend rights should be considered separately as discussed above. In particular under the approach in 4.5.600.50, if the dividend amounts are retained even when vesting conditions are not met, then we believe that no adjustment of the dividend accounting is necessary since the portion of the share-based payment cost related to the non-forfeitable dividend would not be trued up (see 4.5.600.50).

4.5.600.80 In relation to a grant of shares, in our view dividends that are declared during the vesting period but not paid until vesting also should be charged to equity and recognised as a liability when declared. See 4.5.545 for a discussion of the accounting for dividends declared in relation to a grant of share options.

4.5.600.90 In our view, if the share-based payment, and therefore forfeitable dividends thereon, are forfeited due to failure to satisfy a vesting condition, then the return of dividends or reduction in dividend payable should be accounted for as a transaction with a shareholder, i.e. the return of the dividend or reduction in dividend payable should be recognised directly in equity as an adjustment of previously recognised dividends.

4.5.603 *"Shares to the value of"*

4.5.603.10 When a variable number of equity instruments to the value of a fixed amount is granted, commonly known as shares to the value of, then we believe that such an arrangement is an equity-settled share-based payment (see 4.5.310).

4.5.603.20 A question arises as to the measurement of such a grant when the date of delivery of the shares is in the future because there is a service requirement. In our view, there are two acceptable approaches in respect of measurement:

- as a fixed amount of cash that will be received in the future based on its discounted amount, similar to the net present value of a financial liability; or
- as a grant of free shares that are subject only to a service requirement, i.e. reference to the share price, without discounting, because in contrast to a financial liability there is no outflow of resources.

4.5.603.30 We prefer the grant to be measured on a discounted basis if the payment is due to be settled more than 12 months after the end of the reporting period.

4.5.605 *Market condition and variable number of equity instruments*

4.5.605.10 When the number of equity instruments that vest varies with the achievement of a market condition, it is not possible to value an individual equity instrument granted because the number of instruments that vest depends on the achievement of the market condition and the total value is not a fixed amount. Essentially, the recipient has not received an unvested equity instrument, but a right to receive a variable number of equity instruments, whose number and total value both depend on the outcome of the market condition.

4.5.605.20 In our view, the grant-date fair value of the share-based payment for each right should be valued at its expected value by applying a valuation technique that considers the different possible outcomes, such as binomial or Monte Carlo. We believe that the expected value of the share-based payment per right subsequently should not be adjusted for changes in the share price or related to the market condition because it is a share-based payment with a market condition. Changes due to failure to meet a service condition are trued up as required.

4.5.610 *Intrinsic value*

IFRS 2.24 4.5.610.10 In rare cases, when the fair value of the equity instruments cannot be estimated reliably, an intrinsic value method approach is applied. The intrinsic value is remeasured at each reporting date and changes are recognised in profit or loss until the instrument is settled (e.g. until an option is exercised).

4.5.610.20 For example, in an ESPP in which employees pay a monthly contribution of 100 in order to buy shares at the end of the year at a discount of 20 percent of the then-current market price, there is uncertainty at grant date about what the future market price of those shares will be and accordingly how many shares the employees will be entitled to buy. In our view, uncertainty about the future market price is not a reason for not being able to measure the fair value reliably.

4.5.620 **Presentation in financial statements**

4.5.620.10 IFRS 2 does not address specifically the presentation within equity and whether the credit to equity for share-based payment transactions should be accreted only as employee cost is recognised. Alternatively, at inception of the grant, the effect of an equity-settled share-based payment may be presented gross, in which case the total expected cost is recognised within equity (e.g. share options outstanding) with a corresponding and offsetting debit also recognised in equity for services to be received. As services are rendered and the related costs recognised, the offsetting debit for deferred cost is reduced. In our view, two approaches with respect to presentation within equity are acceptable. We prefer to present only the cumulative cost within equity. However, this approach is not required by IFRSs and we believe that a gross presentation within equity also would be permitted.

4.5.620.20 Except for those share-based payment arrangements in which equity instruments of a subsidiary have been granted (see 4.5.1099), IFRSs do not address whether an increase in equity recognised in connection with a share-based payment transaction should be presented in a separate line item within equity or within retained earnings. In our view, either approach would be allowed under IFRSs.

4.5.630 **Cash-settled transactions with employees**

IFRS 2.30 4.5.630.10 Cash-settled share-based payment transactions result in a liability, generally an obligation to make a cash payment, based on the price of the equity instrument (e.g. share price). For cash-settled share-based payment transactions with employees the services received and the liability incurred are measured initially at the fair value of the liability at grant date, and the liability is remeasured until settlement (see 4.5.630.20). The initial measurement of the liability is recognised over the period that services are rendered.

4.5.630.20 At each reporting date, and ultimately at settlement date, the fair value of the recognised liability is remeasured with any changes in fair value recognised in profit or loss. As described in 4.5.630.10, the grant-date fair value is recognised over the vesting period. Remeasurement applies to the recognised amount through the vesting date. The full amount is remeasured from vesting date to settlement date. The total net cost recognised in respect of the transaction will be the amount paid to settle the liability.

IFRS 2.IG   4.5.630.25 Remeasurements during the vesting period are recognised immediately to the
Ex12   extent that they relate to past services and spread over the remaining vesting period to the extent that they relate to future services. That is, in the period of the remeasurement there is a catch-up adjustment for prior periods in order for the *recognised* liability at the end of each reporting period to equal a defined proportion of the *total* fair value of the liability. The recognised proportion is calculated by dividing the period for which services have been provided as of the end of the reporting period by the total vesting period.

IFRS 2.IG19   4.5.630.30 Only the grant-date fair value of the arrangement may qualify for capitalisation under other IFRSs. Accordingly, the remeasurement of the liability is recognised in profit or loss. However, there is no guidance on whether the remeasurement should be presented as an employee cost or as finance income or finance costs. In our view, an entity should choose an accounting policy, to be applied consistently, between both presentations.

4.5.640 *Market conditions and non-market performance conditions*

IFRS 2.33   4.5.640.10 All the terms and conditions should be considered in determining the fair value of a cash-settled share-based payment. However, IFRS 2 does not provide guidance on how to measure the fair value of cash-settled share-based payments with market and/ or non-market performance conditions.

4.5.640.20 It therefore is unclear whether, by analogy to the modified grant-date method for equity-settled share-based payments (see 4.5.430), only market conditions and non-vesting conditions should be taken into account when measuring the fair value of the cash-settled liability or whether all conditions, including service and non-market performance conditions, should be taken into account in determining the fair value.

4.5.640.30 In our view, an entity should choose an accounting policy, to be applied consistently to all cash-settled share-based payments, to measure the fair value of a cash-settled liability taking into account either:

- only market and non-vesting conditions, meaning that service and non-market performance conditions affect the fair value of the liability by adjusting the number of rights to receive cash that are expected to satisfy any service and non-market performance conditions on a best estimate basis; or
- all vesting and non-vesting conditions, including service conditions and non-market performance conditions.

4.5.640.35 [Not used]

IFRS 2.BC
249

4.5.640.40 A cash-settled share-based payment is remeasured to its actual settlement amount; therefore the cumulative cost that ultimately will be recognised under either accounting policy will be equal to the cash payment to the counterparty. This is different from equity-settled transactions for which there is no true up of compensation cost for failure to satisfy a market condition (see 4.5.430.50).

4.5.643 *Non-vesting conditions*

IFRS 2.BC
249

4.5.643.10 In our view, non-vesting conditions also should be taken into account when measuring the fair value of a cash-settled liability, similar to market conditions. We believe that the requirement to remeasure cash-settled share-based payments until and to their ultimate settlement amount overrides the prohibition on true up for failure to satisfy a non-vesting condition. This is consistent with our approach to cash-settled share-based payments with market-performance conditions (see 4.5.640.30).

4.5.645 *Redeemable shares*

4.5.645.10 Grants of equity instruments that are redeemable are classified as cash-settled share-based payments under certain conditions (see 4.5.330). See 4.5.330.25 for a discussion of what is part of the arrangement.

IFRS 2.31

4.5.645.20 In our view, for a grant of options to acquire redeemable shares, the settlement of the share-based payment occurs only upon redemption of the shares and not upon exercise of the options (see 4.5.330.30). We believe that an entity should recognise compensation cost and a corresponding cash-settled liability equal to the grant-date fair value of the options; this liability should be remeasured at each reporting date.

4.5.645.30 Upon exercise of the options, we believe that the entity should remeasure the cash-settled liability to fair value through profit or loss until the shares are redeemed.

4.5.650 **Employee transactions with a choice of settlement**

IFRS 2.34

4.5.650.10 When either the entity or the employee has a choice of settlement, the transaction is accounted for at least in part as a cash-settled transaction if the entity granting the share-based payment will or can be required to settle in cash or other assets.

4.5.660 *Employee's choice*

IFRS 2.35-38

4.5.660.10 When the employee has the choice of settlement, the entity has granted a compound financial instrument that includes a liability component and an equity component. At the measurement date, the fair value of the compound instrument (the value of services to be received) is the sum of the values of the liability component and the equity component. The liability component is measured first. All of the fair value of the grant will be recognised as a liability if the employee would have to surrender the cash settlement right in order to receive the equity alternative. As a result the incremental value of the equity component is zero, unless the employee receives a discount for choosing the equity alternative.

4.5.660.20 Determination of the grant date and vesting date in respect of share-based payment arrangements that provide employees with a choice of cash settlement at one date or shares at a later date can be problematic, as it may not be clear whether the date of cash settlement or the date of issuance of the shares should prevail.

IFRS 2.38, 4.5.660.23 As a consequence of the requirement to account for the cash settlement com-
IU 05-06 ponent and the share component separately, in our view the vesting periods of the two components should be determined separately.

4.5.660.25 In our view, choosing one alternative (i.e. cash settlement or shares) before the end of the vesting period of the other alternative should be treated as a cancellation of the second alternative by one of the parties. We believe that the term *forfeited* used in paragraph 40 of IFRS 2 should not be understood as forfeiture as used in applying the modified grant-date method. In the context of that method forfeiture results in a reversal of previously recognised share-based payment cost. Reversal of the equity component when the cash alternative is selected is not appropriate as services have been provided. Therefore, in our view the equity component should be recognised as long as the required services have been provided to be eligible for cash settlement, notwithstanding the fact that the equity alternative is surrendered when cash settlement is chosen.

4.5.660.27 For example:

- On 1 January 2010 Company R entered into a bonus arrangement with its employees.
- The terms of the arrangement allow employees to choose on 31 December 2010 either:
  - a cash payment equivalent to the increase in share price between 1 January and 31 December 2010 for 100 shares; or
  - shares with a value equivalent to 110 percent of the cash payment.
- If employees choose to receive shares instead of a cash payment, then they are required to work for R until the end of 2012.

IU 05-06 4.5.660.30 At the date that the transaction was entered into, both the employer and employee understood the terms and conditions of the plan, including the formula that would be used to determine the amount of cash to be paid or the number of shares to be delivered to each employee; however, the exact amount of cash or number of shares would be known only at a future point in time. Nonetheless, if the outcome is based on *objective* factors and different knowledgeable parties, independently of each other, would be able to make consistent calculations, then we believe that there is a shared understanding without having specified the actual grant term (see 4.5.490.50). In the example illustrated in 4.5.660.27 we believe that the grant date is 1 January 2010.

IU 05-06 4.5.660.40 Continuing the example in 4.5.660.27, a share-based payment transaction with cash alternatives at the discretion of the employee is treated as a compound instrument with the liability and equity components of the compound instrument accounted for separately. Therefore, in this example we believe that the vesting periods for the liability and equity components would be different: one year for the liability component and three years for the equity component.

IFRS 2.39, 40,   4.5.660.50 In the example in 4.5.660.27, if the grant-date fair value of the liability
IGEx13   component is 500 and the fair value of the equity component is 300, then at the end of year 1 R will have recognised the entire fair value of the cash component of 500 and 100 for the equity component (300 / 3 x 1 = 100). If at the end of year 1 the employee elects to receive the cash payment, then we believe that this election should be treated as a cancellation of the equity component by the counterparty (see 4.5.800).

IFRS 2.35, 44   4.5.660.60 We believe that an arrangement that provides the counterparty a choice of two settlement alternatives that are mutually exclusive and at the discretion of the employee, in which only one of the alternatives would be accounted for under IFRS 2, is in the scope of IFRS 2 (see example in 4.5.210.20). In our view, in that example the requirements for compound instruments are applied by analogy; the liability for the profit-sharing plan embodies the liability component, which should be measured and remeasured in accordance with the requirements of IAS 19. Any incremental fair value of the equity-settled share-based payment over the initial value of the liability component is accounted for as an equity component. Even if there is no equity component to account for, we believe that the disclosure requirements of IFRS 2 should be applied. If and when the choice for the profit-sharing plan is sacrificed, then the liability would be reclassified to equity. If, instead, the option for the profit-sharing plan is exercised, then we believe that the equity component would be treated as cancelled since the equity right had to be surrendered in order to receive the cash alternative.

4.5.670 [Not used]

4.5.680 *Entity's choice*

IFRS 2.41-43   4.5.680.10 When the entity has the choice of settlement, the entity accounts for the transaction either as a cash-settled share-based payment or as an equity-settled share-based payment in its entirety. The entity determines whether it has a present obligation to settle in cash. If it has a present obligation to settle in cash, then it accounts for the transaction as a cash-settled share-based payment; otherwise it accounts for the transaction as an equity-settled share-based payment.

4.5.680.12 Whether or not the entity has a present obligation to settle in cash depends on an assessment of the entity's:

- intent, if any, to settle in cash or in equity instruments;
- past practice, if any, of settling in cash or in equity instruments; and
- ability to settle in equity instruments.

4.5.680.13 If the entity has the *stated intent to settle in equity instruments*, then the entity does not have a present obligation to settle in cash, unless it has a past practice of settling in cash or no ability to settle in equity instruments.

4.5.680.14 An entity has a present obligation to settle in cash if the choice of settlement in equity instruments has no commercial substance, e.g. if the entity legally is prohibited from issuing or buying and reissuing shares. Therefore, in order to classify the share-based payment as equity settled, the entity should have the ability to settle in shares. Otherwise the entity accounts for the arrangement as cash settled.

4.5.680.15 If the entity has the *stated intent to settle in cash*, then the entity has a present obligation to settle in cash, regardless of its past practice.

4.5.680.16 If the entity does *not have a stated intent*, then it classifies the transaction as cash settled if it has either a past practice of settling in cash or no ability to settle in equity instruments; otherwise the transaction is classified as equity settled.

4.5.680.18 The basis of classification of share-based payments when the issuer has a choice of settlement generally differs somewhat from the classification criteria in the financial instruments standards which focus more narrowly on whether the issuer has an obligation without considering its intent in the way that the share-based payment standard does.

4.5.680.20 The classification as equity or cash settled of a transaction in which the entity has the choice of settlement is determined initially at grant date. In our view, an entity should reassess whether it has a present obligation to settle in cash if there is a change in circumstances prior to the settlement date. Examples of changes in circumstances that would indicate that a reassessment of the classification is appropriate include a change in an entity's stated intent or a change in an entity's practice of settlement.

4.5.680.30 In our view, whether or not the change in circumstances would lead to a change in classification of the share-based payment should be assessed based on the specific facts and circumstances of each arrangement. Consider the example of an entity that has the stated intent and ability to settle transactions in equity and has a past practice of doing so; at grant date the arrangement is classified as equity settled. However, if the entity changes its intent to settle in cash and communicates this to employees, then the entity would have a present obligation to settle in cash and therefore it should reclassify the share-based payment arrangement as cash settled.

4.5.680.40 If the entity continues to have a stated policy of settlement in equity but subsequently settles a transaction in cash, then the question arises as to whether the cash settlement results in the entity having a present obligation to settle other transactions in cash. In our view, if the entity's intention is to continue to settle in equity and the cash settlement was limited to an isolated circumstance (e.g. due to an illness in the employee's family), then equity-settled classification may continue to be appropriate. In this case the isolated circumstance of cash settlement generally would not constitute a change in practice and generally would not result in the employees having an expectation that their awards will be settled in cash in the future. However, if the entity settles a number of transactions in cash, then it is more likely that the change in settlement should result in the share-based payment arrangement being reclassified to cash-settled.

4.5.680.50 In our view, if the share-based payment is classified at grant date as cash settled, then it may be more difficult to support a conclusion that a change in circumstances results in the entity no longer having a present obligation to settle in cash. This is because the employees may have an expectation that the previous practice of settlement in cash will continue to be followed until a practice of settlement in equity is established. This is more difficult when the employee's ability to obtain cash by selling the equity instruments received in the share-based payment transaction would not be as easy as cash settlement by the entity; e.g. if there is not an active and liquid market available to the employees in which to sell the entity's equity instruments. For example, an entity has a past practice of settling in cash and, without communicating any change in policy to employees, the entity changes its intent such that it will settle future awards in equity. In our view, prior to the establishment of a practice of settlement in equity, the entity should continue to classify the share-based payment arrangement as cash settled. This is because, in the absence of communication of its change in intent and a change in practice, we believe that the employees will continue to have an expectation that the awards will be settled in cash and therefore the entity continues to have a present obligation to settle in cash.

4.5.680.60 In our view, a change in circumstances that results in a change in classification of a transaction in which the entity has a choice of settlement should be accounted for prospectively. We believe that the change in intent of the entity should be treated as a change in the terms of the award; therefore the change in intent should be treated as a modification that changes the classification of the arrangement (see 4.5.760).

4.5.685 *Cash alternative not share-based*

IU 05-06   4.5.685.10 Some share-based payment arrangements provide the entity rather than the employee with a choice of settlement, but the amount of the settlement of the cash alternative does not vary with changes in the share price of the entity.

4.5.685.20 We believe that such a transaction is in the scope of IFRS 2 (see 4.5.260.10). In our view, the measurement principles of IAS 19 should apply to the non-share-based cash alternative, as for similar compound instruments in which the employee has the choice of settlement (see 4.5.660.50). Measurement principles under IAS 19 include discounting other long-term employee benefits (see 4.4.990).

4.5.690 Modifications and cancellations of employee transactions

4.5.690.10 The accounting for a modification depends on whether or not the modification changes the classification of the arrangement and whether or not the changes are beneficial to the counterparty.

4.5.700 **Modifications that do not change the classification of an arrangement**

IFRS 2.27, 4.5.700.10 Modifications to equity-settled share-based payment transactions that *decrease*
B43(a) the fair value of the grant generally are ignored. When the fair value of the grant *increases*
due to a modification, then the incremental fair value of the modified grant is accounted
for in addition to the original grant.

IFRS 2.27, 4.5.700.20 The incremental fair value is the difference between the fair value of the
B43(a) modified share-based payment and that of the original share-based payment, both
measured at the date of the modification. In our view, when determining these fair
values the same requirements as for determining the grant-date fair value apply, i.e.
service conditions and non-market performance conditions are not taken into account
in determining the fair value (see 4.5.430.60). If, for example, a share-based payment
arrangement with a non-market performance condition is modified such that only the
non-market performance target is modified, and all other terms and conditions remain
the same, then the incremental fair value is zero. This is because the fair value measured
on an IFRS 2 basis, i.e. without adjustments for service and non-market performance
conditions, is the same before and after the modification.

IFRS 2.B43 4.5.700.30 The accounting treatment for any incremental fair value or other modification
(a), (c) depends on the nature of the modification. If the modification increases the fair value
of the share-based payment granted, then the incremental fair value is recognised over
the remaining modified vesting period while the balance of the grant-date fair value is
recognised over the remaining original vesting period. If the modification changes a
market condition, then the impact of the change is treated as a change in the fair value
of the award. However, if the modification changes a service condition or non-market
performance condition in a way that is beneficial to an employee, then the remaining
grant-date fair value is recognised using the revised vesting expectations with true up
to actual outcomes (see 4.5.720).

4.5.710 *Business combinations*

4.5.710.10 [Not used]

4.5.710.20 See 4.5.1090 for guidance on replacements of share-based payment awards
in a business combination.

4.5.720 *Modification of a service condition*

IFRS 2.27, 4.5.720.10 If a share-based payment transaction contains a service condition, then the
B42, B43(c) award is forfeited if employment is terminated prior to the service condition being met.
In our view, if upon termination of employment the employer accelerates the vesting
period such that the employee receives the award despite not having completed the
requisite service period, then this is a modification of the award and not a forfeiture of
the original award (forfeiture would result in true up to zero) and a grant of a new award
(recognise the new grant-date fair value immediately as no further services provided).

This is because IFRS 2 illustrates an acceleration of the vesting period as an example of a modification that is beneficial to an employee. The accounting would be the same if the acceleration of vesting were treated as the forfeiture of the original grant and a grant of a replacement award. This is because the grant of a replacement award also is treated as a modification (see 4.5.810). Under modification accounting, at a minimum the original grant-date fair value is recognised over the vesting period of the share-based payment.

IFRS 2.B43 (c), IGEx1   4.5.720.20 If a service period is reduced, then the entity takes the modified vesting period into account when applying the requirements of the modified grant-date method. For example, Company S grants an equity-settled share-based payment with a grant-date fair value of 1,000 subject to a five-year service period. At the end of year 3 the service period is reduced to four years. In this case, S calculates the cumulative amount to be recognised at the end of year 3 based on the new vesting period and recognises the difference to the amounts recognised in previous years in year 3 ((1,000 x 3/4) - 400 = 350).

4.5.730 Modification of a market condition

IFRS 2.B43(c)   4.5.730.10 Under the modified grant-date method, a market condition is reflected in the fair value of an equity-settled share-based payment (see 4.5.430.50); this is referred to below as the adjusted fair value. If an award that contains a market condition is modified by an entity to make the market condition easier to meet, then this is a modification of a vesting condition that is beneficial to employees. The original market condition is taken into account in estimating the adjusted fair value of the original grant at the date of modification. If it is unlikely that the original market condition will be met at the date of modification, then the adjusted fair value of the original award at the date of modification may be significantly lower than the adjusted fair value of the original award as determined at grant date.

4.5.730.20 For example, at grant date an equity-settled share-based payment that contains a market condition has a fair value of 100. For illustrative purposes it is assumed that the probability at grant date of meeting the market condition is 55 percent and the grant-date fair value is adjusted accordingly; in practice the fair value adjustment to reflect a market condition is not necessarily a probability adjustment. After taking into account the market condition, the adjusted fair value of the award is 55 (100 x 55%). Subsequently the entity modifies the market condition to increase the likelihood that it will be met. At the date of modification the modified award has a fair value of 120, the probability of meeting the new market condition is 90 percent, and the probability of meeting the original market condition has decreased to 30 percent. After taking into account the new market condition the probability-adjusted fair value of the modified award is 108 (120 x 90%) and the probability-adjusted fair value of the original award is 36 (120 x 30%). In this situation the total compensation cost that will be recognised for the award is 127, being the original probability-adjusted fair value of 55 plus the incremental fair value of the modified award of 72 (108 - 36). The total compensation cost that will be recognised of 127 is greater than the unadjusted fair value of the modified award of 120.

4.5.740 *Modification of a non-market performance condition*

4.5.740.10 A change in the performance conditions of a share-based payment arrangement might be considered a modification. For example, an entity grants employees a share-based payment, the vesting of which depends upon the company's relative position within a comparator group of companies. The entity's relative position within this comparator group is based on market share determined with respect to revenue (a non-market performance condition). The agreement specifies that should one of the comparator group companies need to be deleted from the list for reasons outside the control of the company (e.g. delisting of a competitor such that financial information no longer is available), then it will be replaced by the next company in a predetermined list. In our view, any change in the comparator group is not a modification because the composition of the group, including the method of making changes, was pre-defined as part of the terms and condition of the original grant (see 4.5.506 and 508). However, if the agreement does not specify how a company in the comparator group will be replaced and the revision to the comparator group is a free choice or the change is made at the discretion of the entity, then we believe that this should be accounted for as a modification due to the subjectivity involved (see 4.5.508.10).

4.5.750 *Give-and-take modifications*

4.5.750.10 A package of modifications might include several changes to terms of a grant, some of which are favourable to the employee while other changes are not. For example, a share option grant can be modified by reducing the exercise price (give) and simultaneously reducing the number of granted options (take). In our view, it is appropriate to net the effects of both modifications, provided that both modifications are agreed as part of a package. This is because the employee realises the net change rather than being able to earn the enhanced benefit of the reduction of the exercise price without suffering the loss in the total number of options. If the net effect is beneficial, then we believe that this net effect is accounted for by applying the requirements for beneficial modifications.

4.5.760 **Modifications that change the classification of an arrangement**

4.5.770 *Change from equity settled to cash settled*

IFRS 2.27,
IGEx9 4.5.770.10 A modification may lead to a change in the classification of a share-based payment transaction. For example, a modification may change the classification from equity settled to cash settled. Such a modification leads to a reclassification, at the date of modification, of an amount equal to the fair value of the liability from equity to liability.

4.5.770.20 In our view, if the amount of the liability recognised is less than the amount previously recognised as an increase in equity, then no gain is recognised in profit or loss. The entity still should recognise, as a minimum, the grant-date fair value of equity instruments granted as the cost of the share-based payment. However, any subsequent remeasurement of the liability (from the date of modification until settlement date) is recognised in profit or loss.

4.5.770.30 If the amount of the liability recognised is higher than the amount previously recognised as an increase in equity, then in our view two approaches are acceptable with respect to recognising the excess liability. We believe that an entity should choose an accounting policy, to be applied consistently, to either:

- recognise the excess as a cost in profit or loss at the modification date; or
- recognise the entire liability as a reclassification from equity and not recognise any loss in profit or loss.

IU 11-06 4.5.770.40 The approach of recognising the excess as an item in profit or loss in effect transfers an amount to a liability equal to the amount recognised in equity in respect of the share-based payment and then remeasures that amount, through profit or loss, to its current fair value. The approach of recognising the entire amount of the liability as a reduction in equity is consistent with the treatment applied when the liability is less than the amount recognised in equity in that no gain is recognised for the difference between the amount recognised to date in equity and the apportioned fair value of the liability.

4.5.780 Change from cash-settled to equity-settled

4.5.780.10 The standard is silent on how to account for a new equity-settled share-based payment arrangement that is identified as a replacement of a cash-settled share-based payment arrangement (equivalent to reclassification from cash-settled to equity-settled). In our view, the principles for modification and cancellation should be applied by analogy to such changes in classification.

4.5.780.20 Accordingly, we believe that a modification of an existing cash-settled arrangement in which the classification is changed from cash-settled to equity-settled should be accounted for as follows:

- Distinguish between the grant-date fair value of the original cash-settled share-based payment arrangement (first component) and the remeasurement of that liability (second component).
- At the date of modification, the liability as of that date is reclassified to equity (the recognised proportion of the first and second components).
- At the date of modification, the incremental fair value of the modification is calculated as:
  - the fair value of the new grant, measured at the date of modification; less
  - the fair value of the original grant, measured at the date of modification; and
  - any payments made to the employees on cancellation of the original grant.
- Recognise the remaining grant-date fair value of the original grant (unrecognised portion of the first component only) in addition to the incremental fair value, if any, over the remaining vesting period.

1166

4.5.780.30 The normal principles would apply to such a transaction, for example true up for forfeiture due to service conditions and non-market performance conditions not being met.

4.5.790 *Modifications that change the nature of an arrangement*

4.5.790.10 A modification may change the nature of an arrangement from a share-based payment transaction to an employee benefit within the scope of IAS 19. In our view, the accounting for modifications that change the classification of an equity-settled share-based payment arrangement to a cash-settled share-based payment arrangement should be applied by analogy to account for an IAS 19 employee benefit that is identified as a replacement of an equity-settled share-based payment arrangement. However, some adjustments should be made to reflect the fact that the new award is not a cash-settled share-based payment but an IAS 19 employee benefit, e.g. it may be necessary to change from a straight-line attribution method to a projected unit credit method. The employee benefit should be measured and recognised based on the general requirements of IAS 19 applicable to the type of employee benefit issued (see 4.4).

4.5.800 *Cancellations, replacements, settlements*

IFRS 2.28(a),
IGEx9A 4.5.800.10 Cancellations or settlements of equity-settled share-based payments during the vesting period by the entity or by the counterparty are accounted for as accelerated vesting and therefore the amount that otherwise would have been recognised for services received is recognised immediately.

4.5.800.20 A voluntary cancellation by the employee of an unvested share-based payment is accounted for as a cancellation. For example, a CEO may want to waive the entitlement to share options as a gesture in difficult economic times. Even though this change is initiated by the employee and no compensation for waiving the entitlement is received, cancellation accounting still is applied.

4.5.800.30 See 4.5.430.70 for a discussion of a failure to provide service due to the termination of an employee's employment by the employer.

4.5.805 *Accelerated amount*

IFRS 2.28(a) 4.5.805.10 As indicated in 4.5.800.10, the amount recognised when a share-based payment is cancelled is the amount that otherwise would have been recognised over the remainder of the vesting period if the cancellation had not occurred. The standard is not clear about what is meant by "the amount that otherwise would have been recognised for services received over the remainder of the vesting period", i.e. whether it refers to the number of instruments that could have vested (see 4.5.805.30) or that were expected to vest (see 4.5.805.40).

4.5.805.20 In our view, an entity should choose an accounting policy, to be applied consistently, to follow either of the approaches in 4.5.805.30 and 40.

4.5.805.30 Under the first approach the share-based payment should be recognised as if the service and the non-market performance conditions were met for the cancelled awards, i.e. those not forfeited already. This approach is supported by the wording in paragraph 27 of IFRS 2, which requires recognition for those equity instruments that were granted unless those equity instruments do not vest.

4.5.805.40 Under the second approach the amount that would have been recognised should be based on an estimate on the date of cancellation, i.e. estimating how many instruments are expected to vest at the original (future) vesting date. This approach is supported by the fact that on an ongoing basis the entity would have recognised only the grant-date fair value of those instruments that were expected to vest.

4.5.810 *Replacements*

IFRS 2.28(c)   **4.5.810.10** In practice, entities are able to determine whether to account for replacement plans as modifications. If an entity identifies a new equity-settled arrangement as a replacement for a cancelled equity-settled arrangement, then the entity accounts for the grant of replacement equity instruments as a modification of the original arrangement. If the entity does not make this identification, then both plans are accounted for separately. For example, if a new equity-settled share-based payment is offered and an old equity-settled share-based payment is cancelled, but the new plan is not identified as a replacement plan for the cancelled plan, then the new grant is recognised at its grant-date fair value and the original grant is accounted for as a cancellation.

4.5.810.20 An entity may create a new, more beneficial share-based payment plan as a replacement for an old plan, but not formally cancel the old plan, for example because it would be disadvantageous for tax purposes to do so. Employees are expected to, and do, cancel their participation in the old plan and join the new one. Together the entity and the employees are able to identify the new plan as a replacement, but the issue is whether or not it is eligible to be accounted for as a replacement when the old plan continues to exist. If there is sufficient evidence to establish a clear link between the entity's and employees' cancellation of the share-based payment in the old plan and acceptance of the share-based payment under the new plan, then in our view it is acceptable to apply replacement accounting.

4.5.820 **Group share-based payment arrangements**

4.5.830 *Scope of group share-based payment arrangements*

4.5.830.10 Sometimes share-based payment arrangements involve entities that are outside the reporting entity. Share-based payment arrangements that involve other group entities outside the reporting entity are referred to as group share-based payment arrangements. The standard contains the notions of the receiving entity and the settling entity (see 4.5.20.07). To help describe the scope and classification of group share-based payments, in this chapter the term "reference entity" is used to describe the entity whose equity instruments are granted or on whose equity instruments a cash payment is based. See 4.5.120.10 for the definition of a group.

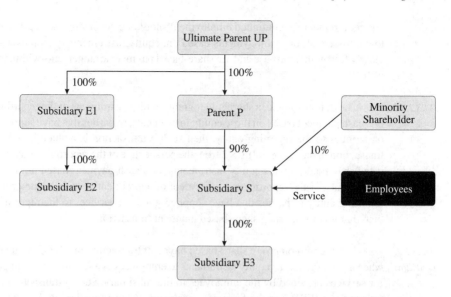

4.5.830.20 For example, in the diagram above, examples of a share-based payment arrangement that involves two entities include:

- Parent P grants its own equity instruments or a cash payment based on its own equity instruments to the employees of Subsidiary S; or
- S grants equity instruments of P or a cash payment based on the equity instruments of P to its own employees.

4.5.830.30 P is not part of the reporting entity when S prepares its separate or consolidated financial statements. Share-based payment arrangements that involve entities outside the reporting entity are referred to as "group share-based payment arrangements", if the other entity is, from the perspective of Ultimate Parent UP, in the same group as the reporting entity (see 4.5.20.100).

IFRS 2.IN2, 4.5.830.40 The definition of a share-based payment arrangement can seem unclear, as it
A refers to an arrangement that "entitles the other party to receive cash or other assets *of the entity* for amounts that are based on the price (or value) of equity instruments (including shares or share options) of the entity or another group entity..." (emphasis added). The question is whether, under this definition, group cash-settled share-based payment transactions also are required to be attributed to the entity receiving services. In our view, "of the entity" should be read as including other group entities and shareholders.

4.5.840 *Share-based payments granted by shareholders*

IFRS 2.3A, 4.5.840.10 The standard excludes from its scope only those transactions that are clearly
BC22 for a purpose other than payment for goods or services supplied to the entity receiving them. In our view, the requirement for the transfer of, or a cash payment based on, equity instruments clearly to be for another purpose is a high threshold. We believe that

any requirement for continued employment should be considered persuasive evidence that transfers of, or cash payments based on, equity instruments to employees are not clearly for another purpose and are share-based payment arrangements within the scope of IFRS 2.

IFRS 2.3A   4.5.840.20 If, for example, a shareholder grants equity instruments of the reporting entity, or a cash payment based on those equity instruments, to parties that have supplied goods or services to the reporting entity, then such a transaction is a share-based payment transaction in the scope of IFRS 2 from the perspective of the reporting entity. Similarly, if the shareholder grants equity instruments, or a cash payment based on those equity instruments, of the reporting entity's parent or another entity in the same group as the reporting entity to parties that have supplied goods or services to the reporting entity, then that grant is a group share-based payment transaction.

IFRS 2.2,   4.5.840.30 A common group share-based payment transaction involving shareholders is
B52(a)   when a parent grants its equity instruments to employees of a subsidiary as compensation for services provided by the employees to the subsidiary. Such a transaction is within the scope of IFRS 2 in the financial statements of the subsidiary and in the scope of IFRS 2 from the perspective of the parent (see 4.5.860.10).

4.5.850 *Share-based payments involving equity instruments of other group entities*

IFRS 2.B52   4.5.850.10 If a reporting entity, rather than, for example the shareholder, grants equity
(b)   instruments of its parent or equity instruments of another entity in the same group as the reporting entity (or a cash payment based on those equity instruments) to parties that have supplied goods or services to the reporting entity, then such a transaction is a share-based payment transaction in the scope of IFRS 2 from the perspective of the reporting entity.

4.5.860 *Share-based payments involving own equity instruments granted by the reporting entity or its shareholders to suppliers (including employees) of other group entities*

IFRS 2.2   4.5.860.10 If a reporting entity grants its own equity instruments, or a cash payment based on those equity instruments, to parties that have supplied goods or services to another entity in the group, then such a transaction is in the scope of IFRS 2 from the perspective of the reporting entity. For example, a transaction in which a parent grants its own equity instruments, or a cash payment based on those equity instruments, to the employees of a subsidiary is within the scope of IFRS 2 from the perspective of the parent. In this case, it also is in the scope of IFRS 2 from the perspective of the subsidiary (see 4.5.840.30).

IFRS 2.2   4.5.860.20 IFRS 2 also applies to transactions in which the reporting entity grants equity instruments of the entity's parent or another entity in the same group as the reporting entity to parties that have supplied goods or services to another party in the group.

4.5.870 [Not used]

4.5.873 *Share-based payments involving equity instruments of non-group entities*

IFRS 2.A 4.5.873.10 The requirement to treat transactions involving instruments of another entity as a share-based payment applies only to transactions involving equity instruments of a group entity (see 4.5.120.10 and 830.40). Therefore, a transaction in which the reporting entity receives services from its employees and the employees receive equity instruments of a shareholder that is not a group entity, or a cash payment based on those equity instruments, would be outside the scope of IFRS 2 from the perspective of the reporting entity.

IAS 27.4 4.5.873.20 A transaction in which the reporting entity receives services from its employees and the employees receive equity instruments of a joint venture or of an associate also would be outside the scope of IFRS 2 from the perspective of the reporting entity because neither joint ventures nor associates are part of a group.

4.5.873.30 However, when a grant of equity instruments of a joint venture or of an associate is provided by the reporting entity directly to its employees, then in our view the transaction is an employee benefit within the scope of IAS 19 to be accounted for by the reporting entity.

4.5.877 *Share-based payment settled by external shareholder when the reference entity is in the same group as the receiving entity*

IFRS 2.3A 4.5.877.10 If a shareholder that is not a group entity settles by granting equity instruments of the receiving entity (or a cash payment based on those equity instruments), then the transaction is in the scope of IFRS 2 from the perspective of the receiving entity.

IFRS 2.3A(b), 4.5.877.20 However, in our view the transaction described in 4.5.877.10 is not a share-
B50 based payment in the scope of IFRS 2 from the perspective of the shareholder. This is because the scope requirement refers to those entities that have an obligation to settle when another entity in the same group receives the goods or services, which is not the case from the perspective of the external shareholder.

4.5.880 *Intermediate parents*

4.5.880.10 A shareholder may grant a share-based payment to employees of a subsidiary that is owned through an intermediate parent. For example, the ultimate parent (UP) in a group may grant an equity-settled share-based payment to employees of Subsidiary S that is held through Holding Company P; the share-based payment is recognised by the subsidiary in its financial statements (see 4.5.840.10 - 30). In our view, either of the following two approaches can be applied in the financial statements of the intermediate parent (P) in respect of the group share-based payment transaction.

4.5.880.20 We believe that P can conclude that it does not have a share-based payment to recognise in its separate financial statements, because P, as the intermediate parent, is neither the receiving nor the settling entity in respect of the share-based payment.

Under this approach, the share-based payment effectively is being accounted for as if UP holds the investment in S directly.

4.5.880.30 Alternatively, we believe that P could recognise the share-based payment in its financial statements. Under this approach, attribution is appropriate as UP has only an indirect investment in S and can realise the benefits of the contribution only via P.

IFRS 2.43B   4.5.880.40 If P chooses to account for the transaction, then P classifies the transaction as
(b)   equity settled in both its separate financial statements and its consolidated financial statements, if prepared. This is because P directly or indirectly receives the services without having an obligation to settle the transaction. By recognising a capital contribution from UP and an increase in investment in S, P mirrors the capital contribution recognised by the subsidiary and reflects the increase in investment by UP.

4.5.890 *Classification of group share-based payment arrangements*

4.5.900 – 910 [Not used]

4.5.912 *Classification principles*

IFRS 2.43A-C   4.5.912.10 Classification of the share-based payment transaction depends on the nature of the award granted and whether the entity has an obligation to settle the transaction. If the entity either has an obligation to settle in its own equity instruments or has no obligation to settle, then the transaction is accounted for as equity settled. A settling entity that is not a receiving entity classifies a share-based payment transaction as equity settled if it settles in its own equity instruments; otherwise it classifies the transaction as cash settled.

4.5.912.20 A share-based payment transaction is classified from the perspective of each reporting entity rather than by making a single group-wide classification determination. In a typical group share-based payment arrangement involving the parent and the subsidiary, three separate classification assessments are needed for a single transaction: from the perspective of the consolidated financial statements of the parent, the separate financial statements of the parent and the separate financial statements of the subsidiary. Therefore a single share-based payment transaction could be classified as equity settled in the financial statements of a subsidiary that receives the services and cash settled in the group's consolidated financial statements, or vice versa.

4.5.912.30 From the perspective of the separate financial statements of the reporting entity, equity instruments of another entity in the group of the ultimate parent would be classified as "cash or other assets". In contrast, from the group perspective equity instruments of an entity of that group are considered to be equity instruments.

4.5.912.40 The scope assessment differs from the classification assessment. In the scope assessment, focus is placed on whether the reference entity is in or outside the group of the *ultimate parent* (see 4.5.830.30); in the classification assessment, focus is placed on whether the equity instruments are those of the *reporting entity*.

1172

4.5.920 – 940 [Not used]

4.5.945 *Accounting for a group share-based payment arrangement*

4.5.946 *Accounting by a receiving entity with no obligation to settle*

IFRS 2.B53   4.5.946.10 A receiving entity that has no obligation to settle the transaction with the counterparty to the share-based payment transaction accounts for the transaction as equity settled and recognises an expense, unless the goods or services received qualify for recognition as an asset, and an increase in its equity for the contribution received from the parent.

4.5.947 *Accounting by a direct parent that settles*

4.5.947.10 A settling entity recognises an increase in equity or liabilities, depending on the classification of the share-based payment transaction. However, there is no explicit guidance on how a settling entity that is different from a receiving entity accounts for the debit entry.

IFRS 2.13A   4.5.947.20 When a parent grants rights to its equity instruments to employees of a subsidiary, the identifiable consideration received by the parent from the perspective of its separate financial statements for the equity instruments may be zero. When the identifiable consideration received is less than the fair value of the equity instruments granted (or liability incurred), there is an indication that other consideration has been or will be received.

4.5.947.30 In our view, when a parent grants rights to its equity instruments to employees of a subsidiary, the parent receives goods or services indirectly through the subsidiary in the form of an increased investment in the subsidiary, i.e. the subsidiary receives services from employees that are paid for by the parent, thereby increasing the value of the subsidiary. Therefore, we believe that the parent should recognise in equity the equity-settled share-based payment with a corresponding increase in its investment in the subsidiary in its separate financial statements. The amount recognised as an additional investment is based on the grant-date fair value of the share-based payment. In our view, the increase in investment and corresponding increase in equity for the equity-settled share-based payment should be recognised by the parent over the vesting period of the share-based payment. In recognising these amounts the normal requirements for accounting for forfeitures should be applied.

4.5.947.40 Accounting for a share-based payment transaction that has been classified as cash settled in the parent's separate financial statements is more complex than for one classified as an equity-settled share-based payment. Assuming that an investment in a subsidiary is not different from any other asset measured on a cost basis, the same principles of recognition of the increase in the carrying amount of the asset for the services received in a cash-settled share-based payment apply, i.e. a parent would capitalise the grant-date fair value of the liability. Depending on the entity's accounting policy choice

1173

on how to measure the liability (see 4.5.640.30) the effects of changes in the estimated and actual outcome of certain conditions either adjust the cost of investment or are part of the remeasurement to be recognised in profit or loss.

4.5.948 *Accounting by an ultimate parent that settles*

4.5.948.10 In some cases the ultimate parent grants a share-based payment to a subsidiary in the group.

4.5.948.20 For example, Ultimate Parent UP grants a share-based payment to the employees of Subsidiary S and will settle the transaction in its own equity instruments. S is held indirectly by UP via parent P. Our view that P as an intermediate parent should choose an accounting policy regarding whether or not to recognise a share-based payment in its separate financial statements is discussed in 4.5.880. In our view, regardless of whether P recognises the transaction, the value of UP's investment in P increases by granting the share-based payment arrangement to S's employees, and therefore we believe that UP should recognise the cost of the share-based payment as a cost of investment in P.

4.5.949 *Accounting by an other group entity that settles*

4.5.949.10 In our view, a settling entity with no direct or indirect investment in the entity receiving the services in a group share-based payment arrangement should recognise the cost of the share-based payment in equity as a distribution to its parent over the vesting period. This is because the entity could be seen to be settling the transaction on behalf of its parent. For example, Parent P has two subsidiaries, Q and R. Q grants a share-based payment to the employees of R and will settle the transaction in its own equity instruments. As Q neither receives services nor has an investment in R, we believe that Q should recognise the cost of the share-based payment in equity as a distribution to P over the vesting period.

4.5.950 **Accounting for transfers of employees**

4.5.950.10 Employees may transfer within the group during the vesting period of a share-based payment arrangement. In some circumstances, the share-based payment may lapse or vest and the employee may be offered a new share-based payment. In such cases the normal requirements for employees leaving and joining share-based payment arrangements usually apply from the perspective of each entity (see accounting for forfeitures in 4.5.430.70).

IFRS 2.B59, 4.5.950.20 In other circumstances, a parent (or another group entity) may grant rights
61 to its equity instruments to employees of a subsidiary that are conditional on the employee providing service within the group for a specified period of time. In such arrangements the transfer of the employee will have no effect on the vesting of the share-based payment from the employee's point of view.

4.5.950.30 If the subsidiaries have no obligation to settle the transaction with their employees, then the transaction is accounted for as equity settled. Each subsidiary measures the services received from the employee by reference to the parent's grant-date fair value of the equity instruments. If an employee subsequently fails to satisfy a vesting condition other than a market condition, such that there is true up of the share-based payment at the group level, then each subsidiary adjusts the amount previously recognised in its financial statements. If the employee transfers between two group entities during the vesting period, then this is not deemed to be a forfeiture from the perspective of the separate financial statements of the former employer or a new grant by the new employer.

4.5.960 *Recharge arrangements*

4.5.960.10 When a parent grants rights to its equity instruments (e.g. share options) to employees of a subsidiary, the parent may require the subsidiary to make a payment to reimburse it for the granting of these rights. A common type of intra-group payment arrangement, or "recharge arrangement", is when the amount recharged is equal to the difference between the exercise price of the options granted and the market price of the parent's shares on the exercise date (i.e. exercise date intrinsic value recharge arrangement). However, in practice many types of recharges may exist.

IFRS 2.43D, 4.5.960.20 IFRSs do not address specifically the accounting for recharge arrangements
B45 related to share-based payment transactions involving group entities or external shareholders. However, a receiving entity with no obligation to settle the transaction classifies the share-based payment in accordance with the normal classification requirements irrespective of the existence of any recharge arrangement. Therefore, the existence of a recharge arrangement between a parent and a subsidiary does not mean that in substance it is the subsidiary that has the obligation to the employees.

4.5.960.30 Paragraphs 4.5.970 and 980 address the accounting in the financial statements of the subsidiary and the parent for recharge arrangements levied in respect of share-based payment arrangements that are classified as equity settled in both the consolidated financial statements of the parent and the financial statements of the subsidiary (see 4.5.900). The guidance also may be applied by analogy to other share-based payment arrangements, for example, to those that are classified as cash settled in the consolidated financial statements of the parent.

4.5.970 *Determining "linked clearly" recharge arrangements*

4.5.970.10 Determining the appropriate accounting treatment for a recharge arrangement will require judgement based on the terms and conditions of each arrangement. In our view, if the recharge is linked clearly to the share-based payment arrangement (see 4.5.970.20 – 50), then it should be accounted for separately from the share-based payment, but as an adjustment of the capital contribution recognised in respect of the share-based payment. In our view, when the recharge is settled in cash, based on the share price of equity instruments of a group entity, the recharge transaction should be recognised and measured by analogy to the requirements for cash-settled share-based payment transactions (see 4.5.630). As the subsidiary recognises a capital contribution as part of the share-based payment arrangement (see 4.5.900.10), we believe that it also is appropriate for the subsidiary to recognise its reimbursement of the capital contribution to the parent as an adjustment of that capital contribution. The subsidiary therefore should recognise a recharge liability and a corresponding adjustment (debit) in equity for the capital contribution recognised in respect of the share-based payment. Similarly, as the parent recognises its capital contribution to the subsidiary as an increase in its investment in the subsidiary (see 4.5.900.20), we believe that it is appropriate for the parent to account for the reimbursement by the subsidiary of this capital contribution by analogy to the requirements for cash-settled share-based payment transactions. The parent therefore should recognise a recharge asset and a corresponding adjustment (credit) to the carrying amount of the investment in the subsidiary.

4.5.970.15 In our experience, recharges from the parent settling the transaction to the subsidiary receiving the services usually are settled in cash. See 4.5.1020 for discussion of the requirements when the recharge is settled by the subsidiary in shares of the parent rather than in cash.

4.5.970.20 In our view, in assessing whether a recharge is linked clearly to the share-based payment arrangement, the primary determinant should be whether the amount of the payment is based on the value of the share-based payment. The following are examples of situations in which we believe that a recharge generally would be considered to be linked clearly to the share-based payment:

- a payment based on the grant-date fair value of the equity-settled share-based payment (IFRS 2 charge);
- a payment based on the cost of the treasury share programme of the parent (parent's cost of acquiring the shares to settle its obligation to the employees of the subsidiary); or
- a payment based on the difference between the exercise price of the options and the market price of the parent's shares on exercise date (intrinsic value recharge).

4.5.970.30 We believe that a recharge that is linked clearly to the share-based payment arrangement also could include, for example, some stated proportion of these bases.

4.5.970.40 In addition, if a recharge that is based on the value of a share-based payment also is based on the number of awards that vest or are exercised, then we believe that this provides additional evidence that the recharge is linked clearly to the share-based payment arrangement.

4.5.970.50 In our view, the timing of a recharge payment should not be a primary determinant as to whether it is linked clearly to the share-based payment arrangement. However, if the parent articulates in advance of or at the same time as the grant that a recharge that is based on the value of the share-based payment is in respect of the share-based payment arrangement, then we believe that this provides evidence that the

1176

recharge is linked clearly. If a parent levies a recharge well after the grant date (e.g. only when the options are exercised) with no prior communication of this intent and the parent having no history of having done so, then the timing of the recharge may weaken its link to the share-based payment arrangement.

4.5.980 *Recognition and measurement of linked clearly recharge arrangements*

4.5.980.10 For recharges accounted for by analogy to the requirements for cash-settled share-based payments (see 4.5.970.10), we believe that the recharge should be accounted for when the parent and the subsidiary have a shared understanding of the terms and conditions of the contract; often this will be prior to the subsidiary making a payment to the parent to settle its obligation under the recharge arrangement. We believe that the subsidiary and parent should measure the fair value of the recharge liability and asset initially at the date that the arrangement is entered into and, similar to the treatment of a share-based payment, the initial measurement of the recharge should be recognised as the services are provided in respect of the share-based payment.

4.5.980.20 Additional complexities arise with regard to the accounting for a recharge in which the amount of the recharge varies, e.g. the amount recharged under an exercise date intrinsic value recharge arrangement varies with changes in share price (see 4.5.960.10). Continuing to apply the guidance for cash-settled share-based payments by analogy, if such a recharge that is linked clearly to a share-based payment is recognised prior to the subsidiary making a cash payment to the parent to settle its obligation, then the asset and liability arising from the recharge arrangement should be remeasured at each reporting date until settlement for changes in fair value (see 4.5.630.20). In our view, changes in the fair value of a linked recharge that is accounted for by analogy to the requirements for cash-settled share-based payments should not be recognised through profit or loss. This is because we believe that it is the nature of the payment that should determine the accounting treatment. We believe that the nature of a linked recharge is that of a reimbursement of a capital transaction and therefore that changes in the fair value of the recharge liability and asset from initial recognition to settlement should be treated as a true up of the initial estimate of the net capital contribution.

4.5.980.30 If a recharge liability is denominated in a currency that is not the functional currency of the subsidiary, then in our view IAS 21 *The Effects of Changes in Foreign Exchange Rates* should be applied. As a result foreign exchange gains and losses that result from changes in the exchange rate should be recognised in profit or loss.

4.5.990 *Excess recharges*

4.5.990.10 The amount recharged may be greater than the increase in the investment recognised by the parent in respect of the share-based payment. In our view, the excess should be treated by the subsidiary as a net capital distribution. In our view, in the absence of specific guidance in IFRSs, more than one approach to the accounting by the parent for the excess may be acceptable. We believe that the parent should choose an accounting policy, to be applied consistently, with respect to the treatment of the excess of a recharge over the capital contribution recognised in respect of the share-based payment in its separate financial statements. Following are examples of accounting policies that we believe are acceptable.

4.5.1000 Approach 1 – Adjustment of capital contribution

4.5.1000.10 Under this approach, the entire amount of the recharge, including the excess, is treated by the parent as an adjustment of the capital contribution to the subsidiary.

4.5.1000.20 If the recharge is greater than the recognised investment in the subsidiary, then we believe that the amount of the recharge in excess of the capital contribution recognised in respect of a share-based payment that is linked clearly to the recharge could be recognised as a return of capital. Under this approach, the initial recognition and subsequent remeasurement of that recharge both would be recognised as a reduction in the cost of the investment in the subsidiary and the excess of the recharge will cause a reduction in the net investment in the subsidiary.

4.5.1010 Approach 2 – Dividend income

4.5.1010.10 Under this approach, the excess is treated by the parent as dividend income.

4.5.1010.20 If the recharge is greater than the increase in the investment in the subsidiary, then we believe that the amount of the recharge in excess of the capital contribution recognised in respect of the linked clearly share-based payment could be recognised as dividend income. For example, on a cumulative basis Parent P recognises an increase in its investment in Subsidiary S under a share-based payment of 100 and, as settlement of its recharge liability, S makes a payment to the parent of 150. Prior to settling the recharge, P's cost of investment in the subsidiary, including the increase recognised in respect of the share-based payment, is 200. Under this approach, on a cumulative basis the parent recognises a reduction of the investment in the subsidiary of 100; the excess of 50 (150 - 100 = 50) is recognised in its entirety as dividend income. The determination of the excess that ultimately will be recognised as dividend income should be made on a grant-by-grant, employee-by-employee basis.

4.5.1020 *Alternative approaches for recharge arrangements that are settleable in shares of the parent*

4.5.1020.10 If the subsidiary is required to settle with the parent a recharge arrangement that is linked clearly to a share-based payment using the parent's shares rather than with cash, then in our view it is acceptable to account for the recharge arrangement by analogy to the requirements of the financial instruments standards rather than by analogy to share-based payment accounting.

4.5.1020.20 In this case, the subsidiary recognises a financial liability by applying IAS 39 *Financial Instruments: Recognition and Measurement* by analogy when the entity becomes a counterparty to the recharge agreement, i.e. the entire fair value of the liability is recognised at once rather than spread over the vesting period. The debit is recognised in equity as an adjustment to the capital contribution, that is recognised under the share-based payment arrangement.

4.5.1020.30 Under this approach, subsequent changes in the fair value of the liability that are due to changes in estimates regarding employees not meeting the service or non-market performance conditions are recognised in equity. All other changes, such as unwinding the discount effect or changes in the value of the shares, are recognised in profit or loss.

4.5.1020.40 If, for example, the subsidiary has purchased its parent's shares at grant date in order to have an economic hedge of its exposure to changes in the value of its parent's shares, then the investment in its parent's shares would be accounted for as a financial asset either at fair value through profit or loss or as available for sale.# As a result of applying a financial instruments approach to account for changes in the liability for the recharge that are due to share prices movements, any fair value changes or impairments in respect to the financial asset that are recognised in profit or loss are mirrored by a change in the value of the financial liability, and also are recognised in profit or loss. The net effect of the effects reflects the natural hedge of the transaction.

4.5.1023 *Forthcoming requirement*

4.5.1023.10 In December 2009 the IASB issued IFRS 9 which amends the measurement categories for financial assets. Under IFRS 9 financial assets are measured either at amortised cost or fair value; the IAS 39 categories of held to maturity, loans and receivables and available for sale are eliminated. See 3.6A for further details.

4.5.1025 *Recognition and measurement of recharge arrangements that are not linked clearly*

4.5.1025.10 Recharge arrangements that are not linked clearly also are accounted for separately from the share-based payment arrangement. An entity considers whether such an arrangement is in the scope of another standard, in particular the financial instruments standards, and whether it is a transaction with a shareholder.

4.5.1030 [Not used]

4.5.1040 *Employee benefit trusts*

4.5.1050 *Scope issues*

4.5.1050.10 A plan sponsor may transfer or sell sufficient shares to enable a trust to meet obligations under share-based payment arrangements not only for current periods but also for future periods. In our view, the transfer of shares to an employee benefit trust does not represent a share-based payment transaction. Rather, the share-based payment arrangement is the arrangement between the employer and employees for which a grant date needs to be identified. Therefore, we believe that the grant date generally will be determined based on the date that the sponsor enters into an agreement with the employees. The fact that the agreement will be satisfied by the trust, or even that, nominally, it is the trust that enters into the agreement with the employees, does not, in our view, shift the grant date to the date of transfer or sale of shares to the trust. We believe that a trust that would be required to be consolidated usually should be seen as an extension of the sponsor and therefore it may be appropriate to view actions that nominally are those of the trust as actions of the sponsor.

4.5.1060 *Sponsor accounting*

4.5.1060.10 IFRSs do not provide specific guidance on the treatment in the entity's separate financial statements of transfers of cash to the trust to enable the trustee to purchase shares of the entity on the market or from the entity. The share-based payment arrangement to the employee is accounted for by the entity under IFRS 2. In our view, from the perspective of the entity's separate financial statements, the entity should choose an accounting policy, to be applied consistently, as follows:

- *Treat the trust as a branch/agent of the entity.* Consequently, the assets and liabilities of the trust are accounted for as assets and liabilities of the entity on the basis that the trust merely is acting as an agent of the entity. Under this treatment, the accounting in the entity's separate financial statements will be the same as the accounting in the consolidated financial statements.
- *Account for the trust as a legal entity separate from the entity but as a subsidiary of the entity.* Any loan from the entity to the trust is accounted for as a loan in accordance with its terms (see 3.6.460). If the trust is funded by the entity making an investment in the trust, then the entity would recognise the investment in the subsidiary as an asset. The purchase of own shares in the market by the trust has no effect on the financial statements of the entity. However, when the trust transfers those shares to employees, this is considered to be in substance two transactions: a distribution of the shares from the trust back to the entity as treasury shares, followed by a distribution of those shares to the employees.

4.5.1060.20 Our view that an entity should choose an accounting policy to treat the trust as a branch/agent of the entity was developed for application to arrangements in which IFRS 2 requires the sponsor to recognise an expense in relation to shares held in trust for employees and should not be applied by analogy to other trust arrangements.

4.5.1065 *Repurchase by the parent*

4.5.1065.10 A parent may be required to repurchase shares of a subsidiary that were acquired by employees of the subsidiary through a share-based payment arrangement. For example, a subsidiary issues options to its employees that it settles by issuing its own shares. Upon termination of employment the parent entity is required to purchase the shares of the subsidiary from the former employee. In our view, the classification of the share-based payment in the financial statements of the subsidiary should be based on the subsidiary's perspective. We believe that the repurchase arrangement is separate from the subsidiary's arrangement with its employees and therefore should not be considered in determining the classification of the share-based payment by the subsidiary. As the subsidiary only has an obligation to deliver its own equity instruments, we believe that the arrangement should be classified as equity settled in its financial statements. However, the arrangement should be classified as cash settled in the consolidated financial statements of the parent since the parent has an obligation to settle in cash based on the subsidiary's shares. This approach is consistent with the requirements for accounting for redeemable shares (see 4.5.330).

4.5.1070 [Not used]

4.5.1080 *Replacements*

4.5.1080.10 In our view, a share-based payment involving equity instruments of one group entity offered in exchange for a share-based payment arrangement of another group entity outside a business combination may be identified as a replacement plan in the consolidated financial statements of the group. For example, if Company P grants options over its shares to employees of Subsidiary Q in exchange for their options over shares of Q, then we believe that the grant of replacement options, if identified as such, should be accounted for in the consolidated financial statements of P as a modification of the original grant of options over shares of Q. This is because the shares in Q form part of the non-controlling interest in P and therefore are considered to be equity for the purposes of the consolidated financial statements of the group.

4.5.1080.20 P accounts for the replacement as described in 4.5.1080.10 in its separate financial statement as an increase in the cost of investment and an increase in equity based on modification-date fair value. From the date of modification Q accounts for the transaction in its separate financial statements by recognising both the original cost at grant-date fair value attributable to future services and the incremental value as a capital contribution from the parent.

4.5.1090 *Replacement awards in a business combination*

4.5.1093 *Consolidated financial statements of the acquirer*

IFRS 3.
B56-B62 4.5.1093.10 IFRS 3 provides guidance with respect to the accounting for the replacement of share-based payment awards held by the acquiree's employees (acquiree awards) in a business combination when the acquirer is obliged to issue share-based payment replacement awards (replacement awards) or when it chooses to replace awards that expire as a result of the business combination. To the extent that the replacement awards relate to past services, they are included in the consideration transferred; to the extent that they require future services, they are not part of the consideration transferred and instead are treated as post-combination remuneration cost. If they relate to both past and future services, then the market-based measure (fair value as measured under IFRS 2) of the

1181

replacement award is allocated between consideration transferred and post-combination remuneration cost (see 2.6.440).#

4.5.1093.20 Neither IFRS 2 nor IFRS 3 provide clear guidance on to how to account for the amount allocated to post-combination service. In our view, an entity should choose an accounting policy, to be applied consistently, to account for the recognition of the remuneration cost in post-combination periods using the new grant approach (see 4.5.1093.30) or the modification approach (see 4.5.1093.40).

4.5.1093.30 *New grant approach.* Under this approach, the replacement award is treated as a new grant, since the shares underlying the replacement award are the acquirer's shares, and not the acquiree's shares. Under the new grant approach, in line with the basic attribution principle in IFRS 2, the amount attributed to post-combination service would be recognised over the vesting period of the replacement award. Although this may appear to be a practical and logical approach, it could be considered not to be fully consistent with the reference in paragraph B56 of IFRS 3 to account for such replacements as "modifications of share-based payment awards in accordance with IFRS 2".

4.5.1093.40 *Modification approach.* Under this approach, the modification accounting principles of IFRS 2 (modification approach) are applied. The modification approach is complex because some of the requirements for modification accounting in IFRS 2 appear to conflict with the requirements regarding replacement awards in IFRS 3. Paragraph B43(a) of IFRS 2 requires the incremental fair value, estimated at the date of modification, to be recognised in addition to the grant-date fair value of the original equity instruments. However, this requirement effectively is overridden by paragraph B59 of IFRS 3 that prescribes how to determine the amount of the replacement award allocated to post-combination services. Under IFRS 3 the amount attributed to post-combination services includes any incremental fair value and the unrecognised amount of the acquisition-date market-based measure of the original award.

4.5.1093.50 As a result of the requirement of paragraph B59 of IFRS 3, the cumulative amount recognised should be the same under the two approaches outlined in 4.5.1093.30 and 40. However, application of IFRS 2's requirements for modifications may lead to a different pattern of attribution in the post-combination periods. For example, in order to apply modification accounting the acquirer would have to determine whether the terms of the replacement award, as compared to the terms of the acquiree award, are beneficial to the employee. If the replacement is considered to be non-beneficial (e.g. replacement with no incremental value and an extension of the vesting period), then the amount allocated to the post-combination services would be recognised over a shorter period under the modification approach than under the new grant approach.

4.5.1093.60 See 2.6.480 for guidance on how a change-in-control clause may affect the attribution of the market-based measure of a replacement award to pre-combination and post-combination services.

4.5.1093.70 See 3.13.630 for a discussion of income taxes related to replacement awards.

4.5.1095 *Separate financial statements of the acquirer*

4.5.1095.10 The requirements in IFRS 3 for attribution of the market-based measure of replacement awards were developed as part of the requirements for acquisition accounting in consolidated financial statements of the acquirer. It is not clear how replacement awards should be accounted for in the separate financial statements of the acquirer.

4.5.1095.20 In our view, one acceptable approach would be to follow the attribution guidance in IFRS 3 by analogy. This is on the basis that, from the point of view of the separate financial statements, the issue of a replacement award may be considered to have been exchanged for two different items:

- as part of the cost of obtaining a controlling interest in the acquiree; and
- for post-acquisition services to be rendered by the acquiree's employees.

4.5.1095.30 The amounts recognised under this view would be added to the cost of the investment in the subsidiary (see 4.5.947):

- in respect of the cost of obtaining control of the acquiree, at the acquisition date (see 2.6.260); and
- in respect of post-acquisition services, as those services are received (see 2.6.340).#

4.5.1098 *Forthcoming requirement*

4.5.1098.10 As a result of the *Improvements to IFRSs 2010*, the attribution guidance contained in IFRS 3 with respect to allocating the market-based measure of a replacement award to pre-combination service and post-combination service also will apply to acquiree awards that the acquirer is not obliged to replace. In addition, attribution guidance for unreplaced acquiree awards has been added to IFRS 3 (see 2.6.510).

4.5.1099 *Presentation in equity*

IAS 27.4   4.5.1099.10 When equity instruments of a subsidiary have been granted to a counterparty in a share-based payment arrangement, the credit entry in equity in the consolidated financial statements of the parent is allocated to non-controlling interest. This is because the definition of non-controlling interest in IAS 27 refers to "the equity in a subsidiary not attributable, directly or indirectly, to a parent."

4.5.1100 Share-based payments with non-employees

IFRS 2.11, A   4.5.1100.10 The requirements for transactions with employees also are applied to transactions with individuals who may not be an employee, but provide services similar to those provided by an employee. This includes non-executive directors.

IFRS 2.13 4.5.1100.20 For equity-settled share-based payment transactions with non-employees there is a rebuttable presumption that the fair value of the goods or services received can be measured reliably. If the presumption is rebutted, then the entity measures the fair value of the goods or services received by reference to the fair value of the equity instruments granted (i.e. like an employee grant). However, unlike an employee grant, the fair value of goods or services received is measured when the goods are obtained or services are rendered. As a result, a single agreement for payment may have multiple measurement dates (i.e. one for each date that goods or services are received) rather than being measured only once at the original grant date.

IFRS 2.30 4.5.1100.30 For cash-settled share-based payment transactions the goods or services received are measured at the fair value of the liability. The liability is remeasured at each reporting date and at the date of settlement in the same way as with cash-settled transactions with employees.

4.5.1110 Other application issues in practice

4.5.1120 *Employee benefit trusts*

SIC-12 4.5.1120.10 Application of the criteria for consolidation of an SPE often would require consolidation of a trust holding shares to meet obligations under a share-based payment arrangement (see 2.5.150). See 4.5.1040 for guidance on how to account for employee benefits trusts in separate financial statements.

4.5.1130 *Hedging of share-based payment transactions*

4.5.1130.10 An entity may purchase treasury shares or derivative instruments as an economic hedge of the risk of share price fluctuations. Such arrangements raise the issue of whether hedge *accounting* can be applied.

4.5.1130.20 In our view, it is not possible to apply hedge accounting for the obligation to issue shares or other equity instruments to settle equity-settled share-based payment transactions. This is because market fluctuations in share price do not affect profit or loss (see 3.7.290).

IAS 39.72 4.5.1130.30 It may, in principle, be possible to apply cash flow hedge accounting for cash-settled share-based payment transactions. However, in practice it may be difficult to meet the hedging requirements, and hedge accounting cannot be applied if the hedging instrument is itself equity (see 3.11.280.20).

4.5.1140 *Tax consequences related to share-based payments*

4.5.1140.10 See 3.13.630 for guidance on the classification and presentation of tax consequences related to share-based payment transactions.

4.5.1150 *Unvested shares and EPS calculation*

4.5.1150.10 See 5.3.80.30 for the impact of unvested shares on the calculation of basic and diluted EPS.

4.5.1160 **Transitional requirements**

4.5.1165 *Modifications of unrecognised otherwise exempt equity-settled share-based payments*

IFRS 2.57   4.5.1165.10 If an unrecognised grant is modified *after* the effective date of the standard, then the entity accounts for the modification by applying paragraphs 26 – 29 of IFRS 2. In our view, this requirement should be interpreted such that the original grant-date fair value remains unrecognised and only the incremental fair value, if any, is accounted for. See 4.5.720 for a discussion of how to determine the incremental fair value. We do not believe that these requirements should be applied to the original share-based payment as paragraph 57 specifically refers to accounting for "the modification".

4.5.1175 *Transitional issues related to the amendments in respect of group cash-settled share-based payment transactions*

4.5.1175.10 When another group entity has the obligation to settle a share-based payment transaction in cash, the entity receiving the services does not recognise any liability because it accounts for the transaction as equity settled. Therefore, the transitional requirements related to liabilities for cash-settled share-based payments in paragraph 58 of IFRS 2 do not seem to be applicable. In addition, no equity instrument of the receiving entity is granted, therefore the transitional requirements related to grants of equity instruments in equity-settled share-based payments in paragraph 53 of IFRS 2 also do not seem to apply. In our view, a subsidiary that accounts for a transaction as equity settled should apply the transitional requirements related to grants of equity instruments in paragraph 53 of IFRS 2 even if the share-based payment is settled by another entity in cash. Applying paragraph 53 of IFRS 2 to this fact pattern is consistent with the general principle of applying the requirements for equity-settled share-based payment transactions. The consequences of this view are that the cut-off date for recognition by the entity receiving the services is the vesting date rather than the date of settlement by the other group entity.

4.5.1175.20 It is unclear from the amendments how the reference to the effective date of IFRS 2 should be read. When the transitional requirements of IFRS 2 refer to the effective date of IFRS 2, in our view the amendments refer to the effective date of the original IFRS 2, i.e. 1 January 2005 rather than to the effective date of the amendments, i.e. 1 January 2010. Accordingly, the amendments would be applied retrospectively to all share-based payments to which IFRS 2 has been applied.

IFRS 2.BC   4.5.1175.30 There is no guidance on situations in which information necessary to apply
310A   the amendment retrospectively is not available. However, the potential problem of using

hindsight if a group share-based payment transaction had not been recognised previously in the financial statements of a subsidiary is acknowledged in the standard. As discussed in 2.8.50, IAS 8 *Accounting Policies, Changes in Accounting Estimates and Errors* includes guidance on when retrospective application is impracticable. In our view, information should be considered not available and retrospective application therefore to be impracticable only if the share-based payment was not measured previously and not able to be measured without the use of hindsight.

4.5.1180 **Future developments**

4.5.1180.10 In June 2005 the IASB published an ED *Proposed Amendments to IAS 37 Provisions, Contingent Liabilities and Contingent Assets and IAS 19 Employee Benefits* (the 2005 ED) and in January 2010 the IASB published ED/2010/1 *Measurement of Liabilities in IAS 37* (the 2010 ED), which is a limited re-exposure of the 2005 ED (see 3.12.880.10 – 30). The proposed standard may result in significant changes in the accounting for reimbursement rights. A final standard is scheduled for the first half of 2011.

4.6 Finance income and finance costs
(IAS 18, IAS 23, IAS 39)

4.6   Finance income and finance costs
(IAS 18, IAS 23, IAS 39)

> **Overview of currently effective requirements**
>
> - Interest income and interest expense are calculated using the effective interest method, based on estimated cash flows which consider all contractual terms of the financial instrument at the date that the instrument is recognised initially, or at the date of any modification.
>
> - Incremental transaction costs directly related to acquiring a financial asset or issuing a financial liability generally are included in the initial measurement of the instrument. However, if the instrument is classified as at fair value through profit or loss, then such costs are recognised in profit or loss.
>
> - Interest, which is calculated using the effective interest method is expensed, except borrowing costs related to qualifying assets which are capitalised if certain conditions are met.

Currently effective requirements

This publication reflects IFRSs in issue at 1 August 2010. The currently effective requirements cover annual periods beginning on 1 January 2010. The requirements related to this topic are derived mainly from IAS 18 *Revenue*, IAS 23 *Borrowing Costs* and IAS 39 *Financial Instruments: Recognition and Measurement*.

Forthcoming requirements and future developments

When a currently effective requirement will be changed by a new requirement that is issued but is not yet effective, it is marked with a # as a **forthcoming requirement** and the impact of the change is explained in the accompanying boxed text. In respect of this topic no forthcoming requirements are noted.

When a significant change to the currently effective or forthcoming requirements is expected, it is marked with a * as an area that may be subject to **future developments** and a brief outline of the relevant project is given in 4.6.560.

4.6.10 Introduction

4.6.10.10 This section provides guidance on determining finance income and finance costs and capitalising borrowing costs, and addresses certain issues related to the presentation of finance income and finance costs. See 3.6 and 3.7 for guidance on how to measure and when to recognise gains and losses on financial instruments, 2.7 for guidance on how to measure and recognise foreign exchange gains and losses and 5.6 for further guidance on presentation.

4.6.20 **Interest income and expense**

IAS 18.29,
30(a), 32,
A14(a), 39.9,
AG5-AG8

4.6.20.10 Interest income and expense is recognised using the effective interest method.

4.6.30 *Effective interest rate calculation**

4.6.40 *Method*

IAS 39.9   4.6.40.10 The *effective interest method* is a method of calculating the amortised cost of a financial asset or financial liability and allocating the interest income or expense over the relevant period. The effective interest method differs from the straight-line method in that the amortisation under the effective interest method reflects a constant periodic return on the carrying amount of the asset or liability.

IAS 18.30,   4.6.40.20 The *effective interest rate* is the rate that exactly discounts the estimated stream
39.9,   of future cash payments or receipts, without consideration of future credit losses, over
AG5-AG8   the expected life of the financial instrument or through to the next market-based repricing date, to the net carrying amount of the financial asset or financial liability on initial recognition.

4.6.40.30 The effective interest rate is calculated on initial recognition of an instrument. For floating rate financial instruments, periodic re-estimation of cash flows to reflect movements in market rates of interest alters the effective interest rate. To calculate the effective interest in each relevant period, the effective interest rate is applied to the amortised cost of the asset or liability at the end of the previous period.

4.6.40.40 The difference between the calculated effective interest for a given period and the instrument's coupon is the amortisation (or accretion) during that period of the difference between the initial measurement of the instrument and the maturity amount.

4.6.40.50 For example, Company Y grants a five-year loan of 50,000 to Company Z on 1 January 2010. There is an annual coupon of 10 percent paid on the last day of each year. Z pays an upfront fee of 1,000 and the net loan proceeds are 49,000. The effective interest rate is calculated by solving for x in the following equation:

$$49,000 = 5,000 / (1 + x) + 5,000 / (1 + x)^2 + 5,000 / (1 + x)^3 + 5,000 / (1 + x)^4 + 55,000 / (1 + x)^5.$$

4.6.40.60 Therefore the effective interest rate is 10.53482 percent. The interest and amortised cost are as follows:

Date	Interest (10.53482%)	Coupon	Amortised cost
1 January 2010	-	-	49,000
31 December 2010	5,162	5,000	49,162
31 December 2011	5,179	5,000	49,341
31 December 2012	5,198	5,000	49,539
31 December 2013	5,219	5,000	49,758
31 December 2014	5,242	5,000	50,000
Total	26,000	25,000	

4.6.50 *Contractual or estimated cash flows*

IAS 39.9   4.6.50.10 The calculation of the effective interest rate takes into account the *estimated* cash flows, which consider all contractual terms of the financial instrument (e.g. prepayment, call and similar options), but without inclusion of future credit losses. In those rare cases when it is not possible to make a reliable estimate of the cash flows or the expected life of the financial instrument, or a group of financial instruments, the contractual cash flows over the full contractual term are used.

IAS 39.9   4.6.50.20 In determining the effective interest rate, all contractual terms of an instrument are considered, including any embedded derivatives (e.g. prepayment options) that are not subject to separation (see 3.6.260). In our view, when an instrument gives either the issuer or the holder the option to require the instrument to be redeemed or cancelled early, and the terms of the instrument are such that it is not certain whether the option will be exercised, then the probability of the option being exercised should be assessed in determining the estimated cash flows.

IAS 39.49   4.6.50.30 However, for financial liabilities with a demand feature (e.g. a demand deposit) the fair value is not less than the amount payable on demand, discounted from the first date that the amount could be required to be paid. Therefore, for example, a non-interest-bearing or low-interest financial liability for which the holder can demand immediate repayment is not discounted, even if the issuer does not expect repayment of the liability in the near future. The impact of this requirement is that interest expense would be recognised at the coupon rate for a low-interest financial liability.

IAS 39.9   4.6.50.40 The calculation of the effective interest rate includes all fees and points paid or received between parties to the contract that are an integral part of the effective interest rate (see 4.6.310), transaction costs (see 4.6.150), and all other premiums or discounts.

IAS 39.9,   4.6.50.50 Future credit losses are not taken into account as this would be a departure from AG5-AG8 the incurred loss model for impairment (see 3.6.1370). In some cases, for example, when a financial asset is acquired at a deep discount, credit losses already have occurred and are reflected in the purchase price (see 5.6.170.20). Such credit losses are included in the estimated cash flows when computing the effective interest rate. Any adjustments arising from revisions to estimated cash flows subsequent to initial recognition, are recognised as part of the carrying amount of the financial asset with a corresponding amount recognised in profit or loss.

IAS 39.9   4.6.50.60 There is a presumption that future cash flows and the expected life can be estimated reliably for most financial instruments. In the rare case when it is not possible to estimate the timing or amount of future cash flows reliably, the entity should use the contractual cash flows over the full contractual term of the financial instrument.

4.6.60 *Changes in timing or amount of estimated cash flows*

IAS 39.AG8   4.6.60.10 If there is a change in the timing or amount of estimated future cash flows (other than due to impairment), then the carrying amount of the instrument (or group of financial instruments) is adjusted in the period of change to reflect the actual and/ or revised estimated cash flows with a corresponding gain or loss being recognised in profit or loss. The revised carrying amount is recalculated by discounting the revised estimated future cash flows at the instrument's original effective interest rate or, when applicable, the revised effective interest rate calculated in accordance with paragraph 92 of IAS 39 in relation to the amortisation of the fair value hedge adjustment in the case of fair value hedges. In our view, this approach on changes in estimated cash flows should apply to changing prepayment expectations but not to a renegotiation of the contractual terms of an instrument.

IAS 39.AG8   4.6.60.15 An entity may reclassify certain financial assets out of the fair value through profit or loss category and/or the available-for-sale category in certain circumstances (see 3.6.850). If a financial asset is so reclassified and the entity subsequently increases its estimates of future cash receipts as a result of increased estimates of recoverability of those cash receipts, then the effect of that increase is recognised as an adjustment to the effective interest rate from the date of the change in estimate rather than as an adjustment to the carrying amount of the asset at the date of the change in estimate, i.e. any increase in estimated future cash receipts is not recognised immediately as a gain.

IAS 39.9   4.6.60.20 The use of estimated cash flows specifically excludes the effect of expected future credit losses. Therefore the amortised cost calculation cannot be used to remove credit spread from interest income to cover future losses.

4.6.60.30 Contractual terms of some financial instruments may be linked to the performance of other assets. For example, assume that a special purpose entity (SPE) holds a portfolio of loans and receivables and have issued notes to investors collateralised by those loans. The contractual terms of the notes are such that the SPE only has an obligation to pay cash on its notes to the extent that it receives cash from its loan and receivable assets. Assume also that the notes do not contain embedded derivatives requiring separation (see 3.6.400) and, at the measurement date, the portfolio of loans and receivables held by the SPE include:

- actual defaults by the debtors of 10;

- incurred losses calculated in accordance with IAS 39 of 15; and
- expected losses of 20 (including 15 of incurred losses).

4.6.60.40 In our view, there are two acceptable approaches to estimating cash flows on the notes issued

- *Incurred loss method.* The incurred loss method, on the basis that taking into account losses incurred on the underlying loan assets is consistent with the requirements that an entity should estimate cash flows considering all contractual terms of an instrument but not future credit losses. Therefore, expected cash flows would be reduced by 15.
- *Expected loss method.* The expected loss method, on the basis that the requirements preclude consideration of future credit losses for financial assets only and the best estimate of the future cash flows payable in respect of the notes includes current expectation of all future, not just already incurred, losses. Therefore, expected cash flows would be reduced by 20.

4.6.60.50 We believe that estimating cash flows for the notes taking into account only actual defaults by the debtors is not consistent with the requirements of the standard.

4.6.70 *Floating rate financial assets and liabilities*

IAS 39.AG7   4.6.70.10 The periodic re-estimation of determinable cash flows to reflect movements in market rates of interest will change the effective interest rate of a floating rate financial asset or liability. However, if the floating rate financial asset or liability is recognised initially at an amount equal to the principal receivable or payable on maturity, then this periodic re-estimation does not have a significant effect on the carrying amount of the asset or liability.

IAS 39.AG7   4.6.70.20 Therefore, in such cases for practical reasons the carrying amount of a floating rate instrument generally would not need to be adjusted at each repricing date as the impact generally would not be significant. In this case interest income or expense is recognised based on the current market rate. For a floating rate financial asset or liability that is recognised initially at a discount or premium, the interest income or expense is recognised based on the current market rate plus or minus amortisation or accretion of the discount or premium (see 4.6.110.30).

4.6.70.30 In our view, this approach also could be applied for a floating rate instrument that includes embedded derivatives that are not separated, e.g. an instrument on which the interest rate is subject to market indices such as inflation.

4.6.70.40 IAS 39 does not prescribe any specific methodology for how transaction costs should be amortised for a floating rate loan, except as discussed in 4.6.110. In our view, any consistent methodology that would establish a reasonable basis for amortisation of the transaction costs may be used. For example, it would be reasonable to determine an amortisation schedule of the transaction costs based on the interest rate in effect at inception.

4.6.80 *Restructuring of a financial liability*

4.6.80.10 If the terms of a financial liability are modified substantially, resulting in an extinguishment of the old financial liability, then the old liability is derecognised and the restructured financial instrument is treated as a new financial liability (see 3.6.1340).

IAS 39.41, 4.6.80.20 If a modification of a financial liability results in derecognition of the financial
AG62 liability, then the effective interest rate of the new financial liability is calculated based on the revised terms of the financial liability at the date of the modification. In this case any costs or fees incurred are recognised as part of the gain or loss on extinguishment and do not adjust the carrying amount of the new liability. Accordingly, in our view no transaction costs are included in the initial measurement of the new liability unless it can be demonstrated incontrovertibly that they relate solely to the new liability instrument and in no way to the modification of the old liability. This usually would not be possible but might apply to taxes and registration fees payable on execution of the new liability instrument.

IAS 39.41, 4.6.80.30 If the exchange or modification is not accounted for as an extinguishment, then
AG62 any costs and fees incurred are recognised as an adjustment to the carrying amount of the liability and amortised over the remaining term of the modified instrument by recomputing the effective interest rate on the instrument.

4.6.90 *Instruments acquired in a business combination*

4.6.90.10 All financial instruments that are acquired as part of a business combination are measured initially by the acquirer at their fair value at the acquisition date (see 2.6.600).

4.6.90.20 At the acquisition date, the fair value of the instrument and the total cash flows expected over the remaining term of the instrument are used by the acquirer to calculate a new original effective interest rate for the instrument. The new original effective interest rate should be used to determine the interest income or expense in the consolidated financial statements but has no impact on the acquiree's accounting.

IAS 39.AG5, 4.6.90.30 As assets of the acquiree are measured in the consolidated accounts at fair value
IFRS 3.B41 at the acquisition date, the acquirer does not recognise a separate valuation allowance to reflect any credit losses incurred at that date. In our view, for an instrument that is impaired at the acquisition date (see 3.6.1370), the estimated cash flows should be determined on the basis of the expected receipts as reduced by those incurred credit losses, rather than on the basis of the cash flows that would arise if the borrower complied with the contractual terms. Generally, the expected cash flows should exclude any future credit losses. In practice, it may be difficult to make a distinction between incurred and future losses, it is considered that the borrower will not be able to meet the contractual terms in full. However, to the extent that the distinction can be made, future losses should be excluded from the estimates.

IAS 39.AG8 4.6.90.40 Continuing the example in 4.6.90.30, if expected cash flows from that asset subsequently are revised upwards due to an improvement in the debtor's credit quality, then in our view the upward revision is recognised in profit or loss but should not be presented as a recovery of impairment. This is because no impairment loss had been recognised in the consolidated financial statements on the asset subsequent to initial recognition and therefore there is no impairment to reverse.

4.6.100 *Hedged item in a fair value hedge*

IAS 39.89(b)   4.6.100.10 An interest-bearing instrument that is the hedged item in a fair value hedge is remeasured to fair value in respect of the risk being hedged during the period of the hedge relationship (see 3.7.50), even if the item normally is measured at amortised cost.

IAS 39.92   4.6.100.20 When hedge accounting is discontinued, the carrying amount of the instrument and the total payments to be made over the remaining term of the instrument are used to calculate a revised effective interest rate for the instrument. The revised effective interest rate is used to determine interest income or expense in subsequent periods.

4.6.110 *Discounts and premiums and pre-acquisition interest*

IAS 39.AG6   4.6.110.10 The straight-line amortisation of discounts or premiums is not permitted. Instead, discounts and premiums (including fees, points paid or received and transaction costs) generally are recognised over the expected life of the related instrument using the effective interest rate at the date of initial recognition of the instrument. However, in some cases a shorter period should be used if this is the period to which such discounts and premiums relate (e.g. when the variable is repriced to market rates before the expected maturity of the instrument).

4.6.110.20 Therefore, for a group of prepayable mortgage loans, any discount, transaction costs and related fees may be required to be amortised over a period shorter than the contractual maturity. Historical prepayment patterns would be used to estimate expected lives, and revised prepayment estimates will give rise to gains and losses that are recognised in profit or loss.

IAS 39.AG6   4.6.110.30 If a discount or premium arises on the acquisition of a floating rate instrument, then it is important to identify the reason for that discount or premium. For example, if a premium or discount on a floating rate instrument reflects *changes in market rates* since the floating interest instrument was last repriced, then it will be amortised to the next repricing date. Alternatively, if the premium or discount results from a change in the credit spread over the floating rate specified in the instrument as a result of a *change in credit risk*, then it is amortised over the expected life of the instrument.

4.6.110.40 When an interest-bearing instrument is acquired between interest payment dates, normally the buyer has an obligation to pay the accrued interest to the seller when it is received, or pays a higher price for the instrument to reimburse the seller for the accrued interest that will be paid to the buyer.

IAS 18.32 4.6.110.50 Interest that has accrued on an interest-bearing investment before it is acquired is not recognised as income. If there is an obligation to pay the accrued interest to the seller, then a receivable and a corresponding payable are recognised in respect of the accrued interest.

4.6.110.60 The amortisation of discounts or premiums is included in interest income or expense and is not required to be disclosed separately.

4.6.120 *Unwinding of the discount on impaired financial assets*

IAS 39.AG93 4.6.120.10 Once an impairment loss has been recognised on a financial asset, interest income is recognised based on the rate of interest that was used to discount future cash flows for the purpose of measuring the impairment loss (see 3.6.1440).

4.6.130 **Low-interest loans and receivables**

IAS 39.43, AG64 4.6.130.10 If, at the time of initial recognition, a loan or other debt instrument does not bear interest at a market rate, then the instrument initially is measured at its fair value determined by discounting the expected future cash flows at a market interest rate (see 3.6.740).

4.6.130.20 For financial assets measured at amortised cost, interest is accrued on the instrument over the period to maturity, using the effective interest method. Unless the instrument is modified (see 4.6.80), the effective interest rate is not revised for fixed rate debt instruments based on subsequent changes in market interest rates.

4.6.130.30 For example, Company L receives an interest-free loan of 900. The loan is repayable in five years. A market interest rate for a similar loan at the date the loan is granted is 5 percent. The fair value of the loan at initial recognition is 705 (the cash flow of 900 in five years discounted at 5 percent). Therefore, the loan is recognised initially at 705. The difference of 195 is recognised immediately as income, liability, or equity (see 3.6.760). In each of the five years that the loan is outstanding, interest is accrued on the carrying amount of the loan at 5 percent. Therefore, in the first year the interest expense is 35 (705 x 5%). In the second year the interest expense is 37 ((705 + 35) x 5%). At the end of five years, the carrying amount of the loan will be 900.

4.6.140 **Stepped interest**

IAS 39.9, IGB.27 4.6.140.10 Sometimes entities purchase or issue debt instruments with a predetermined rate of interest that increases or decreases progressively (stepped interest) over the term of the debt instrument. In this case the entity should use the effective interest method to allocate the interest income or expense over the term of the debt instrument to achieve a level yield to maturity that is a constant interest rate on the carrying amount of the instrument in each period.

4.6.140.20 For example, on 1 January 2010 Bank B takes a five-year deposit from a customer with the following rates of interest specified in the agreement: 2.0 percent in 2010,

2.1 percent in 2011, 2.2 percent in 2012, 2.4 percent in 2013 and 3.0 percent in 2014. The effective interest rate for this instrument is approximately 2.33 percent. Therefore interest is accrued using the 2.33 percent rate.

4.6.140.30 [Not used]

4.6.140.40 If B expects the deposit to be withdrawn after four years without penalty, then this expectation should be taken into account when calculating the instrument's effective interest rate. In this circumstance, the resulting effective interest rate would be approximately 2.17 percent, which should be used to accrue interest expense over the deposit's expected life.

4.6.140.50 A similar approach should be adopted from the perspective of the holder of a financial instrument, i.e. the holder should take into consideration all contractual terms and the probability of any prepayment and call and similar options being exercised.

4.6.140.60 In respect of mortgage loans and credit cards that are issued with a low initial rate of interest in order to attract new customers, an issue similar to stepped interest arises. After the initial period typically the interest rate returns to a standard market rate so that the lender is able to recover the discount over the remaining estimated life of the instrument. Normally any initial discount that is offered widely to market participants should be recognised as part of the effective yield over the estimated life of the instrument. Alternatively, in our view the fair value of such an initial discount might be considered as a cost of attracting new business and recognised immediately as an expense. In our view, any discount that is not offered widely and is therefore in excess of that offered to all market participants should be recognised immediately as an expense (see 3.6.730).

4.6.150 *Transaction costs*

IAS 39.43, IGE.1.1   4.6.150.10 A financial asset or financial liability is recognised initially at its fair value plus, in the case of a financial asset or financial liability not at fair value through profit or loss, transaction costs that are directly attributable to the acquisition or issue of the financial instrument.

4.6.150.20 For example, Company K issues debt of 100,000 at par and incurs direct incremental issue costs of 5,000. The debt will be redeemed at par. Ignoring interest, there is a difference of 5,000 between the net proceeds of 95,000 and the redemption amount of 100,000. This difference represents the transaction costs and is recognised as an expense over the period that the debt is outstanding using the effective interest method.

4.6.150.30 Transaction costs on financial instruments at fair value through profit or loss are charged immediately to profit or loss.

IAS 32.38   4.6.150.32 Transaction costs that relate to the issuance of a compound instrument are allocated to the liability and equity components of the instrument in proportion to the allocation of proceeds.

4.6.150.34 In our view, an entity should choose an accounting policy, to be applied consistently, to allocating transaction costs that relate to a hybrid (combined) instrument which includes a non-derivative host contract and an embedded derivative that is accounted for at fair value through profit or loss:

- Allocate the transaction costs to the non-derivative host contract and embedded derivative components of the instrument in proportion to the allocation of the proceeds, by analogy to the allocation of transaction costs that relate to a compound instrument (see 4.6.150.32). Under this approach, the amount of transaction costs allocated to the embedded derivative will be charged immediately to profit or loss (see 4.6.150.30).
- The embedded derivative is measured at fair value on initial recognition, and the carrying amount of the non-derivative host contract at initial recognition is the difference between the fair value plus transaction costs of the hybrid instrument and the fair value of the embedded derivative (see 3.6.440). Under this approach, all the transaction costs will be allocated to and included in the carrying amount of the non-derivative host contract on initial recognition.

4.6.150.36 We prefer the second approach in 4.6.150.34.

4.6.150.40 Any transaction costs that do not qualify to be included in the initial measurement of an instrument should be expensed as incurred. These costs normally are included in the finance costs line item.

IAS 39.9, 4.6.150.50 Only transaction costs that are related directly to originating or acquiring a
AG13 financial instrument, and that would have been avoided if the instrument had not been originated or acquired, are included as transaction costs in the initial measurement of the instrument, e.g. fees and commissions paid to agents (including employees acting as selling agents), advisers, brokers and dealers, levies by regulatory agencies and securities exchanges, transfer taxes and duties, credit assessment, registration charges and similar costs.

IAS 39.9, 4.6.150.60 Transaction costs do not include debt premiums or discounts, financing costs
AG13 or internal administrative or holding costs. Service fees are not directly attributable to the acquisition of an asset or liability and should be expensed as incurred. Similarly, costs of researching or developing an instrument or assessing alternatives with a number of parties should be expensed as incurred.

4.6.150.70 Transaction costs generally are included in the initial measurement of instruments on an individual basis. This means that the transaction costs should be identifiable with the acquisition or incurrence of each individual instrument. However, in our view it may be appropriate to accumulate the incremental costs attributable to the acquisition or incurrence of individual contracts within a portfolio of instruments and then allocate these costs to items in the portfolio using a method that produces results that are not materially different from a situation in which the amounts are identified with individual items. It is necessary to make such an allocation to individual balances in order for unamortised transaction costs to be associated correctly with items that are repaid early, are sold or become impaired. This approach would be appropriate only when the portfolio comprises homogenous items.

4.6.160 *Internal costs*

IAS 39.AG13   4.6.160.10 In our view, the only internal transaction costs allowed to be included in the initial measurement of a financial instrument are commissions, bonuses and other payments that are made to employees only on completion of each individual transaction. We believe that internal semi-variable costs, for example, the costs of marketing a new product or of employing additional staff to deal with an increase in the volume of transactions, do not qualify as transaction costs.

4.6.170 *Facility or commitment fees paid*

4.6.170.10 An issue that often arises is how to treat facility fees (i.e. initial fees to cover negotiation and arrangement of a facility and periodic fees to compensate the financier for keeping funds available).

4.6.170.20 In our view, if it is probable that a facility will be drawn down, then an initial facility fee typically is, in substance, an adjustment to the interest cost and therefore the fee should be deferred and treated as an adjustment to the instrument's effective interest rate and recognised as an expense over the instrument's estimated life. However, if it is not probable that a facility will be drawn down, then the fee is considered a service fee and recognised as an expense on a straight-line basis over the commitment period.

IAS 18.IE14   4.6.170.30 The above accounting treatment would result in mirror accounting adopted by a borrower and a lender (see 4.6.300).

4.6.180 – 190 [Not used]

4.6.200 **Dividends on shares classified as liabilities**

IAS 32.35   4.6.200.10 Interest, dividends, losses and gains are reported in a way that is consistent with the classification of an instrument as a liability or equity (see 3.11.10). Therefore dividends on shares classified as liabilities are reported in the statement of comprehensive income as finance costs using the effective interest method, as are any gains or losses arising on their early redemption or refinancing.

4.6.210 **Impairment**

IAS 39.63   4.6.210.10 If the terms of an instrument classified as loans and receivables or held to maturity (see 3.6.460) are renegotiated or otherwise modified because of financial difficulties of the borrower or issuer, then an entity (creditor) considers whether an impairment loss on the financial asset has been incurred. If the creditor concludes that an asset is impaired, then the creditor measures the loss as the difference between the asset's carrying amount and the present value of estimated cash flows discounted at the financial asset's original effective interest rate before the modification of terms (see 3.6.1440).

IAS 39.AG93 4.6.210.20 After an impairment loss has been recognised in profit or loss, interest income is recognised based on the rate used to discount the future cash flows when measuring the amount of the impairment loss (see 3.6.1440).

IAS 39.AG93 4.6.210.30 It is inappropriate simply to suspend interest recognition on a non-performing interest-bearing instrument, such as a loan and receivable. Future interest receipts should be taken into account when the entity estimates the future cash flows of the instrument. If no contractual interest payments will be collected, then the only interest income recognised is the unwinding of the discount on those cash flows expected to be received.

4.6.210.40 See 3.6.1370 for a more detailed discussion of the impairment of financial instruments.

4.6.220 Net gains and net losses

4.6.230 *Disposals of assets and liabilities*

IAS 39.56 4.6.230.10 For financial assets and financial liabilities measured at amortised cost (e.g. loans and receivables), a gain or loss is recognised in profit or loss when the financial asset or liability is derecognised or remeasured for exchange differences. Currently there is no specific guidance on the presentation of these gains and losses in the statement of comprehensive income. In our view, gains and losses should be reported in the most appropriate line item based on their nature.

IAS 21.28, 4.6.230.20 For example, an entity may present foreign currency gains and losses on *39.46, 56* financial assets and liabilities that arise from operating activities (e.g. payables arising on the purchase of goods) as part of income and expenses before finance costs, and foreign currency gains and losses related to financing activities as part of finance income and finance costs (see 4.6.540 and 2.7.160.20). In the case of a disposal of financial assets and liabilities (including trade receivables), in our view the gains and losses always should be presented within finance income and finance costs as the decision to dispose of financial assets and liabilities is, we believe, always a financing decision.

IAS 39.55 4.6.230.30 For available-for-sale financial assets, the cumulative gain or loss recognised previously in equity is reclassified to profit or loss when the asset is derecognised.

4.6.240 *Net gains and losses on financial assets or liabilities at fair value through profit or loss*

IAS 1.35, 99 4.6.240.10 The net fair value changes (i.e. gains and losses) on each financial asset or liability at fair value through profit or loss usually are classified as finance income or finance costs. They are presented separately if material.

1200

4.6.240.20 IFRS 7 *Financial Instruments: Disclosures* requires net gains and losses to be disclosed separately for each category of financial asset and liability: held-to-maturity investments, loans and receivables, available-for-sale financial assets, financial liabilities measured subsequently at amortised cost, financial instruments held for trading, and financial instruments designated as at fair value through profit or loss. See 5.6.220 for further discussion of the presentation of gains and losses on financial instruments at fair value through profit or loss.

4.6.250 [Not used]

4.6.260 Dividend income

4.6.270 *Recognition of dividend income*

IAS 18.30   4.6.270.10 Dividend income is recognised when the shareholder's right to receive payment is established (see 3.11.450).

4.6.270.20 In our view, the shareholder's right to receive payment of dividends on *quoted* investments normally is established on the date that the security trades ex-dividend. At this date the fair value of the security decreases by approximately the dividend amount. Therefore, recognising a dividend on the ex-dividend date will avoid double counting, which would occur if the dividend was included both as income and in the measurement of the fair value of the investment. The ex-dividend date is the first date when a sale of the instrument would not settle before the record date. The record date is the date when shareholders have to be included in the register of shareholders in order to receive the dividend. Calculation of the ex-dividend date will depend upon local trading and settlement practices.

4.6.270.30 In our view, for dividends on *unquoted* investments, the shareholder's right to receive payment normally is established when the shareholders have approved the dividends. However, if the relevant law provided that a board decision or announcement required no further approval *and* was binding on the declaring entity, then the dividend is recognised on a board decision or announcement (see also 3.11.450.25). When determining the fair value of such investments, care should be taken to avoid double counting dividends as both receivables and as part of the fair value estimate.

4.6.270.40 For example, Company P's directors declare a dividend on 10 March. The dividend is approved by shareholders on 25 March and will be paid to shareholders of record (i.e. in the shareholders' register) on 31 March. If P's shares are listed in a market that has three-day settlement, then the shares would trade ex-dividend from 28 March (assuming all are business days). Therefore, we believe that dividend income should be recognised on 28 March. If P's shares are not listed and the right to receive dividends is established when the shareholders have approved it, then we believe that the dividends should be recognised when they are approved (i.e. 25 March). Thereafter the dividends should be excluded when estimating the fair value of the shares.

IAS 27.38A,
36.12(h)

4.6.270.50 An entity should recognise a dividend from a subsidiary, jointly controlled entity or associate in profit or loss in its separate financial statements when its right to receive the dividend is established. However, the receipt of dividend income may be an indicator of impairment of the investment in the subsidiary, jointly controlled entity or associate (see 3.10.600.30).

4.6.280 *Share dividends*

4.6.280.10 In some cases shareholders may receive or choose to receive dividends in the form of additional shares rather than cash. These may be referred to as scrip, stock or share dividends. In our view, the accounting treatment of share dividends depends on whether the investor has a cash alternative (i.e. a right to demand a cash payment representing the fair value of the shares).

4.6.280.20 In our view, the substance of share dividends with a cash alternative is the payment of a cash dividend, with reinvestment of the cash in additional shares. Therefore we believe that dividend income should be recognised for the amount of the cash dividend alternative. The corresponding debit should be treated as an additional investment.

IU 01-10

4.6.280.30 In other cases an entity may receive bonus shares or other equity instruments on a *pro rata* basis with other ordinary shareholders with no cash alternative. Share investments generally are categorised as available-for-sale financial assets or as at fair value through profit or loss and therefore always are measured at fair value (see 3.6.460). If all ordinary shareholders receive bonus shares or other equity instruments in proportion to their shareholdings, then the fair value of each shareholder's interest should be unaffected by the bonus issue. In our view, in such circumstances, dividends are not recognised as revenue because it is not probable that there is an economic benefit associated with the transaction that will flow to the investor.

4.6.280.40 If only certain shareholders are granted additional shares, then the fair value of the interests of those shareholders will increase. In this case, in our view it is most appropriate to measure the shares received at their fair value and recognise a corresponding amount of finance income.

4.6.290 [Not used]

4.6.300 **Fee income**

4.6.300.10 The recognition of revenue for fees depends on the nature of the fees and the basis of accounting for any associated financial instrument.

IAS 18.IE14,
39.AG64

4.6.300.20 As the description of financial service fees may not be indicative of the nature and substance of the services provided, it is necessary to distinguish between fees that are an integral part of the effective interest rate of an associated financial instrument, fees that are earned as services are provided and fees that are earned on the execution of a significant act. The accounting treatment of fee income related to interest-bearing instruments depends on whether the fees are an integral part of the effective yield of the instrument.

4.6.310 *Fees that are an integral part of the effective interest rate*

4.6.310.10 Fees earned in relation to the recognition of a financial asset in most instances results in an adjustment of the effective interest rate. Examples of such fees include:

- origination or commitment fees (when it is probable that an entity will enter into a specific lending agreement);
- compensation from the borrower for transaction costs (see 4.6.150) incurred by the lender; and
- appraisal fees for evaluating collateral (e.g. for mortgage loans).

IAS 18.IE14   4.6.310.20 However, if the financial instrument is measured at fair value through profit or loss, then the fees are recognised as revenue upon initial recognition of the instrument.

4.6.320 *Fees earned as services are provided*

IAS 18.IE14,   4.6.320.10 Some financial service fees are not an integral part of the effective yield of an
39.47(d)   associated financial instrument and are recognised as the related services are provided (i.e. normally on a time-proportionate basis). Examples of such financial service fees include:

- fees charged for servicing a loan;
- commitment fees to originate loans when it is unlikely that a specific lending arrangement will be entered into and the loan commitment is outside the scope of IAS 39 (most loan commitments within the scope of IAS 39 are accounted for as derivatives and are measured at fair value); and
- investment management fees.

4.6.330 *Fees that are earned on the execution of a significant act*

IAS 18.IE14   4.6.330.10 Some fees may be related to the execution of a significant act, rather than to the effective interest rate of an associated financial instrument or to a specific service period. Such fees are earned when the related significant act has been completed. Examples include a commission earned on the allotment of shares to a client, placement fees for arranging a loan and loan syndication fees received by an entity that arranges a loan and retains no part of the loan package for itself (or retains a part at the same effective interest rate for comparable risk as other participants).

4.6.330.20 In some cases it may be difficult to determine whether an amount charged to a customer at the inception of a loan represents a fee for structuring the loan or part of the transaction price representing the fair value of the financial asset.

4.6.330.30 For example, a bank structures a transaction, using its expertise and experience ("intellectual capital") for a particular customer and often facilitates the initial steps required, e.g. consultations with experts, valuations, registration and drafting legal documentation. The customer is charged a fee upfront for the structuring service.

4.6.330.40 If the fee is regarded as a structuring fee, then revenue would be recognised immediately under IAS 18. However, if the fee is regarded as part of the initial fair value of the loan, then IAS 39 would preclude recognition of revenue unless fair value is determined using a valuation technique whose variables include only data from observable markets.

4.6.330.50 In our view, a bank should recognise fee income immediately only if the fair value of the loan can be measured reliably using data from observable markets and if it can be demonstrated that the amount of revenue recognised is consistent with the effort and expertise provided for the structuring service, i.e. that it approximates fair value for the service provided.

IFRS 7.20(c)   4.6.330.60 IFRS 7 requires the disclosure of fee income or expense arising from financial instruments that are not at fair value through profit or loss, and from trust or other fiduciary activities, other than for amounts included in the effective interest (see 5.6.230).

4.6.340 [Not used]

4.6.350 **Capitalisation of borrowing costs**

IAS 23.8, 9   4.6.350.10 Borrowing costs that are directly attributable to the acquisition, construction, or production of a qualifying asset form part of the cost of that asset.

IAS 23.4   4.6.350.20 This general requirement to capitalise directly attributable borrowing costs is not required to be applied to:

- qualifying assets measured at fair value; or
- inventories that are manufactured or produced in large quantities on a repetitive basis.

4.6.350.30 See 5.11.120 for a discussion of the capitalisation of borrowing costs related to exploration and evaluation assets.

4.6.350.40 See 5.12.110 for a discussion of the capitalisation of borrowing costs related to service concession arrangements.

4.6.360 *Qualifying assets*

IAS 23.5   4.6.360.10 A qualifying asset is one that necessarily takes a substantial period of time to be made ready for its intended use or sale. Qualifying assets generally are those that are subject to major development or construction projects.

IAS 23.7   4.6.360.20 Investments, including, in our view investments in associates, jointly controlled entities and subsidiaries, are not qualifying assets. However, investment property may be a qualifying asset.

1204

IAS 23.7 4.6.360.30 An asset that is ready for its intended use or sale when acquired is not a qualifying asset, even if expenditure subsequently is incurred on the asset.

4.6.360.40 There is no specific guidance on how long a "substantial period of time" is, but in our view it is a period well in excess of six months.

IAS 23.7 4.6.360.50 Inventories that take a long time to produce (e.g. whisky or property) can be qualifying assets.

IAS 23.5 4.6.360.60 The term "necessarily" is included in the definition of a qualifying asset to indicate that the nature of the asset should be such that it takes a long time to get it ready for its intended use or sale. Therefore, in our view an asset that takes a long time to prepare for use or sale only because of inefficiencies in the development process is not a qualifying asset.

4.6.370 *Refurbishment*

4.6.370.10 There is no guidance in IFRSs regarding whether an asset that is being refurbished can be a qualifying asset. In our view, an asset being refurbished can be a qualifying asset if the refurbishment costs qualify for capitalisation (see 3.2.290), and the refurbishment will take a substantial period of time. For example, an entity owns and manages a hotel. The hotel is closed down for a major refurbishment. The refurbishment costs will be capitalised and the refurbishment will take 18 months. We believe that the borrowing costs related to the refurbishment should be capitalised as the refurbishment takes a substantial period of time.

4.6.380 *Redevelopment*

IAS 23.18 4.6.380.10 Expenditures on a qualifying asset include only those expenditures that have resulted in payments of cash, transfers of other assets or the assumption of interest-bearing liabilities. Therefore, any previously capitalised interest and fair value adjustments should not be included in a qualifying asset.

4.6.380.20 For example, an investor has a property with a fair value of 100 and a historical cost of 60. Interest was capitalised on the historical cost of 60 during the construction of the property. The construction had since been completed and the capitalisation of interest had ceased. To increase its return the investor decides to redevelop the property substantially. The cost of the redevelopment is assumed to be 30. We prefer to capitalise interest only for the incremental cost of redevelopment, which is 30. Alternatively, we believe that an entity also could recommence capitalisation of interest, on the historical cost of 60, if the original loan that was taken at the time of the property's initial construction and interest on that loan still are outstanding.

4.6.390 **Borrowing costs eligible for capitalisation**

IAS 23.6 4.6.390.10 Borrowing costs eligible for capitalisation may include:

- interest expense calculated using the effective interest method (see 4.6.30);
- finance charges in respect of finance leases (see 5.1.300); and
- exchange differences to the extent that they are regarded as an adjustment to interest costs (see 4.6.420).

4.6.390.15 [Not used]

IAS 23.9, 10   4.6.390.20 The borrowing costs that are capitalised are those that otherwise would have been avoided if the expenditure on the qualifying asset had not been made. This includes interest on borrowings made specifically for the purpose of obtaining the qualifying asset (specific borrowings) and the cost of other borrowings that could have been repaid if expenditure on the asset had not been incurred (general borrowings).

4.6.390.30 In our view, adjustments to the carrying amount of borrowings resulting from re-estimation of expected cash flows under the contract (see 4.6.60) are an integral part of interest expense and so are eligible for capitalisation.

4.6.400 *Interest rate swaps*

4.6.400.10 IFRSs are silent on whether interest rate swaps that effectively alter borrowing costs should be considered in determining the amount of borrowing costs to capitalise.

4.6.400.20 In our view, accruals under interest rate swaps entered into as a hedge of eligible borrowing costs may be included in determining the amount of borrowing costs to capitalise, based on the principle that borrowing costs should include those costs that could have been avoided if expenditures on the qualifying asset had not been made. However, in our view it is not acceptable to consider the changes in fair value of interest rate swaps as a borrowing cost. The fair value of an interest rate swap is the present value of expected future cash flows, discounted at market rates, and it does not represent borrowing costs incurred.

4.6.410 *Tax*

4.6.410.10 In our view, the amount of borrowing costs to be capitalised is calculated on a pre-tax basis. Borrowing costs that are capitalised may give rise to deferred tax (see 3.13).

4.6.420 *Foreign exchange differences*

IAS 23.6   4.6.420.10 Borrowing costs may include foreign exchange differences to the extent that these differences are regarded as an adjustment to interest costs. There is no further guidance on the conditions under which foreign exchange differences may be capitalised and in practice there are different views about what is acceptable.

4.6.420.20 In our view, foreign exchange differences on borrowings can be regarded as an adjustment to interest costs only in very limited circumstances. Exchange differences should not be capitalised if a borrowing in a foreign currency is entered into to offset another currency exposure. Interest determined in a foreign currency already reflects the exposure to that currency. Therefore, the foreign exchange differences to be capitalised should be limited to the difference between interest accrued at the contractual rate and the interest that would apply to a borrowing with identical terms in the entity's functional currency. Any foreign exchange differences arising from the notional amount of the loan should be recognised in profit or loss.

4.6.420.30 – 40 [Not used]

4.6.420.50 When exchange differences qualify for capitalisation, in our view both exchange gains and losses should be considered in determining the amount to capitalise.

4.6.430 *Dividends*

IAS 32.18(a), 4.6.430.10 In our view, distributions and similar payments on instruments classified as 20 liabilities, e.g. dividends on preference shares that are classified as a liability (see 3.11.170), are eligible for capitalisation.

4.6.440 *Imputed interest on non-financial liabilities*

4.6.440.10 In our view, imputed interest on non-financial liabilities (e.g. the unwinding of the discount effect on provisions) may not be capitalised.

IFRIC 1.8 4.6.440.20 Capitalising interest expense recognised from unwinding a discount on decommissioning or restoration provisions is not permitted.

4.6.450 **Calculating the amount of borrowing costs to capitalise**

4.6.460 **Specific borrowings**

IAS 23.12 4.6.460.10 The amount of specific borrowing costs capitalised is net of the investment income on any temporary investment of the funds pending expenditure on the asset.

4.6.470 *General borrowings*

IAS 23.14 4.6.470.10 To the extent that the interest costs to be capitalised relate to financing that is part of the entity's general borrowings, the weighted average interest cost (excluding the interest on any borrowings specific to any qualifying assets) is applied to the expenditures on the asset. The objective is to capitalise borrowing costs that would have been avoided if expenditures on the asset had not been incurred. In our view, an entity should determine general borrowings by excluding borrowings used to finance specific assets that are qualifying assets. However, we would not preclude the use of judgement in determining whether general borrowings include or exclude borrowings used to finance specific assets that are non-qualifying assets.

4.6 Finance income and finance costs

4.6.470.20 In our view, the weighted average accumulated expenditures on the asset during the period, reduced by any progress payments or grants received in respect of the asset, may be used in calculating the amount on which interest is capitalised. The amount capitalised may not exceed the actual interest incurred by the entity.

4.6.480 Calculation in the consolidated financial statements

4.6.480.10 There is no specific guidance in IFRSs related to the calculation in consolidated financial statements beyond the comment that in some cases the amount of borrowing costs to capitalise is based on a weighted average borrowing rate applicable for a group rather than a weighted average rate applicable to an individual entity's borrowings.

4.6.480.20 In our view, the approach adopted for consolidated financial statements should be one that reflects the borrowing costs attributable to a particular qualifying asset. Entity-specific rates are likely to be the most appropriate for an individual entity within a group that is financed independently. For an entity that is financed largely by internal borrowings, a group borrowing rate is more appropriate. Only external borrowings should be considered in calculating a weighted average group borrowing rate.

4.6.490 Calculation in separate financial statements

4.6.490.10 In our view, only borrowing costs incurred by the group entity that has incurred expenditures on a qualifying asset are eligible for capitalisation in the entity's separate financial statements. For example, Parent H borrows funds on behalf of Subsidiary S. H makes an equity investment in S so that S can use the capital to construct a qualifying asset. H cannot capitalise the borrowing costs incurred on the financing in its separate financial statements, as it does not have a qualifying asset. Similarly, S does not have eligible borrowing costs and cannot capitalise borrowing costs as part of the cost of the asset. However, in the consolidated financial statements borrowing costs should be capitalised if the other criteria for capitalisation are met.

4.6.500 *Period of capitalisation*

4.6.510 Commencement

4.6.510.10 Capitalisation begins when:

- expenditures for the asset are being incurred;
- borrowing costs are being incurred; and
- activities that are necessary to prepare the asset for its intended use or sale are in progress.

4.6.510.20 If funds are raised in advance to finance a major capital project, then capitalisation of borrowing costs cannot begin until the project starts. Capitalisation is limited to interest costs incurred after expenditures are incurred.

IAS 23.19 4.6.510.30 Activities that are necessary to get an asset ready may include technical and administrative work before construction begins, such as obtaining permits. Therefore, in the case of property constructed on purchased land, finance costs are capitalised in respect of the land once technical and administrative activities are in progress.

4.6.520 *Suspension*

IAS 23.20 4.6.520.10 Capitalisation of interest is suspended during extended periods in which active development is interrupted. For example, capitalisation is suspended if development of a qualifying asset is suspended because an entity is waiting for parts to arrive.

4.6.520.20 There is no guidance on what length of time is considered an extended delay.

IAS 23.21 4.6.520.30 Capitalisation may continue during a temporary delay that is caused by an external event, such as rain or flooding that is common in the region; or during an interruption caused by technical or legal obstacles that are a typical part of the process. Capitalisation also may continue during a period when active development is interrupted in order for *substantial* administrative or technical work to be carried out. In our view, if the administrative or technical work is not significant, then capitalisation should be suspended.

4.6.530 *Cessation*

IAS 23.22 4.6.530.10 Capitalisation ceases when the activities necessary to prepare the asset for its intended use or sale are substantially complete. For example:

- Company V has constructed a chemical plant. Construction is complete but minor modifications to the plant are required to meet the user's specifications before it is brought into use. We believe that capitalisation should stop when the construction is complete.
- Company W has developed a residential property to lease out. The development process is complete, but the property requires minor decoration before it is leased out. We believe that capitalisation should stop when the development process is complete.

4.6.540 **Presentation and disclosure**

IAS 1.82, 85, 97, 18.35(b) 4.6.540.10 A separate line item is required in the statement of comprehensive income for finance costs. There is no requirement to present finance income in the statement of comprehensive income unless such presentation is relevant to an understanding of the entity's financial performance. Significant categories of revenue, including interest and dividends, are disclosed in the financial statements.

4.6.540.20 There is no guidance in IFRSs as to what should be included in finance income and finance costs. In our view, when financial activities are incidental to an entity's principal activities, finance income and finance costs should include the following items:

- interest income and expense, including the amortisation of discounts and premiums (see 4.6.110);
- dividend income;
- foreign exchange gains and losses arising from investing and financing activities, such as exchange gains and losses on financial investments or exchange gains and losses on foreign currency borrowings (see 2.7);
- gains and losses on derivatives related to investing and financing activities, for example, gains and losses on interest rate swaps or gains and losses on foreign currency forward contracts that hedge foreign currency borrowings (see 3.7.50);
- gains and losses on the derecognition of financial investments;
- gains and losses on trading activities involving financial instruments;
- gains and losses on financial instruments designated as at fair value through profit or loss;
- impairment losses and reversals of impairment losses on financial investments;
- unwinding of discounts on non-financial assets and liabilities; and
- gains and losses on the derecognition of financial liabilities.

4.6.540.30 Interest income and expense includes interest that is recognised in respect of an asset or liability that is measured at a discounted amount, e.g. the interest expense that arises on a provision that initially is measured at a discounted amount (see 3.12.120) or the interest that is imputed on the cost of an asset when payment for the asset is deferred beyond normal credit terms (see 3.8.150 and 4.2.20).

IAS 1.82(a)   4.6.540.40 If one of an entity's principal sources of revenue is interest or dividend income, then interest or dividend income is presented as revenue separately in the statement of comprehensive income.

IAS 1.32, 82   4.6.540.50 In our view, finance costs and finance income should not be presented on a net basis (e.g. as "net finance costs") in the statement of comprehensive income without presenting an analysis of the finance costs and finance income. However, this does not preclude presentation of finance income followed immediately by finance costs and a subtotal (e.g. net finance costs) in the statement of comprehensive income.

IAS 21.52   4.6.540.60 There is no specific guidance regarding which line items in the statement of comprehensive income should include foreign exchange gains and losses, although the total amount of exchange differences recognised in profit or loss should be disclosed (except for those arising on financial instruments at fair value through profit or loss). There also is no guidance on the presentation of gains and losses on derivatives (see 5.6.220.80 and 270.30). In practice some entities present foreign exchange gains and losses and gains and losses on derivatives related to operating activities (e.g. those related to foreign currency sales and purchases) in income before finance costs, and the other exchange gains and losses and gains and losses on derivatives in finance income or finance costs. Other entities present all foreign exchange gains and losses and gains and losses on derivatives in the finance income and finance costs line items. In our view, either of these approaches is acceptable as long as it is applied consistently and, when amounts are material, the policy is disclosed.

4.6.540.70 In our view, expenses related to shares that are classified as a liability, for example, dividends on redeemable preference shares, may be included with interest on other liabilities or presented separately within finance costs.

4.6.540.80 – 90 [Not used]

4.6.540.100 The statement of comprehensive income of banks and similar financial institutions comprises mainly finance income and finance costs. The presentation and disclosure for financial institutions is illustrated in KPMG's series of illustrative financial statements.

4.6.550 [Not used]

4.6.560 Future developments

4.6.560.10 The IASB is working on a project that will ultimately replace IAS 39 (see 3.6.1360.10). The IASB's project includes the following phases:

- classification and measurement (see 3.6A and 5.6.530.20);
- impairment (see 4.6.560.20); and
- hedging (see 3.7.900.20).

4.6.560.20 In November 2009 the IASB published ED/2009/12 *Financial Instruments: Amortised Cost and Impairment*, which proposes to replace the incurred loss method for impairment of financial assets with a method based on expected losses (i.e. expected cash flow or ECF approach) and to provide a more principles-based approach to measuring amortised cost. The proposals in the ED would apply to all financial instruments within the scope of IAS 39 that are measured at amortised cost. A final standard is scheduled for the second quarter of 2011.

4.6.560.30 Except for the presentation of changes in the fair value of financial liabilities due to own credit risk (see 5.6.530.20), the IASB has decided generally to retain the current requirements in IAS 39 in respect of the classification and measurement of financial liabilities. A final standard is scheduled for the second quarter of 2011.

5.1 Leases
(IAS 17, IFRIC 4, SIC-15, SIC-27)

Chapter 5

5. Special topics

5.1 Leases
(IAS 17, IFRIC 4, SIC-15, SIC-27)

Overview of currently effective requirements

- An arrangement that at its inception can be fulfilled only through the use of a specific asset or assets, and which conveys a right to use that asset or assets, is a lease or contains a lease.

- A lease is classified as either a finance lease or an operating lease.

- Lease classification depends on whether substantially all of the risks and rewards incidental to ownership of the leased asset have been transferred from the lessor to the lessee.

- Lease classification is made at inception of the lease and is not revised unless the lease agreement is modified.

- Under a finance lease, the lessor recognises a finance lease receivable and the lessee recognises the leased asset and a liability for future lease payments.

- Under an operating lease, both parties treat the lease as an executory contract. The lessor and the lessee recognise the lease payments as income/expense over the lease term. The lessor recognises the leased asset in its statement of financial position, while the lessee does not.

- A lessee may classify a property interest held under an operating lease as an investment property. If this is done, then the lessee accounts for that lease as if it were a finance lease and it measures investment property using the fair value model.

- Lessors and lessees recognise incentives granted to a lessee under an operating lease as a reduction in lease rental income/expense over the lease term.

- A lease of land and a building is treated as two separate leases, a lease of the land and a lease of the building; the two leases may be classified differently.

- **In determining whether the lease of land is an operating lease or a finance lease, an important consideration is that land normally has an indefinite economic life.**

- **Immediate gain recognition from the sale and leaseback of an asset depends on whether the leaseback is classified as an operating or finance lease and, if the leaseback is an operating lease, whether the sale takes place at fair value.**

- **A series of linked transactions in the legal form of a lease is accounted for based on the substance of the arrangement; the substance may be that the series of transactions is not a lease.**

- **Special requirements for revenue recognition apply to manufacturer or dealer lessors granting finance leases.**

Currently effective requirements

This publication reflects IFRSs in issue at 1 August 2010. The currently effective requirements cover annual periods beginning on 1 January 2010. The requirements related to this topic are derived mainly from IAS 17 *Leases* and IFRIC 4 *Determining whether an Arrangement contains a Lease*.

Forthcoming requirements and future developments

When a currently effective requirement will be changed by a new requirement that is issued but is not yet effective, it is marked with a # as a **forthcoming requirement** and the impact of the change is explained in the accompanying boxed text. In respect of this topic no forthcoming requirements are noted.

When a significant change to the currently effective or forthcoming requirement is expected, it is marked with a * as an area that may be subject to **future developments** and a brief outline of the relevant projects is given in 5.1.530.20. In addition, a brief outline of a further project is given in 5.1.530.10 and 15 that affects several aspects of accounting for leases.

5.1.10 **Introduction**

5.1.10.10 The accounting treatment of a lease does not depend on which party has legal ownership of the leased asset, but rather on which party bears the risks and rewards incidental to ownership of the leased asset.

IAS 17.4, 6, 5.1.10.20 A lease is an agreement whereby the lessor conveys to the lessee the right
IFRIC 4.4 to use an asset for an agreed period of time in return for a payment or series of payments. The definition of a lease includes contracts that sometimes are referred to as hire or hire-purchase contracts. While legal definitions of a lease, hire or hire-purchase agreements may vary between different legal jurisdictions, IFRSs focus on the economic

substance of the agreement. Therefore, lease accounting is applicable to contracts that meet the definition of a lease under IFRSs and that are not exempt from IAS 17 or IFRIC 4, regardless of their legal name or definition.

5.1.10.30 Under IFRSs each lease is classified as either a finance lease or an operating lease; the classification determines the accounting treatment to be followed by the lessor and the lessee.

5.1.10.40 A lease is a finance lease when substantially all of the risks and rewards incidental to ownership of the leased asset are transferred from the lessor to the lessee by the agreement. Typical indicators assessed to determine whether substantially all of the risks and rewards are transferred include the present value of the minimum lease payments that the lessee is required to make in relation to the fair value of the leased asset at the inception of the lease, the duration of the lease in relation to the economic life of the leased asset, and whether the lessee will obtain ownership of the leased asset. A lease that is not a finance lease is an operating lease.

5.1.15 *Scope*

IAS 17.2, 3   5.1.15.10 Leases to explore for or use minerals, oil, natural gas and similar non-regenerative resources and licensing agreements for such items as motion picture films, video recordings, plays, manuscripts, patents and copyrights are excluded from the scope of IAS 17 (see 3.3.30.15).

IAS 17.3   5.1.15.20 IAS 17 applies only to agreements or components of agreements that transfer the right to use assets. It does not apply to agreements that are contracts for services that do not transfer the right to use assets from one contracting party to the other.

IAS 17.2   5.1.15.30 IAS 41 *Agriculture* (see 3.9) applies to the measurement of biological assets held by lessees under finance leases and for biological assets provided by lessors under operating leases; however, the requirements of IAS 17 are applied for all other aspects of lease accounting for those assets.

IAS 17.2   5.1.15.40 IAS 40 *Investment Property* (see 3.4) applies to the measurement of investment property provided by lessors under operating leases and for property held by lessees that is accounted for as investment property (see 5.1.250.10). However, the requirements of IAS 17 are applied for all other aspects of lease accounting for those assets. For example, the accounting for lease incentives will be according to IAS 17 and SIC-15 *Operating Leases – Incentives* requirements (see 5.1.310.30 and 40). However, when the investment property is measured at fair value, an entity should not double count assets or liabilities that are recognised as separate assets or liabilities (see 3.4.160.80 – 100).

5.1.20 *Definitions*

5.1.20.10 The definitions in IAS 17 are important in determining classification as a finance lease or as an operating lease. This classification is the basis for subsequent accounting for the lease by both the lessee and lessor.

5.1.30 *Minimum lease payments*

IAS 17.4 5.1.30.10 Minimum lease payments are those payments that the lessee is, or can be, required to make to the lessor over the lease term. From the lessee's point of view, minimum lease payments also include any amount guaranteed by the lessee or a party related to the lessee (e.g. residual value guarantee). From the lessor's point of view, minimum lease payments also include residual value guarantees by any third party unrelated to the lessor provided that party is financially capable of fulfilling the obligations under the guarantee.

5.1.30.13 Both a lessee and a lessor include in minimum lease payments the exercise price of a purchase option over the leased asset held by the lessee only if it is reasonably certain at inception of the lease that the purchase option will be exercised. In addition, if the lease includes a put option under which the lessor can require the lessee to purchase the asset at the end of the lease, then the lessee and the lessor include the exercise price of the put option in the minimum lease payments. This is because the put option functions economically as a residual value guarantee and the exercise price of the option is an amount that the lessee can be required to pay to the lessor.

5.1.30.17 Minimum lease payments do not include contingent rent amounts, costs for services and taxes to be paid by and reimbursed to the lessor.

IAS 17.4 5.1.30.20 Amounts owed by a lessee to a lessor may include charges for repairs and maintenance or for other services. Similarly, payments due under a lease may include charges that are reimbursements for expenditures paid by the lessor on behalf of the lessee (e.g. taxes, insurance). When there are service elements or other reimbursements included in a single payment, these elements should be separated from the minimum lease payments that relate to the right of use of the leased asset. When calculating the present value of minimum lease payments to evaluate lease classification, such service charges and reimbursements are excluded as they are not part of the minimum lease payments.

IFRIC 4.12-15 5.1.30.30 As described in 5.1.510.50, IFRIC 4 provides guidance on the allocation of payments between lease payments and payments related to other elements of the arrangement. In our view, as IFRIC 4 is an interpretation of IAS 17 and the most recent guidance on the allocation of lease payments, the allocation into the two components (right of use and other services/reimbursement) should be based on the guidance in IFRIC 4; therefore, it is based on the components' relative fair values. In some cases, the allocation will require:

- the use of an estimation technique for the fair value of the components, e.g. by reference to a lease agreement for a comparable asset that contains no other components; or
- estimating the payments for the other components by reference to the cost of those components together with a reasonable profit.

5.1.30.40 In our view, the specific nature of the guidance in IFRIC 4 overrides the general revenue allocation criteria discussed at 4.2.60.20 – 60.

5.1.40 *Inception date and commencement date of a lease*

5.1.40.10 A distinction is made between the inception and commencement of the lease.

IAS 17.4 5.1.40.20 The inception of the lease is the earlier of the date of the lease agreement and the date of commitment by the parties to the principal terms of the lease. At this date:

- a lease is classified as either an operating or a finance lease; and
- in the case of a finance lease, the amounts to be recognised at the commencement of the lease are determined.

5.1.40.30 The commencement of the lease term (also referred to as the commencement date) is the date from which the lessee is entitled to exercise its right to use the leased asset. This is the date of initial recognition of the lease. In other words, recognition of the lease takes place at the commencement date based on the amounts determined at the inception date.

IAS 17.4, 5 5.1.40.40 A significant amount of time may pass between the inception date and the commencement date; for example, when parties commit to lease an asset that has not been constructed. In such cases a calculation of the present value of minimum lease payments prepared to assist in determining the classification of the lease covers all lease payments made from the commencement of the lease term. In respect of the period between the inception date and the commencement date in such cases, an acceptable approach is for the calculation of minimum lease payments for both classification and measurement purposes to not take into account the time value effect of the period between the inception date and the commencement date (i.e. at the commencement date the lease is recognised based on the present value of the minimum lease payments as at the commencement date, using the discount rate at the inception date). However, if the lease payments are adjusted for changes in the construction or acquisition cost of the leased asset, general price levels, or the lessor's costs of financing the lease between the inception and commencement dates, then the effect of such changes is deemed to have taken place at inception.

5.1.40.45 For example, Company B entered into a binding agreement on 1 January 2008 to lease a building from Company C. B will have the right to occupy the building from 1 January 2011, once C has completed construction of the building. The estimated fair value of the building on 1 January 2008, assuming that construction was completed at that date, was 11,000. The lease agreement states that the annual lease payments will be 10 percent of the construction costs incurred by C. The expected construction cost of the building is 9,000, such that the expected annual lease rental is 900 (9,000 x 10%). B commences occupation of the building on 1 January 2011 as planned. The actual fair value of the building on this date is 13,000 and C's actual construction costs were 10,000, such that the annual lease payment is 1,000 (10,000 x 10%).

5.1.40.46 We believe that in order to assess the classification of the lease at inception, an acceptable approach is for B to consider the fair value of the building at inception of

11,000 and calculate the minimum lease payments using the actual construction costs of 10,000 discounted back to commencement date only, i.e. 1 January 2011, using the discount rate at inception date. The minimum lease payments need not be discounted back to the inception date of 1 January 2008. If B assesses that the lease is a finance lease, then B will recognise the building as an asset on 1 January 2011, measured at the lower of 11,000 and the present value of the annual lease payments of 1,000 at 1 January 2011 using the discount rate at inception date.

5.1.50 *Lease term*

IAS 17.4   5.1.50.10 The lease term commences when the lessee is entitled to start using the leased asset. This date may be earlier than when actual use begins. For example, the lease term for a retail property may commence on 1 May 2010, but the lessee needs to customise the interior of the property before opening and operating its retail store on 1 July 2010. Even if the tenant could not start customisation until 1 June 2010, the commencement date of the lease is 1 May 2010 because this is the date that the lessee is *entitled* to use the leased asset.

IAS 17.4   5.1.50.20 The lease term includes the *non-cancellable* period of the contract and also any further periods for which the lessee has an option to continue to lease the asset and, at the time of inception of the lease, it is judged reasonably certain that the lessee will exercise that option. For example, if the lease term is nine years but the lessee can cancel the lease without penalty at the end of the third and sixth years, then the non-cancellable period of the contract would be three years, unless at the time of inception of the lease, it is judged reasonably certain that the lessee will not cancel the lease at the end of three years.

5.1.50.30 IFRSs do not provide specific guidance on how to assess when it should be considered "reasonably certain" that a lessee would exercise an option to renew the lease. The assessment of the degree of certainty should be based on facts and circumstances at the inception of the lease rather than being based on the lessee's intentions. Factors relevant to the assessment may include, for example, the amount of the rentals payable in the secondary lease period compared to expected market rates for a similar asset during that period, the significance of continued use of the asset to the lessee's business model, and the ability of the lessee to recover costs that it incurs improving the leased asset. In our view, if it is believed that a lessee will be economically compelled to renew a lease, then this indicates that renewal is reasonably certain. Conversely, if the lessee benefits from a modest discount on market rents in the secondary lease period, then this may increase the likelihood that the lessee will renew but, in the absence of other factors, rarely will demonstrate that renewal is reasonably certain.

5.1.60 *Economic life and useful life*

IAS 17.4,28   5.1.60.10 A leased asset's *economic* life is the period over which the asset is expected to be usable (e.g. by the current lessee and any subsequent user). The economic life is used when comparing the lease term to the asset's life in order to evaluate whether the lease is an operating or a finance lease. A leased asset's *useful* life, which may be shorter than its remaining *economic* life, is the period over which the economic benefits of the asset are expected to be consumed by the lessee. A lessee depreciates an asset capitalised under a finance lease over the shorter of the *lease term* or the asset's *useful* life, unless it is reasonably certain that the lessee will obtain ownership by the end of the lease term, in that case the depreciation period is the useful life.

IAS 17.4   5.1.60.20 In our view, when an asset that previously was leased subsequently becomes the subject of a new lease, the economic life of the asset for purposes of assessing the lease classification of the new lease is the *remaining* economic life of the asset measured from the *commencement date* of the new lease. For example, a new asset with an economic life of 10 years was leased under a five-year lease. At the end of the lease term the remaining economic life of the asset is assessed as seven years. Following expiry of the initial lease, the lessor grants a new five-year lease over the asset. We believe that the *economic* life for purposes of classifying the second lease is seven years and the *useful* life is five years.

5.1.70 *Residual values*

IAS 17.4   5.1.70.10 There are two types of residual value to be considered by the parties to a lease contract: *guaranteed* residual value and *unguaranteed* residual value. A guaranteed residual value is the fixed or determinable amount that is required to be paid to the lessor at the end of the lease term or on disposal of the leased asset. An unguaranteed residual value is the amount that the lessor expects to recover from the leased asset following the end of the term; however, realisation of that amount is not assured by a party external to the lessor.

IAS 17.4   5.1.70.20 The amount of the minimum lease payments reflects whether the residual value is guaranteed or unguaranteed. The lessor includes any guaranteed residual value by the lessee, a party related to the lessee or a third party unrelated to the lessor that is financially capable of discharging the obligations under the guarantee in the determination of the minimum lease payments. The lessee only includes a guaranteed residual value in the determination of the minimum lease payments if the lessee or a party related to the lessee has guaranteed the residual value. An unguaranteed residual value always is excluded from the determination of the minimum lease payments, but is nevertheless part of the lessor's gross investment in a finance lease (see 5.1.330.10).

5.1.80 *Contingent rent*

IAS 17.4   5.1.80.10 *Contingent rent* is the portion of lease payments that is "not fixed in amount". This definition specifically refers to *future* amounts that are not fixed because they are potential incremental payments linked to future changes in indices, sales, usage of equipment etc. In our view, lease payments that are based on a variable rate of interest or that are indexed to inflation are not themselves contingent rents, but the future changes (i.e. the incremental changes) in these lease payments resulting from changes in interest rates or inflation are contingent rents. The calculation of minimum lease payments includes the lease payments that are known as of the lease inception date, based on the then current variable market rate or current price level.

5.1.90 *Initial direct costs*

5.1.90.10 Directly attributable incremental costs often are incurred, by either the lessor or the lessee, in negotiating and arranging a lease. These are referred to as "initial direct costs". See 5.1.340 for accounting for initial direct costs incurred by manufacturer or dealer lessors.

IAS 17.4, 38   5.1.90.20 Examples of initial direct costs include commissions, legal fees and internal costs that are incremental and directly attributable to negotiating and arranging a lease. Items that are not considered to be initial direct costs include allocations of internal overhead costs, such as those incurred by a sales and marketing team.

5.1.90.30 The initial recognition of and the subsequent accounting for initial direct costs depends on the classification of the lease.

IAS 17.38   5.1.90.40 For a transaction that is a finance lease, a lessor includes the initial direct costs in the initial measurement of the finance lease receivable. As a result the amount of interest income recognised over the lease term will be reduced. The interest rate implicit in the lease is defined in such a way that this is done automatically, so there is no need to add these costs separately. However, a manufacturer or dealer lessor should recognise directly attributable incremental costs incurred in negotiating and arranging a lease as an expense when the selling profit is recognised, which for a finance lease is the commencement date of the lease.

IAS 17.20   5.1.90.50 The lessee adjusts the carrying amount of the leased asset under a finance lease by the initial direct costs, which will affect the future depreciation of that asset.

IAS 17.52   5.1.90.60 For a transaction that is an operating lease, the lessor adds initial direct costs to the carrying amount of the asset under the lease and recognises them as an expense over the lease term on the same basis as the lease income, which usually will be on a straight-line basis.

5.1.90.70 In our view, in the case of an operating lease the lessee may either recognise the initial direct costs as an asset and expense them over the lease term, or expense them immediately.

5.1.100 **Classification of a lease**

IAS 17.7, 8   5.1.100.10 A *finance lease* is a lease that transfers substantially all of the risks and rewards incidental to ownership of the leased asset from the lessor to the lessee; title to the asset may or may not transfer under such a lease. An *operating lease* is a lease other than a finance lease.

5.1.100.13 For example, in a simple lease arrangement in which Company V leases an asset to Company W and no other parties are involved, the analysis will focus on the transfer of risks and rewards from V as lessor to W as lessee. Additional factors may need to be considered in more complex, multi-party arrangements. For example, suppose that Company G leases an asset to Company K and G also enters into an agreement with Company Z whereby Z guarantees the residual value of the asset. As Z is unrelated to K, the residual value is included in the minimum lease payments by G, but not by K. Depending on the facts and circumstances, this may result in G accounting for the arrangement as a finance lease and K accounting for the arrangement as an operating lease (see 5.1.160.50).

5.1.100.15 Only risks and rewards incidental to ownership of the leased asset during the lease period should be considered when determining lease classification. Relevant risks include the possibility of losses from idle capacity or technological obsolescence and from decreases in the value of the asset; relevant rewards may include the gain from the increase in value of the asset or realisation of the residual value at the end of the lease. Conversely, risks associated with construction of the asset prior to lease commencement, financing such construction and the costs of providing services using the leased asset, are not incidental to ownership of the leased asset during the lease period and, in our view generally should be disregarded in evaluating the classification of the lease.

IAS 17.13 5.1.100.20 The classification of a lease is determined at the inception of the lease and is not revised unless the lease agreement is modified (see 5.1.270).

5.1.110 *Indicators of a finance lease*

5.1.120 *Primary lease classification criteria*

IAS 17.8, 10 5.1.120.10 The following are indicators that normally would lead to a lease being classified as a finance lease and generally the presence of any one indicator would point to classification as a finance lease. Ultimately, the lease classification is based on an overall assessment of whether substantially all of the risks and rewards incidental to ownership of the asset have been transferred from the lessor to the lessee or to the lessee and a third-party residual value guarantor.

5.1.130 *Transfer of ownership*

IAS 17.10(a) 5.1.130.10 If legal ownership of the asset ultimately transfers to the lessee, either during or at the end of the lease term, then the agreement usually will be classified as a finance lease.

5.1.140 *Purchase options*

IAS 17.10(b) 5.1.140.10 The existence of a purchase option that is expected, based on facts and circumstances at inception of the lease, to be exercised means that title to the asset is expected to transfer. Therefore a lease with such an option normally is classified as a finance lease. For example, if the lessee has the option to purchase the leased asset at a price that is expected to be sufficiently lower than the expected fair value of the leased asset at the date the option becomes exercisable and therefore it is reasonably certain, at the inception of the lease, that the option will be exercised, then the agreement should be classified as a finance lease. In our view, if it is believed that a lessee will be economically compelled for business reasons to purchase the asset by exercising the option, and not just to take advantage of a below-market purchase option, then this also indicates that the option is reasonably certain of being exercised.

5.1.150 *Major part of economic life*

IAS 17.10(c) 5.1.150.10 If the lease term is for the major part of the economic life of the leased asset, then the agreement normally would be classified as a finance lease.

5.1.150.20 IFRSs do not define what is meant by the "major part" of an asset's economic life. Practice has been to look to the lease accounting guidance in US GAAP, which has quantitative criteria about what is considered to be the majority of an asset's economic life. US GAAP has a "bright-line" threshold whereby a lease term equivalent to 75 percent or more of the economic life of an asset is considered to be the major part of the asset's economic life. Practice under US GAAP requires a lease that is very close to, but below this bright-line cut-off (e.g. a lease term equivalent to 74 percent of the asset's economic life) to be classified as an operating lease if none of the other criteria for finance (capital) lease classification are met. In our view, while this 75 percent threshold may be a useful reference point, it does not represent a bright-line or automatic cut-off point under IFRSs. We believe that it is necessary to consider all relevant factors when assessing the classification of a lease and it is clear that some leases may be for the major part of an asset's economic life even if the lease term is for less than 75 percent of the economic life of the asset.

5.1.160 *Present value of minimum lease payments equals substantially all of the fair value*

IAS 17.10(d) 5.1.160.10 If at the inception of the lease the present value of the minimum lease payments (see 5.1.30) amounts to substantially all of the fair value of the leased asset, then the agreement normally would be classified as a finance lease.

5.1.160.20 IFRSs do not define what is meant by "substantially all". US GAAP has a bright-line threshold whereby if the present value of the minimum lease payments is 90 percent or more of the fair value of the leased asset at inception of the lease, then the lease should be classified as a finance lease. Practice under US GAAP requires a lease that is very close to this bright-line cut-off (e.g. 89 percent) to be classified as an operating lease if none of the other criteria for finance (capital) lease classification are met. In our view, while the 90 percent threshold may provide a useful reference point, it does not represent a bright-line or automatic cut-off point under IFRSs. We believe that it is necessary to consider all relevant factors when assessing the classification of a lease and it is clear that some leases may meet this criterion even if the present value of the minimum lease payments is less than 90 percent of the fair value of the leased asset at inception of the lease.

IAS 17.20 5.1.160.30 In our view, the discount rate to be used in assessing this criterion should be determined using the guidance for calculating the present value of minimum lease payments when accounting for finance leases. Therefore both the lessor and lessee should use the interest rate implicit in the lease as the discount rate for determining the present value of minimum lease payments for the lease classification test. In many cases the lessee will not have sufficient information about the unguaranteed residual value of the leased asset to determine the lease's implicit interest rate, in which case the lessee should instead use its own incremental borrowing rate as the discount rate. In determining such a rate, in our view the leased asset should be considered as collateral.

5.1.160.40 Certain leases may, for example, have significant tax benefits that are reflected in the lease pricing such that the present value of the rentals, when discounted at the incremental borrowing rate, is less than 90 percent of the asset's fair value, not because the lessor has retained risk of the leased asset to such extent but because the tax benefits are greater than 10 percent. In these cases judgement needs to be applied as to whether or not the lease transfers substantially all the risks and rewards incidental to ownership.

5.1.160.50 When a residual value guarantee is provided by someone other than the lessee or a party related to the lessee, it is included in the calculation of minimum lease payments by the lessor but not by the lessee. This may result in the present value of the minimum lease payments at the inception date amounting to substantially all of the fair value of the leased asset for a lessor but not for a lessee. In some cases this may indicate that substantially all of the risks and rewards were transferred from the lessor but were not passed on solely to the lessee (i.e. other parties also participated in some of the risks and rewards) and may result in a different classification of the lease by the lessor and the lessee (i.e. the lessor may classify the lease as a finance lease and the lessee may classify the lease as an operating lease).

5.1.170 *Specialised nature of the asset*

IAS 17.10(e) 5.1.170.10 If a leased asset is so specialised that only the lessee can use it without major modification, then the agreement normally would be classified as a finance lease. An asset built to the specifications of the lessee may be a specialised asset. However, in our view a machine that could be used by other entities in the same industry as the lessee (e.g. a printing press) would not be considered to be a specialised asset even if it had some degree of customisation.

5.1.180 *Supplemental indicators of a finance lease*

IAS 17.11 5.1.180.10 There are several additional indicators that a contract may be a finance lease. These are:

- if the lessee can cancel the lease but the lessor's losses associated with the cancellation are borne by the lessee;

- gains or losses from the fluctuation in the fair value of the residual fall to the lessee (e.g. in the form of a rent rebate equalling most of the sales proceeds at the end of the lease); or
- the lessee can extend the lease at a rent that is substantially lower than the market rent.

5.1.190 *Assessing the indicators*

IAS 17.12 5.1.190.10 IFRSs do not provide a hierarchy to be applied when evaluating the indicators discussed in 5.1.130 – 180.10, and these indicators may not be conclusive. If there are other facts or features that make it clear that the lease transfers substantially all risks and rewards incidental to ownership of the leased asset from the lessor to the lessee, then the lease should be classified as a finance lease. For example, in many long-term leases it is not uncommon for the lessee to have a cancellation right with some penalty payments. In our view, the calculation of the minimum lease payments should be based on the smaller of the non-cancellable lease payments plus the penalty, and the total minimum lease payment that would arise if the cancellation right is not exercised, taking into account the time value of money.

5.1.200 *Other classification issues*

5.1.210 *Probability-weighted evaluations of risks and rewards*

5.1.210.10 IFRSs do not address how to consider probability when assessing whether a lease transfers substantially all of the risks and rewards incidental to ownership of an asset. One approach would be to make this assessment based solely on the relative proportions of total possible risks and rewards. Another approach would be to make this assessment on a probability-weighted basis. In our view, a probability-weighted basis should be used.

5.1.210.20 For example, an asset is leased for 14 years and has an estimated economic life of 20 years. The fair value of the asset at inception of the lease is 1,000 and its estimated residual value at the end of the lease term is 250. All risks and rewards of ownership are transferred to Lessee M, other than the residual value risk.

5.1.210.30 M agrees to reimburse Lessor R for the first 50 of losses on disposal of the asset at the end of the lease term (based on the estimated residual of 250). Therefore, if the asset is sold for 230, then M will pay 20 to R. If the asset is sold for 200 or less, then M will pay 50 to R. M has an option to purchase the asset for 250, which is not a purchase option that is reasonably certain, at inception of the lease, to be exercised.

5.1.210.40 The present value of the minimum lease payments, *including* the guarantee of the first 50 of residual value, is 85 percent of the fair value of the asset.

5.1.210.50 Historical data suggests that the residual value of the asset at the end of the lease term is highly unlikely to fall below 200. Therefore substantively all of the residual value risk is with M, although M does not bear the risk that the recoverable amount of the leased asset will be below 200 at the end of the lease term. Furthermore M would receive any potential gains as M would be able to exercise the option to purchase the asset for the fixed price of 250 if, at the end of the lease, the actual value was above 250.

5.1.210.60 We believe that the evaluation of the transfer of risks and rewards should reflect the probabilities of the realistically likely range of outcomes. In this example, substantially all of the reasonably possible risks and all rewards incidental to ownership of the asset are transferred to M. R, has only an insignificant risk and no rewards in relation to the residual value. Therefore, in our view the lease should be classified as a finance lease.

5.1.210.70 In another example, Company Q leases a building and is required to replace the building if it is destroyed by an earthquake during the lease term. In our view, the fact that Q bears these "catastrophic" risks does not mean that the lease necessarily is a finance lease. Rather, the risks should be assessed having regard to the probability of their crystallisation. In an area in which earthquakes are very uncommon, Q's commitment to rebuild the building if it is destroyed by earthquake may have little effect on the classification of the lease.

5.1.220 *Leasing transactions undertaken via special purpose entities*

5.1.220.10 Some leasing transactions may involve special purpose entities (SPEs). In our view, when considering whether the lessor has transferred to the lessee substantially all of the risks and rewards incidental to the ownership of the leased asset, consideration should be given to the risks and rewards borne indirectly by the respective parties as a result of their association with the SPE. See 2.5.150 for further discussion of SPEs and structured transactions.

5.1.230 *Leases of land*

IAS 17.15A   5.1.230.10 The classification of a lease of land is assessed based on the general classification guidance. In determining the lease classification an important consideration is that land normally has an indefinite economic life. However, the fact that the lease term normally is shorter than the economic life of the land does not necessarily mean that a lease of land always is an operating lease; the other classification requirements are considered also.

IAS 17.BC8C,   5.1.230.20 For example, in a 999-year lease of land, the lessee is in a position economi-
BC8D   cally similar to an entity that purchased the land. The present value of the residual value of the land is negligible, and although the title of the land is not transferred to the lessee, substantially all risks and rewards are transferred to the lessee. Therefore, the lease is classified as a finance lease.

5.1.230.21 Consistent with the general leasing requirements, the assessment of the land classification is made at the inception of the lease based on the expected conditions and outcomes at that time and is not revised merely because the value of the residual asset at the end of the lease increases over time.

5.1.230.23 Generally where the following conditions exist a finance lease classification is considered:

- lessor is economically indifferent between selling and leasing; and
- lease is automatically renewed at the end of the lease for a minimal payment.

IAS 17.14 5.1.230.25 In some jurisdictions (e.g. Hong Kong) the outright legal ownership of property is rare. Instead, entities buy and sell rights under long-term leases in the same way that entities buy and sell ownership rights in other countries. The lease of land may be classified as a finance lease if the criteria for finance lease classification are met (see 3.4.40.30).

IAS 17.14 5.1.230.30 In our view, an upfront payment made to obtain the right to use the land that is classified as an operating lease should be capitalised as a lease prepayment and recognised over the lease term as an operating lease expense (see 5.1.310).

5.1.240 Land and building leases

IAS 17. 5.1.240.10 In the case of a combined lease of land and buildings, the land and buildings
15A-17, are considered separately to determine the classification, unless the value of the land
BC9-BC11 at the inception of the lease is deemed immaterial or it is clear that both elements are either finance leases or operating leases. In determining the classification, the minimum lease payments at the inception of the lease are allocated to land and buildings in proportion to the relative fair values of the leasehold interests in the land element and the buildings element. If this allocation cannot be done reliably, then the entire lease is classified as a finance lease unless it is clear that both elements qualify as operating leases.

IAS 17. 5.1.240.20 The fair value of the leasehold interest is different from the fair value of the
15A-17, leased asset. An allocation based on the relative fair values of the land and the building
BC9-BC11 elements (rather than based on the relative fair values of the respective *leasehold interests* in the land and building element) generally is not appropriate as the land often has an indefinite economic life, and therefore is likely to maintain its value beyond the lease term. Thus the lessor normally would not need compensation for using up the land. In contrast, the future economic benefits of a building are likely to be used up to some extent over the lease term (which is reflected via depreciation). Therefore, in allocating the minimum lease payments between the land and the building elements, it is reasonable to assume that the lease payments related to the building element (depreciable asset) are set at a level that enables the lessor not only to make a return on initial investment, but also to recover the part of the value of the building used up over the lease term.

5.1.240.30 When a lease contains no contingent rent, lease payments are equal to minimum lease payments. In our view, one method of allocating the minimum lease payments between the land and building elements is to allocate to the land element the portion of the minimum lease payments that represent a financing cost for the land based on the fair value of the land at the inception date of the lease and the lessee's incremental borrowing rate using the land as collateral. The remainder should be allocated to the building element.

5.1.240.40 When a lease contains contingent rent, in our view the contingent rent is allocated to both the land and the building elements of the lease. In our view, it is not appropriate to allocate the minimum lease payments (which do not include contingent rent) to the land element first and then to attribute the remaining minimum lease payments and the entire contingent rent to the building element. However, a significant amount of contingent lease payments might be an indication that the entire lease is an operating lease.

5.1.250 *Classification of property interest held under an operating lease as investment property*

IAS 17.19, 40.6   5.1.250.10 A lessee may elect to classify a property interest held under an operating lease as an investment property, if the property otherwise would meet the definition of an investment property (see 3.4.10), and if the lessee applies the fair value model to all of its investment property. This election is available on a property-by-property basis. If the lessee makes this election for a given property interest, then the lessee accounts for that property interest as if it were a finance lease. For example, a lessee may acquire a 100-year ground lease that is classified as operating lease and otherwise meets the definition of an investment property. In order to classify this leasehold interest as an investment property, the lessee is required to use the fair value model when accounting for all of its investment property. The lessee continues to account for the lease as a finance lease even if a subsequent event changes the nature of the lessee's interest so that it no longer is classified as investment property.

5.1.260 *Multiple leased assets*

IFRIC 4.3   5.1.260.05 The lease classification principles of IFRSs generally should be applied on an asset-by-asset basis. The underlying asset subject to the lease may be either a stand-alone asset, a portion of a larger asset or a part of a single master lease arrangement. In our view, if an underlying identifiable asset would represent a unit of account under either IAS 16 *Property, Plant and Equipment* or IAS 38 *Intangible Assets,* then that asset also should be a separate unit of account under IFRIC 4 and IAS 17.

5.1.260.10 For example, a lessee may enter into an agreement to lease several buildings with varying economic lives and fair values. In our view, it would not be appropriate to determine a weighted average economic life for the group of buildings to compare to the lease term. Further, it would not be appropriate to compare the net present value of the lease arrangement's minimum lease payments to the total fair value of all of the buildings.

IFRIC 4.13   5.1.260.20 The total lease payments are allocated to each leased asset and any other elements of the arrangement on the basis of their relative fair values (see 5.1.510.50).

5.1.265 *Sub-leases and back-to-back leases*

IAS 1.32, 32.42 5.1.265.10 A situation may arise in which an intermediate party is involved in the lease arrangement. The intermediate party may lease an asset from the head lessor and subsequently enter into a sub-lease with a third party, the ultimate lessee. One of the key determinations is whether the intermediate party is acting as principal in its own right as both lessor and lessee or whether it is merely acting as agent for the head lessor or ultimate lessee. If the intermediate party is determined to be the principal, then offsetting the lessor lease receivable and lessee lease liability is unlikely to be appropriate. Lease receivables and payables may be derecognised only when the IAS 39 *Financial Instruments: Recognition and Measurement* criteria are met. Lease receivables and payables may be offset only when the IAS 32 *Financial Instruments: Presentation* criteria are met; IAS 1 *Presentation of Financial Statements* permits offsetting only where specifically permitted by an accounting standard.

5.1.265.20 Determining whether an entity is acting as an agent or principal is based on an evaluation of the risks and responsibilities taken by the entity. Judgement is required and all relevant facts and circumstances are considered. See 4.2.660 for additional guidance on agency relationships and 5.1.500 for guidance on linked transactions in the legal form of a lease.

5.1.270 *Subsequent changes to classification*

5.1.270.05 The following decision tree summarises the accounting for lease modifications:

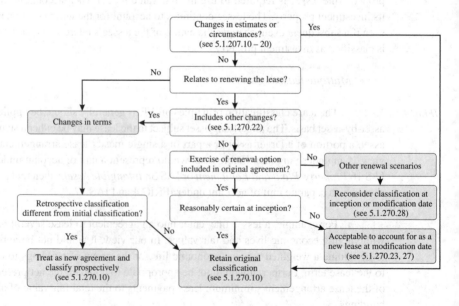

IAS 17.13 5.1.270.10 Leases are not reclassified for changes in estimates (e.g. of the economic life or the residual value of the asset) or changes in circumstances (e.g. default by the lessee). If the terms of the lease are modified other than by renewing the lease (see 5.1.270.21),

then the modified agreement may have to be treated as a new lease agreement, which may be classified differently from the original agreement. To determine whether a modification results in a new lease agreement, the test is whether the lease would have been classified differently if the modified terms had been in effect at the inception of the lease. If the modified terms would have resulted in a different classification based on the original estimates and circumstances, then the modified agreement is regarded as a new lease agreement and classified in accordance with its modified terms, based on estimates determined at the modification date.

5.1.270.20 A lease is not reclassified due to a subsequent change in the likelihood that the lessee will renew a lease. For example, a lease may have a term of five years with a renewal option at the end of five years at a market rate. At inception of the lease, the lessee concluded that exercise of the renewal option was not reasonably certain, and therefore based its lease classification on the minimum lease payments and circumstances of the initial lease term only. If the lessee determines later that it is likely to renew the lease for an additional five years, this would not, in itself, trigger a need to review the classification of the initial lease as it is a change in estimate, not a change in the provisions of the lease. However, see 5.1.270.23 for a discussion of when the renewal option is exercised.

IAS 17.13 5.1.270.21 An exception from the requirement to reconsider the classification of a lease at inception of the original lease when there is a change in the provisions of the lease (see 5.1.270.10) is when there is a renewal of the lease. However, difficulties may arise in applying this exception, resulting from either:

- a lack of clarity with respect to the meaning of "renewing the lease"; or
- a lack of guidance with respect to the required accounting when renewing the lease and meeting the exception to the modification accounting.

5.1.270.22 Determining when the exception applies may be difficult, as the term *renewing the lease* is not defined. In our view, this exception applies whenever a lessee exercises a renewal option that exists in a lease agreement in accordance with the provisions existing in the original lease agreement. Conversely, in our view if a lessee and lessor agree to renew a lease but also to change other provisions of the lease at the same time, then this exception does not apply. For example, Company V leases a building from Company W under an operating lease with an initial term of ten years, renewable for a further ten years. During the ninth year of the lease, V and W agree to extend the lease for another ten years at a new annual rental different from that in the original lease agreement. We believe that the exception from the need to reconsider the lease classification at inception of the original lease is not applicable, as there has been a change to other provisions of the original lease.

5.1.270.23 The standard also does not specify the required accounting when the exception is applicable. Consider, for example, a lessee that exercises a renewal option included in the original lease agreement and thereby agrees to lease an asset for a secondary lease period that was not considered part of the lease term at inception. In some cases the lessee may be required to give notice before the end of the initial lease term that it will exercise the renewal option. Although the standard is silent on the required accounting, in such a case an option has been replaced by a commitment and therefore the economic positions of the lessee and lessor have changed. Therefore, we prefer to account for the secondary lease period as a new lease. In that case, it is acceptable to account for the new lease, beginning on either the date on which the lessee commits to exercise the renewal option or the first day of the secondary lease period (i.e. when the new lease period commences). The classification of this new lease may be different from the original lease classification.

5.1.270.27 For example, Company G enters into a lease of an asset with an economic life of 10 years. The primary lease period is six years and G may extend the lease for a further three years at the original annual rent, provided that it exercises the renewal option by the end of year five. At inception it is not reasonably certain that the lessee will exercise the renewal option. Based on the criteria in IAS 17 G concludes that the lease should be classified as an operating lease at inception. Shortly before the end of year five, G exercises the renewal option and agrees to continue to lease the asset in years seven to nine. We prefer to account for the secondary lease period as a new lease. In that case, it is acceptable for G to account for the new lease starting either at the end of year five or at the beginning of year seven, and ending at the end of year nine. In our view, G should apply a consistent approach to similar transactions.

5.1.270.28 More complex situations may arise in practice, for example, a secondary lease period may be added to a lease agreement that did not contain a renewal option originally, or the term of a secondary lease period may be lengthened or shortened. In such cases, we prefer that an entity reconsider the classification of the lease based on its new provisions, either at inception of the original lease or at the date the change is made to the lease agreement. Under the first alternative, to determine whether the modification results in a new lease agreement, the two-step test described in paragraph 5.1.270.10 should be used.

5.1.270.30 In our view, if a lease agreement contains a purchase option and is classified as an operating lease at its inception, then the lease should be reclassified as a finance lease when the lessee gives notice that it will exercise the option prior to it actually being exercised. This is because the option in the lease agreement has been replaced by a commitment, thereby changing the economic position of the lessee and lessor, and the general requirement to reconsider the classification of the lease if there is a modification to its terms applies.

5.1.270.40 For example, Company H leases an asset from Company J for 10 years. The lease includes a purchase option under which H may purchase the asset from J at the end of the lease. The exercise price under the purchase option, set at inception of the lease, is the expected market price of the asset at the end of the lease. H may give notice that it intends to exercise the option no later than at the end of the eighth year of the lease. At inception, H classifies the lease as an operating lease. By the end of the eighth year of the lease, H serves notice that it will purchase the asset, at which time the lease agreement should be reclassified as a finance lease.

5.1.280 **Accounting for leases**

5.1.290 *Lessee*

5.1.300 *Finance lease*

5.1.300.10 At commencement of the finance lease, the leased asset and the lease liability are recorded at the lower of:

- the fair value of the leased asset at the inception date; and
- the present value of the minimum lease payments at the inception date.

IAS 17.20   5.1.300.20 The discount rate to be used in determining the present value of the minimum lease payments is the interest rate implicit in the lease. The minimum lease payments include the exercise price of options expected, at inception of the lease, to be exercised and predetermined increases in the lease payments (see 5.1.80 in respect of contingent rents).

IAS 17.4   5.1.300.30 The interest rate implicit in the lease is the discount rate that, at the inception of the lease, causes the aggregate present value of the minimum lease payments and the unguaranteed residual value to be equal to the fair value of the leased asset plus any initial direct costs of the lessor. If the rate implicit in the lease cannot be determined, then the lessee's incremental borrowing rate is used. Initial direct costs incurred are capitalised as an addition to the cost of the asset.

IAS 17.25   5.1.300.40 The periodic lease payments are split into two components: the interest charge for the period and the reduction (redemption) of the lease liability. The interest charge is determined so that a constant periodic rate of interest is recognised on the outstanding balance of the liability. Interest and redemption are determined on an effective interest rate basis, whereby the interest amount generally decreases over the lease term and the redemption amount generally increases each period.

5.1.300.50 In our view, subsequent accounting for the asset under a finance lease should be similar to other owned assets, and assets under finance leases cannot be considered to be a separate class of asset solely on the basis that they were acquired under finance leases. For example, if a lessee has an accounting policy under which all property, plant and equipment is revalued (see 3.2.300), then this policy also should be applied to similar assets leased under finance leases. However, the lessee is required to provide additional disclosure (see 5.1.520).

IAS 17.27   5.1.300.60 The asset under a finance lease is depreciated in accordance with the depreciation policy used for comparable owned assets (see 3.2.140 and 3.3.210), over the shorter of the period of the asset's useful life and the lease term. An interest in land held under a finance lease should be depreciated over the life of the lease. However, if at inception of the lease it is reasonably certain that the lessee will obtain ownership of the asset by the end of the lease term, then the asset should be depreciated over the expected useful life of the asset.

IAS 17.29 5.1.300.70 The reduction of the lease liability is recognised using the effective interest method (see 4.6.30). However, depreciation of the asset is recognised on a different basis (e.g. straight-line (see 3.2.160)). Consequently, the amounts included in the statement of financial position for the leased asset and the related liability are unlikely to be equal after commencement of the lease. In our view, the lessee cannot use a depreciation method such as annuity depreciation to reflect consumption of the asset on an after-interest basis (see 5.1.360).

5.1.310 Operating lease

5.1.310.10 A lessee under an operating lease does not recognise the leased asset in its statement of financial position, nor does it recognise a liability for rentals in respect of future periods, except for a property interest held under an operating lease that is accounted for as investment property (see 5.1.250.10, 3.4.40.20).

IAS 17.33 5.1.310.20 A lessee under an operating lease recognises rent expense on a straight-line basis over the lease term (i.e. between the commencement date and the end of the lease term), or on another systematic basis if it is more representative of the pattern of benefits to the lessee over time. When the timing of lease payments does not represent the time pattern of the lessee's benefits under the lease agreement, prepaid rent or accrued liabilities for rental payments is recognised.

SIC-15.3, 5 5.1.310.30 Sometimes lessors provide incentives for the lessee to enter into a lease agreement; such incentives may include the reimbursement of relocation costs or costs associated with exiting existing lease agreements, or initial periods that are rent-free or at a reduced rate. These incentives are an integral part of the net consideration agreed for the use of the asset. Incentives granted to the lessee to enter into the operating lease are spread over the lease term using the same recognition basis as the rental payments (i.e. on a straight-line basis unless another systematic basis is representative of the time pattern over which the benefit of the leased asset is diminished).

5.1.310.40 If, for instance, a rent-free period of two years is agreed in a lease agreement covering ten years at an annual amount of 1,000 for years three to ten, then the lessee (and the lessor) would recognise the net consideration of 8,000 systematically over the ten-year lease term. Alternatively, if a lease agreement is for ten years and the annual lease payment equals 800 in the first five years and 1,000 in years six to ten, then the lessee (and the lessor) would recognise the net consideration of 900 systematically over the ten-year lease term. Assuming that the benefit is the same in each of the ten years, the lessee would recognise rent expense of 900 in the first year and accrued rent of 100 at the end of the first year, while the lessor would recognise 900 of lease income and 100 of accounts receivable.

5.1.310.50 In some jurisdictions where longer term leases are common, there may be periodic rent reviews to adjust the lease payments up to the prevailing market rates. In our view, for leases that are subject to these periodic adjustments, the lease incentive, if any, should be spread over the *entire* lease term rather than the shorter period until the next market adjustment.

5.1.320 *Lessor*

5.1.320.10 The definitions of finance and operating leases are the same for lessors as for lessees. However, the definition of minimum lease payments for a lessor also includes any residual value guaranteed by a financially capable independent third party, whereas the lessee includes only amounts guaranteed by the lessee and parties related to the lessee (see 5.1.30).

5.1.330 *Finance lease*

IAS 17.36-38   5.1.330.10 Initially the lessor records a finance lease receivable at the amount of its net investment, which comprises the present value of the minimum lease payments and any unguaranteed residual value accruing to the lessor. The present value is calculated by discounting the minimum lease payments due and any unguaranteed residual value, at the interest rate implicit in the lease (see 5.1.300.30). Initial direct costs are included in the calculation of the finance lease receivable, because the interest rate implicit in the lease, used for discounting the minimum lease payments, takes initial direct costs incurred into consideration (see 5.1.90).

5.1.330.15 The lessor derecognises the leased asset and recognises the difference between the carrying amount of the leased asset and the finance lease receivable in profit or loss when recording the finance lease receivable. This gain or loss is presented in profit or loss in the same line item in which the lessor presents gains or losses from sales of similar assets. See 5.1.340 for manufacturer or dealer lessors.

IAS 17.39, 40   5.1.330.20 Over the lease term the lessor accrues interest income on the net investment. The receipts under the lease are allocated between reducing the net investment and recognising finance income, so as to produce a constant rate of return on the net investment.

5.1.340 *Manufacturer or dealer lessors*

IAS 17.38, 42   5.1.340.10 In some industries (e.g. office products, automotive), manufacturers or dealers often act as lessors of their products, either directly or through a finance entity subsidiary. A finance lease of an asset by a manufacturer or dealer results in two types of income: initial selling profit; and finance income over the lease term. Manufacturer or dealer lessors recognise the selling profit or loss in the statement of comprehensive income, for the period in accordance with the entity's normal accounting policy for outright sales. Costs incurred in connection with negotiating and arranging a lease (initial direct costs) are recognised as an expense when the selling profit is recognised, which generally is at the commencement date of the lease term.

IAS 17.45   5.1.340.20 If manufacturer or dealer lessors quote below-market interest rates (e.g. as a marketing tool), then selling profit is restricted to that which would have been earned if a market rate of interest was charged. Using the lower rate would not be appropriate since it would overstate the selling profit and understate the financial income in subsequent periods.

5.1.350 *Operating lease*

IAS 17.49   5.1.350.10 If, prior to lease commencement, a lessor recognises an asset in its statement of financial position and leases that asset to a lessee under an operating lease, then the lessor does not derecognise the asset on lease commencement. Generally, future contractual rental payments from the lessee are recognised as receivables over the lease term as the payments become receivable. The asset subject to the operating lease is presented in the lessor's statement of financial position according to the nature of the asset (e.g. equipment).

IAS 17.50,   5.1.350.20 Generally lease income from operating leases is recognised by the lessor in
SIC-15.3, 4   income on a straight-line basis over the lease term. It may be possible to recognise lease income using another systematic basis if that is more representative of the time pattern in which the benefit of the leased asset is diminished.

5.1.350.30 Similarly, increases (or decreases) in rental payments over a period of time, other than contingent lease payments, should be reflected in the determination of the lease income, which is recognised on a straight-line basis. For example, a contractual 3 percent per annum escalation of rents over the lease term is anticipated from commencement of the lease. Consequently, the lessor recognises lease income in excess of cash lease payments received in early periods of the lease and the opposite effect in later years.

IAS 17.52   5.1.350.40 Initial direct costs incurred by the lessor in arranging an operating lease are added to the carrying amount of the leased asset and cannot be recognised immediately as an expense. These initial direct costs are recognised as an expense on the same basis as the lease income. This will not necessarily be consistent with the basis on which the leased asset is depreciated.

SIC-15.3, 4   5.1.350.50 Incentives granted to the lessee in negotiating a new or renewed operating lease are recognised as an integral part of the net consideration agreed for the use of the asset. They are recognised as a reduction of rental income over the lease term using the same recognition basis as for the lease income (i.e. on a straight-line basis unless another systematic basis is representative of the time pattern over which the benefit of the leased asset is diminished).

IAS 17.53   5.1.350.60 The lessor depreciates the asset subject to the lease over the asset's useful life in a manner that is consistent with the depreciation policy that the entity applies to similar owned assets (see 3.2.140 and 3.3.210).

5.1.360 *Annuity depreciation*

5.1.360.10 "Annuity depreciation" refers to depreciation methods under which the depreciation charge is adjusted to reflect the time value of money. Such depreciation methods result in lower depreciation charges in initial periods, and larger depreciation amounts in later periods. These methods are used under some national accounting practices by lessors in order to recognise a level profit, after considering financing costs related to the leased asset, over the lease term. In our view, the way that an asset is financed should not impact the selection of a depreciation policy. IFRSs require depreciation to reflect the consumption of the economic benefits of an asset. We believe that this does not extend to consideration of the time value of money or inflation adjustments.

5.1.370 **Other issues**

5.1.380 *Security deposits and minimum lease payments*

5.1.380.10 In some jurisdictions the terms of property leases normally require the lessee to pay security deposits and advance rentals. The security deposit is held by the lessor throughout the term of the lease and is refunded in full to the lessee at the end of the lease term (if the lessee has performed fully and observed all of the conditions or provisions in the lease). However, the lessor may apply the security deposit to remedy the breach of any provisions in the lease contract and to indemnify any consequential costs and losses related to the leased property that are properly chargeable to the lessee under the contract. Normally the security deposits do not carry any interest or the interest rate received is less than market interest rates.

5.1.380.20 In our view, the security deposit itself is not part of the lease payments and therefore is within the scope of IAS 39 (see 3.6.10). Therefore the security deposit should be measured at fair value at initial recognition. In our view, the difference between the initial fair value and the nominal value of the deposit is an additional lease payment made by the lessee.

5.1.390 *Contingent rent*

5.1.390.10 Contingent rent (as defined in 5.1.80) should be included in profit or loss using the same presentation as for non-contingent rental income or expense. For example, a lease payment may be partially fixed, with additional rent based on total sales volume generated at the leased property. In our view, the fixed and contingent rent should be included in the lessee's financial statements as an expense. Even though it might be appropriate to consider the contingent rent amount as a cost of sales, it would not be appropriate to present the contingent rent as a reduction of sales revenue in the lessee's financial statements.

IAS 34.B7 5.1.390.20 Often leases to retailers include contingent rental payments, for example 1 percent of sales in excess of 5,000 but less than 10,000, and 2 percent of sales of 10,000 or more. Limited guidance is provided in IAS 34 *Interim Financial Reporting* on a lessee's accounting for contingent lease obligations. This standard requires recognition of an obligation before the minimum sales level is met if the required level of sales (5,000 and 10,000 in this example) is expected to be met over the measurement period for which rent payments are calculated.

5.1.390.30 IFRSs do not contain specific guidance on how to account for rent that was considered contingent at inception of the lease but is confirmed subsequently (e.g. following an upwards-only rent review on a property lease). We prefer to account for such a change prospectively by revising the minimum lease payments over the remaining term of the lease. This adjustment would impact both disclosure of minimum lease payments and revenue and expense recognition. It would not trigger reconsideration of the lease classification. Alternatively, the confirmed rentals may be accounted for in the periods in which they are incurred. In our view, either of these alternative approaches can be applied regardless of whether a confirmed contingent rent results in an increase or a decrease in future lease payments. In our view, an entity should choose an accounting policy for the treatment of contingent rent (either prospective adjustment or accrual basis), to be applied consistently to all similar leases with contingent rent provisions, including those with upwards only adjustments and those under which future changes can be either upwards or downwards. The policy also should be applied to tax variation clauses when the additional rentals are considered to be contingent rent (see 5.1.460).

5.1.400 *Derecognition of finance lease receivables**

IAS 39.2(b)(i), 15-37   5.1.400.10 The derecognition of finance lease receivables is covered by the general derecognition guidance in IAS 39 (see 3.6.1070). In order for lease receivables to qualify for derecognition by the lessor, in full or in part, the transfer of the lease receivables needs to meet the derecognition criteria specified in IAS 39. Depending on whether (part of) a financial asset has been transferred, the level of risks and rewards transferred and the extent to which control has been transferred, the transaction could result in full derecognition, partial derecognition under the continuing involvement approach or no derecognition of the transferred lease receivables.

5.1.410 *Derecognition of finance lease payables*

5.1.410.05 The following chart summarises the accounting for a finance lease modification:

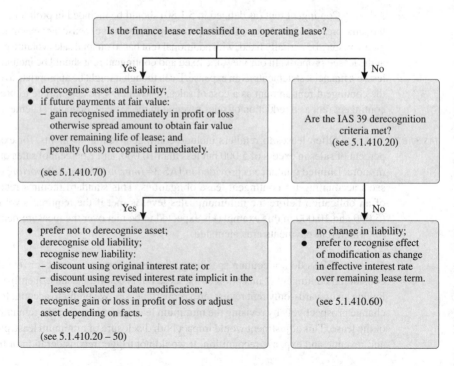

IAS 39.2(b)(ii) 5.1.410.10 Finance lease payables recognised by a lessee are subject to the derecognition provisions of IAS 39 (see 3.6.1330). Finance lease payables are derecognised only when the lessee's obligation in terms of the lease contract is extinguished (i.e. the obligation is discharged, cancelled or expires).

IAS 39.2(b) 5.1.410.20 In our view, a finance lease modification that does not change the finance lease classification but results in a change to the contractual cash flows from those at inception, will trigger the application of the requirements of IAS 39 (see 3.6.1340) for derecognition of the financial liability. In that case, we prefer that the leased asset not be derecognised, even if the IAS 39 derecognition requirements will be met in respect of the lease liability, as the lease arrangement was not terminated or reclassified as an operating lease under the modification accounting.

IAS 39.AG62 5.1.410.30 When meeting the derecognition requirement of IAS 39 for a lease modification (e.g. cash flows have changed by more than 10 percent) that remains classified as a finance lease, it is unclear how the new lease liability should be measured. In our view, an entity should choose an accounting policy, to be applied consistently, either to:

- discount the revised cash flows using the original interest rate implicit in the lease; or
- discount the revised cash flows using the revised interest rate implicit in the lease (or incremental borrowing rate, if applicable), determined, as at the date the new finance lease liability is recognised.

5.1.410.40 In our view, the difference between the finance lease liability that was derecognised and the new finance lease liability should be either recognised immediately in profit or loss or will be recognised as part of the leased asset, depending on the specific facts and circumstances of the modification agreement.

5.1.410.50 For example, a modification of a lease as a result of a substantial change in the fair value of the leased asset or a substantial change to the lease term may indicate that the gain or loss resulting from the lease modification should adjust the carrying amount of the leased asset. Conversely, a modification of a lease as a result of change in the market interest rate may indicate that the gain or loss resulting from the lease modification should be recognised immediately in profit or loss.

5.1.410.60 When the modification does not change the finance lease classification and does not meet the IAS 39 derecognition criteria, in our view the liability should not be remeasured. We prefer that the changes to the lease payments be treated as a change to the effective interest rate over the remaining lease term, consistent with lease incentives and sale and leaseback accounting. This would also be consistent with the accounting treatment for a debt modification not accounted for as an extinguishment (see 3.6.1340).

5.1.410.70 When the modification changes the classification of the lease from a finance lease to an operating lease, the leased asset and the finance lease liability will be derecognised. In our view, any resulting loss should be recognised immediately in profit or loss and, any resulting gain that results from the derecognition of the finance lease balances, should be recognised immediately to the extent that the operating lease transaction is at fair value, otherwise the gain should be recognised over the operating lease period.

5.1.420 *Embedded derivatives*

IAS 39.2(b),
AG33(f)

5.1.420.10 If a lease contract contains terms or conditions with the characteristics of a derivative instrument, then the parties to the lease contract evaluate whether this embedded derivative component of the lease needs to be separated from the lease contract and accounted for separately (see 3.6.260). Examples of terms that may require separate recognition of an embedded derivative include leverage features built into the lease payments, or lease payments that are based on an index that is unrelated to the lease contract. However, an embedded purchase option for a leased asset included in a lease contract should not be separated since such an option is accounted for as part of the lease (see 3.6.270.40).

5.1.430 *Impairment*

5.1.430.10 The impairment of leased assets is dealt with in the same manner as the impairment of other non-financial assets (see 3.10).

IAS 17.30, 54

5.1.430.20 In the case of an operating lease, impairment of the leased asset would be relevant to the lessor, unless the leased asset is an investment property that the lessor measures using the fair value model. Impairment of the asset under a finance lease would be relevant to the lessee.

5.1.430.30 Receivables due from the lessee under an operating lease are financial assets subject to the impairment requirements of IAS 39 (see 3.6.1370).

IAS 39.2(b),
AG9

5.1.430.40 For a finance lease, the lessor recognises lease receivables rather than the leased asset itself. As lease receivables are financial instruments, the lessor applies IAS 39 to determine whether there is any impairment of the receivables that is recognised (see 3.6.1370). The lessor's impairment assessment for a finance lease should be based on the lessor's primary risk exposure, which normally is to the creditworthiness of the lessee as opposed to potential decreases in value of the leased asset, which can be considered as collateral.

5.1.440 *Tax issues in finance leases*

5.1.450 *Post-tax methods of recognising finance income*

5.1.450.10 As noted above (see 5.1.330), a lessor recognises finance income from finance leases based on a pattern reflecting a constant periodic rate of return on its net investment in the lease. In our view, this calculation should be based on the carrying amount of the lease. The lessor may not adjust finance income to achieve a constant rate of return on the net cash investment, and thereby recognise a constant rate of return on a post-tax basis. IFRSs do not specifically prohibit use of the net cash method. However, while recognition of finance income based on the net cash investment previously was permitted by IFRSs, that option was removed in the 1997 revisions to IAS 17.

5.1.450.20 A finance lease may have significant tax benefits that are considered in the pricing of the lease transaction. This could result in a situation in which the finance income from the lease is negative due to the present value of the minimum lease payments being less than the cost of the leased asset. On a pre-tax basis the lease results in a loss. However, on a post-tax basis the lease would be profitable. In our view, the negative finance income should be spread over the lease term and recognised in line with the net investment in the lease. We believe that the pre-tax loss should not be recognised immediately.

5.1.460 *Tax variation clauses*

5.1.460.10 Some finance leases allow the lessor to obtain a tax benefit that is passed to the lessee in the form of reduced lease rentals. Virtually all such lease agreements contain a tax variation clause. Normally these clauses are structured so that any tax disadvantage suffered by the lessor as a result of a change in tax rates or rules will be compensated by an increase in future lease payments.

5.1.460.20 IFRSs do not have any guidance regarding the triggering of tax variation clauses. For example, the lessor may view the triggering of the tax variation clause as a contingency and recognise the contingent cash flows on a prospective basis over the remaining life of the lease. Alternatively, the lessor may determine that the trigger should be treated as a "catch up" in profit or loss. In our view, the method applied by the lessor should reflect the nature of the clause and whether the effect of the tax change is retrospective or prospective. The approach adopted for each type of variation clause should be applied consistently.

5.1.460.30 For example, Lessor T borrows 1,000 at 6 percent to purchase an asset. The asset is leased under a 20-year finance lease at an implicit interest rate of 5 percent. T is able to earn a small profit because tax cash flows allow T to repay the borrowing before the end of the lease term, generating interest cost savings.

5.1.460.40 After 10 years the tax legislation changes, and T is required to reimburse the tax authorities for the full amount of tax benefits previously obtained, including interest. Under the tax variation clause, the lease income over the remaining 10 years of the lease increases to 7 percent. Over the entire lease term, T achieves a return of 6 percent, the rate that would have applied to a loan with no particular tax advantages.

5.1.460.50 There are three possible ways to account for the triggering of the tax variation clause:

- prospectively, recognising future lease income at 7 percent; or
- retrospectively, by restating the net investment in the lease, with a credit to income at the "trigger" date, by discounting future lease rentals either at:

> – 5 percent (the original rate implicit in the lease); or
>
> – 6 percent (the rate that would have applied had the tax benefit never been available to the lessee).

5.1.460.60 If the additional rentals are considered as "contingent rent", then the additional rental payments should be recognised prospectively, once the lessee is obligated to make them (see 5.1.80). Retrospective adjustment as described in the second alternative would be consistent with viewing the net investment in the lease as a financial asset and applying the guidance for changes in cash flow estimates under the effective yield method used to calculate returns on financial assets (see 4.6.60). The third alternative results in the matching (to a degree) of the tax cost incurred by the lessor at the trigger date with the reimbursement of the related tax benefits recovered from the lessee.

5.1.460.70 In practice, tax variation clauses may take many forms. Changes in tax legislation also can take many forms. In some cases rentals would be adjusted for any change in the tax rate applied to T; in others T's tax benefit may be removed or adjusted prospectively. In our view, the first or the third method may be appropriate depending on the circumstances. An entity should apply its chosen method consistently to similar circumstances. The second method has the effect of recognising future income at the date that the change in future terms comes into effect, which in our view would not be appropriate.

5.1.470 Sale and leaseback transactions

5.1.470.10 A sale and leaseback transaction has two components: the sale of the asset from the seller to the lessor, and the leaseback of the asset from the buyer/lessor to the seller/lessee. Under IFRSs the two components each are accounted for rather than the seller/lessee accounting for the net effect of the combined transaction.

IAS 17.4, 59 5.1.470.20 For example, a sale and leaseback transaction may result in a leaseback that is classified as a finance lease. IFRSs require sale and finance leaseback transactions to be accounted for as a sale and a lease even though the net effect of the two transactions is that the seller retains substantially all of the risks and rewards of the asset, and therefore the net effect of the transaction as a whole would not satisfy the revenue recognition criteria in IFRSs (e.g. for sales of real estate (see 4.2.450)).

5.1.470.30 In our view, sale and leaseback transactions bypass the assessment of the *sale* transaction against the revenue recognition criteria. Therefore, we believe that the classification of the leaseback as an operating or finance lease should reflect not only the terms of the *lease* but also the risks and rewards retained by the seller/lessee under the sale agreement.

IAS 17.58 5.1.470.40 In a sale and leaseback transaction, the periodic lease payments usually are highly dependent upon the sale price of the asset. The accounting for the gain or loss on the sale component of the transaction depends in part on the classification of the leaseback.

5.1.480 *Sale and finance leaseback*

IAS 17.59, 60 5.1.480.10 When a sale and leaseback results in a finance lease, any gain on the sale is deferred and recognised as income over the lease term. In our view, it is acceptable that the amortisation of the deferred gain be presented as depreciation expense as the transaction is in substance a finance transaction. No loss is recognised unless the asset is impaired.

5.1.490 *Sale and operating leaseback*

IAS 17.61, 63 5.1.490.10 If the leaseback is classified as an operating lease, then any gain is recognised immediately if the sale and leaseback terms clearly are at fair value. Otherwise, the sale and leaseback are accounted for as follows:

- If the sale price is at or below fair value then the gain or loss is recognised immediately. However, if a loss is compensated for by future rentals at a below-market price, then the loss is deferred and amortised over the period that the asset is expected to be used. In our view, the loss that is deferred cannot exceed the amount equal to the present value of the difference, i.e. rental savings, between the below-market rents and the fair market rents over the period in which such differences exist, as determined at inception of the lease.
- If the sale price is above fair value, then any gain is deferred and amortised over the useful life of the asset.
- If the fair value of the asset is less than the carrying amount of the asset at the date of the transaction, then that difference should be recognised immediately as a loss on the sale.

5.1.500 **Linked transactions in the legal form of a lease**

SIC-27 5.1.500.10 A series of linked transactions that take the legal form of a lease should be accounted for in accordance with their economic substance. This situation may occur, for example, when a transaction is in the form of a lease but does not transfer the right of use of the asset from the lessor to the lessee. These transactions may be entered into in order to generate a tax saving (often cross-border) or to generate fees. Transactions in the legal form of a lease are considered to be "linked" when the individual transactions cannot be understood without reference to the series as a whole. In this case the series of transactions should be accounted for as one transaction. Therefore the net effect of the transaction is accounted for, rather than accounting separately for each component of the transaction.

5.1.500.20 For example, Company P purchased an airplane from Company L and leases it back to L under a finance lease. Most of the payment to L for the airplane was paid into a trust account securing lease payments to be made by L to P. P is entitled to significant tax deductions due to accelerated tax depreciation on the airplane.

5.1.500.30 P has no residual or credit risks arising from the lease transaction as the lease payment is secured by the trust accounts. Therefore, the risk and rewards of the leased assets have in substance not been transferred to P; the reason for the transaction is merely to achieve a tax benefit since in substance P pays a fee to the lessee to obtain tax benefits. Therefore the transactions are included in the scope of SIC-27 *Evaluating the Substance of Transactions Involving the Legal Form of a Lease* and should be accounted for as linked transactions based on the economic substance.

5.1.510 **Lease transactions not in the form of a lease**

IFRIC 4.6   5.1.510.10 An arrangement may contain a lease even though the agreement is not in the legal form of a lease. For example, outsourcing arrangements may contain a lease of the underlying assets. The assessment of the substance of agreements should be analysed at their inception. The assessment depends on whether:

- fulfilment of the arrangement is dependent on the use of a specific asset or assets; and
- the arrangement conveys a right to use the asset(s).

IFRIC 4.4   5.1.510.15 This assessment does not apply to arrangements that are excluded from the scope of IAS 17 or are within the scope of IFRIC 12 *Service Concession Arrangements* (see 5.12.01 – 45).

IFRIC 4.6-8   5.1.510.20 The asset under the arrangement may be identified explicitly in the arrangement or it may be specified implicitly; for example, if the supplier owns or leases only one asset with which to fulfil the obligation, and it is not economically feasible or practicable for the supplier to use alternative assets to fulfil the arrangement.

IFRIC 4.9   5.1.510.30 The arrangement conveys the right to use the asset if the buyer (lessee) obtains the ability or right to control the use of a specific asset. IFRIC 4 clarifies that the right to use an asset is transferred, if any of the following conditions are met:

- The buyer has the ability or right to control the asset including to direct how others should operate the asset, and at the same time obtaining or controlling more than an insignificant amount of the asset's output.
- The buyer has the ability or right to control physical access to the asset, while obtaining or controlling more than an insignificant amount of the asset's output.
- The possibility that another party will take more than an insignificant amount of the asset's output during the term of the arrangement is remote, and the price paid by the buyer for the output is neither a contractually fixed price per unit of output nor the market price per unit of output.

IFRIC 4.9(a)   5.1.510.31 If a buyer agrees to purchase 100 percent of the output of a specified asset and requires the asset to be operated at full capacity, then in our view there is a strong presumption that the buyer has effective control over the asset and therefore that arrangement is or contains a lease.

5.1.510.32 In our view, this presumption can be rebutted only when the operator, although obligated to operate at maximum capacity, retains significant operational flexibility to influence the profitability of the arrangement, for example, the mix of product quality/composition can be varied at the operator's discretion.

IFRIC 4.9(c),   5.1.510.33 Generally under IFRIC 4 a buyer controls an asset and a lease exists when
BC35-BC39   the buyer is taking substantially all of the output, as others cannot obtain the output from the specified asset. However, an exemption was incorporated in paragraph 9(c) of IFRIC 4 so that arrangements in which the price is either contractually fixed per unit of output or equal to the market price per unit of output at the time of delivery of the output are not accounted for as leases. In our view, this exemption for fixed or market prices should be applied narrowly and only for arrangements in which a buyer clearly pays for the actual output. Therefore, except in the limited circumstances discussed in 5.1.10.37 – 39, if any variability is introduced to the price per unit (other than for unit pricing at a market rate at the time of delivery), then in our view such an arrangement does not meet the exemption for fixed or market prices.

IFRIC 4.BC   5.1.510.34 For example, Company D enters into an arrangement to supply Company B
36(c)   with energy and builds a specific power plant to service this arrangement. It is remote that any other party will take more than an insignificant amount of D's plant output. Under the arrangement B will pay D for each megawatt-hour (MWh) produced based on the current selling price per unit. As the price is contractually fixed, and does not vary with output, the arrangement meets the exemption in paragraph 9(c) of IFRIC 4 and does not contain a lease.

5.1.510.35 Modifying the example, B now makes pricing payments to D based on a set recovery of 90 percent of the monthly total operating costs of the plant plus a 25 percent profit mark up for each MWh purchased. This price is set in order to recover a portion of D's capital investment in the plant originally built to service the arrangement with B. In substance the payment reflects a variable allocation per MWh of the ongoing cost of the asset (i.e. the plant), rather than the cost of conversion for the MWh produced. The unit price of output is variable, and not reflective of current market price for the MWh, and accordingly does not meet the exemption in paragraph 9(c) of IFRIC 4. It also may be persuasive evidence that it is remote that parties other than B will take more than an insignificant amount of output of D's plant.

5.1.510.36 In our view, there is a strong presumption that any variability in the price per unit that depends on the volume of output of the asset means that the arrangement does not meet the exemption for fixed or market prices. For example, Company B agrees to purchase all of the electricity generated by a wind farm. B pays 10 per MWh generated, unless the actual electricity generated is 20 percent higher than forecast, in which case the unit price is reduced by 10 percent. We believe that this arrangement does not meet the exemption for fixed prices, as the price to be paid for each unit of output is not determined at the commencement of the arrangement. Similarly, we believe that arrangements in which the unit price is subject to caps, floors or stepped adjustments that depend on the volume of output do not meet the exemption for fixed or market prices.

5.1.510.37 However, in our view the exemption for fixed prices may be met in certain limited circumstances. We believe that if the total volumes and total price for a contract are fixed (predetermined at inception of the contract), then regardless of how the pricing for the individual units occurs, the arrangement meets the exemption for fixed price, as the price per unit is fixed on a total contract basis.

5.1.510.38 We believe that if the buyer agrees to pay different prices at different times during the term of the arrangement and such a pricing structure is consistent with payments for output, then the arrangement meets the exemption for fixed prices, on the basis that the changes were predetermined at inception of the contract. For example, Company C agrees to purchase all of the electricity generated by a wind farm. C pays 8 per MWh generated in the summer months and 12 per MWh generated in the winter months. We believe that this arrangement meets the exemption for fixed prices as the price to be paid for each unit of output is determined at the commencement of the arrangement and the pricing structure is consistent with payments for output.

5.1.510.39 In our view, if an initial fixed price per unit is adjusted under the terms of the contract by reference to a general inflation index such that the price is fixed in real terms, then the arrangement meets the exemption for fixed prices. Reference to a specific inflation index (e.g. a specific commodity index related to the asset) would not satisfy the exemption as the price is not fixed in "real terms".

IFRIC 4.11   5.1.510.40 The entity reassesses the classification of the arrangement only when there is a change in the terms of the arrangement (see 5.1.270), a substantial change to the asset or a change in the determination of whether fulfilment of the arrangement is dependent upon a specific asset.

IFRIC 4.12-   5.1.510.50 If an arrangement contains a lease, then the requirements of IAS 17 are ap-
15   plied only to the lease element of the arrangement. At the inception of such arrangement, payments required by the arrangement are split into lease payments and payments related to the other elements of the arrangement based on their relative fair values. In some cases the separation of such payments will require the use of an estimation technique, e.g. by reference to a lease agreement for a comparable asset that contains no other elements, or by estimating the payments for the other elements by reference to comparable agreements and then deducting these payments from total payments required. If it is impracticable to separate the lease payments, then:

- if the lease arrangement is a finance lease, then the lessee recognises an asset and a liability at an amount equal to the fair value of the asset that is identified as being the subject of the lease; or
- if the lease arrangement is an operating lease, then the lessee classifies all payments as lease payments in order to meet the disclosure requirements of IAS 17.

5.1.510.60 For example, Company L enters into an agreement with Company B to build, and then to own and operate for 25 years, a water and power plant. B will make a fixed monthly payment and a variable payment based on actual output from the water and power plant to L. Ninety percent of the output from the water and power plant will be obtained by B.

5.1.510.70 Both B and L should conclude that the arrangement contains a lease agreement according to IFRIC 4 because:

- the agreement is based on a specific asset;
- the presence of the fixed monthly payment means that the amount B pays is not fixed per unit of output or equal to the market price; and
- B takes a high proportion of the output, making it remote that another party will take more than an insignificant part of the output.

5.1.510.80 Furthermore, the arrangement contains a service element and therefore the payments are allocated between the lease and the service elements.

5.1.520 **Presentation and disclosure**

IAS 32.7 5.1.520.10 Lease receivables and lease payables are financial instruments and are treated as such for disclosure and presentation purposes (see 5.6).

5.1.520.20 For operating leases, a lessee presents its lease payments as expenses in profit or loss. A lessor presents the lease payments received as part of revenue in profit or loss. In our view, a lessee may not separate a finance component of its operating lease payment to present that component as part of interest expense.

IAS 17.31, 5.1.520.30 In addition, lessors and lessees provide a general description of significant
35, 47, 56 leasing arrangements. For lessees this includes information about the basis on which contingent rent payments are determined, the existence and terms of renewal or purchase options, and escalation clauses and restrictions imposed by lease arrangements, such as those concerning dividends, additional debt and further leasing.

IAS 17.35, 56 5.1.520.40 For operating leases, both the lessor and the lessee disclose the non-cancellable minimum lease payments to be received or paid, respectively, over the remaining term of the lease.

5.1.530 **Future developments**

5.1.530.10 In July 2006 the IASB announced a project to reconsider the accounting requirement for leasing arrangements. The project is being conducted jointly with the FASB. In March 2009 the IASB and FASB published a DP *Leases – Preliminary Views*. The DP proposes, for lessees, to eliminate the requirement to classify a lease contract as an operating or finance lease, and to require a single accounting model to be applied to all leases. The DP proposes that a lessee recognise in its financial statements a "right-of-use" asset representing its right to use the leased asset, and a liability representing its obligation to pay lease rentals. The DP includes a high-level discussion of lessor accounting issues but expresses no preliminary views on lessor accounting.

5.1.530.15 An ED is scheduled for the third quarter of 2010. Unlike the DP, the ED is expected to address both lessee and lessor accounting. The proposals for lessee accounting will reflect the "right-of-use" model described in the DP. The proposals for lessor accounting will feature a "hybrid" approach under which a lessor will account for leases using either the performance obligation model or the partial derecognition model, depending on the nature of the lease. Under the performance obligation model, the lessor will continue to recognise the leased asset and will also recognise an asset for its right to receive lease rentals and a liability for its obligation to allow the lessee to use the leased asset. Under the derecognition model, the lessor will derecognise the leased asset and recognise an asset for its right to receive lease rentals and a residual value asset representing its interest in the leased asset at the end of the lease term. The IASB proposes an exemption from these requirements for lessors of investment property measured at fair value.

5.1.530.20 In March 2009 the IASB published ED/2009/3 *Derecognition*. The proposals in the ED aimed to simplify the derecognition model for financial assets. However, except for the proposed disclosure requirements, the IASB has decided not to proceed with the ED at this point in time (see 5.6.530.20).

5.2 Operating segments
(IFRS 8)

5.2 Operating segments
(IFRS 8)

Overview of currently effective requirements

- IFRS 8 sets out requirements for segment disclosures by entities whose debt or equity instruments are traded in a public market or that file, or are in the process of filing, their financial statements with a securities commission or other regulatory organisation for the purpose of issuing any class of instruments in a public market.

- IFRS 8 introduces the "management approach", which requires segment disclosures based on the components of the entity that management monitors in making decisions about operating matters.

- Such components (operating segments) are identified on the basis of internal reports that the entity's chief operating decision maker (CODM) reviews regularly in allocating resources to segments and in assessing their performance.

- The aggregation of operating segments is permitted only when the segments have "similar" economics and meet a number of other specified criteria.

- Reportable segments are identified based on quantitative thresholds of revenue, profit or loss, or assets.

- The amounts disclosed for each reportable segment are the measures reported to the CODM, which are not necessarily based on the same accounting policies as the amounts recognised in the financial statements.

- Because IFRS 8 requires disclosure of segment profit or loss, segment assets and segment liabilities as reported to the CODM rather than as they would be reported under IFRSs, it also requires disclosure of how these amounts are measured for each reportable segment.

- IFRS 8 requires reconciliations between total amounts for all reportable segments and financial statements amounts with a description of all material reconciling items.

- IFRS 8 requires general and entity-wide disclosures, including information about products and services, geographical areas (including country of domicile and individual foreign countries, if material), major customers and factors used to identify an entity's reportable segments. Such disclosures are required even if an entity only has one segment.

> • **Comparative information normally is restated for changes in operating segments.**

Currently effective requirements

This publication reflects IFRSs in issue at 1 August 2010. The currently effective requirements cover annual periods beginning on 1 January 2010. The requirements related to this topic are derived mainly from IFRS 8 *Operating Segments*.

Forthcoming requirements and future developments

When a currently effective requirement will be changed by a new requirement that is issued but is not yet effective, it is marked with a # as a **forthcoming requirement** and the impact of the change is explained in the accompanying boxed text. The forthcoming requirements related to this topic are derived from the revised IAS 24 *Related Party Disclosures* (2009). A brief outline of the impact of IAS 24 (2009) is given in 5.2.232.

When a significant change to the currently effective or forthcoming requirements is expected, it is marked with a * as an area that may be subject to **future developments**. In respect of this topic no future developments are noted.

5.2.10 **Scope**

IFRS 8.2   5.2.10.10 The disclosure of segment information is required only by those entities whose debt or equity instruments are traded in a public market (a domestic or foreign stock exchange or an over-the-counter market, including local and regional markets) or that file, or are in the process of filing, their financial statements with a securities commission or other regulatory organisation for the purpose of issuing any class of instruments in a public market. Other entities are encouraged, but not required, to disclose segment information. Segment disclosures should be made within the financial statements.

5.2.10.12 IFRS 8 does not provide a definition for "traded in a public market". In our view, determining what is meant by traded in a public market depends on facts and circumstances, and can vary based on local requirements from securities commissions and/or regulators. We believe that if a buyer or a seller can contact a broker and obtain a quoted price, then this is an indicator that the debt or equity instruments are publicly traded. This is without regard to how often the instrument is traded.

5.2.10.13 The following factors may indicate that a fund is not traded in a public market:

- The fund is listed at a stock exchange for convenience listing or marketing purposes only, and cannot be traded on the stock market.
- The fund's shares are traded through a fund agent/administrator only, i.e. the subscriptions and redemptions of units are handled by a transfer agent/administrator directly associated with the fund.

- Buyer and seller set up prices based on the fund prospectus valuation principles and therefore prices would not be established by trading in a market.

5.2.10.14 The factors mentioned in 5.2.10.13 are not exhaustive and judgement will be required when assessing if a fund falls within the scope of IFRS 8.

5.2.10.15 Segment information is required when an entity is in the process of issuing listed securities. In our view, segment information will be required only when the entity has taken active steps to obtain a listing, rather than simply planning the listing. When an entity prepares financial statements for inclusion in a prospectus in preparation for a listing, segment information should be included in those financial statements.

IFRS 8.4 5.2.10.20 If an entity presents a financial report that includes both the consolidated financial statements of a parent that is required to present segment information and the parent's separate financial statements, then the segment disclosures are required only in the consolidated financial statements.

IFRS 8. *BC23* 5.2.10.25 The consolidated financial statements of a group in which the parent is unlisted but has a listed non-controlling interests or a subsidiary with listed debt or equity instrument are not within the scope of IFRS 8.

IFRS 8.3 5.2.10.30 When an entity that is not required to provide segment information wishes to do so, but is unable to obtain all of the required information or wishes to disclose only limited information, such information is not described as segment information.

5.2.10.40 Companies also may present information in the management commentary (or director's report) accompanying the financial statements similar to or related to its operating segments disclosures. Such information should, in all material respects, be consistent with the IFRS 8 disclosures in the financial statements (see 5.8.20.50).

5.2.20 Core principle

IFRS 8.1 5.2.20.10 The core principle of IFRS 8 is the disclosure of information that enables users of an entity's financial statements to evaluate the nature and financial effects of the business activities in which it engages and the economic environment in which it operates. The core principle is considered when forming judgements about how and what information is disclosed.

5.2.30 Management approach

IFRS 8.BC4, *BC10* 5.2.30.10 IFRS 8 requires segment disclosure based on the components of the entity that management monitors in making decisions about operating matters (the "management approach"). Such components (operating segments) are identified on the basis of internal reports that the entity's CODM reviews regularly in allocating resources to segments and in assessing their performance.

IFRS 8.BC4,
BC10 5.2.30.20 The management approach is based on the way in which management organises the segments within the entity for making operating decisions and in assessing performance. Consequently, the segments are evident from the structure of the entity's internal organisation and the information reported internally to the CODM. The adoption of the management approach results in the disclosure of information for segments in substantially the same manner as they are reported internally and used by the entity's CODM for purposes of evaluating performance and making resource allocation decisions. In that way, financial statements users are able to see the entity "through the eyes of management".

5.2.35 Five step approach

5.2.35.10 The practical approach to segment reporting under IFRS 8 includes five steps, as presented in the chart below.

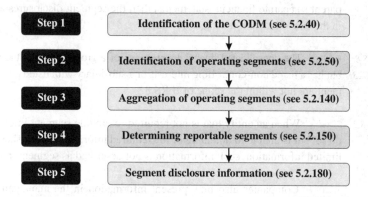

5.2.40 Identification of the chief operating decision maker (Step 1)

IFRS 8.7 5.2.40.10 The term chief operating decision maker (CODM) refers to a function, rather than to a specific title. The function of the CODM is to allocate resources to the operating segments of an entity and to assess the operating segments' performance. The CODM usually is the highest level of management (e.g. CEO or Chief Operating Officer (COO)), but the function of the CODM may be performed by a group rather than by one person (e.g. a board of directors, an executive committee or a management committee).

IFRS 8.7 5.2.40.15 Lower level of management may make decisions about resource allocation that relate to less than the whole of entity. These lower levels management can not be the CODM of the entity. However, they may be the segment manager for an operating segment (see 5.2.50.20).

IFRS 8.7 5.2.40.20 An entity cannot have more than one CODM.

5.2.40.25 For example, an entity has a CEO, a COO and a president. These individuals comprise the executive committee. The responsibility of the executive committee is to assess performance and to make resource allocation decisions related across the whole entity; each of these individuals has an equal vote. The executive committee is the CODM because the committee is the highest level of management that performs these functions. The segment financial information provided to and used by the executive committee to make resource allocation decisions and to assess performance is the segment information that would be the basis for disclosure for external financial reporting purposes.

5.2.40.30 In our view, the mere existence of an executive committee, management committee or other high-level committee does not necessarily mean that one of those committees constitutes the CODM.

5.2.40.35 Assume the same fact pattern as in the example in 5.2.40.25 except that the CEO can override decisions made by the executive committee. Because the CEO essentially controls the committee and therefore has control over the operating decisions that the executive committee makes, in our view the CEO will be the CODM for purposes of applying IFRS 8.

5.2.50 Identification of operating segments (Step 2)

IFRS 8.5 5.2.50.10 The operating segments are identified based on the way in which financial information is organised and reported to the CODM. An operating segment is identified by IFRS 8 as a component of an entity:

- that engages in business activities from which it may earn revenues and incur expenses, including revenues and expenses related to transactions with other components of the same entity;
- whose operating results are reviewed regularly by the entity's CODM in order to allocate resources and assess its performance; and
- for which discrete financial information is available.

IFRS 8.9 5.2.50.20 An operating segment generally has a segment manager. Essentially, the segment manager is directly accountable for the functioning of the operating segment and maintains regular contact with the CODM to discuss operating activities, forecasts and financial results. Like the CODM, a segment manager is a function, rather than a specific title.

5.2.50.30 There is no requirement to disaggregate information for segment reporting purposes if it is not provided to the CODM in a disaggregated form on a regular basis.

5.2.60 *Types of operating segments*

5.2.60.10 Under IFRS 8 operating segments are the individual operations that the CODM reviews for purposes of assessing performance and making resource allocation decisions. Operating segments could be identified on a number of different bases, including:

- products
- services
- customers

- geography
- legal entity
- individual plant (e.g. automotive supplier)
- individual property (e.g. real estate investment trust).

5.2.60.20 The operating segments and, ultimately, the reportable segments identified might not necessarily result in a single basis of segmentation (e.g. all geographic or all products).

5.2.60.25 For example, Company M has six business components (A, B, C, D, E and F). Three of these business components (A, B and C) are located in Germany and each manufactures and sells a different product to customers in Germany. The CEO (who has been identified as the CODM) assesses performance, makes operating decisions and allocates resources to these business components based on the financial information presented on a product-line basis. The remaining three business components are located in the United States (D, E and F). These business components are organised to mirror the German operations (i.e. each manufactures and sells its products but to customers located in the United States). However, the CODM assesses performance, makes operating decisions and allocates resources based on the financial information presented for the US operations as a whole. M's president of the US operations is responsible for assessing performance, making operating decisions and allocating resources to the business components in the United States and is directly accountable to the CODM.

5.2.60.27 In our view, M has four operating segments: A, B and C, which are determined on a product-line basis, and a segment representing the US operations, which consists of business components D, E and F and is determined on a geographic basis.

5.2.60.30 Determination of the *industry* in which a business component of an entity operates generally is not decisive for purposes of identifying all of the operating segments under IFRS 8.

5.2.60.35 For example, Company N operates in the mining industry and presents financial information in its management commentary and press releases on the following business components: gold, copper and coal. N determines that the CODM makes resource allocation decisions based on the financial performance of each of these three business components. In our view, each of the three business components is an operating segment under IFRS 8, despite the fact that they all are in the mining industry.

IFRS 8.5 5.2.60.40 Operating segments can include, but are not limited to, start-up operations, vertically integrated operations, and jointly controlled entities and associates.

5.2.70 *Start-up operations*

IFRS 8.5 5.2.70.10 An operating segment may engage in business activities for which it has yet to earn revenue. Despite a lack of revenue, a start-up operation may qualify as an operating segment in accordance with IFRS 8.

5.2.70.20 For example, Company L produces various lawn and garden products such as swing seats, utility sheds and lawn mowers, which comprise its operating segments. During December 2009 L began construction of a new plant for the purpose of producing barbecue grills. Production is expected to begin in the first quarter of 2010 and management expects the barbecue operation to be the entity's second largest business component, in terms of revenue, within two years. Discrete financial information about the operation is being provided to and used by the CODM. In our view, the barbecue grill operation, even though in a start-up stage, is an operating segment.

5.2.80 *Vertically integrated operations*

IFRS 8.5(a) 5.2.80.10 In certain vertically integrated businesses (e.g. oil and gas entities) information about the components engaged in each stage of production might be useful for the users of financial statements, as different activities within the entity might have significantly different prospects for future cash flows. Under IFRS 8 the definition of an operating segment includes components of an entity that sell primarily or exclusively to other operating segments of the entity if the entity is managed in that way.

5.2.80.20 The fact that an entity has vertically integrated operations does not necessarily mean that each of these individual operations will be considered separate operating segments for purposes of IFRS 8. This will depend on how the business is managed and how the financial information is organised and reported to the CODM.

5.2.80.30 For example, the CODM of an entity receives financial information organised by the following business components:

- Component A designs, manufactures, assembles and markets motorcycles;
- Component B provides consumer financial services such as financing and leasing for new motorcycle purchases;
- Component C provides dealer financing; and
- Component D designs advanced technology electronic systems for the telecommunications industry.

5.2.80.35 Component A contains four separate operations that: (a) design the motorcycles; (b) manufacture the necessary components; (c) assemble the motorcycles; and (d) market the motorcycles to consumers. Component A is essentially a vertically integrated operation. No disaggregated information is provided to the CODM on the separate operations of Component A, and the CODM assesses operating performance and makes resource decisions about Component A based on the combined results of these operations.

5.2.80.40 In this example the *combined* operations of Component A constitute an operating segment. However, if the fact pattern in the example in 5.2.80.30 and 35 is changed so that the disaggregated information on separate operations of Component A is regularly provided to and reviewed by the CODM to assess the separate operation's performance and to allocate resources, then in our view such operations would be separate operating segments.

IFRS 8.5(a)   5.2.80.50 Situations might exist in which an entity consists of vertically integrated operations, but no revenues are allocated to those different activities. To satisfy the definition of an operating segment under IFRS 8 a component of an entity has to engage in business activities from which it *may* earn revenues and incur expenses. It is the ability of a segment to earn revenues rather than the mere existence or an allocation of revenue that is determinative (see 5.2.90.40).

5.2.85 *Jointly controlled entities and associates*

IFRS 8.5   5.2.85.10 A jointly controlled entity, jointly controlled operation or an associate (the "investee") could qualify as an operating segment under IFRS 8. Unilateral control over the investee's activities or control over the performance of the investee is not required in order to satisfy the definition of an operating segment under IFRS 8. Management might review regularly the operating results and performance of the investee for purposes of evaluating whether to retain the investor-investee relationship. IFRS 8 does not require that the CODM be responsible for making decisions about resources to be allocated within the segment, but rather for resources to be allocated to the segment.

5.2.85.20 To determine if an investee qualifies as an operating segment, an entity should consider whether or not the CODM is responsible for making resource allocation decisions (i.e. whether to make additional investments, loans or advances to the investee or to sell any portion of its interest in the investee) and for evaluating the financial performance of the investment. In our view, if the primary responsibility for either of these functions resides at a lower level within the entity's organisation, then the investment might not necessarily qualify as an operating segment.

5.2.90 *Functions and departments*

IFRS 8.6   5.2.90.10 Under IFRS 8 not every part of an entity has to meet the definition of an operating segment or part of an operating segment. A corporate headquarters likely would carry out some, or all, of the functions in the treasury, legal, accounting, information systems and human resources areas. In certain situations these corporate activities might even be reflected as a separate business unit for internal reporting purposes. However, corporate activities generally would not qualify as operating segments under IFRS 8, because typically they are not business activities from which the entity may earn revenues.

IFRS 8.6   5.2.90.20 For purposes of IFRS 8, an entity's pension and other post-employment benefit plans are not considered operating segments.

IFRS 8.16   5.2.90.30 Assuming that amounts related to corporate activities are not allocated to operating segments (i.e. are not included in the measure of operating segment profit or loss reported to the CODM), the amounts for these activities would be reported in the reconciliation of the total reportable segment amounts to the financial statements (see 5.2.160.40).

IFRS 8.5, 9 5.2.90.40 Situations might exist in which a corporate activity may qualify as an operating segment. For example, if sufficient and discrete financial information exists for an R&D activity and is reviewed by the CODM; the R&D activity has a segment manager; the R&D activity is not incidental to the entity; and the R&D activity is capable of earning revenues, then the R&D activity or function may qualify as an operating segment. However, it is not essential for the R&D activity to earn revenue to qualify as an operating segment, as long as it is capable of doing so.

5.2.100 *Information reviewed by the CODM to make decisions*

IFRS 8.5(b) 5.2.100.10 Under IFRS 8 entities are required to consider all types of information provided to the CODM when identifying operating segments. In addition, in our view if revenue and profitability information is released to analysts, the financial press or via an entity's website, then such information could be considered as well. Other forms of information to consider can include:

- management planning and budgeting materials;
- board of directors' reports; and
- media statements about how an entity operates its business, including information posted on its website.

5.2.110 *Discrete and sufficient financial information*

IFRS 8.5(c) 5.2.110.10 In order to assess performance and to make resource allocation decisions, the CODM requires regular financial information about the business component. This information should be *sufficiently detailed* to allow the CODM to assess performance and to make resource allocation decisions.

5.2.120 *Identification of operating segments when multiple types of segment information exist*

IFRS 8.8 5.2.120.10 Identifying the appropriate operating segments is not always obvious. Many entities, particularly multinational companies with diverse operations, organise and report financial information to the CODM in more than one way. As a result, operating segments might not be evident.

IFRS 8.10 5.2.120.20 Judgement will be necessary in determining the single set of operating segments, and will depend on the individual facts and circumstances of the entity. In such situations the entity determines which set of components constitutes the operating segments by reference to the core principle of IFRS 8 (see 5.2.20.10). The following additional factors can be considered in determining the appropriate operating segments:

- the nature of the business activities of each component;
IFRS 8.9 - the existence of managers responsible for the components;
IFRS 8.10 - information presented to the board of directors;
- information provided to external financial analysts and on the entity's website; and

- information presented in the front/end of financial statements, e.g. director's report.

5.2.130 *Matrix organisations*

IFRS 8.10 5.2.130.10 Some entities use a "matrix" form of organisation, whereby business components are managed in more than one way. For example, some entities have segment managers who are responsible for geographic regions, and different segment managers who oversee products and services. If the entity generates financial information about its business components based on both geography and products or services (and the CODM reviews both types of information, and both have segment managers), then the entity determines which set of components constitutes the operating segments by reference to the core principle.

5.2.140 **Aggregation of operating segments (Step 3)**

IFRS 8.12 5.2.140.10 Under IFRS 8 two or more operating segments may be aggregated into a single operating segment when the operating segments have characteristics so similar that they can be expected to have essentially the same future prospects. Aggregation is *permitted* only if segments are similar in each of the following respects:

- it is consistent with the core principle of IFRS 8 (see 5.2.20.10);
- the segments have similar economic characteristics; and
- the segments are similar in each of the following respects:
    - the nature of products and services;
    - the nature of the production processes;
    - the type or class of customer for their products and services;
    - the methods used to distribute their products or provide their services; and
    - if applicable, the nature of the regulatory environment, e.g. banking, insurance or public utilities.

IFRS 8.IG7 5.2.140.15 The aggregation of operating segments is performed before determining which segments are reportable; therefore, operating segments may be aggregated even though individually they may exceed the quantitative thresholds for determining which ones are reportable (see 5.2.150.10).

5.2.140.20 The aggregation criteria are applied as tests and not as indicators. The ability to meet the criteria will depend on the individual facts and circumstances. A significant amount of judgement will be required when applying the aggregation tests.

IFRS 8.12 5.2.140.30 In determining similar economic characteristics, as an example, IFRS 8 refers only to similar long-term average gross margins. However, we believe that other economic factors also could be used to determine if two or more operating segments have similar economic characteristics. Those factors should be entity-specific and should be based on the primary factors that the CODM uses in reviewing the performance of and allocating resources to individual segments. Key performance indicators or other measures used in the industry or by the CODM might be more relevant than gross margins.

5.2.141 *Aggregation of investee operating segments*

5.2.141.10 In our experience, it may be difficult to satisfy the criteria under IFRS 8 to aggregate an investee operating segment with another operating segment. Accordingly, in our view generally it will be inappropriate to aggregate an investee operating segment with another operating segment, including other investee operating segments. If the investee operating segment does not qualify as a reporting segment, then we believe it should be included in the "all other" category.

5.2.142 *Consistency with the core principle of IFRS 8*

IFRS 8.1,
BC32   5.2.142.10 When an entity has very few operating segments, it may be evident that the operating segments also are reportable segments. To be consistent with the core principle of IFRS 8, entities should not apply the aggregation provisions when the result would significantly impact the user's ability to understand the entity's performance, its prospects for future cash flows or the user's decisions about the entity as a whole.

5.2.142.20 For example, Company T is a tour operator providing services in three neighbouring European countries, each of which is determined to be an operating segment. The CODM reviews the operating results of each operation separately to assess the individual performance of and to allocate resources to each one. Although aggregation may be permitted, doing so would reduce the users' ability to understand the entity's performance, its prospects for future cash flows and decisions about the entity as a whole. In our view, T should disclose three reportable segments, which is consistent with the reason that the CODM needs information organised by each operating segment to manage T's business activities.

5.2.143 *Similar economic characteristics*

IFRS 8.12   5.2.143.10 In determining similar economic characteristics, as an example, IFRS 8 refers only to similar long-term average gross margins. However, in our view it may be appropriate to use other economic factors to determine if two or more operating segments have similar economic characteristics. Those factors should be entity-specific and should be based on the primary factors that the CODM uses in reviewing the performance of, and allocating resources to, individual segments. Key performance indicators or other measures used in the industry or by the CODM might be more relevant than gross margins.

5.2.143.20 Useful measures to determine economic similarity may include:

- sales metrics (e.g. sales by square meters)
- trends in sales growth
- return on assets
- levels of capital investments
- operating cash flows.

5.2.143.30 In addition to quantitative performance indicators, in our view the competitive and operating risks, currency risks, and economic and political conditions associated with each operating segment may be considered. Appropriate weight should be given to each of the various factors based on the individual facts and circumstances.

5.2.143.40 In our view, in assessing the similarity of economic characteristics criterion consideration should be given not only to the current measures, but also to future prospect. Operating segments that historically have been aggregated might not have similar economic characteristics in the current period. Management should analyse whether this is due to temporary or abnormal circumstances. If the operating segments are expected to have similar economic characteristics in the foreseeable future, then the segments may be aggregated. In our view, if operating segments historically did not have similar economic characteristics, but do in the current year, although it is not expected that they will continue to have similar economic characteristics in the future, then it may not be appropriate to aggregate the segments for the current year.

5.2.144 *Nature of the products and services*

IFRS 8.12(a) 5.2.144.10 When determining whether the nature of the product or service is similar, it might be necessary to consider how broadly or narrowly the internal financial reporting and overall operations of an entity are defined. For example, an entity with a relatively narrow product range may consider two products not to be similar, while an entity with a broad product range may consider those same two products to be similar. Another factor to be considered is whether products and services have similar degrees of risk, opportunities for growth and end uses.

5.2.145 *Nature of the production process*

IFRS 8.12(b) 5.2.145.10 In our view, the production processes of two or more operating segments may be considered similar if they share, or are able to share, common or interchangeable facilities and employees and use similar raw materials. The amount of capital vs labour intensiveness also should be considered.

5.2.145.20 For example, an automotive supplier produces two types of seats for a particular customer. Although the seats are manufactured through the same process, one is a bench seat for a van and the other is a bucket seat for a luxury coupe. Both products use similar raw materials, require the same amount of capital and labour intensiveness, can be produced interchangeably by existing employees and facilities and use the same manufacturing machinery and equipment. In this case the production process could be viewed as similar. However, all of the other aggregation criteria still need to be met in order to aggregate operating segments.

5.2.146 *Type or class of customer for products and services*

IFRS 8.12(c) 5.2.146.10 There are a number of factors to consider when assessing similarity of type or class of customers; including for example similarity of marketing or promotion methods, geographic areas and the nature and use of sales forces could be relevant factors.

5.2.146.20 For example, an entity manufactures and sells a basic cleaning solution, but in two mixtures; one for home use and the other for commercial use. The commercial customer buys regularly in bulk orders, based on personal contact with entity's sales representatives. The home customers buy products in small quantities and infrequently via website order system. Even though the nature of the products and production process may be viewed as similar, it may be difficult to conclude that the type or class of customer is similar in order to aggregate operating segments.

5.2.147 *Methods used to distribute products or provide services*

IFRS 8.12(d) 5.2.147.10 Whether methods used to distribute products or provide services are considered similar depends on how a particular entity is structured.

5.2.147.20 For example, a retailer sells its products through entity-owned stores located in shopping malls throughout Europe and also through the use of catalogues. The Director of Store Sales is responsible for all store operations and activities; the Director of Catalogue Sales is responsible for all catalogue sales. Separate financial information is reported by each Director to the CODM on a regular basis. The CODM assesses performance and makes resource allocation decisions based on the separate financial information. The methods used to distribute products are not similar, therefore such operating segments would not be aggregated.

5.2.148 *Nature of the regulatory environment*

IFRS 8.12(e) 5.2.148.10 Even when all other criteria for two operating segments are determined to be similar, they may operate in different regulatory environments. When effect of different regulatory environments is that operating segments are not similar, they should not be aggregated.

5.2.148.20 Regulatory environment does not mean regulatory body. Regulatory bodies can be different but still relate to a similar regulatory environment.

5.2.150 **Determining reportable segments (Step 4)**

IFRS 8.13 5.2.150.10 Under IFRS 8 an operating segment is required to be reported separately if any of the following quantitative thresholds is met:

- The segment's reported revenue (external sales and inter-segment transfers) is 10 percent or more of the combined revenue (internal and external) of all operating segments.
- The absolute amount of the segment's reported profit or loss is 10 percent or more of the greater, in absolute amount, of (1) the combined reported profit of all operating segments that did not report a loss; and (2) the combined reported loss of all operating segments that reported a loss.
- The segment's assets are 10 percent or more of the combined assets of all operating segments.

5.2.150.20 The term "combined" in each of the three tests in 5.2.150.10 means the total amounts for all operating segments before the elimination of intra-group transactions and balances (i.e. not the entity's financial statement amounts). It does not include reconciling items and activities that do not meet the definition of an operating segment under IFRS 8 (e.g. corporate activities).

IFRS 8.15   5.2.150.25 Entities are required to ensure that the total external revenue of the identified reportable segment constitutes 75 percent or more of total consolidated revenue. If not, additional operating segments are required to be reported separately until at least 75 percent of total consolidated revenue is accounted for by the reportable segment.

IFRS 8.25   5.2.150.30 The measures of the segment amounts used for these tests are based on the amounts reported to the CODM. As a result, these measures might not necessarily be in accordance with IFRSs (e.g. information based on an adjusted operating profit, EBITDA or on a cash basis), and should not be conformed to IFRSs for purposes of applying the tests.

IFRS 8.26   5.2.150.40 If the CODM uses more than one measure of a segment's profit or loss, or more than one measure of a segment's assets or a segment's liabilities, then the measure disclosed in reporting segment profit or loss, or segment assets or liabilities, should be the measure that management believes is determined in accordance with the measurement principle most consistent with that which is used for the corresponding amounts in the entity's financial statements.

IFRS 8.13   5.2.150.50 Operating segments that do not meet any of the quantitative thresholds may be considered reportable, and disclosed separately, if management believes that information about the segment would be useful to readers of the financial statements or more reportable segments need to be identified to meet the 75 percent test (see 5.2.160.30).

IFRS 8.18   5.2.150.60 After applying the quantitative tests, an operating segment might be determined to be a reportable segment even though it was not considered to be a reportable segment in a previous period (e.g. a specific operating segment grew from 5 percent of total combined segment revenue in the previous period to 13 percent in the current period). In this situation the entity discloses this operating segment as a reportable segment and restates all prior period segment information to be consistent with the current period's segment presentation, unless the information is not available and the cost to develop it would be excessive; in this case that fact is disclosed.

IFRS 8.17   5.2.150.70 Conversely, an operating segment that historically has been a reportable segment might not exceed any of the quantitative thresholds in the current period. In this situation, if management expects it to be a reportable segment in the future, then the entity continues to treat that operating segment as a reportable segment in order to maintain the inter-period comparability of segment information. An operating segment that exceeds one of the quantitative tests (as a result of another operating segment dropping below the thresholds because of temporary or abnormal circumstances) would be a reportable segment.

5.2.155 *Quantitative tests*

5.2.156 *Revenue test*

IFRS 8.13(a)   5.2.156.10 The numerator in the revenue test is the revenue reported to the CODM attributable to the operating segment. The denominator is the combined revenue of all identified operating segments as reported to the CODM. The sum of all combined operating segment revenue might not necessarily equal consolidated revenue because of intersegment sales and/or reconciling items. The term "all operating segments" refers to the total of all operating segments reviewed by the CODM and should not be confused with reportable segments.

5.2.156.15 For example, after applying the aggregation criteria, Company X has four operating segments. The revenue test is applied as follows:

	Revenues		
	External	*Internal*	*Total*
Segments A, B and C (aggregated)	4,000	1,000	5,000
Segment D	200	2,000	2,200
Segment E	500	100	600
Segment F	700	-	700
Combined	5,400	3,100	8,500
Reconciling items and eliminations	(300)	(3,100)	(3,400)
Consolidated	**5,100**	**-**	**5,100**

5.2.156.20 Reconciling items and eliminations in 5.2.156.15 include differences in revenue recognition policies between the measures of revenue reported to the CODM and the measures of revenue in the entity's financial statements, and the elimination of intersegment sales. The threshold for the revenue test is 850 (8,500 x 10%). Therefore, Segment A, B and C (aggregated) and Segment D exceed the quantitative revenue threshold and are reportable segments. Segments E and F would be further evaluated to determine if they meet either the profit or loss or the asset quantitative threshold tests.

5.2.156.25 Situations might exist in which certain revenue relates to a business activity that is not an operating segment. In our view, it is not appropriate to include such revenue amounts in the denominator used to perform the segment revenue test. This could, in certain cases, result in additional operating segments being reported.

5.2.157 *Profit or loss test*

IFRS 8.13(b)   5.2.157.10 To perform the profit or loss test, an entity uses the same measure of profit or loss as used by the CODM to allocate resources and to assess performance. The test is 10 percent or more of the greater of, in absolute amounts: (1) the combined reported profit of all operating segments that did not report a loss; and (2) the combined reported loss of all operating segments that did not report a profit.

5.2.157.15 For example, Company Y has five operating segments. The measure of segment profit or loss reported to and used by the CODM is profit before tax. The operating segment results are as follows:

	Profit or (loss) before tax
Segment A	10,800
Segment B	8,100
Segment C	(3,700)
Segment D	2,400
Segment E	(800)
Combined	16,800
Reconciling items and eliminations	(1,800)
Consolidated	**15,000**

5.2.157.20 Reconciling items and eliminations in 5.2.157.15 include corporate expenses and the elimination of intersegment profits. The absolute amount of the combined segment profit for all operating segments that did not report a loss is 21,300 (10,800 + 8,100 + 2,400) of which 10 percent is 2,130. The absolute amount of the combined segment loss for all operating segments that did not report a profit is 4,500 (3,700 + 800) of which 10 percent is 450. As 2,130 is the greater of the two amounts, this amount is the quantitative threshold used in the segment profit or loss test. Therefore, Segments A, B, C and D are reportable operating segments. Segment E would be further evaluated to see if it meets either the revenue or asset quantitative threshold tests.

5.2.157.30 Situations might exist in which certain profits or losses relate to a business activity that is not an operating segment (e.g. incidental revenue and expenses). In our view, it is not appropriate to include such profits or losses in the denominator used to perform the segment profit or loss test. This could, in certain cases, result in additional operating segments being reported.

5.2.158 *Asset test*

IFRS 8.13(c) 5.2.158.10 All assets identifiable with an operating segment need not be included for purposes of performing the segment assets test. Only those assets included in the measure of segment assets reported to and used by the CODM for purposes of assessing performance and making resource allocation decisions are included in the asset test.

5.2.158.15 For example, Company S has 10 operating segments. The CODM receives and uses only receivables and inventory information in the measure of segment assets for purposes of assessing performance and making resource allocation decisions. While it is evident which other assets (e.g. property, plant and equipment) could be identified with each of these specific operating segments, the measure of segment assets for purposes of the asset test is the total of segment receivables and inventory.

5.2.158.20 Assume the same facts as in 5.2.158.15 except that the segment receivables and inventory information is not reviewed or used by the CODM for purposes of assessing performance and making resource allocation decisions, although it is reported to the CODM. For purposes of applying the asset test, the entity includes the segment assets reported to the CODM, even if the information is not reviewed or used by the CODM. In this example, segment asset information also is required to be disclosed. The disclosure of segment assets would be the total of receivables and inventory, and is described as such.

5.2.160 Remaining operating segments

IFRS 8.14 5.2.160.10 An entity might be able to aggregate information about operating segments that fall below the quantitative thresholds based on the additional aggregation provisions stated in IFRS 8. Under IFRS 8 an entity is allowed to combine information about two or more such operating segments that do not meet the quantitative thresholds to produce a reportable segment only if the operating segments share a majority of the aggregation criteria listed in 5.2.140.10, provided that the aggregation is consistent with the core principle of IFRS 8 and the segments have similar economic characteristics.

5.2.160.20 [Not used]

IFRS 8.15 5.2.160.30 IFRS 8 requires that if the total of external revenue reported by operating segments constitutes less than 75 percent of total revenue reported in the entity's financial statements, then additional operating segments are identified as reportable segments (even if they do not meet the quantitative threshold criteria) until at least 75 percent of the total revenue reported in the financial statements is included in reportable segments.

5.2.160.35 When complying with the consolidated revenue test in 5.2.160.30, in our view entities have flexibility in determining which additional segments will be reported separately. We believe that the next largest operating segment is not required to be reported. Consideration should be given to reporting the additional segments that will be most useful to financial statements users, consistent with the core principle of IFRS 8.

IFRS 8.16 5.2.160.40 IFRS 8 requires that information about other business activities and operating segments that are not reportable be combined and disclosed in an "all other segments" category separate from other reconciling items in the reconciliations required by paragraph 28 of IFRS 8 (see 5.2.210). The sources of the revenue included in the all other segments category should be described.

5.2.170 Changes in the composition of operating segments

5.2.170.10 Events might occur (e.g. a significant internal reorganisation or implementation of a new financial reporting system) that change the composition of the operating segments. In these cases the financial results may be grouped and reported differently to the CODM.

IFRS 8.29   5.2.170.20 Following a change in the composition of an entity's operating segments that in turn results in a change in reportable segments, IFRS 8 requires previously reported segment information (including interim periods) to be restated, unless the information is not available and the cost to develop it would be excessive. The entity should determine whether these limitations apply for each individual item of disclosure. The entity also should disclose whether it has restated the comparative items of segment information for earlier periods.

IFRS 8.30   5.2.170.30 If previously reported segment information is not restated, then IFRS 8 requires the entity to disclose current period segment information on both the old and new basis of segmentation in the year of change, and subsequently until all periods can be presented on the new basis.

5.2.180 Segment disclosure information (Step 5)

5.2.190 *Annual disclosures*

IFRS 8.21   5.2.190.10 IFRS 8 requires an entity to disclose for each period for which a statement of comprehensive income is presented:

- general information about factors used to identify the entity's reportable segments and types of products and services from which each reportable segment generates its revenues;
- information about profit or loss, assets and liabilities; and
- reconciliation disclosures.

5.2.200 *Information about profit or loss, assets and liabilities*

IFRS 8.23   5.2.200.10 IFRS 8 requires an entity to report a measure of profit or loss for each reportable segment, and a measure of total assets and liabilities for each reportable segment if such amounts are provided regularly to the CODM. It also requires that an entity disclose the following about each reportable segment if the specified amounts are included in the measure of segment profit or loss reviewed by the CODM or are otherwise provided regularly to the CODM, even if not included in that measure of segment profit or loss:

- revenues from external customers;
- revenues from transactions with other operating segments of the same entity;
- interest revenue;
- interest expense;
- depreciation and amortisation;
- material items of income and expense disclosed in accordance with IAS 1 *Presentation of Financial Statements*;
- equity accounted earnings;
- income tax; and

- material non-cash items other than depreciation and amortisation.

IFRS 8.23   5.2.200.20 If the amounts specified in 5.2.200.10 are inherent in the measure of segment profit or loss used by the CODM, then those amounts are required to be disclosed even if they are not provided explicitly to the CODM. IFRS 8 requires that the items listed in 5.2.200.10 be disclosed if they are provided regularly to the CODM, even if they are not included in the measure of segment profit or loss that is reviewed by the CODM.

IFRS 8.25   5.2.200.30 Adjustments and eliminations made in preparing the entity's financial state-ments, as well as allocations of revenue, expenses, gains or losses, are included in the reported segment profit or loss only if these items are included in the segment profit or loss measure used by the CODM. Additionally, the allocation of amounts included in the measure of segment profit or loss are made on a reasonable basis.

IFRS 8.20,   5.2.200.35 To help users of financial statements understand an entity's segment disclos-
27, BC.A90 ures, the entity shall provide sufficient explanation of the basis on which the informa-tion reported to the CODM was prepared. That disclosure includes differences in the basis of measurement between the consolidated amounts and the segment amounts and indicates whether allocations of items were made symmetrically.

IFRS 8.23, 25   5.2.200.40 IFRS 8 requires that a measure of total assets be disclosed for each reportable segment only if such information is regularly reported to the CODM. Total segment assets or total identifiable assets by segment are not necessarily measures used by the CODM to assess performance and to make resource allocation decisions. Therefore, only those assets that are included in the measure of the segment's assets that is used by the CODM should be reported for that segment.

IFRS 8.24   5.2.200.50 The following information should be disclosed by each reportable segment if the specified amounts are included in the determination of segment assets reviewed by the CODM, or are otherwise provided regularly to the CODM even if not included in the determination of segment assets:

- equity accounted investees; and
- additions to non-current assets (including tangible and intangible assets) other than financial instruments, deferred tax assets, post-employment benefit assets and rights under insurance contracts.

IFRS 8.27(f)   5.2.200.60 It is possible that a component of an entity could qualify as an operating segment and have no asset information about it reported to the CODM. If no asset information is provided for a reportable segment, then in our view that fact and the reason should be disclosed. IFRS 8 requires disclosure of the nature and effect of any asymmetrical allocation, e.g. if depreciation expense is included in the measure of segment profit or loss, but the related items of property, plant and equipment are not included in the measure of segment assets.

5.2.203 *Jointly controlled entities and associates*

IFRS 8.23, 24, 28   5.2.203.10 The segment information to be disclosed for an investee that is a reportable segment should be consistent with the concept of the management approach and the core principle of IFRS 8. Therefore the segment information that is disclosed should be determined on the same basis as it is reported to the CODM.

5.2.203.20 In situations in which the investee is identified as a reportable segment and the CODM receives financial statements of the investee, the entity discloses the investee's revenue, a measure of profit or loss, assets and other amounts required by IFRS 8, as reported in the investee's financial statements. The difference between the amounts reported in the segment disclosure to the proportionate amounts reported in the entity's financial statements will be included in the reconciliation items.

5.2.203.30 In contrast, there might be situations in which the CODM only receives information about the investee that represents the entity's proportionate share in the investee's revenue, profits and loss, assets and other information. In those instances, in our view the entity discloses the segment information of the investee using the proportionate amounts.

5.2.205 **Lack of a competitive harm exemption**

IFRS 8.BC43-BC45   5.2.205.10 IFRS 8 does not provide any exemption from the required disclosures due to "competitive harm".

5.2.210 *Reconciliation disclosures*

IFRS 8.28   5.2.210.10 An entity is required to provide reconciliations of:

IFRS 8.28(a)   • the total of the reportable segments' revenues to the entity's revenues in the financial statements;

IFRS 8.28(b)   • the total of the reportable segments' measures of profit or loss to the entity's profit or loss before income tax and discontinued operations in the financial statements; however, if an entity allocates to reportable segments items such as income tax, then the entity may reconcile the total of the segments' measures of profit or loss to the entity's profit or loss after those items;

IFRS 8.28(c)   • the total of the reportable segments' assets to the entity's assets in the financial statements;

IFRS 8.28(d)   • the total of the reportable segments' liabilities to the entity's liabilities in the financial statements if segment liabilities are reported to the CODM; and

IFRS 8.28(e)   • the total of the reportable segments' amounts for every other material item of information disclosed to the corresponding amount in the entity's financial statements.

IFRS 8.28   5.2.210.20 IFRS 8 requires that all material reconciling items be identified and described separately, e.g. the amount of each material adjustment to reconcile accounting policies used in determining segment profit or loss to the entity's amounts is identified and described separately.

5.2.210.30 Reconciliations of profit or loss amounts for reportable segments to the amounts reported in the entity's financial statements are required for each period for which a statement of comprehensive income is presented.

5.2.210.40 Reconciliations of statement of financial position amounts for reportable segments to the amounts reported in the entity's financial statements are required for each date for which a statement of financial position is presented.

IFRS 8.27
(b)-(d), (f)
5.2.210.50 If a reconciling item results from an accounting policy used by an operating segment different from that used in the preparation of the entity's financial statements, then additional disclosures about the accounting policies used by the operating segment are required. Similarly, if a reconciling item results from an allocation method that is used by the entity, then additional disclosures about the nature and effect of any asymmetrical allocation to the operating segment are required.

5.2.220 *Interim disclosures*

IAS 34.16
5.2.220.10 The following segment information is required to be disclosed in an entity's interim report only if the entity is within the scope of IFRS 8 for the purposes of its annual financial statements:

- revenues from external customers, if included in the measure of segment profit or loss reviewed by the CODM or otherwise provided regularly to the CODM;
- inter-segment revenues, if included in the measure of segment profit or loss reviewed by the CODM or otherwise provided regularly to the CODM;
- a measure of segment profit or loss;
- total assets for which there has been a material change from the amount disclosed in the last annual financial statements (see 5.2.220.30 and 40);
- a description of any differences from the last annual financial statements in the basis of segmentation or in the basis of measurement of segment profit or loss; and
- a reconciliation of the total of the reportable segments' measures of profit or loss to the entity's profit or loss before income tax and discontinued operations.

5.2.220.20 However, if an entity allocated to reportable segments items such as income tax, then the entity may reconcile the total of the segments' measures of profit or loss to profit or loss after those items. Material reconciling items are separately identified and described in the reconciliation.

5.2.220.30 While IAS 34 *Interim Financial Reporting* states that an entity discloses total assets for which there has been a material change from the amount disclosed in the last annual financial statements, in our view an entity would disclose whether there has been a material change in *segment* assets.

5.2.220.40 Also, it is not clear whether, in the first year of application of IFRS 8, the interim financial statements would need to disclose information about segment assets given that segment assets would not have been presented in the last annual financial statements in accordance with IFRS 8 requirements. We prefer that information about segment assets be disclosed in the first interim financial statements in the first year of application of IFRS 8, if such information is provided regularly to the CODM.

5.2.230 *Entity-wide disclosures#*

IFRS 8.31-34 5.2.230.10 Entity-wide disclosures related to the following items are required, regardless of whether the information is used by the CODM in assessing segment performance:

- products and services
- geographic areas
- non-current assets other than financial instruments
- deferred tax assets
- post-employment benefit assets
- rights arising from insurance contracts.

IFRS 8.33 5.2.230.13 The information in 5.2.230.10 is provided by both: the entity's country of domicile; and by foreign individual country, if material. In our view, disclosing such information by region, e.g. Europe or Asia, does not meet the requirement to disclose information by individual foreign country, if material. Such information should be disclosed by individual foreign country, e.g. France, the Netherlands, Singapore, when material. These disclosures apply to all entities subject to IFRS 8, including entities that have only one reportable segment. However, information required by the entity-wide disclosures need not be repeated if it is included already in the segment disclosures.

IFRS 8.33(a) 5.2.230.15 An entity may allocate revenue from external customers to geographic areas as it deems most appropriate (e.g. by selling location, customer location or the location to which the product is transported, which might differ from the location of the customer). Regardless, the selected method is applied consistently and disclosed in the financial statements.

5.2.230.20 Some entities' segments may report revenues from a broad range of essentially different products and services, or more than one of the reportable segments might provide essentially the same products and services. Similarly, an entity's segments may hold assets in different geographic areas and report revenues from customers in different geographic areas, or more than one of its segments might operate in the same geographic area. These disclosures need to be provided only if they are not disclosed already as part of the reportable operating segment information required by IFRS 8.

IFRS 8.32, 33 5.2.230.30 The entity-wide disclosures should be based on the same financial information that is used to produce the entity's financial statements (i.e. not based on the management approach). Accordingly, the revenue reported for these disclosures should equal the entity's total revenue.

5.2.230.40 IFRS 8 does not provide materiality thresholds for determining the entity-wide disclosures, other than for major customer information as described in 5.2.230.45. As a result, when otherwise not specified by the standard, judgement needs to be used to determine material items for entity-wide disclosure purposes. In our view, quantitative thresholds and qualitative reasons are to be considered when determining material items for entity-wide disclosures.

IFRS 8.34 5.2.230.45 Revenues from an individual external customer that represent 10 percent or more of an entity's total revenue are disclosed. Specifically, the total amount by significant customer and the identity of the segment that includes the revenue is disclosed. However, IFRS 8 does not require the identity of the customer or the amount of revenues that each segment reports from that customer to be disclosed.

5.2.232 *Forthcoming requirements*

5.2.232.10 IAS 24 (2009) amended IFRS 8 so that all government-related entities are no longer considered as a "single customer" by default for IFRS 8 disclosure purposes. Under the revised standard judgement is necessary in assessing whether a government, including government agencies and similar bodies whether local, national or international, and entities known to the reporting entity to be under the control of such government are considered a single customer. The amendment is applied for annual periods beginning on or after 1 January 2011. If the entity applies IAS 24 (2009) for an earlier period, it also applies the amendments to IFRS 8 for that earlier period.

5.2.235 *Currency of segment disclosures*

5.2.235.10 Segment information may be reported internally to the CODM in a currency that is different from the presentation currency used in the entity's financial statements. In our view, it would be more useful to the users if segment information is disclosed using the same presentation currency as the entity's financial statements, even if a different currency is used for internal management reporting.

5.2.250 **Comparative information**

IFRS 8.29, 5.2.250.10 IFRS 8 requires segment information for earlier periods presented to be
30, 36 restated in certain circumstances. Such circumstances include changes in the composition of operating segments (see 5.2.170) and the initial year of application of IFRS 8. Comparative segment information for the initial year of application is required to be restated to conform to the requirements of IFRS 8, unless the information is not available and the cost to develop it would be excessive; in this case that fact is disclosed.

5.2.250.20 IFRS 8 does not provide guidance on whether prior year amounts in entity-wide disclosures (see 5.2.230) need to be restated if there is a change in the current year (e.g. a previously immaterial country representing 3 percent of the external revenues included in the entity-wide geographic disclosures now represents 15 percent of external revenues). In our view, the prior year information should be restated, if practicable, so that the disclosures from year to year are comparable.

5.2.260 **Allocation of goodwill for impairment testing purposes**

IAS 36.80(b) 5.2.260.10 IAS 36 *Impairment of Assets* requires that each unit or group of units to which goodwill is allocated cannot be larger than an operating segment before aggregation (see 3.10.460.10 and 5.2.140).

5.2.270 **Presentation of a third statement of financial position and related notes**

5.2.270.10 See 2.1.35 for the consideration of whether a third statement of financial position and related notes is required on adoption of IFRS 8.

5.3 Earnings per share
(IAS 33)

5.3 Earnings per share
(IAS 33)

Overview of currently effective requirements

- Basic and diluted earnings per share (EPS) is presented by entities whose ordinary shares or potential ordinary shares are traded in a public market or that file, or are in the process of filing, their financial statements for the purpose of issuing any class of ordinary shares in a public market.

- Basic and diluted EPS for both continuing and total operations are presented in the statement of comprehensive income, with equal prominence, for each class of ordinary shares.

- Separate EPS data is disclosed for discontinued operations, either in the statement of comprehensive income or in the notes to the financial statements.

- Basic EPS is calculated by dividing the earnings attributable to holders of ordinary equity of the parent by the weighted average number of ordinary shares outstanding during the period.

- To calculate diluted EPS, profit or loss attributable to ordinary equity holders, and the weighted average number of shares outstanding, are adjusted for the effects of all dilutive potential ordinary shares.

- Potential ordinary shares are considered dilutive only when they decrease earnings per share or increase loss per share from continuing operations. In determining if potential ordinary shares are dilutive, each issue or series of potential ordinary shares is considered separately rather than in aggregate.

- Contingently issuable ordinary shares are included in basic EPS from the date that all necessary conditions are satisfied and, when not yet satisfied, in diluted EPS based on the number of shares that would be issuable if the end of the reporting period were the end of the contingency period.

- When a contract may be settled in either cash or shares at the entity's option, it is treated as a potential ordinary share.

- When a contract may be settled in either cash or shares at the holder's option, the more dilutive of cash and share settlement is used to calculate diluted EPS.

- **For diluted EPS, diluted potential ordinary shares are determined independently for each period presented.**

- **When the number of ordinary shares outstanding changes, without a corresponding change in resources, the weighted average number of ordinary shares outstanding during all periods presented is adjusted retrospectively.**

- **Adjusted basic and diluted EPS based on alternative earnings measures may be disclosed and explained in the notes to the financial statements.**

Currently effective requirements

This publication reflects IFRSs in issue at 1 August 2010. The currently effective requirements cover annual periods beginning on 1 January 2010. The requirements related to this topic are derived mainly from IAS 33 *Earnings per Share*.

Forthcoming requirements and future developments

When a currently effective requirement will be changed by a new requirement that is issued but is not yet effective, it is marked with a # as a **forthcoming requirement** and the impact of the change is explained in the accompanying boxed text. In respect of this topic, no forthcoming requirements are noted.

The currently effective requirements may be subject to **future developments** and a brief outline of the relevant project is given in 5.3.380.

5.3.10 **Scope**

IAS 33.2, 5.3.10.10 Basic and diluted EPS are presented in the statement of comprehensive
3, 4A income by entities whose ordinary shares or potential ordinary shares are traded in a public market (a domestic or foreign stock exchange or an over-the-counter market, including local and regional markets) or that file, or are in the process of filing, their financial statements with a securities commission or other regulatory organisation for the purpose of issuing any class of ordinary shares in a public market. An entity presenting a statement of comprehensive income using the two-statement approach (see 4.1.10) discloses the basic and diluted EPS in the statement displaying components of profit or loss. When an entity voluntarily presents EPS data, that data is calculated and presented in accordance with IAS 33 (see 5.3.370.05).

5.3.10.20 IAS 33 does not provide a definition for "traded in a public market". In our view, determining what is meant by traded in a public market depends on facts and circumstances, and can vary based on local requirements from securities commissions and/or regulators. We believe that if a buyer or a seller can contact a broker and obtain a quoted price, then this is an indicator that ordinary shares or potential ordinary shares are publicly traded. This is without regard to how often the share is traded.

5.3.10.25 The following factors may indicate that a fund is not traded in a public market:

- The fund is listed at a stock exchange for convenience listing or marketing purposes only, and cannot be traded on the stock market.
- The fund's shares are traded through a fund agent/administrator only, i.e. the subscriptions and redemptions of units are handled by a transfer agent/administrator directly associated with the fund.
- Buyer and seller set up prices based on the fund prospectus valuation principles and therefore prices would not be established by trading in a market.

5.3.10.27 The factors mentioned in 5.3.10.25 are not exhaustive and judgement will be required when assessing if a fund falls within the scope of IAS 33.

5.3.10.30 [Not used]

5.3.10.40 In our view, an entity is in the process of issuing ordinary shares or potential ordinary shares only when the entity has taken active steps to obtain a listing, rather than simply planning the listing. We also believe that "issuing" shares includes listing (registering) shares already in issue. When an entity prepares a prospectus in preparation for listing, EPS data should be included in the financial statements included in the prospectus. When an entity's ordinary shares or potential ordinary shares are untraded at the end of the reporting period but are publicly traded by the time that the financial statements are authorised for issue, in our view the entity should disclose EPS data in its financial statements. This is because the entity generally would have had to provide financial statements to complete the listing and IFRSs would require those financial statements to include EPS data.

5.3.10.50 An entity's ordinary shares or potential ordinary shares may be publicly traded for only a portion of the current period, for example because the entity's ordinary shares or potential ordinary shares were listed for the first time during the period. In our view, the entity is required to present EPS data for all periods in which statements of comprehensive income are presented, and not only for the periods that the entity's ordinary or potential ordinary shares were publicly traded.

IAS 33.4 5.3.10.60 If both separate financial statements and consolidated financial statements are prepared (see 2.1.70), then EPS disclosures are required to be provided only on the basis of consolidated information. However, if an entity decides to provide EPS amounts based on its separate financial statements, then it presents this on the face of its own separate statement of comprehensive income.

IAS 34.11 5.3.10.70 An entity is required to present basic and diluted EPS in its interim financial statements only when the entity is within the scope of IAS 33 (see 5.9.50).

IAS 32.16A-F 5.3.10.80 In our view, puttable instruments that qualify for equity classification instead of financial liability classification under IAS 32 *Financial Instruments: Presentation* (see 3.11.48) are not ordinary shares for the purposes of IAS 33. We believe that it is not appropriate to apply by analogy the limited scope exemption under IAS 32 for EPS calculation purposes. Accordingly, we believe the EPS presentation is not required for, or as a result of the existence of, such instruments. However, the terms of such instruments should be evaluated to determine if they are participating instruments, in which case a two-class calculation may be required (see 5.3.50).

5.3.20 Entities with more than one class of equity

IAS 33.6, 66 5.3.20.10 When an entity has more than one class of ordinary shares, EPS is disclosed for each class of ordinary shares. Ordinary shares of the same class are those shares that have the same right to receive dividends. When an entity has shares with different rights it considers whether the shares are in fact ordinary shares. An *ordinary share* is an equity instrument that is subordinate to all other equity shares.

5.3.20.20 For example, an entity has two classes of ordinary shares, A and B. The holders of class B shares are entitled to dividends equal to 50 percent of any dividends declared on the class A shares, but otherwise are identical to class A shares. Therefore, in our view both class A and B shares are ordinary shares as both classes are subordinate to all other classes of equity instruments with respect to participation in profit, despite the difference in entitlement to dividends.

5.3.20.30 In our view, an entity is not required to present separate EPS data for participating preference shares that are not considered to be a separate class of ordinary share. For example, an entity has two classes of shares, X and Y. Shareholders of class X are entitled to a fixed dividend per share and have the right to participate in any additional dividends declared. The class Y shareholders participate equally with class X shareholders with respect to the additional dividends only. We believe, even if both classes participate equally in residual assets on dissolution, class X shares are not considered to be ordinary, as the fixed entitlement creates a preference over the class Y shares, and the class Y shareholders are subordinate to the class X shareholders. The class Y shares are the only class of ordinary shares, and therefore the only class of shares for which disclosure of EPS is required. However, the participating rights of each class of these shares should be considered in determining earnings attributable to ordinary equity holders (see 5.3.50).

5.3.30 Basic earnings per share

IAS 33.9, 19, 5.3.30.10 Basic EPS is the profit or loss attributable to ordinary equity holders of the
66 parent entity for the period, divided by the weighted average number of ordinary shares outstanding during the period. Presentation of EPS is required in the statement of comprehensive income for the profit or loss from both continuing and total operations for the period. The EPS data is presented with equal prominence for each class of ordinary shares.

IAS 33.68, 68A   5.3.30.20 In addition, disclosure of separate EPS data is required for discontinued operations, either in the statement of comprehensive income or in the notes to the financial statements.

5.3.30.30 The table below summarises the impact on basic EPS of various instruments with differing conditions including passage of time, service or other.

Instrument \ Condition	None	Passage of time	Service	Other
Ordinary shares	Include in the calculation of basic EPS from the date the corresponding consideration is receivable (which is generally the date the shares are issued) (see 5.3.65.20).	Treat as outstanding for purposes of calculating basic EPS from the date the right to the shares comes into existence (see 5.3.80.20).	Include in the calculation of basic EPS as the services are rendered considering related terms and conditions of the agreement (see 5.3.80.30).	Include from the date the corresponding consideration is receivable (which is generally the date the shares are issued) (see 5.3.60.20).
Unvested shares	These instruments are considered potential ordinary shares and are not considered in basic EPS (see 5.3.80.30).			
Share options and warrants	These instruments are considered potential ordinary shares and are not considered in basic EPS (see 5.3.60).			

5.3.40 *Earnings*

IAS 33.12-18   5.3.40.10 The profit or loss attributable to ordinary equity holders of the parent entity is the profit or loss, adjusted for the post-tax amounts of dividends on preference shares. Profit or loss also is adjusted for gains or losses on the settlement of preference shares, and other similar effects of preference shares classified as equity, including the amortisation of the premium or discount on the original issue of preference shares and payments to induce conversion.

IAS 33.A14(a)   5.3.40.20 The post-tax amount of preference dividends is deducted to arrive at the profit or loss attributable to ordinary equity holders, as those dividends represent income that is not attributable to ordinary equity holders. Cumulative preference dividends are deducted, whether declared or not. Non-cumulative dividends are not deducted unless they have been declared by the end of the reporting period. In our view, when dividends on non-cumulative preference shares are declared after the end of the reporting period, the profit or loss attributable to ordinary equity holders should not be adjusted for these dividends even if these dividends relate to the reporting period. This is consistent with the requirement that dividends declared after the end of the reporting period are non-adjusting events in accordance with IAS 10 *Events after the Reporting Period* as no obligation exists at the end of the reporting period (see 2.9.30).

IAS 33.17, 18   5.3.40.30 An entity may wish to induce early conversion of convertible preference shares by either favourably amending the original conversion terms or paying additional consideration to the preference shareholders. The early conversion inducement is included in determining the profit or loss of the entity. If the fair value of the ordinary shares or other consideration paid exceeds the fair value of the ordinary shares issuable under the original conversion terms, then this excess is a return to preference shareholders and is deducted in calculating profit or loss attributable to the ordinary equity holders of the entity. When the carrying amount of the preference shares exceeds the fair value of the consideration paid to redeem them early, this difference is added in the calculation of profit or loss attributable to the ordinary equity holders.

5.3.40.40 In our view, in determining profit or loss attributable to ordinary equity holders, an entity also should consider any obligations to cover losses attributable to a non-controlling interest (NCI) regardless of the entity's accounting policy choice for how it accounts for these obligations (see 2.5.330).

5.3.40.50 For example, Company P owns 80 percent of Company S. P provides a guarantee to the NCI of S that it will cover any losses of S attributable to the NCI. P's consolidated profit for the year excluding S is 1,000 and S incurs a loss of 150. P has 100 ordinary shares outstanding throughout the year. If P was not obligated to cover the losses attributable to the NCI, P would disclose EPS of 8.80 ((1,000 - 150 x 80%) / 100). However, since P agreed to cover the losses attributable to the NCI, P discloses EPS of 8.50 ((1,000 - 150) / 100).

5.3.50 *Participating equity instruments*

IAS 33.A14   5.3.50.10 Participating equity instruments are instruments that either are a separate class of ordinary shares (e.g. with different dividends rights) or instruments that participate in dividends along with ordinary shares based on a predetermined formula. To determine the profit or loss attributable to ordinary equity holders, profit or loss for the period is allocated to the different classes of ordinary shares and participating equity instruments. This allocation is made in accordance with the rights of the other class to participate in distributions if the entire profit or loss was distributed.

5.3.50.20 For example, an entity has two classes of shares, X and Y; each class has 100 shares outstanding. Equity holders of class X are entitled to a fixed dividend per share and have the right to participate in any additional dividends declared. The class Y shareholders participate equally with class X shareholders with respect to the additional dividends only. Net profit for the period is 2,000 and preference dividends of 100 are paid to the X shareholders. Even though the entity has no intention to pay additional dividends, to calculate the profit or loss attributable to the Y shares, the undistributed earnings of 1,900 should be allocated to both the X and Y shares in accordance with their participation.

Profit for the period attributable to equity holders of the parent	2,000	
Preference dividends paid	(100)	
Undistributed earnings	1,900	
Earnings attributable to ordinary shareholders of the parent (class Y)	950	(1,900 / 2)
Earnings attributable to participating preference shareholders (class X)	1,050	(1,900 / 2 + 100)

IAS 33.A13, A14 5.3.50.30 In another example, an entity has two classes of ordinary shares, A and G; class A has 30,000 shares outstanding and class G has 10,000 shares outstanding. Class A shareholders participate in dividends at a rate of 1 percent more than class G shareholders. Net profit attributable to all shareholders for the period is 100,000. The entity has not declared or paid any dividends for the period. To calculate the profit or loss attributable to each class of shareholders, the net profit for the period is allocated to the class A and class G shareholders in accordance with their rights to participate in these undistributed earnings since there is a predetermined formula for dividend participation.

X represents the dividend per share to class G shareholders.		
The undistributed net profit for the period is 100,000 attributable to the two classes of shareholders as follows:		
(X x 10,000) + (X x 1.01 x 30,000) = 100,000		
X = 2.48 (rounded)		
Earnings attributable to class G shareholders	24,814	(2.48 x 10,000)
Earnings attributable to class A shareholders	75,186	(2.48 x 1.01 x 30,000)

IAS 33.10, 24, A13 5.3.50.40 In our view, for purposes of calculating basic EPS, the profit or loss should be adjusted for any dividends and undistributed earnings attributable to ordinary shares that are contingently returnable to the entity (i.e. shares subject to recall (see 5.3.100)). This is because the numerator of basic EPS is intended to reflect amounts attributable to ordinary equity holders of the parent entity and shares subject to recall are not considered to be outstanding ordinary shares. Therefore, in calculating basic EPS, dividends on shares subject to recall should be deducted from profit or loss to the extent that they are not already classified as finance costs, e.g. because the instrument subject to recall is classified as a financial liability. We believe that undistributed earnings should be allocated to ordinary shares and shares subject to recall, in accordance with their respective rights to participate in dividends.

5.3.60 *Weighted average number of shares outstanding*

IAS 33.19 5.3.60.10 When calculating basic EPS, the denominator is the weighted average number of ordinary shares outstanding during the period.

IAS 33.20, **5.3.60.20** The following summary of transactions demonstrates an example calculation
IE2 of the weighted average number of ordinary shares outstanding in a year:

Date	Transaction	Shares issued	Treasury shares (see 5.3.70)	Shares out-standing
1 January 2010	Balance at beginning of year	1,500	250	1,250
31 March 2010	Purchase of treasury shares for cash	-	250	1,000
30 June 2010	Issue of new shares to settle a liability	1,000	-	2,000
31 December 2010	Balance at end of year	2,500	500	2,000

The weighted average number of ordinary shares outstanding for 2010 is calculated as:

- $(1,250 \times 3/12) + (1,000 \times 3/12) + (2,000 \times 6/12) = 1,562.5$ shares; or
- $(1,250 \times 12/12) - (250 \times 9/12) + (1,000 \times 6/12) = 1,562.5$ shares.

IAS 33.21-23 **5.3.60.30** Shares are considered outstanding for purposes of determining the weighted
average number of ordinary shares outstanding from the date the corresponding consideration is receivable. For example, ordinary shares issued:

- for cash are included when the cash is receivable;
- for an asset other than cash are included from the time the asset is recognised;
- to settle a liability are included from the settlement date;
- upon conversion of a debt instrument are included from the date that interest ceases to accrue;
- in lieu of interest or principal on other financial instruments are included from the date that interest ceases to accrue;
- on the voluntary reinvestment of dividends are included from the date the dividends are reinvested;
- as compensation for services received are included as the services are rendered;
- as consideration in a business combination are included from the acquisition date; and
- upon mandatory conversion of a convertible instrument are included from the date that the contract is entered into.

5.3.60.40 For example, an entity with an annual reporting period ending 31 December
has share options outstanding with its employees. The options were issued three years
ago with a exercise price equal to the market price of the entity's shares at the time (i.e.
the options represent potential ordinary shares). All vesting conditions were satisfied
during the year; however, the employees did not exercise the options. Although all vest-

ing conditions were met during the year, the options are still potential ordinary shares outstanding (see 5.3.120.10) at the end of the reporting period and therefore the shares are not considered outstanding for the purposes of basic EPS.

5.3.70 *Treasury shares*

IAS 33.IE2   5.3.70.10 Treasury shares are not treated as outstanding ordinary shares. Assets held by employee benefit plans may include an entity's own shares (see 4.4.410) and, if consolidated, the entity's own shares are regarded as treasury shares. However, the requirement to consolidate special purpose entities (SPEs) does not apply to post-employment benefit plans or other long-term employee benefit plans for which offset rather than consolidation applies (see 4.4.420 and 4.5.1120.10). Therefore an entity's own shares that are qualifying plan assets held by an employee benefit plan and netted against the employee benefit obligation are not treasury shares, and in our view would be considered outstanding for the calculation of EPS. However, if shares do not meet the definition of plan assets, then they are presented as treasury shares, even though the plan is not consolidated by the employer (see 4.4.430), and therefore we believe would not be considered as outstanding for the purposes of calculating EPS.

IAS 32.4(f),   5.3.70.20 An SPE established in connection with an equity compensation plan falls
33, 34   under the consolidation requirements for SPEs because the net presentation require-
ments for employee benefit plans do not apply to equity compensation plans. When such an SPE is required to be consolidated, shares of the reporting entity held by that SPE would be treasury shares, which are not treated as outstanding shares for the EPS calculation.

5.3.80 *Contingently issuable ordinary shares*

IAS 33.5, 24   5.3.80.10 Contingently issuable ordinary shares are ordinary shares that are issuable for little or no cash or other consideration upon the satisfaction of specified conditions in a contingent share agreement. Such contingently issuable ordinary shares are included in the calculation of the weighted average number of shares outstanding for purposes of calculating basic EPS from the date that the conditions are met and not from any later date of actually being issued.

IAS 33.24   5.3.80.20 Shares that are issuable solely after the passage of time are treated as outstanding for purposes of calculating basic EPS from the date that the right to the shares comes into existence (i.e. not at the end of the passage of time). They are not considered contingently issuable as the passage of time is a certainty.

IAS 33.21(g),   5.3.80.30 Unvested shares are treated similarly to potential ordinary shares and therefore
24, 48   are included only in calculating diluted EPS (see 5.3.170 and 220). Contingently is-
suable shares for which services required for vesting have been received already are included in the weighted average shares outstanding for purposes of calculating basic EPS.

5.3.80.35 For example, assume that a share-based payment arrangement consists of 15,000 unvested shares granted to employees; the award vests ratably in three tranches of 5,000 after each year of service. In our view, for the basic EPS computation for the second year of the three-year service period, the weighted average shares outstanding would include 5,000 shares being the first tranche that vested at the end of year one (the second tranche of 5,000 only vested on the last day of the year; hence carries a weighing of 0 / 365 in the second year). Note that this averaging approach differs from the graded vesting approach that is required to be recognised as share-based payment expense (see 4.5.520). Conversely, if the entire award vests only upon completion of three years' employment (i.e. no shares would be awarded if employment terminated before the end of the vesting period), then no shares would be included in the basic EPS computation until the end of the three-year service period.

IAS 33.21(g), 24, 48 5.3.80.40 The effect of service-based vesting conditions is calculated differently with respect to ordinary shares from potential ordinary shares, such as options and warrants. Unvested shares subject to service-based vesting conditions are excluded from the calculation of basic EPS. They are included in basic EPS as the required services are received. In contrast, *employee share options* with only a service-based vesting condition are considered outstanding (and not contingently issuable) potential ordinary shares, as such share options generally are not issuable for little or no cash or other consideration. Therefore such share options are included in diluted EPS (if dilutive) from the grant date, even if no services have been received (see 5.3.190). This inconsistency arises from inconsistent specific requirements in IAS 33 related to the impact of unvested shares on basic EPS and the impact of unvested options on diluted EPS.

5.3.90 *Partly-paid shares*

IAS 33.A15 5.3.90.10 When ordinary shares are not fully paid, they are treated as a fraction of ordinary shares for the purposes of basic EPS. The fraction is calculated as the degree to which they are entitled to participate in dividends during the period relative to the dividend participation rights of a fully paid ordinary share. To the extent that partly-paid shares are not entitled to participate in dividends during the period, such partly-paid shares are treated as options or warrants (see 5.3.180).

5.3.100 *Ordinary shares subject to recall*

IAS 33.24 5.3.100.10 When ordinary shares are subject to recall, they are not considered as outstanding and are excluded from the calculation of basic EPS until the date that they are no longer subject to recall.

5.3.100.20 In our view, shares that are subject to repurchase due to a written put option or a forward purchase contract should be excluded from the basic EPS calculation, similar to shares subject to recall. An adjustment to the numerator may be required for any dividends and undistributed earnings attributable to these shares (see 5.3.50.40). However, the calculation of diluted EPS may require adjustment for the written put or forward (see 5.3.170.110).

5.3.110 *Restatement*

IAS 33.26, 29, 64   5.3.110.10 The number of ordinary shares outstanding may be increased or decreased without a corresponding change in resources, e.g. as a result of a bonus issue, share dividend or a share consolidation. When there is a change in the number of shares outstanding without a corresponding change in resources, the weighted average number of shares outstanding for the entire period is adjusted as if the change had occurred at the beginning of the first period of EPS data presented (see 5.3.360).

IAS 33.29   5.3.110.20 However, when there is a change in the number of shares outstanding with a corresponding change in resources (e.g. a share consolidation combined with a special dividend), the weighted average number of shares outstanding is adjusted from the date the change in resources is recognised.

5.3.120 **Diluted earnings per share**

IAS 33.30, 31   5.3.120.10 To calculate diluted EPS, an entity adjusts profit or loss attributable to ordinary equity holders of the parent entity (numerator), and the weighted average number of shares outstanding (denominator) for the effects of all dilutive potential ordinary shares. Potential ordinary shares are contracts that may entitle its holder to ordinary shares. Examples include:

- convertible debt or preference shares (except for mandatorily convertible debt);
- share warrants or options; and
- shares that would be issued upon satisfaction of certain conditions resulting from contractual arrangements, such as the purchase of a business that occurs before the end of the reporting period.

IAS 33.36, 38   5.3.120.20 Potential ordinary shares that were cancelled, have lapsed or have been converted to ordinary shares during the reporting period are reflected in the diluted EPS calculation, if they are dilutive, from the first day of the reporting period to the day that they lapsed or were converted or cancelled. Potential ordinary shares issued during the reporting period are included in the diluted EPS calculation, if they are dilutive, from the day that they are issued.

IAS 33.41   5.3.120.30 The effects of potential ordinary shares are reflected in diluted EPS only when their inclusion in the calculation would decrease EPS, or increase the loss per share (i.e. would be dilutive), from *continuing* operations.

IAS 33.42, 44   5.3.120.40 When considering whether potential ordinary shares are dilutive or anti-dilutive, each type of potential ordinary share is considered separately rather than in aggregate. The goal in computing diluted EPS is to calculate the maximum dilutive effect, and therefore each type of potential ordinary share should be considered in sequence from the most dilutive to the least dilutive. To determine the sequence it is necessary to calculate the effect that the conversion of the potential ordinary shares would have on both earnings from continuing operations and the number of shares.

5.3 Earnings per share

IAS 33.37 5.3.120.50 Dilutive potential ordinary shares are determined independently for each period presented. The number of dilutive potential ordinary shares included in the annual (or year-to-date) period is not equal to a weighted average of the dilutive potential ordinary shares included in each interim computation.

5.3.130 Adjustments to basic EPS

5.3.140 Earnings

IAS 33.33-35 5.3.140.10 To calculate diluted earnings, the numerator used for the calculation of basic EPS is adjusted for the post-tax effect of any dividends, interest and other profit or loss items related to the dilutive potential ordinary shares. Examples of expenses that may result from the conversion of potential ordinary shares include transaction costs incurred on a conversion. The conversion of convertible debt may result in lower interest expense and therefore higher net profit. All these impacts are included in the adjustment to the numerator if they are consequential changes in profit or loss of the assumed conversion.

IAS 33.58, 59 5.3.140.20 The numerator is not adjusted for share-based payment costs when calculating diluted EPS (see 5.3.250). However, when there is a remeasurement expense from a liability of a cash-settled share-based payment, in our view the numerator is adjusted for such an amount when calculating diluted earnings (see 5.3.210.10 and 260.30).

5.3.150 Consequential changes in profit or loss

5.3.150.10 In our view, in order for an item to be treated as having a consequential effect on profit or loss as a result of the assumed conversion, there should be a direct or automatic adjustment to profit or loss. For example, an entity issues share options to employees. Consider the following two methods that the entity uses to fulfil its obligations to deliver the shares:

(1) The entity enters into an agreement for Bank B to purchase shares in the market and deliver them to employees upon exercise of the options by the employees. The entity will pay to Bank B any positive difference between the market price of the shares purchased by Bank B and the exercise price.

In our view, the call option that the entity has with Bank B is not a derivative as the value of the option will not change in response to some underlying variable because the shares are purchased at market price (see 3.6.180). Therefore the call option has no effect on profit or loss and no adjustment will be made to the numerator in a diluted EPS calculation.

(2) The entity enters into a share-swap with Bank C to reduce the entity's exposure to an increase in the market price of its shares when the options become exercisable. The share-swap has the following characteristics:

1288

- The entity takes a notional loan from Bank C with the principal amount equal to the purchase price of a notional number of shares at a notional share price.
- The entity pays interest on the notional loan and Bank C pays dividends on the notional number of shares when the entity declares dividends.
- The entity may change the number of notional shares implicit in the notional loan by notifying the bank in advance, and the entity has the intention of reducing the number of notional shares in line with the reduction in share options outstanding. The difference between the notional price and the market price of shares is refunded by Bank C if the number of shares decreases and vice versa.

5.3.150.20 In our view, while the entity may intend to adjust the notional amount under the swap arrangement to hedge the share-based payment liability, the adjustment is not automatic and the entity has the discretion to adjust its exposure. Therefore we believe that there is insufficient linkage between the swap arrangement with Bank C and the exercise of options in order to consider changes in the swap arrangement with Bank C to be a consequential change to profit or loss.

5.3.150.30 Therefore, neither of the arrangements in 5.3.150.10 results in a consequential change to profit or loss and the numerator in the diluted EPS calculation is not adjusted.

5.3.160 *Weighted average number of shares*

IAS 33.36   5.3.160.10 The denominator (the weighted average number of ordinary shares) used for the calculation of basic EPS is adjusted for the weighted average number of ordinary shares that would have been issued on the conversion or issue of the dilutive potential ordinary shares.

IAS 33.64   5.3.160.20 The diluted EPS calculation may be affected if the number of ordinary shares outstanding is increased or decreased without a corresponding change in resources, e.g. as a result of a bonus issue or share dividend. Each potential ordinary share in issue at the time of such a change in the number of ordinary shares may be required to be adjusted for the effect of this share issue. See 5.3.360 for further detail on how to determine whether such share issues will impact the dilutive effect of each potential ordinary share.

5.3.170 **Options, warrants and other potential ordinary shares**

5.3.170.10 Typical potential ordinary shares are options, warrants, convertible debt securities and convertible preference shares.

IAS 33.45-47   5.3.170.20 To calculate diluted EPS, the entity assumes that dilutive options and warrants are exercised. For options and similar instruments, dilution is computed using the treasury share method. According to this method only the bonus element of the issue is reflected in diluted EPS. The bonus element is calculated by regarding the options as comprising: a contract to issue ordinary shares equal to the proceeds (exercise price multiplied by the number of options) divided by the average market price for the period; and a contract to issue the remaining shares for no consideration. The bonus element is the difference between the number of ordinary shares that would be issued at the exercise price and the number of ordinary shares that would have been issued at the average market price. This difference is added to the number of ordinary shares outstanding in the calculation of diluted EPS. See 5.3.270 for a worked example illustrating the application of the treasury share method.

5.3.170.30 Options, warrants and other potential ordinary shares issued subject to conditions, for example, performance-based employee share options, may be contingently issuable potential ordinary shares (see 5.3.190 and 220).

5.3.170.40 The average market price of an ordinary share is required to determine the bonus element of warrants and options and other potential ordinary shares when the treasury stock method is used to calculate diluted EPS. The average market price should be determined based on the full reporting period, or in our view the period for which the potential ordinary shares are outstanding, if shorter (see 5.3.170.60). For example, if options are outstanding only for four months of the reporting period, then in determining the bonus element the average market price is based on the average market price during that four-month period.

5.3.170.50 In some cases there may not be a quoted market price for the ordinary shares for the full period, for example because the entity does not have ordinary shares or potential ordinary shares that are publicly traded and the entity elects to disclose EPS, or the entity's ordinary shares or potential ordinary shares were not listed for the full period. For example, an entity with an annual reporting period ending on 31 December lists its ordinary shares on 7 November, so that it has a quoted market price for its shares only during the period from 7 November to 31 December. The entity has ordinary shares outstanding during the current and comparative periods.

IAS 39.AG74- 5.3.170.60 In our view, if the average market price of the shares is necessary to
AG79 calculate diluted EPS (e.g. because the entity has outstanding warrants or options), then the average market price used should be a meaningful average for the full reporting period or the period that the potential ordinary shares are outstanding, if shorter. We do not believe that an average market price for approximately two months, as in the example in 5.3.170.50, would be meaningful for potential ordinary shares outstanding for the full year. In our view, when there is no active market for a financial instrument, an entity should determine fair value using valuation techniques. We believe that an entity should apply the guidance for measuring the fair value of financial instruments to determine the fair value of unquoted equity instruments (see 3.6.950) in order to estimate the average market price for the ordinary shares.

5.3.170.70 Specialist expertise may be required in this assessment, and in our view the method used to determine the average market value should be disclosed in the notes to the financial statements.

5.3.170.80 Options that require an entity to issue shares also may be present in agreements other than written options. For example, Company G and Company B enter into an agreement whereby each company contributes a certain portion of their businesses to Newco. G holds 45 percent of Newco and B holds 55 percent. The ordinary shares of B are quoted. B grants a put option to G, whereby G can put its 45 percent interest in Newco to B in exchange for 500 worth of B's ordinary shares.

5.3.170.90 This put option would be considered in B's calculation of diluted EPS. To determine if it would be dilutive, B would need to reflect G's 45 percent share of Newco as the proceeds that B would receive from the issue of 500 of value of its ordinary shares. If the value of the 45 percent share of Newco is less than 500, then the put option is dilutive. If not, then it is anti-dilutive and would not be reflected in the diluted EPS calculation, but B would be required to disclose information about the existence and the effects of the anti-dilutive put option.

IAS 33.62   5.3.170.100 When an entity has purchased options on its own shares, these are excluded from diluted EPS because it is assumed that these options would be exercised only when they are in the money and therefore anti-dilutive. Written put options and forward purchase contracts are included in diluted EPS if dilutive (i.e. if they are in the money).

IAS 33.24,   5.3.170.110 When an entity has written put options, or entered into a forward contract, 63, A10   on its own shares, in our view the shares subject to the put or forward should be excluded from the denominator used to calculate basic EPS (see 5.3.100). However, we believe that even though the shares subject to repurchase should be excluded from basic EPS, the potentially dilutive effect of the written forward contracts should be considered in the calculation of diluted EPS.

IAS 33.63,   5.3.170.115 The dilutive effect of written put options and forward purchase contracts A10   is calculated as the difference between the number of shares that would have to be issued at the average market price during the period in order to raise sufficient proceeds to fulfil the contract, and the number of shares that would be repurchased with these proceeds under the terms of the contract.

5.3.170.120 Forward purchase contracts on an entity's own shares that are entered into in conjunction with arrangements which involve lending of an entity's own shares (share lending arrangements) at the same time, in our view could be considered linked transactions, depending on the substance of the transactions, when determining the impact on diluted EPS.

5.3.170.130 For example, Company C lends its own shares to Bank G for cash at a market price of 5 and agrees to buy back the shares from G for cash at a price of 5 in 22 months. The forward purchase contract is for the return of a fixed amount of shares at a fixed price and is with the same counterparty, G, as the share lending arrangement. The forward purchase contract and the share lending arrangement were entered into at the same time and in contemplation of each other. G enters into this arrangement because it earns dividends on the shares. In our view, the transactions need to be considered together when determining the impact on diluted EPS for C, and therefore there would be no adjustment to the denominator for calculating diluted EPS in this circumstance.

5.3.180 *Partly-paid shares*

IAS 33.A16   5.3.180.10 To the extent that partly-paid shares are not entitled to participate in dividends during the period, such partly-paid shares are treated as options or warrants. The unpaid balance of such shares is regarded as the proceeds from issuing shares. These proceeds are assumed to be used to purchase ordinary shares at the average market price for the period. The number of shares included in diluted EPS is the difference between the number of unpaid shares not included in basic EPS and the number of shares assumed to be purchased with the remaining purchase consideration, if dilutive.

5.3.190 *Vesting conditions*

IAS 33.48   5.3.190.10 Employee share options with fixed or determinable terms and unvested ordinary shares are treated as outstanding options in the calculation of diluted EPS, even though they may be subject to vesting. Instruments with vesting conditions may appear to be contingently issuable. However, employee options that have only service- (time-) based vesting conditions are not treated as contingently issuable shares. Instead, they are treated as outstanding potential ordinary shares from the grant date. In contrast, grants of employee share options and shares with performance conditions other than time-based service, or instruments with market conditions, are treated as contingently issuable options and shares when their issue is contingent upon satisfaction of specified conditions in addition to the passage of time (see 5.3.220).

5.3.200 *Share-based payment arrangements*

IAS 33.47A,   5.3.200.10 For share options and other share-based payment arrangements to which
IE5A   IFRS 2 *Share-based Payment* applies, in calculating diluted EPS an entity adjusts the exercise price of potential ordinary shares to include the fair value of goods or services that will be recognised as a cost in future periods, i.e. the future share-based payment arrangements are included within assumed proceeds. See 5.3.270 for a worked example.

5.3.205 *Potential ordinary shares of a subsidiary, associate or jointly controlled entity*

IAS 33.40,   5.3.205.10 Potential ordinary shares that are issued by a subsidiary, associate
A11, IE10   or jointly controlled entity are included in the calculation of diluted EPS if their effect is dilutive. The dilutive effect of potential ordinary shares of a subsidiary, associate or jointly controlled entity is determined by first calculating the diluted EPS of a subsidiary, associate or jointly controlled entity and then including that diluted EPS in the consolidated entity's diluted EPS based on the entity's ownership of the instruments of the subsidiary, associate or jointly controlled entity. In our view, the same guidance applies if options or warrants that entitle the holder to the ordinary shares of a subsidiary are issued by the parent rather than by the subsidiary itself.

5.3.205.20 For example, Company S, a subsidiary of Company P, has 10,000 ordinary shares and 1,000 options outstanding, of which P owns 9,000 and 500, respectively. The options have an exercise price of 40, while the average market value of S's ordinary share was 50 in 2010. P has 5,000 ordinary shares outstanding. In 2010 P's profit (excluding any distributed and undistributed earnings of subsidiaries) was 7,000. S's profit in 2010 was 30,000.

5.3.205.30 In order to determine diluted EPS of P, diluted EPS of S should be calculated first:

S's diluted EPS = $30,000^1 / (10,000^2 + 200^3) = 2.94$

(1) S's earnings for the period
(2) Weighted average ordinary shares
(3) Incremental shares related to weighted average options outstanding. All options are dilutive because their exercise price is below the average market value of S's ordinary shares for the period. The incremental shares are calculated as follows:

Shares issued upon assumed exercise of options	1,000
Less: shares that would be issued at average market price	$(800)^{(i)}$
Incremental shares	200

Notes
(i) Assumed proceeds from exercise of 40,000 (40 x 1,000), divided by average market price of 50.

5.3.205.40 Assuming the options outstanding are dilutive at P's level (i.e. at the parent level), S's diluted EPS then is included in P's diluted EPS based on P's ownership of S's equity instruments:

P's Diluted EPS = $(7,000^1 + 26,460^2 + 294^3) / 5,000^4 = 6.75$

Notes
(1) P's earnings for the period
(2) P's share of S's earnings attributable to ordinary shares = (9,000 / 10,000) x (2.94 x 10,000)
(3) P's share of S's earnings attributable to options = (500 / 1,000) x (2.94 x 200)
(4) P's weighted average ordinary shares outstanding

5.3.210 ***Contracts that may be settled in ordinary shares or cash***

IAS 33.58, 59   5.3.210.10 When an entity issues a contract that may be settled in ordinary shares or cash at the *entity's* option, the entity presumes that the contract will be settled in ordinary shares. This assumption is independent of the classification of the contract as debt or equity or, if it is a share-based payment, as a cash or equity-settled arrangement (see 4.5). If the resulting potential ordinary shares are dilutive, then they are included in diluted EPS. Such a contract may have been classified either as a financial asset or financial liability or as a compound instrument. Therefore instances may arise in which share-based payments are considered potential ordinary shares even though they are classified as cash-settled share-based payment transactions. It is necessary to adjust the numerator in the diluted EPS calculation for any changes in profit or loss that would have resulted from classifying the contract as an equity instrument in its entirety.

IAS 33.60 5.3.210.20 For contracts that may be settled in ordinary shares or cash at the holder's option, the entity uses the more dilutive of cash settlement and share settlement in calculating diluted EPS. Therefore the EPS settlement assumption may not be consistent with the classification of the share-based payment (see 5.3.350).

IAS 33.60 5.3.210.30 Continuing with the example in 5.3.170.80, if upon exercise of the put option by G, B has a choice to settle either in cash or by issuing shares, then B would presume that it will settle the contract by issuing shares and then determine whether the impact is dilutive. However, if the election to receive cash or shares was at G's option, then B would evaluate which is the more dilutive of cash or equity settlement and assume that option is used in the calculation of diluted EPS.

5.3.210.40 See 5.3.250 for a discussion of the interaction of EPS with IFRS 2.

5.3.220 *Contingently issuable ordinary shares*

IAS 33.21(g), 5.3.220.10 When ordinary shares are issued and are not subject to conditions, they are
48, 52, 57 included in basic EPS from the date consideration is receivable. In other cases, when the issue of shares is subject to conditions, they are considered to be contingently issuable shares unless they are contingently issuable solely on the passage of time (see 5.3.80) or are shares subject only to service conditions (see 4.5 and 5.3.250) issued in a share-based payment. Shares issued subject to service-based vesting conditions are included in basic EPS as the services are rendered (see 5.3.80). Share options, warrants or equivalents issued in a share-based payment transaction in which the only vesting condition is completion of future employment service are not contingently issuable ordinary shares; rather, they are potential ordinary shares. Other contingently issuable ordinary shares are included only in diluted EPS (if dilutive), based on the number of shares that would be issuable if the end of the reporting period were the end of the contingency period.

IAS 33.57 5.3.220.15 In our view, IAS 33 is not clear on how to treat instruments with conditions that cause them to be contingently issuable *potential* ordinary shares. We believe that the guidance in paragraphs 52 – 56 of IAS 33 on contingently issuable shares is used *only* to determine whether or not an entity has a situation in which the instruments would impact the number of shares outstanding, i.e. whether the entity has an instrument that can be assumed to be issuable. The *impact* on diluted EPS is then determined based on the relevant guidance in IAS 33 as follows:

- for options or warrants an entity refers to paragraphs 45 – 48 of IAS 33 (see 5.3.170);

- for convertible instruments an entity refers to paragraphs 49 – 51 of IAS 33; and
- for contracts that may be settled in ordinary shares or cash an entity refers to paragraphs 58 – 61 of IAS 33 (see 5.3.210).

5.3.220.16 For example, an entity has an IFRS 2 share option plan with a three-year service and market condition. At the end of year one, the entity *determines* based on paragraphs 52 – 56 of IAS 33 that all conditions would be met if the end of the first reporting period was the end of the contingency period. However, the number of contingently issuable potential ordinary shares to be included in diluted EPS is determined based on the guidance for options or warrants within IAS 33 (see 5.3.170).

5.3.220.20 Another example of contingently issuable potential ordinary shares is when a loan agreement allows the lender to convert the loan into ordinary shares of the borrowing entity under certain conditions, for example on default by the borrower or a credit rating downgrade of the borrower (triggering events).

IAS 33.IE7   5.3.220.30 The loan clause gives rise to contingently issuable potential ordinary shares. If the borrower defaults during the period, then the conversion option would be exercisable. The number of shares to be included in the diluted EPS computation would be based on the number of shares that would be issuable if the end of the reporting period were the end of the contingency period. If a triggering event has occurred, then the ordinary shares would be considered in the calculation of diluted EPS from the date of the triggering event (or from the date of the loan agreement, if later), and not from the beginning of the reporting period.

IAS 33.24   5.3.220.40 If the option has been exercised, then the ordinary shares would be outstanding and would be included in the calculation of basic EPS from the exercise date, even if the shares had not been issued yet. This is because there are no further conditions or payments required and the issue of shares is contingent on the passage of time.

5.3.220.50 Another example of a contingently issuable potential ordinary share is a share-based payment arrangement in which the employees should complete three years of employment and achieve a 20 percent increase in net income of the entity over this same period for the shares to vest, i.e. a performance condition is included within the share-based payment arrangement. The number of contingently issuable ordinary shares included in diluted EPS (if dilutive) is based on the number of shares that would be issuable if the end of the reporting period were the end of the contingency period. See 5.3.230 and 240 for further discussion of the impact (if any) on the diluted EPS calculation.

5.3.230 *Contingencies related to earnings targets*

IAS 33.53   5.3.230.10 If shares are contingently issuable based on achieving or maintaining a specified amount of earnings, and the entity attains the specified amount of earnings but also is required to maintain the level of earnings for an additional period, then shares should be considered as outstanding only for purposes of computing diluted EPS. The diluted EPS is based on the number of ordinary shares that would be issued if the amount of earnings at the end of the reporting period were the amount of earnings at the end of the contingency period. These contingent shares are not considered outstanding for basic EPS, unless the earnings have been achieved for the required period.

5.3.230.20 For example, an entity hires a consultant to evaluate the entity's operating costs and recommend ways for the entity to reduce its operating costs. If the operating costs are reduced by 350 per annum, and this cost reduction is sustained for a further year, then the consultant will receive 1 percent of the entity's issued ordinary shares. If costs are reduced by 700 per annum, and this cost reduction is sustained for a further year, then the consultant will receive 2 percent of the entity's issued equity. The consultant has three years to achieve these targets.

5.3.230.30 After one year, the consultant achieves only 200 of cost savings. If this were the end of the contingency period, then no shares would be issued, and therefore there is no impact on either basic or diluted EPS. At the end of the second year, cost savings of 400 have been achieved, but not yet sustained. There is no impact on basic earnings per share, as the cost savings have not been sustained, but the potential ordinary shares (1 percent of the entity's issued ordinary shares) will be included in the calculation of diluted EPS. Once the cost savings have been sustained for one year, the effect of the shares to be issued also will be included in the calculation of basic EPS.

5.3.240 Contingencies related to price levels

IAS 33.54 5.3.240.10 The number of ordinary shares that are contingently issuable may depend on the future market price of the ordinary shares. In this case if the effect is dilutive, then the calculation of diluted EPS should be based on the number of ordinary shares that would be issued if the market price at the end of the reporting period were the market price at the end of the contingency period.

5.3.242 Contingencies related to earnings targets and price levels

IAS 33.55 5.3.242.10 When the number of ordinary shares that are contingently issuable depends on future earnings *and* future prices of the ordinary shares, such shares are included in the diluted EPS calculation only if both conditions are met at the end of the reporting period.

IAS 33.37 5.3.242.20 During any interim reporting period, an entity would have to consider whether the conditions were met at that interim reporting period and whether the contingently issuable shares are dilutive for the calculation of diluted EPS. In our view, this would be necessary even if the share price had declined below the trigger level after the end of the interim reporting period but before the interim financial statements were authorised for issue.

5.3.245 Contracts with multiple conversion features

5.3.245.10 In some cases, an entity may issue a financial instrument with more than one conversion feature. The issue arises as to which conversion feature should be considered when determining the potential ordinary shares for inclusion in the diluted EPS calculation. In general, the goal in computing diluted EPS is to calculate the maximum dilutive effect. Therefore, the entity would be required to calculate diluted EPS under the various conversion features and determine which feature is the most dilutive (see 5.3.120.40).

5.3.245.20 For example, convertible bonds are issued with two conversion features attached to the non-mandatory convertible instruments: an option for early conversion and an option for conversion at the end of a contingent period. In our view, the entity would compute separate diluted EPS calculations for the early conversion feature and the conversion at the end of the contingent period to evaluate which feature is most dilutive. The presentation of the diluted EPS would be based on the most dilutive scenario.

5.3.250 *Interaction of EPS with share-based payment arrangements*

5.3.250.10 Outlined below are key factors to be considered in the calculation of diluted EPS when an entity has share-based payment arrangements outstanding:

IAS 33.IE5A • The fair value of future goods or services are included as part of assumed proceeds when calculating the adjustment to the denominator in a diluted EPS calculation (see 5.3.200). However, in our view the numerator is not adjusted to include the unrecognised share-based payment treated as assumed proceeds. Future services ultimately would result in recognition of an expense; however, the expense will be recognised in the numerator in basic EPS only over the remaining vesting period. In addition the numerator is not adjusted for the share-based payment expenses incurred in the current period. Therefore, we believe that the numerator is not adjusted when calculating diluted EPS.

IAS 33.45, • When the treasury share method (see 5.3.170.20) is used to calculate the impact
47A   on the denominator, the assumed proceeds from the exercise of the instrument (e.g. share option) should be determined. The assumed proceeds for a share-based payment will be affected by the number of employees that will exercise their share options. To determine assumed proceeds, an entity factors the forfeitures into the calculation as forfeitures will impact both the consideration received and the future services under the share-based payment. In our view, the consideration received on the exercise of the options component of the assumed proceeds should be based on the weighted average number of options for the period. IAS 33 is unclear regarding the basis to be used for the future services component and a number of approaches may be acceptable. See 5.3.330.30 and 40 for an illustration of two of these approaches.

5.3.260 *Share-based payment arrangements with the option to settle in ordinary shares or cash*

5.3.260.10 Instances may arise in which the classification of share-based payments under IFRS 2 is different from the classification of share-based payments for the purpose of the calculation of EPS (see 5.3.200). Outlined in 5.3.260.20 – 30 are key factors to be considered in the calculation of diluted EPS when share-based payments are considered potential ordinary shares, even though they are classified as cash-settled share-based payment transactions.

IFRS 2.30, IG19, IAS 33.47A
5.3.260.20 *Adjustments to the denominator using the treasury share method.* An entity recognises a share-based payment cost for unvested cash-settled share-based payments over the remaining period until settlement date, which includes amounts arising from the remeasurement of the liability at the end of each reporting period and finally at the settlement date (see 4.5.630). In our view, the cost resulting from the remeasurement of cash-settled share-based payment arrangements should not be included in assumed proceeds. This view is based on the fact that if the share-based payment is classified as equity-settled, then there is no remeasurement of the share-based payment. Instead, the future services are measured using the grant-date fair value of the cash-settled share-based payment.

5.3.260.30 *Adjustments to the numerator.* When an item is classified as cash-settled under IFRS 2, a remeasurement expense will be incurred that would not have been recognised if the share-based payment was classified as equity-settled. In our view, the remeasurement expense on the liability recognised has a consequential effect on the numerator if the share-based payment were to be classified as equity-settled (for the purposes of the EPS calculation). Therefore, the post-tax remeasurement expense should be reversed from the numerator.

5.3.270 Worked example of a basic and diluted EPS calculation

5.3.270.10 This example illustrates the calculation of basic and diluted EPS for an entity that has a share-based payment arrangement in place for its employees. The example illustrates the application of several principles discussed in 5.3.120, including:

- application of the treasury share method;
- calculation of diluted EPS for contracts that are settled in ordinary shares; and
- the impact of unvested share-based payment arrangements on diluted EPS.

Company M is preparing its financial statements at and for the year ending 31 December 2010 and is calculating its basic and diluted EPS. M granted an option scheme to employees on 1 January 2010 (see 5.3.280).

Profit attributable to ordinary equity holders of M (i.e. profit after recognition of share-based payment, including remeasurement)	900,000
Ordinary shares outstanding at beginning and end of 2010	10,000
Average share price in 2010	44

5.3.280 *Details of the share-based payment arrangement*

- On 1 January 2010 M issued, for no consideration, 100 options to each of 10 employees (i.e. 1,000 options). The arrangement is conditional upon the completion of three years of service, i.e. the options vest on 31 December 2012.
- M anticipates, at both grant date and at the end of the reporting period, that seven employees will provide the requisite service and vest in the shares (i.e. an overall vesting rate of 70 percent). Two employees left on 30 June 2010 (i.e. actual forfeiture rate to date of 20 percent). At 31 December 2010 management continued to estimate that 70 percent of the options would vest, i.e. that overall 30 percent would be forfeited.
- The employees' options settle in shares at the completion of three years of service. The exercise price of the options is 31.50.

IFRS 2.36, 37   - The market price of M's shares is 40 at 1 January 2010 and the grant-date fair value of the employee option is 6.75.

5.3.290 *Grant-date fair value of share-based payment*

5.3.290.10 [Not used]

5.3.290.20 The share-based payment recognised in 2010 using the fair value of the instrument at grant date, the expected vesting rate and the three-year vesting period, is determined as 1,575 (1,000 options x 6.75 grant-date fair value / 3 years x 70% expected vesting rate).

5.3.300 **Basic EPS**

Earnings	900,000	
Weighted average number of ordinary shares outstanding	10,000	
Basic EPS	90	(900,000 / 10,000)

5.3.310 **Diluted EPS**

5.3.310.10 [Not used]

5.3.320 *Equity settlement*

IAS 33.47   5.3.320.10 To calculate diluted EPS, M assumes that any dilutive options are exercised. All of the options would be dilutive if they are in the money or essentially the average market price of shares in 2010 exceeds the exercise price of the options plus the fair value of any goods or services to be supplied to M in the future under any respective IFRS 2 arrangements if applicable (see 5.3.330.10). In this example, a simple way to determine if the options are dilutive is to take the exercise price of 31.50 and add 6.75, the grant-date fair value of the option, to arrive at 38.25; the average market price of shares in 2010 (44) exceeds 38.25, and therefore the options are dilutive.

5.3.330 Denominator adjustment

5.3.330.05 For the purposes of calculating the denominator for the diluted EPS calculation, the denominator used in the basic EPS calculation is increased by the weighted average number of ordinary shares that would be issued on the conversion of all dilutive potential ordinary shares into ordinary shares (see 5.3.160.10). For example, if the potential ordinary shares are cancelled or lapse during the period, then they are included only for the part of the period that they were outstanding.

IAS 33.45-48   5.3.330.10 Furthermore, in the case of options or warrants, the treasury share method is used to calculate the weighted average number of potential ordinary shares that should be added to the denominator used in the basic EPS calculation. That is, the denominator is adjusted only for the bonus element contained in the option or warrant, i.e. the difference between the number of ordinary shares that would be issued at the exercise price and the number of ordinary shares that would have been issued at the average market price (see 5.3.170). In the case of options granted as part of a share-based payment arrangement, the "exercise price" for the purpose of the treasury share method includes the fair value of any goods or services to be supplied to the company in the future under the share option or other share-based payment arrangement as well as the actual exercise price of the option (see 5.3.250).

5.3.330.15 The initial step in the diluted EPS calculation is to determine the assumed proceeds from the exercise of the share option as required by paragraph 45 of IAS 33. Outlined in 5.3.330.30 and 40 are two approaches to computing the assumed proceeds. In our view, there may be other approaches to computing the assumed proceeds, in particular the value of the future services component of the calculation, which may be acceptable under IFRSs.

5.3.330.20 [Not used]

5.3.330.30 In the first approach, the value of the future services component of the assumed proceeds calculation is computed based on the outstanding options at the end of the reporting period, i.e. the unrecognised IFRS 2 charge for the 8 employees that remain at the end of the reporting period.

(1) Assumed proceeds		
(a) Consideration received on exercise of options	(900[i] x 31.50[ii])	28,350
IAS 33.47A *Add:* Future services from share-based payment		
(b) Assumed proceeds from future services[iii]	(5,400 - 1,800)	3,600
Assumed proceeds	(28,350 + 3,600)	31,950

Notes

(i)　Consideration to be received by M is based upon deemed exercise of the weighted average number of options per paragraphs 36 and 48 of IAS 33, being the sum of 1,000 options outstanding at the beginning of the period (i.e. from the date of grant on 1 January 2010) and the 800 options outstanding at the end of the period (i.e. 31 December 2010), giving a weighted average total of 900.

(ii)　The exercise price of the options.

(iii)　Assumed proceeds from future services is based on the unrecognised IFRS 2 charge for 8 employees

Total IFRS 2 charge	(800 x 6.75)	5,400
Less: IFRS 2 charge based on actual forfeiture	(800 x 6.75 x 1/3)	(1,800)
Total unrecognised IFRS 2 charge		3,600

(2)　Shares issued for no consideration (bonus element)

(a)	Shares issued at the average market price	$(31,950 / 44)^{(iv)}$	726
(b)	Bonus element, adjusted in denominator	$(900 - 726)^{(v)}$	174

Notes

(iv)　Assumed proceeds (1) *divided by* average market price.

(v)　Weighted average number of options outstanding during the period (900 options) *less* number of shares issued at average market price (iv).

5.3.330.40 Alternatively, in the second approach, the value of the future services component of the assumed proceeds calculation is computed based on the average unearned compensation for the period. In our view, this approach also is acceptable as using the average unearned compensation for the period is consistent with including *weighted average* options and warrants outstanding *during the period* in diluted EPS (if dilutive) and with the use of the average market price for the period to calculate the bonus element.

(1)　Assumed proceeds

(a)	Consideration received on exercise of options	$(900^{(i)}$ x $31.50^{(ii)})$	28,350
IAS 33.47A	*Add:* Future services from share-based payment		
(b)	Assumed proceeds from future services$^{(iii)}$	((6,750 + 3,600) / 2)	5,175
	Assumed proceeds	(28,350 + 5,175)	33,525

Notes

(i)　Consideration to be received by M is based upon deemed exercise of the weighted average number of options per paragraphs 36 and 48 of IAS 33 being the sum of 1,000 options outstanding at the beginning of the period (i.e. from the date of grant on 1 January 2010) and the 800 options outstanding at the end of the period (i.e. 31 December 2010), giving a weighted average total of 900.

(ii)　The exercise price of the options.

(iii) Assumed proceeds from future services is based on average unearned compensation for the period

Unearned compensation at the beginning of the period	(1,000 x 6.75)	6,750
Unearned compensation at the end of the period	(800 x 6.75 x 2/3)	3,600
Average unearned compensation for the period	((6,750 + 3,600) / 2)	5,175

(2) Shares issued for no consideration (bonus element)

(a) Shares issued at the average market price	$(33,525 / 44)^{(iv)}$	762
(b) Bonus element, adjusted in denominator	$(900 - 762)^{(v)}$	138

Notes

(iv) Assumed proceeds (1) *divided by* average market price.

(v) Weighted average number of options outstanding during the period (900 options) *less* number of shares issued at average market price (iv).

5.3.330.45 As a result of the above two approaches, diluted EPS is calculated as follows:

Diluted EPS based on approach in 5.3.330.30:

Earnings		900,000
Weighted average number of ordinary shares outstanding	(10,000 + 174)	10,174
Diluted EPS	(900,000 / 10,174)	88.46

Diluted EPS based on approach in 5.3.330.40:

Earnings		900,000
Weighted average number of ordinary shares outstanding	(10,000 + 138)	10,138
Diluted EPS	(900,000 / 10,138)	88.77

5.3.340 Numerator adjustment

5.3.340.10 In this example, the numerator is not adjusted. In certain circumstances the numerator is adjusted, e.g. in situations in which the employee has the option to settle in cash or equity (see 5.3.350).

5.3.350 Cash settlement

5.3.350.05 If the employees in this worked example had the ability to settle the options in either cash or equity, then M uses the more dilutive of cash settlement and share settlement in calculating diluted EPS.

5.3.350.10 When calculating diluted EPS under the cash settlement option, there is no adjustment to the denominator as cash settlement does not result in any additional ordinary shares being issued. Nor are there adjustments to the numerator. Diluted EPS *assuming cash settlement* is 90 (900,000 / 10,000); the same as basic EPS.

5.3.350.15 When calculating diluted EPS under the share settlement option, the numerator in the diluted EPS as calculated in 5.3.330.45 is adjusted for the remeasurement expense recognised for the liability component before being used for comparison to the diluted EPS in 5.3.350.10 to determine which is more dilutive.

5.3.360 **Retrospective adjustment**

IAS 33.26,
27, 64, 71
5.3.360.10 The current and prior period figures for basic and diluted EPS are adjusted for transactions that, other than the conversion of potential ordinary shares, adjust the number of shares without a corresponding change in resources. A change in the number of shares without a corresponding change in resources occurs, for example, with a bonus share issue, an issue of warrants with a bonus element, share consolidation or split, or if there is a bonus element in a rights issue. Basic and diluted EPS also are adjusted for a bonus issue, share split or reverse share split that occurs after the end of the reporting period but before the financial statements are authorised for issue. The number of ordinary shares is adjusted as if the event had occurred at the beginning of the earliest period presented.

5.3.360.20 For example, an entity has 700 shares outstanding during the year to 31 December 2010. On 1 January 2011 it issues 300 shares for cash. Subsequent to the share issue, the entity issues bonus shares to its equity holders, who receive one share for every share held immediately before the bonus issue. EPS and diluted EPS data are not restated for the impact of the issue of 300 shares for cash, but restatement of the 31 December 2010 EPS data is required for the subsequent bonus issue of shares, as no additional resources were received by the entity in this regard. The number of shares to be used in the EPS calculation in respect of 2010 would be 1,400 (700 x 2) (and the 2009 comparative EPS data would be restated to give retrospective effect to the bonus issue) and 2,000 (1,000 x 2) shares used in respect of 2011.

5.3.360.25 In our view, when an entity pays a dividend such that shareholders have the option to receive either a cash dividend or a share dividend of equal value (i.e. there is no bonus element to the share dividend), the entity is exchanging shares and receiving a corresponding amount in resources (i.e. shares are issued as a dividend in exchange for an equal value of cash savings). The shareholder has given up the fair value of the cash dividend; therefore we believe that there is a corresponding change in resources. As a result, the shares issued would be factored into the calculation of EPS on a prospective basis with no restatement of prior period EPS. Conversely, we believe that if the fair value of a share dividend received exceeds the fair value of the cash alternative, then there is a bonus element that would need to be considered and EPS would be restated in prior periods for the bonus element portion.

5.3.360.27 For example, Company B grants a dividend whereby B's ordinary shareholders have the option to receive either cash of 2 or additional ordinary shares of B at a rate of 2 / x, whereby x is equal to the market price of B's ordinary shares. B has 100 ordinary shares outstanding with a market price of 5 per share. 30 percent of the ordinary shareholders opt to receive additional ordinary shares. These ordinary shareholders have opted to give up the cash value of 2, which is of equal value to the share dividend received. B therefore includes 12 (2 / 5 x 100 x 30%) additional shares in the calculation of diluted EPS from the dividend payment date.

IAS 33.A2 5.3.360.30 The conversion of potential ordinary shares does not result in a retrospective adjustment to EPS. For example, an entity issues share warrants to its shareholders for no consideration. The exercise price of the warrants is 10, which is equal to the market price of the shares on the date of issue. The warrants are exercised a number of years later when the market price of the shares is 15.

5.3.360.40 In our view, the determination of whether a bonus element exists is made once, at the time that the warrants are issued. At that time, the exercise price was equal to the market price of the shares and therefore there was no bonus element. Therefore, during periods when the market price exceeded the warrant exercise price, the warrants would have been included in the determination of diluted EPS. In the basic EPS calculation, the issue of the ordinary shares on exercise of the warrants will affect only the weighted average number of ordinary shares outstanding during the period, without any further adjustment.

5.3.360.50 Bonus issues and rights issues of warrants that do have a bonus element impact the computation of both basic and diluted EPS. For example, an entity issues bonus warrants on the basis of one bonus warrant for every 10 ordinary shares. Each bonus warrant will entitle the warrant holder to subscribe in cash for one new ordinary share at an exercise price of 2.50 during the exercise period. The market price of the entity's shares at the time the warrant was issued is 6 and therefore there is a bonus element. The bonus element needs to be applied retrospectively (i.e. this would require restatement of the prior year's basic and diluted EPS). The adjustment to the basic EPS is calculated by adjusting the cumulative weighted average number of shares outstanding at the time of the bonus issue. Adjustments may be made to diluted EPS only if the potential ordinary shares are outstanding at the date that the shares with a bonus element are issued. For example, a bonus share issue occurs on 31 March 2010 and options are issued on 30 April 2010; no adjustment to the diluted EPS calculation is made in relation to the options as they were issued after the date of the bonus share issue.

5.3.360.60 When determining whether the weighted average number of potential ordinary shares needs to be adjusted, the terms and conditions underlying the potential ordinary shares should be considered. An assessment should be made as to whether the terms and conditions of potential ordinary share arrangements allow for the exercise price or conversion ratios to adjust automatically for any share issues without a change in resources. Unless the conversion ratio or exercise price adjusts automatically, there will be no adjustment to the diluted EPS calculation.

5.3.360.70 For example, an entity has a share option scheme in place at the time that there is a bonus share issue to shareholders. None of the options have been exercised at the date of the bonus issue, the options are in the money just before the bonus issue, and the market price of the entity's shares decreased following the bonus share issue. If the terms and conditions of the share option scheme are that the exercise price of the options do not adjust automatically for the bonus share issue, then the options may become out of the money and would be anti-dilutive. However, if the terms of the scheme are such that the exercise price is adjusted for bonus issues, i.e. the exercise price will decrease in proportion to the bonus element, then the calculation of the diluted EPS in relation to these options should be adjusted to reflect the effect of the bonus share issue. The weighted average number of options outstanding at the date of the share issue is increased by a bonus factor.

5.3.360.80 Diluted EPS is not restated for any subsequent changes in assumptions made in calculating the effects of conversion of potential ordinary shares, such as the average market price or whether contingently issuable shares will be issued.

IAS 33.64, 70 5.3.360.90 Ordinary share or potential ordinary share transactions, other than those that adjust the number of shares outstanding without a corresponding change in resources, that occur after the end of the reporting period, are not accounted for retrospectively but are disclosed in the financial statements.

5.3.370 Presentation and disclosure

IAS 33.3 5.3.370.05 An entity that otherwise would not be required to present EPS may wish or may be required by local regulations to present basic and/or diluted earnings per share or unit. When an entity voluntarily presents EPS data, that data is calculated and presented in accordance with IAS 33.

IAS 33.67 5.3.370.10 EPS figures are presented for all periods presented, including interim periods. However for interim periods the presentation and disclosure requirements are limited (see 5.9.50).

IAS 33.66, 5.3.370.20 Basic and diluted EPS for both continuing and total operations are presented
67A in the statement of comprehensive income for each class of ordinary shares, with equal prominence for all periods. An entity presenting a statement of comprehensive income using the two-statement approach (see 4.1.10) discloses the information in the statement displaying components of profit or loss.

IAS 33.68, 5.3.370.30 Disclosure of separate EPS data is required for discontinued operations,
68A if relevant, either in the statement of comprehensive income or in the notes to the financial statements.

IAS 33.70 5.3.370.40 An entity provides a reconciliation of the earnings used in the EPS and diluted EPS calculations to profit or loss attributable to the parent entity.

IAS 33.67, 5.3.370.50 In some cases there may be no difference between basic and diluted EPS.
67A, 70 This will occur, for example, when the only potential ordinary shares are anti-dilutive and therefore excluded from the calculation of diluted EPS, or when there are dilutive potential ordinary shares but rounding creates the same amounts for basic and diluted

EPS. In such cases the entity still is required to disclose both basic and diluted EPS. However, this could be achieved by presenting only one line in the statement of comprehensive income, labelled "basic and diluted EPS". In our view, when basic and diluted EPS are equal, the entity would not be required to disclose a reconciliation of the weighted average number of ordinary shares used in the EPS calculation to the diluted EPS calculation, which otherwise would be required. However, if diluted EPS is reported for at least one period, then it should be reported for all periods presented, even if it equals basic EPS. In addition, an entity discloses potential ordinary shares that potentially could dilute EPS in the future, but are anti-dilutive for the current period presented.

IAS 1.107   5.3.370.52 Dividends and the related per-share amounts are disclosed either in the statement of changes in equity or in the notes to the financial statements and not in the statement of comprehensive income (see 2.2.40.40).

IAS 33.73,   5.3.370.55 Entities may wish to present additional EPS based on alternative measures
73A   of earnings, for example an entity may disclose earnings before interest, tax, depreciation and amortisation (EBITDA) per share (see 4.1.130 on the presentation of EBITDA). These should be presented in the notes to the financial statements only and not in the statement of comprehensive income.

IAS 33.73,   5.3.370.60 Both the basic and diluted additional amounts per share are disclosed
73A   in the notes to the financial statements for the alternative performance measure and each should be disclosed with equal prominence. The entity describes the basis for determining the earnings amount, which should be consistent over time, and the earnings used should be reconciled to a line item that is reported in the statement of comprehensive income. The denominator used for the calculation of the additional basic and diluted per share amounts should be the same as the weighted average number of ordinary shares used in the basic and diluted earnings per share calculation.

5.3.380 Future developments

5.3.380.10 In August 2008 the IASB published ED *Simplifying Earnings Per Share – Proposed Amendments to IAS 33*. The ED proposes to simplify the denominator for the EPS calculation. In addition, the IASB decided to propose the use of a fair value model to replace the treasury share method, in certain circumstances, and to require the two-class method for computing basic earnings per share for mandatorily convertible instruments with stated participation rights. The IASB does not expect to discuss this project until the second half of 2010.

5.4 Non-current assets held for sale and discontinued operations
(IFRS 5, IFRIC 17)

5.4 Non-current assets held for sale and discontinued operations
(IFRS 5, IFRIC 17)

Overview of currently effective requirements

- Non-current assets and some groups of assets and liabilities (known as disposal groups) are classified as held for sale when their carrying amounts will be recovered principally through sale.

- Non-current assets and disposal groups held for sale generally are measured at the lower of carrying amount and fair value less costs to sell, and are presented separately on the face of the statement of financial position.

- Assets classified as held for sale are not amortised or depreciated.

- The comparative statement of financial position is not re-presented when a non-current asset or disposal group is classified as held for sale.

- The classification, presentation and measurement requirements that apply to items that are classified as held for sale also are applicable to a non-current asset or disposal group that is classified as held for distribution.

- A discontinued operation is a component of an entity that either has been disposed of or is classified as held for sale.

- Discontinued operations are limited to those operations that are a separate major line of business or geographical area, and subsidiaries acquired exclusively with a view to resale.

- Discontinued operations are presented separately on the face of the statement of comprehensive income, and related cash flow information is disclosed.

- The comparative statement of comprehensive income and cash flow information is re-presented for discontinued operations.

Currently effective requirements

This publication reflects IFRSs in issue at 1 August 2010. The currently effective requirements cover annual periods beginning on 1 January 2010. The requirements related to this topic are derived mainly from IFRS 5 *Non-current Assets Held for Sale and Discontinued Operations*.

Forthcoming requirements and future developments

When a currently effective requirement will be changed by a new requirement that is issued but is not yet effective, it is marked with a # as a **forthcoming requirement** and the impact of the change is explained in the accompanying boxed text. In respect of this topic no forthcoming requirements are noted.

When a significant change to the currently effective or forthcoming requirements is expected, it is marked with a * as an area that may be subject to **future developments** and a brief outline of the relevant projects is given in 5.4.270.

5.4.5 Held for sale or distribution

5.4.10 *General*

IFRS 5.5A,   5.4.10.05 The classification, presentation and measurement requirements for non-
IFRIC 17.3   current assets or disposal groups held for sale apply also to those that are held for distribution to owners acting in their capacity as owners. Therefore, the requirements discussed in this chapter in respect of non-current assets and disposal groups that are classified as held for sale generally apply also to those classified as held for distribution.

5.4.10.10 Classification as held for sale changes the measurement basis of most non-current assets and of disposal groups. Classification as held for sale also determines the presentation in the statement of financial position of such non-current assets and disposal groups.

IFRS 5.A   5.4.10.20 A *disposal group* is a group of assets to be disposed of together, by sale or otherwise, in a single transaction, and liabilities directly associated with those assets that will be transferred in the transaction.

5.4.10.30 Classification as a discontinued operation determines only the presentation of the operation in the statement of comprehensive income, statement of cash flows and notes to the financial statements. There are no recognition or measurement impacts from classifying an operation as discontinued. However, a discontinued operation generally will include non-current assets or a disposal group or groups held for sale.

5.4.20 *Held for sale*

IFRS 5.2   5.4.20.10 The classification and presentation requirements of the standard apply to all non-current assets and to disposal groups that are held for sale.

IFRS 5.2, 5   5.4.20.20 The *measurement* requirements for assets held for sale do not apply to certain assets. These assets are excluded either because measurement would be difficult (e.g. deferred tax assets) or because the assets generally are carried on the basis of fair value with changes in fair value recognised in profit or loss (e.g. investment property measured at fair value (see 3.4.150)).

1310

IFRS 5.4, 18, 5.4.20.30 Excluded assets are *measured* using the standards that normally apply to these
19, 23 items, even if such assets are part of a disposal group. However, the disposal group as a whole is measured in a manner consistent with non-current assets that are held for sale.

5.4.20.40 As a result, non-current assets such as some financial assets may be classified and presented as held for sale but measured in accordance with other standards.

5.4.20.50 In the case of a disposal group, while the group as a whole is measured at the lower of carrying amount and fair value less costs to sell (see 5.4.40), some of the individual assets and liabilities within that disposal group may not be.

5.4.30 *Classification*

IFRS 5.6 5.4.30.10 A non-current asset or disposal group is classified as held for sale when its carrying amount will be recovered principally through a sale transaction.

IFRS 5.7 5.4.30.20 This is the case when the asset is *available for immediate sale* in its present condition subject only to terms that are usual and customary for sales of such assets or disposal groups and its sale is *highly probable*, i.e. when it is significantly more likely than merely probable.

IFRS 5.IG1 5.4.30.30 A need to obtain or construct a replacement asset (e.g. a new headquarters) or to cease operations that will not be transferred with the asset means that the asset is not available for immediate sale. Similarly, in our view if an asset is leased out and cannot be sold until the end of the lease term, then it is not available for immediate sale in its present condition.

IFRS 5.6-9, 5.4.30.40 A sale and operating leaseback results in the recognition of a completed sale
IAS 17.61 of an asset. In our view, the general held-for-sale classification criteria are applied to determine at what point the asset is held for sale. In particular, the likelihood of the planned arrangement being an operating lease and therefore a completed sale is relevant in determining whether and when the related asset could qualify as held for sale.

IFRS 5.8, 5.4.30.50 A sale and finance leaseback does not result in the derecognition of the asset,
IG4 and therefore the asset could not qualify as held for sale as a result of such a transaction.

5.4.30.60 In our view, a reduction in the level of ownership of a subsidiary that does not result in a loss of control is insufficient for the consolidated assets and liabilities to be considered to be recovered principally through a sale transaction and therefore classified as held for sale.

IFRS 5.8A 5.4.30.65 An entity that is committed to a sale plan involving loss of control of a subsidiary classifies all the assets and liabilities of that subsidiary as held for sale in its consolidated financial statements when the criteria for classification as held for sale are met, regardless of whether the entity will retain a non-controlling interest in the subsidiary after the sale.

IFRS 5.8, IG4   5.4.30.70 To be highly probable, there needs to be commitment to a plan to sell by an appropriate level of management and that plan needs to have been initiated. This requires active marketing at a price that is reasonable in relation to the asset's fair value. There is an expectation that the sale will be completed within one year of the classification of assets or a disposal group as held for sale, subject to extension in certain circumstances.

5.4.30.75 For example, Company X has commenced the process of selling an investment in a subsidiary and meets all of the criteria for classifying the assets and liabilities of the subsidiary as held for sale, including actively marketing the investment at a price that is reasonable in relation to the investment's fair value. A buyer is identified and the method of calculating the final agreed price for the investment is determined. However, prior to finalising the sale, financial information regarding the subsidiary emerges that leads X to suspect that the final agreed price will be significantly below the price at which it is willing to sell its investment. Before receiving the results of the calculation, the management of X actively begins to consider alternatives to selling the investment. In our view, in this situation the investment in the subsidiary no longer meets the held-for-sale criteria and should be reclassified as held for use (see 5.4.90.10), as management's consideration of other options is indicative of their unwillingness to sell at the current price.

IFRS 5.IG7   5.4.30.80 In our view, when an active market exists, active marketing at a reasonable price generally will lead quickly to a sale. Accordingly, it is unlikely that a non-current asset with a quoted market price will be classified as held for sale for any significant period of time before disposal.

IFRS 5.8   5.4.30.85 For some entities, the sale of significant non-current assets or disposal groups may be subject to shareholder approval. In our view, the requirement to obtain shareholder approval does not necessarily mean that the criteria for classification as held for sale are met only when shareholder approval is obtained. However, if substantive shareholder approval for a sale is required, then the sale might not be highly probable until shareholder approval is obtained as the need to obtain shareholder approval in such a situation may be considered a significant hurdle.

IFRS 5.8, 9, BI, IG5   5.4.30.87 The sale of significant non-current assets or disposal groups also may be subject to regulatory approval. Depending on particular circumstances, regulatory approval may be considered substantive, or in contrary, viewed as a formality. In our view, if considering all available evidence management concludes that the pending regulatory approval does not prevent the sale from being "highly probable", then it may not necessarily be a substantive hurdle preventing the classification of the non-current assets or disposal groups as held for sale.

IFRS 5.10   5.4.30.90 Exchanges of non-current assets are a sale for the purposes of classification of a non-current asset or disposal group as held for sale, provided that the expected exchange has commercial substance (see 5.7.20).

IFRS 5.13   5.4.30.100 Non-current assets that are to be abandoned or mothballed are not classified as held for sale as they will not be recovered principally through a sale transaction.

IFRS 5.12   5.4.30.110 See 5.4.20 for a discussion of the classification of a non-current asset or a disposal group acquired exclusively with a view to its subsequent disposal. For other non-current assets or disposal groups classification as held for sale is *prohibited* when the criteria are met only *after* the reporting date. Instead, disclosures are required in the notes to the financial statements.

IFRS 5.40   5.4.30.120 Statement of financial position comparatives are not re-presented to reflect the classification as held for sale at the current reporting date.

5.4.35 *Held for distribution*

IFRS 5.5A,   5.4.35.10 The classification as held for distribution is applicable to both consolidated
IFRIC 17.5   and separate financial statements. There are no exemptions from the classification as held for distribution when the criteria are met. For example, unlike the scope exemption of IFRIC 17 *Distribution of Non-cash Assets to Owners* in respect of the liability for the distribution, there is no exemption from the requirements of IFRS 5 for common control distributions.

5.4.37 *Classification*

IFRS 5.12A   5.4.37.10 A non-current asset or disposal group is classified as held for distribution when the entity is committed to distribute the asset or disposal group to its owners.

IFRS 5.7   5.4.37.20 This is the case when the asset is *available for immediate distribution* in its present condition and its distribution is *highly probable*, i.e. when it is significantly more likely than merely probable. The criteria relevant to whether a distribution is highly probable are similar to those for classification as held for sale (see 5.4.30).

IFRS 5.7,   5.4.37.30 An entity may be committed to a distribution even if there is a requirement
5.12A   for shareholder approval of the distribution. The probability of shareholder approval is considered as part of the assessment of whether the distribution is highly probable. Accordingly, in some cases an entity may be committed to distribute an asset and therefore being required to classify it as held for distribution before a liability is recognised for the distribution.

5.4.40 *Measurement**

IFRS 5.5A   5.4.40.10 The measurement requirements of IFRS 5 apply equally to non-current assets and the assets and liabilities in a disposal group that are held for sale or held for distribution.

5.4.50 *Before classification as held for sale or distribution*

IFRS 5.18   5.4.50.10 Before classification as held for sale or distribution, non-current assets and the assets and liabilities in a disposal group are measured in accordance with applicable IFRSs. For example, property, plant and equipment is tested for impairment. In our view, any resulting gains or losses are recognised in accordance with the relevant standards.

5.4.60 *On initial classification as held for sale or distribution*

IFRS 5.15, 5.4.60.10 On *initial classification* as held for sale or distribution, disposal groups and
15A non-current assets are measured at the lower of their:

- carrying amount; and
- fair value less costs to sell (or costs to distribute, as applicable).

IFRS 5A 5.4.60.20 Only incremental, directly attributable costs, excluding finance costs and income tax expense, are included in costs to sell or to distribute.

5.4.60.30 In our view, this principle applies to both external and internal costs. However, internal costs are less likely to be incremental.

IFRS 3.B45 5.4.60.35 In some cases, a disposal group may comprise the assets and liabilities of a subsidiary that is not wholly owned and the individual equity shares of that subsidiary may be quoted on an active market. In our view, in consolidated financial statements the unit of account is the controlled disposal group and it is appropriate to consider whether a control premium should be taken into account when estimating the fair value of that disposal group.

IFRS 5.20, 5.4.60.40 Impairment losses on initial classification of a non-current asset or disposal
IG10 group as held for sale are included in profit or loss even if the asset is or the disposal group includes assets that are measured at a revalued amount. The same applies to gains and losses on subsequent remeasurement (see 5.4.70).

IFRS 5.23 5.4.60.50 Losses on a disposal group are allocated to the non-current assets in the disposal group that are within the scope of the *measurement* requirements of IFRS 5 in the order of allocation required by IAS 36 *Impairment of Assets* (see 3.10). In the case of impairment losses, allocation would be first to goodwill and then to other assets on a *pro rata* basis.

5.4.60.60 For example, a disposal group contains assets and liabilities that are not within the measurement scope of IFRS 5 (excluded assets) with a net carrying amount measured on the basis of the relevant standards of 270 (see 5.4.50). The carrying amount of assets within the measurement scope of IFRS 5 is 900. The fair value less costs to sell of the disposal group as a whole is 1,000. A loss of 170 (1,000 compared with 1,170 (900 + 270)) is allocated to the assets within the measurement scope of IFRS 5 in the order of allocation required by IAS 36. The allocation is not restricted by the value in use or fair value less costs to sell of the individual assets as would be the case with an impairment loss recognised under IAS 36 (see 3.10.410).

IFRS 5.15, 5.4.60.62 The recognition and allocation of an impairment loss to the assets in a disposal
5.23 group may have a consequential effect on the temporary differences and therefore the

deferred taxes related to those assets. Assuming that the deferred tax is itself part of the disposal group, an iterative process will be required to determine the correct impairment loss.

5.4.60.63 For example, a disposal group comprises assets A and B. Asset A has a carrying amount of 2,667 and a tax base of 0; asset B has a carrying amount and a tax base of 400. The tax rate is 40 percent. Only asset A is within the measurement scope of IFRS 5. The disposal group therefore includes a deferred tax liability of 1,067 (2,667 x 40%). The fair value less costs to sell of the disposal group is 1,400. Ignoring the impact of changes in the deferred tax resulting from recording the impairment loss, the impairment loss is 600 ((2,667 + 400 - 1,067) - 1,400). However, in order to arrive at an overall carrying amount for the disposal group of 1,400, the impairment loss needs to be grossed up for the effect of tax; this results in an impairment loss of 1,000 (600 / 60%), and a revised deferred tax liability of 667 ((1,667 - 0) x 40%). The post-impairment carrying amount of the disposal group is 1,400 (1,667 + 400 - 667).

IFRS 5.23   5.4.60.65 In our view, if the fair value less costs to sell of a disposal group is below its carrying amount, but the carrying amount of assets within the measurement scope of IFRS 5 is insufficient to absorb the impairment loss, then the amount of the impairment loss recognised is limited to the carrying amount of assets within the disposal group to which the measurement requirements of IFRS 5 apply.

5.4.60.67 [Not used]

IFRS 5.25   5.4.60.70 A disposal group continues to be consolidated while held for sale or distribution. Accordingly, revenue (e.g. from the sale of inventory) and expenses (including interest) continue to be recognised. However, assets held for sale, including those within a disposal group, are not depreciated or amortised.

IFRS 5.38,   5.4.60.80 Foreign currency translation reserves in respect of a disposal group are trans-
BC58,   ferred to profit or loss when the disposal group is disposed of (see 2.7.320) and not when
IAS 21.48, 49   the disposal group is classified as held for sale or distribution.

5.4.70 On subsequent remeasurement

IFRS 5.15,   5.4.70.10 Subsequent to initial classification as held for sale, disposal groups and non-
20-23,   current assets that are measured at their fair value less costs to sell, are subject to a
IAS 36.122   limit on the amount of any gain that can be recognised as a result of an increase in fair value less costs to sell before disposal. The maximum increase (and therefore gain) that can be recognised is the cumulative amount of impairment losses recognised in accordance with IFRS 5 and previously in accordance with IAS 36. Impairment losses allocated to goodwill are included in determining the maximum increase, and the disposal group as a whole continues to be measured at the lower of its carrying amount and fair value less costs to sell. The reversal of the impairment loss should be allocated

to the assets in the disposal group that are subject to the measurement requirements of IFRS 5, except for goodwill, *pro rata* with the carrying amounts of those assets. In our view, reversals of impairment losses on subsequent remeasurement may result in individual assets in the disposal group being measured at amounts above their carrying amount if the non-current assets had not been classified as held for sale. However, the disposal group as a whole continues to be measured at the lower of its carrying amount and fair value less costs to sell. The allocation of gains and losses to individual assets will impact the amount of any temporary differences for deferred tax purposes (see 3.13, 5.4.60.62 and 63).

IFRS 5.19, 22(b) 5.4.70.15 Additional net assets that become part of a disposal group (e.g. due to profits being generated by the disposal group (see 5.4.60.70)) increase the carrying amount of the disposal group. For example, consider a disposal group that is held at 50, being its carrying amount at the date of classification as held for sale. There has not been an impairment previously for this disposal group. The disposal group recognises a profit of 10, together with an increase in debtors within the disposal group, between the date the disposal group was classified as held for sale and the next reporting date. In our view, at the reporting date the carrying amount would be 60 because there has been a change in the assets and liabilities in the disposal group. Also, in our view in such circumstances the recognition of the profit is not restricted by the absence of a cumulative impairment loss that can be reversed. The disposal group is then measured at the lower of the new carrying amount and its fair value less cost to sell.

IFRS 5.19 5.4.70.20 On subsequent remeasurement of a disposal group, the carrying amount of any assets and liabilities excluded from the measurement requirements of IFRS 5 are remeasured in accordance with other applicable IFRSs. In our view, any gains and losses on this remeasurement are recognised in accordance with the relevant standards.

IFRS 5.37 5.4.70.30 Gains and losses on subsequent remeasurement to fair value less costs to sell are included in profit or loss regardless of whether the asset was, or the disposal group includes assets that were, measured previously based on revalued amounts.

IFRS 5.23 5.4.70.40 Gains and losses from the remeasurement of a disposal group are allocated to the non-current assets in that group that are within the scope of the *measurement* require-ments of IFRS 5 in the order of allocation required by IAS 36 (in the case of losses, first to goodwill and then to other assets on a *pro rata* basis).

IFRS 5.29 5.4.70.50 A disposal group continues to be classified as held for sale even when part of the group (e.g. inventory) is sold separately, as long as the remaining items in the group continue to meet the criteria.

5.4.80 On disposal

IFRS 5.24 5.4.80.10 Any gain or loss not recognised prior to the date of sale is recognised on the derecognition of the non-current asset or disposal group.

IFRIC 17.14   5.4.80.20 In respect of a distribution, any gain or loss will be recognised at the date of settlement of the dividend. The amount recognised in profit or loss will be the difference between the carrying amount of the liability for the dividend payable and the carrying amount of the non-current asset or disposal group.

5.4.80.30 The derecognition of certain assets and liabilities may also result in the reclassification to profit or loss of amounts previously recognised in other comprehensive income, for example, the cumulative amount of exchange differences related to a foreign operation (see 5.4.60.80).

5.4.90 *Reclassification as held for use*

IFRS 5.26   5.4.90.10 Non-current assets and disposal groups are reclassified from held for sale or from held for distribution to held for use if they no longer meet the criteria to be classified as held for sale or distribution.

IFRS 5.27   5.4.90.20 Upon reclassification as held for use, a non-current asset is remeasured at the lower of its recoverable amount and the carrying amount that would have been recognised had the asset never been classified as held for sale or distribution. The calculation of this carrying amount should include any depreciation that would have been recognised had the asset not been classified as held for sale or distribution.

IFRS 5.27,   5.4.90.30 Normally, reversals of impairments of goodwill are prohibited. In our view,
IAS 36.124   reclassification as held for use and the requirement to remeasure upon reclassification may create one of the rare circumstances when reversals of goodwill impairment are recognised. This may occur if the recoverable amount of goodwill exceeds its carrying amount as a result of impairment losses recognised in respect of the held for sale disposal group that were allocated to goodwill.

IFRS 5.28   5.4.90.40 Any resulting adjustment is recognised in profit or loss unless the asset was measured at a revalued amount prior to its classification as held for sale or distribution. In these cases the adjustment is recognised, in whole or in part, as a revaluation increase or decrease (see 3.2.300 and 3.3.280).

5.4.100 *Associates and jointly controlled entities*

IAS 28.15,   5.4.100.10 When an interest in an associate or a jointly controlled entity classified as
31.43   held for sale is reclassified as held for use, the equity method or proportionate consolidation is applied retrospectively from the date of its classification as held for sale. Financial statements for earlier periods that classify the investment as held for sale are amended accordingly. In our view, this amendment is made in the financial statements of the reporting period in which the change of classification occurs. To the extent that the amendment relates to earlier periods, it is recognised as a prior period adjustment (i.e. the amendment is calculated retrospectively) and the opening balance of retained earnings and comparatives are restated (see 2.8).

5.4.110 *Presentation*

IFRS 5.38 5.4.110.10 Non-current assets and the assets of a disposal group classified as held for sale or distribution are presented separately from other assets in the statement of financial position.

IFRS 5.38 5.4.110.20 The liabilities of a disposal group classified as held for sale or distribution are presented separately from other liabilities in the statement of financial position.

IAS 27.33 5.4.110.25 IFRSs do not address specifically the presentation of non-controlling interests in a disposal group classified as held for sale or distribution. In our view, non-controlling interests in a disposal group classified as held for sale or distribution continue to be presented within equity consistent with the requirement in IAS 27 *Consolidated and Separate Financial Statements* and are not reclassified as a liability (see 2.5.335.30).

IAS 1.66 5.4.110.30 In our view, non-current assets, assets of disposal groups and liabilities of disposal groups classified as held for sale or distribution are classified as current in the statement of financial position as they are expected to be realised within 12 months of the date of classification as held for sale or distribution. Consequently presentation of a "three column statement of financial position" with the headings of "Assets/Liabilities not for sale", "Assets/Liabilities held for sale" and "Total" generally would not be appropriate if the assets and liabilities held for sale or distribution continue to be included in non-current line items.

IFRS 5.5B, 5.4.110.35 The disclosure requirements of IFRS 5 apply to non-current assets or disposal
IAS 33.68 groups classified as held for sale. Disclosures required by other IFRSs apply only when the requirements refer specifically to non-current assets (or disposal groups) classified as held for sale; for example, the disclosure of earnings per share for a discontinued operation. Disclosures required by other IFRSs also apply where they relate to assets and liabilities in a disposal group that are not within the measurement scope of IFRS 5 (e.g. investment property measured at fair value) and such disclosures are not already provided in the other notes to the financial statements (see 5.4.20). Additional disclosures may be necessary to comply with the general requirements of IAS 1 *Presentation of Financial Statements*, in particular for a fair presentation and in respect of sources of estimation uncertainty.

5.4.120 **Discontinued operations***

5.4.130 *Classification*

IFRS 5.32 5.4.130.10 The presentation of an operation as a discontinued operation is limited to a component of an entity that either has been disposed of, or is classified as held for sale, and:

- represents a separate major line of business or geographical area of operations;
- is part of a co-ordinated single plan to dispose of a separate major line of business or geographical area of operations; or

- is a subsidiary acquired exclusively with a view to resale.

IFRS 5.31 5.4.130.20 A component of an entity comprises operations and cash flows that can be distinguished clearly, both operationally and for financial reporting purposes, from the rest of the entity. A component that previously was held for use will have been one or more cash-generating units (see 3.10.60). In our view, the disposal of a business that previously was part of an entity considered to be a single cash-generating unit does not qualify as a component of an entity, and therefore is not classified as a discontinued operation if disposed of.

5.4.130.25 It is possible for a component of an entity to be a separate major line of business or geographical area of operations with respect to a subsidiary's but not the parent's operations. In that case the presentation in the subsidiary's financial statements may differ from the presentation in the parent's consolidated financial statements. For example, Subsidiary S cultivates pine trees and produces paper products in New Zealand. S disposes of all of its paper producing facilities. Parent P has other subsidiaries producing paper in New Zealand. As the disposed business is a component of S that represents a separate major line of business, the disposal is presented as a discontinued operation in S's financial statements, but not in P's consolidated financial statements.

IAS 27.4 5.4.130.30 A subsidiary is an entity (including an unincorporated entity) that is controlled, and does not need to be a legal entity. In our view, a division may meet these criteria in some circumstances.

5.4.130.40 It is not clear whether a business that will be disposed of by distribution to owners could be classified as a discontinued operation prior to its disposal. Although IFRS 5 was amended to extend the requirements in respect of non-current assets or disposal groups held for sale to such items held for distribution to owners, the cross-referencing in the amendments does not extend to discontinued operations. In our view, although the definition of a discontinued operation has not been extended explicitly, classification of non-current assets or disposal groups held for distribution to owners as a discontinued operation is appropriate if the remaining criteria of IFRS 5 are met.

5.4.140 *Part of a single plan*

5.4.140.10 An entity needs to have a single overall plan under which all or substantially all of a qualifying component of its operations is discontinued. Under the plan, the component may be disposed of in its entirety or by selling the assets and liabilities on a piecemeal basis.

5.4.140.20 For example, during June 2010 Company D disposed of some of the manufacturing facilities within its kitchen segment. In the following year, other facilities within the segment were disposed of and the remaining operations combined with another business within D. None of the disposals met the criteria separately to be a discontinued operation. While different parts of the kitchen segment were disposed of on a piecemeal basis, in this case there was no single plan to dispose of the segment. Therefore, in our view D's kitchen segment is not a discontinued operation.

5.4.150 *Operating segment that is a separate major line of business or geographical area**

5.4.150.10 In our view, an operating segment (see 5.2.50) normally would represent a separate major line of business or geographical area of operation.

5.4.150.20 For example, Company E has five different operating segments, one of which solely produces cigars. All of the cigar growing and production facilities are situated in Central America. E also has other operations in Central America for other operating segments. In April 2010 E disposed of the cigar segment. In our view, the cigar segment meets the definition of a component of a business and represents a separate major line of business and would qualify for reporting as a discontinued operation.

5.4.160 *Discontinuance of products*

5.4.160.10 Abandoning or discontinuing products in a product line or replacing them with newer products is a part of the normal evolution of a business, and in our view does not constitute a discontinued operation. For example, Company Q has four segments: ice cream, chocolate, beverages and snack foods. Q has discontinued producing some of the chocolate bars containing nuts and instead has decided to add chocolate bars containing fruit to its product range.

5.4.160.20 In our view, ceasing to produce chocolate bars with nuts does not constitute a discontinued operation. Even though there may have been a single plan to cease the production of nut chocolate bars, the nut chocolate bars do not represent a separate major line of business.

5.4.160.30 In our view, the sale of a brand also will not meet the definition of a discontinued operation, unless it represents a separate major line of business of the entity.

5.4.170 *Closure of a facility*

5.4.170.10 Closure of facilities due to productivity or other cost reasons often is a part of the general development within a business and does not necessarily meet the definition of a discontinued operation. For example, Company C has closed one of its seven facilities in North America as it is cheaper to manufacture its products in South East Asia. The facilities are included in the clothing segment together with other facilities in North America, South East Asia and Eastern Europe.

5.4.170.20 In our view, even if the closure of the facility is subject to a single plan, this transaction does not meet the definition of a discontinued operation as the same component of the business will continue to operate using different facilities. However, the closure may require the recognition of impairment charges and provisions triggered by the restructuring (see 3.10.110 and 3.12.230). Further recognition and measurement implications arise if the non-current assets used in this facility meet the definition of held for sale (see 5.4.20) or distribution (see 5.4.35).

5.4.180 *Disposal of a subsidiary**

5.4.180.10 In our view, evaluation of whether an operation is a separate major line of business is based on the nature and organisation of the entity's operations, and does not require alignment with legal entities within the organisation.

5.4.180.20 A subsidiary acquired exclusively for resale may be a discontinued operation (see 5.4.240).

5.4.180.30 In the case of an existing subsidiary, its sale or disposal is not automatically a discontinued operation if that subsidiary is not, on its own, a separate major line of business or geographical area of operation.

5.4.180.40 For example, Company B sells baby clothes, sport clothes, toys and gardening equipment and reports each product group as a separate segment. In July 2010 B disposed of Boom, a significant subsidiary included in the toy segment. B retains other operations in the toy segment.

5.4.180.50 In our view, even though the disposal of Boom may be significant for B, is subject to a single plan, and can be distinguished operationally and for financial reporting purposes, the disposal of Boom should not be classified as a discontinued operation. This is because there are other operations within the same segment producing toys, and therefore Boom on its own does not represent a separate major line of business or geographical area of B.

IAS 1.86 5.4.180.60 However, as the disposal of Boom is significant, the impact of the disposal may require separate disclosure.

5.4.190 *Venture capital investors*

5.4.190.10 Venture capital investors often acquire interests in a variety of businesses. Investments may be held for three to five years and then sold. Venture capital investors are required to consolidate entities that they control (see 2.5.280). Typically, when a new investment is proposed, a key feature of the proposal is the exit strategy. The disposal phase of an investment may be carried out in such a way that it may meet the definition of a discontinued operation.

5.4.190.20 In our view, if the investments to be sold in a particular year are a separate major line of business or geographical area of operations and the disposal is pursuant to a single plan, then the entity should present the disposal as a discontinued operation.

5.4.190.30 However, in our view the component is unlikely to be a discontinued operation from its acquisition date, as the disposal groups are unlikely to be held for sale at the acquisition date (see 5.4.240).

5.4.200 *Timing*

IFRS 5.13, 32   5.4.200.10 Classification as a discontinued operation occurs at the date when an operation meets the criteria to be classified as held for sale, when a group of assets is ceased to be used or when an entity has disposed of an operation.

IFRS 5.6-8,   5.4.200.20 In our view, an operation that will be disposed of by distribution to owners 12A, 32   (e.g. a dividend *in specie* or a spin-off transaction) will not be classified as held for sale as no sale will occur but will instead be classified as held for distribution when it meets the relevant criteria. An operation that meets the criteria to be classified as a discontinued operation that is to be distributed to owners will be classified as discontinued at latest when the distribution occurs.

IFRS 5.34   5.4.200.30 The comparative statement of comprehensive income and cash flow information is re-presented each period on the basis of the classification of operations as discontinued or continuing operations at the current reporting date.

5.4.210 *Measurement*

5.4.210.10 There are no recognition or measurement impacts from classifying an operation as discontinued. However, a discontinued operation generally will include non-current assets held for sale or a disposal group or groups. Therefore the measurement requirements for discontinued operations are those of the individual assets and liabilities or disposal groups that comprise the operation (see 5.4.40).

5.4.210.20 An entity continues to recognise ongoing operating profits and losses from discontinued operations as they are incurred. The general prohibition on the accrual of future operating losses also continues to apply (see 3.12.40.20).

5.4.210.30 When a discontinued operation is disposed of, any profit or loss on the sale is recognised in the period that the sale is recognised.

5.4.220 *Presentation**

IFRS 5.33,   5.4.220.10 The results of discontinued operations are presented separately from continu-
33A,   ing operations in the statement of comprehensive income. Amounts included within
IAS 27.34   profit or loss from discontinued operations are presented separately from other comprehensive income from discontinued operations. In our view, the results of the discontinued operations are not presented net of non-controlling interest because non-controlling interest is not an item of income or expense (see 2.5.335.30). An analysis of this single amount is presented either in the statement of comprehensive income or in the notes to the financial statements.

1322

5.4.220.11 When presenting discontinued operations it may be necessary to reconsider the allocation of revenue or expenses to a segment that is classified as a discontinued operation. In our view, revenue and expenses should not be presented as discontinued unless they will cease to be earned/incurred upon disposal of the discontinued operation. For example, general corporate overhead expenses would not be allocated to a discontinued operation.

5.4.220.12 In some cases there may be transactions between the continuing and discontinued operations, for example, intra-segment sales and purchases. If the transactions between the continuing and discontinued operations are expected to continue after the operations are disposed of, then in our view the presentation of the discontinued operation should reflect the continuance of the relationship as such information enables users of the financial statements to evaluate the financial effects of the discontinued operations.

5.4.220.13 [Not used]

5.4.220.14 For example, Segment G sells a product to Segment B for 10. B sells the product to external customers for 12. The sales, cost of sales and gross margins of G and B are as follows:

Segment	G	B
Sales	10	12
Cost of sales	(6)	(10)
Gross margin	4	2

5.4.220.15 The transfer price between the two segments is on an arm's length basis. Assume that B does not hold any of this inventory at the start or end of the reporting period. B will be discontinued and meets the definition of a discontinued operation, but it is expected that the supply relationship between the segments will continue after the disposal.

5.4.220.16 In our view, if the profit or loss from discontinued operations of B are presented as a single line item in the statement of comprehensive income (i.e. with the supporting disclosures in the notes to the financial statements (see 5.4.220.10)), then the entity should present the statement of comprehensive income by eliminating the sales and cost of sales in B. In our view, this presentation also is appropriate for the disclosures in the notes to the financial statements. The entity should include the gross margin obtained by B from the sales to external customers in discontinued operations since this gross margin will be discontinued after the disposal. The sales and cost of sales in G related to the discontinued B should be retained and shown as part of continuing operations since the supply relationship with B will continue after the disposal.

5.4.220.17 In the example in 5.4.220.14, the entity will show continuing revenues of 10, continuing cost of sales of 6 and discontinued operations as a single amount in the statement of comprehensive income that includes the discontinued gross margin of 2. This allocation of revenue and expenses has the advantage of presenting the appropriate gross margin for the discontinued operations and also the appropriate revenue and expenses for the continuing operations.

5.4.220.20 While IFRS 5 is clear that the results of discontinued operations are presented separately from continuing operations in the statement of comprehensive income as a single amount of profit or loss, it is unclear in the standard how the statement of comprehensive income presentation requirements of IFRS 5 interact with those of IAS 1 *Presentation of Financial Statements*, specifically whether amounts (e.g. of revenue, expenses) related to a discontinued operation are permitted or required to be excluded from the total of these line items presented in the statement of comprehensive income.

IFRS 5.IE11 5.4.220.30 In our view, this single amount of profit or loss for discontinued operations can be presented in different ways. An entity should choose a presentation format, to be applied consistently, to present the profit or loss for discontinued operations. We prefer to include amounts related to discontinued operations only in the single amount of profit or loss for discontinued operations, excluding amounts related to discontinued operations from all other amounts presented before that line. Alternatively, we believe that presenting the total of continuing plus discontinued for each line item also is acceptable in some instances, for example, when a columnar approach is used to present the analysis of continuing and discontinued operations in the statement of comprehensive income. However, when such a presentation is used, the "continuing" amount should be presented separately for each line item.

IFRS 5.33 5.4.220.40 Furthermore, it is not clear in the standard how the cash flow presentation requirements of IFRS 5 interact with those of IAS 7 *Statement of Cash Flows*. IAS 7 requires a statement of cash flows to include all cash flows, therefore including both those from continuing and those from discontinued operations. Consequently, cash and cash equivalents include amounts included in disposal groups classified as held for sale. IAS 7 also requires an analysis of cash flows classified into operating, investing and financing activities, and further analysis of the gross cash flows included in these activities (see 2.3.20). However, IFRS 5 requires presentation of the net cash flows attributable to operating, investing and financing activities of discontinued operations to be presented either in the statement of cash flows or in the notes. In our view, there are numerous ways in which these requirements may be met, including:

- Presenting the statement of cash flows split between continuing and discontinued cash flows with a total of the cash flows. The discontinued cash flows are analysed by operating, investing and financing activities and further analysis of these amounts is presented in the statement of cash flows or disclosed in the notes. This could be done through a columnar presentation showing continuing and discontinued operations with a total of the cash flows.
- Presenting a statement of cash flows that includes an analysis of all cash flows in total (i.e. including both continuing and discontinued operations). Amounts related

to discontinued operations by operating, investing and financing activities are disclosed in the notes. This presentation is illustrated in KPMG's series of illustrative financial statements.

IFRS 5.33   5.4.220.50 The analysis of the result presented in the statement of comprehensive income result and cash flow information is not required for a disposal group that is a newly acquired subsidiary that is classified as held for sale upon acquisition.

IFRS 5.34   5.4.220.60 The comparative statement of comprehensive income and cash flow information is re-presented each period so that comparative information given in respect of discontinued operations includes all operations classified as discontinued at the current reporting date.

5.4.220.70 For example, if Segment D is classified as discontinued in 2010, then the 2009 comparatives are re-presented for the statement of comprehensive income and cash flow information in respect of D as discontinued.

IAS 1.81,   5.4.220.80 The investor's share of the discontinued operations of an associate is presented
28.38   as part of the share of profit or loss of associates and also is disclosed separately. In our view, such amounts are not presented as part of the discontinued operations of the entity, unless they are discontinued operations of that entity itself.

5.4.220.90 In our view, when a disposal or abandonment does not meet the definition of a discontinued operation, an entity still may present additional information about the disposal (i.e. similar information to that required by IFRS 5), but the term "discontinued operation" cannot be used. The amounts are presented in the appropriate line items within continuing operations. Such transactions often will meet the definition of a restructuring, and disclosure about provisions and contingent liabilities also may be required (see 3.12.770 and 3.14.50).

IFRS 5.5B,   5.4.220.100 The disclosure requirements of IFRS 5 apply to non-current assets or
IAS 33.68   disposal groups classified as discontinued operations. Disclosures required by other IFRSs apply when they refer specifically to non-current assets or disposal groups classified as discontinued operations; for example the disclosure of earnings per share for a discontinued operation. Disclosures required by other IFRSs also apply where they relate to assets and liabilities in a disposal group that are not within the measurement scope of IFRS 5 (e.g. investment property measured at fair value) and such disclosures are not already provided in the other notes to the financial statements. Additional disclosures may be necessary to comply with the general requirements of IAS 1, in particular for a fair presentation and in respect of sources of estimation uncertainty.

5.4.230 *Reclassification as continuing*

IFRS 5.36   5.4.230.10 If the component ceases to be classified as held for sale (see 5.4.90), then the related operations are reclassified as continuing. The operations are presented as continuing in the current period and prior periods are re-presented consistently.

5.4.240 **Acquired exclusively with a view to resale**

IFRS 5.11,
BC72

5.4.240.10 A non-current asset or a disposal group acquired exclusively with a view to its subsequent disposal is classified as held for sale if it meets the held-for-sale criteria or if it is "highly probable" that it will meet those criteria within a short period after acquisition (usually three months). In our view, any non-current asset or a disposal group that satisfies the criteria to be classified as held for sale at the date of its acquisition may be assumed to have been acquired exclusively with a view to its subsequent disposal.

IFRS 5.16

5.4.240.20 A non-current asset or a disposal group acquired exclusively with a view to its subsequent disposal is measured on initial recognition at the lower of:

- carrying amount had the asset or disposal group not been classified by the buyer as held for sale (e.g. cost); and
- fair value less costs to sell.

5.4.250 *Subsidiaries**

IAS 27.13

5.4.250.10 Subsidiaries are consolidated even if they are held exclusively with a view to subsequent disposal and classified as held for sale.

IFRS 3.36,
5.33(b),
IAS 39.IG13

5.4.250.20 Consolidation requires the application of acquisition accounting, including an acquisition-date fair value exercise (see 2.6.260, 600 and 1050). Disclosure exemptions for disposal groups that are newly acquired subsidiaries and are classified as held for sale may simplify the application of these requirements. These exemptions allow certain analyses of statement of comprehensive income and statement of financial position amounts to be omitted, reducing the need to determine the acquisition date fair values of individual assets and liabilities. However, the acquisition-date fair value of certain non-current assets and liabilities outside the measurement scope of IFRS 5 still may have to be determined (e.g. a financial asset that is measured at fair value with changes recognised in other comprehensive income, and defined benefit post-employment benefits).

5.4.260 *Associates and jointly controlled entities*

IFRS 5.11,
IAS 28.13(a),
14, 31.42

5.4.260.10 An investment in an associate or jointly controlled entity is classified as held for sale on acquisition if the classification criteria are met. It is not equity accounted or proportionately consolidated.

5.4.270 **Future developments**

5.4.270.10 The overall objective of the comprehensive financial statement presentation project is to establish a global standard that prescribes the basis for presentation of financial statements of an entity that are consistent over time, and that promote comparability between entities. The financial statement presentation project is conducted in three phases:

- Phase A was completed in September 2007 with the release of a revised IAS 1;
- Phase B is in progress and addresses the more fundamental issues related to financial statement presentation; and
- Phase C has not been initiated, but is expected to address issues related to interim financial statements.

5.4.270.20 In July 2010 the IASB posted a staff draft of a proposed ED reflecting tentative decisions made to date in respect of phase B to obtain further stakeholder feedback. An ED is scheduled for the first quarter of 2011.

5.4.270.30 In October 2008 the IASB issued an ED *Discontinued Operations – Proposed Amendments to IFRS 5* which contained a new definition of discontinued operations. In considering the responses to the ED, the IASB and FASB decided to adopt a common definition of a discontinued operation based on the current definition in IFRS 5, and decided to re-expose their proposals, including related disclosures, for public comment. In May 2010, the IASB and FASB decided to align the project timetable with the main financial statement presentation project (see 5.4.270.10 and 20). An ED is scheduled for the first quarter of 2011.

5.4.270.40 In May 2009 the IASB published ED/2009/5 *Fair Value Measurement* (the 2009 ED). The proposals in the 2009 ED are intended to replace the fair value measurement guidance contained in individual IFRSs with a single, unified definition of fair value, as well as provide further authoritative guidance on the application of fair value measurement in inactive markets. The 2009 ED proposes a framework for measuring fair value and disclosures about fair value measurements. The proposals in the 2009 ED explain how to measure fair value when it already is required or permitted by existing IFRSs; they do not introduce new fair value measurements, nor do they eliminate the practicability exceptions to fair value measurements that exist currently in certain standards.

5.4.270.50 In June 2010 the IASB published ED/2010/7 *Measurement Uncertainty Analysis Disclosure for Fair Value Measurements* (the 2010 ED). The 2010 ED expands on the proposal in the 2009 ED for an entity to disclose a measurement uncertainty analysis (or sensitivity analysis) for assets and liabilities measured at fair value categorised within Level 3 of the fair value hierarchy. The 2010 ED proposes that an entity consider the effect of correlation between unobservable inputs, if relevant.

5.4.270.60 A final standard on fair value measurement and disclosure, which is expected to be converged with a forthcoming amended standard under US GAAP, is scheduled for the first quarter of 2011.

5.5 Related party disclosures
(IAS 24)

5.5 Related party disclosures
(IAS 24)

Overview of currently effective requirements

- **Related party relationships are those involving control (direct or indirect), joint control or significant influence.**

- **Key management and their close family members are parties related to an entity.**

- **There are no special recognition or measurement requirements for related party transactions.**

- **The disclosure of related party relationships between a parent and its subsidiaries is required, even if there have been no transactions between them.**

- **No disclosure is required in the consolidated financial statements of intra-group transactions eliminated in preparing those statements.**

- **Comprehensive disclosures of related party transactions are required for each category of related party relationship.**

Currently effective requirements

This publication reflects IFRSs in issue at 1 August 2010. The currently effective requirements cover annual periods beginning on 1 January 2010. The requirements related to this topic are derived mainly from IAS 24 *Related Party Disclosures*.

Forthcoming requirements and future developments

When a currently effective requirement will be changed by a new requirement that is issued but is not yet effective, it is marked with a # as a forthcoming requirement and the impact of the change is explained in the accompanying boxed text. The forthcoming requirements related to this chapter are derived from the revised version of IAS 24 *Related Party Disclosures* (2009), which is effective for annual periods beginning on or after 1 January 2011 (see 5.5A).

When a significant change to the currently effective or forthcoming requirements is expected, it is marked with a * as an area that may be subject to **future developments**. In respect of this topic no future developments are noted.

5.5.10 **Scope#**

IAS 24.3   5.5.10.10 Related party disclosure requirements apply to all entities, including parent entities, investors and joint venturers, in their consolidated, separate and individual financial statements (see 2.1.50, 60 and 70). There are no exemptions from the disclosure of intra-group transactions in the separate financial statements of a parent or of its subsidiaries.

5.5.10.20 A state-controlled entity that applies IFRSs is not exempt from providing related party disclosures. Therefore, a state-controlled entity discloses, as related party transactions, its transactions with the state and also with other state-controlled entities, as the parties are under common control and therefore meet the definition of related parties (see 5.5.70 and 130).

5.5.10.30 Local rules and regulations often require an entity to provide certain related party information, for example, directors' individual remuneration or golden parachute agreements. Specific legal requirements may supplement but cannot waive any requirement to provide related party disclosures under IFRSs (see 5.5.80.10).

5.5.15 *Forthcoming requirements*

5.5.15.10 Instead of a state-controlled entity, IAS 24 (2009) uses the term "government-related entities" and modifies the related party disclosure requirements for government-related entities (see 5.5A.10).

5.5.20 **Recognition and measurement**

5.5.20.10 IAS 24 does not establish any recognition or measurement requirements for related party transactions. Related party transactions are accounted for in accordance with the requirements of relevant IFRSs. For example, in an entity's separate financial statements, loans to other group entities are recognised and measured in accordance with IAS 39 *Financial Instruments: Recognition and Measurement* (see 3.6), and the disclosures required for financial instruments (see 5.6) are provided in addition to those required for related party transactions.

IFRS 2.3,   5.5.20.20 Other IFRSs may require attribution of cost. For example, if a parent transfers
IFRIC 11.8   its equity instruments directly to employees of a subsidiary as compensation for services provided to the subsidiary, then IFRS 2 *Share-based Payment* requires recognition of the share-based payment compensation at the subsidiary level (see 4.5.820).

IAS 24.10   5.5.20.30 Consistent with the identification of related party relationships, in our view the accounting for related party transactions should take into account their substance in addition to their legal form. For example, when a shareholder forgives a loan to the entity, in most cases this would be accounted for as a capital contribution to the entity and not as a gain on extinguishment of a liability (see 3.11.230).

5.5.30 **Identification of related parties#**

IAS 24.9 5.5.30.10 The definition of related parties includes relationships involving direct and indirect control, including common control, joint control and significant influence.

5.5.30.20 The definition is not restricted to entities; it also includes individuals, key management personnel and post-employment benefit plans. For example, entities that are under the common control of the same non-corporate shareholder, (e.g. an individual, a group of individuals acting together or a trust), are related parties, even if the shareholder does not prepare consolidated financial statements.

IAS 24.9 5.5.30.30 The definition of related parties also includes close members of the family of an individual who is a related party. Close family members are those who may be expected to influence, or be influenced by, the individual in their dealings with the entity. They may include an individual's children or domestic partner, children of the individual's domestic partner, and dependants of the individual or the individual's domestic partner. In our view, it is difficult to rebut the presumption that children of the individual are related parties, as they generally are expected to influence, or be influenced by, the individual.

5.5.30.40 Examples of some related party relationships are illustrated below:

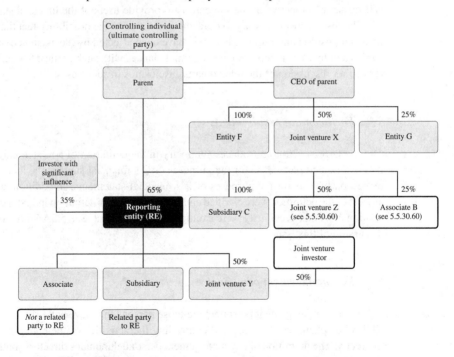

5.5.30.50 [Not used]

IAS 24.9 5.5.30.60 The definition of a related party does not include an entity that is a joint venture or an associate of the parent or ultimate parent of the reporting entity (i.e. Joint venture

Z and Associate B in the diagram in 5.5.30.40). However, an entity that is an associate or joint venture of key management of the parent or ultimate parent is a related party under IFRSs. Therefore, in our view joint ventures and associates of the parent or ultimate parent should be treated as related parties, unless it is clear that the relationship has no current or potential impact on the entity's operations or results.

5.5.30.70 For example, when the parent in the diagram in 5.5.30.40 has the ability to influence decisions and therefore the pricing of transactions between the reporting entity and B, we believe that disclosure of those transactions as related party transactions should be provided.

5.5.30.80 Although a branch is not defined formally in IFRSs, generally it is understood to be an extension of an entity's activities. In our view, if a branch of an entity prepares separate financial statements, then it should disclose related party transactions and relationships, including those with its head office.

IAS 24.1 5.5.30.90 An entity or an individual may become, or cease to be, a related party during the period covered by the financial statements. In our view, the determination of whether an entity or an individual is a related party should be made considering their relationship during the reporting period and not just the relationship at the reporting date. This is because the objective of the standard is to provide users of the financial statements with the disclosures necessary to draw their attention to the possibility that the entity's financial position and profit or loss may have been affected by the existence of related parties and by transactions and outstanding balances with such parties. See 5.5.100.30 for further discussion of the related party disclosures in such cases.

5.5.35 *Forthcoming requirements*

5.5.35.10 IAS 24 (2009) introduces symmetry in the definition of a related party, i.e. if B is a related party of C for the purposes of C's financial statements, then C is a related party of B for the purposes of B's financial statements. In addition, certain aspects of the definition were clarified and therefore the new definition includes certain relationships that previously were excluded and vice versa. See 5.5A.30 for further discussion of this issue.

5.5.40 *Key management personnel*

IAS 24.9 5.5.40.10 Key management personnel are those persons that have authority and responsibility for planning, directing and controlling the activities of the entity, directly or indirectly. The definition of key management personnel includes directors (both executive and non-executive) of an entity. In our view, the term also includes directors of any of the entity's parents to the extent that they have authority and responsibility for planning, directing and controlling the activities of the entity. In our view, an entity's parent includes the immediate, intermediate or ultimate parent.

5.5.40.15 In our view, an individual may be key management personnel of an entity even if that entity does not pay for the services received. For example, a director of Parent B that also acts as a director of Subsidiary C is key management personnel of C, regardless of whether C reimburses B for the services received.

5.5.40.20 In practice, an entity may have more than one level of management. For example, there may be a supervisory board whose members have responsibilities similar to those of non-executive directors, a board of directors that sets the overall strategy under which an entity operates, and a management team that implements those strategies within the authority delegated to it by the board. In many cases any member of either board, including non-executive directors, will be considered to be key management.

IAS 24.9 5.5.40.30 However, key management is not limited to directors; in our view other members of the management team also may be key management. We believe that an individual with significant authority and responsibility for planning, directing and controlling the activities of the entity should be considered to be key management personnel.

5.5.40.33 The role of key management personnel of a group of entities is performed by those who assume the authority and responsibility for planning, directing and controlling the activities of each separate entity in the group. Therefore, in our view in the consolidated financial statements of a group, key management personnel is not limited to the key management personnel of the parent entity, but may include key management personnel of entities of the group, such as of subsidiaries.

IAS 24.9(f) 5.5.40.35 In our view, the definition of key management personnel in IAS 24 specifies a *role*. In our experience, the authority and responsibility for planning, directing and controlling the activities of an entity in some cases is assigned to an entity rather than an individual. For example, a bank might act as an investment manager for an investment fund and in doing so assume the roles and responsibilities of key management personnel. In our view, key management personnel is not limited to individuals, and therefore an entity that assumes the role of key management personnel should be considered a related party of the reporting entity. However, from the perspective of the entity that assumes the role of key management personnel, that relationship does not in itself cause the entity under its management to be a related party. Therefore, unless the managed entity is a related party of the managing entity for another reason (e.g. because of a parent/subsidiary relationship), an entity assuming the role of key management personnel is in our view not required to provide related party disclosures in respect of parties for which it is acting as key management personnel.

IAS 24.9(f) 5.5.40.40 Entities under control, joint control or significant influence of key management personnel (or their close family members) also are related parties of the entity. For example, Mrs Z is a director of Company G and considered to be key management personnel of G. Mrs Z has joint control over Joint Venture H and therefore H is considered to be a related party of G. This also would be the case if a close family member of Mrs Z had joint control over H.

5.5 Related party disclosures

IAS 24.11 5.5.40.50 However, two entities are not related parties simply because they have a director, or other member of key management, in common. In the example in 5.5.40.40, if Mrs Z was a director of H, but as an individual did not have joint control or significant influence over H, then G and H would not be related parties solely because Mrs Z is a director of both.

5.5.50 *Post-employment benefit plans#*

IAS 24.9 5.5.50.10 Related parties include post-employment benefit plans that benefit an entity's employees or the employees of any entity that is a related party of the entity. For example, Company B has significant influence over Company C. B and C each have a pension plan for the benefit of their respective employees. In addition, C transacts with B's pension plan in the ordinary course of business. In this example both pension plans are related parties of C and accordingly, C discloses transactions with:

- Its own pension plan because it provides benefits to its employees; and
- B's pension plan because it provides benefits to the employees of a related party (being B).

IAS 24.9(g) 5.5.50.15 It is not clear whether a multi-employer plan that also benefits employees of unrelated parties should be included in the definition of a related party. The only condition in IAS 24 for the post-employment benefit plan to be regarded as a related party of the entity is that it benefits the employees of the entity, or of any entity that is a related party of the entity. It does not require a specific level of influence or control. Therefore, in our view a multi-employer plan of which a reporting entity is one of the sponsoring entities is related to the reporting entity even in cases when the reporting entity does not have significant influence or control over the multi-employer plan.

5.5.50.20 In certain jurisdictions the trustees of post-employment benefit plans are entirely separate from the sponsoring entity. In our view, these plans are related parties of the sponsoring entity.

5.5.51 *Forthcoming requirements*

5.5.51.10 Consistent with the previous definition of a related party, the revised definition of a related party includes post-employment benefit plans for the benefit of employees of either the reporting entity or an entity related to the reporting entity. Therefore any changes to an entity's list of related parties as a result of the application of IAS 24 (2009), would require a consequential reassessment of the post-employment benefit plans that may be related parties of the entity. The revised definition specifically includes the sponsoring employers of a post-employment benefit plan (see 5.5A.50.15).

5.5.60 *Economic dependence*

IAS 24.11 5.5.60.10 An entity may be dependent, economically or operationally, on another party, e.g. a major customer or supplier. This dependency does not itself create a related party relationship. However, additional information about these relationships and transactions may be relevant to the reader of the financial statements.

IAS 24.11 5.5.60.20 Providers of finance and similar entities are not related parties by virtue of their normal dealings with an entity, even though these parties may limit the actions of an entity or participate in its decision-making process. However, transactions in the ordinary course of business between related parties are disclosed. For example, a banking entity would be required to disclose transactions with its finance provider that is part of the same banking group even if these services are provided on the same terms as to unrelated customers.

5.5.70 *State-controlled entities#*

5.5.70.10 For entities operating in an environment in which state control is pervasive, many counterparties also are state-controlled, and therefore are related parties. For example, a state-controlled utility may buy most of its fuel from a state-controlled coal mine.

5.5.70.20 In our view, any entity in which the state has a controlling interest should be considered to be state-controlled, even if the state does not participate actively in the management of the entity. This is consistent with our view that it is the ability to control, rather than the exercise of that ability, that determines whether an entity is a subsidiary (see 2.5.30). As fellow subsidiaries also are related parties, we believe that all entities that the state can control, whether or not the state exercises that control, are related parties.

IAS 24.9(a)(i) 5.5.70.30 The meaning of "state controlled" will vary between jurisdictions, but in our view identification of related parties should not be limited to a sub-unit of a single government entity, e.g. different ministries of a single federal government should be viewed as part of a single government. However, in our view different governments (e.g. federal and regional governments) within a single country are not necessarily part of a single government entity, and therefore the identification of related parties of a state-controlled entity may be limited to other entities controlled by the same government.

5.5.70.40 See 5.5.130 for a discussion of the extent of disclosures required in respect of transactions between state-controlled entities.

5.5.75 *Forthcoming requirements*

5.5.75.10 IAS 24 (2009) introduces the term "government-related entities" and modifies the disclosure requirements for such entities to enable them to limit the extent of disclosures about related party transactions with the government or other government-related entities.

5.5.80 **Disclosure**

5.5.80.10 Legal requirements and other IFRSs may allow for certain disclosures, which are similar to those required by IAS 24, to be provided outside the financial statements while IAS 24 does not allow specifically the disclosures required by this standard to be provided outside the financial statements.

5.5.90 *Control relationships*

IAS 1.138(c),   5.5.90.10 An entity discloses the name of its parent and ultimate controlling party if
24.12, 15   different. It also discloses the name of its ultimate parent if not disclosed elsewhere in information published with the financial statements. In our view, the *ultimate parent* and the *ultimate controlling party* are not necessarily synonymous. This is because the definition of parent refers to an entity. Accordingly, an entity may have an ultimate parent and an ultimate controlling party. Therefore if the ultimate controlling party in the entity is an individual or a group of individuals, then the identity of that individual or the group of individuals and that relationship should be disclosed.

IAS 24.13, 14   5.5.90.15 Parent and subsidiary relationships are disclosed regardless of whether there
27.42, 43   have been any transactions between the parties. In practice many entities include a list of significant subsidiaries in their consolidated statements similar to that required for separate financial statements by IAS 27 *Consolidated and Separate Financial Statements*.

IAS 24.15   5.5.90.20 If neither the entity's parent nor the ultimate controlling party produces consolidated financial statements available for public use, then an entity discloses the name of the parent that is next most senior to the entity's parent that produces financial statements available for public use.

IAS 24.17   5.5.90.30 While parent and subsidiary relationships are disclosed regardless of whether transactions between the parties occurred, an entity is not required to disclose related party relationships with other entities in a group. For example, Company M and Company B are owned and controlled by the same individual, X, and have the same directors. Both M and B have numerous subsidiaries. B holds shares in M, but not enough to give B control over M; M does not hold any shares in B. In M's separate financial statements, it discloses only its relationships with X and with M's own subsidiaries. M is not required to describe its *relationship* with B or any of B's subsidiaries if there have been no transactions with these entities. However, any *transactions* with B or its subsidiaries are disclosed as related party transactions.

IAS 1.31,   5.5.90.40 The separate financial statements of a parent entity include disclosures of
27.42   relationships with all subsidiaries, including sub-subsidiaries, except those that are immaterial on both a quantitative and qualitative basis.

5.5.100 *Transactions and balances#*

IAS 24.9   5.5.100.10 Related party transactions that involve a transfer of resources, services or obligations are disclosed regardless of whether a price is charged. Therefore, disclosure is required in respect of guarantees, gifts or other non-reciprocal transfers of assets or services, asset swaps or other similar transactions between related parties.

5.5.100.20 For example, Company E and Company F are related parties. F's business activities include providing fund raising and promotional activities and F makes use of E's employees to arrange these events. E does not charge F for these services. Accordingly, in both E's and F's financial statements, the nature and the extent of the use of E's employees by F should be disclosed as a related party transaction.

IAS 24.1 5.5.100.30 In our view, related party disclosures should cover the period during which transactions could have been affected by the existence of the related party relationship (see 5.5.30.90). We believe that the disclosure of transactions occurring after parties cease to be related parties is not required.

5.5.110 *Key management personnel compensation*

IAS 19.7, 5.5.110.10 Key management personnel compensation, including that of non-executive
24.9, 16 directors, is disclosed in total and analysed into its components (short-term, post-employment, other long-term, termination and share-based benefits (see 4.4.1135.10)). Compensation amounts should relate to services rendered to the entity. For example, an entity should disclose the cost of goods or services recognised in relation to share-based benefits, and short-term employee benefits should be disclosed on an accruals basis. In our experience, disclosure of key management personnel compensation generally is aggregated rather than presented separately for each individual unless it is otherwise required, for example by local statutory or regulatory requirements.

IAS 24.BC4- 5.5.110.20 In our view, materiality considerations cannot be used to override the explicit
BC6 requirements for the disclosure of elements of key management personnel compensation. We believe that the nature of the key management personnel compensation always makes it material qualitatively.

IAS 24.9 5.5.110.30 Compensation is not limited to amounts given by the entity. Instead, it includes all amounts paid, payable or provided by the entity, or on behalf of the entity, in return for services received. It will include amounts that are not employee benefits of the entity, e.g. compensation paid by a parent entity to key management personnel of a subsidiary.

5.5.110.40 Payments by an entity may relate to services provided to third parties, and not to the paying entity. If an entity acts as an agent and makes payments to an individual on behalf of another party, then in our view the entity is required to disclose only compensation paid as consideration for services rendered *to the entity*.

5.5.110.50 For example, Mr Y is a director of Parent Z. In addition to providing services to Z, Mr Y provides services to Subsidiary B. Mr Y is compensated by Z for the services performed for Z (in the amount of 800) as well as those performed for B (in the amount of 200). B reimburses Z for the amounts paid to Mr Y on its behalf. The relationships and payments can be illustrated as follows:

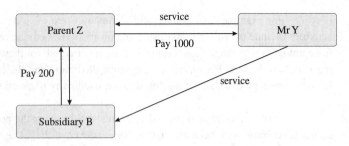

IAS 24.16, 17   5.5.110.60 In our view, B discloses in its own financial statements the amount of 200 paid to Z in respect of the services provided by Mr Y to B as key management personnel compensation even though B pays this compensation to Z and not directly to Mr Y. In Z's separate financial statements, we believe that disclosure of key management compensation should include only the amount paid to Mr Y for services provided to Z i.e. 800 (1000 - 200). Z also discloses the reimbursement received from B for Mr Y's services as a related party transaction.

IAS 24.16, 17   5.5.110.70 Consider the same example as in 5.5.110.50 except that B does not reimburse Z for the services provided by Mr Y to B. In our view, B discloses in its own financial statements the apportioned amount of the compensation paid by Z for the service received by B from Mr Y (i.e. 200) and that the amount paid by B for these services was zero. In Z's separate financial statements, we believe that disclosure of key management personnel compensation should include only the amount paid to Mr Y for services provided to Z (i.e. 800). Z also discloses the amount of the compensation paid for the services provided by Mr Y to B and that no consideration was received, as a related party transaction.

5.5.110.80 In the consolidated financial statements, Mr Y is considered to be key management personnel for both Z and for the group as a whole. The compensation paid by Z therefore relates to the services performed for the group, and therefore Mr Y's total compensation for services to both B and Z, i.e. 1000 is disclosed.

5.5.110.90 In another example, Mrs B is a director of Company X (the reporting entity) and a partner of a legal firm that provides legal services to X. X and the legal firm are not related parties. Mrs B is acting in two capacities in relation to X, as:

- a director; and
- a partner of a legal firm providing services to X.

IAS 24.10, 16, 17   5.5.110.100 This raises the issue of what is included as key management personnel compensation in the financial statements of X in relation to Mrs B. In our view, X should include within its disclosure of key management personnel compensation only the benefits provided to Mrs B in her capacity as director. Therefore, we believe that if

1340

Mrs B is involved closely in providing the legal services to X, by providing the services directly on behalf of the legal firm or by supervising the service provided, then Mrs B is acting not only in the capacity as partner in the legal firm; in substance the transaction is no different from a scenario in which Mrs B provides the legal services directly to X. The fees paid for legal services rendered would be disclosed as "other related party transactions" (see 5.5.120). Conversely, if Mrs B did not provide legal services directly on behalf of the legal firm, did not supervise the services and did not have the power to influence the services provided to X, then we believe that the service is not a related party transaction.

IAS 24.17   5.5.110.110 In addition to key management personnel compensation, an entity also discloses information about other transactions with key management personnel, for example personal finance transactions such as loans, current account balances and interest paid or received. For insurance entities, in our view disclosures should include the insurance cover provided to key management personnel by the entity.

5.5.120 *Other related party transactions#*

IAS 24.17, 18   5.5.120.10 As a minimum, the following disclosures are provided if there have been transactions between related parties:

- the nature of the related party relationship and information about transactions;
- the amount of the transactions;
- outstanding balances, their terms and conditions (including whether outstanding balances are secured);
- the nature of the consideration to be provided and details of guarantees given or received; and
- any allowance for doubtful debts and any amounts written off during the period.

5.5.120.20 [Not used]

IAS 24.4   5.5.120.30 In the consolidated financial statements, intra-group transactions and the profit on transactions with associates or joint ventures to the extent of the investor's interest (see 2.5.370 and 3.5.430) are eliminated. In our view, an entity still is required to disclose the portions of transactions with joint ventures or associates that are not eliminated on proportionate consolidation or equity accounting.

IAS 24.18   5.5.120.40 Disclosure is provided separately for each category of related party. For example, sales to subsidiaries are not aggregated with sales to joint ventures.

IAS 24.22   5.5.120.50 Items of a similar nature may be disclosed in aggregate as long as aggregation does not obscure the importance of individually significant transactions. For example, in the separate financial statements of a subsidiary, regular purchases or sales with other fellow subsidiaries may be aggregated. However, in our view details of a significant disposal of property, plant and equipment to a subsidiary should not be included in an aggregate disclosure of regular sales of goods to subsidiaries as they are not similar in nature.

5.5 Related party disclosures

IAS 24.21 5.5.120.60 Related party transactions are required to be disclosed regardless of whether they are entered into on terms equivalent to those in an arm's length transaction. An entity may include in its financial statements a statement that related party transactions were made on terms equivalent to those that prevail in an arm's length transaction only if that statement can be substantiated.

5.5.120.70 In other situations it is difficult to assess what information about transactions with related parties is required to be disclosed:

- For example, a mutual fund appoints an administrator to provide management services. In our view, the fund should disclose as a minimum: information about the services provided by the administrator, including the terms and conditions of the management agreement; the amount of the management fee paid to the administrator during the period; how the fee is calculated; and any fees outstanding at the reporting date.
- In another example, a parent entity may establish a captive insurance entity to provide self-insurance for the group. The captive insurance entity then may transfer the risk of losses to a third-party insurer. In our view, the relationship between the parent entity and the captive insurance entity should be disclosed in the financial statements of the captive insurance entity, including information about the nature of the insurance contracts, any outstanding balances and revenues arising from those insurance contracts. We believe that the role of the third-party insurer also should be disclosed. See 3.12.410 regarding the accounting for captive insurance entities.

5.5.125 *Forthcoming requirements*

5.5.125.10 IAS 24 (2009) includes a reference to "commitments" whenever it refers to transactions and balances (see 5.5A.120.20).

5.5.130 *State-controlled entities#*

IAS 1.31 5.5.130.10 In our view, in an environment in which transactions with state-controlled entities are on the same terms and subject to the same review and approval processes as transactions with entities that are not state-controlled, the identification of material (see 1.2.80) transactions should focus on the following:

- Transactions for which the standard terms and conditions have been altered, or for which normal review and approval processes were not applied. As a consequence the pricing of the transactions may not be made on a basis equivalent to those that prevail in arm's length transactions.
- Transactions that represent a significant portion of a type of transaction. For example, in our view items such as insignificant telecommunication expenses provided by a state-controlled telecommunications entity to a state-controlled manufacturing entity under normal terms and conditions are unlikely to be material related party transactions, and therefore no separate disclosure is required.

- Outstanding balances that represent concentrations of credit risks. For example, a loan by one state-controlled entity to another state-controlled entity would be a material related party transaction or balance if the loan is an individually significant item.

IAS 24.8   5.5.130.20 This conclusion reflects, in part, a concern that extensive disclosure about all transactions that are with related parties without determining materiality, considering both quantitative and qualitative characteristics, might mask important information that may affect assessments of the entity's results of operations and financial condition. This being the objective of the requirements to disclose related party transactions, outstanding balances and relationships.

5.5.135 *Forthcoming requirements*

5.5.135.10 IAS 24 (2009) introduces modified disclosure requirements for government-related entities to enable them to limit the extent of disclosures about related party transactions with the government or other government-related entities. The modified requirements are expected to result in disclosure of those transactions in which the relationship with government may have played a role in either the occurrence of the transaction or its terms and conditions. See 5.5A.130 for further discussion of these amendments.

5.5A Related party disclosures
(IAS 24 (2009))

5.5A Related party disclosures
(IAS 24 (2009))

> **Overview of forthcoming requirements**
>
> - **Related party relationships are those involving control (direct or indirect), joint control or significant influence.**
>
> - **Key management personnel and their close family members are parties related to an entity.**
>
> - **There are no special recognition or measurement requirements for related party transactions.**
>
> - **The disclosure of related party relationships between a parent and its subsidiaries is required, even if there have been no transactions between them.**
>
> - **No disclosure is required in the consolidated financial statements of intra-group transactions eliminated in preparing those statements.**
>
> - **Comprehensive disclosures of related party transactions are required for each category of related party relationship.**
>
> - **In certain instances, government-related entities are allowed to provide less detailed disclosures on related party transactions.**

Forthcoming requirements and future developments

In November 2009 the IASB published IAS 24 *Related Party Disclosures* (2009), which supersedes IAS 24 as revised in 2003. The main changes from IAS 24 (2003) are:

- IAS 24 (2009) introduces symmetry in the definition of a related party, i.e. if B is a related party of C for the purposes of C's financial statements, then C is a related party of B for the purposes of B's financial statements. In addition, certain aspects of the definition were clarified and therefore the new definition includes certain relationships that previously were excluded and vice versa (see 5.5A.30).
- IAS 24 (2009) introduces a partial exemption for government-related entities to enable them to limit the extent of disclosures about related party transactions with the government or other government-related entities (see 5.5A.130).

IAS 24.28   IAS 24 (2009) is effective for annual periods beginning on or after 1 January 2011 and is applied retrospectively. Earlier application is permitted, either of the whole standard or of the partial exemption in paragraphs 25 – 27 of IAS 24 (2009) available to government-related entities (see 5.5A.130).

When a significant change to the forthcoming requirements is expected, it is marked with a * as an area that may be subject to future developments. In respect of this topic no future developments are noted.

5.5A.10 Scope

IAS 24.3, 4   5.5A.10.10 Related party disclosure requirements apply to all entities, including parent entities, investors and joint venturers, in their consolidated, separate and individual financial statements (see 2.1.50 – 70). There are no exemptions from the disclosure of intra-group transactions in the separate financial statements of a parent or in the financial statements of subsidiaries.

IAS 24.25, 26   5.5A.10.20 A government-related entity (see 5.5A.70.10) that applies IFRSs is not exempt from providing related party disclosures. Therefore, a government-related entity discloses, as related party transactions, its transactions with the government and also with other government-related entities, as the parties are under common control and therefore meet the definition of related parties. However, a government-related entity can elect to reduce the level of disclosure that otherwise would be required by IAS 24 (2009) (see 5.5A.130).

5.5A.10.30 Local rules and regulations often require an entity to provide certain related party information, for example directors' individual remuneration or golden parachute agreements. Specific legal requirements may supplement but cannot waive any requirement to provide related party disclosures under IFRSs (see 5.5A.80.20).

5.5A.20 Recognition and measurement

5.5A.20.10 IAS 24 (2009) does not establish any recognition or measurement requirements for related party transactions. Related party transactions are accounted for in accordance with the requirements of relevant IFRSs. For example, in an entity's separate financial statements, loans to other group entities are recognised and measured in accordance with IAS 39 *Financial Instruments: Recognition and Measurement* (see 3.6), and the disclosures required for financial instruments (see 5.6) are provided in addition to those required for related party transactions.

IFRS 2.3A,   5.5A.20.20 Other IFRSs may require the attribution of cost. For example, if a parent
43A-43D   transfers its equity instruments directly to employees of a subsidiary as compensation for services provided to the subsidiary, then IFRS 2 *Share-based Payment* requires recognition of the share-based payment compensation at the subsidiary level (see 4.5.820).

IAS 24.10   5.5A.20.30 Consistent with the identification of related party relationships, in our view the accounting for related party transactions should take into account their substance in addition to their legal form. For example, when a shareholder forgives a loan to the entity, in most cases this would be accounted for as a capital contribution to the entity and not as a gain on extinguishment of a liability (see 3.11.230).

5.5A.30 **Identification of related parties**

5.5A.30.10 Examples of some related party relationships are illustrated below:

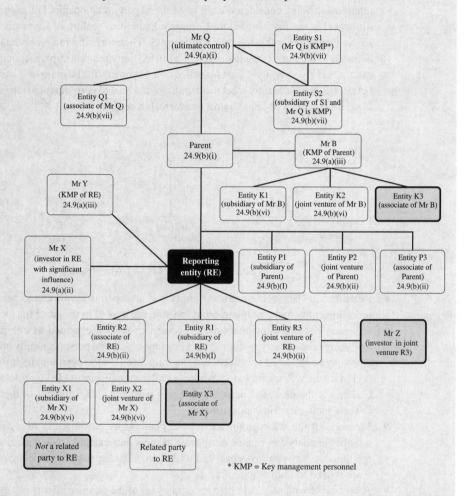

5.5A.30.20 The definition of a related party is not restricted to entities; it also includes persons, key management personnel and post-employment benefit plans. For example, entities that are under the common control of the same non-corporate shareholder (e.g. a person, a group of persons acting together or a trust) are related parties, even if the shareholder does not prepare consolidated financial statements.

IAS 24.9, 11, 12 5.5A.30.30 The following are some of the key principles applied in the identification of related party relationships:

- Related party relationships are symmetrical, i.e. if B is related to C for the purposes of C's financial statements, then C is related to B for the purposes of B's financial statements.
- The definition includes relationships involving direct and indirect control, including common control, joint control and significant influence.
- When analysing indirect relationships, control or joint control in one leg of the relationship being considered leads to a related party relationship. For example, as illustrated in the diagram below, Company J is a joint venture of Company H and H has significant influence over Company S. Therefore, the *indirect* relationship between J and S meets the definition of a related party relationship. In a contrasting example, H also has significant influence over Company T. The indirect relationship between S and T does not meet the definition of a related party relationship because there is no control or joint control between H, S or T.

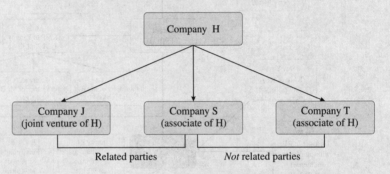

- Relationships between a reporting entity and a corporate investor, and between a reporting entity and a non-corporate investor, are treated in the same manner.
- A person and close members of that person's family are treated as one party in analysing related party relationships. Close members of a person's family are those who may be expected to influence, or be influenced by, the person in their dealings with the entity. They include a person's children and spouse or domestic partner, children of the person's spouse or domestic partner, and dependants of the person or their spouse or domestic partner.
- Members of the same group (i.e. a parent and all its subsidiaries) are considered together in analysing related party relationships. For example, when assessing the relationship between Investor P and its Associate B, any member of B's group and P are related to each other.
- A post-employment benefit plan for employees of the reporting entity or any entity that is a related party of the reporting entity is considered to be a related party of the reporting entity.
- Significant influence as defined in IAS 28 *Investments in Associates* is equivalent to the relationship that exists between an entity and its key management personnel. For the purpose of determining related party relationships, these types of relationships are not as close as a relationship of control or joint control.

5.5A.30.40 Although a branch is not defined formally in IFRSs, in our experience generally it is understood to be an extension of an entity's activities. In our view, if a branch of an entity prepares its own financial statements, then it should disclose related party transactions and relationships, including those with its head office.

IAS 24.1 5.5A.30.50 An entity or a person may become, or cease to be, a related party during the period covered by the financial statements. In our view, the determination of whether an entity or a person is a related party should be made considering their relationship during the reporting period, and not just the relationship at the reporting date. This is because the objective of the standard is to provide users of the financial statements with the disclosures necessary to draw their attention to the possibility that the reporting entity's financial position and profit or loss may have been affected by the existence of related parties and by transactions and outstanding balances, including commitments, with such parties. See 5.5A.100.30 for further discussion of the related party disclosures in such cases.

5.5A.40 *Key management personnel*

IAS 24.9 5.5A.40.10 Key management personnel are those persons that have the authority and responsibility for planning, directing and controlling the activities of the entity, directly or indirectly. The definition of key management personnel includes directors (both executive and non-executive) of an entity. In our view, the term also includes directors of any of the entity's parents to the extent that they have authority and responsibility for planning, directing and controlling the activities of the entity. In our view, an entity's parent includes the immediate, intermediate and ultimate parent.

5.5A.40.20 In our view, a person is key management personnel of an entity even if that entity does not pay for the services received from the person. For example, a director of Parent B that also acts as a director of Subsidiary C is key management personnel of C, regardless of whether C reimburses B for the services received.

5.5A.40.30 In practice, an entity may have more than one level of management. For example, there may be a supervisory board whose members have responsibilities similar to those of non-executive directors, a board of directors that sets the overall strategy under which an entity operates, and a management team that implements those strategies within the authority delegated to it by the board. The members of either board, including non-executive directors, will be considered to be key management personnel.

IAS 24.9 5.5A.40.40 However, key management personnel is not limited to directors; in our view, other members of the management team also may be key management personnel. We believe that a person with significant authority and responsibility for planning, directing and controlling the activities of the entity should be considered to be key management personnel.

5.5A.40.50 The role of key management personnel of a group of entities is performed by those who assume the authority and responsibility for planning, directing and controlling the activities of each separate entity in the group. Therefore, in our view in the consolidated financial statements of a group, key management personnel is not limited to the key management personnel of the parent entity, but may include key management personnel of other entities of the group, such as of subsidiaries. For example, the management of Parent C directs the investment activities of the group, while the management of Subsidiary D, a significant operating subsidiary, directs the operations of D with minimal involvement from C's management. Since D contributes significantly to the group result, we believe its key management personnel should be included as key management personnel of the group.

5.5A.40.60 In our view, the definition of key management personnel in IAS 24 (2009) specifies a *role* and is not limited to a person. In our experience, the authority and responsibility for planning, directing and controlling the activities of an entity in some cases is assigned to an entity rather than a person. For example, a bank might act as an investment manager for an investment fund and in doing so assume the roles and responsibilities of key management personnel. We believe that an entity that assumes the role of key management personnel should be considered a related party of the reporting entity.

IAS 24.9(b)
(vii)
5.5A.40.70 Entities under the control or joint control of key management personnel (or their close family members) also are related parties of the reporting entity. For example, Mrs Z is a director of Company G and considered to be key management personnel of G. Mrs Z has joint control over Joint Venture H and therefore H is considered to be a related party of G. This also would be the case if a close family member of Mrs Z had joint control over H.

IAS 24.11
5.5A.40.80 However, two entities are not related parties simply because they have a director or other member of key management personnel in common, or because a member of key management personnel of one entity has significant influence over the other entity. In the example in 5.5A.40.70, if Mrs Z was a director of H, but as a person did not have control or joint control over H, then G and H would not be related parties solely because Mrs Z is a director of both.

5.5A.50 *Post-employment benefit plans*

IAS 24.9(b)(v)
5.5A.50.10 Related parties include post-employment benefit plans that benefit an entity's employees or the employees of any entity that is a related party of the reporting entity. For example, Company B has significant influence over Company C. B and C each have a pension plan for the benefit of their respective employees. In addition, C transacts with B's pension plan in the ordinary course of business. In this example, both pension plans are related parties of C and, accordingly, C discloses transactions with:

- its own pension plan because it provides benefits to its employees; and
- B's pension plan because it provides benefits to the employees of a related party (being B).

IAS 24.9(b)(v)
5.5A.50.15 If the reporting entity is itself such a benefit plan, then the sponsoring employers also are related to the reporting entity.

5.5A.50.20 It is not clear whether a multi-employer plan that also benefits employees of unrelated parties should be included in the definition of a related party. The only condition in IAS 24 (2009) for the post-employment benefit plan to be regarded as a related party of the reporting entity is that it benefits the employees of the reporting entity, or of any entity that is a related party of the reporting entity. It does not require a specific level of influence or control. Therefore, in our view a multi-employer plan of which a reporting entity is one of the sponsoring entities is related to the reporting entity even when the reporting entity does not have significant influence or control over the multi-employer plan.

5.5A.60 *Economic dependence*

IAS 24.11   5.5A.60.10 An entity may be dependent, economically or operationally, on another party, e.g. a major customer or supplier. This dependency does not itself create a related party relationship. However, additional information about these relationships and the resulting transactions may be relevant to the reader of the financial statements.

IAS 24.11   5.5A.60.20 Providers of finance and similar entities are not related parties by virtue of their normal dealings with an entity, even though these parties may limit the actions of an entity or participate in its decision-making process. However, transactions in the ordinary course of business between related parties are disclosed. For example, a banking entity discloses transactions with its finance provider that is part of the same banking group even if these services are provided on the same terms as to unrelated customers.

5.5A.70 *Government-related entities*

IAS 24.9   5.5A.70.10 *Government* refers to a government, government agencies and similar bodies whether local, national or international, and a *government-related entity* is an entity that is controlled, jointly controlled or significantly influenced by a government. The definition of government is consistent with the one in IAS 20 *Accounting for Government Grants and Disclosure of Government Assistance*.

5.5A.70.20 For entities operating in an environment in which government control is pervasive, many counterparties also are government-related and therefore are related parties. For example, a government-related utility may buy most of its fuel from a government-related coal mine.

5.5A.70.30 See 5.5A.130 for a discussion of a partial disclosure exemption for government-related entities.

5.5A.80 **Disclosure**

IAS 24.1, 5-8   5.5A.80.10 It is the nature of related party relationships and transactions with such parties rather than merely the size of related party transactions that determines the materiality of related party disclosures.

5.5A.80.20 Legal requirements and other IFRSs may allow for certain disclosures, which are similar to those required by IAS 24 (2009), to be provided outside the financial statements while IAS 24 (2009) does not allow specifically the disclosures required by this standard to be provided outside the financial statements.

5.5A.90 *Control relationships*

IAS 1.138(c), 24.13 **5.5A.90.10** A reporting entity discloses the name of its parent and ultimate controlling party, if different. It also discloses the name of its ultimate parent if not disclosed elsewhere in information published with the financial statements. In our view, the *ultimate parent* and the *ultimate controlling party* are not necessarily synonymous. This is because the definition of parent refers to an *entity*. Accordingly, an entity may have an ultimate parent and an ultimate controlling party. Therefore, if the ultimate controlling party of the reporting entity is a person or a group of persons, then the identity of that person or the group of persons and that relationship should be disclosed.

IAS 24.13-15, 27.42, 43 **5.5A.90.20** Parent and subsidiary relationships are disclosed regardless of whether there have been any transactions between the parties. Although not explicitly required by IAS 24 (2009), in practice many entities include a list of significant subsidiaries in their consolidated statements similar to that required for separate financial statements by IAS 27 *Consolidated and Separate Financial Statements*.

IAS 24.13, 16 **5.5A.90.30** If neither the reporting entity's parent nor the ultimate controlling party produces consolidated financial statements available for public use, then a reporting entity discloses the name of the parent that is next most senior to the reporting entity's parent that produces financial statements available for public use.

5.5A.90.40 While parent and subsidiary relationships are disclosed regardless of whether transactions between the parties occurred, a reporting entity is not required to disclose related party relationships with other entities in a group. For example, Company M and Company B are owned and controlled by the same person, X, and have the same directors. Both M and B have numerous subsidiaries. B holds shares in M, but not enough to give B control over M; M does not hold any shares in B. In M's own financial statements, it discloses only its relationships with X and with M's own subsidiaries. M is not required to describe its *relationship* with B or any of B's subsidiaries if there have been no transactions with these entities. However, any *transactions* with B or its subsidiaries are disclosed as related party transactions.

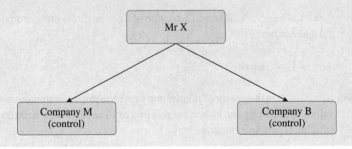

5.5A.100 *Transactions and balances, including commitments*

IAS 24.6, 18   5.5A.100.10 Related party transactions that involve a transfer of resources, services or obligations are disclosed regardless of whether a price is charged. Therefore, disclosure is required in respect of guarantees, gifts or other non-reciprocal transfers of assets or services, asset swaps or other similar transactions between related parties.

5.5A.100.20 For example, Company E and Company F are related parties. F's business activities include providing fundraising and promotional activities and F makes use of E's employees to arrange these events. E does not charge F for these services. Accordingly, in both E's and F's financial statements, the nature and the extent of the use of E's employees by F should be disclosed as a related party transaction.

IAS 24.1   5.5A.100.30 In our view, related party disclosures should cover the period during which transactions could have been affected by the existence of the related party relationship; the disclosure of transactions occurring after parties cease to be related parties is not required (see 5.5A.30.70).

5.5A.110 *Key management personnel compensation*

IAS 19.7,
24.9, 17   5.5A.110.10 Key management personnel compensation, including that of non-executive directors, is disclosed in total and analysed into its components (short-term, post-employment, other long-term, termination and share-based benefits). Compensation amounts relate to services rendered to the reporting entity. For example, a reporting entity discloses the cost of goods or services recognised in relation to share-based payments and short-term employee benefits on an accruals basis. In our experience, disclosure of key management personnel compensation generally is aggregated rather than presented separately for each person unless it is otherwise required, for example by local statutory or regulatory requirements.

IAS 24.BC7-
BC9   5.5A.110.20 In our view, materiality considerations cannot be used to override the explicit requirements for the disclosure of elements of key management personnel compensation. We believe that the nature of the key management personnel compensation always makes it material qualitatively.

IAS 24.9   5.5A.110.30 Compensation is not limited to amounts given by the reporting entity. Instead, it includes all amounts paid, payable or provided by the reporting entity, or on behalf of the reporting entity, in return for services received. Therefore, it includes employee benefits provided to the key management personnel but that are not recognised by the reporting entity in its financial statements, e.g. compensation paid by a parent entity to key management personnel of a subsidiary.

5.5A.110.40 Payments by an entity may relate to services provided to third parties, and not to the paying entity. If an entity acts as an agent and makes payments to a person on behalf of another party, then in our view the reporting entity is required to disclose only compensation paid as consideration for services rendered *to the entity*.

5.5A.110.50 For example, Mr Y is a director of Parent Z. In addition to providing services to Z, Mr Y provides services to Subsidiary B. Mr Y is compensated by Z for the services provided to Z (in the amount of 800) as well as those provided to B (in the amount of 200). B reimburses Z for the amounts paid to Mr Y on its behalf. The relationships and payments can be illustrated as follows:

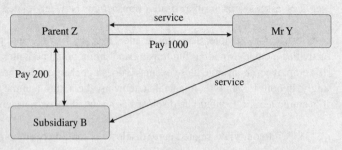

IAS 24.17, 18   5.5A.110.60 In our view, B discloses in its own financial statements the amount of 200 paid to Z in respect of the services provided by Mr Y to B as key management personnel compensation even though B pays this compensation to Z and not directly to Mr Y. In Z's separate financial statements, we believe that disclosure of key management personnel compensation should include only the amount paid to Mr Y for services provided to Z, i.e. 800 (1,000 - 200). Z also discloses the reimbursement received from B for Mr Y's services as a related party transaction.

IAS 24.17, 18   5.5A.110.70 Consider the same example as in 5.5A.110.50 except that B does not reimburse Z for the services provided by Mr Y to B. In our view, B discloses in its own financial statements the apportioned amount of the compensation paid by Z for the service received by B from Mr Y (i.e. 200) and that the amount paid by B for these services was zero. In Z's separate financial statements, we believe that disclosure of key management personnel compensation should include only the amount paid to Mr Y for services rendered to Z (i.e. 800). Z also discloses the amount of the compensation paid for the services provided by Mr Y to B and that no consideration was received, as a related party transaction.

IAS 24.17   5.5A.110.80 In the consolidated financial statements, Mr Y is considered to be key management personnel for both Z and for the group as a whole. The compensation paid by Z therefore relates to services performed for the group, and therefore Mr Y's total compensation for services to both B and Z, i.e. 1,000 is disclosed.

5.5A.110.90 In another example, Mrs B is a director of Company X and a partner of a legal firm that provides legal services to X. X and the legal firm are not related parties. Mrs B is acting in two capacities in relation to X, as:

- a director; and
- a partner of a legal firm providing services to X.

IAS 24.11, 17, 18   5.5A.110.100 This raises the issue of what is included as key management personnel compensation in the financial statements of X in relation to Mrs B. In our view, X should

1356

include within its disclosure of key management personnel compensation only the benefits provided to Mrs B in her capacity as director. Therefore, we believe that if Mrs B is involved closely in providing the legal services to X, by providing the services directly on behalf of the legal firm or by supervising the service provided, then Mrs B is acting not only in the capacity as partner in the legal firm; in substance the transaction is no different from a scenario in which Mrs B provides the legal services directly to X. The fees paid for legal services rendered would be disclosed as "other related party transactions" (see 5.5A.120). Conversely, if Mrs B did not provide legal services directly on behalf of the legal firm, did not supervise the services and did not have the power to influence the services provided to X, then we believe that the service is not a related party transaction.

IAS 24.18 5.5A.110.110 In addition to key management personnel compensation, a reporting entity also discloses information about other transactions with key management personnel, for example personal finance transactions such as loans, current account balances and interest paid or received. For insurance entities, in our view disclosures should include the insurance cover provided to key management personnel by the reporting entity.

5.5A.120 *Other related party transactions*

IAS 24.18, 19 5.5A.120.10 As a minimum, the following disclosures are provided if there have been transactions between related parties:

- the nature of the related party relationship and information about transactions;
- the amount of the transactions;
- outstanding balances, including commitments, their terms and conditions (including whether outstanding balances are secured);
- the nature of the consideration to be provided and details of guarantees given or received; and
- any allowance for doubtful debts and any amounts written off during the period.

IAS 24.21(i), 39.9 5.5A.120.20 Commitments to do something if a particular event occurs or does not occur in the future, including executory contracts (recognised or unrecognised), are disclosed if they are with a related party. Commitments are not defined in IFRSs. However, in IAS 39 a *firm commitment* is a binding agreement for the exchange of a specified quantity of resources at a specified price on a specified future date or dates. It might be useful for management to agree on a working definition for commitments, taking into account all types of commitments, not only those that might result in an outflow of resources.

IAS 24.4 5.5A.120.30 In the consolidated financial statements, intra-group transactions and the profit on transactions with associates or joint ventures to the extent of the investor's interest (see 2.5.370 and 3.5.430) are eliminated. In our view, a reporting entity still is required to disclose the portions of transactions with joint ventures or associates that are not eliminated on proportionate consolidation or equity accounting.

IAS 24.19 5.5A.120.40 Disclosure is provided separately for each category of related party. For example, sales to subsidiaries are not aggregated with sales to joint ventures.

IAS 24.24 5.5A.120.50 Items of a similar nature may be disclosed in aggregate as long as aggregation does not obscure the importance of individually significant transactions. For example, a subsidiary's own financial statements, regular purchases or sales with other fellow subsidiaries may be aggregated. However, in our view details of a significant disposal of property, plant and equipment to a subsidiary should not be included in an aggregate disclosure of regular sales of goods to subsidiaries as they are not similar in nature.

IAS 24.23 5.5A.120.60 Related party transactions are required to be disclosed regardless of whether they are entered into on terms equivalent to those in an arm's length transaction. A reporting entity may include in its financial statements a statement that related party transactions were made on terms equivalent to those that prevail in an arm's length transaction only if that statement can be substantiated.

5.5A.120.70 In other situations it is difficult to assess what information about transactions with related parties is required to be disclosed:

- For example, a mutual fund appoints an administrator to provide management services. In our view, the fund should disclose the following as a minimum: information about the services provided by the administrator, including the terms and conditions of the management agreement; the amount of the management fee paid to the administrator during the period; how the fee is calculated; and any fees outstanding at the reporting date.
- In another example, a parent entity may establish a captive insurance entity to provide self-insurance for the group. The captive insurance entity then may transfer the risk of losses to a third-party insurer. In our view, the relationship between the parent entity and the captive insurance entity should be disclosed in the captive insurance entity's own financial statements, including information about the nature of the insurance contracts, any outstanding balances, and revenues arising from those insurance contracts. We believe that the role of the third-party insurer also should be disclosed. See 3.12.410 for a discussion of the accounting for captive insurance entities.

IAS 21.22, 5.5A.120.80 IAS 24 (2009) includes, as an example of a related party transaction, participation by a parent or subsidiary in a defined benefit plan that shares risks between group entities. In addition, IAS 19 requires certain disclosures for such defined benefit plans, including detail about the contractual agreement or stated policy for charging the net defined benefit cost or the fact that there is no such policy and the policy for determining the contribution to be paid by the entity.

5.5A.130 *Government-related entities*

IAS 24.25, IE3 5.5A.130.10 IAS 24 (2009) allows a reporting entity to reduce the level of disclosures about transactions and outstanding balances, including commitments, with:

- a government that has control, joint control or significant influence over the reporting entity; and

- another entity that is a related party because the same government has control, joint control or significant influence over both the reporting entity and the other entity.

5.5A.130.15 The following diagram highlights the government-related entities, which might be in the scope of the exemption:

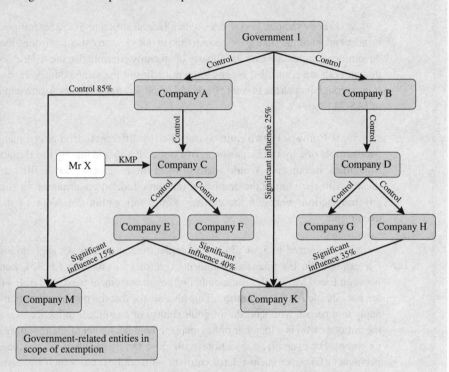

IAS 24.BC37, IE1, IE2   5.5A.130.20 The exemption from the full related party disclosures could be a far-reaching exemption as a result of the broad definition of government-related entities (see 5.5A.70.10), and the interrelationship with the general definition of a related party as it applies to indirect relationships. For example, in the diagram in 5.5A.130.15, it seems Company E is in the scope of the exemption because Government 1 has indirect control over it. Therefore, direct or indirect government control, joint control or significant influence could bring entities in the scope of the exemption regardless of any other related party relationships between them.

5.5A.130.30 However, the partial exemption does not apply to the relationships between an entity and a person in their capacity as an investor or as key management personnel. Continuing the example in 5.5A.130.20, this could mean that in E's financial statements, the partial exemption applies to transactions with Government 1, Companies A, B, C, D, F, G, H, M and K. The partial exemption would not apply to transactions with Mr X.

IAS 24.25   5.5A.130.40 In almost all countries there will be multiple levels of governing public bodies, e.g. at city, provincial, state and perhaps federal levels. However, there may be significant differences from one country to the next as to the relationships between these bodies and the extent to which one body is said to be under the control, joint control or significant influence of another body in the same country. Given this, the identification of entities that are related to the "same government" may not be straightforward.

5.5A.130.50 For example, in countries with a federal structure, if the federal government is independent of the state government, then in our view an entity controlled by the state government might not be a related party of an entity controlled at the federal level, even though both are controlled by government bodies in the same country. In such cases, transactions between the two entities would be subject to the full disclosure requirements of IAS 24 (2009).

IAS 24.25 5.5A.130.60 Conversely, two entities controlled by different federal government bodies, for example one by the Department of Public Health and one by the Department of Education, in our view would seem to meet the criteria set out in the standard as these entities are under the control of the same federal government. In such cases, any transactions between the entities would fall within the scope of the partial exemption.

IAS 24.9, 18, 25, IE2 5.5A.130.70 As stated in 5.5A.130.20, the partial exemption does not apply to individuals. For example, in E's financial statements (see diagram in 5.5A.130.15), transactions between E and Mr X, who is a member of key management personnel of E's parent C, are not eligible for the exemption. This also means that the partial exemption does not apply to a person who has control, joint control or significant influence over a reporting entity or who is a member of key management personnel of the reporting entity or its parent. For example, transactions with close family members of key management personnel of a government-related entity or with entities over which key management personnel have at least joint control would be subject to the full disclosure requirements by that government-related entity.

IAS 24.26, BC43 5.5A.130.80 The partial exemption set out in paragraph 26 of IAS 24 (2009) is intended to meet the objective of IAS 24 (2009) by putting users of the entity's financial statements on notice that certain transactions or relationships could have an impact on the entity's operations or performance. They are not intended to require the reporting entity to identify every government-related entity nor to quantify every transaction with such entities as this would defeat the purpose of the exemption.

IAS 24.26, BC44-46 5.5A.130.90 The following disclosures are required when an reporting entity applies the partial exemption:

- the name of the government and the nature of its relationship with the reporting entity (i.e. control, joint control or significant influence); and
- the following information in sufficient detail to enable users of the entity's financial statements to understand the effect of related party transactions on its financial statements:

- nature and amount of each *individually significant* transaction; and
- for other transactions that are *collectively, but not individually, significant*, a qualitative or quantitative indication of their extent.

IAS 24.27   5.5A.130.100 There are no quantitative indications or bright lines concerning the meaning of significant. It might be useful for entities to establish criteria that they would apply consistently in order to determine whether transactions are individually or collectively significant. At a minimum, the reporting entity considers the closeness of the related party relationship and other factors relevant in establishing the level of significance of the transaction, such as whether it is:

- significant in terms of size;
- carried out on non-market terms;
- outside normal day-to-day business operations, such as the purchase and sale of businesses;
- disclosed to regulatory or supervisory authorities;
- reported to senior management; and/or
- subject to shareholder approval.

IAS 24.IE3   5.5A.130.110 Entities need to exercise judgement in deciding how much quantitative or qualitative information to disclose when transactions are collectively, but not individually, significant. For example, collectively significant sales of goods and purchases of raw materials between government-related entities could be disclosed as follows:

- A large portion of Company B's sales of goods and purchases of raw materials are with entities controlled by Government G; or
- About 50 percent of Company B's sales of goods and about 35 percent of its purchases of raw materials are with entities controlled by Government G.

5.5A.130.120 Both disclosures give an indication of the extent of these collectively significant transactions, but arguably the version with percent amounts is more informative for the user. As a result, management needs to determine how much quantitative or qualitative information is sufficient for the user in order to enable them to understand the effect of related party transactions on the entity's financial statements.

5.5A.130.130 In our view, generally the more clearly significant the transactions are to the entity, and/or the greater the likelihood that the transactions were affected by the existence of the related party relationship, the greater the need for more detailed information.

5.5A.130.140 For example, Company E could make the following disclosure in its financial statements about an individually significant transaction because of the size of the transaction:

> The Company is controlled indirectly by Government X and in 2009 X entered into a procurement agreement with the Company, such that the Company would act as the sole supplier of electronic equipment to X's various agencies and departments for a term of three years from 2010 to 2012, with an agreed bulk discount of 10 percent compared to list prices that the Company generally would charge on individual orders. The aggregate sales value under the agreement for the year ended 31 December 2011 amounted to 350, and 280 for the year ended 31 December 2010. As at 31 December 2011, the aggregate amounts due from X amounted to 100 and 50 as at 31 December 2010. These balances are payable under normal credit terms of 30 days' credit.

5.5A.130.150 Entities qualifying for the partial exemption are required to disclose the name of the related government. The disclosure relates to the basis on which the entity considers itself to be government-related, being the same basis on which it judges whether other entities are related to it by virtue of being related to that same government. In our view, the disclosure therefore should focus on identifying the highest level of government that has control, joint control or significant influence over the entity. In practice, judgement may be required when identifying the relevant government when the entity operates in a country with multiple levels of government.

5.6 Financial instruments: presentation and disclosure
(IFRS 7, IAS 1, IAS 32)

5.6 Financial instruments: presentation and disclosure
(IFRS 7, IAS 1, IAS 32)

Overview of currently effective requirements

- A financial asset and a financial liability are offset only when there is a legally enforceable right to offset, and an intention to settle net or to settle both amounts simultaneously.

- Disclosure is required in respect of:
  - the significance of financial instruments for the entity's financial position and performance; and
  - the nature and extent of risks arising from financial instruments and how the entity manages those risks.

- For disclosure of the significance of financial instruments, the overriding principle is to disclose sufficient information to enable users of financial statements to evaluate the significance of financial instruments for an entity's financial position and performance. Specific details required include disclosure of fair values and assumptions behind the calculations, information on items designated at fair value through profit or loss and on reclassification of financial assets between categories, and details of accounting policies.

- Risk disclosures require both qualitative and quantitative information.

- Qualitative disclosures describe management's objectives, policies and processes for managing risks arising from financial instruments.

- Quantitative data about the exposure to risks arising from financial instruments should be based on information provided internally to key management. However, certain disclosures about the entity's exposures to credit risk, liquidity risk and market risk arising from financial instruments are required, irrespective of whether this information is provided to management.

Currently effective requirements

This publication reflects IFRSs in issue at 1 August 2010. The currently effective requirements cover annual periods beginning on 1 January 2010. The requirements related to this topic are derived mainly from IFRS 7 *Financial Instruments: Disclosures*, IAS 1 *Presentation of Financial Statements* and IAS 32 *Financial Instruments: Presentation.*

Forthcoming requirements and future developments

When a currently effective requirement will be changed by a new requirement that is issued but is not yet effective, it is marked with a # as a **forthcoming requirement** and the impact of this change is explained in the accompanying boxed text. The forthcoming requirements related to this topic are derived from:

- IFRS 9 *Financial Instruments: Classification and Measurement* which is effective for annual periods beginning on or after 1 January 2013. A brief outline of the impact of IFRS 9 is given in 3.6A.
- *Improvements to IFRSs 2010* which are effective for annual periods beginning on or after 1 January 2011. A brief outline of the impact of the *Improvements to IFRSs 2010* on this topic is given in 5.6.520 and a brief outline of the annual improvements process is given in 1.1.85.

When a significant change to the currently effective or forthcoming requirements is expected, it is marked with a * as an area that may be subject to **future developments** and a brief outline of the relevant projects is given in 5.6.530.

5.6.10 **Overview**

5.6.10.10 IFRS 7 sets out the disclosure requirements for all financial instruments. The objective of the disclosures is to enhance financial statement users' understanding of the significance of financial instruments to an entity's overall financial position and performance and the risk exposures resulting from such financial instruments.

5.6.20 **Scope**

IFRS 7.3, 4 5.6.20.10 IFRS 7 applies to *all* entities and to all types of recognised and unrecognised financial instruments (e.g. loan commitments). The only exemptions are:

- interests in subsidiaries, associates and joint ventures accounted for in accordance with IAS 27 *Consolidated and Separate Financial Statements*, IAS 28 *Investments in Associates* and IAS 31 *Interests in Joint Ventures*; however, when the interest in a subsidiary, associate or joint venture is accounted for in accordance with IAS 39 *Financial Instruments: Recognition and Measurement* (see 3.6.60), then the disclosure requirements of IFRS 7 apply in addition to those in IAS 27, IAS 28 and IAS 31;
- employers' rights and obligations arising from employee benefit plans accounted for under IAS 19 *Employee Benefits* (see 4.4);
- insurance contracts as defined in IFRS 4 *Insurance Contracts* (see 3.6.30), except for certain derivatives embedded in those contracts and financial guarantee contracts to which IAS 39 *Financial Instruments: Recognition and Measurement* is applied (see 3.6.35);
- financial instruments, contracts and obligations under share-based payment transactions to which IFRS 2 *Share-based Payment* applies (see 4.5); and

- instruments that are required to be classified as equity instruments in accordance with paragraphs 16A and 16B or paragraphs 16C and 16D of IAS 32 (see 3.11.48).

5.6.30 Presentation – general considerations

5.6.40 *Statement of financial position*

IAS 1.54 5.6.40.10 IAS 1 requires that, at a minimum, financial assets are presented in the statement of financial position, with separate presentation of cash and cash equivalents, trade and other receivables, and investments accounted for under the equity method. IAS 1 also requires that financial liabilities are presented in the statement of financial position, with separate presentation of trade and other payables. Additional line items may be presented.

IFRS 7.8, 5.6.40.20 The use of different measurement bases for different classes of assets suggests
IAS 1.59 that their nature or function differs; therefore, generally instruments that are measured at cost or amortised cost and those that are measured at fair value are presented as separate line items. However, in our view in certain cases instruments with different measurement bases may be included in the same line item, for example a financial instrument host contract that is carried at amortised cost and a separable embedded derivative (see 3.6.260), or an instrument normally carried at amortised cost that is the hedged item in a fair value hedge and other similar instruments that are not hedged. In these cases the notes to the financial statements should disclose the carrying amounts of each category of financial instruments that are combined in a single line item in the statement of financial position.

5.6.50 *Classes vs categories of financial instruments*

IAS 39.9 5.6.50.10 Some of the disclosure requirements of IFRS 7 mandate disclosure by "category" of financial instruments, whereas others are by "class" of financial instruments. *Categories of financial instruments* are:

- financial assets or financial liabilities at fair value through profit or loss;
- held-to-maturity investments;
- loans and receivables;
- available-for-sale financial assets; and
- other liabilities.

IFRS 7.6, B3 5.6.50.20 There is no specific guidance on what comprises a class except that financial instruments are grouped into classes that are appropriate to the nature of the disclosure and take into account the characteristics of those financial instruments. Cash and cash equivalents, unsecured bank facilities and convertible notes (liability) represent some examples of classes of financial instruments. In determining classes the entity, as a minimum, distinguishes instruments measured at amortised cost from those measured at fair value, and treats financial instruments outside the scope of IFRS 7 as a separate class. The entity determines that the level of detail provided strikes an appropriate balance between too much and too little detail and should be sufficient to allow a reconciliation to the statement of financial position.

5.6.60 *Current and non-current classification of financial instruments*

IAS 1.60, 61 5.6.60.10 If an entity makes a distinction between current and non-current assets and liabilities in the statement of financial position (classified statement of financial position (see 3.1.10)), then instruments within the financial instrument classes are classified as current or non-current in accordance with their expected realisation (financial assets) or settlement date (financial liabilities).

IAS 1.66 5.6.60.20 In particular, an asset is classified as current when it is:

- expected to be realised in the entity's normal operating cycle;
- held primarily for the purpose of being traded;
- expected to be realised within 12 months after the reporting date; or
- cash or a cash equivalent as defined by IAS 7 *Statement of Cash Flows*, other than cash that is restricted for at least 12 months after the reporting date (see 2.3.10).

IAS 1.69 5.6.60.30 A liability is classified as current when it is:

- expected to be settled in the entity's normal operating cycle;
- held primarily for the purpose of being traded;
- due to be settled within 12 months after the reporting date; or
- due to be settled because the entity does not have an unconditional right to defer settlement for at least 12 months after the reporting date.

IAS 1.BC38C 5.6.60.40 Derivatives generally are classified as current or non-current based on their outstanding maturities. For example, derivatives with maturities exceeding 12 months that the entity intends to hold for more than 12 months from the end of the reporting period are classified as non-current assets or liabilities.

IAS 1.68 5.6.60.50 The "at fair value through profit or loss" category includes assets and liabilities held primarily for the purpose of being traded (for example certain financial assets classified as held for trading), which are classified as current, and assets and liabilities of longer duration (for example those that were designated upon initial recognition into this category). In our view, such assets and liabilities of longer duration should be presented as non-current to the extent that they are not expected to be realised, or are not due to be settled, within 12 months of the reporting date.

5.6.60.60 In our view, this current vs non-current distinction that is made for assets designated upon initial recognition as at fair value through profit or loss also applies to available-for-sale financial assets.

5.6.70 [Not used]

5.6.80 *Statement of comprehensive income**

5.6.80.10 Currently there is no specific guidance on the statement of comprehensive income presentation of gains and losses on financial instruments. In our view, gains and losses on financial instruments should be reported in the most appropriate line item according to their nature.

5.6.80.20 See 5.6.210 for further discussion of specific presentation issues arising from the application of IFRS 7.

5.6.90 *Offsetting*

IAS 32.42   5.6.90.10 Financial assets and liabilities are offset and the net amount reported in the statement of financial position only if both of the following conditions are met:

- the entity currently has a legally enforceable right to set off the recognised amounts; and
- the entity has the intention to settle on a net basis or to realise the asset and settle the liability simultaneously.

IAS 32.45   5.6.90.20 These requirements may apply to instruments such as receivables and payables with the same counterparty if a legal right of offset is agreed to between the parties. Generally it would not be appropriate to offset assets and liabilities that the entity has with unrelated counterparties. To consider offset there would have to be an agreement in place between the all parties, which would be unusual. Also, practically it may be difficult to demonstrate the intention for net settlement by all parties to the arrangement. Consequently, it is unlikely that either of the conditions for offset will be met.

IAS 32.49(a)   5.6.90.30 Individual instruments that, when viewed together, form a synthetic instrument, usually do not qualify for offset. For example, in the case of a fixed rate liability and a fixed-to-floating interest rate swap that together form a synthetic floating rate liability, generally there is no legal right to offset the swap cash flows and the interest payments on the liability as the settlement of the liability and the realisation of the swap do not occur simultaneously.

IAS 32.42   5.6.90.40 When a transfer of financial assets does not qualify for derecognition (see 3.6.1070), the associated liability and the corresponding assets are not offset.

5.6.90.50 Derivative assets and liabilities usually are presented on a gross basis as separate line items in the statement of financial position as generally they do not meet the offset criteria. This is because usually they are entered into with different counterparties and therefore there is no right to offset the recognised amounts. Even if they are entered into with the same counterparty, the derivative assets and liabilities often have different settlement dates or cash flow structures and therefore normally it is difficult to identify matching cash flows that could be offset at a specific date, even if this was allowed by the contractual relationships. In addition, a legal right to offset often may be conditional on a specified future event, in which case there is no *current* legally enforceable right to offset.

IAS 32.50   5.6.90.60 For example, an entity that undertakes a number of financial instrument transactions with a single counterparty may enter into a master netting arrangement with that counterparty. Such an agreement provides for a single net settlement of all financial instruments covered by the agreement in the event of default on any one contract. A master netting arrangement commonly creates a right of offset that becomes enforceable and affects the realisation or settlement of individual financial assets and financial liabilities only following a specified event of default. A master netting arrangement does not provide a basis for offsetting unless both of the offsetting criteria are met (i.e. there is a legally enforceable right and an intention to settle net or simultaneously).

IAS 32.48   5.6.90.70 In another example, an entity may be a member of a clearing house whereby transactions entered into with other members of the clearing house are novated such that the clearing house is the legal counterparty to the entity for all such transactions. Cash margins are payable or receivable between the entity and the clearing house based on the fair value of outstanding transactions and only one net cash payment or receipt, which covers final settlement of maturing transactions, periodic payments on existing transactions, and net payment or receipt of cash margin, occurs each day between the entity and the clearing house. In our view, the cash flows arising from each daily settlement are, in effect, net settlements and, accordingly, offsetting is appropriate in these circumstances when the entity has the current legally enforceable right to offset and the intention to settle net or simultaneously.

IAS 32.49   5.6.90.80 Further examples of situations in which offsetting usually is not appropriate:

- financial or other assets are pledged as collateral for non-recourse financial liabilities;
- financial assets are set aside in a trust by a debtor for the purpose of discharging an obligation without those assets having been accepted by the creditor in settlement of the obligation; and
- an entity incurs an obligation as a result of certain loss events, which it expects to recover through a claim made under an insurance contract.

5.6.100 Significance of financial instruments for financial position and performance

IFRS 7.7   5.6.100.10 The general disclosure principle in IFRS 7 requires an entity to make sufficient disclosures to enable users of the financial statements to evaluate the significance of financial instruments to the entity's financial position and performance. In order to satisfy this principle, IFRS 7 lists specific disclosure requirements (see 5.6.110 – 310).

5.6.110 *Statement of financial position*

5.6.120 *Carrying amount*

IFRS 7.8   5.6.120.10 The carrying amount of the following categories of financial assets and financial liabilities are disclosed either in the statement of financial position or the notes:

- financial assets at fair value through profit or loss;
- held-to-maturity investments;
- loans and receivables;
- available-for-sale financial assets;
- financial liabilities at fair value through profit or loss; and
- financial liabilities measured at amortised cost.

5.6.120.20 [Not used]

IFRS 7.8   5.6.120.30 The carrying amount of instruments that are designated as at fair value through profit or loss are disclosed separately from the carrying amount of instruments held for trading purposes.

5.6.120.40 In our view, derivative assets and liabilities should be presented in separate line items in the statement of financial position if they are significant. If derivative instruments are not significant, then they may be included within other financial assets and other financial liabilities, respectively, with additional details disclosed in the notes to the financial statements.

5.6.130 *Financial assets or financial liabilities at fair value through profit or loss*

5.6.130.10 As noted in 3.6.490, entities may designate financial assets and financial liabilities into the financial assets or financial liabilities at fair value through profit or loss category.

IFRS 7.9   5.6.130.20 If the entity has designated a loan or receivable as at fair value through profit or loss, then it discloses:

- the maximum exposure to credit risk of that loan or receivable at the reporting date;
- the amount by which this risk is mitigated by credit derivatives or similar instruments;
- for both the period and cumulatively, the amount of change in the fair value of the loan or receivable that is attributable to changes in credit risk; and
- for both the period and cumulatively since the loan or receivable was designated, the amount of change in the fair value of any related credit derivative or similar instrument.

IFRS 7.10   5.6.130.30 If the entity has designated a financial liability as at fair value through profit or loss, then it discloses:

- for both the period and cumulatively, the amount of change in the fair value of the financial liability that is attributable to changes in credit risk; and
- the difference between the carrying amount of the financial liability and the amount that the entity will be contractually required to pay at maturity.

5.6.130.40 In our view, the amount that the entity is *contractually required to pay at maturity* should be the undiscounted amount payable at maturity. Furthermore, when the amount payable at maturity is not fixed, e.g. in the case of a liability containing an embedded derivative that modifies the principal amount payable at maturity, the amount disclosed should be based on conditions existing at the reporting date.

IFRS 7.9(c), 5.6.130.50 In the case of both a loan or receivable and a financial liability, the change in
10(a), 11 the instrument's fair value attributable to changes in credit risk is determined either as the amount of the change in its fair value not attributable to changes in market conditions, or using an alternative method that represents more faithfully the amount of the change in fair value attributable to credit risk. In this regard an entity discloses:

- the methods used to determine the change in fair value attributable to changes in credit risk; and
- if the entity does not believe that the information provided in order to comply with the standard faithfully represents the change in the instrument's fair value attributable to credit risk, then the reasons for reaching this conclusion and the factors that the entity considers relevant.

5.6.140 *Reclassification*

IFRS 7.12 5.6.140.10 If an entity reclassifies a financial asset into or out of either the cost or amortised cost category or the fair value category, with the exception of those reclassifications permitted by paragraphs 50B ("rare circumstances") or 50D (assets that would have met the definition of loans and receivables and are intended to be held for the foreseeable future or to maturity) of IAS 39 (see 3.6.850), then the amount reclassified and the reason for the reclassification are disclosed. This would be relevant for held-to-maturity investments being reclassified from the available-for-sale category because the two-year tainting period has expired (see 3.6.570); it also would apply in exceptional circumstances in which a fair value measure for a financial asset no longer is available.

IFRS 7.12A 5.6.140.20 If an entity reclassifies a financial asset out of fair value through profit or loss or available-for-sale as permitted by paragraphs 50B or 50D of IAS 39 (see 3.6.850), then it discloses:

- the amount reclassified into and out of each category;
- for each reporting period until derecognition of the reclassified financial assets, the carrying amounts and fair values of all financial assets that have been reclassified in the current and previous reporting periods;
- if the financial asset was reclassified due to rare circumstances, then the facts and circumstances indicating that the situation was rare;
- for the reporting period in which the financial asset was reclassified, the fair value gain or loss on the financial asset recognised in profit or loss or other comprehensive income in both that reporting period and in the previous reporting period;
- for each reporting period following the reclassification, including the reporting period in which the financial asset was reclassified, until derecognition of the financial asset:
  - the fair value gain or loss that would have been recognised in profit or loss or other comprehensive income if the financial asset had not been reclassified; and

- the gain, loss, income and expense recognised in profit or loss; and
- the effective interest rate and the estimated amounts of cash flows the entity expects to recover, as at the date of reclassification of the financial asset.

5.6.150 *Derecognition**

IFRS 7.13   5.6.150.10 If an entity has transferred a financial asset in a way that does not qualify for derecognition, for example where it has transferred a financial asset but continues to recognise that asset in its entirety, or to the extent of the entity's continuing involvement (see 3.6.1240), then it discloses:

- the nature of the asset;
- the nature of the risks and rewards of ownership to which the entity remains exposed;
- when the entity continues to recognise the full amount of the asset, the carrying amount of the asset and of the associated liability; and
- when the entity recognises the asset to the extent of its continuing involvement, the total carrying amount of the original asset, the amount of the asset that the entity continues to recognise and the carrying amount of the associated liability.

5.6.150.20 If the terms of a financial liability are modified substantially, resulting in an extinguishment of the old financial liability, then the old liability is derecognised and the restructured financial instrument is treated as a new financial liability (see 3.6.1340). In our view, any gains or losses arising as a result of the derecognition of the old financial liability (including any unamortised discount or premium) should be presented as a separate line item within the disclosure of finance income or expense, respectively.

5.6.160 *Collateral*

IFRS 7.14   5.6.160.10 An entity that has pledged financial assets as collateral for liabilities and contingent liabilities discloses the carrying amount of these assets pledged as collateral, as well as the terms and conditions related to the pledge.

IFRS 7.15   5.6.160.20 When an entity has accepted collateral that it is entitled to sell or repledge in the absence of default by the owner, it discloses:

- the fair value of the collateral held (financial and non-financial assets);
- the fair value of such collateral sold or repledged and whether the entity has an obligation to return it; and
- any terms and conditions associated with its use of this collateral.

5.6.170 *Allowance account for credit losses*

IFRS 7.16,   5.6.170.10 If an entity recognises an impairment of financial assets resulting from credit
BC27   losses in a separate account, then the entity discloses a reconciliation of changes in that account, during the period for each class of financial asset. In the rare circumstances

that an entity does not utilise such an account, then there is no requirement to produce equivalent information.

IFRS 3.B41,
IAS 39.43

5.6.170.20 In our view, it is not appropriate to set up an impairment allowance account on the initial recognition of a financial asset. Financial instruments are measured on initial recognition at fair value plus transaction costs if appropriate. Impairment of a financial asset is recognised only if there is objective evidence of impairment as a result of events that occur after the initial recognition of an asset (see 3.6.1400.20). In addition IFRS 3 *Business Combinations* (2008) provides specific guidance related to business combinations, under which the acquirer in a business combination does not recognise a separate valuation allowance as of the acquisition date for assets acquired in a business combination that are measured at their acquisition date fair values because the uncertainty about future cash flows is included in the fair value measurement.

5.6.180 *Compound financial instruments with multiple embedded derivatives*

IFRS 7.17,
BC29-BC31

5.6.180.10 If an entity issues a compound financial instrument that contains multiple embedded derivative features whose values are interdependent, then it discloses the existence of these features. For example, a callable convertible debt instrument has more than one embedded derivative feature and the value of the call option depends on both interest rates and equity prices. The dependency on both interest rates and equity prices is disclosed.

5.6.190 *Defaults and breaches*

IFRS 7.18, 19

5.6.190.10 If the entity has defaulted during the period on the principal, interest, sinking fund or redemption provisions of a loan payable (i.e. a financial liability, other than a short-term trade payable on normal credit terms) recognised in the statement of financial position, or if during the period there were breaches that were not remedied or the terms were not renegotiated before the reporting date, such that the lender could demand accelerated repayment, then the entity discloses:

- details of the default or breach;
- the amount recognised in respect of the loans payable on which the default or breach occurred; and
- with respect to the above amounts, whether the default or breach was remedied or the terms of the loans payable renegotiated before the financial statements were authorised for issue.

5.6.200 *Embedded derivatives*

IAS 39.11

5.6.200.10 There is no specific guidance on the presentation of embedded derivatives and the related host contracts (see 3.6.450.10).

5.6.200.20 In our view, when an embedded derivative is not required to be accounted for separately (see 3.6.260), the embedded derivative is presented in the same line item as the host contract.

IAS 39.11 5.6.200.30 When an embedded derivative is accounted for separately, an issue arises as to whether the embedded derivative should be included in the same line item as the host contract, on the basis that the two instruments are subject to the same contract, or whether the derivative should be presented separately, together with other derivative instruments. IFRSs do not address whether an embedded derivative should be presented separately in the statement of financial position and therefore the general presentation rules in IAS 1 and IAS 32 are applicable (see 3.1). In our view, if the host contract is a financial instrument and the offsetting criteria are met for the host and the embedded derivative, then a separable embedded derivative and the host contract should be presented on a net basis (see 5.6.90).

5.6.210 *Statement of comprehensive income#*

5.6.220 *Items of income, expense, gains or losses*

IFRS 7.20(a) 5.6.220.10 Net gains or losses on the following are disclosed either in the statement of comprehensive income or in the notes:

- financial assets or financial liabilities at fair value through profit or loss, separately for those that are designated as such on initial recognition and those classified as held for trading;
- available-for-sale financial assets, showing separately the amount of gain or loss recognised in other comprehensive income during the period and the amount reclassified from other comprehensive income to profit or loss for the period;
- held-to-maturity investments;
- loans and receivables; and
- financial liabilities measured at amortised cost.

5.6.220.20 For financial assets and financial liabilities at fair value through profit or loss, there is no need to distinguish between the fair value changes and interest income and dividend or expense. However, fair value changes (net gains or net losses) on such instruments should be presented separately, if material. In addition, the entity should disclose within its accounting policies whether or not interest income and expense on items at fair value through profit or loss are separated.

IAS 1.82(g) 5.6.220.30 Each component of other comprehensive income classified by nature is presented as a separate line item in the statement of comprehensive income. This would include the net change in fair value on available-for-sale financial assets, the effective portion of the net gain or loss on hedges of net investments in foreign operations and the effective portion of changes in fair value in respect of hedging instruments in cash flow hedges.

IAS 1.93, 94 5.6.220.40 Separate components of other comprehensive income are created in accordance with the requirements of IAS 39, which also determine how and when these components should be reclassified to profit or loss. Reclassification adjustments are included with the related component of other comprehensive income in the period that the adjustment is reclassified to profit or loss. They may be presented in the statement of comprehensive income or in the notes. At any point in time the balance on these separate components of other comprehensive income represents a cumulative gain or loss that will be reclassified to profit or loss at some future date. In our view, it would not be appropriate for an entity to reduce or increase these components of other comprehensive income for any reasons other than for those as allowed under IAS 39 (except for related tax effects under IAS 12 *Income Taxes* (see 3.13.390)).

IFRS 7.20(b),
IG13
5.6.220.50 Total interest income and total interest expense for financial assets or financial liabilities that are not at fair value through profit or loss, calculated using the effective interest method, are disclosed either in the statement of comprehensive income or in the notes. Total interest expense disclosed forms part of finance costs, which is required by paragraph 82(b) of IAS 1 to be presented separately in the statement of comprehensive income. The line item for finance costs also may include amounts associated with non-financial liabilities.

IFRS 7.B5(e),
BC34,
IAS 1.35, 82,
5.6.220.60 For non-derivatives at fair value through profit or loss, an entity may either present foreign exchange gains and losses and/or interest income and expense separately from other fair value changes, or present the entire fair value change on a net basis as a single amount. If presented separately, in our view any foreign exchange gains and losses that arise from operating activities should be presented as part of operating income, and exchange gains and losses related to financing activities as part of finance income and finance costs. In addition, if interest is presented separately, then it should be measured on an effective interest basis and presented as interest income or expense.

IFRS 7.20(b)
5.6.220.70 If interest income or expense includes both amounts from instruments at fair value through profit or loss and from instruments not at fair value through profit or loss, then the disclosure of total interest income and total interest expense for financial assets that are not at fair value through profit or loss is required.

5.6.220.80 For derivatives, in our view the presentation of gains and losses depends on whether or not those derivatives are used as hedging instruments for accounting purposes or whether an entity applies the fair value option to a related non-derivative item as an alternative to hedge accounting.

5.6.220.90 If an entity uses derivatives as hedging instruments for accounting purposes, or applies the fair value option to a non-derivative as an alternative to hedge accounting (see 3.6.490), then in our view gains or losses on both the non-derivative, being the item that is economically hedged or subject to hedge accounting, and the derivative, may be split for presentation purposes in order to reflect best the impact on profit or loss of the economics of the relationship. For example, if a bank applies the fair value option to a portfolio of fixed rate loans that are hedged economically using a portfolio of interest rate swaps, then we believe that it is appropriate to separate accrued interest, measured on an effective interest basis, from other fair value changes on both the loans and the swaps and to present the accrued amounts in interest income. See 5.6.270.30 – 60 for further discussion of the presentation of gains and losses on derivatives which are hedging instruments.

5.6.220.100 However, in our view gains and losses arising on derivatives other than those resulting from qualifying hedging instruments, or derivatives economically hedging a financial instrument designated as at fair value through profit or loss, should be presented in their entirety in a single line in the statement of comprehensive income. For example, the changes in fair value of an interest rate swap include accrued interest and gains and losses arising from changes in interest rates. We believe that the entire fair value change on a derivative should be presented on a net basis; the accrual component of the fair value change should not be presented separately.

5.6.220.110 If hedge accounting is not applied to a derivative instrument that is entered into as an economic hedge, then we prefer that the gains or losses on the derivative instrument not be presented as an adjustment to revenues, cost of sales or other line items related to the hedged item. However, in our view derivative gains and losses may be shown in the statement of comprehensive income as either operating or financing items depending on the nature of the item being economically hedged.

5.6.220.120 In our view, the possibilities for the presentation in the statement of comprehensive income also apply to the presentation in the statement of cash flows (see 2.3.60).

5.6.230 *Fee income and expense*

IFRS 7.20(c)   5.6.230.10 Fee income and expense arising from financial assets that are not at fair value through profit or loss, and from trust or other fiduciary activities, are disclosed. The amounts disclosed should exclude amounts included in calculating the effective interest rate.

5.6.240 *Interest income*

IFRS 7.20(d)   5.6.240.10 Interest income on impaired financial assets is disclosed. In our view, when impairment testing is carried out on a portfolio basis (see 3.6.1420) and the portfolio is found to be impaired, the interest income disclosure should be consistent with the portfolio approach used for impairment testing.

IFRS 7.20(e)   5.6.240.20 For each class of financial asset, the amount of any impairment loss is disclosed.

5.6.245 *Forthcoming requirements*

IFRS 9.C12   5.6.245.10 IFRS 9 introduces consequential amendments to IAS 1 that require two additional line items to be presented separately in the statement of comprehensive income:

- gains or losses arising from the derecognition of financial assets measured at amortised cost; and
- gains or losses, arising from re-measurement to fair value of financial assets due to a reclassification.

5.6.245.20 See 3.6A for further details.

5.6.250 *Other disclosures#*

5.6.260 *Accounting policies*

IFRS 7.21,   5.6.260.10 The summary of accounting policies includes disclosure with respect to the
IAS 1.117   measurement basis (or bases) used in preparing the financial statements. Any other accounting policies that are relevant to the understanding of the financial statements also
are disclosed. As an example, the disclosure may include:

- the nature of financial assets and financial liabilities designated as at fair value through profit or loss;
- the criteria for designating financial assets and financial liabilities as at fair value through profit or loss;
- how the entity satisfied the criteria, contained in paragraphs 9, 11A and 12 of IAS 39, for designating financial assets and financial liabilities as at fair value through profit or loss;
- the criteria for designating financial assets as available for sale;
- whether regular way transactions are accounted for using trade or settlement date accounting (see 3.6.220);
- when an impairment allowance account for credit losses is used, the criteria for determining when this account is used in place of reducing the carrying amount of the impaired asset directly;
- when an impairment allowance account for credit losses is used, the criteria for writing off amounts charged to the allowance account against the carrying amount of the impaired financial asset;
- for each category of financial instruments, how the net gains and losses are determined; for example, for items at fair value through profit or loss whether the entity includes interest or dividend income;
- the criteria for determining that there is objective evidence that an impairment loss has occurred; and
- when terms of the financial assets that would otherwise be past due or impaired have been renegotiated, the accounting policies for financial assets that are the subject of renegotiated terms.

5.6.270 *Hedge accounting**

IFRS 7.22-24   5.6.270.10 An entity is required to make specific disclosures about its outstanding hedge
accounting relationships. The following disclosures are made separately for fair value
hedges, cash flow hedges and hedges of net investments in foreign operations:

- a description of each type of hedge;
- a description of the financial instruments designated as hedging instruments for the hedge and their fair values at the reporting date;
- the nature of the risks being hedged;
- in a fair value hedge, gains or losses on the hedging instrument and the hedged item;
- ineffectiveness recognised in profit or loss arising from cash flow hedges; and

- ineffectiveness recognised in profit or loss arising from hedges of net investments in foreign operations.

IFRS 7.23 5.6.270.20 In addition, for a cash flow hedge the entity discloses:

- the periods in which the transactions are expected to occur, and when they are expected to affect profit or loss;
- a description of any forecast transactions that were hedged but are no longer expected to occur;
- the amount recognised in other comprehensive income during the period;
- the amount reclassified from equity to profit or loss during the period, showing the amount included in each line item in the statement of comprehensive income; and
- the amount removed from equity and added to the initial measurement of a non-financial asset or non-financial liability during the period.

5.6.270.30 Gains and losses on derivative hedging instruments have three possible elements: (1) the effective portion; (2) the ineffective portion; and (3) the portion excluded from the assessment of effectiveness.

5.6.270.40 As IFRSs are silent as to the presentation of financial instrument gains and losses in the statement of comprehensive income, there are several alternatives to consider when presenting such gains and losses. The following alternatives relate to a fair value hedge:

- Present the entire change in fair value of the derivative hedging instrument in the same line item as gains and losses from the hedged item.
- Present the effective and ineffective portions of the derivative hedging instrument in the same line item as gains and losses from the hedged item. Present the portion excluded from the assessment of hedge effectiveness in the same line item as gains or losses on non-hedging derivative instruments.
- Present only the effective portion of the derivative hedging instrument in the same line item as the hedged item. Present the ineffective portion and the excluded portion in the same line item as gains or losses on non-hedging derivative instruments.

5.6.270.50 Of the alternatives noted in 5.6.270.40, we prefer the third method.

5.6.270.60 The same possibilities exist for a cash flow hedge, although the timing of recognition of the effective portion of the hedging instrument would be different.

5.6.270.70 There are no specific requirements in IFRSs addressing the presentation of gains and losses on derivatives. However, in our view it would be inappropriate to separate and present gains and losses on derivatives using a method different from one of the three described in 5.6.270.40 or as discussed in 5.6.220.90.

5.6.270.80 In our view, when hedge accounting is not applied, either because an entity chooses not to apply hedge accounting, or because the criteria for hedge accounting are not met, information should be provided to explain the relationship between the derivatives and the transactions for which there are an economic hedge. We believe that this should be done to enable users of the financial statements to understand the extent to which risk is mitigated through the use of the derivatives.

5.6.280 *Fair value**

IFRS 7.25-30   5.6.280.10 For each class of financial asset and financial liability, an entity discloses the fair value in a manner that allows for it to be compared to its carrying amount. Such a disclosure is not required:

- if the carrying amount is a reasonable approximation of the fair value;
- for an investment in equity instruments that do not have a quoted market price in an active market and for derivatives linked to such equity instruments that are measured at cost because fair value cannot be determined reliably; and
- for a contract containing a discretionary participation feature when the fair value of the feature cannot be measured reliably.

IFRS 7.29   5.6.280.20 The carrying amounts of short-term receivables and payables are likely to approximate their fair values in a low interest rate environment in which the effect of discounting is not material. In such cases it is not necessary to disclose these instruments' fair values. However, the fair values of long-term liabilities and receivables carried at amortised cost should be disclosed as the effect of discounting is expected to be material.

IFRS 7.30   5.6.280.30 As described in 3.6.790, IAS 39 presumes that a reliable fair value can be determined for almost all financial instruments. The only exception to this is certain unquoted equity instruments or derivatives linked to and to be settled by delivery of such equity instruments, and contracts containing discretionary participation features for which a reliable fair value cannot be obtained. If any such instruments are not stated at fair value, then the entity discloses:

- the fact that these instruments cannot be measured reliably;
- a description of the financial instruments;
- the carrying amount;
- an explanation of why fair value cannot be measured reliably;
- information about the market for the instruments;
- information about whether and how the entity intends to dispose of the instruments; and
- if the instrument is derecognised, the fact that the fair value could not be measured reliably, the carrying amount at the time of derecognition and the amount of the gain or loss recognised.

IFRS 7.26   5.6.280.40 The fair value disclosures are based on financial asset and financial liability classes. Offsetting is permissible only to the extent that their carrying amounts are offset in the statement of financial position (see 5.6.90).

IFRS 7.27 5.6.280.50 For each class of financial instruments, disclosure is required of the methods used and, when a valuation technique is used, the assumptions applied in determining fair values. This includes:

- assumptions used in a valuation technique, e.g. prepayment rates, rates of estimated credit losses and interest or discount rates; and
- if there has been a change in valuation technique, then the change, and the reasons for making it.

IFRS 7.27B 5.6.280.60 An entity whose fair value measurements are recognised in the statement of financial position discloses for each class of financial instruments the level in the fair value hierarchy (see 5.6.280.70) into which the fair value measurements are categorised in their entirety.

IFRS 7.27A 5.6.280.70 The fair value hierarchy is defined as follows:

- *Level 1*. Fair values measured using quoted prices (unadjusted) in active markets for identical assets or liabilities.
- *Level 2*. Fair values measured using inputs other than quoted prices included within Level 1 that are observable for the asset or liability, either directly (i.e. as prices) or indirectly (i.e. derived from prices).
- *Level 3*. Fair values measured using inputs for the asset or liability that are not based on observable market data (i.e. unobservable inputs).

5.6.280.80 See 3.6.940 for a discussion of the concept of fair value, including whether a market is active and whether an input is observable, is discussed in 3.6.940. This section focuses on issues related to the fair value hierarchy disclosures.

5.6.280.90 The flowchart below outlines an approach to determining the classification of fair value measurements within the fair value hierarchy:

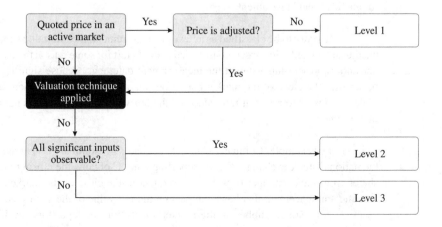

5.6.290 Level 1

IFRS 7.
27A(a),
IAS 39.AG71

5.6.290.10 A fair value measurement for a financial instrument is classified in Level 1 of the fair value hierarchy if the fair value is determined as the unadjusted quoted price for an identical instrument in an active market.

5.6.290.20 For example, Company B holds units in an open-ended unlisted investment fund. The units in the fund are often bought and sold but only by or to the fund or fund manager, i.e. the units are not traded on a stock exchange and cannot be sold to third parties. As the fund is not listed, the fund calculates the price of the units only at a specific time each day to facilitate the purchase and sale of the units. The transactions take place only at this time on each day and at the price so determined by the fund manager. The fair value of the units is determined to be the price calculated by the fund manager. Whether this is a Level 1 measurement will depend upon the number of trades that occur in the units and whether this qualifies as "regularly occurring transactions", and on whether the fund manager's daily pricing is sufficient to meet the "regularly available" criterion. Daily pricing is likely to constitute evidence of regularly available prices. If the number of trades occurring is sufficient for the market in these units to be considered an active market then, notwithstanding that the units are being purchased and sold by the fund and are not being traded between unrelated third-party market participants, a fair value measurement of the units using the unadjusted daily price for the reporting date would be a Level 1 measurement.

IAS 39.AG73

5.6.290.30 It is important to note that to be classified as a Level 1, the measurement should be the quoted price of an identical instrument and not a measurement based on a quoted rate or index to be used as an input into a valuation model to calculate the fair value of the instrument. If a rate (rather than a price) is quoted in an active market, the entity uses that market-quoted rate as an input into a valuation technique to determine fair value. It is explicit in the concept of a Level 1 measurement that the instrument being valued is the same as other existing instruments of the same type. Over-the-counter derivative contracts are individual agreements between specific counterparties and therefore cannot be the subject of a Level 1 measurement as there is unlikely to be an active market for an "identical" instrument.

5.6.290.40 In order to be classified as a Level 1 measurement, the fair value should be the unadjusted quoted price observed in an active market. If for some reason the quoted price does not represent fair value at the measurement date, e.g. because significant events occur after the close of the market but before the measurement date, then the quoted price is adjusted to arrive at fair value and the fair value measurement is not a Level 1 measurement.

5.6.290.50 For example, Company C invests in shares of Company D that are listed on the national stock exchange. On the reporting date, C obtains the closing price of the shares from the exchange. However, subsequent to the close of the market, D makes a public announcement that has an impact on the fair value of the shares as evidenced by prices for a small number of aftermarket transactions in depository receipts on the shares of D that are traded in another jurisdiction. In this case, C uses the aftermarket prices to make appropriate adjustments to the closing price from the exchange to arrive at the fair value of the shares at the measurement date. As the adjustment is derived from observed market prices, the resulting fair value measurement will be a Level 2 measurement.

5.6.290.60 In some cases, conditions attached to a financial instrument may not be reflected in the quoted active market price and, in our view this may justify an adjustment to the quoted price to arrive at the instrument's fair value. For example, assume that an investor is contractually bound by lock-up provisions that prohibit or restrict the sale of the instrument for a specified period. If, in light of these restrictions, the investor determines that the instrument held is not the same as the one with the quoted market price due to the contractual lock-up provisions (i.e. the instruments are not identical), then a valuation technique may be required in order to make adjustments to the quoted active market price to arrive at fair value. As the investor has concluded that the instruments are not identical, the fair value measurement would not qualify as a Level 1 measurement.

IAS 39.AG71 5.6.290.70 There may be other circumstances in which the fair value measurement of an investment that is quoted in an active market may appropriately be categorised as Level 2. For example, an investment is regarded as quoted in an active market if quoted prices representing actual transactions are "readily and regularly available" from a dealer, broker or pricing service. However, the requirement to use a particular price for measurement purposes is limited to "published price quotations." Therefore, there may be circumstances in which quoted prices are readily available from dealers or brokers, if specific enquiry is made of them, but these prices are not "published." If the reporting entity holds a large number of such investments, then the entity may utilise a pricing service which does not rely exclusively on quoted prices for each identical investment (i.e. a matrix pricing methodology) as a practical expedient on cost/benefit grounds provided it has obtained evidence that provides reasonable assurance that the resulting value represents fair value, that is the evidence supports a conclusion that there would be no more than trivial differences between the prices utilised and the quoted prices that would be obtained from a relevant broker or dealer. If the fair value measurement of such an investment is determined using a matrix pricing methodology, then that fair value measurement would not be Level 1 even though the investment is regarded as quoted in an active market.

5.6.300 Level 2 and Level 3

IAS 39.48A 5.6.300.10 Level 2 and Level 3 fair value measurements for financial instruments are determined using valuation techniques. This includes valuing an instrument using a current price for an identical instrument if there is not an active market for that instrument.

IFRS 7.27A 5.6.300.20 The level in the hierarchy into which a financial instrument's fair value measurement is classified in its entirety is determined by reference to the observability and significance of the inputs used in the valuation model. Valuation techniques often incorporate both observable inputs and unobservable inputs. Fair value measurements determined using valuation techniques are classified in their entirety in either Level 2 or Level 3 based on the lowest level input that is significant to the measurement. That is, if a valuation model uses both observable and unobservable inputs, the fair value measurement is classified in Level 3 if the unobservable inputs are significant to the fair value measurement in its entirety. This assessment is made independently of the number or quality of the Level 2 inputs used in the model. Differentiating between Level 2 and Level 3 fair value measurements, i.e. assessing whether inputs are observable and whether the unobservable inputs are significant, may require judgement and a careful analysis of the inputs used to measure fair value, including consideration of factors specific to the asset or liability.

5.6.300.30 An input is observable if it can be observed as a market price or can be derived from an observed market price. In each case, it is not necessary that the market is active. Examples of observable inputs might include:

- transaction prices in markets that are not active for identical instruments;
- quoted prices in active markets for similar, but not identical, instruments;
- transaction prices in markets that are not active for similar, but not identical, instruments;
- interest rates derived from quoted bond prices;
- quoted foreign exchange and interest rates (e.g. forward currency rates and swap rates);
- implied volatilities derived from quoted option prices; and
- credit spreads derived from quoted credit default swap prices.

5.6.300.40 Examples of unobservable inputs include:

- interest rates in a currency that are not observable and cannot be corroborated by observable market data for the term of the financial instrument being valued; and
- volatility for a share option derived from the share's historical prices, as it does not generally represent current market expectations about future volatility.

IFRS 7.27A 5.6.300.50 Assessing significance requires judgement, considering factors specific to the asset or liability. When a fair value measurement is developed using inputs from multiple levels of the fair value hierarchy, the inclusion of a lower level input in an entity's measurement may indicate that the input is significant because the entity's decision to include the lower level input provides evidence that the entity considers the input to be significant to the overall measurement of fair value. However, the final determination of whether inputs are significant is a matter of judgement that will require entities to consider the importance of an input to the overall fair value measurement, including the quantitative effect of an input on the overall fair value measurement.

5.6.300.60 In instances where multiple unobservable inputs are used, in our view the unobservable inputs should be considered in total for purposes of determining their significance. In instances where factors such as volatility inputs are used, an entity could apply some form of comparability methodology (for example, a stress test on an option's volatility input or a "with and without" comparison) to assist in determining significance.

5.6.300.70 An entity may obtain prices from a third-party pricing service or broker as inputs to a fair value measurement. Whether those prices represent observable or unobservable inputs depends on their nature or source.

5.6.300.80 The use of a pricing service does not change the analysis of the categorisation of the inputs in the fair value hierarchy. Also, prices obtained from a pricing service are not considered observable simply because they were obtained from a third party. Rather, an entity using a pricing service should obtain an understanding of the source of the inputs received by the pricing service to properly classify any fair value measurements based on those inputs. For example, if a pricing service provides an unadjusted quoted price from an active market for an identical instrument, then a fair value measurement based only on that price would be a Level 1 measurement. Alternatively, if the pricing service provides prices based on models generated by the pricing service, then any resulting fair value measurement would be a Level 2 or Level 3 measurement depending on the significance of the inputs used.

5.6.300.90 Consensus pricing services obtain information from multiple subscribers who each submit prices to the pricing service. The pricing service returns consensus prices to each subscriber based on the data received. When assessing consensus data it is important to understand what the prices submitted represent. If the estimates provided to the service do not represent executable quotes or are not based on observable prices, then a fair value measurement derived from the consensus price would be a Level 3 measurement. However, if the inputs to the price received from the pricing service are Level 1 or Level 2 inputs, then the use of those prices may result in a higher level measurement than Level 3.

5.6.300.100 Similar considerations apply to prices obtained from brokers. A broker quote generally is not a binding offer. Even if it is, it may not represent the price at which an orderly transaction would take place between market participants. Where a broker quote reflects actual current market transactions in an identical instrument, it may represent a Level 1 or Level 2 input. However, where a broker quote is an indicative price based on the broker's valuation models, then it may represent a Level 2 or Level 3 input.

IFRS 7.27
B(c), (d), (e) 5.6.300.110 For fair value measurements in Level 3 of the fair value hierarchy, the entity discloses for each class of financial instruments:

- a reconciliation from the beginning balances to the ending balances for each period, disclosing separately the changes in the period attributable to the following:
  - total gains or losses for the period recognised in profit or loss and a description of where they are presented in the statement of comprehensive income or separate income statement;
  - total gains or losses recognised in other comprehensive income;

- purchases, sales, issues and settlements (each type of movement disclosed separately); and
- transfers into or out of Level 3 (e.g. transfers attributable to changes in the observability of market data) and the reasons for those transfers; for significant transfers, transfers into Level 3 are distinguished from transfers out of Level 3;

- the amount of total gains or losses for the period included in profit or loss that are attributable to gains or losses related to assets and liabilities held at the end of the reporting period, and a description of where they have been presented in the statement of comprehensive income or separate income statement; and
- the effect, if significant on the fair value, of changing one or more of the inputs used in fair value measurement to another reasonably possible assumption, and also how the effect of such changes is calculated. For this purpose, significance is judged with respect to profit or loss, and total assets or total liabilities, or, when changes in fair value are recognised in other comprehensive income, total equity.

5.6.300.120 The entity also discloses any significant transfers between Level 1 and Level 2 and the reasons for those transfers. For this purpose significance is judged with respect to profit or loss, and total assets or liabilities. Transfers into each level are to be disclosed and discussed separately from transfers out of each level.

5.6.300.130 Instruments may be transferred into or out of Level 3 for a number of reasons, e.g. changes in the inputs used in a valuation, refinements in modelling techniques, the initiation or cessation of market transactions in similar instruments or the passage of time.

5.6.300.140 For example, Company E has an over-the-counter contract to purchase natural gas every month for the next 30 months. The contract is being accounted for as a derivative instrument and is measured at fair value on the statement of financial position. Quoted natural gas prices are available for the next 24 months after the current reporting date. For the remaining six months of the term, the company uses internally developed estimates of future natural gas prices. As market prices are not available for substantially the entire term of the contract and the impact of the unobservable inputs is significant, the fair value measurement of this contract is classified as a Level 3 measurement. In the following year, if quoted natural gas prices continue to be available for the following 24 months, the fair value measurement might be classified as a Level 2 measurement.

5.6.300.150 IFRS 7 does not discuss at which point in time the transferred financial instrument should be measured for the purpose of disclosure of the transfers into or out of a level in the fair value hierarchy. Where practicable, we prefer for an entity to record the transfer at the fair value on the date of transfer. However, it may be difficult for entities to identify the precise date at which non-observable inputs for a fair value measurement of an instrument became or ceased to be significant, particularly as they might not perform fair value measurements on a daily or weekly basis. In our view, an entity should choose an accounting policy, to be applied consistently, to record transfers based on the fair value measurement at the beginning or the end of the relevant interim or annual period, depending on the period for which the disclosure is made.

IFRS 7.27B(c)   5.6.300.160 An entity discloses the changes in fair value of Level 3 instruments recognised in profit or loss and in other comprehensive income (see 5.6.300.110) irrespective of whether they are due to the effect of changes in observable inputs or unobservable inputs.

5.6.300.170 Entities may disclose additional information if they consider it helpful to users of the financial statements. For example, an entity may:

- separate the Level 3 fair value gains and losses into amounts due to changes in observable inputs and amounts due to changes in unobservable inputs; or
- for a Level 3 instrument that is economically hedged by an instrument with a fair value measurement in Level 1 or Level 2, disclose the extent to which the fair value movements offset or correlate.

IFRS 7.27B(e)   5.6.300.180 For Level 3 instruments, if the effect of changing one or more inputs to reasonably possible alternative assumptions would result in a significant change to the fair value measurement, disclosure is required, by class of financial instruments. An entity discloses how these effects have been calculated. For the purpose of this disclosure, significance is judged with respect to profit or loss, and total assets or total liabilities, or, when changes in fair value are recognised in other comprehensive income, total equity.

5.6.300.190 In our view, reasonably possible alternative assumptions are assumptions that could reasonably have been included in the valuation model at the reporting date based on the circumstances at the reporting date. We do not believe that this disclosure is intended to be a forward looking sensitivity analysis for market risk variables or otherwise intended to describe the effect of possible future changes in market conditions.

5.6.310 *Day one profit or loss*

IFRS 7.28   5.6.310.10 When a financial instrument is measured at fair value using a valuation technique that uses unobservable inputs, IAS 39 precludes the recognition of a gain on initial recognition (see 3.6.710.20). For each class of financial asset and financial liability to which this requirement applies, the following is disclosed:

- the accounting policy for recognising the difference subsequently in profit or loss; and
- the aggregate difference yet to be recognised in profit or loss at the beginning and end of the period, and a reconciliation of changes in this difference during the period.

5.6.320 **Nature and extent of risks arising from financial instruments***

IFRS 7.31   5.6.320.10 The general disclosure principle in IFRS 7 requires an entity to make qualitative and quantitative disclosures that enable users of its financial statements to evaluate the nature and the extent of risks arising from financial instruments to which the entity is exposed at the reporting date and how they have been managed. The extent of disclosure depends on the extent of the entity's exposure to risks arising from financial instruments. The types of risks covered by the disclosures include, but are not limited to, credit risk, liquidity risk and market risk.

IFRS 7.B6   5.6.320.20 The disclosures are included either within the financial statements or within another statement such as a management commentary or risk report. The location of the disclosures may be limited by local laws. If the disclosures are made outside the financial statements, then the financial statements are cross-referenced to this information (see 5.8.10.65). The disclosures are made available to users on the same terms and timing as the financial statements.

IFRS 7 B2(b)   5.6.320.30 IFRS 7 addresses risks arising from financial instruments only. Consequently, exposures from commodity contracts that meet the "own use" exemption (see 3.6.90.20), purchase and sale contracts for non-financial items which are to be settled in a foreign currency, highly probable forecasted transactions (see 3.7.230) etc. are excluded from the scope of IFRS 7 even though they may give rise to financial risk for the entity. If an entity manages its financial risk based on its total exposure, i.e. including risk arising from those items not included within the scope of IFRS 7 and such exposures are included in reports to key management personnel, then in our view IFRS 7 does not prohibit an entity from providing additional disclosures about its total financial risk exposure rather than just the risk arising from financial instruments. However, all such additional disclosures should be clearly separated from those required by IFRS 7.

5.6.330 *Qualitative disclosures*

IFRS 7.33   5.6.330.10 An entity discloses the following, for each type of risk arising from financial instruments:

- the exposure to the risk and how it arises;
- the entity's objectives, policies and processes for managing the risk; and
- the methods used to measure the risk.

IFRS 7.33(c)   5.6.330.20 If there are any changes to the factors described in 5.6.330.10 from the previous period, then the reason for the change is disclosed. The changes may be due to changes in exposures themselves or the way in which the entity manages them.

5.6.340 *Quantitative disclosures#*

IFRS 7.34   5.6.340.10 An entity discloses summary quantitative data about its exposure to each risk arising from its financial instruments at the reporting date. The disclosure is based on information that is provided internally to key management personnel of the entity, for example, the board of directors or the chief executive officer. If an entity uses several methods to manage risk, then the disclosure is based on the method that provides the most relevant and reliable information. The quantitative disclosures described in 5.6.350 – 510 are required, if not already provided as part of the summary quantitative data based on information that is provided internally to key management personnel of the entity.

IFRS 7.35   5.6.340.20 When the quantitative data disclosed at the reporting date is not representative of the risk exposure over the course of the reporting period, the entity provides additional disclosure that is representative.

5.6.350 *Concentrations of risk*

IFRS 7.34(c)   5.6.350.10 An entity discloses concentrations of risk.

IFRS 7.B8   5.6.350.20 Concentrations of risk arise from financial instruments that have similar characteristics and are affected in a similar manner when there are changes in economic or other conditions. Identifying concentrations of risk is a matter of judgement and therefore an entity discloses:

- a description of how management determines concentrations;
- a description of the shared characteristics that identify each concentration (e.g. counterparty, geographical area, currency or market); and
- the amount of the risk exposure associated with financial instruments sharing that characteristic.

5.6.360 *Credit risk#**

IFRS 7 A   5.6.360.10 Credit risk is the risk that one party to a financial instrument will cause a financial loss for the other party by failing to discharge an obligation. In our view, the credit risk disclosure requirements are not required for investments in equity instruments as these do not impose an obligation on the issuer to make any payments to the holder and, consequently, the holder is not exposed to the risk of the issuer failing to discharge an obligation.

IFRS 7.36(a),   5.6.360.20 An entity discloses, by class of financial instrument, the amount that best
B9, B10(c)   represents the entity's maximum exposure to credit risk. The amount does not take into account any collateral held or other credit enhancements. For example, the amount for a financial asset typically would be the gross carrying amount less any required offset (in accordance with IAS 32) and any impairment losses recognised.

IFRS 7.36(b)   5.6.360.30 With respect to the amount that best represents the entity's credit risk exposure, the entity discloses a description of any collateral held and other credit enhancements.

IFRS 7.36(c)   5.6.360.40 The entity discloses information about the credit quality of financial assets (by class) that are neither past due nor impaired.

IFRS 7.36(d)   5.6.360.50 For each class of financial asset, an entity discloses the carrying amount of the financial assets that would be past due or impaired had the terms not been renegotiated. In our view, the carrying amounts of such renegotiated financial assets would continue to be disclosed, as long as the asset is recognised in the statement of financial position.

5.6.370 Financial assets that are either past due or impaired

IFRS 7.37(a)   5.6.370.10 For each class of financial asset an entity discloses an ageing analysis of financial assets that are past due but not impaired as at the reporting date.

IFRS 7.37(b) 5.6.370.20 For each class of financial asset an analysis of financial assets that are individually determined to be impaired as at the reporting date, and the factors considered by the entity in determining that the financial asset was impaired.

IFRS 7.37(c) 5.6.370.30 For each class of financial asset that is past due (but not impaired) or individually impaired, the entity discloses any collateral or credit enhancements held in respect of these assets. Unless impracticable, the fair value of the collateral and credit enhancements are be disclosed.

5.6.380 Collateral and other credit enhancements

IFRS 7.38 5.6.380.10 When an entity obtains financial or non-financial assets under collateral and credit enhancement arrangements, and those assets meet the recognition criteria (see 3.6), the entity discloses the nature and the carrying amount of the assets held. In addition, when such assets are not readily convertible into cash, the entity discloses its policies for using the assets in its operations or disposing of them.

5.6.390 *Liquidity risk*

IFRS 7.A 5.6.390.10 Liquidity risk is the risk that an entity will encounter difficulty in meeting the obligations associated with its financial liabilities that are settled by delivering cash or another financial asset.

IFRS 7.39(a), 5.6.390.20 An entity discloses a maturity analysis for:
(b), B11B,
IG30
- non-derivative financial liabilities, including issued financial guarantee contracts, showing their remaining contractual maturities; and
- derivative financial liabilities, including the remaining contractual maturities for those derivative financial liabilities for which contractual maturities are essential for an understanding of the timing of the cash flows (e.g. loan commitments and interest rate swaps designated in a cash flow hedge relationship).

5.6.390.30 In our view, the maturity analysis should include *all* derivative financial liabilities, but contractual maturities only are required for those essential for an understanding of the timing of the cash flows.

5.6.390.40 In determining what is "essential" for an understanding of the cash flows, judgement should be exercised as to what is appropriate based on management's liquidity risk management strategy and the facts and circumstances of each entity. For example, most non-trading "risk management" derivatives might be expected to be held to maturity, and most hedging strategies will not involve closing out a derivative prior to maturity. However, some "trading" derivatives (e.g. interest rate swaps that a bank executes with corporate counterparties) might be expected to be held until maturity whereas some hedging strategies may involve closing out a derivative prior to maturity.

IFRS 7.39(c), B11E   5.6.390.50 An entity explains how it manages the liquidity risk inherent in the maturity analyses described in 5.6.390.20. This includes a maturity analysis for financial assets it holds as part of managing liquidity risk (e.g. financial assets that are expected to generate cash inflows to meet cash outflows on financial liabilities) if such information is necessary to enable financial statement users to evaluate the nature and extent of liquidity risk. In addition, disclosure of collateral pledged which are financial assets, for example cash collateral and securities under repurchase transactions, may be considered "necessary" if such information is provided internally to key management personnel.

IFRS 7.B11A   5.6.390.60 In disclosing the maturity analyses described in 5.6.390.20, an entity does not separate an embedded derivative from a hybrid (combined) financial instrument. For such an instrument the entity applies the disclosure requirements for non-derivative financial liabilities, i.e. it discloses the remaining contractual maturities.

5.6.390.70 IFRS 7 does not define contractual maturities. It therefore leaves open to interpretation the amounts that need to be included in the maturity analysis for certain types of financial liabilities, such as derivatives and perpetual instruments. In our view, both the interest and principal cash flows should be included in the analysis as this best represents the liquidity risk being faced by the entity. The principal amount of the perpetual instrument represents the present value of the payments of the interest stream. As a minimum, for such an instrument, the principal amount should be disclosed, and sufficient appropriate narrative disclosures should be provided, in order to present a meaningful picture of the entity's liquidity exposures.

IFRS 7.B11   5.6.390.80 IFRS 7 does not mandate the number of time bands to be used in the analysis but rather requires the entity to use its judgement to determine an appropriate number of time bands.

IFRS 7.B11 C(a), BC57   5.6.390.90 When the creditor can choose when an amount is paid, the liability is included in the time band that represents the earliest date at which the entity could be required to pay. The intention of this disclosure is to show the worst case scenario from the perspective of the entity. For example, a demand deposit would be included in the earliest time band.

IFRS 7.B11D   5.6.390.100 The amounts disclosed are the contractual undiscounted cash flows. In our view, generally the amounts disclosed will be gross unless the liabilities will be settled net. These amounts will differ from the amounts included in the statement of financial position, as those amounts are based on discounted cash flows.

IFRS 7.B11D   5.6.390.110 When the amount payable is not fixed, the amount to be disclosed is determined by reference to conditions existing at the reporting date. For example, for a floating rate bond with interest payments indexed to three-month Euribor, in our view the amount to be disclosed should be based on forward rates rather than spot rates prevailing at the reporting date as the spot interest rates do not represent the level of the index based on which the cash flows will be payable. Rather, the forward interest rates better describe the level of the index in accordance with the conditions existing at the reporting date.

IFRS 7.B11
C(c)

5.6.390.120 In the case of issued guarantees that meet the definition of a financial guarantee contract under IAS 39 (see 3.6.35), the maximum amount of the guarantee is disclosed in the earliest period in which the guarantee could be called.

IFRS 7.34(a),
B10A

5.6.390.130 In disclosing summary quantitative data about exposure to liquidity risk on the basis of information provided internally to key management, an entity explains how this data is determined. If the outflows included in the data could occur either significantly earlier, or at significantly different amounts, then the entity is required to disclose that fact and provide further quantitative information to enable users to evaluate the extent of this risk, unless such information is included in the contractual maturity analysis required by the standard. Disclosure on the basis of information provided internally to key management should be clearly separated from that required under paragraph 39 of IFRS 7.

5.6.400 *Market risk*

IFRS 7.A,
IG32

5.6.400.10 Market risk is the risk that the fair value or future cash flows of a financial instrument will fluctuate because of changes in market prices. Market risk comprises of three types of risk: currency risk, interest rate risk and other price risk.

IFRS 7.40

5.6.400.20 An entity presents a sensitivity analysis for each type of market risk that it is exposed to as at the reporting date, including the methods and assumptions used in preparing the analysis. If the methods and assumptions used in preparing the analysis change from one period to another, then an entity discloses such changes together with the reason.

IFRS 7.B23

5.6.400.30 An entity may hold an investment in an equity instrument quoted in a foreign currency. In our view, the entity is not required to split the currency risk from other price risk for an equity instrument. However, for a debt instrument as a minimum, the split between currency risk and interest rate risk is presented.

IFRS 7.40(a),
B18, B19

5.6.400.40 The sensitivity analysis reflects the impact, on profit or loss and equity, of changes in the relevant risk variables that are reasonably possible at the reporting date. The reasonably possible change does not include remote or worst case scenarios, or stress tests. The sensitivity calculation assumes that the reasonably possible change occurred at the reporting date and had been applied to the risk exposures at that date.

IFRS 7.41,
B21

5.6.400.50 The sensitivity analysis described in 5.6.400.20 is not required if the entity already prepares an analysis that reflects interdependencies between risk variables, for example, a value at risk (VAR) approach, and uses it to manage its financial risk. If the entity uses this analysis to fulfil its disclosure requirements, then it explains the method used in preparing the analysis, including the main parameters and assumptions underlying the data. Furthermore, the entity explains the objective of the method used and any limitations that may result in the method not fully capturing the risk exposure arising from the underlying assets and liabilities. If an entity uses such an analysis to fulfil its disclosure requirements, then it does not need to disclose additional sensitivity analyses as per paragraph 40 of IFRS 7. However, if the entity applies VAR to only a part of its financial instruments portfolio, then it provides a separate sensitivity analysis in accordance with paragraph 40 of IFRS 7 for those financial instruments not included in the VAR analysis.

5.6.500.60 In our view, the sensitivity analysis includes financial assets and financial liabilities measured at amortised cost as well as those financial instruments measured at fair value through profit or loss.

IFRS 7.B21   5.6.500.70 The sensitivity analysis is provided for the whole of the entity's business, e.g. in the case of a bank this will include both its trading and non-trading books. The entity also may provide different types of analysis for different classes of financial instruments.

5.6.500.80 In our view, "translation risk", arising from translating the financial statements of a foreign operation into the presentation currency of the group, does not meet the definition of currency risk as defined in IFRS 7 and consequently, in our view should not be included in the sensitivity analysis on a consolidated basis. In our view, in consolidated financial statements the sensitivity analysis should address each currency to which an entity in the group has significant exposure based on each entity's functional currency (see 5.6.400.20).

5.6.500.90 When the functional currency of an entity is different from that of its foreign operation, the resulting economic exposure usually can be hedged (see 3.7.620). Therefore, in our view an entity may include net investments in foreign operations in the sensitivity analysis in consolidated financial statements if, and only if, that net investment has been hedged, and only to the extent that it has been hedged.

5.6.510 *Other market risk disclosures*

IFRS 7.42   5.6.510.10 If an entity believes that the sensitivity analysis is not representative of a risk inherent in a financial instrument, then it discloses this fact. This may be the case, for example, when the reporting date risk exposure is not representative of the risk exposure during the year.

IFRS 7.B28   5.6.510.20 Financial instruments that are classified as equity of the entity do not impact profit or loss or equity as they are not remeasured. Therefore no sensitivity analysis is required.

5.6.520 *Forthcoming requirements*

IFRS 9.C8   5.6.520.10 IFRS 9 introduces consequential amendments to IFRS 7. The amendments reflect the changes in the categories of financial assets and therefore delete references to available-for-sale financial assets, loans and receivables and held-to-maturity investments. The amendments also require specific disclosures about equity investments designated as at fair value through other comprehensive income, about reclassified financial assets and of the impact of first application of IFRS 9.

IFRS 9.C8. 5.6.520.20 When an entity first applies IFRS 9, it is required to provide quantitative
44I and qualitative information. The quantitative information includes, for each class of financial assets:

- the original category and carrying amount under IAS 39;
- the new category and carrying amount under IFRS 9; and
- the amount of any financial assets previously designated as at fair value through profit or loss, but for which the designation has been revoked, distinguishing between mandatory and elective de-designations.

IFRS 9.C8. 5.6.520.30 The qualitative information provided enables users to understand:
44J
- how the entity applied the classification requirements in IFRS 9 to those financial assets whose classification has changed; and
- the reasons for any designation or de-designation of financial instruments as measured at fair value through profit or loss.

5.6.520.40 IFRS 7 is amended by the *Improvements to IFRSs 2010* to add an explicit statement that the interaction between qualitative and quantitative disclosures better enables users to evaluate an entity's exposure to risks arising from financial instruments.

5.6.520.50 The existing disclosure requirements of IFRS 7 are amended as follows:

- Disclosure of the amount that best represents an entity's maximum exposure to credit risk without considering any collateral held is required only if the carrying amount of a financial asset does not reflect such exposure already.
- The financial effect of collateral held as security and other credit enhancements in respect of a financial instrument is required to be disclosed in addition to the existing requirement to describe the existence and nature of such collateral.
- The requirement to disclose the nature and carrying amounts of collateral obtained, including policies for using the financial and non-financial assets when they cannot be converted into cash immediately, applies only to collateral held at the end of the reporting period.

5.6.520.60 The following requirements have been removed from IFRS 7:

- The requirement to disclose the carrying amount of financial assets that are not past due or are not impaired as a result of their terms having been renegotiated.

- The requirement to provide a description of collateral held as security and other credit enhancements in respect of financial assets that are past due or individually determined to be impaired, including an estimate of their fair value.

5.6.520.70 Additionally, the clause stating that quantitative disclosures are not required when a risk is not material has been removed from IFRS 7.

5.6.530 Future developments

5.6.530.10 The IASB is working on a project that will ultimately replace IAS 39 and introduce consequential amendments to IFRS 7 (see 3.6.1360.10). The IASB's project includes the following phases:

- classification and measurement (see 3.6A and 5.6.530.20);
- impairment (see 4.6.560.20); and
- hedging (see 3.7.900.20).

5.6.530.20 In May 2010 the IASB published ED/2010/4 *Fair Value Option for Financial Liabilities*, which proposes to amend the fair value option so that changes in the fair value of financial liabilities due to own credit risk are not reflected in profit or loss. The final standard to replace IAS 39 as a whole is scheduled for the second quarter of 2011.

5.6.530.30 In March 2009 the IASB published ED/2009/3 *Derecognition*. The proposals in the ED aimed to simplify the derecognition model for financial assets. In June 2010 the IASB decided that its near-term priority should be on increasing the transparency and comparability of its standards by improving and converging US GAAP and IFRS disclosure requirements for financial assets transferred to another entity. As a result, the IASB plans to finalise the disclosure requirements that were included in the ED. The final revised disclosure requirements are scheduled for the third quarter of 2010.

5.6.530.40 In early 2010, in response to stakeholder concerns, the IASB and the FASB added a joint project to address differences between IFRSs and US GAAP for balance sheet offsetting of derivative contracts and other financial instruments that can result in material differences in financial reporting by financial institutions. This project is still in its preliminary stages and therefore no significant decisions have been made. An ED is scheduled for the fourth quarter of 2010.

5.6.530.50 In May 2009 the IASB published ED/2009/5 *Fair Value Measurement* (the 2009 ED). The proposals in the 2009 ED are intended to replace the fair value measurement guidance contained in individual IFRSs with a single, unified definition of fair value, as well as provide further authoritative guidance on the application of fair value measurement in inactive markets. The 2009 ED proposes a framework for measuring fair value and disclosures about fair value measurements. The proposals in the 2009 ED explain how to measure fair value when it already is required or permitted by existing IFRSs; they do not introduce new fair value measurements, nor do they eliminate the practicability exceptions to fair value measurements that exist currently in certain standards.

5.6.530.60 In June 2010 the IASB published ED/2010/7 *Measurement Uncertainty Analysis Disclosure for Fair Value Measurements* (the 2010 ED). The 2010 ED expands on the proposal in the 2009 ED for an entity to disclose a measurement uncertainty analysis (or sensitivity analysis) for assets and liabilities measured at fair value categorised within Level 3 of the fair value hierarchy. The 2010 ED proposes that an entity consider the effect of correlation between unobservable inputs, if relevant.

5.6.530.70 A final standard on fair value measurement and disclosure, which is expected to be converged with a forthcoming amended standard under US GAAP, is scheduled for the first quarter of 2011.

5.7 Non-monetary transactions
(IAS 16, IAS 18, IAS 38, IAS 40, IFRIC 18, SIC-31)

5.7 Non-monetary transactions
(IAS 16, IAS 18, IAS 38, IAS 40, IFRIC 18, SIC-31)

Overview of currently effective requirements

- Generally, exchanges of assets are measured at fair value and result in the recognition of gains or losses rather than revenue.

- Exchanged assets are recognised based on historical cost if the exchange lacks commercial substance or the fair value cannot be measured reliably.

- Revenue is recognised for barter transactions unless the transaction is incidental to the entity's main revenue-generating activities or the items exchanged are similar in nature and value.

- Property, plant and equipment that is used to provide access to a supply of goods or services is recognised as an asset if it meets the definition of an asset and the recognition criteria for property, plant and equipment.

- Other donated assets may be accounted for in a manner similar to government grants unless the transfer is, in substance, an equity contribution.

Currently effective requirements

This publication reflects IFRSs in issue at 1 August 2010. In the absence of specific IFRS on non-monetary transactions the requirements related to this topic are derived mainly from IAS 16 *Property, Plant and Equipment,* IAS 18 *Revenue,* IAS 38 *Intangible Assets,* IAS 40 *Investment Property,* IFRIC 18 *Transfers of Assets from Customers* and SIC-31 *Revenue – Barter Transactions Involving Advertising Services.*

Forthcoming requirements and future developments

When a currently effective requirement will be changed by a new requirement that is issued but is not yet effective, it is marked with a # as a **forthcoming requirement** and the impact of the change is explained in the accompanying boxed text. In respect of this topic no forthcoming requirements are noted.

When a significant change to the currently effective or forthcoming requirements is expected, it is marked with a * as an area that may be subject to **future developments** and a brief outline of the relevant projects is given in 5.7.100.

5.7.10 **Introduction**

5.7.10.05 When addressing non-monetary transactions, the two most typical issues generally are:

- whether to measure the exchange based on historical cost or fair value; and
- whether to recognise revenue, gains or losses.

5.7.10.10 Guidance on certain specific non-monetary transactions is provided in other topics: business combinations, (see 2.6.390); non-monetary contributions to jointly controlled entities (see 3.5.460); share-based payment transactions (see 4.5); the issue of shares for non-cash consideration (see 3.11.200 and 450); and distribution of non-cash assets to owners and distributions in which the owners may elect to receive either the non-cash asset or a cash alternative (IFRIC 17 *Distributions of Non-cash Assets*) (see 3.11.452).

5.7.10.20 [Not used]

5.7.10.30 Revenue recognition for other non-monetary transactions generally is accounted for under IAS 18 (see 4.2).

5.7.20 **Exchanges of assets held for use**

IAS 16.24, 38.45, 40.27   5.7.20.10 All property, plant and equipment, intangible assets and investment property received in exchange for non-monetary assets are measured at fair value unless the exchange transaction lacks commercial substance or the fair value of neither the asset received nor the asset given up is reliably measurable.

IAS 16.25, 38.46, 40.28   5.7.20.20 Commercial substance is assessed by considering the extent to which future cash flows are expected to change as a result of the transaction. More specifically, an exchange transaction has commercial substance if the configuration of the cash flows (i.e. the amount, timing and uncertainty) of the assets received and transferred are different, or if the entity-specific value of the portion of the entity's operation affected by the transaction changes as a result of the exchange. The difference in both of the above situations should be significant when compared to the fair value of the assets exchanged.

IAS 16.26, 18.7, 12, 38.45-47, 40.29   5.7.20.30 Measurement of an exchange at fair value will result in the recognition of a gain or loss based upon the carrying amount of the asset surrendered. Whether or not revenue will be recognised depend upon whether:

- the transaction is incidental to the main revenue-generating activities of the entity; and
- the assets exchanged are similar in nature and value (see 5.7.30).

IAS 16.26, 38.47, 40.29   5.7.20.40 IAS 16, IAS 38 and IAS 40 contain guidance as to when the fair value of an asset is reliably measurable if a comparable market transaction does not exist. If a fair value can be determined reliably for either the asset received or the asset given up, then the fair value of the asset given up should be used unless the fair value of the asset received is more clearly evident.

5.7.20.60 In our view, the commercial substance test (see 5.7.20.20) applies only when assets held for use are exchanged. See 5.4.30.90 for a discussion of situations that involve non-current assets held for sale.

5.7.30 Exchange of goods and services*

5.7.40 *Barter transactions*

IAS 18.7, 12 5.7.40.10 Revenue is recognised by an entity when goods or services are sold in exchange for dissimilar goods or services, unless the transaction is incidental to the entity's main revenue-generating activities. Revenue is measured at the fair value of the goods or services received, adjusted by any cash or cash equivalents received or paid, unless the fair value cannot be measured reliably. In such cases the revenue is measured at the fair value of the goods or services given up, adjusted by any cash or cash equivalents received or paid.

IAS 1.34, 5.7.40.20 When goods or services are exchanged for goods or services that are similar in
18.12 nature and value, the exchange is considered to be a transaction that does not generate revenue.

5.7.40.30 Non-monetary transactions include barter transactions, typical examples of which include transactions involving commodities such as wheat or oil, or advertising barter transactions.

5.7.40.40 For example, a natural gas company might sell gas to another company and receive in exchange a quantity of steel tubing. In this case the items exchanged are dissimilar and the natural gas company recognises revenue for gas sales equal to the fair value of the steel tubing received, if it can be measured reliably. If the fair value of the tubing received cannot be determined reliably, then the revenue is measured by reference to the fair value of the gas delivered.

IAS 18.12 5.7.40.50 In our view, items are similar when they have a similar use in the same line of business and have a similar value.

5.7.40.60 In our view, when a group of items is exchanged, similarity is assessed based on whether each of the significant components of the group is similar to a component of the other group. The assessment of similarity should not be made with respect to the group as a whole, e.g. total fair value received and delivered.

5.7.50 *Advertising barter transactions*

SIC-31.2 5.7.50.10 In some cases advertising services are exchanged without any cash or other consideration, or in which equal or approximately equal consideration is exchanged. In such barter transactions revenue is not recognised when the advertising services exchanged are of a similar value and nature. For example, an exchange of banners between two travel agent websites is likely to be considered an exchange of similar services that does not qualify for revenue recognition.

5.7.50.20 In our view, if exchanged advertising services share some, but not necessarily all, of the following characteristics, then the transactions normally are considered to be similar and revenue would not be recognised:

- target groups;
- prominence (page on website, location of page, size of advertisement etc.);
- length of time that the advertisement is displayed;
- timing (season of year, time of day, times per week etc.); and
- exposure.

5.7.50.30 In our view, advertising services involving different media generally would be considered dissimilar. Therefore, we believe that a barter of airtime (advertising space) between a TV channel and a radio channel generally is considered as an exchange of dissimilar services.

5.7.50.40 In our view, another example of advertising services generally considered dissimilar is a barter of airtime between TV channels with different audiences (e.g. different target groups or geographical areas).

SIC-31.5, 9 5.7.50.50 Revenue from a barter transaction involving advertising cannot be measured reliably at the fair value of the advertising services *received*. Therefore, advertising revenue obtained in an exchange of dissimilar advertising services is measured at the fair value of the advertising services *given*, provided that the fair value of those services given can be measured reliably. The measurement of advertising services given is considered to be reliable if it is determined by reference to non-barter transactions that:

- involve advertising similar to that in the barter transaction;
- occur frequently;
- represent a predominant number of transactions and amount compared to all transactions to provide advertising that are similar to the advertising in the barter transaction;
- involve cash or other consideration that has a reliably measurable fair value (e.g. not only a swap of cash); and
- do not involve the same counterparty as in the barter transaction.

5.7.50.60 When an entity meets the above criteria, revenue is recognised when the advertisement appears before the public, i.e. when the commercial is broadcast.

5.7.50.70 For example, a radio station enters into an agreement with a television station. The radio station will run three advertisements for the television station on its radio station (for which a third party would have had to pay 15,000), while the television company will broadcast two advertisements on the television channel. The normal cost of the television advertisements also is 15,000. Further to the guidance set out in 5.7.50.35, we believe that these are dissimilar services and both parties should recognise revenue.

5.7.50.80 At the end of the reporting period, both advertisements had been broadcast on the television channel, but only two of the advertisements had been broadcast on the radio station. The third radio advertisement, with a value of 5,000, will be broadcast in the following period. The radio station makes the following accounting entries:

	Debit	Credit
Advertising expense	15,000	
Barter advertising revenue		10,000
Deferred revenue		5,000
To recognise barter transaction		

5.7.50.90 During the following period, when the third advertisement is broadcast on the radio station, the radio station will recognise the deferred amount of 5,000 as revenue.

5.7.60 Donated assets

5.7.70 *General**

5.7.70.10 An entity may receive assets from third parties for no consideration. When assets are transferred to the entity by the government, these transfers normally meet the definition of a government grant (see 4.3.10). However, entities also should consider the requirements of IFRIC 12 *Service Concession Arrangements* as certain assets transferred by the government would not necessarily be government grants. IFRIC 12 provides guidance to private sector entities on certain recognition and measurement issues that arise in accounting for public-to-private service concession arrangements (see 5.12).

F.70(a) 5.7.70.20 Assets or resources transferred to an entity by a shareholder for no consideration normally are equity contributions that would be accounted for directly in equity (see 3.11.230).

5.7.70.30 With the exception of assets or resources transferred to an entity by a shareholder or a government (via government grant), or arrangements within the scope of IFRIC 18, there is no guidance on assets or resources received from other third parties. Gifts without conditions are likely to be rare in an arm's length relationship. In our view, if conditions are attached to a non-reciprocal transfer (see 5.7.80.30), then generally it is not appropriate to recognise a gain immediately; instead, any gain should rather be deferred until the conditions are satisfied.

5.7.70.40 In our view, even though these transactions do not meet the definition of a government grant, government grant accounting should be applied by analogy to non-reciprocal non-monetary contributions by third parties other than sharehold-ers or governments (see 4.3), or those arrangements within the scope of IFRIC 18 (see 5.7.90). The donation is recognised in profit or loss over the periods that the entity recognises as expenses the related costs that the contribution is intended to compensate.

IAS 20.23, 24   5.7.70.50 Therefore, we believe that an entity should choose an accounting policy, to be applied consistently, to measure transferred or donated assets either at the fair value of the assets received or at the nominal amount paid. We prefer to measure these transac-tions at fair value. The resulting income should be deferred and recognised in profit or loss on a systematic basis.

5.7.80 *Not-for-profit entities*

5.7.80.10 Donations often are received by charitable organisations and may be in the form of cash, goods, services or pledges (promises to pay at a future date). Donations may be "earmarked", e.g. when the donor requests that the donation be used for a particular purpose.

5.7.80.20 There is no specific guidance in IFRSs on contributions received by not-for-profit entities. In our view, guidance may be obtained from the accounting for government grants related to biological assets measured at fair value less costs to sell (see 4.3.60), or from the general requirements for other assets (see 4.3.10 – 50).

5.7.80.30 Non-reciprocal transfers are transfers of resources from one party to another when the transferors do not receive approximately equal value in return. Non-reciprocal transfers include transfers such as gifts, donations, government grants and taxes. They may be received as cash, as other assets, or as reductions in liabilities (e.g. forgiven loans), and may or may not have conditions or restrictions attached.

5.7.80.40 In our view, non-reciprocal transfers without conditions attached should be recognised by recipients as assets at the earlier of receipt of the asset or the existence of an enforceable right to receive future delivery of the asset, or as reduced liabilities when the transferor waives its right to receive a future payment.

5.7.80.50 – 60 [Not used]

5.7.80.70 In our view, if an entity elects an accounting policy for non-reciprocal transfers similar to the accounting for government grants related to biological assets measured at fair value less costs to sell (see 4.3.60), then transfers without conditions from non-shareholders should be recognised in profit or loss once such transfers become receivable. The amounts should be recognised as revenue if they arise in the course of the ordinary activities, or as other income if they do not arise in the course of ordinary activities. Transfers with conditions should be recognised by recipients as a liability (deferred revenue or deferred income) until such time as the conditions are met, at which point they should be recognised as revenue or other income.

5.7.80.80 In our view, if an entity elects an accounting policy similar to the accounting for other government grants (see 4.3.10 – 50), then non-reciprocal transfers should be recognised in profit or loss on a systematic basis over the periods that the entity recognises as expenses the related costs that they are intended to compensate.

5.7.90 Transfers of assets from customers*

IFRIC 18.4 5.7.90.10 IFRIC 18 provides guidance on transfers of property, plant and equipment for entities that receive such contributions from their customers where the contributed property, plant and equipment are used by the entity to provide access to a supply of goods or services, either by providing a connection and/or by providing ongoing access to a supply of goods or services. IFRIC 18 addresses the accounting only by the entity receiving contributions, and not by the contributor (see 4.2.640).

IFRIC 18.3 5.7.90.20 In some cases, the party contributing the asset (the transferor) may be different from the party that will receive the access to a supply of goods or services (the ultimate customer). This fact does not affect the accounting outcome under IFRIC 18.

IAS 16.7, 24, 5.7.90.30 An entity that has received a contribution within the scope of the interpretation
IFRIC 18.9, recognises the contribution as an asset only if it determines that the item contributed
11 meets both the definition of an asset as set out in the Framework (see 1.2.30.10) and the recognition criteria for property, plant and equipment set out in IAS 16 (see 3.2.20).

IAS 18.13, 5.7.90.40 When an asset is recognised (at fair value) by the entity that receives the con-
IFRIC 18.13, tribution, a corresponding amount is recognised as revenue in accordance with IAS 18.
14 The timing of revenue recognition is based on the entity's performance obligations following the receipt of the asset, which will depend on the facts and circumstances of each particular arrangement. The entity identifies the separately identifiable performance obligations included in the arrangement (see 4.2.50).

5.7.100 Future developments

5.7.100.10 In May 2009 the IASB published ED/2009/5 *Fair Value Measurement* (the 2009 ED). The proposals in the 2009 ED are intended to replace the fair value measurement guidance contained in individual IFRSs with a single, unified definition of fair value, as well as provide further authoritative guidance on the application of fair value measurement in inactive markets. The 2009 ED proposes a framework for measuring fair value and disclosures about fair value measurements. The proposals in the 2009 ED explain how to measure fair value when it already is required or permitted by existing IFRSs; they do not introduce new fair value measurements, nor do they eliminate the practicability exceptions to fair value measurements that exist currently in certain standards.

5.7.100.20 In June 2010 the IASB published ED/2010/7 *Measurement Uncertainty Analysis Disclosure for Fair Value Measurements* (the 2010 ED). The 2010 ED expands on the proposal in the 2009 ED for an entity to disclose a measurement uncertainty analysis (or sensitivity analysis) for assets and liabilities measured at fair value categorised within

Level 3 of the fair value hierarchy. The 2010 ED proposes that an entity consider the effect of correlation between unobservable inputs, if relevant.

5.7.100.30 A final standard on fair value measurement and disclosure, which is expected to be converged with a forthcoming amended standard under US GAAP, is scheduled for the first quarter of 2011.

5.7.100.40 The IASB and the FASB are working on a joint project to develop a comprehensive set of principles for revenue recognition. In June 2010 the IASB published ED/2010/6 *Revenue from Contracts with Customers,* which would replace IAS 11, IAS 18 and a number of interpretations, including IFRIC 18 and SIC-31. The ED proposes a single revenue recognition model in which an entity recognises revenue as it satisfies a performance obligation by transferring control of promised goods or services to a customer. The ED does not propose to retain current requirements that revenue is not recognised if the goods or services exchanged are of a similar nature and value. The model would be applied to all contracts with customers except leases, financial instruments, insurance contracts and non-monetary exchanges between entities in the same line of business to facilitate sales to customers other than the parties to the exchange. A final standard is scheduled for the second quarter of 2011.

5.8 Accompanying financial and other information
(IAS 1)

5.8 Accompanying financial and other information
(IAS 1)

Overview of currently effective requirements

- **Supplementary financial and operational information may be presented, but is not required.**

- **An entity considers its particular legal or securities listing requirements in assessing what information is disclosed in addition to that required by IFRSs.**

Currently effective requirements

This publication reflects IFRSs in issue at 1 August 2010. The currently effective requirements cover annual periods beginning on 1 January 2010. The requirements related to this topic are derived mainly from IAS 1 *Presentation of Financial Statements*.

Forthcoming requirements and future developments

When a currently effective requirement will be changed by a new requirement that is issued but is not yet effective, it is marked with a # as a **forthcoming requirement** and the impact of the change is explained in the accompanying boxed text. In respect of this topic no forthcoming requirements are noted.

The currently effective requirements may be subject to **future developments** and a brief outline of the relevant project is given in 5.8.40.

5.8.10 General

IAS 1.13 5.8.10.10 In addition to disclosing additional information in the financial statements to achieve a fair presentation (see in particular 1.1.130), many entities provide additional information to accompany the financial statements. Accompanying information may be provided either voluntarily or because of regulatory requirements.

5.8.10.20 IFRSs are not based on a particular legal or listing framework; they also do not contain any requirements for management discussion and analysis, either as part of or outside of the financial statements. However, an entity applying IFRSs may be subject to national, regional or securities exchange requirements or recommendations regarding the presentation of financial and/or non-financial information. For example, in Europe the Committee of European Securities Regulators has issued recommendations in respect of "alternative performance measures" (APMs or non-GAAP measures) presented in the financial statements (see 4.1.120), and accompanying information such as a management commentary and press releases, other than those presented in a prospectus.

5.8.10.30 Accompanying information generally is presented outside of the financial statements, for example, in a narrative section of the annual report, but may be presented within the financial statements if appropriate. Factors that determine whether it is appropriate to present accompanying information within the financial statements include: whether the information is required specifically by regulation; the nature and purpose of the information; its relationship to IFRSs; and whether it is intended to be covered by the auditor's report.

5.8.10.40 For example, it may be appropriate to provide accompanying information within the financial statements when it is intended to provide further explanation of specific financial statement items presented in accordance with IFRSs.

IFRS 8.3   5.8.10.50 Alternatively, it may be inappropriate to provide accompanying information within the financial statements when it is provided voluntarily and is presented in a manner that could lead a user to conclude that it is in accordance with IFRSs when in fact it is not. For example, if an unlisted entity wishes to provide segment information (see 5.2), but is unable to obtain all of the required information, or wishes to disclose only limited segment information, then in our view that segment information should be presented outside of the financial statements (e.g. as part of the directors' report). The discussion that accompanies the segment information should not imply that the information is prepared in accordance with IFRSs when in fact it is not.

IAS 1.49, 50   5.8.10.60 When accompanying information is presented outside of the financial statements, it is important that it is presented in a manner that differentiates it clearly from the financial statements especially when, unlike the financial statements, such information is intended to be unaudited.

IFRS 4.1G62,   5.8.10.65 Both IFRS 4 *Insurance Contracts* and IFRS 7 *Financial Instruments:*
7.B6   *Disclosures* allow certain specific disclosures to be presented outside of the financial statements with a cross-reference to those disclosures from the financial statements, as long as the accompanying information is available to users of the financial statements on the same terms as the financial statements and at the same time. However, we prefer all IFRS disclosures to be included within the financial statements themselves because this assists users in differentiating between disclosures that are required by IFRSs and other information. In our view, if such information is presented outside of the financial statements, then it should be marked clearly as being part of the disclosures required by IFRSs and cross-referenced to the financial statements. We prefer such information to be identified as, for example, "information that is an integral part of the audited financial statements" or "disclosures that are required by IFRSs" rather than simply as "audited".

5.8.10.70 Accompanying information normally will be of interest to a wide range of users, but often is aimed at the needs of investors. In our view, an entity should apply the same guiding principles as set out in the Framework (see 1.2) to ensure that the accompanying information is understandable, relevant, reliable, comparable, complete and free from bias.

5.8.10.80 See 2.1.80 for a discussion of *pro forma* information.

5.8.20 Accompanying financial and non-financial information

IAS 1.13 5.8.20.10 IFRSs note that many entities present, outside of the financial statements, a financial review by management that describes and explains the main features of the entity's financial performance and position, and the principal uncertainties that it faces.

5.8.20.20 Such additional information often is presented in the directors' report, chairman's report or other accompanying information, and may include a review of:

- the main factors and influences affecting the entity's performance, including changes in the environment in which the entity operates, the entity's response to those changes and their effect, and its policy for investment to maintain and enhance performance, including its dividend policy;
- the entity's sources of funding, the policy on gearing (borrowing levels) and its risk management policies; and
- the entity's strengths and resources whose value is not reflected in the statement of financial position under IFRSs (e.g. internally generated brands and trademarks).

IAS 1.14 5.8.20.30 Some entities also present additional reports and statements, such as environmental reports and value-added statements, if management believes that this additional information will assist in making investment decisions or that it will be of interest to other users.

5.8.20.40 In addition to the above, the directors' report or other accompanying information also may include:

- General information:
  - principal activities of the reporting entity;
  - mission statement and values;
  - list of directors and officers; and
  - chairman and chief executive officer's statements.

- Business review:
  - operating results for the period;
  - market and product development, including research activities and competitor information;
  - expectations regarding future developments;
  - acquisitions and disposals of businesses; and
  - a general description of the risks facing the entity.

- Financial review:
  - capital structure and financial position;
  - stock exchange information, including share prices, dividends, and shareholder information and profiles;

- tables of financial data and key figures for periods in addition to those covered in the financial statements and comparative periods (e.g. for the last five or ten years); and
- information about risk management and the sensitivity of key assumptions (in addition to the disclosures required by IFRSs (see 5.6.320)).

- Other items:
  - directors' interests and management philosophy;
  - events subsequent to the reporting date;
  - agenda for the annual general meeting;
  - information technology policies and significant investments; and
  - specific disclosures required by laws and regulations.

5.8.20.50 An entity may wish to discuss some of the above areas on a segment basis. IFRS 8 *Operating Segments* introduced the "management approach", which requires disclosures about components of the entity that management monitors in making decisions about operational matters. Accordingly, an entity ensures that the information provided in the management commentary (or directors' report) is, in all material respects, consistent with the IFRS 8 disclosures in the financial statements.

IAS 1.138   5.8.20.60 Disclosure of the country of incorporation of the entity, address of the registered office (or principal place of business), information about the length of the entity's life (if it is a limited-life entity), a description of the nature of the entity's operations and its principal activities often is provided outside of the financial statements. If not, then the entity should provide these disclosures in the financial statements.

IAS 21.57   5.8.20.70 IFRSs do not prohibit an entity from providing a convenience translation as supplementary information, i.e. to present financial statements or selected information in a currency other than its presentation currency (currencies) as a convenience to users. A convenience translation is prepared using a translation method other than that required by IFRSs, and is identified clearly as supplementary information distinguished from the information that complies with IFRSs (see 2.7.330.20).

5.8.20.80 Supplementary information that an entity may wish to present might include the following:

- information about the effects of changing prices on a current cost basis when an entity's functional currency is not hyperinflationary (see 2.4.140.10); and
- consolidated information when the entity disposed of its last subsidiary during the reporting period and, accordingly, is not required to issue consolidated financial statements at the reporting date (see 2.1.50.90 and 5.9.10.40).

5.8.30 **Corporate governance**

5.8.30.10 IFRSs do not provide guidance on the disclosure of corporate governance information. Often a local legal or securities exchange requirement specifies what corporate governance information should be disclosed and where such information should be presented (see 5.8.10.30).

5.8.30.20 Examples of corporate governance disclosures include:

- composition of the board of directors, including their responsibilities, criteria for election, term of office and frequency of, and attendance at, board meetings;
- if there is a supervisory board, then the names of members of this board and a report of the supervisory board may be included in the annual report;
- names and responsibilities of the chief executive officer and president;
- identification and responsibilities of executive and other management groups;
- identification, composition and responsibilities of various committees and sub-boards, for example advisory board, personnel committee, audit committee, nomination committee and other entity-specific committees, such as a research and development committee or environmental committee;
- details of the remuneration of individual directors, including share or other incentive schemes;
- insider trading policies and practices;
- risk management disclosures, including board accountability and systems of control;
- sustainability disclosures including social, ethical, safety, health and environmental policies and practices;
- a description of information technology governance;
- management's assertion on effectiveness of internal controls; and
- a description or confirmation of compliance with rules, laws, codes and standards and reporting of any exceptions.

5.8.40 **Future developments**

5.8.40.10 In June 2009 the IASB published ED/2009/6 *Management Commentary*, which proposes a framework to assist in the preparation of management commentary that accompanies financial statements prepared in accordance with IFRSs. The proposals in the ED will not result in an IFRS. Completed guidance is expected in the second half of 2010.

5.9 Interim financial reporting
(IAS 34, IFRIC 10)

5.9 Interim financial reporting
(IAS 34, IFRIC 10)

Overview of currently effective requirements

- Interim financial statements contain either a complete or a condensed set of financial statements for a period shorter than a financial year.

- The following, as a minimum, are presented in condensed interim financial statements: condensed statement of financial position; condensed statement of comprehensive income, presented as either a condensed single statement or a condensed separate income statement and a condensed statement of comprehensive income; condensed statement of cash flows; condensed statement of changes in equity; and selected explanatory notes.

- Items, other than income tax, generally are recognised and measured as if the interim period were a discrete period.

- Income tax expense for an interim period is based on an estimated average annual effective income tax rate.

- Generally, the accounting policies applied in the interim financial statements are those that will be applied in the next annual financial statements.

Currently effective requirements

This publication reflects IFRSs in issue at 1 August 2010. The currently effective requirements cover annual periods beginning on 1 January 2010. The requirements related to this topic are derived mainly from IAS 34 *Interim Financial Reporting* and IFRIC 10 *Interim Financial Reporting and Impairment*.

Forthcoming requirements and future developments

When a currently effective requirement will be changed by a new requirement that is issued but is not yet effective, it is marked with a # as a **forthcoming requirement** and the impact of the change is explained in the accompanying boxed text. The forthcoming requirements related to this topic are derived from the *Improvements to IFRSs 2010*, for which the amendments to IAS 34 are effective for annual periods beginning on or after 1 January 2011; earlier application is permitted. A brief outline of the impact of the *Improvements to IFRSs 2010* on this topic is given in 5.9.65, and a brief outline of the annual improvements is given in 1.1.85.

The currently effective or forthcoming requirements may be subject to **future developments** and a brief outline of the relevant project is given in 5.9.240.

In addition, a brief outline on a further project is given in 5.9.240.10 – 40 that may affect several aspects of interim financial reporting.

5.9.10 **Scope and basis of preparation**

IAS 34.1   5.9.10.10 IFRSs do not require the presentation of interim financial statements. Publicly-traded entities are encouraged to provide interim financial statements at least for the first six months of their financial year. Regulators may require interim financial statements to be prepared and also may specify the frequency of preparation (e.g. quarterly or half-yearly). An entity is not required to prepare interim financial statements in accordance with IAS 34 in order for its annual financial statements to comply with IFRSs.

IAS 1.4, 16, 5.9.10.20 If an entity prepares interim financial statements, then IAS 34 may be applied
34.1-3, 7, 9, in their preparation and presentation. The interim financial statements should state that
19 they comply with IAS 34 if this is the case. When compliance with IAS 34 is claimed, the interim financial statements should comply with all of the requirements of the standard.

5.9.10.25 An entity may prepare condensed interim financial statements. Alternatively, an entity may prepare a complete set of financial statements covering the interim period. In this case, the interim financial statements should state that they comply with IFRSs and a complete set of financial statements is presented that complies with all requirements set out in IFRSs including those of IAS 1 *Presentation of Financial Statements* in addition to the measurement and any supplementary disclosure requirements of IAS 34.

IAS 1.4, 5.9.10.30 IAS 34 provides guidance on the structure and content of condensed interim
15-35 financial statements. The overall considerations for preparing annual financial statements also are applicable to condensed interim financial statements. These include guidance on fair presentation and compliance with IFRSs, the accrual basis of accounting, materiality and aggregation, offsetting and going concern.

IAS 34.23-25 5.9.10.31 Specific guidance in respect of materiality and its application to interim financial statements is included in IAS 34. Materiality is relevant to the recognition and measurement of items in interim financial statements (see 5.9.80.20) and the presentation and disclosure of items in those interim financial statements (see 5.9.60). Materiality is assessed based on information related to the interim period and not to the full year period. For example, an impairment charge may be material for the interim period even if it is expected not to be material for the annual period.

IAS 1.4, 25, 5.9.10.32 When making an assessment of uncertainties associated with an entity's
26 going concern assumption, management takes into account all available information for a period of at least 12 months from the date of the interim financial statements. For example, an entity with a calendar year end that prepares half-yearly interim financial statements should, for the purpose of preparing its 30 June 2010 condensed interim financial statements, consider information about a future period through, but not limited to, 30 June 2011 when assessing whether the going concern assumption is appropriate.

IAS 1.4, 25, 26, 10.16(b) 5.9.10.34 If management determines that a material uncertainty relative to an entity's ability to continue as a going concern exists at the date at which interim financial statements are authorised for issue, then such uncertainty is disclosed in those interim financial statements, whether or not it was disclosed in the most recent annual financial statements.

5.9.10.36 If management determined that a material uncertainty existed at the date of authorisation for issue of its most recent annual financial statements and provided such disclosure in those financial statements, but no material uncertainty is identified at the date of authorisation for issue of subsequent interim financial statements, then the entity provides disclosure about such a change in circumstances.

IAS 34.14 5.9.10.40 Generally, the interim financial statements are prepared on a consolidated basis if the most recent annual financial statements were prepared on that basis. In our view, this approach is not required if an entity disposes of its last subsidiary during the interim reporting period. In this case, as the entity no longer is a parent at the end of the interim reporting period, consolidated financial statements are no longer required unless otherwise prescribed, for example by a local regulator (see 2.1.50). In such cases, we believe that interim financial statements, including the comparatives, should be presented as unconsolidated financial statements and identified as such. Disclosure of the previously reported consolidated information as supplementary information may be useful (see 5.8).

5.9.10.50 We prefer that the interim financial statements, including the comparative information, be included in one section in an interim report. However, there is no requirement in IFRSs that prevents presentation or disclosure in another manner, as may be prescribed by local regulatory requirements or in response to other factors.

5.9.20 Form and content

5.9.30 *Minimum components*

IAS 34.10, 15 5.9.30.10 Interim financial statements may be prepared in a condensed format, omitting most disclosures that are required to comply with IFRSs when publishing a complete set of IFRS financial statements. Condensation and the omission of disclosures are permitted assuming that the financial statement user will have access to the most recent annual financial statements. Therefore, in our view the interim financial statements should focus on changes since the last annual financial statements. However, an entity should consider whether information disclosed in the last annual financial statements remains relevant. When changes in circumstances have made significant disclosures in the last annual financial statements less relevant, then in our view an entity should consider whether additional supplementary interim disclosures should be provided.

5.9.30.20 Condensed interim financial statements include at least:

- a condensed statement of financial position at the end of the current interim period and at the end of the immediately preceding financial year;

- a condensed statement of comprehensive income for the current interim period and cumulatively for the year-to-date, and for the comparable interim periods (current and cumulative) of the immediately preceding financial year;
- a condensed statement of changes in equity, cumulatively for the current year-to-date and for the comparable year-to-date period of the immediately preceding financial year;
- a condensed statement of cash flows, cumulatively for the current year-to-date and for the comparable year-to-date period of the immediately preceding financial year; and
- certain explanatory notes (see 5.9.60).

IAS 1.BC33, 34.5, 9, 16(a) 5.9.30.22 Unlike a complete set of interim financial statements, which in certain circumstances is required to include a statement of financial position as at the beginning of the earliest comparative period presented (see 2.1.10.10), there is no requirement to present an additional statement of financial position in condensed interim financial statements. However, disclosure is required in respect of a change of accounting policy or a material prior period error (see 5.9.60.20).

IAS 34.5, 8, 9, 10 5.9.30.23 Additionally, if an entity prepares a complete set of interim financial statements, then the (primary) financial statements are not condensed and full notes are required.

IAS 34.8, 20 5.9.30.25 A condensed statement of comprehensive income is presented as either:

- a condensed single statement; or
- a condensed separate income statement (displaying components of profit or loss) and a condensed separate statement of comprehensive income (beginning with profit or loss and displaying components of other comprehensive income).

IAS 34.8A 5.9.30.27 The same approach as adopted for the annual financial statements regarding the presentation of the condensed statement of comprehensive income as a single statement or as two statements is followed in the condensed interim financial statements.

5.9.30.30 [Not used]

IAS 34.4, 20, 22, A.A2 5.9.30.40 IAS 34 defines an interim period as a "financial reporting period shorter than a full financial year". In our view, this means the period between the end of the last reporting period and the end of the current reporting period when an entity reports more than once during the financial year. An entity may not, for example, define an interim period as a year-to-date period to the end of the current reporting period, and on that basis prepare a condensed statement of comprehensive income for the year-to-date period only. For example, we believe that an entity reporting quarterly and claiming compliance with IAS 34 should present in its half-year report interim a statement of comprehensive income for each of the three months and the six months ending on the end of the current reporting period, as well as for the comparable periods of the immediately preceding financial year.

1420

5.9.40 *Format of condensed interim financial statements*

IAS 34.10 5.9.40.10 Condensed interim financial statements include, at a minimum, each of the headings and subtotals that were included in the most recent annual financial statements. Additional line items are included if their omission would make the financial statements misleading.

5.9.40.20 Although not required by IAS 34, in our view if an entity has operations that are discontinued at the end of the interim reporting period or are disposed of during the interim period, then these operations should be presented separately in the condensed interim statement of comprehensive income following IFRS 5 *Non-current Assets Held for Sale and Discontinued Operations* (see 5.4.120). In addition, in our view if an entity has non-current assets or a disposal group classified as held for sale or distribution at the end of the interim reporting period, then we believe that these should be presented separately from other assets and liabilities in the condensed interim statement of financial position (see 5.4.110).

5.9.50 *Earnings per share in condensed interim financial statements*

IAS 34.10, 5.9.50.10 When an entity is within the scope of IAS 33 *Earnings per Share* it presents
11, 11A basic and diluted earnings per share (EPS (see 5.3)) in the statement displaying the components of profit or loss. Although not required explicitly by IAS 34, EPS for continuing operations may be material to an understanding of the interim period, in which case it would be disclosed in condensed interim financial statements.

5.9.60 *Explanatory notes in condensed interim financial statements*

IAS 34.15 5.9.60.10 Entities are not required to repeat or provide insignificant updates to information already reported in the most recent annual financial statements.

IAS 34.16, 21 5.9.60.20 Explanatory notes to the condensed interim financial statements include at least the following information, unless it is immaterial or disclosed elsewhere in the interim report (see 5.9.10.50):#

- *Changes in accounting policies.* An entity discloses the nature and effect of any change in accounting policy, or provides a statement that the interim financial statements reflect the same accounting policies as in the most recent annual financial statements (see 5.9.230).
- *Description of seasonality of activities.* An entity explains the reasons for any seasonal fluctuations in its operations. Entities with highly seasonal activities also are encouraged to supplement the required disclosures with information for the 12-month period ending on the interim reporting date, as well as comparatives. There is no guidance on what additional information might be provided, and in our view such information may be limited to the information that is affected by seasonality, e.g. revenue and gross margin.
- *Unusual items.* An entity discloses the nature and amount of items affecting assets, liabilities, equity, net income or cash flows that are unusual because of their nature, size or incidence.

- *Changes in estimates.* An entity discloses the nature and amount of material changes in estimates of amounts reported in prior interim periods or in prior financial years (see 5.9.210).
- *Debt and equity transactions.* An entity discloses issues, repurchases and repayments of debt and equity securities, and dividends paid for ordinary and other shares.
- *Segment information.* If an entity is required to disclose segment information in its annual financial statements in accordance with IFRS 8 *Operating Segments*, then in its condensed interim financial statements it discloses (see 5.2.220):
  - a measure of segment profit or loss;
  - if included in the measure of segment profit or loss reviewed by, or otherwise provided regularly to, the chief operating decision maker:
    - revenues from external customers; and
    - inter-segment revenues;
  - total assets for which there has been a material change from the amount disclosed in the last annual financial statements;
  - any change in the basis of segmentation or the basis of measuring segment profit or loss; and
  - a reconciliation between the total of the reportable segments' measures of profit or loss in respect of continuing operations and the profit or loss in the financial statements; this reconciliation generally excludes income tax expense.
- *Subsequent events.* An entity discloses material events that occurred subsequent to the end of the interim reporting period and that are not reflected in the interim financial statements.
- *Effects of changes in the composition of an entity.* The disclosure of changes in composition includes business combinations, acquisitions and disposals of subsidiaries and long-term investments, restructurings and discontinued operations. In respect of business combinations, an entity is required to disclose in its interim financial statements the information required by IFRS 3 *Business Combinations* (see 5.9.63).
- *Changes in contingent assets and liabilities since the end of the last annual reporting period.*

5.9.60.25 Unlike in a complete set of financial statements, for condensed interim financial statements there is no explicit requirement to disclose the date that the condensed interim financial statements were authorised for issue and who gave such authorisation (see 2.9.15). We prefer that an entity discloses the date of authorisation since it is relevant to a user's understanding, as any event that occurs after that date is not disclosed or adjusted in the condensed financial statements of the current interim period.

IAS 34.16 5.9.60.30 The entity also provides a description of any other transactions and events that may be material to an understanding of the current interim period. Some items may be considered material because of their nature rather than their size (e.g. individually material items (see 4.1.82)).

IAS 34.17 5.9.60.40 Paragraph 17 of IAS 34 contains the following list of disclosures, together with the statement that they are examples of the kinds of disclosures required by paragraph 16 of IAS 34. In our view, these disclosures are required only if they are material to an understanding of the current interim period:

- inventory write-downs and their reversal, and the recognition and reversal of impairment losses on any other assets (see 5.9.80);
- acquisitions, disposals and commitments for the purchase of property, plant and equipment;
- litigation settlements and the reversal of restructuring provisions;
- any loan default or breach of a loan agreement that was not remedied on or before the end of the interim reporting period;
- correction of prior period errors; and
- related party transactions.

IAS 34.16, 17   5.9.60.50 In respect of related party transactions, care should be taken in determining the level of disclosure that is necessary in condensed interim financial statements. If the nature and amounts of related party transactions are consistent with those reported previously, then no disclosure may be necessary in the condensed interim financial statements. However, if related party transactions are significant, then disclosure may be necessary even if the nature and amounts of those transactions are consistent with previous periods.

5.9.60.60 In our view, an entity generally does not have to update the disclosure of related party relationships unless there has been a significant change, such as a change in the controlling investor.

5.9.60.70 Other examples of items that may be material to an understanding of the interim period include:

- disclosures required by IAS 8 *Accounting Policies, Changes in Accounting Estimates and Errors* in respect of a change in accounting policy;
- changes in significant judgements and assumptions made by management, as well as areas of estimation uncertainty;
- disclosures required by IFRS 7 *Financial Instruments: Disclosures,* if changes in an entity's financial risk management objectives and policies or in the nature and extent of risks arising from financial instruments occur during the interim period;
- disclosures required by IAS 36 *Impairment of Assets*, if an entity's annual impairment testing of goodwill and intangible assets with indefinite useful lives occurs during an interim period;
- significant changes in the effective income tax rate;
- significant changes in the carrying amounts of assets and liabilities measured at fair value;
- disclosures required by IFRS 2 *Share-based Payment,* if an entity grants a share-based payment award during the current interim period;
- disclosures required by IFRS 5, if an entity has operations that are discontinued at the end of the interim reporting period or are disposed of during the interim period, or non-current assets or a disposal group classified as held for sale at the end of the interim reporting period;

- acquisitions, disposals and commitments for the purchase of significant categories of non-current assets, in addition to property, plant and equipment, which is addressed in 5.9.60.40; and
- material movements in provisions during the interim period.

IAS 34.26   5.9.60.80 Any significant changes in estimates made during the final interim period should be disclosed in the annual financial statements, unless separate interim financial statements are published for this period.

5.9.60.90 Additional disclosures are required in the interim financial statements in the year that an entity adopts IFRSs (see 6.1.1670).

5.9.63 Business combinations

IFRS 3.59-63,   5.9.63.10 Following the adoption of IFRS 3 (2008), the minimum disclosures in
IAS 34.16(i)   condensed interim financial statements in respect of changes in composition have been extended to include all of the disclosures required by IFRS 3.

IAS 34.16(h),   5.9.63.20 IAS 34 requires IFRS 3 disclosures to be given in respect of changes in
(i)   composition, including business combinations that occur during the interim reporting period. IAS 34 also requires disclosure of material events subsequent to the end of the interim period. A business combination that occurs after the end of the interim period may be an example of a material event subsequent to the end of the interim period.

5.9.65 Forthcoming requirements

5.9.65.10 The *Improvements to IFRSs 2010* amended IAS 34 to add further examples of events or transactions that may require disclosure under IAS 34:

- changes in an entity's business or economic circumstances that have an impact on the fair value of financial items in the statement of financial position, regardless of whether such items are accounted for at fair value;
- transfers of financial instruments between levels of the fair value hierarchy; and
- changes in financial assets' classification (e.g. from available for sale to held to maturity) as a result of changes in their purpose or use.

5.9.70 Comparative information

IAS 34.20, 1.4   5.9.70.05 An entity that prepares a complete set of interim financial statements (see 5.9.10.25) includes comparative information in accordance with the specific requirements of IAS 34 (see 5.9.30.20) and the general requirements of IAS 1. See 2.1.30 for further discussion of the requirements of IAS 1 in respect of quantitative and narrative comparative information.

IAS 1.4   5.9.70.10 An entity that prepares condensed interim financial statements is not required to apply the requirements of IAS 1 in respect of quantitative and narrative comparative information.

IAS 34.20   5.9.70.20 IAS 34 itself contains specific requirements for the comparative primary statements (see 2.1.10.20) that are included in the condensed (and complete) interim financial statements (see 5.9.30.20). For example, in an initial public offering a set of half-yearly interim financial statements may be presented in addition to the most recent annual financial statements, which include comparative information. If the interim financial statements claim compliance with IFRSs (for a complete set of financial statements) or IAS 34 (for condensed interim financial statements), then presentation of the comparative interim period also is required.

IAS 34.6, 15,   5.9.70.30 However, IAS 34 is less specific in respect of the comparative information
16   (both quantitative and narrative) that should be included in the selected explanatory notes. In our experience, entities generally include both quantitative and narrative comparative information in the explanatory notes because the disclosure is of continuing relevance to the current interim period. In our view, management should exercise judgement to decide what comparative information should be included in the explanatory notes. In some circumstances it may be appropriate to omit certain disclosures related to the comparative period that were disclosed in the condensed interim financial statements of the comparative interim period and/or in the last annual financial statements. For example, a business combination occurred and was finalised during the previous annual period and was disclosed in accordance with IFRS 3 in the last annual financial statements. It may be appropriate to exclude from the condensed financial statements of the current interim period some of the disclosures in respect of the prior year business combination; however, certain information may need to be disclosed if necessary for the understanding of the current interim period.

5.9.80 Recognition and measurement

IAS 34.29, 30   5.9.80.10 Generally items are required to be recognised and measured as if the interim period were a discrete stand-alone period. However, the tax charge is based on the estimated weighted average effective tax rate for the full year (see 5.9.160).

IAS 34.23   5.9.80.20 The determination of materiality should be made in relation to the interim period financial information, rather than in relation to the prior or current annual period.

IAS 34.37, 39   5.9.80.30 The conditions for recognising expenses and provisions are the same for interim financial statements as for annual financial statements. Therefore, losses, expenses and income are recognised as incurred or earned and may not be anticipated (see 3.12.330). Similarly, costs and income that are incurred or earned unevenly during the financial year are anticipated or deferred at the end of the interim reporting period if, and only if, it also would be appropriate to anticipate or defer that type of cost or income at the end of the annual reporting period.

5.9.90 *Inventory losses and manufacturing variances*

IAS 34.B26, B28   5.9.90.10 Losses on inventories and interim period manufacturing cost variances are recognised using the same procedures as would be used at the end of the annual reporting period. Therefore, they cannot be deferred on the basis that they are expected to be restored or absorbed by the end of the financial year.

5.9.100 *Volume rebates and discounts*

IAS 34.B23   5.9.100.10 Volume rebates and discounts often are granted by a supplier to a buyer on a "stepped" basis, and calculated based on the volume or value of purchases during a certain period, for example a full year. Both buyers and sellers should anticipate volume rebates and other contractual price adjustments if it is probable that these will be earned (see 4.2.420).

5.9.100.20 – 40 [Not used]

IAS 34.B23   5.9.100.50 Discretionary rebates and discounts are not anticipated.

5.9.110 *Seasonal results*

IAS 34.37, 38   5.9.110.10 Revenue that is received seasonally or occasionally within a financial year is not anticipated or deferred, but is recognised when it is earned.

5.9.110.20 For example, an entity makes and sells printed directories. Income is earned primarily from advertisements placed in the directories and is recognised as revenue when the directories are delivered to the users (see 4.2.630).

5.9.110.30 In our view, revenue that has been earned may not be deferred, and revenue that has not been earned may not be anticipated at the end of the interim reporting period, and therefore cannot be spread over the annual reporting period.

IAS 34.39   5.9.110.40 Any related expenses, such as costs to produce the directories, are capitalised as inventory or work in progress to the extent permitted (see 3.8) until the revenue and the related cost of sales is recognised. Expenses that cannot be capitalised as part of inventory are expensed as incurred.

5.9.120 *Amortisation charges*

IAS 34.39, B24   5.9.120.10 Intangibles with finite useful lives often are amortised on a straight-line basis. In our view, the recognition of amortisation on a straight-line basis means evenly throughout the year. We believe that it is not acceptable to allocate amortisation to interim periods on the basis of seasonal revenues when an entity's accounting policy is to amortise intangible assets on a straight-line basis.

5.9.120.20 In our view, this treatment also is applied to other assets that are depreciated on a straight-line basis, for example property, plant and equipment.

5.9.130 *Major planned periodic maintenance or overhauls*

IAS 34.B2 5.9.130.10 Costs of planned or periodic maintenance or overhauls are not anticipated for interim reporting purposes unless the requirements to recognise a provision are met at the end of the interim reporting period (see 3.12.30). Similarly, other planned or budgeted (but not yet incurred) costs, for example employee training costs, are not anticipated.

5.9.130.20 For example, Company B produces canned food using fresh vegetables. B's annual reporting period ends on 31 December. Production takes place from 1 January to 30 June and most workers are temporary. From 1 July to 31 December the plant is closed and maintenance work is performed.

5.9.130.30 Direct costs (labour) are incurred largely over the first six-month period, but other significant costs are incurred during the second six-month period, for example cleaning and maintenance of the factory. Depreciation of the machinery and plant are direct costs of production.

5.9.130.40 Maintenance and repair costs are recognised as incurred. B does not recognise a provision for the costs to be incurred during the second half of the year at the end of the first six-month period. However, B should consider whether these costs should be either expensed as incurred or capitalised as a separate component of the plant (see 3.2.230).

5.9.130.50 Depreciation of the operating assets should be allocated on a systematic basis that reflects the pattern in which the asset is used in production. In our view, a unit-of-production method may be appropriate for operating assets (such as plant and production equipment). If so, then the annual depreciation charges related to these assets would be spread over the first six months of the year. The planned maintenance shut down for the second six months means that a straight-line time-based charge over the 12 months is unlikely to be appropriate for such assets.

5.9.140 *Assets and liabilities measured at fair value*

IAS 34.C7 5.9.140.10 The carrying amount of assets that are measured at fair value, for example investment property, should be determined at the end of the interim reporting period. The fair value assessment may involve a higher degree of estimation than is used for the annual financial statements. In our experience, external valuers often are not used at the end of the interim reporting period, and in our view extrapolations based upon the balance at the end of the previous annual reporting period may be appropriate for interim financial statements.

5.9.140.20 The fair value of liabilities for cash-settled share-based payment transactions is remeasured at the end of each reporting period (see 4.5.630.20), often involving the use of valuation techniques (see 4.5.580.10). In our view, in assessing whether an updated valuation is required to be performed at the end of the interim reporting period, an entity should consider the complexity of the valuation and the sensitivity of the fair value to changes in key inputs (e.g. the share price and interest rate risk) used in the valuation technique. While we do not believe that a complete new valuation is required at the end of the interim reporting period in all cases, the most recent valuation should be updated such that measurement of the obligation is not materially different from the measurement that would result if a new valuation were obtained at the end of the interim reporting period.

5.9.150 *Employee benefits*

IAS 34.B9, C4 5.9.150.10 Amounts recognised in respect of employee benefit obligations in the statement of financial position at the end of an interim reporting period generally are determined by adjusting the opening statement of financial position for the current service cost, interest cost, expected return on assets, amortisation of actuarial gains and losses, and contributions to the plan. Generally it does not involve obtaining an updated actuarial valuation.

IAS 34.B9 5.9.150.20 However, material changes to the plan, such as a curtailment or settlement or unexpected significant changes in market conditions, are adjusted for in the interim calculation. In our view, if there have been significant changes in the plan, or events such as significant investment gains or losses, then an updated actuarial valuation should be obtained at the end of the interim reporting period.

IAS 19.110 5.9.150.30 In addition, IFRSs specifically require the remeasurement of plan assets and obligations when a curtailment or settlement is recognised.

5.9.150.40 Entities may choose to update their actuarial valuation more frequently than required by IFRSs. In our view, entities may update this calculation at regular intervals (e.g. 30 June, 31 December) provided that the valuations are obtained at the same time each year.

5.9.150.50 In our view, when it is necessary to update the actuarial valuation at the end of the interim reporting period and internal expertise is not available to do so, an actuary should perform the updated valuation.

IAS 19.93A 5.9.150.60 An entity may elect to recognise actuarial gains and losses in other comprehensive income in the periods in which they occur (see 4.4.510). If an entity elects to recognise actuarial gains and losses in other comprehensive income and does not update its actuarial valuation at the end of the interim reporting period, then there would be no actuarial gains or losses to recognise during the interim period. In our view, entities that choose to recognise actuarial gains and losses in other comprehensive income do not need to update their actuarial valuation, unless otherwise required by IFRSs (e.g. there have been material changes to the plan or to market conditions since the last actuarial valuation). However, we believe that such entities should disclose the reason why no actuarial gains or losses are recognised in the interim financial statements.

5.9.160 *Income tax expense*

IAS 34.30(c), B12-B16 5.9.160.10 The income tax expense recognised in each interim period is based on the best estimate of the weighted average annual income tax rate expected for the full year applied to the pre-tax income of the interim period.

5.9.160.20 This effective rate reflects enacted or substantively enacted changes in tax rates that are expected to take effect later in the year. Amounts accrued in one interim period may need to be adjusted in a subsequent interim period if the estimate of the annual effective tax rate changes (see 5.9.210). The income tax expense for an interim period comprises both current tax and deferred tax.

IAS 34.B19 5.9.160.30 Anticipated tax benefits from tax credits generally are reflected in computing the estimated annual effective tax rate when the credits are granted and calculated on an annual basis. However, if the credits relate to a one-off event, then they are recognised in the interim period in which the event occurs.

IAS 34.30(c), B19 5.9.160.35 A change in tax rate that is substantively enacted in an interim period is analogous to a tax credit granted in relation to a one-off event. As such, we prefer that an entity recognise the effect of the change immediately in the interim period in which the change occurs. However, another acceptable approach would be to spread the effect of a change in the tax rate over the remainder of the annual reporting period via an adjustment to the estimated annual effective income tax rate.

IAS 34.B14 5.9.160.40 If different income tax rates apply to different categories of income, for example capital gains, or to different tax jurisdictions, then a separate rate is applied to each category in the interim period, to the extent practicable. However, a weighted average rate across jurisdictions and income categories may be used if it is a reasonable approximation of the effect of using more specific rates.

5.9.160.50 For example, Companies A and B, two subsidiaries within a group, have different effective tax rates. While B's activities are not seasonal, A has seasonal activities. The expected results for the full year are as follows:

	A	B	Total
Pre-tax profit (loss) – first six months	(100)	60	(40)
Pre-tax profit – second six months	200	60	260
Total profit before tax	100	120	220
Expected tax expense	(33)	(12)	(45)
Effective tax rate	**33%**	**10%**	**20.5%**

5.9.160.60 In our view, it is not appropriate to use an annual consolidated effective tax rate of 20.5 percent to estimate the interim period tax expense. This is because it is unlikely that this weighted average rate will be a reasonable approximation of the result of using separate rates for each component, due to the impact of the seasonality of A's operations and the difference in effective rates of A and B.

5.9.160.70 We believe that the effective rate for each subsidiary should be applied to interim pre-tax profit (loss) to determine the interim income tax expense for the group, as follows:

First six months	A	B	Total
Pre-tax profit (loss)	(100)	60	(40)
Income tax benefit (expense)	33	(6)	27
Effective tax rate	**(33%)**	**10%**	**(67.5%)**
Second six months	*A*	*B*	*Total*
Pre-tax profit	200	60	260
Income tax expense	(66)	(6)	(72)
Effective tax rate	**33%**	**10%**	**27.7%**

5.9.160.80 There may be cases when a reliable estimate of the annual effective tax rate cannot be made. That situation may arise, for example, when relatively small changes in estimated pre-tax accounting income would produce a large change in the estimated annual effective tax rate. In our view, if a reliable estimate of the annual effective tax rate cannot be made, then the actual effective rate based on a year-to-date actual tax calculation may represent the best estimate of the annual effective tax rate.

5.9.170 Non-tax deductible items

5.9.170.10 The average annual effective tax rate is based on the estimated pre-tax profit (loss) for the year. It is unclear whether the estimated pre-tax profit (loss) for the year should be adjusted to exclude non-tax deductible items.

5.9.170.20 For example, Group X is required to prepare quarterly interim financial statements in accordance with IAS 34. To estimate the amount of its income tax expense for the first quarter of 2010 X has prepared annual projections of income and tax.

5.9.170.30 X has made the following assumptions:

- the average enacted tax rate applicable to the group is 40 percent;
- no temporary difference will exist at the end of the financial year; and
- the only non-tax deductible item at the end of the year will be amortisation of an intangible asset.

Estimation of the average effective tax rate	
	End of 2010
Projected annual profit before tax and amortisation	1,200
Projected annual amortisation	(600)
Projected annual pre-tax profit	600
Projected annual income tax expense (1,200 x 40%)	480

There are two different approaches to estimating both the average annual effective tax rate and the income tax expense for the interim periods.

	Tax rate
Method 1: (480 / 1,200)	40%
Method 2: (480 / 600)	80%

5.9.170.40 In method 1, X calculates the average annual effective tax rate by adjusting the reported income for the effect of the amortisation that is not tax deductible.

5.9.170.50 In method 2, X does not adjust the reported income for the non-tax deductible amortisation, resulting in the estimated average annual effective tax rate of 80 percent. This expected annual effective tax rate differs from the average enacted tax rate due to the significance of the amortisation.

5.9.170.60 The following illustrates the impact of applying either method 1 or 2 in the interim financial statements when pre-amortisation profit is earned unevenly during the year:

Income tax expense estimation	*Q1*	*Q2*	*Q3*	*Q4*	*2010*
Profit before tax and					
amortisation (a)	50	350	400	400	1,200
Amortisation	(150)	(150)	(150)	(150)	(600)
Pre-tax profit (loss) (b)	(100)	200	250	250	600
Income tax expense –					
Method 1: (a) x 40 percent	(20)	(140)	(160)	(160)	(480)
Effective tax rate					80%
Income tax benefit (expense) –					
Method 2: (b) x 80 percent	80	(160)	(200)	(200)	(480)
Effective tax rate					80%

5.9.170.70 In our view, X should choose an accounting policy, to be applied consistently, to calculate the annual effective tax rate.

- We prefer that an entity use the estimated pre-tax income (loss) for the year without adjustment to exclude non-tax deductible items. In this example, an effective tax rate of 80 percent is applied to the pre-tax accounting profit during each interim period (method 2).
- However, another acceptable approach is to calculate the effective income tax rate based on the estimated *taxable* profit for the interim period. Under this approach the accounting profit is adjusted for non-tax deductible items (e.g. non-tax deductible amortisation). In this example, an effective tax rate of 40 percent is applied to the accounting profit *after* the adjustment for the effect of the amortisation (method 1). This approach treats identifiable non-tax deductible expenses (or non-taxable income) in a similar way to different categories of income (e.g. capital gains) to which a different tax rate is applied. In our view, this approach would be appropriate only when the amounts are significant and separately identifiable, different tax rates are applied to *each* separate category of income, and an entity applies the same level of analysis to identify, in each tax jurisdiction, items taxed at both higher and lower rates.

5.9.180 *Tax losses*

5.9.180.10 Tax losses may be carried forward from previous reporting periods or may be created during an interim period and reversed in subsequent interim periods.

IAS 34.B20-B22 5.9.180.20 The effect of any tax loss carried forward, originating in previous or current reporting periods, is considered in computing the average annual effective tax rate. The general criteria for recognition of a deferred tax asset are applied at the end of each interim reporting period (see 3.13.170). The entity assesses the probability of generating enough taxable profits in future periods to utilise the tax benefit.

5.9.180.30 For example, in its first quarter Company B incurs a tax loss as a result of poor trading conditions, but anticipates making a profit for the year and paying tax for the full year. B estimates its tax expense for the year taking into account the losses in the first period and utilisation thereof in later interim periods. The effective tax rate is applied to the pre-tax loss and a deferred tax asset is recognised at the end of the first quarter.

IAS 34.B20 5.9.180.40 If a tax loss arising in an interim period is available for a tax loss carry-back, then the related benefit is reflected in the interim period in which the loss is incurred.

5.9.180.50 If management's estimate of the recoverability of unused tax losses changes during an interim period, then in our view it is acceptable for this change to be reflected in calculating the expected annual effective tax rate and apportioned between the interim periods.

5.9.180.60 For example, assume that at the beginning of the year Company X has unrecognised tax losses of 20,000. Profit for the first half year is 4,000 and estimated profit for the second half year is 6,000; total 10,000 for the year. At the end of the half-year interim reporting period, X reassesses the recoverability of the tax losses and believes that the entire tax loss will be utilised in current and future periods. Therefore previously unrecognised tax losses of 8,000 would be allocated to the first half year (20,000 x (4,000 / 10,000)).

5.9.180.70 The change in the estimate of recoverability of the tax loss carried forward may result in a change in the expected annual tax rate as compared to previous interim periods of the same financial year, e.g. if the entity reports quarterly. In this case previous interim periods are not restated, but the cumulative adjustment (calculation applied in 5.9.180.60 less the amount which has been recognised in previous interim periods) is recognised in the current interim period. This is consistent with the accounting for a change in estimate and the requirement in IAS 34 that amounts reported in interim financial statements be measured on a year-to-date basis (see 5.9.160.10, 210.10 and 30).

5.9.190 *Current and deferred tax*

5.9.190.10 Although IAS 34 provides guidance on how the income tax expense should be determined, it does not specify how the total amount should be split between current and deferred tax. An example of an appropriate method may be to split current and deferred tax based on the relative proportions expected at the end of the financial year. In our experience, most entities do not show this split.

5.9.190.20 As the income tax expense is calculated by applying the estimated annual effective tax rate to the pre-tax profit for the interim period, the resulting deferred tax asset or liability does not reflect the effect of temporary differences that do not impact profit or loss (e.g. temporary differences on the revaluation of property, plant and equipment). In our view, if material temporary differences arise in an interim period due to items of income and expense recognised directly in equity or in other comprehensive income, then deferred tax also should be calculated and recognised for these items. In our view, it would be appropriate in such cases to measure deferred tax using the same principles as would apply as of the end of the annual period, i.e. based on the temporary difference between the item's tax base and its carrying amount, and the tax rate expected to apply when the underlying asset/liability is recovered/settled (see 3.13.220).

5.9.200 *Impairment*

IAS 34.B35, B36   5.9.200.10 Reviews for indicators of impairment and any resulting impairment tests are performed at the end of the interim reporting period in the same manner as at the end of the annual reporting period.

5.9.210 *Estimates*

IAS 34.41, C1-C9   5.9.210.10 While measurements in both annual and interim financial statements often are based on reasonable estimates, the preparation of interim financial statements generally will require a greater use of estimation than annual financial statements. Changes to accounting estimates are applied to the current and future periods and do not involve the restatement of results for either the prior year or prior interim periods in the current financial year (see 2.8.60).

5.9.210.20 For example, Company D prepares quarterly interim financial statements. The carrying amount of one of its assets is 100,000, with the asset's useful life initially estimated to be 10 years. The resulting depreciation expense is 10,000 for the year and 2,500 for the first quarter. Subsequently there is a change to the estimated useful life of the asset, which, at the beginning of the second quarter, is revised to be five years from that date. In our view, the depreciable amount at the end of the first quarter of 97,500 is depreciated over the remaining useful life of five years because the change in estimate is applied prospectively. Therefore depreciation of 4,875 will be recognised for each quarter (97,500 / 20 quarters) over the remaining useful life of the asset.

IAS 34.28,   5.9.210.30 The measurement of annual results should not be affected by the frequency
IFRIC 10.8   of an entity's financial reporting (i.e. annual, half-yearly or quarterly) and amounts reported in interim financial statements are measured on a year-to-date basis. However, as an exception, an entity is prohibited from reversing an impairment loss recognised in a previous interim period in respect of goodwill, an investment in an equity instrument classified as available for sale or a financial asset carried at cost (not amortised cost). This specific prohibition should not be applied by analogy to other transactions and events.

5.9.210.40 Generally, in our view separate transactions and events should be accounted for as such during an interim period. For example, Company P recognises an impairment loss in its interim financial statements for the first quarter. The asset is sold during a subsequent interim period and a gain is realised. In the above example, the impairment loss should not be reclassified and offset against the gain on disposal merely because they occurred in two interim periods of a single year. In addition, the gain does not lead automatically to the reversal of the earlier impairment loss. Instead, each of the impairment loss, any possible reversal of that loss and the gain on disposal are dealt with separately, in accordance with individual requirements of the standard applicable to the underlying item. However, recognition of a gain shortly after a loss may be an indicator that either the event giving rise to the impairment has reversed or that the estimates used should be reconsidered and, if necessary, revised.

5.9.210.50 Certain impairment losses may not be reversed if they have been recognised in interim financial statements that state compliance either with IFRSs or with IAS 34 (see 5.9.10.20 – 25 and 210.30). It is not clear whether the requirements described in 5.9.210.30 apply when no such interim financial statements are prepared, but when an entity has prepared selected information in respect of an earlier interim period in which that impairment was recognised. In our view, judgement is needed and it may be relevant to consider whether the users of the selected interim financial information would have concluded that the impairment has been recognised in accordance with

IFRSs. For example, if the interim financial information is described as being prepared in accordance with the recognition and measurement principles of IFRSs and includes a financial measure that reflects the impairment loss, then we believe that it may be appropriate not to reverse the impairment loss in the financial statements of subsequent interim (or annual) periods.

5.9.220 [Not used]

5.9.230 **Accounting policies**

IAS 34.28   5.9.230.10 The accounting policies followed in the interim report generally will be the same as those applied in the previous annual financial statements, except for changes in accounting policies made during the current financial year.

IAS 34.43   5.9.230.20 Any change in accounting policy on adoption of a new or revised standard is accounted for in accordance with the transitional requirements specified in the relevant IFRSs if such guidance is provided. Otherwise, the change in accounting policy is accounted for in accordance with the general guidance on changes in accounting policies in IAS 8 (see 2.8.10).

5.9.230.30 The recognition and measurement requirements of any new standards should be applied to all interim periods within the annual period in which the new standards first are adopted unless the transitional requirements of a standard permit or require different transition. For example, if an entity's annual reporting period ends on 31 December 2010, then it should apply any new standards that are effective for periods commencing on or after 1 January 2010 in its interim financial statements at 31 March 2010, 30 June 2010 and 30 September 2010. The entity should not apply earlier versions of the standards in the interim financial statements and then change to the new standards for the annual financial statements.

IFRS 8.22(a),   5.9.230.35 The presentation and disclosure requirements of any new standards and inter-
IAS 34.16(a),   pretations are not directly applicable to the preparation of condensed interim financial
(g)   statements unless those new requirements amend IAS 34 itself. However, an entity is required to describe the nature and effect of any change, which may result in further disclosure, even in condensed interim financial statements. For example, an entity applies IFRS 8 in its condensed interim financial statements. IAS 34 sets out the minimum disclosure requirements in respect of segment information in condensed interim financial statements (see 5.9.60.20). However, in order to explain the nature and effect of the change, the entity includes additional disclosure, for example of the factors used to identify the reportable segments.

5.9.230.40 Changes in accounting policy adopted after the first interim period normally are presented by restating the financial statements for prior interim periods of the current financial year and comparative interim periods presented. This may occur, for example, if a new or revised standard is published during the year and the entity early adopts the new standard.

5.9.240 **Future developments**

5.9.240.10 The overall objective of the comprehensive financial statement presentation project is to establish a global standard that prescribes the basis for presentation of financial statements of an entity that are consistent over time, and that promote comparability between entities. The financial statement presentation project is conducted in three phases:

- Phase A was completed in September 2007 with the release of a revised IAS 1 *Financial Statement Presentation*;
- Phase B is in progress and addresses the more fundamental issues related to financial statement presentation; and
- Phase C has not been initiated, but is expected to address issues related to interim financial statements.

5.9.240.20 In July 2010 the IASB posted a staff draft of a proposed ED reflecting tentative decisions made to date in respect of phase B to obtain further stakeholder feedback. An ED is scheduled for the first quarter of 2011.

5.10 Insurance contracts
(IFRS 4)

5.10 Insurance contracts
(IFRS 4)

Overview of currently effective requirements

- Generally, entities that issue insurance contracts are required to continue their existing accounting policies with respect to insurance contracts except when IFRS 4 requires or permits changes in accounting policies.

- An insurance contract is a contract that transfers significant insurance risk. Insurance risk is significant if an insured event could cause an insurer to pay significant additional benefits in any scenario, excluding those that lack commercial substance.

- A financial instrument that does not meet the definition of an insurance contract (including investments held to back insurance liabilities) is accounted for under the general recognition and measurement requirements for financial instruments.

- Financial instruments that include discretionary participation features may be accounted for as insurance contracts although these are subject to the general financial instrument disclosure requirements.

- In some cases a deposit element should be "unbundled" (separated) from an insurance contract and accounted for as a financial instrument.

- Some derivatives embedded in insurance contracts should be separated from their host insurance contract and accounted for as if they were stand-alone derivatives.

- Changes in existing accounting policies for insurance contracts are permitted only if the new policy, or a combination of new policies, results in information that is more relevant or reliable, or both, without reducing either relevance or reliability.

- The recognition of catastrophe and equalisation provisions is prohibited for contracts not in existence at the reporting date.

- A liability adequacy test is required to ensure that the measurement of an entity's insurance liabilities considers all contractual cash flows, using current estimates.

- The application of "shadow accounting" for insurance liabilities is permitted for consistency with the treatment of unrealised gains or losses on assets.

> - **An expanded presentation of the fair value of insurance contracts acquired in a business combination or portfolio transfer is permitted.**
>
> - **Significant disclosures are required of the terms, conditions and risks related to insurance contracts, consistent in principle with those required for financial assets and liabilities.**

Currently effective requirements

This publication reflects IFRSs in issue at 1 August 2010. The currently effective requirements cover annual periods beginning on 1 January 2010. The requirements related to this topic are derived mainly from IFRS 4 *Insurance Contracts*.

Forthcoming requirements and future developments

When a currently effective requirement will be changed by a new requirement that is issued but is not yet effective, it is marked with a # as a **forthcoming requirement** and the impact of the change is explained in the accompanying boxed text. The forthcoming requirements related to this topic are derived from IFRS 9 *Financial Instruments* and a brief outline of the impact is given in 5.10.95.

The currently effective or forthcoming requirements may be subject to **future developments** and a brief outline of the relevant projects is given in 5.10.160.

5.10.10 Introduction

5.10.10.10 IFRS 4 represents the completion of the first phase of the IASB's project on accounting for insurance contracts. The IASB, in developing this standard, sought to minimise the amount of change required from current accounting policies and practices and to avoid changes that may be reversed in the second phase of the IASB's insurance project. Therefore, entities generally are required to continue most of their existing accounting policies for insurance contracts and restrictions are placed on the introduction of new policies.

5.10.20 Scope

IFRS 4.2-4, 5.10.20.10 IFRS 4 applies to insurance contracts (including reinsurance contracts) that
6 an entity issues and reinsurance contracts that it holds (i.e. to the contractual rights and obligations arising from these contracts). In addition, the scope of IFRS 4 also includes *financial instruments* with a discretionary participation feature that an entity issues (see 5.10.110). It does not address other aspects of accounting by insurers, for example accounting for financial instruments, which are in the scope of IAS 39 *Financial Instruments: Recognition and Measurement* (see 3.6), or other assets and liabilities of insurance entities. It does not address accounting for insurance contracts by policyholders, other than holders of reinsurance contracts.

IFRS 4.4, B18, B19 5.10.20.20 IFRS 4 focuses on types of contracts rather than types of entities. Therefore, it applies to both entities regulated as insurance entities and all other entities. Insurers are subject to the requirements of other applicable IFRSs in respect of products or components of products that are not insurance contracts. For example, IAS 18 *Revenue* applies to fees and related costs on investment management contracts (see 4.2.610). In addition, some contracts that may meet the definition of insurance contracts are excluded from the scope of the standard, such as product warranties issued directly by a manufacturer or retailer, employers' assets and liabilities under employee benefit plans, some financial guarantees and contingent consideration payable or receivable in a business combination. Rights and obligations excluded from IFRS 4 may be dealt with specifically in another standard; for example, assets and liabilities under employee benefit plans are covered by IAS 19 *Employee Benefits* (see 4.4); financial instruments, including certain financial guarantees, are covered by IAS 39 (see 3.6); and provisions, contingent liabilities and contingent assets are covered by IAS 37 *Provisions, Contingent Liabilities and Contingent Assets* (see 3.12 and 3.14).

IFRS 4.4, B18 5.10.20.30 Although financial guarantee contracts meet the definition of an insurance contract, generally they are outside the scope of IFRS 4 and are accounted for under IAS 39 (see 3.6.35). However, if an entity issuing such contracts has previously asserted explicitly that it regards financial guarantee contracts as insurance contracts and has accounted for them as such, then it may apply IFRS 4 to such contracts. For an insurer, it is likely to be clear from previous practices, contract documents etc. whether issued financial guarantee contracts have been regarded as and accounted for as insurance contracts. For entities that write financial guarantee contracts that are incidental to their main business, for example, to support borrowings of subsidiaries or of customers, it may be less clear whether the entity has made such an explicit assertion. For such entities, in our view it is not necessary that insurance contract terminology be used in documenting its financial guarantee contracts. The explicit assertion may be apparent from information in previous financial statements and other published information.

5.10.30 *Definition of an insurance contract*

IFRS 4.A 5.10.30.10 An insurance contract is a contract under which the insurer accepts significant insurance risk from the policyholder by agreeing to compensate the policyholder if a specified uncertain future event adversely affects the policyholder. This specified uncertain future event is known as the "insured event".

IFRS 4.B2 5.10.30.20 Some guidance is provided to clarify the definition in 5.10.30.10. One of the central characteristics of an insurance contract is the specified uncertain future event. Uncertainty (or risk) is the essence of an insurance contract. Therefore, uncertainty is required at the inception of an insurance contract regarding: (1) whether an insured event will occur; (2) when it will occur; or (3) how much the insurer will need to pay if it occurs.

IFRS 4.A, B 5.10.30.30 The specified uncertain future event that is covered by an insurance contract creates "insurance risk". Insurance risk is any risk, other than financial risk, *transferred* from the holder to the issuer of a contract. Financial risk is the risk of a possible future change in a specified interest rate, financial instrument price, commodity price, foreign exchange rate, index of prices or rates, credit rating or credit index or other variable, provided, in the case of a non-financial variable, that it is not specific to a party to the contract. Risks to the holder such as death, illness, disability, loss of property due to damage, theft etc. are each an insurance risk because they are specific to a party to the contract.

5.10.30.40 When a contract refers to a variable that determines significant cash flows under that contract, is non-financial and is specific to a party to the contract, that variable is considered to give rise to insurance risk, assuming it is a *transferred* risk, rather than to financial risk. For example, if a contract written by a manufacturer or dealer guarantees the residual value of a vehicle owned by the holder of the contract, and the amount payable under the guarantee will vary significantly depending on the specific condition of the vehicle at the date of sale, then the contract is an insurance contract. Conversely, if the owner is required to restore the vehicle to a specified condition before disposal in the marketplace, such that the guarantee is of a market value that is not dependent on the condition of the vehicle, then in our view the contract is not an insurance contract.

5.10.30.50 Similarly, if the holder of an asset value guarantee uses the asset in its business and can only exercise the guarantee by returning the asset to the guarantor, then the holder's decision to exercise the guarantee will be influenced not only by the market price of the asset but also by its value in use, and the availability of alternative assets for use in the business. In our view, it would be reasonable to conclude in such cases that the underlying variable that drives the value of the guarantee to the holder is specific to the holder of the guarantee. Therefore the contract would be an insurance contract even if the holder is required to restore the asset to a specified condition before returning it.

IFRS 4.B12, 5.10.30.60 Lapse or persistency risk (i.e. the risk that the counterparty will cancel the
B15, B16 contract earlier or later than the issuer had expected in pricing the contract) or expense risk (i.e. the risk of unexpected increases in the administrative costs associated with the servicing of a contract, rather than in costs associated with insured events) are not insurance risks because they are not risks that are transferred by the counterparty to the contract issuer and also because they do not adversely affect the counterparty. However, if the issuer of a contract exposed to lapse, persistency or expense risk (but not, from the perspective of the issuer, insurance risk) mitigates those risks by using a second contract to transfer all or part of those risks to another party, then the second contract exposes that other party to significant insurance risk and is therefore an insurance contract from the perspective of that other party (issuer). However, the holder (transferor of insurance risk) is the policyholder of that second contract and therefore does not apply IFRS 4 to that contract.

IFRS 4.B22- 5.10.30.70 A contract that exposes the issuer to financial risk without significant insurance
B28 risk is not an insurance contract and therefore the contract is accounted for as a financial instrument (see 3.6). Insurance risk is significant when there is at least one scenario that has commercial substance in which the insurer would suffer a significant loss as

a result of an insured event taking place. A loss event has commercial substance if it has a discernible effect on the economics of the transaction, so that the insurer would be required to pay additional significant benefits to the policyholder beyond those that would be paid if the insured event does not occur. It does not matter that the insured event is extremely unlikely or that the expected present value of contingent cash flows is a small proportion of the expected present value of all of the remaining contractual cash flows. The additional benefits referred to above can include a requirement to pay a benefit earlier (e.g. upon death) than if the policyholder survives for a longer period. For example, an investment contract that pays a fixed amount at maturity, but also pays the same amount in the case of death during the term of the contract, is an insurance contract as long as the death benefit, in present value terms, could significantly exceed the present value of the amount payable at maturity.

IFRS 4.B25,
IGE.1.5

5.10.30.80 Insurance risk is assessed in relation to the individual contract and without considering portfolio effects. Therefore, the insurance risk on an individual contract may be significant even if material losses are not expected in a portfolio of contracts (i.e. gains on some contracts in a portfolio offset the losses on other contracts in the portfolio). However, if a relatively homogeneous book of small contracts is known to consist of contracts that all transfer insurance risk, then an insurer need not examine each contract within this book to identify a few non-derivative contracts that transfer insignificant insurance risk. For example, the significance of insurance risk in endowment contracts typically depends on the age of the policyholder at the outset of the contract or on the contract duration. Where insurance risk is known generally to be significant based on these factors, the few contracts with an unusually low entry age or unusually short duration, forming part of a portfolio of endowment contracts, need not be considered separately.

IFRS 4.B29,
IGE.1.7

5.10.30.90 Some contracts do not transfer any insurance risk to the issuer at inception, although they do transfer insurance risk at a later time. In these cases, the contract is not considered an insurance contract until the risk transfer occurs. For example, a contract may provide a specified investment return and also specify that the policyholder will receive, or can elect to receive, a life-contingent annuity at current annuity rates determined by the insurer when the annuity begins. Such a contract is not an insurance contract at the outset. For such a contract to be an insurance contract at the outset, it is necessary that the annuity rate or the determination basis is fixed at that time.

5.10.30.95 Once a contract has qualified as an insurance contract it remains an insurance contract until all rights and obligations are extinguished or expired. Therefore, an insurance contract is not reclassified as an investment contract during its life even if insurance risk becomes insignificant or non-existent.

5.10.30.100 Because of the requirements for "significant insurance risk" under IFRS 4, it may be the case that a contract accounted for as a financial instrument under previous GAAP is an insurance contract under IFRSs. In our view, the previous accounting for that contract should continue under IFRSs unless a change in accounting policy can be justified as an improvement (see 5.10.90). It would not be appropriate to change previous GAAP accounting for the contract (e.g. to apply previous GAAP insurance accounting) simply because the definition of an insurance contract under IFRSs is met. The additional requirements of IFRS 4 with respect to the liability adequacy test, unbundling and embedded derivatives also would apply.

5.10.30.110 Conversely, if a contract is not an insurance contract under IFRS 4 but did qualify for insurance accounting under previous GAAP, then for IFRS accounting purposes the contract is not an insurance contract and should be accounted for under IAS 39 or other relevant standards. The continuation of previous GAAP is prohibited for a contract that does not qualify as an insurance contract under IFRS 4.

5.10.40 *Deposit components and embedded derivatives in insurance contracts*

5.10.40.10 Some insurance contracts contain a deposit component, which is a component that would, if it were a stand-alone instrument, be a financial instrument (see 3.6). The deposit component is required to be "unbundled" and accounted for as a financial instrument if the rights or obligations under that component otherwise would not be recognised under the insurer's accounting policies. If, for example, an insurer's liability adequacy test is sufficient to ensure that the full obligation under a deposit component, including any guaranteed amounts, is recognised, then unbundling is not required.

IFRS 4.10   5.10.40.20 An insurer nevertheless may choose to unbundle a deposit component, provided the deposit component can be measured separately from the insurance component. For example, certain reinsurance contracts specify that any compensation received from the reinsurer for losses will be reimbursed to the reinsurer by increases in future reinsurance premiums. Because the repayment is not contingent, the obligation arises from a deposit component and the deposit obligation is required to be unbundled and accounted for separately as a financial liability, provided that it can be measured separately, unless the accounting policies of the holder of the reinsurance contract otherwise would require recognition of the repayment obligation.

IFRS 4.IGE.2   5.10.40.30 Components of insurance contracts that meet the definition of a derivative are within the scope of IAS 39 (see 3.6) and are therefore subject to the general requirements for embedded derivatives, with two exceptions as noted in 5.10.40.50.

IAS 39.10, 11   5.10.40.40 IAS 39 requires an embedded derivative to be separated from the host contract and accounted for as a stand-alone derivative if the following conditions are met:

- the economic characteristics and risks of the embedded derivative are not closely related to those of the host contract;
- a separate instrument with the same terms as the embedded derivative would meet the definition of a derivative; and
- the hybrid instrument is not measured at fair value with changes in fair value recognised in profit or loss.

IFRS 4.7-9   5.10.40.50 IFRS 4 provides two significant exemptions to the general requirements for the separation of embedded derivatives. These exemptions apply to:

- components that meet the definition of an insurance contract (e.g. they have significant insurance risk); and
- surrender options with fixed terms.

5.10.40.60 As insurance contracts are not within the scope of IAS 39, the requirements in that standard to separate embedded derivatives (see 3.6.260) are not applicable to insurance contracts embedded in a host contract. A component meeting the definition of an insurance contract does not need to be separated from its host contract. For example, an option to take a life-contingent annuity contract would not be separated from a host insurance contract.

5.10.40.70 An insurer is not required to separate a fixed-price surrender option from a host insurance liability, or a surrender option based on a fixed amount and an interest rate. Even though the surrender value may be viewed as a deposit component, IFRS 4 does not require unbundling of a contract if all obligations arising under the deposit component are recognised.

IAS 39.AG33   5.10.40.80 Since liabilities under unit-linked contracts generally are measured at their current unit values, there is no need to separate a host deposit contract and an embedded derivative for such contracts.

5.10.45 *Contracts containing guaranteed minimum death and/or survival benefits*

5.10.45.10 Some unit-linked savings contracts include a guaranteed minimum benefit that is payable, *either* upon the death of the policyholder *or* upon maturity of the contract, if the guaranteed minimum benefit is higher than the bid value of the units (the unit value) at the time that a claim is made. If the contract is surrendered, then the policyholder receives cash for the value of the units surrendered (less surrender penalties). Therefore, the benefit payable on death or maturity may exceed the benefit paid upon surrender of the contract. If the guaranteed minimum benefits are larger, in present value terms, than the unit value payable on surrender (before consideration of surrender penalties), then these contracts transfer insurance risk because additional amounts are payable if the insured event (either death or survival, depending on the terms of the contract) occurs. For these types of contracts, the issuer determines whether insurance risk is significant taking into account both the probability of the insured event taking place and, if the insured event takes place, the probability of the unit value being significantly below the guaranteed amount at that time. If this insurance risk is significant, then the contract should be classified as an insurance contract.

5.10.45.20 In the scenario described in 5.10.45.10, there are two triggers needed to cause a significant additional benefit: (1) the bid value of the units must fall below the guaranteed minimum benefit (financial risk); and (2) the insured event has to occur (insurance risk). The first trigger is a pre-condition for the existence of insurance risk in the contract. Insurance risk exists only if financial risk already has resulted in losses when the insured event takes place.

5.10.45.30 The classification of a savings contract containing guarantees of this type should be determined on its own merits by considering the level of the guaranteed minimum payments and the likelihood that the bid price of the units will fall below that level. In order for this financial risk to be significant, as a precursor for the existence of insurance risk, in our view it should be *reasonably possible*, based on historical and expected volatility in similar investments, that unit values could fall significantly below the guaranteed amount during the term of the contract.

5.10.45.40 In many cases with investments of high volatility and a guarantee close to the initial investment, an insurance contract classification will be appropriate. However, if the term of the contract is relatively short, the volatility of the units is relatively low, or the level of the guaranteed minimum benefit is relatively low compared to the initial investment, then it might be more difficult for an insurer to justify an insurance contract classification.

5.10.45.50 If the guarantee applies to *both* a death benefit and survival benefit, in our view the amount subject to insurance risk is the difference between the amount payable on death and the amount payable on survival, in present value terms, considering the time value of money and any premium payable in future for continuing the rights under the contract. We believe that the lower surrender value is not relevant in this case because absent a policyholder election to surrender the policy, which is not an insurable event, either death or survival to maturity is certain.

5.10.50 **Recognition and measurement**

5.10.60 *Accounting policies for insurance contracts*

IFRS 4.13   5.10.60.10 In order to allow an insurer to continue using its existing accounting practices for insurance contracts as far as possible, entities are exempted from applying certain portions of the hierarchy for selecting accounting policies (see 2.8.6) to insurance contracts. Specifically, in developing accounting policies under IFRSs for insurance contracts written and reinsurance contracts held, an insurer generally is not required to consider whether the resulting information would be relevant and reliable using the qualitative characteristics in the *Framework for the Preparation and Presentation of Financial Statements*; nor is it required to consider the requirements of other IFRSs by analogy. It is this exemption that largely permits an insurer to continue its existing practices for insurance contracts. Without this exemption, an insurer adopting IFRSs would have needed to assess whether its accounting policies for insurance contracts comply with the hierarchy requirements, in particular the Framework and all other IFRSs, including IAS 37 (see 3.12).

IFRS 4.25, 26   5.10.60.20 While the continuation of many existing practices is permitted, the introduction of some practices as changes in accounting policies is prohibited. For example, an entity is not required to eliminate excessive prudence in accounting for insurance contracts nor is it required, on consolidation, to apply consistent accounting policies to insurance contracts held by each entity within a group. There also is no requirement to use discounting in the measurement of insurance liabilities. However, these policies may not be adopted if they were not used prior to adopting IFRS 4. For example, an entity that did not use excessive prudence may not adopt a policy of doing so on or after adopting IFRS 4.

IFRS 4.14   5.10.60.30 Nevertheless, the impact of the exemption from portions of the hierarchy is limited by five specific requirements. An insurer *does not*:

- recognise as a liability any provisions for possible future claims under insurance contracts if those contracts are not in existence at the reporting date, such as catastrophe and equalisation provisions; or
- offset reinsurance assets against the related insurance liabilities or offset reinsurance income and expenses against expenses or income from the related insurance contracts.

5.10.60.40 An insurer:

- derecognises an insurance liability only when the obligation specified in the contract is discharged, cancelled or expires;
- considers whether its reinsurance assets are impaired; and
- carries out a liability adequacy test.

IAS 18.A14   5.10.60.50 With the exception of insurance assets (e.g. salvage and subrogation, and premium receivables), deferred acquisition costs related to insurance contracts, present value of future profits (PVFP) (see 5.10.100) and reinsurance assets, an insurer's accounting for its assets will follow other applicable IFRSs. As deferred acquisition costs on investment management contracts are accounted for in accordance with IAS 18 (see 4.2), in our view these costs are not within the scope of IAS 38 *Intangible Assets*.

5.10.70 *Liability adequacy test*

IFRS 4.15   5.10.70.10 An insurer assesses at each reporting date whether its recognised insurance liabilities (less related deferred acquisition costs and related intangible assets) are adequate, using current estimates of future cash flows under the insurance contracts. Any shortfall is recognised in profit or loss.

IFRS 4.16-18   5.10.70.20 At a minimum, the assessment of the adequacy of the liability should consider current estimates of all contractual cash flows and of related cash flows such as claim handling costs, as well as cash flows resulting from embedded options and guarantees. If an insurer's existing accounting policies include an assessment that meets this requirement, then no further test is required. If they do not, then IAS 37 (see 3.12) should be applied to determine whether the recognised liabilities are adequate. IFRS 4 does not specify whether, in performing the liability adequacy test, cash flows should be discounted or, if discounting is applied, what discount rate should be used. However, if the assessment shows that the liability is inadequate, then the shortfall is recognised in profit or loss.

5.10.70.30 In our view, if an insurer's liability adequacy test takes into account amounts recoverable under reinsurance contracts, then that practice may be continued under IFRS 4.

However, the resulting net liability should be presented gross in the statement of financial position by separating the amount recognised for the reinsurance asset from the insurance liability. In our view, such a change in presentation would not be a change in accounting policy. In our view, in performing such a liability adequacy test it would not be appropriate, however, to include estimated reinsurance recoveries from contracts that are not in force at the reporting date.

5.10.80 *Reinsurance*

5.10.80.10 IFRS 4 applies to all insurance contracts (including reinsurance contracts) that an entity issues and also to reinsurance contracts that an entity holds. Reinsurance contracts that an entity holds are an exception to the general scope of IFRS 4, which otherwise excludes accounting by policyholders. Therefore, there are separate requirements for the cedant's reinsurance assets as set out in 5.10.80.20 – 40.

IFRS 4.14(d),   5.10.80.20 The general requirements of IFRSs (see 5.6.90) prohibit the offsetting of
BC106   assets and liabilities as well as income and expenses except in certain defined circumstances. An entity is prohibited from offsetting reinsurance assets against the related insurance liabilities and income or expenses from reinsurance contracts against expenses or income from the related insurance contracts. Even if offsetting is permitted or required under existing accounting policies, an entity should change its policies in these respects.

IFRS 4.14(e),   5.10.80.30 The cedant considers at each reporting date whether its reinsurance assets are
BC107,   impaired. In our view, the impairment test to be applied is based on the impairment test
BC108   applied to financial assets and the guidance in IAS 39 should therefore be applied (see 3.6.1370). The focus of the test is credit risk, which arises from the risk of default by the reinsurer and also from disputes over coverage, and not on matters arising from the measurement of the underlying direct insurance liabilities.

IFRS 4.20   5.10.80.40 A reinsurance asset is considered impaired if there is objective evidence that the cedant may not receive all amounts due to it under the terms of the contract, as a result of an event that occurred after initial recognition of the reinsurance asset. Additionally, the impact of that event on the amounts that the cedant will receive from the reinsurer should be reliably measurable. An impairment may not be recognised for estimates of credit losses expected to arise from future events. In our view, it is unlikely that an insurer's reinsurance assets would be sufficiently similar in terms of nature and risk such that a portfolio-based impairment test could be applied. Therefore, we believe any impairment is likely to be based on specific credit events related to each individual reinsurer.

5.10.90 *Changes in accounting policies*

IFRS 4.22   5.10.90.10 An entity is permitted to make changes in its accounting policies for insurance contracts as long as the change improves either the relevance or the reliability of its financial statements without reducing either.

5.10.90.20 The assessment of relevance and reliability is judged by the criteria in the hierarchy for selecting accounting policies (see 2.8.6) without the need to achieve full compliance with those criteria. This limit on voluntary changes in accounting policies applies both to changes made by an insurer that already applies IFRSs and to a first-time adopter of IFRSs (see 6.1).

IFRS 4.24,
27, 30,
BC180

5.10.90.30 An insurer is permitted, for example, to change a policy in order to:

- remeasure some insurance liabilities (but not necessarily all of them) to reflect changes in current market interest rates; at that time measurement can be changed to reflect other current estimates and assumptions as well;
- switch to a comprehensive, widely-used, investor-oriented model for insurance policy liabilities, even if this means a move towards recognising future investment margins. However, such margins can be included only if this change is made as part of an overall switch to an investor-oriented model and not as an isolated change; or
- apply "shadow accounting" to remeasure insurance liabilities to reflect recognised but unrealised gains and losses on related financial assets, classified as available for sale (see 3.6.640), in the same way that realised gains or losses are reflected. Under shadow accounting the effect of unrealised losses and gains on an insurance liability is recognised in other comprehensive income consistent with the recognition of those unrealised gains and losses on the related financial assets. Shadow accounting also may be applied to insurance liabilities with payments that are linked contractually to the carrying amount of owner-occupied properties. Shadow accounting also may be applied to deferred acquisition costs and certain intangible assets related to these insurance liabilities.#

5.10.90.35 When an entity applies its existing accounting policies to insurance contracts under IFRS 4, it applies the policies based on GAAP existing at the date that the entity adopts IFRS 4. In our view, if after IFRS 4 is adopted changes occur to the previous GAAP upon which an insurer's existing policies were based, then the entity may amend its policies in line with those previous GAAP changes only if the entity can demonstrate that the changes fulfil the criteria specified in 5.10.90.10 and 20. That is, in our view the entity is not required to adopt changes in the previous GAAP, and indeed can only do so when it demonstrates that the criteria in 5.10.90.10 and 20 are met. Accordingly, in some circumstances the entity may not be able to do so and will be required to apply the "frozen" previous GAAP.

5.10.90.40 In our view, an entity that is intending to move from its existing regulatory-based approach towards US GAAP for its insurance contract liabilities would satisfy the requirements for accounting policy selection with respect to a comprehensive, widely-used, investor-oriented model for insurance contracts. However, entities applying US GAAP may do so only for their insurance contracts, as defined under IFRSs, and cannot also apply other specialised industry accounting practices for items covered by other IFRSs.

5.10.90.50 An entity may wish to change its accounting policy for the measurement of insurance liabilities by moving from a contract-by-contract assessment to a portfolio-based measurement of the liability. Since IAS 37 would apply in the absence of a liability adequacy test that meets the minimum requirements, in our view a change in accounting policy that moves towards the requirements of IAS 37 generally would be considered to increase the relevance of the financial information presented. In our view, such a change would not meet the requirement to increase relevance without impairing the reliability of the resulting information if it results in offsetting gains and losses on dissimilar contracts. However, the requirement could be met to the extent, for example, that the previous contract-by-contract measurement resulted in excessive prudence.

IFRS 4.18,   5.10.90.60 When an entity applies the IAS 37 model with respect to a liability
BC100   adequacy test, IFRS 4 requires the test to be applied at the level of a portfolio of contracts that are subject to broadly similar risk. In deliberating IFRS 4, the IASB noted that there is no conceptual justification for offsetting a loss on one contract against a gain on another contract. Therefore, in our view a change to a portfolio-based approach would not be appropriate if it results in the offsetting of gains and losses from dissimilar contracts, e.g. if expected losses on contracts with a 5 percent guaranteed return were offset against potential gains arising on contracts with a 2 percent guaranteed return. In order to increase the relevance of the resulting information, we believe a change to a portfolio-based measurement should define portfolios sufficiently narrowly that such offsetting effects are eliminated.

IFRS 4.45   5.10.90.70 To avoid artificial accounting mismatches when an insurer changes its accounting policies for insurance liabilities, such as remeasuring the insurance liabilities to reflect current market interest rates and recognising the changes in insurance liabilities in profit or loss, an insurer is permitted to reclassify some or all of their financial assets as at fair value through profit or loss. This reclassification is treated as a change in accounting policy (see 2.8.10).

5.10.95 *Forthcoming requirements*

5.10.95.10 See 3.6A for forthcoming requirements with respect to accounting for financial instruments. In applying IFRS 9, an entity may elect to present gains and losses on some investments in equity instruments measured at fair value in other comprehensive income. The gains and losses on these investments are not reclassified from equity to profit or loss on disposal of the investment. In our view, paragraph 30 of IFRS 4 allows the use of shadow accounting through other comprehensive income for the remeasurement of liabilities to reflect gains and losses that are not recognised in profit or loss upon disposal of the related assets. The relevant criterion in paragraph 30 of IFRS 4 is that unrealised gains or losses on the investment are recognised in other comprehensive income. The standard does not specify where realised gains or losses should be recognised. In our view, if shadow accounting is applied, then remeasurement of the liabilities reflecting gains and losses on these assets should be recognised in other comprehensive income as unrealised gains and losses are recognised on the investment and should not be reclassified to profit or loss upon derecognition of the investment.

5.10.100 Insurance contracts acquired in a business combination

IFRS 3.24   5.10.100.10 When an entity acquires another entity in a business combination, the acquirer measures, at the date of exchange, the identifiable assets acquired, the liabilities and contingent liabilities assumed, and equity instruments issued at fair value (see 2.6.600).

IFRS 4.31   5.10.100.20 Therefore, at the acquisition date, an insurer measures at fair value the assets and liabilities arising under insurance contracts acquired in a business combination. An insurer is permitted, but not required, to use an expanded presentation that splits the fair value of acquired insurance contracts into two components:

- a liability measured in accordance with the insurer's existing accounting policies, which generally would be larger than the fair value of the acquired contracts; and
- an intangible asset, representing the difference between the fair value of the acquired insurance contracts and the larger reported amount under the first component.

IFRS 4.BC   *147(b)*   5.10.100.30 This intangible asset often is described as the present value of in-force business, PVFP or value of business acquired. For a non-life insurance business a similar presentation may be used, for example, if acquired claim liabilities are not discounted.

IFRS 4.33,   *BC149*   5.10.100.40 The recognised acquired intangible asset is excluded from the scope of the general standard on intangibles (see 3.3). This was done to permit insurers to continue to use their existing method of amortisation. That measurement should be consistent with the measurement of the related insurance liability. In our view, this means that, unlike goodwill, this intangible asset generally is amortised over the estimated life of the contracts or a run-off period of insurance contract provisions. Since these intangible assets related to insurance liabilities are covered by the liability adequacy test (as to insurance liabilities related intangible assets), these assets also are excluded from the scope of the general standard on impairment (see 3.10).

IFRS 4.32   5.10.100.50 An insurer acquiring a portfolio of insurance contracts (portfolio transfer), outside a business combination, also may use the expanded presentation described in 5.10.100.20.

IFRS 4.BC   *150*   5.10.100.60 However, IAS 36 *Impairment of Assets* and IAS 38 apply to intangible assets such as customer lists and customer relationships because such assets do not represent contractual insurance rights and contractual insurance obligations that existed at the date of a business combination (value of future business).

IFRS 3.I   *E.30(d)*   5.10.100.70 An illustrative example published with IFRS 3 *Business Combinations* deals with customer relationships acquired together with a portfolio of one-year motor contracts that are cancellable by policyholders. Because an insurer establishes its relationships with policyholders through insurance contracts, the customer relationship with policyholders meets the contractual-legal criterion for identification as an intangible asset and is recognised separately from goodwill.

5.10.110 **Contracts with discretionary participation features**

IFRS 4.A, 5.10.110.10 A discretionary participation feature (DPF) is a contractual right of the
IU 01-10 investor or policyholder to receive, as a supplement to guaranteed benefits, additional
benefits. In our view, both the DPF and the guaranteed benefits should be present at the
inception of the contract to fall into the scope of IFRS 4 as there must be a guaranteed
benefit to the holder for the definition of a DPF to be met. The amount or timing of
the additional benefits received by the policyholder contractually is at the discretion
of the issuer. These additional benefits generally are based on the performance of a
specified pool of contracts, on the realised and/or unrealised investment returns on a
designated pool of assets or on the profit or loss of the entity. When a contract stipulates
that unrealised gains become payable to the policyholder when they are realised, then
in our view the policyholder's right to these gains meets the definition of a DPF if
the timing of realisation of the gains is at the discretion of the insurer. To fall within
the definition of a DPF, the additional benefits should be a significant portion of the
total contractual benefits. Such contracts may be insurance contracts or investment
contracts, and often are described as "participating" or "with profits" contracts.

5.10.110.20 In our view, the amount of a DPF is limited to the amount of discretionary
benefit that is referred to either in the contract or in related law. If a contract establishes
a minimum share of a surplus (up to 100 percent of the surplus) that will, subject to discretion over timing, be paid under the DPF, then in our view the entire surplus is part of
the DPF because the timing of any payments is discretionary with respect to the whole
surplus. However, if a contract establishes a right to share in a specified amount of the
surplus, subject to discretion over timing and with no further rights beyond the specified
amounts, then we believe only the specified amount meets the definition of a DPF (i.e.
any additional amounts that are paid voluntarily by the insurer do not meet the definition).

5.10.110.25 If a contract establishes a right to share in surplus but specifies neither a minimum
nor a specified share in a surplus, then in our view the entire surplus is part of the DPF.
However, if a contract, including any applicable law, contains no mention whatsoever of
additional amounts that may be payable beyond a specified amount, so that any additional
amount paid by the insurer is paid despite no contractual right of the policyholder, then
we believe that such additional amount that is paid is not part of a DPF. The classification
also is valid regardless of the amounts paid in practice (e.g. paid because of competitive
considerations). However, in certain cases application of the liability adequacy test considering all the expected cash flows under the contract may result in the measurement of
the liability exceeding the amount that meets the definition of a DPF.

IFRS 4.34 5.10.110.30 Any guaranteed amount to which the policyholder has an unconditional
right should be classified as a liability by the entity issuing the policy. The amount
payable under the DPF, if measured separately from the guaranteed amount, may be
classified as a liability or as a separate component of equity. It may not be classified in
an intermediate (mezzanine) category that is neither liability nor equity. The standard
does not specify how the classification should be determined; however, it does require
that the presentation adopted be applied consistently.

IFRS 4.35 5.10.110.40 When a contract, classified as a financial instrument, contains a DPF, the contract falls into the scope of IFRS 4 and the guidance of IFRS 4 for insurance contracts also applies. If the entire DPF within the investment contract is classified as a liability, then the liability adequacy test should be applied to the whole contract. If some or all of the DPF is classified as equity, then the liability amount includes, as a minimum, the amount that would be recognised for the guaranteed element under IAS 39. However, if the recognised liability clearly is higher, then the issuer does not need to determine the amount that would result from applying IAS 39 to the guaranteed element.

5.10.110.43 When a DPF amount is classified as a liability, it is considered in applying the liability adequacy test. In our view, amounts that the policyholder could enforce at the reporting date also should be included in applying the liability adequacy test even if that portion of the DPF is classified as equity. For example, amounts that would be required to be paid in the event that a surrender option is exercised should be included in applying the liability adequacy test.

5.10.110.45 In a contract that establishes the policyholder's right to receive a share of the surplus and the insurer classifies this DPF as a liability, the insurer may expect to pay an amount less than the entire difference between the guaranteed amount and the specified share of surplus. In our view, notwithstanding the insurer's expectation of paying a lower amount, the entire difference between the guaranteed amount and the specified share of accumulated surplus should be included in the measurement of the DPF liability.

5.10.110.47 In our view, if a DPF amount that is presented as equity is subject to a constructive obligation (see 3.12.60), then as a minimum, the nature of the equity amount should be described, including the nature of the constraints over the entity's discretion.

IFRS 4.34(c) 5.10.110.50 Premiums received may be recognised as revenue for both insurance contracts and investment contracts containing a DPF. However, the portion of profit or loss attributable to the equity component is presented as an allocation of profit or loss (in a manner similar to the presentation of non-controlling interests), and not as expense or income.

5.10.110.60 See 5.10.150 regarding the disclosure of financial instruments with a DPF.

5.10.112 Investment contracts with the option to switch between unit-linked funds and funds with discretionary participation features

5.10.112.10 Investment contracts often give an investor the option to invest in both a range of unit-linked funds and funds with DPFs. Investment contracts such as unit-linked products are accounted for under IAS 39, whereas investment contracts with DPFs are within the scope of IFRS 4.

5.10.112.20 Investment contracts may provide the investor with the option of switching from one fund or product to another, e.g. from a unit-linked product to a product with a DPF. Switches may happen at any time during the term of a contract, with the ability to switch sometimes unrestricted and sometimes limited. Although investment contracts with the option to switch are usually financial instruments under IAS 39, IFRS 4 applies to financial instruments with a DPF and so the appropriate accounting treatment is not always immediately apparent.

5.10.114 *Classification*

5.10.114.10 A contract (or group of contracts) would be classified as DPF from its inception when, at inception, historical data suggests it is likely that investors will switch a significant portion of their investments into DPF funds for a sufficiently long period during the life of the contract, and that the investment returns (surplus) arising on the DPF component is significant compared to the entire investment returns under the contract. In our view, the assessment of significance should consider both the amounts and timing of expected cash flows. If these requirements are not met, then a contract (or group of contracts) would not be classified as DPF even if investments are placed in a DPF fund at inception. In our view, whether or not the definition is met may be assessed based on portfolios of similar contracts.

5.10.116 *Reclassification as a result of changes in investor behaviours*

5.10.116.10 Since the definition of a contract is based on the probability of switching and the significance of DPF-type benefits over the life of the contract, the decision of an investor to switch between funds will not impact the classification of a contract. However, an entity would need to consider changing the classification of a contract, or a group of contracts, if there is a significant change in investor behaviour such that either it becomes less likely or more likely that investors will invest in DPF funds for significant periods during the life of the contract. In our view, the classification and accounting for such contracts should be changed prospectively from the date that the expectations change.

5.10.118 *Reclassification when the DPF option is no longer available*

5.10.118.10 In some cases, the investor's option to switch between DPF and unit-linked funds may expire during the life of a contract. In our view, the expiry of an option to switch would not, on its own, lead to a reclassification, although changing expectations with regard to behaviour before the option expires may cause a change in classification. For example, a contract (or group of contracts) in which investments are held in unit-linked funds and the option to switch to DPF funds no longer exists nevertheless should be classified as DPF if the amount of historical DPF-type benefits is sufficient that it still is likely that DPF benefits will be a significant portion of total contractual benefits. Similarly, a contract (or group of similar contracts) in which funds are invested in a DPF fund with no further option to switch into a unit-linked fund should be classified as DPF only if it still is expected that historical and future DPF-type benefits will be a significant portion of total contractual benefits.

5.10.120 **Presentation and disclosures**

5.10.130 *Self insurance/captive insurance*

5.10.130.10 A number of entities within a group may insure certain risks with a third party insurer under an arrangement in which another entity within the group (a captive reinsurer) takes some or all of that risk back into the group. The question that then arises is whether and to what extent the amounts in the statement of comprehensive income and the statement of financial position, in respect of the insurance and reinsurance contracts with the third-party insurer, should be eliminated or offset in consolidated financial statements.

IFRS 4.B25   5.10.130.20 IFRS 4 notes that (for the purpose of assessing the significance of insurance risk) contracts entered into simultaneously with a single counterparty (or contracts that are otherwise interdependent) form a single contract. This approach is consistent with the requirements for financial instruments (see 3.6.690) whereby two transactions would be considered as a single contract when they are entered into at the same time, in contemplation of each other, with the same counterparty and when there is no substantive business reason for undertaking the two transactions separately.

5.10.130.30 In our view, the amounts in the statement of financial position in respect of premiums and claims payable to and receivable from the captive reinsurer should not be offset unless the strict offsetting requirements are met (see 5.6.90). In our view, it may be appropriate to offset premium and claims expenses and income in the statement of comprehensive income, but only if the third-party insurer is acting as a conduit for the captive reinsurer, in other words if the contracts are interdependent. This would sometimes be the case if the captive reinsurer does not have the regulatory approval required to issue a direct insurance contract. We believe that a primary indicator that the third-party insurer is acting as a conduit rather than as a principal in the transaction would be that the insurer is not exposed to credit risk from the captive reinsurer. For example, the third-party insurer may not be required to pay claims unless and until it has received payment from the captive reinsurer. If the third party is exposed to the credit risk of the captive, then in our view this would indicate that the transactions are not interdependent and no offsetting in the statement of comprehensive income should be permitted.

5.10.140 *Presentation of premium income as revenue*

5.10.140.10 In some jurisdictions practice has been to present insurance premiums received as revenue, with a deduction for unearned premiums presented elsewhere in the statement of comprehensive income. In our view, consistent with the definition of revenue in IAS 18, revenue on insurance contracts represents premiums earned for insurance cover provided during the period. Therefore, premiums received should not be described as revenue. However, we believe this does not preclude the presentation of premiums received as additional information in the statement of comprehensive income as long as this amount is not described as revenue.

5.10.150 *Disclosures*

IFRS 4.36,
38

5.10.150.10 Disclosures are required that explain the amounts in the financial statements arising from insurance contracts. Disclosure of information that enables a user to evaluate the nature and extent of risks arising from insurance contracts also is required.

IFRS 4.37

5.10.150.20 An insurer is required to disclose:

- its accounting policies for insurance contracts;
- the amounts of the recognised assets, liabilities, income and expense arising from insurance contracts;
- how the most significant assumptions used to measure those amounts are determined (and if practicable, the assumptions themselves); and
- information about the effect of changes in assumptions.

IFRS 4.37

5.10.150.30 An insurer also discloses the reconciliations of changes in insurance liabilities, reinsurance assets and related deferred acquisition costs.

IFRS 4.39

5.10.150.40 In addition to the disclosure requirements in 5.10.150.10 – 30, an insurer is required to disclose:

- its risk management objectives, policies and methods for managing insurance risk;
- the sensitivity to insurance risk;
- concentrations of insurance risk (e.g. low-frequency, high-severity risks such as earthquakes or cyclical risks);
- claims development information, covering all periods for which material claims (for which uncertainty remains) are outstanding, up to a maximum of ten years; and
- information about credit, liquidity and market risks of insurance contracts as if the insurance contracts were within the scope of IFRS 7 *Financial Instruments: Disclosures*.

IFRS 4.IG11-
IG71

5.10.150.50 The implementation guidance suggests extensive *possible* disclosures. However, an insurer decides in light of its circumstances how much detail has to be given to satisfy the disclosure requirements, how much emphasis it places on different aspects and how it aggregates information to portray the overall picture without combining information that has materially different characteristics.

IFRS 4.2,
7.29(c)

5.10.150.60 Since financial instruments with a DPF are financial instruments, the disclosure requirements for financial instruments (see 5.6) also apply. However, there is some additional relief regarding the requirement to disclose fair values, if the fair value cannot be measured reliably.

5.10.160 Future developments

5.10.160.10 In July 2010 the IASB issued ED/2010/8 *Insurance Contracts* as part of its joint project with the FASB to develop a common, high-quality standard that will address recognition, measurement, presentation and disclosure requirements for insurance contracts. The key proposals in the ED include:

- scope that focuses on insurance contracts, financial guarantees and certain investment contracts with a discretionary participation feature;
- a fulfilment value-based net measurement approach for insurance and reinsurance contracts, which incorporates an estimate of future cash flows including incremental acquisition costs, the effect of the time value of money, an explicit risk adjustment and a residual margin;
- an unearned premium approach for short duration contracts which requires discounting if the effect is material;
- new unbundling criteria for non-derivative components;
- revised accounting guidance for business combinations and portfolio transfers; and
- insurance liabilities would not be permitted to be measured through other comprehensive income.

5.10.160.20 The ED does not address policyholder accounting other than in the context of reinsurance contracts.

5.10.160.30 Given the current divergent accounting practices related to insurance contracts, any final standard resulting from this project will have a significant impact. The final standard is scheduled for the second quarter of 2011.

5.11 Extractive activities
(IFRS 6)

5.11 Extractive activities
(IFRS 6)

Overview of currently effective requirements

- Entities identify and account for pre-exploration expenditure, exploration and evaluation (E&E) expenditure and development expenditure separately.

- Each type of E&E cost can be expensed as incurred or capitalised, in accordance with the entity's selected accounting policy.

- Capitalised E&E costs are segregated and classified as either tangible or intangible assets, according to their nature.

- The test for recoverability of E&E assets can combine several cash-generating units, as long as the combination is not larger than an operating segment.

- There is no specific guidance on the recognition or measurement of pre-exploration expenditure or development expenditure. Pre-E&E expenditure generally is expensed as incurred.

Currently effective requirements

This publication reflects IFRSs in issue at 1 August 2010. The currently effective requirements cover annual periods beginning on 1 January 2010. The requirements related to this topic are derived mainly from IFRS 6 *Exploration for and Evaluation of Mineral Resources*.

Forthcoming requirements and future developments

When a currently effective requirement will be changed by a new requirement that is issued but is not yet effective, it is marked with a # as a **forthcoming requirement** and the impact of the change is explained in the accompanying boxed text. In respect of this topic no forthcoming requirements are noted.

The currently effective or forthcoming requirements may be subject to **future developments** and a brief outline of the relevant projects is given in 5.11.400.

5.11.10 Scope

IFRS 6.3, 4   5.11.10.10 IFRSs provide specific extractive industry guidance only for the recognition, measurement and disclosure of expenditure incurred on the exploration for and evaluation of mineral resources.

5.11.10.20 E&E expenditure does not include amounts incurred in activities that precede the exploration for and evaluation of mineral resources (pre-exploration activities), such as expenditure incurred before obtaining the legal rights to explore a specific area.

IFRS 6.5   *5.11.10.30* Similarly, E&E expenditure does not include expenditure incurred after the technical feasibility and commercial viability of extracting a mineral resource are demonstrable (development activities).

IFRS 6.7, 18   *5.11.10.40* IFRS 6 provides limited relief from the requirement to select accounting policies in accordance with the hierarchy for their selection (see 2.8.6), and from the general requirements for impairment testing (see 5.11.170). However, no such relief is provided for either pre-exploration activities or development activities; therefore, in our view these activities should comply fully with IFRSs, including the hierarchy for the selection of accounting policies.

5.11.20 Exploration and evaluation (E&E) expenditure

5.11.30 Accounting policy on recognition and measurement

IFRS 6.5   *5.11.30.10* An entity determines which of its expenditure meets the definition of E&E expenditure. E&E expenditure does not include pre-exploration expenditure or development expenditure (see 5.11.240 and 270 respectively).

IFRS 6.9   *5.11.30.20* For each type of E&E expenditure, an entity chooses an accounting policy, to be applied consistently, of either immediate expense or capitalisation as an E&E asset.

IFRS 6.9   *5.11.30.30* The policy of expense or capitalisation reflects the extent to which the type of E&E expenditure can be associated with finding specific mineral resources. In our view, the more closely an expenditure relates to a specific mineral resource, the more likely that its capitalisation will result in relevant and reliable information.

IFRS 6.6, 7,   *5.11.30.40* In developing an accounting policy for E&E expenditure, an entity need not
IAS 8.11, 12   consider other IFRSs (by analogy) and need not refer to the definitions contained in the Framework, i.e. an entity need not apply the hierarchy for the selection of accounting policies.

5.11.40 E&E assets

IFRS 6.9   *5.11.40.10* Types of expenditure that may be included in the initial measurement of an E&E asset include:

- acquisition of rights to explore (e.g. exploration licences)
- topographical, geological, geochemical and geophysical studies
- exploratory drilling
- trenching
- sampling

- activities in relation to evaluating the technical feasibility and commercial viability of extracting a mineral resource.

IAS 8.13 5.11.40.20 In some countries an entity may make a contribution to the local community within which it wishes to commence E&E activities (e.g. a payment to relocate a village or to provide enhanced community services), to facilitate the acquisition of permission to operate. In our view, these types of contributions may be capitalised as E&E assets as part of the cost of acquisition if an entity elects a policy of capitalising this type of E&E expenditure. The entity's accounting policy to capitalise or immediately expense each *type* of E&E expenditure is applied consistently to similar items and activities.

5.11.40.30 In our view, the cost of similar activities is not different in type solely because the probability of them leading to a project that is technically feasible and commercially viable is different. For example, an entity undertakes exploratory drilling activities across several regions of a country. The entity has identified that some regions have a high probability of success and others a low probability of success. The exploratory drilling activities should be accounted for consistently based on the accounting policy (i.e. either expensed or capitalised). The geographical location and the probability of whether the exploration will result in a project that is technically feasible and commercially viable is not a consideration in determining the recognition criteria.

5.11.50 *E&E expenses*

IFRS 6.9 5.11.50.10 E&E expenditure that is not recognised as an E&E asset is expensed as incurred.

5.11.50.20 E&E expenditure of a type that is not sufficiently closely related to a specific mineral resource to support capitalisation also is expensed as incurred. For example, general seismic data costs might not be sufficiently closely related to finding a specific mineral resource to be capitalised as an E&E asset.

5.11.60 *Classification*

IFRS 6.15 5.11.60.10 An entity should classify each E&E asset as tangible or intangible based on the nature of the asset. Therefore, it is not possible to choose a single accounting policy with respect to the classification of all E&E expenditure.

5.11.60.20 E&E assets include:

- *Identifiable assets used for E&E.* These include tangible items of property, plant and equipment such as exploration drilling rigs used only for E&E, and identifiable intangible assets such as exploratory licences. These items are depreciated or amortised as they are used for E&E activities.
- *Costs incurred in connection with E&E activities that an entity elects to capitalise as E&E assets.* These costs might include, for example, labour costs, as well as the depreciation and amortisation of identifiable assets used for E&E.

1463

5.11.60.30 Many identifiable E&E assets clearly will be tangible (e.g. vehicles, drilling rigs) and others clearly intangible (e.g. exploration licences). It is likely that there also will be a residual E&E asset that is less easily classified, and that a significant component of the residual E&E asset will consist of costs incurred in constructing exploratory wells or mines.

5.11.60.40 In our view, determining whether the nature of E&E assets is tangible or intangible should reflect whether the cost contributes to an item that is a physical (tangible) asset that itself will be used or, alternatively, to intangible knowledge about where, ultimately, to build a physical asset. For example, a well that will be used to extract reserves may be a tangible asset. However, an exploratory well may result only in knowledge. We prefer costs related to the building of exploratory wells or geological and geophysical activities to be classified as intangible E&E assets.

5.11.60.50 The classification of E&E assets as tangible or intangible is the basis for accounting policy choices for both the subsequent measurement of the assets and for disclosure purposes.

5.11.70 *Intangible assets*

IFRS 6.15   5.11.70.10 Examples of E&E assets that may be classified as intangible include:

- drilling rights
- acquired rights to explore
- costs of conducting topographical, geological, geochemical and geophysical studies
- exploratory drilling costs
- trenching costs
- sampling costs
- costs of activities in relation to evaluating technical feasibility and commercial viability of extracting a mineral resource.

5.11.80 *Tangible assets*

5.11.80.10 IFRSs do not define "tangible". However, most tangible assets will be identifiable items of property, plant and equipment (see 3.2.10).

5.11.80.20 Examples of E&E assets that may be classified as tangible assets include:

- equipment used in exploration, such as vehicles and drilling rigs
- piping and pumps
- tanks.

IFRS 6.16   5.11.80.30 To the extent that a tangible asset is consumed in developing an intangible asset, the amount reflecting that consumption is part of the cost of the intangible asset created. However, the asset being used remains a tangible asset.

5.11.80.40 For example, even if a drilling rig is used only in the exploratory phase, the equipment is a tangible asset. The depreciation expense recognised on the drilling rig is a cost of developing an intangible E&E asset, being the exploratory well. The depreciation is capitalised as part of the cost of the related E&E asset, which is the exploratory mine shaft or well.

5.11.90 *Initial recognition and measurement*

IFRS 6.8   5.11.90.10 If an entity elects to capitalise E&E expenditure as an E&E asset, then that asset is measured initially at cost.

5.11.100 *Administrative and other general overhead costs*

IFRS 6.BC28   5.11.100.10 An entity chooses an accounting policy, to be applied consistently, of either expensing administrative and other general overhead costs, or capitalising those costs associated with finding specific mineral resources in the initial recognition and measurement of an E&E asset. In our view, the selected policy of expensing or capitalising administrative and other general overhead costs should comply, by analogy, with the guidance for capitalising similar costs incurred in relation either to inventories (see 3.8.120), intangible assets (see 3.3.90) or property, plant and equipment (see 3.2.20).

5.11.100.20 In our view, if an entity elects to capitalise administrative and other general overhead costs associated with finding specific mineral resources, then the following costs may qualify for inclusion as an E&E asset:

- payroll-related costs attributable to personnel working directly on a specific project, including the costs of employee benefits and share-based compensation for such personnel;
- certain management costs if their roles are specific to a project;
- sign-up bonuses paid to contractors involved in a particular project;
- legal or other professional costs specific to the project, for example, costs in respect of obtaining certain permits and certifications; and
- general office overheads for an office that is set up specifically to support E&E activities.

5.11.110 *Licence acquisition costs*

IFRS 6.BC12   5.11.110.10 In accordance with its accounting policy, an entity may recognise an exploration licence as an E&E asset. In our view, the cost of that licence includes the directly attributable costs of its acquisition. We believe that entities should apply the guidance on costs that are directly attributable to intangibles (see 3.3.90). Examples of such costs may include non-refundable taxes and professional and legal costs incurred in obtaining the licence.

5.11.120 *Borrowing costs*

IAS 23.8, 9   5.11.120.10 IAS 23 *Borrowing Costs* requires the capitalisation of borrowing costs as part of the cost of qualifying assets (see 4.6.350). However, it is unclear how the requirements of IAS 23 interact with the requirements of IFRS 6.

IFRS 6.A   5.11.120.15 In our view, the requirements of IAS 23 do not override the exception in IFRS 6 that allows an entity a choice of either expensing or capitalising each type of E&E expenditure (see 5.11.30.20); this is because IFRS 6 defines E&E expenditure as expenditure incurred "in connection with" E&E activities, which is broad enough to cover the related financing of such activities. Accordingly, we believe that an entity may choose to expense borrowing costs related to E&E assets.

5.11.130 *Decommissioning liabilities*

IFRS 6.11   5.11.130.10 Many entities in the extractive industries incur an obligation in relation to site restoration and decommissioning as a result of undertaking E&E activities. A provision is recognised for the costs of any obligations for removal and restoration that are incurred as a consequence of having undertaken E&E activities (see 3.12.450). For example, a provision is recognised for the expected cost of dismantling a test drilling rig when it is installed.

IAS 37.IE.   5.11.130.20 Obligations that result from production, i.e. the extraction of reserves, are
A.Ex3   recognised only as extraction occurs.

5.11.130.30 In our view, the cost of a decommissioning liability should be treated consistently with the treatment of the E&E expenditure that gave rise to the obligation. For example, if a decommissioning liability arises in relation to drilling test bores and expenditure incurred for test bores is capitalised as an intangible E&E asset, then the initial estimate of a decommissioning liability should be treated as part of the cost of the intangible asset. As entities may have differing treatments for different types of E&E expenditure, this may result in the cost of some decommissioning liabilities being recognised as part of the cost of the related E&E asset (whether classified as tangible or intangible), while the cost of other liabilities is recognised immediately in profit or loss.

5.11.140 *Subsequent measurement*

IFRS 6.12   5.11.140.10 After recognition, an entity applies either the cost model or the revaluation model, as appropriate, to each of tangible and intangible E&E assets.

5.11.150 *Cost model*

IAS 16.6, 53,   5.11.150.10 Tangible assets used for E&E (and intangible assets with a finite life used for
38.100   E&E) are depreciated (amortised) over their useful lives. The depreciable amount of a tangible asset (or an intangible asset with a finite useful life) is its cost less its residual value. The residual value of a tangible asset is the amount that an entity could receive for the asset at the reporting date if the asset were in the condition that it will be when the entity expects to dispose of it. The residual value of an intangible asset with a finite useful life is assumed to be zero unless certain criteria are met (see 3.3.220).

IAS 38.88   5.11.150.20 In our view, it will be uncommon for an intangible asset used for E&E to be assessed as having an indefinite useful life.

IFRS 6.16, 5.11.150.30 Depreciation or amortisation of a tangible or intangible asset commences
IAS 16.49, only when the asset is available for use (see 3.2.220 and 3.3.240). Certain E&E assets
38.99 (e.g. a vehicle or a drilling rig) may be available for use immediately; accordingly, such
assets are depreciated or amortised during the E&E phase. Other E&E assets may not
be available for use until a later date, for example when the mine or oil field is ready to
commence operations. In that case, in our view there are two acceptable approaches to
determining when depreciation/amortisation should commence:

- The first approach is to commence depreciation/amortisation of the E&E assets
  once when the mine or oil field is ready to commence operations, since in effect it
  is from this point that the entity will realise the future economic benefits embodied
  in the E&E assets.
- The second approach is to commence depreciation/amortisation during the E&E phase
  since the assets are available for use when considered on a stand-alone basis; however,
  such depreciation/amortisation is capitalised to the extent that the E&E assets are used
  in the development of other assets (see, for example, 5.11.80.30 and 40).

IAS 38.97, 98 5.11.150.40 Regarding the method of amortisation, the unit-of-production method may
be more reflective of the pattern in which an intangible E&E asset's future economic
benefits are expected to be consumed by the entity than the straight-line method.

IAS 36.2 5.11.150.50 Both tangible and intangible E&E assets are tested for impairment in some
circumstances (see 5.11.170).

5.11.160 *Revaluation model*

5.11.160.10 If an entity elects to apply the revaluation model, then the model applied is
consistent with the classification of the assets as tangible or intangible. Tangible E&E
assets are revalued using the property, plant and equipment model (see 3.2.300) and
intangible E&E assets using the intangible asset model (see 3.3.280).

IFRS 6.25 5.11.160.20 E&E assets are treated as a separate class of assets for disclosure purposes. IFRSs
generally define a class of assets as a grouping of items that have a similar nature and use in
an entity's operations. A policy of revaluation is applied to all assets in a class (see 3.2.300).

IFRS 6.25 5.11.160.30 In our view, tangible and intangible E&E assets are two separate classes of
assets. We believe that generally all tangible assets used for E&E will form a separate
class and a policy of cost or revaluation should be applied consistently to all assets in
that class. We believe that it is acceptable to apply the revaluation model to tangible E&E
assets and the cost model to intangible E&E assets.

5.11.160.40 Intangible E&E assets may be revalued to fair value only when an active
market exists (see 3.3.280). In our experience, it will be very rare for an intangible E&E
asset to meet this criterion.

IAS 16.31, 32 5.11.160.50 Tangible E&E assets may be revalued to fair value, provided that fair value
can be measured reliably.

5.11.160.60 In our experience, difficulties are likely to arise in determining fair value for tangible E&E assets. For example, there may be a lack of evidence of market value as the assets generally are specialised and rarely sold except as part of a continuing business, or when the design of equipment is specially adapted for a well with particular characteristics. In addition, there may be difficulties in finding an observable market that may serve as a basis for estimating market value.

IAS 16.33   *5.11.160.70* If there is no market-based evidence of fair value, then depreciated replacement cost or an income approach may be used to estimate fair value. In our view, as the income (cash flows) that may be generated in the future by an E&E asset are highly uncertain, it is unlikely that an income approach will provide a reliable estimate of the fair value of a tangible E&E asset.

5.11.160.80 Due to the difficulties in determining fair values for tangible E&E assets, in our experience, the use of the revaluation model is rare.

5.11.160.90 The frequency of revaluation will depend on the volatility of the fair value of the E&E asset being valued. In our view, if the E&E assets that are being revalued experience significant and volatile changes in fair value, then revaluation should be performed at least on an annual basis.

5.11.165 *Statement of cash flows*

IAS 7.16   *5.11.165.10* An entity presents cash flows during the period classified by operating, investing and financing activities in the manner most appropriate to its business (see 2.3.20). When an entity elects to expense E&E expenditure as incurred (see 5.11.30.20), the related cash flows are classified as operating activities. Cash flows from investing activities include only expenditure that results in the recognition of an asset.

5.11.170 **Impairment**

IFRS 6.18   *5.11.170.10* The general impairment standard is applied to measure, present and disclose the impairment of E&E assets (see 3.10).

IFRS 6.18, 19   *5.11.170.20* Relief is provided from the general requirements of IFRSs in assessing whether there is any indication of impairment for E&E assets. Also, the level at which any impairment assessment is performed is specified and may be at a more aggregated level than would be required for non-E&E assets. The assessment of impairment then is performed in accordance with general impairment requirements.

5.11.180 *Indicators of impairment*

IFRS 6.17, 18,   *5.11.180.10* E&E assets are assessed for impairment only when facts and circumstances
BC39   suggest that the carrying amount of an E&E asset may exceed its recoverable amount, and upon the transfer of E&E assets to development assets. Unlike other assets, there is no requirement to assess whether an indication of impairment exists at each reporting

date until an entity has sufficient information to reach a conclusion about commercial viability and the feasibility of extraction.

IFRS 6.20   5.11.180.20 IFRS 6 includes industry-specific examples of facts and circumstances that, if one or more are present, indicate that an entity should test an E&E asset for impairment. One such indicator is that an entity's right to explore in the specific area has expired or will expire in the near future, and is not expected to be renewed.

5.11.180.30 "Near future" is not defined under IFRSs. In our view, near future should be a period sufficiently short such that no significant doubt exists as to whether the area can be developed and any reserves extracted so as to recover the carrying amount of E&E assets before the right to explore lapses. In our view, the recoverable amount should be measured for any areas for which the rights to explore are due to expire within 12 months of the reporting date and the rights are not subject to a perfunctory renewal right. Other E&E assets are reviewed against the following list of indicators:

- Substantive expenditure on further exploration and evaluation activities in the specific area is neither budgeted nor planned.
- The entity has not discovered commercially viable quantities of mineral resources as a result of E&E activities in the area to date, and the entity has decided to discontinue such activities in the specific area.
- Even if development is likely to proceed, the entity has sufficient data indicating that the carrying amount of the asset is unlikely to be recovered in full from successful development or by sale.

5.11.180.40 These indicators are based on management information or intentions and decisions with respect to a given area of exploration.

5.11.180.50 In our view, the identification of the specific area being monitored is likely to be a significant factor in the frequency with which indicators exist and therefore when it is necessary to review the recoverable amount of E&E assets. In practice it may be preferable for the level at which indicators are monitored and the level of E&E assets for which the recoverable amount is reviewed to be consistent.

5.11.180.60 The list of impairment indicators is not exhaustive, and there may be additional facts and circumstances that would suggest that an entity should review E&E assets for impairment. Other impairment indicators may include, for example, significant adverse changes in commodity prices and markets or changes in the taxation or regulatory environment. In assessing whether an entity has sufficient cash to fund future planned or budgeted substantive exploration and evaluation, the entity's capacity to raise future cash is considered if cash is not on hand currently.

5.11.190 *Level of impairment assessment*

IFRS 6.21, 22   5.11.190.10 An entity chooses an accounting policy, to be applied consistently, for allocating E&E assets to cash-generating units (CGUs) or groups of CGUs for the purpose of assessing E&E assets for impairment. Entities allocate potentially impaired E&E assets to the carrying amount of other E&E assets (or to the carrying amount of producing assets) in the same CGU or operating segment and to test the combined carrying amount for impairment (see 3.10).

5.11.190.20 An entity may be able to identify E&E assets for internal management purposes at a low level, for example at the level of a specific geological structure thought to contain hydrocarbons or a contiguous ore body. Although an entity may choose to assess impairment at this level, impairment is not required to be assessed at such a low level. Instead, entities are permitted to combine one or more CGUs for the purpose of testing E&E assets for impairment.

5.11.190.30 Entities should consider the level of impairment assessment to avoid assets being carried forward that would, if not aggregated with other assets, be impaired. For example, continuing to aggregate E&E costs for an area that will not be developed with other CGUs may result in knowingly carrying forward costs associated with assets when a decision has been taken not to develop those mineral resources. In our view, a policy of recognising an impairment loss in respect of the capitalised costs of E&E assets that relate to a specific area identified as not being capable of being developed into a producing asset is consistent with the encouragement to consider additional indicators of impairment, and therefore may be appropriate.

IFRS 6.21 5.11.190.40 An entity is permitted to aggregate CGUs to form a group of units for the purposes of impairment testing of E&E assets, but the CGUs or group of units cannot be at a level of aggregation larger than that of the operating segment to which the CGU belongs (see 5.2.50).

5.11.190.50 In our view, the requirement that each CGU (or group of units) may not be larger than an operating segment is not considered in absolute terms such as segment profit or loss or total assets. Instead, we believe that impairment testing may not be performed at a level that results in the aggregation of E&E assets or CGUs belonging to different operating segments.

5.11.190.60 The identification of CGUs or groups of units requires judgement and may be one of the most difficult areas of impairment testing for E&E assets. Its interaction with the indicators of impairment based upon a specific area will require consideration.

5.11.190.70 Upon determination of an accounting policy for the allocation of E&E assets to CGUs or groups of units, this policy should be applied consistently from period to period for the same types of assets. A change in accounting policy would be permitted only if the criteria for a voluntary change in accounting policy are met (see 5.11.350).

5.11.200 *Assessment of recoverable amount*

IFRS 6.18, 5.11.200.10 When facts and circumstances suggest that the carrying amount of a CGU
IAS 36.18   of E&E assets (or a group of such units) may exceed its recoverable amount, an entity

measures the recoverable amount of the E&E assets. The recoverable amount is the higher of the asset's fair value less costs to sell and its value in use.

5.11.200.20 It is likely that many entities first will determine the value in use of a potentially impaired asset, as the information from which to perform this assessment will be available more readily than fair value less costs to sell. Only if this assessment highlights a potential impairment loss will the entity then be required to determine fair value less costs to sell. If the fair value less costs to sell cannot be estimated, then the recoverable amount is measured at the value in use amount. See 3.10.180 – 350 for further guidance on measuring impairment.

5.11.210 *Value in use*

IAS 36.33, 35 5.11.210.10 Cash flow projections to determine value in use generally are based on budgets approved by management that do not exceed five years (see 3.10.230). For most extractive activities, detailed budgets are prepared covering a period significantly in excess of five years, typically for the estimated field or mine life, which generally is based on resource and reserve reports; therefore, the period could be 20 years or more. In our view, when these are considered reliable, cash flow projections may be based on these longer budget periods.

5.11.220 *Capital expenditure*

IAS 36.42, 44 5.11.220.10 When assessing impairment using a value in use model, future cash flows are estimated for the asset in its current condition (see 3.10.250). In the case of an asset that is not yet ready for use, estimates include cash outflows expected to be incurred to bring the asset into use. In our view, the same approach of including expected cash outflows to bring the asset to its intended use is appropriate in the case of an E&E asset or CGU that is not yet in use, for example an E&E asset that has not reached development stage yet.

5.11.230 *Reversal of impairment*

IAS 36.110 5.11.230.10 Partial or full reversals of impairments of assets, other than impairments of goodwill, are recognised if there is a change in the estimate of the recoverable amount (see 3.10.420).

5.11.240 **Pre-exploration expenditure**

5.11.240.10 Entities are required to identify and account for pre-exploration expenditure separately from E&E expenditure.

5.11.250 *Identifying pre-exploration expenditure*

IFRS 6.5(a) 5.11.250.10 Pre-licence costs are excluded from the scope of E&E costs. In our view, this exclusion implies that E&E activities commence upon the acquisition of legal rights to undertake exploration activities in a certain area.

5.11.250.20 Activities prior to the acquisition of an exploration licence are pre-exploration. Costs incurred in relation to these activities will need to be identified separately. Pre-exploration expenditure typically includes the acquisition of speculative seismic data and expenditure on the subsequent geological and geophysical analysis of this data.

5.11.250.30 A formal process of bidding for licences may help the separate identification of activities that precede obtaining the licence. However, in some regions the licence process is less formal. For example, in certain areas in Africa it is not uncommon for a significant amount of E&E activity to commence whilst finalising the formalities of obtaining a licence and government approval, based on a valid expectation of a licence being granted. In our view, when the grant of the licence is subject only to administrative processes that are not substantive, the licence may be deemed to have been granted. It is necessary to consider the nature of the regulatory approval in each case as this determination is a matter of fact rather than accounting policy. Accordingly, it may be appropriate in some circumstances to capitalise E&E expenditure incurred prior to obtaining the licence, subject to an entity's accounting policies for such expenditure.

5.11.260 *Accounting for pre-exploration expenditure*

5.11.260.10 The recognition and measurement of pre-exploration expenditure is not addressed by IFRSs and therefore entity should choose an accounting policy, to be applied consistently, using the hierarchy for the selection of accounting policies (see 2.8.6).

IFRS 6.BC13 5.11.260.20 Generally, pre-exploration expenditure cannot be associated with any specific mineral resources as usually it is speculative in nature, for example costs incurred in reassessing previous seismic data. In our view, such expenditure should be expensed as incurred.

IFRS 6.BC13 5.11.260.30 There may be some cases in which expenditure incurred in the pre-licence phase gives rise to an item that is an asset, notwithstanding that it relates to E&E activities; for example, the purchase of seismic data or analysis from a third party.

5.11.260.40 In addition, to the extent that pre-licence prospecting and exploration costs give rise to proprietary information that the entity has the ability to control, these costs may qualify for recognition as an intangible asset.

5.11.270 **Development expenditure**

5.11.270.10 Entities are required to identify and account for development expenditure separately from E&E expenditure.

5.11.280 *Identification of development expenditure*

IAS 38.8, 58 5.11.280.10 IFRSs do not contain a definition of development activities or expenditure. Normally (accounting) development in the context of research and development is "the application of research findings or other knowledge to a plan or design for the production of new or substantially improved materials, devices, products, processes, systems or services before the start of commercial production or use". Examples of (accounting) development expenditure include costs related to the design, construction and operation of a pilot plant that is not of a scale economically feasible for commercial production.

IFRS 6.5(b) 5.11.280.20 In the extractive industries, often "development" refers to the phase in which the technical feasibility and commercial viability of extracting a mineral resource have been demonstrated and an identified mineral reserve is being prepared for production (e.g. construction of access to the mineral reserves). In our view, these development activities are more akin to the construction of an asset to be used in commercial production than to expenditure incurred for (accounting) development activities.

5.11.280.30 [Not used]

5.11.280.40 A significant factor in determining technical feasibility and commercial viability is likely to be the existence of proven and probable reserves. Entities will be making such assessments based on either their in-house, operators' or third-party reserve evaluations. In our view, in assessing commercial viability an entity will need to consider whether they have access to adequate resources to proceed with development activities.

5.11.290 *Accounting for development expenditure*

IFRS 6.10 5.11.290.10 Once the technical feasibility and commercial viability of extracting a mineral resource are demonstrable, expenditure related to the development of that mineral resource should not be recognised as E&E assets.

5.11.290.20 IFRSs do not specify requirements for costs incurred on the development and extraction of mineral resources. IFRSs do not prescribe when the technical feasibility and commercial viability of extracting a mineral resource are demonstrable and therefore an entity should choose an accounting policy, to be applied consistently, using the accounting policy hierarchy (see 2.8.6).

IFRS 6.BC27 5.11.290.30 If an entity identifies an (accounting) development phase once E&E activities have concluded, then generally it can identify an intangible asset and demonstrate that the asset will generate probable future economic benefits. In our view, to the extent that an entity incurs expenditure of an (accounting) development nature, the capitalisation of that expenditure as an intangible asset may be appropriate.

5.11.290.40 Alternatively, an entity may conclude that there is no (accounting) development phase between the determination of technical feasibility and commercial viability and activities that are in preparation for production or extraction of a specific mineral reserve (extractive industry development activities). In this case it may be appropriate to capitalise development expenditure as part of the cost of an item of property, provided that those costs otherwise qualify as part of cost.

5.11.300 *Reclassification of E&E assets*

IFRS 6.17   5.11.300.10 When the technical feasibility and commercial viability of extracting a mineral resource are demonstrable, an entity (1) stops capitalising E&E costs for that area; (2) tests recognised E&E assets for impairment; and (3) ceases classifying any unimpaired E&E assets (tangible and intangible) as E&E.

IFRS 6.17   5.11.300.20 For E&E assets reclassified to development assets an entity chooses an ac-counting policy, to be applied consistently, to classify such assets either as tangible or intangible development assets. Intangible E&E assets may be reclassified into tangible development assets or intangible development assets and vice versa.

5.11.310 *Identifiable E&E assets*

5.11.310.10 Identifiable tangible assets that cease to be classified as E&E assets gener-ally will be classified as tangible development assets, e.g. a vehicle that will be used in production. Identifiable intangible E&E assets, e.g. an exploratory licence, may continue to be classified as an intangible asset, or may be reclassified as a tangible asset if the intangible asset is considered to be integral to the tangible development asset and the tangible element of the asset is more significant.

5.11.320 *Non-identifiable E&E assets*

5.11.320.10 Generally, when commercial and technical feasibility are demonstrable, a specific mineral reserve will have been identified for development. In practice, mineral reserves are classified as either property assets (i.e. tangible) or intangible assets. In our view, an entity should choose an accounting policy, to be applied consistently, to classify mineral reserves either as tangible or as intangible assets. We prefer mineral reserves, and by association the non-identifiable E&E assets, to be classified as tangible development assets.

IFRS 6.6, 7,   5.11.320.20 Mineral reserves are excluded from the scope of both the intangible asset and
IAS 16.3(c),   the property, plant and equipment standards, and they are not within the scope of any
38.7   other standard. Therefore, an entity chooses an accounting policy for mineral reserves, to be applied consistently, by applying the hierarchy for the selection of accounting policies (see 2.8.6). The limited relief from this hierarchy introduced by IFRS 6 (see 5.11.30) does not apply to mineral reserves that are not subject to E&E activities.

5.11.330 *Depreciation (amortisation)*

5.11.330.10 Upon reclassification of E&E assets, an entity depreciates (amortises) the resulting tangible development assets (and intangible developments assets with a finite life) over their useful lives. For both tangible and intangible development assets, the unit-of-production method may be an appropriate method.

5.11.340 *Impairment testing*

IFRS 6.17   5.11.340.10 Prior to reclassification, E&E assets are assessed for impairment and any impairment loss is recognised in profit or loss. This impairment assessment is required regardless of whether facts and circumstances indicate that the carrying amount of the E&E asset is in excess of its recoverable amount. In our view, E&E assets can continue to be tested as part of the CGUs to which they have been included previously, as described in 5.11.170. This is because we believe that these assets are E&E assets to which the special aggregation relief applies.

5.11.340.20 This impairment testing will be performed in accordance with the general impairment testing requirements (see 3.10). This will require an entity to develop additional accounting policies for the allocation of assets to CGUs and the assessment of recoverable amounts for these assets.

5.11.350 **Changes in accounting policies**

IFRS 6.6, 7,   5.11.350.10 IFRSs provide some relief from the standard hierarchy selection of accounting
9, 10,   policies regarding E&E expenses and assets. The modifications to the general guidance
IAS 8.10   on changes in accounting policy relate only to E&E expenditure. Changes in accounting policies for pre-exploration activities and development expenditure are subject to the general requirements of IFRSs for changes in accounting policy (see 2.8.10).

IFRS 6.13   5.11.350.20 An entity may change its existing IFRS accounting policy for E&E expenditure if, and only if, the change makes the financial statements more relevant to the economic decision-making needs of users and no less reliable, or more reliable and no less relevant to those needs, judged by the criteria for voluntary changes in accounting policies (see 2.8.30).

5.11.350.30 In our view, the requirement that a change in accounting policy should bring the financial statements closer to meeting the criteria in 5.11.350.20 prohibits entities changing between certain policies used in current practice. For example, we believe that this requirement would preclude entities in the oil and gas sector that account for exploration and development activities under IFRSs using the successful-efforts method from changing to the full-cost method (see 5.11.370). Successful-efforts accounting refers to a practice of capitalising costs on a field-by-field basis with an assessment of commercial viability of the fields performed on a periodic basis. We believe that such a change in policy is not considered to result in more relevant and/or reliable information to the user of the financial statements as it may result in capitalisation of unsuccessful costs; for example, costs related to dry wells that do not represent future economic benefits.

5.11.350.40 Similarly, a mining company that currently expenses E&E costs would, in our view, be precluded from changing to a policy of capitalisation of all such costs. This is because, absent the temporary exemption from the accounting policy hierarchy, it would be difficult to demonstrate the probability of future economic benefits from

E&E expenditure (see 5.11.10), and therefore we believe that such a change in policy is not considered to result in more relevant and/or reliable information to the users of the financial statements.

5.11.350.50 Conversely, we believe that a change in policy from the full-cost method to one based upon the successful-efforts method or from capitalisation of all E&E expenditure to expensing (at least some) costs as incurred would be acceptable. In our view, expensing many such costs is more consistent with the Framework because it is difficult to demonstrate that these costs meet the definition of an asset, and therefore expensing these costs as incurred may be viewed as more reliable.

5.11.360 Specific application issues*

5.11.370 *Compatibility of full-cost accounting with IFRSs*

5.11.370.10 "Full-cost accounting" is a phrase used in the extractive industries to refer to a practice of capitalising a range of costs for a field or area under exploration. In our view, certain aspects of full-cost accounting are not fully compatible with IFRSs. Examples of aspects of full-cost accounting that we believe may be inconsistent with IFRSs include:

- capitalising all pre-licence acquisition costs (see 5.11.240); and
- not disaggregating cost pools to a level that will enable identification of when E&E for a particular resource ceases and also allow impairment testing to be performed (see 5.11.170).

5.11.380 *Royalties and taxes*

5.11.380.10 Levies imposed on entities that are not calculated based on taxable profit are prevalent in the extractive industries; these levies may take the form of royalties, extraction taxes and corporate taxes, or a combination thereof. The form and complexity of these arrangements will vary from country to country or even within a country.

5.11.380.20 For example, in the oil and gas industry, royalties may be imposed based on a fixed percentage of gross production, either by reference to physical quantities or monetary values. Alternatively these levies, sometimes referred to as Petroleum Resource Taxes (PRTs), may be based on a percentage of operating profit as determined on a mine-by-mine or field-by-field basis, after allowing for the deduction of certain expenses. In other cases PRTs are imposed in a way that may be viewed as creating a joint venture between the producing entity and the government. In other cases they may, in substance, be an operating expense.

5.11.380.30 Many of these tax and royalty arrangements have been classified as income taxes under previous national GAAP. In our view, the classification of arrangements such as PRT is not an accounting policy choice. See 3.13.10 for a discussion of the classification of such arrangements.

5.11.390 *Extraction rights*

IAS 17.2, 38.2 5.11.390.10 In some jurisdictions entities may be required to pay royalties to land owners for the right to extract mineral resources located on the land. Such royalty payments are not within the scope of IFRS 6 as the technical feasibility and commercial viability of extracting the mineral resources already would have been demonstrated (see 5.11.10.30). Such royalties also are excluded from the scope of both IAS 17 *Leases* and IAS 38 *Intangible Assets*. However, as extraction rights do not fall under the scope of other IFRSs, in our view an entity may account for the royalties by analogy to either IAS 17 or IAS 38 under the hierarchy for the selection of accounting policies (see 2.8.6).

5.11.390.20 The fee to be paid for the extraction rights (royalties) may be calculated under a variety of payment structures. Analysis may be required to determine whether the royalties are in substance a payment for the right to use the land (i.e. more like a lease agreement under IAS 17) or are a payment for the right to extract mineral resources. Indicators that the royalties represent a right to extract mineral resources include calculations based on the quantity of resources extracted or cancellation clauses triggered by a reason related to the mineral resources, such as arrangements that are cancellable if the quality of the mineral deposit prevents exploration or if the mineral resource is exhausted.

5.11.390.30 If the royalties are not analogous to payments for the right to use the land, then a portion of these payments may qualify for capitalisation by analogy to IAS 38. In our view, if the extraction rights meet the definition of an intangible asset (see 3.3.30), then the present value of any non-refundable upfront payments, and non-refundable annual minimum payments, may be capitalised as an intangible asset. This is because the entity has a contractual obligation to make these payments and therefore these payments meet the definition of a financial liability when the contract is entered into (see 3.6.150.60).

5.11.390.40 In our view, variable payments should not be recognised until the obligating event occurs (e.g. as mineral reserves are extracted) because there is no contractual or present obligation before such time. Such payments generally are recognised in profit or loss as incurred unless they qualify for capitalisation, for example as part of the cost of inventory (see 3.8.120).

5.11.395 **Going concern**

5.11.395.10 The requirements of IFRS 6 are applied in the context of an entity preparing its accounts on a going concern basis (see 2.4.15). However, when an entity has only E&E activities, for example a junior explorer, and there is no planned or budgeted substantive exploration and evaluation, it may raise questions about the entity's ability to continue as a going concern (see 2.9.55). In such circumstances, it may also be relevant to consider access to capital and any reduction of planned capital expenditure.

5.11.400 **Future developments**

5.11.400.10 The IFRS Interpretations Committee is preparing a draft interpretation on deferred stripping costs incurred in surface mining activity during the production phase of a mine; the draft is expected to propose that such costs be accounted for as a component (see 3.2.230) of the related asset. The draft is expected to be issued in the third quarter of 2010.

5.11.400.20 In April 2010 the IASB published a DP *Extractive Activities*, which is based on the work of a group of national standard-setters. The proposals focus on upstream activities for minerals, oil and natural gas, addressing the following principal topics:

- definitions of reserves and resources for financial reporting
- asset recognition criteria for exploration assets
- unit of account selection for asset recognition
- asset measurement of exploration assets
- impairment testing requirements for exploration assets
- disclosure requirements
- "publish what you pay" disclosure proposals.

5.11.400.30 A decision whether to add this project to the IASB's active agenda is expected no earlier than the first half of 2011.

5.11.400.40 A final standard on *Joint Arrangements* is scheduled for the third quarter of 2010. Many extractive entities operate through joint arrangements and may be impacted by the changes (see 3.5.880.10).

5.11.400.50 In January 2010 the IASB published ED/2010/1 *Measurement of Liabilities in IAS 37*, which is a limited re-exposure of the proposed measurement requirements for liabilities not covered by another standard. Many extractive entities have significant decommissioning and environmental liabilities and will be impacted if the proposals are finalised in their current form (see 3.12.880.10). A final standard is scheduled for the first half of 2011.

5.12 Service concession arrangements
(IFRIC 12, SIC-29)

5.12 Service concession arrangements
(IFRIC 12, SIC-29)

Overview of currently effective requirements

- IFRIC 12 provides guidance on the accounting by private sector entities (operators) for public-to-private service concession arrangements.

- IFRIC 12 applies only to those service concession arrangements in which the public sector (the grantor) controls or regulates the services provided with the infrastructure and their prices, and controls any significant residual interest in the infrastructure.

- In these circumstances the operator does not recognise the infrastructure as its property, plant and equipment if the infrastructure is existing infrastructure of the grantor, or if the infrastructure is constructed or purchased by the operator as part of the service concession arrangement. Depending on the conditions of the arrangement, the operator recognises either a financial asset or an intangible asset, or both, at fair value as compensation for any construction or upgrade services that it provides.

- If the grantor provides other items to the operator that the operator may retain or sell at its option, then the operator recognises those items as its assets together with a liability for unfulfilled obligations.

- The operator recognises and measures revenue for providing construction or upgrade services in accordance with IAS 11 and revenue for other services in accordance with IAS 18.

- The operator recognises consideration receivable from the grantor for construction or upgrade services, including upgrades of existing infrastructure, as a financial asset and/or an intangible asset.

- The operator recognises a financial asset to the extent that it has an unconditional right to receive cash (or another financial asset) irrespective of the usage of the infrastructure.

- The operator recognises an intangible asset to the extent that it has a right to charge for usage of the infrastructure.

- Any financial asset recognised is accounted for in accordance with the relevant financial instruments standards, and any intangible asset in accordance with IAS 38. There are no exemptions from these standards for operators.

> - **The operator recognises and measures obligations to maintain or restore infrastructure, except for any construction or upgrade element, in accordance with IAS 37.**
>
> - **The operator generally is required to capitalise attributable borrowing costs incurred during construction or upgrade periods to the extent it has a right to receive an intangible asset. Otherwise the borrowing costs are expensed as incurred.**

Currently effective requirements

This publication reflects IFRSs in issue at 1 August 2010. The currently effective requirements cover annual periods beginning on 1 January 2010. The requirements related to this topic are derived mainly from IFRIC 12 *Service Concession Arrangements* and SIC-29 *Service Concession Arrangements: Disclosures.*

Forthcoming requirements and future developments

When a currently effective requirement will be changed by a new requirement that is issued but is not yet effective, it is marked with a # as a **forthcoming requirement** and the impact of the change is explained in the accompanying boxed text. In respect of this topic no forthcoming requirements are noted.

The currently effective requirements may be subject to **future developments** and a brief outline of the relevant project is given in 5.12.240.

5.12.01 Scope

5.12.05 *Introduction*

IFRIC 12.1-3 5.12.05.10 IFRIC 12 focuses on arrangements in which a private sector entity (the operator) constructs or upgrades public service infrastructure. The operator typically receives cash, either from the public sector body that awards the concession (the grantor) or users, only once the infrastructure is available for use.

IFRIC 12.5-9 5.12.05.20 The scope of IFRIC 12 is public-to-private service concession arrangements in which the public sector controls or regulates the services provided with the infrastructure and their prices, and controls any significant residual interest in the infrastructure. IFRIC 12 does not address all forms of infrastructure service arrangements (see 5.12.10.20) and does not address accounting by grantors.

5.12.05.30 The determination of whether an arrangement is within the scope of IFRIC 12 affects the recognition and measurement of assets by the operator, notably whether the operator recognises service concession infrastructure as property, plant and equipment.

IFRIC 12 includes the following guidance that may be relevant to the determination of whether an arrangement is within its scope:

IFRIC 12.1-3 ● a description of the typical features of public-to-private service concession arrangements;

IFRIC 12.5-9 ● specific scope criteria related to control of the service concession infrastructure;

IFRIC 12.AG 1-8 ● application guidance related to the scope criteria, which forms an integral part of the interpretation;

IFRIC 12.IN2 ● an information note referring to the IFRSs that apply to typical types of public-to-private service arrangements, which accompanies but is not part of IFRIC 12; and

IFRIC 12. BC2-BC19 ● explanatory material in the Basis for Conclusions, which accompanies but is not part of IFRIC 12.

IFRIC 12.B2 5.12.05.40 The key requirements of the guidance in 5.12.05.30 are discussed below. In addition, IFRIC 12 consequentially amends IFRIC 4 *Determining whether an Arrangement contains a Lease* such that any service concession arrangements within the scope of IFRIC 12 are excluded from the scope of IFRIC 4 (see 5.1.510).

5.12.10 *Public-to-private service concession arrangements*

IFRIC 12.3 5.12.10.10 While IFRIC 12 does not define "public-to-private service concession arrangements", it does describe the typical features of such arrangements. Typically a public-to-private service concession arrangement within the scope of IFRIC 12 will involve most of the following:

● *Infrastructure used to deliver public services*. The infrastructure can take many forms and may be transport-related (e.g. roads, bridges, tunnels), a type of building (e.g. hospitals, prisons), utility-related (e.g. water distribution network, electricity supply plant), or be specialist plant or equipment (e.g. medical equipment, vehicles). The infrastructure may include moveable and immoveable items, e.g. it may include a hospital building and related plant and equipment.

● *A contractual arrangement between the grantor and the operator*. This arrangement is referred to as a "concession agreement". The concession agreement specifies the services that the operator is to provide to the grantor and governs the basis upon which the operator will be remunerated. Arrangements of this nature can vary greatly in duration, but terms of 30 years or more are not unusual.

● *Supply of services by the operator*. These services may include the construction or upgrade of the infrastructure and the operation and maintenance of that infrastructure. Service concessions involving a significant construction or upgrade element are sometimes called "build-operate-transfer" or "rehabilitate-operate-transfer" arrangements. Often the construction or upgrade services are provided during the early years of the concession, but they also may be provided in stages during the concession period.

● *Payment of the operator over the term of the arrangement*. In many cases the operator will receive no payment during the initial construction or upgrade phase. Instead, the operator will be paid by the grantor directly or will charge users during the period that the infrastructure is available for use.

- *Return of the infrastructure to the grantor at the end of the arrangement.* For example, if the operator has legal title to the infrastructure during the term of the arrangement, then legal title may be transferred to the grantor at the end of the arrangement, often for no additional consideration.

5.12.10.20 The features in 5.12.10.10 give a broad indication of the types of arrangements to which the interpretation may relate. A wide variety of service concession arrangements exist in practice and not all of the arrangements that are within the scope of IFRIC 12 will have all of the features listed in 5.12.10.10.

5.12.15 *Scope criteria*

IFRIC 12.5 5.12.15.10 The scope of IFRIC 12 is defined by reference to control of the infrastructure. An arrangement is within the scope of the interpretation if:

- the grantor controls what services the operator must provide with the infrastructure (control of services);
- the grantor controls to whom it must provide them (control of services provided);
- the grantor controls at what price services are charged (control of pricing); and
- the grantor controls through ownership, beneficial entitlement or otherwise, any significant residual interest in the infrastructure at the end of the term of the arrangement (control of the residual interest).

5.12.15.20 For example, Grantor G awards a concession to Operator O to build and operate a new road. G transfers to the operator the land on which the road is to be constructed, together with adjacent land that O may redevelop or sell at its discretion. Construction is expected to take five years, after which O will operate the road for 25 years. During these 25 years O has a contractual obligation to perform routine maintenance on the road and to resurface it as necessary, which is expected to be three times. At the end of the arrangement the road will revert to G. The road is to be used by the general public. Tolls for use of the road are set annually by G.

5.12.15.30 This arrangement is a public-to-private service concession arrangement as described in 5.12.10.10 as the road is constructed pursuant to general transport policy and is to be used by the public. The arrangement is within the scope of IFRIC 12 as:

- the grantor controls the services to be provided using the infrastructure and the price charged for those services, i.e. the grantor requires the infrastructure to be used as a road available to the public and sets the tolls; and
- the grantor controls the significant residual interest in the infrastructure, as the road reverts to the grantor at the end of the arrangement.

5.12.15.40 Conversely, a public-to-private service concession arrangement may contain some of the features indicated in 5.12.15.10 and not be within the scope of IFRIC 12.

5.12.15.50 For example, Company R, a private sector company, enters into a contract with the Transport Ministry (the grantor) of Country S to acquire the right to operate the civil air navigation system in S. Under this contract the grantor sells the air navigation system to R, which R is required to upgrade and operate. Upon the acquisition of the air navigation system R will charge users based on rates negotiated directly by R with individual users; there is no price cap mechanism imposed by S. The contract is for an indefinite period of time and does not require R to transfer the air navigation system back to the grantor.

5.12.15.60 This arrangement has many characteristics of a public-to-private service concession arrangement, e.g. the grantor is a public sector body, the operator is a private sector body, the operator is responsible for the upgrade and operation of the service concession infrastructure, and the infrastructure is used pursuant to public policy. However, under the terms of the contract the grantor does not control prices or any significant residual interest in the infrastructure. Therefore, the contract is not within the scope of IFRIC 12.

5.12.20 *Scope criteria: control of services*

IFRIC 12.5, 5.12.20.10 The grantor may control the services to be provided by the operator in a
AG2 number of different ways. For example, the services may be specified through the terms of the concession agreement and/or a licence agreement and/or some other form of regulation. All of these forms of control are consistent with the scope criteria of IFRIC 12.

5.12.20.20 Furthermore, the degree of specification of the services may vary in practice. In some cases the grantor will specify the services to be provided in detail and by reference to specific tasks to be undertaken by the operator (e.g. build a hospital according to the design and timetable in schedule A; or complete the cleaning tasks in schedule B in each ward each evening etc.). In other cases the grantor will specify the services that the infrastructure should have the capacity to deliver (e.g. provide hospital accommodation suitable to support delivery of acute healthcare services to a local population of 10,000). In our view, the latter approach, using what sometimes is called an "output specification", also is consistent with the scope criteria of IFRIC 12.

5.12.30 *Scope criteria: control of pricing*

IFRIC 12.5, 5.12.30.10 The grantor may control or regulate the pricing of the services to be
AG3, provided using the infrastructure in a variety of ways. In our view, any substantive
IU 05-09 reviews or approvals by the grantor required by the service concession arrangement generally would meet this criterion in IFRIC 12. See 5.12.30.20 – 40 for examples of price control, including price-setting by an independent economic regulator.

5.12.30.20 In some cases, particularly when the grantor pays the operator directly, prices (or a price formula) may be set out in the concession agreement. In other cases prices may be re-set periodically by the grantor, or the grantor may give the operator discretion to set unit prices but set a maximum level of revenue or profits that the operator may retain. All of these forms of arrangement are consistent with the control criteria in IFRIC 12.

5.12.30.30 In some cases prices may be indexed by, or re-set periodically by reference to, a factor that is outside the control of the grantor. For example, prices may be indexed annually by a consumer price index (CPI), or a regulator may establish a price formula that depends on the value of an index, e.g. the regulator may specify that prices may rise by a maximum of CPI less X, with X being a value that is re-set periodically by the regulator. Although the grantor cannot control the value of CPI, the grantor is controlling the framework in which the price is set. In our view, such price-setting mechanisms constitute price regulation that is consistent with the scope criterion in IFRIC 12.

IFRIC 12. 5.12.30.40 An arrangement may be within the scope of IFRIC 12 when either the services
AG2 to be provided or pricing is controlled by an economic regulator acting in the public interest. For example, when the operator is a monopoly supplier of services in a geographic area, an "independent economic regulator" may be established to set prices and to monitor the operator's compliance with the conditions of its licence. The duties and powers of the regulator may be set out in legislation that requires the regulator to act in the public interest and also constrains the ability of the government to direct the operations of the regulator.

5.12.30.50 If an entity operates in a regulated industry and has a legal right to charge a price based on a cost-plus model, then other considerations may apply. See 3.3.180 and 3.12.720 for a discussion of regulatory assets and liabilities.

5.12.40 *Scope criteria: control of the residual interest*

IFRIC 12.3, 5 5.12.40.10 The simplest way in which the grantor may control the residual is for the concession agreement to require the operator to return all concession assets to the grantor, or to transfer the infrastructure to a new operator, at the end of the arrangement for no consideration. Such a requirement is a common feature of service concession arrangements involving concession assets with long useful lives, such as road and rail infrastructure. However, other forms of arrangements also are within the scope criteria of IFRIC 12.

5.12.40.20 The residual interest criterion may be met when the grantor holds an option to acquire the infrastructure assets at the end of the concession. Such an option gives the grantor the ability to control the use of the asset at the end of the concession period and restricts the operator's practical ability to sell or pledge any significant interest in the infrastructure. For example, an operator may acquire a site and develop a building that is to be used as a public healthcare facility. At the end of the arrangement the grantor may have an option to acquire the site for its then fair value. This is an example of an arrangement in which the grantor controls the residual interest in the infrastructure but the operator bears residual value risk.

IFRIC 12.
AG4 5.12.40.25 The residual interest criterion also may be met when the concession agreement establishes that the grantor holds the right to stipulate to whom the operator should transfer the assets at the end of the concession agreement. In our view, such a right effectively restricts the ability of the operator to sell or pledge the assets and gives the grantor control of the residual interest in the infrastructure.

IFRIC 12.6,
AG4, AG6 5.12.40.30 "Whole-of-life" arrangements, that is, arrangements for which the residual interest in the infrastructure is not significant, are within the scope of IFRIC 12 if the other scope criteria are met. The application guidance to IFRIC 12 states that the residual interest in the infrastructure is the estimated current value of the infrastructure as if it were already of the age and in the condition expected at the end of the period of the arrangement. For example, service concession arrangements for providing specialist medical equipment or IT infrastructure may have terms equivalent to the expected economic life of the equipment. Even if the operator retained ownership of the equipment at the end of the arrangement, the arrangement would be within scope as the equipment is not expected to have a significant residual value at the end of the arrangement.

5.12.45 *Other service arrangements*

IFRIC 12.
BC14 5.12.45.10 IFRIC 12 applies directly to public-to-private service concession arrangements. IFRIC 12 does not define "public sector" or "private sector"; such terms also are not defined elsewhere in IFRSs. Application by analogy of IFRIC 12 to private-to-private service arrangements would be appropriate under the hierarchy in IAS 8 *Accounting Policies, Changes in Accounting Estimates and Errors*. However, IFRIC 12 is silent on application to public-to-public service arrangements.

5.12.45.20 Consider the following example. Government in Country X has established a limited liability company, Company B, to act as the operator in a service concession arrangement. B's management has been recruited from the private sector and are encouraged to manage the day-to-day operations of B as if it were a commercial organisation. However, the Government owns 100 percent of B's equity and controls 100 percent of the voting rights in B. For the purpose of this example all scope criteria in paragraph 5(a) and (b) of IFRIC 12 are met. The diagram below illustrates the relationship of the entities in the service concession arrangement.

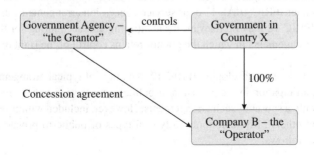

5.12.45.30 In our view, as the operator is 100 percent owned and controlled by the Government, the arrangement is a public-to-public service concession arrangement and so is not directly within the scope of IFRIC 12.

IAS 8.11 5.12.45.40 Nevertheless, in accordance with IAS 8, B's management should use its judgement to develop and apply appropriate accounting policies. This will include considering the guidance and requirements in current accounting standards and interpretations dealing with similar and related issues and the *Framework for the Preparation and Presentation of Financial Statements*. Therefore, depending on the facts and circumstances, in our view application of IFRIC 12 by analogy may be appropriate.

5.12.45.50 If in a subsequent accounting period the government sells a controlling interest in B to a private sector entity, then in our view B should reconsider its accounting treatment for the service concession arrangement, which may fall within the scope of IFRIC 12 directly at that time. Furthermore, if the operator is in the process of listing on a stock exchange or otherwise being privatised, it should consider the application of IFRIC 12 under the hierarchy for selecting accounting policies. In both circumstances described above, we prefer that the operator use the accounting requirements set out in IFRIC 12.

5.12.45.60 In other cases, it may be appropriate to apply IFRIC 12 to some private-to-private arrangements. The Basis for Conclusions to IFRIC 12 states that application by analogy to private-to-private arrangements would be appropriate for arrangements that:

- meet the requirements set out in paragraph 5, i.e. meet the scope criteria that establish that the grantor controls the use of the infrastructure; and
- have the characteristics described in paragraph 3, i.e. have the general features of service concession arrangements described in that paragraph.

5.12.45.70 IFRIC 12 identifies types of arrangements that may be very similar to leases. In some cases the accounting by operators would be significantly different under IFRIC 4/ IAS 17 *Leases* and IFRIC 12. However, the scope of IFRIC 12 defines the border between leases and service concession arrangements that are within its scope: leases convey a right to control the use of an asset whereas the grantor retains control of the right to use the infrastructure in arrangements that are within the scope of IFRIC 12.

5.12.45.80 In our view, the reference in IFRIC 12 to application by analogy is not intended to signify a free choice as to whether to account for other arrangements either under IFRIC 4/IAS 17 or as service concession arrangements under IFRIC 12. Rather, IFRIC 12 may be relevant for identifying and accounting for those private-to-private arrangements in which the grantor retains control of the right to use the infrastructure.

IFRIC 12.IN2, 5.12.45.90 In developing IFRIC 12, the range of typical arrangements for private sector
BC13 participation in the provision of public services were considered; IFRIC 12 addresses only a subset of such arrangements. However, included within IFRIC 12 are references to other IFRSs that apply to typical types of public-to-private service arrangements, as follows:

Category	Lessee	Service provider			Owner	
Typical arrangement types	Lease (e.g. Operator leases assets from grantor)	Service and/or maintenance contract (specific tasks e.g. debt collection)	Rehabilitate-operate-transfer	Build-operate-transfer	Build-own-operate	100% Divestment/ Privatisation/ Corporation
Asset ownership	Grantor				Operator	
Capital investment	Grantor		Operator			
Demand risk	Shared	Grantor	Operator and/or Grantor		Operator	
Typical duration	8 – 20 years	1 – 5 years	25 – 30 years		Indefinite (or may be limited by licence)	
Residual interest	Grantor				Operator	
Relevant IFRSs	IAS 17	IAS 18	IFRIC 12		IAS 16	

IFRIC 12.IN2   5.12.45.100 Such references represent a subset of the spectrum of such arrangements; no bright lines exist between the accounting requirements for different types of service concession arrangements.

5.12.50 Key requirements

5.12.60 *The operator's rights over the infrastructure*

IFRIC 12.11   5.12.60.10 The operator does not recognise public service infrastructure within the scope of IFRIC 12 as its property, plant and equipment, as the operator is considered to have a right of access rather than a right of use. This requirement applies to existing infrastructure of the grantor and also to infrastructure that the operator constructs or acquires for the purposes of the concession.

5.12.60.15 For example, Company C enters into a service concession arrangement with the government of Country Y to build and operate a hydroelectric power plant. C is responsible for purchasing the land on which the power plant will be constructed and other assets used in the construction. As the land and the other assets used in the construction were not existing assets of C but rather were purchased to build the power plant under the terms of the service concession agreement, they are not recognised as assets of C.

IFRIC 12.8   5.12.60.20 IFRIC 12 does not apply to existing property, plant and equipment of the operator. The operator applies the derecognition criteria of IAS 16 *Property, Plant and Equipment* to assess whether it should derecognise existing property, plant and equipment that it held and recognised before entering the service concession arrangement and uses to fulfil its obligations under the arrangement.

5.12.70 *Recognition of construction or upgrade revenue*

IFRIC 12.
13-15

5.12.70.10 IFRIC 12 characterises operators as "service providers", who should recognise revenue and costs related to construction or upgrade services in accordance with IAS 11 *Construction Contracts* and revenue and costs related to operation services in accordance with IAS 18 *Revenue*. Revenue recognised in accordance with IAS 11 is based on the stage of completion of the services and is measured by reference to the fair value of the consideration receivable.

IFRIC 12.13,
BC 30,
IAS 18.9

5.12.70.15 Generally the operator should measure revenue at the fair value of the consideration received. However, in practice the fair value of the construction services delivered may be the most appropriate method of establishing the fair value of the consideration received for the construction services.

5.12.70.17 For example, under the terms of a service concession arrangement, Company Q constructs a toll road to a new development area. As consideration for constructing the toll road, Q receives a right to collect tolls from users of the road for 25 years. The value of this intangible asset will depend, *inter alia*, on the expected number of users of the toll road. Traffic consultants have reported that the expected usage of the road is uncertain and have prepared two projections: a high and a low level of usage. A valuation of the intangible asset using the high level of usage suggests that the fair value of the intangible asset is 1,000; a valuation using the low level of usage suggests the fair value is 800. Based on its experience of completing other roads, Q considers that the fair value of the construction services it performs constructing this toll road is 950. In our view, Q should measure the intangible asset at 950 on initial recognition.

IFRIC 12.
BC34

5.12.70.18 The consideration received/receivable by the operator may comprise a financial asset, an intangible asset, or both. In cases in which the operator receives an intangible asset, the total revenue recognised by the operator over the concession term exceeds the total cash received by the operator over the concession term. This is because the revenue recognised by the operator includes construction revenue for which the consideration received is non-cash, i.e. an intangible asset.

5.12.70.20 There may be situations in which an operator provides more than one service. In such situations, the operator may need to exercise considerable judgement in determining the amount to be recorded as construction or upgrade revenue. In many cases the concession agreement will not specify an amount of consideration for construction or upgrade services. Instead, the concession agreement will specify the total consideration to be received by the operator during the concession period. In such cases the operator will need to allocate the total consideration receivable over the concession period to determine the amount to be recognised as construction or upgrade revenue.

IFRIC 12.
BC31

5.12.70.25 In order to assess whether a service concession agreement contains more than one service, the operator first applies the criteria in IAS 18 to identify separate components of the contract. Subsequently, if any construction element is identified, the segmenting criteria in IAS 11 are applied. As a result, the operator may recognise different margins on different components of a service concession arrangement, even if the total arrangement does not meet the segmentation criteria in IAS 11. This is because services that are separately identifiable are required to be accounted for separately under IAS 18. The operator then will apply the requirements of IAS 11 to the separately identifiable components of the arrangement, if applicable.

IAS 18.A11, 5.12.70.30 When the operator provides more than one service, the consideration received is allocated between services "by reference to the relative fair values of the services delivered when the amounts are separately identifiable". The allocation is performed by reference to the fair values of the services provided even if the concession agreement stipulates individual prices for certain services. This is because the amounts specified in the concession agreement may not necessarily be representative of the fair values of the services provided or the prices that would be charged if the services were sold on a stand alone basis. In practice the operator might estimate the relative fair values of the services by reference to the costs of providing each service plus a reasonable profit margin.

5.12.70.35 The requirement for the allocation of the consideration received based on the relative fair value of the services delivered is:

- more specific than IAS 18, which does not mandate a single method for allocating revenue between different components of an arrangement; and
- more specific than IFRIC 13 *Customer Loyalty Programmes*, which requires an entity to allocate consideration to award credits by reference to their fair value.

IAS 18.11 5.12.70.40 In addition, when determining the fair value of the total consideration to be allocated, future cash receipts are discounted using an imputed rate of interest in accordance with IAS 18. That standard defines an imputed rate of interest as the more clearly determinable of either (1) the prevailing rate of lending for a similar instrument to a borrower with a similar credit rating; or (2) the rate of interest that discounts nominal amounts receivable to the current sales price of the goods or services. Accordingly, in practice total consideration receivable may be discounted to the amount equal to the total fair value of services rendered, or it may be discounted using a prevailing rate of lending to the grantor with the resulting amount allocated in a manner proportionate to the estimated fair values of the services rendered.

IAS 18.13, 5.12.70.50 Judgement may be required to determine margins to be recognised as
A11, services are provided. In particular, an operator may have to recognise different
IFRIC 12. margins for providing construction and operation services under a single concession
BC31 agreement, even if the concession agreement does not meet the conditions for the segmentation of construction contracts in IAS 11, as indicated in 5.12.70.25.

5.12.70.55 For example, under the terms of a service concession arrangement, Company P constructs and operates a prison. The grantor pays P a fixed amount of cash for performing construction and operating services. The fair value of the total consideration is 1,100. P concludes that the service concession arrangement contains two components under paragraph 13 of IAS 18: a construction component and an operation component. P estimates that:

- the fair value of the construction services it performs is 900 and the cost of construction services is 800; and
- the fair value of the operation services is 300 and the cost of the operation services is 250.

5.12.70.60 P accounts for the arrangement by first allocating the total consideration between construction and operation services according to the relative fair values of the individual services. That is, P allocates revenue of 825 ((900 / (900 + 300) x 1,100) to construction services and revenue of 275 ((300 / (900 + 300) x 1,100) to operation services. On this basis, P expects to recognise a margin of 3 percent on performing construction services and a margin of 10 percent on performing operation services.

5.12.70.70 Service concession agreements may have different structures, and facts and circumstances of the specific agreement will have to be considered when allocating margin among the entities in the agreement. In some jurisdictions, it is common for a joint venture to be formed to undertake a specific service concession arrangement. The joint venture partners typically are a construction entity, a service provider and a financial institution. The joint venture partners may sub-contract certain services required under the terms of the concession agreement to investors in the joint venture.

5.12.70.75 For example, Company B is a joint venture formed to act as the operator in a service concession arrangement to build and operate a hospital. B's investors include Company C, a construction company. B sub-contracts construction of the hospital to C. The key terms of the construction contract between B and C mirror the sections of the concession agreement dealing with construction of the hospital.

5.12.70.80 In our view, B should estimate an appropriate construction margin applying the principles outlined above to the facts and circumstances of the specific arrangement. An appropriate construction margin is likely to reflect, when applicable:

- the work performed by B to co-ordinate the various construction services required to be performed under the terms of the service concession arrangement; and
- the construction risks retained by B which have not been passed on to C or other sub-contractors.

5.12.80 *Recognition of consideration receivable for construction or upgrade revenue*

IFRIC 12.15   5.12.80.10 The operator recognises consideration received or receivable for providing construction or upgrade services as:

IFRIC 12.16   - a financial asset to the extent that it has an unconditional right to receive cash irrespective of usage of the infrastructure; and/or

IFRIC 12.17 • an intangible asset to the extent that its consideration is dependent on usage of the infrastructure.

IFRIC 12.16, 5.12.80.20 The operator recognises a financial asset only when its right to receive cash
BC42, BC47, is not dependent upon the usage of the infrastructure. That is, the nature of the asset
BC48, BC52 recognised by the operator will depend on the allocation of the demand risk between the operator and the grantor. In simple cases the operator recognises a financial asset to the extent that the grantor bears the demand risk, and an intangible asset to the extent that it bears the demand risk. The nature of the asset recognised by the operator depends on the allocation of the demand risk, not the significance of the demand risk in the context of the arrangement as a whole.

5.12.80.30 For example, suppose Operator O enters into two separate concession agreements, each involving the construction and operation of a hospital. In the first case (Hospital K), O receives fixed payments from the grantor during the concession period. In this case the grantor bears the demand risk, as the cash flows of O do not depend on the usage of the hospital. O therefore recognises a financial asset as the consideration received for its construction services. In the second case (Hospital L) the grantor pays O an amount calculated by reference to the average number of beds occupied by patients each month, i.e. the payment is calculated as the average occupancy multiplied by a rate per bed. In this case O bears the demand risk as the cash flows of O depend on the usage of Hospital L. Therefore, O recognises an intangible asset as the consideration received for its construction services.

5.12.80.40 In more complex cases the operator may recognise both a financial asset and an intangible asset. For example, Operator O constructs and operates a hospital for the grantor, Hospital M. In this case Hospital M pays O based on occupancy as for Hospital L in 5.12.80.30 except that the monthly payment is subject to a minimum level: the monthly payment by the grantor is calculated as the higher of (1) average occupancy multiplied by a rate per bed; and (2) a fixed monetary amount. In this case O recognises a financial asset representing the right to receive the fixed monetary amount and an intangible asset representing the right to charge for the usage of the hospital above this fixed monetary amount.

IFRIC 12. 5.12.80.50 The identity of the party that makes payments to the operator once the infra-
BC39, structure is available for use does not affect how the operator classifies consideration
BC40 receivable for construction or upgrade services. Consider two separate concession agreements in which the operator constructs and operates a road. In the first case users of the road pay tolls to the operator based on usage. In the second case the grantor makes payments to the operator based on the number of users of the road; sometimes such an arrangement is described as a "shadow toll". In both cases the operator bears the demand risk and does not have an unconditional right to receive cash irrespective of usage; therefore the operator recognises an intangible asset as consideration for construction services.

IFRIC 12. 5.12.80.60 The operator's right to receive cash is considered unconditional even when
BC44 payment is contingent upon the operator meeting future quality or efficiency perform-

ance requirements. For example, an operator may have a right to receive fixed amounts of cash from the grantor in return for the construction services, subject to deductions if the infrastructure is not available for use or is operating below a specified standard. In this case the operator recognises a financial asset even though its right to receive cash is contingent upon the satisfaction of other contractual conditions.

IFRIC 12.
BC52 5.12.80.70 Some service concession agreements incorporate contractual clauses designed to eliminate substantially all variability in the operator's return. In such cases it remains necessary to apply the criteria in 5.12.80.10 to determine whether the operator should recognise a financial asset and/or an intangible asset. This is because the fact that the operator's asset is low risk does not give the operator the unconditional contractual right to receive cash.

5.12.80.80 For example, Operator T enters in a service concession agreement with Country W to construct and operate a toll bridge. The amounts receivable by T depend on the usage of the bridge and will be paid directly by the users. The grantor regulates the toll prices that T may charge users based on a targeted rate of return (i.e. rate is reset to reach an average return in the contract). In this situation, as indicated in 5.12.80.70, although T has a substantial fixed return established in the service concession agreement it does not give rise to a financial asset as T does not have an unconditional right to receive cash. Rather, T will recognise an intangible asset.

5.12.90 *Payments from the operator to the grantor*

5.12.90.10 IFRIC 12 addresses scenarios in which the operator receives consideration from the grantor for construction or upgrade services. In addition, in some cases the operator may make payments to the grantor at the inception of a service concession arrangement or over the concession period. In our view, the operator should recognise and measure any assets arising from such payments according to their substance, having regard to the terms of the arrangement as a whole.

5.12.90.20 For example, Operator S makes a payment to Grantor H at inception of a service concession arrangement related to an existing toll road. S has the right to collect tolls from users from commencement of the arrangement and also an obligation to upgrade sections of the road in later years. In this case it appears that the initial payment by S is made as consideration for the right to collect tolls on the existing toll road. S should recognise an intangible asset at inception of the arrangement; the subsequent performance of upgrade services may result in an enhancement of this intangible asset (see 5.12.170.13).

5.12.90.22 In some cases an operator may be required to make a combination of fixed and variable payments over the concession period in order to acquire the right to collect tolls in this manner. In our view, the operator should include the fair value of the fixed element of the payments in the cost of the intangible asset and recognise a corresponding financial liability at inception of the agreement. Variable payments are discussed in 3.3.100.55 and, we believe that generally they would be expensed as incurred.

5.12.90.25 In another example, Operator R transfers to Grantor M, at inception of a service concession arrangement for a toll road, options to acquire equity instruments and other participation rights. The transfer is made as consideration for the right to charge the users for usage of the road. In that case, we believe that the fair value of the items transferred should be recognised as part of the cost of the intangible asset at inception of the arrangement; the options to acquire equity instruments should be accounted for under IFRS 2 *Share-based Payment* (see 4.5); and other participation rights which are not share-based payment should be accounted for under IAS 39 *Financial Instruments: Recognition and Measurement* (see 3.6).

5.12.90.30 In a contrasting example, Operator M makes a payment to Grantor L at inception of a service concession arrangement related to a new hospital. Under the terms of the arrangement M is required to construct a new hospital building. Once the hospital is available for use M will receive monthly payments from L that do not depend on usage of the hospital. The total cash receivable from L exceeds the fair value of the construction and operation services to be provided by M. In this case the initial payment by M forms part of the financial asset receivable by M from L.

5.12.90.40 In another example, Operator P enters into a 15-year contract to operate an airport terminal. P is required to provide routine maintenance and operate terminal services (e.g. duty free shops, catering and hotel services, ground handling services). P earns revenue from retail sales to passengers and receives additional fees from the Grantor N based on the number of passengers using the airport. P is required to make annual payments to N over the concession period as it delivers operating services. In our view, P should recognise the payments as incurred to the extent that they represent the cost of delivering operating services; P should not recognise a financial or intangible asset since there are no construction or upgrade services identified in this agreement.

5.12.100 *Timing of recognition*

IFRIC 12. 5.12.100.10 In accordance with general practice for executory contracts, the opera-
BC67, tor recognises consideration receivable as it performs the construction or upgrade
BC68 services. Generally the nature of the asset(s) that the operator recognises once the infrastructure is available for use determines the nature of the asset(s) that the operator recognises as it performs construction or upgrade services. For example, when the operator receives a licence to charge users once the infrastructure is available for use, IFRIC 12 concludes that the asset that the operator recognises as it performs construction or upgrade services is itself an intangible asset.

5.12.110 **Borrowing costs**

IAS 23.4, 10, 5.12.110.10 If the operator receives a right to charge for usage of the public service
IFRIC 12.22, infrastructure, then the operator generally is required to capitalise attributable
BC58 borrowing costs for qualifying assets incurred during the construction or upgrade phase. Otherwise, the operator expenses borrowing costs as incurred. Capitalisation of attributable borrowing costs will be relevant only in respect of intangible assets, since a financial

asset cannot be a qualifying asset. See 4.6.350 for a discussion of the capitalisation of borrowing costs.

5.12.120 *Items provided by the grantor*

IFRIC 12.27   5.12.120.10 If the grantor provides items to the operator that the operator may retain or sell at its discretion, and those items form part of the consideration for the services provided, then the operator recognises those items as assets. The operator measures the items at fair value on initial recognition, recognising a corresponding liability representing the obligation to provide services in the future. Such "keep or deal" items should be distinguished from items that the grantor provides to the operator with conditions attached for use in the service concession arrangement, which the operator recognises as a financial and/or intangible asset (see 5.12.80.10). They also should be distinguished from government grants (see 4.3), which are accounted for either at fair value or at nominal value.

5.12.130 *Operation revenue*

IAS 18.9,   5.12.130.10 The operator should recognise and measure revenue related to operation
IFRIC 12.20   services in accordance with IAS 18. The general principle in IAS 18 is for revenue to be measured at the fair value of consideration received or receivable for services provided.

IAS 18.9, 20   5.12.130.20 When the operator recognises an intangible asset during the construction phase (i.e. it receives a right to collect fees that are contingent upon the extent of use of the public service), it recognises operation revenue as it is earned. For example in a case of a toll road constructed by the operator in which the operator receives the right to collect tolls from the users, the operator recognises toll revenue as the road is used.

IAS 18.9, 20   5.12.130.30 When the operator recognises a financial asset during the construction phase (i.e. it receives an unconditional right to receive cash that is not dependent upon the extent of use of the public service), a portion of payments received during the operation phase is allocated to reduce this financial asset. The operator recognises revenue from operation services and the resulting financial asset as revenue is earned, and measures revenue at the fair value of consideration received or receivable.

IFRIC 12.18,   5.12.130.40 Further complexities may arise in service concession arrangements in
IE27   which the operator recognises an intangible asset and a financial asset. In such cases the fair value of consideration receivable under the arrangement will be allocated between a financial asset and an intangible asset. Revenue is recognised as earned at the fair value of consideration received or receivable. A portion of payments collected is allocated to the repayment of the financial asset. This is illustrated in the worked example in 5.12.180.

5.12.140 *Maintenance obligations and upgrade services*

5.12.140.10 Typically service concession agreements require the operator to maintain the infrastructure such that the infrastructure can deliver a specified standard of service at all times. In addition, generally service concession arrangements other than "whole-of-life" arrangements require the operator to hand back the infrastructure to the grantor or another party in a specified state at the end of the concession period.

IFRIC 12.21 5.12.140.20 The operator recognises and measures contractual obligations to maintain or restore infrastructure in accordance with IAS 37 *Provisions, Contingent Liabilities and Contingent Assets* (see 3.12), except for any upgrade element for which the operator should recognise revenue and costs in accordance with IAS 11.

IFRIC 12.IE4, 5.12.140.30 Judgement may be required to determine whether a particular activity to be
IE19, IE35 undertaken by an operator under the contract is an obligation arising under the terms of its licence to be recognised under IAS 37 or if it is a service provided under the terms of the arrangement and therefore a revenue generating activity. The illustrative examples in IFRIC 12 demonstrate situations in which major maintenance is accounted for as a provision, and when it is accounted for as a revenue-generating activity. For example, in a case in which the operator is required to resurface a road at a specified time during the concession period, the resurfacing work is viewed as a revenue-generating activity and is accounted for as a revenue component of the arrangement (see 5.12.70). In cases in which the operator is required to maintain the road in a specified condition, but the exact nature and extent of work is not specified but varies according to use, the obligation to resurface the road is measured and recognised in accordance with IAS 37. In our view, the most appropriate accounting treatment of such activities will depend on the facts and circumstances of each arrangement, not on whether the operator recognises a financial asset or an intangible asset as consideration for construction or upgrade services.

5.12.140.35 For example, Company H builds and operates a toll road and recognises an intangible asset. The service concession agreement requires that H maintain the toll road and, in practice, H expects to resurface the toll road every seven years. However, H has no contractual right to increase unit tolls on the road after it completes the resurfacing. In our view, it would not be appropriate for H to treat the resurfacing activity as construction or enhancement revenue and record an increase in the carrying amount of the intangible asset in this case, as H does not receive an additional right to charge users of the road when it resurfaces the road.

5.12.140.40 Judgement will be required in measuring an obligation to maintain or restore a concession asset and in determining the timing of its recognition. Generally IAS 37 requires a provision to be measured at the estimated amount at which it could be settled or transferred at the reporting date. Often it will be appropriate to recognise a provision for an obligation to restore a concession asset as the asset deteriorates. In such a case the provision is likely to be measured at the estimated costs expected to be incurred to perform maintenance or restoration work, discounted using a rate that reflects the time value of money and the risks involved (see 3.12.620).

IFRIC 12. 5.12.140.50 As mentioned in 5.12.140.30 judgement will be required in measuring an obli-
BC68 gation to maintain or restore a service concession asset and in determining the timing of its recognition. Agreements within the scope of IFRIC 12 generally are executory when

signed, and should not be recognised to the extent that they are executory. However, if the facts and circumstances indicate that the operator accepts an obligation at inception of the service concession agreement as consideration for the rights it acquires, then the operator will recognise a provision at inception of the service concession agreement, recognising the corresponding debit as part of the cost of the intangible asset.

5.12.140.60 For example, Company R enters into a concession agreement contract to operate and maintain the existing water distribution network into Country S. There was no upfront fee paid by R; however, at the inception of the contract R assumes an obligation to maintain and rehabilitate the existing water distribution network in order to reach certain standards of serviceability. Prices charged by R to the customers are established by S at the inception of the contract and are not subject to increases upon the conclusion of rehabilitation activity.

5.12.140.70 The intangible asset and the provision for the obligation assumed would be recognised at inception of the agreement based on the present value of the expected future restoration costs (e.g. the present value of the contractual minimum amount based on the best estimate of the time schedule of the expenditures over the contract period), and would be reassessed at each reporting date.

5.12.140.80 There may be situations in which the operator is reimbursed for some costs incurred in upgrading the service concession asset. If the operator concludes that the requirement to enhance the physical infrastructure is a revenue generating service, then the operator will recognise construction revenue and construction costs as it performs the construction work. Under this approach, the amount to be reimbursed by the grantor will form part of the consideration receivable for performing the construction services.

5.12.140.90 For example, suppose that the initial estimate of the fair value of the construction services required to complete the upgrade is 100, Operator C earns a gross margin on sales of 5 percent and the grantor agrees to reimburse 20 percent. C records the following entry:

	Debit	Credit
Financial asset (95 x 20%)	19	
Intangible asset	81	
Construction revenue		100
Cost of sales	95	
Cash		95
To recognise upgrade work		

5.12.140.100 Conversely, if C concludes that the requirement is an obligation arising under the terms of the licence, then C will recognise a provision under IAS 37. Under this approach the amount to be reimbursed by the grantor will form a right to be considered under paragraphs 53 – 58 of IAS 37. In particular the reimbursement will be recognised when, and only when it is virtually certain that reimbursement will be received if C settles the obligation (i.e. upgrade) and shall be recognised as a separate asset.

5.12.140.110 Using the same figures and in the example in 5.12.140.90, C would recognise a reimbursement asset of 19 and a provision of 95. These balances should be shown separately in the statement of financial position.

5.12.150 *Subsequent accounting for financial and intangible assets*

IFRIC 12.23, 26 5.12.150.10 The operator accounts for any financial asset it recognises in accordance with IAS 39 (see 3.6); the operator accounts for any intangible asset it recognises in accordance with IAS 38 *Intangible Assets* (see 3.3). There are no exemptions from these standards for operators.

5.12.160 *Financial assets*

IFRIC 12.24 5.12.160.10 IFRIC 12 requires the operator to classify the financial asset as a loan or receivable, available for sale, or at fair value through profit or loss if so designated and the designation criteria are met. The operator classifies financial assets on an asset-by-asset basis; there is no requirement for an entity that recognises a number of financial assets arising from different service concession arrangements to apply the same classification in all cases.

5.12.170 *Intangible assets*

IAS 38.97 5.12.170.10 IAS 38 requires an intangible asset to be amortised over its expected useful life. The useful life of an intangible asset recognised in a service concession arrangement is the concession period. In our view, amortisation should begin when the asset is available for use, i.e. when the operator is able to charge the public for use of the infrastructure.

5.12.170.13 For example, Company D signs a service concession arrangement with the government of Country Z to construct and operate a toll road. The concession agreement is for a 30 year period commencing with the granting of the concession. The concession agreement requires D to construct the infrastructure in discrete sections allowing D to operate the individual sections of the road upon completion of the construction services and start generating revenues by charging the users for the use of these sections, while other sections are still under construction. As the concession agreement is represented by a series of intangible assets, in our view, D should commence amortisation of the intangible asset(s) on a phased basis as each individual section begins operations.

IAS 38.98, IFRIC 12. 5.12.170.20 No specific method of amortisation is required to be used, and the straight-line method, the diminishing (or reducing balance) method and the unit-of-production

BC64, method are cited as possible approaches; these methods are illustrated in 3.2.160. If
BC65 the pattern in which the asset's economic benefits are consumed cannot be determined
reliably, then the straight-line method is used. IAS 38 and IFRIC 12 do not allow the
use of "interest" methods of amortisation, including the "annuity method", which take
into account the time value of money.

IAS 38.98 5.12.170.30 While the straight-line method may be appropriate for many service concession arrangements, other methods also may be acceptable as illustrated in the following
examples.

5.12.170.33 For example, Company E constructs and operates a toll road between two
established population centres in a country with a stable economy. Tolls remain fixed
for the duration of the concession. Traffic forecasts based on studies of other similar
projects in the country predict that usage of the road will rise rapidly in the years following construction until the road reaches its capacity, and will remain stable for the
remainder of the concession term. In our view, the use of a unit-of-production method
of amortisation (in which the unit of production would be the number of users of the
toll road) is acceptable as the company has developed a reliable estimate of expected
traffic over the life of the concession arrangement.

5.12.170.35 In another example, Company F constructs and operates a toll bridge. The
concession has a variable term and ends when the total revenues collected by F from
users of the bridge reaches a predetermined level established in the concession contract.
In our view, a revenue-based method of amortisation is acceptable as it represents the
pattern in which the intangible asset's economic benefits are consumed.

IAS 38.111 5.12.170.40 Intangible assets with finite useful lives are tested for impairment using the
general impairment requirements (see 3.10.110).

5.12.180 **Worked example**

5.12.180.10 This simple worked example illustrates the mechanics of applying the key
requirements of IFRIC 12 regarding the recognition and measurement of revenue,
and recognition and measurement of the consideration for construction services. For
simplicity it does not illustrate the other requirements of IFRIC 12.

5.12.180.20 Municipality M (the grantor) contracts with Company B (the operator) to build
diagnostic medical equipment (a scanner) that will be used in providing public health
services. The scanner will take one year to build. After its construction the operator
will provide maintenance services and make the scanner available to the public health
service facility for a period of five years. The operator does not expect major repairs
to be necessary during the concession period. At the end of the concession period the
operator must return the scanner to the grantor for no additional consideration. The
patient will pay the operator 100 each time that the scanner is used, with the grantor
guaranteeing a minimum annual payment of 60,000.

5.12.180.30 The operator also sells similar scanners in the normal course of business and estimates that the fair value of services provided in building the scanner is 350,000. The estimated interest rate of lending to M for a similar instrument is 5 percent.

5.12.190 *Asset recognition*

5.12.190.10 In exchange for construction services, B receives a right to a fixed and determinable amount of cash of 60,000 per year for five years. B also receives a right to charge patients for the use of the scanner and to retain the amount collected over and above the annual minimum. Therefore B receives a financial asset and an intangible asset.

5.12.200 *Measuring the financial asset*

5.12.200.10 B classifies the financial asset received in the arrangement as a receivable under IAS 39, and accordingly measures it initially at fair value and subsequently at amortised cost. Fair value at the end of the first year (upon completion of construction) is estimated by discounting the guaranteed future cash flows of 60,000 per year for five years at a discount rate of 5 percent per annum (i.e. rate of lending for similar service concession agreement). The amount of consideration allocated to the financial asset is 259,769 (see 5.12.70.40).

5.12.210 *Measuring the intangible asset*

IFRIC 12. 5.12.210.10 The fair value of an intangible asset can be difficult to measure; therefore,
BC30 in practice, the fair value of the construction services may be the most appropriate way of measuring the fair value of the consideration received. When both financial and intangible assets are recognised, the fair value of the intangible asset can be measured as the difference between the fair value of the total consideration for the construction services (i.e. no elements of the cash flows received from M relates to operating services) and the fair value of the financial asset received in the arrangement.

5.12.210.20 The total revenue from construction services will be equal to the fair value of the construction services, i.e. 350,000. The amount of 259,769 of consideration is received in the form of a financial asset (see 5.12.200.10). In this example, the remaining balance of 90,231 is allocated to the intangible asset, representing the right to charge patients.

IFRIC 12. 5.12.210.30 In this example, B performs construction services only in the first year and
IE23 therefore recognises the financial asset and intangible asset in full by the end of the first year. In more complex arrangements it is likely that the operator will be required to perform construction services over the course of several years. In such cases the operator will recognise revenue, and will build up the financial asset and the intangible asset receivable, as it performs the construction services (see illustrative example 3 of IFRIC 12).

5.12.220 *Accounting for revenue*

5.12.220.10 Revenue for services provided is accounted for in accordance with IAS 11 and IAS 18. In year 1 B recognises revenue from construction services of 350,000.

5.12.220.20 Assume that actual demand for the scanner over the five years of operation is as follows:

	Year 2	Year 3	Year 4	Year 5	Year 6
Number of times used	480	780	960	840	900

5.12.220.30 Based on the illustrative examples in IFRIC 12, in our view the cash receipts should be allocated between repayment of the receivable and revenue as follows:

	Year 2	Year 3	Year 4	Year 5	Year 6
Usage x 100	48,000	78,000	96,000	84,000	90,000
Amount received (subject to 60,000 minimum)	60,000	78,000	96,000	84,000	90,000
Allocated to receivable paydown	60,000	60,000	60,000	60,000	60,000
Allocated to revenue from operation	-	18,000	36,000	24,000	30,000

5.12.220.40 Relevant amounts in the statement of comprehensive income and statement of financial position over the concession period are as follows:

	Year 1	Year 2	Year 3	Year 4	Year 5	Year 6
Revenue	350,000	-	18,000	36,000	24,000	30,000
Finance income[1]	-	12,988	10,638	8,170	5,578	2,857
Amortisation expense[2]	-	(18,046)	(18,046)	(18,046)	(18,046)	(18,047)
Receivable[3]	259,769	212,757	163,395	111,565	57,143	-
Intangible asset	90,231	72,185	54,139	36,093	18,047	-

Notes
(1) Receivable at the end of the previous period x 5 percent
(2) Intangible asset's initial carrying amount / five years
(3) Receivable at the end of the previous period + finance income for the period - payments for the period

5.12.230 **Disclosures**

IFRIC 12.28, SIC-29 5.12.230.10 Disclosure requirements applicable to service concession arrangements are contained in SIC-29. SIC-29 applies to both grantors and operators in service concession arrangements in which the operator receives a right and assumes an obligation to provide services to the public.

5.12.240 **Future developments**

5.12.240.10 In July 2009 the IASB issued ED/2009/8 *Rate-regulated Activities*, which proposes definitions of regulatory assets and regulatory liabilities, and that regulatory assets and regulatory liabilities are measured at the present value of expected future cash flows, both on initial recognition and for subsequent remeasurement.

5.12.240.20 In the ED, the IASB noted that an entity with an arrangement within the scope of IFRIC 12 would have to consider whether it has rate-regulated activities that are under the scope of the proposed standard. If it does, the entity would apply both IFRIC 12 and the proposed standard on rate-regulated activities. The requirements of the proposed ED are applicable solely to the operational phase of the concession agreement in which rates charged by the operator will be regulated and may create additional assets/ liabilities. There are no changes in the requirements of IFRIC 12 for the recognition of the revenues for the construction services. A final standard is scheduled for the first half of 2011.

5.13 Common control transactions and Newco formations

5.13 Common control transactions and Newco formations

> **Overview of currently effective requirements**
>
> - In our view, the acquirer in a common control transaction has a choice of applying either book value accounting or IFRS 3 accounting in its consolidated financial statements.
>
> - In our view, the transferor in a common control transaction that is a demerger has a choice of applying either book value accounting or fair value accounting in its consolidated financial statements. In other disposals, in our view judgement is required in determining the appropriate consideration transferred in calculating the gain or loss on disposal.
>
> - In our view, generally an entity has a choice of accounting for a common control transaction using book value accounting, fair value accounting or exchange amount accounting in its separate financial statements when investments in subsidiaries are accounted for at cost.
>
> - Common control transactions are accounted for using the same accounting policy to the extent that the substance of the transactions is similar.
>
> - If a new parent is established within a group and certain criteria are met, then the cost of the acquired subsidiaries in the separate financial statements of the new parent is determined by reference to its share of total equity of the subsidiaries acquired.
>
> - Newco formations generally fall into two categories: formations to effect a business combination involving a third party; or formations to effect a restructuring amongst entities under common control.
>
> - In a Newco formation to effect a business combination involving a third party, generally acquisition accounting applies.
>
> - In a Newco formation to effect a restructuring amongst entities under common control, in our view often it will be appropriate to account for the transaction using book values.

Currently effective requirements

This publication reflects IFRSs in issue at 1 August 2010. The currently effective requirements cover annual periods beginning on 1 January 2010.

This chapter deals with business combinations amongst entities under common control. It does not deal with the wider issue of common control transactions, e.g. the transfer of a single item of property, plant and equipment between fellow subsidiaries.

The issues dealt with in this chapter are not covered explicitly in any of the standards. However, the following standards are relevant in understanding the accounting for common control transactions and Newco formations: IFRS 3 *Business Combinations*, IAS 27 *Consolidated and Separate Financial Statements* and IFRIC 17 *Distributions of Non-cash Assets to Owners*.

Forthcoming requirements and future developments

When a currently effective requirement will be changed by a new requirement that is issued but is not yet effective, it is marked with a # as a **forthcoming requirement** and the impact of the change is explained in the accompanying boxed text. In respect of this topic no forthcoming requirements are noted.

The currently effective requirements may be subject to **future developments** and a brief outline of the relevant project is given in 5.13.240.

5.13.10 **Common control transactions**

IFRS 3.B1 5.13.10.10 A business combination involving entities or businesses under common control is a business combination in which all of the combining entities or businesses ultimately are controlled by the same party or parties both before and after the combination, and that control is not transitory.

IFRS 3.B2 5.13.10.20 A group of individuals is regarded as controlling an entity when, as a result of contractual arrangements, they collectively have the power to govern its financial and operating policies so as to obtain benefits from its activities. In our view, the requirement for there to be a contractual arrangement should be applied strictly and is not overcome by an established pattern of voting together.

5.13.10.30 For example, Company X and Company Y are owned by shareholders B, C, D and E, each of whom hold 25 percent of the shares in each company. B, C and D have entered into a shareholders' agreement in terms of which they exercise their voting power jointly. Therefore, both X and Y are under the control of the same group of individuals (B, C and D), and are under common control.

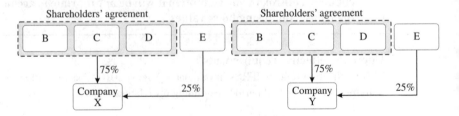

5.13.10.40 In another example, Company Y and Company Z are owned by members and close relatives of a single family. The father owns 40 percent of the shares in each entity, each of his two brothers owns another 15 percent of the shares, and his son owns the remaining 30 percent of the shares. However, there are no agreements between the family members that they will exercise their voting power jointly. Therefore, even though the shares are held within a single family who may have an established pattern of voting together, this group of individuals does not have a contractual arrangement to exercise control collectively over either company, and Y and Z are not under common control.

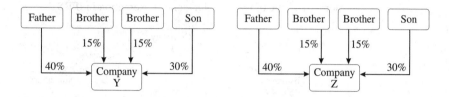

5.13.10.50 Continuing the example in 5.13.10.40, a different conclusion might be reached if, for example, the son were a child. However, judgement would be required to assess the facts and circumstances of each case.

IFRS 3.B3 5.13.10.60 In determining whether the combination involves entities under common control, it is not necessary that an individual, or a group of individuals acting together under a contractual arrangement to control an entity, be subject to the financial reporting requirements of IFRSs. Also, the entities are not required to be part of the same consolidated financial statements.

IFRS 3.B4 5.13.10.70 The extent of non-controlling interests in each of the combining entities before and after the business combination is not relevant in determining whether the combination involves entities under common control. However, transactions that affect the level of non-controlling interests are discussed in 5.13.60.60 – 80.

5.13.20 *Scope of the common control exemption*

IAS 27.38 5.13.20.10 In general IFRSs do not make specific provision for the accounting for common control transactions in the separate financial statements (see 2.1.70) when the entity elects to account for investments in subsidiaries at cost in accordance with IAS 27. The only exception is the establishment of a new parent in certain circumstances (see 5.13.150). In our view, an entity may apply the common control scope exclusion in IFRS 3 by analogy to the accounting for common control transactions in separate financial statements. When the entity elects to account for investments in subsidiaries in accordance with IAS 39, the common control exemption is not relevant and the requirements of IAS 39 apply (see 3.6).

IAS 28.20, 5.13.20.20 In our view, the common control exemption in accounting for business com-
31.33 binations also applies to the transfer of investments in associates and jointly controlled entities between investors under common control. Although neither IAS 28 *Investments in Associates* nor IAS 31 *Interests in Joint Ventures* includes an explicit exemption for common control transactions, both equity accounting and proportionate consolidation

follow the methodology of acquisition accounting. Therefore, we believe that it is appropriate to extend the application of the common control exemption.

5.13.20.30 For example, in the following group structure the 30 percent investment in Associate C is transferred from Subsidiary S1 to Subsidiary S2, both of which are controlled by Company P. Accordingly, we believe that the transfer of C, compared with the acquisition of an associate from a third party, is outside the scope of the IFRS 3 methodology by virtue of the common control exemption in IFRS 3.

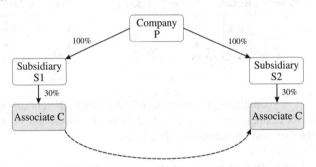

IAS 39.BC 5.13.20.40 Questions have been raised about whether the view in 5.13.20.20 can continue *24D* to apply following comments made by the Board in amending the scope of IAS 39 *Financial Instruments: Recognition and Measurement* in respect of forward contracts to enter into a business combination (see 3.6.65). The Board noted that the exemption in respect of forward contracts to enter into a business combination had not been extended to forward contracts in relation to associates and joint ventures, and therefore the scope exemption could not be inferred to extend to IAS 28. This was on the basis that the linkage between acquisition accounting and equity accounting is only in respect of accounting methodology and not the *principles* of the accounting. However, we believe that the extension of the common control exemption is a matter of accounting methodology and therefore that the common control exemption in IFRS 3 applies.

5.13.30 *Transitory common control*

5.13.30.10 The term "transitory" is not defined under IFRSs. In our view, the notion of transitory is included in the common control definition as an anti-abuse measure to deal with so-called "grooming" transactions, i.e. transactions structured to achieve a particular accounting treatment. Therefore, acquisition accounting should be applied to those transactions that look as though they are combinations involving entities under common control, but which in fact represent genuine substantive business combinations with unrelated parties.

5.13.30.20 In our view, the requirement that control not be transitory should be applied narrowly in order to give effect to its intention. We believe that transitory common control is relevant only when there is an intention to avoid applying acquisition accounting by sequencing an acquisition to place entities under common control before effecting the business combination.

5.13.30.30 For example, Company P has a subsidiary B. P acquires all of the shares of Company C. Next P combines the activities of B and C by transferring the shares in C to B. The question arises as to how the transfer of C into B should be accounted for in the consolidated financial statements of B.

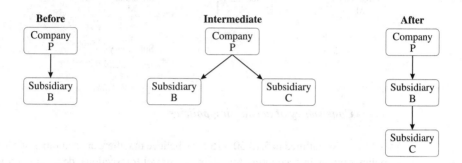

5.13.30.40 In this example, if the intermediate step had been omitted and instead B had been the P group's vehicle for the acquisition of C (i.e. going straight to the "after" position), then B would have been identified as the acquirer. Since B and C are under common control, initially it appears that acquisition accounting would not be required because of the common control scope exemption. However, we believe that B should be identified as the acquirer and should account for its combination with C using acquisition accounting. This is because B would have applied acquisition accounting for C if B had acquired C directly rather than through P. Acquisition accounting cannot be avoided in the financial statements of B simply by placing B and C under the common control of P shortly before the transaction in what is a grooming transaction.

5.13.30.50 An assessment of whether control is transitory may require consideration of a wider series of transactions of which the business combination, which looks as though it involves entities under common control, is only one element.

5.13.30.60 Another issue with respect to common control transactions is whether an intention to dispose of a restructured or internally-created group means that post-combination control is transitory and therefore that common control accounting does not apply to a restructuring within a group in preparation for disposal. In our view, an intention to dispose of restructured or internally-created entities does not in itself result in control of the combined entities being transitory. See 5.13.200.100 for a discussion of the formation of a Newco prior to a disposal.

5.13.30.70 For example, Parent P has two subsidiaries, Company M and Company V. Both subsidiaries have been part of the group for many years. P intends to combine the activities of M and V by transferring the shares in V to M, and then to sell the M sub-group. We believe that control by P over M and V is not transitory because M and V were part of the group for many years. Therefore, we believe that the common control exemption applies.

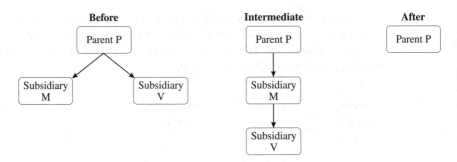

5.13.40 *Consistency of accounting policies*

5.13.40.10 As outlined in 5.13.50 – 150, we believe that there are a number of accounting policy options in accounting for common control transactions, depending on whether the financial statements are consolidated or separate.

IAS 8.13, 5.13.40.20 IFRSs require the application of consistent accounting policies for similar
27.34 transactions. Accordingly, common control business combinations are accounted for using the same accounting policy in the consolidated financial statements to the extent that the substance of the transaction is similar.

IAS 8.13 5.13.40.30 Similarly, common control transactions are accounted for using the same accounting policy in the separate financial statements, independently of the choice for the entity's consolidated financial statements, to the extent that the substance of the transaction is similar. This applies to both the accounting for acquisitions and disposals.

IAS 8.13 5.13.40.40 Judgement is required in assessing the substance of a common control transaction to determine whether the specific facts and circumstances of a case warrant an accounting treatment that differs from that applied to previous common control transactions.

5.13.40.50 However, in our view the nature of the investee does not affect the choice of accounting policy. For example, if the acquisition of a subsidiary in a common control transaction was accounted for previously using book value accounting (see 5.13.60), then we believe that the fact that a subsequent common control transaction involves the acquisition of an associate is not sufficient in itself to support a different accounting policy being applied.

5.13.50 *Common control transactions in the consolidated financial statements of the acquirer*

5.13.50.10 In the following group structure, if Company IP2 were to transfer its investment in Company S4 to Company S3, then S3 would be the acquirer for the purpose of applying the guidance that follows.

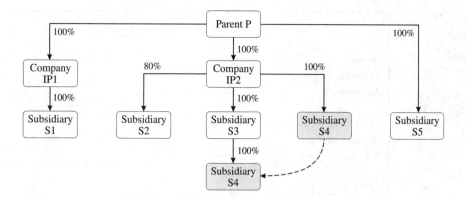

5.13.50.20 In our view, the acquirer in a common control transaction should choose an accounting policy in respect of its consolidated financial statements, to be applied consistently to all similar common control transactions (see 5.13.40), to use:

- *book value (carry-over basis) accounting* on the basis that the investment simply has been moved from one part of the group to another; or
- *IFRS 3 accounting* on the basis that the acquirer is a separate entity in its own right, and should not be confused with the economic group as a whole.

5.13.50.30 In addition, the accounting policy choice in 5.13.50.20 applies also in the acquirer's separate financial statements when it acquires assets and liabilities constituting a business under IFRS 3 (from an entity under common control) rather than acquiring shares in that business.

5.13.60 *Book value accounting*

5.13.60.10 In our view, in applying book value accounting, the acquirer should choose an accounting policy, to be applied consistently, in recognising the assets acquired and liabilities assumed using the book values in the financial statements of:

- the transferor (IP2 in 5.13.50.10);
- the entity transferred (S4 in 5.13.50.10);
- the ultimate parent (P in 5.13.50.10); or
- any intermediate parent (IP2 in 5.13.50.10).

5.13.60.20 Continuing the example in 5.13.50.10, assume that S3 pays 2,000 to IP2 to acquire all of the shares in S4 on 1 July 2010. Based on the book values in the consolidated financial statements of IP2, the transferor (see 5.13.60.10), the following illustrates the consolidated position of S3 and S4 at the transaction date.

Financial information at 1 July 2010, the date on which the transaction occurs:

	S3	S4[1]
Assets	11,000	9,000
Liabilities	(5,000)	(6,000)
Net assets	6,000	3,000
Share capital	1,500	0[2]
Retained earnings	4,500	1,800[3]
Total equity	6,000	1,800[4]

Notes

(1) As represented in the consolidated financial statements of IP2, i.e. including the effects of IP2's acquisition accounting.
(2) Eliminated on consolidation into IP2.
(3) Represents post-acquisition earnings for IP2.
(4) The difference (1,200) between the net assets of 3,000 and total equity of 1,800 is the capital and pre-acquisition earnings of S4 eliminated on consolidation by IP2 plus fair value adjustments made by IP2.

Consolidated financial position of S3 at 1 July 2010 after accounting for the acquisition of S4:

	S3
Assets	18,000[5]
Liabilities	(11,000)
Net assets	7,000
Share capital	1,500
Other equity	(800)[6]
Retained earnings	6,300
Equity	7,000

Notes

(5) Adjusted for the amount paid by S3 of 2,000.
(6) Represents the IP2 pre-acquisition position and fair value adjustments of 1,200 (see note 4 above) less the amount paid of 2,000.

5.13.60.30 In our view, in its consolidated financial statements the acquirer is permitted, but not required, to restate its comparatives and adjust its current year prior to the date of the transaction as if the combination had occurred prior to the start of the earliest period presented. However, this restatement should not, in our view, extend to periods during which the entities were not under common control.

5.13.60.40 For example, Company D acquired Company E in a common control transaction on 1 June 2010; D's annual reporting date is 31 December. Both D and E have been owned by a single shareholder, X, since their incorporation many years ago. On that basis we believe that D may elect to restate its 2009 consolidated financial statements as if the acquisition had occurred prior to 1 January 2009. Additionally, the results of E will be included in D's financial statements for the period from 1 January to 1 June 2010.

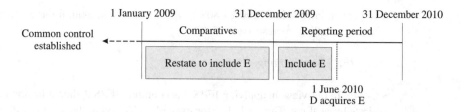

5.13.60.50 In another example, Company G acquired Company H in a common control transaction on 1 June 2010; G's annual reporting date is 31 December. Both G and H are owned by a single shareholder, X; X acquired its investment in G in 2003, and its investment in H on 1 July 2009. On that basis we believe that G may elect to restate its 2009 consolidated financial statements as if the acquisition had occurred on 1 July 2009, but not earlier. Additionally, the results of H will be included in G's financial statements for the period from 1 January to 1 June 2010.

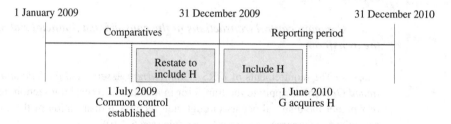

5.13.60.60 In our view, to the extent that the common control transaction involves transactions with non-controlling interests, the changes in non-controlling interests should be accounted for as acquisitions and/or disposals of non-controlling interests on the date that the changes occur (see 2.5.380).

5.13.60.70 For example, using the group structure below, 100 percent of the shares in Company S2 are transferred to Company S4 and the previous non-controlling shareholders in S2 obtain shares in S4; as a result, Company IP2's interest in S4 falls to 90 percent.

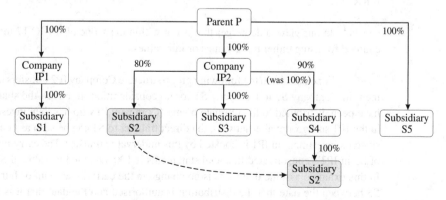

5.13.60.80 Therefore, IP2 has sold a 10 percent interest in S4 (100% - 90%), which IP2 should account for as a disposal without the loss of control (see 2.5.380); and has acquired a 10 percent interest in S2 (90% - 80%), which it should account for as an acquisition of non-controlling interests (see 2.5.380).

5.13.70 *IFRS 3 accounting*

5.13.70.10 In our view, in applying IFRS 3 accounting, IFRS 3 should be applied in its *entirety* by analogy. This includes, for example, identifying the acquirer, identifying and measuring the consideration transferred, identifying and measuring the identifiable assets and liabilities and recognising goodwill.

5.13.70.20 However, to the extent that the acquisition accounting gives rise to an apparent gain on a bargain purchase, in our view such amount should be recognised in equity as a capital contribution from the shareholders of the acquirer. This is on the basis that the profit relates to a transaction with shareholders acting in their capacity as shareholders.

5.13.80 *Common control transactions in the consolidated financial statements of the transferor*

5.13.80.10 The requirements of IFRS 5 *Non-current Assets Held for Sale and Discontinued Operations* apply to the transferor in a common control transaction, regardless of whether the disposal occurs through non-reciprocal distribution of the shares in a subsidiary (a demerger or spin-off) or a sale (see 5.4.10).

5.13.90 *Demergers*

IAS 27.BC57, 5.13.90.10 While IAS 27 deals with the loss of control in general, it does not deal with
IFRIC 17.5 the loss of control through a demerger. Instead, in general demergers are dealt with in IFRIC 17. However, the scope of IFRIC 17 excludes distributions in which the asset distributed ultimately is controlled by the same party or parties before and after the distribution; therefore common control transactions are excluded from the scope of IFRIC 17.

5.13.90.20 In our view, a demerger that is not within the scope of IFRIC 17 may be accounted for using either book values or fair values.

5.13.90.30 For example, in the following group structure Company IP2 transfers its investment in Company S3 to Company S1 for no consideration. In effect, the shares in S3 have been distributed to the ultimate owner (Company P) who has then invested them in the IP1 sub-group; alternatively, the direct transfer to S1 can be seen as benefiting P since its investment in IP1 is boosted by this undervalue transfer. The carrying amount of S3 in IP2's consolidated financial statements is 100, and the fair value of S3 is 130. In this example assume that there is no change in the carrying amount or fair value of S3 between the date that the distribution is authorised and the date that it is effected; see 3.11.452.60 for the implications of a distribution that is authorised and effected in different reporting periods.

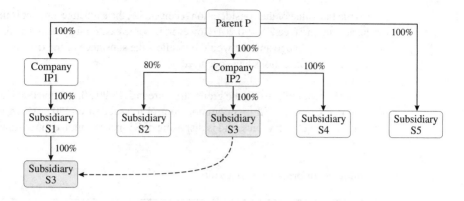

5.13.90.40 If IP2 elects to account for the demerger using fair values, then it will record the following entries, which are consistent with the accounting under IFRIC 17 (see 3.11.452):

	Debit	Credit
Equity	130	
Liability for distribution		130
To recognise liability at fair value of S3		
Liability for distribution	130	
Net assets of S3		100
Profit or loss		30
To derecognise liability and net assets of S3		

5.13.90.50 If IP2 elects to account for the demerger using book values, then it will record the following entries with no impact on profit or loss:

	Debit	Credit
Equity	100	
Liability for distribution		100
To recognise liability at book value of S3		
Liability for distribution	100	
Net assets of S3		100
To derecognise liability and net assets of S3		

5.13.100 *Other disposals*

5.13.100.10 Other disposals that result in the loss of control fall within the scope of IAS 27. In applying IAS 27, on the face of it the gain or loss on disposal is calculated by reference to the fair value of the consideration received, i.e. the exchange amount is the basis for the accounting (see 2.5.490.20). However, in some cases it may be determined that the use of the exchange amount would not reflect the substance of the transaction, and that in fact two transactions have occurred.

5.13.100.20 For example, using the group structure in 5.13.90.30, assume that Company IP2 acquired Company S3 in a common control transaction in 2009, which was accounted for using book values, and is disposing of S3 in a common control transaction in 2010.

The following information is relevant:

	At acquisition date	At disposal date
Book value of S3	100	120
Fair value of S3	130	160
Consideration paid (received)	130	(160)

5.13.100.30 Because IP2 accounted for the acquisition of S3 using book values (see 5.13.60), the gain recognised on disposal will be 40 (160 consideration received - 120 book value at date of disposal). However, if IFRS 3 had been applied to the acquisition (see 5.13.70), then the gain recognised on disposal would have been 10 (160 consideration received - (130 consideration paid + (120 - 100 increase in book values since acquisition date))).

5.13.100.40 Therefore, depending on the facts and circumstances, an entity should consider whether, in substance, a contribution or distribution has been made in addition to the disposal of the subsidiary. Continuing the example in 5.13.100.20 and 30, IP2 concludes that two transactions have in effect occurred:

- a disposal of S3 for consideration equal to the carrying amount of S3, i.e. 120, which results in no gain or loss on disposal; and
- a capital contribution of 40 from P for the difference between the actual consideration received of 160 and the carrying amount of S3 of 120.

5.13.110 *Common control transactions in separate financial statements*

5.13.110.10 When a common control transaction is effected through the acquisition of assets and liabilities constituting a business under IFRS 3 (from an entity under common control) rather than by acquiring shares in that business, the acquirer accounts for the transaction in its separate financial statements in accordance with the guidance in 5.13.50 in respect of consolidated financial statements.

IAS 27.38(a) 5.13.110.20 The guidance that follows applies when an entity accounts for investments in subsidiaries under a cost policy in its separate financial statements.

5.13.110.30 In our view, each of the acquirer and the transferor in a common control transaction should choose an accounting policy in respect of their separate financial statements, to be applied consistently to all similar common control transactions (see 5.13.40), to use:

- *book value accounting* on the basis that the entities are part of a larger economic group, and that the figures from that larger group are the relevant ones. In applying book value accounting, no entries are recognised in profit or loss; instead, the result of the transaction is recognised in equity as arising from a transaction with shareholders. In our view, the relevant book value is the carrying amount of the investee in the separate financial statements of the transferor;
- *fair value accounting* on the basis that the parties are separate entities in their own right and that the accounting for the transaction should be as if it had been carried out on an arm's length basis; or
- *exchange amount accounting* on the basis that the parties are separate entities in their own right and that the accounting should reflect the actual terms of the transaction.

5.13.110.40 In the following paragraphs we consider the application of these views to sideways transfers (see 5.13.120), downstream transfers (see 5.13.130) and upstream transfers (see 5.13.140).

5.13.120 Sideways transfers

5.13.120.10 In a "sideways transfer", a subsidiary is transferred to a fellow subsidiary such that the transferor loses control of the subsidiary. In the following transaction, Company S1 pays 80 to Company IP2 to acquire all of the shares in Company S3. The book value of IP2's investment in S3 is 100, and the fair value of S3 is 130.

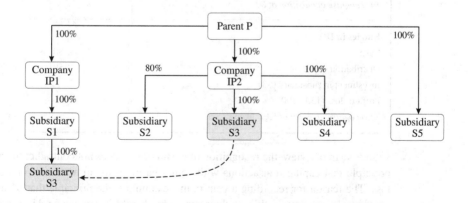

5.13.120.20 In applying *book value accounting*, the acquirer (S1) and the transferor (IP2) record the following entries, recognising the difference between the book value of the transferee (S3) and the consideration paid/received as an equity transaction with the shareholder (P), i.e. as if S3 had been purchased for its book value of 100 and the difference of 20 paid back as a distribution made/contribution received:

	Debit	Credit
Entries in S1		
Investment in subsidiary (S3)	100	
Cash		80
Contribution (equity)		20
To recognise acquisition of S3		
Entries in IP2		
Cash	80	
Distribution (equity)	20	
Investment in subsidiary (S3)		100
To recognise disposal of S3		

5.13.120.30 In applying *fair value accounting*, the acquirer (S1) and the transferor (IP2) record the following entries, recognising the difference between the fair value of the transferee (S3) and the consideration paid/received as an equity transaction with the shareholder (P), i.e. as if S3 had been purchased for its fair value of 130 and the difference of 50 paid back as a distribution made/contribution received:

	Debit	Credit
Entries in S1		
Investment in subsidiary (S3)	130	
Contribution (equity)		50
Cash		80
To recognise acquisition of S3		
Entries in IP2		
Cash	80	
Distribution (equity)	50	
Investment in subsidiary (S3)		100
Profit or loss (130 - 100)		30
To recognise disposal of S3		

5.13.120.40 In our view, the recognition of a gain or loss does not contradict the general principle that capital transactions with equity participants do not result in a gain or loss. The reason for recording a gain in this example is the principle that S1 and IP2 are viewed as separate entities in their own right; therefore, a gain would be recognised as if the transaction had been entered into with a third party.

5.13.120.50 In applying *exchange amount accounting*, the acquirer (S1) and the transferor (IP2) record the following entries, in the same way as if the transaction had been with a third party for the actual price paid:

	Debit	Credit
Entries in S1		
Investment in subsidiary (S3)	80	
Cash		80
To recognise acquisition of S3		
Entries in IP2		
Cash	80	
Profit or loss	20	
Investment in subsidiary (S3)		100
To recognise disposal of S3		

5.13.130 *Downstream transfers*

5.13.130.10 In a "downstream transfer", a direct subsidiary of the transferor becomes an indirect subsidiary. In the following transaction, Company S3 acquires all of the shares in Company S4 from Company IP2. The book value of IP2's investment in S4 is 100, and the fair value of S4 is 130.

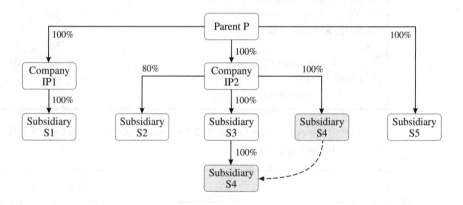

5.13.130.20 In a downstream transfer, the accounting in the acquirer's (S3's) separate financial statements is unchanged from the accounting in a sideways transfer (see 5.13.120.20 and 50).

5.13.130.30 However, the accounting in the transferor's (IP2's) separate financial statements is affected because the transferor does not lose its investment in the transferee (S4). Instead, the transferee (S4) is now an indirect rather than a direct subsidiary of the transferor (IP2). In our view, there is no loss on such a transaction as the transferor does not lose any value. Accordingly, we believe that the transaction is accounted for as follows:

- A surplus or deficit is computed in the same way as for a sideways transfer (see 5.13.120).

- The actual price received and the benchmark are compared with any surplus (of the former) being recognised as a dividend received and any deficit being recorded as an additional investment in the acquirer (S3).

5.13.130.40 We believe that IP2 would record the following entries in the example in 5.13.130.10 if the consideration paid by S3 was 80:

	Debit	Credit
Book value accounting		
Cash	80	
Investment in subsidiary (S3)	20	
Investment in subsidiary (S4)		100
To recognise disposal of S4		
Fair value accounting		
Cash	80	
Investment in subsidiary (S3)	50	
Investment in subsidiary (S4)		100
Profit or loss (130 - 100)		30
To recognise disposal of S4		
Exchange amount accounting		
Cash	80	
Investment in subsidiary (S3)	20	
Investment in subsidiary (S4)		100
To recognise disposal of S4		

5.13.130.50 If the consideration was 120 instead of 80, then we believe that IP2 would record the following entries:

	Debit	Credit
Book value accounting		
Cash	120	
Investment in subsidiary (S4)		100
Dividend received (profit or loss)		20
To recognise disposal of S4		
Fair value accounting		
Cash	120	
Investment in subsidiary (S3)	10	
Investment in subsidiary (S4)		100
Profit or loss (130 - 100)		30
To recognise disposal of S4		

	Debit	Credit
Exchange amount accounting		
Cash	120	
Investment in subsidiary (S4)		100
Dividend received (profit or loss)		20
To recognise disposal of S4		

5.13.140 *Upstream transfers*

5.13.140.10 In an "upstream transfer", an indirect subsidiary becomes a direct subsidiary. In the following transaction, Company P pays 80 to Company IP1 to acquire all of the shares in Company S1. The book value of IP1's investment in S1 is 100, and the fair value of S1 is 130.

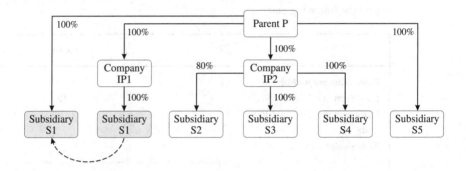

5.13.140.20 In an upstream transfer, the accounting in the transferor's (IP1's) separate financial statements is unchanged from the accounting in a sideways transfer (see 5.13.120.20 and 50).

5.13.140.30 However, the accounting in the acquirer's (P's) separate financial statements is affected because P already holds an investment in the transferee (S1), although indirect. In our view, the transaction is accounted for as if it had taken place at an amount set as the benchmark chosen (i.e. at book value, fair value or exchange amount), with any excess consideration being recognised as an additional investment and any deficit being recorded as a dividend received.

5.13.140.40 Accordingly, we believe that P would record the following entries in the example in 5.13.140.10 if it paid consideration of 80 to IP1:

	Debit	Credit
Book value accounting		
Investment in subsidiary (S1)	100	
Dividend received (profit or loss)		20
Cash		80
To recognise acquisition of S1		

	Debit	Credit
Fair value accounting		
Investment in subsidiary (S1)	130	
Dividend received (profit or loss)		50
Cash		80
To recognise acquisition of S1		
Exchange amount accounting		
Investment in subsidiary (S1)	80	
Cash		80
To recognise acquisition of S1		

5.13.140.50 If the consideration was 120 instead of 80, then we believe that P would record the following entries:

	Debit	Credit
Book value accounting		
Investment in subsidiary (S1)	100	
Investment in subsidiary (IP1)	20	
Cash		120
To recognise acquisition of S1		
Fair value accounting		
Investment in subsidiary (S1)	130	
Dividend received (profit or loss)		10
Cash		120
To recognise acquisition of S1		
Exchange amount accounting		
Investment in subsidiary (S1)	120	
Cash		120
To recognise acquisition of S1		

5.13.140.60 Additionally, following the transaction the acquirer (P) should consider whether there are any indications that the carrying amount of its investment in the transferor (IP1) may not be recoverable (see 3.10.120). However, in our view in general any resulting impairment "loss" should first reduce to zero any entry for a dividend received with the remainder being added to the carrying amount of the transferring entity (S1) because it is in effect a contribution to that investment. Overall the transaction has moved investments and cash around the acquirer's group and there has been no loss of value; accordingly, in general we believe that it would be inappropriate to recognise a loss in profit or loss.

5.13.150 *Establishment of a new parent*

IAS 27.38B,   5.13.150.10 IAS 27 specifies the accounting in the *separate* financial statements of a newly
38C   formed entity that becomes the new parent entity of another entity in a group when:

- the new parent entity issues equity instruments as consideration in the reorganisation;
- there is no change in the group's assets or liabilities as a result of the reorganisation; and
- there is no change in the interest of the shareholder, either absolute or relative, as a result of the reorganisation.

IAS 27.38   5.13.150.20 In such cases, if the new parent entity elects to measure the investment in the subsidiary at cost, then cost is determined as its share of total equity shown in the separate financial statements of the subsidiary at the date of the reorganisation. This represents a specific approach to determining cost and effectively rules out the application of fair value accounting in these circumstances.

5.13.160 Common control transactions in the financial statements of a common controller that is not a party to the transaction

5.13.160.10 If the common control transaction does not involve non-controlling interests, then in most cases neither the consolidated nor the separate financial statements of a common controller that is not a party to the transaction are affected. Using the group structure below, if Company IP2 were to transfer its investment in Company S4 to Company S3, then neither the consolidated nor the separate financial statements of P would be affected by the transaction.

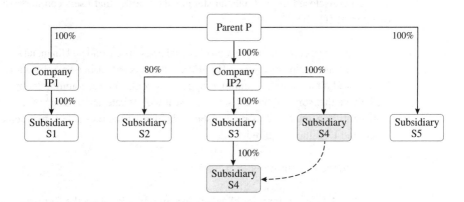

5.13.160.20 If the common control transaction involves non-controlling interests and the common controller's interest in the subsidiary is diluted, then the requirements of IAS 27 in respect of transactions with non-controlling interests apply (see 2.5.380).

5.13.160.30 For example, using the group structure below, 100 percent of the shares in Company S2 are transferred to Company S4 and the previous non-controlling shareholders in S2 obtain shares in IP2; as a result, Company P's interest in IP2 falls to 98 percent. Therefore, P accounts for the dilution in IP2 as a transaction with non-controlling interests in its consolidated financial statements.

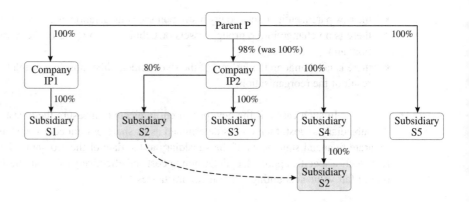

5.13.170 *Disclosure*

IAS 1.10(e) 5.13.170.10 In our view, an entity should disclose its accounting policy for common control transactions.

IAS 1.15 5.13.170.20 An entity provides additional disclosures in the financial statements when necessary for users to understand the effect of specific transactions. In our view, in order to meet this requirement, sufficient information about common control transactions should be disclosed in the financial statements in order that users can understand the effect thereof.

IFRS 3.59-63 5.13.170.30 In respect of the acquisition of subsidiaries in consolidated financial statements, in our view the disclosures required by IFRS 3 in respect of business combinations should be followed if fair value accounting is applied. If book value accounting is applied, then we believe that some of these disclosures still will be relevant to users of the financial statements, e.g. the amounts recognised at the date of the transaction for each class of assets and liabilities acquired.

5.13.180 **Newco formations**

5.13.180.10 A "Newco formation" is a transaction that involves the formation of a new entity for the purpose of effecting a business combination or a transaction that purports to be a business combination. Generally there is no guidance in IFRSs on the accounting for such transactions in the financial statements of the newly formed entity (Newco); however, see 5.13.150 in relation to the *separate* financial statements of a new parent established in a group structure. The discussion that follows relates to consolidated financial statements.

5.13.180.20 In our view, the primary step in analysing how a Newco formation should be accounted for is establishing whether IFRS 3 applies by identifying the party on whose behalf the Newco has been formed, i.e. the instigator of the transaction(s). This analysis involves understanding the economic drivers and rationale behind the transaction(s), which will vary from case to case. Common drivers include tax considerations or a restructuring of business activities prior to a listing. In effect, as the accounting outlined in 5.13.190 – 200 illustrates, the driving factor in the analysis of a Newco formation is establishing whether a business combination has occurred (see 2.6).

5.13.180.30 Newco formations generally fall into two categories. They are either used in a restructuring amongst entities under common control, or to effect a business combination involving a third party.

5.13.180.40 For example, Company G is incorporated in Singapore and wishes to move its operations to Australia. G's shares are held widely and there is no controlling shareholder or group of shareholders. G incorporates a Newco in Australia; Newco issues one share for every share held in G, with the same rights and interests. Ownership of G's net assets is transferred to Newco. In this example it is clear that Newco was formed solely for the benefit of G and that no other parties are involved. This is an example of a Newco formation used in a restructuring.

5.13.180.50 In another example, Company X is a private equity fund seeking to acquire retail operations that meet specified investment criteria. X identifies the retail operations of Company R as a suitable target, and forms a Newco to effect the acquisition. The retail operations of R are transferred to Newco in return for cash. In this example Newco was formed for the benefit of X in effecting a business combination by a third party (X).

5.13.180.60 Not all situations are as clear as the examples in 5.3.180.40 and 50, and judgement may be required in determining the party for whom Newco acts.

5.13.190 *Newco formations to effect a business combination involving a third party*

5.13.190.10 The first issue in any Newco formation is establishing whether IFRS 3 applies.

5.13.190.20 For example, Company P forms a Newco, which then acquires Company S from a third party in exchange for cash.

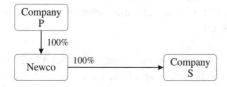

5.13.190.30 In this example, Newco is identified as the acquirer because Newco was used by P to acquire a business from a third party. Therefore, Newco will apply acquisition accounting as the acquirer.

5.13.190.40 In a more complex example, Newco is formed by a venture capital company (VCO), which transfers cash to Newco in exchange for a 52 percent equity interest in Newco. Company Q transfers Subsidiary S1 to Newco in exchange for a 25 percent interest in Newco, and Company R transfers Subsidiary S2 to Newco in exchange for a 23 percent interest in Newco. Through its 52 percent equity interest, VCO has the ability to appoint a voting majority of the board of directors of Newco. There are no other factors that indicate which of the combining entities is the acquirer (see 2.5.20).

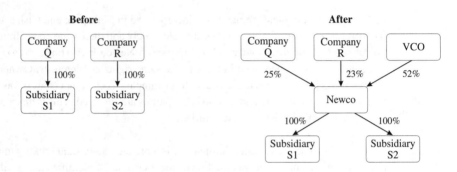

5.13.190.50 In this example VCO is the acquirer in a business combination in which it has acquired control of S1 and S2 through Newco.

5.13.190.60 At the Newco level, Newco is identified as the acquirer since it is the vehicle used by VCO to effect the acquisition; the number of shares in Newco issued to VCO exceeds the number of shares issued to the former owners of S1 and S2. Accordingly, the assets and liabilities of both S1 and S2 will be subject to acquisition accounting.

5.13.190.70 In their consolidated financial statements, Q and R will account for the loss of control in S1 and S2, respectively, with a gain or loss being recognised in profit or loss (see 2.5.490); and will subsequently account for S1 and S2 as associates (assuming that significant influence exists (see 3.5.30)).

5.13.190.80 If in this example Q, R and VCO had received equal shareholdings in Newco, then further analysis of the facts and circumstances would be required in order to identify the acquirer, or to determine whether Newco is in fact a jointly controlled entity (see 3.5.90).

5.13.190.90 Although in the examples in 5.3.190.20 – 80 Newco is identified as the acquirer for the purpose of its own consolidated financial statements, this may not always be the case. Modifying the example in 5.13.190.40 to remove VCO, Company Q contributes wholly-owned subsidiary S1, and Company R contributes wholly-owned subsidiary S2, to Newco. In exchange, Q receives a 52 percent equity interest in Newco and as a result has the ability to appoint a voting majority of the board of directors of Newco. R receives the remaining 48 percent equity interest in Newco. There are no other factors that indicate which of the combining entities is the acquirer (see 2.5.20).

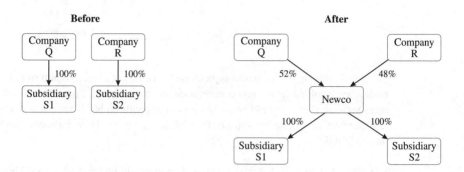

5.13.190.100 At the Newco level, S1 is identified as the acquirer because S1's parent (Q) received a 52 percent equity interest in Newco and there are no other factors that indicate which of the combining entities is the acquirer. Because S1 is the acquirer, its assets and liabilities will be recognised on a carry-over basis, i.e. at their pre-combination carrying amounts, and the assets and liabilities of S2 will be subject to acquisition accounting.

5.13.190.110 In this example Q, through its vehicle Newco, is the acquirer from the perspective of Q's consolidated position because it has effectively acquired control of S2 (by acquiring a 52 percent equity interest in Newco) in exchange for a non-controlling interest in S1 (through the 48 percent non-controlling interest in Newco acquired by R). In Q's consolidated financial statements, it continues to recognise the assets and liabilities of S1 at their pre-combination carrying amounts, and the assets and liabilities of S2 will be subject to acquisition accounting.

5.13.190.120 In R's consolidated financial statements, it has lost control of its former subsidiary, S2, and will recognise a gain or loss in profit or loss (see 2.5.490). R also will account for its investment in the Newco group as an associate (assuming that significant influence exists (see 3.5.30)).

5.13.200 *Newco formations used in a restructuring*

5.13.200.10 When a Newco is established by a parent to effect a restructuring and no independent parties are involved, in our experience usually it is appropriate to conclude that no business combination has occurred.

5.13.200.20 For example, Parent P forms a Newco, which then acquires Company X, an existing operating subsidiary of P, in exchange for shares of Newco. X meets the definition of a business (see 2.6.20).

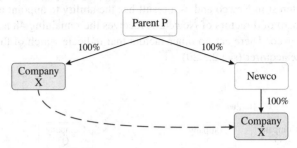

5.13.200.30 Although X is a business, because Newco is not a business and no independent parties are involved, a business combination has not occurred. This is because if IFRS 3 were applied, then X would be identified as the acquirer, but Newco is not a business and therefore cannot be the acquiree (see 2.6.20); accordingly, no business combination has occurred.

5.13.200.40 We believe that the same conclusion would be reached even if Newco borrowed funds from a third party, for example from a bank, and subsequently paid cash to acquire X. We do not believe that financing from a third party changes the economics of the transaction as no independent party has acquired X. In our view, Newco was formed simply for the purpose of a restructuring amongst entities under common control and therefore there is no business combination involving a third party and therefore IFRS 3 is not applicable.

5.13.200.50 Accordingly, we believe that Newco should use book value accounting in its consolidated financial statements on the basis that there has been no business combination and in substance nothing has occurred.

5.13.200.60 In a more complex example, Parent P forms a Newco, which then acquires Company X in exchange for shares of Newco. X is an existing subsidiary of P and comprises a group of three operating companies (A, B and C). The following diagram illustrates the transaction.

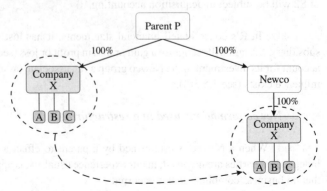

5.13.200.70 Similarly to the example in 5.13.200.20, in our view Newco could account for the restructuring using book value accounting in its consolidated financial statements on the basis that there has been no business combination and in substance nothing has occurred.

5.13.200.80 However, an issue arises as to whether this is the only accounting that Newco could apply in its consolidated financial statements, i.e. is it possible to conclude that a business combination has occurred and therefore that acquisition accounting should be applied to part of the X group? In this example, in our view the entire X group would be identified as the acquirer if IFRS 3 were applied. However, because Newco is not a business, it cannot be the acquiree and therefore no business combination has occurred. Accordingly, we believe that acquisition accounting should not be applied.

5.13.200.90 The conclusion in 5.13.200.80 that the entire X group would be identified as the acquirer is based on the analysis that would be made under IFRS 3 if two independent groups of entities came together in a business combination. In that case one of the groups would be identified as the acquirer; a single entity within one of the groups would not be identified as the acquirer with acquisition accounting applied to the rest of that group plus the entire other group.

5.13.200.100 The conclusion in 5.13.200.80 would be the same if the transaction was structured differently such that the X group of companies was transferred under the control of Newco in consecutive stages rather than as a single transfer. In that case we believe that the guidance on the linkage of transactions contained in IAS 27 (see 2.5.500) is relevant.

5.13.200.110 In referring to book values in 5.13.200.50 and 70, an issue arises as to whose book values should be used: those of the transferring entity (X) or those of the parent. The appropriate book values to use will depend on the facts and circumstances of each case. However, judgement is required to ensure that the resulting outcome is an appropriate presentation of the financial statements of the transferring entity/group of entities.

5.13.210 Legal mergers and amalgamations following a Newco formation

5.13.210.10 For purposes of the discussion that follows, a merger is a transaction that involves the combination of two or more entities in which one of the legal entities survives and the other ceases to exist, or in which both existing entities cease to exist and a new legal entity comes into existence.

5.13.210.20 A merger can occur for a number of reasons, including achieving a tax benefit or to facilitate a listing.

5.13.210.30 For example, Parent P forms a Newco and acquires Company S from a third party in exchange for cash. S is a holding company and the only asset that it holds is a

100 percent investment in operating Company X. Shortly after the acquisition, Newco and S merge. The following diagram illustrates the structure of the transaction.

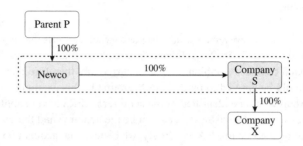

5.13.210.40 A merger can occur in numerous ways. For example, in the diagram in 5.13.210.30 S could merge into Newco, which commonly is referred to as an upstream merger; in this case S legally disappears and the legal entity that continues to exist is Newco. Alternatively, Newco could merge into S, which commonly is referred to as a downstream merger; in this case Newco legally disappears and the legal entity that continues to exist is S.

5.13.210.50 In some jurisdictions the merger between Newco and S may result in a new entity, different from both Newco and S, legally surviving after the merger; sometimes this is referred to as an amalgamation. Judgement is required in assessing whether the form of the merger, which can vary from jurisdiction to jurisdiction, should result in a different accounting outcome.

5.13.210.60 Regardless of the nature of the merger, either upstream, downstream or as a new surviving entity, the result economically is the same as the merged entity will have identical net assets.

5.13.220 *Consolidated financial statements*

5.13.220.10 The issue that arises in a merger is determining which entity is the continuing entity for accounting purposes. Continuing the example in 5.13.210.30, should the consolidated financial statements of the newly merged entity represent a continuation of the consolidated financial statements of S, or of the consolidated financial statements of Newco?

5.13.220.20 In our view, the legal form of the transaction is less important for the consolidated financial statements, because the focus in consolidated financial statements is the economic entity rather than the legal entity. Therefore, based on the example in 5.13.210.30, in our view in respect of its consolidated financial statements the merged entity can do either of the following:

• Use Newco consolidated as the consolidated financial statements of the newly merged entity on the basis that Newco was the acquirer in the business combination and therefore the newly merged entity should be a continuation of Newco consolidated. This is our preferred approach.

- Use S consolidated as the consolidated financial statements of the newly merged entity on the basis that S continues to reflect the operations of the merged entity; from S's point of view there has simply been a change in shareholding.

5.13.230 *Separate financial statements*

5.13.230.10 Unlike in the consolidated financial statements, in our view the legal form of a merger is more important in the context of separate financial statements as these have a different purpose, being the financial statements of a legal entity.

5.13.230.20 Legal form can have a range of consequences. For example, in certain jurisdictions the form of the merger (upstream, downstream or a new surviving entity) can result in different tax consequences, which represent different economic outcomes. In some jurisdictions, legal requirements mean that only one form of merger is available. Therefore, in our view the legal form of the transaction should guide the accounting in the separate financial statements.

5.13.230.30 Continuing the example in 5.13.210.30, if the merger of Newco and S takes the legal form of an upstream merger, then because the legal entity that continues to exist is Newco, in our view it is appropriate for the merged entity's statement of financial position to reflect the carrying amounts of the assets on Newco's statement of financial position.

5.13.230.40 However, if the merger of Newco and S takes the legal form of a downstream merger, then because the legal entity that continues to exist is S, in our view it is appropriate for the merged entity's statement of financial position to reflect the carrying amounts of the assets on S's statement of financial position.

5.13.230.50 If the merger of Newco and S takes the legal form of a new surviving entity (an amalgamation), then based on the example in 5.13.210.30, in our view in respect of its separate financial statements the merged entity can do either of the following:

- Use Newco as the separate financial statements of the newly merged entity on the basis that Newco was the acquirer in the business combination and therefore the newly merged entity should be a continuation of Newco. This is our preferred approach.
- Use S as the separate financial statements of the newly merged entity on the basis that S continues to reflect the operations of the merged entity; from S's point of view there has simply been a change in shareholding.

5.13.240 **Future developments**

5.13.240.10 The IASB's project on common control is expected to examine the definition of common control and the methods of accounting for business combinations amongst entities under common control. This project is intended to provide guidance in respect of the consolidated and separate financial statement of the acquiring entity. The project will also consider the accounting for demergers. Work on this project has been suspended while the IASB completes its work on other projects.

6.1 First-time adoption of IFRSs
(IFRS 1)

Chapter 6

6. First-time adoption of IFRSs

6.1 First-time adoption of IFRSs
(IFRS 1)

Overview of currently effective requirements

- IFRSs include a specific standard that sets out all transitional requirements and exemptions available on the first-time adoption of IFRSs.

- An opening statement of financial position is prepared at the date of transition, which is the starting point for accounting in accordance with IFRSs.

- The date of transition is the beginning of the earliest comparative period presented on the basis of IFRSs.

- Accounting policies are chosen from IFRSs in effect at the first annual reporting date.

- Generally those accounting policies are applied retrospectively in preparing the opening statement of financial position and in all periods presented in the first IFRS financial statements.

- A number of exemptions are available from the general requirement for retrospective application of IFRS accounting policies.

- Retrospective application of changes in accounting policy is prohibited in some cases, generally when doing so would require hindsight.

- At least one year of comparative financial statements are presented on the basis of IFRSs, including the opening statement of financial position.

- Detailed disclosures on the first-time adoption of IFRSs include reconciliations of equity and profit or loss from previous GAAP to IFRSs.

- The transitional requirements and exemptions on first-time adoption of IFRSs are applicable to both annual and interim financial statements.

Currently effective requirements

This publication reflects IFRSs in issue at 1 August 2010. The currently effective requirements cover annual periods beginning on 1 January 2010. The requirements related to
this topic are derived mainly from IFRS 1 *First-time Adoption of International Financial
Reporting Standards.*

KPMG's publication *IFRS Handbook: First-time adoption of IFRS* provides a comprehensive analysis of IFRS 1 and addresses practical application issues that a first-time
adopter could expect to encounter when transitioning to IFRSs. In addition to including
additional clarification of the requirements of IFRS 1 and of our interpretative guidance, the Handbook includes extensive illustrative examples to elaborate or clarify the
practical application of IFRS 1, and as such is more in-depth than this chapter.

Forthcoming requirements and future developments

When a currently effective requirement will be changed by a new requirement that is
issued but is not yet effective, it is marked with a # as a **forthcoming requirement** and
the impact of the change is explained in the accompanying boxed text. The forthcoming
requirements related to this topic are derived from:

- *Improvements to IFRSs 2010*. A brief outline of the impact of the *Improvements to
  IFRSs 2010* on this topic is given in 6.1.270, 320, and 1720, and a brief outline of
  the annual improvements process is given in 1.1.85.
- *Limited Exemption from Comparative IFRS 7 Disclosures for First-time Adopters
  – Amendment to IFRS 1*, which is effective for annual periods beginning on or after
  1 July 2010; earlier application is permitted. A brief outline of the impact of this
  amendment to IFRS 1 is given in 6.1.260.
- IFRS 9 *Financial Instruments*, which will supersede IAS 39 *Financial Instruments:
  Recognition and Measurement* on classification and measurement of financial assets
  is effective for annual periods beginning on or after 1 January 2013; earlier application is permitted. Entities that adopt the standard early are required to disclose
  that fact and apply all the consequential amendments to other standards at the same
  time. A brief outline of the impact of the new standard is given in 6.1.235, 280, 740,
  825 and 1660, and a more detailed discussion of the impact is given in 3.6A.490.

When a significant change to the currently effective or forthcoming requirements is
expected, it is marked with a * as an area that may be subject to **future developments**
and a brief outline of the relevant project is given in 6.1.1730.

6.1.10 **General requirements**

6.1.10.10 IFRS 1 contains all of the transitional recognition, measurement, presentation
and disclosure requirements applicable for a first-time adopter preparing its first annual
and interim financial statements in accordance with IFRSs. A first-time adopter does

not apply the transitional requirements of individual standards or interpretations unless required specifically to do so.

IFRS 1.9 6.1.10.20 Entities already applying IFRSs should refer to the transitional requirements of individual standards and interpretations and to the general requirements applicable to changes of accounting policy (see 2.8.10). IFRS 1 does not apply to entities already reporting under IFRSs that comply for the first time with a new standard.

6.1.20 *Key terms*

6.1.20.10 A number of terms have been introduced in the context of the adoption of IFRSs as an entity's reporting framework and are used throughout this chapter.

IFRS 1.A 6.1.20.20 The following terms are applicable on first-time adoption of IFRSs:

- The *date of transition* is the beginning of the earliest period for which an entity presents full comparative information under IFRSs in its first IFRS financial statements.
- An entity's *first IFRS financial statements*, is the first annual financial statements in which the entity adopts IFRSs and in which it makes an explicit and unreserved statement of compliance with IFRSs.
- The *first IFRS reporting period* is the latest reporting period covered by an entity's first IFRS financial statements.
- A *first-time adopter* is an entity that presents its first IFRS financial statements (see 6.1.30).
- The *opening IFRS statement of financial position* is an entity's statement of financial position at the date of transition (see 6.1.130.10).

6.1.20.30 For example, Company X plans to present its first IFRS financial statements for the year ending 31 December 2010, i.e. X will be a first-time adopter in 2010. X will present one year of comparative information. The following diagram illustrates the key dates and periods in relation to X's adoption of IFRSs:

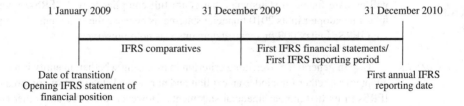

6.1.20.40 In the diagram in 6.1.20.30 the first-time adopter is presenting only one year of comparative information on the basis of IFRSs and therefore has a date of transition of 1 January 2009. IFRSs require that comparative information be disclosed in respect of at least one previous reporting period (see 2.1.30). However, IFRS 1 does not prohibit presenting more than one year of comparative information. In such cases the first-time adopter's date of transition would be at the start of the earliest comparative period presented on the basis of IFRSs.

IFRS 1.A 6.1.20.50 The following terms relate to other aspects of the adoption of IFRSs:

- *Deemed cost* is an amount used as a surrogate for cost or depreciated cost at a given date. Subsequent depreciation or amortisation assumes that the first-time adopter had initially recognised the asset or liability at the given date and that its cost was equal to the deemed cost.
- *Fair value* is the amount for which an asset could be exchanged, or a liability settled, between knowledgeable, willing parties in an arm's length transaction.
- *Previous GAAP* is the basis of accounting that a first-time adopter used immediately before adopting IFRSs (see 6.1.120).

6.1.30 *Statement of compliance with IFRSs*

IFRS 1.2, A 6.1.30.10 A first-time adopter is an entity that presents its first annual financial statements that include an explicit and unreserved statement of compliance with IFRSs. The first-time adoption requirements apply also to interim financial statements prepared in accordance with IFRSs (see 5.9) for part of a period that will be covered by an entity's first IFRS financial statements.

IAS 1.16 6.1.30.20 A first-time adopter does not describe financial statements as complying with IFRSs unless it complies with all of the requirements of IFRSs applicable to the first-time adopter.

6.1.30.30 For example, Company X prepares its financial statements in accordance with previous GAAP. In 2010 X will stop preparing its financial statements in accordance with previous GAAP and instead will prepare them in accordance with IFRSs. In 2010 X will be a first-time adopter if it makes an explicit and unreserved statement of compliance with IFRSs in its 2010 financial statements.

6.1.30.35 In another example, Company S's financial statements for the year ended 31 December 2009 claimed compliance with IFRSs except for IAS 39 (see 3.6). In 2010 S will prepare financial statements that claim full compliance with IFRSs. S will be a first-time adopter in its 2010 financial statements because the statement of compliance with IFRSs in its 2009 financial statements was not unreserved.

IAS 1.3 6.1.30.40 In general the overriding criterion in assessing whether an entity is a first-time adopter is whether it includes an explicit and unreserved statement of compliance with IFRSs in its first annual financial statements. However, there are also other common situations that arise in practice that are interrelated to this overriding criterion, some of which are discussed in 6.1.30.50 –120.

6.1.30.50 Each entity that prepares financial statements, i.e. each reporting entity, can be a first-time adopter. In our view, financial statements that are prepared for a part of the reporting entity do not make the entity as a whole a first-time adopter.

6.1.30.60 For example, Company Y prepares its financial statements in accordance with previous GAAP. In 2010 Y will stop preparing its financial statements in accordance with previous GAAP and instead will prepare them in accordance with IFRSs. However, for the year ended 31 December 2009 Y prepared a set of financial statements in accordance with IFRSs for a single division of the company that it was planning to sell; these financial statements were presented to prospective buyers. In our view, the IFRS financial statements of the division as a separate reporting entity do not mean that Y as a whole has adopted IFRSs for the first time. Instead, in 2010 the reporting entity, that is Y, will be a first-time adopter if it makes an explicit and unreserved statement of compliance with IFRSs in its 2010 financial statements.

IFRS 1.3(a)(i), 6.1.30.70 Even if previous GAAP is very similar to IFRSs, or IFRSs are referred to when
(iv) national GAAP is silent, this is not sufficient to conclude that the entity already is applying IFRSs.

6.1.30.80 For example, Company Z prepares its financial statements in accordance with previous GAAP. In accordance with the requirements of previous GAAP, Z accounts for investment property following IAS 40 *Investment Property* (see 3.4) because previous GAAP has no specific guidance on that topic. However, previous GAAP is not necessarily consistent with IFRSs in other respects. In 2010 Z will stop preparing its financial statements in accordance with previous GAAP and instead will prepare them in accordance with IFRSs. In 2010 Z will be a first-time adopter if it makes an explicit and unreserved statement of compliance with IFRSs in its 2010 financial statements.

IFRS 1.3(a)(v) 6.1.30.90 In some cases previous GAAP may require a reconciliation of key figures in the financial statements, e.g. profit or loss, to what they would have been if prepared in accordance with IFRSs. However, because the entity does not fully comply with all of the requirements of IFRSs, the reconciliation is not sufficient to conclude that the entity already is applying IFRSs.

6.1.30.100 For example, Company P prepares its financial statements in accordance with previous GAAP. Although not required by previous GAAP, P reconciles its profit or loss under previous GAAP to IFRSs in accordance with the requirements of the local stock exchange. In 2010 P will stop preparing its financial statements in accordance with previous GAAP and instead will prepare them in accordance with IFRSs. In 2010 P will be a first-time adopter if it makes and explicit and unreserved statement of compliance with IFRSs in its 2010 financial statements. Its previous reconciliation of profit or loss to IFRSs did not constitute the adoption of IFRSs.

IFRS 1.4(c) 6.1.30.110 An entity is a first-time adopter when, for the first time, its annual financial statements include an explicit and unreserved statement of compliance with IFRSs; it is not relevant whether or not the audit report (if any) is qualified.

6.1.30.120 For example, Company T's financial statements for the year ended 31 December 2009 contained an explicit and unreserved statement of compliance with IFRSs; however, the audit report was qualified because T did not comply with certain requirements of IAS 39. In 2010 T will prepare financial statements that fully comply with IFRSs and it expects to receive an unqualified audit report. T will not be a first-time adopter in its 2010 financial statements because the statement of compliance with IFRSs in its 2009 financial statements was unreserved; the fact that T received a qualified audit report is not relevant to the determination of whether T is a first-time adopter.

6.1.40 Dual compliance and implicit compliance

IFRS 1.A 6.1.40.10 Some jurisdictions use the term "IFRSs" as a starting point for describing their own GAAP. For example, European Union (EU) member states describe their national GAAP as "IFRSs as adopted by the EU" or "EU IFRSs". The IFRSs referred to in IFRS 1 are IFRSs as issued by the IASB.

IFRS 1.4(a) 6.1.40.20 An entity may make an explicit and unreserved statement of compliance with both IFRSs and another GAAP, such as EU IFRSs. Such dual statements of compliance do not impact the assessment of whether an entity is a first-time adopter; the only test is whether the financial statements include an explicit and unreserved statement of compliance with IFRSs. If in a subsequent year the entity drops the reference to its national GAAP while keeping its statement of compliance with IFRSs, then the entity is not a first-time adopter in that year. This is because the most recent previous annual financial statements included an explicit and unreserved statement of compliance with IFRSs.

6.1.50 Reinstating the reference to IFRSs

6.1.50.10 When an entity previously included an explicit and unreserved statement of compliance with both IFRSs and another GAAP, and then subsequently drops the reference to IFRSs from its statement of compliance even though it continues to comply in full with IFRSs, then in our view either of the following approaches is acceptable if the entity subsequently reinstates the statement of compliance with IFRSs:

- *Approach 1*. The entity is a first-time adopter. This is because the definition of a first-time adopter is predicated on an entity stating explicit compliance with IFRSs. The omission of a statement of compliance with IFRSs would result in the entity being a first-time adopter *again* when it subsequently reinstates compliance with IFRSs.
- *Approach 2*. The entity is not a first-time adopter if it is determined that compliance with IFRSs could have been made. The entity would need to assess, and make a determination of, whether it could have asserted dual compliance with both IFRSs and its other GAAP. If it is determined that dual compliance could have been possible, then the entity would not be a first-time adopter when it subsequently reinstates compliance with IFRSs.

6.1.60 Previous omission of a statement of compliance with IFRSs

6.1.60.10 A question also arises as to whether an entity is a first-time adopter when previously the entity only included an explicit and unreserved statement of compliance with an IFRS equivalent, e.g. EU IFRSs, and subsequently includes an explicit and unreserved statement of compliance with IFRSs for the first time. In our view, the two approaches noted in 6.1.50.10 also are available in this situation.

6.1.70 Subsidiary, associate or joint venture adopting IFRSs before or after its parent/ investor

6.1.70.10 IFRSs include specific requirements, some of which are mandatory, when a subsidiary (or associate or joint venture) becomes a first-time adopter later than its parent and when an entity becomes a first-time adopter later than its subsidiary (or associate or joint venture) (see 6.1.1360 and 1440). The question that arises is whether these requirements are applicable also when the relevant group entity has included previously an explicit and unreserved statement of compliance with an IFRS equivalent, but did not include a dual statement of compliance.

6.1.70.20 In our view, the same approaches that are available for an entity in assessing whether it is a first-time adopter when reinstating the reference to IFRSs (see 6.1.50.10) also extends to situations in which entities within a group adopt IFRSs at different dates. See 6.1.1500 for further discussion of this topic.

6.1.80 *First-time adopter more than once by different reporting entities*

IFRS 1.D16, 6.1.80.10 An entity is a first-time adopter in relation to a set of financial statements, e.g.
D17 consolidated, separate or individual, rather than in relation to the entity. Therefore, it is possible for an entity, through its different reporting entities, to be a first-time adopter more than once over a number of years, in respect of each of its separate, and its individual or consolidated financial statements. IFRS 1 includes specific requirements in respect of separate and consolidated financial statements when IFRSs are adopted in each of the statements in different years (see 6.1.1370).

6.1.80.20 In our view, it is possible for an entity to be a first-time adopter in respect of the same set of financial statements more than once over several years. This is because IFRS 1 refers to an explicit and unreserved statement of compliance with IFRSs being included in an entity's *most recent* previous annual financial statements. The statement of compliance may have been omitted in the most recent financial statements by choice or necessity.

6.1.80.30 For example, Company B's financial statements for the year ended 31 December 2008 contained an explicit and unreserved statement of compliance with IFRSs, although the audit report was qualified for non-compliance with IAS 39. B's financial statements for the year ended 31 December 2009 still did not comply with IAS 39, and therefore B decided not to include a statement of compliance with IFRSs in the financial statements. B plans to comply fully with IFRSs in its 2010 financial statements and will include an explicit and unreserved statement of compliance with IFRSs in those statements. Accordingly, B will be a first-time adopter in 2010 because its most recent

1543

previous financial statements did not include an explicit and unreserved statement of compliance with IFRSs.

6.1.80.40 However, in our view IFRS 1 cannot be applied more than once in respect of the same set of financial statements prepared for the same reporting period. In our experience, this issue is most likely to arise in connection with regulatory requirements dealing with the number of years of comparative information required to be included in the financial statements. Since IFRSs themselves only require one year of comparatives plus a statement of financial position at the date of transition, i.e. any additional comparatives are presented on a voluntary basis, we believe that any such issue should be discussed with the relevant regulator.

6.1.80.50 For example, Company C will prepare its first financial statements in accordance with IFRSs for the year ending 31 December 2010; the financial statements will include one year of comparative information, plus a statement of financial position at the date of transition of 1 January 2009. These financial statements will be filed with the securities regulator in Country M.

6.1.80.60 In early 2011 C plans to undertake an initial public offering in Country G. Under Country G's applicable regulatory requirements, C is required to file, in its offering document, its most recent financial statements prepared in accordance with IFRSs, and those financial statements must include two years of comparative information. In order to satisfy Country G's regulatory requirements, C would have to prepare 2010 IFRS financial statements with two years of comparative information, which would mean that C would have a date of transition of 1 January 2008.

6.1.80.70 On the face of it, these two requirements mean that C requires two sets of first IFRS financial statements for the year ending 2010, which would show different results and financial positions because of the different starting points in preparing the financial statements: 1 January 2008 vs 1 January 2009. We believe that this would not be appropriate and the date of transition in respect of C's first IFRS financial statements for the year ending 31 December 2010 should be either 1 January 2008 or 1 January 2009.

6.1.80.80 However, if the 2010 financial statements in 6.1.80.50 already have been filed with the securities regulator, i.e. made publicly available, in Country M, then these are C's first IFRS financial statements. Since C already made its first IFRS financial statements publicly available in Country M, C would not be able to have a second set of *first* IFRS financial statements under Country G's regulatory requirements; the date of transition will be 1 January 2009. However, the financial statements may include additional information to satisfy the requirements in Country G.

6.1.90 *Financial statements for internal use only*

IFRS 1.3(b) 6.1.90.10 Financial statements may be prepared for internal use only, without being distributed to external parties. In such cases the entity, even if the financial statements include an explicit and unreserved statement of compliance with IFRSs, has not adopted IFRSs.

6.1.90.20 For example, Company D prepares financial statements in accordance with previous GAAP. For the year ended 31 December 2009 D prepared an additional set of financial statements in accordance with IFRSs to assist management in assessing the potential impact of adopting IFRSs in the future. The IFRS financial statements were not distributed to D's shareholders or to any other external parties. Although D may have complied with IFRS 1 on a voluntary basis in preparing the IFRS financial statements, it is not a first-time adopter for the purpose of those financial statements because they were not distributed externally. However, to avoid repeating the effort involved in preparing the opening statement of financial position when IFRSs are adopted the following year, i.e. for the year ending 31 December 2010, D can elect to present two years of comparative information in its first IFRS financial statements in order to preserve the date of transition of 1 January 2008 (see 6.1.20.40).

6.1.90.30 In another example, Company E prepares financial statements in accordance with previous GAAP. For the year ended 31 December 2009 E prepared an additional set of financial statements in accordance with IFRSs to assist management in assessing the potential impact of adopting IFRSs in the future. The IFRS financial statements were not distributed to E's shareholders, but they were given to a bank that requested IFRS financial information in assessing a new loan facility for E. Because the IFRS financial statements were distributed to an external party, the bank, E is a first-time adopter for the purpose of those financial statements.

6.1.90.40 If in 2010 E is required to publish IFRS financial statements for statutory reporting purposes, then E would not be a first-time adopter and therefore would not be required to disclose, for example, an explanation of the impact of its transition from previous GAAP to IFRSs (see 6.1.1650). Such disclosures would have been included in E's 2009 IFRS financial statements, which were not distributed to E's shareholders. In such cases E may consider providing additional voluntary disclosure, e.g. similar disclosures as provided in its 2009 IFRS financial statements, to assist the users of its 2010 IFRS statutory financial statements in understanding its transition from previous GAAP to IFRSs.

6.1.100 *Group reporting packages*

IFRS 1.3(c)   6.1.100.10 A group reporting package that is prepared for the first time in accordance with IFRSs for consolidation purposes, but which is not a complete set of financial statements in accordance with IAS 1 *Presentation of Financial Statements* (see 2.1), does not result in the entity being a first-time adopter.

6.1.100.20 Even if the group reporting package were to comprise a complete set of financial statements, if distribution is only to the parent for consolidation purposes, then in our view the entity is not a first-time adopter because the financial statements have not been distributed to a party external to the group (see 6.1.90).

6.1.110 *No previous financial statements*

IFRS 1.3(d)   6.1.110.10 An entity is a first-time adopter when it did not present financial statements for previous periods. In our view, this requirement of IFRS 1 applies only when the entity existed in previous periods, but did not present financial statements; it does not mean that all new entities should apply IFRS 1 when they prepare their first financial statements.

6.1.110.20 However, when a new entity is formed and pre-existing businesses are trans-ferred to the new entity as part of a restructuring that is accounted for on a book value basis, then in our view the new entity can be a first-time adopter in respect of those businesses. This is because book value accounting in this type of transaction assumes that the pre-existing business (entity) is continued.

6.1.120 *Previous GAAP*

6.1.120.10 A first-time adopter could have prepared more than one set of financial state-ments of the same type for the same period, e.g. two sets of consolidated financial statements for the same annual period using different bases of accounting, e.g. US GAAP or Brazilian GAAP. The question that arises is which basis of accounting meets the definition of previous GAAP.

6.1.120.20 In our view, when assessing previous GAAP in these circumstances, it is necessary to consider the following:

- which financial statements are being replaced (see 6.1.120.30); and
- what will be more meaningful to the recipients of the IFRS financial statements (see 6.1.120.40).

6.1.120.30 For example, previously Company T prepared statutory financial statements in accordance with Brazilian GAAP and non-statutory US GAAP financial statements. T is adopting IFRSs in its 2010 statutory financial statements. T's Brazilian and US GAAP financial statements both are publicly available, although the US GAAP financial statements are the more widely distributed set of financial statements. We believe that Brazilian GAAP is previous GAAP for purposes of the first-time adoption of IFRSs if the IFRS financial statements now being prepared are the statutory financial statements. We believe that previous GAAP is that GAAP applied in preparing the same financial statements published immediately preceding the period. We do not believe that IFRS 1 draws any distinction based upon how widely distributed the previous GAAP financial statements were, provided that they were publicly available.

6.1.120.40 In another example, Company G prepares statutory financial statements in accordance with Indian GAAP as well as non-statutory US GAAP financial statements. G is adopting IFRSs in 2010 for non-statutory reporting purposes but will continue to prepare statutory financial statements in accordance with Indian GAAP. Previously G's non-domestic investors were provided only with G's US GAAP financial statements. We believe US GAAP is *previous GAAP* for purposes of G's first-time adoption of IFRSs for its non-statutory financial statements. We believe that if an entity's first IFRS financial statements are prepared for non-statutory purposes, then the accounting framework used immediately before the adoption of IFRS for its non-statutory filings would be the previous GAAP for such purposes. We believe that the users of G's first IFRS financial statements would be the same users of G's US GAAP financial statements prepared for the preceding year, and therefore would benefit most by assessing the effects of G's transition from US GAAP to IFRSs rather than from Indian GAAP to IFRSs. In our view, if G's non-domestic investors had access to both Indian and US GAAP financial statements, then it would be possible for G to select either Indian or US GAAP as previous GAAP for the purpose of adopting IFRSs in the non-statutory financial statements. G would apply judgement in making a final determination.

6.1.130 **Overview of IFRS 1**

6.1.130.10 The starting point for an entity's adoption of IFRSs is the creation of a statement of financial position at the entity's date of transition. This involves the steps outlined below.

IFRS 1.10(a)   6.1.135 ***Recognise all assets and liabilities whose recognition is required by IFRSs***

6.1.135.10 Assets and liabilities that were not recognised under previous GAAP at the date of transition, but which meet the requirements for recognition under IFRSs, are recognised in the opening IFRS statement of financial position; for example:

- defined benefit plan assets or liabilities;
- deferred tax assets or liabilities;
- provisions for restoration costs in respect of non-current assets; and
- amounts received that do not qualify for recognition as revenue (i.e. deferred income).

IFRS 1.10(b)   6.1.140 ***Derecognise all assets or liabilities whose recognition is not allowed by IFRSs***

6.1.140.10 Assets and liabilities that were recognised under previous GAAP at the date of transition, but which do not meet the requirements for recognition under IFRSs, are derecognised from the opening IFRS statement of financial position; for example:

- intangible assets that do not qualify for recognition, e.g. some internally generated intangible assets, all internally generated goodwill, capitalised start-up costs or research expenditure (see 3.3.110); and
- liabilities for restructuring that do not meet the recognition requirements for a provision (see 3.12.230).

IFRS 1.10(c)   6.1.150 ***Reclassify assets, liabilities or components of equity as necessary***

6.1.150.10 Reclassification is required for items that were recognised under previous GAAP as one type of asset, liability or component of equity, but which are a different type of asset, liability or component of equity under IFRSs; for example:

- some intangibles are reclassified as goodwill and *vice versa*;
- some equity items are reclassified as liabilities and *vice versa*; and
- reserves related to revaluations made under previous GAAP may be reclassified as retained earnings.

IFRS 1.10(d) 6.1.160 **Apply IFRSs in measuring all recognised assets and liabilities**

6.1.160.10 Assets and liabilities in the opening IFRS statement of financial position are remeasured in accordance with relevant IFRSs; for example:

- provisions are measured on a discounted basis (see 3.12.120);
- deferred tax liabilities and assets are measured on an undiscounted basis (see 3.13.350); and
- investment property is measured at fair value, when applicable (see 3.4.140).

6.1.160.20 The measurement of assets and liabilities is in accordance with IFRSs even if an item is measured under both previous GAAP and IFRSs on a cost basis, i.e. the measurement requirements of IFRSs are applied at a detailed level. For example, IFRSs do not permit inventories to be measured under the last-in, first-out (LIFO) method and require the same inventory cost formula to be applied by the entire reporting entity for inventories having a similar nature and use to the entity (see 3.8.280).

6.1.170 *Choice of accounting policies*

IFRS 1.7, 8 6.1.170.10 In preparing its first IFRS financial statements, a first-time adopter selects accounting policies based on IFRSs that are effective as at the first annual IFRS reporting date; this may include the early adoption of new standards or interpretations that are not effective for the first IFRS reporting period but for which early adoption is permitted (see 6.1.1700.20). A first-time adopter does not apply earlier versions of standards that no longer are effective.

IFRS 1.7 6.1.170.20 Generally those policies are applied consistently at the date of transition to fully restate on a retrospective basis the opening statement of financial position on an IFRS basis, and in each of the periods presented in the first IFRS financial statements; this is the case even if a particular standard does not require retrospective application for existing users of IFRSs. The retrospective application of IFRSs effectively requires a first-time adopter to re-measure all transactions and events as of the date that they arose originally using IFRSs effective as at the entity's first annual IFRS reporting date. The mandatory exceptions and optional exemptions in IFRS 1 provide relief from these general principles (see 6.1.230 and 240).

IFRS 1.5(a), 6.1.170.30 In choosing its accounting policies that will be used on an ongoing basis, a
27, IAS 8.29 first-time adopter has a free choice. The restrictions that apply to an existing user of IFRSs in respect of voluntary changes in accounting policy, as set out in IAS 8 *Accounting Policies, Changes in Accounting Estimates and Errors,* do not apply to a first-time adopter. A first-time adopter can adopt an accounting policy without the explicit need for the new policy to be more relevant and reliable than any alternative policies not adopted, provided that the policy complies with IFRSs. Consequently certain restrictions, for example on the change from the fair value model to the cost model for investment property under IAS 40, do not apply to a first-time adopter. Therefore, the transition from previous GAAP to IFRSs provides a first-time adopter with the opportunity to evaluate

its accounting policies under IFRSs and to take a "clean sheet of paper" approach to selecting its IFRS accounting policies and practices.

IFRS 1.5, 9 6.1.170.40 Unless specifically allowed otherwise by IFRS 1, the transitional requirements of the standards and interpretations that apply to existing users of IFRSs do not apply to first-time adopters; instead IFRS 1 includes specific guidance, or refers to specific transitional guidance in certain standards and interpretations.

6.1.180 ***Estimates***

IFRS 1.14-16 6.1.180.10 The preparation of financial statements requires management to make judgements about estimates. IFRS 1 includes specific guidance on how to deal with changes in estimates that applies across all standards and interpretations. Essentially the guidance is a modification of IAS 10 *Events after the Reporting Period.*

IFRS 1.17, 6.1.180.20 The guidance in IFRS 1 applies from the date of transition to the first annual
BC84 reporting date, i.e. the guidance covers all periods presented in a first-time adopter's first IFRS financial statements. In developing the guidance on estimates, the IASB considered it more helpful for changes in estimates to be recognised when they were made, rather than pushing them back to the date of transition. This approach also reduces the ability of a first-time adopter to use hindsight when preparing its opening IFRS statement of financial position and IFRS comparatives.

6.1.190 *Estimates made under previous GAAP*

IFRS 1.14, 15 6.1.190.10 Estimates made by an entity in preparing its first IFRS financial statements (i.e. at the date of transition, and in the comparative and current reporting periods) are consistent with estimates made under previous GAAP. Therefore, estimates are not updated for information received at a later date. When changes in estimates are appropriate, they are accounted for prospectively.

IFRS 1.14, 6.1.190.20 The following are the only exceptions to this requirement:
IAS 8.5

- The estimate and related information under previous GAAP no longer are relevant because the entity elects a different accounting policy upon the adoption of IFRSs.
- There is objective evidence that the estimate under previous GAAP was in error. A prior period error is an omission or misstatement arising from the failure to use, or the misuse of, reliable information that was available when financial statements for those periods were authorised for issue, and could reasonably be expected to have been obtained and taken into account.

6.1.190.30 For example, Company Y is a first-time adopter in 2010. At 31 December 2008 Y recognised a provision of 100 under previous GAAP in connection with a legal claim. The provision is calculated in the same way as under IFRSs except that the provision is not discounted to its present value (see 3.12.110). The estimate of the provision under previous GAAP is not changed under IFRSs except that the amount is discounted to its present value. In determining an appropriate discount rate, Y uses a discount rate that reflects market conditions at the date of transition, 1 January 2009, even if market conditions changed after that date.

6.1.200 *Estimates not made under previous GAAP*

IFRS 1.16   6.1.200.10 When a first-time adopter needs to make an estimate under IFRSs that was not required under previous GAAP, the estimate reflects conditions that existed at the relevant reporting date (i.e. the date of transition, the end of the comparative period(s) and/or the latest reporting date). These estimates cannot reflect conditions that arose after the relevant reporting date, including changes in market prices, interest rates or foreign exchange rates.

6.1.210 **Mandatory exceptions and optional exemptions**

IFRS 1.18, B   6.1.210.10 IFRS 1 includes numerous mandatory exceptions (see 6.1.230) and optional exemptions (see 6.1.240) from the requirements of the standards and interpretations that apply to existing users of IFRSs. In general the purpose of the exceptions and exemptions is to ensure that the cost incurred by an entity in preparing its first IFRS financial statements does not exceed the benefits thereof. These exceptions and exemptions cannot be applied by analogy to any other items.

6.1.220 **Adjustments from previous GAAP to IFRSs**

IFRS 1.11,   6.1.220.10 In preparing its opening IFRS statement of financial position, a first-time
C4(g)   adopter typically will generate a series of adjustments. In certain cases these adjustments are recognised in goodwill. Otherwise the adjustments generally are recognised in the appropriate component of equity in the opening IFRS statement of financial position, which often will be opening retained earnings.

6.1.220.20 For example, Company X measured an unquoted financial asset (a security) at cost under previous GAAP and the carrying amount at the date of transition is 90. Under IFRSs the financial asset is classified as available for sale (see 6.1.730.20) and has a fair value of 110 at the date of transition; under IFRSs the amount recorded upon initial recognition would have been 90. Had IFRSs always been applied, changes in fair value would have been recognised in a separate component of equity; therefore, the adjustment of 20 on transition is recognised in a separate component of equity.

6.1.230 **Mandatory exceptions#**

6.1.230.10 Retrospective application of some aspects of IFRSs is prohibited. Unlike the optional exemptions (see 6.1.240), first-time adopters are required to use these exceptions from the general requirement for retrospective application.

IFRS 1.14-17,   6.1.230.20 The following table summarises the mandatory exceptions that are required
B   to be applied by a first-time adopter.

Mandatory exception	Exception applies to	Discussed in
Estimates	All estimates in the opening statement of financial position and IFRS comparative period.	6.1.180
Derecognition of financial instruments	Financial assets and liabilities derecognised under previous GAAP prior to 1 January 2004.	6.1.810
Hedge accounting	Hedging relationships accounted for as hedges under previous GAAP that still exist at the date of transition.	6.1.860
Non-controlling interests	All subsidiaries.	6.1.1290
Assets and liabilities of subsidiaries, associates and joint ventures	Parent/investor that adopts IFRSs *after* a subsidiary, associate or joint venture.	6.1.1380
Assets and liabilities of a parent	The separate and consolidated financial statements of all parent entities.	6.1.1370

6.1.230.30 The last two mandatory exceptions noted in the table in 6.1.230.20, and discussed in 6.1.1360 and 6.1.1370 respectively, are listed in Appendix D of IFRS 1, which describes all of the optional exemptions that a first-time adopter may elect on transition to IFRSs. However, these two exceptions are not exemptions that an entity may elect to apply; rather if a first-time adopter meets the relevant criteria to which these exceptions apply, then it applies the exceptions.

6.1.235 *Forthcoming requirements*

6.1.235.10 IFRS 9 includes consequential amendments to IFRS 1, which include a mandatory exception from retrospective application of IFRS 9 (see 3.6A.490.10 and 20).

6.1.240 **Optional exemptions#**

6.1.240.10 Entities may elect to use one or more of the voluntary exemptions from the general requirement for retrospective application of IFRSs. Some of these need to be applied to classes of items or transactions; others may be elected on an item-by-item basis.

IFRS 1.D1 6.1.240.20 These elections may not be applied to other items by analogy.

IFRS 1. C, D 6.1.240.30 The following table summarises the optional exemptions available to a first-time adopter.

Optional exemption	Exemption applies to	Discussed in
Business combinations	All business combinations that occurred prior to the date of transition, or prior to an earlier date if so elected. Applies also to acquisitions of associates and interests in joint ventures.	6.1.1120
Share-based payment transactions	Equity instruments granted on or before 7 November 2002, equity instruments granted after 7 November 2002 that vested prior to the date of transition, and liabilities for cash-settled awards that were settled prior to the date of transition.	6.1.1030
Insurance contracts	Insurance contracts, financial assets related to insurance contracts, and claims development information.	6.1.1600
Fair value or revaluation as deemed cost	Items of property, plant and equipment, investment property measured under the cost model and certain intangible assets.	6.1.330, 530, 590
	All assets and liabilities following a remeasurement event.	6.1.310
Deemed cost for oil and gas assets	Oil and gas properties accounted for in cost centres that included all properties in a large geographic area (often referred to as "full cost accounting").	6.1.1610
Arrangements containing a lease	All arrangements outstanding at the date of transition.	6.1.1520 and 1530
Employee benefits	All post-employment benefit plans for which unrecognised actuarial gains and losses exist at the date of transition.	6.1.990
Cumulative translation differences	All cumulative translation differences existing at the date of transition.	6.1.1320
Investments in subsidiaries, associates and jointly controlled entities	Separate financial statements of a parent/investor.	6.1.1630
Assets and liabilities of subsidiaries, associates and joint ventures	Subsidiary, associate or joint venture that adopts IFRSs *after* the parent/investor.	6.1.1440
Compound financial instruments	All compound financial instruments in respect of which the liability component has been settled prior to the date of transition.	6.1.830

Optional exemption	Exemption applies to	Discussed in
Designation of previously recognised financial instruments	All financial instruments.	6.1.760
Fair value measurement of financial assets and financial liabilities at initial recognition	Certain financial assets or liabilities arising from transactions entered into after 25 October 2002 or 1 January 2004.	6.1.800
Decommissioning liabilities	All decommissioning liabilities that will be included in the carrying amount of property, plant and equipment.	6.1.960
Decommissioning liabilities related to oil and gas assets	Decommissioning liabilities related to oil and gas assets in the development or production phases for which the deemed cost exemption is used.	6.1.1610
Service concession arrangements	All service concession arrangements outstanding at the date of transition.	6.1.1570
Borrowing costs	Borrowing costs incurred on qualifying assets for which the commencement date for capitalisation is on or after the date of transition, or 1 January 2009 if later.	6.1.630
Transfers of assets from customers	Transfers of assets from customers received on or after the date of transition or 1 July 2009, whichever is later.	6.1.510

6.1.250 *Forthcoming requirements*

6.1.260 *Limited exemption from comparative IFRS 7 disclosures*

6.1.260.10 An amendment to IFRS 1, published in January 2010, provides a short-term optional exemption for first-time adopters from the requirement to provide comparative period disclosures for the information required to be presented by *Improving Disclosures about Financial Instruments – Amendments to IFRS 7*, published in March 2009. A first-time adopter may apply the optional exemption for any interim or annual comparative period for which the reporting date is before 31 December 2009.

6.1.270 *Deemed cost for rate-regulated operations*

6.1.270.10 An amendment to IFRS 1, published in May 2010, provides an additional optional deemed cost exemption. In particular for items of property, plant and equipment or intangible assets used in certain rate-regulated activities, the carrying amounts determined under previous GAAP may include amounts that do not qualify for capitalisation under IFRSs. The amendment results in such carrying amounts being permitted to be used as deemed cost at the date of transition to IFRSs. This exemption may be applied on an item-by-item basis, provided that each item to which this exemption is applied is tested for impairment in accordance with IAS 36 *Impairment of Assets* at the date of transition. Use of this exemption and the basis on which carrying amounts were determined under previous GAAP are required to be disclosed.

6.1.280 *Consequential amendments to IFRS 1 as a result of IFRS 9*

6.1.280.10 IFRS 9 includes consequential amendments to IFRS 1, which include some optional exemptions from retrospective application of IFRS 9 (see 3.6A.490.30).

6.1.290 *Combining exceptions and exemptions*

6.1.290.10 More than one exemption may be applied to a particular asset or liability. For example, a first-time adopter that elects not to restate a past business combination (see 6.1.1120) also may choose to apply the fair value or revaluation as deemed cost exemption (see 6.1.330) to an item of property, plant and equipment acquired in an unrestated business combination. Under the business combination exemption, the previous initial measurement at acquisition of the assets and liabilities acquired in the business combination becomes their deemed cost under IFRSs at the acquisition date (see 6.1.1180.10). However, the additional application of the deemed cost exemption, at a date later than when the asset was acquired in the unrestated business combination, means that the valuation at that later date is adopted as the asset's deemed cost in the opening IFRS statement of financial position.

6.1.290.20 However, certain exemptions may not be combined. For example, the requirements of IFRS 1 in respect of the assets and liabilities of subsidiaries that have adopted IFRSs before a parent requires that the items be measured in the consolidated financial statements at the same carrying amounts as in the subsidiary's financial statements after adjusting for consolidation and the effects of the business combination (see 6.1.1380). In our view, this requirement generally prevents the use of another exemption that would alter these carrying amounts (e.g. the deemed cost exemption).

6.1.300 **Application issues**

6.1.310 *Event-driven fair value#*

6.1.310.10 The "event-driven fair value" optional exemption in IFRS 1 is unlike other optional exemptions in that it may be applied selectively to some or all assets and liabilities of a first-time adopter if specific criteria are met, i.e. the exemption is not limited to a particular asset or liability. For example, unlike the fair value or revaluation as deemed cost optional exemption that only is applicable to property, plant and equipment (see 6.1.330), investment property (see 6.1.580) and certain intangible assets (see 6.1.530), in our view the event-driven fair value optional exemption may be applied to some or all of the assets and liabilities to which the event-driven fair values relate.

IFRS 1.D8 6.1.310.20 A first-time adopter may have established a deemed cost in accordance with previous GAAP for some or all of its assets and liabilities by measuring them at their fair value at one particular date because of an event such as a privatisation or initial public offering. It may use such event-driven fair value measurements as deemed cost for IFRSs at the date of that measurement.

IFRS 1.19, 6.1.310.30 In our view, the reference in the exemption to fair value is interpreted in accord-
D8 ance with the definition in IFRS 1 (see 6.1.20.50), i.e. the amount for which an asset could be exchanged, or a liability settled, between knowledgeable, willing parties in an arm's length transaction. Therefore, we believe that only remeasurements that could be referred to as fair value under IFRSs qualify for the exemption. This is stricter than the "previous GAAP revaluation as deemed cost" exemption that applies to property, plant and equipment (see 6.1.360), intangible assets (see 6.1.530.20) and investment property (see 6.1.590.20) because that exemption explicitly provides more flexibility in determining fair value.

6.1.310.40 In our view, the reference in the exemption to "established a deemed cost in accordance with previous GAAP" and "by measuring them at their fair value" means that the fair values should have been recognised in the first-time adopter's previous GAAP financial statements. Therefore, for example, fair value information disclosed in the notes to the financial statements would not be sufficient to qualify for the exemption.

6.1.310.50 Although the wording of the exemption implies that the remeasurement event is infrequent or non-routine, in our view privatisations and initial public offerings are just two examples of the events that qualify for the exemption.

6.1.310.60 We believe that other acceptable remeasurement events include, but are not limited to, fair values recognised by a company emerging from bankruptcy, and fair values recognised in applying acquisition accounting that were pushed down into the financial statements of the first-time adopter (acquiree). However, in the latter example we believe that the exemption would not apply if the acquisition accounting recognised by the parent had not been pushed down into the first-time adopter's (acquiree's) financial statements; this is because the fair values were not recorded in the first-time adopter's financial statements. Notwithstanding the fact that the fair values were pushed down into the financial statements of the first-time adopter (acquiree), the first-time adopter would not be permitted to recognise assets or liabilities that in themselves would not qualify for recognition in accordance with IFRSs in the separate financial statements of the first-time adopter, e.g. acquirer's goodwill, intangible assets and contingent liabilities recognised using business combination accounting principles.

6.1.310.70 For example Company P is a first-time adopter in 2010. P was privatised in 2007 and at the date of privatisation the carrying amounts of P's assets and liabilities were established by reference to their fair value. This exercise included the recognition of internally generated goodwill attributable to the business that was privatised as P. At its date of transition of 1 January 2009, P wishes to continue to recognise the internally generated goodwill and to establish the carrying amount of property, plant and equipment using the fair value established in the privatisation, adjusted for depreciation between the date of privatisation and the date of transition. Therefore, the gross carrying amount of the property, plant and equipment in P's opening IFRS statement of financial position will be its fair value at the date of privatisation, with the subsequent depreciation representing the balance of accumulated depreciation at the date of transition. Depreciation recognised under previous GAAP was consistent with that required under IFRSs.

6.1.310.80 However, we believe that P should not recognise the goodwill recognised in the privatisation in its opening IFRS statement of financial position as internally generated goodwill does not qualify for recognition under IFRSs.

6.1.320 *Forthcoming requirements*

6.1.320.10 The *Improvements to IFRSs 2010* amended IFRS 1 to extend the scope of paragraph D8 so that a first-time adopter is permitted to use an event-driven fair value measurement as deemed cost for some or all of its assets (e.g. revaluation of certain assets on the occurrence of an initial public offering) when such revaluation occurred *during* the reporting periods covered by its first IFRS financial statements. Currently such a revaluation is permitted only when the revaluation occurs *at or prior to* the date of transition. The event-driven fair value measurement would be recognised at the date that the event triggering such a revaluation occurred. In addition, the first-time adopter also will be required to determine an IFRS cost or deemed cost using paragraphs D5 – D7 of IFRS 1 as at the date of transition.

6.1.325 *Property, plant and equipment*

6.1.330 Optional exemption to use fair value or revaluation as deemed cost

6.1.330.10 [Not used]

IFRS 1.D5, 6.1.330.20 The "fair value or revaluation as deemed cost" optional exemption (also referred
D6, D8 to as the "deemed cost exemption") permits the carrying amount of an item of property, plant and equipment to be measured at the date of transition based on a deemed cost. If elected, the deemed cost exemption may be based on any of the following:

Measurement basis	At what date?
Fair value (see 6.1.350 and 510)	Date of transition or, for assets transferred from customers, later of 1 July 2009 and date of transition.

Measurement basis	At what date?
A previous GAAP revaluation that broadly was on a basis comparable to fair value under IFRSs (see 6.1.360)	Date of revaluation, which is on or before the date of transition.
A previous GAAP revaluation, based on a cost or depreciated cost measure broadly comparable to IFRSs adjusted to reflect, e.g. changes in a general or specific price index (see 6.1.360)	Date of revaluation, which is on or before the date of transition.
An event-driven valuation, e.g. when an entity was privatised and at that point valued and recognised some or all of its assets and liabilities at fair value (see 6.1.310)	Date of valuation, which is on or before the date of transition.

IFRS 1.IG9   6.1.330.30 When the deemed cost exemption is used to establish the cost of an item of property, plant and equipment, the deemed cost becomes the new IFRS cost basis at that date; any accumulated depreciation recognised under previous GAAP prior to that date is set to zero.

IFRS 1.IG9   6.1.330.40 If deemed cost is measured at a revalued or other fair value-based amount under previous GAAP prior to the date of transition, then the measurement of that asset between that date and the date of transition complies with IFRSs.

IFRS 1.D5, D6, D8   6.1.330.50 A first-time adopter does not have to apply the deemed cost exemption to all classes of property, plant and equipment or to all items within a class of property, plant and equipment; rather the exemption may be applied to individual items of property, plant and equipment.

6.1.330.60 The election of the deemed cost exemption is independent of the first-time adopter's accounting policy choice for the subsequent measurement of property, plant and equipment, i.e. a first-time adopter that elects to apply the deemed cost exemption is not required to apply the revaluation model subsequently.

6.1.340 [Not used]

6.1.350 *Fair value as deemed cost at the date of transition*

IFRS 1.A   6.1.350.10 In addition to the IFRS definition of fair value, in our view in determining fair value a first-time adopter also should have regard to the specific guidance in IAS 16 *Property, Plant and Equipment*, which means that fair value at the date of transition may be determined using the methodology that is most appropriate to a first-time adopter's specific facts and circumstances.

IAS 16.32, 33   6.1.350.20 IAS 16 states that the fair value of property, plant and equipment usually is determined by reference to its market value or market-based information as determined by appraisal. Generally this is done by looking at the highest possible price that could be obtained for the item, without regard to its existing use. However, when there is no observable evidence of market value, property, plant and equipment may be measured using an income or depreciated replacement cost (DRC) approach (see 3.2.330); this might be appropriate when the asset is particularly specialised and rarely sold except as part of a continuing business.

6.1.360 *Previous GAAP revaluation as deemed cost*

IFRS 1.D6   6.1.360.10 A first-time adopter may use a previous GAAP revaluation as the deemed cost of an item of property, plant and equipment if the revaluation under previous GAAP was broadly comparable to:

- fair value; or
- cost or depreciated cost under IFRSs adjusted, e.g. for changes in a general or specific price index.

6.1.360.20 In our view, the reference in IFRS 1 to a previous GAAP revaluation means that the exemption is available only if the previous GAAP revaluation was reflected in the first-time adopter's financial statements. Further, in our view the deemed cost is based on the most recent revaluation under previous GAAP on or before the date of transition.

6.1.360.30 By using the phrase "broadly comparable", IFRS 1 allows some flexibility in allowing a deemed cost that is not identical to the amount that would have been determined if IFRSs had been applied, or if an index had been applied to a fully IFRS-compliant cost. However, no further guidance is provided and the degree of acceptable flexibility is assessed based on a first-time adopter's specific facts and circumstances.

6.1.370 *Depreciation*

6.1.370.10 The requirements of IFRSs in respect of depreciation are relevant to each item of property, plant and equipment as follows:

- from the acquisition date if the first-time adopter does not elect the deemed cost exemption;
- from the date of transition if the first-time adopter elects the deemed cost exemption and deemed cost is determined at the date of transition; or
- from the date of the revaluation or other determination of fair value if the first-time adopter elects the deemed cost exemption and deemed cost is determined prior to the date of transition.

IFRS 1.IG7   6.1.370.20 Estimates of depreciation made under previous GAAP may not be revised at the date of transition or in the first IFRS financial statements unless it is determined that they were made in error. On transition to IFRSs, if errors are discovered with respect to depreciation recognised under previous GAAP, then those errors are corrected in the opening IFRS statement of financial position and disclosed separately in the reconciliations required from previous GAAP to IFRSs (see 6.1.1650.60).

6.1.370.30 Depreciation is an accounting estimate and therefore changes in the depreciation method or changes in the estimate of useful lives normally are dealt with prospectively. However, if a first-time adopter previously depreciated an item of equipment based, e.g. on tax allowances, without reference to the useful life of the asset or to its residual value as required by IFRSs, then an adjustment to measure depreciation based on the useful life of the asset or its residual value is recognised as an adjustment to opening retained earnings.

6.1.370.40 In our view, when depreciation recognised in accordance with previous GAAP is not consistent with a method of depreciation permitted under IFRSs, disclosure of the adjustment to cumulative depreciation does not result in disclosure of an error; this is because the depreciation recognised was in accordance with previous GAAP.

6.1.380 *Component accounting*

IFRS 1.IG12   6.1.380.10 There are no exemptions available from identifying components of property, plant and equipment that are required to be depreciated separately under IFRSs. The identification and separate recognition of the depreciation of components is required in the opening IFRS statement of financial position. For example, IFRSs require major inspections and overhauls to be identified and depreciated as a separate component of the asset. Component depreciation affects the subsequent accounting for both cost and depreciation. Accordingly, both cost and accumulated depreciation are allocated to identified components separately.

6.1.380.20 When the original cost of a major inspection or overhaul is not available, the expected cost of the next overhaul may be used as the best estimate of the cost of the component. In our view, a similar approach is acceptable for measuring major inspection and overhaul costs in the opening IFRS statement of financial position.

6.1.390 *Revaluation surplus under previous GAAP*

IAS 16.29   6.1.390.10 The treatment of any revaluation surplus under previous GAAP depends on whether the first-time adopter will apply the cost or revaluation model under IFRSs subsequent to the date of transition.

IFRS 1.11   6.1.390.20 If a revaluation model was used under previous GAAP but the cost model will be used under IFRSs, then any existing revaluation surplus at the date of transition is either reclassified as a separate component of equity, not described as a revaluation reserve, or transferred to retained earnings.

IFRS 1.IG10   6.1.390.30 If a first-time adopter elects the revaluation model under IFRSs, then the revaluation surplus at the date of transition is measured as the difference between the carrying amount of the asset at that date and its cost or deemed cost.

6.1.390.40 For example, Company B has an owner-occupied property with a cost of 60 under previous GAAP and of 55 under IFRSs. Before the date of transition, the property was revalued to a fair value of 85 and a revaluation reserve of 25 was recognised under previous GAAP. Its fair value is 100 at the date of transition. Depreciation is ignored for the purpose of this example. B elects as its accounting policy under IFRSs to measure the class of asset that includes this property on a fair value basis (see 3.2.300). Therefore, the carrying amount of the property at date of transition will be 100.

6.1.390.50 Depending upon the exemptions chosen by B, the IFRS revaluation reserve at the date of transition will be as follows:

- If the deemed cost exemption is not elected, then the IFRS revaluation reserve will be 45 (100 - 55), based on the IFRS cost of the asset.
- If the deemed cost exemption is applied on the basis of the fair value at the date of transition, then the IFRS revaluation reserve will be zero (100 - 100).
- If the deemed cost exemption is applied on the basis of the earlier revaluation, then the IFRS revaluation reserve at the date of transition will be 15 (100 - 85), based on that earlier revaluation as deemed cost.

6.1.400 *Deemed cost for property, plant and equipment held under a finance lease*

6.1.400.10 A first-time adopter applies the leasing requirements of IFRSs to classify any leases in effect at its date of transition as operating or finance leases (see 5.1). Assets held under finance leases are accounted for as own assets, e.g. as property, plant and equipment, subject to the additional leasing requirements regarding initial recognition, measurement of cost and depreciation.

6.1.400.20 In our view, the deemed cost exemption for property, plant and equipment also may be applied to an asset acquired under a finance lease.

6.1.410 – 490 [Not used]

6.1.500 *Deemed cost for property, plant and equipment acquired in a business combination*

6.1.500.10 In our view, the deemed cost exemption may be chosen by a first-time adopter that acquired an item of property, plant and equipment in a business combination that is not restated upon transition to IFRSs.

6.1.510 *Optional exemption for transfers of assets from customers*

IFRS 1.D24 6.1.510.10 IFRS 1 includes an optional exemption that allows a first-time adopter to elect to apply the transitional requirements set out in IFRIC 18 *Transfers of Assets from Customers*. IFRIC 18 provides guidance on transfers of property, plant and equipment (or cash to acquire such property, plant and equipment) for entities that receive such contributions from their customers, and requires such assets to be measured at fair value (see 4.2.640). The optional exemption permits a first-time adopter to measure at fair value assets transferred from customers on or after:

- the later of 1 July 2009 and the date of transition; or
- any date chosen by the first-time adopter before the date of transition.

6.1.510.20 A first-time adopter that elects to apply the optional exemption in respect of transfers of assets from customers does so on a consistent basis across all relevant assets; the exemption cannot be applied on an asset-by-asset basis. If a first-time adopter elects not to apply the optional exemption, then full retrospective application of IFRIC 18 is required.

6.1.520 *Intangible assets and goodwill*

6.1.530 *Optional exemption to use fair value or revaluation as deemed cost*

IFRS 1.D7(b) 6.1.530.10 The "fair value or revaluation as deemed cost" optional exemption (also referred to as the "deemed cost exemption") permits the carrying amount of an intangible asset to be measured at the date of transition based on a deemed cost. However, the exemption, which applies on an asset-by-asset basis, is available only when the following criteria are met:

- the asset qualifies for recognition under IAS 38 *Intangible Assets*; and
- the asset meets the criteria in IAS 38 for revaluation (see 3.3.280).

IFRS 1.IG50 6.1.530.20 To the extent that an active market exists and the deemed cost exemption is available for an intangible asset, the exemption applies in the same way as it does to property, plant and equipment. This means that deemed cost may be either fair value at the date of transition or a previous GAAP revaluation that meets certain criteria, with deemed cost determined at the date of the previous GAAP revaluation (see 6.1.330.20).

6.1.540 *Internally generated intangible assets*

IFRS 1.IG44, 6.1.540.10 A first-time adopter recognises in its opening IFRS statement of financial posi-
IG47 tion all internally generated intangible assets that qualify for recognition under IAS 38; similarly, it derecognises internally generated intangible assets that do not qualify for recognition.

IFRS 1.IG46, 6.1.540.20 In accordance with IAS 38, expenditure is capitalised only from the date that
IG47 the recognition criteria in the standard are met, i.e. prospectively; these criteria cannot be assessed using the benefit of hindsight. Therefore, in order to capitalise costs at the date of transition that were expensed under previous GAAP, it is required that the criteria for capitalisation were met at the time that the costs were incurred and that a system that measured such costs reliably was in place.

6.1.540.30 In our view, the interaction of the prohibition on the use of hindsight with the requirements for the first-time adoption of IFRSs should be interpreted as requiring either:

- contemporaneous evidence that all of the recognition requirements of IFRSs were considered at the time that the expenditure was incurred. Expenditure should be capitalised only from the date that it can be demonstrated that this information was available; or
- the existence of a process or control system to ensure that no expenditure of this nature is incurred without all recognition requirements having been considered. This might be the case, for example, if the first-time adopter had a well-managed product development programme that considered all of the recognition criteria and there is no reason to believe that the normal process or control system was not followed.

6.1.540.40 First-time adopters with extensive development programmes may have control procedures in place to assess the probability of future economic benefits periodically. In our view, if a first-time adopter has such a monitoring system, and if the costs incurred were measured reliably, then this information is likely to satisfy the requirements of IFRSs for contemporaneous assessment of the probability of future economic benefits.

6.1.550 *Intangible asset acquired separately*

IFRS 1.IG48 6.1.550.10 The considerations in 6.1.540 in respect of the recognition of an internally generated intangible asset apply equally to an intangible asset acquired separately, i.e. outside of a business combination. However, in that case generally the criteria are easier to satisfy because a transaction involving a party separate from the first-time adopter occurred.

6.1.560 *Intangible assets acquired in a business combination*

6.1.560.10 The requirements of IFRS 1 in respect of intangible assets acquired in a business combination are discussed in 6.1.1190.10.

6.1.570 *Amortisation*

6.1.570.10 The general requirements related to the amortisation of intangible assets are discussed in 3.3.200 and 210 and are relevant to a first-time adopter in relation to each intangible asset as follows:

- from the acquisition date if the first-time adopter does not elect the deemed cost exemption;
- from the date of transition if the first-time adopter elects the deemed cost exemption and deemed cost is determined at that date; or
- from the date of the revaluation or other determination of fair value if the first-time adopter elects the deemed cost exemption and deemed cost is determined prior to the date of transition.

IFRS 1.IG51 6.1.570.20 Estimates of amortisation made under previous GAAP may not be revised at the date of transition or in the first IFRS financial statements unless it is determined that they were made in error. On transition to IFRSs, if errors are discovered with respect to amortisation recognised under previous GAAP, then those errors are corrected in the opening IFRS statement of financial position and disclosed separately in the reconciliations required from previous GAAP to IFRSs.

IFRS 1.IG51　6.1.570.30 Amortisation is an accounting estimate and therefore changes in the amortisation method or changes in the estimate of useful lives normally are dealt with prospectively. However, if a first-time adopter previously amortised an intangible asset based, for example, on tax allowances, without reference to the useful life of the asset, then an adjustment to measure amortisation based on the useful life of the asset is recognised as an adjustment to opening retained earnings.

IFRS 1.26　6.1.570.40 In our view, when amortisation recognised in accordance with previous GAAP is not consistent with a method of amortisation permitted under IFRSs, disclosure of the adjustment to cumulative amortisation does not result in disclosure of an error; this is because the amortisation recognised was in accordance with previous GAAP.

6.1.580 *Investment property*

6.1.590 *Optional exemption to use fair value or revaluation as deemed cost*

IFRS 1.D5-　6.1.590.10 The "fair value or revaluation as deemed cost" optional exemption (also
D8　referred to as the "deemed cost exemption") permits the carrying amount of investment property to be measured at the date of transition based on a deemed cost. However, the fair value or revaluation as deemed cost exemption for investment property is relevant only when a first-time adopter elects to use the cost model.

6.1.590.15 The deemed cost exemption can be elected to be applied to individual investment properties on an item-by-item basis.

IFRS 1.IG50　6.1.590.20 The deemed cost exemption applies in the same way as it does to property, plant and equipment. This means that deemed cost may be either fair value at the date of transition or a previous GAAP revaluation that meets certain criteria, with deemed cost determined at the date of the previous GAAP revaluation (see 6.1.330.20).

6.1.590.30 If a first-time adopter elects to measure investment property using the fair value model, then all investment property at the date of transition would be measured at fair value in accordance with IAS 40 and the deemed cost exemption does not apply. This is because the first-time adopter's chosen accounting policy of fair value requires investment property to be measured at fair value, determined in accordance with IAS 40, at the date of transition.

6.1.600 *Depreciation*

6.1.600.10 If the cost model is applied subsequent to initial recognition, then investment property is accounted for in accordance with the cost model for property, plant and equipment. In such cases the relevant requirements of IFRS 1 on transition to IFRSs in respect of depreciation of property, plant and equipment as discussed in 6.1.370 also are relevant to the depreciation of investment property.

6.1.600.20 If the fair value model is applied subsequent to initial recognition, then fair value changes at each reporting date are recognised in profit or loss and the investment property is not separately depreciated (see 3.4).

6.1.610 *Deemed cost for investment property acquired in a business combination*

6.1.610.10 In our view, the deemed cost exemption may be chosen by a first-time adopter that acquired an investment property in a business combination that is not restated upon transition to IFRSs.

6.1.620 **Borrowing costs**

6.1.630 *Optional exemption for borrowing costs*

IFRS 1.D23,
IAS 23.27, 28

6.1.630.10 A first-time adopter is permitted to apply the transitional requirements of IAS 23 *Borrowing Costs*. To the extent that the adoption of IAS 23 upon transition is a change in accounting policy, these transitional requirements provide a first-time adopter relief from applying the standard retrospectively. Instead, IAS 23 is applied to qualifying assets for which the commencement date for capitalisation is on or after:

- the later of 1 January 2009 and the date of transition; or
- an earlier date chosen by the first-time adopter.

6.1.630.20 A first-time adopter that elects to apply the optional exemption in respect of borrowing costs is required to do so on a consistent basis across all relevant assets; the exemption cannot be applied on an asset-by-asset basis. If a first-time adopter does not elect to apply the optional exemption, then full retrospective application of IAS 23 is required.

6.1.640 *Unit of account*

IAS 23.27,
BC15, BC17

6.1.640.10 Under the transitional requirements of IAS 23, an entity capitalises borrowing costs related to qualifying assets for which the commencement date for capitalisation is on or after the effective date. In our view, the unit of account in applying the transitional requirements of IAS 23 is the qualifying asset rather than the borrowing costs because the intended accounting is clear from the discussion in the basis for conclusions to IAS 23.

6.1.640.20 For example, Company Y is a first-time adopter in 2010. Y commenced the construction of an office building, a qualifying asset, in June 2008. Y had a policy under previous GAAP of expensing borrowing costs as incurred. Since the office building is the unit of account rather than the borrowing costs, the borrowing costs incurred in respect of the qualifying asset will continue to be expensed because construction of the asset commenced prior to the date of transition, 1 January 2009. However, as an alternative Y could elect to apply the requirements of IAS 23 from June 2008 (see 6.1.630.10).

6.1.650 *Treatment of borrowing costs under previous GAAP*

6.1.660 Change in accounting policy upon the adoption of IFRSs

6.1.660.10 The prospective application of IAS 23 is permitted only when it represents a change in accounting policy (see 6.1.630.10). Some previous GAAPs may permit or require entities to capitalise borrowing costs using a methodology that is not consistent with the requirements of IAS 23. Therefore, an issue arises as to whether a change in methodology is a change in accounting policy that would allow a first-time adopter to take advantage of the transitional requirements of IAS 23 upon the adoption of IFRSs.

IAS 8.5   6.1.660.20 In our view, a change in the method of calculating capitalised borrowing costs is a change in accounting policy. This is because *accounting policies* are the specific principles, bases, conventions, rules and practices applied by an entity in *preparing* and presenting its financial statements. Therefore, we believe that a first-time adopter that capitalised borrowing costs under previous GAAP is able to apply the requirements of IAS 23 prospectively if the methodology under previous GAAP is not consistent with the requirements of IFRSs in this regard.

6.1.660.30 In addition, when a first-time adopter capitalised borrowing costs under previous GAAP using a methodology that was not consistent with IAS 23, it also considers whether such borrowing costs need to be reversed upon the adoption of IFRSs.

IAS 23.BC15   6.1.660.40 In our view, when IAS 23 is not applied retrospectively, a first-time adopter should expense borrowing costs incurred and capitalised in a manner inconsistent with IFRSs on qualifying assets for which construction commenced before the date of applying IAS 23. This is because the transitional requirements of IAS 23 provide relief from retrospective application for a first-time adopter that expensed borrowing costs previously; it does not provide relief from a method of capitalisation that is inconsistent with the methodology in IAS 23. Additionally, IFRS 1 generally requires the opening IFRS statement of financial position to be prepared in accordance with IFRSs, and the standard is explicit when an optional exemption permits the "grandfathering" of previous GAAP. As the optional exemption for borrowing costs does not permit explicitly the grandfathering of borrowing costs capitalised under previous GAAP, we believe that an adjustment should be made to reverse borrowing costs capitalised in a manner inconsistent with IFRSs under previous GAAP prior to the date of transition.

6.1.660.50 Therefore, for construction of a qualifying asset that:

- is completed before the date of transition, we believe that the carrying amount of the qualifying asset should be adjusted to reverse borrowing costs capitalised prior to the date of transition using a methodology that is inconsistent with IAS 23;

1565

- is not completed before the date of transition, we believe that the carrying amount of the qualifying asset should be adjusted to reverse borrowing costs capitalised prior to the date of transition using a methodology that is inconsistent with IAS23, and that borrowing costs incurred after the date of transition in respect of that asset should not be capitalised (see 6.1.640.10); and
- commences after the date selected in 6.1.630.10, borrowing costs are capitalised in accordance with IAS 23 (see 6.1.640.10).

6.1.670 Interaction with other requirements and exemptions

IFRS 1.D23, **6.1.670.10** The optional exemption in respect of borrowing costs is not relevant for a
IG23 particular qualifying asset when the carrying amount of that asset is determined by reference to a deemed cost at the date of transition, e.g. when the carrying amount of property, plant and equipment is determined by reference to fair value (see 6.1.330.20), or the carrying amount of an intangible asset is determined under the optional exemption for service concession arrangements (by reference to the carrying amount of property, plant and equipment under previous GAAP) (see 6.1.1570). In such circumstances the carrying amount is reset for the purpose of accounting subsequent to the date of transition.

6.1.670.20 For example, Company B is a first-time adopter in 2010. B commenced a significant construction project in 2008 that represents a qualifying asset. B elects to apply IAS 23 as of 1 January 2008 (see 6.1.630.10) and capitalises 40 of IAS 23-compliant borrowing costs in the period from 1 January 2008 to 31 December 2008. At the date of transition, 1 January 2009, B elects to use the fair value as deemed cost optional exemption (see 6.1.330.20) and determines the fair value of the construction project to be 2,000. In our view, at the date of transition B would recognise the construction project at 2,000 and subsequent to the date of transition capitalise borrowing costs on the construction project in accordance with IAS 23. Therefore, B should not adjust the fair value of 2,000 at the date of transition to incorporate the borrowing costs of 40 capitalised during the period prior to the date of transition.

6.1.680 Impairment of non-financial assets

6.1.690 Impairment testing at the date of transition

6.1.690.10 At the date of transition a first-time adopter should perform impairment tests in accordance with IAS 36 as follows:

IFRS 1. - Goodwill that was acquired in an unrestated business combination (see 6.1.1190.10)
C4(g)(ii) is tested for impairment regardless of whether there is an indication of impairment. While there is no specific requirement in IFRS 1, we prefer that goodwill acquired in a restated business combination also be tested for impairment at the date of transition (see 6.1.1240).
IFRS 1.C5 - In our view, goodwill that arose from the acquisition of an associate or joint venture that is not restated (i.e. for which the business combinations exemption is applied) (see 6.1.1350.20) is tested for impairment regardless of whether there is an indica-

tion of impairment. This is because the optional exemption for such investments requires application of all elements of the optional exemption for past business combinations, i.e. including the mandatory impairment test for goodwill that is not restated at the date of transition. However, for investments in associates and jointly controlled entities that are equity accounted, the impairment testing is performed on the carrying amount of the investment as a whole.

IFRS 1.IG39 • For other assets, detailed impairment testing is carried out at the date of transition if there is an indication of impairment.

6.1.690.20 Any impairment losses and reversals of impairment losses recognised at the date of transition are charged or credited to retained earnings unless another component of equity is appropriate. The latter would be the case, for example when a revaluation surplus exists in respect of an item of property, plant and equipment, and the revaluation model will continue to be applied subsequent to transition (see 6.1.390).

6.1.700 *Reversal of impairment*

IFRS 1.IG43. 6.1.700.10 At the date of transition a first-time adopter assesses whether there is an
IAS 36.110 indication that a previously recognised impairment loss has reversed. If there is such an indication and the recoverable amount of the impaired asset or cash generating unit subsequently increases, then the impairment loss generally is reversed (see 3.10.420). If there is no such indication, then the first-time adopter carries forward the previous GAAP carrying amount at the date of transition; it does not seek to recalculate the amount of the previous impairment loss.

6.1.700.20 However, impairment losses are not reversed if a first-time adopter elected to measure the related asset based on deemed cost (see 6.1.330, 530 and 590) at a date after the original impairment.

6.1.700.30 In practice often the accounting will be more complex when previous GAAP differs from IFRSs, e.g. the first-time adopter may have capitalised costs that would have been expensed under IFRSs. Therefore, the reversal of any impairment loss requires careful consideration.

6.1.710 *Estimates made under previous GAAP*

IFRS 1.IG40 6.1.710.10 Impairment testing typically requires the use of significant estimates. As discussed in 6.1.180, previous GAAP estimates made at the date of transition and at the end of the comparative period are not changed (except for the effect of differences between previous GAAP and IFRSs), unless there is objective evidence that those estimates were in error. This prohibition on revising estimates applies to cash flow estimates that are the basis for impairment testing under IFRSs, except when there is a difference between previous GAAP and IFRSs regarding the composition and estimation of those cash flows.

IFRS 1.IG41 6.1.710.20 Complying with IAS 36 may require a first-time adopter to make estimates that were not required under its previous GAAP; for example, a first-time adopter might be determining value in use for the first time. In such cases the additional estimates required by IFRSs reflect conditions at the date of transition. They cannot reflect conditions that arose after the date of transition.

6.1.720 *Financial instruments#*

6.1.730 *Classification on transition*

6.1.730.10 For existing users of IFRSs, financial assets are classified on *initial* recognition into one of four categories, and financial liabilities are classified on *initial* recognition into one of two categories (see 3.6.460); subsequent reclassification is limited to specific circumstances (see 3.6.850).

6.1.730.20 The following table summarises the classification requirements that apply to a first-time adopter, which include some relief from the normal classification requirements of IFRSs.

	Category	Description
	Fair value through profit or loss	Fair value through profit or loss comprises a held-for-trading category and a fair value option category.
		The held-for-trading category comprises financial instruments that are:
IFRS 1. IG56(d)(i) *IFRS 1. IG56(d)(ii)*		• acquired or incurred principally for the purpose of selling or repurchasing in the near term. A first-time adopter applies this classification test as of the date of initial recognition of a financial instrument because there is no specific relief provided from retrospective application; • at the date of transition, part of a portfolio of identified financial instruments that are managed together and for which there is evidence of a recent actual pattern of short-term profit taking; or • derivatives, except for derivatives that are designated and effective hedging instrument.
IFRS 1.D19(b), IG56(d)(iii), IAS 39.AG4B-AG4K		Under the fair value option a first-time adopter may, on an instrument-by-instrument basis, designate financial instruments as at fair value through profit or loss at the date of transition. Such classification is permitted only if, at the date of transition:
IFRS 1.D19(b), IG56(d)(iii), IAS 39.9(b)(i), 9(b)(ii), 11A		• the instrument is a hybrid instrument that contains an embedded derivative that can significantly modify the cash flows of the hybrid and it is clear with little or no analysis that separation of the embedded derivative is not prohibited; • the classification is for a portfolio of financial assets and/or financial liabilities that are managed and evaluated together on a fair value basis; or • the classification eliminates or significantly reduces a measurement or recognition inconsistency (also referred to as an accounting mismatch).

	Category	Description
IFRS 1. *IG56(a)*	Held to maturity	A first-time adopter may, on an instrument-by-instrument basis, designate financial assets as held to maturity at the date of transition if it has the intent and ability at that date to hold such securities until maturity.
IFRS 1. *IG56(b)*	Loans and receivables	Loans and receivables are non-derivative financial assets with fixed or determinable payments, except for those loans and receivables that are classified as held for trading or available for a sale, or are designated upon initial recognition as at fair value through profit or loss. A first-time adopter applies this classification test as of the date of initial recognition of a financial asset because there is no specific relief provided from retrospective application.
IFRS 1. *D19(a),* *IG56(e)*	Available for sale	Financial assets, including non-marketable equity securities that do not fall into any of the other categories, are classified as available for sale. Also, a first-time adopter may designate, on an instrument-by-instrument basis, financial assets, other than those classified as held for trading, as available for sale at the date of transition, including a loan and receivable or a financial asset that the investor intends to hold to maturity.
	Other financial liabilities	Financial liabilities that do not fall into the fair value through profit or loss categories, are classified as other financial liabilities.

IFRS 1.IG35, 6.1.730.30 Instruments issued by a first-time adopter are classified as equity or as liabilities
IAS 32.15 in accordance with the specified criteria in 3.11.10. In determining the appropriate classification a first-time adopter considers the facts and circumstances when an instrument was issued or at the date of any later change to the terms of the instrument, and not the facts and circumstances at the date of transition. Other than in respect of compound financial instruments (see 6.1.830) there are no exemptions from this requirement.

6.1.740 *Forthcoming requirements*

6.1.740.10 The requirements of IFRS 9 retain but simplify the mixed measurement model and establish two primary measurement categories for financial assets: amortised cost and fair value. The basis of classification depends on the entity's business model and the contractual cash flow characteristics of the financial asset. The IAS 39 categories of held-to-maturity, loans and receivables and available-for-sale are eliminated and so are the existing tainting provisions for disposals before maturity of certain financial assets. See 3.6A.30 for a further discussion of classification.

6.1.750 *Designation*

IAS 39.AG4C 6.1.750.10 The term "designate" is used when referring to designating items as at fair value through profit or loss, or as available for sale or as held to maturity. The term is not defined in IFRSs, although the financial instruments standards do state that such designation for a financial asset or a financial liability as at fair value through profit or loss is similar to an accounting policy choice. However, unlike an accounting policy choice it is not required to be applied consistently to all similar transactions.

6.1.750.20 In our view, designation of a financial instrument as at fair value through profit or loss or available for sale at the date of transition need not be a formal exercise; the designation could be informal and undocumented and, for example, could be evidenced at the date of transition by the following:

- inclusion of the item in a particular general ledger account;
- presentation as such in published financial statements under previous GAAP; or
- an appropriate description in the accounting policies published under previous GAAP.

6.1.760 *Optional exemption for designation as at fair value through profit or loss or as available for sale*

IFRS 1.D19 6.1.760.10 An optional exemption in IFRS 1 allows a first-time adopter to designate at the date of transition any financial asset or financial liability as at fair value through profit or loss provided that the relevant criteria to qualify for classification as at fair value through profit or loss are met at that date. The same relief allows a first-time adopter to designate at the date of transition any financial asset, other than those that are classified as held for trading, as available-for-sale. This is regardless of the classification under previous GAAP.

6.1.770 *Designation after the date of transition has passed*

6.1.770.10 The classification relief in IFRS 1 relies on the first-time adopter making a designation at the date of transition. However, the practical availability of this relief depends on a first-time adopter knowing of, and planning its adoption of, IFRSs in advance of its date of transition, which will not always be the case. When an entity decides to adopt IFRSs after its date of transition has passed, it may appear that the relief effectively is no longer available. For example, a first-time adopter who has passed its date of transition and under previous GAAP designated a financial asset as available for sale would not be permitted to retrospectively designate the financial asset as at fair value through profit or loss.

6.1.770.20 In our view, designation under IFRSs at the date of transition is not required when such designation was made under previous GAAP, as long as the other designation criteria under IFRSs are met at the date of designation under previous GAAP. We believe that this approach is acceptable only if based on information available at the date of transition without the use of hindsight. Therefore, we believe that designation after the date of transition has passed is acceptable under IFRSs in the following circumstances:

- Like IFRSs, designation was required under previous GAAP at the later of the effective date of the previous GAAP standard and the initial recognition of the instrument, even if the effective date under previous GAAP differed from that under IAS 39 (periods beginning on or after 1 January 2006).

1570

- The classification requirements under previous GAAP were less strict than those under IFRSs. However, for the specific instrument being designated at the date of transition, the classification criteria of IFRSs were met at the date of designation under previous GAAP.

6.1.770.30 However, we believe that a first-time adopter should not use the benefit of hindsight to designate retrospectively only selected financial instruments in order to achieve a particular financial statement result, e.g. only electing to designate retrospectively financial instruments designated as at fair value through profit or loss under previous GAAP that at the date of transition would result in fair value gains being recognised in profit or loss subsequent to the date of transition. We believe that such selective application of the designation criteria is the reason why the classification relief in IFRS 1 generally relies on the first-time adopter making a designation at the date of transition.

6.1.770.40 For example, Company G is a first-time adopter in 2010; its financial statements will include two years of comparative information. Therefore, G's date of transition of 1 January 2008 has passed and G is unable to make the optional elective designations in respect of its financial instruments into the fair value through profit or loss category at that date.

6.1.770.50 G's previous GAAP included a fair value through profit or loss category that differed from the IFRS fair value through profit or loss category as follows:

- under previous GAAP any financial asset or financial liability could be designated into the fair value through profit or loss category, i.e. there were no specific criteria to be met; and
- differences in transitional requirements.

6.1.770.60 G designated certain financial instruments as at fair value through profit or loss under previous GAAP as at 1 January 2007, the effective date of its previous GAAP financial instruments standard.

6.1.770.70 We believe that *only* those financial instruments that G designated into the fair value through profit or loss category under previous GAAP that met the criteria for fair value through profit or loss designation under IFRSs at that date, i.e. the date of designation under previous GAAP, may be designated by G as at fair value through profit or loss in its opening IFRS statement of financial position.

6.1.780 *Designation as held to maturity*

IAS 39.9, 51 6.1.780.10 The designation of financial assets as held to maturity reflects the first-time adopter's intent and ability to hold the investments to maturity. For existing users of IFRSs, an entity generally is prohibited from classifying any financial assets as held to maturity if, in the current or previous two years, the entity has sold, reclassified, transferred or exercised a put option on more than an insignificant amount of held to maturity assets (known as the tainting rules) (see 3.6.570).

IFRS 1.
IG56(a)
6.1.780.20 However, for a first-time adopter, designation as held to maturity reflects the first-time adopter's intent and ability at the date of transition. Therefore, any sales or transfers occurring prior to the date of transition do not trigger the tainting rules in IFRSs, even if the sale or transfer resulted in a held-to-maturity portfolio being tainted under previous GAAP.

IFRS 1.
IG56(a)
6.1.780.30 Although IFRS 1 refers to "designating" a financial asset as held to maturity at the date of transition, such designation is not a requirement for existing users of IFRSs. In our view, IFRS 1 permits a first-time adopter to classify financial assets as held to maturity as of the date of transition even if the date of transition has passed, i.e. this classification can be made on a retrospective basis. However, we believe that this approach is acceptable only if based on information available at the date of transition without the use of hindsight.

6.1.800 *Optional exemption for fair value measurement at initial recognition*

IFRS 1.D20
6.1.800.10 IFRS 1 provides relief from the retrospective application of the requirements in respect of the recognition of "day one" gains or losses (see 3.6.710.10 – 20). Under the optional exemption, the criteria for the recognition of gains and losses subsequent to the initial recognition of a financial asset or liability only need to be applied prospectively to transactions entered into:

- after 25 October 2002; or
- after 1 January 2004.

6.1.810 *Mandatory exception for the derecognition of financial instruments*

6.1.810.10 A first-time adopter needs to assess the characteristics of its financial instruments recognised under previous GAAP carefully, and consider:

- whether it should recognise financial assets at the date of transition that qualify for recognition in accordance with IFRSs, but which were derecognised under previous GAAP; and
- whether it should derecognise financial assets at the date of transition that qualify for derecognition in accordance with IFRSs, but which continued to be recognised under previous GAAP.

IFRS 1.B2
6.1.810.20 An exception from applying the general requirements of IFRSs in respect of the recognition/derecognition of financial instruments at the date of transition applies to transactions that took place before 1 January 2004. Under a mandatory exception in IFRS 1, a first-time adopter applies the derecognition requirements of IFRSs prospectively to transactions occurring on or after 1 January 2004 in respect of all non-derivative financial assets and liabilities. Under this exception, the previous GAAP accounting for transfers of financial assets and liabilities before 1 January 2004 is not altered, which means that the opening IFRS statement of financial position is not adjusted in respect of such transactions.

6.1.810.30 There are no exceptions for transactions occurring on or after 1 January 2004 and therefore such transactions that resulted in the derecognition of one or more financial instruments under previous GAAP are re-evaluated under IFRSs. If the instruments would not have been derecognised under IFRSs, then they are reinstated in the opening IFRS statement of financial position and are subject to other relevant transition adjustments as necessary.

IFRS 1.B3 6.1.810.40 Notwithstanding this mandatory exception, a first-time adopter may elect to apply the derecognition requirements of IFRSs retrospectively from any date prior to 1 January 2004, provided that the information required to do this was obtained at the time of initially accounting for those transactions.

6.1.810.50 In our view, the exception from retrospective application of the derecognition requirements applies equally to financial instruments that would have qualified for derecognition under IFRSs, but which were not derecognised under previous GAAP.

6.1.810.60 The derecognition requirements of IFRSs are particularly relevant when analysing the transfer of assets in a securitisation arrangement. Importantly, if assets are transferred to a special purpose entity (SPE) and IFRSs are being adopted in the consolidated financial statements, then derecognition is not achieved if the SPE is consolidated (see 2.5.150).

6.1.810.70 For example, in March 2003 Company T transferred a portfolio of long-term receivables to an SPE. To finance the purchase of the receivables, the SPE issued notes to third-party investors. Under its previous GAAP, T derecognised the receivables from its statement of financial position and the SPE was not consolidated. When applying the requirements of IFRS 1:

- T does not reinstate the receivables onto its separate (i.e. unconsolidated) opening IFRS statement of financial position. T does not consider whether the derecognition requirements of IFRSs are met because of the mandatory exception in respect of derecognition transactions occurring before 1 January 2004.
- T determines that the SPE is consolidated under IFRSs. As a result, T's consolidated financial statements will include the SPE and also will include the receivables that had been derecognised under previous GAAP.

6.1.820 *Derivatives#*

IFRS 1.B4(a), 6.1.820.10 Consistent with the general requirement of the financial instruments standards,
IG53, all derivatives within the scope of IAS 39, including embedded derivatives, are measured
IG56(c), at fair value in the opening IFRS statement of financial position. The only exceptions
IAS 39.2(e), relate to derivatives that are linked to and settled by delivery of unquoted equity instru-
46(c) ments whose fair value cannot be measured reliably.

IFRS 1.IG55 6.1.820.20 A first-time adopter assesses whether an embedded derivative is required to be separated from its host contract and accounted for as a derivative on the basis of the conditions that existed when it first became a party to the contract. The initial carrying amounts of the host contract and embedded derivatives are determined based on the circumstances at the date when the entity first became a party to the contract.

IFRS 1.IG55,
IAS 39.13 6.1.820.30 If the fair value of the embedded derivative cannot be determined reliably at the date of initial recognition, then it can be calculated as the difference between the fair value of the hybrid instrument and the fair value of the host contract. If the fair value of the embedded derivative cannot be determined using this technique, then the entire instrument is classified as held for trading and is measured at fair value.

6.1.825 **Forthcoming requirements**

6.1.825.10 Under IFRS 9 embedded derivatives with host contracts that are financial assets within the scope of IAS 39 are not separated; instead, the hybrid financial instrument is assessed as a whole for classification under IFRS 9. Hybrid instruments with host contracts that are not financial assets within the scope of IAS 39 (e.g. financial liabilities and non-financial host contracts) are outside the scope of IFRS 9. See 3.6A.210 for a further discussion of the accounting requirements under IFRS 9 related to embedded derivatives.

6.1.830 *Optional exemption for compound financial instruments*

IFRS 1.IG35,
IAS 32.28 6.1.830.10 A compound instrument is a financial instrument that, from the issuer's perspective, includes both a liability and an equity component. For a compound instrument in which the liability component still is outstanding at the date of transition, a first-time adopter identifies separately the liability and equity components. The equity component is split between the retained earnings component, i.e. cumulative interest on the liability portion, and the "true" equity component. The allocation between liabilities and equity is based on the circumstances at the date of issue of the instrument and the subsequent interest expense on the liability component is calculated using the effective interest method required by IFRSs.

IFRS 1.D18,
IG36 6.1.830.20 If the liability component in a compound instrument no longer is outstanding at the date of transition, then IFRS 1 contains an optional exemption that permits a first-time adopter to ignore the above split between retained earnings and true equity.

6.1.830.30 For example, Company Q is a first-time adopter in 2010. On 1 January 2005 Q issued an instrument for net proceeds of 1,000 with the following terms:

- a notional value of 1,000;
- a 5 percent coupon rate, payable at the end of each year;
- a maturity date of 31 December 2009; and
- the holder has an option to convert the instrument into a specified number of Q's shares at any time during 2009.

6.1.830.40 At the date of issue of 1 January 2005 the same instrument without the conversion feature would have had a fair value of 950. At the date of transition the liability still is outstanding and therefore Q separately identifies and recognises a liability component and an equity component. At the date of issue the liability component would be recognised at its fair value of 950, and the residual of 50 would be allocated to the equity component.

6.1.830.50 Under previous GAAP interest is recognised on the notional amount of 1,000 at a constant rate of 5 percent over the term of the instrument and the carrying amount would remain at 1,000 at each reporting date. Under IFRSs, interest is accrued on the liability component of 950 using the effective interest method over the term and the interest and liability carrying amounts at each reporting date are calculated as follows:

	Carrying amount at 1 January	Interest accrued at 6.0175%	Interest paid	Carrying amount at 31 December
2005	950	57	(50)	957
2006	957	58	(50)	965
2007	965	58	(50)	973
2008	973	59	(50)	982

6.1.830.60 Therefore the adjustment at the date of transition is recorded as follows:

	Debit	Credit
Liability (1,000 – 982)	18	
Retained earnings	32	
Equity – conversion option		50
To recognise compound instrument on transition		

6.1.830.70 In our view, this election may be made on an instrument-by-instrument basis.

6.1.840 [Not used]

6.1.850 *Impairment of financial instruments*

6.1.850.10 There is no exemption in IFRS 1 from the IAS 39 impairment requirements for financial assets and therefore such financial assets are required to be tested for impairment retrospectively under IFRSs. This requires a first-time adopter to assess whether any impairment losses, provisions or general reserves recognised under previous GAAP should be reversed at the date of transition and whether any new impairment losses or reversals of such losses should be provided for in accordance with IFRSs. Any such adjustments are recognised against retained earnings unless another component of equity is appropriate (see 3.6.1370). The latter would be the case, for example, when a reserve exists in respect of an investment classified as available for sale.

IFRS 1.IG58 6.1.850.20 IFRS 1 clarifies that a first-time adopter's estimates of loan impairments at the date of transition are consistent with estimates made for the same date in accordance with previous GAAP, after adjustments to reflect any differences in accounting policies. The only exception is if there is objective evidence that those assumptions were in error under previous GAAP. Therefore, it is only the method of calculating impairment that changes to take into account the requirements of IFRSs. Any later revisions to those estimates are recognised as impairment losses or reversals of impairment losses in the period in which the revision occurs.

6.1.850.30 IFRS 1 does not provide any specific guidance on applying the impairment requirements retrospectively to financial assets. In rare cases, a first-time adopter may not be able to apply retrospectively such requirements to financial assets without the use of hindsight. This is because a first-time adopter firstly would need to have all of the appropriate information available for each financial instrument for each relevant reporting date under previous GAAP. Secondly, assuming that all such information is available, it may prove difficult to make a reasonable assessment of whether there existed objective evidence of impairment of a financial asset at some date in the past, without using hindsight.

6.1.850.40 In our view, in rare cases that a first-time adopter is unable to apply the impairment requirements of IAS 39 retrospectively to financial assets, it is acceptable to apply such impairment requirements at the date of transition. We believe that this assessment should be made on an instrument-by-instrument basis.

6.1.860 Hedge accounting

6.1.870 Mandatory exception on hedge accounting

IFRS 1.B6 6.1.870.10 To prevent a first-time adopter from using hindsight to achieve a specific hedging result, a mandatory exception in IFRS 1 prohibits a first-time adopter from retrospectively designating derivatives and other qualifying instruments as hedges. Accordingly, the exception requires a first-time adopter to apply hedge accounting prospectively from the date of transition if the criteria for hedge accounting in IFRSs are met.

IFRS 1.B4-B6 6.1.870.20 At the date of transition a first-time adopter follows these steps:

- measure all derivatives at fair value;
- in the opening IFRS statement of financial position, derecognise any deferred gains and losses related to derivatives that were reported as assets and liabilities under previous GAAP;
- in respect of hedging relationships for which hedge accounting is to be applied prospectively from the date of transition, ensure that these hedging relationships meet, on or before the date of transition, the conditions for hedge accounting, including designation, documentation and effectiveness testing, as specified in IAS 39; and
- in respect of hedging relationships designated under previous GAAP prior to transition that are of a type that qualify for hedge accounting under IAS 39, adjust the previous GAAP carrying amounts of assets and liabilities and the components of equity in the statement of financial position at the date of transition as explained in 6.1.910.

6.1.880 *Measure all derivatives at fair value*

IFRS 1.B4(a)   6.1.880.10 All derivatives are measured at fair value in the opening IFRS statement of financial position, with certain exceptions (see 6.1.820).

6.1.890 *Derecognise deferred gains and losses that were previously reported as assets and liabilities*

IFRS 1.B4(b)   6.1.890.10 Any assets and liabilities at the date of transition that represent deferred gains and losses on derivatives under previous GAAP are removed from the opening IFRS statement of financial position.

6.1.900 *Identify and designate IFRS hedging relationships*

IFRS 1.IG60   6.1.900.10 A first-time adopter may apply hedge accounting from the date of transition only to hedging relationships that comply with the hedge accounting requirements of IFRSs at that date. These requirements include the need for contemporaneous documentation.

6.1.900.20 For certain hedges designated under previous GAAP, although the hedging relationship is of a type that qualifies for hedge accounting under IFRSs, the first-time adopter may have performed no effectiveness testing or performed effectiveness testing that does not comply with the IAS 39 effectiveness assessment requirements. In such cases, provided that on or before the date of transition the first-time adopter documents an effectiveness testing method for the hedge relationship that complies with IAS 39, and tests effectiveness to demonstrate that the hedge is expected to be highly effective, then in our view the existing hedge relationship may continue on transition.

6.1.900.30 For example, Company B is a first-time adopter in 2010 and its date of transition is 1 January 2009. On 1 October 2008, B designated a one-year interest rate swap as the hedging instrument in a cash flow hedge of the variability in interest payments attributable to changes in LIBOR on a floating rate bond. Under its previous GAAP, since the critical terms of the swap and the bond were matched, B was permitted to assume perfect effectiveness without performing any effectiveness assessment. On 31 December 2008 the deferred balance in equity comprising the entire cumulative gain on the interest rate swap, is 1,000. On 1 January 2009 B adjusts its existing hedge documentation to specify that it would assess effectiveness, both prospectively and retrospectively, using the offset method (see 3.7.500.40). B also performs effectiveness testing under the documented offset method and the hedge is expected to be highly effective.

6.1.900.40 We believe that in this example there is no requirement for the first-time adopter to de-designate the existing hedging relationship and re-designate a new hedging relationship on account of the adjustment to the hedge documentation to specify the method of assessing hedge effectiveness. Accordingly, as the existing hedge relationship continues after transition, for the purpose of testing effectiveness and computing ineffectiveness to be recognised in profit or loss subsequent to transition, B would take into account the original hedge designation date. Therefore, if B decides to use the hypothetical derivative method for measuring effectiveness (see 3.7.545), then the terms of the hypothetical derivative could be determined as of 1 October 2008.

IFRS 1.B5   6.1.900.50 When the hedging relationship designated under previous GAAP is not of a type that qualifies for hedge accounting under IAS 39, e.g. the use of a written option as the hedging instrument or, perhaps more commonly, the hedge of a net position, then such hedging relationship is not reflected in the opening IFRS statement of financial position, except as explained in 6.1.900.60.

6.1.900.60 When a first-time adopter has designated a net position as the hedged item under previous GAAP, it may reflect the hedging relationship in its opening IFRS statement of financial position, only if the first-time adopter designates a gross exposure comprised within that net position as a hedged item in accordance with IFRSs and it does so no later than the date of transition.

6.1.900.70 For example, Company Y is a first-time adopter in 2010. Y's functional currency is FC. Y has certain cash inflows and outflows in a foreign currency (AC) related to the sale of its products and payments for goods, respectively. Y monitors its foreign currency risk exposure by analysing its AC inflows and outflows within cash flow time bands of three months (i.e. on a quarter-by-quarter basis). The cash flows within such time bands relate to either highly probable or committed transactions.

6.1.900.80 Sales and purchases within the three months ended 31 March 2009 are expected to result in cash inflows of AC 1,000 and cash outflows of AC 700. As permitted under previous GAAP, Y designates as the hedged item its expected net inflows of AC during the three months ended 31 March 2009.

6.1.900.90 The net exposure designated as the hedged item under previous GAAP would not qualify for designation as a hedged item under IFRSs.

6.1.900.100 To achieve hedge accounting under IFRSs, Y could, for example, designate as the hedged item as at 1 January 2009 the first AC 300 of highly probable or committed sales in AC for the three months ending 31 March 2009. In this situation, although Y continues to economically hedge a net exposure arising from future sales and purchases in AC, for accounting purposes Y documents the hedged item as a gross amount of sales. The highly probable sales should be designated with sufficient specificity so that it is possible to determine which transactions are the hedged sales transactions when they occur (see 3.7.200.70).

6.1.910 *Adjust previous GAAP carrying amounts*

6.1.920 Fair value hedging relationships

IFRS 1.IG60A   6.1.920.10 For a fair value hedging relationship that is of a type that qualifies for hedge accounting under IFRSs, and for which under previous GAAP gains and losses have either been deferred or not recognised, the first-time adopter adjusts the carrying amount of the hedged asset or liability on the date of transition by the lower of:

- the portion of the cumulative change in the fair value of the hedged item since inception of the hedge that is due to the hedged risk and was not recognised under previous GAAP; and
- the portion of the cumulative change in fair value of the hedging instrument that relates to the designated hedged risk and, under previous GAAP, was either not recognised or was deferred in the statement of financial position as an asset or liability.

6.1.920.20 For example, on 1 January 2007 Company G issued non-cancellable five-year bonds for 500. The interest rate on the bonds is fixed at the then market rate of 6 percent per annum and the bonds were issued at par. G's desired risk management policy is to have variable rate funding and therefore, on 1 January 2007 G also entered into a five-year interest rate swap with a notional amount of 500. The swap pays a floating interest rate based on LIBOR and receives a 6 percent fixed interest rate. Under previous GAAP G had designated the swap as the hedging instrument in a fair value hedge of the exposure to changes in the fair value of the bonds attributable to changes in LIBOR. However, under previous GAAP fair value changes related to the swap were not recognised in G's financial statements and the carrying amount of the bond was recognised at cost. Assume that, ignoring the effects of hedge accounting, on the date of transition the carrying amount of the bond under both previous GAAP and IFRSs is 500.

6.1.920.30 At the date of transition, 1 January 2009, G documents the earlier hedge designation, i.e. the interest rate swap as a fair value hedge of interest rate risk for the issued bonds, and ensures that the hedging relationship meets the conditions for hedge accounting under IAS 39, including effectiveness testing. The hedging relationship is determined to be effective based on the offsetting of the fair value change of the swap and the fair value changes of the bond attributable to changes in LIBOR.

6.1.920.40 On 1 January 2009 the fair value of the bonds is 480. The change in fair value of 20 since inception comprises 15 related to changes in LIBOR and 5 related to changes in G's credit risk. The fair value of the swap as at 1 January 2009 is a liability of 18, all of which relates to changes in LIBOR.

6.1.920.45 When adjusting the carrying amount of the hedged liability at the date of transition, the carrying amount of the bond (liability) is reduced by 15, which is the lower of the cumulative change in the fair value of the hedged item since inception of the hedge due to the hedged risk (15) and the cumulative change in fair value of the hedging instrument (18) (see 6.1.920.10). When recognising the interest rate swap at the date of transition, the interest rate swap liability is reflected at 18.

6.1.920.50 In our view, the carrying amount of the hedged asset or liability to which the adjustment under 6.1.920.10 is applied is arrived at as follows:

(1) Determine the carrying amount of the hedged item under IFRSs on the date of transition as if hedge accounting never was applied. For example, a financial liability classified as other financial liabilities is measured at amortised cost using the effective interest method.

(2) The amount in (1) is then adjusted for the fair value hedge adjustments, if any, that were recognised under previous GAAP.

6.1.920.60 IFRS 1 does not appear to contemplate situations in which a first-time adopter applied fair value hedge accounting under previous GAAP in a manner similar to that required under IAS 39, i.e. by adjusting the carrying amount of the hedged item for fair value changes attributable to the hedged risk. In our view, if the fair value hedge accounting applied under previous GAAP results in substantially the same outcome as if IAS 39 had been applied, then either of the following approaches, applied on a consistent basis, is acceptable at the date of transition to determine the carrying amount of the hedged asset or liability:

- the amount determined in accordance with 6.1.920.50 above; or
- the amount determined in (1) in 6.1.920.50 above, adjusted for the lower of the cumulative change in the fair value of the hedging derivative and the cumulative change in the fair value of the hedged item attributable to the hedged risk.

6.1.920.70 If the hedge accounting applied under previous GAAP does not qualify for hedge accounting under IFRSs, then the hedged item is recognised in accordance with the IFRSs that apply to that item, in which case it is likely that any adjustments to the hedged item under previous GAAP will be reversed.

6.1.930 Cash flow hedging relationships

IFRS 1.IG60B 6.1.930.10 When the hedged item is a forecast transaction, that on the date of transition no longer is highly probable to occur but is still expected to occur, then any deferred gain or loss recognised under previous GAAP is transferred to a separate component of equity, typically referred to as a cash flow hedging reserve. This amount remains in equity until:

IAS 39.97
- the forecast transaction subsequently results in the recognition of a financial asset or financial liability, in which case the amount continues to be held in equity and is transferred to profit or loss when the hedged cash flow affects profit or loss;

IAS 39.98
- the forecast transaction subsequently results in the recognition of a non-financial asset or non-financial liability, at which time the entity should choose an accounting policy, to be applied consistently, either to: (1) continue to hold the amount in equity and transfer it to profit or loss when the related non-financial asset or non-financial liability affects profit or loss; or (2) include the amount in the initial cost or carrying amount of the non-financial asset or non-financial liability (also known as a basis adjustment);

IAS 39.100
- the forecast transaction affects profit or loss, at which time the amount is transferred to profit or loss; or

IAS 39.101(c) • subsequent circumstances indicate that the forecast transaction is no longer expected to occur, in which case the amount is transferred to profit or loss.

IFRS 1. 6.1.930.20 The requirements in 6.1.930.10 mean that any cumulative ineffectiveness prior
IG60B, to the date of transition that was recognised as deferred gains or losses may be recognised
IAS 39.95(b) in the cash flow hedging reserve. However, hedge ineffectiveness arising after the date of transition will be recognised immediately in profit or loss (see 3.7.510.20).

6.1.930.30 To the extent that the related forecast transaction is no longer expected to occur, any deferred gain or loss recognised under previous GAAP is transferred to retained earnings in the opening IFRS statement of financial position.

6.1.940 Net investment hedging relationships

6.1.940.10 Net investment hedging relationships are not dealt with specifically by IFRS 1. However, because IFRSs account for net investment hedges in a manner similar to cash flow hedges, in our view the same basic process as set out in 6.1.930 should be followed.

6.1.940.20 However, when advantage is taken of the transitional relief included in IFRS 1 to set the cumulative translation reserve to zero at the date of transition (see 6.1.1320), the related hedge reserve also will be set at zero with any adjustment arising from the recognition of the derivative or non-derivative hedging instrument being recognised in opening retained earnings.

6.1.950 *Provisions*

6.1.950.10 Generally provisions for repairs and maintenance are derecognised in the opening IFRS statement of financial position (see 3.12.540). In our view, the dere-cognition of such a provision is an indication that a component of the relevant asset may need to be depreciated separately (see 3.2.230). See 6.1.380 for discussion of the identification of components of property, plant and equipment on the first-time adoption of IFRS.

6.1.960 *Optional exemption for changes in decommissioning liabilities included in the cost of property, plant and equipment*

IFRS 1. 6.1.960.10 When an obligation to restore the environment or dismantle an asset arises
IG201, upon the initial recognition of an item of property, plant and equipment, the correspond-
IG202, ing debit is treated as part of the cost of the related asset. This cost includes not only
IAS 16.16(c) the initial estimate of the costs related to dismantlement, removal or restoration of the asset at the time of installing the item, but also amounts recognised during the period of use. Changes in the amount of the provision, other than those related to the production of inventories or the unwinding of the effect of discounting the provision, are adjusted against the carrying amount of property, plant and equipment, and the adjusted depreciable amount is depreciated prospectively over the remaining useful life of the asset.

IFRS 1.D21, 6.1.960.20 IFRS 1 includes an optional exemption that allows a first-time adopter to
IG203 calculate the amount of the provision capitalised in property, plant and equipment in its
opening IFRS statement of financial position using the following steps:

(1) calculate the provision at the date of transition as if the obligation arose at that date,
discounted using a current market-based discount rate;
(2) discount the provision back to the date that the obligation first arose, using the
first-time adopter's best estimate of the historical risk-adjusted discount rate(s) that
would have applied between that date and the date of transition; and
(3) depreciate the resulting present value from the date that the obligation first arose to
the date of transition.

6.1.960.30 For example, on 1 January 2004 Company H acquired a manufacturing plant
at a cost of 900. The plant has a useful life of 30 years and at the end of its useful life
H will be required to decommission the plant in accordance with local regulations; the
obligation arose as a result of the plant being built.

6.1.960.40 Under previous GAAP there is no requirement to recognise a provision for
decommissioning, and the carrying amount of the plant is 750 at the date of transition,
being 1 January 2009. H elects to use the optional exemption in IFRS 1 and as of 1 January 2009 H estimates that a decommissioning provision of 20 should be recognised,
which is the present value, using a current market-based discount rate at that date, of
the estimated amount that will be incurred when decommissioning occurs in 2034.

6.1.960.50 H discounts the 20 back five years to 1 January 2004, using a historical risk-
adjusted discount rate, which results in an amount of 15. H then calculates depreciation
based on the useful life of the plant of 30 years, arriving at an adjusted amount of 12.5
(15 - (15 / 30 x 5)) at the date of transition.

6.1.960.60 H records the following adjustment on transition:

	Debit	Credit
Manufacturing plant	15	
Retained earnings	7.5	
Accumulated depreciation		2.5
Decommissioning liability		20
To recognise decommissioning liability at date		
of transition		

6.1.970 Interaction with the deemed cost exemption

6.1.970.10 A first-time adopter considers the interaction between the decommissioning
provision and the fair value as deemed cost exemption (see 6.1.350), if elected, to establish the opening balance for property, plant and equipment at the date of transition.
When fair value is used as deemed cost, the valuation is grossed up for any provision

for decommissioning, if the valuation reflects the price that a third party would pay for the asset and assume the related obligation to decommission the asset, i.e. the amount of the asset less the provision is what the third party would pay. The decommissioning liability is measured in accordance with IFRSs and the resulting adjustment is recognised in opening retained earnings.

6.1.970.20 If the valuation does not reflect the price that a third party would pay for the asset and assume the related liability, then the difference between the fair value of the asset and the previous GAAP carrying amount is recognised as an adjustment to opening retained earnings. The decommissioning liability is measured in accordance with IFRSs and the resulting adjustment also is recognised in opening retained earnings.

6.1.970.30 Modifying the example in 6.1.960.30, H chooses to apply the fair value as deemed cost exemption at the date of transition (see 6.1.350). The fair value of the plant at the date of transition is 850, which reflects the price a third party would pay for the asset and assume the restoration obligation. At the date of transition, H records the following adjustment:

	Debit	Credit
Accumulated depreciation	150	
Manufacturing plant		150
To reverse accumulated depreciation at date of transition		
Manufacturing plant (850 - 750)	100	
Retained earnings		100
To recognise plant at fair value at date of transition		
Manufacturing plant	20	
Provision for restoration		20
To recognise restoration provision at date of transition		

IFRS 1.D21A 6.1.970.40 If a first-time adopter uses the deemed cost exemption for oil and gas assets in the development or production phases (see 6.1.1610), then the amount of any adjustments required to measure decommissioning, restoration and similar liabilities in accordance with IAS 37 *Provisions, Contingent Liabilities and Contingent Assets* at the date of transition is recognised directly in retained earnings rather than adjusting the carrying amount of the underlying assets.

6.1.980 *Employee benefits*

6.1.990 *Retrospective calculation of the "corridor" for defined benefit plans**

IFRS 1.D10, 6.1.990.10 In the absence of a specific exemption, a first-time adopter would be required to
IAS 19.155 recalculate all actuarial gains and losses from inception of each post-employment defined benefit plan if it intended to use a "corridor" approach to recognising actuarial gains and losses.

IFRS 1.D10   6.1.990.20 Alternatively, in respect of actuarial gains and losses for a defined benefit plan, a first-time adopter may elect to apply the exemption to recognise all cumulative actuarial gains and losses at the date of transition as an adjustment to opening retained earnings. This option is available even if the first-time adopter will apply the corridor approach thereafter or elect to recognise actuarial gains and losses using a method that results in faster recognition in profit or loss than the corridor method after the date of transition.

IFRS 1.D10   6.1.990.30 An election to use the first-time adoption exemption is applied to all defined benefit plans and cannot be applied on a plan-by-plan basis.

6.1.1000 *Estimates*

IFRS 1.14,   6.1.1000.10 The measurement of employee benefit obligations under IFRSs requires an
IAS 19.72   entity to make demographic assumptions, for example to select mortality tables. A first-time adopter's estimates under IFRSs at the date of transition are consistent with estimates made for the same date under previous GAAP (after adjustments to reflect any difference in accounting policies), unless there is objective evidence that those estimates were in error (see 6.1.180). In our view, if the assumptions made under previous GAAP are consistent with the methodologies and assumptions required under IFRSs, then the same mortality tables should be used to determine the defined benefit obligation, unless there is objective evidence that those estimates were in error.

IFRS 1.IG20   6.1.1000.20 However, IFRSs may require a first-time adopter to make actuarial assumptions that were not required under previous GAAP, or were made using assumptions different from those under IFRSs. For example, IAS 19 *Employee Benefits* may require the use of a discount rate that is different from previous GAAP. In such cases the first-time adopter uses estimates that reflect conditions at the date of transition; they cannot reflect conditions that arose after that date (see 6.1.180).

6.1.1010 *Disclosure of experience*

IFRS 1.D11   6.1.1010.10 A first-time adopter may elect to provide the following information in respect of its defined benefit plans for the current and four previous periods prospectively from its date of transition:

- the present value of the defined benefit obligation, fair value of plan assets and the surplus/deficit in the plan; and
- experience adjustments arising on plan assets (liabilities) expressed as either an amount or as a percentage of plan assets (liabilities).

6.1.1020 **Share-based payment transactions**

6.1.1030 *Transitional requirements and optional exemption*

IFRS 1.D2,   6.1.1030.10 The requirements of IFRS 1 in respect of share-based payment transactions
D3, IG65   match the transitional requirements that applied to existing users of IFRSs when IFRS 2

1584

Share-based Payment came into effect in 2005. A first-time adopter is *required* to apply IFRS 2 to:

- equity instruments that were granted after 7 November 2002 that will vest *after* the date of transition;
- liabilities arising from cash-settled share-based payment transactions that will be settled *after* the date of transition; and
- awards that are modified *on or after* the date of transition, even if the original grant of the award is not accounted for in accordance with IFRS 2.

IFRS 1.D2, D3, IG64   6.1.1030.20 Additionally, a first-time adopter is *encouraged*, but not required, to apply IFRS 2 retrospectively to:

- equity instruments that were granted on or before 7 November 2002, or equity instruments that were granted after 7 November 2002 that vested before the date of transition. However, such application is allowed only if the first-time adopter had publicly disclosed the fair value of such awards determined at the measurement date in accordance with IFRS 2; and
- liabilities arising from cash-settled share-based payment transactions that were set-tled before the date of transition.

6.1.1030.30 Awards for which retrospective application of IFRS 2 is encouraged but not required are referred to in this chapter as "otherwise exempt awards". The optional exemption in IFRS 1 in respect of share-based payment transactions permits a first-time adopter to elect to not apply IFRS 2 to otherwise exempt awards.

6.1.1030.40 The following table demonstrates how application of the optional exemption impacts grants of equity-settled share-based payments made by entities with their first IFRS reporting date on 31 December 2010 or 30 June 2011:

Reporting date	Date of transition	Grant date	Vesting date	Treatment
31 December 2010	1 January 2009	On or before 7 November 2002	Before or after 1 January 2009	No share-based payment cost recognised*
		After 7 November 2002	Before 1 January 2009	No share-based payment cost recognised*
			On or after 1 January 2009	Recognise share-based payment cost for 31 December 2010 and 31 December 2009; and adjust 1 January 2009 retained earnings

Reporting date	Date of transition	Grant date	Vesting date	Treatment
30 June 2011	1 July 2009	On or before 7 November 2002	Before or after 1 July 2009	No share-based payment cost recognised*
		After 7 November 2002	Before 1 July 2009	No share-based payment cost recognised*
			On or after 1 July 2009	Recognise share-based payment cost for 30 June 2011 and 30 June 2010; and adjust 1 July 2009 retained earnings

> *   Only a modification to the terms of the award on or after the date of transition would result in the recognition of share-based payment cost (see 6.1.1060), unless the first-time adopter applies IFRS 2 retrospectively to an otherwise exempt award (see 6.1.1040).

6.1.1040 *Retrospective application to otherwise exempt equity-settled awards*

IFRS 1.D2   6.1.1040.10 A first-time adopter may apply the recognition and measurement requirements of the share-based payment standard retrospectively to equity instruments for which it is otherwise not required to do so *only* if:

- the first-time adopter had disclosed publicly the fair value of those equity instruments, measured in a manner consistent with IFRS 2; and
- the fair value was determined at the measurement date, as defined in IFRS 2.

6.1.1040.20 In our view, retrospective application of the recognition and measurement requirements of the share-based payment standard to otherwise exempt awards may be applied on a grant-by-grant basis. We believe that a grant-by-grant election is possible since application of the standard to otherwise exempt awards is encouraged when possible and the availability of the required fair value data may vary for grants made at different dates.

IFRS 1.D2   6.1.1040.30 The publicly disclosed fair value should have been determined on the measurement date required by, and following the valuation methodology of, IFRS 2.

6.1.1040.40 In our view, the fair value should have been disclosed prior to publication of the first IFRS financial statements; however, it does not have to have been disclosed publicly at the time that the award was granted.

6.1.1040.50 If the first-time adopter previously has disclosed publicly fair value information at an aggregated level and that fair value is supported by sufficiently detailed calculations to permit estimates of the fair values of the separate share-based payment plans to be determined, then in our view the disclosure requirements for previous public disclosure have been met for the separate awards.

IFRS 1.D2, 2.44, 45   6.1.1040.60 Certain of the disclosure requirements that apply to share-based payment transactions also apply to grants of equity instruments to which the recognition and measurement requirements of IFRS 2 have not been applied.

6.1.1050 Awards to which the recognition and measurement requirements of the standard have not been applied

6.1.1050.10 IFRSs do not specifically address the treatment in the opening IFRS statement of financial position of share-based payment cost recognised under previous GAAP for awards to which the recognition and measurement requirements of IFRS 2 are not applied (see 6.1.1030.20). For example, under its previous GAAP a first-time adopter may have accounted for equity-settled share-based payment awards by debiting share-based payment cost in profit or loss and crediting a separate category of equity, such as contributed surplus or additional paid-in-capital. As a result, for such equity-settled share-based payment awards which are effectively "grandfathered", it is unclear as to what, if any, adjustments should be made at the date of transition.

6.1.1050.20 In our view, a first-time adopter should choose one of the following accounting approaches to be applied consistently at the date of transition:

- *Approach 1.* Share-based payment cost recognised in equity under previous GAAP is reversed in the opening IFRS statement of financial position. This is because IFRS 1 generally requires the opening IFRS statement of financial position to be prepared in accordance with IFRSs, and the standard usually is explicit when an optional exemption permits the "grandfathering" of previous GAAP. As the optional exemption for share-based payment transactions does not permit explicitly the grandfathering of share-based payment cost recognised under previous GAAP, a first-time adopter may reverse the accounting under previous GAAP.
- *Approach 2.* Share-based payment cost recognised under previous GAAP is not reversed. This is because the circumstances in which IFRS 1 permits explicitly the grandfathering of previous GAAP generally relate to the accounting for assets and liabilities, and not to items of equity. This approach results in no adjustment at the date of transition, which may be seen as more in line with the objective of the share-based payment standard, i.e. that a first-time adopter recognises in profit or loss, and thereby equity, the effects of share-based payment transactions.

6.1.1050.30 For example, Company X is a first-time adopter in 2010. In 2005 X granted share options to its employees; each option vests after a three-year service period. The aggregate fair value of the awards under previous GAAP was 200.

6.1.1050.40 By 1 January 2009 all of the awards have vested and share-based payment cost of 200 was recognised in profit or loss under previous GAAP, with the corresponding credit being recognised as contributed surplus, which is a separate component of equity. As the awards vested prior to X's date of transition, X is not required to apply IFRSs to these awards.

6.1.1050.50 Under Approach 1 in 6.1.1050.20, X reverses the share-based payment cost recognised under previous GAAP at the date of transition by reallocating 200 from the contributed surplus to retained earnings.

6.1.1050.60 Under Approach 2 in 6.1.1050.20, X makes no accounting entry at the date of transition in respect of the share-based payment cost recognised under previous GAAP.

6.1.1060 *Modification of awards*

6.1.1060.10 An entity may modify the terms and conditions of a share-based payment arrangement, e.g. it may reduce the exercise price of the options granted, which would increase the fair value of those options.

IFRS 1.D2   6.1.1060.20 Modifications to the terms or conditions of a grant of equity instruments will affect a first-time adopter as follows:

- *Modifications occurring before the date of transition.* The recognition and measurement requirements of IFRS 2 are not required to be applied when the original grant is not accounted for in accordance with IFRS 2.
- *Modifications occurring on or after the date of transition.* The recognition and measurement requirements of IFRS 2 are applied, even if the original grant was not accounted for in accordance with IFRS 2. However, in our view the modification accounting should be applied to the modification but not to the original grant, i.e. the original grant-date fair value should remain unrecognised and only the incremental fair value, if any, should be accounted for; this is because paragraph 57 of IFRS 2 specifically refers to the accounting for the modification.

6.1.1060.30 If an entity elects to apply IFRS 2 retrospectively to otherwise exempt equity-settled or cash-settled awards (see 6.1.1030.30), then in our view any modifications to those awards before the date of transition also should be accounted for in accordance with IFRS 2.

6.1.1060.40 An equity-settled share-based award granted after 7 November 2002 with a vesting date after the date of transition is required to be accounted for in accordance with IFRS 2 (see 6.1.1030.10). However, if such a grant is modified before the date of transition so that the instruments vest fully before this date, then in our view the transaction is not required to be accounted for under IFRS 2.

6.1.1070 *Adjustments on transition for awards to which the recognition and measurement requirements of IFRS 2 are applied*

6.1.1070.10 If the requirements of IFRS 2 are applied (see 6.1.1030.10) or the first-time adopter applies IFRS 2 to otherwise exempt awards (see 6.1.1030.20), then the recognition and measurement requirements of IFRS 2 are applied retrospectively. Any differences arising from this accounting at the date of transition generally are recognised in opening retained earnings.

6.1.1080 *Share-based payment exemption and deferred taxes*

IAS 12.9, 68B 6.1.1080.10 In some jurisdictions entities receive a tax deduction based on the intrinsic value of equity-settled share-based payment transactions (e.g. share options) when the employees exercise their options and receive the equity instruments. IAS 12 *Income Taxes* provides specific guidance regarding the accounting for any tax deductions available on share-based payment transactions within the scope of IFRS 2 (see 3.13.630.10). In respect of options issued after 7 November 2002, a temporary difference arises between the tax base (based on the future tax deductions) of the share option and its carrying amount in the opening IFRS statement of financial position (zero because the IFRS 2 share-based payment cost is offset by a corresponding credit entry in equity). A resulting deferred tax asset is recognised if the recognition criteria in IAS 12 are met.

IAS 12.68C, 6.1.1080.20 However, neither IFRS 1 nor IAS 12 provides specific guidance regarding
IEB.Ex5 the treatment of taxes on share-based payment transactions outside the scope of IFRS 2, e.g. equity-settled share-based payment transactions granted before 7 November 2002. One approach is to identify the difference between the tax base of the share options and their carrying amount of zero as a temporary difference on which a deferred tax asset should be recognised, subject to recoverability (see 3.13.170). In accordance with the principle in IAS 12 that the tax consequences of a transaction are recognised in a manner consistent with the accounting for the transaction itself, the deferred tax asset will be recognised in equity because the underlying transaction will affect equity upon exercise of the options and issue of the shares. The initial recognition exemption in IAS 12 is not available as the difference only develops over time. Alternatively, the first-time adopter may elect not to identify a temporary difference and consequently not to recognise any deferred tax on the basis that the share-based payments granted prior to 7 November 2002 have not been recognised in the IFRS financial statements and hence there is no carrying amount, rather than a carrying amount of zero, recognised for accounting purposes (see 3.13.630.40).

6.1.1085 *Deferred tax*

6.1.1090 *Recognition of transition adjustments*

6.1.1090.10 [Not used]

IFRS 1.C4(k) 6.1.1090.20 Deferred tax assets and liabilities are adjusted to reflect any adjustments to book value recognised as a result of adopting IFRSs; and to measure deferred tax assets and deferred tax liabilities in accordance with the requirements of IFRSs (see 3.13).

IFRS 1.IG5 6.1.1090.30 If there is a taxable temporary difference in the opening IFRS statement of financial position, then a deferred tax liability is recognised in that opening IFRS statement of financial position. Adjustments to the balance of deferred tax at the date of transition are recognised in equity, generally in retained earnings, except in the following circumstances:

- If a business combination is restated, then the balance of deferred tax at the acquisition date is determined as part of the reconstruction of the acquisition accounting (see 6.1.1230). The corresponding adjustment is against goodwill at the acquisition date.
- If a business combination is not restated but an intangible asset is either subsumed into goodwill or is recognised separately from goodwill at the date of transition, then any related adjustment to deferred tax is recognised against goodwill.

6.1.1090.40 A first-time adopter should take particular care to distinguish the adjustment for deferred tax made in the second bullet in 6.1.1090.30 (related to a goodwill adjustment for an intangible asset) from any adjustment to deferred tax related to an unadjusted intangible asset. If deferred tax is recognised in relation to an intangible asset recognised under previous GAAP that was not adjusted in an unrestated business combination, then the adjustment is to retained earnings and not to goodwill.

6.1.1100 *Subsequent measurement*

IAS 12.61A   6.1.1100.10 Generally changes in the carrying amount of deferred tax that relate to changes in the related temporary differences are recognised in profit or loss. Other changes, for example resulting from changes in tax rates, are recognised in profit or loss unless they relate to items previously recognised in other comprehensive income or directly in equity (see 3.13.360).

6.1.1100.20 In our view, the first-time adopter should recognise any subsequent changes in deferred taxes in a manner consistent with how the deferred tax originally would have been recognised if the first-time adopter had been an existing user of IFRSs.

6.1.1100.30 [Not used]

6.1.1100.40 In our view, the principle of recognising changes in deferred tax in accordance with IAS 12 subsequent to the date of transition applies equally to deferred tax arising in a business combination, regardless of whether or not the business combination was restated (see 6.1.1110).

6.1.1100.50 See 6.1.1080 for a discussion of deferred taxes related to share-based payment transactions.

6.1.1110 *Business combinations*

6.1.1120 *Optional exemption for business combinations*

IFRS 1.C1   6.1.1120.10 IFRS 1 provides an optional exemption whereby a first-time adopter may elect not to apply IFRSs retrospectively to business combinations that occurred prior to the date of transition. However, all business combinations occurring on or after the date of transition are required to be accounted for in accordance with IFRSs.

IFRS 1.C1   6.1.1120.20 For business combinations that occurred before the date of transition, entities have the following choices:

- restate all of these business combinations;
- restate all business combinations after a particular date; or
- do not restate any of these business combinations.

6.1.1120.30 If one business combination that is not required to be restated is restated voluntarily, then all subsequent business combinations and acquisitions are restated.

IFRS 1.C1   6.1.1120.40 If business combinations are not restated, then the previous acquisition accounting remains unchanged. However, some adjustments, for example to reclassify intangibles and goodwill, may be required (see 6.1.1140).

IFRS 1.C5   6.1.1120.50 The business combinations exemption applies equally to acquisitions of investments in associates and interests in joint ventures that occurred prior to the date of transition. If a first-time adopter chooses to restate business combinations that occurred after a particular date prior to the date of transition, then that cut-off date applies equally to acquisitions of investments in associates and interests in joint ventures (see 6.1.1350).

6.1.1130 Definition of a business combination

6.1.1130.10 In our view, the business combination exemption is available to all transactions that would be considered to be a business combination under IFRSs (i.e. to all business combinations as defined in IFRS 3), regardless of how the transaction was accounted for under previous GAAP. We believe that the business combinations exemption is not available for transactions that are described as business combinations under previous GAAP, but which do not meet the definition of a business combination under IFRSs. In our view, the exemption is available even if the business combination is outside the scope of IFRS 3 (e.g. a common control transaction or the formation of a jointly venture).

6.1.1130.20 For example, Company S's controlling shareholder, X, owns controlling interests in a number of other companies. In 2008 S acquired all of the shares in Company V, another operating company owned by X and in which S had no interest prior to the transaction. The transaction was a combination of businesses under common control. In assessing business combinations under previous GAAP, S applies the definition of a business combination in IFRS 3, i.e. a transaction or other event in which an acquirer obtains control of one or more businesses. Since V is a business, the definition of a business combination is met and the exemption can be applied to the acquisition of V even though common control transactions are outside the scope of IFRS 3.

6.1.1130.30 When a first-time adopter refers to the definition of a business combination in IFRSs to determine whether the exemption applies, an issue arises as to which version of the business combinations standard is relevant. Over the years successive standards have included slightly different definitions of a business combination. In particular, IFRS 3 (2008), which applies to business combinations in annual periods beginning on or after 1 July 2009, includes a more restrictive definition than IFRS 3 (2004).

6.1.1130.40 In our view, each business combination under previous GAAP should be assessed using the definition in the standard effective as at the first annual IFRS reporting date. For example, a first-time adopter with a first annual IFRS reporting date of 31 December 2009 would be required to use the definition of a business combination in IFRS 3 (2004), unless the first-time adopter chose to early adopt IFRS 3 (2008). However, a first-time adopter with a first annual IFRS reporting date of 31 December 2010 uses the definition of a business combination in IFRS 3 (2008).

IFRS 1.B7 6.1.1130.50 In our view, the exemption also extends to any additional interest acquired between the date of the unrestated business combination and the date of transition. For example, Company P is a first-time adopter in 2010. In 2005 P acquired 65 percent of Company S, and in 2007 acquired the remaining 35 percent. P elects not to restate business combinations that occurred prior to its date of transition, 1 January 2009. In our view, the business combination exemption is applied to the 100 percent interest in the assets and liabilities of S.

6.1.1140 *Accounting for unrestated business combinations*

6.1.1140.10 Once a first-time adopter has determined which business combinations under previous GAAP will not be restated upon the adoption of IFRSs, the following steps are relevant:

(1) maintain previous GAAP classification;
(2) determine whether any additional assets or liabilities are recognised;
(3) determine whether any recognised assets or liabilities are derecognised;
(4) remeasure the assets and liabilities subsequent to the business combination if appropriate;
(5) adjust the measurement of goodwill if appropriate;
(6) eliminate any balance of negative goodwill.

6.1.1140.20 Although not specifically mentioned in the section that follows, a first-time adopter considers the consequential effects on deferred tax and non-controlling interests whenever an adjustment is made.

6.1.1150 Maintain previous GAAP classification

IFRS 1.C4(a), 6.1.1150.10 If a first-time adopter does not apply IFRSs retrospectively to past
IG22 Ex 2 business combinations, then it keeps the same classification of the business combination as under previous GAAP. For example, if under previous GAAP a business combination was treated as an acquisition by the legal acquirer, then this classification is maintained even if the transaction would have been classified as a reverse acquisition under IFRSs.

6.1.1160 Determine whether any additional assets or liabilities are recognised

IFRS 1.C4(b), 6.1.1160.10 Even if the accounting for a business combination is carried forward from
C4(f) previous GAAP, the general requirements of IFRS 1 in respect of the recognition of
assets and liabilities still apply (see 6.1.135). This requirement to assess recognition
means, for example that an asset cannot be omitted from the opening IFRS statement
of financial position simply on the basis that it was not recognised in the accounting for
the business combination under previous GAAP.

IFRS 1.C4(b) 6.1.1160.20 However, an asset, including goodwill, is not recognised in the first-time
(ii), C4(f) adopter's statement of financial position unless it would be recognised in the acquiree's
own statement of financial position if it were prepared in accordance with IFRSs.

6.1.1160.30 For example, Company H will be a first-time adopter in 2010. H acquired
subsidiary M in 2006 in a transaction that would be a business combination under
IFRSs. H elects not to restate the acquisition of M. As part of the accounting for the
business combination under previous GAAP, a lease that had been entered into by M
was classified as an operating lease and no asset or liability related to the lease was
recognised in H's consolidated statement of financial position. However, under IFRSs
the lease would have been classified as a finance lease in M's statement of financial
position based on an assessment of the facts and circumstances at inception of the
lease. The lease remains in force at 1 January 2009. Therefore, in order to comply with
the recognition requirements of IFRS 1, the leased asset and the finance lease liability
will be recognised in H's opening IFRS statement of financial position (see 6.1.1550).

IFRS 1.C4(b) 6.1.1160.40 An asset is not recognised in the parent's opening IFRS statement of financial
(i) position if it would be subject to the mandatory exception in IFRS 1 in respect of the
derecognition of financial assets (see 6.1.810). In other words, the mandatory exception
overrides the business combinations exemption.

IFRS 1.IG22 6.1.1160.50 If an asset or liability acquired in an unrestated business combination is
Ex 2, Ex 5, recognised for the first time as a result of applying this exemption, then it is measured
Ex 7 at the amount that would have been recognised in the acquiree's own IFRS financial
statements. Unless otherwise indicated, the resulting adjustment is recognised in opening retained earnings.

6.1.1160.60 Continuing the example in 6.1.1160.30, H determines the adjustments required
to its opening IFRS statement of financial position as follows:

- The leased asset is an item of property, plant and equipment. Therefore, H applies the
  guidance in respect of such assets (see 6.1.325) to determine the appropriate carrying amount at the date of transition. H elects to apply the fair value as deemed cost
  exemption at the date of transition. As a result, the asset has a deemed cost of 100.
- H applies the guidance in respect of finance leases (see 6.1.1550) to determine
  the appropriate carrying amount of the lease liability at the date of transition. H
  determines a carrying amount of 80, which is the amount of the lease liability that

would have been recognised in M's own IFRS financial statements if the lease had been classified as a finance lease at its inception.

6.1.1170 Determine whether any recognised assets or liabilities are derecognised

IFRS 1.C4(c), IG22 Ex 3, Ex 4 6.1.1170.10 Assets and liabilities recognised in an unrestated business combination under previous GAAP are eliminated from the opening IFRS statement of financial position if they do not qualify for recognition under IFRSs.

6.1.1170.20 For example, Company R is a first-time adopter in 2010. R acquired Subsidiary Y in 2008 in a transaction that would be a business combination under IFRSs. R elects not to restate the acquisition of Y. As part of the accounting for the business combination under previous GAAP, R recognised a provision related to the future restructuring of Y's activities and the amount is still outstanding at 1 January 2009. This restructuring liability does not qualify for recognition under IFRSs at the acquisition date in the financial statements of Y (see 3.12.230). Therefore, the liability is eliminated from R's opening IFRS statement of financial position.

6.1.1180 Remeasure the assets and liabilities subsequent to the business combination if appropriate

IFRS 1.C4(e) 6.1.1180.10 The carrying amount under previous GAAP of assets acquired and liabilities assumed in an unrestated business combination immediately after the business combination becomes their deemed cost at that date, even if a different amount would have been assigned under IFRSs.

IFRS 1.C4(f) 6.1.1180.20 The only exception to this principle is in the case of assets or liabilities that were assigned a deemed cost of zero and which are recognised because they would be recognised in the acquiree's statement of financial position if it were prepared in accordance with IFRSs.

6.1.1180.30 In our view, the phrase "immediately after the business combination" includes adjustments made to the carrying amounts of the assets and liabilities acquired during the measurement period under previous GAAP, i.e. for the period during which the business combination accounting is kept open for adjustments under previous GAAP. This would be the case even if the measurement period under previous GAAP ends after the date of transition.

6.1.1180.40 For example, Company X is a first-time adopter in 2010. X acquired Subsidiary B in 2007 in a transaction that would be a business combination under IFRSs. X elects not to restate the acquisition of B. Under previous GAAP X was allowed, until 31 December 2008, to finalise the amounts assigned provisionally to the assets and liabilities acquired. During 2008 an appraisal report on the acquisition was completed, and it indicated that certain of the equipment acquired had a fair value 20 higher than the amount assigned provisionally by X. Under previous GAAP X adjusted the business combination accounting by increasing the carrying amount of equipment at the acquisition date, with a corresponding adjustment to goodwill. In our view, the costs of equipment and goodwill immediately after the business combination are the adjusted amounts following receipt of the appraisal report.

IFRS 1.C4(d), 6.1.1180.50 Having established deemed cost at the acquisition date, the measurement
(e), IG22 requirements of IFRSs are applied subsequent to that date. Therefore, property, plant
Ex 2 and equipment is depreciated using a method and rate that is appropriate under IFRSs and component accounting is applied (see 6.1.380). Similarly, investment property that the first-time adopter elects to measure using the fair value model is recognised at fair value in the opening IFRS statement of financial position (see 6.1.590).

6.1.1180.60 If the asset or liability qualifies for the fair value or revaluation as deemed cost exemption, then in our view this exemption also is available at the date of transition (see 6.1.330, 530 and 590).

6.1.1190 Adjust the measurement of goodwill if appropriate

IFRS 1.C4(b), 6.1.1190.10 The balance of goodwill at the date of transition, arising from an unrestated
C4(c)(i), business combination, is adjusted only in respect of the following:
C4(g)

IFRS 1. • to recognise separately certain intangible assets that were subsumed within goodwill
C4(g)(i) under previous GAAP, including any consequential effect on deferred tax and non-controlling interests (see 6.1.1090 and 6.1.1300);

IFRS 1. • to subsume within goodwill certain intangible assets that were recognised separately
C4(g)(i) under previous GAAP, including any consequential effect on deferred tax and non-controlling interests (see 6.1.1090 and 6.1.1300);

IFRS 1.14 • to correct any errors discovered upon the transition to IFRSs; and

IFRS 1.C4(g) • to recognise any impairment loss on goodwill at the date of transition (see 6.1.690).
(ii)

IFRS 1.C4(h), 6.1.1190.20 No other adjustments to the balance of goodwill at the date of transition are
IG22 Ex 2 made. This is the case even if goodwill was accounted for under previous GAAP, between the date of the business combination and the date of transition, using a method that did not comply with IFRSs. For example, under previous GAAP goodwill may have been amortised, which is prohibited under IFRSs.

IFRS 1.C4(c) 6.1.1190.30 The above discussion assumes that goodwill was recognised as an asset under
(ii), C4(i), previous GAAP. If, for example goodwill was written off against equity on the date of
IG22 Ex 5 the business combination, then no adjustments are made that would create a goodwill balance at the date of transition. Instead, all adjustments are made against retained earnings. Additionally, in this example the goodwill cannot be reclassified to profit or loss as part of the gain or loss upon disposal of the subsidiary.

6.1.1190.40 When a subsidiary was accounted for using the equity method under previous GAAP, the balance of goodwill would have been embedded in the carrying amount of the investee. That amount becomes the carrying amount of goodwill for the purpose of applying IFRS 1, i.e. the amount embedded in the carrying amount of the investee previously is presented separately when the subsidiary is consolidated under IFRSs.

IFRS 1.C4(g) 6.1.1190.50 Goodwill acquired in an unrestated business combination is tested for impair-
(ii) ment at the date of transition in accordance with IFRSs, with any resulting impairment loss recognised directly in retained earnings. This mandatory impairment testing is required regardless of whether there is any indication that the goodwill may be impaired.

6.1.1200 Gain on a bargain purchase

IFRS 3.34-36 6.1.1200.10 When a gain on a bargain purchase arises in a business combination under IFRSs, the acquirer reassesses the procedures on which its acquisition accounting is based and whether amounts included in the acquisition accounting have been appropriately determined. Any amount remaining after this reassessment is recognised immediately in profit or loss at the acquisition date (see 2.6.900). Consistent with IFRSs, the balance of any gain on a bargain purchase that is still recognised in the first-time adopter's statement of financial position at the date of transition is eliminated against retained earnings.

IFRS 1.C4(e) 6.1.1200.20 Under previous GAAP a gain on a bargain purchase arising in a business combination may have been used to reduce the carrying amount of some or all of the assets acquired. In our view, the carrying amounts of any such assets should not be adjusted at the date of transition. This is because the carrying amount under previous GAAP of assets acquired and liabilities assumed in an unrestated business combination immediately after the business combination becomes their deemed cost at that date (see 6.1.1180.10).

6.1.1210 Contingent consideration not recognised under previous GAAP

6.1.1210.10 IFRSs do not specifically address the treatment in the opening IFRS statement of financial position of contingent consideration that was not recognised under previous GAAP in an unrestated business combination and which remains outstanding at the date of transition. See 2.6.1010 for a discussion of contingent consideration.

6.1.1210.20 In our view, contingent consideration that was not recognised in an unrestated business combination and is determined to be liability-classified at the date of transition in accordance with IFRSs, should be recognised in the opening IFRS statement of financial position with a corresponding adjustment to retained earnings. The measurement of the liability-classified contingent consideration, both at the date of transition and subsequently, is based on the relevant IFRS, e.g. IAS 39 or IAS 37, or another relevant standard. Any changes in the measurement of the liability-classified contingent consideration after the date of transition generally are recognised in profit or loss.

6.1.1210.30 If liability-classified contingent consideration was recognised under previous GAAP and also meets the recognition criteria under IFRSs at the date of transition, but was measured differently, then in our view the transition adjustment to reflect the measurement difference at the date of transition would be recorded against opening retained earnings.

6.1.1210.40 IFRSs prohibit the remeasurement of equity-classified contingent considera-tion that arises in a business combination subsequent to the acquisition date. Therefore if, in an unrestated business combination, equity-classified contingent consideration was not recognised, then it is unclear as to what, if any, adjustment is made at the date of transition.

6.1.1210.50 In our view, an entity should choose one of the following accounting approach-es, to be applied consistently, in respect of equity-classified contingent consideration at the date of transition, if the recognition criteria under IFRSs have been met at that date:

- *Approach 1*. The equity-classified contingent consideration is not recognised at the date of transition in the opening IFRS statement of financial position. This is because IFRSs do not permit subsequent remeasurement of such equity instruments and IFRS 1 does not include a specific requirement to adjust for such instruments in an unrestated business combination at the date of transition.
- *Approach 2*. The equity-classified contingent consideration is measured in accord-ance with IFRSs at the date of transition in the opening IFRS statement of financial position. This is because non-recognition of such instruments would go against the general principle of recording assets and liabilities that qualify for recognition in the opening IFRS statement of financial position. Even though the general principle relates to assets and liabilities, we believe that it also would be appropriate to ex-tend this principle to equity-classified contingent consideration in such situations. Under this approach, the corresponding adjustment on the date of transition would be recorded against opening retained earnings, and the equity-classified contingent consideration would not be remeasured subsequently.

6.1.1220 Subsidiary not consolidated under previous GAAP

6.1.1220.10 Depending on the requirements of previous GAAP, a subsidiary might be consolidated for the first time at the date of transition. This might occur, for example because previous GAAP did not require the preparation of consolidated financial state-ments or because of a specific exclusion from the scope of consolidation.

6.1.1220.20 When a subsidiary is being consolidated for the first time, IFRS 1 includes a mandatory formula for the calculation of goodwill. See 6.1.1260 for a discussion of the requirements related to previously unconsolidated subsidiaries, and the implications thereof.

6.1.1230 *Accounting for restated business combinations*

6.1.1230.10 IFRS 1 permits a first-time adopter to restate past business combinations retrospectively in accordance with IFRSs (see 6.1.1120). However, retrospective restate-ment may be a very difficult and onerous exercise, and in fact may prove impracticable in certain circumstances. This is primarily due to the requirement that the information available to restate the past business combination is required to be available at the time of the acquisition; the use of hindsight is prohibited. This may cause a practical difficulty for a first-time adopter as they may not have been aware of all of the information to be collected at the acquisition date in order to record the business combination on a basis consistent with IFRSs.

6.1.1230.20 Some of the general issues that may be encountered are:

- calculating the consideration transferred in the business combination in accordance with IFRSs and assessing whether any contingent consideration should be recognised without the use of hindsight;
- assessing whether to recognise contingent liabilities at the acquisition date, again without the use of hindsight; and
- measuring the fair value of assets acquired and liabilities assumed at the acquisition date on a basis consistent with IFRSs.

6.1.1240 Testing goodwill for impairment in a restated business combination

IFRS 1.BC39, 6.1.1240.10 There is no specific requirement in IFRSs that goodwill acquired in a restated
BC40 business combination be tested for impairment at the date of transition. However, IFRSs provide some guidance that suggests that the impairment standard in IFRSs is applied at the date of transition in determining whether any impairment loss exists at that date.

6.1.1240.20 If goodwill acquired in a restated business combination is not tested for impairment at the date of transition, then such goodwill would be required to be tested for impairment at some point during the first IFRS comparative period, unless there was an indication that a possible impairment existed at the date of transition (see 6.1.690).

6.1.1240.30 We prefer that a first-time adopter tests all goodwill for impairment at the date of transition even if there is no indication that an impairment exists at the date of transition. This is particularly important when the impairment requirements of previous GAAP differ significantly from the impairment requirements of IFRSs.

6.1.1250 Goodwill and fair value adjustments of foreign operations

IAS 21.47, 6.1.1250.10 IFRSs require any goodwill and fair value adjustments arising on the
IG21A acquisition of a foreign operation to be treated as part of the assets and liabilities of the foreign operation and translated at the closing exchange rate at the reporting date.

IFRS 1.C2 6.1.1250.20 A first-time adopter is not required to apply this requirement between the acquisition date in a business combination and the date of transition, regardless of whether or not the business combination is restated. Instead, the first-time adopter treats any goodwill and fair value adjustments as assets of the parent.

IFRS 1.C3 6.1.1250.30 However, a first-time adopter may apply this requirement retrospectively to:

- all business combinations; or
- all business combinations that are being restated (see 6.1.1230).

6.1.1260 *Consolidation*

6.1.1270 *Previously unconsolidated subsidiaries*

6.1.1270.10 IFRSs require the consolidation of all subsidiaries (see 2.5). However, a first-time adopter's previous GAAP may not have required consolidation of an entity that is considered a subsidiary under IFRSs. This may occur because:

- previous GAAP did not require the consolidation of certain subsidiaries, e.g. because the subsidiary had dissimilar operations to the parent, or the subsidiary was held for sale;
- previous GAAP did not require the consolidation of subsidiaries held by venture capital or investment companies, or similar entities; or
- previous GAAP did not require the consolidation of a subsidiary acquired and to be disposed of in the "near future".

IFRS 1.C2(j) 6.1.1270.20 For example, a subsidiary may have been classified as an investment in associate or a joint venture under previous GAAP because the definitions under previous GAAP of subsidiaries, associates and joint ventures are different from the definitions of those entities under IFRSs (see 2.5 and 3.5). The exemption from the restatement of past business combinations applies also to past acquisitions of investments in associates and of interests in joint ventures. However, this exemption covers only the initial acquisition transaction. All subsidiaries are consolidated in the opening IFRS statement of financial position.

6.1.1280 Requirements on first-time consolidation of previously unconsolidated subsidiaries

6.1.1280.10 [Not used]

IFRS 1.C4(j), 6.1.1280.20 When a subsidiary is being consolidated for the first time, the following steps
IG22 Ex6, are followed at the date of transition:
IG27

(1) Measure the assets and liabilities of the subsidiary in the parent's opening IFRS consolidated statement of financial position based on the amounts that would be recognised in the subsidiary's financial statements if the subsidiary were applying IFRSs.
(2) Measure goodwill at the date of transition as the difference between:
  – the parent's interest in the amounts ascribed to the assets and liabilities of the subsidiary in (1) above; and
  – the cost of the investment in the subsidiary as it would be reflected in the parent's separate financial statements, if prepared.

6.1.1280.30 This calculation effectively increases goodwill by the amount of any post-acquisition losses, and reduces goodwill by the amount of any post-acquisition profits.

6.1.1280.40 In our view, in determining the carrying amounts of the assets and liabilities of the subsidiary in (1) in 6.1.1280.20, the exceptions and exemptions in IFRS 1 apply as if the subsidiary were a first-time adopter.

6.1.1280.50 For example, Company L is a first-time adopter in 2010. L acquired all of the shares in Company J in 2005. J was not consolidated by L under previous GAAP because its business activities were dissimilar from those of the rest of the group. L acquired J for 100, which is the cost of the subsidiary in L's separate financial statements. The carrying amount of J's net assets is 60, which includes property, plant and equipment with a carrying amount of 35. As part of determining the carrying amount of J's assets and liabilities on an IFRS basis, L uses the fair value as deemed cost exemption (see 6.1.350) to measure property, plant and equipment at its fair value of 55. When recording its investment in J at the date of transition, L recognises various assets and liabilities at 80 (60 + 55 - 35), the cost of investment in J at 100, and goodwill as the difference of 20 (100 - 80).

IFRS 3.34 6.1.1280.60 In many cases applying the above formula for the calculation of goodwill will result in a gain on a bargain purchase at the date of transition. In that case the difference will be recognised in opening retained earnings because negative goodwill is recognised in profit or loss immediately under IFRSs (see 6.1.1200).

IFRS 1.C4(j) 6.1.1280.70 IFRS 1 is very specific in referring to the "cost" of the investment in the
(ii) subsidiary as the basis for the calculation of goodwill. Therefore, in our view any additional amounts included in the carrying amount of the investee in the parent's separate financial statements, e.g. fair value changes, will be eliminated against retained earnings at the date of transition.

6.1.1280.80 In our view, if a first-time adopter elected to measure its investment in subsidiary at a deemed cost at the date of transition, then this is the cost of the investment in subsidiary used in the calculation referred to in (2) in 6.1.1280.20 (see 6.1.1630).

IFRS 1.IG27 6.1.1280.90 The calculation of deemed goodwill applies to previously unconsolidated
(c) subsidiaries that were acquired in a business combination. If a subsidiary was not acquired in a business combination, i.e. the subsidiary was created by the first-time adopter, then no goodwill is recognised. In such cases, when the adjusted net assets of the subsidiary are less than the cost of the investment in the parent's separate financial statements, the resulting adjustment does not create goodwill, but rather is a debit to retained earnings.

6.1.1290 *Non-controlling interests*

6.1.1295 *Business combinations restated*

IFRS 1.B7 6.1.1295.10 If a first-time adopter elects to restate any or all business combinations (see 6.1.1230), then the balance of non-controlling interests at the date of transition related to all such subsidiaries is determined retrospectively, taking into account the impact of other elections made as part of the adoption of IFRSs. In this case IAS 27 *Consolidated and Separate Financial Statements* is applied (see 2.6.840), regardless of its application date for existing users of IFRSs.

6.1.1300 *Business combinations not restated*

6.1.1300.10 – 20 [Not used]

IFRS 1.B7, IG28

6.1.1300.30 In respect of business combinations that are not restated upon the adoption of IFRSs (see 6.1.1120), the balance of non-controlling interests under previous GAAP is not changed other than for adjustments made as part of the transition to IFRSs. This means that the following specific requirements of IFRSs in relation to non-controlling interests are applied prospectively from the date of transition:

IAS 27.28 • the attribution of total comprehensive income between non-controlling interests and the owners of the parent;

IAS 27.30, 31 • the accounting for changes in ownership interests without the loss of control; and

IAS 27.34-37 • the accounting for the loss of control in a subsidiary.

6.1.1300.40 If a subsidiary is being consolidated for the first time, then non-controlling interests are recognised as part of the initial consolidation adjustment.

6.1.1300.50 For example, Company X is a first-time adopter in 2010. X acquired 80 percent of the shares in Company Z in 2007. Z was not consolidated by X under previous GAAP because its business activities were dissimilar from those of the rest of the group. X acquired Z for 100, which is the cost of the subsidiary in X's separate financial statements. The carrying amount of Z's net assets on an IFRS basis would be 60. To consolidate Z at the date of transition, X records its investment in Z in its opening IFRS consolidated statement of financial position as follows:

	Debit	Credit
Various assets and liabilities	60	
Goodwill (100 - (60 x 80%))	52	
Non-controlling interests		12
Cost of investment in Z		100
To consolidate Z at date of transition		

6.1.1310 *Agreements to acquire non-controlling interests*

6.1.1310.10 Agreements may be entered into as part of a business combination whereby a parent entity commits to acquire the shares held by the non-controlling interests in a subsidiary, or whereby the non-controlling interest in a subsidiary holds a put option that would require the parent to purchase its non-controlling interests in the future. This is an area that requires careful analysis on transition to IFRSs. See 2.5.300 and 460 for a further discussion of the accounting treatment for such agreements.

6.1.1315 *Foreign currency translation*

6.1.1320 *Optional exemption for cumulative foreign currency translation differences*

6.1.1320.10 [Not used]

IFRS 1.D13 (a) BC53- BC55 6.1.1320.20 IFRSs require that cumulative translation differences arising on the translation of a foreign operation be recognised as a separate component of equity (see 2.7.230). A first-time adopter may either:

- apply IAS 21 *The Effects of Changes in Foreign Exchange Rates* retrospectively to determine the cumulative translation differences for each foreign operation that should be recognised as a separate component of equity at the date of transition; or
- deem the cumulative translation differences to be zero at the date of transition, and reclassify any amounts recognised in accordance with previous GAAP at that date as retained earnings.

IFRS 1.D13 (a) 6.1.1320.30 The optional exemption is applied consistently to all foreign operations, including interests in joint ventures and investments in associates that are foreign operations. The gain or loss on the subsequent disposal of any foreign operation *excludes* translation differences that arose before the date of transition if a first-time adopter elected to reset the cumulative foreign currency translation differences to zero at the date of transition. The optional exemption is not relevant for the translation of foreign currency transactions in which such exchange differences generally are recognised in profit or loss.

IAS 21.39 6.1.1320.40 Cumulative foreign currency translation differences also arise when a first-time adopter presents its financial statements in a presentation currency that is different from its functional currency. This is because the translation procedures are the same as those for translating foreign operations. In our view, the optional exemption to deem cumulative foreign currency translation differences to be zero also applies to cumulative foreign currency translation differences that arise on translating financial statements from a first-time adopter's functional currency to a different presentation currency (see 2.7.290), even though such translation differences do not relate to foreign operations and will not reclassified to profit or loss.

6.1.1330 Determination of functional currency

6.1.1330.10 IAS 21 includes specific requirements for the selection of an appropriate functional currency under IFRSs (see 2.7.400). These requirements may differ from previous GAAP, for example when previous GAAP assumes a first-time adopter's functional currency of the country in which the first-time adopter is domiciled.

6.1.1330.20 There is no optional exemption in IFRS 1 that allows a first-time adopter to determine its functional currency at the date of transition, and to simply translate its opening IFRS statement of financial position into the functional currency using the spot rate at the date of transition. Therefore, a first-time adopter is required to consider the appropriate functional currency since inception because otherwise the carrying amount of non-monetary assets may be misstated in the opening IFRS statement of financial position. This may be another reason for a first-time adopter to consider using the deemed cost exemption for property, plant and equipment, intangible assets and investment property (see 6.1.330, 530 and 590, respectively). If the exemption is elected, then the deemed cost is translated into the first-time adopter's functional currency at the date of its determination. The following example illustrates the difficulty of determining the appropriate functional currency retrospectively.

6.1.1330.30 For example, under previous GAAP Company X's functional currency was euro. However, under IFRSs it is determined that X's functional currency always would have been US dollars (USD). Therefore, X reconstructs the carrying amount of property, plant and equipment on an IFRS basis at the date of transition, which is 1 January 2009, as follows:

Transaction	Euro	Rate	USD
Acquisition[1]	1,000	1.50	1,500
Depreciation[2]	(100)	1.45	(145)
Additions[1]	270	1.78	481
Depreciation[2]	(130)	1.30	(169)
Carrying amount	1,040		1,667

Notes
(1) The historical exchange rate at the acquisition date.
(2) The average exchange rate for each year.

6.1.1330.40 The above example shows that if USD had been used as X's functional currency since the acquisition of the asset, then its carrying amount at the date of transition would have been USD 1,667.

6.1.1330.50 Assuming that the spot rate at 1 January 2009, is 1.35, then a different result is obtained if the first-time adopter simply takes the carrying amount of the property, plant and equipment at the date of transition in euro and translates it to USD; in that case the carrying amount would be USD 1,404, which would be inappropriate because, under IFRSs, the carrying amount of non-monetary assets is not restated at the latest exchange rate at each reporting date.

6.1.1340 Hyperinflationary economies

IFRS 1.IG33, 6.1.1340.10 IFRS 1 does not provide relief to first-time adopters from the ret-
IG34, BC67 rospective application of IAS 29 *Financial Reporting in Hyperinflationary Economies*. Therefore, when an entity prepares its first IFRS financial statements, IAS 29 is applied to any periods during which the economy of the functional currency of the entity or

any of its investees was hyperinflationary. See 2.4.20 for a discussion of the accounting treatment for hyperinflation.

6.1.1340.20 A first-time adopter not only considers whether such economies are hyperinflationary at the date of transition, but also whether any of these economies were ever hyperinflationary in the past. If this is the case, then IAS 29 is applied retrospectively to those past periods.

6.1.1340.30 In order to avoid some of the effort required to apply IAS 29 retrospectively, a first-time adopter may consider using the deemed cost exemption for property, plant and equipment, intangible assets and investment property (see 6.1.330, 530 and 590 respectively). If the deemed cost exemption is elected, then the requirements of IAS 29 are applied to these non-monetary assets only after the date for which the fair value or revaluation amount was established, to the extent that the economy still is considered to be hyperinflationary, which could result in less effort upon transition.

6.1.1350 *Investments in associates and interests in joint ventures*

6.1.1350.10 In the absence of any exemptions, a first-time adopter would be required to apply equity accounting, on an IFRS basis, to investments in associates from their acquisition date. The difficulties associated with this approach are the same as those that apply to business combinations.

6.1.1350.20 In order to avoid such a process, the following requirements in respect of investments in subsidiaries also apply to investments in associates and interests in joint ventures:

IFRS 1.C5 ● The optional exemption for business combinations also applies to acquisitions of investments in associates and interests in joint ventures before the date of transition (see 6.1.1120). If a first-time adopter chooses to restate business combinations that occurred after a particular date prior to the date of transition, then that cut-off date applies equally to associates and joint ventures.

IFRS 1.D16, D17 ● The requirements that apply when a first-time adopter transitions to IFRSs either before or after its parent (investor) also apply to associates and joint ventures (see 6.1.1360).

IFRS 1.D14, D15 ● The optional exemption for investments in subsidiaries in the separate financial statements of a parent also applies to associates and jointly controlled entities (see 6.1.1630).

6.1.1350.30 Additionally, the exemptions that apply to the assets and liabilities of a first-time adopter or its subsidiaries also apply to the assets and liabilities of an associate or jointly controlled entity for the purpose of applying the equity method of accounting (or proportionate consolidation in case of a jointly controlled entity). For example, the carrying amount of the property, plant and equipment of an associate at the date of transition can be based on its fair value (see 6.1.330).

IFRS 1.C2, 6.1.1350.40 Goodwill recognised under previous GAAP in respect of an unrestated busi-
C3 ness combination is required to be tested for impairment at the date of transition
(see 6.1.690.10). For acquisitions of associates or jointly controlled entities that occurred
before the date of transition and for which the business combination exemption is applied, goodwill recognised under previous GAAP is included in the carrying amount
of the investment in the associate or jointly controlled entity (if entity accounting is
applied); and is not presented separately from the investment (see 3.5.330).

6.1.1350.50 See 6.1.690 for impairment testing of goodwill at the date of transition in
respect of an unrestated acquisition of an associate.

6.1.1360 *Assets and liabilities of subsidiaries, associates and joint ventures*

IFRS 1.D16, 6.1.1360.10 See 6.1.30 for guidance on determining when an entity has adopted IFRSs
D17 for the first time. It is possible that individual entities in a group (i.e. a parent and its
subsidiaries) or their associates and joint ventures will adopt IFRSs at different dates
(i.e. each may have a different date of transition). There are special requirements and
exemptions when this is the case.

6.1.1360.20 The exemptions and related requirements apply to subsidiaries, associates
and joint ventures.

6.1.1370 *Adoption in parent's separate and consolidated financial statements*

IFRS 1.D17 6.1.1370.10 When a parent adopts IFRSs in its separate financial statements earlier or
later than in its consolidated financial statements, it measures its assets and liabilities
at the same amounts in both sets of financial statements, except for consolidation
adjustments.

6.1.1370.20 In our view, consolidation adjustments include accounting policy alignments,
as explained in 6.1.1390 and 6.1.1460 in relation to a parent adopting IFRSs later or
earlier than a subsidiary.

6.1.1380 *Parent/investor becomes a first-time adopter later than its subsidiary, associate or joint venture*

IFRS 1.D17 6.1.1380.10 The discussion that follows refers to a parent and its subsidiary. However,
the requirements apply equally to an investor and its associate or joint venture.

IFRS 1.D17 6.1.1380.20 There are no optional exemptions available to a parent that adopts IFRSs in
its consolidated financial statements later than a subsidiary with respect to the measurement of assets and liabilities of the subsidiary that will be included in the parent's first
IFRS consolidated financial statements. In the consolidated financial statements of the
parent, the assets and liabilities of the subsidiary are measured at the same carrying
amounts as in the financial statements of the subsidiary, after adjusting for the effects
of consolidation procedures and business combination accounting.

6.1.1380.30 In our view, the requirement for the parent to use amounts included in the financial statements of the subsidiary applies regardless of the subsidiary's basis of conversion to IFRSs; for example, the subsidiary might have applied SIC-8 *First-time Application of IASs as the Primary Basis of Accounting*, which preceded IFRS 1.

6.1.1380.40 In general the exceptions and exemptions in IFRS 1 are not applicable to the parent in respect of the measurement of the assets and liabilities of the subsidiary. However, there are circumstances in which the parent is not required to measure the assets and liabilities of the subsidiary in this manner:

- the parent elects accounting policies in its IFRS consolidated financial statements different from those used by the subsidiary in its IFRS financial statements (see 6.1.1390); and/or
- in the business combination accounting in which the subsidiary was acquired (see 6.1.1400).

6.1.1390 Consolidation adjustments

6.1.1390.10 The consolidation adjustments required prior to incorporating the subsidiary's assets and liabilities into the parent's opening IFRS statement of financial position include the elimination of intra-group balances, transactions and accounting policy alignments (see 6.1.1370.20).

6.1.1390.20 In our view, when consolidation adjustments include the alignment of accounting policies, then the optional exemptions in Appendix D are available to the parent in respect of the assets and liabilities of the subsidiary. This is because we believe that the availability of the optional exemptions overrides the requirement regarding subsidiaries when dealing with the alignment of accounting policies; otherwise there would be no relief provided by IFRS 1.

6.1.1400 Business combinations accounting

IFRS 1.D17   6.1.1400.10 When recognising the subsidiary's assets and liabilities in the parent's opening IFRS statement of financial position, the parent is required to consider the effects of the business combination in which it acquired the assets, and assumed the liabilities, of the subsidiary.

IFRS 1.D17   6.1.1400.20 The mandatory requirements when a parent adopts IFRSs later than its subsidiary do not override the requirements in IFRS 1 with respect to past business combinations (see 6.1.1120). Therefore, a parent would apply Appendix C of IFRS 1 to account for the assets acquired and liabilities assumed in the business combination in which it acquired the subsidiary.

IFRS 1.IG   6.1.1400.30 However, for new assets acquired and liabilities assumed by the subsidiary
30(a)   after the business combination that are still held by the subsidiary at the parent's date of transition, generally the parent uses the carrying amounts in the IFRS financial statements of the subsidiary.

6.1.1400.40 This means that it will be necessary for the parent to separate the assets and liabilities of the subsidiary at its date of transition into two categories:

- assets acquired and liabilities assumed in the business combination in which the subsidiary was acquired; and
- assets acquired and liabilities assumed by the subsidiary subsequent to the business combination.

6.1.1410 Interaction with the deemed cost exemption

6.1.1410.10 A first-time adopter is able to elect to recognise certain assets at deemed cost at the date of transition (see 6.1.330, for example). However, in our view, in general a parent may not apply the deemed cost exemption to establish the carrying amount of an asset of a subsidiary if the subsidiary adopted IFRSs before the group. This is because the parent is required to measure the assets and liabilities of the subsidiary at the same carrying amounts as in the financial statements of the subsidiary.

6.1.1410.20 However, if a parent adopts a policy of revaluing property, plant and equipment, and the subsidiary has a policy of cost, then in our view this overrides the requirement regarding subsidiaries because it constitutes an accounting policy alignment (see 6.1.1390.10).

6.1.1410.30 Alternatively, if the subsidiary adopts a policy of revaluing property, plant and equipment, and the parent has a policy of cost, then in our view the deemed cost exemption is available to the parent with respect to the property, plant and equipment of the IFRS reporting subsidiary (see 6.1.1390.20).

6.1.1420 Interaction with the optional exemption for actuarial gains and losses

6.1.1420.10 A first-time adopter is able to elect to recognise cumulative actuarial gains and losses directly in opening retained earnings at the date of transition (see 6.1.990.20). If the parent elects this optional exemption, then it is applied to all defined benefit plans. However, when a subsidiary adopts IFRSs before its parent, the parent is required to measure the assets and liabilities of the subsidiary at the same carrying amounts as in the financial statements of the subsidiary.

6.1.1420.20 If the subsidiary has unrecognised actuarial gains or losses at the parent's date of transition, then there is a conflict between the requirement for the parent to measure the assets and liabilities of the subsidiary based on the carrying amounts in the financial statements of the subsidiary, and the ability to apply the optional exemption for actuarial gains and losses to all defined benefit plans.

6.1.1420.30 In our view, the requirement regarding subsidiaries overrides the ability to apply the optional exemption for actuarial gains and losses to all defined benefit plans. Accordingly, the unrecognised actuarial gains and losses related to the defined benefit plan of the subsidiary should not be recognised in opening retained earnings at the parent's date of transition. This is because we believe that the optional exemptions themselves are not accounting policy choices.

6.1.1420.40 However, if a parent adopts a policy of recognising all actuarial gains and losses as incurred, either in profit or loss or in other comprehensive income, then in our view this overrides the requirement regarding subsidiaries because it constitutes an accounting policy alignment (see 6.1.1390.20).

6.1.1420.50 Alternatively, if a subsidiary adopts a policy of recognising all actuarial gains and losses as incurred, either in profit or loss or in other comprehensive income, and the parent adopts a policy of recognising actuarial gains and losses using the corridor method, then in our view the optional exemption for actuarial gains and losses (see 6.1.990.20) is available to the parent with respect to the defined benefit plan of the subsidiary.

6.1.1420.60 For example, Company P has one subsidiary, Company X. Both entities have post-employment defined benefit plans. P is a first-time adopter in 2010 and elects the optional exemption to recognise cumulative actuarial gains and losses in opening re-tained earnings and subsequently applies the corridor method for recognising actuarial gains and losses under IFRSs. X, which had a date of transition of 1 January 2004 elected to recognise actuarial gains and losses immediately in other comprehensive income in its IFRS financial statements. Therefore, at P's date of transition of 1 January 2009 the cumulative unrecognised actuarial gains and losses of X are zero.

6.1.1420.70 Absent the availability of the optional exemption, P would be required to apply the corridor method retrospectively to determine the cumulative unrecognised actuarial gains and losses of X at its date of transition. However, the optional exemption applies also to the defined benefit plan of X, and therefore P is not required to apply this policy retrospectively in respect of X. Therefore, P recognises the cumulative actuarial losses in equity at the date of transition.

6.1.1430 Interaction with the optional exemption for cumulative foreign currency transla-tion differences

6.1.1430.10 A first-time adopter is able to deem cumulative translation differences to be zero at the date of transition, and reclassify any such amounts determined in accordance with previous GAAP at that date to retained earnings. The optional exemption, when elected, is applied consistently to all foreign operations (see 6.1.1320).

6.1.1430.15 In our view, when a parent is a first-time adopter later than its subsidiary, the parent can elect to deem the cumulative foreign currency translation differences to be zero, and reclassify any amounts recognised in accordance with previous GAAP at that date as retained earnings, even if the subsidiary did not make this election in respect of its own IFRS financial statements. This is because the requirement to measure all assets and liabilities of the subsidiary at the same carrying amount as in the financial statements of the subsidiary is not affected by the cumulative translation adjustment exemption, which is a component of equity.

6.1.1430.20 For example, Company P has three subsidiaries, Companies X, Y and Z, which are foreign operations from the perspective of P. The investment in Z is held by Y. Y was a first-time adopter in 2007 and elected to recognise the cumulative foreign currency translation differences related to Z under previous GAAP in opening retained earnings.

6.1.1430.30 P elects to reset the cumulative foreign currency translation differences related to X, Y and Z to zero at the date of transition. This includes the cumulative translation differences for X and Y as determined under previous GAAP, as well those for Z that have arisen between Y's date of transition of 1 January 2006 and P's date of transition of 1 January 2009, as determined under IFRSs.

6.1.1440 *Subsidiary, associate or joint venture becomes a first-time adopter later than its parent/investor*

IFRS 1.D16   6.1.1440.10 The discussion that follows refers to a subsidiary and its parent. However, the requirements apply equally to an associate or joint venture and its investor.

6.1.1440.20 A subsidiary may adopt IFRSs later than its parent and also may have been reporting previously to the parent on an IFRS basis for group reporting purposes without presenting a full set of IFRS financial statements. Without any relief, the subsidiary would be required to keep two sets of parallel accounting records: one set for group reporting purposes based on the parent's date of transition; and one set for the subsidiary's own financial statements based on its own date of transition.

IFRS 1.D16,   6.1.1440.30 When a subsidiary adopts IFRSs later than its parent, the subsidiary may
BC60   measure its assets and liabilities at either:

- the amounts included in the consolidated financial statements of the parent, based on the parent's date of transition, excluding the effects of consolidation procedures and the business combination in which the parent acquired the subsidiary; or
- the carrying amounts required by IFRS 1 based on the subsidiary's own date of transition.

IFRS 1.BC61   6.1.1440.40 The optional election to measure the assets and liabilities of the subsidiary based on the parent's date of transition provides relief in that it reduces, but does not eliminate, differences between the subsidiary's IFRS financial statements and the group reporting package. For example, as a reporting package does not constitute a full set of financial statements, the parent may have recorded certain material IFRS adjustments centrally, e.g. pension cost adjustments. Therefore, additional IFRS adjustments still may be required even when the subsidiary elects to measure its assets and liabilities based on the parent's date of transition.

IFRS 1.IG31   6.1.1440.50 In addition, the group materiality threshold likely will be higher for group reporting than required for the subsidiary's own financial statements. When the materiality threshold for group reporting is well in excess of that in the financial statements of the subsidiary, it may be particularly onerous for the subsidiary to determine all of the adjustments required when preparing its opening IFRS statement of financial position that were not recognised in its IFRS reporting package. The required adjustments also would need to be determined relative to the parent's date of transition, and then rolled forward from the parent's date of transition to the subsidiary's date of transition. In these cases, the subsidiary effectively may be precluded from electing the optional exemption altogether on practical grounds.

6.1.1445 Subsidiary elects to use IFRS 1 based on its own date of transition

IFRS 1.D16
(b)
6.1.1445.10 If the subsidiary chooses to measure its assets and liabilities in accordance with IFRS 1 based on its own date of transition, then the subsidiary applies the requirements of IFRS 1 without regard to the parent. In such cases it is likely that the subsidiary will need to maintain two sets of parallel accounting records: one set for group reporting purposes based on the parent's date of transition; and one set for the subsidiary's own financial statements based on its own date of transition. However, this option provides the subsidiary with additional flexibility to select optional exemptions that otherwise would not be available.

6.1.1450 Subsidiary elects to use IFRS 1 based on its parent's date of transition

6.1.1450.10 – 20 [Not used]

6.1.1450.30 In our view, the optional exemption for the subsidiary to use amounts included in the consolidated financial statements of the parent is available regardless of the parent's basis of conversion to IFRSs; for example, the parent might have applied SIC-8, which preceded IFRS 1.

IFRS 1.D16
(a)
6.1.1450.40 The requirement regarding subsidiaries means that a subsidiary, at its date of transition, is required to measure its assets and liabilities using the same carrying amounts as in the IFRS consolidated financial statements of the parent, after adjusting for the effects of consolidation procedures and the business combination in which the subsidiary was acquired.

6.1.1450.50 When the subsidiary elects the optional exemption, the other exceptions and exemptions in IFRS 1 generally are not applicable to the subsidiary. However, there are circumstances in which the subsidiary is not required to measure its assets and liabilities in this manner:

- the subsidiary elects accounting policies in its IFRS financial statements different from those used by the parent in its IFRS consolidated financial statements (see 6.1.1460); and/or
- the assets and liabilities of the subsidiary were part of the net assets of the subsidiary at the time of the business combination in which the subsidiary was acquired by the parent.

6.1.1460 Consolidation procedures

6.1.1460.10 The consolidation adjustments required prior to incorporating the carrying amount of the subsidiary's assets and liabilities in the parent's consolidated financial statements into the subsidiary's opening IFRS statement of financial position include the elimination of intra-group balances, transactions and accounting policy alignments (see 6.1.1370.20).

6.1.1460.20 In our view, when consolidation adjustments include the alignment of accounting policies, then the optional exemptions are available to the subsidiary in respect of its assets and liabilities. This is because we believe that the availability of the optional exemptions overrides the requirement regarding the parent when dealing with the alignment of accounting policies; otherwise there would be no relief provided by IFRS 1.

6.1.1470 Business combination accounting

6.1.1470.10 The requirements of IFRS 1 in respect of a subsidiary transitioning to IFRSs later than its parent are complex, particularly for groups with numerous subsidiaries and in different jurisdictions.

IFRS 1.D16 (a), IG30(a) 6.1.1470.20 In order to apply the requirements of IFRS 1, it is necessary to understand the timing of the business combination in which the parent acquires the subsidiary and the subsidiary's acquisition of any subsidiaries in relation to the parent's date of transition and its own date of transition.

6.1.1480 Business combination in which the parent acquires the subsidiary

IFRS 1.D16 (a) 6.1.1480.10 When recognising the assets and liabilities in the subsidiary's opening IFRS statement of financial position, the subsidiary is required to eliminate the effects of the business combination in which it was acquired by the parent.

IFRS 1.IG30 (a) 6.1.1480.20 Adjusting for the effect of the business combination in which the parent acquired the subsidiary effectively means that in effect the requirements of paragraph D16(a) do not apply to assets acquired and liabilities assumed prior to the date on which the parent acquired the subsidiary. Accordingly, the mandatory exceptions and optional exemptions apply to such assets and liabilities (see 6.1.230 and 240).

6.1.1490 Business combinations after the parent acquires the subsidiary

IFRS 1.IG30 (a) 6.1.1490.10 After its acquisition by the parent but prior to its date of transition, a subsidiary that is transitioning to IFRSs may have completed its own acquisitions of subsidiaries. In our view, when the subsidiary elects to use the carrying amounts in the financial statements of the parent, the requirements of Appendix C of IFRS 1 do not override the requirements for the subsidiary to measure its assets and liabilities at the carrying amounts in the parent's consolidated financial statements.

6.1.1490.20 However, if the subsidiary's acquisition of its own subsidiaries during this period is prior to the parent's transition to IFRSs, then the accounting for the acquisition in the subsidiary's IFRS consolidated financial statements will reflect the choices that the parent made in respect of accounting for the business combination in preparing its opening IFRS consolidated statement of financial position.

6.1.1490.30 For example, Company S was acquired by Parent P on 1 July 2007 and Company T was acquired by S on 1 January 2003. Costs of 150 were incurred in respect of the restructuring of T in 2003 and goodwill of 650 was recognised. P elected to not restate the business combination in which S was acquired upon its adoption of IFRSs. As the acquisition of T occurred prior to P's date of transition of 1 January 2004, it was accounted for in P's consolidated financial statements under previous GAAP in the same manner as it was accounted for in the financial statements of S. In addition, as P elected not to restate the acquisition in which S was acquired, the carrying amounts assigned to the assets and liabilities under previous GAAP became their deemed cost immediately after the acquisition date.

6.1.1490.40 Therefore, P did not recognise an adjustment to goodwill in respect of the acquisition of T in its opening IFRS statement of financial position, even though goodwill under previous GAAP of 650 includes an amount of 150 that would not have been recorded in acquisition accounting under IFRSs (see 6.1.1190). As S is required to measure its assets and liabilities at the carrying amounts in the consolidated financial statements of P, the business combination exemption is not relevant to S, and S measures the goodwill of T in its opening IFRS statement of financial position at 650.

6.1.1490.50 If the subsidiary's acquisition of its own subsidiaries during this period is subsequent to the parent's transition to IFRSs, then the accounting for the acquisition in the subsidiary's IFRS consolidated financial statements will be in accordance with IFRSs.

6.1.1500 *Dual compliance and implicit compliance*

6.1.1500.10 An entity is a first-time adopter when, for the first-time, its annual financial statements include an explicit and unreserved statement of compliance with IFRSs (see 6.1.30 – 70).

6.1.1500.20 When a subsidiary, associate or joint venture adopting IFRSs before or after its parent/investor includes an explicit and unreserved statement of compliance with an IFRS equivalent, and not IFRSs as issued by the IASB, then in our view either of the following approaches, applied on a consistent basis, is acceptable:

- *Approach 1.* The requirements in IFRS 1 when a subsidiary, associate or joint venture adopts IFRSs before or after its parent/investor are not applicable. This is because such requirements are predicated on an entity stating explicit compliance with IFRSs. The omission of a statement of compliance with IFRSs would result in the relevant group entity not having to follow such requirements.
- *Approach 2.* The requirements in IFRS 1 when a subsidiary, associate or joint venture adopts IFRSs before or after its parent/investor are applicable if it is determined that compliance with IFRSs could have been made. The entity would need to assess, and

make a determination of, whether the relevant group entity who previously adopted the IFRS equivalent could also have asserted dual compliance with both IFRSs and its IFRS equivalent. If it is determined that dual compliance could have been possible, then the relevant group entity adopting IFRSs would be required to follow the requirements in IFRSs when a subsidiary, associate or joint venture adopts IFRSs before or after its parent/investor.

6.1.1510 *Leases*

6.1.1520 *Optional exemption for arrangements containing a lease*

6.1.1520.10 IFRIC 4 *Determining whether an Arrangement contains a Lease* requires an entity to assess whether an arrangement contains a lease at the inception of the arrangement. Arrangements are reassessed only if certain criteria are met. Any reassessment is based on the facts and circumstances at the date of assessment (see 5.1).

IFRS 1.D9, 6.1.1520.20 An existing user of IFRSs need not perform an assessment retrospectively
IFRIC 4.17 at the date of inception. Instead, it may apply the interpretation to arrangements existing at the start of the earliest period for which comparative information is presented, based on the facts and circumstances existing at that date. First-time adopters may apply the transitional provisions in IFRIC 4, i.e. to arrangements existing at the date of transition, based on facts and circumstances at that date.

6.1.1530 *Optional exemption on reassessment of lease determination*

IFRS 1.IG205, 6.1.1530.10 In some jurisdictions, a first-time adopter's previous GAAP may have had
BC63DA the same accounting requirements as that required by IFRSs; the only difference being the effective date of the standard, differences in transitional requirements and/or slight differences in wording. The IASB recognised this to be the case with respect to IFRIC 4. Without any specific relief, a first-time adopter that had the equivalent standard as IFRIC 4 in its previous GAAP, and elected the optional exemption for arrangements containing a lease, would be required to reassess its lease determination at the date of transition, even though it already would have performed such an assessment under previous GAAP.

IFRS 1.D9A, 6.1.1530.20 IFRS 1 includes an optional exemption that if a first-time adopter made the
IG206 same determination of whether an arrangement contains a lease under previous GAAP as that required by IFRIC 4 but at a date other than that required by IFRIC 4, then the first-time adopter need not reassess that determination for such arrangements when it adopts IFRSs. For a first-time adopter to have made the same determination under previous GAAP as that under IFRSs, the determination is required to give the same outcome as applying IAS 17 *Leases* and IFRIC 4.

IFRS 1.BC 6.1.1530.30 In our view, the exemption is available even when the date on which an
63DA arrangement was assessed under previous GAAP was the same as the date that would have been required if IFRIC 4 had been applied, notwithstanding the phrase "at a date

other than that required by IFRIC 4". We believe that interpreting the requirement literally as requiring the assessment to have been made at a date *other than that required by IFRIC 4* would be inconsistent with the intention of the IASB in providing relief.

IFRS 1.D9A, 6.1.1530.40 In our view, application of the exemption does not rely on the first-time
IFRIC 4.BC adopter having applied the same accounting to the lease under previous GAAP as it
13 would have done under IAS 17. We believe that the reference in the exemption to "the same outcome as that resulting from applying IAS 17 and IFRIC 4" refers to the scope of IAS 17 rather than the accounting. This is consistent with the objective of IFRIC 4, which is to determine whether an arrangement falls within the scope of IAS 17. Interpreting IFRS 1 to require the same accounting as under IAS 17 would be inconsistent with the idea that, after applying this exemption, a first-time adopter goes on to apply the classification and accounting requirements of IAS 17 to leases at the date of transition.

6.1.1540 *Classification*

IFRS 1.7, 6.1.1540.10 A first-time adopter, at the date of transition, classifies leases as operating or
IG14 finance leases based on circumstances existing at the inception of the lease (unless the agreement is changed). The classification is based on IFRSs effective at the reporting date for its first IFRS financial statements.

IFRS 1.IG14 6.1.1540.20 If a lease agreement is changed between the inception of the lease and the date of transition, then the classification of the lease under IFRSs is tested using both the original and the revised terms based on the circumstances (and therefore the assumptions and estimates that were, or would have been used) at the inception of the original lease. If the revisions would result in a different classification using the original assumptions, then the revisions are treated as a new lease from the modification date, and the classification, recognition and measurement of the lease are determined using assumptions that were, or would have been, used as of the modification date.

IFRS 1.IG14 6.1.1540.30 However, changes in estimates, e.g. changes in estimates of the economic life or of the residual value of the leased asset, or changes in circumstances such as default by the lessee, do not result in reclassification of leases.

6.1.1550 *Accounting for leases*

6.1.1550.10 With respect to finance leases, a lessee recognises, at the date of transition:

- the carrying amount of the leased asset determined as if IFRSs had been applied from inception of the lease, subject to the requirements and/or optional exemptions of IFRS 1. For example, in our view the deemed cost exemption for property, plant and equipment may be applied to an asset acquired under a finance lease (see 6.1.330); and
- the carrying amount of the lease liability is a progression of the amount that would have been recognised at commencement of the lease, taking into account accrued interest and repayments.

IFRS 1.IG15, 6.1.1550.20 A lessor recognises a finance lease receivable in the statement of financial
IAS 17.36 position at the amount of its net investment, which comprises the present value of the
minimum lease payments and any unguaranteed residual value accruing to the lessor. If
the lessor recognised the leased asset under previous GAAP, then it is derecognised at
the date of transition. The carrying amount of the lease receivable at the date of transition is a progression of the amount that would have been recognised at commencement
of the lease, taking into account accrued interest and repayments.

IFRS 1.IG16, 6.1.1550.30 With respect to operating leases, a lessee (lessor) recognises rent expense
IAS 17.33, 50 (income) on a straight-line basis over the lease term, or on another systematic basis
if appropriate. Lease incentives are taken into account in determining the total lease
expense (income) that is spread over the relevant period.

6.1.1560 *Land and buildings*

IAS 17.7-19 6.1.1560.10 A lease of both land and building is treated as two leases, one for the land and
one for the building, with each lease classified separately under IFRSs (see 5.1.240).

6.1.1570 *Service concession arrangements*

IFRS 1.D22 6.1.1570.10 Full retrospective application of the measurement requirements of IFRIC 12
Service Concession Arrangements may be impracticable for service concession arrangements that have been in existence for a long period of time. For example, obtaining
information about construction costs incurred and estimating what would have been an
appropriate service margin on construction services may be difficult for arrangements
that started many years ago. IFRIC 12 provides transition relief to existing users of
IFRSs. IFRS 1 also makes this relief available, but not mandatory, to first-time adopters.

IFRIC 12.30 6.1.1570.20 If retrospective application of IFRIC 12 at the date of transition is impracticable for any service concession arrangement, then the operator:

- reclassifies assets recognised previously under the service concession arrangement
  as a financial asset or an intangible asset at the date of transition, measured at the
  previous GAAP carrying amount; and
- tests those assets for impairment at the date of transition, or if impracticable, at the
  start of the current reporting period.

IFRIC 12.30 6.1.1570.30 The impairment test is undertaken, in accordance with either IAS 36 (for an
intangible asset) or IAS 39 (for a financial asset).

6.1.1570.40 Neither IFRIC 12 nor IFRS 1 specifies how the operator should account for a
financial asset recognised on transition at the carrying amount of the assets recognised
previously.

6.1.1570.50 There also is no explicit guidance in IFRIC 12 when an operator recognises both
a financial asset and an intangible asset on transition to IFRSs and how an allocation of

the previous GAAP carrying amount should be made. In our view an entity should choose one of the following methods, to be applied consistently to all such allocations. One acceptable method is to allocate the carrying amount to the financial asset and the intangible asset based on their relative fair values. Another method is to measure the financial asset by discounting the future guaranteed payments using a reasonable rate of lending to the grantor, and assigning the remainder of the carrying amount to the intangible asset.

6.1.1580 *Interaction with other requirements and exemptions*

6.1.1580.10 In our view, the exemption in respect of service concessions takes precedence over other requirements and exemptions in IFRS 1. Therefore, a first-time adopter that follows the specific transitional requirements for service concession requirements does not further restate the previous GAAP carrying amount of the asset for elements that do not otherwise comply with IFRSs, e.g. for borrowing costs included in the carrying amount.

6.1.1590 **Insurance contracts**

6.1.1600 *Optional exemption for insurance contracts*

IFRS 1.D4, 4.41, 41A   6.1.1600.10 A first-time adopter is permitted to apply the transitional requirements of IFRS 4 *Insurance Contracts*. Instead of applying the standard retrospectively, the transitional requirements allow a first-time adopter to apply the standard prospectively to reporting periods beginning on or after 1 January 2005. In addition, subsequent amendments to IFRS 4 in respect of financial guarantee contracts may be applied prospectively to reporting periods beginning on or after 1 January 2006 (see 5.10).

6.1.1610 **Extractive Activities**

6.1.1610.10 There is no relief from the requirements of IFRS 6 *Exploration and Evaluation of Mineral Resources* for first-time adopters. The accounting for extractive activities under IFRSs differs depending on the stage of activity in which the expenditure was incurred (see 5.11).

IFRS 1.BC 47A   6.1.1610.20 IFRS 1 includes an optional exemption that is applicable *only* to entities in the oil and gas industry that under previous GAAP accounted for exploration and development costs for properties in the development or production phases in cost centres that included all properties in a large geographic area; this often is referred to as full cost accounting. Generally under full cost accounting, the historical information available under previous GAAP would have been aggregated at a much higher unit of account than the acceptable unit of account under IFRSs. For many of these assets, the information available to recreate an IFRS-compliant carrying amount at the date of transition may not be available or, if available, then the recreation of an IFRS-compliant carrying amount at the date of transition would result in significant costs to preparers.

IFRS 1.D8A   6.1.1610.30 An optional exemption permits applicable first-time adopters to measure:

- exploration and evaluation assets at the carrying amount at the date of transition under previous GAAP; and
- assets in the development or production phases at amounts determined based on the related cost centre under previous GAAP, which is then allocated on a *pro rata* basis to the cost centre's underlying assets using reserve volumes or reserve values at the date of transition.

IFRS 1.D8A   6.1.1610.40 If a first-time adopter elects to apply the optional exemption, then an impairment test of the assets to which the exemption is applied is required at the date of transition. For exploration and evaluation assets, a first-time adopter would perform the impairment test in accordance with IFRS 6; for assets in the development or production phases, a first-time adopter would perform the impairment test in accordance with IAS 36 (see 3.10).

IFRS 1.D21A   6.1.1610.50 For oil and gas assets in the development or production phases, a consequential amendment was made to the exemption in IFRS 1 in respect of decommissioning, restoration and similar liabilities (see 6.1.960). If a first-time adopter uses the deemed cost exemption for oil and gas assets in the development or production phases, then the amount of any adjustments required to measure decommissioning, restoration and similar liabilities in accordance with IAS 37 at the date of transition are recognised directly in retained earnings rather than adjusting the carrying amount of the underlying assets.

6.1.1620 *Separate financial statements*

6.1.1630 *Optional exemption for investments in subsidiaries, jointly controlled entities and associates*

IAS 27.38   6.1.1630.10 Investments in subsidiaries, jointly controlled entities and associates are accounted for either at cost or in accordance with the requirements of IAS 39.

IFRS 1.D15 *(a), (b)*   6.1.1630.20 If a first-time adopter chooses to measure any of these categories of investments at cost, then it may choose to measure the carrying amount of any such investments at the date of transition at an amount equal to:

- cost, determined in accordance with IAS 27; or
- deemed cost, which is either fair value, determined in accordance with IAS 39, or the previous GAAP carrying amount of the investment.

IFRS 1.D15   6.1.1630.30 The deemed cost exemption is available on an investment-by-investment basis.

6.1.1630.40 For example, in accordance with local laws, Company J presents separate financial statements in addition to consolidated financial statements. J is a first-time adopter in 2010. J acquired 80 percent of the shares in Company H for 40 in 2008. J financed the acquisition through the issue of debt securities, and 2 of issue costs incurred were capitalised as part of the carrying amount of the investment in H. Accordingly, at the date of transition, 1 January 2009, the carrying amount of H is 42 in J's separate financial statements.

6.1.1630.50 If IFRSs were applied retrospectively, then the issue costs would be adjusted against the carrying amount of the debt securities. However, J elects to apply the deemed cost exemption and to state its investment in H at its carrying amount under previous GAAP at the date of transition, i.e. 42.

6.1.1630.60 See 6.1.1260 for guidance on consolidation.

6.1.1640 Presentation and disclosure#

6.1.1650 *First IFRS financial statements*

IFRS 1.6, 21   6.1.1650.10 An entity's first IFRS financial statements include presentation of the opening statement of financial position. Therefore an entity in its first IFRS financial statements will present three statements of financial position, i.e. as of the current reporting date; as of the previous annual reporting date; and as of the date of transition.

6.1.1650.20 In addition to presenting a third statement of financial position as at the date of transition, IFRS 1 also requires the presentation of "related notes". In our view, this requirement should be interpreted as requiring disclosure of those notes that are relevant to an understanding of how the transition from previous GAAP to IFRSs affected the first-time adopter's financial position at the date of transition, i.e. not all notes related to the third statement of financial position are required in every circumstance. A first-time adopter might approach its decision about the relevant note disclosures by first assuming all notes are necessary, and then considering which note disclosures are not relevant to an understanding of the effect of the transition to IFRSs and may be omitted. In deciding which notes and other comparative information to omit, regard is given to materiality and the particular facts and circumstances of the first-time adopter, including legislative and other requirements of the jurisdiction in which the first-time adopter operates.

6.1.1650.30 For example, a first-time adopter may decide to include all of the notes disaggregating the line items in the statement of financial position at the date of transition, but to omit selected supporting (or descriptive) comparative information that it considers is not relevant to an understanding of the effect of transition at that date, e.g. the contractual maturity analysis for financial liabilities and the sensitivity analyses required by IFRS 7.

6.1.1650.40 The disclosure in the notes need not include information that relates to the period before the date of transition. For example, a first-time adopter presents a statement of financial position at its date of transition of 1 January 2009. The notes to the statement of financial position include the gross carrying amount and accumulated depreciation of each class of property, plant and equipment at that date and the amount of expenditure in the carrying amount of an item of property, plant and equipment in the course of its construction. However, a reconciliation of the carrying amount of property, plant and equipment in the period from 1 January 2008 to 31 December 2008 would not be required to be presented.

6.1.1650.50 Extensive disclosures are required in the first IFRS financial statements to explain how the transition from previous GAAP to IFRSs affected the reported financial position, financial performance and cash flows of the first-time adopter. These disclosures include reconciliations of equity and reported profit or loss at the date of transition and at the end of the comparative period.

6.1.1650.60 The reconciliations show the material adjustments made to amounts reported under previous GAAP in order to determine corresponding amounts presented under IFRSs, together with explanations of the reconciling items. The correction of errors made under previous GAAP is identified separately.

IFRS 1.25 6.1.1650.70 A first-time adopter that presented a statement of cash flows under previous GAAP also explains the material adjustments to its statement of cash flows, if any.

6.1.1650.80 In our view, it is not sufficient to include a cross reference to previously published disclosures of the impact of the transition to IFRSs in the first IFRS financial statements. A reference to previously published additional voluntary information (e.g. a more detailed analysis) is permitted, but should not call into question whether the information in the financial statements complies fully with IFRSs or the level of assurance provided on the previously published additional information.

6.1.1650.90 Some entities may have been required to prepare only separate (i.e. unconsolidated) financial statements under previous GAAP, but under IFRSs are required to prepare consolidated financial statements. In our view, the non-preparation of consolidated financial statements is not a prior period error. We believe that amounts reported under previous GAAP are those of the separate financial statements of the parent and IFRS 1 treats the transition to IFRSs of an entity in its separate financial statements as a different transition to the same entity's transition in its consolidated financial statements. As we have previously taken the view that reconciliations generally would be to the amounts reported in the same set of financial statements (see 6.1.80.10), in our view there is no relevant previous GAAP financial statements from which the first-time adopter is transitioning, and therefore no reconciliations in the consolidated first-time adoption IFRSs to the previous GAAP separate financial statements are required.

IFRS 1.36 6.1.1650.100 The comparatives in a first-time adopter's first IFRS financial statements may be for a period shorter or longer than 12 months, but are for the same period as the previous GAAP financial statements. This also applies if the first-time adopter changes its annual reporting date during the period in which IFRSs are adopted. For example, Company B's previous GAAP comparative financial statements are for the 12-month period ended 30 June 2008; after 1 July 2008 B decides to change its annual reporting date from 30 June 2009 to 31 December 2008. Therefore, B's first IFRS financial statements are for the six-month period ended 31 December 2008 with comparatives for the 12-month period ended 30 June 2008, provided that this is in accordance with local laws and regulations.

6.1.1650.110 For examples of disclosures in a first-time adopter's first annual IFRS financial statements, see KPMG's series of illustrative financial statements.

6.1.1660 *Forthcoming requirements*

6.1.1660.10 If a first-time adopter adopts IFRSs for an annual period beginning before 1 January 2012 and chooses to apply IFRS 9, then comparative information in the first IFRS financial statements does not have to be restated in accordance with IFRS 9. This exemption also includes IFRS 7 disclosures related to assets in the scope of IAS 39. If this option is taken:

- with respect to the application of IFRS 9, the *date of transition* is the beginning of the first IFRS reporting period;
- for assets in the scope of IAS 39, previous GAAP is applied in comparative periods (rather than IFRS 9 or IAS 39);
- the fact that the exemption is applied, as well as the basis of preparation of the comparative information, is disclosed; and
- the differences arising on adopting IFRS 9 are treated as a change in accounting policy; all adjustments resulting from applying IFRS 9 are recognised in the statement of financial position at the beginning of the first IFRS reporting period and certain disclosures required by IAS 8 are given.

6.1.1660.20 See 3.6A.490.50 and 60 for further discussion of the impact on first-time adopters.

6.1.1670 *Interim financial statements*

6.1.1680 *Form, content and disclosures in the interim IFRS financial statements*

IAS 34.10   6.1.1680.10 If a first-time adopter publishes a set of condensed interim financial statements in accordance with IFRSs, then these financial statements contain, as a minimum, each of the headings and subtotals that were included in its most recent annual financial statements, together with selected notes required by IAS 34 *Interim Financial Reporting* (see 5.9). In our view, a first-time adopter applies this requirement by including at least all of the headings and subtotals that are expected to be included in its first annual IFRS financial statements.

IFRS 1.32(b)   6.1.1680.20 The extensive disclosures required in the first IFRS financial statements (see 6.1.1650) also are provided in any interim financial statements prepared in accordance with IFRSs (see 5.9) for part of the period covered by the first IFRS financial statements. Alternatively, the interim financial statements include a cross reference to another published document that contains those disclosures.

IFRS 1.32(a)   6.1.1680.30 In addition, if the first-time adopter presented an interim financial report for the comparable interim period of the immediately preceding financial year, additional reconciliations are included in its first IFRS interim financial statements. These are reconciliations of its equity at the end of that comparable interim period and profit or loss for that comparable interim period (current and year to date).

6.1.1680.40 Unlike for the first IFRS financial statements, when a first-time adopter publishes its first IFRS condensed interim financial statements, IFRSs are not explicit on whether to present the third statement of financial position as a primary financial statement or in the notes. We prefer that a first-time adopter presents the third statement of financial position as a primary financial statement.

6.1.1680.50 In our view, a first-time adopter that presents comparative information in its first IFRS interim financial statements on the basis of previous GAAP will need to provide additional information to explain its transition to IFRSs. We believe that a first-time adopter should consider providing in its first interim IFRS financial statements the information required to be given in its first annual IFRS financial statements.

6.1.1680.60 In our view, when a first-time adopter prepares interim financial statements that claim compliance with IAS 34, these first interim IFRS financial statements should include a complete set of significant accounting policies. Significant judgement is then required in determining other areas that may require additional disclosure; these may include, but are not limited to:

- significant judgements made in applying accounting policies and key sources of estimation uncertainty
- operating segments
- non-current assets held for sale and discontinued operations
- income tax expense
- earnings per share
- employee benefits
- financial instruments.

6.1.1680.70 In our view, having included extensive disclosures in the first interim financial statements presented, it may be appropriate for subsequent interim financial statements for part of the period covered by its first IFRS financial statements to include a cross-reference to the first interim financial statements, if the additional disclosures would not be material to an understanding of the subsequent interim financial statements. However, including extensive disclosures in interim financial statements is not a substitute for the required disclosures in the first annual IFRS financial statements and therefore a cross-reference in the first annual IFRS financial statements to an interim financial statement would not be permitted (see 6.1.1650.80).

6.1.1680.80 For example, Company M's most recent annual financial statements under previous GAAP were prepared for the year ended 31 December 2009. M is required to prepare quarterly interim IFRS financial statements in the year of adoption and M also prepared quarterly interim financial statements under previous GAAP throughout 2009.

6.1.1680.90 In its *first* interim IFRS financial statements, for the three months ending 31 March 2010, M will disclose the following reconciliations:

- Reconciliations of equity under previous GAAP to equity under IFRSs at:
  - the date of transition, being 1 January 2009;
  - the end of the comparative interim period, being 31 March 2009; and
  - the end of comparative annual period, being 31 December 2009.
- Reconciliations of total comprehensive income under previous GAAP to total comprehensive income under IFRSs for:
  - the comparative interim period, being the three months ended 31 March 2009; and
  - the comparative annual period ending 31 December 2009.

6.1.1680.100 In its interim IFRS financial statements for the six months ending 30 June 2010, M will disclose the following reconciliations:

- Reconciliation of equity under previous GAAP to equity under IFRSs at the end of the comparative interim period, being 30 June 2009.
- Reconciliations of total comprehensive income under previous GAAP to total comprehensive income under IFRSs for:
  - the comparative interim period, being the three months ended 30 June 2009; and
  - the comparative cumulative interim period, being the six months ended 30 June 2009.

6.1.1680.110 For examples of disclosures in a first-time adopter's first interim IFRS financial statements, see KPMG's series of illustrative financial statements.

6.1.1690 [Not used]

6.1.1700 Changing accounting policies in the year of adoption#

6.1.1700.10 In our view, it is acceptable for a first-time adopter to adopt an accounting policy in its first annual IFRS financial statements that differs from an accounting policy applied in any interim IFRS financial statements published previously. We also believe that it is acceptable for a first-time adopter to adopt different accounting policies between sets of interim IFRS financial statements prior to the issue of the first annual IFRS financial statements. We believe that this is acceptable because IFRS 1 governs the selection of accounting policies in the first annual IFRS financial statements, and therefore the general requirements of IAS 8 in respect of a voluntary change in accounting policy do not apply.

6.1.1700.20 In some circumstances this might arise because a new IFRS is issued between the interim and annual reporting dates and the first-time adopter elects to early adopt that pronouncement in its first annual IFRS financial statements. In rare circumstances a first-time adopter might decide to change an accounting policy voluntarily.

6.1.1700.30 However, in such cases we prefer that a first-time adopter in its first annual IFRS financial statements include sufficient disclosure about the change to ensure that readers of the financial statements have a full understanding of the policies adopted upon transition to IFRSs. Therefore, it may be appropriate to disclose details of the change in accounting policy in its first annual IFRS financial statements, together with the information about the impact of the change.

6.1.1700.40 Notwithstanding our view that changes in accounting policies between a first-time adopter's IFRS interim and first annual IFRS financial statements are not within the scope of IAS 8, some regulators may consider that the policies adopted in the first annual financial statements are more appropriate, e.g. on the basis of evolving best practice. When considering whether the policy is more appropriate, the criteria for voluntary changes in accounting policy in IAS 8 may be useful guidance (see 2.8.30).

6.1.1710 Changing optional exemptions in the year of adoption#

6.1.1710.10 In our view, it is acceptable for a first-time adopter to elect an optional exemption in its first annual IFRS financial statements that differs from the election made in any interim IFRS financial statements published previously. This is because the use of the optional exemptions in IFRS 1 is closely tied to a first-time adopter's overall selection of accounting policies.

6.1.1710.20 Similar to changes in accounting policies in 6.1.1700, we prefer that a first-time adopter in its first annual IFRS financial statements include sufficient disclosure about the change, i.e. from an election made in any interim IFRS financial statements published previously to a different election made in its first annual IFRS financial statements, to ensure that readers of the financial statements have a full understanding of the optional exemptions used upon transition to IFRSs. Therefore, it may be appropriate to disclose details of the change in its first annual IFRS financial statements, together with the information about the impact of the change.

6.1.1720 *Forthcoming requirements*

6.1.1720.10 The *Improvements to IFRSs 2010* amended IFRS 1 to clarify that IAS 8 does not apply to the changes in accounting policies that occur during the period covered by their first IFRS financial statements. In addition, the amendment provides guidance for entities that publish interim financial information under IAS 34 and change their accounting policies or use of the IFRS 1 optional exemptions during the period covered by their first IFRS financial statements. The amendment clarifies that:

- the entity should explain any such changes between the first interim and the first annual financial statements; and
- the entity should update reconciliations from previous GAAP to IFRSs included in the previous interim financial information for those changes in the interim period when the change is made.

6.1.1720.20 The amendment applies for annual periods beginning on or after 1 January 2011; early application is permitted.

6.1.1730 Future developments

6.1.1730.10 In April 2010 the IASB published ED/2010/3 *Defined Benefit Plans – Proposed Amendments to IAS 19* as part of the first phase of the project to revisit fundamentally the accounting for employee benefits under IAS 19. The ED proposes significant changes to the recognition, presentation and disclosure of defined benefit plans and also changes to their measurement, including to remove the option of using the "corridor method" for recognising actuarial gains and losses, i.e. all changes in the value of the defined benefit obligation and in the value of plan assets would be recognised in the financial statements in the period in which they occur. A final standard on this initial phase of the employee benefits project is scheduled for the first quarter of 2011.

Currently effective and forthcoming requirements

Below is a list of standards and interpretations, including the latest amendment to the standards and interpretations, in issue at 1 August 2010 that are effective for annual reporting periods beginning on 1 January 2010. The list notes the principal related chapter(s) within which the requirements are discussed. It also notes forthcoming requirements in issue at 1 August 2010 that are effective for annual reporting periods beginning after 1 January 2010.

Standard	Principal related chapter(s)	Latest effective amendment	Forthcoming requirements
IFRS 1 *First-time Adoption of International Financial Reporting Standards*	6.1	*Additional Exemptions for First-time Adopters* (Amendments to IFRS 1) *Issued:* July 2009 *Effective:* 1 January 2010	*Improvements to IFRSs 2010* *Issued:* May 2010 *Effective:* 1 January 2011 *Limited Exemption from Comparative IFRS 7 Disclosures for First-time Adopters* (Amendment to IFRS 1) *Issued:* January 2010 *Effective:* 1 July 2010 IFRIC 19 *Extinguishing Financial Liabilities with Equity Instruments* *Issued:* November 2009 *Effective:* 1 July 2010 IFRS 9 *Financial Instruments* *Issued:* November 2009 *Effective:* 1 January 2013
IFRS 2 *Share-based Payments*	4.5	*Group Cash-settled Share-based Payment Transactions* (Amendments to IFRS 2) *Issued:* June 2009 *Effective:* 1 January 2010	-

Appendix I

Standard	Principal related chapter(s)	Latest effective amendment	Forthcoming requirements
IFRS 3 *Business Combinations* Issued: January 2008 Effective: 1 July 2009	2.6, 3.3, 5.13	-	*Improvements to IFRSs 2010* Issued: May 2010 Effective: 1 July 2010
IFRS 4 *Insurance Contracts*	5.10	*Improving Disclosures about Financial Instruments* (Amendments to IFRS 7) Issued: March 2009 Effective: 1 January 2009	-
IFRS 5 *Non-current Assets Held for Sale and Discontinued Operations*	5.4	*Improvements to IFRSs 2009* Issued: April 2009 Effective: 1 January 2010	-
IFRS 6 *Exploration for and Evaluation of Mineral Resources*	5.11	*Improvements to IFRSs 2009* Issued: April 2009 Effective: 1 January 2010	-
IFRS 7 *Financial Instruments: Disclosures*	5.6	*Improving Disclosures about Financial Instruments* (Amendments to IFRS 7) Issued: March 2009 Effective: 1 January 2009	*Improvements to IFRSs 2010* Issued: May 2010 Effective: 1 July 2010 and 1 January 2011 IFRS 9 *Financial Instruments* Issued: November 2009 Effective: 1 January 2013
IFRS 8 *Operating Segments*	5.2	*Improvements to IFRSs 2009* Issued: April 2009 Effective: 1 January 2010	IAS 24 *Related Party Disclosures* (2009) Issued: November 2009 Effective: 1 January 2011
IAS 1 *Presentation of Financial Statements*	1.1, 2.1, 2.2, 2.4, 2.8, 2.9, 3.1, 4.1, 5.6, 5.8	*Improvements to IFRSs 2009* Issued: April 2009 Effective: 1 January 2010	*Improvements to IFRSs 2010* Issued: May 2010 Effective: 1 January 2011 IFRS 9 *Financial Instruments* Issued: November 2009 Effective: 1 January 2013

Standard	Principal related chapter(s)	Latest effective amendment	Forthcoming requirements
IAS 2 *Inventories*	3.8	*Improvements to IFRSs 2008* Issued: May 2008 Effective: 1 January 2009	-
IAS 7 *Statement of Cash Flows*	2.3	*Improvements to IFRSs 2009* Issued: April 2009 Effective: 1 January 2010	-
IAS 8 *Accounting Policies, Changes in Accounting Estimates and Errors*	2.8	*Improvements to IFRSs 2008* Issued: May 2008 Effective: 1 January 2009	-
IAS 10 *Events after the Reporting Period*	2.9	IFRIC 17 *Distributions of Non-cash Assets to Owners* Issued: November 2008 Effective: 1 July 2009	-
IAS 11 *Construction Contracts*	4.2	IAS 1 *Presentation of Financial Statements* Issued: September 2007 Effective: 1 January 2009	-
IAS 12 *Income Taxes*	3.13	IFRS 3 *Business Combinations* Issued: January 2008 Effective: 1 July 2009	-
IAS 16 *Property, Plant and Equipment*	3.2, 5.7	*Improvements to IFRSs 2008* Issued: May 2008 Effective: 1 January 2009	-
IAS 17 *Leases*	3.4, 5.1	*Improvements to IFRSs 2009* Issued: April 2009 Effective: 1 January 2010	-
IAS 18 *Revenue*	4.2, 4.6, 5.7	*Improvements to IFRSs 2009* Issued: April 2009 Effective: April 2009	-
IAS 19 *Employee Benefits*	4.4	*Improvements to IFRSs 2008* Issued: May 2008 Effective: 1 January 2009	-

Standard	Principal related chapter(s)	Latest effective amendment	Forthcoming requirements
IAS 20 *Accounting for Government Grants and Disclosure of Government Assistance*	4.3	*Improvements to IFRSs 2008* Issued: May 2008 Effective: 1 January 2009	-
IAS 21 *The Effects of Changes in Foreign Exchange Rates*	2.4, 2.7, 3.6	*Cost of an Investment in a Subsidiary, Jointly Controlled Entity or Associate* (Amendments to IFRS 1 and IAS 27) Issued: May 2008 Effective: 1 July 2009	*Improvements to IFRSs 2010* Issued: May 2010 Effective: 1 July 2010
IAS 23 *Borrowing Costs*	4.6	*Improvements to IFRSs 2008* Issued: May 2008 Effective: 1 January 2009	-
IAS 24 *Related Party Disclosures*	5.5, 5.5A	IAS 1 *Presentation of Financial Statements* Issued: September 2007 Effective: 1 January 2009	IAS 24 *Related Party Disclosures* (2009) Issued: November 2009 Effective: 1 January 2011
IAS 26 *Accounting and Reporting by Retirement Benefits Plans*	Not covered; see *About this publication.*		
IAS 27 *Consolidated and Separate Financial Statements*	2.1, 2.5, 5.13	*Improvements to IFRSs 2008* Issued: May 2008 Effective: 1 January 2009	-
IAS 28 *Investments in Associates*	3.5	*Improvements to IFRSs 2008* Issued: May 2008 Effective: 1 January 2009	*Improvements to IFRSs 2010* Issued: May 2010 Effective: 1 July 2010
IAS 29 *Financial Reporting in Hyperinflationary Economies*	2.4, 2.7	*Improvements to IFRSs 2008* Issued: May 2008 Effective: 1 January 2009	-
IAS 31 *Interests in Joint Ventures*	3.5	*Improvements to IFRSs 2008* Issued: May 2008 Effective: 1 January 2009	*Improvements to IFRSs 2010* Issued: May 2010 Effective: 1 July 2010

Standard	Principal related chapter(s)	Latest effective amendment	Forthcoming requirements
IAS 32 *Financial Instruments: Presentation*	3.6, 3.11, 5.6	*Improvements to IFRSs 2008* *Issued:* May 2008 *Effective:* 1 January 2009	*Improvements to IFRSs 2010* *Issued:* May 2010 *Effective:* 1 July 2010 *Classification of Rights Issues* (Amendment to IAS 32) *Issued:* October 2009 *Effective:* 1 February 2010
IAS 33 *Earnings per Share*	5.3	IFRS 3 *Business Combinations* and IAS 27 *Consolidated and Separate Financial Statements* *Issued:* January 2008 *Effective:* 1 July 2009	-
IAS 34 *Interim Financial Reporting*	5.9	*Improvements to IFRSs 2008* *Issued:* May 2008 *Effective:* 1 January 2009	*Improvements to IFRSs 2010* *Issued:* May 2010 *Effective:* 1 January 2011
IAS 36 *Impairment of Assets*	3.10	*Improvements to IFRSs 2009* *Issued:* April 2009 *Effective:* 1 January 2010	-
IAS 37 *Provisions, Contingent Liabilities and Contingent Assets*	3.12, 3.14	IFRS 3 *Business Combinations* *Issued:* January 2008 *Effective:* 1 July 2009	-
IAS 38 *Intangible Assets*	3.3, 5.7	*Improvements to IFRSs 2009* *Issued:* April 2009 *Effective:* 1 July 2009	-
IAS 39 *Financial Instruments: Recognition and Measurement*	3.6, 3.6A, 3.7, 3.11, 4.6	*Improvements to IFRSs 2009* *Issued:* April 2009 *Effective:* 1 January 2009 and 2010	*Improvements to IFRSs 2010* *Issued:* May 2010 *Effective:* 1 July 2010 IFRS 9 *Financial Instruments* *Issued:* November 2009 *Effective:* 1 January 2013

Standard	Principal related chapter(s)	Latest effective amendment	Forthcoming requirements
IAS 40 *Investment Property*	3.4, 5.7	*Improvements to IFRSs 2008* Issued: May 2008 *Effective:* 1 January 2009	-
IAS 41 *Agriculture*	3.9, 4.3	*Improvements to IFRSs 2008* Issued: May 2008 *Effective:* 1 January 2009	-
IFRIC 1 *Changes in Existing Decommissioning, Restoration and Similar Liabilities*	3.2, 3.12	IAS 1 *Presentation of Financial Statements* Issued: September 2007 *Effective:* 1 January 2009	-
IFRIC 2 *Members' Shares in Co-operative Entities and Similar Instruments*	3.11	*Puttable Financial Instruments and Obligations Arising on Liquidation* (Amendments to IAS 32 and IAS 1) Issued: February 2008 *Effective:* 1 January 2009	-
IFRIC 4 *Determining whether an Arrangement contains a Lease*	5.1	IFRIC 12 *Service Concession Arrangements* Issued: November 2006 *Effective:* 1 January 2008	-
IFRIC 5 *Rights to Interests arising from Decommissioning, Restoration and Environmental Rehabilitation Funds*	3.12	IAS 1 *Presentation of Financial Statements* Issued: September 2007 *Effective:* 1 January 2009	-
IFRIC 6 *Liabilities arising from Participating in a Specific Market – Waste Electrical and Electronic Equipment* Issued: September 2005 *Effective:* 1 December 2005	3.12	-	-

Standard	Principal related chapter(s)	Latest effective amendment	Forthcoming requirements
IFRIC 7 *Applying the Restatement Approach under IAS 29 Financial Reporting in Hyperinflationary Economies*	2.4	IAS 1 *Presentation of Financial Statements* *Issued:* September 2007 *Effective:* 1 January 2009	-
IFRIC 9 *Reassessment of Embedded Derivatives*	3.6	*Improvements to IFRSs 2009* *Issued:* April 2009 *Effective:* 1 July 2009	-
IFRIC 10 *Interim Financial Reporting and Impairment*	3.10, 5.9	IAS 1 *Presentation of Financial Statements* *Issued:* September 2007 *Effective:* 1 January 2009	-
IFRIC 12 *Service Concession Arrangements*	5.12	IAS 1 *Presentation of Financial Statements* *Issued:* September 2007 *Effective:* 1 January 2009	-
IFRIC 13 *Customer Loyalty Programmes* *Issued:* June 2007 *Effective:* 1 July 2008	4.2	-	*Improvements to IFRSs 2010* *Issued:* May 2010 *Effective:* 1 January 2011
IFRIC 14 *The Limit on a Defined Benefit Asset, Minimum Funding Requirements and their Interaction*	4.4	IAS 1 *Presentation of Financial Statements* *Issued:* September 2007 *Effective:* 1 January 2009	*Prepayments of a Minimum Funding Requirement* (Amendments to IFRIC 14) *Issued:* November 2009 *Effective:* 1 January 2011
IFRIC 15 *Agreements for the Construction of Real Estate* *Issued:* July 2008 *Effective:* 1 January 2009	4.2	-	-
IFRIC 16 *Hedges of a Net Investment in a Foreign Operation*	3.7	*Improvements to IFRSs 2009* *Issued:* April 2009 *Effective:* 1 July 2009	-
IFRIC 17 *Distributions of Non-cash Assets to Owners* *Issued:* November 2008 *Effective:* 1 July 2009	3.11, 5.4, 5.13	-	-

Standard	Principal related chapter(s)	Latest effective amendment	Forthcoming requirements
IFRIC 18 *Transfers of Assets from Customers* *Issued:* January 2009 *Effective:* 1 July 2009	3.2, 4.2, 5.7	-	-
-	3.6, 3.11	-	IFRIC 19 *Extinguishing Financial Liabilities with Equity Instruments* *Issued:* November 2009 *Effective:* 1 July 2010
SIC-7 *Introduction of the Euro*	none	IAS 27 *Consolidated and Separate Financial Statements* *Issued:* January 2008 *Effective:* 1 July 2009	-
SIC-10 *Government Assistance – No Specific Relation to Operating Activities*	4.3	IAS 1 *Presentation of Financial Statements* *Issued:* September 2007 *Effective:* 1 January 2009	-
SIC-12 *Consolidation – Special Purpose Entities*	2.5	IFRIC Amendment to SIC-12 *Scope of SIC-12* Consolidation – Special Purpose Entities *Issued:* November 2004 *Effective:* 1 January 2005	-
SIC-13 *Jointly Controlled Entities – Non-Monetary Contributions by Venturers*	3.5	IAS 1 *Presentation of Financial Statements* *Issued:* September 2007 *Effective:* 1 January 2009	-
SIC-15 *Operating Leases – Incentives*	5.1	IAS 1 *Presentation of Financial Statements* *Issued:* September 2007 *Effective:* 1 January 2009	-
SIC-21 *Income Taxes – Recovery of Revalued Non-Depreciable Assets*	3.13	IAS 1 *Presentation of Financial Statements* *Issued:* September 2007 *Effective:* 1 January 2009	-
SIC-25 *Income Taxes – Changes in the Tax Status of an Entity or its Shareholders*	3.13	IAS 1 *Presentation of Financial Statements* *Issued:* September 2007 *Effective:* 1 January 2009	-

Standard	Principal related chapter(s)	Latest effective amendment	Forthcoming requirements
SIC-27 *Evaluating the Substance of Transactions Involving the Legal Form of a Lease*	4.2, 5.1	IAS 1 *Presentation of Financial Statements* *Issued:* September 2007 *Effective:* 1 January 2009	-
SIC-29 *Service Concession Arrangements: Disclosures*	5.12	IAS 1 *Presentation of Financial Statements* *Issued:* September 2007 *Effective:* 1 January 2009	-
SIC-31 *Revenue – Barter Transactions Involving Advertising Services*	4.2, 5.7	IAS 8 *Accounting Policies, Changes in Accounting Estimates and Errors* *Issued:* December 2003 *Effective:* 1 January 2005	-
SIC-32 *Intangible Assets – Web Site Costs*	3.3	IAS 1 *Presentation of Financial Statements* *Issued:* September 2007 *Effective:* 1 January 2009	-

Appendix II

Table of concordance (moved paragraphs and changed paragraph numbers)

This table shows the paragraphs that have either been moved or have changed in numbering from the 2009/2010 edition to this edition of this publication.

2009/10 Edition Reference 6th edition	Current Reference 7th edition	2009/10 Edition Reference 6th edition	Current Reference 7th edition
1.1.20.20	1.1.5.10	3.6.35.190	3.6.37.70
1.1.25.10	1.1.5.20	3.6.35.200	3.6.38.10, 20
1.1.140	2.8.6	3.6.280.27	3.6.280.28
2.1.35.50	2.1.30.30, 40	3.6.1040.70	3.6.1020.40
2.4.160	2.8.7	3.6.1220.10 – 50	3.6.1210.50 – 90
2.7.320.20	2.7.320.110	3.6.1310.80	3.6.1317.10
2.7.320.30	2.7.320.160	3.6.1310.90	3.6.1317.20
2.7.320.40	2.7.320.190	3.6.1310.100	3.6.1317.30
2.7.320.50	2.7.320.200	3.7.10.10	3.7.10.10, 14
2.7.320.80	2.7.320.210	3.7.490.50	3.7.490.10
2.7.320.90	2.7.320.220	3.8.330.20	3.8.335.10, 20
3.1.40.100	3.1.40.57	3.9.60.45	3.9.10.70
3.3.70.30	3.3.70.10	3.11.50	3.11.45
3.4.20.40	3.4.20.40, 50	3.11.51	3.11.48
3.6.35.20	3.6.36.10	3.11.52	3.11.50
3.6.35.30	3.6.36.20	3.11.53.10 – 50	3.11.51
3.6.35.40	3.6.36.30	3.11.53.60	3.11.53.10
3.6.35.50	3.6.36.40	3.11.53.70	3.11.53.20
3.6.35.60	3.6.36.50	3.13.670	3.13.1000
3.6.35.70	3.6.36.60	4.1.82.60	4.1.20.40
3.6.35.75	3.6.36.70	4.2.60.50	4.2.60.100
3.6.35.80	3.6.36.90	4.2.180.30	4.2.180.20
3.6.35.90	3.6.36.100	4.2.210.50	4.2.210.30
3.6.35.100	3.6.36.110	4.2.210.60	4.2.210.40
3.6.35.110	3.6.36.120	4.2.210.70	4.2.210.50
3.6.35.120	3.6.36.130	4.2.210.80	4.2.210.60
3.6.35.130	3.6.36.140	4.2.210.90	4.2.210.70
3.6.35.140	3.6.37.20	4.2.640.20	4.2.642.10
3.6.35.150	3.6.37.30	4.3.90.20	4.3.90.50
3.6.35.160	3.6.37.40	4.3.150.10	4.3.150.10, 20
3.6.35.170	3.6.37.50	4.4.29	4.4.28
3.6.35.180	3.6.37.60	4.4.260	4.4.265

2009/10 Edition Reference 6th edition	Current Reference 7th edition	2009/10 Edition Reference 6th edition	Current Reference 7th edition
4.4.400.10	4.4.400.10, 30	5.7.50.30	5.7.50.20
4.4.400.20	4.4.400.40	5.7.50.20, 40	5.7.50.30
4.4.400.30	4.4.400.50	5.10.20.40	5.10.20.30
4.4.570.10	4.4.570.20	5.12.10.05	5.12.05.10
4.4.570.20	4.4.572.10	5.12.10.10	5.12.05.20
4.4.570.30	4.4.572.20	5.12.10.20	5.12.10.10
4.4.900.20	4.4.900.40	5.12.10.30	5.12.10.20
4.4.900.30	4.4.900.50	5.12.10.40	5.12.15.10
4.4.900.40	4.4.900.60	5.12.10.50	5.12.15.20
4.4.900.50	4.4.900.70	5.12.10.60	5.12.15.30
4.5.150.10	4.5.150.10 – 15	5.12.90.20	5.12.90.20, 22
4.5.180.10	4.5.180.10, 20		
4.5.290.10	4.5.290.20, 30		
4.5.440.10	4.5.445.10		
4.5.440.30	4.5.445.20 – 30		
4.5.440.40 – 50	4.5.445.40		
4.5.440.60	4.5.448.10		
4.5.450.30	4.5.443.10		
4.5.500.20	4.5.503.10		
4.5.500.30	4.5.505.10		
4.5.500.40	4.5.508.10		
4.5.540.40	4.5.540.55		
4.5.600.60	4.5.600.60 – 65		
4.5.640.50	4.5.643.10		
4.5.660.20	4.5.660.20, 27		
4.5.680.10	4.5.680.10, 12, 14, 18		
4.5.820.10	4.5.830.10		
4.5.900.20	4.5.947.20, 30		
4.5.920	4.5.1065		
4.5.960.10	4.5.960.10 – 30		
4.6.470.30	4.6.470.10		
5.1.510.33	5.1.510.31		
5.1.510.35	5.1.510.32		
5.1.510.37	5.1.510.33, 36, 39		
5.2.80.30	5.2.80.50		
5.2.230.10	5.2.230.10, 13		
5.3.240.20	5.3.242.10		
5.3.240.30	5.3.242.20		
5.5.40.10	5.5.40.10, 15		
5.5.90.10	5.5.90.10, 15		
5.7.10.20	5.7.10.05		
5.7.30.10	5.7.20.60		

Chapters 3.5 *Investments in associates and joint ventures*, 3.10 *Impairment of non-financial assets*, 5.6 *Financial instruments: presentation and disclosure* and 6.1 *First-time adoption of IFRSs* and sections of chapters 2.5 *Consolidation* and 3.13 *Income taxes*, have been restructured; therefore nearly all paragraphs of these chapters or sections have moved from the 2009/10 edition to this edition of this publication. Such changes are not reflected in this table of concordance.

In addition, the 2009/10 edition of this publication contained forthcoming requirement chapter 2.6A *Business combinations* of which the related requirements have become currently effective in this edition of this publication. The majority of the paragraphs in chapter 2.6A moved to chapters 2.6 *Business combinations* or 5.13 *Common control transactions and Newco formations*. Such changes are not reflected in this table of concordance.

Index

A

C

F

Notes

Notes

Notes

Notes

Notes

Notes

Notes

Notes

Notes

Notes